Praise for Ian Kershaw's *Hitler*

"As close to definitive as anything we are ever likely to see."
—Jane Kramer, *The New Yorker*

"Kershaw is able to clarify, perhaps better than any biographer who preceded him, what made Hitler's dictatorial power possible."
—Walter Reich, *New York Times Book Review*

"Massive, extensively researched, extraordinarily balanced, and remarkably judicious. . . . Highly readable, often exciting. . . . [A] rich and nuanced interpretation of the manner in which Hitler attained, exercised, and held on to power."
—Omer Bartov, *The New Republic*

"Will become the classic Hitler biography of our time. . . . [Kershaw has] significantly altered the perspective from which Hitler and his actions have been seen by previous biographers."
—Gordon A. Craig, *New York Review of Books*

"The most astute assessment of Hitler's bond with the German people yet written."
—*Wall Street Journal*

"A staggering achievement. . . . Allows us to view Hitler not so much as a creation of Germany's past but as a figure who looms over our present and all our futures."
—Richard Gott, *New Statesman*

"A much needed, readable, up-to-date biography."
—*Washington Post*

"Ian Kershaw has written the Hitler biography for the twenty-first century. It is cool, judicious, factually reliable and intelligently argued. . . . Will immediately take its place as the standard work to which all others in future will have to refer."
—Richard J. Evans, Cambridge University

"Kershaw demonstrates brilliantly and painstakingly how, step by step, hate and fear were brought about, and so horrifyingly used. . . . [Kershaw is] a historian of a new generation and a new century."
—Gitta Sereny, *The Times* (London)

"*Nemesis* is an achievement of the very highest order, by the historian who is Britain's uncontested expert on Nazi Germany. . . . It will be some decades before anyone will need to shine a searching light once more into the rank darkness of that German bunker."
—Michael Burleigh, *Financial Times*

"Ian Kershaw's two volumes on Hitler must rank as one of the greatest scholarly and biographical achievements of our time."
—David Cesarani, *Literary Review*

'The Hitler Myth': Image and Reality in the Third Reich
Popular Opinion and Political Dissent in the Third Reich, Bavaria 1933–45
The Nazi Dictatorship: Problems and Perspectives of Interpretation
(Edited) Weimar: Why Did German Democracy Fail?
Hitler: A Profile in Power
(Edited, with Moshe Lewin) Stalinism and Nazism: Dictatorships in Comparison
Hitler 1889–1936: Hubris

HITLER

1936–45: NEMESIS

Ian Kershaw

W. W. NORTON & COMPANY

NEW YORK • LONDON

The text and display of this book are composed in Sabon.
Manufacturing by the Haddon Craftsmen, Inc.

Library of Congress Catalog Card Number: 98-29569

ISBN 0-393-04994-9
ISBN 0-393-32252-1 pbk.

W. W. Norton & Company, Inc.
500 Fifth Avenue, New York, N.Y. 10110
www.wwnorton.com

W. W. Norton & Company Ltd.
Castle House, 75/76 Wells Street, London W1T 3QT

5 6 7 8 9 0

CONTENTS

LIST OF ILLUSTRATIONS

Every effort has been made to contact all copyright holders. The publishers will be glad to make good in future editions any errors or omissions brought to their attention. (Photographic acknowledgements are given in brackets.)

LIST OF MAPS

PREFACE

The first part of this study, *Hitler, 1889–1936: Hubris,* tried to show how the people of a highly cultured, economically advanced, modern state could allow into power and entrust their fate to a political outsider with few, if any, special talents beyond undoubted skills as a demagogue and propagandist.

By the time his Chancellorship was devised through the intrigues of influential individuals close to Reich President von Hindenburg, Hitler had been able in free elections to garner the votes of no more than a good third of the German electorate. Another third – on the Left – stood implacably opposed, though internally in disarray. The remainder were often sceptical, expectant, hesitant, and uncertain. By the end of the first volume we had traced the consolidation of Hitler's power to the point where it had become well-nigh absolute. Internal opposition had been crushed. The doubters had been largely won over by the scale of an internal rebuilding and external reassertion of strength which, almost beyond imagination, had restored much of the lost national pride and sense of humiliation left behind after the First World War. Authoritarianism was seen by most as a blessing; repression of those politically out of step, disliked ethnic minorities, or social misfits approved of as a small price for what appeared to be a national rebirth. While the adulation of Hitler among the masses had grown ever stronger, and opposition had been crushed and rendered inconsequential, powerful forces in the army, the landed aristocracy, industry, and high ranks of the civil service had thrown their weight behind the regime. Whatever its negative aspects, it was seen to offer them much in advancing their own interests.

Hitler, by the time the first volume drew to a close with the remilitarization of the Rhineland in 1936, enjoyed the support of the overwhelming mass of the German people – even most of those who had not voted for him before he became Chancellor. From the depths of national degradation, most Germans were more than content to share the new-found national pride. The sense that Germany was well on its way to becoming the dominant power in Europe was widespread. Hitler's own profound sense of personal degradation, felt in his Vienna years, had long since been supplanted by a gathering sense of political mission – that of Germany's redeemer from chaos and champion against the dark and menacing forces challenging the nation's very existence. By 1936, his narcissistic self-glorification had swollen immeasurably under the impact of the near-deification projected upon him by his followers. By this time, he thought himself infallible; his self-image had reached the stage of outright hubris.

The German people had shaped this personal hubris of the leader. They were about to enter into its full expression: the greatest gamble in the nation's history – to acquire complete dominance of the European continent. They would have to live with the consequences. The size of the gamble itself implied an implicit willingness to court self-destruction, to invite the nemesis which was seen by a prescient few as likely to follow hubris on such a scale.

In Greek mythology, Nemesis is the goddess of retribution, who exacts the punishment of the gods for the human folly of overweening arrogance, or hubris. The English saying 'pride comes before a fall' reflects the common-place occurrence. History has no shortage of examples among the high and mighty, though 'nemesis' tends to be a more political than moral judgement. The meteoric rise of rulers, politicians, or domineering court favourites has so often been followed by an arrogance of power leading to an equally swift fall from grace. Usually, it afflicts an individual who, like a shooting star, flashes into prominence then fades rapidly into insignificance leaving the firmament essentially unchanged.

Very occasionally in history, the hubris of the individual reflects more profound forces in society and invites more far-reaching retribution. Napoleon, arising from humble origins amid revolutionary upheavals, taking power over the French state, placing the imperial crown upon his own head, conquering much of Europe, and ending in defeat and exile with his empire displaced, dismantled, and discredited, provides a telling example. But Napoleon did not destroy France. And important strands of his legacy remained intact. A national administrative structure, educational system, and legal code form three significant positive remnants. Not least, no moral opprobrium is attached to Napoleon. He can be, and often is, looked upon with pride and admiration by modern-day Frenchmen.

Hitler's legacy was of a totally different order. Uniquely in modern times – perhaps Attila the Hun and Ghengis Khan offer faint parallels in the distant past – this legacy was one of utter destruction. Not in architectural remains, in artistic creation, in political structures, or economic models, least of all in moral stature was there anything from Hitler's Reich to commend to future generations. Big improvements in motorization, aviation, and technology generally did, of course, take place – in part forced through the war. But these were occurring in all capitalist countries, most evidently in the USA, and would undoubtedly have taken place in Germany, too, without a Hitler. Most significantly, unlike Napoleon, Hitler left behind him an immense moral trauma, such that it is impossible even decades after his death (other than for a residue of fringe support) to look back upon the German dictator and his regime with approval or admiration – in fact with anything other than detestation and condemnation.

Even in the cases of Lenin, Stalin, Mao, Mussolini, or Franco the level of condemnation is not so unanimous or so morally freighted. Hitler, when he realized the war was irrevocably lost, looked to his place in history, at the highest seat in the pantheon of Germanic heroes. Instead, he stands uniquely as the quintessential hate-figure of the twentieth century. His place in history has certainly been secured – though in a way he had not anticipated: as the embodiment of modern political evil. However, evil is a theological or philosophical, rather than a historical, concept. To call Hitler evil may well be both true and morally satisfying. But it explains nothing. And unanimity in condemnation is even potentially an outright barrier to understanding and explanation. As I hope the following chapters make abundantly plain, I personally find Hitler a detestable figure and despise all that his regime stood for. But that condemnation scarcely helps me to understand why millions of German citizens who were mostly ordinary human beings, hardly innately evil, in general interested in the welfare and daily cares of themselves and their families, like ordinary people everywhere, and by no means wholly brainwashed or hypnotized by spellbinding propaganda or terrorized into submission by ruthless repression, would find so much of what Hitler stood for attractive – or would be prepared to fight to the bitter end in a terrible war against the mighty coalition of the world's most powerful nations arrayed against them. My task in this volume, as in the first part of this study, has been, therefore, not to engage in moral disquisitions on the problem of evil in a historical personality, but to try to explain the grip Hitler had on the society which eventually paid such a high price for its support.

For, ultimately, Hitler's nemesis as retribution for unparalleled hubris would prove to be not just a personal retribution, but the nemesis of the Germany which had created him. His own country would be left in ruins – much of Europe with it – and divided. What was formerly central Germany – 'Mitteldeutschland' – would experience for forty years the imposed values of the Soviet victor, while the western parts would eventually revive and thrive under a 'pax americana'. A new Austria, having experienced Anschluß under Hitler, would prove in its reconstituted independence to have lost once and for all any ambitions to be a part of Germany. The eastern provinces of the Reich would have gone forever – and along with them dreams of eastern conquest. The expulsion of the German ethnic minorities from those provinces would remove – if at a predictably harsh price – the irredentism which had plagued the inter-war years. The big landed estates in those provinces, basis of the influence of the Junker aristocracy, would also be swept away. The Wehrmacht, the final representation of German military might, would be discredited and disbanded. With it would go the state of Prussia, bulwark of the economic and political power of the Reich since Bismarck's day. Big industry, it is true, would survive sufficiently intact to rebuild with renewed strength and vigour – though it would now be increasingly integrated into a west-European and Americanized set of economic structures.

All this was to be the outcome of what the second part of this study attempts to grasp: how Hitler could exercise the absolute power which he had been permitted to acquire; how the most mighty in the land became bound still further to a highly personalized form of rule acclaimed by millions and exceptional in a modern state, until they were unable to extricate themselves from the will of one man who was taking them unerringly down the road to destruction; and how the citizens of this modern state became complicitous in genocidal war of a character hitherto unknown to mankind, resulting in state-sponsored mass murder on a scale never previously witnessed, continent-wide devastation, and the final ruination of their own country.

It is an awesome story of national as well as individual self-destruction, of the way a people and their representatives engineered their own catastrophe – as part of a calamitous destruction of European civilization. Though the outcome is known, how it came about perhaps deserves consideration once more. If this book contributes a little to deepen understanding, I will be well satisfied.

Ian Kershaw
Manchester/Sheffield, April 2000

ACKNOWLEDGEMENTS

It is with the greatest of pleasure that I use this opportunity to add to the expressions of thanks which I made on concluding the first volume of this study. All the debts of gratitude – institutional, intellectual, and personal – owed two years ago apply now in equal, or even greater, measure. I hope those mentioned there will accept on this occasion my renewed, most sincere thanks even if I do not list them all once more by name. In some cases, however, my gratitude has to be explicitly reinforced. And in other instances new debts have been incurred.

For help with archival material specifically related to this volume, I am most grateful to the Directors, archivists, and staff of: the Bayerisches Hauptstaatsarchiv; the Berlin Document Center; the Bibliothek für Zeitgeschichte (Stuttgart); Birmingham University Library; the Borthwick Institute (York); the Bundesarchiv, Berlin (formerly Koblenz); the Bundesarchiv/Militärarchiv, Potsdam (formerly Freiburg i.B.); the Gumberg Library, Duquesne University, Pittsburgh; the former Institut für Marxismus-Leninismus, Zentrales Parteiarchiv, East Berlin (GDR); the Library of Congress, Washington DC; the National Archives, Washington DC; Princeton University Library; the Public Record Office, London; the Franklin D. Roosevelt Library, Hyde Park, New York; the 'Special Archiv', Moscow; the Wiener Library, London; the former Zentrales Staatsarchiv, Potsdam (GDR); and, not least, to Frau Regnauer, Director of the Amtsgericht Laufen, who went beyond the call of duty in giving me access to post-war testimony of some of the key witnesses to the events in the bunker in 1945.

Above all, as with the previous volume, I have been able to depend upon the indispensable expert assistance from the renowned Institut für Zeitgeschichte in Munich. I would like once more to voice my warmest thanks to the Director, Professor Dr Horst Möller, to all colleagues and friends at the Institut, and, quite especially, to the library and archive staff who performed wonders in attending to my frequent and extensive requests. Singling out individuals is invidious, but I must nevertheless mention that Hermann Weiß, as with the first volume, gave most generously of his time and archival expertise. And with her unrivalled knowledge of the Goebbels diaries, Elke Fröhlich was of great help, not least in dealing with a query regarding one important but difficult point of transcription of Goebbels's awful handwriting.

Numerous friends and colleagues have supplied me at one time or another with valuable archival material or allowed me to see so far unpublished work they had written, as well as sharing views on evidence, scholarly literature, and points of interpretation. For their kindness and assistance in this regard, I am extremely grateful to: David Bankier, Omer Bartov, Yehuda Bauer, Richard Bessel, John Breuilly, Christopher Browning, Michael Burleigh, Chris Clarke, François Delpla, Richard Evans, Kent Fedorowich, Iring Fetscher, Conan Fischer, Gerald Fleming, Norbert Frei, Mary Fulbrook, Dick Geary, Hermann Graml, Otto Gritschneder, Lothar Gruchmann, Ulrich Herbert, Edouard Husson, Anton Joachimsthaler, Michael Kater, Otto Dov Kulka, Moshe Lewin, Peter Longerich, Dan Michmann, Stig Hornshøh-Møller, Martin Moll, Bob Moore, Stanislaw Nawrocki, Richard Overy, Alastair Parker, Karol Marian Pospieszalski, Fritz Redlich, Steven Sage, Stephen Salter, Karl Schleunes, Robert Service, Peter Stachura, Paul Stauffer, Jill Stephenson, Bernd Wegner, David Welch, Michael Wildt, Peter Witte, Hans Woller, and Jonathan Wright.

A special word of thanks is owing to Meir Michaelis for his repeated generosity in providing me with archival material drawn from his own researches. Gitta Sereny, likewise, not only offered friendly support, but also gave me access to valuable papers in her possession, related to her fine study of Albert Speer. A good friend, Laurence Rees, an exceptionally gifted producer from the BBC with whom I have had the pleasure and privilege of cooperating on the making of two television series connected with Nazism, and also Detlef Siebert and Tilman Remme, the able and knowledgeable heads of the research teams on the programmes, have helped greatly, both with probing inquiries and with material derived from the films they helped create. Two outstanding German historians of the Third Reich, whose own interpretations of Hitler differ sharply, have been of singular importance to this study. Eberhard Jäckel has given great support as well as expert advice throughout, and Hans Mommsen, friend of many years, has been unstinting in his help, generosity, and encouragement. Both have also made unpublished work available to me. Finally, I am most grateful to two British experts on Nazi Germany, Ted Harrison and Jeremy Noakes, for reading and commenting on the completed typescript (though, naturally, any errors remaining are my own responsibility). The particular inspiration I derived from Jeremy's work I was keen to acknowledge in the first volume, and am equally keen to underline on this occasion.

In a different way, I would like to express my thanks to David Smith, Director of the Borthwick Institute in York (where papers on Lord Halifax's meeting with Hitler sitting alongside archival deposits from medieval York-shire correspond to my intellectual schizophrenia as a historian of Nazi Germany who still dabbles in the history of monasticism in Yorkshire during the Middle Ages). Through the generous offer of his time and expertise, it has proved possible to see through the press our edition of the thirteenth-and fourteenth-century account-book of Bolton Priory without interrupting the work needed to complete this volume. Without David's help and input, this would not have been feasible.

Given the need to accommodate the writing of this book to my normal duties at the University of Sheffield, I have had to make notable demands on the patience of my editors, both at Penguin and abroad. I have been most fortunate in my editor at Penguin, Simon Winder, who has been an unfailing source of cheerful encouragement and optimism, as well as a perceptive reader and critic. I am extremely grateful to Simon, also for his advice on the photographic material and maps for the book, and to Cecilia Mackay for searching out and assembling the photographs. In this connection, I would also like to thank Joanne King of the BBC, and, for the notable assistance provided by the Bibliothek für Zeitgeschichte in Stuttgart, its Director, Dr Gerhard Hirschfeld (excellent scholar and long-standing friend), and Irina Renz, who supervises its extensive photographic collection. In preparing the lengthy text for the printers, I owe a large debt of gratitude, as with the first volume, to the expert copy-editing of Annie Lee, the superb indexing skills of Diana LeCore, and the great help and support of all the excellent publishing team at Penguin.

Outside Britain, I am hugely indebted to Don Lamm, my editor at Norton in the USA, who never ceased to keep me on my toes with his extensive knowledge, his many insights, and his inexhaustible queries. To Ulrich Volz and Michael Neher at Deutsche Verlags-Anstalt, and to my editors at Flammarion, Spektrum, and Ediciones Peninsula, who either did not panic or concealed their panic from me when delivery of a lengthy typescript still needing translation became delayed, I offer my gratitude for their patience and forbearance. And to the translators of the German, French, Dutch, and Spanish editions who worked miracles to enable the simultaneous appearance of the book in those languages, my warm thanks for their efforts are combined with my utmost admiration for their skills.

As with the previous volume, much of the checking of the extensive references provided in the notes had to be undertaken in a highly concentrated spell at the Institut für Zeitgeschichte in Munich. This time, thanks to Penguin and DVA, I could make use of invaluable assistance from Wenke Meteling (during a break in her own promising historical studies at the University of Tübingen); from my niece Charlotte Woodford (who took time out from her own doctoral research on early-modern German literature at Oxford University, was of great help also in subsequently locating a number of arcane works which I needed, and, not least, compiled so thoroughly and meticulously the List of Works Cited); and from my elder son, David, who, as two years earlier, generously took a week's holiday from his work in the airline business – somewhat to the amazement of his colleagues – to come to Munich to check references for me. I am deeply grateful to all three of them. Without them, I would have been quite unable to complete the work in time.

As with the preparation of the first volume, the incomparable Alexander von Humboldt-Stiftung in Bonn-Bad Godesberg offered to support the month's stay in Munich while the references were checked. I would like to express my sincere gratitude for this support, and for all the generosity from which I have been privileged to benefit since I first became a Fellow of the Alexander von Humboldt-Stiftung in the mid-1970s.

I would also like to thank most warmly a long-standing friend, Traude Spät, whose great skills as a language-teacher set me on the path many years ago to research on the darkest chapter in the history of her country, and who provided not only hospitality but also continuing encouragement of my work when, during my time in Munich, I was able to stay at her home.

In the flourishing Department of History at the University of Sheffield, I have at times had to rely more than I would have wished on the tolerance as well as good services of my colleagues and the patience of my students. I would like to thank them all most sincerely for their support, encouragement, and forbearance, and some colleagues quite especially for easing my path through taking on and efficiently carrying out sometimes quite onerous Departmental duties.

Most of all I have to thank Beverley Eaton, whose efficient help and encouragement in ten years of working as my secretary and personal assistant have been of immeasurable value in enabling the completion of this book in the face of many other pressing duties. More than anyone she has borne the brunt of the work – in the day-to-day running of a busy Department, in handling an extensive and mounting correspondence, and in coping with a variety of other tasks – which spilled over from my attempts to combine writing a biography of Hitler with being a professor at a university in a British system currently choking under the weight of its own bureaucracy. She has also been a constant source of support during the entire period of the writing of this work.

Finally, on home ground in Manchester, the Convenor and Fellows of SOFPIK, the club of which I am most proud to be a member, have shown their friendship and support for even longer than it has taken to write these two volumes on Hitler. I can never forget, though it is now many years ago, the sacrifices made by my mother and late father, who lived through Hitler's war, to give me and my sister, Anne, the priceless opportunity to study at university. And, meanwhile, not just Betty, David, and Stephen, but now also as the years roll on Katie, Becky, and – though she is not yet aware of it – Sophie have lived in the shadow of a biography of Hitler for too long. I hope we can soon move out of this shadow and into the sunlight again. But I would like to thank them all as much as words can express for the different ways in which they have contributed to the making of this work.

I.K.

April 2000

Legend:
- Territory lost by Germany
- Territory lost by USSR
- Austria-Hungary in 1914
- Post First World War Boundaries

NORWAY
Oslo
SWEDEN
Stockholm
FINLAND
Helsinki
Leningrad
Tallinn
ESTONIA
DENMARK
Copenhagen
Riga
LATVIA
SOVIET
UNION
Danzig (League of Nations Free City)
Memel
LITHUANIA
Kaunas (Kovno)
Vilna
Polish Corridor
EAST PRUSSIA
Hamburg
Berlin
Warsaw
Brest-Litovsk
GERMANY
POLAND
Kiev
Cologne
Weimar
SILESIA
Prague
Teschen
GALICIA
CZECHOSLOVAKIA
LORRAINE
ALSACE
Munich
Vienna
BESSARABIA
SWITZ-ERLAND
AUSTRIA
Budapest
HUNGARY
TRAN-SYLVANIA
ROMANIA
Locarno
TRENTINO
Trieste
Fiume
ITALY
Bucharest
DOBRUJA
Belgrade
CORSICA (France)
YUGOSLAVIA
MONTE-NEGRO
Sofia
BULGARIA
Rome
ALBANIA

1. The legacy of the First World War.

3. The Western offensive, 1940: the Sichelschnitt attack.

DENMARK

Schleswig-
Holstein

Mecklenburg

Hamburg
Hamburg

Weser-Ems

East
Hanover

NETHERLANDS

Magdeburg-
Anhalt

North
Westphalia

South
Hanover-
Brunswick

Essen
Cologne
Düsseldorf

South
Westphalia

Halle-
Merseburg

BELGIUM

Cologne-
Aachen
Koblenz

Kurhessen

Thuringia

Hesse-
Nassau

Main-
Franconia

Moselland

Westmark

Franconia

Bayerische
Ostmark

FRANCE

Wurttemberg-
Hohenzollern

Baden

Swabia

Munich

Munich-
Upper Bavaria

SWITZERLAND

Tirol-
Vorarlberg

Salzburg

ITALY

Occupied territory

German satellite state

4. The German Reich of 1942: the Nazi Party Gaue.

Konigsberg

Danzig-
West Prussia

East Prussia

Pomerania

Berlin

Mark
Brandenburg

Wartheland

Warsaw

erlin

Lower Silesia

P O L A N D

Dresden

Saxony

Upper
Silesia

Protectorate of
Bohemia and
Moravia

Lower Danube

S L O V A K I A

Upper
Danube

Vienna

Vienna

Styria

H U N G A R Y

Carinthia

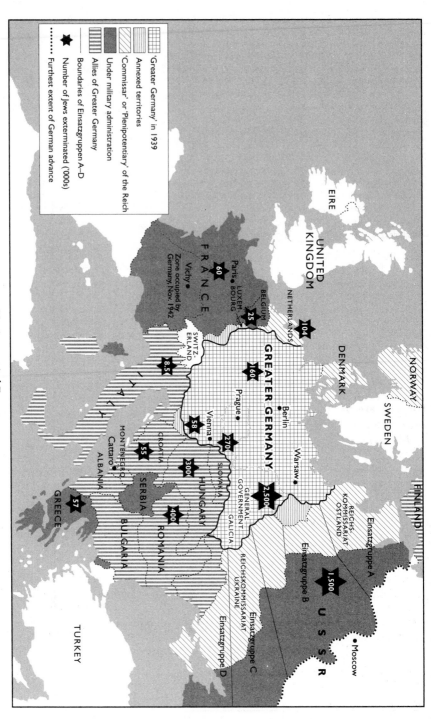

5. Nazi occupied Europe.

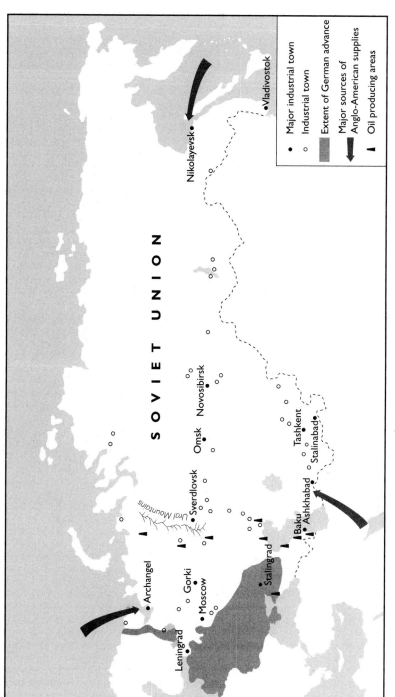

6. Limits of the German occupation of the USSR.

7. The Western and Eastern fronts, 1944–5.

SWEDEN

Tallinn •

Riga •

28 July 1944

Danzig •

Minsk •

15 December 1944

R. Bug

rlin •

R. Oder

Warsaw •

SOVIET UNION

Dresden •

Breslau •

Lublin •

Kiev •

GREATER

Russian forces,
19 April 1945

Prague •

GERMANY

22 June 1944

SLOVAKIA

Vienna •

15 December 1944

Budapest •

HUNGARY

15 September 1944

Zagreb •

ROMANIA

Belgrade •

Bucharest •

R. Danube

YUGOSLAVIA

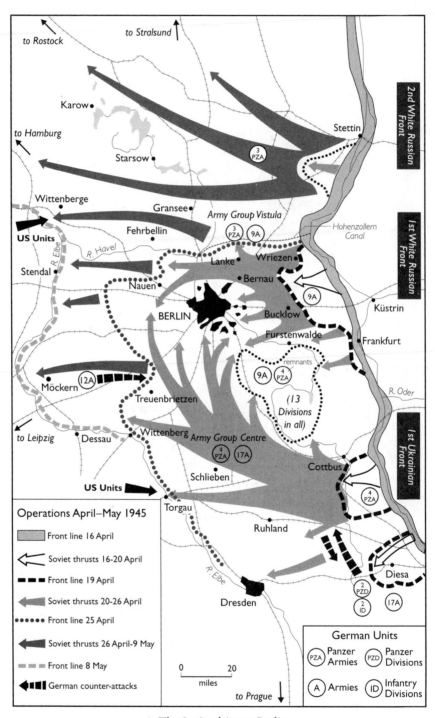

to Rostock
to Stralsund
2nd White Russian Front
Karow
Stettin
to Hamburg
Starsow
Wittenberge
Gransee
Army Group Vistula
Hohenzollern Canal
Fehrbellin
3 PZA
9A
1st White Russian Front
R. Havel
Lanke
Wriezen
US Units
R. Elbe
Stendal
Nauen
Bernau
9A
Küstrin
BERLIN
Bucklow
Furstenwalde
Frankfurt
remnants
9A
4 PZA
R. Oder
Möckern
12A
(13 Divisions in all)
Treuenbrietzen
to Leipzig
Dessau
Wittenberg
Army Group Centre
4 PZA
17A
Cottbus
1st Ukrainian Front
Schlieben
4 PZA
US Units
Torgau
Ruhland
Diesa

Operations April–May 1945

	Front line 16 April
	Soviet thrusts 16–20 April
	Front line 19 April
	Soviet thrusts 20–26 April
	Front line 25 April
	Soviet thrusts 26 April–9 May
	Front line 8 May
	German counter-attacks

R. Elbe

Dresden

2 PZD
2 ID
17A

0   20
miles

to Prague

German Units

| PZA Panzer Armies | PZD Panzer Divisions |
| A Armies | ID Infantry Divisions |

8. The Soviet drive to Berlin.

1936: HITLER TRIUMPHANT

'That this new deed of Hitler is another milestone on the way to the hell's jaws of destruction seems hardly to have entered the consciousness of anyone.'

'Germany Report' of the Sopade, April 1936

I

'After three years, I believe that, with the present day, the struggle for German equal rights can be regarded as closed.' The day was 7 March 1936. The words were those of Hitler addressing the Reichstag as German troops, defying the western democracies, crossed into the demilitarized Rhineland. 'Great are the successes which Providence has let me attain for our Fatherland in these three years,' Hitler continued. 'In all areas of our national, political, and economic life, our position has been improved . . . In these three years, Germany has regained its honour, found belief again, overcome its greatest economic distress and finally ushered in a new cultural ascent.' In this paean to his own 'achievements', Hitler also explicitly stated that 'we have no territorial claims to make in Europe'. He ended with an appeal – received to rapturous acclaim – to support him in new 'elections' (though only one party, the Nazi Party, was standing), set for 29 March.[1] The outcome of these 'elections' was a vote of 98.9 per cent backing Hitler. But however 'massaged' the figures had been, whatever the combined weight of propaganda and coercion behind them, there can be no doubt that the overwhelming mass of the German people in March 1936 applauded Hitler's recovery of German sovereignty in the Rhineland (as they had his earlier steps in throwing off the shackles of Versailles). It was a major triumph for Hitler, both externally and internally. It was the culminating point of the first phase of his dictatorship.

Hitler's triumph also marked the plainest demonstration of the weakness of France and Great Britain, the dominant powers in Europe since the First World War. Hitler had broken with impunity the treaties of Versailles and Locarno, the main props of the post-war peace-settlement. And he had signalled Germany's reassertiveness and new importance in international affairs.

Within Germany, by this point, Hitler's power was absolute. The largest, most modern, and most thrusting nation-state in central Europe lay at his feet, bound to the 'charismatic' politics of 'national salvation'. His position as Dictator was unchallenged. No serious threat of opposition faced him.

The mood of national exhilaration whipped up by the Rhineland spectacular was, it is true, of its nature short-lived. The worries and complaints of daily life returned soon enough. Worker discontent about low wages and poor work conditions, farmer resentment at the 'coercive economy' of the Food Estate, the grumbling of small tradesmen about economic difficulties, and ubiquitous consumer dissatisfaction over prices continued unabated. The behaviour and corruption of party functionaries was as much a source of grievance as ever. And in Catholic areas, where the 'Church struggle' had intensified, the party's attacks on the Church's practices and institutions, the assault on denominational schooling, and the harassing of clergy (including highly publicized trials of members of religious orders for alleged foreign-currency smuggling and sexual impropriety) left the mood extraordinarily sour. But it would be as well not to overestimate the significance of the discontent. None of it was translated into political opposition likely to cause serious trouble to the regime.

Oppositional forces on the Left, the Communists and Socialists, were crushed, cowed, and powerless – dismayed at the supine acquiescence of the western democracies as Hitler continued to upturn the post-war international order. The propaganda image of a statesman of extraordinary boldness and political genius seemed as a consequence of weakness of the western powers to match reality in the eyes of millions. Under threat of draconian recrimination, the perilous illegal work of undercover resistance had continued, even revived, for a brief period in late 1935 and early 1936 as foodstuff shortages led to rising unrest in industrial areas, and was never halted. But following a huge onslaught by the Gestapo to crush all indications of a short-lived Communist revival, any threat of resistance from below by illegal organizations was effectively ruled out.[2] Resistance cells, especially those of the Communists, were constant prey to Gestapo informers, and were as a result frequently penetrated, the members arrested and interned in prisons or concentration camps. It has been estimated that around one in two of the 300,000 Communist Party members of 1932 was imprisoned at some stage during the Third Reich – a statistic of unrelenting attritional repression.[3] Even so, new cells invariably sprang up. Those risking liberty, even life, showed great courage. But they lacked any semblance of power or influence, had no contacts in high places, and consequently lacked all opportunity to overthrow the regime. By this time, they could pose no real threat to Hitler. Opposition endangering his dictatorship – leaving aside the unpredictable actions of an outsider acting alone, as would occur in 1939 – could now in practice only come from within the regime itself.[4]

Meanwhile, the pillars of the regime – armed forces, Party, industry, civil service – were loyal in their support.

The national-conservative élites who had helped Hitler into power in 1933, imagining that they would be able to control and manipulate him, had largely swallowed their differences. Disquiet in such circles had been marked especially during the gathering internal crisis of spring and summer 1934, which had been ended by the massacre of the stormtroopers' leadership (and the liquidation of numerous other genuine or presumed opponents) in the 'Night of the Long Knives' on 30 June 1934. But whatever their continuing misgivings about anti-capitalistic tendencies in the Party, the high-handed behaviour of Party bosses, attacks on the Christian Churches, the lawlessness of Party formations, and other disquieting aspects of the regime, the conservative élites had by early 1936 not distanced themselves from Hitler in any serious fashion.

The armed forces, though the officer corps often turned up their noses at the vulgar upstarts now running the country, had fewer grounds than most for dissatisfaction. The tensions with the SA which had preoccupied the military leaders in the early months of the regime were now long past. The political murder of two generals, the former Reich Chancellor Kurt von Schleicher and Major-General Ferdinand von Bredow, in the 'Night of the Long Knives' had seemed a small price to pay for removing the scourge of SA leader Ernst Röhm and his associates. Meanwhile, military leaders had seen their aim of rebuilding a powerful Wehrmacht, cherished even in the dark days of the 1920s, fully backed.[5] The army had been delighted when general conscription, despite the prohibition under the Versailles Treaty, had been reintroduced (as the basis of a greatly expanded thirty-six-division peacetime army) in March 1935. In line with Hitler's promise in February 1933 'that for the next 4–5 years the main principle must be: everything for the armed forces',[6] rearmament was now rapidly gathering pace. The existence of the Luftwaffe – a further flouting of Versailles – had been announced, without recrimination, in March 1935. And, remarkably, Great Britain had proved a willing accomplice in the undermining of Versailles in its willingness in June 1935 to conclude a naval treaty with the Reich allowing Germany to attain 35 per cent of the strength of the British Navy. With the remilitarization of the Rhineland Hitler had then accomplished a cherished desire of the military leadership long before they had contemplated such a move being possible. He was doing all that the leaders of the armed forces wanted him to do – and more. There could be few grounds for complaint.

Leaders of big business, though often harbouring private concerns about current difficulties and looming future problems for the economy, were, for their part, grateful to Hitler for the destruction of the left-wing parties and trade unions. They were again 'masters in their house' in their dealings with their work-force. And the road to massively increased profits and dividends was wide open. Even where Party interference was criticized, problems of export trade or shortage of raw materials were raised, or worries about the direction of the economy voiced, no industrialist advocated, even in private, a return to the 'bad' old democratic days of the Weimar Republic.

Some individuals from within the national-conservative élite groups – mainly in the leadership of the army and the upper echelons of the state bureaucracy – would some two years later at first gradually and falteringly begin to feel their way towards fundamental opposition to the Nazi regime. But at this time, they still saw their own interests, and what they took to be the national interest, served by the apparently successful policies of national assertiveness and reconstruction embodied in the figure of Hitler.

Only the intensified 'Church Struggle', causing heightened friction between clergy and churchgoers on the one side and Party activists on the other, cast a substantial shadow, notably in Catholic rural districts where the influence of the clergy remained unbroken, over what amounted otherwise to an extensive prevailing consensus (in part, of course, manufactured through a mixture of repression and propaganda). But the stance of both major Christian denominations was riddled with ambivalence. Though still wielding considerable influence over the churchgoing population, the clergy felt they had to tread warily in public pronouncements, particularly where religious matters were not directly concerned. In some ways, they were led by public opinion more than they were willing or able to lead it. They had to take account of the fact that Hitler's national 'successes', most of all his triumph in remilitarizing the Rhineland, were massively popular even among the same members of their flocks who harshly criticized the Nazi attacks on the Churches.

The unrest stirred up by the 'Church Struggle' was extensive. But it was largely compartmentalized. It seldom equated with fundamental rejection of the regime, or with any commitment to active and outright political opposition. Fierce defence of traditional observances, customs, and practices against Nazi chicanery was compatible with support for Hitler personally, with approval for his assault on the Left, with applause for his national 'triumphs', with readiness to accept his discriminatory measures against Jews, with most measures, in fact, which did not directly impinge on Church affairs. Catholic bishops had, in the very first weeks of Hitler's chancellorship, exhorted their charges to obedience to the new regime.[7] And even at the height of the 'Church Struggle', they publicly endorsed its stance against 'atheistic' Bolshevism and affirmed their loyalty to Hitler.[8] The brutality of the concentration camps, the murder in 1934 of the SA leaders, and the mounting discrimination against the Jews had brought no official protests or opposition. Similarly in a Protestant Church divided within itself, unease, criticism, or dissent over Nazi high-handedness towards the Church and interference in its affairs, practices, structures, and doctrine coexisted – apart from the examples of a few exceptional individuals – with official avowals of loyalty and a great deal of genuine approval for what Hitler was doing.

Underpinning Hitler's unchallenged authority in spring 1936 was the adulation of the masses. Large sections of the population simply idolized him. Even his opponents acknowledged this. 'What a fellow, Hitler. He had the courage to risk something,' was a sentiment frequently recorded at the time by the underground socialist opposition. 'The spirit of Versailles is hated by all Germans. Hitler has now torn up this accursed treaty and thrown it at the feet of the French,' was the reason given for the upsurge of support for the Dictator even among those who up to then had been less than enthusiastic about him.[9] In 1936, the German people – at any rate the vast majority of them – revelled in the national pride that Hitler (almost single-handedly, it often seemed, in the relentless trumpetings of effusive propaganda) had restored to the country.

The backing of a huge mass movement, the mainstay of his plebiscitary support, guaranteed that the flow of adulation was never stemmed. But the support for Hitler was genuine enough, and massive in extent. Most

Germans, whatever their grumbles, were at least in some respects Hitler supporters by summer 1936. Unquestionably, the foreign-policy triumphs had united the overwhelming majority of the population behind his leadership. Admiration for the Führer was widespread. Indeed, at the level of humdrum daily life, too, many were prepared to credit Hitler with bringing about a change in Germany that seemed to them little short of miraculous. For most of those who did not belong to a persecuted minority, remain firm adherents of the suppressed Social Democrats or Communists, or feel wholly alienated by the attacks on the Churches, things seemed incomparably better than they had been when Hitler took over. Unemployment, far from increasing again (as the Jeremiahs had predicted), had practically been wiped out. Modestly, but noticeably, living standards were beginning to improve. More consumer goods were becoming available. The 'people's radio' (*Volksempfänger*) was spreading to more and more households.[10] Leisure pursuits, entertainment, and minor forms of tourism were expanding. The cinemas and dance-halls were full. And even if the much-trumpeted 'glamour' trips to Madeira or Norway on cruise-ships run by 'Strength Through Joy' (the leisure organization of the German Labour Front) remained the preserve of the privileged and made little real dent on class divisions, far more people were able to take advantage of days out in the country or visits to theatres and concerts.[11] For many, even looking back long after the war, these were the 'good times'.[12]

In a mere three years, Hitler appeared to have rescued Germany from the miseries and divisions of Weimar democracy, and to have paved the way for a grandiose future for the German people. The demagogue and political firebrand had apparently been transformed into a statesman and national leader of a stature to match that of Bismarck. That the the national revival had been accompanied by rigid authoritarianism, loss of civil rights, brutal repression of the Left, and intensifying discrimination against Jews and others thought unfit to belong to the 'national community' was seen by most as at least a price worth paying – by many as positively welcome.

Few at this stage had the foresight to imagine what would come – that Germany's new international standing in spring 1936 would prove the prelude to boundless expansion, world war bringing slaughter on an immeasurable scale, unparalleled genocide, and the eventual destruction of the Reich itself. 'That this new deed of Hitler is another milestone on the way to the hell's jaws of destruction,' the same perceptive report of the exiled Social Democratic movement added, 'seems hardly to have entered the consciousness of anyone.'[13]

II

For most dictators, the acquisition of unrivalled power over the state would have been enough. For Hitler, this was no end in itself. In his thinking, power served a twin ideological purpose: destroying the Jews – for him, Germany's mortal enemy; and, through their destruction, acquiring mastery over the entire continent of Europe – a platform for subsequent world dominance. Both interlocking aims, resting on a 'world-view' that saw racial struggle and survival of the fittest as the key determinants in human history, had been central to his thinking since the 1920s. However uncharted the route to attaining them, these basic ideas, once formed, never left him.

The obsessiveness and tenacity with which he held to these fixed ideas were part of Hitler's unique role in steering Germany, Europe, and the world to disaster. However, relatively few of the millions of followers attracted to Nazism on its road to power saw matters precisely as Hitler did, or were drawn by fanatical adherence to the fixed points of the personal 'world-view' that constituted his own prime ideological driving-force.[14] The growing appeal of Hitler as an alternative to Weimar democracy rested to a far greater extent on the forcefulness of his uncompromising, frontal assault on a visibly failing political system undermined in high places and increasingly haemorrhaging mass support. During his rise to power, his central ideological tenets had been embedded within the general, all-embracing armoury of hate-filled tirades against the Weimar 'system' and within the appealing counter-image he conjured up of national rebirth once the 'criminals' who had instigated defeat and revolution, with catastophic consequences, had been destroyed. His success as a demagogue lay in his ability to say what the disaffected masses wanted to hear, to speak their language – to capture and exploit a psychology of despair and invest it with new hope for a phoenix-like resurgence of the nation. He was able as no one else to give voice to popular hatreds, resentments, hopes, and expectations. He spoke more stridently, more vehemently, more expressively and appealingly than any of those with a similar ideological message. He was the mouthpiece of the nationalist masses at a decisive time of all-embracing national crisis.

And in showing that he could galvanize the nationalist masses as no one else could, he made himself an increasingly attractive proposition to those with power and influence, who saw him and his rapidly expanding Movement as an indispensable weapon in the fight against 'Marxism' (code not just for attacks on the Communists, but on the Social Democrats, the trade unions, and the democratic system itself), which the conservative élites had done everything possible to undermine. Through their help, in the final stage of the collapse of the Weimar Republic, Hitler was at last given what he had long striven for: control over the German state. Their fatal error had been to think that they could control Hitler. Too late, they discovered how disastrously they had underestimated him.

By the time he was levered into power, the 'redemptive' politics which Hitler preached – the overturning of the defeat and revolution of 1918 at their heart – had won the support of over 13 million Germans, among them an activist base of well over a million members of the various branches of the Nazi Movement. Hitler embodied their expectations of national salvation. The pseudo-religious strains of the cult built up around him – in an era when popular piety was still strong – had been able to portray him as a secular 'redeemer'. A lost war, national humiliation, profound economic and social misery, lack of faith in democratic institutions and politicians, and readiness to look to a 'strong man' able to overcome through force the apparently insurmountable acute political chasms prevailing in a comprehensive state crisis, had all contributed to drawing large sections of the masses towards seductive slogans of national salvation.

But not only the politically naïve had been attracted. The deep cultural pessimism widespread in neo-conservative and intellectual circles could also find appeal in the idea of 'national rebirth', however much the vulgarity of Hitler and his followers might be disparaged. Already before the First World War, the sense of unstoppable cultural decline – often directly coupled with increasingly fashionable views on the allegedly inexorable growth of racial impurity – was gathering pace.[15] In the aftermath of the war, the mood of cultural despair gripped ever more tightly among conservative intellectuals. Oswald Spengler's Decline of the West, with its melancholy prognosis of unstoppable cultural decay, was highly influential.[16] Abstract art and modern theatre could be vilified as 'Jewish' and not truly German. Syncopated hot jazz – labelled 'nigger music' – seemed to epitomize the inevitable coming Americanization of not only music, but all walks of life, in the land of Bach and Beethoven.[17]

Germany's cultural descent seemed mirrored in politics. Where only decades earlier Bismarck had bestridden the political stage as a giant, the country's representatives now appeared reduced to squabbling pygmies, the irredeemably divided Reichstag a reflection of an irredeemably divided Germany – irredeemable, that is, unless a new national hero creating (if need be by force) new unity should emerge. Hopes could be invested only in the vision of such a hero – warrior, statesman, and high priest rolled into one – who would arise from the ashes of national humiliation and post-war misery to restore national pride and greatness.[18] The seeds of subsequent intellectual backing for Hitler and his Movement were fertilized in such soil – however distant reality proved to be from the ideal.

The shrill antisemitism of the Nazis was no barrier to such support. The Jews – less than 1 per cent of the population, the vast majority more than anxious to be seen as good, patriotic German citizens – had few friends. Even those who might criticize overt Nazi violence and the frequent outrages which the Jewish community had to suffer during the Weimar Republic were often infected by some form of resentment, envy, or suspicion of the Jews. Though relatively few were drawn to the outright violence against Jews (which was nonetheless commonplace in Weimar Germany), latent or passive antisemitism was widespread.[19] As incessant Nazi agitation shored up layers of animosity already intensified by the search for scapegoats for a lost war, revolution, mounting political crisis, and deep social misery, prejudice intensified. Allegations that Jews were disproportionately wealthy, harmfully dominant in the economy, and unhealthily influential in the cultural sphere proliferated. The sense, in other words, that Jews were different (however much they strove to prove the opposite) and were responsible for Germany's ills was spreading fast even before Hitler took power.

Once he had done so, the anti-Jewish premises of Nazism were able to build on such negative feelings, permeate the entire regime and, magnified by incessant propaganda, touch all levels of society. The intention of 'removing' the Jews from Germany, as a basis of national renewal resting upon racial 'purification', was therefore guaranteed to prompt initiatives from every corner of the regime. And among the many who felt unease or disquiet at the ferocity of antisemitism in the new state, widespread latent dislike of Jews and moral indifference to discrimination offered no barriers to spiralling persecution.

The restraining of open aggression towards the Jews in the Olympic year of 1936 was regarded by activists as a mere temporary device, and simply kept the pressure for further discriminatory measures simmering below the surface. Social resentment, malice, and greed, as well as outright hatred and ideological correctness made sure the screw of persecution did not loosen. By late 1937 the 'aryanization' of the economy was starting to advance rapidly. By 1938, open assaults on the Jewish community were again commonplace. The internal dynamics of an ideologically driven police force with its own agenda, on the look-out for new racial target-groups, searching for fresh possibilities of 'solving the Jewish Question', additionally meant that radicalism in the fight against the 'racial enemy' mounted, rather than subsided, in the 'quiet years' of 1936 and 1937.

Gradually, then, the 'removal of the Jews', which Hitler as early as 1919 had advanced as the necessary aim of a national government, began to seem like a realizable aim.[20]

In the other sphere most closely linked with Hitler's own ideological obsessions, the expansion of Germany's borders, radicalizing forces were also at work. If Hitler was the chief, most single-minded, and most unscrupulous exponent of the German expansionist drive, the dream of mastery in Europe was far from his dream alone. Rooted in certain strains of German imperialist ideology,[21] it had been embedded as a key component in Hitler's thinking by the mid-1920s at the latest. It had then gained momentum as the Nazi Movement itself had gained momentum and swollen massively in size in the early 1930s. It had formed part of the great 'mission' of 'national redemption' embodied in Hitler's utopian 'vision' of a glorious German future. However unreal acquisition of 'living space' in eastern Europe at the expense of the Soviet Union 'by the sword' (as Hitler had repeatedly stated in the later 1920s) might have seemed in conditions of unprecedented impoverishment and enfeeblement of the German state in the early 1930s, the vaguely expressed Hitlerian 'vision' of mastery in Europe had the great advantage that it could encompass (while not being identical with) long-held and differing conceptions of the revival of German dominance close to the hearts of powerful groups within the leadership of the army, in the upper echelons of the Foreign Ministry, in some prominent business circles, and among many intellectuals. As self-confidence returned during the first years of the Hitler dictatorship, as the economy recovered, as rearmament began to gather pace, and as the regime swept from one diplomatic triumph to another, the varying ideas of German expansion and dominance began gradually to congeal and to seem increasingly realistic.

Expansion, moreover, began to appear not just ideologically desirable as the fulfilment of the reborn nation, the culmination of the 'national salvation' which Hitler had preached; it was more and more seen to be desirable – even necessary – on economic and military grounds.

For businessmen, Hitler's idea of 'living space' blended easily into their notions of a 'greater economic sphere' (*Großraumwirtschaft*), even if they favoured expansion to recover traditional German dominance in south-eastern Europe rather than looking to the brutal colonization of Russia. As thoughts of economic recovery turned to thoughts of economic domination, and as the pressures of an increasingly armaments-orientated economy laid bare the mounting shortages of labour and raw materials, the attractiveness of expansion became all the more evident. The economic balancing-act of accommodating the demands of both consumer and armaments spending urgently needed a solution. The eventual setting of priorities in favour of an armaments economy effectively set the points for expansion. Indeed, for those sections of the economy aligned to armaments production, fervent backing for the regime's expansionist programme was the certain route to soaring profits.

For the military, forced to bide its time as long as Germany had been shackled by the terms of the Versailles Treaty and the burden of reparations imposed on the country after the First World War (and effectively written off in 1932), the aim of restoring the army to its former stature in order to regain the lost territories and to establish dominance in central Europe was long-standing.[22] The speed of the rebuilding of the armed forces after 1933 and the evident reluctance and inability of the western democracies to counter it now produced their own momentum. Not just to Hitler, but to some military leaders, too, it seemed opportune to take advantage of circumstances which could rapidly become less favourable once Britain and France entered an arms race to counter Germany's rearmament. The international instability following the break-up of the post-Versailles order, the weakness of the western democracies, and the incipient arms-race all suggested that the time was more propitious than it might ever be again to establish Germany's dominant role on the European continent. It was an argument that Hitler could often deploy with effect when addressing his generals. The proximity of potentially hostile neighbours in Poland and Czechoslovakia, prospects of conflict at some future point with France and Britain, and, above all, the fears – whatever the perception of current weakness – of Bolshevism to the east all added to the allure of expansionism and, in so doing, helped to tie the military to Hitler and to his own dreams of domination in Europe.

In such ways, Hitler's fixed points of ideology – 'removal of the Jews' and preparations for a future titanic struggle to attain 'living-space' – acted as such broad and compelling long-term goals that they could easily embrace the differing interests of those agencies which formed the vital pillars of the Nazi regime. As a result, the instruments of a highly modern state – bureaucracy, economy, and, not least, army – in the heart of Europe increasingly bound themselves to Hitler's 'charismatic' authority, to the politics of national salvation and the dream of European mastery embodied in the personalized 'vision' and power of one man. Hitler's essential, unchanging, distant goals had inexorably become the driving-force of the entire Nazi regime, constituting the framework for the extraordinary energy and dynamism that permeated the entire system of rule. It was a dynamism which knew no terminal point of domination, no moment where power-lust could be satiated, where untrammelled aggression could lapse into mere oppressive authoritarianism.

The 'good times' which the first three years of Hitler's dictatorship had seemingly brought to Germany – economic revitalization, order, prospects of prosperity, restored national pride – could not last indefinitely. They were built on sand. They rested on an illusion that stability and 'normality' were within reach. In reality, the Third Reich was incapable of settling into 'normality'. This was not simply a matter of Hitler's personality and ideological drive – though these should not be underestimated. His temperament, restless energy, gambler's instinctive readiness to take risks to retain the initiative, were all enhanced through the gain in confidence that his triumphs in 1935 and 1936 had brought him. His expanding messianism fed itself on the drug of mass adulation and the sycophancy of almost all in this company. His sense that time was against him, the impatience to act, were heightened by the growing belief that he might not have much longer to live. But beyond these facets of Hitler's personality, more impersonal forces were at work – pressures unleashed and driven on by the chiliastic goals represented by Hitler. A combination of both personal and impersonal driving-forces ensured that in the 'quiet' two years between the march into the Rhineland and the march into Austria the ideological dynamism of the regime not only did not subside but intensified, that the spiral of radicalization kept turning upwards.

The triumph of 1936, which had given Hitler's own self-confidence such a huge boost, proved in this way not an end but a beginning. Most dictators would have been content to relish such a momentous triumph – and to draw the line. For Hitler, the remilitarization of the Rhineland was merely an important stepping-stone in the quest for mastery in Europe. The months that followed paved the way for the sharp radicalization of all aspects of the regime that became noticeable from late 1937 onwards, and which would take Germany and Europe two years later into a second cataclysmic conflagration.

I

CEASELESS RADICALIZATION

'The showdown with Bolshevism is coming. Then we want to be prepared. The army is now completely won over by us. Führer untouchable . . . Dominance in Europe for us is as good as certain. Just let no chance pass by. Therefore rearm.'

'The Jews must get out of Germany, yes out of the whole of Europe. That will still take some time. But it will and must happen. The Führer is firmly decided on it.'

Goebbels's diary entries of 15 November 1936 and
30 November 1937, indicating Hitler's views

I

Hitler was more convinced than ever, following the Rhineland triumph, that he was walking with destiny, guided by the hand of Providence. The plebiscite of 29 March 1936 was both at home and outside Germany a demonstration of Hitler's enhanced strength. He could act with new confidence. During the summer, the international alignments that would crystallize over the next three years began to form. The balance of power in Europe had unmistakably shifted.[1]

Characteristically, Hitler's first step after his 'election' success was to present a 'peace plan' – generous in his own eyes – to his coveted allies, the British. On 1 April, his special envoy in London, Joachim von Ribbentrop, the former champagne salesman who had become his most trusted adviser in foreign affairs, passed on the offer Hitler had drafted the previous day to the British government. It included a four-month moratorium on any troop reinforcements in the Rhineland, together with an expression of willingness to participate in international talks aimed at a twenty-five-year peace pact, restricting production of the heaviest forms of artillery alongside bans on the bombing of civilian targets and usage of poison-gas, chemical, or incendiary bombs.[2] The seemingly reasonable 'offer' had arisen from the serious diplomatic upheaval following the German march into the Rhineland, when belated French pressure for action against Germany had prompted British attempts to gain a commitment from Hitler to refrain from any increase in troop numbers on the Rhine and from fortifying the region.[3] Naturally, on these concrete points Hitler had made no concessions. The reply of 6 May 1936 from the British Foreign Secretary, Anthony

Eden, left the door open for improved relations through new international agreements to replace the now defunct Locarno settlement of 1925. But for all its diplomatic language, the reply was essentially negative. Eden informed the German Foreign Minister, Konstantin Freiherr von Neurath, that 'His Majesty's Government regret that the German Government have not been able to make a more substantial contribution towards the re-establishment of the confidence which is such an essential preliminary to the wide negotiations which they both have in view.'⁴ With this, the British government's distrust of Hitler was plain. It would sit ever more uneasily alongside the determination, at practically any cost, to prevent Britain once more being embroiled in war.⁵ As Stanley Baldwin, the British Prime Minister, had put it at the end of April: 'With two lunatics like Mussolini and Hitler you can never be sure of anything. But I am determined to keep the country out of war.'⁶

If Hitler was to encounter increased difficulties in attaining his desired alliance with Great Britain, his Rhineland triumph opened up new opportunities elsewhere. Italy, taken up since the previous autumn with the repercussions of the invasion of Abyssinia, now heading to a belatedly victorious conclusion for Mussolini, was more than content to see the attention of the western powers diverted by the remilitarization of the Rhineland. More than that: the diplomatic fall-out from the invasion of Abyssinia had forged better relations between Italy and Germany. As Mussolini had signalled earlier in the year, Italy's interest in protecting Austria from German inroads had sharply diminished in return for Germany's support in the Abyssinian conflict. The way was opening for the eventual emergence of the Berlin–Rome 'axis' towards the end of the year. Meanwhile, the inevitable consequence of the removal of any protection from Italy was that Austria was forced to acknowledge – as would be the case in a one-sided agreement in July – that the country had now fallen within Germany's orbit.

Within a fortnight of the Austrian agreement, the diplomatic fault-lines in Europe would widen still further with Hitler's decision to commit Germany to intervention in what would rapidly emerge as the Spanish Civil War – a baleful prelude to the catastrophe soon to engulf the whole of Europe. To shrewd observers, it was becoming clear: Hitler's Rhineland coup had been the catalyst to a major power-shift in Europe; Germany's ascendancy was an unpredictable and highly destabilizing element in the international order; the odds against a new European war in the foreseeable future had markedly shortened.

To the German public, Hitler once more professed himself a man of peace, cleverly insinuating who was to blame for the gathering storm-clouds of war. Speaking to a vast audience in the Berlin Lustgarten (a huge square in the city centre) on 1 May – once an international day of celebration of labouring people, now redubbed 'National Labour Day' – he posed the rhetorical question: 'I ask myself,' he declared, 'who are then these elements who wish to have no rest, no peace, and no understanding, who must continually agitate and sow mistrust? Who are they actually?' Immediately picking up the implication, the crowd bayed: 'The Jews.' Hitler began again: 'I know . . . ,' and was interrupted by cheering that lasted for several minutes. When at last he was able to continue, he picked up his sentence, though – the desired effect achieved – now in quite different vein: 'I know it is not the millions who would have to take up weapons if the intentions of these agitators were to succeed. Those are not the ones . . .'[7]

The summer of 1936 was, however, as Hitler knew only too well, no time to stir up a new antisemitic campaign. In August, the Olympic Games were due to be staged in Berlin. Sport would be turned into a vehicle of nationalist politics and propaganda as never before. Nazi aesthetics of power would never have a wider audience. With the eyes of the world on Berlin, it was an opportunity not to be missed to present the new Germany's best face to its hundreds of thousands of visitors from across the globe. No expense or effort had been spared in this cause. The positive image could not be endangered by putting the 'dark' side of the regime on view. Open anti-Jewish violence, such as had punctuated the previous summer, could not be permitted. With some difficulties, antisemitism was kept under wraps. Manifestations thought distasteful for foreign visitors, such as anti-Jewish notices – 'Jews not wanted here', and other vicious formulations – at the roadside at the entry to towns and villages, had already been removed on Hitler's orders at the insistence of Count Henri Baillet-Latour, the Belgian President of the International Olympic Committee, before the commencement the previous February of the Winter Olympics in the Bavarian alpine resort of Garmisch-Partenkirchen.[8] The antisemitic zealots in the Party had temporarily to be reined in. Other objectives were for the time being more important. Hitler could afford to bide his time in dealing with the Jews.

Frenetic building work, painting, renovation, and refurbishment aimed at offering the most attractive appearance possible to Berlin, the city of the Games.[9] The centre-point was the new Olympic Stadium. Hitler had angrily denounced the original plans of the architect Werner March as a 'modern glass box', and, in one of his usual childlike temper tantrums, had threatened to call off the Olympics altogether. It was probably a device to make sure he got his own way. And like pandering to a spoilt child, those around him made sure he was not disappointed. Speer's rapidly sketched more classically imposing design immediately won his favour.[10] Hitler was more than assuaged. Now fired with enthusiasm, he demanded at once that it should be the biggest stadium in the world – though even when under construction, and outstripping the size of the previous largest stadium at Los Angeles, built for the 1932 Games, he complained that everything was too small.[11]

The whole of Berlin was wreathed in swastika banners on 1 August as the arrival of the Olympic torch signalled, amid spectacular ceremonial, the commencement of the XIth modern Olympiad – Hitler's Olympics. Overhead, the massive airship *Hindenburg* trailed the Olympic flag. In the stadium, a crowd of 110,000 people had assembled in great expectation. Over a million others, it was estimated, unable to get tickets, lined the Berlin streets for a glimpse of their Leader as a cavalcade of black limousines conveyed Hitler with other dignitaries and honoured guests to the newly designed high temple of sport. As he entered the great arena that afternoon, a fanfare of thirty trumpets sounded. The world-famous composer Richard Strauß, clad in white, conducted a choir of 3,000 in the singing of the national anthem, 'Deutschland, Deutschland über alles', and the Nazi Party's own anthem, the 'Horst-Wessel-Lied', before conducting the new 'Olympic Hymn' which he had composed specially for the occasion. As the music faded, the giant Olympic bell began to toll, announcing the parade of the competing athletes that then followed. Many national delegations offered the Nazi salute as they passed Hitler's dais; the British and Americans demonstrably refrained from doing so.[12] All around the stadium, cameras whirred. The camera teams of Leni Riefenstahl, the talented director who, after her success in filming the 1934 Party Rally, had been commissioned to produce a film on the Olympics, had been installed in numerous strategic positions, accumulating their material for a celluloid record of the stirring events.[13]

At last, the opening ceremonials out of the way, the Games were under way. During the following two weeks, a glittering display of sporting prowess unfolded. Amid the notable achievements in the intense competition, none compared with the towering performance of the black American athlete Jesse Owens, winner of four gold medals. Hitler, famously, did not shake Owens's hand in congratulation. It had not, in fact, been intended that he should congratulate Owens or any other winners. He had indeed, though this had apparently not been foreseen by the organizers, shaken the hands of the medal winners on the first day – Finnish and German. Once the last German competitors in the high jump had been eliminated that evening, he had left the stadium in the gathering dusk before completion of the event, which had been delayed and was running late. Whether a deliberate snub or not, this prevented him having to decide whether to shake the hands of Cornelius Johnson and David Albritton, two black Americans who came first and second in the high jump. But Jesse Owens did not compete in a final that day. And before he won any of his medals, Count Baillet-Latour had politely informed Hitler that as a guest of honour of the Committee, if the most important one, it was not in line with protocol for him to congratulate the winners. Thereafter, he congratulated none.[14] He was, therefore, in no position to offer a direct affront to Owens when the American sprinter won the first of his gold medals next day for the 100 metres dash. That he would nevertheless have been prepared to snub Owens can be inferred from what he apparently said to Baldur von Schirach, the Hitler Youth leader: that the Americans should be ashamed at letting their medals be won by negroes, and that he would never have shaken hands with one of them. At Schirach's suggestion that he be photographed alongside Jesse Owens, Hitler was said to have exploded in rage at what he saw as a gross insult.[15]

Alongside the sporting events, the Nazi leadership lost no opportunity to impress prominent visiting dignitaries with extravagant shows of hospitality. Joachim von Ribbentrop, just appointed by Hitler to be the new Ambassador in London, entertained hundreds of important foreign guests in lavish style at his elegant villa in Dahlem. Reich Propaganda Minister Joseph Goebbels threw a huge reception with an Italian theme and spectacular fireworks display for over 1,000 notable visitors – more than half of them from abroad – on the lovely Pfaueninsel (Peacock Island) in the Havel (the wide expanse of water to the west of Berlin), linked for the occasion to the mainland by specially built pontoon bridges. Hermann Göring, head of the Luftwaffe and recognized as the second man in the state, outdid all others in his festive extravaganza. The well-heeled and highly impressionable British Conservative Member of Parliament Sir Henry 'Chips' Channon, then in his late thirties, attended an unforgettable party: 'I don't know how to describe this dazzling crowded function,' he confided to his diary. 'We drove to the Ministerium' – the Air Ministry in Berlin, where Göring's own palatial residence was housed – 'and found its great gardens lit up and 700 or 800 guests gaping at the display and the splendour. Goering, wreathed in smiles and orders and decorations received us gaily, his wife at his side . . . Towards the end of dinner a corps de ballet danced in the moonlight: it was the loveliest coup-d'œil imaginable, and there were murmurs of delighted surprise from all the guests . . . The end of the garden was in darkness, and suddenly, with no warning, it was floodlit and a procession of white horses, donkeys and peasants, appeared from nowhere, and we were led into an especially built Luna Park. It was fantastic, roundabouts, cafés with beer and champagne, peasants dancing and "schuhplattling" vast women carrying bretzels and beer, a ship, a beerhouse, crowds of gay, laughing people, animals . . . The music roared, the astonished guest[s] wandered about. "There has never been anything like this since the days of Louis Quatorze," somebody remarked. "Not since Nero," I retorted . . .'[16]

However magnificent the stadium, however spectacular the ceremonials, however lavish the hospitality, it would have been embarrassing for Hitler, and for national pride, had the German performance at the Games been a poor one. There was no need for concern. The German athletes – much to Hitler's delight – turned the Games into a national triumph. They won more medals than the athletes of any other country.[17] This did nothing to harm the nation's belief in its own superiority.[18]

Above all, the Olympics were an enormous propaganda success for the Nazi regime. Hitler attended almost every day – underlining the significance of the Games – the crowd rising in salute each time he entered the stadium.[19] The German media coverage was massive. Over 3,000 programmes were transmitted worldwide in around fifty languages; over 100 radio stations in the USA alone took transmission; they were even the first Games to be shown on television – though the coverage, confined to Berlin, gave out only fuzzy pictures.[20] Almost 4 million spectators had watched the games (spending millions of Reich Marks for the privilege).[21] Many more millions had read reports of them, or seen newsreel coverage. And of paramount importance: Hitler's Germany had been open to viewing for visitors from all over the world. Most of them went away mightily impressed.[22] 'I'm afraid the Nazis have succeeded with their propaganda,' noted the American journalist William Shirer. 'First, they have run the games on a lavish scale never before experienced, and this has appealed to the athletes. Second, they have put up a very good front for the general visitors, especially the big businessmen.'[23] An outsider within Germany, the Jewish philologist Victor Klemperer, living in Dresden, took a similarly pessimistic view. He saw the Olympics as 'wholly and entirely a political affair . . . It's incessantly drummed into the people and foreigners that here you can see the revival (*Aufschwung*), the blossoming, the new spirit, the unity, the steadfastness, the glory, naturally too the peaceful spirit of the Third Reich lovingly embracing the whole world.' The anti-Jewish agitation and warlike tones had disappeared from the newspapers, he noted, at least until 16 August – the end of the Games. Guests were repeatedly reminded of the 'peaceful and joyful' Germany in stark contrast to the pillage and murder carried out (it was claimed) by 'Communist hordes' in Spain.[24] The enthusiastic Hitler Youth activist Melita Maschmann later recalled young people returning to their own countries with a similar positive and peaceful image of Germany. 'In all of us,' she remembered, 'there was the hope in a future of peace and friendship.'[25] In her eyes and those of the many sharing her enthusiasm, it was a future which had no place for the Victor Klemperers and others regarded as racial misfits. In any case, the expectations of peaceful coexistence would reveal themselves only too soon as no more than pipe-dreams.

Away from the glamour of the Olympic Games and out of the public eye, the contrast with the external image of peaceful goodwill was sharp. By this time, the self-induced crisis in the German economy arising from the inability to provide for both guns and butter – to sustain supplies of raw materials both for armaments and for consumption – was reaching its watershed. A decision on the economic direction the country would take could not be deferred much longer. The outcome in the summer of 1936 was an economic policy geared inexorably to expansion, making international conflict all the more certain. By then, the outbreak of the Spanish Civil War had already started to move Europe closer towards explosion.

II

By the spring, it had become clear that it was no longer possible to reconcile the demands of rapid rearmament and growing domestic consumption. Supplies of raw materials for the armaments industry were by then sufficient for only two months.[26] Fuel supplies for the armed forces were in a particularly critical state.[27] Economics Minister Hjalmar Schacht was by now thoroughly alarmed at the accelerating tempo of rearmament and its inevitably damaging consequences for the economy. Only a sharp reduction in living standards (impossible without endangering the regime's stability) or a big increase in exports (equally impossible given the regime's priorities, exchange rate difficulties, and the condition of external markets) could in his view provide for an expanding armaments industry. He was adamant, therefore, that it was time to put the brakes on rearmament.[28]

The military had other ideas. The leaders of the armed forces, uninterested in the niceties of economics but fully taken up by the potential of modern advanced weaponry, pressed unabatedly for rapid and massive acceleration of the armaments programme. Within weeks of the reoccupation of the Rhineland, General Ludwig Beck, Chief of the General Staff of the army, had come up with plans to expand the thirty-six divisions envisaged in March 1935, when military service was reintroduced, into forty-one divisions. By the summer, the projections had been worked out for an army to be bigger in 1940 than the Kaiser's war army had been in 1914.[29]

The army leaders were not acting in response to pressure from Hitler. They had their own agenda. They were at the same time 'working towards the Führer', consciously or unconsciously acting 'along his lines and towards his aim' (in phrases tellingly used by one Nazi official in a speech two years earlier, hinting at how the dynamic of Nazi rule operated)[30] in the full knowledge that their rearmament ambitions wholly coincided with Hitler's political aims, and that they could depend upon his backing against attempts to throttle back on armament expenditure. Reich War Minister Werner von Blomberg, Colonel-General Werner Freiherr von Fritsch, Commander-in-Chief of the Army, and his Chief of Staff, Beck, were thereby paving the way, in providing the necessary armed might, for the later expansionism which would leave them all trailing in Hitler's wake.[31]

Even so, the economic impasse seemed complete. Huge increases in allocation of scarce foreign currency were demanded by both the Ministry of Food and the Ministry of Armaments.[32] The position could not be sustained. Fundamental economic priorities had to be established as a matter of urgency. Autarky and export lobbies could not both be satisfied. Hitler remained for months inactive. He had no patent solution to the problem. The key figure at this point was Göring.

Several factors contributed to Göring's arrival centre-stage in the arena of economic policy: his own insatiable drive to aggrandizement of power; his involvement the previous autumn when acting as Hitler's troubleshooter in a dispute between Schacht and Richard Walther Darré, Reich Minister for Food and Agriculture, over the allocation of scarce foreign currency to import food products in short supply instead of for raw materials needed by the expanding armaments industries; Schacht's attempt to use him as a barrier against Party intrusions into the economic sphere; the increasing desperation of Blomberg about the raw-materials crisis in armaments production which eventually forced him to back the power pretensions of the Luftwaffe chief; and not least Hitler's patent reluctance to become involved, especially if it meant taking decisions in opposition to Party demands.[33] Blomberg had been pressing for months for a 'Fuel Commissar'. Schacht's repeated rejection of the proposition, realizing the threat to his own sphere of competence, opened the door for Göring, as Air Minister and head of the Luftwaffe, to demand that the Fuel Commissar be answerable to him. Then in March 1936, as the fuel shortage reached crisis-point, Göring decided to put himself forward as 'Fuel Dictator'.[34] Keen for different reasons to block Göring's ambitions, Schacht and Blomberg tried to tie him down within the framework of a four-man commission involving the three of them and Reich Minister Hanns Kerrl (a close ally of Göring to whom Hitler had assigned a role in economic affairs in spring 1936) to tackle the foreign-exchange crisis.[35] Hoping to keep the party off his back, Schacht helped persuade Hitler to install Göring at the beginning of April as Plenipotentiary for the Securing of the Raw Materials and Foreign Exchange Demands of the Reich. Göring's brief was to overcome the crisis, get rearmament moving again, and force through a policy of autarky in fuel production.[36] But by now Göring was in the driving-seat. Schacht was rapidly becoming yesterday's man. In May, shocked at the new power-base that his own Machiavellian manoeuvrings had unwittingly helped to create for Göring, the Economics Minister protested to Hitler. Hitler waved him away. He did not want anything more to do with the matter, he was reported as telling Schacht, and the Economics Minister was advised to take it up with Göring himself.[37] 'It won't go well with Schacht for much longer,' commented Goebbels. 'He doesn't belong in his heart to us.' But Göring, too, he thought would have difficulties with the foreign-exchange and raw-materials issue, pointing out: 'He doesn't understand too much about it.'[38]

It was not necessary that he did. His role was to throw around his considerable weight, force the pace, bring a sense of urgency into play, make things happen. 'He brings the energy. Whether he has the economic know-how and experience as well? Who knows? Anyway, he'll do plenty of bragging,' was Goebbels's assessment.[39]

Göring soon had a team of technical experts assembled under Lieutenant-Colonel Fritz Löb of the Luftwaffe. In the research department of Löb's planning team, run by the chemical firm IG Farben's director Karl Krauch, solutions were rapidly advanced for maximizing production of synthetic fuels and rapidly attaining self-sufficiency in mineral-oil extraction.[40] By midsummer, Löb's planners had come up with a detailed programme for overcoming the unabated crisis. It envisaged a sharp tilt to a more directed economy with distinct priorities built on an all-out drive both to secure the armaments programme and to improve food provisioning through maximum attainable autarky in specific fields and production of substitute raw materials such as synthetic fuels, rubber, and industrial fats.[41] It was not a war economy; but it was on the road to becoming the nearest thing to a war economy in peacetime.

At the end of July, while Hitler was in Bayreuth and Berchtesgaden, Göring had a number of opportunities to discuss with him his plans for the economy. On 30 July he obtained Hitler's agreement to present them with a splash at the coming Reich Party Rally in September. 'A big speech of the Colonel-General at the Party Congress' was envisaged, according to a note in Göring's desk-diary.[42] Göring intended to reap the glory. The new economic programme would dominate the Rally. That was what the Luftwaffe chief had in mind. But when it came to propaganda, Hitler, sniffing another chance to enhance his image through the major announcement of a 'Four-Year Plan', was unwilling as ever to concede the star-role. He decided to deliver the key speech himself.[43]

Hitler had meanwhile become increasingly preoccupied with the looming threat, as he saw it, from Bolshevism, and with the prospect that the mounting international turmoil could lead to war in the nearer rather than more distant future.[44] Whatever tactical opportunism he deployed, and however much he played on the theme for propaganda purposes, there is no doubt that the coming showdown with Bolshevism remained – as it had been since the mid-1920s at the latest – the lodestar of Hitler's thinking on foreign policy. In 1936, this future titanic struggle started to come into sharper focus.

At his private meeting with the former British Air Minister Lord Londonderry in February 1936, Hitler had concentrated on what he described as 'the growing menace to the world of Bolshevism'. He was, he said, destined to play the part of the prophet internationally, as he had done within Germany some fifteen years earlier. He understood the dangers of Bolshevism better than other European statesmen, he went on, since 'his political career had grown out of a struggle against Bolshevist tendencies'. Continental Europe was unbalanced and unstable, he claimed. Most governments were weak and short-lived. The continent was living 'from hand to mouth'. The 'extraordinary development of Soviet power' had to be seen against this background of 'decay'. Moreover, he added, playing up the bogey of Bolshevism to his British guest, the Soviet Union was not merely the greatest military power on the continent, but also 'the embodiment of an idea'. He went on to provide Lord Londonderry with facts and figures on Soviet military and economic might. The admission of Russia to the League of Nations reminded him of the fable of Reynard the Fox – overcoming the suspicion of the other animals, then devouring them one after another. 'Just in the same way as one does not allow germ-carriers in ordinary life to frequent the society of healthy people, so we must keep Russia at a distance,' he maintained. But if the decomposition of Europe and the strengthening of the Soviet Union continued, he asked, 'what will the position be in ten, twenty, or thirty years?'[45]

Hitler had visualized for Lord Londonderry the prospect of war between the Soviet Union and Japan, with defeat for the Japanese opening the path for Soviet domination also of the Far East. After meeting the Japanese ambassador in Berlin early in June, Hitler repeated his view that deepening conflict was on the way in the Far East, though he now thought that Japan would 'thrash' Russia. At that point, 'this colossus will start to totter (*ins Wanken kommen*). And then our great hour will have arrived. Then we must supply ourselves with land for 100 years,' he told Goebbels. 'Let's hope we're ready then,' the Propaganda Minister added in his diary notes, 'and that the Führer is still alive. So that action will be taken.'[46]

Holidaying in Berchtesgaden in mid-July, Hitler told Goebbels that 'the next Party Rally will again be against the Bolsheviks'.[47] A few days later in Bayreuth, where as usual he was attending the Wagner Festival, he warned two of his most ardent English devotees, the good-looking daughters of the British aristocrat Lord Redesdale, Unity Valkyrie Mitford (who said that sitting next to Hitler was 'like sitting beside the sun')[48] and her sister Diana (divorced from a member of the wealthy Guinness family and on the verge of marrying – in a ceremony attended by Hitler and Goebbels – the leader of the British Union of Fascists, Oswald Mosley), of the 'Jewish and Bolshevik danger'.[49] By this time, events in Spain were also focusing Hitler's attention on the threat of Bolshevism. Until then, he had scarcely given a thought to Spain. But on the evening of 25 July, following a performance of *Siegfried* conducted by Wilhelm Furtwängler, his decision – against the advice of the Foreign Office – to send aid to General Franco committed Germany to involvement in what was rapidly to turn into the Spanish Civil War.[50]

The refusal of the Spanish Right to accept the narrow victory of the left-wing Popular Front in the elections of February 1936 had left Spain teetering on the brink of civil war. During late spring and early summer, horror stories of terroristic outrages, political murders, violent attacks on clergy, and burning churches had started to pour out of a country rapidly descending into political chaos. Europe was alarmed. For the Spanish Right,

there was little difficulty in portraying it as the work of Marxist revolution-
aries and evoking the image of a country on the verge of Communist
takeover.[51] Between May and July, army plans for a coup took shape.[52]
On 17 July army garrisons in Spanish Morocco rose against the elected
government. The Commander-in-Chief of the army in Morocco, General
Francisco Franco, put himself next morning at the head of the rebellion. But
a mutiny of sailors loyal to the Republic denied him the transport facilities
he needed to get his army to the mainland, most of which remained in
Republican hands. The few planes he was able to lay hands upon did not
amount to much in terms of an airlift.[53] In these unpropitious circumstances,
Franco turned to Mussolini and Hitler. It took over a week to overcome
Mussolini's initial refusal to help the Spanish rebels. Hitler was persuaded
within a matter of hours. Ideological and strategic considerations – the
likelihood of Bolshevism triumphing on the Iberian peninsula – were uppermost in his mind. But the potential for gaining access to urgently needed
raw materials for the rearmament programme – an aspect emphasized by
Göring – also appears to have played its part in the decision.[54]

Good luck was on Franco's side in his approach to Germany to send
transport planes. His initial request for German aid had been coolly received
by the Foreign Office. He decided to make a direct appeal to Hitler. A
German businessman, Johannes Bernhardt, the head of an export firm which
had close dealings with the Spanish army in Morocco and a member of the
Nazi Party Foreign Organization (the Auslandsorganisation, or AO), had
offered his help in mediation to Franco. As late as 22 July, Franco had not
had a plane at his disposal capable of reaching Germany. But the following
day a Lufthansa Junkers Ju-52/3m mail plane, sequestered by the rebels in
Las Palmas amid German protests, arrived in Morocco, carrying the rebel
General Orgaz. Franco now took up Bernhardt's offer of help. Carrying a
written request from Franco to Hitler – and in all probability a similar one
to Göring[55] – Bernhardt flew to Berlin, accompanied by the sixty-year-old
branch leader of the AO in Tetuán, Adolf Langenheim, arriving on the
evening of 24 July at Tempelhof aerodrome.[56]

Meanwhile, the German Foreign Office had been increasingly worried
about the deteriorating situation in Spain. A number of attacks on German
citizens by Communists and anarchists led to two warships being dispatched
into Spanish coastal waters. Concern grew that a victory of the government
forces would pave the way for a Communist takeover. The prospect of
Bolshevik dominance also in the south-west of Europe – compounding the
victory of the left-wing Popular Front in France earlier in the year – seemed

a real one.[57] Even so, the Foreign Office thought direct involvement in Spain too risky. Gauleiter Ernst Wilhelm Bohle, the head of the AO, who had advanced the case of Franco's emissaries, was told in no uncertain terms to take the matter no further.[58] Ignoring the warning, however, Bohle telephoned Rudolf Heß, Deputy Head of the Party, who immediately arranged for the emissaries to fly in his personal plane to meet him in Thuringia. After a two-hour discussion, Heß rang Hitler. A meeting with the Führer was fixed for the evening of the following day, 25 July, in Bayreuth.[59]

It was close to ten o'clock in the evening when Bernhardt and Langenheim were ushered into Hitler's presence in the Wagner residence, 'Haus Wahnfried'. Hitler had by then been well briefed on the situation in Spain. He knew the rebels' position had worsened. The last report from the German Embassy in Madrid that morning had warned that a long civil war was in prospect, and that a Republican victory would have damaging consequences for German interests. The report raised the spectre of a Spanish soviet regime closely bound into the French-Soviet alliance.[60] Göring had by this time also had the opportunity to brief Hitler on the economic advantages to be gained from supporting Franco, were the rebel cause to succeed.[61]

That, however, was far from a foregone conclusion. Bernhardt reinforced the message that Franco's struggle against Communism was lost without German aid.[62] The talk moved on to the question of payment for the aid. Noticing that Hitler looked 'somewhat shocked' when he mentioned purely nominal sums, Bernhardt stressed the 'rich sources' to be gained from Andalusia, almost certainly going on to indicate benefits to Germany from increased raw material imports in exchange for armaments.[63] Hitler was still hesitant. But once he had turned the audience into another lengthy monologue, in which he praised the idealism of Spanish nationalists and ranted endlessly about the dangers of Bolshevism, the outcome was little in doubt. In contrast to the position of the Foreign Ministry, he had convinced himself that the dangers of being sandwiched between two Bolshevik blocs outweighed the risks of German involvement in the Spanish crisis – even if, as seemed likely, it should turn into full-blown and protracted civil war. War against the Soviet Union – the struggle for Germany's 'living space' – was, in his view, at some point inevitable. The prospect of a Bolshevik Spain was a dangerous complication.[64] He decided to provide Franco with the aid requested. It was an indication both of Hitler's own greatly increased self-confidence and of the weakened position of those who had advised him on international affairs that he took the decision alone. Possibly, knowing the reluctance of the Foreign Office to become involved, and aware that

Göring, for all his interest in possible economic gains, shared some of its reservations, Hitler was keen to present doubters with a *fait accompli*.[65] Possibly, too, Hitler was also still under the influence of Wagner's *Siegfried*, which he had come from earlier in the evening. At any rate, the operation to assist Franco came to be dubbed '*Unternehmen Feuerzauber*' ('Operation Magic Fire'), recalling the heroic music accompanying Siegfried's passage through the ring of fire to free Brünnhilde.[66]

Only after Hitler had taken the decision were Göring and Blomberg summoned. Göring, despite his hopes of economic gains from intervention, was initially 'horrified' about the risk of international complications through intervention in Spain. But faced with Hitler's usual intransigence, once he had arrived at a decision, Göring was soon won over.[67] Blomberg, his influence – not least after his nervousness over the Rhineland affair – now waning compared with the powerful position he had once held, went along without objection.[68] Ribbentrop, too, when he was told on arrival in Bayreuth that Hitler intended to support Franco, initially warned against involvement in Spain. But Hitler was adamant. He had already ordered aircraft to be put at Franco's disposal. The crucial consideration was ideological: 'If Spain really goes communist, France in her present situation will also be bolshevised in due course, and then Germany is finished. Wedged between the powerful Soviet *bloc* in the East and a strong communist Franco-Spanish *bloc* in the West, we could do hardly anything if Moscow chose to attack us.'[69] Hitler brushed aside Ribbentrop's weak objections – fresh complications with Britain, and the strength of the French bourgeoisie in holding out against Bolshevism – and simply ended the conversation by stating that he had already made his decision.[70]

Twenty Junkers Ju-52 transport planes – ten more than Franco had asked for – supported by six Heinkel He 51 fighters were to be provided and were soon *en route* to Spanish Morocco and to Cádiz, in southern Spain, which had rapidly fallen to the insurgents. Subsequent aid was to follow through a barter system of German equipment for Spanish raw materials under cover of two export companies, one German and one Spanish.[71] Despite the warnings he had received that Germany could be sucked into a military quagmire, and however strongly ideological considerations weighed with him, Hitler probably intervened only on the assumption that German aid would tip the balance quickly and decisively in Franco's favour. 'We're taking part a bit in Spain. Not clear. Who knows what it's good for,' commented Goebbels laconically the day after the decision to help Franco had been taken.[72] Short-term gains, not long-term involvement, were the premiss of Hitler's impulsive decision. Significant military and economic involvement in Spain began only in October.[73] By then, Göring – spurred by his role as head of the new Four-Year Plan as well as chief of the Luftwaffe – was the driving-force. Hitler agreed to substantial increases in German military assistance to Spain. Fighters, bombers, and 6,500 military personnel – the future Legion Condor (a mixed Luftwaffe unit assigned to support for the Spanish nationalists) – were dispatched to take part in what was rapidly developing into a rehearsal for a general showdown between the forces of Fascism and Communism.[74]

The ideological impetus behind Hitler's readiness to involve Germany in the Spanish maelstrom – his intensified preoccupation with the threat of Bolshevism – was not a cover for the economic considerations that weighed so heavily with Göring.[75] This is borne out by his private as well as his public utterances. Publicly, as he had told Goebbels the previous day would be the case, in his opening proclamation to the Reich Party Rally in Nurem-berg on 9 September, he announced that the 'greatest world danger' of which he warned for so long – the 'revolutionizing of the continent' through the work of 'Bolshevik wire-pullers' run by 'an international Jewish revolu-tionary headquarters in Moscow' – was becoming reality. Germany's mili-tary rebuilding had been undertaken precisely to prevent what was turning Spain into ruins from taking place in Germany.[76] Out of the public eye, his sentiments were hardly different when he addressed the cabinet for three hours on the foreign-policy situation at the beginning of December. He concentrated on the danger of Bolshevism. Europe was divided into two camps. There was no more going back. He described the tactics of the 'Reds'. Spain had become the decisive issue. France, ruled by Prime Minister Léon Blum – seen as an 'agent of the Soviets', a 'Zionist and world-destroyer' – would be the next victim. The victor in Spain would gain great prestige. The consequences for the rest of Europe, and in particular for Germany and for the remnants of Communism in the country, were major ones. This was the reason, he went on, for German aid in armaments to Spain. 'Germany can only wish that the crisis is deferred until we are ready,' he declared. 'When it comes, seize the opportunity (*zugreifen*). Get into the paternoster lift at the right time. But also get out again at the right time. Rearm. Money can play no role.'[77] Only two weeks or so earlier, Goebbels had recorded in his diary: 'After dinner I talked thoroughly with the Führer alone. He is very content with the situation. Rearmament is proceeding. We're sticking in fabulous sums. In 1938 we'll be completely ready. The showdown with Bolshevism is coming. Then we want to be prepared. The army is now completely won over by us. Führer untouchable . . . Dominance in Europe for us is as good as certain. Just let no chance pass by. Therefore rearm.'[78]

III

The announcement of the Four-Year Plan at the Nuremberg Party Rally in September had by then pushed rearmament policy on to a new plane. Priorities had been established. They meant in practice that balancing consumer and rearmament spending could only be sustained for a limited period of time through a crash programme which maximized autarkic potential to prepare Germany as rapidly as possible for the confrontation which Hitler deemed inevitable and other leading figures in the regime thought probable, if not highly likely, within the following few years. Through the introduction of the Four-Year Plan, Germany was economically pushed in the direction of expansion and war. Economics and ideology were by now thoroughly interwoven. Even so, the decision to move to the Four-Year Plan was ultimately an ideological one. Economic options were still open – even if the policies of the previous three years meant they had already narrowed sharply. Schacht, Goerdeler, and others, backed by important sectors of industry, favoured a retreat from an armaments-led economy to a re-entry into international markets. Against this, the powerful IG-Farben lobby, linked to the Luftwaffe, pushed for maximizing production of synthetic fuels. The stalemate persisted throughout the summer. The economic crisis which had dogged Germany during the previous winter and spring was unresolved. With no end to the dispute in sight, Hitler was pressed in late August to take sides. The preoccupation with Bolshevism, which had weighed heavily with him throughout the summer, was decisive in his own inimitable approach to Germany's economic problems.

The driving-force behind the creation of what came to be known as the Four-Year Plan was not, however, Hitler but Göring. Following their discussions in Berchtesgaden and Bayreuth in July, Hitler had requested reports from Göring on the economic situation, and how the problems were to be overcome. At the beginning of August Göring had in turn demanded memoranda from different branches of the economy to be sent to him as rapidly as possible. The timing was determined by propaganda considerations, not economic criteria: the proximity of the Reich Party Rally in early September was what counted. The complex reports could not be put together as swiftly as Göring had wanted. By the time he travelled to Berchtesgaden at the beginning of the last week in August, he only had a survey from his Raw Materials and Currency staff about the possibilities of synthetic raw-material production within Germany to hand.[79] He had meanwhile been encountering powerful opposition to his economic plans from Schacht, who was voicing feelings in some important sectors of business and industry, such as those of one of the most important Ruhr industrialists, Albert Vögler, head of the biggest steel concern in Europe, the Vereinigte Stahlwerke, who had strongly backed a Hitler Chancellorship in the final phase of the Weimar Republic. Carl Goerdeler, too, Lord Mayor of Leipzig, who had served Hitler as Reich Price Commissioner and would eventually become a leading opponent of the regime, joined in the criticism towards the end of the month.[80] It was in these circumstances that Hitler was persuaded during the last week of August to dictate a lengthy memorandum on the future direction of the economy – one of the extremely rare occasions in the Third Reich (leaving aside formal laws, decrees, and directives) that he put forward his views in writing.

Most likely, the memorandum, containing neither title nor signature and possibly completed only on 2 September, two days before it was presented to government ministers, was compiled at Göring's suggestion.[81] The Luftwaffe chief stood to gain most directly from it in the power-struggle with Schacht for dominance over the economy. 'The lack of understanding of the Reich Economics Ministry and the resistance of German business to all large-scale (*großzügigen*) plans prompted him to compose this memorandum on the Obersalzberg,' Hitler told his Armaments Minister Albert Speer, when handing him a copy eight years later.[82] The only two copies of the memorandum originally distributed went to Göring himself, and to his ally against Schacht, War Minister Blomberg. The Economics Minister himself was not shown a copy of the memorandum, and in fact only heard as late as 2 September of Hitler's intention to proclaim a new economic policy at the Reich Party Rally.[83]

The memorandum fell into two parts. The first, on 'the political situation', was pure Hitler. It was couched exclusively in ideological terms. The 'reasoning' was, as it had been in *Mein Kampf* and the *Second Book*, social-Darwinist and racially determinist. 'Politics are the conduct and course of the historical struggle for life of peoples,' he began. 'The aim of these struggles is the assertion of existence.' The world was moving towards a new conflict, centred upon Bolshevism, 'whose essence and aim . . . is solely the elimination of those strata of mankind which have hitherto provided the leadership and their replacement by world-wide Jewry'.

Germany would be the focus of the inevitable showdown with Bolshevism. 'It is not the aim of this memorandum to prophesy the time when the untenable situation in Europe will become an open crisis. I only want, in these lines, to set down my conviction that this crisis cannot and will not fail to arrive,' he asserted. 'A victory of Bolshevism over Germany would lead not to a Versailles Treaty but to the final destruction, indeed to the annihilation, of the German people . . . In face of the necessity of defence against this danger, all other considerations must recede into the background as being completely irrelevant.' The defensive capacity of the German people had been greatly strengthened under National Socialism. The level of ideological solidarity was unprecedented. But making the German Army 'into the first army in the world, in training, in the raising of units, in armaments, and, above all, in spiritual education (*in der geistigen Erziehung*)' was vital. If this did not happen, then 'Germany will be lost,' he declared.[84]

The second part of the memorandum, dealing with 'Germany's economic situation', and offering a 'programme for a final solution of our vital need', bore unmistakable signs of Göring's influence, resting in turn on the raw material programmes drawn up by his planning staff, with significant input by IG Farben.[85] The resemblance to statements on the economy put forward by Göring earlier in the summer suggests that Hitler either had such statements before him when compiling his memorandum, or that his Raw Materials Commissar worked alongside him in preparing the memorandum.[86] The tone was nonetheless classically Hitlerian – down to the threat of a law 'making the whole of Jewry liable for all damage inflicted by individual specimens of this community of criminals upon the German economy', a threat put into practice some two years later.

A temporary solution to the economic problems was to be found in partial autarky. Maximizing domestic production wherever possible would allow for the necessary food imports, which could not be at the cost of rearmament. Fuel, iron, and synthetic-rubber production had to be stepped up. Cost was irrelevant. Objections – and the opposition voiced in the previous weeks – were taken on board and brushed aside. The nation did not live for the economy; rather, 'finance and the economy, economic leaders and theories must all exclusively serve this struggle for self-assertion in which our people are engaged'. The Ministry of Economics had simply to set the national economic tasks; private industry had to fulfil them. If it could not do so, the National Socialist state, Hitler threatened, would 'succeed in carrying out this task on its own'. In typical fashion, he couched his threat in stark alternatives: 'The German economy will either grasp the new economic tasks or else it will prove itself quite incompetent to survive in this modern age when a Soviet State is setting up a gigantic plan. But in that case it will not be Germany that will go under, but, at most, a few industrialists.' Though Germany's economic problems, the memorandum asserted, could be temporarily eased through the measures laid down, they could only finally be solved through the extension of 'living space'. It was 'the task of the political leadership one day to solve this problem'. Again this was redolent of *Mein Kampf* and the *Second Book*. But it also matched Göring's aggressive tone in his economic statements earlier in the summer. Only nuances separated Göring's more pragmatic nationalist-imperialism from Hitler's race-determined version. Both variants implied war at some point in the future – when economic mobilization, wrote Hitler, would become 'solely a question of will'. The memorandum closed by advocating a 'Several Years Plan' – the term 'Four-Year Plan' was not mentioned in the document – to maximize self-sufficiency in existing conditions and make it possible to demand economic sacrifices of the German people. Opportunities had been missed during the previous four years; in the next four years, the German army had to be made operational, the economy made ready for war.[87]

Even in the economic sections, few concrete details were offered. No organizational structure was laid down. The economic ideas mooted in the second part were in themselves not new. But the drive for maximum autarky in the interests of a forced rearmament drive was now taken on to a new plane, and established as the outright priority.[88] Hitler's economic notions were confined, as always, to an ideological imperative. The memorandum was wholly programmatic. The more pragmatic expansionist notions of Göring and Blomberg both in the military and in the economic sphere were accommodated within the Hitlerian ideological vision. Moreover, Hitler's way of argumentation was characteristic. The inflexibility of its ideological premises coupled with the very broadness of its dogmatic generalities made it impossible for critics to contest it outright without rejection of Hitler himself and his 'world-view'. This 'world-view', whatever tactical adjustments had proved necessary, showed again its inner consistency in the central place assigned to the coming showdown with Bolshevism – an issue which, as we have seen, preoccupied Hitler throughout 1936.

Göring got what he wanted out of Hitler's memorandum. Armed with Hitler's backing he was able to determine his supremacy in the central arena of the armaments economy.[89] Schacht recognized the scale of the defeat he had suffered.[90] Hitler was reluctant to drop him because of the standing he enjoyed abroad.[91] But his star was now waning fast. Alternative policies to that advanced in Hitler's memorandum could now be condemned out of hand. Goerdeler's memorandum rejecting the autarkic programme and arguing for curtailment of rearmament in favour of re-entry into the international market economy was peremptorily dismissed by the new armaments supremo. The dictatorial style in which he conducted the meeting of the Prussian Ministerial Council on 4 September was that of the victor in the power-struggle, basking in the certainty of control over the massive economics empire now opening up before him.[92]

The growth of this huge domain did not derive from a clearly conceived notion of economic planning. Hitler – in so far as he had given any consideration at all to organizational matters – had, it appears, simply imagined that Göring would work through only a small bureaucracy and function as an overlord in coordinating economic policy with the relevant ministries, which would retain their specific responsibilities.[93] Instead, Göring rapidly improvised a panoply of 'special commissioners' (Sonderbeauftragte), each backed by their own bureaucratic apparatus, for different facets of the Four-Year Plan, often without clear lines of control, not infrequently overlapping or interfering with the duties of the Ministry of Economics, and all of course answerable to Göring himself. It was a recipe for administrative and economic anarchy.

But the momentum created by the Four-Year Plan was immense. All areas of the economy were affected in the following peacetime years. The resulting pressures on the economy as a whole were not sustainable indefinitely. The economic drive created its own dynamic which fed directly into Hitler's ideological imperative. The ambitious technocrats in the offices and sub-organizations of the Four-Year Plan, not least the leaders of the rapidly expanding chemicals giant IG Farben, were in their own way – whatever their direct motivation – also 'working towards the Führer'. Territorial expansion became necessary for economic as well as for ideological reasons. And racial policy, too, was pushed on to a new plane as the spoils to be gained from a programme of 'aryanization' were eagerly seized upon as easy pickings in an economy starting to overheat under its own, self-manufactured pressures.

When Hitler drew up his memorandum in late August 1936 all this was in the future. Hitler had no clear notion himself of how it would all unfold. Nor was he specially interested in such questions. Propaganda concerned him more immediately than economics in drawing up the memorandum. He needed the new economic programme as the cornerstone of the Party

Rally. His big speech there on the economy – which, as we have seen, Göring had initially wanted to deliver – was closely based, occasionally word for word, on his August memorandum.[94] He now spoke publicly for the first time of a 'new Four-Year Programme' (recalling his initial 'four-year plan' put forward immediately after his appointment as Chancellor in 1933).[95] A planned economy sounded modern. A 'Five-Year Plan' had already been taken up in the Bolshevik state at which German preparations were ultimately targeted.[96] The designation 'Four-Year Plan' rapidly caught on in the German press. It became officially so called some weeks later, on 18 October, with Hitler's 'Decree for the Implementation of the Four-Year Plan'.[97]

IV

In the foreign-policy arena, the shifts which had begun during the Abyssinian crisis were hardening across the summer and autumn of 1936. Clearer contours were beginning to emerge. Diplomatic, strategic, economic, and ideological considerations – separable but often closely interwoven – were starting to take Germany into more dangerous, uncharted waters. The possibility of a new European conflagration – however unimaginable and horrifying the prospect seemed to most of the generation that had lived through the last one – was starting to appear a real one.

The long-desired alliance with Britain, which had seemed a real possibility in June 1935 at the signing of the Naval Pact, had remained elusive. It was still a distant dream. The Abyssinian crisis and the reoccupation of the Rhineland, now the Spanish Civil War, had all provided hurdles to a closer relationship despite German efforts to court those they imagined had power and influence in Britain and some British sympathizers in high places.[98] Ribbentrop, appointed in the summer an unwilling Ambassador to London with a mandate from Hitler to bring Britain into an anti-Comintern pact, had since his triumph with the Naval Treaty become increasingly disillusioned about the prospects of a British alliance.[99] Hitler pointed out to Mussolini in September that Ribbentrop's appointment marked the last attempt to win over Great Britain.[100] But the new 'Ambassador Brickendrop', as he was lampooned on account of the innumerable *faux pas* (such as saluting the King with the 'Hitler Greeting') for which he became renowned in London diplomatic circles, or 'Half-Time Ambassador' because of his frequent absences, in any case made his own personal contribution to the growing alienation felt in Britain towards the Third Reich.[101] Hitler saw the abdication on 11 December 1936 of King Edward VIII, in the face of opposition in Britain to his proposed marriage to a twice-divorced American, Mrs Wallis Simpson, as a victory for those forces hostile to Germany.[102] Ribbentrop had encouraged him in the view that the King was pro-German and anti-Jewish, and that he had been deposed by an anti-German conspiracy linked to Jews, freemasons, and powerful political lobbies.[103]

By the end of the year (according to a reported indication of his view), Hitler had become more lukewarm about a British alliance, claiming – whether with total conviction may be doubted – that it would at best bring some minor colonial gains but would, on the other hand, hinder Germany's plans for expansion in central and south-eastern Europe. The reason he gave was that Italy would, through an Anglo-German alliance which undermined its policy in the Mediterranean, be forced on to the side of France, leading to a block by the two countries on any attempt at a new order in south-eastern Europe. Germany, he concluded, had its interests better served by close ties with Italy.[104]

The rapprochement with Italy – slow and tenuous in the first half of 1936 – had by then come to harden into a new alliance of the two fascist-style militaristic dictatorships dominating central and southern Europe. The Abyssinian crisis, as we have noted, had turned Italy towards Germany. The repercussions on Austria were not long in the waiting. Deprived *de facto* of its Italian protector, Austria was swept inevitably further into the German slipstream.[105] Encouraged by the Italians as well as put under pressure by the Germans, Austria was ready by 11 July 1936 to sign a wide-ranging agreement with Germany, improving relations, ending restrictions placed upon the German press, and upon economic and cultural activities within Austria.[106] Though recognizing Austrian independence, the agreement in reality turned the Reich's eastern neighbour into an economic and foreign-policy dependency.[107] It was a development which by this time suited both Germany and Italy.[108] And within weeks, the aid provided by the two dictatorships to the nationalist rebels in Spain, and the rapidly deepening commitment to the Spanish Civil War, brought Italy and Germany still closer together. German and Italian pilots in Spain were soon operating in unison.[109] The annihilation of the small Basque market town of Guernica, leaving over 2,500 citizens dead or injured, in a devastating three-hour bombing raid on the afternoon of 26 April 1937 by combined German and Italian forces, immortalized in Picasso's famous painting, would become an emblem of the horror of the Spanish Civil War, and of innocent civilians defenceless against the new menace of terror from the skies.[110]

The diplomatic benefits from closer ties with Italy were reinforced in Hitler's own eyes by the anti-Bolshevik credentials of Mussolini's regime. In his August memorandum on the economy, Hitler had highlighted Italy as the only European country outside Germany capable of standing firm against Bolshevism.[111] In September, he made overtures to Mussolini through his envoy Hans Frank, inviting the Duce to visit Berlin the following year – an invitation readily accepted.[112] Mussolini's son-in-law, the vain Count Ciano – the 'Ducellino' – arranged matters with Neurath in mid-October. There was agreement on a common struggle against Communism, rapid recognition of a Franco government in Spain, German recognition of the annexation of Abyssinia, and Italian 'satisfaction' at the Austro-German agreement.[113]

Hitler was in effusive mood when he welcomed Ciano to Berchtesgaden on 24 October. He described Mussolini as 'the leading statesman in the world, to whom none may even remotely compare himself'.[114] In a conversation of two and a quarter hours, Hitler, noted Ciano, 'talked slowly and in a low voice', with 'violent outbursts when he spoke of Russia and Bolshevism. His way of expressing himself was slow and somewhat verbose. Each question was the subject of a long exposition and each concept was repeated by him several times in different words . . . The principal topics of his conversation were Bolshevism and English encirclement.'[115] Ciano had drawn Hitler's attention to a telegram, which had fallen into Italian hands, to the Foreign Office in London from the British Ambassador in Berlin, Sir Eric Phipps, stating that the Reich government was in the hands of dangerous adventurers. Hitler's furious response was that 'England, too, was led by adventurers when she built the Empire. Today it is governed merely by incompetents.' Germany and Italy should 'go over to the attack', using the tactic of anti-Bolshevism to win support from countries suspicious of an Italo-German alliance. There was no clash of interests between Italy and Germany, he declared. The Mediterranean was 'an Italian sea'. Germany had to have freedom of action towards the East and the Baltic.[116] He was convinced, he said, that England would attack Italy, Germany, or both, given the opportunity and likely chances of success. A common anti-Bolshevik front, including powers in the East, the Far East, and South America, would however act as a deterrent, and probably even prompt Britain to seek an agreement. If Britain continued its offensive policy, seeking time to rearm, Germany and Italy had the advantage both in material and psychological rearmament, he enthused. In three years, Germany would be ready, in four years more than ready; five years would be better still.[117]

In a speech in the cathedral square in Milan a week later, Mussolini spoke of the line between Berlin and Rome as 'an axis round which all those European States which are animated by a desire for collaboration and peace can revolve'.[118] A new term was coined: 'Axis' – whether in a positive or negative sense – caught the imagination. In Italian and German propaganda, it evoked the might and strength of two countries with kindred philosophies joining forces against common enemies. For the western democracies, it raised the spectre of the combined threat to European peace by two expansionist powers under the leadership of dangerous dictators.

The menacing image became global when, within weeks of the formation of the Axis, Hitler entered a further pact with the one power outside Italy he had singled out in his August memorandum as standing firm against Bolshevism: Japan.[119] Hitler had told Ciano in September that Germany had already made considerable progress towards an agreement with Japan within the framework of an anti-Bolshevik front. The anti-British thrust had been explicit.[120] The driving force behind the pact, from the German side, had from the beginning been Ribbentrop, operating with Hitler's encouragement.[121] The professionals from the German Foreign Office, far more interested in relations with China, found themselves largely excluded as a new body of 'amateurs' from the Dienststelle Ribbentrop (Ribbentrop Bureau) – the agency for foreign affairs founded in 1934, by now with around 160 persons working for it, upon which Hitler was placing increasing reliance – made the running.[122] Neurath was not alone in disapproving of the overtures to Tokyo (once he had belatedly come to learn of them).[123] Schacht, Göring, and Blomberg, along with leading industrialists (including the Ruhr armaments magnate Krupp von Bohlen), were also among those keen not to damage relations with China – a source of extensive deliveries of indispensable raw materials for the armaments industry, notably manganese ore and tungsten.[124] In 'official' German foreign policy, Japan was still little more than a sideshow. But in the 'alternative' foreign policy being conducted by Ribbentrop, keen to establish his credentials as Hitler's spokesman in international affairs and attuned to Hitler's ideological interest in a symbolic anti-Bolshevik agreement, Japanese relations had a far higher profile.

Ribbentrop used his intermediary, Dr Friedrich Wilhelm Hack, who had good connections to the Japanese military and important industrial circles, to put out feelers in January 1935. The Japanese military leaders saw in a rapprochement with Berlin the chance to weaken German links with China and to gain a potential ally against the Soviet Union.[125] The prime initiative during the second half of 1935 appears, in fact, to have been taken by the Japanese military authorities, through Hack, in close collaboration with Ribbentrop.[126] Proposals for an anti-Soviet neutrality pact were put forward in October by the Japanese Military Attaché in Berlin, Hiroshi Oshima. Ribbentrop took the proposals – couched as a pact against the Comintern, not directly against the Soviet Union – to Hitler in late November, and gained his approval. Internal upheaval in Japan in the wake of a military revolt of February 1936, and the rapidly changing international situation, led to almost a year's delay before the pact finally came to fruition.[127] On 27 November 1936 Hitler approved what became known as the Anti-Comintern Pact (which Italy joined a year later), under whose main provision – in a secret protocol – neither party would assist the Soviet Union in any way in the event of it attacking either Germany or Japan.[128] The pact was more important for its symbolism than for its actual provisions: the two most militaristic, expansionist powers in the world had found their way to each other. Though the pact was ostensibly defensive, it had hardly enhanced the prospects for peace on either side of the globe.[129]

In his Reichstag speech on 30 January 1937, celebrating the fourth anniversary of his takeover of power, Hitler announced that 'the time of the so-called surprises' was over. Germany wished 'from now on in loyal fashion' as an equal partner to work with other nations to overcome the problems besetting Europe.[130] This pronouncement was soon to prove even more cynical than it had appeared at the time. That further 'surprises' were inevitable – and not long postponed – was not solely owing to Hitler's temperament and psychology. The forces unleashed in four years of Nazi rule – internal and external – were producing their own dynamic. Those in so many different ways who were 'working towards the Führer' were ensuring, directly or indirectly, that Hitler's own ideological obsessions served as the broad guidelines of policy initiatives. The restlessness – and recklessness – ingrained in Hitler's personality reflected the pressures for action emanating in different ways from the varied components of the regime, loosely held together by aims of national assertiveness and racial purity embodied in the figure of the Leader. Internationally, the fragility and chronic instability of the post-war order had been brutally exposed. Within Germany, the chimeric quest for racial purity, backed by a leadership for which this was a central tenet of belief, could, if circumstances demanded, be contained temporarily, but would inevitably soon reassert itself to turn the screw of discrimination ever tighter. The Nazi regime could not stand still. As Hitler himself was to comment before the end of the year, the alternative to expansion – and to the restless energy which was the regime's lifeblood – was what he called 'sterility', bringing in its wake, after a while, 'tensions of a social kind', while failure to act in the near future could bring internal crisis and a 'weakening point of the regime'.[131] The bold forward move (*Flucht nach vorne*), Hitler's trademark, was, therefore, intrinsic to Nazism itself.

V

To most observers, both internal and external, after four years in power the Hitler regime looked stable, strong, and successful. Hitler's own position was untouchable. The image of the great statesman and national leader of genius manufactured by propaganda matched the sentiments and expectations of much of the population. The internal rebuilding of the country and the national triumphs in foreign policy, all attributed to his 'genius', had made him the most popular political leader of any nation in Europe. Most ordinary Germans – like most ordinary people anywhere and at most times – looked forward to peace and prosperity. Hitler appeared to have established the basis for these. He had restored authority to government. Law and order had been re-established. Few were concerned if civil liberties had been destroyed in the process. There was work again. The economy was booming. What a contrast this was to the mass unemployment and economic failure of Weimar democracy. Of course, there was still much to do. And many grievances remained. Not least, the conflict with the Churches was the source of great bitterness. But Hitler was largely exempted from blame. Despite four years of fierce 'Church struggle', the head of the Protestant Church in Bavaria, Bishop Meiser, publicly offered prayers for Hitler, thanking God 'for every success which, through your grace, you have so far granted him for the good of our people'.[132] The negative features of daily life, most imagined, were not of the Führer's making. They were the fault of his underlings, who frequently kept him in the dark about what was happening.

Above all, even critics had to admit, Hitler had restored German national pride. From its post-war humiliation, Germany had risen to become once more a major power. Defence through strength had proved a successful strategy. He had taken risks. There had been great fear that these would lead to renewed war. But each time he had been proved right. And Germany's position had been inordinately strengthened as a consequence. Even so, there was widespread relief at the indication, in Hitler's speech of 30 January 1937, that the period of 'surprises' was over. Hitler's comment was seized upon throughout the land as a sign that consolidation and stability would now be the priorities.[133] The illusion would not last long. The year 1937 was to prove the calm before the storm.[134]

Not only ordinary people were taken in by Hitler. And not only through the imagery of the mass media was the impression created that the leader of the Third Reich was a man of unusual talent and vision. No less a figure than David Lloyd George – product of Welsh radical traditions, former Liberal Party leader, and British Prime Minister at the time of the Versailles Treaty – came away from a three-hour meeting with Hitler at the Berghof at the beginning of September 1936 (at which the old adversaries had exchanged memories of the First World War) enormously impressed, convinced that the German leader was 'a great man'.[135] Even more remarkably, the British Labour Leader and famed pacifist George Lansbury – whose crumpled suit and woolly sweater prompted the introduction of a new dress-code for audiences with the Führer – went away from his meeting with Hitler in mid-April 1937 firmly convinced that the latter was prepared to do what was necessary to avoid war.[136] He had been so enthused at the meeting that he had not noticed how bored Hitler had been, and how vague and non-committal were his unusually monosyllabic responses to Lansbury's own idealistic plans for peace.[137] Other eminent foreign visitors who met Hitler also took away positive impressions. 'He did not only spread fear or aversion,' recalled the French Ambassador François-Poncet. 'He excited curiosity; he awakened sympathy; his prestige grew; the force of attraction emanating from him had an impact beyond the borders of his country.'[138]

Even for those within Germany known to be critical of the regime, Hitler could in a face-to-face meeting create a positive impression. He was good at attuning to the sensitivities of his conversation-partner, could be charming, and often appeared reasonable and accommodating. As always, he was a skilled dissembler. On a one-to-one basis, he could pull the wool over the eyes even of hardened critics. After a three-hour meeting with him at the Berghof in early November 1936, the influential Catholic Archbishop of Munich-Freising, Cardinal Faulhaber – a man of sharp acumen, who had often courageously criticized the Nazi attacks on the Catholic Church – went away convinced that Hitler was deeply religious. 'The Reich Chancellor undoubtedly lives in belief in God,' he noted in a confidential report. 'He recognizes Christianity as the builder of western culture.'[139]

Few, even of those who were daily in his company – the regular entourage of adjutants and secretaries – and those with frequent, privileged access, could claim to 'know' Hitler, to get close to the human being inside the shell of the Führer figure. Hitler himself was keen to maintain the distance. 'The masses need an idol,' he was later to say.[140] He played the role not just to the masses, but even to his closest entourage. Despite the torrents of words he poured out in public, and the lengthy monologues he inflicted upon those in his circle, he was by temperament a very private, even secretive, individual. A deeply ingrained sense of distrust and cynicism meant he was unwilling and unable to confide in others. Behind the public figure known to millions, the personality was a closed one. Genuine personal relations were few. Most even of those who had been in his immediate company for years were kept at arm's length. He used the familiar '*Du*' form with a mere handful of people. Even when his boyhood friend August Kubizek met him again the following year, following the Anschluß, Hitler used the formal '*Sie*' mode of address.[141] The conventional mode of addressing Hitler, which had set in after 1933, 'Mein Führer', emphasized the formality of relations. The authority of his position depended upon the preservation of the nimbus attached to him, as he well realized. This in turn demanded the distance of the individual even from those in his immediate *familia*. The 'mystery' of Hitler's personality had important functional, as well as temperamental, causes. Respect for his authority was more important to him than personal warmth.

Hitler's dealings with his personal staff were formal, correct, polite, and courteous. He usually passed a pleasant word or two with his secretaries when any engagements in the late morning were over, and often took tea with them in the afternoons and at night.[142] He enjoyed the joking and songs (accompanied on the accordion) of his chef and *Hausintendant* or major-domo Arthur Kannenberg.[143] He could show sympathy and understanding, as when his new Luftwaffe adjutant, Nicolaus von Below, had – to his embarrassment – to ask to leave for his honeymoon immediately on joining Hitler's service.[144] He sent Christa Schroeder, one of his secretaries, presents when she was ill and visited her in hospital.[145] He enjoyed giving presents to his staff on their birthdays and at Christmas, and paid personal attention to selecting appropriate gifts.[146]

But genuine warmth and affection were missing. The shows of kindness and attentiveness were superficial. Hitler's staff, like most other human beings, were of interest to him only as long as they were useful.[147] However lengthy and loyal their service, if their usefulness was at an end they would be dispensed with. His staff, for their part, admired 'the Boss' (*der Chef*) as they called him. They respected, at times feared, him. His authority was unquestioned and absolute. Their loyalty to him was equally beyond question. But whether they genuinely liked him as a person is doubtful. There was a certain stiffness about the atmosphere whenever Hitler was present. It was difficult to relax in his company. He was demanding of his staff, who had to work long hours and fit into his eccentric work habits.[148] His secretaries were often on duty in the mornings, but had to be prepared to take dictation of lengthy speeches late at night or into the early hours.[149] Patronizingly complimentary to them on some occasions, on others he would scarcely notice their existence.[150] In his own eyes, more even than in the eyes of those around him, he was the only person that mattered. His wishes, his feelings, his interests alone counted. He could be lenient of misdemeanours when he was unaffected. But where he felt a sense of affront, or that he had been let down, he could be harsh in his treatment of those around him. He was brusque and insulting to the lady-friend, of whom he disapproved, of his Chief Adjutant Wilhelm Brückner, a massive figure, veteran of the SA in the party's early days, and participant in the Beerhall Putsch of 1923. A few years later he was peremptorily to dismiss Brückner, despite his lengthy and dutiful service, following a minor dispute.[151] On another occasion he dismissed his valet Karl Krause, who had served him for several years, again for a trivial matter.[152] Even his jovial hospitality manager, Arthur Kannenberg, who generally enjoyed something of the freedom of a court jester, had to tread carefully. Always anxious at the prospect of any embarrassment that would make him look foolish and damage his standing, Hitler threatened him with punishment if his staff committed any mistakes at receptions.[153]

Hitler strongly disliked any change in the personnel of his immediate entourage. He liked to see the same faces around him. He wanted those about him whom he was used to, and who were used to him. For one whose lifestyle had always been in many respects so 'bohemian', he was remarkably fixed in his routines, inflexible in his habits, and highly reluctant to make alterations to his personal staff.[154]

In 1937 he had four personal adjutants: SA-Gruppenführer Wilhelm Brückner (the chief adjutant); Julius Schaub (formerly the head of his bodyguard, a Putsch veteran who had been in prison in Landsberg with Hitler and in his close attendance ever since, looking after his confidential papers, carrying money for the 'Chief's' use, acting as his personal secretary, general factotum, and 'notebook'); Fritz Wiedemann (who had been Hitler's direct superior in the war); and Albert Bormann (the brother of Martin, with whom, however, he was not on speaking terms).[155] Three military adjutants – Colonel Friedrich Hoßbach for the army, Captain Karl-Jesko Otto von Puttkamer for the navy, and Captain Nicolaus von Below for the Luftwaffe – were responsible for Hitler's links with the leaders of the armed forces. Secretaries, valets (one of whom had to be on call at all moments of the day), his pilot Hans Baur, his chauffeur Erich Kempka, the head of the Leibstandarte-SS Adolf Hitler and long-standing Hitler trustee Sepp Dietrich, the leaders of the bodyguard and criminal police attachments, and the doctors who, at different times, attended upon him all formed part of the additional personal staff.[156]

By 1937, Hitler's day followed a fairly regular pattern, at least when he was in Berlin. Late in the morning, he received a knock from his valet, Karl Krause, who would leave newspapers and any important messages outside his room. While Hitler took them in to read, Krause ran his bath and laid out his clothes. Always concerned to avoid being seen naked, Hitler insisted upon dressing himself, without help from his valet.[157] Only towards midday did he emerge from his private suite of rooms (or 'Führer apartment') – a lounge, library, bedroom, and bathroom, together with a small room reserved for Eva Braun – in the renovated Reich Chancellery.[158] He gave any necessary instructions to, or received information from, his military adjutants, was given a press summary by Otto Dietrich, and was told by Hans Heinrich Lammers, head of the Reich Chancellery, of his various engagements. Meetings and discussions, usually carried out while Hitler walked backwards and forwards with his discussion partner in the 'Wintergarten' (or conservatory) looking out on the garden, generally filled the next couple of hours – sometimes longer – so that lunch was frequently delayed.[159]

The spacious and light dining-room had a large round table with a dozen chairs in the centre and four smaller tables, each with six chairs, around it. Hitler sat at the large table with his back to the window, facing a picture by Kaulbach, *Entry of the Sun Goddess*.[160] Some of the guests – among them Goebbels, Göring, and Speer – were regulars. Others were newcomers or were seldom invited. The talk was often of world affairs. But Hitler would tailor the discussion to those present. He was careful in what he said. He consciously set out to impress his opinion on his guests, perhaps at times to gauge their reaction. Sometimes he dominated the 'conversation' with a monologue. At other times, he was content to listen while Goebbels sparred with another guest, or a more general discussion unfolded. Sometimes the table talk was interesting. New guests could find the occasion exciting and Hitler's comments a 'revelation'. Frau Below, the wife of the new Luftwaffe-Adjutant, found the atmosphere, and Hitler's company, at first exhilarating and was greatly impressed by his knowledge of history and art.[161] But for the household staff who had heard it all many times, the midday meal was often a tedious affair.[162]

After lunch there were usually further meetings in the Music Salon with ambassadors, generals, Reich Ministers, foreign dignitaries, or personal acquaintances such as the Wagners or Bruckmanns. Such meetings seldom lasted longer than an hour, and were arranged around tea. Thereafter, Hitler withdrew to his own rooms for a rest, or went for a stroll round the park attached to the Reich Chancellery.[163] He spent no time at all during the day at his massive desk, other than hurriedly to attach his signature to laws, letters of appointment, or other formal documents placed before him. Beyond his major speeches, letters to foreign heads of state, and the occasional formal note of thanks or condolence, he dictated little or nothing to his secretaries.[164] Apart from his temperamental aversion to bureaucracy, he was anxious to avoid committing himself on paper. The consequence was that his adjutants and personal staff often had the task of passing on in written form directives which were unclear, ill-thought-out, or spontaneous reactions. The scope for confusion, distortion, and misunderstanding was enormous. What Hitler had originally intended or stated was, by the time it had passed through various hands, often open to different interpretation and impossible to reconstruct with certainty.[165]

The evening meal, around 8p.m., followed the same pattern as lunch, but there were usually fewer present and talk focused more on Hitler's favourite topics, such as art and history. During the meal, Hitler would be presented by one of the servants (most of whom were drawn from his bodyguard, the Leibstandarte) with a list of films, including those from abroad and German films still unreleased, which Goebbels had provided. (Hitler was delighted at his Christmas present from Goebbels in 1937: thirty feature films of the previous four years, and eighteen Mickey Mouse cartoons.)[166] After the meal, the film chosen for the evening would be shown in the Music Salon. Any members of the household staff and the chauffeurs of any guests present could watch. Hitler's secretaries were, however, not present at the meals in the Reich Chancellery, though they were included in the more relaxed atmosphere at the Berghof. The evening ended with conversation stretching usually to about 2 a.m. before Hitler retired.[167]

In this world within the Reich Chancellery, with its fixed routines and formalities, where he was surrounded by his regular staff and otherwise met for the most part official visitors or guests who were mainly in awe of him, Hitler was cocooned within the role and image of the Führer which had elevated him to demi-god status. Few could behave naturally in his presence. The rough 'old fighters' of the Party's early days now came less frequently. Those attending the meals in the Reich Chancellery had for the most part only known him since the nimbus of the 'great leader' had become attached to him.[168] The result only reinforced Hitler's self-belief that he was a 'man of destiny', treading his path 'with the certainty of a sleepwalker'.[169] At the same time, he was ever more cut off from real human contact, isolated in his realm of increasing megalomania. Aways glad to get away from Berlin, it was only while staying with the Wagners during the annual Bayreuth Festival and at his alpine retreat 'on the mountain' above Berchtesgaden that Hitler relaxed somewhat.[170] But even at the Berghof, rituals were preserved. Hitler dominated the entire existence of his guests there too. Real informality was as good as impossible in his presence. And Hitler, for all the large numbers of people in attendance on him and paying court to him, remained impoverished when it came to real contact, cut off from any meaningful personal relationship through the shallowness of his emotions and his profoundly egocentric, exploitative attitude towards all other human beings.

It is impossible to be sure of what, if any, emotional satisfaction Hitler gained from his relationship with Eva Braun (whom he had first met in 1929 when, then aged seventeen, she worked in the office of his photographer, Heinrich Hoffmann). It could not have been much. For prestige reasons, he kept her away from the public eye. On the rare occasions she was in Berlin, she was closeted in her little room in the 'Führer Apartment' while Hitler attended official functions or was otherwise engaged.[171] Even in his close circle she was not permitted to be present for meals if any important guests were there. She did not accompany Hitler on his numerous journeys, and had to stay for the most part either in his flat in Munich or at the Berghof, the only place where she could emerge as one of the extended 'family'.[172] Even there, however, she was hidden away during receptions for important guests.[173] Hitler often treated her abysmally when she was present, frequently humiliating her in front of others.[174] The contrast with the olde-worlde charm – kissing hands, linking arms, cupping elbows – that he habitually showed towards pretty women in his presence merely rubbed salt in the wounds.[175] That Eva had long suffered from Hitler's neglect of her is evident from her plaintive diary entries two years earlier, in 1935.[176] Her deep unhappiness had culminated in her second suicide attempt in the May of that year – an overdose of sleeping tablets that amounted, like her first attempt (with a revolver) in 1932, to a *cri de cœur* rather than a serious effort to kill herself.[177]

Probably the closest that Hitler came to friendship was in his relations with Joseph Goebbels and, increasingly, with his court architect and new favourite, Albert Speer, whom in January 1937 he made responsible for the rebuilding of Berlin.[178] Hitler frequently sought out their company, liked their presence, was fond of their wives and families, and could feel at ease with them. The Goebbels home was a frequent refuge in Berlin. Lengthy talks with Speer about the rebuilding of the capital city amounted to the nearest thing Hitler had to a hobby, a welcome respite from his otherwise total involvement in politics. At least in Goebbels's case there were elements of a father-son relationship.[179] A rare flicker of human concern could be glimpsed when Hitler asked Goebbels to stay for an extra day in Nuremberg after the Rally in September 1937, since (according to the Propaganda Minister) he did not like him flying at night.[180] Hitler was the dominant figure – the father figure. But he may have seen something of himself in each of his two protégés – the brilliant propagandist in Goebbels, the gifted architect in Speer.

In the case of Speer, the fascination for architecture provided an obvious bond. Both had a liking for neo-classical buildings on a monumental scale. Hitler was impressed by Speer's taste in architecture, his energy, and his organizational skill. He had rapidly come to see him as the architect who could put his own grandiose building schemes, envisaged as the representation of Teutonic might and glory that would last for centuries, into practice. But other architects, some better than Speer, were available. The attractiveness of Speer to Hitler went beyond the building mania that linked them closely to each other. Nothing homoerotic was involved – at least not consciously. But Hitler perhaps found in the handsome, burningly ambitious, talented, and successful architect an unconsciously idealized self-image.[181] What is plain is that both Goebbels and Speer worshipped Hitler. Goebbels's adoration of the father-figure Hitler was undiminished since the mid-1920s. 'He is a fabulous man' was merely one of his effusions of sentiment in 1937 about the figure who was the centre-point of his universe.[182] For Speer, as he himself later recognized, his love of Hitler transcended the power-ambitions that his protector and role-model was able to satisfy – even if it originally arose out of them and could never be completely separated from them.[183]

In earlier years, Hitler had invariably spoken of his own 'mission' as the mere beginning of Germany's passage to world domination. The whole process would take generations to complete.[184] But, flushed with scarcely imaginable triumphs since 1933 and falling ever more victim to the myth of his own greatness, he became increasingly impatient to see his 'mission' fulfilled in his lifetime.

Partly, this was incipient megalomania. He spoke on numerous occasions in 1937 about building plans of staggering monumentality.[185] At midnight on his birthday, he, Goebbels, and Speer stood in front of plans for rebuilding Berlin, fantasizing about a glorious future.[186] Hitler even thought for a while of creating a new capital city on the Müritzsee in Mecklenburg, eighty miles or so north-west of Berlin, but eventually dropped an idea which was patently absurd.[187] 'The Führer won't speak of money. Build, build! It will somehow be paid for!' Goebbels has him saying. 'Frederick the Great didn't ask about money when he built Sanssouci.'[188]

In part, too, it was prompted by Hitler's growing preoccupation with his own mortality and impatience to achieve what he could in his lifetime. Before the mid-1930s, his health had generally been good – astonishingly so given his lack of exercise, poor diet (even before his cranky vegetarianism following the death in 1931 of his niece, Geli Raubal), and high expenditure of nervous energy. However, he already suffered from chronic stomach pains which, at times of stress, became acute spasms.[189] A patent medicine he took – an old trench remedy with a base in gun-cleaning oil – turned out to be mildly poisonous, causing headaches, double vision, dizziness, and ringing in the ears.[190] He had been worried in 1935 that a polyp in his throat (eventually removed in the May of that year) was cancerous.[191] It turned out to be harmless. During 1936, a year of almost continual tension, the stomach cramps were frequently severe, and Hitler also developed eczema on both legs, which had to be covered in bandages.[192] At Christmas 1936, Hitler asked Dr Theodor Morell, a physician who had successfully treated his photographer Heinrich Hoffmann, to try to cure him. Morell gave him vitamins and a new patent remedy for intestinal problems.[193] Goebbels mentioned in June, and again in August 1937, that Hitler was unwell.[194] But by September, Morell's treatment had apparently made a difference. At any rate, Hitler was impressed. He felt fit again, his weight was back to normal, and his eczema had vanished.[195] His belief in Morell would last down to the bunker in 1945. From late 1937 onwards, his increasing hypochondria made him ever more reliant on Morell's pills, drugs, and injections.[196] And the fear of cancer (which had caused his mother's death) never left him. At the end of October, he told a meeting of propaganda leaders that both his parents had died young, and that he probably did not have long to live. 'It was necessary, therefore, to solve the problems that had to be solved (living-space) as soon as possible, so that this could still take place in his lifetime. Later generations would no longer be able to accomplish it. Only his person was in the position to bring it about.'[197]

Hitler was seldom out of the public eye in 1937. No opportunity was missed to drive home to the German public an apparently endless array of scarcely credible 'achievements' at home and the glories of his major 'triumphs' in foreign policy. Flushed with success and certain of the adulation of the masses, he wanted to be seen. The bonds between the Führer and the people – the cement of the regime, and dependent upon recurring success and achievement – were thereby reinforced. And for Hitler the ecstasy of his mass audiences provided each time a new injection of the drug to feed his egomania.

A constant round of engagements ensured that he was ever visible. By 1937 the Nazi calendar, revolving around Hitler's major speeches and appearance at parades and rallies, was well established, the rituals firmly in place. A speech to the Reichstag on 30 January (the anniversary of his appointment as Chancellor), speeches to the Party's 'Old Fighters' on 24 February (the anniversary of the promulgation of the 1920 Party Programme) and 8 November (the anniversary of the 1923 putsch), taking the salute at big military parades on his birthday on 20 April, a speech at the huge gathering (estimated at 1,200,000 in 1937) in Berlin's Lustgarten on the 'National Day of Celebration of the German People' (1 May), and, of course, the week of the Reich Party Rally at Nuremberg in the first half of September all formed fixed points of the year. Other public appearances in 1937 included: the opening of the International Car Exhibition in Berlin on 20 February, next day laying a wreath at the Berlin cenotaph and reviewing troops on 'Heroes' Memorial Day', the launch of the 'Strength Through Joy' ship *Wilhelm Gustloff* (intended as a cruise-ship for German workers) on 5 May, the opening of the Reich Food Estate's Agricultural Exhibition in Munich on 30 May, a speech to 200,000 people at the Gau Party Rally of the Bayerische Ostmark (Bavarian Eastern Marches) in Regensburg on 6 June, and to a further mass rally of the Gau Unterfranken (Lower Franconia) on 27 June, a speech at the festive opening of the 'House of German Art' (the imposing new art gallery designed by one of Hitler's early favourite architects, Paul Ludwig Troost) in Munich on 19 July, an address to half a million attending the Festival of the League of German Singers in Breslau on 1 August, five days of Mussolini's state visit to Germany between 25 and 29 September, speeches in early October at the harvest festival on the Bückeberg, near Hanover, and in Berlin at the opening of the 'Winter Aid' campaign (the annual collection, initially established in 1933 to help the unemployed over the winter months), a speech to the Party faithful in Augsburg on 21 November, and a speech at the laying of the foundation stone of the Military Technical Faculty of Berlin's Technical University on 27 November. In all, Hitler held some twenty-six major speeches during the course of the year (thirteen alone at the Nuremberg Rally), apart from lesser addresses, and appearances at parades and other meetings where he did not speak.[198]

As always, the effect of his speeches depended heavily upon the atmosphere in which they were held. The content was repetitive and monotonous. The themes were the familiar ones. Past achievements were lauded, grandiose future plans proclaimed, the horrors and menace of Bolshevism emphasized. But there was no conflict between propaganda and ideology. Hitler believed what he was saying.

The 'nationalization of the masses' – the prerequisite for German power and expansion, which he had posited since the early 1920s – he thought well on the way to being accomplished. At his three-hour speech to the Reichstag on 30 January 1937, the anniversary of the takeover of power, giving account of his first four years in office, he claimed he had restored German honour through the reintroduction of conscription, the creation of the Luftwaffe, the rebuilding of the navy, and the reoccupation of the Rhineland, and announced that he was solemnly withdrawing the German signature from the admission of war-guilt in the Versailles Treaty, 'wrung out of a then weak government'.[199] On 1 May, he lauded Germany as a classless society where individuals from all backgrounds had a chance to rise to the top through their own achievements – as long as they were in the collective interest of the nation, and as long as the total subservience such as he had himself practised for almost six years as a soldier was forthcoming.[200] Wholly detached from the practical considerations of day-to-day politics, he held out a breathtaking vision of German grandeur, power, and dominance enshrined in heroic art and architecture which would monumentalize Teutonic cultural achievements for 1,000 years. 'The building of a temple' for 'a true and eternal German art' was how he described the 'House of German Art' at its opening in July.[201] Presenting 'a thousand-year people with a thousand-year historical and cultural past' with a fitting 'thousand-year city' was what he foresaw in November as the task of turning Berlin into the world-capital 'Germania'.[202] At the Reich Party Rally at Nuremberg in early September, the themes of great national and social achievements in the past years were coupled with the aims of a racial revolution whose profound consequences would 'create the new man' (*Menschen*).[203] His lengthy concluding speech to the Party Congress was an onslaught on 'Jewish Bolshevism'.[204] In passages at times reminiscent of *Mein Kampf*, and in his fiercest public attack on the Jews for many months, he portrayed them as the force behind Bolshevism and its 'general attack on the present-day social order', and spoke of 'the claim of an uncivilized Jewish-Bolshevik international guild of criminals to rule Germany, as an old cultural land of Europe, from Moscow'.[205] This is what the Party faithful wanted to hear. But it was far more than window-dressing. Even in private, dictating the speeches to his secretary, when it came to passages on Bolshevism Hitler, red-faced and eyes blazing, would work himself to a frenzy, bellowing at full volume his thunderous denunciations.[206]

VI

Away from the continual propaganda activity revolving around speeches and public appearances, Hitler was largely preoccupied in 1937 with keeping a watchful eye on the changing situation in world affairs and with his gigantic building plans. The continuing conflict with both the Catholic and Protestant Churches, radical though his own instincts were, amounted to a recurrent irritation, especially in the first months of the year, rather than a priority concern (as it was with Goebbels, Rosenberg, and many of the Party rank-and-file). With regard to the 'Jewish Question' – to go from the many private discussions with Goebbels which the Propaganda Minister reported in his diary notes – Hitler, unchanged though his views were, showed little active interest and seldom spoke directly on the subject. But however uninvolved Hitler was, the radicalization of the regime continued unabated, forced on in a variety of ways by Party activists, ministerial bureaucracy, economic opportunists, and, not least, by an ideologically driven police.

In February 1937 Hitler made it plain to his inner circle that he did not want a 'Church struggle' at this juncture. The time was not ripe for it. He expected 'the great world struggle in a few years' time'. If Germany lost one more war, it would mean the end.[207] The implication was clear: calm should be restored for the time being in relations with the Churches. Instead, the conflict with the Christian Churches intensified. The anti-clericalism and anti-Church sentiments of the grass-roots Party activists simply could not be eradicated. Provincial Nazi leaders such as the Gauleiter of Upper Bavaria (and Bavarian Education and Interior Minister) Adolf Wagner were often only too keen to keep the conflict on the boil.[208] The eagerness of Party activists and local leaders (a disproportionate number of whom were teachers) to break the Christian influence reinforced through denominational schools sustained the momentum at grass-roots level. It was met by determined (if ultimately unsuccessful) rearguard action of the clergy and churchgoing population.[209] The stranglehold that the Churches maintained over the values and mentalities of large sections of the population was an obvious thorn in the side of a Movement with its own highly intolerant 'world-view', which saw itself as making a total claim on soul as well as body. The assault on the practices and institutions of the Christian Churches was deeply embedded in the psyche of National Socialism. Where the hold of the Church was strong, as in the backwaters of rural Bavaria, the conflict raged in villages and small towns with little prompting from on high.[210]

At the same time, the activists could draw on the verbal violence of Party leaders towards the Churches for their encouragement. Goebbels's orchestrated attacks on the clergy through the staged 'immorality trials' of Franciscans in 1937 – following usually trumped-up or grossly exaggerated allegations of sexual impropriety in the religious orders – provided further ammunition.[211] And, in turn, however much Hitler on some occasions claimed to want a respite in the conflict, his own inflammatory comments gave his immediate underlings all the licence they needed to turn up the heat in the 'Church struggle', confident that they were 'working towards the Führer'.

Hitler's impatience with the Churches prompted frequent outbursts of hostility. In early 1937, he was declaring that 'Christianity was ripe for destruction' (*Untergang*), and that the Churches must yield to the 'primacy of the state', railing against any compromise with 'the most horrible institution imaginable'.[212] In two conferences he summoned in February to try to end the damaging consequences of the conflict which Church Minister Kerrl had done nothing to solve, he eagerly seized upon Goebbels's suggestion for new elections – to be publicized as 'the peace move of the Führer in the Church Question'.[213] However, he indicated that at some point in the future Church and state would be separated, the Concordat of 1933 between the Reich and the Vatican dissolved (to provide the regime with a free hand), and the entire force of the Party turned to 'the destruction of the clerics (*Pfaffen*)'.

For the time being it was necessary to wait, see what the opponents did, and be tactically clever. Everything was a means to an end – 'the life of the people'. He expected in five or six years' time 'a great world showdown (*Auseinandersetzung*)'. In fifteen years, he would have liquidated the Peace of Westphalia – the treaty of 1648 which had brought religious accord in the German states, ending the Thirty Years War. 'A grandiose outlook for the future,' Goebbels called it.[214]

Addressing the Gauleiter in mid-March, Hitler announced that he wanted 'no ordinary victory' over the Churches. Either one should keep quiet about an opponent (*totschweigen*), or slay him (*totschlagen*), was how he put it.[215] In April, Goebbels reported with satisfaction that the Führer was becoming more radical in the 'Church Question', and had approved the start of the 'immorality trials' against clergy.[216] Goebbels noted Hitler's verbal attacks on the clergy and his satisfaction with the propaganda campaign on several subsequent occasions over the following few weeks.[217] Much of the ranting was probably at Goebbels's prompting. But Hitler was happy to leave the Propaganda Minister and others to make the running. In as divisive an issue as this, Goebbels himself fully recognized that what must be avoided at all costs was 'to send the Führer into the field'.[218] Hitler was nevertheless again in the glare of world publicity about the persecution of the clergy when, in early July, Pastor Martin Niemöller, the leading voice of the 'Confessing Church', was arrested as part of an assault on 'disloyal' Protestant churchmen.[219] But, if Goebbels's diary entries are a guide, Hitler's interest and direct involvement in the 'Church struggle' declined during the second half of the year. Other matters were by now occupying his attention.

The 'Jewish Question' does not appear to have figured prominently among them. Goebbels, who saw Hitler almost on a daily basis at this time and who noted the topics of many private conversations they had together, recorded no more than a couple of instances where the 'Jewish Question' was discussed. On the first day of the Party Rally in Nuremberg, Hitler talked in his hotel to Goebbels about 'race questions'. 'There too there's a lot still to be clarified,' commented the Propaganda Minister.[220] At the end of November, among 'a thousand things talked about' over lunch was the 'Jewish Question'. The discussion appears to have been prompted by Goebbels's preparations for legislation to ban Jews from attending theatres and cultural events. 'My new law will soon be ready,' he wrote.[221] 'But that is not the goal. The Jews must get out of Germany, yes out of the whole of Europe. That will still take some time. But it will and must happen. The Führer is firmly decided on it.'[222] It was a statement of belief, not a political decision resting on clearly thought-out strategy. Anti-Jewish policy, as we have seen, had gathered pace since 1933 without frequent or coherent central direction. It was no different in 1937. Hitler's views, as his comment to Goebbels makes clear, remained unchanged since his first statement on the 'Jewish Question' back in September 1919. He gave a clear indication to a gathering of some 800 district leaders (*Kreisleiter*) in April 1937 of his tactical caution but ideological consistency in the 'Jewish Question'. Though he made plain to his enemies that he wanted to destroy them, the struggle had to be conducted cleverly, and over a period of time, he told his avid listeners. Skill would help him manoeuvre them into a corner. Then would come the blow to the heart.[223] It was in line with these precepts that he now sanctioned, following the prompting in June 1937 of the Reich Doctors' Leader Gerhard Wagner, measures (eventually coming into effect in 1938) to ban all Jewish doctors from medical practice – a step he had regarded as inopportune when the issue had been raised in late 1933.[224]

But this was a rare instance of direct involvement around this time. For the most part, he was content to remain for the time being inactive in the 'Jewish Question'. His tacit approval was all that was required. And no more was needed than his tirade against 'Jewish Bolshevism' at the Party Rally in September to act as a green light inviting the new antisemitic wave – even fiercer than that of 1935 – that was to unfold throughout 1938.[225]

After two relatively quiet years, discrimination against the Jews again intensified. Increasingly radical steps were initiated to eliminate them from the economy, and from more and more spheres of social activity. The Security Service (Sicherheitsdienst, SD), whose 'Jewish Section' (Judenreferat) was run by the ambitious Adolf Eichmann, had in fact since the start of the year been advocating renewed pressure on the Jews to force them out of the economy and speed up their emigration from Germany.[226] The manufacture of a 'popular mood hostile to Jews' and the deployment of illegal 'excesses' – mob violence, which was seen as particularly effective – were recommended.[227] By autumn, the climate was becoming more hostile than ever for the Jewish population.[228] Schacht's loss of influence, and finally his departure from the Economics Ministry on 27 November, now removed an obstacle to the 'aryanization' of the economy. Pressure to fulfil this aspect of the Party's Programme mounted.[229] Göring, by this time in effect in charge of the economy, was more than ready to push forward the 'aryanization'. The upswing of the economy made big business, losing the uncertainties of the first years of Nazi rule, willing partners, eager to profit from the takeover of Jewish firms at knock-down prices.[230] By April 1938 more than 60 per cent of Jewish firms had been liquidated or 'aryanized'.[231] From late 1937 onwards, individual Jews also faced an expanding array of discriminatory measures, initiated without central coordination by a variety of ministries and offices – all in their way 'working towards the Führer' – which tightened immeasurably the screw of persecution.[232] Hitler's own contribution, as usual, had largely consisted of setting the tone and providing the sanction and legitimation for the actions of others.

In world affairs, events beyond Hitler's control were causing him to speculate on the timing and circumstances in which the great showdown would occur. By the end of 1937, the signs were that radicalization was gathering pace not just in anti-Jewish policy (and, largely instigated by the Gestapo, in the persecution and repression of other ethnic and social minorities), but also in foreign policy.[233]

Hitler began the year by expressing his hope to those at his lunch table that he still had six years to prepare for the coming showdown. 'But, if a very favourable chance comes along,' commented Goebbels, 'he also doesn't want to miss it.' Hitler stressed Russian strength and warned against under-estimating the British because of their weak political leadership. He saw opportunities of winning allies in eastern Europe (particularly Poland) and the Balkans as a consequence of Russia's drive for world revolution.[234] Hitler's remarks followed a long briefing by Blomberg earlier that morning in the War Ministry about the rapid expansion of rearmament and the Wehrmacht's preparations for 'Case X' – taken to be Germany, together with its fascist allies against Russia, Czechoslovakia, and Lithuania. The question of German occupation was evidently raised. Hitler, Goebbels, and Blomberg discussed the installation of senior Gauleiter as Civilian Commissars. Hitler was satisfied with what he had heard.[235]

A foretaste of what might be expected from the German leadership in war followed the dropping of two 'red bombs' on the battleship *Deutschland*, stationed off Ibiza, by a Spanish Republican plane on the evening of 29 May, killing twenty-three and injuring over seventy sailors. Admiral Raeder, Commander-in-Chief of the Navy, was dispatched by Blomberg to Munich to bear the brunt of Hitler's fury. Hitler's immediate reaction, 'fuming with rage', as Goebbels put it, was to bomb Valencia in reprisal. But after a hastily arranged conference with Blomberg, Raeder, Göring, and von Neurath, he ordered instead the cruiser *Admiral Scheer* to fire on the southern Spanish harbour town of Almería. Hitler, seething but nervous at the outcome, paced up and down his room in the Reich Chancellery until three o'clock in the morning. The shelling of Almería for an hour left twenty-one civilians dead, fifty-three injured, and destroyed thirty-nine houses. Hitler was satisfied. He had seen it as a prestige question. Prestige had now been restored.[236]

He had by this time lost faith in Spain becoming a genuinely fascist country. He saw Franco as a Spanish variant of General Seeckt (the former 'strong man' in the German army in the 1920s) – a military man without any mass movement behind him.[237] Despite his worries about Spain, however, he had no regrets about ordering German intervention, and pointed to the many advantages which Germany had drawn from its involvement.[238] Goebbels's diary notes reflect Hitler's wider perceptions of world affairs during the latter half of 1937, and his watchful eye on opportunities for German expansion. The radicalization in foreign policy which brought the Anschluß with Austria and then the Sudeten crisis in Czechoslovakia in 1938 were foreshadowed in Hitler's musings on future developments during these months.

The arch-enemy, the Soviet Union, was in Hitler's eyes weakened both by its internal turmoils and by Japanese triumphs in the war against China.[239] He was puzzled by the Stalinist purges. 'Stalin is probably sick in the brain (*gehirnkrank*),' Goebbels reported him as saying. 'His bloody regime can otherwise not be explained. But Russia knows nothing other than Bolshevism. That's the danger we have to smash down some day.'[240] A few months later, he was repeating the view that Stalin and his followers were mad. 'Must be exterminated (*Muß ausgerottet werden*)' was his sinister conclusion.[241] He was anticipating that the opportunity might arise following a Japanese victory over China. Once China was smashed, he guessed, Tokyo would turn its attention to Moscow. 'That is then our great hour,' he predicted.[242]

Hitler's belief in an alliance with Britain had by now almost evaporated. His attitude towards Britain had come to resemble that of a lover spurned.[243] Contemptuous of the British government, he also saw Britain greatly weakened as a world power.[244] Egged on by Ribbentrop, by now aggressively anti-British, and diverging sharply from the more cautious Foreign Office line that looked to a negotiated settlement in time with Britain (involving territorial revision and concession of colonies), his hopes now rested – too strongly for Goebbels's liking – on his new friend Mussolini.[245]

Nothing was spared in the preparations for a huge extravaganza with all conceivable pomp and circumstance to make the maximum impact on the Duce during his state visit to Germany between 25 and 29 September. Hitler even had an aeroplane dispatched to fetch ripe pears for the Duce, concerned that there was not a sufficiently wide choice of fruit to offer his guest from southern Europe.[246] Not even the torrential rain that drenched the hundreds of thousands assembled at Tempelhof on 28 September to hear speeches from the two dictators, and made it difficult for Mussolini to read his prepared German text, could damage the impression that the visit made on the Duce.[247] He took home with him an image of German power and might – together with a growing sense that Italy's role in the Axis was destined to be that of junior partner. Hitler was also overjoyed at the outcome. There had been agreement on cooperation in Spain, and on attitudes towards the war in the Far East. Hitler was certain that Italian friendship was assured, since Italy had in any case little alternative. Only the 'Austrian Question', on which Mussolini would not be drawn, remained open. 'Well, wait and see,' commented Goebbels.[248]

From remarks recorded by Goebbels, it is clear that Hitler was already by summer 1937 beginning to turn his eyes towards Austria and Czechoslovakia, though as yet there was no indication of when and how Germany might move against either state. Nor were ideological or military-strategic motives, however important for Hitler himself, the only ones influencing notions of expansion in central Europe. Continuing economic difficulties, especially in fulfilling the Wehrmacht's demands for raw materials, had been the main stimulus to increased German pressure on Austria since the successful visit by Göring to Italy in January.[249] Gold and foreign-currency reserves, labour supplies, and important raw materials were among the lure of a German takeover of the alpine Republic.[250] Not surprisingly, therefore, the office of the Four Year Plan was at the forefront of demands for an Anschluß as soon as possible. The economic significance of the 'Austrian Question' was further underlined by Hitler's appointment in July 1937 of Wilhelm Keppler, who had served before 1933 as an important link with business leaders, to coordinate Party affairs regarding Vienna.[251] Further concessions to follow on those of the 1936 agreement – including the ending of censorship on *Mein Kampf* – were forced on the Austrian government in July. 'Perhaps we're again coming a step further,' mused Goebbels.[252] 'In Austria, the Führer will some time make a *tabula rasa*,' the Propaganda Minister noted, after a conversation with Hitler at the beginning of August. 'Let's hope we can all still experience it,' he went on. 'He'll go for it then. (*Er geht dann aufs Ganze.*) This state is not a state at all. Its people belong to us and will come to us. The Führer's entry into Vienna will one day be his proudest triumph.'[253] At the end of the Nuremberg Rally, a few weeks later, Hitler told Goebbels that the issue of Austria would some time be resolved 'with force'.[254] Before the end of the year, Papen was unfolding to Hitler plans to topple the Austrian Chancellor Schuschnigg.[255] Göring and

Keppler were by then both convinced that Hitler would tackle the question of Austria during the spring or summer of 1938.[256]

In the case of Czechoslovakia, too, Hitler's intentions were unmistakable to Goebbels. 'Czechia (*die Tschechei*) is also no state,' he noted in his diary in August. 'It will one day be overrun.'[257] The refusal by Czech authorities to allow children from the Sudeten area to go for holidays to Germany was used by Goebbels as the pretext to launch the beginning of a vitriolic press campaign against the Czechs.[258] Göring had by this time been stressing to the British Ambassador, Nevile Henderson – who gave the air of being more accommodating to German claims than his predecessor Sir Eric Phipps, whom he had replaced in April, had been – Germany's rights to Austria and the Sudetenland (in due course also to revision of the Polish border). To a long-standing British acquaintance, the former air attaché in Berlin, Group Captain Christie, he went further: Germany must have not simply the Sudetenland, but the whole of Bohemia and Moravia, Göring asserted.[259] By mid-October, following the demands of Konrad Henlein, the Sudeten German leader, for autonomy, Goebbels was predicting that Czechoslovakia would in the future 'have nothing to laugh about'.[260]

On 5 November 1937 the Propaganda Minister lunched, as usual, with Hitler. The general situation was discussed. The Czech question was to be toned down for the time being because Germany was still not in a position to take any action. The issue of colonies was also to be taken more slowly, so as not to awaken false expectations among the population. In the run-up to Christmas, the heat had, too, to be turned down on the 'Church struggle'. The long-running saga of Schacht was nearing its dénouement. Schacht had to go, it was agreed. But the Führer wanted to wait until after the Party's ritual Putsch commemoration on 9 November before taking any action. In the afternoon, Goebbels went home to continue work. The Führer, he noted, had 'General Staff talks'.[261]

VII

In the gloom of late afternoon, the chiefs of the army, Luftwaffe, and navy, together with War Minister Blomberg, made their way to the Reich Chancellery for a meeting, as they thought, to establish the allocation of steel supplies to the armed forces. The reason for the meeting dated back to late October, when Admiral Raeder, increasingly concerned about Göring's allocation of steel and the preferential treatment of the Luftwaffe, had posed an ultimatum to Blomberg indicating that no expansion of the navy was possible without additional steel supplies. Raeder was unwilling to make concessions. He thought an immediate decision by the Führer was necessary.[262] With the dispute among the branches of the armed forces simmering and the prospect of the arms drive stagnating, Blomberg pressed Hitler for clarification. Eventually, Hitler agreed to the meeting. Blomberg, not Hitler, sent out the invitations to discuss 'the armaments situation and raw materials demands' to the chiefs of the three armed forces' branches.[263] The military leaders had a surprise when they reached the Reich Chancellery at 4p.m. to find present, alongside Hitler and his military adjutant, Colonel Hoßbach, also the Foreign Minister von Neurath. Another surprise was waiting for them when, instead of dealing with the issue of raw materials allocation (which was discussed relatively briefly only towards the end of the lengthy meeting), Hitler, speaking from prepared notes, launched into a monologue lasting over two hours on Germany's need to expand by use of force within the following few years.[264]

He began by emphasizing the importance of what he had to say. He wanted, he said, to explain his thinking on foreign policy. In the event of his death, what he had to say ought to be viewed as his 'testamentary legacy'. No arrangements had been made for minutes to be taken, but Hoßbach, sitting opposite Hitler at the table, decided that what he was about to hear might be of some moment and started to scribble notes in his diary. He was sure his mentor, the increasingly critical General Beck, would be interested.[265]

Hitler launched into a familiar theme: the need to expand German 'living space'. Without this expansion, 'sterility', leading to social disorder, would set in – an argument reflecting Hitler's premiss that permanent mobilization and ever new goals, foreign and domestic, were necessary to ensure the popular support of the regime. In characteristic vein, he raised alternatives to expansion of 'living space', only to dismiss them. Only limited autarky could be achieved. Food supplies could not be ensured by this route. Dependence on the world economy could never bring economic security, and would leave Germany weak and exposed. Here, Hitler was attacking the views associated with Schacht, whose departure as Economics Minister had already been decided. Schacht had also been a strong proponent of a colonial policy. Hitler dismissed the 'liberal capitalist notions in the exploitation of colonies'. The return of colonies would only come about, argued Hitler, once Britain was seriously weakened and Germany more powerful. 'Living space', he asserted, meant territory for agricultural production in Europe, not acquisition of overseas colonies. Britain and France, both implacably hostile, stood in Germany's way. But Britain and its Empire were weakened. And France faced internal difficulties. His conclusion to the first part of his address was that Germany's problem could only be solved by the use of force, which was always accompanied by risks. Only the questions 'when?' and 'how?' remained to be answered.

He went on to outline three scenarios. Typically, he first argued that time was not on Germany's side, that it would be imperative to act by 1943-5 at the latest. The relative strength in armaments would decrease. Other powers would be prepared for a German offensive. Alluding to the problems of 1935-6, he raised the prospect of economic difficulties producing a new food crisis without the foreign exchange to master it – a potential 'weakening-point (*Schwächungsmoment*) of the regime'. Declining birthrates, falling living standards, and the ageing of the Movement and its leaders were added points to underline what he declared was his 'unalterable determination to solve the German problem of space by 1943-5 at the latest'.

In the other two scenarios, Hitler outlined circumstances in which it would be necessary to strike before 1943-5: if France became so enveloped by internal strife, or embroiled in war with another power, that it was incapable of military action against Germany. In either case the moment would have arrived to attack Czechoslovakia. A war of France and Britain against Italy he saw as a distinct possibility arising from the protracted conflict in Spain (whose prolongation was in Germany's interest). In such an eventuality, Germany must be prepared to take advantage of the circumstances to attack the Czechs and Austria without delay – even as early as 1938. The first objective in any war involving Germany would be to overthrow Czechoslovakia and Austria simultaneously to protect the eastern flank for any possible military operation in the west. Hitler conjectured that Britain, and probably France as well, had already written off Czechoslovakia. Problems within the Empire – Hitler had in mind here primarily the growing pressure for independence in India – and reluctance to become embroiled in a long European war would, he thought, prove decisive in deterring Britain from involvement in a war against Germany. France was unlikely to act without British support. Italy would not object to the elimination of Czechoslovakia. Its attitude towards Austria could not at the moment be determined. It would depend on whether Mussolini were still alive – another implied argument for avoiding delay. Poland would be too concerned about Russia to attack Germany. Russia would be preoccupied with the threat from Japan. The incorporation of Austria and Czechoslovakia would improve the security of Germany's borders, freeing up forces for other uses, and would allow the creation of a further twelve divisions. Assuming the expulsion of 3 million from the two countries, their annexation would mean the acquisition of foodstuffs for 5 to 6 million people. Hitler ended by stating that when the moment arrived the attack upon the Czechs would have to be carried out 'lightning fast' ('*blitzartig schnell*').[266]

Hitler's comments to his chiefs of staff were in line with what he had been saying for weeks to Goebbels and other Party leaders. He wanted to use the occasion of the meeting about raw materials allocation to impress similar arguments upon his military leaders. His disdain for the caution of the military leadership had grown alongside his own self-confidence. The *Deutschland* affair had increased his contempt. He wanted to see how the chiefs of staff would react to the bold ideas for expansion that he put forward.[267] It would have been surprising had the military high command not got wind of Hitler's heavy hints of expansion directed at Austria and Czechoslovakia, been aware of his disillusionment with Britain and his views that the weakness of the Empire made Italy a preferable ally, known of his opinion that the threat from Russia (mentioned only in passing at the meeting on 5 November) had receded, and that sustained conflict in the Mediterranean involving the major powers was in Germany's interest.[268] But the meeting on 5 November was the first time that the chiefs of staff had been explicitly told of Hitler's thoughts on the likely timing and circumstances of German expansion into Austria and Czechoslovakia.[269]

Hitler's arguments did not convince most of his small audience. He was under no illusion at the negative response to his comments.[270] It was perhaps out of pique that he more than once refused to read the memorandum of the meeting that Hoßbach had constructed five days later out of the notes he had jotted down at the time.[271] Blomberg, Fritsch, and Neurath in particular were alarmed at what they heard. It was not the aim of expansion that concerned them. There was no disagreement here with Hitler. His familiar racial interpretation of *Lebensraum* had a different emphasis, but accorded well enough with military-strategic interests in German supremacy in central Europe, and with Göring's aims of economic dominance in south-eastern Europe. Nor did talk of the annexation of Austria and destruction of Czechoslovakia worry them. That both would happen at some point was by late 1937 largely taken for granted.[272] Even General Beck's sharp criticism of Hitler's statement, when he read an account some days later, did not dispute 'the expediency of clearing up (*bereinigen*) the case of

Czechia (*Tschechei*) (perhaps also Austria) if the opportunity presents itself'.[273]

What did shock them was the prospect of the early use of force, and with that the grave danger that Germany would be plunged into war with Britain and France. Hitler, they thought, was taking foolhardy risks. They raised objections. Neurath saw an expansion of the Mediterranean conflict, in the way Hitler had conceived it, as highly unlikely. The generals pointed to deficiencies in Hitler's military analysis.[274] On no account must Germany find itself at war with Britain and France was the essence of their remarks.[275] Even Göring, though he kept quiet until the discussion moved on to armaments matters, still favoured trying to reach agreement with Britain.[276] Only Raeder, who had wanted the meeting in the first place, seemed unperturbed. If his later testimony is to be believed, he did not take Hitler's remarks seriously, other than as a vehicle to spur on the army to speed up its armaments. Possible future conflict with Britain was, for Raeder, an inevitable component of planning for naval expansion. But an imminent conflict in the present state of Germany's armaments was, in his view, such 'complete madness' that it could not be envisaged as a serious proposition.[277]

Others were less relaxed. Fritsch had to be reassured by Hitler at the end of the meeting that there was no immediate danger of war, and no need to cancel his planned leave.[278] General Beck, shown a copy of Hoßbach's record of the meeting, found Hitler's remarks 'crushing' (*niederschmetternd*).[279] It was not the prospect of expansion into Austria and Czechoslovakia and attainment of German dominance in central Europe, once military strength had been consolidated, that appalled him, but the irresponsibility and dilettantism with which Hitler was prepared to run the risk of involving Germany in a catastrophic war with the western powers. His own, detailed and devastating ten-point critique of Hitler's statement, probably drawn up as the basis of comments to be made to Blomberg, indicated how seriously he viewed the danger and how far he was estranged from the high-risk policy of the head of state and supreme commander of the armed forces.[280] Neurath, who had arranged with Beck and Fritsch that he would speak to Hitler, had the opportunity to do so in mid-January 1938. Hitler's policies, he warned, meant war. Many of his plans could be attained by more peaceful methods, if somewhat more slowly. Hitler replied that he had no more time.[281]

Blomberg's own doubts expressed at the November meeting were, as usual, short-lived. The pliant War Minister was soon conveying Hitler's wishes to the upper echelons of the Wehrmacht. Within weeks, without

Hitler having to give any express order, Chief of Defence Staff Colonel Alfred Jodl, recognizing what was needed, had devised a significant alteration to the previous mobilization plans against Czechoslovakia, aimed at preventing Czech intervention in the event of a war against France. The new directive included the sentence: 'Once Germany has attained its full war preparedness in all spheres, the military basis will have been created to conduct an offensive war (*Angriffskrieg*) against Czechoslovakia and thereby also to carry the German space problem to a triumphant conclusion, even if one or other great power intervenes against us.'[282]

Externally as well as internally, the Third Reich was entering a new, more radical phase. The drift of Hitler's thinking was plain from the November meeting, and from his comments earlier in the autumn. Nothing had been decided, no plans laid, no programme established. It was still 'wait and see'. But Hitler's hand became further strengthened at the end of January and beginning of February 1938 by a chance set of events – a personal scandal involving the War Minister Werner von Blomberg.

VIII

Blomberg was not popular in the top leadership of the army. He was seen as too much Hitler's man and too little the army's. A friendly word from Hitler or touch of pathos in a speech could move him to tears.[283] Behind his back, some generals called him 'Hitlerjunge Quex' after the Hitler Youth hero of a propaganda film, prepared to sacrifice his life for his belief in the Führer.[284] They thought his admiration of Hitler clouded his professional judgement. For Fritsch, his immediate superior was too impulsive, too open to influence, too weak in his own judgement.[285] The snobbish and conservative officer corps also thought him too close to the Party bigwigs whom they commonly held in contempt. That Blomberg wore the Golden Party Badge on his uniform and marched each year at the celebration of the Putsch was scarcely held to his credit.[286] When his personal life led to professional trouble in late January 1938, he had no friends to count upon. But until then, until he was struck down by the scandal he had brought upon himself, his position as Hitler's right hand in all matters to do with the Wehrmacht was secure. As he later acknowledged, he remained firmly behind Hitler, 'would have gone the Führer's way to Austria', and was expecting a period of ten years in order to build up the armed forces for the war he recognized as inevitable.[287] For Hitler's part, as he had done since

1933, he continued to look to Blomberg to prepare for him the war machine he intended to use, as he had indicated in November, well before the decade envisaged by Blomberg had passed. To be rid of his War Minister at this juncture was not remotely on his agenda.

On a September morning in 1937, walking in the Tiergarten, the Field-Marshal, widowed with five grown-up children, met the woman who would change his life and, unwittingly, usher in the biggest internal crisis in the Third Reich since the Röhm affair in the summer of 1934. Blomberg, a lonely and empty individual, rapidly became totally besotted with his new lady-friend, Fräulein Margarethe Gruhn, thirty-five years younger than he was, and from a crassly different social background. Within weeks he had asked her to marry him. He needed the consent of Hitler, as supreme commander of the Wehrmacht. He hinted that his fiancée was a typist, a simple 'girl from the people', and that he was concerned about the response of the officer class to his marriage to someone below his status. Hitler immediately offered to be a witness to the marriage to emphasize his rejection of such outmoded class snobbery, and recommended Göring as the second witness.[288] The wedding was prepared in great secrecy. Even Blomberg's adjutant knew nothing of it until the previous afternoon. The ceremony, attended only by Blomberg's five children and the bride's mother, apart from the wedding couple and the witnesses, Hitler and Göring, took place in the War Ministry on 12 January. There were no celebrations. The simplest note of the wedding was published in the newspapers.[289]

Blomberg had good reason for wanting to keep his bride out of the public eye. She had a past. Around Christmas 1931, then aged eighteen, she had posed for a number of pornographic photos which had come into the hands of the police. The following year the police officially registered her as a prostitute. In 1934 she had again come to the attention of the police, accused of stealing from a client.[290] Now, within days of the wedding, Berlin prostitutes started talking about 'one of them' rising so far up the social ladder that she had married the War Minister. An anonymous phone-call tipped off the head of the army, Colonel-General Fritsch.[291] The Gestapo had by this time also picked up the rumours. The Berlin Police Chief, Wolf Heinrich Graf von Helldorff, was put in the picture and, aware of the political sensitivity of what he saw on the card registering her as a prostitute, immediately took the matter to Blomberg's closest colleague, Head of the Wehrmacht Office, General Wilhelm Keitel, to ascertain that the woman with the police record was indeed identical with the wife of the War Minister. Keitel, who had seen Fräulein Gruhn on only one occasion, heavily veiled at the funeral of Blomberg's mother, could not help Helldorf, but referred him to Göring, who had been a witness at the wedding. Göring established the identity on 21 January. Three days later, Göring stood nervously in the foyer of the Reich Chancellery, a brown file in his hand, awaiting the return of Hitler from a stay in Bavaria.[292]

Hitler was stunned at the news that awaited him. Prudery and racial prejudice went hand in hand when he heard that the indecent photos of Blomberg's bride had been taken by a Jew of Czech origin, with whom she was cohabiting at the time. Scurrilous rumours had it that Hitler took a bath seven times the next day to rid himself of the taint of having kissed the hand of Frau Blomberg. What concerned him above all, however, was the blow to prestige which would follow; that, as a witness at the wedding, he would appear a laughing-stock in the eyes of the world. All night long, as he later recounted, he lay awake, worrying how to avoid a loss of face.[293] The next day, as his adjutant Fritz Wiedemann recalled, he paced up and down his room, his hands behind his back, shaking his head and muttering, ' "If a German Field-Marshal marries a whore, anything in the world is possible." '[294] Goebbels and Göring tried to cheer him up over lunch.[295] That morning, Hitler had spoken for the first time to his military adjutant Colonel Hoßbach about the matter. He praised Blomberg's achievements. But the Field-Marshal had caused him great embarrassment through not telling him the truth about his bride and involving him as a witness at the wedding. He expressed his sadness at having to lose such a loyal colleague. But because of his wife's past, Blomberg had to go as War Minister.[296] 'Blomberg can't be saved,' noted Goebbels. 'Only the pistol remains for a man of honour . . . The Führer as marriage witness. It's unthinkable. The worst crisis of the regime since the Röhm affair . . . The Führer looks like a corpse.'[297]

Presuming that Blomberg was ignorant of his wife's shady past, and hoping to hush the matter up and prevent a public scandal, Göring hurried to persuade the Field-Marshal to have his marriage immediately annulled. To the astonishment and disgust of Göring and of Hitler, Blomberg refused. On the morning of 27 January, Hitler had his last audience with Blomberg. It began in heated fashion, but became calmer, and ended with Hitler offering Blomberg the prospect of rejoining him, all forgotten, if Germany should be involved in war. A day later, Blomberg was gone – over the border to Italy to begin a year's exile, sweetened by a 50,000 Mark 'golden handshake' and his full pension as a Field-Marshal.[298]

The crisis for Hitler had meanwhile deepened. On the very evening, 24 January, that he was recoiling from the shock of the news about his War

Minister, and in a bleak mood, he remembered the whiff of a potential scandal two years earlier concerning the head of the army, Colonel-General von Fritsch. Himmler had presented him at the time, in the summer of 1936, with a file raising suspicions that Fritsch had been blackmailed by a Berlin rent-boy by the name of Otto Schmidt on account of alleged homosexual practices in late 1933. Hitler had refused to believe the allegations, had rejected out of hand any investigation, said he never wanted to hear any more of the matter, and ordered the file destroyed. Now, he told Himmler that he wanted the file reconstructed as a matter of urgency. The reconstruction posed no difficulties since, counter to Hitler's express orders to destroy it, Reinhard Heydrich, head of the Security Police, had had the file put in a safe. Within hours, by 2.15a.m. in the early morning of 25 January, the file was on Hitler's desk.[299]

Hitler had not summoned the file as part of a well-thought-out strategy to be rid of Fritsch as well as Blomberg. In fact, he was apparently still thinking of Fritsch on the morning of 26 January, a day after he had seen the 'reconstructed' file, as Blomberg's possible successor as War Minister.[300] Fritsch had presumably been thought of by Hitler in this capacity immediately on realization that Blomberg had to go. In the light of the shock he had just received, and his immediate loss of confidence in his leading officers, Hitler now wanted assurance that no further scandals were likely to be forthcoming.[301] But just as the Blomberg case was unexpected, so were developments in the Fritsch case to unfold in an unpredictable fashion. Without the Blomberg affair, Hitler is said subsequently to have told his army adjutant Major Gerhard Engel, the Fritsch case would never have come up again.[302] The second crisis arose from the first.

On the morning of 25 January, in his state of depression over Blomberg, Hitler gave the thin file on Fritsch to Hoßbach with instructions for absolute secrecy. Hoßbach was horrified at the implications for the Wehrmacht of a second scandal. He thought Fritsch, whom he greatly admired, would easily clear up the matter – or would know what to do.[303] Either way, the honour of the army would be preserved. In this frame of mind, he disobeyed Hitler's express order and informed Fritsch about the file.[304] It was a fateful step.

Fritsch, when Hoßbach broke the news of the file on the evening of 25 January, reacted with anger and disgust at the allegations, declaring them a pack of lies. Hoßbach reported back to Hitler. The Dictator showed no sign of anger at the act of disobedience. In fact, he seemed relieved, commenting that since everything was in order, Fritsch could become War Minister.[305] However, Hitler added that Hoßbach had done him a great disservice in destroying the element of secrecy.[306] In fact, Hoßbach had unwittingly done Fritsch an even greater disservice.

When he heard from Hoßbach what was afoot, Fritsch not unnaturally brooded for hours about the allegations. They must have something to do, he thought, with the member of the Hitler Youth with whom he had lunched, usually alone, in 1933–4, in a willingness to comply with the request of the Winter Aid Campaign to provide free meals for the needy. He presumed that malicious tongues had manufactured an illicit relationship out of harmless acts of charity. Thinking he could clear up a misunderstanding, he sought out Hoßbach the following day, 26 January. All he did, however, was to raise the private doubts of Hitler's military adjutant. Hoßbach did not think to indicate to Fritsch that to mention the Hitler Youth story might not be tactically the best way to convince Hitler of his innocence.[307]

During the afternoon, Hitler conferred with Himmler, Reich Justice Minister Gürtner, and Göring (who saw Fritsch as his rival for Blomberg's post as War Minister).[308] There was a general air of mistrust. By early evening, Hitler was still wavering. Göring pressed him to come to a decision. Hoßbach chose the moment to suggest that Hitler speak directly about the matter to Fritsch. After some hesitation, Hitler agreed.[309] In the meantime, four Gestapo officers had been sent to the Börgermoor internment camp in the Emsland to fetch Otto Schmidt to Berlin.[310] In Hitler's private library in the Reich Chancellery that evening a remarkable scene ensued: the head of the army, in civilian clothing, was confronted by his accuser, an internee of proven ill-repute, in the presence of his Supreme Commander and head of state, and the Prussian Minister President Göring.

Hitler looked despondent to Fritsch. But he came straight to the point. He wanted, he said, simply the truth. If Fritsch acknowledged his guilt, he was prepared to have the matter hushed up and send him well away from Germany. He had contemplated the possibility of Fritsch perhaps serving as military adviser to Chiang Kai-shek.[311] Fritsch vehemently professed his innocence. He then made the mistake of telling Hitler about the harmless episode of the Hitler Youth boy. It had precisely the opposite effect to that hoped for by Fritsch. Hitler's suspicions rose immediately. He now gave Fritsch the file. While he was reading it, Fritsch's alleged blackmailer was brought in. Otto Schmidt, who had proved a reliable witness in a number of other cases where he had blackmailed individuals, insisted that he recognized Fritsch as the man in question. Fritsch repeated several times, in a cool and collected manner, that he had never seen the man in his life before and gave Hitler his word of honour that he had nothing to do with the entire affair.

Hitler had expected, so he told his generals a few days later, that Fritsch would have thrown the file at his feet. His subdued behaviour did not impress Hitler as an impassioned display of injured innocence.[312] Fritsch for his part found it difficult to believe that Hitler and Göring retained their suspicions and simply ignored the word of honour of a high-ranking German officer.[313] The reality, as Goebbels recognized, was that Hitler had by now lost faith in Fritsch.[314]

The Gestapo's interrogation of Fritsch on the morning of 27 January, when he again faced his tormentor Schmidt, was inconclusive. Schmidt remained adamant in his accusations, Fritsch indignantly vehement in his denial of any involvement. The level of detail in the accuser's story seemed telling. But as Fritsch pointed out, though to no avail, the detail was erroneous. The alleged meeting with Fritsch was said to have taken place in November 1933. Schmidt claimed to have remembered it as if it had been the previous day. Yet he had Fritsch smoking (which he had not done since 1925), wearing a fur coat (such as he had never possessed), and – Schmidt was repeatedly pressed on this point – announcing himself as 'General of the Artillery von Fritsch', a rank he had attained only on 1 February 1934.[315] The inconsistency in evidence was not picked up or acted upon. It remained a matter of word against word.

Meanwhile, Hitler had given the Fritsch file to Justice Minister Franz Gürtner, and asked for his views. Goebbels had little confidence in the outcome. 'Gürtner has now still to write a legal report,' he wrote. 'But what use is all that. The porcelain is smashed.'[316] Gürtner's report, delivered before the end of the month, was damning. Upturning conventional legal notions, Gürtner stated that Fritsch had not proved his innocence and regarded the issue of the Hitler Youth boy as damaging to his case.[317] But Gürtner insisted upon a legal trial for Fritsch in front of a military court. The military leadership backed the demand. Even if reluctantly, in the case of so prominent a person as the head of the army Hitler had little choice but to concede.[318]

The double scandal of Blomberg and Fritsch had left the Nazi leadership with a major public relations problem. How was it all to be explained to the people? How was a serious blow to prestige and standing to be avoided? On Thursday 27 January, Hitler, looking pale and grey, decided to cancel his big speech to the Reichstag on the anniversary of the 'seizure of power'. The meeting of the Reich cabinet was also cancelled. Goebbels suggested that a way out of the political crisis would be for Hitler himself to take over the whole of the Wehrmacht, with the different sections of the armed forces turned into separate ministries. 'And then comes the most difficult question,' he added: 'how to put it to the people (*wie dem Volke sagen*). The wildest rumours are circulating. The Führer is at the end of his tether (*ganz erledigt*). None of us has slept since Monday.'[319]

Goebbels's suggestion – if indeed it originally came from him – for restructuring the Wehrmacht leadership entirely was at least in part taken up.[320] It offered a neat way out of a choice of successor for Blomberg. Göring's self-evident ambitions for this post were never seriously entertained by Hitler. Blomberg, Keitel, and Wiedemann all spoke out in Göring's favour. Göring himself would have been prepared to give up his control of the Four Year Plan in return for the War Ministry. Hitler was, however, dismissive of his military abilities. He was not even competent, Hitler scoffed, in running the Luftwaffe, let alone the whole of the armed forces. For the army and the navy, the appointment of Göring (who had in his regular military career never had a rank higher than that of captain) would have been insulting. More than that, it would have amounted for Hitler to a heavy concentration of military command in the hands of one man.[321] Heinrich Himmler also cherished ambitions – though always wholly unrealistic ones for a police chief who headed a small rival military force to that of the army in what would develop into the Waffen-SS, who had not served in the First World War, and who, in the later disparaging comment of one general, scarcely knew how to drive a fire-engine. Hitler told his generals on 5 February that rumours of Himmler taking over had been 'insane twaddle' (*wahnsinniges Geschwätz*). A third ambitious hopeful, General Walter von Reichenau, was seen as far too close to the Party and too untraditionalist to be acceptable to the army.[322]

In fact, already on 27 January, picking up a suggestion made by Blomberg at his farewell audience, Hitler had decided to take over the Wehrmacht leadership himself, appointing no successor to the War Ministry.[323] Within hours, he was initiating General Keitel (scarcely known to him to this point, but recommended by Blomberg) in his – that is to say, initially Blomberg's – ideas for a new organizational structure for the Wehrmacht. Keitel, he said, would be his sole adviser in questions relating to the Wehrmacht.[324] With one move, this shifted the internal balance of power within the armed forces from the traditionalist leadership and general staff of the army (as the largest sector) to the office of the Wehrmacht, representing the combined forces, and directly dependent upon and pliant towards Hitler.[325] In a statement for army leaders on 7 February, explaining the changes that had taken place, it was claimed that Hitler's takeover of the Wehrmacht command 'was already intended in his programme, but for a later date'.[326] In reality, it was a rapidly taken decision providing a way out of an embarrassing crisis.

His removal for days a matter of little more than timing, Fritsch was asked by Hitler on 3 February for his resignation.[327] By then, an increasingly urgent answer – given the rumours now circulating – to the presentational problem of how to explain the departure of the two most senior military leaders had been found: 'In order to put a smoke-screen round the whole business, a big reshuffle will take place,' noted Goebbels.[328] In a two-hour discussion, alone with Goebbels in his private rooms, Hitler went over the whole affair – how disillusioned he had been by Blomberg, whom he had trusted blindly; how he disbelieved Fritsch despite his denials – 'these sort of people always do that'; how he would take over the Wehrmacht himself with the branches of the armed forces as ministries; and the personnel changes he intended to make, particularly the replacement of Neurath by Ribbentrop at the Foreign Office.[329] 'Führer wants to deflect the spotlight from the Wehrmacht, make Europe hold its breath,' recorded Colonel Jodl in his diary. The Austrian Chancellor Schuschnigg, he added ominously, should be 'trembling'.[330]

Within four days the reshuffle was in place. Twelve generals (apart from Blomberg and Fritsch) were removed, six from the Luftwaffe; fifty-one other posts (a third in the Luftwaffe) were also refilled.[331] Fritsch's post was given to Walther von Brauchitsch – a compromise candidate suggested by Blomberg and Keitel to keep out Reichenau.[332] The navy was left alone. Raeder had, according to Goebbels's report of Hitler's views, 'behaved splendidly during the entire crisis and everything is in order in the navy'. Göring was given a Field-Marshal's baton as consolation prize for missing the War Ministry.[333] Major changes were also undertaken in the diplomatic service. Neurath, having to make way for his arch-rival Ribbentrop, was 'elevated' to a pseudo-position as head of a 'privy council' (*Geheimer Kabinettsrat*) of ministers which was never to meet.[334] The key ambassadorial posts in Rome, Tokyo, London, and Vienna were given new occupants. Schacht's replacement by Funk at the Ministry of Economics was also announced as part of the general reshuffle.[335]

Blomberg and Fritsch were said to have retired 'on health grounds'.[336] Blomberg would survive the war, still praising the 'genius' of the Führer but dismayed that Hitler had not called upon his services once more, and would die, shunned to the last by his former army comrades, in prison in Nuremberg in March 1946.[337] Fritsch's innocence – the victim of mistaken identity –

would be established by a military court in Berlin on 18 March 1938.[338] Though his name had been cleared, he did not gain the rehabilitation he hoped for. Deeply depressed and embittered, but still claiming to be 'a good National Socialist',[339] he volunteered for his old artillery regiment in the Polish campaign and would fall fatally wounded on the outskirts of Warsaw on 22 September 1939.[340]

A communiqué on the sweeping changes – said to be in the interest of the 'strongest concentration of all political, military, and economic forces in the hand of the supreme leader' – was broadcast on the evening of 4 February.[341] The sensational news covered page after page of the following day's news-papers. Great surprise, worries about the likelihood of war, and a flurry of the wildest rumours – including an attack on Hitler's life, mass shootings and arrests, attempts to depose Hitler and Göring and proclaim a military dictatorship, war-plans opposed by the dismissed generals – were common reactions over the next days.[342] The real reasons were kept dark. 'Praise God the people know nothing of it all and would not believe it,' Goebbels reported Hitler as saying. 'Therefore greatest discretion.' Hitler's way to handle it was to emphasize the concentration of forces under his leadership and 'let nothing be noticed'.[343]

The following afternoon, 5 February, a pallid and drawn-looking Hitler addressed his generals. He described what had happened, cited from the police reports, and read out sections of Gürtner's damning assessment on Fritsch. The assembled officers were benumbed. No objections were raised. Hitler's explanations appeared convincing. No one believed that he could have acted differently.[344] As one of those present, General Curt Liebmann, acknowledged, 'the impression of these disclosures, both over Blomberg and over Fritsch, was downright crushing, especially because Hitler had described both matters so clearly that there could be scarcely any remaining doubt about the actual guilt. We all had the feeling that the army – in contrast to the navy, Luftwaffe, and Party – had suffered a devastating (vernichtenden) blow . . .'[345] At a crucial moment, the undermining of the moral codex of the officer corps by its leading representatives had weakened the authority of the military leadership and in so doing had considerably strengthened Hitler's position. That evening, Hitler spoke in an emotional tone for an hour to the cabinet, unfolding the drama once more, finding words of praise for Blomberg, Fritsch, and especially Neurath, explaining the need to stick to the official version of events, and recalling with much pathos his own feelings of despair during the crisis.[346] It proved to be the last cabinet meeting in the Third Reich. Afterwards, Hitler told Goebbels he felt in the same position with regard to the Wehrmacht that he had been in regarding the German people in 1933. 'He would first have to fight for his position. But he would soon succeed.'[347]

Two weeks later, on 20 February, Hitler addressed the Reichstag. His extraordinarily lengthy speech – replacing the one he ought to have given on 30 January – predictably had nothing new to offer on the Blomberg–Fritsch crisis.[348] In countering rumours of rifts between Party and Wehrmacht, he returned to the 'two pillars' notion of political and military props of the state. To the careful listener, it was, however, plain. Any semblance that the Wehrmacht was a power in its own right, standing above politics, had now vanished. 'In this Reich, everyone in any responsible position is a National Socialist,' Hitler intoned. Party and Wehrmacht simply had separate functions, both of which were united in his undisputed leadership.[349]

Though the crisis was unforeseen, not manufactured, the Blomberg–Fritsch affair engendered a key shift in the relations between Hitler and the most powerful non-Nazi élite, the army. At precisely the moment when Hitler's adventurism was starting to cause shivers of alarm, the army had demonstrated its weakness and without a murmur of protest swallowed his outright dominance even in the immediate domain of the Wehrmacht. Hitler recognized the weakness, was increasingly contemptuous of the officer corps, and saw himself more and more in the role not only of Head of State, but of great military leader.

The outcome of the Blomberg–Fritsch affair amounted to the third stepping-stone – after the Reichstag Fire and the 'Röhm-Putsch' – cementing Hitler's absolute power and, quite especially, his dominance over the army. With the military emasculated and the hawkish Ribbentrop at the Foreign Office, Hitler's personal drive for the most rapid expansion possible – blending with the expansionist dynamic coming from the economy and the arms race – was unshackled from the forces which could have counselled caution. In the months that followed, the radical dynamic that had been building up through 1937 would take foreign and domestic developments into new terrain. The threat of war would loom ever closer. Racial persecution would again intensify. Hitler's ideological 'vision' was starting to become reality. The momentum which Hitler had done so much to force along, but which was driven too by forces beyond his personality, was carrying him along with it. 'Vision' was beginning to overcome cold, political calculation. The danger-zone was being entered.

2

THE DRIVE FOR EXPANSION

'Perhaps I'll appear some time overnight in Vienna; like a
spring storm.'   *Hitler to Kurt Schuschnigg,*
                    the Austrian Chancellor, 12 February 1938

'I am utterly determined that Czechoslovakia should disappear from the map.'
                    Hitler, addressing his generals on 28 May 1938

'If you recognize the principle of self-determination for the
treatment of the Sudeten question, then we can discuss how
to put the principle into practice.'
                    Hitler to Neville Chamberlain,
                    the British Prime Minister, 15 September 1938

'I got the impression that here was a man who could be
relied upon when he had given his word.'
        Chamberlain, in a private letter of 19 September 1938,
                    on return from his first meeting with Hitler

Hitler's 'mission' since he entered politics had been to undo the stain of defeat and humiliation in 1918 by destroying Germany's enemies – internal and external – and restoring national greatness. This 'mission', he had plainly stated on many occasions during the 1920s, could only be accomplished through 'the sword'.[1] It meant war for supremacy. The risk could not be avoided. 'Germany will either be a world power, or there will be no Germany,' he had written in *Mein Kampf*.[2] Nothing had changed over the years in his fanatical belief in this 'mission'. He had made necessary dove-like noises for international consumption. And his early speeches and writings had often been dismissed as no more than wild rantings which had little to do with the practical realities of international diplomacy and were not to be taken over-seriously as true expressions of intent.[3] But, whatever the public rhetoric, the first five years since he became Chancellor had in fact over and again confirmed the belief of a Leader becoming ever more convinced of his own messianism, certain that his 'mission' was on course to fulfilment. His own actions – decisions such as those in 1936 to remilitarize the Rhineland and to introduce the Four-Year Plan – had been instrumental in making the 'mission' seem more realizable.

Powerful forces beyond 'triumph of the will' had made those actions possible. The final decision had invariably been Hitler's. He had determined the timing of the critical moves in foreign policy. But the significant steps taken since 1933 had in every case been consonant with the interests of the key agencies of power in the regime, above all with those of the Wehrmacht.[4] Hitler's own obsessively held convictions had served as a spur to, and blended in with, the ambitious armaments plans of the armed forces, varying notions of restoration of hegemony in Europe entertained by the Foreign

Office (along with the 'amateur' agencies involved in international affairs), and autarkic aims of big industrial firms. His vision of Germany's greatness through racial purity, strength of arms, and national rebirth had proved an inspiration for hundreds of thousands of fervent activist followers, anxious to put his maxims into practice and forcing along the pace of radicalization by 'working towards the Führer'. Not least, the ideological fanaticism which Hitler embodied had been institutionalized in the massive Party and its affiliate organizations, above all in the growing power of the SS. Controlling the German police and entertaining unconcealed military ambitions, the SS had become the key organization behind the regime's ideological dynamism.

By the end of 1937, as his remarks at the 'Hoßbach meeting' showed, Hitler acutely sensed that time was not on Germany's side. The Reich, he had concluded, could not simply wait passively on international developments; by 1943–5 at the latest it had to be prepared to take military action, sooner if circumstances presented themselves. His keenness to accelerate the momentum of expansionism was partly sharpened by his growing feeling that he might not have long to live in order to accomplish his aims.[5] But beyond that it reflected an awareness that the pressures accumulating could not be contained without the expansion which he in any case strove after, and a recognition that Germany's current advantage in armaments build-up would be lost as other countries undertook their own armaments programmes. At precisely this juncture, with Hitler already in such a frame of mind, the Blomberg–Fritsch affair served to underline his absolute supremacy, to highlight the compliance of the army, and further to weaken the lingering influence of the diminishing number of voices advising caution.

Before the reverberations of the crisis had subsided, a fatal miscalculation by the Austrian Chancellor Kurt Schuschnigg over a plebiscite to back Austrian independence gave Hitler a welcome opportunity to turn the spotlight away from his domestic troubles – as Jodl had hinted he would like to do – through the drama of the Anschluß.[6] It amounted to a defining moment in the Third Reich. Even more than following the Rhineland triumph two years earlier, Hitler felt after the Anschluß that he could take on the world – and win. And both internally and externally, the impetus to radicalization provided by the Anschluß formed a crucial link in the chain of events that eventually plunged Europe into a new war in September 1939.

I

Since his boyhood days in Linz, Hitler had seen the future of Austria's German-speaking population lying in its incorporation in the German Reich. Like many in his part of Austria, he had favoured the ideas of Georg Schönerer, the Pan-Germanist leader, rejecting the Habsburg monarchy and looking to union with the Wilhelmine Reich in Germany. Defeat in the First World War had then brought the dismembering of the sprawling, multi-ethnic empire of the Habsburgs. The new Austria, the creation of the victorious powers at the Treaty of St Germain in September 1919, was no more than a mere remnant of the former empire. The small alpine republic now had only 7 million citizens (compared with 54 million in the empire), 2 million of them in Vienna itself. It was wracked by daunting social and economic problems, and deep political fissures, accompanied by smouldering resentment about its loss of territory and revised borders. The new Austria was, however, almost entirely German-speaking. The idea of union (or Anschluß) with Germany now became far more appealing and was overwhelmingly supported in plebiscites in the early 1920s. Hitler's rise to power in Germany changed this. It accentuated the already acute divisions between socialists, pan-Germans, and Catholic-conservatives (with their own Austrian-nationalist brand of fascism). Only for the pan-Germans, by now entirely sucked into the Austrian Nazi Movement, was an Anschluß with Hitler's Germany an attractive proposition.[7] But, despite the ban on the Nazi Party in Austria following the German-inspired assassination of the Austrian Chancellor Engelbert Dollfuß in July 1934, the increasing might of the Third Reich and the growing exposure of Austria to German dominance as Italy's protection waned in the wake of the Abyssinian conflict kept the Anschluß hopes alive among one sizeable part of the Austrian population.

For Hitler's regime in Germany, meanwhile, the prospects of attaining the union with Austria implicit in the first point of the Nazi Party Programme of 1920, demanding 'the merger of all Germans . . . in a Greater Germany',[8] had become much rosier in the changed diplomatic circumstances following Italy's embroilment in Abyssinia and then the triumphant remilitarization of the Rhineland. Hitler had written on the very first page of *Mein Kampf*: 'German-Austria must return to the great German mother-country, and not because of any economic considerations. No, and again no: even if such a union were unimportant from an economic point of view; yes, even if it were harmful, it must nevertheless take place. One blood demands one Reich.'[9] Ideological impulses were, however, far from alone in driving on the quest to bring Austria under German sway. Whatever his emphasis in *Mein Kampf*, by the late 1930s Austria's geographical position, straddling strategically vital stretches of central Europe, and the significant material resources that would accrue to Germany's economy, hard-pressed in the push to rearm as swiftly as possible under the Four-Year Plan, were the key determinants in forcing the pace of policy towards the Reich's eastern neighbour.

On a number of occasions during the second half of 1937, as we have noted, Hitler had spoken in imprecise but menacing terms about moving against Austria. During the summer he had bound the Austrian Nazi Party closer to Berlin through the appointment of his economic adviser Wilhelm Keppler to run party affairs in Vienna.[10] Alongside the direct reporting to Hitler of Franz von Papen – the former Vice-Chancellor in the Reich Cabinet who had been sent as a special envoy to Vienna to pour oil on troubled waters following Dollfuß's assassination, and had been appointed Ambassador after the signing of the Agreement of July 1936 – this provided a further channel of information on developments inside Austria. The effect was to lessen even more the influence of the German Foreign Ministry.[11] In September Hitler had sounded out Mussolini about a likely Italian reaction, but received inconsequential, if not discouraging, replies. At the beginning of November, at the 'Hoßbach meeting', he had strongly intimated early action to destroy Austria. The visit to Germany in mid-November by Lord Halifax, Lord Privy Seal and President of the Council in the British Government, close to the recently appointed British Prime Minister Neville Chamberlain and soon to become his Foreign Secretary, had confirmed in Hitler's mind that Britain would do nothing in the event of German action against Austria.[12]

The questions of Austria, Czechoslovakia, and Danzig, Lord Halifax had told Hitler, 'fell into the category of possible alterations in the European order which might be destined to come about with the passage of time'. (In his diary entry on the discussion, Halifax had noted telling Hitler that 'on all these matters we were not necessarily concerned to stand for the status quo as today, but we were concerned to avoid such treatment of them as would be likely to cause trouble'.) Hitler had responded by stating that 'the Agreement of July 11th [1936] had been made with Austria and it was to be hoped that it would lead to the removal of all difficulties'. Halifax's subsequent confidential memorandum on the meeting noted Hitler as saying:

'Germany did not want to annex Austria or to reduce her to political dependence – her desire was to bring about by peaceful means full economic, cultural, commercial, and possibly monetary and currency union with Austria and to see in Austria a Government really friendly to Germany and ready to work hand in hand for the common welfare of both branches of the Teutonic race.'[13]

A few days earlier, Hitler had told the Danzig Gauleiter Albert Forster that he wanted Danzig kept quiet from January onwards to allow for concentration on Austria.[14] In December, he informed von Papen, who had talked of ways of toppling Schuschnigg, that he wanted to avoid force in the Austrian matter as long as this were desirable to prevent international repercussions.[15] Göring and Keppler both had the impression that Hitler would act on Austria in spring or summer 1938.[16]

Plainly, Hitler had moved during the second half of 1937, despite his express disavowal to Lord Halifax, to a readiness to end Austria's independence within the foreseeable future. He was, however, in this fully in line with other forces in the Third Reich. The Austro-German treaty of 11 July 1936 together with improved relations with Italy had inevitably brought greater German pressure on Austria. Only increasingly fragile reliance on Italy and recognizably unrealistic hopes placed in the western powers could hinder the relentless squeeze on Austria's exposed position in central Europe. Papen and Foreign Minister Neurath exerted their own influence where possible, the former largely through direct links with Hitler, the latter through official Foreign Office channels; the growing numbers of Austrian Nazis unfolded a ceaseless clamour of agitation; the bosses of the Four-Year Plan and leaders of the ferrous industries cast envious eyes on Austria's iron-ore deposits and other sources of scarce raw materials; above all, it was Hermann Göring, at this time close to the pinnacle of his power, who, far more than Hitler, throughout 1937 made the running and pushed hardest for an early and radical solution to the 'Austrian Question'.

Göring was not simply operating as Hitler's agent in matters relating to the 'Austrian Question'. His approach differed in emphasis in significant respects.[17] As with Hitler, anti-Bolshevism was central to his thinking. But Göring's broad notions of foreign policy, which he pushed to a great extent on his own initiative in the mid-1930s, drew more on traditional pan-German concepts of nationalist power-politics to attain hegemony in Europe than on the racial dogmatism central to Hitler's ideology. Return of colonies (never a crucial issue for Hitler), the alliance with Britain (which he continued to strive for long after Hitler's ardour had cooled), and an emphasis on domination in south-eastern Europe to ensure German raw material supplies from a huge economic sphere of exploitation (*Großraumwirtschaft*, a notion that differed from Hitler's racially determined emphasis on Lebensraum), were the basic props of his programme to ensure Germany's hegemony.[18] Within this framework, Austria's geography and raw materials gave it both strategically and economically a pivotal position.[19]

Göring was increasingly determined, now as supremo of the Four-Year Plan, in the face of Germany's mounting problems of securing raw material supplies, to press for what he called the 'union' or 'merger' (*Zusammenschluß*) of Austria and Germany – even, if necessary, at the expense of the alliance with Italy on which Hitler placed such store.[20] Göring had come close to offending Mussolini on his visit to Rome in January 1937 with his brusque demands for Italy's need to come to terms with the fact that Austria would eventually have to fall to Germany. But by the time he had next broached the topic to the Duce four months later, Mussolini had appeared tacitly to recognize that the Anschluß was purely a matter of time. A month before his second (nominally private) visit to Italy that year, in April, amid severe blockages in Germany's raw material supplies, Göring had told leaders of the iron industry in confidence that the rich iron ores of Austria must come to Germany.[21] No time-scale was envisaged. But in view of the pressing economic difficulties, it was plain that Göring did not have the distant future in mind.

As diplomatic feelers, also put out by Neurath and Papen, appeared to be fruitless, Göring's impatience for a more radical solution to the 'Austrian Question' grew. Before Mussolini's visit to Germany in September, Hitler gave Göring instructions to tread delicately with his important guest on matters relating to Austria. He wanted Mussolini to understand that Germany had no intention in the foreseeable future of bringing the Austrian problem to a head, but that German intervention would be possible should a crisis be otherwise provoked in Austria. By whom or in what circumstances was left to the imagination. How much notice Göring took of Hitler's instructions was plain when, on the Duce's visit to Carinhall, he showed him a map of Europe which had Austria already incorporated within Germany. The lack of any negative reaction from Mussolini was taken by his host as a sign that Italy would not object to an Anschluß.[22] Göring showed the same map in November to Guido Schmidt, state secretary in the Austrian Foreign Ministry, and his guest at an international hunting exhibition. Good huntsmen knew no boundaries, a grinning Göring told him.[23] It was an attempt to bully Schmidt into accepting the inevitability of a currency union between Germany and Austria which, it was plain, was meant to evolve over time into a full merger of the two countries.[24] Göring assured Lord Halifax (whose visit to Germany he had instigated) later the same month that German intentions towards Austria were not aggressive, and that relations between the two countries could be settled by diplomatic means.[25] At the same time, he took additional steps to isolate Austria still further in south-east Europe.[26]

By the beginning of 1938, the noose had tightened around Austria's neck. Göring was pushing hard for currency union. But with Austria stalling for time, and Italy's reactions uncertain, immediate results through diplomatic channels seemed unlikely. An Anschluß resulting from German intervention through force in the imminent future appeared improbable.

At this unpromising juncture, the idea emerged of a meeting between Hitler and the Austrian Chancellor, Schuschnigg. Such a meeting may well have formed part of Papen's scheme for bringing down the Austrian Chancellor, noted by Goebbels in mid-December 1937.[27] According to Papen's own later account, he had suggested such a meeting to the Austrian Chancellor in December – in accordance with Schuschnigg's own expressed wish that month for personal discussions with Hitler (which the Austrian Chancellor naïvely saw as the only hope of stabilizing his country's deterio-rating situation by reaffirming its independence and the terms of the agree-ment of July 1936). He had then put the same suggestion to Neurath and Hitler.[28] He repeated the suggestion to Guido Schmidt on 7 January, indicating Hitler's readiness to have a meeting towards the end of the month. Schuschnigg agreed the date.[29] Hitler had then had the meeting postponed because of the Blomberg–Fritsch crisis. It was eventually rearranged for 12 February.[30] For Hitler, looking, as Jodl had intimated, for a foreign-policy deflection from the internal problems which had dominated the previous weeks, the meeting with the Austrian Chancellor offered the pros-pect of winning Austrian concessions, giving him something tangible to include in his speech to the Reichstag, rescheduled from 30 January to 20 February.

The Austrians had meanwhile uncovered documents embarrassing to the German government, revealing the plans of the Austrian NSDAP for serious disturbances (including, as a provocation, the murder of Papen by Austrian Nazis disguised as members of the Fatherland Front) aimed at bringing down Schuschnigg.[31] At the same time, Schuschnigg was trying to win over Arthur Seyß-Inquart – an Austrian lawyer and Nazi sympathizer who had kept his distance from the rowdier elements within the NSDAP – to incorporate the Nazis in a united patriotic Right in Austria which would appease Berlin but preserve Austrian independence.[32] Seyß was, however, in Hitler's pocket, betraying to Berlin exactly what Schuschnigg was prepared to concede.[33] The terms forced upon Schuschnigg by Hitler at the meeting on 12 February were in essence an expanded version of those which the Austrian Chancellor himself had put to Seyß – and were already fully known in Berlin prior to the meeting.[34] The main difference was nevertheless a significant one: that Seyß be made Minister of the Interior, and that his powers should be extended to include control of the police.[35]

At 11a.m. on 12 February, Papen met the Austrian Chancellor, in the company of Guido Schmidt and an adjutant, on the German–Austrian border at Salzburg, where they had spent the night. The Austrian visitors were not enamoured at hearing that three German generals would be among the party awaiting them at the Berghof.[36] Nicolaus von Below, Hitler's Luftwaffe adjutant, had been told to make sure Keitel was present, and in addition one or two generals of particularly 'martial' demeanour. Below's recommendation of the commanding generals of army and Luftwaffe in Munich, Walter von Reichenau (one of the most thoroughly nazified generals) and Hugo Sperrle (who the previous year had commanded the Legion Condor, the squadrons sent to aid the nationalists in Spain), had met with Hitler's enthusiastic approval. Keitel had arrived that morning from Berlin, along with Ribbentrop. The two generals had travelled from Munich. They were told by Hitler that their presence was purely intended to intimidate Schuschnigg by the implied threat of military force.[37]

Hitler, tense and keyed up, received Schuschnigg on the steps of his alpine retreat with due politeness.[38] However, as soon as they entered the great hall, with its breathtaking view over the mountains, Hitler's mood abruptly changed. When Schuschnigg remarked on the beauty of the panorama, Hitler snapped: 'Yes, here my ideas mature. But we haven't come together to talk about the beautiful view and the weather.'[39]

Hitler took Schuschnigg into his study while Papen, Schmidt, Ribbentrop, and the others remained outside. Once inside he launched into a ferocious attack, lasting till lunchtime, on Austria's long history of 'treason' against the German people. 'And this I tell you, Herr Schuschnigg,' he reportedly threatened. 'I am firmly determined to make an end of all this . . . I have a historic mission (*Auftrag*), and this I will fulfil because Providence has destined me to do so . . . You don't believe you can hold me up for half an hour, do you? Who knows? Perhaps I'll appear some time overnight in Vienna; like a spring storm. Then you'll see something.'[40]

Meanwhile, Ribbentrop had presented Guido Schmidt with Hitler's ulti-matum: an end to all restrictions on National Socialist activity in Austria, an amnesty for those Nazis arrested, the appointment of Seyß-Inquart to the Ministry of the Interior with control over the security forces, another Nazi sympathizer, Edmund Glaise-Horstenau (a former military archivist and historian), to be made War Minister, and steps to begin the integration of the Austrian economic system with that of Germany.[41] The demands were to be implemented by 15 February – timing determined by Hitler's major speech on foreign policy, set for 20 February.[42]

The negotiations were initially intended to last only until lunchtime. But the first session had been taken up almost solely with Hitler's rantings. It would be evening before the Austrian visitors could depart. At lunch, however, Hitler was as if transformed – once more the genial host. The generals were brought in. They told Schmidt they had no idea why they had been invited. Conversation avoided the Austrian question. It was mostly small-talk, apart from Sperrle speaking of his experiences in the Spanish Civil War, which gave Hitler the opportunity to turn to a pet theme: the dangers of Bolshevism.[43] It was late afternoon when Schuschnigg, now apprised by Schmidt of the text of the German demands, returned to Hitler's study. Hitler threatened to march into Austria if his demands were not met in full. Schuschnigg refused to buckle to the threats. Only the Austrian President, he declared, could make cabinet appointments and grant an amnesty. He could not guarantee that such action would be taken. As Schuschnigg was retreating for further discussions with Schmidt, Hitler's bellow for Keitel to come immediately could be heard throughout the house. When the general, arriving at the double in Hitler's study, asked what was required of him, he was told: 'Nothing. Sit down.' After ten minutes of inconsequential chat, he was told to go.

But the impact of the charade on Schuschnigg was not lost.[44] The threat of military invasion seemed very real. Eventually, Papen brokered a number of alterations in the German demands and, under pressure, the Austrians finally accepted the chief difficulty, the appointment of Seyß-Inquart. Hitler told Schuschnigg: 'For the first time in my life I have made up my mind to reconsider a final decision.'[45] With a heavy heart, Schuschnigg signed.

It was by now late evening. The Austrians, browbeaten and depressed after subjection to such merciless bullying, preferred to travel back hungry than accept Hitler's invitation to dinner. They returned to Salzburg in complete silence. Only Papen spoke. 'Now you have some idea, Herr Bundeskanzler, how difficult it is to deal with such an unstable person,' he remarked, adding that next time it would be different and that the Führer could be 'distinctly charming.'[46]

Keitel returned to Berlin early next morning to organize fake military manoeuvres near the Austrian border to exert further pressure on the Reich's eastern neighbours.[47] There was no question of genuine military preparations for an invasion. Keitel had to report to the newly appointed supreme commander of the army, von Brauchitsch, that Hitler was not thinking of a military conflict.[48]

Hitler was dissatisfied at the outcome of the meeting with Schuschnigg.[49] But he told Goebbels that his threats of force had had their effect: 'cannons always speak a good language'.[50] Only when Schuschnigg had complied with his demands, on 15 February, did Hitler's mood improve.[51] 'The world press rages. Speaks of rape. Not entirely without justification,' wrote Goebbels.[52] Hitler spent the next days largely withdrawn in his private quarters in the Berghof, preparing drafts of his big speech on the 20th, and dictating it to the two secretaries working in rotation on the typewriter.[53] In his speech, he thanked the Austrian Chancellor 'for the great understanding and warmhearted readiness' in accepting his invitation to talks and his efforts to find a way of serving 'the interest of both countries'.[54]

Two weeks after the notorious meeting at the Berghof, when laying down directives for the restless Austrian NSDAP, which had threatened to upset developments through its own wild schemes for disturbances, Hitler emphasized, according to Keppler's notes of the meeting, that he wanted to proceed along 'the evolutionary way whether or not the possibility of success could be envisaged at present. The protocol signed by Schuschnigg,' he went on, 'was so far-reaching that if implemented in full the Austrian Question would automatically be solved. A solution through force was something he did not now want if it could in any way be avoided, since for us the foreign-policy danger is diminishing from year to year and the military strength becoming year by year greater.'[55] Hitler's approach was at this time still in line with Göring's evolutionary policy. He plainly reckoned that the tightening of the thumbscrews on Schuschnigg at the February meeting had done the trick. Austria was no more than a German satellite. Extinction of the last remnants of independence would follow as a matter of course. Force was not necessary.

In line with the 'Trojan horse' policy of eroding Austrian independence from the inside, following the Berchtesgaden meeting Hitler had complied with demands from Seyß-Inquart – matching earlier representations by Schuschnigg himself – to depose Captain Josef Leopold, the leader of the unruly Austrian National Socialists, and his associates.[56] Even so, the meeting at the Berghof and Hitler's speech on 20 February, his first broadcast in full on Austrian radio – stating that 'in the long run' it was 'unbearable' for Germans to look on the separation of 10 million fellow Germans by borders imposed through peace treaties – had given the Austrian Nazis a new wind.[57] Disturbances mounted, especially in the province of Styria, in the south-east of the country, where resentment at the loss of territory to the new state of Yugoslavia after the First World War had helped fuel the radicalism that had turned the region into a hotbed of Austrian Nazism.[58] The situation was by now highly volatile, the Nazis barely controllable by Austrian state forces. Schuschnigg's own emotional appeals to Austrian patriotism and independence had merely exacerbated the tension within the country and further irritated Hitler.[59] At the same time, Schuschnigg, evidently impressed by Hitler's threats to use force and anxious to avoid anything that might occasion this, was reassuring Britain, France, and Italy that he had the situation in hand rather than rousing foreign sympathy at German strong-arm tactics.[60] The resignation as Foreign Secretary on 21 February of Anthony Eden, despised by the German leadership, and his replacement by Lord Halifax – known particularly since his visit to Germany the previous November to favour a conciliatory approach to revisionist demands in the interests of preserving peace in Europe and preventing a conflict which could threaten Great Britain's position as a world power – was meanwhile seen in Berlin as a further indication of British appeasement.[61]

The same tone came across in comments of Sir Nevile Henderson, the British Ambassador in Berlin, when he met Hitler on 3 March. Hitler, in a vile mood, was unyielding. If Britain opposed a just settlement in Austria, where Schuschnigg had the support of only 15 per cent of the population, Germany would have to fight, he declared. And if he intervened, he would do so like lightning (*blitzschnell*). His aim was nevertheless 'that the just interests of the German Austrians should be secured and an end made to oppression by a process of peaceful evolution'.[62] However inadequately the undermining of the Austrian state from within through a combination of infiltration and agitation, backed by German bullying, could be described as 'peaceful evolution', pressure-tactics, not armed takeover, still formed the preferred solution to the Austrian Question.

Such notions were thrown overboard by Schuschnigg's wholly unexpected decision, announced on the morning of 9 March, to hold a referendum on Austrian autonomy four days later. The Nazis themselves had been pressing for years for a plebiscite on Anschluß, confident that they would gain massive support for an issue backed by large numbers of Austrians since 1919.[63] But Schuschnigg's referendum, asking voters to back 'a free and German, independent and social, Christian and united Austria; for freedom and work, and for the equality of all who declare for race and fatherland', was couched in a way that could scarcely fail to bring the desired result. It would be a direct rebuff to union with Germany.[64] German plans were immediately thrown into disarray. Hitler's own prestige was at stake. The moves that followed, culminating in the German march into Austria and the Anschluß, were all now improvised at breakneck speed.

The German government was completely taken aback by Schuschnigg's gamble. For hours, there was no response from Berlin. Hitler had not been informed in advance of Schuschnigg's intentions, and was at first incredulous. But his astonishment rapidly gave way to mounting fury at what he saw as a betrayal of the Berchtesgaden agreement.[65] Goebbels recorded the decision to hold an Austrian plebiscite in his diary, though initially without further commentary.[66] In the evening, when he was address- ing a gathering of newspaper editors at a reception in the Propaganda Ministry, he was suddenly summoned to Hitler's presence. Göring was already there. He was told of Schuschnigg's move – 'an extremely dirty trick' (ganz gemeinen Bubenstreich) to 'dupe' (übertölpeln) the Reich through 'a stupid and idiotic plebiscite'. The trio were still unsure how to act. They considered replying either by Nazi abstention from the plebiscite (which would have undermined its legitimacy), or by sending 1,000 aeroplanes to drop leaflets over Austria 'and then actively intervening'.[67] For the time being, the German press was instructed to publish nothing at all about Austria.[68]

By late at night, perhaps egged on by Göring, Hitler was warming up. Goebbels was again called in. Glaise-Horstenau (along with Seyß-Inquart a Nazi sympathizer in the Austrian cabinet), on a visit in southern Germany when suddenly summoned to Berlin by Göring, was also present. 'The Führer drastically outlines for him his plans,' Goebbels recorded. 'Glaise recoils from the consequences.' But Hitler, who went on to discuss the situation alone with Goebbels until 5a.m., was now 'in full swing' and showing 'a wonderful fighting mood'. 'He believes the hour has arrived,' noted Goebbels. He wanted to sleep on it. But he was sure that Italy and England would do nothing. Action from France was possible, but not likely. 'Risk not so great as at the time of the occupation of the Rhineland,' was the conclusion.[69]

Just how unprepared the German leadership had been was shown by the fact that the Foreign Minister, Ribbentrop, was in London, Reichenau had to be recalled from Cairo, and General Erhard Milch (Göring's right-hand man in the Luftwaffe) was summoned from holiday in Switzerland.[70] Göring himself was scheduled to preside over the military court to hear the Fritsch case, meeting for the first time on 10 March. The hearing was abruptly adjourned when a courier brought a message demanding Göring's presence in the Reich Chancellery.[71] Goebbels had also been called there, arriving to find Hitler deep in thought, bent over maps. Plans were discussed for transporting 4,000 Austrian Nazis who had been exiled to Bavaria, together with a further 7,000 paramilitary reservists.[72]

The Wehrmacht leadership was taken completely by surprise through Hitler's demand for plans for military intervention. Keitel, abruptly ordered to the Reich Chancellery on the morning of 10 March, spinelessly suggested calling in Brauchitsch and Beck, knowing full well that no plans existed, but wishing to avoid having to tell this to Hitler. Brauchitsch was not in Berlin. Beck despairingly told Keitel: 'We have prepared nothing, nothing has happened, nothing.' But his objections were dismissed out of hand by Hitler. He was sent away to report within hours on which army units would be ready to march on the morning of the 12th.[73]

By this time, Goebbels had again had intensive discussions alone with Hitler. It seems to have been Goebbels who came up with the idea of having the two Nazi supporters in the Austrian cabinet, Seyß-Inquart and Gleise-Horstenau, demand the referendum should follow the procedures laid down for the Saar plebiscite in 1935. Should Schuschnigg refuse, as was to be expected, the two ministers would resign and 600–800 German planes would shower Austria with leaflets on the Saturday, exhorting the people to resistance against their government. The people – meaning the Nazi activists – would rise in revolt. And on the Sunday, 13 March, the day of the referendum, the Wehrmacht followed by the Austrian 'Legionaries' – exiled paramilitaries based in Bavaria – would march in. The SA-Obergruppenführer Hermann Reschny, leader of the Austrian stormtroopers, thought that the Austrian army would open fire. This, too, had to be reckoned with. But Mussolini was unable and London unwilling to act, while Paris was handicapped by a government crisis. 'So it must be risked. In any case, prepare everything. The Führer works out the military plans . . . March was always the Führer's lucky month.'[74]

Around midnight Goebbels had once more been called to see Hitler. 'The die is cast,' he noted. 'On Saturday march in. Push straight to Vienna. Big aeroplane action. The Führer is going himself to Austria. Göring and I are to stay in Berlin. In 8 days Austria will be ours.' He discussed the propaganda arrangements with Hitler, then returned to his Ministry to work on them until 4a.m. No one was now allowed to leave the Ministry till the 'action' began. The activity was feverish. 'Again a great time. With a great historical task . . . It's wonderful,' he wrote.[75]

After three hours' sleep, Goebbels was back with Hitler by 8a.m. dictating leaflets for distribution in Austria.[76] An hour later, when Papen arrived post-haste from Vienna, he found the Reich Chancellery in a frenzy of activity. Apart from Goebbels and his propaganda team, Neurath, Frick (with several officials from the Ministry of the Interior), Himmler ('surrounded by a dozen giant SS officers'), Brauchitsch, Keitel, and their adjutants were all in attendance. Ribbentrop was missing – sidelined in London, where he was making his official farewells as former ambassador, his recall to Berlin now hindered by Göring.[77]

Prominent in Hitler's mind that morning was Mussolini's likely reaction. Around midday, he sent a handwritten letter, via his emissary Prince Philipp of Hessen, telling the Duce that as a 'son of this [Austrian] soil' he could no longer stand back but felt compelled to intervene to restore order in his homeland, assuring Mussolini of his undiminished sympathy, and stressed that nothing would alter his agreement to uphold the Brenner border.[78] But whatever the Duce's reaction, Hitler had by then already put out his directive for 'Case Otto', expressing his intention, should other measures – the demands put by Seyß-Inquart to Schuschnigg – fail, of marching into Austria. The action, under his command, was to take place 'without use of force in the form of a peaceful entry welcomed by the people'.[79]

Hitler, when Papen was ushered in to see him that morning, was 'in a state bordering on hysteria'.[80] During the course of the day, Göring (so he claimed), rather than Hitler, made most of the running. 'It was not the Führer so much as I, myself, who set the pace and, even overruling the Führer's misgivings, brought everything to its final development,' he proudly insisted at his Nuremberg trial, anxious to establish his own 'Göring myth' for posterity.[81] 'Without actually discussing it with the Führer,' he recalled, 'I demanded spontaneously the immediate resignation of Chancellor Schuschnigg. When this was approved, I put the next demand, so that now the entire business was ready for the Anschluß.'[82] This was something of an over-simplification.

Hitler had put the first ultimatum around 10a.m., demanding Schuschnigg call off the referendum for two weeks to allow a plebiscite similar to that in the Saarland in 1935 to be arranged – the idea that Goebbels had raised the previous day. Schuschnigg was to resign as Chancellor to make way for Seyß-Inquart. All restrictions on the National Socialists were to be lifted.[83] It was when Schuschnigg, around 2.45p.m., accepted the postponement of the plebiscite but rejected the demand to resign that Göring acted on his own initiative in repeating the ultimatum for the Chancellor's resignation and replacement by Seyß. Göring reported back to the Reich Chancellery: Seyß had to be named Chancellor by 5.30p.m., the other conditions of the original ultimatum accepted by 7.30p.m.[84] He had simply overridden the objections of Seyß himself, who was still hoping to avoid a German invasion and preserve some shreds of Austrian independence.[85] Looking harassed and tense, Seyß put the ultimatum to the Austrian cabinet, remarking that he was no more than 'a girl telephone switchboard operator'.[86] At this point, the military preparations in Germany were continuing, 'but march in still uncertain', recorded Goebbels. Plans were discussed for making Hitler Federal President, to be acclaimed by popular vote, 'and then eventually (*dann so nach und nach*) to complete the Anschluß'.[87] In the immediate future, the 'coordination' (*Gleichschaltung*) of Austria, not the complete Anschluß, was what was envisaged.[88]

Then news came through that only part of the second ultimatum had been accepted. Schuschnigg's desperate plea for British help had solicited a telegram from Lord Halifax, baldly stating: 'His Majesty's Government are unable to guarantee protection.'[89] About 3.30p.m. Schuschnigg resigned.[90] But President Wilhelm Miklas was refusing to appoint Seyß-Inquart as Chancellor.[91] A further ultimatum was sent to Vienna, expiring at 7.30p.m.[92] By now Göring was in full swing. Returning to the Reich Chancellery in the early evening, Nicolaus von Below found him 'in his element', constantly on the phone to Vienna, the complete 'master of the situation'.[93] Just before 8.00 that evening, Schuschnigg made an emotional speech on the radio, describing the ultimatum. Austria, he said, had yielded to force. To spare bloodshed, the troops would offer no resistance.[94]

By now, Nazi mobs were rampaging through Austrian cities, occupying provincial government buildings. Local Nazi leaders were hoping for *Gleichschaltung* through a seizure of power from within to forestall an invasion from Germany.[95] Göring pressed Seyß-Inquart to send a prearranged telegram, dictated from Berlin, asking the German government for help to 'restore order' in the Austrian cities, 'so that we have legitimation', as Goebbels frankly admitted.[96] Keppler rang at 8.48p.m. to inform Göring that Seyß was refusing to send the telegram. Göring replied that the telegram need not be sent; all Seyß needed do was to say 'agreed'.[97] Eventually,

Keppler sent the telegram, at 9.10p.m. It was irrelevant. Twenty-five minutes earlier, persuaded by Göring that he would lose face by not acting after putting the ultimatum, Hitler had already given the Wehrmacht the order to march.[98] Brauchitsch had left the Reich Chancellery, the invasion order in his pocket, depressed and worried about the response abroad.[99] Just before 10.30p.m. Hitler heard the news he had been impatiently awaiting: Mussolini was prepared to accept German intervention. 'Please tell Mussolini I will never forget him for it, never, never, never, come what may,' a hugely relieved Hitler gushed over the telephone to Philipp of Hesse. 'If he should ever need any help or be in any danger, he can be sure that do or die I shall stick by him, come what may, even if the whole world rises against him,' he added, carried away by his elation.[100]

At midnight, President Miklas gave in. Seyß-Inquart was appointed Federal Chancellor.[101] All German demands had now been met. But the invasion went ahead. As the American journalist William Shirer, observing the scenes in Vienna, cynically commented: with the invasion Hitler broke the terms of his own ultimatum.[102] A last attempt by Seyß-Inquart, at 2.30a.m., to have the invasion stopped was brusquely rejected by Hitler: the military intervention could no longer be halted.[103] Keitel did not dare pass on a plea he received at 4a.m. from General Max von Viebahn, in the Wehrmacht Head Office, imploring him to intervene with the Führer to desist from the invasion. Had Hitler known of the request, Keitel claimed, he would have been utterly contemptuous of the army leadership.[104] That, in Keitel's eyes, had to be avoided at all costs in the light of the events of the previous weeks. The 'friendly visit' of German troops began at 5.30a.m.[105]

Later that morning, Hitler, accompanied by Keitel, landed in Munich, *en route* for his triumphal entry into Austria, leaving Göring to serve as his deputy in the Reich.[106] By midday, the cavalcade of grey Mercedes, with open tops despite the freezing weather, had reached Mühldorf am Inn, close to the Austrian border. General Fedor von Bock, Commander-in-Chief of the newly formed 8th Army, hastily put together in two days out of troop units in Bavaria, reported to Hitler. The motorized Leibstandarte-SS Adolf Hitler had joined them from Berlin. Bock could tell Hitler that the German troops had been received with flowers and jubilation since crossing the border two hours earlier. Hitler listened to the report of reactions abroad by Reich Press Chief Otto Dietrich. He did not expect either military or political complications, and gave the order to drive on to Linz.[107]

Back in Berlin, Frick was drafting a set of laws to accommodate the

German takeover in Austria. A full Anschluß – the complete incorporation of Austria, marking its disappearance as a country – was still not envisaged; at any rate, not in the immediate future. Elections were prescribed for 10 April, with Austria 'under Germany's protection'. Hitler was to be Federal President, determining the constitution. 'We can then push along the development as we want,' commented Goebbels.[108] Hitler himself had not hinted at an Anschluß in his proclamation, read out at midday by Goebbels on German and Austrian radio, stating only that there would be a 'true plebiscite' on Austria's future and fate within a short time.[109]

Shortly before 4p.m. that afternoon, Hitler crossed the Austrian border over the narrow bridge at his birthplace, Braunau am Inn. The church-bells were ringing. Tens of thousands of people (most of them from outside Braunau), in ecstasies of joy, lined the streets of the small town. But Hitler did not linger. Propaganda value, not sentiment, had dictated his visit. Braunau played its brief symbolic part. That sufficed. The cavalcade passed on its triumphal progression to Linz.

Progress was much slower than expected because of the jubilant crowds packing the roadsides. It was in darkness, four hours later, that Hitler eventually reached the Upper Austrian capital. Seyß-Inquart, Glaise-Horstenau, Himmler, and other leading Nazis had long been waiting for him.[110] So had an enormous crowd, gathered on the marketplace. The cars could go no further. Hitler's bodyguards pushed a way through the crowd so that he could go the last few yards to the town hall on foot.[111] Peals of bells rang out; the ecstatic crowd was screaming 'Heil'; Seyß-Inquart could hardly make himself heard in his introductory remarks. Hitler looked deeply moved.[112] Tears ran down his cheeks.[113] In his speech on the balcony of the Linz town hall, he told the masses, constantly interrupting him with their wild cheering, that Providence must have singled him out to return his homeland to the German Reich. They were witnesses that he had now fulfilled his mission. 'I don't know on which day you will be called,' he added. 'I hope it is not far off.' This somewhat mystical remark seemed to indicate that even up to this point, he was not intending within hours to end Austria's identity by incorporating the country into Germany.[114]

Once more, plans were rapidly altered. He had meant to go straight on to Vienna. But he decided to stay in Linz throughout the next day, Sunday the 13th, and enter Vienna on the Monday.[115] To the accompaniment of unending cries of 'One people, one Reich, one Leader' ('*ein Volk, ein Reich, ein Führer*'), his party took up rooms in the Hotel Weinzinger on the banks of the Danube. Beds were hastily allocated. The restaurant could not cope with the food requirements. The single telephone in the hotel had to be reserved solely for Hitler's use.[116] The extraordinary reception had made a huge impact on him. He was told that foreign newspapers were already speaking of the 'Anschluß' of Austria to Germany as a *fait accompli*. It was in this atmosphere that the idea rapidly took shape of annexing Austria immediately.

In an excited mood, Hitler was heard to say that he wanted no half-measures. Stuckart, from the Reich Ministry of the Interior, was hurriedly summoned to Linz to draft legislation.[117] In an interview he gave to the British journalist Ward Price in the Hotel Weinzinger, Hitler hinted that Austria would become a German province 'like Bavaria or Saxony'.[118] He evidently pondered the matter further during the night.[119] The next day, 13 March – the day originally scheduled for Schuschnigg's referendum on Austrian independence – the Anschluß, not intended before the previous evening, was completed.[120] Hitler's visit to Leonding, where he laid flowers on his parents' grave and returned to the house where the family had lived, meeting some acquaintances he had not seen for thirty years, perhaps reinforced the belief, stimulated the previous evening by his reception in Linz, that Providence had predestined him to reunite his homeland (*Heimat*) with the Reich.[121]

At some point during the day Hitler contacted Mussolini to assure himself of the Duce's acceptance of the final move to full Anschluß. On hearing the news he wanted, he dispatched an effusive telegram, in the same vein as his telephone message two days earlier: 'Mussolini, I will never forget you for this!'[122] The Duce's reply the following day, addressed simply to 'Hitler. Vienna', was less emotional: 'My stance is determined by the friendship between our two countries sealed in the axis,' he wrote.[123]

Stuckart had meanwhile arrived overnight and sat in the Hotel Weinzinger on the morning of the 13th drafting the 'Law for the Reunion of Austria with the German Reich'.[124] This was put together in all haste through much toing and froing between Stuckart in Linz and Keppler in Vienna.[125] Hitler told a group of surprised and jubilant Austrian Nazi leaders, invited to lunch in the Hotel Weinzinger, around 3p.m. that 'an important law' announcing Austria's incorporation within the German Reich was about to appear.[126] Around 5p.m. the Austrian Ministerial Council – a body by now bearing scant resemblance to the cabinet under Schuschnigg – unanimously accepted Stuckart's draft with one or two minor reformulations. The meeting lasted a mere five minutes and ended with the members of the Council rising to their feet to give the 'German Greeting'. The Austrian President,

Wilhelm Miklas, laid down his office at about the same time, refusing to sign the reunion law and handing his powers over to Seyß-Inquart. That evening, Seyß-Inquart and Keppler drove to Linz to confirm that the law had been accepted. Hitler signed the law before the evening was out.[127] Austria had become a German province.[128] Göring, who before the events triggered by the Berchtesgaden meeting had, as we have seen, been the one most strongly pressing for the union of the two countries, was taken by surprise – astonished at the manner in which the actual Anschluß had come about.[129]

Immediately, the Austrian army was sworn in to Hitler. In a surprise move, Gauleiter Josef Bürckel, a trusted 'old fighter' of the Movement but with no connections with Austria, was brought in from the Saar to reorganize the NSDAP.[130] Hitler was well aware of the need to bring the Party in Austria fully into line as quickly as possible, and not to leave it in the hands of the turbulent, ill-disciplined, and unpredictable Austrian leadership.

In mid-morning on 14 March, Hitler left Linz for Vienna. Cheering crowds greeted the cavalcade of limousines – thirteen police cars accompanied Hitler's Mercedes – all the way to the capital, where he arrived, again delayed, in the late afternoon.[131] On the orders of Cardinal Innitzer, Archbishop of Vienna, all the Catholic churches in the city pealed their bells in Hitler's honour and flew swastika banners from their steeples – an extraordinary gesture given the 'Church struggle' which had raged in the Reich itself over the previous years.[132] The scenes of enthusiasm, according to a Swiss reporter who witnessed them, 'defied all description'.[133] An English observer of the scene commented: 'To say that the crowds which greeted [Hitler] along the Ringstraße were delirious with joy is an understatement.'[134] Hitler had to appear repeatedly on the balcony of the Hotel Imperial in response to the crowd's continual shouts of 'We want to see our Führer.'[135] Keitel, whose room faced the front of the hotel, found it impossible to sleep for the clamour.[136]

The next day, 15 March, in beautiful spring weather, Hitler addressed a vast, delirious crowd, estimated at a quarter of a million people, in Vienna's Heldenplatz. The Viennese Nazi Party had been impatiently expecting him to come to the capital for three days.[137] They had had time to ensure the preparations were complete. Work-places were ordered to be closed (though employees were still to be paid – some compensation for the hours spent standing and waiting for Hitler's speech); many factories and offices had marched their employees as a group to hear the historic speech; schools had not been open since the Saturday; Hitler Youth and girls from the Bund

Deutscher Mädel were bussed in from all parts of Austria; party formations had turned out in force.[138] But for all the organization, the wild enthusiasm of the immense crowd was undeniable – and infectious. Those less enthusiastic had already been cowed into submission by the open brutality of the Nazi hordes, exploiting their triumph since the weekend to inflict fearful beatings or to rob and plunder at will, and by the first waves of mass arrests (already numbering between 10,000 and 20,000 in the early days) orchestrated by Himmler and Heydrich, who had arrived in Vienna on 12 March.[139]

Ominous in Hitler's speech was his reference to the 'new mission' of the 'Eastern Marches (*Ostmark*) of the German People' (as the once independent country of Austria was now to be known) as the 'bulwark' against the 'storms of the east'.[140] He ended, to tumultuous cheering lasting for minutes, by declaring 'before history the entry of my homeland into the German Reich'.[141]

After attending a military parade in the afternoon, Hitler had a short but important audience, arranged by Papen, with the Austrian primate, Cardinal Innitzer.[142] The Cardinal assured Hitler of the loyalty of Austria's Catholics, the overwhelming body of the population.[143] Three days later, along with six other Austrian bishops and archbishops, he put his signature to a declaration of their full support and blessing for the new regime in Austria and their conviction 'that through the actions of the National Socialist Movement the danger of godless Bolshevism, which would destroy everything, would be fended off'.[144] Cardinal Innitzer added in his own hand: 'Heil Hitler.'[145]

In the early evening, Hitler left Vienna and flew to Munich, before returning next day to Berlin to another 'hero's welcome'.[146] Two days later, on 18 March, a hastily summoned Reichstag heard his account of the events leading up to what he described as the 'fulfilment of the supreme historical commission'.[147] He then dissolved the Reichstag and set new elections for 10 April. On 25 March, in Königsberg, he began what was to prove his last 'election' campaign, holding six out of fourteen major speeches in the former Austria.[148] In both parts of the extended Reich, the propaganda machine once more went into overdrive. Newspapers were prohibited from using the word '*ja*' in any context other than in connection with the plebiscite.[149] When the results were announced on 10 April, 99.08 per cent in the 'Old Reich', and 99.75 per cent in 'Austria' voted 'yes' to the Anschluß and to the 'list of the Führer'.[150] Goebbels's Propaganda Ministry congratulated itself. 'Such an almost 100 per cent election result is at the same time a badge of honour for all election propagandists,' it concluded.[151]

From Hitler's perspective, it was a near-perfect result. Whatever the undoubted manipulative methods, ballot-rigging, and pressure to conform which helped produce it, genuine support for Hitler's action had unquestionably been massive.[152] Once again, a foreign-policy triumph had strengthened his hand at home and abroad. For the mass of the German people, Hitler once more seemed a statesman of extraordinary virtuoso talents. For the leaders of the western democracies, anxieties about the mounting instability of central Europe were further magnified.

The Austrian adventure was over. Hitler's attentions were already moving elsewhere. Within days of returning from Vienna, he was poring over maps together with Goebbels. 'First comes now Czechia (*Tschechei*),' the Propaganda Minister recorded. '. . . And drastically (*rigoros*), at the next opportunity . . . The Führer is wonderful . . . A true genius. Now he sits for hours over the map and broods. Moving, when he says he wants to experience the great German Reich of the Teutons (*Germanen*) himself.'[153]

The Anschluß was a watershed for Hitler, and for the Third Reich. The backcloth to it had been one of domestic crisis. Yet almost overnight any lingering threat in the Blomberg–Fritsch affair had been defused by a triumph greater than any that Hitler had enjoyed before. The overwhelming reception he had encountered on his grandiose procession to Vienna, above all his return to Linz, had made a strong impression on the German Dictator. The intoxication of the crowds made him feel like a god. The rapid improvisation of the Anschluß there and then, fulfilling a dream he had entertained as a young Schönerer supporter all those years earlier, proved once more – so it seemed to him – that he could do anything he wanted. His instincts were, it seemed, always right. The western 'powers' were powerless. The doubters and sceptics at home were, as always, revealed as weak and wrong. There was no one to stand in his way. As Papen later put it: 'Hitler had brought about the Anschluß by force; in spite of all warnings and prophecies, his own methods had proved the most direct and successful. Not only had there been no armed conflict between the two countries, but no foreign power had seen fit to intervene. They adopted the same passive attitude as they had shown towards the reintroduction of conscription in Germany and the reoccupation of the Rhineland. The result was that Hitler became impervious to the advice of all those who wished him to exercise moderation in his foreign policy.'[154]

Hitler had, with the Anschluß, created 'Greater Germany' ('*Großdeutschland*'), now incorporating his homeland. As Goebbels's diary entry, just noted, indicates, he was impatient for more. He had once seen himself as the 'drummer', paving the way for the 'great leader' to follow. He had then come to see himself as that 'great leader', rebuilding Germany, 'nationalizing' the masses for the great future conflict. Would he live to see the creation of the Great Germanic Reich, embracing all Germans and dominating the continent of Europe, himself? He had doubted it. Perhaps a later 'great leader' would be needed to complete the task. But from 1936 onwards, he was sure, Europe was 'on the move'; the conflict would not be long delayed. By late 1937 he was envisaging expansion in the foreseeable future. The Anschluß now suggested to him that the Great Germanic Reich did not have to be a long-term project. He could create it himself. But it had to be soon. The incorporation of Austria had seriously weakened the defences of Czechoslovakia – the Slav state he had detested since its foundation, and one allied with the Bolshevik arch-enemy and with France. The next step to German dominance on the European continent beckoned.

The Anschluß did not just set the roller-coaster of foreign expansion moving. It gave massive impetus to the assault on 'internal enemies'. Early arrivals in Vienna had been Himmler and Heydrich. The repression was ferocious – worse even than it had been in Germany following the Nazi takeover in 1933. The Austrian police records fell immediately into the Gestapo's hands. Supporters of the fallen regime, but especially Socialists, Communists, and Jews – rounded up under the aegis of the rising star in the SD's 'Jewish Department', Adolf Eichmann – were taken in their thousands into 'protective custody'.[155]

Many other Jews were manhandled, beaten, and tortured in horrific ordeals by Nazi thugs, looting and rampaging. Jewish shops were plundered at will. Individual Jews were robbed on the open streets of their money, jewellery, and fur coats. Groups of Jews, men and women, young and old, were dragged from offices, shops, or homes and forced to scrub the pavements in 'cleaning squads', their tormentors standing over them and, watched by crowds of onlookers screaming 'Work for the Jews at last,' kicking them, drenching them with cold, dirty water, and subjecting them to every conceivable form of merciless humiliation.[156]

The pent-up fury of the Nazi mobs threatened to explode into a full-scale pogrom. The Daily Telegraph's long-standing correspondent in Vienna, G.E.R. Gedye, described the menacing atmosphere: 'As I crossed the Graben [one of the main streets in the centre of Vienna] to my office, the Brown flood was sweeping through the streets. It was an indescribable witches' sabbath – stormtroopers, lots of them barely out of the schoolroom, with cartridge belts and carbines, the only other evidence of authority being swastika brassards, were marching side by side with police turncoats, men and women shrieking or crying hysterically the name of their leader, embracing the police and dragging them along in the swirling stream of humanity, motor-lorries filled with stormtroopers clutching their long-concealed weapons, hooting furiously, trying to make themselves heard above the din, men and women leaping, shouting, and dancing in the light of the smoking torches which soon began to make their appearance, the air filled with a pandemonium of sound in which intermingled screams of: "Down with the Jews! Heil Hitler! Heil Hitler! Sieg Heil! Perish the Jews! . . ." '[157]

'Hades had opened its gates and released its basest, most despicable, most unpure spirits,' was how the esteemed playwright and writer Carl Zuckmayer, his own works banned in Germany since 1933, described the scene. Vienna had transformed itself, in his eyes, 'into a nightmare painting of Hieronymus Bosch'.[158]

One seventeen-year-old Jew later recalled his own experience, only a short few weeks after being part of a fun-loving crowd enjoying the dancing, drinking, and merriment of the Viennese carnival: 'I rushed to the window and looked out into Nußdorferstraße . . . Then the first lorry came into sight. It was packed with shouting, screaming men. A huge swastika flag fluttered over their heads . . . Now we could hear clearly what they were shouting: "Ein Volk, ein Reich, ein Führer!" they were chanting in chorus, followed by "Ju-da verr-rrecke! Ju-da verr-rrecke!" ("Per-rish Judah!") . . . I was still looking out into Nußdorferstraße when I suddenly heard a muffled shout from right below our window. I craned my neck and saw an Austrian policeman, a swastika brassard already over his dark green uniform sleeve, his truncheon in his fist, lashing out with berserk fury at a man writhing at his feet. I immediately recognized that policeman. I had known him all my life . . .'[159]

Thousands tried to flee. Masses packed the railway stations, trying to get out to Prague. They had the few possessions they could carry with them ransacked by the squads of men with swastika armbands who had assembled at the stations, 'confiscating' property at will, entering compartments on the trains and dragging out arbitrarily selected victims for further mishandling and internment. Those who left on the 11.15p.m. night express thought they had escaped. But they were turned back at the Czech border. Their ordeal was only just beginning. Others tried to flee by road. Soon, the roads to the Czech border were jammed. They became littered with abandoned cars as their occupants, realizing that the Czech authorities were turning back refugees at the borders, headed into the woods to try to cross the frontier illegally on foot.[160]

For many, there was only one way out. Suicide among the Viennese Jewish community became commonplace in these terrible days.[161]

The quest to root out 'enemies of the people', which in Germany had subsided in the mid-1930s and had begun to gather new pace in 1937, was revitalized through the new 'opportunities' that had opened up in Austria. The radicalized campaign would very quickly be reimported to the 'Old Reich', both in the new and horrifying wave of antisemitism in the summer of 1938, and – behind the scenes but ultimately even more sinister – in the rapid expansion of the SS's involvement in looking for solutions to the 'Jewish Question'.[162]

After the tremors of the Blomberg–Fritsch affair, Hitler's internal position was now stronger than ever. His leadership was absolute. The officer corps of the army, deeply angered at the treatment of Fritsch, had had the wind taken out of their sails by the Anschluß triumph. For a small number of officers, the seeds of resistance had been sown which would eventually germinate into a conspiracy that would nearly take Hitler's life on 20 July 1944. But at this stage the bitter animosity was directed largely against Himmler, Heydrich, and Göring, not Hitler. And they recognized that there were no forces capable of carrying through a putsch since, as Major-General Friedrich Olbricht put it, 'the people are behind Hitler'.[163] Nor was the reception accorded to the German troops on the Austrian roads lost on them. The vast majority of officers were, as regards the Anschluß, of one mind with the people: they could only approve and – if sometimes begrudgingly – admire Hitler's latest triumph.

Among the mass of the population, 'the German miracle' brought about by Hitler released what was described as 'an elemental frenzy of enthusiasm' – once it was clear that the western powers would again stand by and do nothing, and that 'our Führer has pulled it off without bloodshed'.[164] It would be the last time that the German people – now with the addition of their cousins to the east whose rapid disillusionment soon dissipated the wild euphoria with which many of them had greeted Hitler[165] – would feel the threat of war lifted so rapidly from them through a foreign-policy coup completed within days and presented as a *fait accompli*. The next crisis, over the Sudetenland, would drag over months and have them in near-panic over the likelihood of war. And if Hitler had had his way, there would have been war.

I I

The crisis over Czechoslovakia in the summer of 1938 took Germany's expansionist drive on to a new plane. This crisis was different from those which had preceded it in a number of significant ways. Down to the Anschluß, the major triumphs in foreign policy had been in line with the revisionist and nationalist expectations of all powerful interests in the Reich, and quite especially those of the army. The withdrawal from the League of Nations in 1933, the reintroduction of general military service in 1935, the reoccupation of the Rhineland in 1936, and probably the Anschluß, too, would have been sought by any nationalist government in Germany at the time. The methods – on which the army, the Foreign Office, and others often looked askance – were Hitlerian. The timing had been determined by Hitler. The decisions to act were his alone. But in each case there had been powerful backing, as well as some hesitancy, among his advisers. And in each case, he was reflecting diverse currents of revisionist expression. The immense popularity of his triumphs in all sections of the political élite and among the masses of the population testified to the underlying consensus behind the revisionism. The earlier crises had also all been of brief duration. The tension had in each case been short-lived, the success rapidly attained. And in each case, the popular jubilation was in part an expression of relief that the western powers had not intervened, that the threat of another war – something which sent shivers of horror down the spines of most ordinary people – had been averted. The resulting popularity and prestige that accrued to Hitler drew heavily upon his 'triumphs without bloodshed'.[166] In reality, as we have seen, there had in every instance been little chance of allied intervention, even to counter the reoccupation of the Rhineland. The weakness and divisions of the western powers had in each case been the platform for Hitler's bloodless coups.

For the first time, in the summer of 1938, Hitler's foreign policy went beyond revisionism and national integration, even if the western powers did not grasp this. Whatever his public veneer of concern about the treatment of the Sudeten Germans,[167] there was no doubt at all to the ruling groups in Germany aware of Hitler's thinking – his comments at the 'Hoßbach meeting' had already made it plain – that he was aiming not just at the incorporation of the Sudetenland in the German Reich, but at destroying the state of Czechoslovakia itself. By the end of May this aim, and the timing envisaged to accomplish it, had been outlined to the army leadership. It meant war – certainly against Czechoslovakia, and probably (so it seemed to others), despite Hitler's presumption of the contrary, against the western powers. Hitler, it became unmistakably plain, actually wanted war. 'Long live war – even if it lasts from two to eight years,' he would proclaim to the Sudeten leader Konrad Henlein in September, at the height of the crisis.[168] 'Every generation must at one time have experienced war,' his adjutant Fritz Wiedemann recalled him commenting around the same time.[169] Whatever the warnings, he was even prepared for war (though he did not think it likely at this juncture) against Britain and France.

The sheer recklessness of courting disaster by the wholly unnecessary (in their view) risk of war at this time against the western powers – which they thought Germany in its current state of preparation could not win – appalled and horrified a number of those who knew what Hitler had in mind.

It was not the prospect of destroying Czechoslovakia that alienated them. The state that had been founded in 1918 out of the ruins of the Habsburg empire had sustained its democracy despite German, Hungarian, Polish, and Ruthenian minorities alongside Czechs and Slovaks (though since Hitler's assumption of power in Germany the German ethnic minority, over 3 million strong, had proved increasingly restless). The country had a strong industrial base, and had expanded its defence capabilities until its army had to be regarded as a force to be reckoned with. Given that its long north and south borders abutted Germany, Austria, Hungary, Romania, the Ukraine, and Poland, the emphasis on defence was scarcely surprising. Czechoslovakia looked to Germany's arch-enemies – not just to France, but also to the Soviet Union – for support, and Communism had a sizeable following in the country. To German nationalist eyes, therefore, Czechoslovakia could only be seen as a major irritant occupying a strategically crucial area. Coloured in addition by anti-Slav prejudice, there was little love lost for a democracy, hostile to the Reich, whose destruction would bring major advantages for Germany's military and economic dominance of central Europe. The army had already planned in 1937 for the possibility of a pre-emptive strike against Czechoslovakia – 'Case Green' – to counter the possibility of the Czechs joining in from the east if their allies, the French, attacked the Reich from the west.[170] As the prospect of a war with the French, something taken extremely seriously in the mid-1930s, had receded, 'Case Green' had been amended a month after the 'Hoßbach meeting' to take account of likely circumstances in which the Wehrmacht could invade Czechoslovakia to solve the problem of 'living space'.[171]

In economic terms, too, the fall of Czechoslovakia offered an enticing prospect. Göring, his staff directing the Four-Year Plan, and the leaders of the arms industry, were for their part casting greedy eyes on the raw materials and armaments plants of Czechoslovakia. The problems built into an economy so heavily tilted towards armaments production but still heavily dependent upon costly imports of food and raw materials, facing too an increasingly acute labour shortage, and with an agricultural sector strained to the limit, were – as countless reports indicated – mounting alarmingly.[172] The economic pressures for expansion accorded fully with the power-political aims of the regime's leadership. Those who had argued for an alternative economic strategy, most of all of course Schacht, had by now lost their influence. Göring was the dominant figure. And in Göring's dreams of German dominion in south-eastern Europe, the acquisition of Czechoslovakia was plainly pivotal.

But neither military strategy nor economic necessity compelled a Czech crisis in 1938. It is true that Beck, the Chief of Staff, could state in late May 1938 that 'Czechia (die Tschechei) in the form that the Versailles Diktat compelled it to take is intolerable for Germany', so that 'a way must be found to eliminate it as a danger-spot for Germany, if necessary through a military solution'. He nevertheless took the lead in the army in opposing what he saw as a catastrophic step in involving the Reich in conflict with the west.[173] Göring, the arch-bully of the Austrian government during the Anschluß crisis, whose rapaciousness was second to no one's, shared Beck's forebodings, and pressed for territorial concessions from the western powers in Czechoslovakia in order to avoid what he saw as the disaster of war with Britain. There were few keener than he was to see the end of the Czech state. But his views on how that end should come about – gradual liquidation over time through relentless pressure – were closer to those of the national-conservatives than to Hitler's intention to achieve it through military might in the near future. As war with Britain seemed increasingly likely, Göring's feet became ever colder. At the peak of the crisis, he would push for peace at Munich rather than Hitler's preferred military aggression against the Czechs. It did not enhance his standing as a foreign-policy adviser with a disappointed Hitler. His political influence would never again be as high after Munich.[174]

It was the vision of national disaster that led for the first time to the tentative emergence of significant strands of opposition to what was regarded as Hitler's madness. In the army leadership (still smarting from the Fritsch scandal), in the Foreign Office, and in other high places, the germs of resistance were planted among those certain that Germany was

being driven headlong into catastrophe.[175] In the military, the leading opponents of Hitler's high-risk policy emerged as Colonel-General Beck, who
resigned as Chief of Staff in the summer, and Admiral Wilhelm Canaris,
head of the Abwehr (military intelligence).[176] In the Foreign Office, the State
Secretary Ernst von Weizsäcker was at the forefront of those in opposition
to the policy supported avidly by his immediate superior, Foreign Minister
von Ribbentrop.[177] Among civilians with inside knowledge of what was
going on, Carl Goerdeler, the former Reich Price Commissar, used his
extensive foreign contacts to warn about Hitler's aims.[178]

Nor was there any popular pressure for a foreign adventure, let alone one
which was thought likely to bring war with the western powers. Among
ordinary people, excluded from the deliberations in high places which kept
Europe on the thinnest of tightropes between war and peace in September,
the long-drawn-out crisis over Czechoslovakia, lasting throughout the late
spring and summer, unlike earlier crises allowed time for the anxieties about
war to gather momentum. The acute tension produced what was described
as a 'real war psychosis'.[179] No love was lost on the Czechs. And the relentless
propaganda about their alleged persecution of the German minority was
not without impact. There were indeed some feelings of real gung-ho
aggression, though these were largely confined to gullible younger Germans,
who had not lived through the World War. The overwhelming sentiment
was a fervent desire that war should be avoided and peace preserved. For
the first time there was a hint of lack of confidence in Hitler's policy. Most
looked to him to preserve peace, not take Germany into a new war.[180] But
this time, both to the leading actors in the drama and to the millions looking
on anxiously, war looked a more likely outcome than peace.

Among those with power and influence, the most forthright supporter of
war to destroy Czechoslovakia was the new Foreign Minister, Joachim von
Ribbentrop, an entirely different entity to the displaced conservative, von
Neurath. Ribbentrop was more than keen to stamp his imprint on the
Foreign Office – and to make up for the embarrassment he had sustained
when, largely at Göring's doing, he had been sidelined in London and
allowed to play no part in the Austrian triumph that his arch-rival in foreign
policy had been instrumental in orchestrating.[181] He provided Hitler with
his main backing in these months. His hatred of Britain – the country which
had spurned and ridiculed him – as well as his fawning devotion to the
Führer made him the most hawkish of the hawks, a warmonger second only
to Hitler himself. When he was not directly spurring on Hitler, he was doing
his utmost to shore up the conviction that, when it came to it, Britain would

not fight, that any war would be a localized one. State Secretary von Weizsäcker was sure of Ribbentrop's baleful influence on Hitler in this respect. When, in the middle of August, Weizsäcker contradicted Ribbentrop's assertion that the western powers would not act, the Foreign Minister retorted that 'the Führer had so far never made a mistake; his most difficult decisions and actions (Rhineland occupation) were already behind him. One had to believe in his genius, just as he, Ribbentrop, did from long years of experience.' He hoped that Weizsäcker could also come to have 'such blind faith'. The State Secretary would later regret it if that were not the case, and the facts then spoke against him.[182]

For all Ribbentrop's influence, however, there could be no doubt that the crisis that brought Europe to the very brink of war in the summer of 1938 was instigated and directed by Hitler himself. And unlike the rapid improvisation and breakneck speed which had characterized previous crises, this one was consciously devised to escalate over a period of months.

Until 1938, Hitler's moves in foreign policy had been bold, but not reckless. He had shown shrewd awareness of the weakness of his opponents, a sure instinct for exploiting divisions and uncertainty. His sense of timing had been excellent, his combination of bluff and blackmail effective, his manipulation of propaganda to back his coups masterly. He had gone further and faster than anyone could have expected in revising the terms of Versailles and upturning the post-war diplomatic settlement. From the point of view of the western powers, his methods were, to say the least, unconventional diplomacy – raw, brutal, unpalatable; but his aims were recognizably in accord with traditional German nationalist clamour. Down to and including the Anschluß, Hitler had proved a consummate nationalist politician. During the Sudeten crisis, some sympathy for demands to incorporate the German-speaking areas in the Reich – for another Anschluß of sorts – still existed among those ready to swallow Goebbels's propaganda about the maltreatment of the Sudeten Germans by the Czechs, or at any rate prepared to accept that a further nationality problem was in need of resolution. It took the crisis and its outcome to expose the realization that Hitler would stop at nothing. Some of the shame felt at the Munich settlement in the western democracies as soon as the elation at the salvation of peace had evaporated was that they had merely bought off Hitler for a time through sacrificing Czechoslovakia. Before that point was reached, there had been increasing incomprehension among western statesmen during the course of the summer about Hitler and his aims. Some of the comments doubting his sanity reflect the sense of British statesmen at the time that they were dealing with someone who had crossed the bounds of rational behaviour in international politics. In the view of the British Ambassador, Nevile Henderson, Hitler had 'become quite mad' and, bent on war at all costs, had 'crossed the borderline of insanity'.[183]

They were not far wrong. The spring of 1938 marked the phase in which Hitler's obsession with accomplishing his 'mission' in his own lifetime started to overtake cold political calculation. As Goebbels had put it in the passage already cited, Hitler wanted to experience the 'Great Germanic Reich' himself.[184] Probably, as we have already noted, his increased health worries and preoccupation with his own mortality played their part in heightening his sense of urgency. A deep-seated hatred of the Czechs – a legacy of his Austrian upbringing (when rabid hostility towards the Czechs had been endemic in the German-speaking part of the Habsburg Empire) – added a further personal dimension to the drive to destroy a Czechoslovakian state allied with the arch-enemies of the USSR in the east and France in the west. Prestige – as always – also came into it. He was to feel slighted and embarrassed at the diplomatic outfall from sudden Czech military mobilization in May (generally, though mistakenly, believed to have been in response to initial threatening moves by Germany).[185] This at the very least reinforced his decision to act with speed to crush Czechoslovakia by the autumn.[186] Finally, the sense of his own infallibility, massively boosted by the triumph of the Anschluß, underscored his increased reliance on his own will, matched by his diminished readiness to listen to countervailing counsel. That he had invariably been proved right in his assessment of the weakness of the western powers in the past, usually in the teeth of the caution of his advisers in the army and Foreign Office, convinced him that his current evaluation was unerringly correct. He had come during 1937 to be dismissive about the strength and will to fight both of Britain, which had spurned his advances, and of France, wracked by internal divisions. Partly prompted, and at any rate greatly amplified, by Ribbentrop, his views had hardened to the point where he felt the western powers would do nothing to defend Czechoslovakia. At the same time, this strengthened his conviction that the Reich's position relative to the western powers could only worsen as their inevitable build-up of arms began to catch up with that of Germany. To remain inactive – a recurring element in the way he thought – was, he asserted, not an option: it would merely play into the hands of his enemies. Therefore, he characteristically reasoned: act without delay to retain the initiative.

These various strands of his thinking came together in the conclusion that the time was ripe to strike against Czechoslovakia. Until Czechoslovakia was eliminated – this was the key strategic element in Hitler's idea – Germany would be incapable of taking action either in the east or in the west. He had moved from a position of a foreign policy supported by Great Britain to one where he was prepared to act without Britain, and, if need be, against Britain. Despite the forebodings of others, war against Czechoslovakia in his view carried few risks. And if the western powers, contrary to expectation, were foolish enough to become involved, Germany would defeat them.

More important even than why Hitler was in such a hurry to destroy Czechoslovakia is why he was by this time in a position to override or ignore weighty objections and to determine that Germany should be taken to the very brink of general European war. Decisive in this was the process, which we have followed, of the expansion of his power, relative to other agencies of power in the regime, to the point where, by spring 1938, it had freed itself from all institutional constraints and had established unchallenged supremacy over all sections of the 'power cartel'.[187] The five years of Hitler's highly personalized form of rule had eroded all semblance of collective involvement in policy-making. This fragmentation at one and the same time rendered the organization of any opposition within the power-élite almost impossible – not to speak of any attached dangers to life and liberty – and inordinately strengthened Hitler's own power. The scope for more cautious counsel to apply the brakes had sharply diminished. The constant Hobbesian 'war of all against all', the competing power fiefdoms that characterized the National Socialist regime, took place at the level below Hitler, enhancing his extraordinary position as the fount of all authority and dividing both individual and sectional interests of the different power entities (the Movement, the state bureaucracy, the army, big business, the police, and the sub-branches of each). Hitler was, therefore, as the sole linchpin, able internally to deal, as in foreign policy, through bilateral relations – offering his support here, denying it there, remaining the sole arbiter, even when he preferred (or felt compelled) to let matters ride and let his subordinates battle it out among themselves. It was less a planned strategy of 'divide and rule' than an inevitable consequence of Führer authority. Without any coordinating bodies to unify policy, each sectional interest in the Third Reich could thrive only with the legitimacy of the Führer's backing. Each one inevitably, therefore, 'worked towards the Führer' in order to gain or sustain that backing, ensuring thereby that his power grew still further and that his own ideological obsessions were promoted.

The inexorable disintegration of coherent structures of rule was therefore not only a product of the all-pervasive Führer cult reflecting and embellishing Hitler's absolute supremacy, but at the same time underpinned the myth of the all-seeing, all-knowing infallible Leader, elevating it to the very principle of government itself. Moreover, as we have witnessed throughout, Hitler had in the process swallowed the Führer cult himself, hook, line, and sinker. He was the most ardent believer in his own infallibility and destiny. It was not a good premiss for rational decision-making.

The compliance of all sections of the regime in the growth of the Führer cult, the exemption made for Hitler himself even by vehement internal critics of the Party or Gestapo, and the full awareness of the immense popularity of the 'great Leader', all contributed to making it extraordinarily difficult by summer 1938 – the first time that deep anxieties about the course of his leadership surfaced – now to contemplate withdrawing support, let alone take oppositional action of any kind.

In any case, the extent of opposition to plans for an assault on Czechoslovakia should not be exaggerated. From within the regime, only the army had the potential to block Hitler. The Blomberg–Fritsch affair had certainly left a legacy of anger, distaste, and distrust among the army leadership. But this was directed less at Hitler personally, than at the leadership of the SS and police. Even Beck, by far the most vehement critic of the regime among the top military leadership, went out of his way – and not for tactical reasons – to emphasize that the resistance needed towards the methods of the SS and the corrupt Party 'bigwigs' was a 'fight *for* the Führer' and that there should not be even the 'slightest presumption of anything like a plot' against him.[188]

Following the changes of February 1938, the army's own position, in relation to Hitler, had weakened. In the process, the army leadership had, as has been claimed, been transformed from a 'power-élite' into a 'functional élite' – an adjunct of Hitler's power rather than the 'state within the state' which it had effectively been since Bismarck's era.[189] The Anschluß had then further bolstered Hitler's supremacy. By the summer of 1938, whatever the anxieties about the risk of war with the western powers, the leadership of the armed forces was divided within itself. Hitler could depend upon unquestioning support from Keitel and Jodl in the Supreme Command of the Wehrmacht. Brauchitsch could be relied upon to keep the army in line, whatever the reservations of some of the generals. Raeder was, as always, fully behind Hitler and already preparing the navy for eventual war with Britain. The head of the Luftwaffe, Göring, fearful of such a war and seeing it as the negation of his own conception of German expansionist policy, nevertheless bowed axiomatically to the Führer's superior authority at all points where his approach started to diverge from Hitler's own. When Beck felt compelled to resign as Chief of Staff, therefore, he stirred no broad protest within the army, let alone in the other branches of the Wehrmacht. Instead, he isolated himself and henceforth formed his links with equally isolated and disaffected individuals within the armed forces, the Foreign Office, and other state ministries who began to contemplate ways of removing Hitler. They were well aware that they were swimming against a strong tide. Whatever doubts and worries there might be, they knew that the consensus behind Hitler within the power-élites was unbroken. They were conscious, too, that from the masses, despite mounting anxieties about war, Hitler could still summon immense reserves of fanatical support.[190] The prospects of successful resistance were, therefore, not good.

It was scarcely surprising, then, that there would be overwhelming compliance and no challenge to Hitler's leadership, or to his dangerous policy, as the crisis unfolded throughout the summer. Despite reservations, all sections of the regime's power-élite had by this point come to bind themselves to Hitler – whether to flourish or to perish.

III

The international constellation also played completely into Hitler's hands. Czechoslovakia, despite its formal treaties with France and the Soviet Union, was exposed and friendless. France's vacillation during the summer reflected a desperation to avoid having to fulfil its treaty obligations to Czechoslovakia through military involvement for which there was neither the will nor the preparation. The French were fearful of Czechoslovakia coming under German control. But they were even more fearful of becoming embroiled in a war to defend the Czechs.[191] The Soviet Union, in any case preoccupied with its internal upheavals, could only help the defence of Czechoslovakia if its troops were permitted to cross Polish or Romanian soil – a prospect which could be ruled out.[192] Poland and Hungary both looked greedily to the possibility of their own revisionist gains at the expense of a dismembered Czechoslovakia. Italy, having conceded to the rapidly emerging senior partner in the Axis over the key issue of Austria, had no obvious interest in propping up Czechoslovakia.[193] Great Britain, preoccupied with global commitments and problems in different parts of its Empire, and aware of its military unreadiness for an increasingly likely conflict with Germany, was anxious at all costs to avoid prematurely being drawn into a war over a nationality problem in a central European country to which it was bound by no treaty obligations. The British knew the French were not prepared to help the Czechs.[194] The government were still giving Hitler the benefit of the doubt, ready to believe that designs on Sudeten territory did not amount to 'international power lust' or mean that he was envisaging a future attack on France and Britain.[195] Beyond this, it was accepted in London that the Czechs were indeed oppressing the Sudeten German minority.[196] Pressure on the Czechs to comply with Hitler's demands was an inevitable response – and one backed by the French.

On top of its increasingly hopeless international position, Czechoslovakia's internal fragility also greatly assisted Hitler. Not just the clamour of the Sudeten Germans, but the designs of the Slovaks for their own autonomy placed the Czech government in an impossible situation. Undermined from without and within, the only new democracy surviving from the post-war settlement was about to be deserted by its 'friends' and devoured by its enemies.

In the very days before Schuschnigg had prompted the Anschluß crisis, Goebbels had noted, after discussions with Hitler, that Czechoslovakia would 'be torn to pieces (*zerfetzt*) one day'.[197] Even as Göring was reassuring the Czechs that there was no contemplation of military action against them, he was telling the Hungarians that the turn of Czechoslovakia would certainly come once the Austrian question was settled.[198] Hitler himself, according to Jodl, also made similar comments around the same time: 'Austria would have to be digested first.'[199] Within two weeks of the Anschluß, in discussions in Berlin with the Sudeten German leader Konrad Henlein, Hitler was indicating that the Czech question would be solved 'before long'. He also prescribed the general strategy of stipulating demands which the Prague government could not meet – vital to prevent the Czechoslovakian government at any stage falling in line with British pressure to accommodate the Sudeten Germans.[200] Henlein wasted no time in putting forward his demands, amounting to autonomy for Sudeten Germans, on 24 April at the Congress of the Sudeten German Party at Carlsbad (Karlovy Vary).[201] One demand to be kept up Henlein's sleeve, which Hitler was certain from his knowledge of the Austria-Hungarian multinational state could never be accepted, was for German regiments within the Czechoslovakian army.[202] In Germany itself, the strategy was to turn up the volume of propaganda at the alleged oppression of the Sudeten Germans by the

Czechs. If necessary, incidents to fuel the agitation could be manufactured.[203] Militarily, Hitler was hoping to prevent British intervention, and was certain the French would not act alone.[204] A key deterrent, in his view, was the building of a 400-mile concrete fortification (planned to include 'dragon's teeth' anti-tank devices and gun emplacements, with over 11,000 bunkers and reinforced dug-outs) along Germany's western border – the 'Westwall' – to provide a significant obstruction to any French invasion. The direct interest which Hitler took in the Westwall and the urgency in completing the fortifications were directly related to the question of timing in any blow aimed at the Czechs.[205] At this stage, in late March and April 1938, Hitler evidently had no precise time-scale in mind for the destruction of Czechoslovakia.[206]

This was still the case when Hitler instructed Keitel, on 21 April, to draw up plans for military action against Czechoslovakia. According to Keitel's account of the meeting, Hitler mentioned that the problem would have to be solved some time on account of the oppression of the German minority, but especially because of Czechoslovakia's strategic position, which was of immense danger to the Reich in the event of 'the great showdown in the east, not only with the Poles but above all with Bolshevism'.[207] However, Hitler had indicated that he did not intend to attack Czechoslovakia in the near future unless circumstances within the country or fortuitous international developments offered an opportunity. This would then have to be seized so rapidly – military action would have to prove decisive within four days – that the western powers would realize the pointlessness of intervention.[208] Keitel and Jodl were in no hurry to work out the operational plan which, when eventually presented to Hitler in draft on 20 May, still represented what Keitel had taken to be Hitler's intentions a month earlier. 'It is not my intention to smash Czechoslovakia by military action within the immediate future,' the draft began.[209]

In the interim, Hitler had reacted angrily to a memorandum composed on 5 May by army Chief of Staff General Beck, emphasizing Germany's military incapacity to win a long war, and warning of the dangers of British intervention in the event of military action against Czechoslovakia that year.[210] An indication of the divisions within the leadership of the army itself, let alone of the Wehrmacht as a whole, and its enfeebled relations with the Führer, was the decision by Keitel and Brauchitsch, without consulting Beck, not to place the first parts of the memorandum before Hitler since they knew he would dismiss them out of hand and not even read the third part.[211] Hitler was even more scathing when Göring reported to him how little progress had been made on the Westwall (where construction work had been under the direction of Army Group Command 2, headed by General Wilhelm Adam). He accused the General Staff of sabotaging his plans, removed the army's construction chiefs, and put Fritz Todt – his civil engineering expert who, since 1933, had masterminded the building of the motorways – in charge.[212] It was an example of Hitler's increasingly high-handed way of dealing with the army leadership.[213] Hitler still recalled what he saw as the army's obstructionism as late as 1942.[214]

The question of Mussolini's attitude towards German action over Czechoslovakia had been high on Hitler's agenda during his state visit to Italy at the beginning of May. Three special trains, carrying around 500 diplomats, officials, party leaders, security men, and journalists had set off for Rome on 2 May.[215] The return visit, lavish in the extreme in its arrangements, ran less smoothly than Mussolini's state visit to Germany had done the previous September. Hitler was irritated by the fact that King Victor Emmanuel III, not Mussolini, was his host. He felt ill at ease and out of place at the court ceremonials. He sensed, too, not without reason, that he was treated with some disdain by the King and Queen and their court circle.[216] The low-point for Hitler came when, following a gala performance of *Aida* in Naples, he found himself, without prior warning, alongside the King (who was dressed in full uniform), still in his evening dress, right arm outstretched, his left pressed against his waistcoat, coat-tails flapping behind him, inspecting a guard of honour while resembling, in the eyes of his adjutant Fritz Wiedemann, a flustered head-waiter in a restaurant.[217] A furious Hitler vented his wrath on Ribbentrop, who in turn sought a scapegoat and sacked the head of protocol.[218]

Diplomatically, too, there were hiccups. Ribbentrop, clumsy as ever, chose a wholly inopportune moment to press upon the Italians a mutual assistance pact, directed against France and Britain, formalizing the Axis agreement. Ciano was contemptuous about Ribbentrop. Mussolini, interested in the long run in such a pact, told his son-in-law that Ribbentrop 'belongs to the category of Germans who bring misfortune to Germany. He talks left and right all the time about making war, without having a particular enemy or clear objective in view.' He was not to be taken seriously.[219]

Hitler, on the other hand, had done much to dispel any initial coolness towards the visit with his speech in Rome on the evening of 7 May in which he enthused over the natural 'alpine border' providing a 'clear separation of the living spaces of the two nations'.[220] This public renunciation of any claim on the South Tyrol was no more than Hitler had been stating since the mid-1920s. But, coming so soon after the Anschluß, it was important in assuaging the Italians, not least since Hitler was anxious to sound them out over Czechoslovakia. The soundings were, from Hitler's point of view, the most successful part of the visit. He took Mussolini's remarks as encouragement to proceed against the Czechs.[221] State Secretary von Weizsäcker noted that Italy intended to stay neutral in any war between Germany and Czechoslovakia.[222] Reporting on Hitler's visit in a circular to German diplomatic missions, Ribbentrop stated: 'As far as the Sudeten Question is concerned, discussions indicated without further ado that the Italians have understanding for our involvement in the fate of the Sudeten Germans.'[223] Diplomatically, Hitler had achieved what he wanted from the visit.

Before the 'Weekend Crisis' of 20–22 May, no timetable had been established for an attack on Czechoslovakia. Nevertheless, Hitler had plainly become increasingly interested in acting within the foreseeable future. Already in mid-May, he had spoken of solving the 'Sudeten question' by the end of the year, since the international situation might well deteriorate thereafter.[224] At this point the 'Weekend Crisis' intervened.[225]

Reports reaching the French and British embassies and the Prague government on 19–20 May of German troop movements near the Czech border were treated seriously, given the shrill German anti-Czech propaganda and the tension in the Sudetenland on account of the imminent local elections there. The Czechoslovakian government responded to what they took to be a threat of imminent invasion by partially mobilizing their military reserves – close on 180,000 men.[226] Tension rose still further when two Sudeten Germans were killed in an incident involving the Czech police. Meanwhile, Keitel's explicit reassurance to the British Ambassador Henderson, which had been given to the press, that the movements were no more than routine spring manoeuvres, had led to a furious tirade by Ribbentrop, incensed that Henderson had not gone through proper diplomatic channels in publishing the information, and threatening that Germany would fight as it had done in 1914 should war break out.[227]

This had the effect of stirring genuine alarm in the British Ambassador, worried that he had been misled by Keitel, and that a German invasion of Czechoslovakia was imminent. On the afternoon of Saturday, 21 May, Henderson was instructed by the British Foreign Secretary Lord Halifax to inform Ribbentrop that the French were bound to intervene in the event of an attack on Czechoslovakia, and that the Germans should not depend upon the British standing by.[228] Ribbentrop's hysterical reply was scarcely reassuring: 'If France were really so crazy as to attack us, it would lead to perhaps the greatest defeat in French history, and if Britain were to join her, then once again we should have to fight to the death.'[229] By the Sunday, 22 May, however, British reconnaissance on the borders had revealed nothing untoward.[230] It had been a false alarm.

The crisis blew over as quickly as it had started. But reactions abroad, not least in Britain, ran along the lines that German action *had* been intended, and that Hitler had backed down under pressure.[231] According to Jodl's diary notes – though they were compiled some weeks later – Hitler was affronted by the loss of German prestige.[232] Keitel later recalled Hitler stating that he was not prepared to tolerate 'such a provocation' by the Czechs, and demanding the fastest possible preparations for a strike.[233] It was not as a result of the crisis that Hitler resolved to crush Czechoslovakia before the year was out. That, as we have noted, was his intention already before the crisis. But the crisis accelerated matters. The blow to pride reinforced his determination to act as soon as possible. Delay was ruled out. 'After 21 May it was quite clear that this problem had to be solved one way or the other. Every further postponement could only make the question more difficult and the solution thereby bloodier,' was how he himself put it in retrospect.[234]

After days of brooding over the issue at the Berghof, pondering the advice of his military leaders that Germany was ill-equipped for an early strike against the Czechs, Hitler returned to Berlin and summoned a meeting of his top generals, together with leading figures from the Foreign Ministry, for 28 May.[235] The day before the meeting, Hitler had told Raeder to speed up the construction programme for battleships and submarines.[236] The target was plainly Britain. But Hitler did not expect war with the British over Czechoslovakia. The conflict with the west, he declared at the military conference the next day, would come after a further three or four years.[237] Hitler told his generals bluntly: 'I am utterly determined that Czechoslovakia should disappear from the map.'[238] He claimed Germany was stronger than in 1914. He pointed to the train of successes since 1933. But there was no such thing as a lasting state of contentment. Life was a constant struggle. And Germany needed living-space in Europe, and in colonial possessions. The current generation had to solve the problem. France and Britain would remain hostile to an expansion of German power. Czechoslovakia was Germany's most dangerous enemy in the event of conflict with the west. Therefore it was necessary to eliminate Czechoslovakia. He gave the incomplete state of Czech fortifications, the underdeveloped British and French armaments programmes, and the advantageous international situation as reasons for early action. The western fortifications were to be drastically speeded up. These would provide the framework for a 'lightning march into Czechoslovakia'.[239]

Two days later, the revised 'Case Green' was ready. Its basic lines were unchanged from those drawn up earlier in the month by Keitel and Jodl. But the preamble now ran: 'It is my unalterable decision to smash Czechoslovakia by military action in the foreseeable future.' Keitel's covering note laid down that preparations must be complete by 1 October at the latest.[240] From that date on, Hitler was determined to 'exploit every favourable political opportunity' to accomplish his aim.[241] It was a decision for war – if need be, even against the western powers.[242]

Chief of Staff Beck responded with two memoranda of 29 May and 3 June, highly critical both of Hitler's political assumptions with regard to Britain and France, and of the operational directives for 'Case Green'.[243] Even so, as in his earlier memorandum of 5 May, there was significant overlap with Hitler's basic assumptions about the need for 'living-space' (even if Beck had a much more limited conception of what this implied) and to eliminate – if necessary through war – the state of Czechoslovakia. The 'cardinal point' (as he put it) of disagreement was about the prospect of a war against France and Britain which, Beck was certain, Germany would lose.[244] Beck was still at this time labouring under the illusion that Hitler was being badly advised by the *Oberkommando der Wehrmacht* (OKW, High Command of the Wehrmacht). His chief target was less Hitler than what in his view was a malformed structure of military command.[245] What only gradually became clear to Beck was how far he had isolated himself even in the army's own high command. In particular, the head of the army, Brauchitsch, though sharing some of Beck's reservations, would undertake nothing which might appear to challenge or criticize Hitler's plans.[246] The distance between Brauchitsch and Beck became more marked. Increasingly, the head of the army looked to Beck's deputy, General Franz Halder.[247]

At a meeting of around forty army high commanders at Barth in Pomerania on 13 June, Brauchitsch served initially as Hitler's mouthpiece, in a morning session informing the assembled officers, most of whom had until then known nothing of Hitler's directive and were taken completely by surprise, of the decision to solve the Czech problem by force. In such a tense situation, Brauchitsch appealed for, and received, the loyalty of his leading officers. The meeting had been called by Hitler to inform the officers about the Fritsch affair and head off the disaffection about the treatment of the former highly revered army leader which had lingered, and had been growing, since his complete exoneration by a military court.[248] By the time Hitler arrived, around noon, Brauchitsch's surprise announcement about the imminence of war had helped him out of his internal difficulties. Hitler's subsequent skilfully toned 'rehabilitation' of Fritsch – though without restoring him to his office – had then fully warded off the possible crisis of confidence. He ended by taking up the theme introduced by Brauchitsch: in the face of impending danger of war, he appealed to his generals for loyalty.[249] The generals complied. Any hopes that Beck – not present at the meeting – might have cherished of a united rejection by the military leadership of Hitler's Czech adventure were revealed as futile.

Beck's own position, and the force of his operational arguments, weakened notably in mid-June when the results of war games – initiated by the General Staff itself, and requested neither by Hitler nor the OKW – demonstrated, in contrast to Beck's grim prognostications, that Czechoslovakia would in all probability be overrun within eleven days, with the consequence that troops could rapidly be sent to fight on the western front.[250] His differences with Brauchitsch were unmistakably evident at the concluding discussion of the war-games exercise during the second half of June. Even in the General Staff itself, Beck's Cassandra warnings were regarded as exaggerated.[251] Increasingly despairing and isolated, Beck went so far in summer as to advocate collective resignation of the military leadership to force Hitler to give way, to be followed by a purge of the 'radicals' responsible for the high-risk international adventurism.[252] 'The soldierly duty [of the highest leaders of the Wehrmacht],' he wrote on 16 July 1938, 'has a limit at the point where their knowledge, conscience, and responsibility prohibits the execution of an order. If their advice and warnings in such a situation are not listened to, they have the right and duty to the people and to history to resign from their posts. If they all act with a united will, the deployment of military action is impossible. They will thereby have saved their Fatherland from the worst, from destruction (*Untergang*) . . . Extraordinary times demand extraordinary actions.'[253]

It proved impossible to win over Brauchitsch to the idea of any generals' ultimatum to Hitler, even though the Army Commander-in-Chief accepted much of Beck's military analysis and shared his fears of western intervention. At a meeting of top generals summoned for 4 August, Brauchitsch did not deliver the speech which Beck had prepared for him. Instead, distancing himself from the Chief of the General Staff, he had Beck read out his own memorandum of 16 July, with its highly pessimistic assessment of eventualities following an invasion of Czechoslovakia.[254] Most of those present agreed that Germany could not win a war against the western powers. But Reichenau, speaking 'from his personal knowledge of the Führer', warned against individual generals approaching Hitler with such an argument; it would have the reverse effect to that which they wanted. And General Ernst Busch questioned whether it was the business of soldiers to intervene in political matters. As Brauchitsch recognized, those present opposed the risk of a war over Czechoslovakia. He himself commented that a new world war would bring the end of German culture. But there was no agreement on what practical consequences should follow. Colonel-General Gerd von Rundstedt, one of the most senior and respected officers, was unwilling to provoke a new crisis between Hitler and the army through challenging him on his war-risk policy. Lieutenant-General Erich von Manstein, Commander of the 18th Infantry Division, who would later distinguish himself as a military tactician of unusual calibre, advised Beck to rid himself of the burden of responsibility – a matter for the political leadership – and play a full part in securing success against Czechoslovakia.[255]

Brauchitsch, spineless though he was, was plainly not alone in his unwillingness to face Hitler with an ultimatum. The reality was that there was no collective support for a frontal challenge. Brauchitsch contented himself with passing on Beck's memorandum to Hitler via one of his adjutants.[256] When Hitler heard what had taken place at the meeting, he was incandescent. Brauchitsch was summoned to the Berghof and subjected to such a ferocious high-decibel verbal assault, lasting several hours, that those sitting on the terrace below the open windows of Hitler's room felt embarrassed enough to move inside.[257]

Hitler responded by summoning – an unorthodox step – not the top military leadership, but a selective group of the second tier of senior officers, those who might be expecting rapid promotion in the event of a military conflict, to the Berghof for a meeting on 10 August. He was evidently hoping to gain influence over his staff chiefs through their subordinates. But he was disappointed. His harangue, lasting several hours, left his audience – which was fully acquainted with the content of Beck's July memorandum – still unconvinced.[258] Enraged at one point by doubts about the western fortifications, he snarled: 'General Adam said the Westwall would only hold for three days. I tell you, it will hold for three years if it's occupied by German soldiers.'[259] The crisis of confidence between Hitler and the army general staff had reached serious levels. At the same time, the assembled officers were divided among themselves, with some of them increasingly critical of Beck.[260]

Five days later, Hitler attempted once more to counter the effects of
Beck's memorandum on the leading generals during artillery exercises at
Jüterbog, some sixty miles south of Berlin. He rehearsed once more his array
of arguments about the favourable international constellation justifying his
decision to solve the Czech problem by force that autumn. What he could
not dispel was the fear and belief that the west would act to defend Czechoslovakia.[261] Beck made a last attempt to persuade Brauchitsch to take a firm
stance against Hitler.[262] It was whistling in the wind. On 18 August, Beck
finally tendered the resignation he had already prepared a month earlier.[263]
Even then, he missed a last trick. He accepted Hitler's request – 'for
foreign-policy reasons' – not to publicize his resignation. A final opportunity
to turn the unease running through the army, and through the German
people, into an open challenge to the political leadership of the Reich – and
when Beck knew that only Ribbentrop, and perhaps Himmler, fully backed
Hitler – was lost.[264] Beck's path into fundamental resistance was a courageous one. But in summer 1938 he gradually became, at least as regards
political strategy, an isolated figure in the military leadership. As he himself
saw it several months later: 'I warned – and in the end I was alone.'[265]
Ironically, he had been more responsible than any other individual for
supplying Hitler with the military might which the Dictator could not wait
to use.[266]

By midsummer, therefore, Hitler was assured of the compliance of the
military, even if they were reluctant rather than enthusiastic in their backing
for war against the Czechs, and even if relations were tense and distrustful.
And as long as the generals fell into line, his own position was secure, his
policy unchallengeable.

As it transpired, his reading of international politics turned out to be
closer to the mark than that of Beck and the generals. In the guessing- and
second-guessing political poker-game that ran through the summer, the
western powers were anxious to avoid war at all costs, while the east-
European neighbours of Czechoslovakia were keen to profit from any war
but unwilling to take risks. Diplomatic activity, increasingly feverish as the
summer wore on, in any case appeared less and less likely to bear dividends
– not least since the greatest warmonger other than Hitler himself was his
Foreign Minister, Ribbentrop.

Messages, often doom-laden, sometimes conflicting, and invariably
treated with differing degrees of belief and scepticism, were passed from
those close to oppositional sources within Germany.[267] Soundings were
taken by unorthodox routes. Göring put out feelers through a number of

informal links. He let it be known that he would be interested in coming to London himself to carry out discussions about Anglo-German relations at the highest level. Göring was instrumental in the invitation extended by the British government to Fritz Wiedemann, Hitler's adjutant, to come to London.[268]

The ostensible purpose was to discuss the possibility of a future visit by Göring himself. Becoming increasingly estranged from Hitler over the high-risk foreign policy, Wiedemann was particularly anxious to bypass Ribbentrop when he met Lord Halifax in London in mid-July. He had been given his instructions not by Hitler, but by Göring. Hitler had approved the visit, though given Wiedemann no message to convey to London. Wiedemann, connected with Beck, Göring, and others anxious to avoid military conflict, tried to assure the British that Germany wanted a peaceful solution to the Czech crisis. But he himself knew differently. He had been present at Hitler's explicit briefing on 28 May.[269] In any case, Hitler was uninterested in Wiedemann's 'mission'. On his adjutant's return to Berlin, Hitler accorded him a mere five minutes to report, and ruled out any visit by Göring.[270] Ribbentrop's wrath at being bypassed helped discredit Wiedemann in Hitler's eyes, leading to the former adjutant's 'exile' as Consul General in San Francisco.[271]

By midsummer, the German Foreign Minister regarded the die as cast. He told his State Secretary, Ernst von Weizsäcker, 'that the Führer was firmly resolved to settle the Czech affair by force of arms'. Mid-October was the latest possible date because of flying conditions. 'The other powers would definitely not do anything about it and if they did we would take them on as well and win.'[272] Weizsäcker, whose efforts remained urgently concentrated on a diplomatic solution which would concede the Sudeten territory to Germany and at the same time further the 'chemical dissolution process' ('*chemischer Auflösungsprozeß*') of Czechoslovakia, would temporarily find solace in the pact among the leading powers which would be concluded in Munich.[273] But he only gradually realized what he was up against in his own ministry, let alone with Hitler. In post-war reflections on his own behaviour at the time, he candidly admitted: 'I too much wanted to apply the art of the possible and underestimated the value of the irrational.'[274]

Hitler himself spent much of the summer at the Berghof. Despite the Sudeten crisis, his daily routine differed little from previous years: he got up late, went for walks, watched films, and relaxed in the company of his regular entourage and favoured visitors like Albert Speer. Whether on the basis of newspaper reports, or through information fed to him by those able to gain access, he also intervened – sometimes quirkily – in an array of minutiae: punishment for traffic offences, altering the base of a statue, considerations of whether all cigarettes should be made nicotine-free, or the type of holes to be put into flagpoles. He also interfered directly in the course of justice, ordering the death penalty for the perpetrator of a series of highway robberies, and the speediest possible conviction for the alleged serial killer of a number of women.[275]

But the Czechoslovakian crisis was never far away. Hitler was preoccupied with the operational planning for 'Green'. His confidence in his generals dwindled as his anger at their scepticism towards his plans mounted.[276] He also involved himself in the smallest detail of the building of the Westwall – a key component in his plans to overrun the Czechs without French intervention and the bluff to discourage Germany's western neighbours from even attempting to cross the Rhine. He was still expecting the fortifications to be complete by the autumn – by the onset of frost, as he told Goebbels – at which point he reckoned Germany would be unassailable from the west.[277] But the sluggish progress made by the army made him furious. When General Adam claimed that the extra 12,000 bunkers he had ordered were an impossibility, Hitler flew into a rage, declaring that for Todt the word 'impossible' did not exist.[278] He felt driven to dictate a lengthy memorandum, drawing on his own wartime experiences, laying down his notions of the nature of the fortifications to be erected, down to sleeping, eating, drinking, and lavatory arrangements in the bunkers – since new recruits in their first battle often suffered from diarrhoea, he claimed to recall.[279] The Westwall had priority over all other major building projects. By the end of August, 148,000 workers and 50,000 army sappers were stationed at the fortifications. Autobahn and housing construction had been temporarily halted to make use of the workers.[280]

At the end of August, Hitler paid an inspection visit to the western front. General Adam had the unenviable task of informing him that by the end of October no more than around a third of the requirements would be in place – and this only if the promised raw materials arrived. Adam could see that Hitler was close to an explosion. This came when the general remarked that the western powers would, in his view, certainly intervene in the event of a German attack on Czechoslovakia. Hitler fumed: 'We have no time to listen any longer to this stuff. You don't understand that. We produce in Germany 23 million tons of steel a year, the French only 6 millions and the English only 16 millions. The English have no reserves and the French have the greatest internal difficulties. They'll beware of declaring war on us.' More dubious 'facts' followed. Hitler's technique of throwing out a torrent of statistics – correct, fabricated, or embellished – to support an argument made countering it extremely difficult. Adam, struck – so he later claimed – by Hitler's 'lack of education (*Unbildung*)', inability to confront reality, and readiness to resort to lies to get his way, retorted provocatively that if that was the case, there was little point in worrying any longer about the western front. After a tense few moments, during which those present braced themselves for a further violent outburst, Hitler calmed himself, and the inspection continued without further incident.[281]

By this time, the end of August, the crisis was beginning to move towards its climacteric phase. The question of Czechoslovakia now dominated all conversation at midday meals in the Reich Chancellery.[282] 'In the country there is serious unrest on account of the situation,' noted Goebbels. 'Everywhere there's talk of war . . . The hot topic: war and Prague. These questions weigh heavily at present on all.'[283] The Propaganda Minister, unlike some of his immediate subordinates in his ministry, still felt confident that when it came to it Britain, which held the key, would do no more than protest.[284] Hitler, too, when Goebbels saw him on the Obersalzberg on the last day of August, was in a determined and optimistic mood: he did not think Britain would intervene. 'He knows what he wants and goes straight towards his goal,' remarked Goebbels. By this time, Goebbels too knew that the planned time for action was October.[285]

Ordinary people were, of course, wholly unaware of the planned aggression. The weeks of anti-Czech propaganda, often near-hysterical in tone, had shaped the impression that the issue was about the despicable persecution of the German minority, not the military destruction of Czechoslovakia. But whether or not the Sudeten Germans came 'home into the Reich' was, for the overwhelming majority of the population, less important than avoiding the war which Hitler was determined to have. Beck had emphasized the widespread popular opposition to war in his July memoranda.[286] 'In Berlin the best opinion is that Hitler has made up his mind for war if it is necessary to get back his Sudetens,' wrote the American journalist William Shirer in early September. 'I doubt it for two reasons: first, the German army is not ready; secondly, the people are dead against war.'[287] 'The war psychosis is growing,' noted Goebbels. 'A gloomy mood lies over the land. Everyone awaits what is coming.'[288] Reports on popular opinion compiled by the SD and other agencies uniformly registered similar sentiments.[289] Looking for diversions from their worries, many people acted as if there were no tomorrow. 'The theatres are well patronized, the cinemas full, the cafés overcrowded, with music and dancing till the early hours,' ran one report in early September. 'Sunday excursion traffic is setting record figures.' But the mood was depressed. 'There exists in the broadest sections of the population the earnest concern that in the long or short run a war will put an end to the economic prosperity and have a terrible end for Germany.'[290]

I V

During August, the British had indirectly exerted pressure on the Czechs to comply with Sudeten German demands through the mission of Lord Runciman, aimed at playing for time, mediating between the Sudeten German Party and the Prague government, and solving the Sudeten question within the framework of the continued existence of the state of Czechoslovakia.[291] By the end of the month, the British government had learnt from their contacts with oppositional sources in Germany that Hitler intended to attack Czechoslovakia within weeks. The crucial moment, they imagined, would probably follow Hitler's speech to the Reich Party Rally in Nuremberg in mid-September.[292] On 30 August, in an emergency meeting, the British cabinet declined to offer a formal warning to Hitler of likely British intervention in the event of German aggression. Instead, it was decided to apply further pressure on the Czechs, who were effectively given an ultimatum: accept Henlein's programme to give virtual autonomy for the Sudeten Germans within the Czechoslovakian state, as laid down in his Karlsbad speech in April, or be doomed.[293] On 5 September, President Eduard Beneš, faced with such an unenviable choice, bowed to the pressure.[294]

This in fact left Henlein and the Sudeten German leadership in a predicament: entirely against expectations, their demands had been met almost in their entirety.[295] With that, Hitler's pretext for war was undermined. Desperate for an excuse to break off negotiations with the Czechs, the Sudeten Germans grasped at an incident in which the Czech police manhandled three local Germans accused of spying and smuggling weapons.[296] It was enough to keep matters on the boil until Hitler's big speech on 12 September.

Increasingly worried though the Sudeten German leaders themselves were about the prospect of war, Henlein's party was simply dancing to Hitler's tune. Hitler had told Henlein's right-hand man, Karl Hermann Frank, as early as 26 August to instigate provocative 'incidents'.[297] He followed it up with instructions to carry out the 'incidents' on 4 September.[298] He had left

Frank in no doubt at all of his intentions. 'Führer is determined on war,' Frank had reported. Hitler had verbally lashed Beneš, saying he wanted him taken alive and would himself string him up.[299] Three days later, on 29 August, it was known, from what was emanating from Hitler's entourage, that Czech compliance, under British pressure, to the Karlsbad demands would no longer be sufficient. 'So the Führer wants war,' was the conclusion drawn by Helmuth Groscurth, head of Department II of the Abwehr.[300]

When he met Henlein at the Berghof on 2 September, however, Hitler was giving little away. He implied to the Sudeten leader that he would act that month, though specified no date.[301] Knowing that Hitler had a military solution in mind, Henlein nevertheless told his British contact, Frank Ashton-Gwatkin, Runciman's assistant, that the Führer favoured a peaceful settlement – information which further nourished appeasement ambitions.[302] The reality was very different: at a military conference at the Berghof on the day after his meeting with Henlein, Hitler determined details of 'Case Green', the attack on Czechoslovakia, ready to be launched on 1 October.[303]

Hitler was by this stage impervious to the alarm signals being registered in diplomatic circles. When Admiral Canaris returned from Italy with reports that the Italians were urgently advising against war, and would not participate themselves, Hitler took them simply as a reflection of the divisions between the general staff and the Duce, similar to those he was experiencing with the army in Germany.[304] He remained adamant that Britain was bluffing, playing for time, insufficiently armed, and would stay neutral.[305] Warnings about the poor state of the German navy met with the same response.[306] The present time, with the harvest secured, he continued to argue, was the most favourable for military action. By December, it would be too late.[307] He was equally dismissive about warning noises from France. When the German ambassador in Paris, Johannes von Welczek, reported his strong impression that France would reluctantly be obliged to honour the obligation to the Czechs, Hitler simply pushed the report to one side, saying it did not interest him.[308] Hearing of this, Lord Halifax pointed it out to the British cabinet as evidence that 'Herr Hitler was possibly or even probably mad.'[309]

With German propaganda reaching fever-pitch, Hitler delivered his long-awaited and much feared tirade against the Czechs at the final assembly of the Party Congress on 12 September. Venomous though the attacks on the Czechs were, with an unmistakable threat if 'self-determination' were not granted, Hitler fell short of demanding the handing over of the Sudetenland, or a plebiscite to determine the issue.[310] In Germany there was an air of impending war and great tension.[311] The anxious Czechs thought war and peace hung in the balance that day.[312] But in Hitler's timetable, it was still over two weeks too early.[313]

Even so, Hitler's speech triggered a wave of disturbances in the Sudeten region.[314] These incidents, and the near-panic which had gripped the French government, persuaded Neville Chamberlain that, if the German offensive expected for late September were to be avoided, face-to-face talks with Hitler – an idea worked out already in late August – were necessary.[315] On the evening of 14 September, the sensational news broke in Germany: Chamberlain had requested a meeting with Hitler, who had invited him to the Obersalzberg for midday on the following day.[316]

Early on the morning of 15 September, the sixty-nine-year-old British Prime Minister – a prim, reserved, austere figure – took off from Croydon airport in a twin-engined Lockheed, hoping, as he said, to secure peace.[317] He was apprehensive at what lay in store for him; and nervous about flying.[318] It was his first flight, and his first experience of what a later age would call shuttle-diplomacy.

Chamberlain was cheered by the Munich crowds as he was driven in an open car from the airport to the station to be taken in Hitler's special train to Berchtesgaden. Along with his accompaniment of Sir Horace Wilson, his close adviser, and William Strang, head of the central European section of the Foreign Office, the British Ambassador Sir Nevile Henderson, and Ribbentrop, Chamberlain had to watch one troop-transport train after another pass by during the three-hour journey. It was raining, the sky dark and threatening, by the time Chamberlain reached the Berghof.

Hitler was waiting to greet him on the steps. Chamberlain noticed the Iron Cross, First Class, pinned to his uniform. Like all visitors, Chamberlain was impressed by the grandeur of Hitler's alpine residence, regretting that the view of breathtaking mountain scenery from the vast window looking towards Salzburg was spoilt by the low cloud. He was less impressed by the physical appearance of Germany's leader. He found Hitler's expression, he told one of his sisters, Ida, on return to London, 'rather disagreeable . . . and altogether he looks entirely undistinguished. You would never notice him in a crowd . . .'[319]

After some desultory small-talk, Hitler and the British Prime Minister retreated to his study. Ribbentrop, to his intense irritation, was left out of the discussions. Only the interpreter Paul Schmidt was present. For three hours Hitler and Chamberlain talked as the peace of Europe hung in the balance. Hitler paraded the German grievances, with occasional outbursts against Beneš. Chamberlain listened expressionless as the storm outside swelled to match the menacing atmosphere inside the alpine retreat. He said he was prepared to consider any solution to accommodate German interests, as long as force was ruled out. Hitler angrily retorted: 'Who is speaking of force? Herr Beneš is using force against my countrymen in the Sudetenland. Herr Beneš, and not I, mobilized in May. I won't accept it any longer. I'll settle this question myself in the near future one way or another.' 'If I've understood you correctly,' Chamberlain angrily replied, 'then you're determined in any event to proceed against Czechoslovakia. If that is your intention, why have you had me coming to Berchtesgaden at all? Under these circumstances it's best if I leave straight away. Apparently, it's all pointless.' It was an effective counter-thrust to the bluster. Hitler, to Schmidt's astonishment, retreated. 'If you recognize the principle of self-determination for the treatment of the Sudeten question, then we can discuss how to put the principle into practice,' he stated. Chamberlain said he would have to consult his cabinet colleagues. But when he declared his readiness thereafter to meet Hitler again, the mood lifted. Chamberlain won Hitler's agreement to undertake no military action in the meantime. With that, the meeting was over.[320]

During their stay that night in a hotel in Berchtesgaden, before flying back the next day, the British party were refused – a remarkable breach of diplomatic courtesy – a copy of interpreter Schmidt's transcript of the proceedings. The order had come from Hitler himself, not Ribbentrop.[321] He evidently wanted his bargaining position to be kept as open as possible, and to avoid being bound by particular verbal formulations.[322]

Immediately after the meeting, Hitler told Ribbentrop and Weizsäcker what had happened, rubbing his hands with pleasure at the outcome. He claimed he had manoeuvred Chamberlain into a corner. His 'brutally announced intention, even at the risk of a general European war, of solving the Czech question' – he had not spoken of the 'Sudeten question' – along with his concession that Germany's territorial claims in Europe would then be satisfied, had, he asserted, forced Chamberlain to cede the Sudetenland. Hitler had, he went on, been unable to reject the proposal of a plebiscite. If the Czechs were to refuse one, 'the way would be clear for the German invasion'.[323] If Czechoslovakia yielded on the Sudetenland, the rest of the country would be taken over later, perhaps the following spring. In any event, there would have to be a war, and during his own lifetime.[324]

Hitler was clearly satisfied with the way the talks had gone.[325] He spoke to his immediate circle at the Berghof the next day about the discussions.

As the night before, it appeared that he might now after all be prepared to consider a diplomatic solution – at least for the immediate future. Chamberlain's visit had impressed him and, in a way, unsettled him. Dealing at first hand with a democratic leader who had to return to consult with the members of his government, and was answerable to parliament, left a tinge of uncertainty. He was, he said, still basically intending to march on Prague. But for the first time there were signs of wavering. He was starting to look for a possible retreat. Only very unwillingly, he hinted, if it proved unavoidable in the light of the general European situation, would he go along with the British proposal. Beyond that, things could be settled with the Czechs without the British being involved. Czechoslovakia was in any case, he added, difficult to rule, given its ethnic mix and the claims of the other minorities – Poles, Hungarians, and especially the Slovaks. There was, Hitler's immediate circle felt, now a glimmer of hope that war would be avoided.[326]

Chamberlain reported to the British cabinet his belief that he had dissuaded Hitler from an immediate march into Czechoslovakia and that the German dictator's aims were 'strictly limited'. If self-determination for the Sudeten Germans were to be granted, he thought, it would mark the end of German claims on Czechoslovakia.[327] The extent to which Chamberlain had allowed himself to be deluded by the personality and assurances of Germany's dictator is apparent in the private evaluation he offered his sister on returning to England: 'In spite of the harshness and ruthlessness I thought I saw in his face, I got the impression that here was a man who could be relied upon when he had given his word.'[328]

The next days were spent applying pressure to the Czechs to acquiesce in their own dismemberment. Preferably avoiding a plebiscite, the joint approach to Prague of the British and French was to compel the Czechs to make territorial concessions in return for an international guarantee against unprovoked aggression. On 21 September, the Czechs yielded.[329]

Chamberlain's second meeting with Hitler had meanwhile been arranged for 22 September in Bad Godesberg, a quiet spa-resort on the Rhine, just outside Bonn. The Germans had originally contemplated including the French premier Édouard Daladier, but this idea had been discarded.[330] The pressure of the British and the French on the Czechs simply laid bare for Hitler the weakness of the western powers. Serious resistance was not to be expected from Britain; France would do what Britain did; the war was half-won.[331] That was how Hitler saw it. He was uncertain whether the Czechs would resist alone. Goebbels assured him they would not.[332] But

Hitler too was feeling the tension. He relaxed by watching entertainment films. He did not want to see anything more serious.[333] His options remained open. On the day after his meeting with Chamberlain he had ordered the establishment of a Sudeten German Legion, a Freikorps volunteer unit made up of political refugees under Henlein to sustain disturbances and terror attacks.[334] They would serve if need be as a guarantee of the staged provocation which would form the pretext of a German invasion. But Hitler, as his comments following Chamberlain's visit had shown, was now evidently moving away from the all-out high-risk military destruction of Czechoslovakia in a single blow, on which he had insisted, despite much internal opposition, throughout the summer. Instead, there were pointers that he was now moving towards a territorial solution not unlike the one which would eventually form the basis of the Munich Agreement. He did not think he would get the Sudetenland without a fight from the Czechs, though he reckoned the western powers would leave Beneš to his fate. So he reckoned with limited military confrontation to secure the Sudetenland as a first stage. The destruction of the rest of Czechoslovakia would then follow, perhaps immediately, but at any rate within a short time.[335]

On 19 September he showed Goebbels the map that would represent his demands to Chamberlain at their next meeting. The idea was to force acceptance of as broad a demarcation line as possible. The territory to be conceded was to be vacated by the Czechs and occupied by German troops within eight days. Military preparations, as Goebbels was now informed, would not be ready before then. If there was any dispute, a plebiscite by Christmas would be demanded. Should Chamberlain demand further negotiations, the Führer would feel no longer bound by any agreements and would have freedom of action.[336] 'The Führer will show Chamberlain his map, and then – end (Schluß), basta! Only in that way can this problem be solved,' commented Goebbels.[337]

V

On the afternoon of 22 September, Hitler and Chamberlain met again, this time in the plush Hotel Dreesen in Bad Godesberg, with its fine outlook on the Rhine. Chamberlain had flown from England that morning, and was accommodated on the opposite bank of the river at the Petersberg Hotel.[338] When William Shirer, one of the journalists covering the visit, observed Hitler at close quarters in the garden of his hotel, he thought he looked very strained. The dark shadows under his eyes and the nervous twitch of his right shoulder when he walked made Shirer think he was on the edge of a breakdown. Other journalists in the group had started the rumour that in his rages Hitler chewed the edge of the carpet. The term 'carpet-biter', once coined, was to have a long life.[339]

The meeting began with a shock for Chamberlain. He initially reported how the demands raised at Berchtesgaden had been met. He mentioned the proposed British-French guarantee of the new borders of Czechoslovakia, and the desired German non-aggression pact with the Czechs. He sat back in his chair, a self-satisfied look on his face. He was astounded when Hitler retorted: 'I'm sorry Herr Chamberlain that I can no longer go into these things. After the development of the last days, this solution no longer applies.' Chamberlain sat bolt upright, angry and astonished. Hitler claimed he could not sign a non-aggression pact with Czechoslovakia until the demands of Poland and Hungary were met. He had some criticisms of the proposed treaties. Above all, the envisaged time-scale was too long. Working himself up into a frenzy about Beneš and the alleged terroristic repression of the Sudeten Germans, he demanded the occupation of the Sudeten territory immediately. Chamberlain pointed out that this was a completely new demand, going far beyond the terms outlined at Berchtesgaden. He returned, depressed and angry, to his hotel on the other bank of the Rhine.[340]

Chamberlain did not return for the prearranged meeting the next morning. Instead, he sent a letter to Hitler stating that it was impossible for him to approve a plan which would be seen by public opinion in Britain, France, and the rest of the world as deviating from the previously agreed principles. Nor had he any doubts, he wrote, that the Czechs would mobilize their armed forces to resist any entry of German troops into the Sudetenland. Hitler and Ribbentrop hastily deliberated. Then Hitler dictated a lengthy reply – amounting to little more than his verbal statements the previous day and insisting on the immediate transfer of the Sudeten territory to end 'Czech tyranny' and uphold 'the dignity of a great power'. The interpreter Schmidt was designated to translate the four- to five-page letter, and take it by hand to Chamberlain. Chamberlain received it calmly.[341] His own response was given to Ribbentrop within two hours or so. He offered to take the new demands to the Czechs, said he would have to return to England to prepare for this, and requested a memorandum from the German government which, it was agreed, would be delivered later that evening by Hitler.

It was almost eleven o'clock when Chamberlain returned to the Hotel

Dreesen. The drama of the late-night meeting was enhanced by the presence of advisers on both sides, fully aware of the peace of Europe hanging by a narrow thread, as Schmidt began to translate Hitler's memorandum. It demanded the complete withdrawal of the Czech army from the territory drawn on a map, to be ceded to Germany by 28 September.[342] Hitler had spoken to Goebbels on 21 September of demands for eight days for Czech withdrawal and German occupation.[343] He was now, late on the evening of 23 September, demanding the beginning of withdrawal in little over two days and completion in four. Chamberlain raised his hands in despair. 'That's an ultimatum,' he protested. 'With great disappointment and deep regret I must register, Herr Reich Chancellor,' he remarked, 'that you have not supported in the slightest my efforts to maintain peace.'[344]

At this tense point, news arrived that Beneš had announced the general mobilization of the Czech armed forces. For some moments no one spoke. War now seemed inevitable. Then Hitler, in little more than a whisper, told Chamberlain that despite this provocation he would hold to his word and undertake nothing against Czechoslovakia – at least as long as the British Prime Minister remained on German soil. As a special concession, he would agree to 1 October as the date for Czech withdrawal from the Sudeten territory. It was the date he had set weeks earlier as the moment for the attack on Czechoslovakia. He altered the date by hand in the memorandum, adding that the borders would look very different if he were to proceed with force against Czechoslovakia. Chamberlain agreed to take the revised memorandum to the Czechs. After the drama, the meeting ended in relative harmony. Chamberlain flew back, disappointed but not despairing, next morning to London to report to his cabinet.[345]

While Chamberlain was meeting his cabinet, on Sunday 25 September, Hitler was strolling through the gardens of the Reich Chancellery on a warm, early autumn afternoon, with Goebbels, talking at length about his next moves. 'He doesn't believe that Benesch [Beneš] will yield,' noted the Propaganda Minister the following day in his diary. 'But then a terrible judgement will strike him. On 27–28 September our military build-up (*Aufmarsch*) will be ready. The Führer then has 5 days' room for manoeuvre. He already established these dates on 28 May. And things have turned out just as he predicted. The Führer is a divinatory genius. But first comes our mobilization. This will proceed so lightning-fast that the world will experience a miracle. In 8–10 days all that will be ready (*ist das alles fertig*). If we attack the Czechs from our borders, the Führer reckons it will take 2–3 weeks. But if we attack them after our entry (*Einmarsch*), he thinks it will be finished in 8 days. The radical solution is the best. Otherwise, we'll never be rid of the thing.'[346] This somewhat garbled account appears to indicate that Hitler was at this juncture contemplating a two-stage invasion of Czechoslovakia: first the Sudeten area, then at a later, and unspecified, point, the rest of the country. This matches the notion reported by Weizsäcker after the first meeting with Chamberlain.[347] Hitler was not bluffing, therefore, in his plans to take the Sudetenland by force on 1 October if it was not conceded beforehand. But he had retreated from the intention, which had existed since the spring, of the destruction of the whole of Czechoslovakia by a single military operation at the beginning of October.[348]

The mood in London was, meanwhile, changing. Following his experience in Godesberg, Chamberlain was moving towards a harder line, and the British cabinet with him. After talks with the French, it was decided that the Czechs would not be pressed into accepting the new terms. Sir Horace Wilson, Chamberlain's closest adviser, was to go as the Prime Minister's envoy to Berlin to recommend a supervised territorial transfer and at the same time warn Hitler that in the event of German military action against Czechoslovakia France would honour its alliance commitments and Britain would support France.[349]

On the late afternoon of 26 September, Wilson, accompanied by Sir Nevile Henderson and Sir Ivone Kirkpatrick, first secretary in the British embassy, was received by Hitler in his study in the Reich Chancellery. That evening Hitler was to deliver a ferocious attack on Czechoslovakia in the Sportpalast. Wilson had not chosen a good moment to expect rational deliberation of the letter from Chamberlain that he presented to the German dictator. Hitler listened, plainly agitated, to the translation of the letter, informing him that the Czechs had rejected the terms he had laid down at Godesberg. Part-way through he exploded with anger, jumping to his feet, shouting: 'There's no point at all in somehow negotiating any further.' He made for the door, as if ending the meeting forthwith with his visitors left in his own study. But he pulled himself together and returned to his seat while the rest of the letter was translated. As soon as it was over, there was another frenzied outburst. The interpreter, Paul Schmidt, later commented that he had never before seen Hitler so incandescent. Wilson's attempts to discuss the issues rationally and his cool warning of the implications of German military action merely provoked him further. 'If France and England want to strike,' he ranted, 'let them go ahead. I don't give a damn (*Mir ist das vollständig gleichgültig*).' He gave the Czechs till 2.p.m. on Wednesday, 28 September, to accept the terms of the Godesberg Memorandum and

German occupation of the Sudetenland by 1 October. Otherwise Germany would take it by force. He recommended a visit to the Sportpalast that evening to Wilson, so that he would sense the mood in Germany for himself.[350]

The ears of the world were on Hitler's speech to the tense audience of around 20,000 or so packed into the cavernous Sportpalast.[351] The large number of diplomats and journalists present were glued to every word. The American journalist William Shirer, sitting in the balcony directly above the German Chancellor, thought Hitler 'in the worst state of excitement I've ever seen him in'.[352] His speech – 'a psychological masterpiece' in Goebbels's judgement[353] – was perfectly tuned to the whipped-up anti-Czech mood of the Party faithful. He was soon into full swing, launching into endless tirades against Beneš and the Czechoslovakian state. Beneš was determined, he asserted, 'slowly to exterminate Germandom (*das Deutschtum langsam auszurotten*)'.[354] Referring to the memorandum he had presented to Chamberlain, and the 'offer' he had made to the Czechs, he indicated that his tolerance towards the intransigence of Beneš was now at an end.[355] Cynically, he praised Chamberlain for his efforts for peace. He had assured the British Prime Minister, he went on, that he had no further territorial demands in Europe once the Sudeten problem was solved.[356] He had also guaranteed, he stated, that he had no further interest in the Czech state. 'We don't want any Czechs at all,' he declared.[357] The decision for war or peace rested with Beneš: 'He will either accept this offer and finally give freedom to the Germans, or we will take this freedom ourselves!' he threatened. He would lead a united people, different to that of 1918, as its first soldier. 'We are determined. Herr Beneš may now choose,' he concluded.

The masses in the hall, who had interrupted almost every sentence with their fanatical applause, shouted, cheered, and chanted for minutes when he had ended: 'Führer command, we will follow! (*Führer befiehl, wir folgen!*)' Hitler had worked himself into an almost orgasmic frenzy by the end of his speech. When Goebbels, closing the meeting, pledged the loyalty of all the German people to him and declared that 'a November 1918 will never be repeated', Hitler, according to Shirer, 'looked up to him, a wild, eager expression in his eyes . . . leaped to his feet and with a fanatical fire in his eyes . . . brought his right hand, after a grand sweep, pounding down on the table and yelled . . . "Ja". Then he slumped into his chair exhausted.'[358]

Hitler was in no mood for compromise when Sir Horace Wilson returned next morning to the Reich Chancellery with another letter from Chamberlain guaranteeing, should Germany refrain from force, the implementation of the Czech withdrawal from the Sudeten territory. When Wilson asked whether he should take any message back to London, Hitler replied that the Czechs had the option only of accepting or rejecting the German memorandum. In the event of rejection, he shouted, repeating himself two or three times, 'I will smash the Czechs.' Wilson, a tall figure, then drew himself to his full height and slowly but emphatically delivered a further message from Chamberlain: 'If, in pursuit of her Treaty obligations, France became actively engaged in hostilities against Germany, the United Kingdom would feel obliged to support her.'[359] Enraged, Hitler barked back: 'If France and England strike, let them do so. It's a matter of complete indifference to me. I am prepared for every eventuality. I can only take note of the position. It is Tuesday today, and by next Monday we shall all be at war.'[360] The meeting ended at that point. As Schmidt recalled, it was impossible to talk rationally with Hitler that morning.[361]

Still, Wilson's warnings were not lost on Hitler. In calmer mood, he had Weizsäcker draft him a letter to Chamberlain, asking him to persuade the Czechs to see reason and assuring him that he had no further interest in Czechoslovakia once the Sudeten Germans had been incorporated into the Reich.[362]

Late that afternoon a motorized division began its ominous parade through Wilhelmstraße past the government buildings. For three hours, Hitler stood at his window as it rumbled past.[363] According to the recollections of his Luftwaffe adjutant Nicolaus von Below, he had ordered the display not to test the martial spirit of the Berlin people, but to impress foreign diplomats and journalists with German military might and readiness for war.[364] If that was the aim, the attempt misfired. The American journalist William Shirer reported on the sullen response of the Berliners – ducking into doorways, refusing to look on, ignoring the military display – as 'the most striking demonstration against war I've ever seen'.[365] Goebbels, who had been uninvolved in the arrangements, recorded that the display had made 'the deepest impression'.[366] But in contradiction to this comment he apparently acknowledged that people had taken little notice of the parade.[367] Hitler was reportedly disappointed and angry at the lack of enthusiasm shown by Berliners.[368] The contrast with the reactions of the hand-picked audience in the Sportpalast was vivid. It was a glimpse of the mood throughout the country. Whatever the feelings about the Sudeten Germans, only a small fanaticized minority thought them worth a war against the western powers.

But if Hitler was disappointed that the mood of the people did not resemble that of August 1914, his determination to press ahead with military action on 1 October, if the Czechs did not yield, was unshaken, as he made clear that evening to Ribbentrop and Weizsäcker.[369] The Foreign Minister was, if anything, even more bellicose than Hitler. He told Rudolf Schmundt, Hoßbach's successor as Hitler's chief military adjutant, that acceptance by the Czechs of the German ultimatum would be the worst that could happen.[370] But Ribbentrop was by now practically the only hawkish influence on Hitler.[371] From all other sides, pressures were mounting for him to pull back from the brink.

For Hitler, to retreat from an 'unalterable decision' was tantamount to a loss of face. Even so, for those used to dealing at close quarters with Hitler, the unthinkable happened. The following morning of 28 September, hours before the expiry of the ultimatum to Czechoslovakia, he changed his mind and conceded to the demands for a negotiated settlement. 'One can't grasp this change. Führer has given in, and fundamentally,' noted Helmuth Groscurth.[372]

The decisive intervention was Mussolini's. Feelers for such a move had been put out by an increasingly anxious Göring a fortnight or so earlier. Göring had also tried, through Henderson, to interest the British in the notion of a conference of the major powers to settle the Sudeten question by negotiation.[373] Before Mussolini's critical move, the British and French had also applied maximum pressure. Chamberlain had spoken the previous evening on the radio of the absurdity of war on account of 'a quarrel in a faraway country between people of whom we know nothing'.[374] He had followed this up with a reply to Hitler's letter, emphasizing his incredulity that the German Chancellor was prepared to risk a world war perhaps bringing the end of civilization 'for the sake of a few days' delay in settling this long-standing problem'.[375] His letter contained proposals, agreed with the French, to press the Czechs into immediate cession of the Sudeten territory, the transfer to be guaranteed by Britain and to begin on 1 October. An International Boundary Commission would work out the details of the territorial settlement. The British Prime Minister indicated that he was prepared to come to Berlin immediately, together with the representatives of France and Italy, to discuss the whole issue.[376] Chamberlain also wrote to Mussolini, urging agreement with his proposal 'which will keep all our peoples out of war'.[377]

The French, too, had been active. The ambassador in Berlin, André François-Poncet, had been instructed at 4a.m. to put proposals similar to Chamberlain's before Hitler.[378] His request early next morning for an audience with Hitler was not welcomed by Ribbentrop, still spoiling for war.[379] But after intercession by Göring, prompted by Henderson, Hitler agreed to see the French ambassador at 11.15a.m.[380] By then the Reich Chancellery was buzzing with adjutants, ministers, generals, and party bosses, conferring in little groups or scurrying to some hasty discussion with Hitler. To the interpreter Schmidt, the Reich Chancellery resembled an army camp more than a seat of government. Every now and again Hitler would retire with Ribbentrop, Göring, or Keitel to discuss some point or other. But for the most part, he seemed to be passing through the rooms delivering mini Sportpalast harangues to anyone who cared to listen.[381] Before François-Poncet arrived, Göring and Neurath had both urged Hitler to settle by negotiation. Göring and Ribbentrop had a fierce row, though not in Hitler's presence, in which the Foreign Minister was accused of warmongering. *He* knew what war was, shouted Göring. If the Führer ordered it, he would be in the first aeroplane. But he would insist upon Ribbentrop being in the seat next to him.[382]

François-Poncet, when eventually his audience was granted, warned Hitler that he would not be able to localize a military conflict with Czechoslovakia, but would set Europe in flames. Since he could attain almost all his demands without war, the risk seemed senseless.[383] At that point, around 11.40a.m., the discussion was interrupted by a message that the Italian ambassador Bernardo Attolico wished to see Hitler immediately on a matter of great urgency. Hitler left the room with his interpreter, Schmidt. The tall, stooping, red-faced ambassador lost no time in coming to the point. He breathlessly announced to Hitler that the British government had let Mussolini know that it would welcome his mediation in the Sudeten question. The areas of disagreement were small. The Duce supported Germany, the ambassador went on, but was 'of the opinion that the acceptance of the English proposal would be advantageous' and appealed for a postponement of the planned mobilization.[384] After a moment's pause, Hitler replied: 'Tell the Duce I accept his proposal.'[385] It was shortly before noon. Hitler now had his way of climbing down without losing face.[386] 'We have no jumping-off point for war,' commented Goebbels. 'You can't carry out a world war on account of modalities.'[387]

When the British Ambassador Henderson entered at 12.15p.m with Chamberlain's letter, Hitler told him that at the request of his 'great friend and ally, Signor Mussolini', he had postponed mobilization for twenty-four hours. The climax of war-fever had passed. During Henderson's hour-long audience, Attolico interrupted once more to tell Hitler that Mussolini had agreed to the British proposals for a meeting of the four major powers.[388] When the dramatic news reached Chamberlain, towards the end of a speech about the crisis he was making to a packed and tense House of Commons, which was expecting an announcement meaning war, the house erupted. 'We stood on our benches, waved our order papers, shouted until we were hoarse – a scene of indescribable enthusiasm,' recorded one Member of Parliament. 'Peace must now be saved.'[389]

War was averted – at least for the present. 'The heavens are beginning to lighten somewhat,' wrote Goebbels. 'We probably still have the possibility of taking the Sudeten German territory peacefully. The major solution still remains open, and we will further rearm for future eventualities.'[390]

Already early the next afternoon, Hitler, Mussolini, Chamberlain, and Édouard Daladier, the small, quiet, dapper premier of France (who looked somewhat ill at ease at the task of dispensing parts of Czechoslovakia, without even a representative of that country present), together with Ribbentrop, Weizsäcker, Ciano, Wilson, and Alexis Léger, State Secretary in the French Foreign Office, took their seats around a table in the newly constructed Führerbau amid the complex of Party buildings centred around the Brown House – the large and imposing Party headquarters – in Munich. There they proceeded to carve up Czechoslovakia.[391] Chamberlain, who privately wrote on return to England that the day had been for him a 'prolonged nightmare', felt 'instant relief' at Hitler's 'moderate and reasonable' opening remarks.[392] The four heads of government began by stating their relative positions on the Sudeten issue. They all – Hitler, too – spoke against a solution by force. The only lack of harmony occurred when the German dictator launched into ferocious attacks on Beneš, which provoked a spirited counter from the otherwise reserved Daladier, and when Chamberlain irritated Hitler by doggedly insisting upon financial compensation to Czechoslovakia for government property which was now to be transferred to Germany. 'Our time is for me too precious to waste it on such trivialities,' Hitler exploded. After a short break in mid-afternoon, the discussions focused upon the written proposal to settle the Sudeten question, by now translated into all four languages, that Mussolini had delivered the previous day (though the text had actually been sketched out by Göring, then formalized in the German Foreign Office under Weizsäcker's eye with some input by Neurath but avoiding any involvement by Ribbentrop, before being handed to the Italian ambassador). It provided the basis for what would become known as the notorious Munich Agreement. The circle of those involved in discussions had now widened to include Göring and the

Ambassadors of Italy, France, and Great Britain (Attolico, François-Poncet, and Henderson), as well as legal advisers, secretaries, and adjutants. But it was now mainly a matter of legal technicalities and complex points of detail. The main work was done. That evening, Hitler invited the participants to a festive dinner. Chamberlain and Daladier found their excuses. After the dirty work had been done, they had little taste for celebration.[393]

The deliberations had lasted in all for some thirteen hours.[394] But, sensational though the four-power summit meeting was for the outside world, the real decision had already been taken around midday on 28 September, when Hitler had agreed to Mussolini's proposal for a negotiated settlement.[395] Eventually, around 2.30a.m. on the morning of 30 October, the draft agreement was signed.[396] These terms were essentially those of the Godesberg Memorandum, modified by the final Anglo-French proposals, and with dates entered for a progressive German occupation, to be completed within ten days.[397] 'We have then essentially achieved everything that we wanted according to the small plan,' commented Goebbels. 'The big plan is for the moment, given the prevailing circumstances, not yet realizable.'[398]

The following day, Goebbels added: 'We have all walked on a thin tightrope over a dizzy abyss . . . The word "peace" is on all lips. The world is filled with a frenzy of joy. Germany's prestige has grown enormously. Now we are really a world power again. Now, it's a matter of rearm, rearm, rearm . . .'[399] Hitler and Ribbentrop did not share the general elation. Ribbentrop had pushed for war until the last minute. He felt robbed of his humiliation of the British – all the more so since Chamberlain was fêted on his journey through Munich in an open-topped car as the hero of the moment, the actual saviour of Europe's peace.[400] Hitler's own mood had altered overnight. The impressions he had given of savouring his triumph over the western powers had vanished by the next morning.[401] He looked pale, tired, and out of sorts when Chamberlain visited him in his apartment in Prinzregentenplatz to present him with a joint declaration of Germany's and Britain's determination never to go to war with one another again. Chamberlain had suggested the private meeting during a lull in proceedings the previous day. Hitler had, the British Prime Minister remarked, 'jumped at the idea'. Chamberlain regarded the meeting as 'a very friendly and pleasant talk'. 'At the end,' he went on, 'I pulled out the declaration which I had prepared beforehand and asked if he would sign it.'[402] After a moment's hesitation, Hitler – with some reluctance it seemed to the interpreter Paul Schmidt – appended his signature.[403] For him, the document was meaningless. And for him Munich was no great cause for celebration. He felt cheated of the greater triumph which he was certain would have come from the limited war with the Czechs which had been his aim all summer.[404] Even military action for the more restricted goal of attaining the Sudetenland by force had been denied him. He had been compelled, through the readiness of the western powers to make Czechoslovakia concede the Sudetenland, to compromise on the directives that he had upheld since May despite internal opposition. During the Polish crisis the following summer this would make him all the more determined to avoid the possibility of being diverted from war. But when that next crisis came, he was even more confident that he knew his adversaries: 'Our enemies are small worms,' he would tell his generals in August 1939. 'I saw them in Munich.'[405]

Of those in Hitler's immediate entourage, none had done more to bring about the eventual acceptance of a negotiated settlement than Göring. He had ultimately scored a victory over his arch-rival, and leading hawk, Ribbentrop. The draft which formed the basis of the Munich Agreement had been largely Göring's work. His excellent mood at Munich reflected his pleasure that his own approach had ultimately triumphed. But it marked the end of Göring's influence on foreign policy. It was the first, and last, time that he had pressed for a solution which did not meet with Hitler's favour. The Führer's displeasure was apparent to him. His standing with Hitler was diminished. During the following months, he would be totally displaced by Ribbentrop as Hitler's right hand in all matters related to foreign policy. Weakened and depressed, Göring would take himself on an extended holiday in the Mediterranean in early 1939, leaving the way clear for his arch-rival, and would be largely excluded from decisions on the expansionist programme that culminated in the Polish crisis and war.[406]

Hitler was scornful, too, of his generals after Munich.[407] Their opposition to his plans had infuriated him all summer. How he would have reacted had he been aware that no less a person than his new Chief of Staff, General Halder, had been involved in plans for a *coup d'état* in the event of war over Czechoslovakia can be left to the imagination.[408] Whether the schemes of the ill-coordinated groups involved in the nascent conspiracy would have come to anything is an open question. But with the Munich Agreement, the chance was irredeemably gone. Chamberlain returned home to a hero's welcome, proclaiming to cheering crowds from the window of the Prime Minister's residence in 10 Downing Street – choosing words which he associated with Benjamin Disraeli, Prime Minister under Queen Victoria, following the Berlin Conference six decades earlier – that he had brought 'peace with honour' and 'peace for our time'.[409] Distancing itself from the general euphoria, the *Manchester Guardian* shrewdly noted the external consequences: the Czechs could scarcely see the forcible break-up of their country as 'peace with honour'; Czechoslovakia was now 'rendered helpless'; 'Hitler will be able to advance again, when he chooses, with greatly increased power.'[410] The consequences within Germany were also profound. For German opponents of the Nazi regime, who had hoped to use Hitler's military adventurism as the weapon of his own deposition and destruction, Chamberlain was anything but the hero of the hour. 'Chamberlain saved Hitler', was how they bitterly regarded the appeasement diplomacy of the western powers.[411]

Hitler's own popularity and prestige reached new heights after Munich. He returned to another triumphant welcome in Berlin. But he was well aware that the elemental tide of euphoria reflected the relief that peace had been preserved. The 'home-coming' of the Sudeten Germans was of only secondary importance. He was being feted not as the 'first soldier of the Reich', but as the saviour of the peace he had not wanted.[412] At the critical hour, the German people, in his eyes, had lacked enthusiasm for war. The spirit of 1914 had been missing. Psychological rearmament had still to take place. A few weeks later, addressing a select audience of several hundred German journalists and editors, he gave a remarkably frank indication of his feelings: 'Circumstances have compelled me to speak for decades almost solely of peace,' he declared. 'It is natural that such a . . . peace propaganda also has its dubious side. It can only too easily lead to the view establishing itself in the minds of many people that the present regime is identical with the determination and will to preserve peace under all circumstances. That would not only lead to a wrong assessment of the aims of this system, but would also above all lead to the German nation, instead of being forearmed in the face of events, being filled with a spirit which, as defeatism, in the long run would take away and must take away the successes of the present regime.' It was necessary, therefore, to transform the psychology of the German people, to make it see that some things could only be attained through force, and to represent foreign-policy issues in such a way that 'the inner voice of the people itself slowly begins to cry out for the use of force'.[413]

The speech is revealing. Popular backing for war had to be manufactured, since war and expansion were irrevocably bound up with the survival of the regime. Successes, unending triumphs, were indispensable for the regime, and for Hitler's own popularity and prestige on which, ultimately, the regime depended. Only through expansion – itself impossible without war – could Germany, and the National Socialist regime, survive. This was

Hitler's thinking. The gamble for expansion was inescapable. It was not a matter of personal choice.

The legacy of Munich was fatally to weaken those who might even now have constrained Hitler. Any potential limits – external and internal – on his freedom of action instead disappeared. Hitler's drive to war was unabated. And next time he was determined he would not be blocked by last-minute diplomatic manoeuvres of the western powers, whose weakness he had seen with his own eyes at Munich.

3

MARKS OF A GENOCIDAL MENTALITY

'In Germany the Jew cannot hold out. This is a question of years. We will drive them out more and more with an unprecedented ruthlessness.'

Himmler, addressing SS leaders on 8 November 1938

'If the German Reich comes into foreign-political conflict in the foreseeable future, it can be taken for granted that we in Germany will think in the first instance of bringing about a great showdown with the Jews.'

Göring, at a meeting in the Air Ministry, 12 November 1938

'The Jews have not brought about the 9 November 1918 for nothing. This day will be avenged.'

Hitler, speaking to the Czechoslovakian Foreign Minister, Franzisek Chvalkovsky, 21 January 1939

'I want today to be a prophet again: if international finance Jewry inside and outside Europe should succeed in plunging the nations once more into a world war, the result will be not the bolshevization of the earth and thereby the victory of Jewry, but the annihilation of the Jewish race in Europe!'

Hitler, addressing the Reichstag, 30 January 1939

The ideological dynamic of the Nazi regime was a vital component of the drive for expansion. This was by no means solely a matter of Hitler's personalized *Weltanschauung*. In fact, Hitler's ideological aims had so far played only a subordinate role in his expansionist policy, and would not figure prominently in the Polish crisis during the summer of 1939. The Party and its numerous sub-organizations were, of course, important in sustaining the pressure for ever-new discriminatory measures against ideological target-groups. But little in the way of coherent planning could be expected from the central Party office, under the charge of Rudolf Heß, Hitler's deputy in Party affairs.[1] The key agency was not the Party, but the SS.

The interest in expansion was self-evident. Buoyed by their successes in Austria and the Sudetenland, Himmler, Heydrich, and the top echelons of the SS were keen to extend – naturally, under Hitler's aegis – their own empire. Already in August 1938, a decree by Hitler met Himmler's wish to develop an armed wing of the SS. It provided in effect a fourth branch of the armed forces – far smaller than the others, but envisaged as a body of ideologically motivated 'political soldiers' standing at the Führer's 'exclusive disposal'.[2] It was little wonder that Himmler had been one of the hawks during the Sudeten crisis, aligning himself with Ribbentrop, and encouraging Hitler's aggression.[3] The leaders of the SS were now looking to territorial gains to provide them with opportunities for ideological experimentation on the way to the fulfilment of the vision of a racially purified Greater German Reich under the heel of the chosen caste of the SS élite. In a world after Hitler, with 'final victory' achieved, the SS were determined to be the masters of Germany and Europe.

They saw their mission as the ruthless eradication of Germany's ideological enemies, who, in Himmler's strange vision, were numerous and menacing. He told top SS leaders in early November 1938: 'We must be clear that in the next ten years we will certainly encounter unheard of critical conflicts. It is not only the struggle of the nations, which in this case are put forward by the opposing side merely as a front, but it is the ideological (*weltanschauliche*) struggle of the entire Jewry, freemasonry, Marxism, and churches of the world. These forces – of which I presume the Jews to be the driving spirit, the origin of all the negatives – are clear that if Germany and Italy are not annihilated, *they* will be annihilated (*vernichtet werden*). That is a simple conclusion. In Germany the Jew cannot hold out. This is a question of years. We will drive them out more and more with an unprecedented ruthlessness . . .'[4]

The speech was held a day before Germany exploded in an orgy of elemental violence against its Jewish minority in the notorious pogrom of 9–10 November 1938, cynically dubbed in popular parlance, on account of millions of fragments of broken glass littering the pavements of Berlin outside wrecked Jewish shops, 'Reich Crystal Night' (*Reichskristallnacht*).[5] This night of horror, a retreat in a modern state to the savagery associated with bygone ages, laid bare to the world the barbarism of the Nazi regime. Within Germany, it brought immediate draconian measures to exclude Jews from the economy, accompanied by a restructuring of anti-Jewish policy, placing it now directly under the control of the SS, whose leaders linked war, expansion, and eradication of Jewry.

Such a linkage was not only reinforced in the eyes of the SS in the aftermath of 'Crystal Night'. For Hitler, too, the connection between the war he knew was coming and the destruction of Europe's Jews was now beginning to take concrete shape. Since the 1920s he had not deviated from the view that German salvation could only come through a titanic struggle for supremacy in Europe, and for eventual world power, against mighty enemies backed by the mightiest enemy of all, perhaps more powerful even than the Third Reich itself: international Jewry. It was a colossal gamble. But for Hitler it was a gamble that could not be avoided. And for him, the fate of the Jews was inextricably bound up with that gamble.

I

The nationwide pogrom carried out by rampaging Nazi mobs on the night of 9–10 November was the culmination of a third wave of antisemitic violence – worse even than those of 1933 and 1935 – that had begun in the spring of 1938 and run on as the domestic accompaniment to the foreign-political crisis throughout the summer and autumn. Part of the background to the summer of violence was the open terror on the streets of Vienna in March, and the 'success' that Eichmann had scored in forcing the emigration of the Viennese Jews. Nazi leaders in cities of the 'old Reich', particularly Berlin, took note. The chance to be rid of 'their' Jews seemed to open up. A second strand in the background was the 'aryanization' drive to hound Jews out of German economic life.[6] At the beginning of 1933 there had been some 50,000 Jewish businesses in Germany. By July 1938, there were only 9,000 left. The big push to exclude the Jews came between spring and autumn 1938. The 1,690 businesses in Jewish hands in Munich in February 1938, for instance, had fallen to only 666 (two-thirds of them owned by foreign citizens) by October.[7] The 'aryanization' drive not only closed businesses, or saw them bought out for a pittance by new 'aryan' owners. It also brought a new flood of legislative measures imposing a variety of discriminatory restrictions and occupational bans – such as on Jewish doctors and lawyers – even to the extent of preventing Jews from trying to eke out a living as pedlars. It was a short step from legislation to pinpoint remaining Jewish businesses to identifying Jewish persons. A decree of 17 August had made it compulsory for male Jews to add the forename 'Israel', females the forename 'Sara' to their existing names and, on pain of imprisonment, to use those names in all official matters. On 5 October, they were compelled to have a 'J' stamped in their passports.[8] A few days later, Göring declared that 'the Jewish Question must now be tackled with all means available, for they [the Jews] must get out of the economy'.[9]

Alongside the legislation, inevitably, went the violence. Scores of localized attacks on Jewish property and on individual Jews, usually carried out by members of Party formations, punctuated the summer months. Far more than had been the case in the earlier antisemitic waves, attention of Party activists increasingly focused on synagogues and Jewish cemeteries, which were repeatedly vandalized. As an indicator of their mood, and an 'ordered' foretaste of what would follow across the land during 'Crystal Night', the main synagogue in Munich was demolished on 9 June, the first in Germany to be destroyed by the Nazis. During a visit to the city a few days earlier, Hitler had taken objection to its proximity to the Deutsches Künsterlerhaus ('German Artists' House). The official reason given was that the building was a hindrance to traffic. The Jewish Community in Munich was given only hours' notice of the synagogue's destruction.[10] Learning quickly from his master, Julius Streicher, the Nazi Party's Jew-baiter-in-chief soon instigated the demolition of Nuremberg's main synagogue, claiming that the building disfigured 'the beautiful German townscape' (*das schöne deutsche Stadtbild*). Tens of thousands gathered to view the demolition on 10 August.[11]

Hitler saw it as important that he should not be publicly associated with the anti-Jewish campaign as it gathered momentum during 1938. No discussion of the 'Jewish Question' was, for example, permitted by the press in connection with his visits to different parts of Germany in that year.[12] Preserving his image, both at home and – especially in the light of the developing Czech crisis – abroad, through avoiding personal association with distasteful actions towards the Jews appears to have been the motive. Hence, he insisted in September 1938, at the height of the Sudeten crisis, that his signing of the fifth implementation ordinance under the Reich Citizenship Law, to oust Jewish lawyers, should not be publicized at that stage in order to prevent any possible deterioration of Germany's image – clearly meaning his own image – at such a tense moment.[13]

In fact, he had to do little or nothing to stir the escalating campaign against the Jews. Others made the running, took the initiative, pressed for action – always, of course, on the assumption that this was in line with Nazism's great mission.[14] It was a classic case of 'working towards the Führer' – taking for granted (usually on grounds of self-interest) that he approved of measures aimed at the 'removal' of the Jews, measures seen as plainly furthering his long-term goals. Party activists in the Movement's various formations needed no encouragement to unleash further attacks on Jews and their property. 'Aryans' in business, from the smallest to the largest, looked to every opportunity to profit at the expense of their Jewish counterparts. Hundreds of Jewish businesses – including long-established private banks such as Warburg and Bleichröder – were now forced, often through gangster-like extortion, to sell out for a pittance to 'Aryan' buyers. Big business gained most. Giant concerns like Mannesmann, Krupp, Thyssen, Flick, and IG-Farben, and leading banks such as the Deutsche Bank and the Dresdner Bank, were the major beneficiaries, while a variety of business consortia, corrupt Party functionaries, and untold numbers of small commercial enterprises grabbed what they could.[15] 'Aryan' pillars of the establishment like doctors and lawyers were equally welcoming of the economic advantages that could come their way with the expulsion of Jews from the medical and legal professions.[16] University professors turned their skills, without prompting, to defining alleged negative characteristics of the Jewish character and pyschology.[17] And all the time, civil servants worked like beavers to hone the legislation that turned Jews into outcasts and pariahs, their lives into torment and misery.[18] The police, particularly the Gestapo – helped as always by eager citizens anxious to denounce Jews or those seen as 'friends of Jews' (*Judenfreunde*)[19] – served as a pro-active enforcement agency, deploying their 'rational' methods of arrest and internment in concentration camps rather than the crude violence of the Party hotheads, though with the same objective. Not least, the Security Service (the *Sicherheitsdienst*, or SD) – beginning life as the Party's own intelligence organization, but developing into the crucial surveillance and ideological planning agency within the rapidly expanding SS – was advancing on its way to adopting the pivotal role in the shaping of anti-Jewish policy.[20]

Each group, agency, or individual involved in pushing forward the radicalization of anti-Jewish discrimination had vested interests and a specific agenda. Uniting them all and giving justification to them was the vision of racial purification and, in particular, of a 'Jew-free' Germany embodied in the person of the Führer. Hitler's role was, therefore, crucial, even if at times indirect. His broad sanction was needed. But for the most part little more was required.

There is no doubt that Hitler fully approved of and backed the new drive against the Jews, even if he took care to remain out of the limelight. One of the main agitators for radical action against the Jews, Joseph Goebbels, had no difficulty in April 1938 – in the immediate wake of the savage persecution of the Jews in Vienna – in persuading Hitler to support his plans to 'clean up' Berlin, the seat of his own Gau. Hitler's only stipulation was that nothing should be undertaken before his meetings with Mussolini in early May. A successful outcome of his talks with the Duce was of great importance to him, particularly in the context of his unfolding plans regarding Czechoslovakia. Possible diplomatic repercussions provoked by intensified persecution of Jews in Germany's capital were to be avoided. Goebbels had already discussed his own aims on the 'Jewish Question' with Berlin's Police Chief Wolf Heinrich Graf von Helldorf before he broached the matter with Hitler. 'Then we put it to the Führer. He agrees, but only after his trip to

Italy. Jewish establishments (*Judenlokale*) will be combed out. Jews will then get a swimming-pool, a few cinemas, and restaurants (*Lokale*) allocated to them. Otherwise entry forbidden. We'll remove the character of a Jew-paradise from Berlin. Jewish businesses will be marked as such. At any rate, we're now proceeding more radically. The Führer wants gradually to push them all out. Negotiate with Poland and Romania. Madagascar would be the most suitable for them.'[21]

The 'Madagascar solution' – which would be considered seriously for a brief time in 1940 – had been touted among radical antisemites for decades.[22] Reference to it at this juncture seems to signify that Hitler was moving away from any assumption that emigration would remove the 'Jewish problem' in favour of a solution based upon territorial resettlement. He was conceivably influenced in this by Heydrich, reporting the views of the 'experts' on Jewish policy in the SD. The relative lack of success in 'persuading' Jews to emigrate – little short of three-quarters of the Jewish population recorded in 1933 still lived in Germany, despite the persecution, as late as October 1938 – together with the mounting obstacles to Jewish immigration created by other countries had compelled the SD to revise its views on future anti-Jewish policy.[23] By the end of 1937 the idea of favouring a Jewish state in Palestine, which Eichmann had developed, partly through secret dealings with Zionist contacts, had cooled markedly. Eichmann's own visit to Palestine, arranged with his Zionist go-between, had been an unmitigated failure. And, more importantly, the German Foreign Office was resolutely hostile to the notion of a Jewish state in Palestine.[24] However, emigration remained the objective.

Hitler, too, favoured Palestine as a targeted territory. In early 1938, he reaffirmed the policy, arrived at almost a year earlier, aimed at promoting with all means available the emigration of Jews to any country willing to take them, but looking to Palestine in the first instance.[25] But he was alert to the perceived dangers of creating a Jewish state to threaten Germany at some future date. In any case, other notions were being mooted. Already in 1937 there had been suggestions in the SD of deporting Jews to barren, unwelcoming parts of the world, scarcely capable of sustaining human life and certainly, in the SD's view, incompatible with a renewed flourishing of Jewry and revitalized potential of 'world conspiracy'. In addition to Palestine, Ecuador, Columbia, and Venezuela had been mentioned as possibilities.[26] Nothing came of such ideas at the time. But the suggestions were little different in essence from the old notion, later to be revamped, of Madagascar as an inhospitable territory fit to accommodate Jews until, it was implied, they eventually died out.[27] The notion of Jewish resettlement, already aired in the SD, was itself latently genocidal.

Whatever line of policy was favoured, the 'final goal' (as Hitler's comments to Goebbels indicated) remained indistinct, and as such compatible with all attempts to further the 'removal' of the Jews. This eventual 'removal' was conceived as taking a good number of years to complete. Even following 'Crystal Night', Heydrich was still envisaging an 'emigration action' lasting from eight to ten years.[28] Hitler himself had already inferred to Goebbels towards the end of July 1938 that 'the Jews must be removed from Germany in ten years'. In the meantime, he added, they were to be retained as 'surety' (*Pfaustpfand*).[29] He would abandon this 'hostage' idea, characteristic of his mentality, only in December 1941, when the declaration of war on the USA made the notion redundant.[30] By that time, the Reich's Jews were already being deported to the east, to their certain death.

Goebbels, meanwhile, was impatient to make headway with the 'racial cleansing' of Berlin. 'A start has to be made somewhere,' he remarked. He thought the removal of Jews from the economy and cultural life of the city could be accomplished within a few months.[31] The programme devised by mid-May for him by Helldorf, and given his approval, put forward a variety of discriminatory measures – including special identity cards for Jews, branding of Jewish shops, bans on Jews using public parks, and special train compartments for Jews – most of which, following the November Pogrom, came to be generally implemented.[32] Helldorf also envisaged the construction of a ghetto in Berlin to be financed by the richer Jews.[33]

Even if this last aim remained unfulfilled, the poisonous atmosphere stirred by Goebbels's agitation – with Hitler's tacit approval – had rapid results.[34] Already on 27 May, a 1,000-strong mob roamed parts of Berlin, smashing windows of shops belonging to Jews, and prompting the police, anxious not to lose the initiative in anti-Jewish policy, to take the owners into 'protective custody'.[35] When in mid-June Jewish stores on the Kurfürstendamm, the prime shopping street in the west of the city, were smeared with antisemitic slogans by Party activists, and plundering of some shops took place, concern for Germany's image abroad dictated a halt to the public violence. Hitler intervened directly from Berchtesgaden, following which Goebbels ruefully banned all illegal actions.[36] However, Berlin had set the tone. Similar 'actions', initiated by the local Party organizations, were carried out in Frankfurt, Magdeburg, and other towns and cities.[37] The lack of any explicit general ban from above on 'individual actions', as had been imposed in 1935, was taken by Party activists in countless localities as a green light to step up their own campaigns. The touchpaper had been lit to the summer and autumn of violence. As the tension in the Czech crisis mounted, local antisemitic initiatives in various regions saw to it that the 'Jewish Question' became a powder-keg, waiting for the spark.[38]

Hitler's own approval of the antisemitic campaign of the summer may well have been linked to his expectation of a short war to crush Czechoslovakia in the autumn.[39] Successful completion of that enterprise was, it appears, to have been accompanied by the completion of the expropriation of Jewish property and exclusion of Jews from the economy.[40] Hitler had, in the event, no choice but to be content for the time being with the Sudetenland, and the tension had suddenly evaporated. But the triumphalism of the Nazi Movement, the pressures to exclude Jews from the economy as a matter of urgency, the demands to speed up emigration, and the general momentum of violence and discrimination that had built up over the summer meant that the radical tide surged forward. The atmosphere had become menacing in the extreme for the Jews.

Even so, from the perspective of the regime's leadership, how to get the Jews out of the economy and force them to leave Germany still appeared to be questions without obvious answers. As early as January 1937, Eichmann had suggested, in a lengthy internal memorandum, that pogroms were the most effective way of accelerating the sluggish emigration.[41] Like an answer to a prayer, the shooting of the German Third Legation Secretary Ernst vom Rath in Paris by a seventeen-year-old Polish Jew, Herschel Grynszpan, on the morning of 7 November 1938 opened up an opportunity not to be missed. It was an opportunity eagerly seized upon by Goebbels. He had no difficulty in winning Hitler's full backing.

II

Grynszpan had meant to kill the Ambassador. Vom Rath just happened to be the first official he saw. The shooting was an act of despair and revenge for his own miserable existence and for the deportation of his family at the end of October from Hanover – simply deposited, along with a further 18,000 Polish Jews, over the borders with Poland.[42] Two and a half years earlier, when the Jewish medical student David Frankfurter had killed the Nazi leader in Switzerland, Wilhelm Gustloff, in Davos, circumstances had demanded that the lid be kept firmly on any wild response by Party fanatics in Germany. In the menacing climate of autumn 1938, the situation could scarcely have been more different. Now, the Nazi hordes were to be positively encouraged to turn their wrath on the Jews. The death of vom Rath – he succumbed to his wounds on the afternoon of 9 November – happened, moreover, to coincide with the fifteenth anniversary of Hitler's attempted putsch of 1923. All over Germany, Party members were meeting to celebrate one of the legendary events of the 'time of struggle'. The annual commemoration marked a high point in the Nazi calendar. In Munich, as usual, the Party bigwigs were gathering.

On the morning following the fateful shooting, the Nazi press, under Goebbels's orchestration, had been awash with torrents of vicious attacks on the Jews, guaranteed to incite violence.[43] Sure enough, that evening, 8 November, pogroms – involving the burning of synagogues, destruction of Jewish property, plundering of goods, and maltreatment of individual Jews – were instigated in a number of parts of the country through the agitation of local Party leaders without any directives from on high. Usually, the local leaders involved were radical antisemites in areas, such as Hessen, with lengthy traditions of antisemitism.[44] Goebbels noted the disturbances with satisfaction in his diary: 'In Hessen big antisemitic demonstrations. The synagogues are burnt down. If only the anger of the people could now be let loose!'[45] The following day, he referred to the 'demonstrations', burning of synagogues, and demolition of shops in Kassel and Dessau.[46] During the afternoon, news of vom Rath's death came through. 'Now that's done it (*Nun aber ist es g[ar]*),' remarked Goebbels.[47]

The party's 'old guard' were meeting that evening in the Old Town Hall in Munich. Hitler, too, was present. On the way there, with Goebbels, he had been told of disturbances against Jews in Munich, but favoured the police taking a lenient line.[48] He could scarcely have avoided being well aware of the anti-Jewish actions in Hessen and elsewhere, as well as the incitements of the press. It was impossible to ignore the fact that, among Party radicals, antisemitic tension was running high. But Hitler had given no indication, despite vom Rath's perilous condition at the time and the menacing antisemitic climate, of any intended action when he had spoken to the 'old guard' of the Party in his traditional speech at the Bürgerbräukeller the previous evening.[49] By the time the Party leaders gathered for the reception on the 9th, Hitler was aware of vom Rath's death. With his own doctor, Karl Brandt, dispatched to the bedside, Hitler had doubtless been kept well informed of the Legation Secretary's deteriorating condition and had heard of his demise at the latest by 7 o'clock that evening – in all probability by telephone some hours earlier.[50] According to his Luftwaffe adjutant, Nicolaus von Below, he had already been given the news – which he had received without overt reaction – that afternoon while he was engaged in discussions on military matters in his Munich apartment.[51]

Goebbels and Hitler were seen to confer in agitated fashion during the reception, though their conversation could not be overheard. Hitler left shortly afterwards, earlier than usual and without his customary exchanges with those present, to return to his Munich apartment. Around 10p.m. Goebbels delivered a brief but highly inflammatory speech, reporting the death of vom Rath, pointing out that there had already been 'retaliatory' action against the Jews in Kurhessen and Magdeburg-Anhalt. He made it abundantly plain without explicitly saying so that the Party should organize and carry out 'demonstrations' against the Jews throughout the country, though make it appear that they were expressions of spontaneous popular anger.[52]

Goebbels's diary entry leaves no doubt of the content of his discussion with Hitler. 'I go to the party reception in the Old Town Hall. Huge amount going on (Riesenbetrieb). I explain the matter to the Führer. He decides: let the demonstrations continue. Pull back the police. The Jews should for once get to feel the anger of the people. That's right. I immediately give corresponding directives to police and party. Then I speak for a short time in that vein to the party leadership. Storms of applause. All tear straight off to the telephone. Now the people will act.'[53]

Goebbels certainly did his best to make sure 'the people' acted. He put out detailed instructions of what had and had not to be done. He fired up the mood where there was hesitancy.[54] Immediately after he had spoken, the Stoßtrupp Hitler, an 'assault squad' whose traditions reached back to the heady days of pre-putsch beerhouse brawls and bore the Führer's name, was launched to wreak havoc on the streets of Munich. Almost immediately they demolished the old synagogue in Herzog-Rudolf-Straße, left standing after the main synagogue had been destroyed in the summer. Adolf Wagner, Gauleiter of Munich and Upper Bavaria (who as Bavarian Minister of Interior was supposedly responsible for order in the province), himself no moderate in the 'Jewish Question', got cold feet. But Goebbels pushed him into line. The 'capital city of the Movement' of all places was not going to be spared what was happening already all over Germany. Goebbels then gave direct telephone instructions to Berlin to demolish the synagogue in Fasanenstraße, off the Kurfürstendamm.[55]

The top leadership of the police and SS, also gathered in Munich but not present when Goebbels had given his speech, learnt of the 'action' only once it had started. Heydrich, at the time in the Hotel Vier Jahreszeiten, was informed by the Munich Gestapo Office around 11.20p.m., after the first orders had already gone out to the Party and SA. He immediately sought Himmler's directives on how the police should respond. The Reichsführer-SS was contacted in Hitler's Munich apartment.[56] He asked what orders Hitler had for him. Hitler replied – most likely at Himmler's prompting – that he wanted the SS to keep out of the 'action'.[57] Disorder and uncontrolled violence and destruction were not the SS's style. Himmler and Heydrich preferred the 'rational', systematic approach to the 'Jewish Question'. Soon after midnight orders went out that any SS men participating in the 'demonstrations' were to do so only in civilian clothing.[58] At 1.20a.m. Heydrich telexed all police chiefs instructing the police not to obstruct the destruction of the synagogues and to arrest as many male Jews, especially wealthy ones, as available prison accommodation could take.[59] The figure of 20–30,000 Jews had already been mentioned in a Gestapo directive sent out before midnight.[60]

Meanwhile, across the Reich, Party activists – especially SA men – were suddenly summoned by their local leaders and told to burn down synagogues or were turned loose on other Jewish property.[61] Many of those involved had been celebrating at their own commemoration of the Beerhall Putsch, and some were the worse for wear from drink. The 'action' was usually improvised on the spot. The dozen or so men from the SA-Reserve in Marburg, still drinking solidly when they were told, to their surprise, by their Standartenführer that they were to burn down the synagogue that night, could not find anything with which to set the building alight until someone had the idea that there were four large canisters of oil in the nearby theatre.[62] In Tübingen, three Party members making their unsteady way home in the early hours were picked up *en route* by a car containing the District Leader. He told them that he had received a telegram from the Gauleiter in Stuttgart that all the synagogues in the Reich were to be set on fire. They returned with him to their Party headquarters to look for incendiary material. When they arrived at the synagogue, they found it already vandalized. A group of eight SA and SS men had broken in around midnight, smashing the windows and door, and had carried off some of the contents and hurled them in the river Neckar. Only with difficulty, and with the help of a rotting wreath of oak-leaves and some floor-polish, could the Party members get the synagogue to catch fire. Eventually they managed it. The fire-brigade saw to it that the nearby houses were protected. By morning, the synagogue was a burnt-out shell.[63] The pattern, more or less, repeated itself all over Germany.

At midnight, at the Feldherrnhalle in Munich where the attempted putsch in 1923 had met its end, Goebbels had witnessed the swearing-in of the SS to Hitler. The Propaganda Minister was ready to return to his hotel when he saw the sky red from the fire of the burning synagogue in Herzog-Rudolf-Straße.[64] Back he went to Gau headquarters. Instructions were given out that the fire brigade should extinguish only what was necessary to protect nearby buildings. Otherwise they were to let the synagogue burn down. 'The Stoßtrupp is doing dreadful damage,' he commented. Reports came in to him of seventy-five synagogues on fire throughout the Reich, fifteen of them in Berlin. He had evidently by this time heard of the Gestapo directive. 'The Führer has ordered,' he noted, 'that 20–30,000 Jews are immediately to be arrested.' In fact, it had been a Gestapo order with no reference in it to a directive of the Führer. Clearly, however, though he had instigated the pogrom, Goebbels took it that the key decisions came from Hitler.[65] Goebbels went on: 'That will go down (*Das wird ziehen*). They should see that our patience is exhausted.' He went with Julius Schaub, Hitler's general factotum, into the Artists' Club to wait for further news. Schaub was in fine form. 'His old Stoßtrupp past has been revived,' commented Goebbels. He went back to his hotel. He could hear the noise of shattering glass from smashed shop windows. 'Bravo, bravo,' he wrote. After a few hours snatched sleep, he added: 'The dear Jews will think about it in future before they shoot down German diplomats like that. And that was the meaning of the exercise.'[66]

All morning new reports of the destruction poured in. Goebbels assessed the situation with Hitler. 'I weigh up our current measures with the Führer. Allow to strike further or stop. That's now the question.'[67] In the light of the mounting criticism of the 'action', also – though naturally not for humanitarian reasons – from within the top ranks of the Nazi leadership, the decision was taken to halt it.[68] Goebbels prepared a decree to end the destruction, cynically commenting that if it were allowed to continue there was the danger 'that the mob would start to appear'.[69] He reported to Hitler, who was, Goebbels claimed, 'in agreement with everything. His opinions are very radical and aggressive.' 'With minor alterations, the Führer approves my edict on the end of the actions . . . The Führer wants to move to very severe measures against the Jews. They must get their businesses in order themselves. Insurance will pay them nothing. Then the Führer wants gradually to expropriate the Jewish businesses.'[70]

By that time, the night of horror for Germany's Jews had brought the demolition of around 100 synagogues, the burning of several hundred others, the destruction of at least 8,000 Jews' shops and vandalizing of countless apartments. The pavements of the big cities were strewn with shards of glass from the display windows of Jewish-owned stores; merchandise, if not looted, had been hurled on to the streets. Private apartments were wrecked, furniture demolished, mirrors and pictures smashed, clothing shredded, treasured possessions wantonly trashed.[71] The material damage was estimated soon afterwards by Heydrich at several hundred million Marks.[72]

The human misery of the victims was incalculable. Beatings and bestial maltreatment, even of women, children, and the elderly, were commonplace. A hundred or so Jews were murdered. One woman in Innsbruck told despairingly on 10 November of how a troop of young men had broken into the apartment she shared with her husband and four-year-old daughter. They knew none of their assailants. 'What do you want of me?' her husband had asked. He received no answer. Ten minutes later she found him stabbed to death. The Jewish Community was allowed only to enter, as cause of death, 'wound in the chest' (*Brustverletzung*).[73] It was little wonder that suicide was commonplace that terrible night. Some tried, but did not manage, to kill themselves. One Jewish doctor in Vienna, held back from throwing himself from a third-storey window, slit his wrists and throat, but could still not end his own life, and was hauled off to a psychiatric clinic.[74] Many more succumbed to brutalities in the weeks following the pogrom in the concentration camps of Dachau, Buchenwald, and Sachsenhausen, where the 30,000 male Jews rounded up by the police had been sent as a means of forcing their emigration.[75] Hans Berger, a forty-year-old from Wiesbaden, was one of those taken into custody by the Gestapo on 10 November. Like those arrested with him, he was subjected to indescribable sadism and torture by the camp-guards in Buchenwald, where he was interned. To maximize the humiliation, the prisoners – many suffering from chronic diarrhoea – were left to stand in their own excrement. It was as if the dirt and stench were to emphasize the separation of the Jews from the 'healthy', 'clean', and 'wholesome' German 'national community'.[76] Three weeks of hell on earth were finally over for Herr Berger when he was eventually released to emigrate to Brussels, and from there to southern France. He, his wife, and two sons, were presumed to be among those later deported to the death camps.[77]

The scale and nature of the savagery, and the apparent aim of maximizing degradation and humiliation, reflected the success of propaganda in demonizing the figure of the Jew – certainly within the organizations of the

Party itself – and massively enhanced the process, under way since Hitler's takeover of power, of dehumanizing Jews and excluding them from German society – a vital step on the way to genocide.[78]

The propaganda line of a spontaneous expression of anger by the people was, however, believed by no one. 'The public knows to the last man,' the Party's own court later admitted, 'that political actions like that of 9 November are organized and carried out by the party, whether this is admitted or not. If all the synagogues burn down in a single night, that has somehow to be organized, and can only be organized by the party.'[79]

Ordinary citizens, affected by the climate of hatred and propaganda appealing to base instincts, motivated too by sheer material envy and greed, nevertheless followed the Party's lead in many places and joined in the destruction and looting of Jewish property. Sometimes individuals regarded as the pillars of their communities were involved. In Düsseldorf, for example, doctors from a local hospital were said to have taken part in the violence; in the Lower Franconian village of Gaukönigshofen, well-respected farmers smashed the Torah shrine, hurled the Torah Rolls and other sacred objects into the flames enveloping the synagogue, and came with wash-baskets to carry away wine and foodstuffs from Jewish homes.[80] Schoolchildren and adolescents were frequently ready next day to add their taunts, jibes, and insults to Jews being rounded up by the police, who were often subjected to baying, howling mobs hurling stones at them as they were taken into custody.[81] Many young Germans had been fanaticized and inured to the brutality by their years of indoctrination in the Hitler Youth. The BDM functionary Melita Maschmann, for instance, told herself that the Jews were the enemies of the new Germany and had now learnt what that meant. World Jewry had to see what had happened as a warning. If they sowed hatred against Germany, they had to realize 'that hostages of their people found themselves in our hands'.[82]

At the same time, there is no doubt that many ordinary people were appalled at what met them when they emerged on the morning of 10 November. 'All reports agree,' summarized the Sopade – the exiled Social Democratic Party's leadership – in its verdict on the events of 'Crystal Night', 'that the outrages are strongly condemned by the great majority of the German people.'[83] A mixture of motives operated. Some, certainly, felt human revulsion at the behaviour of the Nazi hordes and sympathy for the Jews, even to the extent of offering them material help and comfort. Jews who managed to flee to safety told in later months of how 'Christian neighbours' in Schweinfurt had brought them milk and bedding. In Burgsinn, also in Lower Franconia, Jews were given money, fresh clothing, bread, and other foodstuffs by local inhabitants. Jews from other neighbourhoods had similar stories to tell.[84] Not all motives for the condemnation were as noble. Often, it was the shame inflicted by 'hooligans' on Germany's standing as a 'nation of culture' which rankled. 'One could weep, one must be ashamed to be a German, part of an aryan noble people (*Edelvolk*), a civilized nation guilty of such a cultural disgrace,' wrote one Nazi sympathizer in an anonymous letter to Goebbels.[85] Most commonly of all, there was enormous resentment at the unrestrained destruction of material goods at a time when people were told that every little that was saved contributed to the efforts of the Four-Year Plan. 'On the one hand we have to collect silver paper and empty toothpaste tubes, and on the other hand millions of Marks' worth of damage is caused deliberately,' ran one such bitter complaint.[86]

III

By the morning of 10 November, anger was also rising among leading Nazis responsible for the economy about the material damage which had taken place. Walther Funk, who had replaced Schacht as Economics Minister early in the year, complained directly to Goebbels, but was told, to placate him, that Hitler would soon give Göring an order to exclude the Jews from the economy.[87] Göring himself, who had been in a sleeping-compartment of a train heading from Munich to Berlin as the night of violence had unfolded, was furious when he found out what had happened. His own credibility as economics supremo was at stake. He had exhorted the people, so he told Hitler, to collect discarded toothpaste tubes, rusty nails, and every bit of cast-out material. And now, valuable property had been recklessly destroyed.[88]

When they met at lunchtime on 10 November in his favourite Munich restaurant, the Osteria Bavaria, Hitler made plain to Goebbels his intention to introduce draconian economic measures against the Jews. They were dictated by the perverted notion that the Jews themselves would have to foot the bill for the destruction of their own property by the Nazis. The victims, in other words, were guilty of their own persecution. They would have to repair the damage without any contributions from German insurance firms and would be expropriated. Whether, as Göring later claimed, Goebbels was the initiator of the suggestion to impose a fine of 1,000 million Marks on the Jews is uncertain. More probably Göring, with his direct interest as head of the Four-Year Plan in maximizing the economic exploitation of the Jews, had himself come up with the idea in telephone conversations with Hitler, and perhaps also with Goebbels, that afternoon. Possibly, the idea was Hitler's own, though Goebbels does not refer to it when speaking of his wish for 'very tough measures' at their lunchtime meeting. At any rate, the suggestion was bound to meet with Hitler's favour. He had, after all, in his 'Memorandum on the Four-Year Plan' in 1936 already stated, in connection with accelerating the economic preparations for war, his intention to make the Jews responsible for any damage to the German economy. With the measures decided upon, Hitler decreed 'that now the economic solution should also be carried out', and 'ordered by and large what had to happen'.[89]

This was effectively achieved in the meeting, attended by over 100 persons, which Göring called for the following morning, 12 November, in the Air Ministry. Göring began by stating that the meeting was of fundamental importance. He had received a letter from Bormann, on behalf of the Führer, desiring a coordinated solution to the 'Jewish Question'. The Führer had informed him, in addition, by telephone the previous day that the decisive steps were now to be centrally synchronized. In essence, he went on, the problem was an economic one. It was there that the issue had to be resolved. He castigated the method of 'demonstrations', which damaged the German economy. Then he concentrated on ways of confiscating Jewish businesses and maximizing the possible gain to the Reich from the Jewish misery. Goebbels raised the need for numerous measures of social discrimination against the Jews, which he had been pressing for in Berlin for months: exclusion from cinemas, theatres, parks, beaches and bathing resorts, 'German' schools, and railway compartments used by 'aryans'. Heydrich suggested a distinctive badge to be worn by Jews, which led on to discussion of whether ghettos would be appropriate. In the event, the idea of establishing ghettos was not taken up (though Jews would be forced to leave 'aryan' tenement blocks and be banned from certain parts of the cities, so compelling them in effect to congregate together); and the suggestion of badges was rejected by Hitler himself soon afterwards (presumably to avoid possible recurrence of the pogrom-style violence which had provoked criticism even among the regime's leaders).[90] They would not be introduced in the Reich itself until September 1941.

But 'Crystal Night' had nevertheless spawned completely new openings for radical measures. This was most evident in the economic sphere, to which the meeting returned. Insurance companies were told that they would have to cover the losses, if their foreign business was not to suffer. But the payments would be made to the Reich, not, of course, to the Jews. Towards the end of the lengthy meeting, Göring announced, to the approval of the assembled company, the 'atonement fine' that was to be imposed on the Jews.[91] Later that day, he issued decrees, imposing the billion-Mark fine, excluding Jews from the economy by 1 January 1939, and stipulating that Jews were responsible for paying for the damage to their own property.[92] 'At any rate now a tabula rasa is being made,' commented Goebbels with satisfaction. 'The radical view has triumphed.'[93]

Indeed, the November Pogrom had in the most barbaric way imaginable cleared a pathway through the impasse into which Nazi anti-Jewish policy had manoeuvred itself by 1938. Emigration had been reduced to little more than a trickle, especially since the Evian Conference, where, on the initiative of President Franklin D. Roosevelt, delegates from thirty-two countries had assembled in the French resort, deliberated from 6 to 14 July, then confirmed the unwillingness of the international community to increase immigration quotas for Jews. Moves to remove the Jews from the economy were still proceeding far too slowly to satisfy Party fanatics. And anti-Jewish policy had suffered from complete lack of coordination. Hitler himself had been little involved. Goebbels, a driving-force, as we have noted, in pressing for tougher measures against the Jews since the spring, had recognized the opportunity that vom Rath's assassination gave him. He sniffed the climate, and knew conditions were ripe. In a personal sense, too, the shooting of vom Rath was timely. Goebbels's marital difficulties and relationship with the Czech film actress Lida Baarova had threatened to lower his standing with Hitler.[94] Now was a chance, by 'working towards the Führer' in such a key area, to win back favour.

One consequence of the night of violence was that the Jews were now desperate to leave Germany. Some 80,000 fled, in the most traumatic circumstances, between the end of 1938 and the beginning of the war.[95] Some, like the Fröhlichs, the family of the eminent American historian Peter Gay, were able through daring ingenuity, involving minor but dangerous forms of illegalities in forging documents and smuggling out possessions, to outwit intimidating and obstructive bureaucrats, and to subvert their chicanery in managing, amid constant anxiety and with many travails, to buy exit visas for Cuba, after being denied entry to Great Britain.[96] Countless others were less fortunate – sick with worry at the unknown fate of husbands and fathers marched off by the Gestapo, or taking flight with no more than they could carry with them. Many, with little hope of an official exit route, fled across the borders illegally – 1,500 into the Netherlands alone.[97] Many other Jews pleading for asylum were turned back at the Dutch frontier as border guards were doubled in number to deny entry to the Nazis' victims.[98] By the time the Dutch closed their borders on 17 December, nevertheless, some 7,000 German Jews had, legally or illegally, found refuge there.[99] In the same days, the British government opened the country's doors to 10,000 Jewish children – though it rejected an appeal to allow a further 21,000 Jews to enter Palestine.[100] By whatever desperate means, tens of thousands of Jews were able to escape the clutches of the Nazis and flee across neighbouring borders, to Britain, the USA, Latin America, Palestine (despite British prohibitions), and to the distant refuge with the most lenient policy of all: Japanese-occupied Shanghai.[101]

The Nazis' aim of forcing the Jews out had been massively boosted. Beyond that, the problem of their slow-moving elimination from the economy had been tackled. Whatever his criticism of Goebbels, Göring had wasted no time in ensuring that the chance was now taken fully to 'aryanize' the economy, and to profit from 'Reichskristallnacht'. When he spoke, a week later, of the 'very critical state of the Reich finances', he was able to add: 'Aid first of all through the billion imposed on the Jews and through the profits to the Reich from the aryanization of Jewish concerns'.[102] Others, too, in the Nazi leadership, critical or not of Goebbels, also seized the chance to push through a flood of new discriminatory measures, intensifying the hopelessness of Jewish existence in Germany.[103] Radicalization fed on radicalization.

The radicalization now encountered no opposition of any weight. Any opposition would have had to come from those with access to the levers of power. The ordinary people who expressed their anger, sorrow, distaste, or shame at what had happened were powerless. Those who might have articulated such feelings, such as the leaders of the Christian Churches, among whose precepts was 'love thy neighbour as thyself', kept quiet. Neither major denomination, Protestant or Catholic, raised an official protest or even backing for those courageous individual pastors and priests who did speak out. Within the regime's leadership, those, like Schacht, who had used economic or otherwise tactical objections to try to combat what they saw as counter-productive, wild 'excesses' of the radical antisemites in the party, were now politically impotent. In any case, such economic arguments lost all force with 'Crystal Night'. The leaders of the armed forces, scandalized though some of them were at the 'cultural disgrace' of what had happened, made no public protest. Brauchitsch shrugged his shoulders when outraged comments from generals came to his ears. His gutless response mirrored the broader feeling of powerlessness among an officer corps whose collective strength and moral authority *vis à vis* Hitler had been greatly diminished across the months spanning the Blomberg–Fritsch crisis, the Anschluß, the Sudeten crisis, and now 'Reichskristallnacht'. And despite all that had happened, there was evidently a readiness to believe that Hitler was not responsible, and blame could be attached to Goebbels.[104]

Beyond that, the deep antisemitism running through the armed forces meant that no opposition worth mentioning to Nazi radicalism could be expected from that quarter. Characteristic of the mentality was a letter which the revered Colonel General von Fritsch wrote, almost a year after his dismissal and only a month after the November Pogrom. Fritsch was reportedly outraged by 'Crystal Night'. But, as with so many, it was the method not the aim that appalled him. He mentioned in his letter that after the previous war he had concluded that Germany had to succeed in three battles in order to become great again. Hitler had won the battle against the working class (*Arbeiterschaft*). The other two battles, against Catholic Ultramontanism, and against the Jews, still continued. 'And the struggle against the Jews is the hardest,' he noted. 'It is to be hoped that the difficulty of this struggle is apparent everywhere.'[105]

'Crystal Night' marked the final fling within Germany of 'pogrom antisemitism'. Willing though he was to make use of the method, Hitler had emphasized as early as 1919 that it could provide no solution to the 'Jewish Question'.[106] The massive material damage caused, the public relations disaster reflected in the almost universal condemnation in the international press, and to a lesser extent the criticism levelled at the 'excesses' (though not at the draconian anti-Jewish legislation that followed them) by broad sections of the German population ensured that the ploy of open violence had had its day. Its place was taken by something which turned out to be even more sinister: the handing-over of practical responsibility for a coordinated anti-Jewish policy to the 'rational' antisemites in the SS. On 24 January 1939, Göring established – based on the model which had functioned effectively in Vienna – a Central Office for Jewish Emigration under the aegis of the Chief of the Security Police, Reinhard Heydrich.[107] The policy was still forced emigration, now transformed into an all-out, accelerated drive to expel the Jews from Germany. But the transfer of overall responsibility to the SS nevertheless began a new phase of anti-Jewish policy. For the victims, it marked a decisive step on the way that was to end in the gas-chambers of the extermination camps. Heydrich was to refer back to this commission from Göring when opening the Wannsee Conference, to coordinate extermination measures, in January 1942.[108]

Hitler was directly involved in the shaping of anti-Jewish policy in the weeks following 'Crystal Night'. On 5 December, Göring transmitted to the Gauleiter on his behalf directives on a variety of discriminatory measures relating, for instance, to the banning of Jewish access to hotels and restaurants, but allowing them to shop in 'German' stores. At the end of December, Göring again sought Hitler's views on the restrictions to be placed on Jews, which he passed on to all Party and state offices. These were left as open to interpretation as possible, and were characteristically ill-defined. The radical suggestions put forward by Goebbels and Heydrich at the meeting on 12 November were neither taken up in full, nor completely rejected. Jews were to be banned from railway sleeping- and restaurant-cars, for example, but no special compartments for them were to be erected; they were still to be allowed to use public transport. Or, another example, rent protection for Jews was not to be abolished; but it was nonetheless desirable that they be concentrated in specific apartment blocks. Pensions were not to be taken away from dismissed Jewish civil servants. And a number of exceptions were also made for *Mischlinge* – those deemed to be of mixed Jewish and 'Aryan' descent. These were not signs of any 'moderation' or lack of radicalism on Hitler's part. An indication of his own hard line was his communication to Reich Minister of the Interior Frick in December 1938 that he would no longer make use of the rights he had to exempt individuals from the provisions of the Nuremberg Laws. For the rest, he was prepared, as he had been following previous antisemitic waves in 1933 and 1935, to let the radicalization of anti-Jewish policy develop organically.[109]

IV

The open brutality of the November Pogrom, the round-up and incarceration of some 30,000 Jews that followed it, and the draconian measures to force Jews out of the economy had, Goebbels's diary entries make plain, all been explicitly approved by Hitler even if the initiatives had come from others, above all from the Propaganda Minister himself.

To those who saw him late on the evening of 9 November, Hitler had appeared to be shocked and angry at the reports reaching him of what was happening.[110] Himmler, highly critical of Goebbels, was given the impression that Hitler was surprised by what he was hearing when Himmler's chief adjutant Karl Wolff informed them of the burning of the Munich synagogue just before 11.30 that evening.[111] Nicolaus von Below, Hitler's Luftwaffe adjutant, who saw him immediately on his return to his apartment from the 'Old Town Hall', was convinced that there was no dissembling in his apparent anger and condemnation of the destruction.[112] Speer was told by a seemingly regretful and somewhat embarrassed Hitler that he had not wanted the 'excesses'. Speer thought Goebbels had probably pushed him into it.[113] Rosenberg, a few weeks after the events, was convinced that Goebbels, whom he utterly detested, had 'on the basis of a general decree (*Anordnung*) of the Führer ordered the action as it were in his name'.[114] Military leaders, equally ready to pin the blame on 'that swine Goebbels', heard from Hitler that the 'action' had taken place without his knowledge and that one of his Gauleiter had run out of control.[115]

Was Hitler genuinely taken aback by the scale of the 'action', for which he had himself given the green light that very evening? The agitated discussion with Goebbels in the Old Town Hall, like many other instances of blanket verbal authorization given in the unstructured and non-formalized style of reaching decisions in the Third Reich, probably left precise intentions open to interpretation. And certainly, in the course of the night, the welter of criticism from Göring, Himmler, and other leading Nazis made it evident that the 'action' had got out of hand, become counter-productive, and had to be stopped – mainly on account of the material damage it had caused.

But when he consented to Goebbels's suggestion to 'let the demonstrations continue', Hitler knew full well from the accounts from Hessen what the 'demonstrations' amounted to.[116] It took no imagination at all to foresee what would happen if active encouragement were given for a free-for-all against the Jews throughout the Reich. If Hitler had not intended the 'demonstrations' he had approved to take such a course, what, exactly, had he intended? Even on the way to the Old Town Hall, it seems, he had spoken against tough police action against anti-Jewish vandals in Munich.[117] The traditional Stoßtrupp Hitler, bearing his own name, had been unleashed on Jewish property in Munich as soon as Goebbels had finished speaking. One of his closest underlings, Julius Schaub, had been in the thick of things with Goebbels, behaving like the Stoßtrupp fighter of old. During the days that followed, Hitler took care to remain equivocal. He did not praise Goebbels, or what had happened. But nor did he openly, even to his close circle, let alone in public, condemn him outright or categorically dissociate himself from the unpopular Propaganda Minister. Indeed, within a week Hitler was seen again in Goebbels's presence at a performance of *Kabale und Liebe*

('Intrigue and Love') at the opening of the Schiller Theatre, and stayed that night at the Goebbels' villa at Schwanenwerder. On that occasion, too, he 'spoke harshly about the Jews'. Goebbels had the feeling that his own policy against the Jews met with Hitler's full approval.[118]

None of this has the ring of actions being taken against Hitler's will, or in opposition to his intentions.[119] Rather, it seems to point, as Speer presumed, to Hitler's embarrassment when it became clear to him that the action he had approved was meeting with little but condemnation even in the highest circles of the regime. If Goebbels himself could feign anger at the burning of synagogues whose destruction he had himself directly incited, and even ordered, Hitler was certainly capable of such cynicism.[120] What anger Hitler harboured was purely at an 'action' that threatened to engulf him in the unpopularity he had failed to predict. Disbelieving that the Führer could have been responsible, his subordinate leaders were all happy to be deceived. They preferred the easier target of Goebbels, who had played the more visible role. From that night on, it was as if Hitler wanted to draw a veil over the whole business. At his speech in Munich to press representatives on the following evening, 10 November, he made not the slightest mention of the onslaught against the Jews.[121] Even in his 'inner circle', he never referred to 'Reichskristallnacht' during the rest of his days.[122] But although he had publicly distanced himself from what had taken place, Hitler had in fact favoured the most extreme steps at every juncture.

The signs are that 'Crystal Night' had a profound impact upon Hitler. For at least two decades, probably longer, he had harboured feelings which fused fear and loathing into a pathological view of Jews as the incarnation of evil threatening German survival. Alongside the pragmatic reasons why Hitler agreed with Goebbels that the time was opportune to unleash the fury of the Nazi Movement against Jews ran the deeply embedded ideological urge to destroy what he saw as Germany's most implacable enemy, responsible in his mind for the war and its most tragic and damaging consequence for the Reich, the November Revolution. This demonization of the Jew and fear of the 'Jewish world conspiracy' was part of a world-view that saw the random and despairing act of Herschel Grynszpan as part of a plot to destroy the mighty German Reich. Hitler had by that time spent months at the epicentre of an international crisis that had brought Europe to the very brink of a new war. In the context of continuing crisis in foreign policy, with the prospect of international conflict never far away, 'Crystal Night' seems to have reinvoked — certainly to have re-emphasized — the presumed links, present in his warped outlook since 1918-19 and fully expounded in *Mein Kampf*, between the power of the Jews and war.

He had commented in the last chapter of *Mein Kampf* that 'the sacrifice of millions at the front' would not have been necessary if 'twelve or fifteen thousand of these Hebrew corrupters of the people had been held under poison gas'.[123] Such rhetoric, appalling though the sentiments were, was not an indication that Hitler already had the 'Final Solution' in mind. But the implicit genocidal link between war and the killing of Jews was there. Göring's remarks at the end of the meeting on 12 November had been an ominous pointer in the same direction: 'If the German Reich comes into foreign-political conflict in the foreseeable future, it can be taken for granted that we in Germany will think in the first instance of bringing about a great showdown with the Jews.'[124]

With war approaching again, the question of the threat of the Jews in a future conflict was evidently present in Hitler's mind. The idea of using the Jews as hostages, part of Hitler's mentality, but also advanced in the SS's organ *Das Schwarze Korps* in October and November 1938, is testimony to the linkage between war and idea of a 'world conspiracy'. 'The Jews living in Germany and Italy are the hostages which fate has placed in our hand so that we can defend ourselves effectively against the attacks of world Jewry,' commented *Das Schwarze Korps* on 27 October 1938, under the headline 'Eye for an Eye, Tooth for a Tooth'.[125] 'Those Jews in Germany are a part of world Jewry,' the same newspaper threatened on 3 November, still days before the nationwide pogrom was unleashed. 'They are also responsible for whatever world Jewry undertakes against Germany, and – they are liable for the damages which world Jewry inflicts and will inflict on us.' The Jews were to be treated as members of a warring power and interned to prevent their engagement for the interests of world Jewry.[126] Hitler had up to this date never attempted to deploy the 'hostage' tactic as a weapon of his foreign policy.[127] Perhaps promptings from the SS leadership now reawakened 'hostage' notions in his mind. Whether or not this was the case, the potential deployment of German Jews as pawns to blackmail the western powers into accepting further German expansion was possibly the reason why, when stating that it was his 'unshakeable will' to solve 'the Jewish problem' in the near future, and at a time when official policy was to press for emigration with all means possible, he showed no interest in the plans advanced by South African Defence and Economics Minister Oswald Pirow, whom he met at the Berghof on 24 November, for international cooperation in the emigration of German Jews.[128] The same motive was probably also behind the horrific threat he made to the Czechoslovakian Foreign Minister

Franzisek Chvalkovsky on 21 January 1939. 'The Jews here (*bei uns*) will be annihilated (*vernichtet*),' he declared. 'The Jews had not brought about the 9 November 1918 for nothing. This day will be avenged.'[129]

Again, rhetoric should not be mistaken for a plan or programme. Hitler was scarcely likely to have revealed plans to exterminate the Jews which, when they did eventually emerge in 1941, were accorded top secrecy, in a comment to a foreign diplomat. Moreover, 'annihilation' (*Vernichtung*) was one of Hitler's favourite words. He tended to reach for it when trying to impress his threats upon his audience, large or small. He would speak more than once the following summer, for instance, of his intention to 'annihilate' the Poles.[130] Horrific though their treatment was after 1939, no genocidal programme followed.

But the language, even so, was not meaningless. The germ of a possible genocidal outcome, however vaguely conceived, was taking shape. Destruction and annihilation, not just emigration, of the Jews was in the air. Already on 24 November *Das Schwarze Korps*, portraying the Jews as sinking ever more to the status of pauperized parasites and criminals, had concluded: 'In the stage of such a development we would therefore be faced with the hard necessity of eradicating (*auszurotten*) the Jewish underworld just as we are accustomed in our ordered state (*Ordnungsstaat*) to eradicate criminals: with fire and sword! The result would be the actual and final end of Jewry in Germany, its complete annihilation (*Vernichtung*).'[131] This was not a preview of Auschwitz and Treblinka. But without such a mentality, Auschwitz and Treblinka would not have been possible.

In his speech to the Reichstag on 30 January 1939, the sixth anniversary of his takeover of power, Hitler revealed publicly his implicitly genocidal association of the destruction of the Jews with the advent of another war. The 'hostage' notion was probably built into his comments. And, as always, he obviously had an eye on the propaganda impact. But his words were more than propaganda.[132] They gave an insight into the pathology of his mind, into the genocidal intent that was beginning to take hold. He had no idea how the war would bring about the destruction of the Jews. But, somehow, he was certain that this would indeed be the outcome of a new conflagration. 'I have very often in my lifetime been a prophet,' he declared, 'and was mostly derided. In the time of my struggle for power it was in the first instance the Jewish people who received only with laughter my prophecies that I would some time take over the leadership of the state and of the entire people in Germany and then, among other things, also bring the Jewish problem to its solution. I believe that this once hollow laughter of Jewry in Germany has meanwhile already stuck in the throat. I want today to be a prophet again: if international finance Jewry inside and outside Europe should succeed in plunging the nations once more into a world war, the result will be not the bolshevization of the earth and thereby the victory of Jewry, but the annihilation (*Vernichtung*) of the Jewish race in Europe!'[133] It was a 'prophecy' that Hitler would return to on numerous occasions on several occasions in the years 1941 and 1942, when the annihilation of the Jews was no longer terrible rhetoric, but terrible reality.[134]

4

MISCALCULATION

'I will go down as the greatest German in history.'
Hitler, speaking to his secretaries after imposing
a German Protectorate over the remainder of
Czechoslovakia, 15 March 1939

'In the event of any action which clearly threatened Polish
independence ... His Majesty's Government would feel
themselves bound at once to lend the Polish Government
all support in their power.'
The British Prime Minister, Neville Chamberlain,
addressing the House of Commons, 31 March 1939

'I'll brew them a devil's potion.'
Hitler, on hearing of the British Guarantee to Poland,
31 March 1939

I

After Munich things started to move fast. None but the most hopelessly naïve, incurably optimistic, or irredeemably stupid could have imagined that the Sudetenland marked the limits of German ambitions to expand. Certainly, neither the British nor the French governments thought that to be the case. Chamberlain had been rapidly disabused of his initial naïve belief, following his first meeting with the German Dictator, that Hitler was a man of his word, and of any hopes that the Munich Agreement would bring lasting peace. He and the British government were resigned to Germany's further expansion in south-eastern Europe, but thought that Hitler could be contained for at least two more years.[1] Both France and Britain were now rearming furiously. Fears of an imminent strike against Britain most probably stirred up by Colonel Hans Oster – at the hub of Germany's counter-intelligence service as Chief of Staff at the Abwehr, and a key driving-force in the plot against Hitler that had petered out with the signing of the Munich Agreement – proved groundless.[2] But there was serious and growing concern in London at the prospect of a new 'mad dog act' by Hitler in the near future. Where and when he might strike were matters of guesswork.[3]

The diplomatic turmoil in central Europe certainly opened up further opportunities of revisionism – and not just from Germany. Almost before the ink was dry on the Munich Agreement, Hungary – egged on by Poland, looking to its own interests in a strong central European cordon of states between Germany and the Soviet Union – was eyeing up the eastern tip of Czechoslovakia known as Ruthenia (or the Carpatho-Ukraine), a mountain-ous tract so backward that some of its peasant population had never heard of Hitler.[4] Hungary had disappointed Hitler through its hesitancy during the Sudeten crisis. And it suited Germany at this point to encourage the Ukrainian nationalists in the ethnically divided Ruthenian population.[5] Hungarian hopes of gaining Ruthenia were, therefore, for the time being firmly vetoed.[6] Hitler's own aims for the total destruction of Czechoslovakia had, as we noted, only been temporarily interrupted, not halted, by the Munich settlement.[7] With the dismembered state of Czechoslovakia now friendless and, with its border fortifications lost, exposed, and at Germany's mercy, the completion of the plans made in 1938 for its liquidation was only a matter of time. As we have seen, that had been Hitler's view even before he acceded to the Munich Agreement.

Beyond the rump of Czechoslovakia, German attention was immediately turned on Poland. There was no plan at this stage for invasion and conquest. The aim – soon proving illusory – was to bind Poland to Germany against Russia (thereby also blocking any possibility of an alliance with the French). At the same time, the intention was to reach agreement over Danzig and the Corridor (the land which Germany had been forced to cede to Poland in the Versailles Treaty of 1919, giving the Poles access to the sea but leaving East Prussia detached from the remainder of the Reich).[8] Already by late October, Ribbentrop was proposing to settle all differences between Germany and Poland by an agreement for the return of Danzig together with railway and road passage through the Corridor – not in itself a novel idea – in return for a free port for Poland in the Danzig area and an extension of the non-aggression treaty to twenty-five years with a joint guarantee of frontiers.[9]

The proposal met with a predictably stony response from the Polish government.[10] Most vehement of all was the refusal to join the Anti-Comintern Pact, which would have been tantamount to admitting to a position as Germany's puppet.[11] The obduracy of the Poles, especially over Danzig, rapidly brought the first signs of Hitler's own impatience, and an early indication of preparations to take Danzig by force.[12] Hitler was nevertheless at this point more interested in a negotiated settlement with the Poles. Misleadingly informed by Ribbentrop of Polish readiness in principle to move to a new settlement of the Danzig Question and the Corridor, he emphasized German–Polish friendship during his speech to the Reichstag on 30 January 1939.[13] Some army leaders, a few days earlier, had been more belligerent. In contrast to their overriding fears of western intervention during the Sudeten crisis, a number of generals now argued that Britain and France would remain inactive – a direct reflection of the weakness of the western powers fully revealed at Munich – and that negotiations with the Poles should be abandoned in favour of military measures. A war against Poland, they claimed, would be popular among the troops and among the German people.[14]

Ribbentrop, aided by Göring, played – for strategic reasons – the moderate on this occasion. For him, the main enemy was not Poland, but Britain. He countered that, through a premature attack in 1939 on Poland and Russia, Germany would become isolated, would forfeit its armaments advantage, and would most likely be forced by western strength to give up any territorial gains made. Instead, Germany needed to act together with Italy and Japan, retaining Polish neutrality until France had been dealt with and Britain at least isolated and denied all power on the Continent, if not militarily defeated.[15] War by Germany and Italy to defeat France and leave Britain isolated had been the basis of the military directives laid down by Keitel, in line with Hitler's instructions, in November 1938.[16] The priority which Hitler accorded in January 1939 to the navy's Z-Plan, for building a big battle-fleet directed squarely at British naval power, indicates that he was looking at this stage to an eventual showdown with the western powers as the prime military objective. The construction at the same time of an 'East Wall' – limited defensive fortifications for the event of possible conflict with Poland over Danzig – is a further pointer in that direction.[17] Russia, and the eradication of Bolshevism, could wait. But neither Hitler nor anyone in his entourage expected war with Britain and France to come about in the way that it would do that autumn. Hitler had told Goebbels in October 1938 that he foresaw 'for the more distant future a very serious conflict', to decide European hegemony. This would be 'probably with England'.[18] Göring – who had lost face with Hitler since helping to engineer the Munich Agreement that had thwarted his intention of taking Czechoslovakia by force, and by this time no longer initiated into his plans – had no expectation of any general war before about 1942.[19] Keitel had seen his right-hand man in the High Command of the Wehrmacht, General Jodl, transferred to Vienna at the end of October 1938, a move he later stated he would have prevented had he had any notion that war might have been imminent.[20]

In the late autumn and winter of 1938–9, differing views about foreign-policy aims and methods existed within the German leadership. The army was more ready to turn to military action against Poland than it had been against Czechoslovakia. But the specific measures adopted, particularly the building of the eastern fortifications, were still defensive in nature. The 'Ostwall' comprised little more than basic fortifications – castigated by

Hitler as grossly lacking in fire-power and death-traps for those manning them – along a bend in the river Oder some sixty miles east of Berlin.[21] Long-term military preparations were directed towards eventual confrontation with the West, but it was well recognized that the armed forces were years away from being ready for any conflict with Britain and France.[22] As in 1938, military leaders' prime fear was confrontation being forced on Germany too soon through impetuous actions and an over-risky foreign policy. Göring and Ribbentrop were advocating diametrically opposed policies towards Britain. Göring's hopes still rested on an expansive policy in south-eastern Europe, backed for the foreseeable future by an understanding with Britain.[23] Ribbentrop, by now violently anti-British, was, as we have noted, pinning his hopes on smoothing the problems on Germany's eastern front and tightening the alliance with Italy and Japan to prepare the ground for a move against Britain as soon as was feasible. But at this stage, Göring's star was temporarily on the wane and Ribbentrop's usually clumsy diplomacy was meeting in most instances with little success.[24] Hitler's thoughts, whether or not influenced by Ribbentrop's reasoning, were broadly consonant with those of his Foreign Minister. The coming showdown with Bolshevism, prominent in the foreground in 1936, though certainly not displaced in Hitler's own mind as the decisive struggle to be faced at some point in the future had by now moved again into the shadows. Hitler favoured at this point rapprochement with the Poles, to bring them into the German orbit, and preparations for confrontation with the West (which he continued to indicate would not be before 1943 or 1944).[25] But he was, as usual, content to keep his options open and await developments.

The one certainty was that developments *would* occur, thus providing the opportunity for German expansion. For there was no agency of power or influence in the Third Reich advocating drawing a line under the territorial gains already made. All power-groups were looking to further expansion – with or without war.

Military, strategic, and power-political arguments for expansion were underpinned by economic considerations. By late 1938, the pressures of the forced rearmament programme were making themselves acutely felt. The policy of 'rearm, whatever the cost' was now plainly showing itself to be sustainable only in the short term. Bottlenecks were building up in crucial areas of the economy.[26] Lack of coherent and comprehensive economic planning exacerbated them. Expansion into Austria, with its well developed industrial areas around Vienna and Linz, and the Sudetenland, a relatively well industrialized part of Czechoslovakia, had eased matters somewhat.

The unemployed from these additions to the Reich were swiftly put to work. New sources of skilled labour became available. Existing industrial plant could be extended into armaments factories, as in the huge steel complex erected at Linz by the state-run Reichswerke Hermann Göring. Iron ore from Austria and high-quality lignite from the Sudetenland were valuable for synthetic fuel production. The Sudeten area also yielded stocks of tungsten and uranium ore, which Germany had not previously possessed.[27] In economic terms, expansion in 1938 had given German industry a significant boost. But further expansion was necessary if the tensions built into the overheated armaments-driven economy were not to reach explosion point. The Four-Year Plan had been implicitly directed at offloading the costs of German rearmament on to the areas of Europe to be exploited after a successful war.[28] By 1938–9, it was absolutely evident that further expansion could not be postponed indefinitely if the economic impasses were to be surmounted.

When Göring met the members of the Reich Defence Council (Reichsverteidigungsrat) at its first meeting on 18 November 1938, he told them: 'Gentlemen, the financial situation looks very critical.'[29] The following month, Goebbels noted in his diary: 'The financial situation of the Reich is catastrophic. We must look for new ways. It cannot go on like this. Otherwise we will be faced with inflation.'[30] Indeed, the massive rearmament programme, stimulating increased demand from full employment, but without commensurate expansion of consumer goods, was intrinsically inflationary.[31] Price controls and the threat of draconian punishment had contained inflationary pressures so far. But they could not be kept in check indefinitely. In early January 1939, the Reichsbank Directorate sent Hitler a submission, supported by eight signatories, demanding financial restraint to avoid the 'threatening danger of inflation'.[32] Hitler's reaction was: 'That is mutiny!' Twelve days later, Schacht was sacked as President of the Reichsbank.[33]

But the Cassandra voices were not exaggerating. Nor would the problem go away by sacking Schacht. The insatiable demand for raw materials at the same time that consumer demand in the wake of the armaments boom was rising had left public finances in a desolate state. By the time of Schacht's dismissal, the national debt had tripled since Hitler's takeover of power. The Ministry of Economics concluded that it would simply have to be written off after the war. Hitler was aware of the problem, even if he did not understand its technicalities. He ordered a reduction in the Wehrmacht's expenditure in the first quarter of 1939 – an order which the army simply ignored.[34] A way of addressing the problem through more conventional fiscal policies and a reversal to an export-led re-entry into the international economy could not, of course, be entertained. The decision to reject such a course had been taken in 1936. There was now no turning back.

Beyond the crisis in public finances, the labour shortage which had been growing rapidly since 1937 was by this time posing a real threat both to agriculture and to industry. The repeated plaintive reports of the Reich Minister for Food and Agriculture, Richard Walther Darré, left no doubt of the severity of the difficulties facing farming.[35] There had been a 16 per cent drop in the number of agricultural workers between 1933 and 1938 as the 'flight from the land' to better-paid jobs in industry intensified.[36] No amount of compulsion or propaganda could prevent the drain of labour. Nor was mechanization the answer: scarce foreign exchange was needed for tanks, guns, and planes, not tractors and combine-harvesters. Signs of falling production were noted. That meant further demands on highly squeezed imports.[37] Women, many of them members of the farmer's household, were already employed in great numbers in agricultural work. Girls' labour service on the land and drafting the Hitler Youth in to help with the harvest could help only at the margins.[38] The only remedy for the foreseeable future was the use of 'foreign labourers' that war and expansion would bring. It was little wonder that when the first 'foreign workers' were brought back after the Polish campaign and put mainly into farm work, they were initially regarded as 'saviours in a time of need' ('*Retter in der Not*').[39]

Industry was faring no better than agriculture, despite the influx of labour from the land. By 1938, reports were regularly pouring in from all sectors about mounting labour shortages, with serious implications for the productive capacity of even the most crucial armaments-related industries.[40] A sullen, overworked, and – despite increased surveillance and tough, state-backed, managerial controls – often recalcitrant work-force was the outcome.[41] One indication among many of the dangerous consequences for the regime of the labour shortage was the halt on coal exports and reduction in deliveries to the railways in January 1939 on account of a shortage of 30,000 miners in the Ruhr. By that time, the overall shortage of labour in Germany was an estimated 1 million workers. By the outbreak of war, this had risen still further.[42]

Economic pressures did not force Hitler into war. They did not even determine the timing of the war.[43] They were, as we have noted, an inexorable consequence of the political decisions in earlier years: the first, as soon as Hitler had become Chancellor – naturally, with the enthusiastic backing of the armed forces – to make rearmament an absolute spending priority; the second, and even more crucial one, in 1936 to override the objections of those pressing for a return to a more balanced economy and revived involvement in international markets in favour of a striving for maximum autarky within an armaments-driven economy focused on war preparation. The mounting economic problems fed into the military and strategic pressures for expansion. But they did not bring about those pressures in the first place. And for Hitler, they merely confirmed his diagnosis that Germany's position could never be strengthened without territorial conquest.

I I

Hitler's regrets over the Munich Agreement and feeling that a chance had been lost to occupy the whole of Czechoslovakia at one fell swoop had grown rather than diminished during the last months of 1938.[44] His impatience to act had mounted accordingly. He was determined not to be hemmed in by the western powers. He was more than ever convinced that they would not have fought for Czechoslovakia, and that they would and could do nothing to prevent Germany extending its dominance in central and eastern Europe. On the other hand, as he had indicated to Goebbels in October, he was certain that Britain would not concede German hegemony in Europe without a fight at some time.[45] The setback which Munich had been in his eyes confirmed his view that war against the West was coming, probably sooner than he had once envisaged, and that there was no time to lose if Germany were to retain its advantage.[46]

Already on 21 October 1938, only three weeks after the Munich settlement, Hitler had given the Wehrmacht a new directive to prepare for the 'following eventualities': '1. securing the frontiers of the German Reich and protection against surprise air attacks; 2. liquidation of remainder of the Czech state; 3. the occupation of Memelland.' The third point referred to the district of Memel, a seaport on the Baltic with a largely German population, which had been removed from Germany by the Versailles Treaty. On the key second point, the directive added: 'It must be possible to smash at any time the remainder of the Czech State should it pursue an anti-German policy.'[47] Recognizing the perilous plight they were in, the Czechs in fact bent over backwards to accommodate German interests. *In extremis*, rather than end their existence as a country, the Czechs were prepared to turn themselves into a German satellite.[48] Why, then, was Hitler so insistent on smashing the remnants of the Czech state? Politically it was not necessary. Indeed, the German leadership cannot fail to have recognized that an invasion of Czechoslovakia, tearing up the Munich Agreement and breaking solemn promises given only such a short time earlier, would inevitably have the most serious international repercussions.

Part of the answer is doubtless to be found in Hitler's own personality and psychology. His Austrian background and dislike of Czechs since his youth was almost certainly a significant element. Yet after occupation, the persecution of the Czechs was by no means as harsh as that later meted out to the conquered Poles. 'They must always have something to lose,' commented Goebbels.[49] And, following his victorious entry into Prague, Hitler showed remarkably little interest in the Czechs.

More important, certainly, was the feeling that he had been 'cheated' out of his triumph, his 'unalterable wish' altered by western politicians. 'That fellow Chamberlain has spoiled my entry into Prague,' he was overheard saying on his return to Berlin after the agreement at Munich the previous autumn.[50]

His 'sheer bloodymindedness' – his determination not to be denied Prague – probably also has to be regarded as part of the explanation.[51] And yet, the Goebbels diary entries, which we have noted, indicate plainly that Hitler had decided *before* Munich that he would concede to the western powers at that point, but gobble up the rest of Czechoslovakia in due course, and that the acquisition of the Sudetenland would make that second stage easier.[52] That was Hitler's rationalization at the time of the position he had been manoeuvred into. But it does indicate the acceptance by that date of a two-stage plan to acquire the whole of Czechoslovakia, and does not highlight vengeance as a motive.

There were other reasons for occupying the rump of Czechoslovakia that went beyond Hitler's personal motivation. Economic considerations were of obvious importance. However pliant the Czechs were prepared to be, the fact remained that even after the transfer of October 1938, which brought major raw material deposits to the Reich, immense resources remained in Czecho-Slovakia (as the country, the meaningful hyphen inserted, was now officially called) and outside direct German control.[53] The vast bulk of the industrial wealth and resources of the country lay in the old Czech heartlands of Bohemia and Moravia, not in the largely agricultural Slovakia. An estimated four-fifths of engineering, machine-tool construction, and electrical industries remained in the hands of the Czechs. Textiles, chemicals, and the glass industry were other significant industries that beckoned the

Germans. Not least, the Skoda works produced locomotives and machinery as well as arms. Czecho-Slovakia also possessed large quantities of gold and foreign currency that could certainly help relieve some of the shortages of the Four-Year Plan.[54] And a vast amount of equipment could be taken over and redeployed to the advantage of the German army. The Czech arsenal was easily the greatest among the smaller countries of central Europe.[55] The Czech machine-guns, field-guns, and anti-aircraft guns were thought to be better than the German equivalents. They were all taken over by the Reich, as well as the heavy guns built at the Skoda factories.[56] It was subsequently estimated that enough arms had fallen into Hitler's possession to equip a further twenty divisions.[57] Significantly, Hitler had refused the previous autumn to allow the Poles to occupy the area of Moravská-Ostrava, of importance for its minerals and industries. It was the first area to be taken over by the Germans in March 1939.[58]

But of even greater importance than direct economic gain and exploitation was the military-strategic position of what remained of Czecho-Slovakia. As long as the Czechs retained some autonomy, and possession of extensive military equipment and industrial resources, potential difficulties from that quarter could not be ruled out in the event of German involvement in hostilities. More important still: possession of the rectangular, mountain-rimmed territories of Bohemia and Moravia on the south-eastern edge of the Reich offered a recognizable platform for further eastward expansion and military domination. The road to the Balkans was now open. Germany's position against Poland was strengthened. And in the event of conflict in the west, the defences in the east were consolidated.[59]

By the winter of 1938–9, the Polish Question, its significance growing all the time, was of direct relevance to considerations of how to handle Czecho-Slovakia. According to Below, Hitler regretted not occupying the whole of Czecho-Slovakia the previous autumn because the starting-point for negotiations with the Poles over Danzig and the extra-territorial transit-routes through the Corridor would then have been far more advantageous.[60] As we have seen, German hopes of a peaceful revisionism to acquire Danzig and access through the Corridor while bringing Poland into the German orbit were already running into the sand. The future of the rump state of Czecho-Slovakia featured in the diplomatic manoeuvrings. The Poles had seen the possibility blocked of detaching Ruthenia from the Czech heartlands through cession to Hungary (which from the Polish point of view would have undermined the Ukrainian nationalist movement within Ruthenia, with its obvious dangers for inciting trouble among the sizeable Ukrainian minority within Poland). They had consequently turned their attention to Slovakia. Slovakian autonomy from Prague would, so the Poles reasoned, isolate Ruthenia from Bohemia and thereby attain the same effect as would have been achieved by the Hungarian takeover.[61]

Göring, keen to defend what he could of his waning influence in foreign policy by making the most of his extensive contacts in eastern Europe, was able to persuade Hitler of the advantages of a separate Slovakian state. Göring himself wanted to use Slovakia for German air bases for operations in eastern Europe, especially targeting the Balkans. But the Slovakian solution to Poland's worries about Ukrainian nationalism in Ruthenia could in his view be used as a bargaining-counter to persuade Poland to accept some territorial adjustments in return for former German areas coming back to the Reich.[62] And if the Poles remained intransigent, a Slovakia under German tutelage pursuing an anti-Polish policy could help concentrate their minds.[63]

As late as December 1938, there was no indication that Hitler was preparing an imminent strike against the Czechs. There were hints, however, that the next moves in foreign policy would not be long delayed. Hitler told the German leader in Memel, Ernst Neumann, on 17 December that annexation of Memelland would take place in the following March or April, and that he wanted no crisis in the area before then.[64] Occupation of the Memel, as we noted, had been mentioned in the same military directive in October as the preparations for a strike against Czecho-Slovakia. In mid-January, Hitler indicated to the Hungarian Foreign Minister Count István Csáky that no military action was possible between the previous October and March.[65] On 13 February, Hitler let it be known to a few associates that he intended to take action against the Czechs in mid-March. German propaganda was adjusted accordingly.[66] The French had already gleaned intelligence in early February that German action against Prague would take place in about six weeks.[67]

Hitler's meeting at the Berghof with the Polish Foreign Minister and strong man in the government, Joseph Beck, on 5 January had proved, from the German point of view, disappointing. Hitler had tried to appear accommodating in laying down the need for Danzig to return to Germany, and for access routes across the Corridor to East Prussia. Beck implied that public opinion in Poland would prevent any concessions on Danzig.[68] When Ribbentrop returned empty-handed from his visit to Warsaw on 26 January, indicating that the Poles were not to be moved, Hitler's approach to Poland changed markedly.[69]

From friendly overtures, the policy moved to pressure. Poland was to be excluded from any share in the spoils from the destruction of the Czech state (though Hungary, having been denied benefits the previous autumn, would in due course be granted Ruthenia). And turning Slovakia into a German puppet-state intensified the threat to Poland's southern border. Once the demolition of Czecho-Slovakia had taken place, therefore, the Germans hoped and expected the Poles to prove more cooperative.[70] The failure of negotiations with the Poles had probably accelerated the decision to destroy the Czech state.[71]

In January and February 1939, Hitler gave three addresses – not intended for general public consumption – to groups of officers. Partly, he hoped to repair the poor relations with the army that had prevailed since the Blomberg–Fritsch affair. Partly, he wanted to emphasize the type of mentality he expected in face of the conflicts ahead.

On 18 January, before 3,600 recently promoted younger officers assembled in the Mosaic Hall of Speer's New Reich Chancellery, opened only a few days earlier, in a paean to the virtues of belief, optimism, and heroism in soldiers, Hitler demanded 'the unconditional belief that our Germany, our German Reich, will one day be the dominant power in Europe'. The size and racial stock of the German population, and the overcoming of the 'decomposition' of people and state that had prevailed after 1918, provided the basis for this. Now there was a new spirit in Germany, 'the spirit of the world-view which dominates Germany today . . . a deeply soldierly spirit'. The new Wehrmacht had arisen as the guarantor of the military strength of the state. It was his 'unshakable will', he declared, 'that the German Wehrmacht should become the strongest armed force of the entire world', and it was the task of the young officers to help in constructing it.[72] The responsiveness of his audience – frequently breaking into applause, in contrast to the usual military tradition of listening to his speeches in silence, which he did not like – pleased him. Afterwards, he spent some time sitting and talking with groups of officers. He felt the meeting had gone well. He did not even show displeasure at reports that drunken officers, unable to find the toilets in the brand new building, had vomited in the corners of his new splendrous Mosaic Hall.[73]

A week later, on 25 January, he spoke to 217 officers, including top generals and admirals, underlining his vision of a glorious future, now within reach, built on a return to the heroic values of the past. These had embraced 'brutality, meaning the sword, if all other methods fail'. They also meant the elimination of 'the principles of democratic, parliamentary, pacifistic, defeatist mentality' which had characterized the catastrophe of 1918 and the Republic which had followed Germany's defeat. The British Empire was put forward as a model; but as an example, too, of how empires were destroyed by pacifism. Hitler concluded by holding out an enticing prospect to the young officers listening: when the work of constructing the new society was consolidated in 100 years or so, producing a new ruling élite, 'then the people that in my conviction is the first to take this path will stake its claim to the domination of Europe'.[74]

In a third address, in the Kroll Opera House on 10 February to a large gathering of senior commanders, Hitler forcefully restated his belief that Germany's future could only be secured by the acquisition of 'living space'. He expressed disappointment at the attitude of some officers during the crises of 1938, and sought to convince his audience that all his steps in foreign policy (though not their precise timing) had followed a carefully preconceived plan. The events of 1938 had formed part of a chain, reaching back to 1933, and forwards as a step on a long path. 'Understand, gentlemen,' he declared, towards the end of his lengthy speech, 'that the recent great successes have only come about because I perceived the opportunities . . . I have taken it upon myself . . . to solve the German problem of space. Note that as long as I live this thought will dominate my entire being. Be convinced, too, that, when I think it possible to advance a step at some moment, I will take action at once and never draw back from the most extreme measures (vor dem Äußersten) . . . So don't be surprised if in coming years, too, the attempt will be made to attain some German goal or other at every opportunity, and place yourselves then, I urge you, in most fervent trust behind me.'[75]

Around this time, according to Goebbels, Hitler spoke practically of nothing else but foreign policy. 'He's always pondering new plans,' Goebbels noted. 'A Napoleonic nature!'[76] The Propaganda Minister had already guessed what was in store when Hitler told him at the end of January he was going 'to the mountain' – to the Obersalzberg – to think about his next steps in foreign policy. 'Perhaps Czechia (die Tschechei) is up for it again. The problem is after all only half solved,' he wrote.[77]

III

By the beginning of March, in the light of mounting Slovakian nationalist clamour (abetted by Germany) for full independence from Prague, the break-up of what was left of the state of Czecho-Slovakia looked to close observers of the scene to be a matter of time. German propaganda against Prague was now becoming shrill. Relations between the Czech and Slovak governments were tense. But for all their pressure the Germans were unable to prise out of the Slovakian leaders the immediate proclamation of full independence and request for German aid that was urgently wanted.[78]

When the Prague government deposed the Slovakian cabinet, sent police in to occupy government offices in Bratislava, and placed the former Prime Minister, Father Jozef Tiso, under house arrest, Hitler spotted his moment. On 10 March, he told Goebbels, Ribbentrop, and Keitel that he had decided to march in, smash the rump Czech state, and occupy Prague. The invasion was to take place five days later; it would be the Ides of March. 'Our borders must stretch to the Carpathians,' noted Goebbels. 'The Führer shouts for joy. This game is dead certain.'[79]

Göring, on holiday on the Riviera enjoying the luxury comforts of San Remo, was sent a message telling him not to leave before German troops entered Czecho-Slovakia in order not to stir suspicions abroad.[80] On 12 March orders were given to the army and Luftwaffe to be ready to enter Czecho-Slovakia at 6a.m. on the 15th, but before then not to approach within ten kilometres of the border.[81] German mobilization was by that stage so obvious that it seemed impossible that the Czechs were unaware of what was happening.[82] The propaganda campaign against the Czechs had meanwhile been sharply stepped up.[83] Ribbentrop, Goebbels, and Hitler discussed foreign-policy issues until deep into the night. Ribbentrop argued that conflict with England in due course was inevitable. Hitler, according to Goebbels, was preparing for it, but did not regard it as unavoidable. Goebbels criticized Ribbentrop's inflexibility. 'But the Führer corrects him, for sure.'[84]

That evening, 12 March, Tiso had been visited by German officials and invited to Berlin. The next day he met Hitler. He was told the historic hour of the Slovaks had arrived. If they did nothing, they would be swallowed up by Hungary.[85] Tiso got the message. By the following noon, 14 March, back in Bratislava, he had the Slovak Assembly proclaim independence. The desired request for 'protection' was, however, only forthcoming a day later, after German warships on the Danube had trained their sights on the Slovakian government offices.[86]

Goebbels listened again to Hitler unfolding his plans. The entire 'action' would be over within eight days. The Germans would already be in Prague within a day, their planes within two hours. No bloodshed was expected. 'Then the Führer wants to fit in (*einlegen*) a lengthy period of political calm,' wrote Goebbels, adding that he did not believe it, however enticing the prospect. A period of calm, he thought, was necessary. 'Gradually, the nerves aren't coping.'[87]

On the morning of 14 March, the anticipated request came from Prague, seeking an audience of the Czech State President Dr Emil Hácha with Hitler. Hácha, a small, shy, somewhat unworldly, and also rather sickly man, in office since the previous November, was unable to fly because of a heart complaint.[88] He arrived in Berlin during the course of the evening, after a five-hour train journey, accompanied only by Foreign Minister Chvalkovsky, his secretary, and his daughter. Hitler kept him nervously waiting in the Adlon Hotel until midnight to increase the pressure upon him – 'the old tested methods of political tactics', as Goebbels put it.[89] While Hácha fretted, Hitler amused himself watching a film called *Ein hoffnungsloser Fall* (*A Hopeless Case*).[90]

The fiction of normal courtesies to a visiting head of state was retained. When he arrived at the New Reich Chancellery at midnight, Hácha was first put through the grotesque ceremonial of inspecting the guard of honour. It was around 1a.m. when, his face red from nervousness and anxiety, the Czech President was eventually ushered into the intimidating surrounds of Hitler's grandiose 'study' in the New Reich Chancellery.[91] A sizeable gathering, including Ribbentrop, the head of his personal staff Walther Hewel, Keitel, Weizsäcker, State Secretary Otto Meissner, Press Chief Otto Dietrich, and interpreter Paul Schmidt, were present. Göring, summoned back from holiday, was also there. Hácha's only support was the presence of Chvalkovsky and Dr Voytech Mastny, the Czech Ambassador in Berlin.[92]

Hitler was at his most intimidating. He launched into a violent tirade against the Czechs and the 'spirit of Beneš' that, he claimed, still lived on. It was necessary in order to safeguard the Reich, he continued, to impose a protectorate over the remainder of Czecho-Slovakia. Hácha and Chvalkovsky sat stony-faced and motionless. The entry of German troops was 'irreversible', ranted Hitler. Keitel would confirm that they were already marching towards the Czech border, and would cross it at 6a.m.[93] His Czech 'guests' knew that some had in fact already crossed the border in one place.[94] Hácha should phone Prague at once and give orders that there was to be no resistance, if bloodshed were to be avoided. Hácha said he wanted no bloodshed, and asked Hitler to halt the military build-up. Hitler refused: it was impossible; the troops were already mobilized.[95] Göring intervened to add that his Luftwaffe would be over Prague by dawn, and it was in Hácha's hands whether bombs fell on the beautiful city. In fact, the 7th Airborne

Division detailed for the operation was grounded by snow.[96] But at the threat, the Czech President fainted. If anything happened to Hácha, thought Paul Schmidt, the entire world would think he had been murdered in the Reich Chancellery.[97] But Hácha recovered, revived by an injection from Hitler's personal physician, Dr Morell.

Meanwhile, Prague could not be reached by telephone. Ribbentrop was beside himself with fury at the failings of the German Post Office (though it was established that any difficulty was at the Prague end). Eventually, contact with Prague was made. The browbeaten President went immediately to the telephone and, on a crackly line, passed on his orders that Czech troops were not to open fire on the invading Germans. Just before 4a.m., Hácha signed the declaration, placing the fate of his people in the hands of the Leader of the German Reich.[98]

Overjoyed, Hitler went in to see his two secretaries, Christa Schroeder and Gerda Daranowski, who had been on duty that night. 'So, children,' he burst out, pointing to his cheeks, 'each of you give me a kiss there and there . . . This is the happiest day of my life. What has been striven for in vain for centuries, I have been fortunate enough to bring about. I have achieved the union of Czechia with the Reich. Hácha has signed the agreement. I will go down as the greatest German in history.'[99]

Two hours after Hácha had signed, the German army crossed the Czech borders and marched, on schedule, on Prague. By 9a.m. the forward units entered the Czech capital, making slow progress on ice-bound roads, through mist and snow, the wintry weather providing an appropriate back-cloth to the end of central Europe's last, betrayed, democracy. The Czech troops, as ordered, remained in their barracks and handed over their weapons.[100]

Hitler left Berlin at midday, travelling in his special train as far as Leipa, some sixty miles north of Prague, where he arrived during the afternoon. A fleet of Mercedes was waiting to take him and his entourage the remainder of the journey to Prague. It was snowing heavily, but he stood for much of the way, his arm outstretched to salute the unending columns of German soldiers they overtook. Unlike his triumphal entries into Austria and the Sudetenland, only a thin smattering of the population watched sullenly and helplessly from the side of the road. A few dared to greet with clenched fists as Hitler's car passed by. But the streets were almost deserted by the time he arrived in Prague in the early evening and drove up to the Hradschin Castle, the ancient residence of the Kings of Bohemia.[101] Little was ready for his arrival. The great iron gates to the castle were locked. No food was on hand for the new occupiers as Hitler sat down with Reich Minister of the Interior Frick and his Secretary of State Stuckart to finalize the decree initiating the German Protectorate. The military escort were sent out in the early hours to find bread, ham, and Pilsner. Hitler, too, was given a glass of beer. He tasted it, pulled a face, and put it down. It was too bitter for him.[102] He dictated the preamble to the decree. It stated that 'the Bohemian and Moravian lands had belonged to the living space of the German people for 1,000 years'.[103] The terminology, sounding alien to Prussian ears, hinted at his Austrian origins; the name of the Protectorate was derived from the designations of the old Habsburg imperial crown lands. He spent the night in the Hradschin. When the people of Prague awoke next morning, they saw Hitler's standard fluttering on the castle. Twenty-four hours later he was gone.[104] He showed little further interest in Prague, or the Protectorate. For the Czechs, six long years of subjugation had begun.

Hitler returned to Berlin, via Vienna, on 19 March, to the inevitable, and by now customary, triumphator's reception. Despite the freezing temperatures, huge numbers turned out to welcome the hero. When Hitler descended from his train at the Görlitzer Bahnhof, Göring, tears in his eyes, greeted him with an address embarrassing even by the prevailing standards of sycophancy. Thousands cheered wildly as Hitler was driven to the Reich Chancellery. The experienced hand of Dr Goebbels had organized another massive spectacular. Searchlights formed a 'tunnel of light' along Unter den Linden. A brilliant display of fireworks followed. Hitler then appeared on the balcony of the Reich Chancellery, waving to the ecstatic crowd of his adoring subjects below.[105]

The real response among the German people to the rape of Czecho-Slovakia was, however, more mixed – in any event less euphoric – than that of the cheering multitudes, many of them galvanized by Party activists, in Berlin. This time there had been no 'home-coming' of ethnic Germans into the Reich. The vague notion that Bohemia and Moravia had belonged to the 'German living-space' for a thousand years left most people cold – certainly most north Germans who had traditionally had little or no connection with the Czech lands.[106] For many, as one report from a Nazi District Leader put it, whatever the joy in the Führer's 'great deeds' and the trust placed in him, 'the needs and cares of daily life are so great that the mood is very quickly gloomy again'.[107] There was a good deal of indifference, scepticism, and criticism, together with worries that war was a big step closer. 'Was that necessary?' many people asked. They remembered Hitler's precise words following the Munich Agreement, that the Sudetenland had been his 'last territorial demand'.[108] In the industrial belt of Rhineland-Westphalia, according to a report from the Social Democrat underground movement, there was a good deal of condemnation of the invasion while sympathy for the Czechs was openly expressed in coal-pits, workers' wash-rooms, and on the streets. The Nazi regime was criticized; but there was also contempt for the way France and Britain had let Hitler do what he wanted.[109] Similar sentiments were commonplace among those who detested the Nazis. 'No shot fired. Nowhere a protest,' noted one woman in her diary – adding to her comment the forecast of a friend: 'I bet they now get Danzig and Poland still without war ... and if they're lucky, even the Ukraine.'[110] 'Can't he get enough?' murmured the mother of a fourteen-year-old girl in Paderborn. The young girl herself, who had been appalled the previous summer at the 'outrages' allegedly perpetrated against the German minority in the Sudetenland, now found herself sympathizing with the Czechs, and at the same time asking what Germany was doing in annexing the territory of 'an entirely alien people' who could under no circumstances be 'germanized'. She consoled herself with the thought that no blood had been shed, that it could even be an advantage for a small country to be under the protection of a great power, and that the German people would be 'much more generous, tolerant, and fair' protectors than 'some Slavic people'.[111] It was a reflection of the widespread latent hostility towards Slavs, the impact of propaganda, and of the confused sentiments that continued to accompany Hitler's expansionism. Even opponents of Hitler recognized that moral scruples carried little weight in the face of another major prestige suc-cess. 'Internal opponents, too, are now declaring that he's a great man,' ran a report sent to the exiled Social Democrat leadership in Paris. It indicated the difficulty in challenging those lauding his 'achievements'. Counter-arguments, it was said, were pointless – not least 'the argument that Czecho-Slovakia has been invaded and Hitler has done something wrong'.[112]

Hitler had been contemptuous of the western powers before the taking of Prague. He correctly judged that once more they would protest, but do nothing. However, everything points to the conclusion that he miscalculated the response of Britain and France *after* the invasion of Czecho-Slovakia. The initial reaction in London was one of shock and dismay at the cynical demolition of the Munich Agreement, despite the warnings the British government had received. Appeasement policy lay shattered in the ruins of the Czecho-Slovakian state. Hitler had broken his promise that he had no further territorial demands to make. And the conquest of Czecho-Slovakia had destroyed the fiction that Hitler's policies were aimed at the uniting of

German peoples in a single state. Hitler, it was now abundantly clear – a recognition at last and very late in the day – could not be trusted. He would stop at nothing. Chamberlain's speech in Birmingham on 17 March hinted at a new policy. 'Is this the last attack upon a small State, or is it to be followed by others?' he asked. 'Is this, in fact, a step in the direction of an attempt to dominate the world by force?'[113] British public opinion was in no doubt. Hitler had united a country deeply divided over Munich. On all sides people were saying that war with Germany was both inevitable and necessary. Recruitment for the armed forces increased almost overnight.[114] It was now clear both to the man in the street and to the government: Hitler had to be tackled.

The following day, 18 March, amid rumours circulating that Germany was threatening Romania, the British cabinet endorsed the Prime Minister's recommendation of a fundamental change in policy. No reliance could any longer be placed on the assurances of the Nazi leaders, Chamberlain stated. The old policy of trying to come to terms with the dictatorships on the assumption that they had limited aims was no longer possible. Chamberlain regarded his Birmingham speech, he told the cabinet, 'as a challenge to Germany on the issue whether or not Germany intended to dominate Europe by force. It followed that if Germany took another step in the direction of dominating Europe, she would be accepting the challenge.' Lord Halifax, the Foreign Secretary, underlined the view that 'the real issue was Germany's attempt to obtain world domination, which it was in the interest of all countries to resist'. Britain alone, he argued, could organize such resistance – though he admitted that it was hard to see how Britain could effectively attack Germany – if the Germans invaded Romania or whether they turned on Holland. 'The attitude of the German government was either bluff, in which case it would be stopped by a public declaration on our part; or it was not bluff, in which case it was necessary that we should all unite to meet it, and the sooner we united the better. Otherwise we might see one country after another absorbed by Germany.' The policy had shifted from trying to appease Hitler to attempting to deter him. In any new aggression, Germany would be faced at the outset with the choice of pulling back or going to war. As the Foreign Secretary's comments made clear, the geographical thrust of any new move by Hitler was immaterial to this new strategy. But the Prime Minister had little doubt as to where trouble might next flare up. 'He thought that Poland was very likely the key to the situation . . . The time had now come for those who were threatened by German aggression (whether immediately or ultimately) to get together. We should enquire how far Poland was prepared to go alone these lines.'[115] The British Guarantee to Poland and the genesis of the summer crisis which, this time, would end in war were foreshadowed in Chamberlain's remarks.

Similar reactions were registered in Paris. Daladier let Chamberlain know that the French would speed up rearmament and resist any further aggression. The Americans were told that Daladier was determined to go to war should the Germans act against Danzig or Poland. Even strong advocates of appeasement were now saying enough was enough: there would not be another Munich.[116]

IV

Before the Polish crisis unfolded, Hitler had one other triumph to register – though compared with what had gone before, it was a minor one. As we noted, Hitler had referred in his directive of 21 October 1938 to preparation for 'the occupation of Memelland'.[117] The incorporation of Memelland in the German Reich was now to prove the last annexation without bloodshed. After its removal from Germany in 1919, the Memel district, with a mainly German population but a sizeable Lithuanian minority, had been placed under French administration. The Lithuanians had marched in, forcing the withdrawal of the French occupying force there in January 1923. The following year, under international agreement, the Memel had gained a level of independence, but remained in effect a German enclave under Lithuanian tutelage. Trouble had flared briefly in 1935 when the Lithuanians put 128 Memelland National Socialists on trial, sentencing four of them to death. But other than launch a fierce verbal onslaught on the Lithuanians, Hitler had at the time done nothing. The matter died down as quickly as it had arisen. The Memel question was not raised again for another four years. But in March 1938, the German army had prepared plans to occupy the Memel in the event of war between Poland and Lithuania. Then in October Hitler had included the recovery of the Memel in the directive for taking over Czecho-Slovakia. By the end of the year, interested in agreement with Poland, Hitler had insisted that there should be no agitation from the restless Nazis in the Memel. Early in 1939, anxious to avoid any action which might provoke German intervention, the Lithuanians had yielded to all the wishes of the now largely nazified Memel population.[118]

Politically, the return of the territory to Germany was of no great significance. Even symbolically, it was of relatively little importance. Few ordinary

Germans took more than a passing interest in the incorporation of such a remote fleck of territory into the Reich. But the acquisition of a port on the Baltic, with the possibility that Lithuania, too, might be turned into a German satellite, had strategic relevance. Alongside the subordination to German influence of Slovakia on the southern borders of Poland, it gave a further edge to German pressure on the Poles.[119]

On 20 March, Ribbentrop subjected the Lithuanian Foreign Minister, Joseph Urbsys, to the usual bullying tactics. Kowno would be bombed, he threatened, if Germany's demand for the immediate return of the Memel were not met.[120] Urbsys returned the next day, 21 March, to Kowno. The Lithuanians were in no mood for a fight. They sent in a draft communiqué. It did not suffice and had to be redrafted in Berlin. By then the Lithuanian ministers had gone to bed and had to be awakened by the German ambassador, who had been told, figuratively, to put a pistol to their chest. 'Either-or,' remarked Goebbels.[121] At 3a.m. everything was finally accepted. The revised communiqué arrived about three hours later. A Lithuanian delegation was sent to Berlin to arrange the details. 'If you apply a bit of pressure, things happen,' noted Goebbels, with satisfaction.[122]

Hitler left Berlin that afternoon, 22 March, for Swinemünde, where, along with Raeder, he boarded the cruiser *Deutschland*. Late that evening, Ribbentrop and Urbsys agreed terms for the formal transfer of the Memel district to Germany. Hitler's decree was signed the next morning, 23 March. German troops crossed the bridge near Tilsit and entered the Memel. Squadrons of the Luftwaffe landed at the same time. At 1.30p.m., Hitler was put on shore in the new German territory. He gave a remarkably short speech on the balcony of the theatre. In under three hours he was gone. He was back in Berlin by noon next day. This time, he dispensed with the hero's return.[123] Triumphal entries to Berlin could not be allowed to become so frequent that they were routine. Goebbels was aware of 'the danger that the petty-bourgeois (*Spießer*) think it will go on like this forever. A lot of quite fantastic ideas about the next plans of German foreign policy are being put about.'[124]

According to Goebbels, Hitler repeated what he had said a few days earlier. He now wanted a period of calm in order to win new trust. 'Then the colonial question will be brought up (*aufs Tapet*).' 'Always one thing after another,' added the Propaganda Minister.[125] He did not anticipate things becoming quiet. Hitler, however, was evidently not looking to war with the western powers within a matter of months.

V

His own pressure on Poland forced the issue. Wasting no time, Ribbentrop had pushed Ambassador Lipski on 21 March to arrange a visit to Berlin by Beck. He indicated that Hitler was losing patience, and that the German press was straining at the leash to be turned loose on the Poles – a threat that German feeling could be as easily inflamed against Poland as it had been against Czecho-Slovakia. He repeated the requests about Danzig and the Corridor. In return, Poland might be tempted by the exploitation of Slovakia and the Ukraine.[126]

But the Poles were not prepared to act according to the script. Beck, noting Chamberlain's Birmingham speech, secretly put out feelers to London for a bilateral agreement with Britain.[127] Meanwhile, the Poles mobilized their troops.[128] On 25 March, Hitler still indicated that he did not want to solve the Danzig Question by force to avoid driving the Poles into the arms of the British.[129] He had remarked to Goebbels the previous evening that he hoped the Poles would respond to pressure, 'but we must bite into the sour apple and guarantee Poland's borders'.[130]

However, just after noon on 26 March, instead of the desired visit by Beck, Lipski simply presented Ribbentrop with a memorandum representing the Polish Foreign Minister's views. It flatly rejected the German proposals, reminding Ribbentrop for good measure of Hitler's verbal assurance in his speech on 20 February 1938 that Poland's rights and interests would be respected. Ribbentrop lost his temper. Going beyond his mandate from Hitler, he told Lipski that any Polish action against Danzig (of which there was no indication) would be treated as aggression against the Reich. The bullying attempt was lost on Lipski. He replied that any furtherance of German plans directed at the return of Danzig to the Reich meant war with Poland.[131] Hitler's response can be imagined.[132] Goebbels recorded in his diary: 'Poland still makes great difficulties. The Polacks are and remain naturally our enemies, even if from self-interest they have done us some service in the past.'[133] Beck confirmed the unbending attitude of the Poles to the German ambassador in Warsaw on the evening of 28 March: if Germany tried to use force to alter the status of Danzig, there would be war.[134]

By 27 March, meanwhile, Chamberlain, warned that a German strike against Poland might be imminent, was telling the British cabinet he was prepared to offer a unilateral commitment to Poland, aimed at stiffening Polish resolve and deterring Hitler.[135] The policy that had been developing since the invasion of Czecho-Slovakia found its expression in Chamberlain's statement to the House of Commons on 31 March 1939: 'In the event of any action which clearly threatened Polish independence, and which the Polish Government accordingly considered it vital to resist with their national forces, His Majesty's Government would feel themselves bound at once to lend the Polish Government all support in their power.'[136]

This was followed, at the end of Beck's visit to London on 4–6 April, by Chamberlain's announcement to the House of Commons that Britain and Poland had agreed to sign a mutual assistance pact in the event of an attack 'by a European power'.[137]

On hearing the British Guarantee of 31 March, Hitler fell into a rage. He thumped his fist on the marble-topped table of his study in the Reich Chancellery. 'I'll brew them a devil's potion,' he fumed.[138]

Exactly what he had wanted to avoid had happened. He had expected the pressure on the Poles to work as easily as it had done in the case of the Czechs and the Slovaks. He had presumed the Poles would in due course see sense and yield Danzig and concede the extra-territorial routes through the Corridor. He had taken it for granted that Poland would then become a German satellite – an ally in any later attack on the Soviet Union. He had been determined to keep Poland out of Britain's clutches. All of this was now upturned. Danzig would have to be taken by force. He had been thwarted by the British and spurned by the Poles. He would teach them a lesson.[139]

Or so he thought. In reality, Hitler's over-confidence, impatience, and misreading of the impact of German aggression against Czecho-Slovakia had produced a fateful miscalculation.

The next day, 1 April, speaking in Wilhelmshaven after attending the launch of the *Tirpitz* (the second new modern battleship, following the *Bismarck*, intended to spearhead Germany's challenge to the supremacy of the Royal Navy during the next few years),[140] Hitler used the opportunity to castigate what he claimed was Britain's 'encirclement policy', and to voice scarcely veiled threats at both Poland and Britain. He summarized his brutal philosophy in a single, short sentence: 'He who does not possess power loses the right to life.'[141]

At the end of March Hitler had indicated to Brauchitsch, head of the army, that he would use force against Poland if diplomacy failed. Immediately, the branches of the armed forces began preparing drafts of their own operational plans. These were presented to Hitler in the huge 'Führer type' that he could read without glasses. He added a preamble on political aims. By 3 April the directive for 'Case White' (*Fall Weiß*) was ready.[142] It was issued eight days later.[143] Its first section, written by Hitler himself, began: 'German relations with Poland continue to be based on the principles of avoiding any disturbances. Should Poland, however, change her policy towards Germany, which so far has been based on the same principles as our own, and adopt a threatening attitude towards Germany, a final settlement might become necessary in spite of the Treaty in force with Poland. The aim then will be to destroy Polish military strength, and create in the East a situation which satisfies the requirements of national defence. The Free State of Danzig will be proclaimed a part of the Reich territory by the outbreak of hostilities at the latest. The political leaders consider it their task in this case to isolate Poland if possible, that is to say, to limit the war to Poland only.'[144] The Wehrmacht had to be ready to carry out 'Case White' at any time after 1 September 1939.[145]

Army commanders had been divided over the merits of attacking Czecho-Slovakia only a few months earlier. Now, there was no sign of hesitation. The aims of the coming campaign to destroy Poland were outlined within a fortnight or so by Chief of the General Staff Halder to generals and General Staff officers. Oppositional hopes of staging a coup against Hitler the previous autumn, as the Sudeten crisis was reaching its dénouement, had centred upon Halder. At the time, he had indeed been prepared to see Hitler assassinated.[146] It was the same Halder who now evidently relished the prospect of easy and rapid victory over the Poles and envisaged subsequent conflict with the Soviet Union or the western powers. Halder told senior officers that 'thanks to the outstanding, I might say, instinctively sure policy of the Führer', the military situation in central Europe had changed fundamentally. As a consequence, the position of Poland had also significantly altered. Halder said he was certain he was speaking for many in his audience in commenting that with the ending of 'friendly relations' with Poland 'a stone has fallen from the heart'. Poland was now to be ranked among Germany's enemies. The rest of Halder's address dealt with the need to destroy Poland 'in record speed' ('*einen Rekord an Schnelligkeit*'). The British Guarantee would not prevent this happening. He was contemptuous of the capabilities of the Polish army.[147] It formed 'no serious opponent'. He outlined in some detail the course the German attack would take, acknowledging cooperation with the SS and the occupation of the country by the paramilitary formations of the Party. The aim, he repeated, was to ensure 'that Poland as rapidly as possible was not only defeated, but liquidated', whether France and Britain should intervene in the West (which on balance he deemed unlikely) or not. The attack had to be 'crushing' ('*zermalmend*'). He concluded by looking beyond the Polish conflict: 'We must be finished with Poland within three weeks, if possible already in a fortnight. Then it will depend on the Russians whether the eastern front becomes Europe's fate or not. In any case, a victorious army, filled with the spirit of gigantic victories attained, will be ready either to confront Bolshevism or . . . to be hurled against the West . . .'[148]

On Poland, there was no divergence between Hitler and his Chief of the General Staff. Both wanted to smash Poland at breakneck speed, preferably in an isolated campaign but, if necessary, even with western intervention (though both thought this more improbable than probable). And both looked beyond Poland to a widening of the conflict, eastwards or westwards, at some point. Hitler could be satisfied. He need expect no problems this time from his army leaders.

The contours for the summer crisis of 1939 had been drawn. It would end not with the desired limited conflict to destroy Poland, but with the major European powers locked in another continental war. This was in the first instance a consequence of Hitler's miscalculation that spring. But, as Halder's address to the generals indicated, it had not been Hitler's miscalculation alone.

5

GOING FOR BROKE

'The answer to the question of how the problem "Danzig
and the Corridor" is to be solved is still the same
among the general public: incorporation in the Reich? Yes.
Through war? No.'

Reported opinion in a district of Upper Franconia,
31 July 1939

'When starting and waging a war it is not right that matters,
but victory.'

Hitler to his military leaders, 22 August 1939

'In my life I've always gone for broke.'

Hitler to Göring, 29 August 1939

For 20 April 1939, Hitler's fiftieth birthday, Goebbels had orchestrated an astonishing extravaganza of the Führer cult. The lavish outpourings of adulation and sycophancy surpassed those of any previous 'Führer's Birthday'. The festivities had already begun on the afternoon of the 19th. In mid-evening, followed by a cavalcade of fifty limousines, Hitler was driven along the thronged seven kilometres of the newly opened 'East-West Axis', lit by flaming torches and bedecked with hundreds of banners, built as the main boulevard of the intended new capital of the Nazi empire, 'Germania'. After Albert Speer had declared the new road open, Hitler returned to the Reich Chancellery, watching from the balcony, as Party deputations from all the Gaue wound their way in torchlight procession through the vast, cheering crowd assembled in Wilhelmsplatz. At midnight he was congratulated by all the members of his personal entourage, beginning with his secretaries. Speer, by now the firmly established court favourite, presented a delighted Hitler with a four-metre model of the gigantic triumphal arch that would crown the rebuilt Berlin. Captain Hans Baur, Hitler's pilot, gave him a model of the four-engined Focke-Wulf 200 'Condor', under construction to take service as the 'Führer Machine' in the summer. Row upon row of further gifts – marble-white nude statues, bronze casts, Meissen porcelain, oil-paintings (some valuable, including a Lenbach and even a Titian, but mostly the standard dreary exhibits found in the House of German Art in Munich), tapestries, rare coins, antique weapons, and a mass of other presents, many of them kitsch (like the cushions embroidered with Nazi emblems or 'Heil mein Führer') – were laid out on long tables in the hall where Bismarck had presided over the Berlin Congress of 1878. Hitler admired some, made fun of others, and ignored most.[1]

The central feature of the birthday itself was a mammoth display of the might and power of the Third Reich, calculated to show the western powers what faced them if they should tangle with the new Germany. The ambassadors of Britain, France, and the USA, recalled after the march into Czecho-Slovakia, were absent. The Poles had sent no delegation.[2] The parade on the 'East-West Axis' began at 11a.m. and lasted almost five hours. His secretaries returned to the Reich Chancellery exhausted from the 'dreadfully long' show; but Hitler never tired of being the centre of attraction at propaganda displays, however long he had to stand with his arm raised.[3] The entire parade was recorded on 10,000 metres of film. The image of Hitler the 'statesman of genius' had now to be complemented by the portrayal of the 'future military leader, taking muster of his armed forces'.[4]

'The Führer is fêted like no other mortal has ever been,' effused Goebbels.[5] Hitler's most adoring disciple was scarcely a rational judge. But, elaborately stage-managed though the entire razzmatazz had been, there was no denying Hitler's genuine popularity – even near-deification by many – among the masses. What had been before 1933 bitterly anti-Nazi Communist and Socialist sub-cultures remained, despite terror and propaganda, still largely impervious to the Hitler adulation. Many Catholics, relatively immune throughout to Nazism's appeal, and, in lesser measure, Protestant church-goers had been alienated by the 'Church Struggle' (though Hitler was held less generally to blame than his subordinates, especially Rosenberg and Goebbels). Intellectuals might be disdainful of Hitler, old-fashioned, upper-class conservatives bemoan the vulgarity of the Nazis, and those with remaining shreds of liberal, humanitarian values feel appalled at the brutality of the regime, displayed in full during 'Crystal Night'. Even so, Hitler was without doubt the most popular government head in Europe. The exiled Social Democratic leaders, analysing the Führer cult as reflected in the plethora of letters, poems, and other *devotalia* sent in by ordinary citizens and published in German newspapers around Hitler's fiftieth birthday, admitted that the phenomenon could not be explained by propaganda alone. Hitler, a national leader arising from the lower ranks of society, had tapped a certain 'naïve faith' embedded in lengthy traditions of 'heroic' leadership. Internal terror and the readiness of the western powers to hand Hitler one success after another in foreign policy had undermined the scepticism of many waverers. The result was that, although there was much fear of war, belief in the Führer was extensive.[6] 'A great man, a genius, a person sent to us from heaven,' was one seventeen-year-old girl's naïve impression.[7] She spoke for many.

Whatever the criticisms ordinary people had about everyday life in the Third Reich, its irritations and vexations, the cult constructed around the Führer represented an enormous force for integration. The daily reality of Nazi rule spawned much antagonism. Grandiose Party buildings, erected at vast cost, greatly affronted a hard-pressed and poorly housed working population in the big cities. Massive criticism continued to be heaped on the self-evident corruption, scandalous high-living, and arrogance of Party functionaries. And, though the 'Church struggle' had died down somewhat, compared with intensity of the years 1936 and 1937, the attritional conflict between Party anti-Church fanatics and the churchgoing population remained a source of repeated friction.[8] But Hitler's 'successes' offered a counter – a set of 'achievements', put forward as those of a national, not party, leader, in which almost any German could take pride. 'I have overcome the chaos in Germany,' claimed Hitler in his speech to the Reichstag on 28 April, 'restored order, massively raised production in all areas of our national economy.' His litany of what were advanced as his own, personal accomplishments, continued: 'I have succeeded in completely bringing back into useful production the seven [!] million unemployed who were so dear to all our own hearts, in keeping the German peasant on his soil despite all difficulties and in rescuing it for him, in attaining the renewed flourishing of German trade, and in tremendously promoting transportation. I have not only politically united the German people, but also militarily rearmed them, and I have further attempted to tear up page for page that Treaty, which contained in its 448 articles the most base violations ever accorded to nations and human beings. I have given back to the Reich the provinces stolen from us in 1919. I have led back into the homeland the millions of deeply unhappy Germans who had been torn away from us. I have recreated the thousand-year historic unity of the German living-space, and I have attempted to do all this without spilling blood and without inflicting on my people or on others the suffering of war. I have managed this from my own strength, as one who twenty-one years ago was an unknown worker and soldier of my people.'[9]

People worried how long it could all last. But the contrast with the dark days of economic depression and national humiliation was scarcely credible. What had been achieved seemed staggering. Most people did not want to see it put at risk through external conflict. For those who did not dwell too long on the causes and consequences, one man alone appeared to have masterminded it all. For that man, what had been achieved so far was no more than a preparation for what was to come.

As what was to prove the last peacetime spring and summer wore on, Hitler's subordinates were in no doubt about the difficulties at home, and their impact on large sections of the population. The SD had spoken of a 'mood close to complete despair' among the peasantry at the end of 1938 owing to the 'flight from the land' and ensuing massive labour shortage. The feeling of being crushed, the SD claimed, was partly reflected in resignation, partly in outright revolt against the farmers' leaders.[10] In the first months of 1939, the peasants' mood was said to have deteriorated still further.[11] In Bavaria, it had reportedly reached 'boiling point' ('*Siedehitze*').[12] The SD concluded that the 'production battle' had passed its peak, and was now facing decline, with the extensification of agriculture, and threat to the '*völkisch* substance'.[13] In fact, the whole economic expansion, the SD suggested, had now reached its limits. Further pressure on the work-force would result only in declining performance and production.[14]

'Growing unrest and discontent' as a consequence of living, working, and housing conditions was reported among the working class of one of the most industrialized regions, the Ruhr District, in early 1939.[15] By summer, reports from the same area were pointing to the sharp rise in the cases of sickness among industrial workers in armaments factories and coal-mines – whether, as some claimed, from 'lack of discipline', or, more likely, from genuine overwork, or from a combination of both can only be surmised.[16] By then, the labour situation was described as 'catastrophic'.[17] Yet sullen apathy, not rebelliousness, characterized a work-force worn down by intensified production demands.[18] Even so, if the industrial working class was politically neutralized, its productive capacity had by all accounts reached its peak. This in itself posed an evident threat to any long-term preparations for war.

Hitler showed no interest in the details of economic difficulties pouring in from every part of the Reich. He was sensitive, as he had been in the mid 1930s, to the impact on morale, refusing in 1938 to entertain any rise in food prices.[19] But he had become increasingly preoccupied with foreign policy. Domestic issues were largely pushed to one side. Decisions were left untaken; much business was postponed or neglected; access to him was difficult. Even Lammers, in the absence of cabinet meetings now the sole link with the various government ministers, had been forced to plead with the Führer's chief adjutant, Wilhelm Brückner, on 21 October 1938 for a brief audience with Hitler to discuss urgent business since, because of the demands of foreign policy, he had managed only one short meeting with him since 4 September.[20] The reports of the 'Trustees of Labour' (*Treuhänder der Arbeit*) had normally been passed to Lammers and often brought directly to Hitler's attention in 1937. But in 1938–9, as the labour crisis became acute, Hitler was verbally informed of the content, emphasizing the seriousness of the mounting labour problems, on only one occasion (at the meeting with Lammers in early September 1938) and most of the reports, regarded as highly repetitive, were by now not even reaching Lammers.[21]

With regard to agriculture, Hitler's disinterest was even more marked. He simply refused to accede to Darré's repeated requests for an audience and did not respond to the Agriculture Minister's bombardment of the Reich Chancellery with memoranda about the critical situation. Only in October 1940 was Hitler finally persuaded to comment on the intense bitterness in the farming community about the labour shortage. He replied that their complaints would be attended to after the war.[22]

This reflected a key feature of Hitler's thinking: war as panacea. Whatever the difficulties, they would be – and could only be – resolved by war. He was certainly alert to the dangers of a collapse in his popularity, and the likely domestic crisis which would then occur.[23] The fears of a repeat of 1918 were never far away.[24] He even seemed to sense that his own massive popularity had shaky foundations. 'Since I've been politically active, and especially since I've been leading the Reich,' he told his audience of newspaper editors in November 1938, 'I have had only successes . . . What would then happen if we were some time to experience failure? That, too, could happen, gentlemen.'[25] But he was speaking here of the 'intellectual strata', for whom he felt in any case nothing but contempt. If he took cognizance at all of the reports of poor mood among industrial workers and farmers, they must merely have confirmed his view that he had been correct all along: only war and expansion could provide the answer to Germany's problems.

It is, in fact, doubtful whether he would have believed the accounts of poor morale, even if he had read them. Even three years or so earlier, when his adjutant at the time, Fritz Wiedemann, had tried to summarize the content of negative opinion reports, Hitler had refused to listen, shouting: 'The mood in the people is not bad, but good. I know that better. It's made bad through such reports. I forbid such things in future.'[26] On the day Poland was invaded he would say to members of the Reichstag: 'Don't anyone tell me that in his Gau or his district, or his constituency (Gruppe), or his cell the mood could at some point be bad. You are responsible for the mood.'[27] In April 1939, he took the adulation of the crowds at his fiftieth birthday celebrations, which, he claimed, had given him new strength, as the true indication of the mood of the people.[28] Following one extraordinary triumph upon another, his self-belief had by this time been magnified into full-blown megalomania. Even among his private guests at the Berghof, he frequently compared himself with Napoleon, Bismarck, and other great historical figures.[29] The rebuilding programmes that constantly preoccupied him were envisaged as his own lasting monument – a testament of greatness like the buildings of the Pharaohs or Caesars.[30] He felt he was walking with destiny. Such a mentality allowed little space for the daily worries and concerns of ordinary people. It was much the same when Schacht or Göring brought the deteriorating economic situation to his attention. Such problems were, in his view, a mere passing phenomemon, a temporary irritant of no significance compared with the grandeur of his vision and the magnitude of the struggle ahead. Conventional economics – however limited his under-standing – would, he was certain, never solve the problems. The sword alone, as he had repeatedly advocated since the 1920s, would produce the solution: the conquest of the 'living space' needed for survival. The lands of the East would one day provide for Germany. There would be no economic problems then. The opportunities awaited. But they had to be grasped quickly. His enemies – he had said so after Munich – were puny. But they were gathering strength. There was no time to lose.

It was a bizarre mentality. But in the summer of 1939, such a mentality was driving Germany towards European war. All along the way, Hitler had pushed at open doors. Revanchism and revisionism had given him his platform. Foreign Ministry mandarins, captains of industry, and above all the leaders of the armed forces had done everything – in their own interest – to 'work towards the Führer' in destroying Versailles and Locarno, pushing for economic expansion, building up a war machine. The weakened and divided western powers had given way at every step. They had provided the international backcloth to the expansion of Hitler's power, to the diplomatic triumphs cheered to the echo by millions. The exalting of Hitler's prestige had in turn elevated him to a position where he was held in awe even by his close entourage. The Führer cult removed him more and more from criti-cism, undermined opposition, inordinately strengthened his own hand against those who had done everything to build him up but now found themselves sidelined or bypassed. The traditional national-conservative power-élites had helped to make Hitler. But he now towered above them.[31] The major shifts in personnel in the army leadership and Foreign Ministry in February 1938, and the great foreign-policy triumphs that followed, had removed the last possible constraining influences. Surrounded by lackeys, yes-men, and time-servers, Hitler's power was by this time absolute. He could decide over war and peace.[32]

I

Hitler made public the abrupt shift in policy towards Poland and Great Britain in his big Reichstag speech of 28 April 1939.

The speech, lasting two hours and twenty minutes, had been occasioned by a message sent by President Roosevelt a fortnight earlier.[33] Prompted by the invasion of Czecho-Slovakia, and in direct response to the German dictator's aggressive speech in Wilhelmshaven on 1 April, the President had appealed to Hitler to give an assurance that he would desist from any attack for the next twenty-five years on thirty named countries – mainly European, but also including Iraq, Arabia, Syria, Palestine, Egypt, and Iran. Were such an assurance to be given, the United States, declared Roosevelt, would play its part in working for disarmament and equal access to raw materials on world markets.[34] Hitler was incensed by Roosevelt's telegram. That it had been published in Washington before even being received in Berlin was taken as a slight. Hitler also thought it arrogant in tone.[35] And the naming of the thirty countries allowed Hitler to claim that inquiries had been conducted in each, and that none felt threatened by Germany. Some, such as Syria, however, had been, he alleged, unable to reply, since they were deprived of freedom and under the military control of democratic states, while the Republic of Ireland, he asserted, feared aggression from Britain, not from Germany.[36] Roosevelt's raising of the disarmament issue (out of which Hitler had made such capital a few years earlier) handed him a further propaganda gift. With heavy sarcasm, he tore into Roosevelt, 'answering' his claims in twenty-one points, each cheered to the rafters by the assembled members of the Reichstag, roaring with laughter as he poured scorn on the President.[37]

He returned to the Reich Chancellery drenched in sweat, ready for the hot bath that had been prepared for him.[38] Civil servants in the Foreign Ministry thought he had 'lashed out' (*ausgekeilt*) in all directions, which Hitler took as a compliment. Many German listeners to the broadcast thought it one of the best speeches he had made.[39] William Shirer, the American journalist in Berlin, was inclined to agree: 'Hitler was a superb actor today,' he wrote.[40] The performance was largely for internal consumption. The outside world – at least those countries that felt they had accommodated Hitler for too long – were less impressed.

Preceding the vaudeville, Hitler had chosen the occasion to renounce the Non-Aggression Pact with Poland and the Naval Agreement with Britain.

Memoranda to this effect had been handed over by the German embassies in Warsaw and London to coincide with the timing of the speech. Hitler, repeating his admiration for the British Empire, his search for an understanding, and that his only demand on Britain was the return of the former German colonies, blamed the renunciation of the naval pact on Britain's 'encirclement policy'.[41] In reality, he was complying with the interests of the German navy, which felt its construction plans restricted by the pact and had been pressing for some time for Hitler to renounce it.[42] The intransigence of the Poles over Danzig and the Corridor, their mobilization in March – in Hitler's eyes almost as big an affront as the Czech mobilization the previous May – and the alignment with Britain against Germany were given as reasons for the ending of the Polish pact.[43] The reasons were scarcely regarded as compelling outside Germany.

Since the end of March, which had brought the British guarantee for Poland, followed soon afterwards by the announcement that there was to be a British–Polish mutual assistance treaty, Hitler had, in fact, given up on the Poles. The military directives of early April were recognition of this. The Poles, he acknowledged, were not going to concede to German demands without a fight. So they would have their fight. And they would be smashed. Only the timing and conditions remained to be determined.

Hitler's new aggressive stance towards Poland was certain of a warm welcome throughout the regime's leadership, even among those who had opposed the high risk on Czecho-Slovakia the previous summer, and among broad swathes of the German population. The traditional anti-Polish sentiment in the Foreign Ministry was reflected in the relish with which Weizsäcker had conveyed the news to the Poles in early April that Germany was ending all negotiations.[44] Anti-Polish feeling in the military was also rampant. Military leaders – even those with little time for Hitler – were enthusiastic about a revision of the disputed borders with Poland where they had been cool about Czecho-Slovakia. Ordinary soldiers were raring to be let loose at the Poles.[45] The commanders of the armed forces' branches were, moreover, better integrated from the outset into the military planning on Poland than they had been in the early stages of the Sudeten crisis.[46] Despite the British guarantee, they had greater confidence than the previous year in Hitler pulling off yet another coup, and fewer fears of western involvement.[47]

At a meeting in his study in the New Reich Chancellery on 23 May, Hitler outlined his thinking on Poland and on wider strategic issues to a small group of top military leaders. The main points of his speech were noted down by his Wehrmacht Adjutant Lieutenant-Colonel Rudolf Schmundt. It was a frank address, even if some points (according to the noted record) were left ambiguous. It held out the prospect not only of an attack on Poland, but also made clear that the more far-reaching aim was to prepare for an inevitable showdown with Britain. Unlike the meeting on 5 November 1937 that Hoßbach had recorded, there is no indication that the military commanders were caused serious disquiet by what they heard. As on that occasion, the meeting had been called to deal with questions of raw materials allocation, arising from the priority that had been given in January to the naval Z-Plan.[48] As then, Hitler did not deal with such specifics, but launched into a broad assessment of strategy, this time regarding Poland and the West. Other countries, including the Soviet Union, were scarcely touched upon.

Significantly – and an indication that reports of the mounting difficulties had not passed him by – Hitler began by emphasizing the need to solve Germany's economic problems. His answer was the one he had been rehearsing for over fifteen years, though it was now more plainly stated than it had been in his first speech to military leaders on being appointed Chancellor, over six years earlier. 'This is not possible without "breaking in" to other countries or attacking other people's possessions,' he baldly stated. In characteristic vein he continued: 'Living space proportionate to the greatness of the State is fundamental to every Power. One can do without it for a time, but sooner or later the problems will have to be solved by hook or by crook. The alternatives are rise or decline. In fifteen or twenty years' time the solution will be forced upon us. No German statesman can shirk the problem for longer.'

He turned to Poland. The Poles would always stand on the side of Germany's enemies. The Non-Aggression Treaty had not altered this in the least. He made his intentions brutally clear. 'It is not Danzig that is at stake. For us it is a matter of expanding our living space in the East and making food supplies secure and also solving the problem of the Baltic States. Food supplies can only be obtained from thinly populated areas. Over and above fertility, thorough German cultivation will tremendously increase the produce. No other openings can be seen in Europe.' Colonies were no answer, he averred, since they were always subject to blockade by sea. In the event of war with the West, the territories in the East would provide food and labour.

He moved from economic to strategic considerations. The problem of Poland could not be dissociated from the showdown with the West. The

Poles would cave in to Russian pressure. And they would seek to exploit any German military involvement with the western powers. He drew the conclusion from this that it was necessary 'to attack Poland at the first suitable opportunity. We cannot expect a repetition of Czechia. There will be war. Our task is to isolate Poland. Success in isolating her will be decisive.' He reserved to himself, therefore, the timing of any strike. Simultaneous conflict with the West had to be avoided. Should it, however, come to that – Hitler revealed here his priorities – 'then the fight must be primarily against England and France'. He repeated – directly contradicting himself, if Schmundt's notes are accurate – that the attack on Poland would only be successful if the West were kept out of it, but if that proved impossible 'it is better to fall upon the West and finish off Poland at the same time'.

For the first time, there was less than outright hostility in his comments about the Soviet Union. Economic relations would only be possible, he said, once political relations had improved – an oblique reference to comments made by the new Soviet Foreign Minister Molotov a few days earlier.[49] He did not, as had previously been the case, rule out such an improvement. He even suggested that Russia might be disinterested in the destruction of Poland.

His main concern was the coming showdown with the West, particularly with Britain. He doubted the possibility of peaceful coexistence in the long run. So it was necessary to prepare for conflict. A contest over hegemony, he implied (as he had done privately to Goebbels earlier in the year), was unavoidable. 'Therefore England is our enemy and the showdown with England is a matter of life and death.' He speculated on what the showdown would be like – speculations not remote from what was to happen a year later. Holland and Belgium would have to be overrun. Declarations of neutrality would be ignored. Once France, too, was defeated (which he did not dwell upon as a major difficulty), the bases on the west coast would enable the Luftwaffe and U-boats to effect the blockade that would bring Britain to its knees. The war would be an all-out one: 'We must then burn our boats and it will no longer be a question of right or wrong but of to be or not to be for 80 million people.' A war of ten to fifteen years had to be reckoned with. A long war had, therefore, to be prepared for, even though every attempt would be made to deliver a surprise knock-out blow at the outset – possible only if Germany avoided 'sliding into' war with Britain as a result of Poland. Clearly, Hitler was here, too, envisaging the elimination of Poland *before* any conflict with the West took place.[50]

Decisive in the conflict with Britain – and here Hitler indirectly provided the answer on raw materials allocation, and showed himself at the same time strategically still locked in the past – would not be air-power but the destruction of the British fleet. How, exactly, this would be achieved was not clarified. A special operations staff of the armed forces was to be set up to prepare the ground in detail and keep Hitler informed. 'The aim is always to bring England to its knees,' he stated.

Only Göring responded at the end of the forthright, if rambling, address. Not surprisingly, he wanted to hear something concrete about the priorities for raw materials, and about the likely timing of the conflict with the West. Hitler replied, vaguely, that the branches of the armed forces would determine what was to be constructed. On naval requirements, however, he was adamant, as his remarks had indicated: 'Nothing will be changed in the shipbuilding programme.' To the relief of those present, who took it as an indication of when he envisaged the conflict with the West taking place, he stipulated that the rearmament programmes were to be targeted at 1943–4 – the same time-scale he had given in November 1937. But no one doubted that Hitler intended to attack Poland that very year.[51]

II

Throughout the spring and summer frenzied diplomatic efforts were made to try to isolate Poland and deter the western powers from becoming involved in what was intended as a localized conflict. On the day before Hitler's address to his military leaders, Italy and Germany had signed the so-called 'Pact of Steel', meant to warn Britain and France off backing Poland.[52] The Italians had been soured by being kept in the dark about the invasion of Czecho-Slovakia. 'Every time Hitler occupies a country he sends me a message,' Mussolini had lamented.[53] But Ribbentrop had striven to mend fences. The Italian annexation of Albania in early April – partly to show the Germans they could do it too – had been applauded by Berlin. The Japanese, interested only in an anti-Soviet alliance and keen to avoid any commitments involving the West, adamantly refused to fall in with Ribbentrop's grand plan and establish a tripartite pact.[54] But the pompous German Foreign Minister – even Hitler described him as swollen-headed – duped the Italians into signing a bilateral military pact on the understanding that the Führer wanted peace for five years and expected the Poles to settle peacefully once they realized that support from the West would not be forthcoming.[55]

In the attempt to secure the assistance or benevolent neutrality of a number of smaller European countries and prevent them being drawn into the Anglo-French orbit, the German government had mixed success. In the west, Belgian neutrality – whatever Hitler's plans to ignore it when it suited him – was shored up to keep the western powers from immediate proximity to Germany's industrial heartlands. Every effort had been made in preceding years to promote trading links with the neutral countries of Scandinavia to sustain, above all, the vital imports of iron ore from Sweden and Norway.[56] In the Baltic, Latvia and Estonia agreed non-aggression pacts. But in central Europe, diplomatic efforts had more patchy results. Hungary, Yugoslavia, and Turkey were unwilling to align themselves closely with Berlin. Turkey could not be prevented from siding officially with Britain. But even here, Turkey's need for good relations with Germany meant a willingness to provide the vital supplies of chrome. Economic penetration of the Balkans had, moreover, ensured that copper and other minerals would be forthcoming from Yugoslavia. And persistent pressure had turned Romania into an economic satellite, sealed by treaty in late March 1939, more or less assuring Germany of crucial access to Romanian oil and wheat in the event of hostilities.[57]

The big question-mark concerned the Soviet Union. The regime's antichrist it might be. But it held the key to the destruction of Poland. If the USSR could be prevented from linking hands with the West in the tripartite pact that Britain and France were half-heartedly working towards; better still, if the unthinkable – a pact between the Soviet Union and the Reich itself – could be brought about: then Poland would be totally isolated, at Germany's mercy, the Anglo-French guarantees worthless, and Britain – the main opponent – hugely weakened. Such thoughts began to gestate in the mind of Hitler's Foreign Minister in the spring of 1939.[58] In the weeks that followed, it was Ribbentrop on the German side, rather than a hesitant Hitler, who took the initiative in seeking to explore all hints that the Russians might be interested in a rapprochement – hints that had been forthcoming since March.[59]

Within the Soviet leadership, the entrenched belief that the West wanted to encourage German aggression in the East (that is, against the USSR), the recognition that following Munich collective security was dead, the need to head off any aggressive intent from the Japanese in the east, and above all the desperate need to buy time to secure defences for the onslaught thought certain to come at some time, pushed – if for a considerable time only tentatively – in the same direction.[60] However, Stalin kept his options open.

Not until August was the door finally closed on a pact with the foot-dragging western powers.[61]

Stalin's speech to the Communist Party Congress on 10 March, attacking the appeasement policy of the West as encouragement of German aggression against the Soviet Union, and declaring his unwillingness to 'pull the chestnuts out of the fire' for the benefit of capitalist powers, had been taken by Ribbentrop, so he later claimed, as a hint that an opportunity might be opening up. He showed the speech to Hitler, asking for authorization to check what Stalin wanted. Hitler was hesitant. He wanted to await developments.[62] Ribbentrop nevertheless put out cautious feelers. The unofficial response was encouraging. But Ribbentrop thought Hitler would disapprove, and did not bring it to his attention.[63] By mid-April, however, the Soviet Ambassador was remarking to Weizsäcker that ideological differences should not hinder better relations.[64] Still there was no response from Hitler. He remained unconvinced when Gustav Hilger, a long-serving diplomat in the German Embassy in Moscow, was brought to the Berghof to explain that the dismissal of the Soviet Foreign Minister Maxim Litvinov (who had been associated with retaining close ties with the West, partly through a spell as Soviet Ambassador to the USA, and was moreover a Jew), and his replacement by Vyacheslav Molotov, Stalin's right-hand man, had to be seen as a sign that the Soviet dictator was looking for an agreement with Germany.[65]

Again it was Ribbentrop who was stirred by the suggestion.[66] He heard around the same time from the German ambassador in Moscow, Count Friedrich Werner von der Schulenburg, that the Soviet Union was interested in a rapprochement with Germany.[67] He scented a coup which would dramatically turn the tables on Britain, the country which had dared to spurn him – a coup that would also win him glory and favour in the Führer's eyes, and his place in history as the architect of Germany's triumph. Hitler for his part thought that Russian economic difficulties and the chance spotted by 'the wily fox' Stalin to remove any threat from Poland to the Soviet western borders were at the back of any opening towards Germany. His own interests were to isolate Poland and deter Britain.[68]

Ribbentrop was now able to persuade Hitler to agree to the Soviet requests for resumption of trade negotiations with Moscow, which had been broken off the previous February.[69] Molotov told Schulenburg, however, that a 'political basis' would have to be found before talks could be resumed. He left unclear what he had in mind.[70] Hitler again poured cold water on Ribbentrop's eagerness to begin political talks. Weizsäcker's view was that the Foreign Minister's notions of offering mediation in the Soviet conflict with Japan and hinting at partition of Poland would be rejected 'with a peal of Tartar laughter'.[71] Deep suspicions on both sides led to relations cooling again throughout June. Molotov continued to stonewall and keep his options open. Desultory economic discussions were just kept alive. But at the end of June, Hitler, irritated by the difficulties raised by the Soviets in the trade discussions, ordered the ending of all talks.[72] This time the Soviets took the initiative. Within three weeks they were letting it be known that trade talks could be resumed, and that the prospects for an economic agreement were favourable.[73] This was the signal Berlin had been waiting for. Schulenburg in Moscow was ordered to 'pick up the threads again'.[74]

Four days later, Ribbentrop's Russian expert in the Foreign Ministry's Trade Department, Karl Schnurre, invited the Soviet Chargé d'Affaires Georgei Astakhov and trade representative Evengy Babarin to dinner in Berlin. Acting under detailed instructions from the Foreign Minister himself, he indicated that the trade agreement could be accompanied by a political understanding between Germany and the Soviet Union, taking into account their mutual territorial interests. The response was encouraging.[75] Within three days Ribbentrop was directing Schulenburg to put the same points directly to Molotov. Schnurre wrote himself to Schulenburg: 'Politically, the problem of Russia is being dealt with here with *extreme urgency*.' He was in daily contact with Ribbentrop, he stated, who in turn was in constant touch with the Führer. Ribbentrop was concerned to obtain a breakthrough in the Russian question, to disturb Soviet–British negotiations, but also to bring about an understanding with Germany. 'Hence the haste with which we sent you the last instructions.'[76] Molotov was non-committal and somewhat negative when he met Schulenburg on 3 August. But two days later, through his informal contacts with Schnurre, Astakhov was letting Ribbentrop know that the Soviet government was seriously interested in the 'improvement of mutual relations', and willing to contemplate political negotiations.[77]

Towards the end of July, Hitler, Ribbentrop, and Weizsäcker had devised the basis of an agreement with the Soviet Union involving the partition of Poland and the Baltic states.[78] Hints about such an arrangement were dropped to Molotov during his meeting with Schulenburg on 3 August.[79] But Stalin was in no rush. And by now he had learned what the Germans were up to, and the broad timing of the intended action against the Poles.[80] But for Hitler there was not a moment to lose. The attack on Poland could not be delayed. Autumn rains, he told Count Ciano in mid-August, would turn the roads into a morass and Poland into 'one vast swamp . . . completely unsuitable for any military operations'. The strike had to come by the end of the month.[81]

I I I

Hitler, meanwhile, did everything possible to obscure what he had in mind to the general public in Germany and to the outside world. He had told the NSDAP's press agency in mid-July to publish the dates of the 'Reich Party Rally of Peace' – longer than ever before, and scheduled to take place at Nuremberg on 2–11 September 1939. It was also announced that he would attend a huge gathering, expected to attract 100,000 people, on 27 August to celebrate the twenty-fifth anniversary of the Battle of Tannenberg.[82] By then, detailed military plans to launch the attack to destroy Poland no later than 1 September had been in existence for several weeks.[83]

Remarkably, for the best part of three months during this summer of high drama, with Europe teetering on the brink of war, Hitler was almost entirely absent from the seat of government in Berlin. Much of the time, as always, when not at his alpine eyrie above Berchtesgaden, he was travelling around Germany. Early in June he visited the construction site of the Volkswagen factory at Fallersleben, where he had laid the foundation stone a year or so earlier. From there it was on to Vienna, to the 'Reich Theatre Week', where he saw the première of Richard Strauß's *Friedenstag*, regaling his adjutants with stories of his visits to the opera and theatre there thirty years earlier, and lecturing them on the splendours of Viennese architecture. Before leaving, he visited the grave of his niece, Geli Raubal (who had shot herself in mysterious circumstances in his Munich flat in 1931). He flew on to Linz, where he criticized new worker flats because they lacked the balconies he deemed essential in every apartment. From there he was driven to Berchtesgaden via Lambach, Hafeld, and Fischlham – some of the places associated with his childhood and where he had first attended school.[84]

At the beginning of July, he was in Rechlin in Mecklenburg, inspecting new aircraft prototypes, including the He 176, the first rocket-propelled plane, with a speed of almost 1,000 kilometres an hour. Whenever he expressed particular interest, Göring told him that everything would be done to ensure it would soon be ready for service. No one dared explain that their deployment lay in the distant future.[85]

Then in the middle of the month Hitler attended an extraordinary four-day spectacular in Munich, the 'Rally of German Art 1939', culminating in a huge parade with massive floats and extravagant costumes of bygone ages to illustrate 2,000 years of German cultural achievement.[86] Less than a week later he paid his regular visit to the Bayreuth festival. At Haus Wahnfried, in the annexe that the Wagner family had set aside specially for his use, Hitler felt relaxed. There he was 'Uncle Wolf', as he had been known by the Wagners since his early days in politics. While in Bayreuth, looking self-conscious in his white dinner-jacket, he attended performances of *Der fliegende Holländer*, *Tristan und Isolde*, *Die Walküre*, and *Götterdämmerung*, greeting the crowds as usual from the window on the first floor.[87]

There was also a second reunion (following their meeting the previous year in Linz) with his boyhood friend August Kubizek. They spoke of the old days in Linz and Vienna, going to Wagner operas together. Kubizek sheepishly asked Hitler to sign dozens of autographs to take back for his acquaintances. Hitler obliged. The overawed Kubizek, the archetypal local-government officer of a sleepy small town, carefully blotted every signature. They went out for a while, reminiscing in the gathering dusk by Wagner's grave. Then Hitler took Kubizek on a tour of Haus Wahnfried. Kubizek reminded his former friend of the *Rienzi* episode in Linz all those years ago. (Wagner's early opera, based on the story of a fourteenth-century 'tribune of the people' in Rome, had so excited Hitler that late at night, after the performance, he had hauled his friend up the Freinberg, a hill on the edge of Linz, and regaled him about the meaning of what they had seen.) Hitler recounted the tale to Winifried Wagner, ending by saying, with a great deal more pathos than truth: 'That's when it began.' Hitler probably believed his own myth. Kubizek certainly did. Emotional and impressionable as he always had been, and now a well-established victim of the Führer cult, he departed with tears in his eyes. Shortly afterwards, he heard the crowds cheering as Hitler left.[88]

Hitler spent most of August at the Berghof. Other than when he had important visitors to see, daily life there retained its usual patterns. The routine was more relaxed than in Berlin, but its rituals were equally fixed and tedious. Lengthy midday meals, dominated by the sound of Hitler's voice, the arrival of the press reports (typed in large letters on the special 'Führer typewriter', and usually necessitating the household to search for the misplaced reading glasses that he refused to be seen wearing in public), walks down the hill to the 'Tea House' for afternoon tea or coffee and cakes (usually producing further monologues on favourite themes), an evening snack followed by a film and more late-night talk for those unable to escape. Magda Goebbels told Ciano of her boredom. 'It is always Hitler who talks!'

he recalled her saying. 'He can be Führer as much as he likes, but he always repeats himself and bores his guests.'[89]

If less so than in Berlin, strict formalities were still observed. The atmosphere was stuffy, especially in Hitler's presence. Only Eva Braun's sister, Gretl, lightened it somewhat, even smoking (which was much frowned upon), flirting with the orderlies, and determined to have fun whatever dampening effect the Führer might have on things. What little humour otherwise surfaced was often in dubious taste in the male-dominated household, where the women in attendance, including Eva Braun, served mainly as decoration. But in general, the tone was one of extreme politeness, with much kissing of hands, and expressions of 'Gnädige Frau'.[90] Despite Nazi mockery of the bourgeoisie, life at the Berghof was imbued with the intensely bourgeois manners and fashions of the *arriviste* Dictator.

Hitler's lengthy absence from Berlin, while European peace hung by a thread, illustrates how far the disintegration of anything resembling a conventional central government had gone. Few ministers were permitted to see Hitler. Even the usual privileged few had dwindled in number. Goebbels – the most hated man in Germany according to Rosenberg (who, as the Party's self-professed ideological 'expert' was himself detested so much for his radical attacks on the Christian Churches, and ought to have been a good judge) – was still out of favour following his affair with Lida Baarova.[91] Göring had not recovered the ground he had lost since Munich.[92] Speer enjoyed the special status of the protégé. He spent much of the summer at Berchtesgaden.[93] But most of the time he was indulging Hitler's passion for architecture, not discussing details of foreign policy. Hitler's 'advisers' on the only issue of real consequence, the question of war and peace, were now largely confined to Ribbentrop, even more hawkish, if anything, than he had been the previous summer, and the military leaders. On the crucial matters of foreign policy, Ribbentrop – when not represented through the head of his personal staff, Walther Hewel, far more liked by the Dictator and everyone else than the preening Foreign Minister himself – largely had the field to himself. The second man at the Foreign Ministry, Weizsäcker, left to mind the shop while his boss absented himself from Berlin, claimed not to have seen Hitler, even from a distance, between May and the middle of August. What the Dictator was up to on the Obersalzberg was difficult to fathom in Berlin, Weizsäcker added.[94]

The personalization of government in the hands of one man – amounting in this case to concentration of power to determine over war or peace – was as good as complete.

IV

Danzig, allegedly the issue dragging Europe towards war, was in reality no more than a pawn in the German game being played from Berchtesgaden. Gauleiter Albert Forster – a thirty-seven-year-old former Franconian bank clerk who had learnt some of his early political lessons under Julius Streicher and had been leader of the NSDAP in Danzig since 1930 – had received detailed instructions from Hitler on a number of occasions throughout the summer on how to keep tension simmering without allowing it to boil over. As had been the case in the Sudetenland the previous year, it was important not to force the issue too soon.[95] Local issues had to chime exactly with the timing determined by Hitler. Incidents were to be manufactured to display to the population in the Reich, and to the world outside, the alleged injustices perpetrated by the Poles against the Germans in Danzig. Instances of mistreatment – most of them contrived, some genuine – of the German minority in other parts of Poland, too, provided regular fodder for an orchestrated propaganda campaign which, again analogous to that against the Czechs in 1938, had been screaming its banner headlines about the iniquities of the Poles since May.

The propaganda certainly had its effect. The fear of war with the western powers, while still widespread among the German population, was – at least until August – nowhere near as acute as it had been during the Sudeten crisis. People reasoned, with some justification (and backed up by the German press), that despite the guarantees for Poland, the West was hardly likely to fight for Danzig when it had given in over the Sudetenland.[96] Many thought that Hitler had always pulled it off without bloodshed before, and would do so again.[97] Some had a naïve belief in Hitler. One seventeen-year-old girl recalled much later how she and her friends had felt: 'Rumours of an impending war were spreading steadily but we did not worry unduly. We were convinced that Hitler was a man of peace and would do everything he could to settle things peacefully.'[98] Fears of war were nevertheless pervasive. The more general feeling was probably better summed up in the report from a small town in Upper Franconia at the end of July 1939: 'The answer to the question of how the problem "Danzig and the Corridor" is to be solved is still the same among the general public: incorporation in the Reich? Yes. Through war? No.'[99]

But the anxiety about a general war over Danzig did not mean that there was reluctance to see military action against Poland undertaken – as long as the West could be kept out of it. Inciting hatred of the Poles through propaganda was pushing at an open door. 'The mood of the people can be much more quickly whipped up against the Poles than against any other neighbouring people,' commented the exiled Social Democratic organization, the Sopade. Many thought 'it would serve the Poles right if they get it in the neck'.[100] Other reports from the Sopade's observers, whose anti-Nazi attitude needs no underlining, emphasize the impact the propaganda was having even among those hostile to the regime. Existing anti-Polish feelings were being massively sharpened. 'An action against Poland would be greeted by the overwhelming mass of the German people,' ran one report. 'The Poles are enormously hated among the masses for what they did at the end of the War.'[101] 'If Hitler strikes out against the Poles, he will have a majority of the population behind him,' commented another.[102] In Danzig, too, where, not surprisingly, fear of a war was especially pronounced, the daily reports about 'Polish terror' were manufacturing antagonism among those who had never been 'Pole haters'. Above all, no one, it was claimed, whatever their political standpoint, wanted a Polish Danzig; the conviction that Danzig was German was universal.[103]

The issue which the Danzig Nazis exploited to heighten the tension was the supervision of the Customs Office by Polish customs inspectors. These had indeed sometimes abused their position in the interests of increased Polish control over shipping. But there had been nothing serious, and matters could quite easily have been amicably resolved, or at least a *modus vivendi* reached, if that had been the intention. As it was, the customs officers were increasingly subjected to violent attacks.[104] This had the desired effect of keeping the tension in the Free City at fever pitch. When the customs inspectors were informed on 4 August – in what turned out to be an initiative of an over-zealous German official – that they would not be allowed to carry out their duties and responded with a threat to close the port to foodstuffs, the local crisis threatened to boil over, and too soon. The Germans reluctantly backed down – as the international press noted.[105] Forster was summoned to Berchtesgaden on 7 August and returned to announce that the Führer had reached the limits of his patience with the Poles, who were probably acting under pressure from London and Paris.[106]

This allegation was transmitted by Forster to Carl Burckhardt, the League of Nations High Commissioner in Danzig. Overlooking no possibility of trying to keep the West out of his war with Poland, Hitler was ready to use the representative of the detested League of Nations as his intermediary.[107]

On 10 August, during a dinner in honour of the departing Deputy Representative of Poland in Danzig, Tadeusz Perkowski, Burckhardt was summoned to the telephone to be told by Gauleiter Forster that Hitler wanted to see him on the Obersalzberg at 4p.m. next day and was sending his personal plane ready for departure early the following morning.[108] Following a flight in which he was regaled by a euphoric Albert Forster with tales of beerhall fights with Communists during the 'time of struggle', Burckhardt landed in Salzburg and, after a quick snack, was driven up the spiralling road beyond the Berghof itself and up to the Eagle's Nest (*Adlerhorst*), the recently built spectacular Tea House in the dizzy heights of the mountain peaks.[109]

Hitler was not fond of the Eagle's Nest and seldom went up there. He complained that the air was too thin at that height, and bad for his blood pressure.[110] He worried about an accident on the roads Bormann had had constructed up the sheer mountainside, and about a failure of the lift that had to carry its passengers from the huge, marble-faced hall cut inside the rock to the summit of the mountain, more than 150 feet above.[111] But this was an important visit. Hitler wanted to impress Burckhardt with the dramatic view over the mountain tops, invoking the image of distant majesty, of the dictator of Germany as lord of all he surveyed.[112]

The imperious image had been somewhat dented just after Burckhardt arrived, when one of the serving staff had managed to drop a heavy armchair on Hitler's foot and had him hopping in pain.[113] But he quickly recovered to play every register in driving home to Burckhardt – and through him to the western powers – the modesty and reasonableness of his claims on Poland and the futility of western support. It was a calculated attempt to keep the West out of the coming conflict. His voice rose in a crescendo of anger one moment, fell to feigned sadness and resignation the next. The threats gave way to hopes even at this stage of an arrangement with Britain. Almost speechless with rage, he denounced press suggestions that he had lost his nerve and been forced to give way over the issue of the Polish customs officers. His voice rising until he was shouting, he screamed his response to Polish ultimata: if the smallest incident should take place, he would smash the Poles without warning so that not a trace of Poland remained. If that meant general war, then so be it. He would not fight like Wilhelm II, held back by his conscience, but ruthlessly to the bitter end. He poured out, as usual, an array of facts and figures to demonstrate Germany's superiority in armaments. He could hold the western line, thanks to his fortifications, with seventy-four divisions. The rest of his forces would be hurled against Poland, which would be liquidated within three weeks. All he wanted was land in the east to feed Germany, and a single colony for timber. International trade offered no basis of security. Germany had to live from its own resources. That was the only issue; the rest nonsense. He emphasized more than once that he wanted nothing of the West, but demanded only a free hand in the East. He was ready, he said, to negotiate, but not when he was insulted and confronted with ultimata. He accused Britain and France of interference in the reasonable proposals he had made to the Poles. Now the Poles had taken up a position that blocked any agreement once and for all. His generals, hesitant the previous year, were this time raring to be let loose against the Poles.

Hitler took Burckhardt outside on to the terrace. He had had enough turmoil, he intimated. He needed the peace and quiet that he found there. Burckhardt enjoined that this lay in his hands more than any other person's. This was not so, replied Hitler in a low voice. If he knew that England and France were inciting Poland to war, he would prefer war 'this year rather than next'. But he was coming to the point of Burckhardt's visit. Were the Poles to leave Danzig in peace, he could wait. He was prepared for a pact with Britain, guaranteeing British possessions. For him, he repeated, it was a matter of grain and timber. He was ready for negotiations on this issue. 'But it will be another matter if they revile me and cover me with ridicule as in May last. I do not bluff. If the slightest thing happens in Danzig or to our minorities I shall hit hard.' Again shifting from threats to apparent reason, he suggested that a German-speaking Englishman, possibly General Ironside – tall, handsome, and dashing, but 'more bluff and brawn than brain', who had been dispatched to Poland by the British government for a time in July – should go to Berlin.[114]

Burckhardt, as intended, rapidly passed on to the British and French governments the gist of his talks with Hitler.[115] The dictator had seemed much older than when he had last met him, two years earlier, Burckhardt told his British and French contacts, and had been nervous, even anxious.[116] 'Hitler apparently undecided, rather distracted, rather aged,' was the laconic comment of Sir Alexander Cadogan, head of the Foreign Office.[117] No conclusions were drawn from Burckhardt's report other than to urge restraint on the Poles.[118]

While Hitler and Burckhardt were meeting at the Eagle's Nest on the Kehlstein, another meeting was taking place only a few miles away, in Ribbentrop's newly acquired splendrous residence overlooking the lake in Fuschl, not far from Salzburg. Count Ciano, resplendent in uniform, was learning from the German Foreign Minister, dressed, to his visitors' surprise, in casual civilian dress, that the Italians had been deceived for months about Hitler's intentions. The atmosphere was icy. Ribbentrop told Ciano that the 'merciless destruction of Poland by Germany' was inevitable. The conflict would not become a general one. Were Britain and France to intervene, they would be doomed to defeat. But his information 'and above all his *psychological knowledge*' of Britain, he insisted, made him rule out any intervention. Ciano found him unreasoning and obstinate. Discussion with him was pointless. He evaded all requests for details of Germany's plans by saying 'all decisions were still locked in the Führer's impenetrable bosom'. Dinner passed without a word. Ciano left after ten hours of discussion, greatly depressed, sure 'that he intends to provoke the conflict and will oppose any initiative which might have the effect of solving the present crisis peacefully'.[119] Ciano added in his diary: 'The decision to fight is implacable. He [Ribbentrop] rejects any solution which might give satisfaction to Germany and avoid the struggle.'[120]

The impression was reinforced when Ciano met Hitler at the Berghof the next day. Among the reasons put forward for the need to act, most of which echoed the points that had been made by Ribbentrop, Hitler again revealed the extent to which he was affected by matters of prestige. He claimed that Germany, as a great nation, could not tolerate the continued provocation by Poland 'without losing prestige'. He was convinced that the conflict would be localized, that Britain and France, whatever noises they were making, would not go to war. It would be necessary one day to fight the western democracies. But he thought it 'out of the question that this struggle can begin now'.[121] Ciano noted that he realized immediately 'that there is no longer anything that can be done. He has decided to strike, and strike he will.'[122]

Important news came through for Hitler at the very time that he was underlining to the disenchanted Ciano his determination to attack Poland no later than the end of August: the Russians were prepared to begin talks in Moscow, including the position of Poland. A beaming Ribbentrop took the telephone call at the Berghof. Hitler was summoned from the meeting with Ciano, and rejoined it in high spirits to report the breakthrough.[123] The way was now open.

The idea seems initially to have been to send Hans Frank, the Nazis' chief legal expert, who had been involved in the talks producing the Axis in 1936, to Moscow to conduct negotiations.[124] But by 14 August Hitler had decided to send Ribbentrop.[125] A flurry of diplomatic activity – Ribbentrop pressing with maximum urgency for the earliest possible agreement, Molotov cannily prevaricating until it was evident that Soviet interest in the Anglo-French mission was dead – unfolded during the following days.[126] The text of a trade treaty, under which German manufactured goods worth 200 million Reich Marks would be exchanged each year for an equivalent amount of Soviet raw materials, was agreed.[127] Finally, on the evening of 19 August, the chattering teleprinter gave Hitler and Ribbentrop, waiting anxiously at the Berghof, the news they wanted: Stalin was willing to sign a non-aggression pact without delay.[128]

Only the proposed date of Ribbentrop's visit – 26 August – posed serious problems. It was the date Hitler had set for the invasion of Poland.[129] Hitler could not wait that long. On 20 August, he decided to intervene personally. He telegraphed a message to Stalin, via the German Embassy in Moscow, requesting the reception of Ribbentrop, armed with full powers to sign a pact, on the 22nd or 23rd.[130] Hitler's intervention made a difference. But once more Stalin and Molotov made Hitler sweat it out. The tension at the Berghof was almost unbearable. It was more than twenty-four hours later, on the evening of 21 August, before the message came through. Stalin had agreed. Ribbentrop was expected in Moscow in two days' time, on 23 August. Hitler slapped himself on the knee in delight. Champagne all round was ordered – though Hitler did not touch any. 'That will really land them in the soup,' he declared, referring to the western powers.[131]

The news, announced just before midnight, struck like a bombshell. Most German citizens, once they had adjusted to the surprise, felt simply a sense of relief. The understanding with the unlikely new friends in the east had eliminated the threat of encirclement and a war on two fronts.[132] Older army leaders, schooled in the tradition of Seeckt's Reichswehr of good relations with Russia, felt the same way. Most presumed that Poland would now not dare to fight, and that the conflict would be resolved in much the same way as the Sudeten crisis of the previous year.[133] But reactions were mixed, even among the Nazi leadership. 'We're on top again. Now we can sleep more easily,' recorded a delighted Goebbels.[134] 'The question of Bolshevism is for the moment of secondary importance,' he later added, saying that was the Führer's view, too. 'We're in need and eat then like the devil eats flies.'[135]

For the dyed-in-the-wool old anti-Bolshevik Alfred Rosenberg, who hailed from the Baltic and had personal experience of conditions at the time of the Russian Revolution, the response was predictably different. 'A moral loss of respect in the light of our by now twenty-year long struggle,' was how he described the pact. Even so, he was prepared to attribute Hitler's

180-degree shift – the U-turn of all time – to necessity, and blamed Ribbentrop, whom he believed occupied the post of Foreign Minister that ought to have been his own, for destroying any hopes of the desired alliance with Britain.[136] In his dismay at the pact, but ready as always to place his trust in the Führer's judgement, Rosenberg undoubtedly spoke for most 'old fighters' of the Party.[137] A good number of SA men, veterans of many a street fight with the Communists, had even less sympathy with the dramatic change of course. Voices were heard that it was about time that *Mein Kampf* was taken out of the bookshops since Hitler was now doing the exact opposite of what he had written.[138] Heinrich Hoffmann, according to his later account, raised the reactions of the Party faithful with Hitler. 'My Party members know and trust me; they know I will never depart from my basic principles, and they will realize that the ultimate aim of this latest gambit is to remove the Eastern danger,' Hitler is said to have replied. But next morning the garden of the Brown House was reportedly littered with badges discarded by disillusioned Party members.[139]

Abroad, Goebbels remarked, the announcement of the imminent non-aggression pact was 'the great world sensation'.[140] But the response was not that which Hitler and Ribbentrop had hoped for. The Poles' fatalistic reaction was that the pact would change nothing.[141] In Paris, where the news of the Soviet–German pact hit especially hard, the French Foreign Minister Georges Bonnet, fearing a German–Soviet entente against Poland, pondered whether it was now better to press the Poles into compromise with Hitler in order to win time for France to prepare its defences.[142] But eventually, after dithering for two days, the French government agreed that France would remain true to its obligations.[143] The British cabinet, meeting on the afternoon of 22 August, was unmoved by the dramatic news, even if MPs were asking searching questions about the failure of British intelligence. The Foreign Secretary coolly, if absurdly, dismissed the pact as perhaps of not very great importance.[144] Instructions went out to embassies that Britain's obligations to Poland remained unaltered. Sir Nevile Henderson's suggestion of a personal letter from the Prime Minister to Hitler, warning him of Britain's determination to stick by Poland, was taken up.[145]

Meanwhile, in excellent mood on account of his latest triumph, Hitler prepared, on the morning of 22 August, to address all the armed forces' leaders on his plans for Poland. The meeting, at the Berghof, had been arranged before the news from Moscow had come through.[146] Hitler's aim was to convince the generals of the need to attack Poland without delay.[147] The diplomatic coup, by now in the public domain, can only have boosted his self-confidence. It certainly weakened any potential criticism from his audience.

The generals arrived mainly by plane, landing in Salzburg, Munich, or on the small airfield near Berchtesgaden, from where they were driven during the course of the morning to the Obersalzberg.[148] They were dressed in civilian clothing in order not to arouse particular attention – an objective not best furthered by Göring turning up in outlandish hunting garb.[149] General Liebmann had met Papen on the way through Salzburg. Papen told him that he had spoken with Hitler the previous evening, warning him not to risk war with England, where the chances of winning would be under 50 per cent. He had the feeling that his arguments had made no impression at all.[150] Around fifty officers (including the Führer's adjutants) had assembled in the Great Hall of the Berghof by the time that Hitler began his address at noon.[151] Ribbentrop was also present.[152] The generals were seated on rows of chairs. Hitler, leaning on the grand piano, spoke with barely a glance at the sparse notes he clutched in his left hand.[153] No minutes were taken. Those listening were explicitly told not to make any record of the proceedings.[154] One or two of those present, including Admiral Canaris, head of the Abwehr, ignored the instruction and surreptiously jotted down the main points. Others, including Chief of Staff Colonel-General Halder and Admiral-General Boehm, thought what they heard was so important that they hastily compiled a summary of what had gone on later that day.[155]

'It was clear to me that a conflict with Poland had to come sooner or later,' began Hitler. 'I had already made this decision in the spring, but I thought that I would first turn against the West in a few years, and only after that against the East.' Circumstances had caused him to change his thinking, he went on. He pointed in the first instance to his own importance to the situation. Making no concessions to false modesty, he claimed: 'Essentially all depends on me, on my existence, because of my political talents. Furthermore, the fact that probably no one will ever again have the confidence of the whole German people as I have. There will probably never again in the future be a man with more authority than I have. My existence is therefore a factor of great value. But I can be eliminated at any time by a criminal or a lunatic.' He also emphasized the personal role of Mussolini and Franco, whereas Britain and France lacked any 'outstanding personality'. He briefly alluded to Germany's economic difficulties as a further argument for not delaying action. 'It is easy for us to make decisions. We have nothing to lose; we have everything to gain. Because of our restrictions (*Einschränkungen*) our economic situation is such that we can only hold out for a few more years. Göring can confirm this. We have no other choice. We must act.' He reviewed the constellation of international forces, concluding: 'All these favourable circumstances will no longer prevail in two or three years' time. No one knows how much longer I shall live. Therefore, better a conflict now.'

In typical vein, he continued. It was better to test German arms now. The Polish situation had become intolerable. The initiative could not be handed to others. There was a danger of losing prestige. The high probability was that the West would not intervene. There was a risk, but it was the task of the politician as much as the general to confront risk with iron resolve. He had done this in the past, notably in the recovery of the Rhineland in 1936, and always been proved right. The risk had to be taken. 'We are faced,' he stated with his usual apocalyptic dualism, 'with the harsh alternatives of striking or of certain annihilation sooner or later.' He compared the relative arms strength of Germany and the western powers. He concluded that Britain was in no position to help Poland. Nor was there any interest in Britain in a long war. The West had vested its hopes in enmity between Germany and Russia. 'The enemy did not reckon with my great strength of purpose,' he boasted. 'Our enemies are small fry (*kleine Würmchen*). I saw them in Munich.' The pact with Russia would be signed within two days. 'Now Poland is in the position in which I want her.' There need be no fear of a blockade. The East would provide the necessary grain, cattle, coal, lead, and zinc. His only fear, Hitler said, in obvious allusion to Munich, was 'that at the last moment some swine or other will yet submit to me a plan for mediation'. Hinting at what was in his mind following the destruction of Poland, he added that the political objective went further. 'A start has been made on the destruction of England's hegemony. The way will be open for the soldiers after I have made the political preparations.' Göring thanked Hitler, assuring him that the Wehrmacht would do its duty, and around 1.30p.m. the meeting broke up for a light lunch on the terrace.[156]

After the lunch break, Hitler spoke again for about an hour, partly about operational details.[157] His broader remarks were now largely aimed at boosting fighting morale. Style and diction were inimitable, the sentiments brutally social-Darwinist. He repeated the need for 'iron determination'. The would be 'no shrinking back from anything'. It was a 'life and death struggle'. The destruction of Poland, even if war in the West were to break out, was the priority, and had to be settled quickly in view of the season. The aim was, he stated, somewhat unclearly, if with evident menace, 'to eliminate active forces (*Beseitigung der lebendigen Kräfte*), not to reach a definite line'.[158] He would provide a propaganda pretext for beginning the war, however implausible. He ended by summarizing his philosophy: 'The victor will not be asked afterwards whether he told the truth or not. When starting and waging a war it is not right that matters, but victory. Close your hearts to pity. Act brutally. Eighty million people must obtain what is their right. Their existence must be made secure. The stronger man is right. The greatest harshness.'[159]

The reactions of Hitler's audience were mixed. Some three months later General Liebmann, certainly no Hitler admirer, recalled his own feelings. He had heard some effective speeches by Hitler, he wrote, but this one lacked all objectivity and was full of illusions. 'Its bragging and brash tone was downright repulsive. One had the feeling that here a man spoke who had lost all feeling of responsibility and any clear conception of what a victorious war signified, and who, with unsurpassed wantonness, was determined to leap into the dark.' He thought that many, who left with grave faces or expressions of black humour, felt like he did.[160]

Probably this was the case. But if the generals were not enthused by what Hitler had to say, they posed no objections. The mood was largely fatalistic, resigned. After the war, Liebmann tried to summarize the broad impact of the speech. The assembled generals, he commented, were certain that the picture was less rosy than Hitler's description. But they took the view that it was too late for objections, and simply hoped things would turn out well.[161] No one spoke out against Hitler.[162] Brauchitsch, who ought to have replied if anyone were to do so, said nothing. Any objections on his part, in Liebmann's view, could only have been made as representing all the generals. Evidently he doubted whether Brauchitsch could have spoken for all. In any case, he thought such objections would have to have been raised by spring. By August it was too late. Liebmann added one other telling point. For Hitler it was only a matter of a war against Poland. And the army felt up to that.[163]

The disastrous collapse in the army's power since the first weeks of 1938 could not have been more apparent. Its still lamented former head, Werner von Fritsch, had remarked to Ulrich von Hassell some months earlier: 'This man – Hitler – is Germany's fate for good or evil. If it's now into the abyss, he'll drag us all with him. There's nothing to be done.'[164] It was an indication of the capitulation of the Wehrmacht leadership to Hitler's will. Hitler's own comments after the meeting indicated that, on the eve of war, he had little confidence in and much contempt for his generals.[165]

Towards the end of his speech, Hitler had broken off momentarily to wish his Foreign Minister success in Moscow. Ribbentrop left at that point to fly to Berlin. In mid-evening, he then flew in Hitler's private Condor to Königsberg and, after a restless and nervous night preparing notes for the negotiations, from there, next morning, on to the Russian capital.[166] So large was his retinue of around thirty persons (including Heinrich Hoffmann, to ensure the historic moment was captured on film, and do the profits of his family concern no harm in the process) that a second Condor was needed.[167] Within two hours of landing, Ribbentrop was in the Kremlin. Attended by Schulenburg (the German Ambassador in Moscow), he was taken to a long room where, to his surprise, not just Molotov, but Stalin himself, awaited him. Ribbentrop began by stating Germany's wish for new relations on a lasting basis with the Soviet Union. Stalin replied that, though the two countries had 'poured buckets of filth' over each other for years, there was no obstacle to ending the quarrel. Discussion quickly moved to delineation of spheres of influence. Stalin staked the USSR's claim to Finland, much of the territory of the Baltic states, and Bessarabia. Ribbentrop predictably brought up Poland, and the need for a demarcation line between the Soviet Union and Germany. This – to run along the rivers Vistula, San, and Bug – was swiftly agreed. Progress towards concluding a non-aggression pact was rapid. The territorial changes to accompany it, carving up eastern Europe between Germany and the Soviet Union, were contained in a secret protocol. The only delay occurred when Stalin's claims to the Latvian ports of Libau (Liepaja) and Windau (Ventspils) held up matters for a while. Ribbentrop felt he had to consult.[168]

Nervously waiting at the Berghof, Hitler had by then already had the Moscow embassy telephoned to inquire about progress at the talks.[169] He paced impatiently up and down on the terrace as the sky silhouetted the Unterberg in striking colours of turquoise, then violet, then fiery red. Below remarked that it pointed to a bloody war. If so, replied Hitler, the sooner the better. The more time passed, the bloodier the war would be.[170]

Within minutes there was a call from Moscow. Ribbentrop assured Hitler that the talks were going well, but asked about the Latvian ports. Inside half an hour Hitler had consulted a map and telephoned his reply: 'Yes, agreed.'[171] The last obstacle was removed. Back at the Kremlin in late evening there was a celebratory supper. Vodka and Crimean sparkling wine lubricated the already effervescent mood of mutual self-congratulation. Among the toasts was one proposed by Stalin to Hitler.[172] The texts of the Pact and Protocol had been drawn up in the meantime. Though dated 23 August, they were finally signed by Ribbentrop and Molotov well after

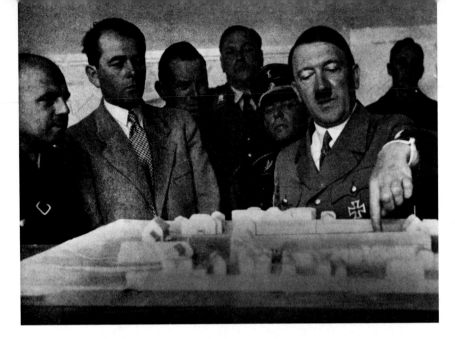

1. (*previous page*) Hitler, September 1936, portrayed wearing a suit and not the usual Party uniform.

2. (*above*) Hitler discussing plans in 1936 for new administrative buildings in Weimar with his up-and-coming favourite architect, Albert Speer. Fritz Sauckel, Reich Governor and Gauleiter of Thuringia, is on Hitler's right.

3. (*below*) The Berlin Olympics, 1936: the crowd salutes Hitler.

4. British Royalty at the Berghof. Hitler meets the Duke and Duchess of Windsor on 22 October 1937, during the visit to Germany of the ex-King Edward VIII and his wife, the former Mrs Wallis Simpson.

5. Field-Marshal Werner von Blomberg in 1937. He was to be dismissed from office as War Minister the following January on account of a scandal concerning his wife.

6. Colonel-General Werner Freiherr von Fritsch, Commander-in-Chief of the Army until his dismissal, in the wake of the Blomberg scandal, at the beginning of February 1938 on trumped-up charges of homosexuality.

7. Hitler addresses the exultant masses in Vienna's Heldenplatz on 15 March 1938, following the Anschluß.

8. (*facing page, above*) The Axis: flanked by Mussolini and King Victor-Emmanuel III, Hitler views a parade of troops in Rome during his visit to Italy in May 1938.

9. (*facing page, below*) Hitler is cheered by crowds of admirers in Florence.

10. Part of the exhibition 'The Eternal Jew', which opened in Munich on 8 November 1937 and ran until 31 January 1938, purporting to show the 'typical external features' of Jews and to demonstrate their supposedly Asiatic characteristics. The exhibition drew 412,300 visitors in all – over 5,000 per day. It helped to promote the sharp growth of anti-Semitic violence in Munich and elsewhere in Germany during 1938.

11. (*below*) 'Jews in Berlin', from the exhibition 'The Eternal Jew', which opened in the Reich capital on 12 November 1938. This was two days after Goebbels had unleashed a nation-wide orgy of violence in which Jewish property was destroyed throughout Germany, leading to mass arrests of Jews and their exclusion from business and commerce.

12. (*left*) The synagogue in Fasenenstraße, Berlin, burns after Nazi stormstroopers set it on fire during the pogrom of 9–10 November 1938.

13. (*right*) The Jewish Community building in Kassel on the morning after the pogrom. Beds, papers, and furniture, thrown out by the Nazi perpetrators, lie on the street. Onlookers and police watch as two people attempt to clear up.

14. Passers-by – some smiling, some looking in apparent bewilderment – outside a demolished and looted Jewish shop in Berlin. The amount of glass smashed by Nazi mobs gave rise to the sarcastic appellation 'Reichskristallnacht'.

15. (*left*) A model family? Reich Propaganda Minister Joseph Goebbels, his wife Magda, and their children Helga, Hilde, and baby Helmut, posing for the camera in 1936.

16. (*below*) Goebbels, broadcasting to the Germans on the eve of Hitler's fiftieth birthday, 20 April 1939. The Propaganda Minister's marriage had been under severe strain during the previous months on account of his affair with the Czech actress Lida Baarova, but for prestige reasons Hitler had insisted that Goebbels and his wife did not separate.

17. An unusual photograph, taken about 1938, of Eva Braun, Hitler's companion since 1932 – a relationship kept secret from the German public until 1945.

18. (*top*) With Hitler looking on, General Wilhelm Keitel, chief of the High Command of the Wehrmacht, greets the British Prime Minister, Neville Chamberlain, at the Berghof on 15 September 1938, during the Sudeten crisis.

19. German troops crossing the Charles Bridge in Prague in March 1939, a few days after Hitler had forced the Czech government to agree to the imposition of a German Protectorate over the country.

20. (*top*) Hitler's imposing 'study' in the Reich Chancellery, used more to impress visitors than for work.

21. Pomp and Circumstance: Hermann Göring addresses Hitler during a ceremonial occasion – probably on Hitler's birthday, 20 April 1939 – in the New Reich Chancellery, designed by Albert Speer and completed in early 1939.

22. (*top*) 'The Führer's birthday': Hitler is amused, on his forty-ninth birthday, 20 April 1938, when Ferdinand Porsche presents him with a model of the Volkswagen, pointing out that the engine is in the boot. None of the 336,000 Germans who ordered and paid for a car partly or in full ever took delivery of a Volkswagen. The vehicles were produced during the war exclusively for military purposes.

23. (*centre*) 'The Führer's birthday': Heinrich Himmler, head of the SS, gives Hitler his present – a valuable equestrian portrait of Frederick the Great by Adolf von Menzel – on the Führer's fiftieth birthday, 20 April 1939, watched by Sepp Dietrich (*centre*), commander of the SS-Leibstandarte Adolf Hitler, and (*extreme right*) Karl Wolff, chief of Himmler's personal staff.

24. (*bottom*) Hitler, in evening dress, walks with Winifred Wagner past cheering crowds during the last Bayreuth Festival before the war, in July 1939.

25. Molotov signs the Non-Aggression Pact of the Soviet Union with Germany in the early hours of 24 August 1939, watched by (*left to right*) Red Army Chief of Staff Marshal Boris S. Shaposhnikov, adjutant to Ribbentrop Richard Schulze, a smug-looking German Foreign Minister Joachim von Ribbentrop, and Joseph Stalin.

26. Hitler in his temporary field-headquarters during the Polish campaign, together with his Wehrmacht adjutants, (*from left to right*) Captain Nicolaus von Below (Luftwaffe), Captain Gerhard Engel (Army), and Colonel Rudolf Schmundt (chief adjutant). Martin Bormann is on Hitler's left.

27. (*top*) Hitler reviewing troops in Warsaw on 5 October 1939 at the conclusion of the victory over Poland.

28. Hitler during his address to the Party's 'Old Guard' in the Bürgerbräukeller in Munich on 8 November 1939. Only minutes after he had left the building, a time-bomb placed by a Swabian joiner, Georg Elser, exploded close to where he had been speaking, killing eight and injuring more than sixty of those present.

29. (*left*) Arthur Greiser, the fanatical Reich Governor and Gauleiter of Reichsgau Wartheland, the annexed part of western Poland, at the celebration for the 'liberation' of the area on 2 October 1939.

30. (*right*) Albert Forster, Gauleiter of Danzig-West Prussia, a rival to Greiser in the brutal attempt to 'germanize' the annexed parts of Poland.

31. (*left and right*) An ecstatic Hitler at his headquarters 'Wolfsschlucht' (Wolf's Gorge), near Bruly de Pêche in Belgium, on hearing the news on 17 June 1940 that France had requested an armistice. Walther Hewel, Ribbentrop's liaison at Führer Headquarters, is on Hitler's right.

32. (*top*) Hitler visiting emplacements on the Maginot Line in Alsace, during his short stay at his headquarters 'Tannenberg', near Freudenstadt in the Black Forest, on 30 June 1940.

33. Hitler in Freudenstadt on 5 July 1940, the last day he was based at 'Tannenberg'.

34. (*overleaf*) An immense crowd gathered on Wilhelmplatz in Berlin on 6 July 1940, wildly cheering the conquering hero on Hitler's return from the triumph over France. Göring is on Hitler's right on the balcony of the Reich Chancellery.

midnight.[173] Hitler and Goebbels had been half-watching a film, still too nervous about what was happening in Moscow to enjoy it. Finally, around 1a.m. Ribbentrop telephoned again: complete success. Hitler congratulated him.[174] 'That will hit like a bombshell,' he remarked.[175]

In fact, the impact abroad was somewhat lessened through the earlier announcement that an agreement was imminent.[176] Even so, the implications were obvious. 'A black day,' noted Sir Alexander Cadogan at the British Foreign Office.[177] Harold Nicolson, a critic of the Chamberlain government, felt 'stunned'.[178] 'A partition of Poland seems inevitable,' remarked the Conservative MP Chips Channon. 'I cannot bear to think that our world is crumbling to ruins.'[179] 'Everybody is agreed that war is unthinkable . . . but the gulf between the British and the Hitlerian viewpoints is so wide that it really seems all but unavoidable,' commented Collin Brooks, a journalist with strong Conservative connections, adding: 'The engines of destruction may become so many and so terrible that there will be no war for generations.'[180]

The Comintern, meanwhile, consoled the shocked members of its constituent Communist parties by interpreting the Pact as the only avenue open to the USSR, given the appeasement of Hitler by the western democracies. There was renewed advocacy of a popular front against Hitlerian aggression, accompanied by the remarkable illusion that the chances of preventing war and rallying Germans to overthrow Hitler might have been enhanced.[181] Falling immediately and predictably in line with Moscow, the exiled leadership of the German Communist Party greeted the Pact as 'a successful act of peace on the part of the Soviet Union', contributing to the defusing of the international situation.[182]

Relief as well as satisfaction was reflected in Hitler's warm welcome for Ribbentrop on the latter's return next day to Berlin.[183] While his Foreign Minister had been in Moscow, Hitler had begun to think that Britain might after all fight.[184] Now, he was confident that prospect had been ruled out.

V

While Ribbentrop had been on his way to Moscow, Sir Nevile Henderson, the British Ambassador in Berlin, was flying to Berchtesgaden to deliver the letter composed by the Prime Minister, Neville Chamberlain, following the cabinet meeting on 22 August. In his letter, Chamberlain emphasized his conviction 'that war between our two peoples would be the greatest calamity that could occur'. But he left Hitler in no doubt about the British position.

A German–Soviet agreement would not alter Great Britain's obligation to Poland. Britain was, however, ready, if a peaceful atmosphere could be created, to discuss all problems affecting relations with Germany. And Britain was anxious for Poland and Germany to cease their polemics and incitement in order to allow direct discussions between the two countries on the reciprocal treatment of minorities.[185]

Accompanied by Weizsäcker and Hewel, Henderson arrived at the Berghof at 1p.m. on 23 August. Hitler was at his most aggressive. 'He made no long speeches but his language was violent and exaggerated both as regards England and Poland,' Henderson reported.[186] The German Chancellor launched into a series of wild tirades about British support of the Czechs the previous year, and now of the Poles, and how he had wanted only friendship with Britain. He claimed Britain's 'blank cheque' to Poland ruled out negotiations. He was recriminatory, threatening, and totally unyielding. He finally agreed to reply to Chamberlain within two hours.[187]

On return to Salzburg, Henderson was rapidly recalled to the Berghof. This time the meeting was shorter – under half an hour. Hitler was now calmer, but adamant that he would attack Poland if another German were to be maltreated there. War would be all Britain's fault. 'England' (as he invariably called Britain) 'was determined to destroy and exterminate Germany,' he went on. He was now fifty years old. He preferred war at this point than in five or ten years' time.[188] Henderson countered that talk of extermination was absurd. Hitler replied that England was fighting for lesser races, whereas he was fighting only for Germany. This time the Germans would fight to the last man. It would have been different in 1914 had he been Chancellor then. His repeated offers of friendship to Britain had been contemptuously rejected. He had come to the conclusion that England and Germany could never agree. England had now forced him into the pact with Russia. Henderson stated that war seemed inevitable if Hitler maintained his direct action against Poland. Hitler ended by declaring that only a complete change of British policy towards Germany could convince him of the desire for good relations.[189] The written reply to Chamberlain that he handed to Henderson was couched in much the same vein. It contained the threat – clear in implication if not expression – to order general mobilization, were Britain and France to mobilize their own forces.[190]

Hitler's tirades were, as so often, theatricals. They were a play-acted attempt to break the British Guarantee to Poland by a calculated demonstration of verbal brutality. As soon as Henderson had left, Hitler slapped his thigh – his usual expression of self-congratulation – and exclaimed to

Weizsäcker: 'Chamberlain won't survive this discussion. His cabinet will fall this evening.'[191]

Chamberlain's government was still there next day. Hitler's belief in his own powers had outstripped realistic assessment. His comment revealed how out of touch he was with the mood of the British government, now fully backed by public opinion, by this time. He was puzzled, therefore, the following day by the low-key response in Britain to the Soviet Pact, and irritated by the speeches made in Parliament by Chamberlain and Halifax reasserting Britain's resolve to uphold its obligations to Poland.[192] Within twenty-four hours Ribbentrop had persuaded him, since wielding the big stick had produced little effect, to dangle the carrot.[193]

At 12.45p.m. on 25 August, Henderson was informed that Hitler wished to see him at 1.30p.m. in the Reich Chancellery. The meeting lasted over an hour. Ribbentrop and the interpreter Paul Schmidt were also present. Hitler was far calmer than he had been in Berchtesgaden. He criticized Chamberlain's speech. But he was prepared to make Britain, he said, 'a large comprehensive offer' and pledge himself to maintain the continued existence of the British Empire once the Polish problem had been solved as a matter of urgency.[194] Hitler was so anxious that his 'offer' be immediately and seriously considered that he suggested that Henderson fly to London, and put a plane at his disposal. Henderson stated that the offer would only be considered if it meant a negotiated settlement of the Polish question. Hitler refused to guarantee this. Hitler ended the interview with pathos: he was by nature an artist not a politician, and once the Polish question were settled he would end his life as an artist.[195] Henderson flew next morning to London.[196] Goebbels expected little to come from it.[197]

The 'offer' to Britain was, in fact, no more than a ruse, another – and by now increasingly desperate – attempt to detach Britain from support for Poland, and prevent the intended localized war from becoming a general European war. How honest Hitler's 'offer' was can be judged from the fact that at the very time that Henderson was talking in the Reich Chancellery, final preparations were being made for the start of 'Case White' next morning, Saturday, 26 August, at 4.30a.m.[198] While Henderson was flying to London in the plane Hitler had put at his disposal, the attack on Poland was meant to be under way. By the time the British government had considered his 'offer', the Wehrmacht ought to have been making devastating inroads into Poland. It would have been another *fait accompli*.[199] As he had told his generals on 22 August, this time he was not going to be deprived of his war through last-minute negotiations.

Already on 12 August, Hitler had set the likely date of the 26th for the invasion of Poland.[200] This had been reaffirmed as the probable start of 'Case White' at the meeting with military leaders on 22 August.[201] Schmundt picked up Hitler's decision confirming this the following afternoon, while Ribbentrop was in Moscow, and after seeing Henderson at the Berghof.[202] Goebbels learnt on the morning of the 25th that the mobilization was due to take place that afternoon. At midday, Hitler then gave him propaganda instructions, emphasizing that Germany had been given no choice but to fight against the Poles, and preparing the people for a war, if necessary lasting 'months and years'.[203] Telephone communications between Berlin and London and Paris were cut off for several hours that afternoon. The Tannenberg celebrations and Party Rally were abruptly cancelled. Airports were closed from 26 August. Food rationing was introduced as from 27 August.[204] By midday on the 25th, however, even while Hitler was giving propaganda directives to Goebbels, Keitel's office was telephoning Halder to find out what was the latest time for the march-order, since there might have to be a postponement. The answer was given: no later than 3p.m. The final order was delayed at 1.30p.m. because Henderson was at that time in the Reich Chancellery. It was then further held back in the hope that Mussolini would have replied to Hitler's communication of earlier that morning. Under pressure from the military timetable, but anxious for news from Rome, Hitler put the attack on hold for an hour. Finally, without awaiting Mussolini's answer, but able to wait no longer, Hitler gave the order at 3.02p.m. Directives for mobilization were passed to the various troop commanders during the afternoon.[205] Then, amazingly, within five hours the order was cancelled.[206] To a great deal of muttering from army leaders about incompetence, the complex machinery of invasion was halted just in time.[207]

Mussolini's reply had arrived at 5.45p.m. At 7.30p.m. Brauchitsch telephoned Halder to rescind the invasion order.[208] A shaken Hitler had changed his mind.

On 24 August Hitler had prepared a lengthy letter for Mussolini, justifying the alliance with the Soviet Union, and indicating that a strike against Poland was imminent.[209] The letter was delivered by the German Ambassador in Rome on the morning of the 25th.[210] Mussolini's answer gave the over-confident Hitler an enormous shock. The Duce did not beat about the bush: Italy was in no position to offer military assistance at the present time.[211] Hitler icily dismissed Attolico, the Italian Ambassador. 'The Italians are behaving just like they did in 1914,' Paul Schmidt heard Hitler remark.[212]

'That alters the entire situation,' judged Goebbels. 'The Führer ponders and contemplates. That's a serious blow for him.'[213] For an hour, the Reich Chancellery rang with comments of disgust at the Axis partner. The word 'treachery' was on many lips.[214] Brauchitsch was hurriedly summoned. When he arrived, around seven that evening, he told Hitler there was still time to halt the attack, and recommended doing so to gain time for the Dictator's 'political game' ('*politisches Spiel*'). Hitler immediately took up the suggestion. Vormann was dispatched at 7.45p.m. with a frantic order to Halder to halt the start of hostilities.[215] Keitel emerged from Hitler's room to tell an adjutant: 'The march order must be rescinded immediately.'[216]

Another piece of bad news arrived for Hitler at much the same time. Minutes before the news from Rome had arrived, Hitler had heard from the French Ambassador Robert Coulondre, that the French, too, were determined to stick by their obligations to Poland.[217] This in itself was not critical. Hitler was confident that the French could be kept out of the war, if London did not enter.[218] Then Ribbentrop arrived to tell him that the military alliance between Great Britain and Poland agreed on 6 April had been signed late that afternoon.[219] This had happened after Hitler had made his 'offer' to Henderson. Having just signed the alliance, it must have been plain even to Hitler that Britain was unlikely to break it the very next day.[220] Yesterday's hero, Ribbentrop, now found himself all at once out of favour and, in the midst of a foreign-policy crisis on which peace hinged, was not in evidence for over two days.[221] Hitler turned again to the Foreign Minister's great rival, Göring.[222]

Immediately, Göring inquired whether the cancellation of the invasion was permanent. 'No. I will have to see whether we can eliminate England's intervention,' was the reply.[223] When Göring's personal emissary, his Swedish friend the industrialist Birger Dahlerus, already in London to belabour Lord Halifax with similar vague offers of German good intent that Henderson would shortly bring via the official route, eventually managed, with much difficulty, to place a telephone call to Berlin, he was asked to report back to the Field Marshal the following evening.[224]

In the meantime, Hitler wrote again to Mussolini, who had indicated that lack of *matériel* prevented Italy from joining Germany's war, to ask what precisely was needed.[225] The reply next day brought a deliberately impossible list of demands. Hitler could do nothing but tell Mussolini that he had understanding for Italy's position, hoped for propaganda support, but would not hold back from solving the eastern question even at the risk of the involvement of the West.[226] Mussolini, 'really out of his wits', was left vainly proposing that there should be a political solution.[227] Hitler's rage was directed at the King of Italy, not at his friend, the Italian dictator. He was glad, he said, that there was no longer a monarchy in Germany.[228]

The mood in the Reich Chancellery had not been improved by the message from Daladier on 26 August underlining France's solidarity with Poland.[229] Things at the hub of the German government seemed chaotic. No one had a clear idea of what was going on. Hewel, head of Ribbentrop's personal staff, though with different views to those of his boss, warned Hitler not to underestimate the British. He was a better judge of that than his Minister, he asserted. Hitler angrily broke off the discussion. Brauchitsch thought Hitler did not know what he should do.[230]

Dahlerus certainly found him in a highly agitated state when he was taken towards midnight to the Reich Chancellery. He had brought with him a letter from Lord Halifax, indicating in non-committal terms that negotiations were possible if force were not used against Poland.[231] It added in reality nothing to that which Chamberlain had already stated in his letter of 22 August.[232] It made an impact on Göring, but Hitler did not even look at the letter before launching into a lengthy diatribe, working himself into a nervous frenzy, marching up and down the room, his eyes staring, his voice at one moment indistinct, hurling out facts and figures about the strength of the German armed forces, the next moment shouting as if addressing a party meeting, threatening to annihilate his enemies, giving Dahlerus the impression of someone 'completely abnormal'.[233] Eventually, Hitler calmed down enough to list the points of the offer which he wanted Dahlerus to take to London. Germany wanted a pact or alliance with Britain, would guarantee the Polish borders, and defend the British Empire (even against Italy, Göring added). Britain was to help Germany acquire Danzig and the Corridor, and have Germany's colonies returned. Guarantees were to be provided for the German minority in Poland.[234] Hitler had altered the stakes in a bid to break British backing for Poland. In contrast to the 'offer' made to Henderson, the alliance with Britain now appeared to be available *before* any settlement with Poland.

Dahlerus took the message to London next morning, 27 August. The response was cool and sceptical. Dahlerus was sent back to report that Britain was willing to reach an agreement with Germany, but would not break its guarantee to Poland. Following direct negotiations between Germany and Poland on borders and minorities, the results would require international guarantee. Colonies could be returned in due course, but not under threat of war. The offer to defend the British Empire was rejected.[235]

Astonishingly, to Dahlerus, back in Berlin late that evening, Hitler accepted the terms, as long as the Poles had been immediately instructed to contact Germany and begin negotiations.[236] Halifax made sure this was done. In Warsaw, Beck agreed to begin negotiations.[237] Meanwhile, the German mobilization, which had never been cancelled along with the invasion, rolled on.[238] On the very day of Dahlerus's shuttling, the Abwehr had word that the new date for the attack was 31 August.[239] Next day, before Henderson arrived back in Berlin to bring the official British response, Brauchitsch informed Halder that Hitler had provisionally fixed the invasion for 1 September.[240]

As Henderson was setting out for Berlin, Hitler was addressing a meeting of SS and Party leaders in the Reich Chancellery. Himmler, Heydrich, Bormann, and Goebbels were among those present. Whatever his state of mind, Hitler could expect nothing but enthusiastic backing from this grouping for whatever hard line he wished to take. He told them he was determined to have the eastern question settled one way or the other. He posed a minimal demand of the return of Danzig and the settling of the Corridor issue. The maximum demand depended upon the military situation. He could not retreat from the minimalist position, and would attain it. 'It has already become a question of honour,' Goebbels noted.[241] If the minimum demands were not met, 'then war: brutal!' The war would be hard, and Hitler did not even rule out eventual failure. But, Halder recorded him saying, 'as long as I am alive, there will be no talk of capitulation'. The agreement with the Soviets had been widely misunderstood in the Party. It was nothing but 'a pact with Satan to cast out the Devil', Hitler declared. He looked worn and haggard to Halder, speaking in a breaking voice. It was said he kept himself completely surrounded by his SS advisers.[242]

Henderson handed Hitler a translation of the British reply to his 'offer' of 25 August at 10.30p.m. that evening, the 28th. Ribbentrop and Schmidt were there.[243] Hitler and Henderson spoke for over an hour. For once, Hitler neither interrupted, nor harangued Henderson. He was, according to the British Ambassador, polite, reasonable, and not angered by what he read.[244] The 'friendly atmosphere' noted by Henderson was so only in relative terms. Hitler still spoke of annihilating Poland.[245] The British reply did not in substance extend beyond the informal answer that Dahlerus had conveyed (and had been composed after Hitler's response to that initiative was known).[246] The British government insisted upon a prior settlement of the differences between Germany and Poland. Britain had already gained assurances of Poland's willingness to negotiate. Depending upon the outcome of any settlement and how it was reached, Britain was prepared to work towards a lasting understanding with Germany. But the obligation to Poland would be honoured.[247] Hitler promised a written reply the next day.[248]

Goebbels quickly learned that Hitler was not satisfied with what he had seen.[249] The Propaganda Minister nonetheless thought he detected a weakening of the British stance, a greater readiness to negotiate. The Führer, he commented, now wanted a plebiscite in the Corridor under international control. He hoped through this device to prise London away from Warsaw 'and to find an occasion to strike'.[250] Hitler planned to ponder his reply overnight, and come up, Himmler noted, with a 'masterpiece of diplomacy (*ein Meisterstück an Diplomatie*)' that would put the British on the spot.[251]

At 7.15p.m. on the evening of 29 August, Henderson, sporting as usual a dark red carnation in the buttonhole of his pin-striped suit, passed down the darkened Wilhelmstraße – Berlin was undergoing experimental blackouts – through a silent, but not hostile, crowd of 300–400 Berliners, to be received at the Reich Chancellery as on the previous night with a roll of drums and guard of honour.[252] Otto Meissner, whose role as head of the so-called Presidential Chancellery was largely representational, and Wilhelm Brück-ner, the chief adjutant, escorted him to Hitler. Ribbentrop was also present. Hitler was in a less amenable mood than on the previous evening. He gave Henderson his reply. He had again raised the price – exactly as Henlein had been ordered to do in the Sudetenland the previous year, so that it was impossible to meet it. Hitler now demanded the arrival of a Polish emissary with full powers by the following day, Wednesday 30 August. Even the pliant Henderson, protesting at the impossible time-limit for the arrival of the Polish emissary, said it sounded like an ultimatum.[253] Hitler replied that his generals were pressing him for a decision. They were unwilling to lose any more time because of the onset of the rainy season in Poland.[254] Henderson told Hitler that the success or failure of any talks with Poland depended upon his good will, or lack of it. The choice was his. But any attempt to use force against Poland would inevitably result in conflict with Britain.[255] Henderson's telegram to the British Foreign Secretary, Lord Hali-fax, early the following afternoon, stated: 'If Herr Hitler is allowed to con-tinue to have the initiative, it seems to me that [the] result can only be either war or once again victory for him by a display of force and encouragement thereby to pursue the same course again next year or the year after.'[256]

When Henderson had left, the Italian Ambassador Attolico was ushered in. He had come to tell Hitler that Mussolini was prepared to intercede with Britain if required. The last thing Hitler wanted, as he had made clear to his generals at the meeting on 22 August, was a last-minute intercession to bring about a new Munich – least of all from the partner who had just announced that he could not stand by the pact so recently signed. Hitler coldly told Attolico that direct negotiations with Britain were in hand and that he had already declared his readiness to accept a Polish negotiator.[257]

Hitler had been displeased at Henderson's response to his reply to the British government. He now called in Göring to send Dahlerus once more on the unofficial route to let the British know the gist of the 'generous' terms he was proposing to offer the Poles – return of Danzig to Germany, and a plebiscite on the Corridor (with Germany to be given a 'corridor through the Corridor' if the result went Poland's way). By 5a.m. on 30 August, Dahlerus was again heading for London in a German military plane.[258] An hour earlier Henderson had already conveyed Lord Halifax's unsurprising response, that the German request for the Polish emissary to appear that very day was unreasonable.[259]

During the day, while talking of peace Hitler prepared for war. In the morning he instructed Albert Forster, a week earlier declared Head of State in Danzig, on the action to be taken in the Free City at the outbreak of hostilities.[260] Later, he signed the decree to establish a Ministerial Council for the Defence of the Reich with wide powers to promulgate decrees. Chaired by Göring, its other members were Heß as Deputy Leader of the Party, Frick as plenipotentiary for Reich administration, Funk as plenipotentiary for the economy, Lammers, the head of the Reich Chancellery, and Keitel, chief of the High Command of the Wehrmacht.[261] It had the appearance of a 'war cabinet' to administer the Reich while Hitler preoccupied himself with military matters. In reality, the fragmentation of Reich government had gone too far for that. Hitler's own interest in preventing any centralized body operating as a possible check on his own power was to mean that the Ministerial Council was destined not to bring even a limited resurrection of collective government.[262]

Hitler spent much of the day working on his 'proposals' to be put to the Polish negotiator who, predictably, never arrived. From the outset it had not been a serious suggestion. But when Henderson returned to the Reich Chancellery at midnight to present the British reply to Hitler's communication of the previous evening, he encountered Ribbentrop in a highly nervous state and in a vile temper. Diplomatic niceties were scarcely preserved. At one point it seemed to the interpreter Paul Schmidt – in attendance though Henderson, as usual, insisted on speaking his less than perfect German – that the German Foreign Minister and the British Ambassador were going to come to blows.[263] After Ribbentrop had read out Hitler's 'proposals' at breakneck speed, so that Henderson was unable to note them down, he refused – on Hitler's express orders – to let the British Ambassador read the document, then hurled it on the table stating that it was now out of date (*überholt*), since no Polish emissary had arrived in Berlin by midnight.[264] Henderson reported to Halifax 'that Herr von Ribbentrop's whole demeanour during an unpleasant interview was aping Herr Hitler at his worst'.[265] In retrospect, Henderson thought that Ribbentrop 'was wilfully throwing away the last chance of a peaceful solution'.[266]

There had, in fact, been no 'last chance'. No Polish emissary had been expected. Ribbentrop was concerned precisely *not* to hand over terms which the British might have passed to the Poles, who might have been prepared to discuss them. Hitler had needed his 'generous suggestion over the regulation of the Danzig and Corridor Question', as Schmidt later heard him say, as 'an alibi, especially for the German people, to show them that I have done everything to preserve peace'.[267] Immediately following Henderson's audience with Ribbentrop, Hitler had told Goebbels that he wanted the document published 'at a suitable opportunity'.[268] It was arranged for a radio broadcast that evening.[269] By then, Göring had heard, unsurprisingly, from his intermediary Dahlerus that there was no further movement in London: the British government insisted, as it had throughout, on peaceful settlement of the Polish question before there could be any negotiations towards a better relationship between Britain and Germany.[270]

The army had been told on 30 August to make all preparations for attack on 1 September at 4.30a.m. If negotiations in London required a postponement, notification would be given before 3p.m. next day. But 2 September was the last day possible for a strike.[271] At 6.30a.m. on the morning of 31 August, within hours of Henderson's departure from the Reich Chancellery after hearing the terms of the German 'offer' to Poland, Halder learnt that Hitler had given the order to attack on 1 September – a day before the deadline ran out.[272] For some reason, Göring, on behalf of the Luftwaffe, had objected to having the timing set for 4.30a.m.[273] By 12.40p.m. the order directive had been completed and signed by Hitler.[274] At 1.50p.m. – still well before the possible cancellation point of 3p.m. – the order was confirmed to go ahead, with the starting time changed to 4.45a.m. 'Armed intervention by Western powers now said to be unavoidable,' noted Halder. 'In spite of this, Führer has decided to strike.'[275]

When informed that Ribbentrop had arrived at the Reich Chancellery, Hitler told him he had given the order, and that 'things were rolling (*die Sache rolle*)'. Ribbentrop wished him luck.[276] 'It looks as if the die is finally cast,' wrote Goebbels.[277]

After making his decision, Hitler cut himself off from external contact.[278] He refused to see the Polish Ambassador, Jozef Lipski, later in the afternoon. Ribbentrop did see him a little later. But hearing that the Ambassador carried no plenipotentiary powers to negotiate he immediately terminated the interview. Lipski returned to find telephone lines to Warsaw had been cut off.[279]

At 9p.m. the German radio broadcast Hitler's 'sixteen-point proposal' which Ribbentrop had so crassly presented to Henderson at midnight.[280] By 10.30p.m. the first reports were coming in of a number of serious border incidents, including an armed 'Polish' assault on the German radio station at Gleiwitz in Upper Silesia. These had been planned for weeks by Heydrich's office, using SS men dressed in Polish uniforms to carry out the attacks. To increase the semblance of authenticity, a number of concentration-camp inmates killed by lethal injections and carried to the sites provided the bodies required.[281]

Throughout Germany, people went about their daily business as normal. But the normality was deceptive. All minds now were fixed on the likelihood of war. A brief war, with scarcely any losses, and confined to Poland, was one thing. But war with the West, which so many with memories of the Great War of 1914–18 had dreaded for years, now seemed almost certain. There was now no mood like that of August 1914, no 'hurrah-patriotism'. The faces of the people told of their anxiety, fears, worries, and resigned acceptance of what they were being faced with. 'Everybody against the war,' wrote the American correspondent William Shirer on 31 August. 'How can a country go into a major war with a population so dead against it?' he asked.[282] 'Trust in the Führer will now probably be subjected to its hardest acid test,' ran a report from the Upper Franconian district of Ebermannstadt. 'The overwhelming proportion of people's comrades expects from him the prevention of the war, if otherwise impossible even at the cost of Danzig and the Corridor.'[283]

How accurate such a report was as a reflection of public opinion cannot be ascertained. The question is in any case irrelevant. Ordinary citizens, whatever their fears, were powerless to affect the course of events. While many of them were fitfully sleeping in the hope that even now, at the eleventh hour and beyond, some miracle would preserve peace, the first shots were fired and bombs dropped near Dirschau at 4.30a.m. And just over quarter of an hour later in Danzig harbour the elderly German battleship *Schleswig-Holstein*, now a sea-cadet training-ship, focused its heavy guns on the fortified Polish munitions depot on the Westerplatte and opened fire.[284]

By late afternoon the army leadership reported: 'Our troops have crossed the frontier everywhere and are sweeping on toward their objectives of the day, checked only slightly by the Polish forces thrown against them.'[285] In Danzig itself, the purported objective of the conflict between Germany and Poland, border posts and public buildings manned by Poles had been attacked at dawn. The League of Nations High Commissioner had been forced to leave, and the swastika banner raised over his building.[286] Gauleiter Albert Forster proclaimed Danzig's reincorporation in the Reich.[287] In the turmoil of the first day of hostilities, probably few people in Germany took much notice.

On a grey, overcast morning Shirer had found the few people on the streets apathetic.[288] There were not many cheers from those thinly lining the pavements when Hitler drove to the Reichstag shortly before 10a.m. A hundred or so deputies had been called up to serve in the army. But Göring saw to it that there were no empty spaces when Hitler spoke. The vacancies were simply filled by drafting in Party functionaries.[289] Hitler, now wearing Wehrmacht uniform, was on less than top form. He sounded strained. There was less cheering than usual.[290] After a lengthy justification of the alleged need for Germany's military action, he declared: 'Poland has now last night for the first time fired on our territory through regular soldiers. Since 5.45a.m.' – he meant 4.45a.m. – 'the fire has been returned. And from now on bomb will be met with bomb.'[291]

Hitler had still not given up hope that the British could be kept out of the conflict. On his return from the Reichstag he had Göring summon Dahlerus to make a last attempt.[292] But he wanted no outside intercession, no repeat of Munich. Mussolini, under the influence of Ciano and Attolico, and unhappy at Italy's humiliation at being unable to offer military support, had been trying for some days to arrange a peace conference. He was now desperate, fearing attack on Italy from Britain and France, to stop the war spreading.[293] Before seeing Dahlerus, Hitler sent the Duce a telegram explicitly stating that he did not want his mediation.[294] Then Dahlerus arrived. He found Hitler in a nervous state. The odour from his mouth was so strong that Dahlerus was tempted to move back a step or two. Hitler was at his most implacable. He was determined to break Polish resistance 'and to annihilate (*vernichten*) the Polish people', he told Dahlerus. In the next breath he added that he was prepared for further negotiations if the British wanted them. Again the threat followed, in ever more hysterical tones. It was in British interests to avoid a fight with him. But if Britain chose to fight, she would pay dearly. He would fight for one, two, ten years if necessary.[295]

Dahlerus's reports of such hysteria could cut no ice in London.[296] Nor did an official approach on the evening of 2 September, inviting Sir Horace Wilson to Berlin for talks with Hitler and Ribbentrop. Wilson replied straightforwardly that German troops had first to be withdrawn from Polish territory. Otherwise Britain would fight.[297] This was only to repeat the message which the British Ambassador had already passed to Ribbentrop the previous evening.[298] No reply to that message was received.[299] At 9a.m. on 3 September, Henderson handed the British ultimatum to the interpreter Paul Schmidt, in place of Ribbentrop, who had been unwilling to meet the British Ambassador.[300] Unless assurances were forthcoming by 11a.m. that Germany was prepared to end its military action and withdraw from Polish soil, the ultimatum read, 'a state of war will exist between the two countries as from that hour'.[301] No such assurances were forthcoming. 'Consequently,' Chamberlain broadcast to the British people then immediately afterwards repeated in the House of Commons, 'this country is at war with Germany.'[302] The French declaration of war followed that afternoon at 5p.m.[303]

Hitler had led Germany into the general European war he had wanted to avoid for several more years. Military 'insiders' thought the army, 2.3 million strong, through the rapidity of the rearmament programme, was less prepared for a major war than it had been in 1914.[304] Hitler was fighting the war allied with the Soviet Union, the ideological arch-enemy. And he was at war with Great Britain, the would-be 'friend' he had for years tried to woo. Despite all warnings, his plans – at every turn backed by his warmongering Foreign Minister – had been predicated upon his assumption that Britain would not enter the war – though he had shown himself undeterred even by that eventuality. It was little wonder that, if Paul Schmidt's account is to believed, when Hitler received the British ultimatum on the morning of 3 September, he angrily turned to Ribbentrop and asked: 'What now?'[305]

VI

'Responsibility for this terrible catastrophe lies on the shoulders of one man,' Chamberlain had told the House of Commons on 1 September, 'the German Chancellor, who has not hesitated to plunge the world into misery in order to serve his own senseless ambitions.'[306] It was an understandable over-simplification. Such a personalized view necessarily left out the sins of omission and commission by others – including the British government and its French allies – which had assisted in enabling Hitler to accumulate such a unique basis of power that his actions could determine the fate of Europe.

Internationally, Hitler's combination of bullying and blackmail could not have worked but for the fragility of the post-war European settlement. The Treaty of Versailles was 'the blackmailer's lucky find'.[307] It had given Hitler the basis for his rising demands, accelerating drastically in 1938–9. It had provided the platform for ethnic unrest, that Hitler could easily exploit, in the cauldron of central and eastern Europe. Not least, it had left an uneasy guilt-complex in the West, especially in Britain. Hitler might rant and exaggerate; his methods might be repellent; but was there not some truth in what he was claiming? The western governments, though Britain more than France, backed by their war-weary populations, anxious more than all else to do everything possible to avoid a new conflagration, their traditional diplomacy no match for unprecedented techniques of lying and threatening, thought so, and went out of their way to placate Hitler. The blackmailer simply increased his demands, as blackmailers do. By the time the western powers fully realized what they were up against, they were no longer in any position to bring the 'mad dog' to heel.

Within Germany, Hitler's personal power had expanded after 1933 at the expense of other power-groups – notably the army – until it was absolute and unchallenged. The year 1938, beginning with the near-showdown with the army over the Blomberg–Fritsch affair, crossing the triumph of the Anschluß, and ending with peace just about saved at Munich – but no thanks to the German army or to those in powerful positions in the regime who opposed Hitler – brought vital steps in this process.

As war loomed in 1939, a number of individuals who had begun to establish contact with each other the previous year and whose disparate approaches and aims would eventually coalesce into the 1944 attempt on Hitler's life – nationalists, with access to the levers of power, horrified at the madness of the risks being taken to court war – had warned the West of the dictator's plans. Colonel Oster of the Abwehr had leaked vital information. Lieutenant-Colonel Gerhard Graf von Schwerin had tried to encourage a greater show of British belligerence to undermine Hitler's claims that Britain would not fight. Adam von Trott zu Solz, former Oxford Rhodes scholar with a wide circle of friends in high places in Britain, had attempted – reflecting Weizsäcker's views – to suggest a deal restoring Czech independence but acceding to German claims over Danzig and the Corridor. The attempts of Hitler's opponents fell on stony ground. The mood in Britain had changed drastically following the march into Czecho-Slovakia. There was too much suspicion of motives, too few certainties that there was any coherent 'opposition' (which there was not), too little clarity of how, if at all, Hitler was to be replaced. Well-intentioned though the efforts were, it was hardly surprising that nothing came of them.[308]

Within Germany in the last days of peace, the conservative opponents of Hitler were uncoordinated, unclear about what was happening, and uncertain how to act themselves. An example was their behaviour when Hitler rescinded his order to attack on 26 August, just hours after it had been given. Hans-Bernd Gisevius, one-time Gestapo officer but by now radically opposed to Hitler, went straight to Schacht, and both had the news confirmed by General Thomas, head of office of the War Economy (*Wehrwirtschaft*). All three now thought the time was ripe to persuade Halder and Brauchitsch to intervene by deposing Hitler. Whether any scheme involving Brauchitsch had a hope of success is highly doubtful. But the matter was never even broached. Oster, second to none in his detestation of the regime, and his boss Canaris thought a putsch would prove unnecessary. Their misunderstanding of political realities was breathtaking. A supreme warlord who rescinds such a decisive order as that over war and peace within a few hours was finished, ran their wildly over-optimistic view.[309] Canaris added: 'He'll never recover from this blow. Peace has been saved for twenty years.'[310] Armed with such 'insights', Hitler's opponents did nothing.

Nor, unless the army leadership could have been stirred into action, could they have achieved anything. But the army leadership, as we have seen, was weakened and divided. We noted something of the feeling among the generals after Hitler's speech at the Berghof on 22 August. The mood was much the same in the tense days that followed. Some leading officers thought Hitler's optimism about the non-intervention of the West was likely to prove false. Others still thought the conflict could be localized. Most were sceptical, anxious even, but fatalistic and in depressed frame of mind. Resignation, not gung-ho enthusiasm for war, prevailed. But it was no platform for opposition.[311] Compliance, even if reluctant on the part of some generals, was all that was needed. Hitler remained unhindered by any action such as that which Beck had mooted at the height of the Sudeten crisis the previous year, by any threat of refusal to collaborate in the destruction of Poland.

Close to the epicentre of power in the Reich, but following a line that differed from that of both Hitler and Ribbentrop, was Göring, now attempting something of a comeback after months in the doldrums. Over the summer he had tried through three intermediaries – the Swedish million-aire Axel Wenner-Gren, his own deputy in the Four-Year Plan organization Helmut Wohltat, and, as we have seen, Birger Dahlerus, also a Swede – to coax the British into negotiations.[312] Predictably, nothing had come of such moves. The mood in the British government was not amenable to initiatives resting on major concessions to Germany, based on unclear authority, and leaving Hitler's power untouched, the future potential for aggression undiminished. Göring was certainly anxious to avoid war with Britain, at least until Germany was ready for the big showdown. His entire political thinking over the previous years had rested on a rapprochement with Britain. This strategy was faced with imminent ruin, a development which Göring blamed exclusively on Ribbentrop. But, ultimately, Göring had no real alternative to offer Hitler. His informal approaches were no more successful than Hitler's threats in severing the British from the Poles. Nor did he have the will to stand up against Hitler. For all the differences in emphasis, Göring remained Hitler's man through and through.[313]

Göring was scarcely alone in blaming the war not on Hitler, but on Ribbentrop. It was the view, among others, of Dahlerus, Hassell, Hewel, Papen, Weizsäcker, and the British Ambassador Henderson.[314] Unques-tionably, Ribbentrop's self-certainty, derived from his 'understanding' of the British and his absolute conviction that in the end they would not fight over Poland, helped to influence Hitler in his miscalculation.[315] Despite the impression he tried to leave behind in his memoirs, Ribbentrop had – as in the previous year – been an outright warmonger, his crass aggression fuelled by smouldering resentment at his treatment in Britain. Alongside Goebbels and Himmler he could always be relied upon to egg on Hitler. While he acted, as always, as an amplifier, it is – given the domineering assertiveness of Hitler and his own fawning subservience – difficult to imagine Ribbentrop as the moving force. Hitler's liaison officer with army command, Nikolaus von Vormann, had in retrospect no doubts about the relationship: 'Hitler did not believe in a war with the western powers because he did not want to believe in it. From the difference in character and on the basis of the entire atmosphere in the Führer headquarters' – he evidently meant, since he was writing of the last days before the war, the Reich Chancellery – he concluded 'that the initiative rested with Hitler and that the essentially submissive (*weiche*) Ribbentrop, who in any case represented no opinion of his own, thought it appropriate and expedient to reinforce him in this view'.[316]

Hitler decided. That much is clear. The fracturing of any semblance of collective government over the previous six years left him in the position where he determined alone. No one doubted – the suffocating effect of years of the expanding Führer cult had seen to that – that he had the right to decide, and that his decisions were to be implemented. His style was not to listen to differing or conflicting advice, weigh up the pros and cons, and arrive at a conclusion. He would ponder things overnight, hit on what he saw as a solution, and put it forward for acclaim.[317] Or he would expound his ideas in endless monologues until he had convinced himself that they were right.[318] In the critical days, he saw a good deal of Ribbentrop, Göring, Goebbels, Himmler, and Bormann. Other leading figures in the Party, government ministers, even court favourites like Speer, had little or no contact with him.[319] He was naturally also in constant touch with the Wehrmacht leadership. But while Goebbels, for instance, only learnt at second hand about military plans, leaders of the armed forces often had less than full information, or were belatedly told, about diplomatic developments. The cabinet, of course, never met. Schacht, still nominally a member of that non-functioning body as Reich Minister without Portfolio, had notions of insisting on it being summoned, since constitutionally any declaration of war had to be preceded by cabinet consultation.[320] It was an empty hope, rapidly discarded. Whichever way one viewed it, and remarkable for a complex modern state, there was no government beyond Hitler and whichever individuals he chose to confer with at a particular time. Hitler was the only link of the component parts of the regime. Only in his presence could the key steps be taken. But those admitted to his presence, apart from his usual entourage of secretaries, adjutants, and the like, were for the most part officers needing operational guidelines or those like Ribbentrop or Goebbels who thought like he did and were dependent on him. Internal government of the Reich had become Führer autocracy.

For those in proximity to Hitler, the personalized decision-making meant anything but consistency, clarity, and rationality. On the contrary: it brought bewildering improvisation, rapid changes of course, uncertainty. Hitler was living off his nerves. That conveyed itself to others around him. 'He was no man of logic or reason (*Raison*),' reflected Ernst von Weizsäcker almost a decade later. This showed, he went on, in the 'bizarre zigzag' of his intentions and actions in those last days of peace: 'On 22 August Hitler indicated in an address to his generals that he was firmly determined to start war in a few days whether or not it remained localized; the day after he reckoned with it being localized, but he could also conduct a European war.' With the Moscow Pact, according to Weizsäcker, Hitler 'crossed the Rubicon'. 'By the 25th at midday he took the West on board; on the 25th in the evening he withdrew the order for attack that had already been given for fear that England would march, but Italy would not. On 31 August neither matters to him any more; he orders the attack on Poland although he knows that nothing has altered, namely that Italy remains out of it and England has firmly promised assistance to the Poles. On 3 September, finally, Hitler is surprised by the British-French declaration of war and at first clueless.'[321] Hitler, Weizsäcker went on to remark, with some insight, was the prisoner of his own actions. The wagon had begun in the spring to roll towards the abyss. In the last days of August, Hitler 'could hardly have turned the carriage around without being thrown off himself'.[322]

External pressures of the course he had embarked upon met Hitler's personal psychology at this point. At the age of fifty, men frequently ruminate on the ambitions they had, and how the time to fulfil them is running out. For Hitler, a man with an extraordinary ego and ambitions to go down in history as the greatest German of all time, and a hypochondriac already prepossessed with his own approaching death, the sense of ageing, of youthful vigour disappearing, of no time to lose was hugely magnified. He had more than hinted as much on 23 August, as we noted, to the British Ambassador, Nevile Henderson.[323] To his own entourage, at the evening meal a few days later, he had said: 'I'm now fifty years old, still in full possession of my strength. The problems must be solved by *me*, and I can wait no longer. In a few years I will be physically and perhaps mentally, too, no longer up to it.'[324] The grandiose parades on 20 April had been held to demonstrate Germany's military strength to the world. To Hitler the celebrations of his fiftieth birthday had merely reminded him how old he was getting.[325]

Between the Hoßbach meeting in November 1937 and the outbreak of war at the start of September 1939, Hitler had constantly felt time closing in on him, under pressure to act lest the conditions became more disadvantageous. He had thought of war against the West around 1943–5, against the Soviet Union – though no time-scale was ever given – at some point after that. He had never thought of avoiding war. On the contrary: reliving the lost first great war made him predicate everything on victory in the second great war to come. Germany's future, he had never doubted and had said so on innumerable occasions, could only be determined through war. In the dualistic way in which he always thought, victory would ensure survival, defeat would mean total eradication – the end of the German people. War – the essence of the Nazi system which had developed under his leadership – was for Hitler inevitable. Only the timing and the direction were at issue. And there was no time to wait. Starting from his own strange premisses, given Germany's strained resources and the rapid strides forward in rearmament by Britain and France, there was a certain contorted logic in what he said.[326] Time was running out on the options for Hitler's war.

This strong driving-force in Hitler's mentality was compounded by other strands of his extraordinary psychological make-up. The years of spectacular successes – all attributed by Hitler to the 'triumph of the will' – and the undiluted adulation and sycophancy that surrounded him at every turn, the Führer cult on which the 'system' was built, had by now completely erased in him what little sense of his own limitations had been present. This led him to a calamitous over-estimation of his own abilities, coupled with an extreme denigration of those – particularly in the military – who argued more rationally for greater caution. It went hand in hand with an equally disastrous refusal to contemplate compromise, let alone retreat, as other than a sign of weakness. The experience of the war and its traumatic outcome had doubtless cemented this characteristic. It was certainly there in his early political career, for instance at the time of the attempted putsch in Munich in 1923. But it must have had deeper roots. Pyschologists might have answers. At any rate the behaviour trait, increasingly dangerous as Hitler's power expanded to threaten the peace of Europe, was redolent of the spoilt child turned into the would-be macho-man. His inability to comprehend the unwillingness of the British government to yield to his threats produced tantrums of frustrated rage.[327] The certainty that he would get his way through bullying turned into blind fury whenever his bluff was called. The purchase he placed on his own image and standing was narcissistic in the extreme. The number of times he recalled the Czech mobilization of May 1938, then the Polish mobilization of March 1939, as a slight on his prestige was telling. A heightened thirst for revenge was the lasting consequence. Then the rescinding of the order to attack Poland on 26 August, much criticized as a sign of incompetence by the military, he took as a defeat in the eyes of his generals, feeling his prestige threatened.[328] The result was increased impatience to remedy this by a new order at the earliest possible moment, from which there would be no retreat, without any alteration to the diplomatic situation. On a broader scale, the same applies to Hitler's reaction to the Munich Settlement the previous year. All his actions during the Polish crisis can be seen as a response to the defeat he felt he had suffered personally in agreeing to pull back at the end of September 1938. His comment to his generals that he wanted at all costs to prevent 'some swine' from interceding this time; his determination to prevent Mussolini mediating; and his increase of the stakes to avoid negotiation at the last were all reflections of his 'Munich syndrome'.

Not just external circumstances, but also his personal psyche, pushed him forwards, compelled the risk. Hitler's reply on 29 August, when Göring suggested it was not necessary to 'go for broke', was, therefore, absolutely in character: 'In my life I've always gone for broke.'[329] There was, for him, no other choice.

The gambler has to think he will win. Hitler's dismay on 3 September at hearing of the British ultimatum quickly gave way to the necessary optimism. Goebbels was with him that evening. Hitler went over the military situation. The Führer 'believes in a potato-war (*Kartoffelkrieg*) in the West,' he wrote. Hearing that Churchill, long seen in Berlin as the leading western warmonger, had been called into the British cabinet as First Lord of the Admiralty, Goebbels was not so sure.[330]

6

LICENSING BARBARISM

'. . . Extensive shootings were planned in Poland and . . . especially the nobility and clergy were to be exterminated.'
Admiral Canaris, seeking clarification from General Keitel, 12 September 1939, about information that had come to his attention

'. . . This matter has already been decided by the Führer.'
General Keitel's reply

'You are now the master race here. Nothing was yet built up through softness and weakness . . . That's why I expect, just as our Führer Adolf Hitler expects from you, that you are disciplined, but stand together hard as Krupp steel. Don't be soft, be merciless, and clear out everything that is not German and could hinder us in the work of construction.'
Ludolf von Alvensleben, head of the 'Volksdeutscher Selbstschutz' ('Ethnic German Self-Protection') militia squads in West Prussia, 16 October 1939

'It was immaterial to him if some time in the future it were established that the methods to win this territory were not pretty or open to legal objection.'
Note by Martin Bormann, 20 November 1940, on Hitler's comments to the Gauleiter of incorporated territories

In war Nazism came into its own.[1] The Nazi Movement had been born out of a lost war. The experience of that war and erasing the stain of that defeat were at its heart. 'National renewal' and preparation for another war to establish the dominance in Europe which the first great war had failed to attain drove it forwards. Mobilizing the people in an attempt at perpetual re-creation of the 'spirit of 1914' was essential preparation for the new conflict.[2] The keynote of the message was 'struggle'. National survival – the future of the German people – its Leader had preached for fifteen years or more, could only be assured through acquiring 'living-space'. And this could only be gained, he had repeatedly stated, 'through the sword'.

Six years of Nazi rule had brought the 'world-view' that Hitler stood for into much sharper focus. Almost imperceptibly at first, restoration of territory taken away from Germany at Versailles had been transformed into a drive for expansion. Hitler had done more than any other individual to bring about this transformation. But it could not have been accomplished without the avid involvement of all ruling groups, but quite especially the armed forces' leadership, in the push for massive and rapid rearmament. And all sections of the regime's élites had supported expansion, baulking only at its speed and what were seen as the unnecessary dangers of conflict with the western powers. Meanwhile, with remarkably little direction from Hitler, other than – though this was crucial – to provide the green light for action at key moments, and sanction for what had been done, the aim of 'racial purification' had been greatly advanced. Traditional social prejudice and resentment had played its part. Widespread denunciation of fellow-citizens by ordinary Germans had kept the mill of discrimination and persecution turning. Obsession with 'law and order' easily slipped into an obsession with the exclusion of 'troublemakers' and 'social outsiders'. Social hygiene fetishism translated readily into pressure for measures to improve 'racial hygiene'.

Victims of social prejudice far from confined to inter-war Germany were readily to hand: prostitutes, homosexuals, Gypsies, habitual criminals, and others seen as sullying the image of the new society by begging, refusing work, or any sort of 'antisocial' behaviour. Beyond these, of course, were the Number One racial and social enemy: the Jews. Where Germany differed from other countries with regard to such 'outsider' groups was that licence was provided from the highest leadership in the land to every agency of control and power to look for radical solutions to 'cleanse' society, offering the widest scope for increasingly inhumane initiatives that could ignore, override, or bypass the constraints of legality. To serve their own organizational vested interests, those agencies most directly involved – the medical and health bureaucracy, legal authorities, and criminal police – did not hesitate to exploit the general remit of the Nazi state's philosophy to lead the drive to rid society of 'racial undesirables', 'elements harmful to the people', and 'community aliens'. Sterilization and eugenics programmes gained in attraction. Not least, as we have seen, the relentless persecution of the Jews, the foremost racial target, had produced even before the war distinct signs of the mentality which would lead to the gas chambers.

The war now brought the circumstances and opportunities for the dramatic radicalization of Nazism's ideological crusade. Long-term goals seemed almost overnight to become attainable policy objectives. Persecution which had targeted usually disliked social minorities was now directed at an entire conquered and subjugated people. The Jews, a tiny proportion of the German population, were not only far more numerous in Poland, but were despised by many within their native land and were now the lowest of the low in the eyes of the brutal occupiers of the country.

As before the war, Hitler set the tone for the escalating barbarism, approved of it, and sanctioned it. But his own actions provide an inadequate explanation of such escalation. The accelerated disintegration of any semblance of collective government, the undermining of legality by an everencroaching and ever-expanding police executive, and the power-ambitions of an increasingly autonomous SS leadership all played important parts. These processes had developed between 1933 and 1939 in the Reich itself. They were now, once the occupation of Poland opened up new vistas, to acquire a new momentum altogether. The planners and organizers, theoreticians of domination, and technocrats of power in the SS leadership saw Poland as an experimental playground. They were granted a *tabula rasa* to undertake more or less what they wanted. The Führer's 'vision' served as the legitimation they needed. Party leaders put in to run the civilian administration of the parts of Poland annexed to the Reich, backed by thrusting and 'inventive' civil servants, also saw themselves as 'working towards the Führer' in their efforts to bring about the speediest possible 'Germanization' of their territories. And the occupying army – officers and rank-and-file – imbued with deep-seated anti-Polish prejudice, also needed little encouragement in the ruthlessness with which the conquered Poles were subjugated.

The ideological radicalization fed back into the home front – one important manifestation being the unfolding of a 'euthanasia action' to eliminate the incurably sick, something which had been put on ice during the peacetime years, but which could now be attempted. And as the war went on in its early stages to produce almost unbelievable military triumphs in the West, so the options for 'solving the Jewish Question' and for tackling the still unresolved 'Church struggle' (which Hitler had wanted dampened down at the start of war) appeared to open up.

But the key area was Poland. The ideological radicalization which took place there in the eighteen months following the German invasion was an essential precursor to the plans which unfolded in spring 1941 as preparation for the war which Hitler knew at some time he would fight: the war against Bolshevik Russia.

I

Towards nine o'clock on the evening of 3 September, Hitler boarded his special armoured train in Berlin's Stettiner Bahnhof and left for the front.[3] For much of the following three weeks, the train – standing initially in Pomerania (Hinterpommern), then later in Upper Silesia – formed the first wartime 'Führer Headquarters'.[4] Among Hitler's accompaniment were two personal adjutants, for the most part Wilhelm Brückner and Julius Schaub, two secretaries (Christa Schroeder and Gerda Daranowski), two man-servants, his doctor, Karl Brandt (or sometimes his deputy, Hans-Karl von Hasselbach), and his four military adjutants (Rudolf Schmundt, Karl-Jesko von Puttkamer, Gerhard Engel, and Nicolaus von Below).[5] Behind Hitler's carriage, the first on the train, containing his spacious 'living-room', sleeping compartment, and bathroom, together with compartments for his adjutants, was the command carriage that held communications equipment and a conference room for meetings with military leaders. In the next carriage Martin Bormann had his quarters.[6] On the day of the invasion of Poland, he had informed Lammers that he would 'continue permanently to belong to the Führer's entourage'.[7] From now on, he was never far from Hitler's side – echoing the Führer's wishes, and constantly reminding him of the need to keep up the ideological drive of the regime.

The Polish troops, ill-equipped for modern warfare, were from the outset no match for the invaders.[8] Within the first two days, most aerodromes and almost the whole of the Polish air-force were wiped out.[9] The Polish defences were rapidly overrun, the army swiftly in disarray. Already on 5 September Chief of Staff Halder noted: 'Enemy practically defeated.'[10] By the second week of fighting, German forces had advanced to the outskirts of Warsaw.[11] Hitler seldom intervened in the military command.[12] But he took the keenest interest in the progress of the war. He would leave his train most mornings by car to view a different part of the front line.[13] His secretaries, left behind to spend boring days in the airless railway carriage parked in the glare of the blazing sun, tried to dissuade him from touring the battle scenes standing in his car, as he did in Germany.[14] But Hitler was in his element. He was invigorated by war.

On 17 September, in the move which Hitler had impatiently awaited, Stalin's army invaded Poland from the east. German generals, kept in the dark until then about the precise details of the demarcation line drawn up in the secret protocol to the Ribbentrop–Molotov pact, did not conceal their anger at having to withdraw from territories way beyond the agreed line that had cost casualties to capture. 'A day of disgrace for the German political leadership' was how Halder recorded it.[15]

Two days later, Hitler entered Danzig to indescribable scenes of jubilation. He took up accommodation for the next week in the Casino-Hotel at the adjacent resort of Zoppot.[16] From there, on the 22nd and again on the 25th, he flew to the outskirts of Warsaw to view the devastation wrought on the city of a million souls by the bombing and shelling he had ordered. By 27 September, when the military commander of Warsaw eventually surrendered the city, he was back in Berlin, returning quietly with no prearranged hero's reception.[17] Poland no longer existed. An estimated 700,000 Polish soldiers were taken prisoners of war.[18] Around 70,000 were killed in action, and a further 133,000 wounded.[19] German fatalities numbered about 11,000, with 30,000 wounded, and a further 3,400 missing.[20]

Among the German dead was Colonel-General Werner von Fritsch, unexpectedly caught in heavy Polish fire on 22 September on an inspection of the front where his artillery regiment was fighting.[21] Typical of the mentality of conservative nationalists who had deep reservations about Hitler but rejoiced in the territorial gains he had brought about, Fritsch had commented in his last letter from the front that victory in the war would bring 'the united states of Central Europe in a strong continental block under Germany's leadership'.[22] Hitler scarcely reacted when informed of Fritsch's death.[23] Publicity was kept to a minimum.[24] On the anniversary of Fritsch's death a year later Hitler expressly banned any floral tributes.[25]

Territorial and political plans for Poland had not been finalized before the invasion. They were improvised and amended as events unfolded in September and October 1939. Hitler had, in fact, shown remarkably little interest in Poland before autumn 1938. As an Austrian, his main anti-Slav antipathies were directed at the Czechs, not the Poles. For Prussians, the age-old antagonisms revolving around the disputed territory on the eastern borders of the Reich tended in the opposite direction. In the face of tra-ditional anti-Polish feeling in the Foreign Ministry and the army, Hitler had pushed through the pact with Poland in 1934 and repeatedly expressed admiration for the Polish head of state, until his death in 1935, Marshal Pilsudski, victor over the Red Army in 1920. Though the pact had obvious tactical value during the build-up of rearmament, and was presumed by many Nazi followers to be merely a ploy with limited life-span, Hitler's preference continued in autumn 1938 and spring 1939, as we have seen, to have Poland as an ally (if now more or less as a German satellite). The British Guarantee had changed all that. But the new aim of destroying Poland by military force in summer 1939 was still not coupled with clear plans for the post-war future of the country. Neither in *Mein Kampf* nor in subsequent writings or speeches had Hitler had much to say about Poland. In his *Second Book* he had indicated that Poles ought to be removed from their property and the land given to ethnic Germans. He rigorously opposed, in this brief passage, the incorporation of Poles in the Reich (as had happened before 1914). 'The *völkisch* state,' he declared, 'must on the contrary take the decision either to seal off these racially alien elements in order not again to allow the blood of our own people to be debased (*zersetzen*), or it must remove them forthwith and transfer the land (*Grund und Boden*) made available to our own people's comrades.'[26] Otherwise, there was remarkably little on Poland. The vast expanses of Russia, as he had often stated, were what he had in mind as the answer to Germany's alleged 'space problem'.

But Hitler had repeatedly shown that he was prepared to put off long-term ideological goals in favour of short-term advantage.

The pact concluded with the Soviet Union in August, and in particular its secret protocol agreeing to partition Poland, naturally altered the situation. 'Living space' further east dropped for the foreseeable future out of the equation. Any resettlement of populations and ethnic experimentation would now have to take place in the former territory of Poland, not farther east. Whether a Polish state should continue in existence had been left open in the secret protocol. A country divided among two occupying powers held little prospect of sustaining even a puppet state. However, the lack of immediate invasion by the Soviets and Hitler's hope even at this point of persuading the West, faced with the *fait accompli* of a Polish defeat, to pull out of the war and strike a deal with him left German plans still uncertain.[27]

On 7 September Hitler had been ready to negotiate with the Poles, recognizing a rump Polish state (with territorial concessions to Germany and breaking of ties with Britain and France), together with an independent western Ukraine.[28] Five days later he still favoured a quasi-autonomous Polish rump state with which he could negotiate a peace in the east, and thought of limiting territorial demands to Upper Silesia and the Corridor if the West stayed out.[29] Another option advanced by Ribbentrop was a division between Germany and Russia, and the creation, out of the rump of Poland, of an autonomous Galician and Polish Ukraine – a proposal unlikely to commend itself to Moscow.[30] The belated Soviet occupation of eastern Poland on 17 September in any case promptly ruled out this possibility. Hitler still left open the final shape of Poland in his Danzig speech on 19 September.[31] During the next days, Stalin made plain his opposition to the existence of a Polish rump state. His initial preference for the demarcation line along the line of the Pissia, Narew, Vistula, and San rivers was then replaced by the proposal to exchange central Polish territories within the Soviet zone between the Vistula and Bug rivers for Lithuania. Once Hitler had accepted this proposal – the basis of the German-Soviet Treaty of Friendship signed on 28 September 1939 – the question of whether or not there would be a Polish rump state was in Berlin's hands alone.[32]

Hitler was still contemplating the possibility of some form of Polish political entity at the end of the month.[33] He held out the prospect of re-creating a truncated Polish state – though expressly ruling out any re-creation of the Poland of the Versailles settlement – for the last time in his Reichstag speech of 6 October, as part of his 'peace offer' to the West.[34] But by then the provisional arrangements set up to administer occupied Poland had in effect already eliminated what remained of such a prospect. Even before the formality of Chamberlain's rejection of the 'peace offer' on 12 October, they had created their own dynamic militating towards a rump Polish territory – the 'General Government', as it came to be known – alongside the substantial parts of the former Polish state to be incorporated in the Reich itself.

By 26 October, through a series of decrees characterized by extraordinary haste and improvisation, Hitler brought the military administration of occupied Poland to an end, replacing it by civilian rule in the hands of tried and tested 'Old Fighters' of the Movement. Albert Forster, Gauleiter of Danzig, was made head of the new Reichsgau of Danzig–West Prussia. Arthur Greiser, former President of the Danzig Senate, was put in charge of the largest annexed area, Reichsgau Posen (or 'Reichsgau Wartheland', as it was soon to be renamed, though generally known simply as the 'Warthegau'). Hans Frank, the Party's legal chief, was appointed General Governor in the rump Polish territory.[35] Other former Polish territory was added to the existing Gaue of East Prussia and Silesia. In each of the incorporated territories, most of all in the Wartheland, the boundaries fixed during the course of October enclosed sizeable areas which had never been part of the former Prussian provinces. The borders of the Reich were thereby extended some 150–200 kilometres to the east. Only in the Danzig area were ethnic Germans in the majority. Elsewhere in the incorporated territories the proportion of Germans in the population seldom reached much over 10 per cent.[36]

It was imperialist conquest, not revisionism. The treatment of the people of the newly conquered territory was unprecedented, its modern forms of barbarism evoking, though in even more terrible fashion, the worst barbaric subjugations of bygone centuries. What was once Poland amounted in the primitive view of its new overlords to no more than a colonial territory in eastern Europe, its resources to be plundered at will, its people regarded – with the help of modern race theories overlaying old prejudice – as inferior human beings to be treated as brutally as thought fit.

In Germany itself, despite new economic restrictions, life went on during the Polish campaign much as normal.[37] Berlin's cafés, restaurants, and bars had been packed, as usual, on the first night of the war.[38] On the evening that the British and French had declared war, William Shirer heard people saying that the 'Polish thing' would soon be over, and that the West would not move. 'There were food cards and soap cards and you couldn't get any petrol and at night it was difficult stumbling around in the blackout,' he reported. 'But the war in the east has seemed a bit far away to them.'[39] A week later, fears of the conflagration in the west had not materialized. Leisure pursuits were not affected by the war raging in the east. Two hundred football matches were played in Germany that weekend. Berliners flocked to cinemas, to the opera to see *Madame Butterfly* and *Tannhäuser*, or to the State Theatre, where Goethe's *Iphigenie* was playing.[40] Shirer listened to a crowd of mainly women who had come out of the opera. They 'seemed oblivious of the fact that a war was on, that German bombs and shells were falling on the women and children in Warsaw', he observed.[41] 'I have still to find a German, even among those who don't like the regime,' he added on 20 September, 'who sees anything wrong in the German destruction of Poland . . . As long as the Germans are successful and do not have to pull in their belts too much, this will not be an unpopular war.'[42] Reports from the exiled Social Democrat leadership (the Sopade), resting on information filtered out from within Germany, told much the same tale.[43] The propaganda version of a war forced on Germany was widely believed. So were lurid stories – mainly wild exaggeration – of Polish atrocities against the ethnic German minority in western Poland. Many approved of the 'rigorous approach' towards the Poles.[44] This stance was given encouragement by letters sent home by soldiers. One, not exceptional, ran: 'Anything more vile than Polish soldiers has never been seen in a war. They've taken hardly any prisoners. Those falling into their hands have been butchered in a horrible fashion, and the Polacks have been treated in such brotherly fashion by us.'[45] People followed the military advance with keen interest.[46] They rejoiced in the victory.[47] But the military triumph in Poland was taken largely for granted. Hitler's popularity was undiminished.[48] Most people hoped that the West would now see sense, and that the war would then be over.

II

The terror unleashed from the first days of the invasion of Poland left the violence, persecution, and discrimination that had taken place in the Reich itself since 1933 – dreadful though that had been – completely in the shade.[49] The orgy of atrocities was unleashed from above, exploiting in the initial stages the ethnic antagonism which Nazi agitation and propaganda had done much to incite. The radical, planned programme of 'ethnic cleansing' that followed was authorized by Hitler himself. But its instigation – everything points to this – almost certainly came from the SS leadership. The SS had readily recognized the opportunities there to be grasped from expansion. New possibilities for extending the tentacles of the police state had opened up with the Anschluß. Einsatzgruppen (task forces) of the Security Police had been used there for the first time. They had been deployed again in the Sudeten territory, then the rest of Czecho-Slovakia, where there was even greater scope for the SS's attack on 'enemies of the state'. The way was paved for the massive escalation of uncontrolled brutality in Poland. Once more, five (later six) Einsatzgruppen were sent into action. They interpreted most liberally their brief to shoot 'hostages' in recrimination for any show of hostility, or 'insurgents' – seen as anyone giving the slightest indication of active opposition to the occupying forces. The need to sustain good relations with the Wehrmacht initially restricted the extent and arbitrariness of the shootings.[50] It probably also at first constrained the 'action' aimed at liquidating the Polish nobility, clergy, and intelligentsia.[51] This 'action' nevertheless claimed ultimately an estimated 60,000 victims.[52] Plainly, with the occupation of Poland, the barbarities of the Einsatzgruppen had moved on to a new plane. The platform was established for what was subsequently to take place in the attack on the Soviet Union in 1941.[53]

There was no shortage of eager helpers among the ethnic Germans in the former Polish territories. The explosion of violence recalled, in hugely magnified fashion, the wild and barbarous treatment of 'enemies of the state' in Germany in spring 1933. But now, after six years of cumulative onslaught on every tenet of humane and civilized behaviour, and persistent indoctrination with chauvinistic hatred, the penned-in aggression could be let loose externally on a downtrodden and despised enemy.

There had been undoubted discrimination against the German minority – around 3 per cent of the total population – in pre-war Poland, mounting sharply during the summer crisis of 1939. The Germans had also been economically disadvantaged. The incorporation of Austria and the Sudetenland had then raised expectations among the Germans in Poland of their own 'return to the Reich'.[54] And, in a climate of mounting ethnic conflict, Goebbels's propaganda, grossly exaggerating or simply fabricating incidents of sporadic violence against the German minority (while of course keeping quiet about worse outrages on the German side), contributed immensely to inciting venomous antagonism towards the Poles.

For their part, immediately following the German invasion the Poles, reacting to real or alleged cases of sabotage by the German minority – taken to be a 'fifth column' – arrested some 10–15,000 ethnic Germans (1–2 per cent of the German minority) and force-marched them eastwards.[55] Though the brutality accompanying the marches was later hugely magnified for propaganda purposes, the prisoners were indeed often beaten, or otherwise maltreated, and subjected to violence by the local population as they passed through Polish towns and villages. In some cases, those unfit to walk any further were shot.[56]

Outrages against the minority German population occurred in numerous places. Most notoriously in Bromberg (Bydgoszcz), attacks on Germans on 3 September had the character of a local pogrom. Precisely how many died at Bromberg has never been satisfactorily established.[57] For German propaganda, the attacks on ethnic Germans were exploited as an apparent justification for a policy of 'ethnic cleansing' that had surpassed in its first days anything that could be regarded as retaliation.[58] The Germans claimed in November 1939 that 5,400 had been killed in the 'September Murders' (including what they dubbed the 'Bromberg Bloody Sunday'). Then, in February 1940, on Hitler's own instructions (it was later claimed) this was simply multiplied by around ten-fold and a figure of 58,000 German dead invented.[59] The most reliable estimates put the total number of ethnic Germans killed in outrages, forced marches, bombing and shelling at around 4,000.[60] Terrible though these atrocities were, they were more or less spontaneous outbursts of hatred that took place in the context of panic and fear following the German invasion. They did not remotely compare with, let alone provide any justification for, the calculated savagery of the treatment meted out by the German masters, directed at wiping out anything other than a slave existence for the Polish people.[61]

Some of the worst German atrocities in the weeks following the invasion were perpetrated by the Volksdeutscher Selbstschutz (Ethnic German Self-Protection), a civilian militia established on Hitler's directions in the first days of September and within little more than a week coming under the control of the SS.[62] Himmler's adjutant, Ludolf von Alvensleben, took over its organization, and later led the Selbstschutz in West Prussia, where the extent of its brutality stood out even in the horrific catalogue of misdeeds of the organization's other branches.[63] Tens of thousands of male ethnic Germans between seventeen and forty-five years of age served in the Selbstschutz.[64] Von Alvensleben told his recruits, at a meeting in Thorn on 16 October: 'You are now the master race here. Nothing was yet built up through softness and weakness . . . That's why I expect, just as our Führer Adolf Hitler expects from you, that you are disciplined, but stand together hard as Krupp steel. Don't be soft, be merciless, and clear out everything that is not German and could hinder us in the work of construction.'[65] Especially in West Prussia, where ethnic conflict had been at its fiercest, the Selbstschutz carried out untold numbers of 'executions' of Polish civilians. On 7 October, von Alvensleben reported that his units had taken the 'sharpest measures' against 4,247 former Polish citizens.[66] When one subordinate Selbstschutz leader reported to von Alvensleben that no executions had been carried out that week, he was asked whether there were no more Poles left at all in his town.[67] The Selbstschutz was eventually wound up – in West Prussia in November, and elsewhere by early 1940 – but only because its uncontrolled atrocities were becoming counter-productive on account of the resulting conflicts with the army and German civil authorities in the occupied areas.[68]

The rampaging actions of the Selbstschutz were only one element of the programme of radical 'ethnic struggle' (*Volkstumskampf*) designed by the SS leadership for the 'new order' in Poland. More systematic 'ethnic cleansing' operations, involving widespread liquidation of targeted groups, were mainly in the hands of the Security Police Einsatzgruppen, following in the wake of the military advance. Already at the end of the first week of the invasion, Heydrich was reported to be enraged – as, apparently, was Hitler too – at the legalities of the military courts, despite 200 executions a day. He was demanding shooting or hanging without trial. 'The nobility, clerics, and Jews must be done away with (*umgebracht*),' were his reported words.[69] He repeated the same sentiments, referring to a general 'ground cleansing' (*Flurbereinigung*), to Halder's Quartermaster-General Eduard Wagner some days later.[70] Reports of atrocities were not long in arriving. By 10–11 September accounts were coming in of an SS massacre of Jews herded into a church, and of an SS shooting of large numbers of Jews.[71] On 12 September Admiral Canaris, chief of the Abwehr, told Keitel that he had heard 'that extensive shootings (*Fusilierungen*) were planned in Poland and that especially the nobility and clergy were to be exterminated (*ausgerottet*)'. Keitel replied 'that this matter had already been decided by the Führer'.[72] Chief of Staff Halder was already by then heard to have said that 'it was the intention of the Führer and of Göring to annihilate (*vernichten*) and exterminate (*auszurotten*) the Polish people', and that 'the rest could not even be hinted at in writing'.[73]

What it amounted to – an all-out 'ethnic cleansing' programme – was explained by Heydrich to the commanders of the Einsatzgruppen on 21 September. The thinking was that the former German provinces would become German Gaue. Another Gau with a 'foreign-speaking population' (*mit fremdsprachiger Bevölkerung*) would be established, with its capital in Cracow. An 'eastern wall' would surround the German provinces, with the 'foreign-speaking Gau' forming a type of 'no man's land' in front of it. The Reichsführer-SS was to be appointed Settlement Commissar for the East (an appointment of vital importance, giving Himmler immense, practically unrestricted powers in the east, confirmed by secret edict of Hitler on 7 October).[74] 'The deportation of Jews into the foreign-speaking Gau, expulsion over the demarcation-line has been approved by the Führer,' Heydrich went on. The process was to be spread over a year. As regards 'the solution of the Polish problem', the 3 per cent at most of the Polish leadership in the occupied territories 'had to be rendered harmless' and put in concentration camps. The Einsatzgruppen were to draw up lists of significant leaders, and of various professional and middle-class groups (including teachers and priests) who were to be deported to the rump territory (soon to be known as the General Government). The 'primitive Poles' were to be used as migrant workers and gradually deported to the 'foreign-speaking Gau'. Poles were to remain no more than seasonal and migrant workers, with their permanent homes in the Cracow region. Jews in urban areas were to be concentrated in ghettos, giving better possibilities of control and readiness for later deportation. Jews in rural areas were to be removed, and placed in towns. Jews were systematically to be transported by goods-train from German areas. Heydrich also envisaged the deportation to Poland of the Reich's Jews, and of 30,000 Gypsies.[75]

Hitler spoke little over a week later to Rosenberg of the Germanization and deportation programme to be carried out in Poland. The three weeks spent in Poland during the campaign had confirmed his ingrained racial prejudices. 'The Poles,' Rosenberg recalled him saying: 'a thin Germanic layer, below that dreadful material. The Jews, the most horrible thing imaginable. The towns covered in dirt. He has learnt a lot in these weeks. Above all: if Poland had ruled for a few decades over the old parts of the Reich, everything would be lice-ridden (*verlaust*) and decayed. A clear, masterful hand was now needed to rule here.' Hitler then referred, along similar lines to Heydrich's address to his Einsatzgruppen chiefs, to his plans for the conquered Polish territories. 'He wanted to divide the now established territory into three strips: 1. between the Vistula and the Bug: the entire Jewry (also from the Reich) along with all somehow unreliable elements. On the Vistula an invincible Eastern Wall – even stronger than in the West. 2. Along the previous border a broad belt of Germanization and colonization. Here there would be a great task for the entire people: to create a German granary, strong peasantry, to resettle there good Germans from all over the world. 3. Between, a Polish "form of state" (*Staatlichkeit*). Whether after decades the settlement belt could be pushed forward will have to be left to the future.'[76]

A few days later, Hitler spoke to Goebbels in similar vein. 'The Führer's judgement on the Poles is annihilatory (*vernichtend*),' Goebbels recorded. 'More animals than human beings . . . The filth of the Poles is unimaginable.' Hitler wanted no assimilation. 'They should be pushed into their reduced state' – meaning the General Government – 'and left entirely among themselves.' If Henry the Lion – the mighty twelfth-century Duke of Saxony and Bavaria, who had resettled peasants on lands in northern and eastern Germany – had conquered the east, the result, given the scope of power available at the time, would have been a 'slavified' German mongrel-race, Hitler went on. 'It's all the better as it is. Now at least we know the laws of race and can act accordingly.'[77]

Hitler hinted in his Reichstag speech of 6 October, though in the vaguest terms for public consumption, at 'cleansing work' (*Sanierungsarbeit*) and massive ethnic resettlement as preparation for the 'new order of ethnographical relations' in former Poland.[78] Only in confidential dealings with those in the regime's leadership who needed to know – a characteristic technique of his rule not to spread information beyond essential limits – did Hitler speak frankly, as he had done to Rosenberg and Goebbels, about what was intended. At a meeting on 17 October in the Reich Chancellery attended by Keitel, Frank, Himmler, Heß, Bormann, Lammers, Frick, and the State Secretary in the Reich Ministry of the Interior, Stuckart, Hitler outlined the draconian policy for Poland.[79] The military should be happy to be freed from administrative responsibility. The General Government was not to become part of the Reich. It was not the task of the administration there to run it like a model province or to establish a sound economic and financial basis. The Polish intelligentsia were to be deprived of any chance to develop into a ruling class.[80] The standard of living was to remain low: 'We only want to get labour supplies from there.' The administration there was to be given a free hand, independent of Berlin ministries. 'We don't want to do anything there that we do in the Reich,' was ominously noted. Carrying out the work there would involve 'a hard ethnic struggle (*Volkstumskampf*) that will not permit any legal restrictions. The methods will not be compatible with our normal principles.' Rule over the area would 'allow us to purify the Reich area too of Jews and Polacks'. Cooperation of the General Government with the new Gaue of Posen and West Prussia was to take place only for resettlement purposes (through Himmler's new role as Commissar for Settlement). 'Cleverness and hardness in this ethnic struggle,' Hitler ended, with usual recourse to national needs as justification, 'must save us from again having to enter the fields of slaughter on account of this land.'[81] 'The devil's work', he called it.[82]

Hitler's approval for what Heydrich had set in motion cannot be doubted.[83] Referring back several months later to the chequered relations of the SS and police in Poland with the army leadership, Heydrich pointed out that the work of the Einsatzgruppen in Poland (as it had been in Austria and Czecho-Slovakia) was 'in accordance with the special order of the Führer'. The 'political activity' carried out in Poland by the Reichsführer-SS, which had caused conflict with some of the army leadership, had followed 'the directives of the Führer as well as the General Field Marshal'. He added 'that the directives according to which the police deployment took place were extraordinarily radical (e.g. orders of liquidation for numerous sectors of the Polish leadership, going into thousands)'. Since the order was not passed on to army leaders, they had presumed that the police and SS were acting arbitrarily.[84]

Indeed, the army commanders on the ground in Poland had been given no explicit instructions about any mandate from Hitler for the murderous 'ethnic cleansing' policy of the SS and Security Police, though Brauchitsch, like Keitel, was well aware of what was intended.[85] This was in itself characteristic of how the regime functioned, and of Hitler's keenness – through keeping full knowledge to the smallest circle possible, and speaking for the most part even there in generalities, however draconian – to cloud his own responsibility. The army's hands were far from unsullied by the atrocities in Poland. Brauchitsch's proclamation to the Poles on 1 September had told them that the Wehrmacht did not regard the population as its enemy, and that all agreements on human rights would be upheld.[86] But already in the first weeks of September numerous army reports recounted plundering, 'arbitrary shootings', 'maltreatment of unarmed, rapes', 'burning of synagogues', and massacres of Jews by soldiers of the Wehrmacht.[87] The army leaders – even the most pro-Nazi among them – nevertheless regarded such repellent actions as serious lapses of discipline, not part of a consistent racially motivated policy of unremitting 'cleansing' to be furthered with all means possible, and sought to punish those involved through the military courts. (In fact, most were amnestied by Hitler through a decree on 4 October justifying German actions as retaliation 'out of bitterness for the atrocities committed by the Poles'.)[88] The commanders on the ground in Poland, harsh though their own military rule was, did not see the atrocities which they acknowledged among their own troops – in their view regrettable, if inevitable, side-effects of the military conquest of a bitter enemy and perceived 'inferior' people – as part of an exterminatory programme of 'ethnic struggle'. Their approach, draconian though their treatment of the Poles was, differed strikingly from the thinking of Hitler, Himmler, and Heydrich.

Gradually, in the second half of September the unease among army commanders in Poland at the savagery of the SS's actions turned to unmistakable criticism.[89] Awareness of this fed complaints from the Nazi leadership about the 'lack of understanding' in the army of what was required in the 'ethnic struggle'.[90] Hitler told Goebbels on 13 October that the military in Poland were 'too soft and yielding' and would be replaced as soon as possible by civil administration. 'Only force is effective with the Poles,' he added. 'Asia begins in Poland.'[91] On 17 October, in a step notably contributing to the extension of the SS's autonomy, Hitler removed the SS and police from military jurisdiction.[92] Two days later an unpublished decree stipulated that military administration of Poland would cease on 25 October, to be replaced by civilian rule. This had already been anticipated a fortnight earlier by Hitler's decision to establish civilian administration in Danzig and West Prussia – a decision directly prompted, it seems, by Forster's complaints about the army's 'lack of understanding' for the measures being taken there.[93]

The transfer of responsibility from the army did little to affect the deteriorating relations between army and SS in Poland. The most forthright – and courageous – denunciations of the continuing horrendous outrages of the SS were made in written reports to Brauchitsch by Colonel-General Johannes Blaskowitz, following the ending of military administration the commander of the army in Poland.[94] His reports condemned the 'criminal atrocities, maltreatment, and plundering carried out by the SS, police, and administration', castigating the 'animal and pathological instincts' of the SS which had brought the slaughter of tens of thousands of Jews and Poles. Blaskowitz feared 'immeasurable brutalization and moral debasement' if the SS were not brought under control – something, he said, which was increasingly impossible within Poland 'since they can well believe themselves officially authorized and justified in committing any act of cruelty'. General Wilhelm Ulex, Commander in Chief of the southern section of the front, reported in similar vein.[95]

The weak-kneed response of army Commander-in-Chief von Brauchitsch

– in effect an apologia for the barbaric 'ethnic cleansing' policy authorized by Hitler – was fateful.[96] It compromised the position of the army, and pointed the way to the accommodation between army and SS about the genocidal actions to be taken in the Soviet Union in 1941. Brauchitsch spoke of 'regrettable mistakes' (*'bedauerliche Mißgriffe'*) in the 'difficult solution' of the 'ethnic-political tasks'. After lengthy discussions with the Reichsführer-SS, he was confident that the future would bring a change. Criticism endangering the 'unity and fighting power of the troops' had to be prohibited. 'The solution of ethnic-political tasks, necessary for securing German living space and ordered by the Führer, had necessarily to lead to otherwise unusual, harsh measures against the Polish population of the occupied area,' he stated. 'The necessarily accelerated execution of these tasks, caused by the imminently decisive struggle of the German people, naturally brought about a further intensification of these measures.'[97] Doubtless anticipating the inevitable explosion at the inadequacies of the army, Brauchitsch did not even deliver Blaskowitz's reports in person to Hitler. As he had done with Beck's memorandum in July 1938, he passed on at least the first report on 18 November 1939 via Hitler's army adjutant Gerhard Engel. At first there was little reaction. Then the expected ferocious denunciation of the 'childish attitudes' in the army leadership inevitably followed. 'You can't wage war with Salvation Army methods,' Hitler raged.[98]

The inquiries Himmler had set in train following the army complaints predictably concluded that it was a matter only of 'trivialities'.[99] But the Reichsführer-SS was angered by the attacks. In March 1940 he eventually sought an opportunity to address the leaders of the army. He accepted responsibility for what had happened, though played down the reports, attributing the accounts of serious atrocities to rumour.[100] According to the memory of one participant, General Weichs, he added that 'he was prepared, in matters that seemed perhaps incomprehensible, to take on responsibility before the people and the world, since the person of the Führer could not be connected with these things'.[101] Another participant, with more cause than most to take a keen interest in Himmler's comments, General Ulex, recalled the Reichsführer-SS saying: 'I do nothing that the Führer does not know about.'[102]

With the sanctioning of the liquidation programme at the core of the barbaric 'ethnic cleansing' drive in Poland, Hitler – and the regime he headed – had crossed the Rubicon. This was no longer a display of outright brutality at home that shocked – as had the massacre of the SA leadership in 1934, or even more so the November Pogrom against the Jews in 1938 – precisely because the structures and traditions of legality in the Reich, whatever the inroads made into them, had not been totally undermined. In what had once been Poland, the violence was unconstrained, systematic, and on a scale never witnessed within the Reich itself. Law, however draconian, counted for nothing. The police were given a free hand. Even the incorporated areas were treated for policing terms as outside the Reich.[103] What was taking place in the conquered territories fell, to be sure, still far short of the all-out genocide that was to emerge during the Russian campaign in the summer of 1941. But it had near-genocidal traits. It was the training-ground for what was to follow.

Hitler's remarks to Rosenberg and Goebbels illustrated how his own impressions of the Poles provided for him the self-justification for the drastic methods he had approved. He had unquestionably been strengthened in these attitudes by Himmler and Heydrich. Goebbels, too, played to Hitler's prejudices in ventilating his own. In mid-October Goebbels told him of the preliminary work carried out on what was to become the nauseating antisemitic 'documentary' film Der ewige Jude (The Eternal Jew). Hitler listened with great interest. What Goebbels said to Hitler might be implied from his own reactions when he viewed the first pictures from what he called the 'ghetto film'. The appearance of the degraded and downtrodden Jews, crushed under the Nazi yoke, had come to resemble the caricature that Goebbels's own propaganda had produced. 'Descriptions so terrible and brutal in detail that your blood clots in your veins,' he commented. 'You shrink back at the sight of such brutishness (Roheit). This Jewry must be annihilated (vernichtet).'[104] A fortnight or so later Goebbels showed Hitler the horrible ritual-slaughter scenes from the film, and reported on his own impressions – already pointing plainly in a genocidal direction – gleaned during his visit to the Lodz ghetto: 'It's indescribable. Those are no longer human beings. They are animals. So it's not a humanitarian but a surgical task. Otherwise Europe will perish through the Jewish disease.'[105]

In a most literal sense, Goebbels, Himmler, Heydrich, and other leading Nazis were 'working towards the Führer', whose authority allowed the realization of their own fantasies. The same was true of countless lesser figures in the racial experiment under way in the occupied territories. Academics – historians at the forefront – excelled themselves in justifying German hegemony in the east.[106] Racial 'experts' in the Party set to work to construct the 'scientific' basis for the inferiority of the Poles.[107] Armies of planners, moved to the east, started to let their imagination run riot in

devising megalomaniac schemes for ethnic resettlement and social restructuring.[108] Hitler had to do no more than provide the general licence for
barbarism. There was no shortage of ready hands to put it into practice.

This began with the heads of the civil administration in occupied Poland.
Forster in Danzig–West Prussia, Greiser in the Warthegau, and Frank in
the General Government were trusted 'Old Fighters', hand-picked for the
task by Hitler. They knew what was expected of them. Regular and precise
directives were not necessary.

The Warthegau provides clear illustration of the ways 'working towards
the Führer' – anticipating Hitler's presumed wishes and intentions – translated into ever more radical actions. Hitler's man in Posen, head of the civil
administration in 'Reichsgau Wartheland' (as it was officially known from
January 1940 onwards), was Arthur Greiser. For Greiser, a native of the
Posen area, the way to Hitler had been the classical one. As with Hitler
himself, the war had been a formative experience. He identified completely
with the 'front-soldier' mentality. Defeat and the loss of his home province
left a searing mark on him. Service in the Freikorps was followed by years
where he scraped by, earning a living as best he could, including running
boat-rides round Danzig harbour.[109] His resentment at his parlous financial
situation doubtless helped drive him further into the *völkisch* camp, then
on into the Nazi Party. He was apparently unemployed when, in 1929, he
was attracted to what he later called 'the solution of the great social question'
– unquestionably synonymous in his mind with the 'ethnic question' in the
former Prussian provinces. He believed that 'in the chaos of party politics,
only Hitler was capable of this solution'.[110]

Greiser was clever and ambitious enough to work his way through the
intrigues of the Danzig Party to become Forster's deputy and President of
the Senate in the Free City, surviving scandals about financial corruption,
his membership of a Freemasons' Lodge in the 1920s, and the stormy
break-up of his first marriage. Greiser's survival owed not a little to his
good connections with Himmler. He was also already prepared to do
anything to retain favour with Hitler. 'For this favour,' recalled Carl Burckhardt, 'no price was too high. A wish expressed by Hitler counted for even
more than an order.'[111] When appointed by Hitler Reich Governor and
Gauleiter of the Warthegau, Greiser's 'gratitude knew no bounds', according
to one contemporary.[112] He lost no opportunity to emphasize 'that he
was *persona gratissima* with the Führer', and also had the ear of the
Reichsführer-SS.[113] He saw his task as working to put into practice the
Führer's 'heroic vision' for the Germanization of the Warthegau, to turn

it into the 'model Gau' of the 'New Order'. He was given full scope to do
so.

The combined headship of state and party in the incorporated area,
following the structure used in the 'Ostmark' and Sudetenland, provided
far greater influence for the Party than was the case in the 'Old Reich'.[114]
Greiser met any obstacles by pointing to 'the special plenipotentiary powers
personally given to me by the Führer' which, he claimed, according to his
mandate had to be more extensive than in other areas of the Reich.[115]

Greiser demanded of his own subordinates that they be 'brutal, harsh,
and again harsh' in the 'ethnic struggle'.[116] Brutality reproduced itself; it
became the norm. Leniency was banned. The climate in the Warthegau can
be gauged from the directive of the head of the constabulary (not the dreaded
Security Police) in one district of the Posen province. Speaking of what he
called the 'Polacks', he laid down that he did not 'want to see any officer
showing mildness to such elements'.[117] The same constabulary chief added,
some months later: 'The Pole is for us an enemy and I expect from every
officer . . . that he acts accordingly. The Poles must feel that they do not
have the right to put themselves on the same level as a people of culture.'[118]
This ethos was passed on to and adopted by practically every one of the
25,000 or so police and 22,500 members of the civil administration – mostly
drawn from the Reich – who controlled the Warthegau.[119]

Hitler's attitude towards policy in the incorporated territories was typical.
He placed great value on giving his Gauleiter the 'necessary freedom of
action' to carry out their difficult tasks. He stressed 'that he only demanded
a report from the Gauleiter after ten years that their area was German, that
is purely German. He would not ask about the methods they had used to
make the area German, and it was immaterial to him if some time in the
future it were established that the methods to win this territory were not
pretty (*unschön*) or open to legal objection.'[120] The inevitable consequence
of this broad mandate – though it was alleged that it ran counter to Hitler's
intention – was competition between Greiser and his arch-rival Forster to
be the first to announce that his Gau was fully Germanized.[121] Greiser and
Forster went about meeting this aim in different ways. While, to Himmler's
intense irritation, Forster swept as many Poles in his area as possible into
the third group of the *Deutsche Volksliste* (German Ethnic List), giving them
German citizenship on approval (constantly subject, that is, to revocation),
Greiser pushed fanatically and ruthlessly for complete *apartheid* – the
maximum separation of the two ethnic groups.[122] While Forster frequently
clashed with Himmler, Greiser gave full support to the policies of the

Reichsführer-SS, and worked in the closest cooperation with the Higher SS-and-Police Chief in the Warthegau, Wilhelm Koppe.

The Warthegau turned years of indescribable torment for the subjugated people into the nearest approximation to a vision of the 'New Order' in the east. The vast deportation and resettlement programmes, the ruthless eradication of Polish cultural influence, the mass-closing of Catholic churches and arrests or murder of clergy, the eviction of Poles from their property, and the scarcely believable levels of discrimination against the majority Polish population – always accompanied by the threat of summary execution – were carried out under the aegis of Greiser and Koppe with little need to involve Hitler. Not least, the vicious drive by the same pairing to rid their Germanized area of the lowest of the low – the Jewish minority in the Warthegau – was to form a vital link in the chain that would lead by late 1941 to the 'Final Solution'.[123]

The rapidity with which the geographical divisions and administrative structure for the occupied territories of former Poland had been improvised, the free hand given to Party bosses, the widespread autonomy which the police had obtained, and the complete absence of legal constraint, had created a power free-for-all in the 'wild east'. But where conflict among the occupying authorities was most endemic, as in the General Government, the greatest concentration of power was plainly revealed to lie in the hands of the Security Police, represented by the Higher SS-and-Police Chief, backed by Himmler and Heydrich. Himmler's 'Black Order', under the Reichs-führer's extended powers as Reich Commissar for the Consolidation of Germandom, and mandated by Hitler's to 'cleanse' the east, had come into its own in the new occupied territories. The unlimited power that war and occupation had brought, and the lessons in barbarism rapidly learnt in former Poland, would be put to immediate use during the onslaught on the Soviet Union in the summer of 1941.

III

Meanwhile, within the Reich itself the beginning of the war had also marked a vital step in the descent into modern barbarism. Here, too, Hitler now authorized mass murder.

Parallel to the murders in occupied Poland, it was an irreversible advance in the direction of genocide. The programme – euphemistically called the 'euthanasia action' – to kill the mentally ill and others incurably sick that he launched in autumn 1939 was to provide a gangway to the vaster extermination programme to come. And, like the destruction of European Jewry, it was evidently linked in his own mind with the war that, he was certain, would bring the fulfilment of his ideological 'mission'.

It was some time in October that Hitler had one of his secretaries type, on his own headed notepaper and backdated to 1 September 1939 – the day that the war had begun – the single sentence: 'Reichsleiter Bouhler and Dr med. Brandt are commissioned with the responsibility of extending the authority of specified doctors so that, after critical assessment of their condition, those adjudged incurably ill can be granted mercy-death.' He took a pen and signed his name below this lapidary, open-ended death-sentence.[124]

By this time, the killing of mental patients, already authorized verbally by Hitler, was well under way. It suited neither Hitler's style nor his instinct to transmit lethal orders in writing. The reason he did so on this one and only occasion was because of the difficulties, in a land where the writ of law was still presumed to run, already being encountered by those attempting, without any obvious authority, to build an organization in conditions of secrecy to implement a murderous mandate.[125] Even then, knowledge of Hitler's written authorization was confined to as few persons as possible. It was ten months later, on 27 August 1940, before even the Reich Minister of Justice, Franz Gürtner, faced with growing criticism of the illegality of what was inevitably leaking more and more into the open, was shown a facsimile of it.[126]

Indeed, there was no basis of legality for what was taking place. Hitler explicitly refused to have a 'euthanasia' law, rejecting the prospect of a cumbersome bureaucracy and legal constraints.[127] Even according to the legal theories of the time, Hitler's mandate could not be regarded as a formal Führer decree and did not, therefore, possess the character of law.[128] But an order from the Führer, whatever its legal status, was nonetheless seen as binding.[129] That applied also to Reich Justice Minister Gürtner. Once he had seen with his own eyes that Hitler's will stood behind the liquidation of the mentally sick, and that it was not the work of Party underlings operating without authority, he gave up his attempts on legal grounds to block or regulate the killings.[130] To a courageous district judge, Lothar Kreyssig, who had written frank protest letters to him about the crass illegality of the action, and on being shown Hitler's authorization had exclaimed that even on the basis of positivist legal theory wrong could not be turned into right, Gürtner gave a simple reply: 'If you cannot recognize the will of the Führer as a source of law, as a basis of law, then you cannot remain a judge.' Kreyssig's notice of retirement followed soon afterwards.[131]

The exchange between Gürtner and Kreyssig shows how far the acceptance of 'Führer power' had undermined the essence of law. The genesis of the 'euthanasia action' that Hitler authorized in writing in October 1939 provides, beyond that, a classic example of the way 'working towards the Führer' converted an ideological goal into realizable policy.

Hitler was indispensable to the process. His well-aired views from the 1920s on 'euthanasia' served after 1933 as an encouragement to those, most notably represented in the National Socialist Doctors' League but by no means confined to fanatical Nazis, anxious to act on the 'problem' of what they described as the 'ballast' of society (Ballastexistenzen).[132]

The notion of the 'destruction of life not worth living' ('Vernichtung lebensunwerten Lebens') had already been the subject of much public debate following the publication in 1920 of a tract by the lawyer Professor Karl Binding and the psychiatrist Dr Alfred Hoche – neither of them a National Socialist – demanding the killing of the incurably sick and insane on request of relatives or the decision of a commission comprising two doctors and two lawyers who had thoroughly investigated the circumstances of a particular case. Among the reasons given for such a policy – later to be voiced by the Nazis – was the need to avoid having to spend money otherwise available for 'productive' purposes on the care of those deemed to be no more than a social burden.[133]

Doctors had, however, overwhelmingly rejected euthanasia during the Weimar era. Psychiatrists began by doing the same, despite arguments already being aired that money spent upon 'idiots' could be put to better use. As professional conditions in psychiatry deteriorated, as pychiatrists' public standing declined – they were often regarded as second-class doctors – and as conditions in the asylums drastically worsened in the wake of severe cuts in public spending by the early 1930s, radical suggestions for reducing the cost of institutionalized support of the mentally ill gained ground. But it was recognized that the public climate for such changes was still not propitious.

Hitler's takeover of power changed that climate – and opened up new possibilities to the medical profession. Some leading psychiatrists were more than ready to exploit them. Hitler's presumed intentions provided guidelines for their endeavours, even if the time was still not deemed right to introduce the programme they wanted. Above all, Hitler's role was decisive in 1938–9 in providing approval for every step that extended into the full 'euthanasia' programme from the autumn of 1939 onwards. Without that approval, it is plain, and without the ideological drive that he embodied, there would have been no 'euthanasia action'.

But the mentality which led to the killing of the mentally sick was no creation of Hitler. Building on foundations firmly laid, especially in the wake of the catastrophic public funding cuts during the Depression years, the erection of the dictatorship had provided licence to the medical and pyschiatric professions after 1933 to think the unthinkable. Minority views, constrained even in a failing democracy, could now become mainstream. The process gathered pace. By 1939, doctors and nurses attached to the asylums were aware of what was required. So was the medical bureaucracy which oiled the wheels of the killing machinery.[134] The climate of opinion among the general public was by this time also not unfavourable. Though there were strong feelings against euthanasia, particularly among those attached to the Churches, others were in favour – notably, it seems, in the case of mentally ill or disabled children – or at least passively prepared to accept it.[135]

Finally, but not least, the point at which, coinciding with the outbreak of war, a secret programme of mass murder could be implemented would have been unimaginable without the progressive erosion of legality and disintegration of formal structures of government that had taken place since 1933.

Hitler had given a strong indication of his own thoughts on how to deal with the incurably ill in *Mein Kampf*, where he advocated their sterilization. His remarks were made in the context of a diatribe on the need to eradicate sexually transmitted diseases from society. He wanted no half-measures. 'It is a half-measure,' he wrote, 'to let incurably sick people steadily contaminate the remaining healthy ones ... The demand that defective people be prevented from propagating equally defective offspring is a demand of the clearest reason ... If necessary, the incurably sick will be pitilessly segregated – a barbaric measure for the unfortunate who is struck by it, but a blessing for his fellow men and posterity.'[136]

For Hitler, typically, when he spoke at the Nuremberg Party Rally in 1929 about how the weakest in society should be handled, the economic argument used by the eugenics lobby in the medical profession and others weighed less heavily than questions of 'racial hygiene' and the 'future maintenance of our ethnic strength (*Volkskraft*), indeed of our ethnic nationhood (*unseres Volkstums*) altogether'.[137] 'If Germany were to have a million children a year,' he declared, 'and do away with (*beseitigen*) 700,000–800,000 of the weakest of them, the result would finally be perhaps even a rise in strength.'[138] This implied racial engineering through mass murder, justified through social-Darwinist ideology, not 'euthanasia' in the conventional sense as the voluntary release from terminal illness.

According to the comments of his doctor, Karl Brandt, in his post-war trial, Hitler was known to favour involuntary euthanasia at the latest from 1933 onwards.[139] Lammers, too, later recalled Hitler musing on the killing of mental patients in 1933 during discussions on the 'Sterilization Law'.[140] But in 1933, German public opinion was nowhere near prepared for such a drastic step. The Nazi regime could not contemplate introducing as controversial a measure as compulsory 'euthanasia' for the incurably sick, certain at the very least at that time to provoke the condemnation of the Catholic Church.

But the idea did not disappear from view. In 1933 a published lengthy memorandum on National Socialist penal law, whose author was the Prussian Minister of Justice, Hanns Kerrl, did not classify voluntary euthanasia, certified by two doctors, as a criminal offence. Kerrl also stated that it would not be an offence, were the state 'legally to order the elimination from life of incurably mentally sick by official organs'.[141] The hierarchy of the Catholic Church responded in predictably hostile manner (though in an unpublished memorandum).[142] In 1935, Gürtner's published report on the work of the commission set up to review the penal code, in direct contrast to Kerrl's line of interpretation, then appeared to rule out explicitly the prospect of any legalization of the killing of the mentally sick.[143] However, Hitler's own position was indicated in his reply in 1935 to the Reich Doctors' Leader Gerhard Wagner (who was instrumental in the drive to introduce an anti-Jewish 'Blood Law'). Evidently, Wagner was pressing for radical measures to bring about the 'destruction of life not worth living'. Hitler reportedly told him that he would 'take up and carry out the questions of euthanasia' in the event of a war. He was 'of the opinion that such a problem could be more smoothly and easily carried out in war', and that resistance, as was to be expected from the Churches, would then have less of an impact than in peacetime. He intended, therefore, 'in the event of a war radically to solve the problem of the mental asylums'.[144]

For the next three years, Hitler had little involvement with the 'euthanasia' issue. Others were more active. Evidently encouraged by Hitler's remarks that he did intend, once the opportunity presented itself through the war for which the regime was preparing, to introduce a 'euthanasia programme', Reich Doctors' Leader Wagner pushed forward discussions on how the population should be prepared for such action. Calculations were published on the cost of upkeep of the mentally sick and hereditarily ill, instilling the impression of what could be done for the good of the people with vast resources now being 'wasted' on 'useless' lives. Cameras were sent into the asylums to produce scenes to horrify the German public and convince them of the need to eliminate those portrayed as the dregs of society for the good of the whole population.[145] The National Socialist Racial and Political Office (NS-*Rasse und Politisches Amt*) produced five silent films of this kind between 1935 and 1937.[146] Hitler himself liked one of them, *Erbkrank* (Hereditarily Ill), made in 1936, so much that he commissioned a sequel with sound, *Opfer der Vergangenheit* (Victims of the Past) and had the film shown in all German cinemas in 1937.[147]

From 1936 onwards, the Churches were forced to transfer the patients in the sanatoria they ran into asylums controlled by the state.[148] These had already had their budgets slashed as the overcrowding grew, and the quality of the staff deteriorated.[149] Rumours circulated that the Reich Ministry of the Interior was pondering the drastic reduction of food-rations for asylum patients in the event of war.[150] In the SS organ *Das Schwarze Korps* a reader's letter in 1937 demanding a law to permit the killing of mentally retarded children, if their parents gave consent, was accompanied by a commentary advocating a law 'that helps nature to its right'. The view that there was no right to kill, the paper declared, could be countered by stating that there was a hundred times less right to defy nature by keeping alive 'what was not born to life'.[151] It was to take away nothing from a seriously brain-damaged child to 'extinguish its light of life'. The 'child-euthanasia' programme was presaged in such sentiments. Murder in the asylums was in the air. It was a matter of time and occasion until it was implemented.

In the interim, the 'Chancellery of the Führer of the NSDAP', the agency which would come to run the 'euthanasia action' from 1939 onwards, was doing all it could to expand its own power-base in the political jungle of the Third Reich. Despite its impressive name, the Führer Chancellery had little actual power. Hitler had set it up at the end of 1934 to deal with correspondence from Party members directed to himself as head of the NSDAP. It was officially meant to serve as the agency to keep the Führer in direct touch with the concerns of his people.[152] Much of the correspondence, as Hitler himself made clear, was a matter of trivial complaints, petty grievances, and minor personal squabbles of Party members. But a vast number of letters to Hitler did pour in after 1933 – around a quarter of a million a year in the later 1930s.[153] And, to preserve the fiction of the Führer listening to the cares of his people, many of them needed attention.

Hitler put the Führer Chancellery under the control of Philipp Bouhler –
a member of the Party's *Reichsleitung* (Reich Leadership) since 1933, a
quiet, bureaucratic type but intensely loyal and deferential. Tenacious and
efficient, Bouhler had been in no small measure responsible for setting up
the Party's administrative organization after its refoundation in 1925.[154]
At the time of his appointment he was thirty-five years old, somewhat
owlish-looking with round, black horn-rimmed spectacles and swept-back
hair. His soft-voiced and polite manner was unusual in the Nazi leadership.
He was a quiet man behind the scenes who, at another time in another
place, might have become a company secretary. But Bouhler, still bearing a
walking disability – and perhaps psychological scars – from the serious
injuries to his legs sustained towards the end of the war which had prevented
him from pursuing an officer's career in the army as his father had done,
was ambitious.[155] He was also, whatever his introverted mannerisms, ideologically fanatical. And exploiting his direct connections with Hitler, the
vagueness of his remit, and the randomness of the business that came the
way of the organization he headed, he was now able to expand his own
little empire – treading on numerous toes along the way. By the time the
Führer Chancellery moved in 1936 into new accommodation close to the
Reich Chancellery, it consisted of six departments, and the original twenty-
six employees had almost doubled, increasing five-fold by 1942.[156] Of the
various departments, the most important was Department (*Amt*) II (from
1939 Main Department – *Hauptamt*) headed by Bouhler's deputy, Viktor
Brack. This Department itself covered a wide range of heterogeneous
business but, in its section 'IIb', under Hans Hefelmann, was responsible
for handling petitions relating to the Reich Ministry of the Interior, including
sensitive issues touching on the competence of the health department of the
Ministry.[157] Brack, five years younger than Bouhler, was, if anything, even
more ambitious than his boss. He had a classical Nazi background: *völkisch*
upbringing, Freikorps, participation in the Beerhall Putsch, study of agricultural economics at the Technische Hochschule in Munich, student activism,
entry into the Party and SS at the age of twenty-five in 1929. His father
was Frau Himmler's doctor. He himself acted for a time as Himmler's
chauffeur.[158] Brack was ideologically attuned to what was wanted. And he
was ready to grasp an opportunity when he saw one.

This came some time in the first months of 1939. Around that time the
father of a severely handicapped child – born blind, with no left forearm
and a deformed leg – in Pomßen, near Leipzig, sent in a petition to Hitler,
asking for the child to be released through mercy-killing. The petition

arrived in Hefelmann's office in the Führer Chancellery.[159] Hefelmann did not consider involving either the Reich Ministry of the Interior or the Reich Ministry of Justice. He thought it should be taken to Hitler himself, to see how the Führer thought it should be handled.[160] This was probably in May or June 1939. Hitler sent his doctor, Karl Brandt, to the University of Leipzig Children's Clinic, to consult the child's doctors with the mandate, and, if the position was as the father had described it, to authorize the doctors in his name to carry out euthanasia.[161] This was done towards the end of July 1939. Soon after Brandt's return, he was verbally empowered by Hitler, as was Bouhler, to take similar action should other cases arise. (The case of the child from Pomßen was evidently not an isolated instance around this time.)[162] Whether Hitler took this step unprompted, or whether it followed a suggestion from Brandt or the ambitious Bouhler is not known. But between February and May 1939 Hefelmann, on Brandt's instructions, carried out discussions with doctors known to be sympathetic and eventually set up a camouflaged organization that was given the title 'Reich Committee for the Scientific Registration of Serious Hereditary and Congenital Suffering' (*Reichsausschuß zur wissenschaftlichen Erfassung erb- und anlagebedingter schwerer Leiden*'). Between 5,000 and 8,000 children are estimated to have been put to death, mostly with injections of the barbiturate luminal, under its aegis.[163]

In July Hitler told Lammers, Bormann, and Dr Leonardo Conti (recently appointed Reich Health Leader and State Secretary for Health in the Reich Ministry of the Interior) that he favoured mercy-killing for seriously ill mental patients. Better use of hospitals, doctors, and nursing staff could be made in war, he stated. Conti was commissioned to investigate the feasibility of such a programme.[164] By then, war was looming. Hitler's own comments showed that he continued to see a 'euthanasia programme' in the context of war. By that time, too, Hitler had probably received the evaluation commissioned around the start of the year by Brack from Dr Joseph Mayer, Professor of Moral Theology at the University of Paderborn. Hitler had been uneasy about likely reaction of the Churches in the event of the introduction of a 'euthanasia programme'. He imagined both the Catholic and Protestant Churches would outrightly oppose it. Mayer, who in 1927 had published a tract in favour of the legal sterilization of the mentally sick, was now asked to assess the attitude of the Catholic Church. He sided with the right of the state to take the lives of the mentally ill. Though this was against orthodox Catholic teaching, Mayer left the impression that unequivocal opposition from the Churches was not to be expected. This was the conclusion which Hitler apparently drew, following further discreet inquiry.[165] The biggest internal obstacle to such a programme appeared to be surmountable. The programme could go ahead.

The organization, set up to deal with the 'euthanasia' of children, was to hand. Brack had heard indirectly of Hitler's instructions to Conti at the July meeting.[166] Spotting his chance, but needing to act without delay, if control were not to be lost to Conti and the Reich Ministry of the Interior, he had Hefelmann draw up a short statistical memorandum on the asylums and took it to Bouhler. The head of the Führer Chancellery had little difficulty in persuading Hitler to extend the authorization he had earlier granted to himself and Brandt to deal with the children's 'euthanasia'. It was in August 1939 that Hitler told Bouhler that he wanted the strictest secrecy maintained, and 'a completely unbureaucratic solution of this problem'. The Reich Ministry of the Interior should be kept out of it as far as possible.[167]

Shortly after this, a sizeable number of doctors were summoned to a meeting in the Reich Chancellery to seek their views on such a programme. They were overwhelmingly in favour and ready to cooperate. They suggested that around 60,000 patients might be 'eligible'.[168] The number involved meant there was a serious problem about maintaining secrecy. Once more, camouflaged organizations were needed. Three were set up to distribute questionnaires to the asylums (the Reich Association of Asylums), handle personnel and finance matters (Community Foundation for the Care of Asylums), and organize transport (Community Patients' Transport). They were based, under Brack's direction, in an unpretentious villa in Berlin-Charlottenburg, Tiergartenstraße 4, from which the entire 'euthanasia action' drew its code-name 'T4'. Apart from Bouhler, Brandt, and Brack the organization comprised 114 persons.[169]

Plainly, the construction of such an organization and the implementation of its gruesome task needed more than simply the verbal authorization that had sufficed for the children's 'euthanasia' up to then. This is what prompted Hitler's almost casual written authorization some weeks later, backdated (as we noted) to 1 September. This formless empowering, and the way the Führer Chancellery had been able, without the ministries of state even being informed, to expropriate control over a programme calculated to bring the deaths of tens of thousands in an action lacking any basis in law, is the clearest indication of how far internal structures of government had been deformed and superseded by executive agencies devoted to implementing what they saw as the will of the Führer. The cloak-and-dagger secrecy –

some leading figures, including Brack, even worked with false names – highlighted the illegality of what was taking place.[170] The regime had taken the step into outright criminality.

The medical staff of the asylums selected their own patients for inclusion in the 'euthanasia action'. They, too, were 'working towards the Führer', whether or not this was their overt motivation. Patients included had their names marked with a red cross. Those to be spared had a blue 'minus' sign against their names.[171] The killing, mostly by carbon monoxide gas administered by doctors under no compulsion to participate, was carried out in selected asylums, the most notorious of which were Grafeneck, Hadamar, Bernburg, Brandenburg, Hartheim, and Sonnenstein.[172]

Alongside the T4 'action', the Gauleiter of Pomerania, Franz Schwede-Coburg, rapidly alerted to the new possibilities, worked closely with the SS in October 1939 to 'clear' the asylums near the coastal towns of Stralsund, Swinemünde, and Stettin to make space for ethnic Germans from the Baltic region (and for an SS barracks at Stralsund). Patients were removed from the asylums, transported to Neustadt, not far from Danzig, and shot by squads of SS men. Gauleiter Erich Koch was quick to follow suit, arranging to pay for the costs of 'evacuating' 1,558 patients from asylums in his Gau of East Prussia, liquidated by an SS squad provided by Wilhelm Koppe, newly appointed Police Chief in Gauleiter Arthur Greiser's Reichsgau Posen. This was the 'Sonderkommando Lange', which was soon put to use in Greiser's own Gau, deploying prototype mobile gas-vans to kill the mentally sick in this part of annexed Poland. By mid-1940, these regional 'actions' had claimed the lives of an estimated 10,000 victims.[173]

By the time 'Aktion-T4' was halted – as secretly as it had begun – in August 1941, the target-figure laid down by the doctors in the late summer had been surpassed. In the T4 'action' alone by this date, between 70,000 and 90,000 patients are reckoned to have fallen victim to Hitler's 'euthanasia programme'.[174] Since the killings were neither confined to the T4 'action', nor ended with the halt to that 'action' in 1941, the total number of victims of Nazism's drive to liquidate the mentally ill may have been close on double that number.[175]

IV

Was there the will to halt the already advanced rupture of civilization and descent into modern barbarism that had so swiftly broken new ground since the start of the war? And even if there were the will, could anything be done?

Given Hitler's outright dominance and unassailable position within the regime, significant change could by this time, autumn 1939, be brought about only through his deposition or assassination. This basic truth had been finally grasped the previous summer, during the Sudeten crisis, by those individuals in high-ranking places in the military, Foreign Ministry, and elsewhere close to the levers of power who had tentatively felt their way towards radical opposition to the regime. For long even some of these individuals had tended to exempt Hitler from the criticism they levelled at others, especially Himmler, Heydrich, and the Gestapo. But by now they were aware that without change at the very top, there would be no change at all. This realization started to forge tighter links between the disparate individuals and groups concerned. Oster, backed by his boss, the enigmatic Canaris, was the driving-force in making the Abwehr the centre of an oppositional network, building on the contacts made and relationships forged the previous summer. Oster placed his most trusted associate, and implacably opposed to Hitler, Lieutenant-Colonel Helmuth Groscurth, as liaison with Chief of Staff Halder at the headquarters of the Army High Command in Zossen, just south of Berlin. He encouraged Weizsäcker to appoint, as the Foreign Office's liaison at army headquarters, another opponent of the regime, Rittmeister (Major in the Cavalry) Hasso von Etzdorf. This was probably done on the initiative of Erich Kordt, head of the Ministerial Bureau who continued, under Weizsäcker's protection, to make the Foreign Office another centre of oppositional contacts, placing sympathizers (including his brother, Theo) in embassies abroad. Oster also appointed to his own staff another individual who would play an energetic role in extending and deepening oppositional contacts while officially gathering foreign intelligence: the able and well-connected lawyer Hans Dohnanyi, for some years a close associate of Reich Justice Minister Gürtner, and who had helped clear former Commander-in-Chief of the Army Fritsch of the trumped-up charges of homosexual relations that had been laid against him. Dohnanyi would regularly drive Oster during autumn 1939 – dismal weeks for those opposed to Hitler – to see the man whom practically all who hoped to see an early end to the Nazi regime regarded as the patron of the oppositional groups, former Chief of the General Staff, Ludwig Beck.[176] Gradually, something beginning to resemble a fundamental, conspiratorial resistance movement among, necessarily, existing or former 'servants' of the regime was in the process of emerging.[177] The dilemma for those individuals, mostly national-conservative in inclination, patriots all, in contemplating the unseating of the head of state was great, and even more acute now that Germany was at war.

The autumn of 1939 would provide a crucial testing-time for the national-conservative resistance. In the end, they would resign themselves to failure. At the centre of their concern was not in the first instance the bestiality in Poland (though the detailed reports of the abominations there certainly served to cement oppositional feeling and the sense of urgency, both for moral reasons and out of a sense of national shame, at the need to be rid of Hitler and his henchmen who were responsible for such criminal acts).[178] Nor was it the 'euthanasia action'. Of the mass murder in the asylums they had not for months any real inkling. At any rate, it was not voiced as a matter of prime concern. The key issue for them, as it had been for two years or so, was the certainty that Hitler was leading Germany to catastrophe through engaging in war with the western powers. Preventing a calamitous attack on France and Britain, and ending the war, was vital. This issue came to a head in the autumn of 1939, when Hitler was determined to press on with an early attack on the West. But even before Hitler pulled back – because of poor weather conditions – from such a risky venture in the autumn and winter, then went on the following spring to gain unimaginable military successes in the western campaign, the fragility, weakness, and divisions of the nascent resistance had been fully laid bare. No attempt to remove Hitler had been made.[179]

Hitler could by late 1939 be brought down in only one of two ways: a *coup d'état* from above, meaning a strike from within the regime's leadership from those with access to power and military might; or, something which the Dictator never ruled out, an assassination attempt from below, by a maverick individual operating entirely alone, outside any of the known – by now tiny, fragmented, and utterly powerless – left-wing underground resistance groups which could so easily be infiltrated by the Gestapo.[180] While generals and leading civil servants pondered whether they *might* act, but lacked the will and determination to do so, one man with no access to the corridors of power, no political links, and no hard-and-fast ideology, a Swabian joiner by the name of Georg Elser, *did* act. In early November 1939

Elser would come closer to destroying Hitler than anyone until July 1944. Only luck would save the Dictator on this occasion. And Elser's motives, built on the naïvety of elemental feeling rather than arising from the tortured consciences of the better-read and more knowledgeable, would mirror not the interests of those in high places but, without doubt, concerns of countless ordinary Germans at the time. We will return to them shortly.

For Hitler, the swift and comprehensive demolition of Poland did not signal a victory to sit upon and await developments. Certainly, he hoped that the West, having now witnessed the might of the Wehrmacht in action, would – from his point of view – see sense, and come to terms with Germany. The peace feelers that he put out in September and October were couched in this vein. As Weizsäcker – reckoning the chances of peace to be no higher than 20 per cent – put it early in October, summarizing what he understood as Hitler's desired outcome, in the somewhat unlikely event that London might agree to a settlement at the expense of Poland, Germany 'would be spared the awkward decision on how England could be militarily forced down'.[181] The western powers had done absolutely nothing militarily to help Poland.[182] Perhaps they could now be persuaded to accept the *fait accompli*, agree to a relatively generous victor's peace, and end the war, giving him the return of former German colonies and, especially, the free hand in the east that he had always demanded.[183] Had the western powers complied with such proposals – and further overtures to Britain would be made during 1940 – it would merely have deferred the inevitable conflict that Hitler had reckoned with since 1937. As it was, Hitler, though his overtures were serious enough, had few expectations that Britain would show interest in a settlement, particularly once the British cabinet had announced that it was preparing for a war that would last at least three years. He was sure that the western powers would try to hold out as long as possible, until their armaments programmes were complete.[184] That would mark a danger-point for Germany. Though – a view not shared by his generals – he held the French military in some contempt, he had a high esteem of British resilience and fighting-power.[185] And behind the British, there was always the threat (which at this time he did not rate highly) that in due course the Americans would intervene. So there was no time to lose. On the very day after his return to Berlin, with the shells still raining down on Warsaw, Hitler told his military leaders to prepare for an attack on the West that very autumn.[186]

'Militarily,' he declared, 'time, especially in the psychological and material sense, works against us.' Victory over Poland had brought a growth in prestige. But, he went on, 'all historical successes come to nothing when they are not continued'. Meanwhile, Germany's enemies were improving their military capacity. If they were to reach the borders of the Reich, it would be too late for a counter-attack. They could destroy the Ruhr. 'Therefore, no delay until the enemy arrives, but, should peaceful efforts fail, direct assault in the West.' He derided the French who, he said, 'have less value than the Poles'. The British, however, 'are deciders'. It was, therefore, 'essential that immediate plans for an attack against France be prepared'. The defeat of France, it was plainly inferred, would force Britain to terms. Hitler brought out obvious objections to an early strike. The rainy season would arrive within a few weeks. The air-force would be better in spring. 'But we cannot wait,' he insisted. If a settlement with Chamberlain were not possible, he would 'smash the enemy until he collapses'. The goal was 'to bring England to its knees; to destroy France'.[187] His favoured time for carrying out the attack was the end of October.[188] The Commanders-in-Chief – even Göring – were taken aback. But none protested. Hitler casually threw his notes into the fire when he had finished speaking.[189]

Two days later, Hitler told Rosenberg that he would propose a major peace conference (together with an armistice and demobilization) to regulate all matters rationally. Rosenberg asked whether he intended to prosecute the war in the West. 'Naturally,' replied Hitler. The Maginot Line, Rosenberg recorded him saying, was no longer a deterrent. If the English did not want peace, he would attack them with all means available 'and annihilate (vernichten) them' – again, his favourite phrase.[190]

Hitler's speech to the Reichstag on 6 October indeed held out, as he had indicated to Rosenberg, the prospect of a conference of the leading nations to settle Europe's problems of peace and security.[191] But a starting-point was that the division of Poland between Germany and the Soviet Union was to remain. There would be no re-creation of the Poland of the Versailles settlement.[192] It would be peace on Hitler's terms, with no concessions on what he had won. He painted a lurid picture of death and destruction if the western powers should decline his 'offer'. He blamed the warmongering on 'a certain Jewish-international capitalism and journalism', implying in particular Churchill and his supporters.[193] If Churchill's view should prevail, he concluded, then Germany would fight. Riding one of his main hobby-horses, he added: 'A November 1918 will never be repeated in German history.'[194] The speech amounted to an olive-branch clenched in a mailed fist.

Hitler's 'offer' was dismissed by Chamberlain in a speech in the House of Commons six days later.[195] It was what Hitler had expected. He had not waited. On the very day of his Reichstag speech, he stressed to Brauchitsch and Halder that a decisive move in the north-west was necessary to prevent a French advance that autumn through Belgium, threatening the Ruhr.[196] Two days later Brauchitsch was informed that Hitler had provisionally set 25 November as the date of attack.[197] One general, Colonel-General Ritter von Leeb, noted in his diary that day that there was evidently a serious intent to carry out 'this mad attack', breaching the neutrality of Holland, Belgium, and Luxemburg, which meant that the Reichstag speech had been 'merely lying to the German people'.[198] On this same day, 9 October, Hitler completed a lengthy memorandum that he had worked on for two nights, outlining and justifying his plans for an attack on the West. He had specifically prepared it because of his awareness of opposition to the idea in the army leadership.[199] Again, he emphasized that time was of the essence. The attack could not begin soon enough. The aim was the complete military defeat of the western powers.[200] He read out the memorandum at a meeting with his military leaders on 10 October.[201] Its contents were embodied in 'Directive No.6 for the Conduct of War' issued later that day (though dated 9 October), stating Hitler's determination 'without letting much time pass by' to take offensive action.[202]

When Hitler heard on 12 October of Chamberlain's rejection of his 'peace offer', he made no effort – as Weizsäcker thought might still have been possible – to probe for feasible openings to defuse the situation, but lost no time in announcing, even without waiting for the full text of Chamberlain's speech, that Britain had spurned the hand of peace and that, consequently, the war continued.[203] On 16 October Hitler told Brauchitsch he had given up hope of coming to an agreement with the West. 'The British,' he said, 'will be ready to talk only after defeats. We must get at them as quickly as possible.' He reckoned with a date between 15 and 20 November.[204] Within a matter of days, Hitler had brought this date forward and now fixed 'Case Yellow', as the attack on the West had been code-named, for 12 November.[205]

Speaking to his generals, Hitler confined himself largely to military objectives. To his trusted circle, and to Party leaders, he was more expressive. Goebbels found him high in confidence on 11 October. Germany's defeat in the last war, he stated, was solely attributable to treachery. This time traitors would not be spared.[206] He responded to Chamberlain's dismissal of his 'peace offer' by stating that he was glad that he could now 'go for England' ('*gegen England losgehen*'). He had given up almost all hope of peace. 'The English will have to learn the hard way,' he stated.[207]

He was in similar mood when he addressed the Reichs- and Gauleiter in a two-hour speech on 21 October. He reckoned war with the West was unavoidable. There was no other choice. But at its end would be 'the great and all-embracing (*umfassende*) German people's Reich (*Volksreich*)'.[208] He would, Hitler told his Party leaders, unleash his major assault on the West – and on England itself – within a fortnight or so. He would use all methods available, including attacks on cities. After defeating England and France he would again turn to the East. Then – an allusion to the Holy Roman Empire of the Middle Ages – he would create a Germany as of old, incorporating Belgium and Switzerland.[209] Hitler was evidently still thinking along such lines when he told Goebbels a few days later he had earmarked Burgundy for the resettlement of the South Tyroleans. 'He's already distributing French provinces,' noted the Propaganda Minister. 'He hurries far ahead of all steps of development. Just like every genius.'[210]

On 6 November Goebbels was again listening to Hitler's views on the war. 'He's of the opinion that England has to get a knock-out blow. That's right. England's power is now simply a myth, not a reality any longer. All the more reason why it must be smashed. Before then there will be no peace in the world. The military say we're not ready. But no army will ever be ready. That's not the point. It's a question of being more ready than the others. And that's the case . . . The strike against the western powers will not have to wait much longer.' 'Perhaps,' added Goebbels, 'the Führer will succeed sooner than we all think in annulling the Peace of Westphalia. With that his historic life will be crowned.'[211] Goebbels thought the decision to go ahead was imminent.[212]

All the signs are that the pressure for an early strike against the West came directly from Hitler, without initiation or prompting from other quarters. That it received the support of Goebbels and the Party leadership was axiomatic. Within the military, as Goebbels's comments hinted, it was a different matter. Hitler could reckon with the backing – or at least lack of objection – of Raeder, Commander-in-Chief of the Navy.[213] And whatever his private anxieties, Göring would never deviate in public from Hitler's line.[214] But, as Hitler recognized, the decision to attack the West already in the autumn set him once more on a collision course with the army leadership, spearheaded by Brauchitsch and Halder. On 14 October, primed by Weizsäcker about Hitler's reaction to Chamberlain's speech rejecting his 'peace offer', the head of the army and his Chief of Staff met to discuss the consequences. Halder noted three possibilities: attack, wait, 'fundamental changes'. None offered prospects of decisive success, least of all the last one 'since it is essentially negative and tends to render us vulnerable'.[215] The qualifying remarks were made by Brauchitsch. The weak, ultra-cautious, and tradition-bound Commander-in-Chief of the army could not look beyond conventional attempts to dissuade Hitler from what he thought was a disastrous course of action. But he was evidently responding to a suggestion floated by Halder, following his discussions with Weizsäcker the previous day, to have Hitler arrested at the moment of the order for attack on the West.[216] The cryptic third possibility signified then no less than the extraordinary fact that in the early stages of a major war the two highest representatives of the army were airing the possibility of a form of *coup d'état* involving the removal of Hitler as head of state.[217]

The differences between the two army leaders were nonetheless wide. And nothing flowed from the discussion in the direction of an embryonic plan to unseat Hitler. Brauchitsch attempted, within the bounds of ortho-doxy, to have favoured generals such as Reichenau and Rundstedt try to influence Hitler to change his mind – a fruitless enterprise.[218] Halder went further. By early November he was, if anything, still more convinced that direct action against Hitler was necessary to prevent the imminent catas-trophe. In this, his views were coming to correspond with the small numbers of radical opponents of the regime in the Foreign Ministry and in the Abwehr who were now actively contemplating measures to remove Hitler.[219]

In the last weeks of October various notions of deposing Hitler – often unrealistic or scarcely thought through – were furtively pondered by the tiny, disparate, only loosely connected oppositional groups. Goerdeler and his main contacts – Hassell, Beck, and Popitz – were one such cluster, weighing up for a time whether a transitional government headed by Göring (whose reluctance to engage in war with Britain was known to them) might be an option.[220] This cluster, through Beck, forged loose links with the group based in the Abwehr – Oster, Dohnanyi, Gisevius, and Groscurth. The latter worked out a plan of action for a coup, involving the arrest of Hitler (perhaps declaring him mentally ill), along with Himmler, Heydrich, Ribbentrop, Göring, Goebbels, and other leading Nazis.[221] Encouraged by their chief, Admiral Canaris, and driven on by Oster, the Abwehr group attempted, though with little success, to gain backing for their ideas from selected officers at General Staff headquarters in Zossen. Their ambivalence about Halder meant that they did not approach him directly. Moreover, they knew nothing of the thoughts he had aired to Brauchitsch on 14 October.[222] A third set of individuals sharing the view that Hitler had to be removed and war with the West prevented centred on Weizsäcker in the Foreign Ministry, and was chiefly represented by Erich Kordt, who was able to utilize his position as head of Ribbentrop's Ministerial Bureau to foster contacts at home and abroad.[223] As we have noted, this grouping had contact to the Abwehr group and to known sympathizers in the General Staff – mainly staff officers, though at this point not Halder himself – through Weizsäcker's army liaison, Legation Secretary Hasso von Etzdorf.[224]

Halder himself (and his most immediate friend and subordinate General Otto von Stülpnagel) came round to the idea of a putsch by the end of the month, after Hitler had confirmed his intention of a strike on 12 November.[225] Halder sent Stülpnagel to take surreptitious soundings among selected generals about their likely response to a coup. The findings were not encouraging. While army-group commanders such as Bock and Rundstedt were opposed to an offensive against the West, they rejected the idea of a putsch, partly on the grounds that they were themselves unsure whether they would retain the backing of their subordinate officers. In addition, Halder established to his own satisfaction, based on a 'sample' of public opinion drawn from the father of his chauffeur and a few others, that the German people supported Hitler and were not ready for a putsch.[226] Halder's hesitancy reflected his own deep uncertainty about the moral as well as security aspect of a strike against the head of state and supreme commander of the armed forces. Others took a bolder stance. But, though loosely bonded through parallel thoughts of getting rid of Hitler, the different oppositional clusters had no coherent, unified, and agreed plan for action. Nor, while now accepting Halder's readiness to act, was there full confidence in the determination of the Chief of Staff, on whom practically everything depended, to see it through.[227]

This was the position around noon on 5 November when Brauchitsch nervously made his way through the corridors of the Reich Chancellery to confront Hitler directly about the decision to attack the West. If the attack were to go ahead on schedule on 12 November, the order to make operational preparations had to be confirmed to the Supreme Commander of the Army by 1p.m. on the fifth. Among the oppositional groups, the hope was that Brauchitsch could finally be persuaded to go along with a putsch if Hitler, as was to be expected, held firm to his decision for an attack. Halder waited in the ante-room while Brauchitsch and Hitler conferred together. Keitel joined them some while later. The meeting was a fiasco. It lasted no longer than twenty minutes. Brauchitsch hesitantly began to tell Hitler that preparations were not sufficiently advanced for an offensive against the West which, therefore, had every chance of proving catastrophic.

He went on to back up his argument by pointing out that the infantry had shown morale and technical weaknesses in the attack on Poland, and that the discipline of officers and men had often been lacking. The Front showed similar symptoms to those of 1917–18, he claimed. This was a bad mistake by Brauchitsch. It diverted from the main issue, and, as Brauchitsch could have anticipated, it provoked Hitler into a furious outburst. He wanted concrete evidence, he fumed, and demanded to know how many death-sentences had been carried out. He did not believe Brauchitsch, and would fly the next night to the Front to see for himself. Then he dismissed Brauchitsch's main point. The army was unprepared, he asserted, because it did not want to fight. The weather would still be bad in the spring – and furthermore bad for the enemy too. He knew the 'spirit of Zossen', he raged, and would destroy it. Almost shaking with anger, Hitler marched out of the room, slamming the door, leaving the head of the army speechless, trembling, face as white as chalk, and broken.[228]

'Any sober discussion of these things is impossible with him,' Halder commented, in something of an understatement.[229] But for Halder the impact of the meeting went further. Talk of destroying the 'spirit of Zossen' suggested to the Chief of Staff that Hitler knew of the plot to unseat him. The Gestapo could turn up in Zossen any time. Halder returned in panic to his headquarters and ordered the destruction of all papers relating to the conspiracy.[230] Next day he told Groscurth that the attack in the West would be carried out. There was nothing to be done. 'Very depressing impression,' recorded Groscurth.[231]

Hitler had given the order for the offensive at 1.30p.m. on 5 November, soon after his interview with Brauchitsch.[232] Two days later the attack was postponed because of poor weather.[233] But the chance to strike against Hitler had been lost. The circumstances would not be as favourable for several years. The order for the attack, meant to be the moment to undertake the proposed coup, had come and gone. Brauchitsch, badly shaken by his audience with Hitler, had indicated that he would do nothing, though would not try to hinder a putsch. Canaris, approached by Halder, was disgusted at the suggestion that he should instigate Hitler's assassination. Other than this suggestion that someone else might take over responsibility for the dirty work, Halder now did little. The moment had passed. He gradually pulled back from the opposition's plans. In the end, he lacked the will, determination, and courage to act. The Abwehr group did not give up. But they acknowledged diminishing prospects of success. Oster's soundings with Witzleben, then with Leeb, Bock, and Rundstedt, produced mixed results.[234]

The truth was that the army was divided. Some generals opposed Hitler. But there were more who backed him. And below the high command, there were junior officers, let alone the rank-and-file, whose reactions to any attempt to stop Hitler dead in his tracks were uncertain. Throughout the conflict with the army leadership, Hitler continued to hold the whip-hand. And he had not yielded in the slightest. Despite repeated postponements because of bad weather – twenty-nine in all – he had not cancelled his offensive against the West.[235] Divisions, distrust, fragmentation, but above all a lack of resolve had prevented the oppositional groups – especially the key figures in the military – from acting.

The plotters in the Abwehr, Foreign Ministry, and General Staff headquarters were as astonished as all other Germans when they heard of an attack on Hitler's life that had taken place in the Bürgerbräukeller on the evening of 8 November 1939. They thought it might have come from someone within their own ranks, or been carried out by dissident Nazis, or some other set of opponents – Communists, clerics, or 'reactionaries' – and that Hitler had been tipped off in time.[236] In fact, Hitler, sitting in the compartment of his special train and discussing with Goebbels how the showdown with the clergy would have to await the end of the war, was wholly unaware of what had happened until his journey to Berlin was interrupted at Nuremberg with the news. His first reaction was that the report must be wrong.[237] According to Goebbels, he thought it was a 'hoax' ('*Mystifikation*').[238] The official version was soon put out that the British Secret Service was behind the assassination attempt, and that the perpetrator was 'a creature' of Otto Strasser.[239] The capture next day of the British agents Major R.H. Stevens and Captain S. Payne Best on the Dutch border was used by propaganda to underpin this far-fetched interpretation.[240]

The truth was less elaborate – but all the more stunning. The attempt had been carried out by a single person, an ordinary German, a man from the working class, acting without the help or knowledge of anyone else.[241] Where generals had hesitated, he had tried to blow up Hitler to save Germany and Europe from even greater disaster.

His name was George Elser. He was a joiner from Königsbronn in Württemberg.[242] At the time that he attempted to kill Hitler he was thirty-six years old, small in stature, with dark, wavy hair brushed back. Those who knew him – they were not many – thought well of him. He was a loner with few friends – quiet, reserved, industrious, and a perfectionist in his work. He had little education to speak of, did not read books, and scarcely bothered with newspapers. Even in the days immediately preceding his assassination attempt, he took so little interest in the news that he did not realize that because of the pressing business of the war – these were, as we have seen, precisely the days when the decision for the western offensive was taken, then rescinded – Hitler had pulled out of giving his usual address to the 'Old Fighters' on the anniversary of the Beerhall Putsch, and was to be replaced by Heß. The bomb-attack would, therefore, have been unnecessary. But Elser knew nothing of this, nor of Hitler's decision then to give the speech after all. Elser was, remarkably enough, not really interested in politics. He took no part in political discussions, and was not ideologically well-versed. He had, it is true, joined the Communist Roter Frontkämpferbund (Red Front Fighters' League), and had been a member of the woodworkers' union, but he had taken an active role in neither. Before 1933 he had supported the KPD in elections, but because in his view it stood for improving the lot of the working classes, not on account of an ideological programme. After 1933 he said he had observed the deterioration in the living-standard of the working class, and restrictions on its freedom. He noticed the anger among workers at the regime. He took part in discussions with workmates about poor conditions, and shared their views. He also shared their anxieties about the coming war which they all expected in the autumn of 1938. After the Munich Agreement he remained convinced, he said, 'that Germany would make further demands of other countries and annex other countries and that therefore a war would be unavoidable'. Prompted by no one, he began to be obsessed by ways of improving the condition of workers and preventing war. He concluded that only the 'elimination' (*Beseitigung*) of the regime's leadership – by which he meant Hitler, Göring, and Goebbels – would bring this about. The idea would not leave him. In autumn 1938 he decided that he himself would undertake 'the elimination of the leadership'.[243]

He read in the newspapers that the next gathering of Party leaders would be in the Bürgerbräukeller in early November and travelled to Munich to assess the possibilities for what he had in mind. The security problems were not great. (Security for the events was left to the Party, not to the police.) He worked out that the best method would be to place a time-bomb in the pillar behind the dais where Hitler would stand. During the next months he stole explosives from the armaments factory where he was currently working, and designed the mechanism for his time-bomb. In early April he travelled again from Königsbronn to Munich and returned to the Bürgerbräukeller. This time he reconnoitred more carefully, making detailed sketches and taking precise measurements. His new work, at a quarry, now enabled him to steal dynamite. In the next weeks he constructed a model of the bomb in the most minute detail and carried out a practical test with the exploding mechanism in his parents' garden. At the beginning of August he returned to Munich. Between then and early November he hid over thirty times during the night in the Bürgerbräukeller, working on hollowing out a cavity in the selected pillar and leaving by a side-door early next morning. So meticulous was he that he even lined the cavity with tin to prevent any hollow sound, should anyone tap on the pillar, or damage the bomb-mechanism by nailing up decorations. The bomb was in place, and set, by 6 November. Elser was leaving nothing to chance. He returned on the night of 7 November to make sure it was functioning properly. He pressed his ear to the side of the pillar, and heard the ticking. Nothing had gone wrong. Next morning he left Munich for Konstanz, *en route* – as he thought – to Switzerland, and safety.[244]

That evening, as always on 8 November, the 'Old Guard' of the Party assembled. Hitler had announced the previous day that he would, after all, give his annual address.[245] Usually, this lasted from about 8.30p.m. until about ten o'clock. It had already been announced that, in the circumstances of the war, this year's meeting would begin earlier and that the two-day commemoration of the Putsch would be shortened.[246] Hitler began his speech soon after his arrival in the Bürgerbräukeller, at 8.10p.m., and finished at 9.07p.m. The speech itself was one long tirade against Britain, highly sarcastic in tone, well tailored to his raucous audience of Party fanatics.[247] Hitler normally spent some time after his speech chatting to the Movement's 'Old Fighters'. This time, escorted by a good number of Party bigwigs, he left immediately for the station to take the 9.31p.m. train back to Berlin.[248]

At twenty past nine the pillar immediately behind the dais where Hitler had stood minutes earlier, and part of the roof directly above, were ripped apart by Elser's bomb. Eight persons were killed in the blast, a further sixty-three injured, sixteen of them seriously.[249] Hitler had been gone no more than ten minutes when the bomb went off.

He attributed his salvation to the work of 'Providence' – a sign that he was to fulfil the task destiny had laid out for him.[250] In its headline on 10 November, the *Völkischer Beobachter* called it 'the miraculous salvation of the Führer'.[251] There was, in fact, nothing providential or miraculous about it. It was pure luck. Hitler's reasons for returning without delay to Berlin were genuine enough. The decision to attack the West had been temporarily postponed on 7 November, with a final decision set for the 9th. Hitler had to be back in the Reich Chancellery by then. It was more important than reminiscing about old times with Party stalwarts in the Bürgerbräukeller.[252] Elser could have known nothing about the reasons for the curtailment of Hitler's quick trip to Munich. It was mere chance that the Swabian joiner did not succeed where the generals had failed even to mount an attempt. Whether the generals would *then* have acted, had Elser's attempt been successful, and once the main object of their putsch plans had been removed, is open to question. But with Elser's failure, the possibility of more 'moderate' forces taking over and pulling back from the brink of all-out war with the West had gone.

Elser himself was already under arrest at the customs post near Konstanz when the bomb went off. He had been picked up trying to cross the Swiss border illegally. It seemed a routine arrest. Only some hours after the explosion did the border officials begin to realize that the contents of Georg Elser's pockets, including a postcard of the Bürgerbräukeller, linked him with the assassination attempt on Hitler. On 14 November, Elser confessed. A few days later he gave a full account of his actions, and the motives behind them. He was interned in Sachsenhausen concentration camp, and treated, remarkably, as a privileged prisoner. Probably Hitler, who continued to believe that Elser was the front-man of an international conspiracy, intended a post-war show-trial to incriminate the British Secret Service. At the end of 1944 or in early 1945 Elser was brought to Dachau. There was to be no show-trial. With the war as good as lost, Elser had no more value to the regime. Shortly before the Americans liberated Dachau, he was taken out and killed.[253]

Elser had acted alone. But the concerns which had motivated him – worries about living-standards, anxieties about extending the war – were widespread in the autumn of 1939. Reports abounded of unrest in the working class around that time. The War Economy Decree of 4 September had brought an instant worsening of living standards, higher taxes, abolition of higher rates for overtime and weekend work, and other restrictions. A wage-freeze had followed.[254] Industrial indiscipline, including absenteeism and refusal of overtime, eventually forced the regime to back down.[255] But longer hours, rises in food prices, and an acute coal shortage affected the poorer in society most of all that autumn. And for those stepping out of line, increased police presence in factories was a constant reminder of the threat of the labour camp.[256]

Euphoria over the victory in Poland had soon faded. Alongside the daily worries were those of an extension of the war. The 'Phoney War' (as American journalists dubbed the autumn and winter months of 1939-40), with no action from the West, raised hopes. Above all else most people wanted the war to be over. In his anxieties about the war, Elser spoke for many. He was on far less sure ground with his attribution of blame for the war to the Nazi leadership. The signs are that propaganda had been successful in persuading most ordinary Germans that the western powers were to blame for the prolongation of a war which Hitler had done all he could to avoid.[257] Whatever criticisms – and they were many and bitter – people had of the Party and the regime, Hitler still retained his massive popularity. The view of one Munich upper-class conservative, antagonized above all by the assault on Christianity, that there was no one in the city who did not regret the failure of Elser's attempt, was no more than wishful thinking.[258] Few would have applauded a successful assassination attempt. Vast numbers would have been appalled. The chances of a backlash, and a new 'stab-in-the-back' legend, would have been great. As it was, the failure of the attempt brought, as could be expected, a new, great upsurge of support for Hitler, accompanied by feelings of intense hatred for Britain, held to be behind the bomb-attack. Not only internal reports stressed that 'the devotion to the Führer has deepened still further'.[259] The underground opponents of the regime also acknowledged that Elser's bomb had brought a 'strengthening of determination'. People were saying that if the attempt had been successful it would have resulted in internal confusion, benefit to Germany's enemies, loss of the war, worse misery than was caused by Versailles, and the upturning of everything achieved since 1933.[260]

Hitler's hold over Germany was as strong as ever. The failure of those in positions of power to move against him and the repercussions of Elser's bomb-attack demonstrated that his authority was unchallengeable from within the regime's élites and that he was still immensely popular with the masses. He played on this latter point when he addressed a gathering of around 200 commanding generals and other senior Wehrmacht officers in the Reich Chancellery at noon on 23 November.

Hitler's speech was remarkable for its frankness. In the light of the conflict with the army leadership in the previous weeks, its aim was to convince the generals of the need to attack the West without delay. First of all he paraded before his audience the successes of the previous years. Then he came to the conflict with Poland. He was, he said, reproached that he wanted to 'fight and fight again'. His next words represented the core of his philosophy: 'In fighting (*Kampf*) I see the fate of all creatures. Nobody can avoid fighting if he does not want to go under.'[261] This led him into the struggle for *Lebensraum*. Again reiterating words which he had repeatedly preached in the late 1920s, he was adamant: 'Solution only with the sword.' The people lacking the strength to fight must yield. The struggle now, he went on, was different than it had been 100 years earlier. 'Today we can speak of a racial struggle.' This had a self-evident material dimension. It was a struggle, he added, for oil-fields, rubber, and mineral wealth.[262]

He went on to review the strategic position. Germany no longer faced a war on two fronts. The West front stood open. But no one knew for how long. He had long pondered whether to strike in the East first, then in the West. 'Basically I did not organize the armed forces in order not to strike. The decision to strike was always in me.'[263] The Polish front could now be held by a few divisions – something long held scarcely attainable. The question was how long Germany could sustain the position in the West. He spoke openly of future policy towards the Soviet Union. Russia, he stated, was currently not dangerous, and was preoccupied with the Baltic. 'We can oppose Russia only when we are free in the West. Further, Russia is seeking to increase her influence in the Balkans and is striving toward the Persian Gulf. That is also the goal of our foreign policy.'[264] He moved on to Italy. There, he said, everything depended on Mussolini. 'Italy will not attack until Germany has taken the offensive against France. Just as the death of Stalin, so the death of the Duce can bring danger to us.' 'How easily the death of a statesman can come about,' he remarked with reference to Elser's near-miss: 'I have myself experienced that recently.'[265] After his *tour d'horizon* he reached the characteristic conclusion: 'Everything is determined by the fact that the moment is favourable now; in six months it might not be so any more.'[266]

He turned to his own role. 'As the last factor I must in all modesty describe my own person: irreplaceable. Neither a military man nor a civilian could replace me. Attempts at assassination may be repeated. I am convinced of my powers of intellect and of decision. Wars are always ended only by the annihilation of the opponent. Anyone who believes differently is irresponsible. Time is working for our adversaries. Now there is a relationship of forces which can never be more propitious for us, but which can only deteriorate. The enemy will not make peace when the relationship of forces is unfavourable for us. No compromises. Hardness towards ourselves. I shall strike and not capitulate. The fate of the Reich depends only on me.'[267]

He underlined Germany's military superiority over Britain and France. He flattered the armed forces' leadership that it was better than that of 1914. But there was unmistakable criticism of army leaders. While there was express praise for the navy, the Luftwaffe, and the army's achievements in Poland, Hitler – in a barbed comment directed straight at Brauchitsch – remarked that he could not 'bear to hear people say the army is not in good order. Everything lies in the hands of the military leader. I can do anything with the German soldier if he is well led.'[268]

Internal conditions also favoured an early strike, he went on. Revolution from within was impossible. And behind the army stood the strongest armaments industry in the world. But Germany had an Achilles' heel: the Ruhr. An advance by Britain and France through Belgium and Holland would imperil the Reich. Once the French army had marched into Belgium it would be too late.[269] He put forward another argument for breaching Dutch and Belgian neutrality. Laying mines off the English coast to bring about a blockade could only be done through occupation of Belgium and Holland. He compared himself – as he would do throughout the war – with Frederick the Great. 'Prussia owes its rise to the heroism of one man. Even there,' Hitler declared, an aside aimed at his army leaders, 'the closest advisers were disposed to capitulation. Everything depended on Frederick the Great.'[270] Hitler said he was now gambling all he had achieved on victory. At stake was who was to dominate Europe in the future.[271] His decision was unalterable, Hitler went on. 'I shall attack France and England at the most favourable and earliest moment. Breach of the neutrality of Belgium and Holland is of no importance. No one will question that when we have won . . . I consider it possible to end the war only by means of an attack . . . The whole thing means the end of the World War, not just a single action. It is a matter of not just a single question but of the existence or non-existence of the nation.'[272] Hitler demanded that the 'spirit of determination' be passed on to the lower ranks.[273]

His final point was the psychological readiness of the German people. He would return to stress this five years later when justifying to his generals the need to go to war in 1939. At that time he would say it was impossible to preserve enthusiasm and readiness for self-sacrifice as if it could be corked up in a bottle.[274] This was not merely a retrospective reflection. With an eye on the possible deterioration of the backing he had from the German people, he now told the military: 'I want to annihilate the enemy. Behind me stands the German people, whose morale can only grow worse.'[275] Here, too, Hitler saw no possibility of waiting. Time was not on Germany's side. Hitler ended with a rhetorical flourish – and with a prophecy: 'If we come through this struggle victoriously – and we shall come through it – our time will go down in the history of our people. I shall stand or fall in this struggle. I shall never survive the defeat of my people. No capitulation to the outside, no revolution from within.'[276]

That evening, at 6p.m., Hitler summoned Brauchitsch and Halder to see him. He berated them once more with the failings of the army leadership, threatening to root out the 'spirit of Zossen' and crush any opposition from the General Staff. Brauchitsch offered his resignation. Hitler refused it. Brauchitsch, he said, should do his duty.[277] Hitler had no need to go further. His speech earlier in the day, with its scarcely veiled criticism of army leaders set against praise for the Luftwaffe and navy, and its threats to destroy any opposing him, had offended some generals. But it had cowed them. None had protested at what Hitler had said. Afterwards, they complained in private but only Guderian could be prevailed upon to voice, and then in mild terms, a few days later their disquiet at Hitler's evident distrust. The radicals in the opposition had meanwhile given up on Halder. And Brauchitsch had been reduced to a withdrawn depressive, prepared to take Hitler's insults and still accept responsibility for the western offensive that he inwardly opposed.[278]

Hitler had been right in his speech: no revolution could be expected from within. Heydrich's police-state ruled that out. But it was not only a matter of repression. Alongside the ruthlessness of the regime towards internal opponents stood the widespread basic consensus reaching across most of society behind much of what the regime had undertaken and, in particular, what were taken to be the remarkable achievements of Hitler himself. This was embodied in the extraordinary adulation of the Leader. Hitler enjoyed a level of popularity exceeded by no other political leader at the time. He was correct in saying that he had the German people – certainly an overwhelming majority of the German people – behind him. This had strengthened him inordinately in his conflicts with the army, and had weakened the resolve of oppositional groups on many occasions. By the end of 1939 his supremacy was assured. Elser's bomb had merely brought a renewed demonstration of his popularity. Meanwhile, the internal opposition was resigned to being unable to act. The navy and Luftwaffe were behind Hitler. The army leadership would, whatever its reservations, fulfil its duty. The division of the generals, coupled with their pronounced sense of duty even when they held a course of action to be disastrous, was Hitler's strength.

Nothing could stop the western offensive. Hitler was by now obsessed with 'beating England'.[279] It was purely a matter of when, not if, the attack on the West would take place. After further short-term postponements, the last of them in mid-January, on 16 January 1940 Hitler finally put it off until the spring.[280]

The war was set to continue, and to widen. Also set to escalate was the barbarism that was an intrinsic part of it. At home the killings in the asylums were mounting into a full-scale programme of mass murder. In Poland, the grandiose resettlement schemes presided over by Himmler and Heydrich were seeing the brutal uprooting and deportation of tens of thousands of Poles and Jews into the 'dumping-ground' of the General Government.[281] Not least, the centre-point of the 'racial cleansing' mania, the 'removal' of the Jews, was farther from solution than ever now that over 2 million Polish Jews had fallen into the hands of the Nazis. In December Goebbels reported to Hitler on his recent visit to Poland. The Führer, he recorded, listened carefully to his account and agreed with his views on the 'Jewish and Polish question'. 'The Jewish danger must be banished from us. But in a few generations it will reappear. There's no panacea.'[282]

Evidently, no 'complete solution' to the 'Jewish problem' was yet in sight. The constant quest to find such a 'panacea' by Nazi underlings working directly or indirectly 'towards the Führer' would nevertheless ensure that, in the conquered and subjugated territories of the east, a 'solution' would gradually begin to emerge before long.

7

ZENITH OF POWER

'The Führer is greatly puzzled by England's persisting unwillingness to make peace . . . He sees the answer (as we do) in England's hope in Russia . . .'

'Decision: Russia's destruction must therefore be made a part of this struggle . . . If we start in May 1941, we would have five months to finish the job.'

Diary entries of General Halder,
Chief of the General Staff, 13 and 31 July 1940

'Only when there's no more going back . . . is the courage found for very big decisions . . . That's how it is, too, in our present situation.' Goebbels was summarizing what Hitler had been saying at lunch on 15 January 1940. Hitler had begun by grumbling about unreliable weather-forecasts; half-decent weather was needed for the offensive, he had stated. He then went on to philosophize about strength in adversity – one of his regular themes, and to become even more repetitive as the war wore on. He referred to the usual heroes in the German pantheon – Bismarck and, even more so, Frederick the Great – adding on examples from his own 'time of struggle' to illustrate how danger brought forth special qualities of courage and boldness in the 'historical genius'. 'The Führer was always greater in adversity than in fortune,' added the impressionable Propaganda Minister. Goebbels had, however, registered the serious point of Hitler's typically narcissistic musings on his own 'greatness': there could be no going back. This imperative had been directly linked to German policy in Poland – an indication that Hitler and Goebbels were only too aware of the Rubicon that had been crossed with the descent into the barbaric treatment of the Poles. 'We simply must not lose the war,' Goebbels summed up. 'And all our thinking and action has to follow from that.'[1]

A characteristic technique that Hitler had of couching his arguments was invariably to pose stark alternatives, one of which he promptly dismissed out of hand or ridiculed. The *fait accompli*, resting on force deriving from underlying strength, was the only bargaining position he recognized. Concession, compromise, retreat were to his mind inconceivable. If the way back was ruled out, only the bold forward move remained. It was how he had acted since his ultimatum demanding the Party leadership in 1921, and his foolhardy launching of the putsch in 1923. By 1940, given the ways in which in particular the army and the Foreign Ministry, over the course of the previous years and especially since early 1938, had allowed themselves to be manoeuvred into near total dependency on Hitler, this way of thinking had drawn inexorably into its slipstream all the agencies of a complex, modern state system. Aided by a good deal of enthusiastic backing and the ineffectiveness of limited, often weak-kneed, resistance, Hitler had brought his own subjective philosophy – that the only way out was through the bold strike, and without delay since time was working against Germany – into near alignment with objective circumstances.

But these circumstances, the conditions in which the crucial decisions of 1940–41 would be taken, had not been shaped by Hitler alone. He had placed the Reich in a quandary. The war could not be ended. That was now a decision out of Germany's control, unless Britain could be forced to the conference table or militarily defeated. But neither militarily, as the chiefs of the armed forces made plain, nor economically, as every indicator demonstrated, was Germany equipped at this stage to fight the long war with which, it was known, the British were already reckoning.[2] The Wehrmacht had entered into hostilities in autumn 1939 with no well-laid plans for a major war, and no strategy at all for an offensive in the West. Nothing at all had been clearly thought through.[3] The Luftwaffe was the best equipped of the three branches of the armed forces. But even here, the armaments programme had been targeted at 1942, not 1939.[4] The navy's operational planning was based upon a fleet that could not be ready before 1943.[5] In fact, the 1939 Z-Plan – halted at the start of the war – would leave Germany with severe limitations at sea until 1946. And within the confines of that plan, the building of U-boats necessary for an economic blockade of Britain was deliberately neglected by Hitler in favour of the interests of the army. However, the army itself lacked even sufficient munitions following the brief Polish campaign (in which some 50 per cent of the tanks and motorized units deployed were no longer serviceable) to contemplate an immediate continuation of the war in the West.[6]

The war could have been over had the French government been bold enough to send at least the forty divisions it had promised the Poles into action against the far smaller German forces left guarding the western front in September 1939.[7] At the outbreak of war the Germans could spare only thirty-two divisions for the western front. The French had at the time ninety-one divisions, though it was reckoned that it would take ten days to mobilize fifty of these divisions.[8] By the end of the Polish campaign it was in any case too late. As it was, the breathing-space that the German army gained during the repeated postponements of the western offensive, much to Hitler's chagrin, in the winter of 1939–40 was crucial in allowing the time and opportunity to put the army in a state of readiness to attack France.[9]

Hitler had to gamble everything on the defeat of France. If Britain could be kept from gaining a foothold on the Continent until this were achieved, Hitler was certain that the British would have to sue for peace. Getting Britain out of the war through isolation after a German defeat of France was Hitler's only overall war-strategy as the abnormally icy winter of 1940 gradually gave way to spring.[10] Ranged against Germany at some point, Hitler was aware, would be the might of the USA. Currently dominated by isolationism, and likely to be preoccupied by the forthcoming presidential elections in the autumn, its early involvement in a European conflict could be discounted. But as long as Britain stayed in the war, the participation – at the very least by benevolent neutrality – of the USA, with its immense economic power, could not be ruled out. And that was a factor that was out of Germany's reach. It was all the more reason, objectively as well as simply in Hitler's manic obsession with time, to eliminate Britain from the war without delay.[11]

The East was at this point at the back of Hitler's mind – though not out of it. Mussolini had written to Hitler at the beginning of January, exhorting him not to relinquish his long-standing principles of anti-Bolshevism (and antisemitism) for tactical purposes.[12] In his reply, sent over two months later, Hitler claimed, somewhat disingenuously, that Stalin had transformed Bolshevism into 'a Russian-national state ideology and economic idea', which Germany had no interest in combating.[13] Privately, he was saying something different. Bolshevism, he commented over lunch on 12 January, was the form of 'state organization' that matched the Slavs. He likened Stalin to a modern Ivan the Terrible, who had done away with the traditional ruling class and replaced it with Slavs. That was good for Germany. 'Rather a weak partner as neighbour than an alliance treaty, however good,' he cynically added.[14] In his memorandum the previous October he had already remarked that Soviet neutrality could be reckoned with at present, but that no treaty or agreement could guarantee it in the future. 'In eight months, a year, let alone a few years this could all be different,' he had said.[15] 'If all treaties concluded were held to,' he told Goebbels, 'mankind would no longer exist today.'[16] Hitler presumed that the Russians would break the non-aggression pact when it suited them to do so. For the time being they were militarily weak – a condition enhanced by Stalin's inexplicable purges; they were preoccupied with their own affairs in the Baltic, especially the troublesome Finnish war; and they posed, therefore, no danger from the East. They could be dealt with at a later stage. Their current disposition provided still further evidence for Hitler that his attack on the West, and the elimination of Britain from the war, could not wait.

There was a certain logic in the presumption that, following a defeat of France and the offer of 'reasonable' terms, Britain would bow to the inevitable in its own self-interest. There continued to be strong lobbies in Britain that thought along those lines. There was nothing inexorable about Britain's decision to 'go it alone' in the summer of 1940. But that decision, when it came, would vitiate the one strategy Hitler had. In his assumption that immediate self-interest was the only maxim of war and peace, he crassly underestimated the resilience and idealism that had arisen in Britain following the march into Prague in 1939 and which, in summer 1940, the new Prime Minister, Winston Churchill, was able to evoke among the British people. The 'duel' between Hitler and his arch-enemy Churchill would dominate the summer. Its outcome would in many ways determine the further course of the war.[17]

Hitler was in 1940–41 at the zenith of his power. But despite his spectacular triumph over France, he could not bring the war in the West to the conclusion he wanted. His inability to do this would shape the rest of the war. The decision to open the war in the East with the war in the West unfinished would take away from Germany what room for manoeuvre remained. And by the winter of 1941 it would become plain just how catastrophic that decision had been.[18]

I

It became clear in early 1940 that, before the western offensive could be launched, it was imperative to secure control over Scandinavia and the northern sea passages. A key consideration was the safeguarding of supplies of Swedish iron-ore, vital for the German war-economy, which were mainly shipped through the port of Narvik in the north of Norway. Hitler had acknowledged to Raeder as early as 1934 how essential it would be for the navy to guarantee the iron-ore imports in the event of war.[19] But he had shown no actual strategic interest in Scandinavia until the first months of 1940. Alongside the need to secure the supplies of ore went, in Hitler's mind, the aim of keeping Britain off the European continent.[20] The navy itself had developed no operational plans for Scandinavia before the outbreak of war. But as the prospect of war with Britain began to take concrete shape in the later 1930s, naval planners started to weigh up the need for bases on the Norwegian coast.[21]

Once war had started, the navy leadership, not Hitler, took the initiative in pressing for the occupation of Denmark and Norway. In October, and again in early December 1939, Raeder, elevated the previous April to the rank of Grand-Admiral, stressed to Hitler the importance to the war-economy of occupying Norway. Eventually, after introducing him to Norwegian nationalist leader Vidkun Quisling on 12 December, Raeder persuaded Hitler to agree to an exploratory study by the High Command of the Wehrmacht for the occupation of Norway. Increasingly worried by the possibility of being pre-empted by British occupation (under the pretext of assisting the Finns in the war against the Soviet Union), Raeder continued to lobby Hitler for early action. In January, he instructed the naval leadership to prepare an operational plan. Hitler became seriously alerted to the danger of Allied intervention in Norway after the *Altmark*, carrying around 300 Allied merchant seamen captured in the south Atlantic, had been raided on 16 February in Norwegian waters by a boarding-party from the British destroyer *Cossack*, and the prisoners freed.[22] Now the matter became urgent for him. Five days later he sent for General von Falkenhorst, known to have experience of Finland from the First World War. This sufficed for Hitler to put him in charge of the preparations for 'Weser Exercise'. To retain maximum secrecy, Falkenhorst was initially given no documents or maps to help him plan the operation. Instead, he bought himself a Baedecker of Norway, retired to a hotel room, and returned in the afternoon with proposals that Hitler accepted.[23] Rumours, passed on by the German embassy in Stockholm, of a major British action in the near future, made plain that there was no time to lose. On 1 March Hitler put out the directive for '*Weserübung*' ('Weser Exercise').[24] Two days later, he underlined the urgency of action in Norway. He wanted an acceleration of preparations, and ordered 'Weser Exercise' to be carried out a few days before the western offensive.[25] As fears of a British occupation mounted throughout March, Raeder finally persuaded Hitler, towards the end of the month, to agree to set a precise date for the operation. When he spoke to his commanders on 1 April, Hitler closely followed Raeder's lines of argument. The next day, the date for the operation was fixed as 9 April.[26] Within forty-eight hours it was learnt that British action was imminent. On 8 April British warships mined the waters around Narvik.[27] The race for Norway was on.[28]

The Allied mine-laying gave Germany the pretext it had been waiting for. Hitler called Goebbels, and explained to him what was afoot while they walked alone in the grounds of the Reich Chancellery in the lovely spring sunshine. Everything was prepared. No worthwhile resistance was to be expected. He was uninterested in America's reaction. Material assistance from the USA would not be forthcoming for eight months or so, manpower not for about one and a half years. 'And we must come to victory in this year. Otherwise the material supremacy of the opposing side would be too great. Also, a long war would be psychologically difficult to bear,' Hitler conceded. He gave Goebbels an insight into his aims for the conquest of the north. 'First we will keep quiet for a short time once we have both countries' – Denmark and Norway – 'and then England will be plastered (*bepflastert*). Now we possess a basis for attack.' He was prepared to leave the kings of Denmark and Norway untouched, as long as they did not create trouble. 'But we will never again give up both countries.'[29]

Despite the warnings by the Swedes of a build-up of troops and ships in the Baltic, poised ready to take Scandinavia, the German strike took the British by surprise.[30] Landings by air and sea took place in Denmark in the early morning of 9 April. A German warship entered Copenhagen harbour; the Danish navy had not even been put on the alert. The aerodrome at Aalborg in the north of Jutland fell to a parachute landing of German troops. The Danish army briefly opened fire in North Schleswig. But the Danes swiftly decided to offer no resistance. The Norwegian operation went less smoothly. Narvik and Trondheim were taken. But the sinking of the *Blücher*, by a single shell from an ancient coastal battery that landed in the ammunition hold of the new cruiser as it passed through the narrows near Oscarsborg, forced the accompanying ships to turn back and delayed the occupation of Oslo for the few hours that allowed the Norwegian royal family and government to leave the capital. Despite sturdy resistance by the Norwegians and relatively high naval losses at the hands of the British fleet, air superiority, following the swift capture of the airfields, rapidly helped provide the German forces with sufficient control to compel the evacuation of the British, French, and Polish troops who had landed in central Norway by the beginning of May. The Allies eventually took Narvik later in the month, after a protracted struggle, only to be pulled out again by Churchill in early June on account of the mounting danger to Britain from the German offensive in the West. The last Norwegian forces capitulated on the tenth.

'Weser Exercise' had proved a success. But it had been at a cost. Much of the surface-fleet of the German navy had been put out of action for the rest of 1940. Running the occupied parts of Scandinavia from now on sucked in on a more or less permanent basis around 300,000 men, many of them engaged in holding down a Norwegian population bitterly resentful at a German administration that was aided and abetted by Quisling's movement.[31] And there was a further consequence which would turn out to be to Germany's disadvantage and have major significance for the British war-effort. Blame for the Allied fiasco in Norway was attributed by the British public not to Churchill, the minister directly responsible, but to the Prime Minister, Chamberlain. Indirectly, the British failure led to the end of the Chamberlain government and brought into power the person who would prove himself Hitler's most defiant and unrelenting foe: Winston Churchill.[32]

The eventual success of 'Weser Exercise' concealed to all but the armed forces' leadership Hitler's serious deficiencies as a military commander. The lack of coordination between the branches of the armed forces; the flawed communications between the OKW and the heads of the navy and, especially, army and Luftwaffe (leading to the need for alterations to directives already signed and issued); Hitler's own reluctance, in larger briefing meetings, to oppose either Raeder or Göring, though advocating a tough line in private; and his constant interference in the minutiae of operations control: all provided for serious complications in the execution of 'Weser Exercise'.[33] And for all his talk of keeping strong nerves, Hitler betrayed signs of panic and dilettante military judgement when things started to go wrong in Narvik in mid-April. General Walter Warlimont, observing Hitler at close quarters in these days, later recounted 'the impression of truly terrifying weakness of character on the part of the man who was at the head of the Reich'. Citing Jodl's diary entries, he pointed to 'a striking picture of agitation and lack of balance'. He recalled on one occasion having to see Jodl, whom Warlimont credited as largely responsible for the success of the operation, in the Reich Chancellery: 'and there was Hitler hunched on a chair in a corner, unnoticed and staring in front of him, a picture of brooding gloom. He appeared to be waiting for some new piece of news which would save the situation . . .'[34] On this occasion, the crisis soon passed. Hitler could bask in the glory of another triumph. But when the victories ran out, the flaws in his style of military leadership would prove a lasting weakness.

For now, however, he could turn his full energies to the long-awaited western offensive.

The repeated postponements of 'Case Yellow' (as the western offensive had come to be called), probably a reflection of Hitler's own uncertainty as well as poor weather conditions and concerns about the transport situation, provided not just the opportunity to build up the army after the Polish campaign but also time to rethink operational plans.[35] In Poland, Hitler had kept out of involvement in military operations. Now, in the preparation of the western offensive, he intervened directly for the first time.[36] It set the pattern for the future. Already in the autumn he was uneasy about the directives coming from the Army High Command. Some of the top commanders were equally unconvinced.[37] The plans seemed too conventional. They were what the enemy would expect. Even after modifications they remained less than satisfactory.[38] They envisaged the decisive thrust coming from the north, either side of Liège. Hitler wanted something more daring, something which would retain the crucial element of surprise. His own ideas were still embryonic. They favoured a main line of attack further south – though the Army High Command thought this too risky since it involved attacking across the difficult wooded terrain of the Ardennes, with obvious problems for tank operations. Hitler did not know for some weeks that similar ideas were being more thoroughly worked out by Lieutenant-General von Manstein, chief of staff of Army Group A. Manstein was among those generals concerned at the unimaginative strategy of the Army High Command. Discussions with Guderian, the general with greatest expertise in tank warfare, led him to conclude that the Ardennes posed no insuperable barrier to a Panzer thrust. General von Rundstedt, Manstein's immediate superior, also supported the bolder plan. However, Manstein was unable to persuade Army High Command to adopt his plan. Brauchitsch was adamantly opposed to any alteration to the established strategy and not even prepared to discuss Manstein's plan. Halder at least agreed to take all operational proposals into account in a series of war games. These eventually, by February, were to make him more amenable to the Manstein plan. In January, however, Brauchitsch still refused to take Manstein's operational draft to Hitler, and had the persistent general moved to a new command post in Stettin. Hitler had, even so, been made aware of the basic lines of Manstein's plan in the second half of December. The postponement until spring of 'Yellow' that followed in January then gave him the opportunity to state that he wanted to give the operation a new basis, and above all to ensure absolute secrecy and the element of surprise. His 'Basic Order' of 11 January, to be hung up in every military office, was framed in this context.[39] Reflecting one of Hitler's most prevalent instincts, the 'Basic Order' stated: 'No one: no office, no officer may learn of something to be kept secret if they don't absolutely have to have knowledge of it for official reasons'. They should also learn only as much as was necessary to carry out their tasks, and then no earlier than need be.[40]

In mid-February the operational plan for 'Yellow' was still not definitively agreed. Hitler was said to have described the existing planning of the Army High Command as the 'ideas of a military cadet' ('*Gedanken eines Kriegsschülers*').[41] But nothing had as yet taken their place. At this point, Hitler's Wehrmacht adjutant Schmundt took the initiative and arranged for a meeting with Manstein on 17 February. By this time, Jodl had been informed that Hitler favoured a thrust of the motorized units on the southern flank, towards Sedan, where the enemy would least expect them. The army leadership, taking these wishes of Hitler on board and also bearing in mind the outcome of the war games, had already adjusted its strategic thinking when, on 18 February, Hitler spoke of the favourable impression he had gained of Manstein's plan the day before.[42] The die was now cast. By chance, the basic thoughts of the amateur had coincided with the brilliantly unorthodox planning of the professional strategist. Further refined by the OKH, the Manstein plan gave Hitler what he wanted: a surprise assault in the most unexpected area which, though not without risk, had the boldness of genius. The famous 'sickle cut' – though the designation was not a contemporary one – was incorporated in the new directive of 24 February.[43] While the Allied forces countered the expected German attack through Belgium, armoured units of Army Group A would rapidly drive through the Ardennes and into the lowlands of northern France towards the coast, scything through Allied forces and pushing them into the path of Army Group B, advancing from the north.[44]

No strategic information was, of course, passed to Mussolini when the dictators met, for the first time since the Munich Conference, on the Brenner Pass on 18 March 1940. But Hitler was keen to clarify relations with his Italian ally before the big western offensive started. It was snowing heavily when Hitler's Special Train pulled into the small station, some 4,000 feet above the Italian–German border. Mussolini and Ciano greeted Hitler and Ribbentrop on the platform. Then the dictators and their foreign ministers stepped into Mussolini's Special Train on the adjacent platform. The lines through the Brenner were blocked while the dictators talked. Neither passenger trains nor goods trains carrying crucial cargoes of coal, desperately needed in the hard winter, were allowed through.[45]

The talks lasted two-and-a-half hours. There was no doubt now who was the dominant partner. Mussolini said remarkably little. He listened, almost deferentially, as Hitler spoke almost the whole time. He said he had come, before the big showdown, to give the Duce an overview of the situation from the German standpoint. He sought to justify the timing of the attack on Poland, underlining how disadvantageous it would have been to wait. With scarcely concealed conceit he described the military achievement in Poland, and how bad weather had prevented him from attacking the West straight away. He bombarded Mussolini and the accompanying Ciano with facts and figures on German military strength. He was confident, he said, of dealing with his enemies by the autumn. He came to the point of the meeting: to persuade Italy to enter the war. If Italy was satisfied with being a second-rate Mediterranean power, he remarked, she needed to do nothing. But England and France would always block her ambitions to become a first-class power. Should Germany win the war, it would need to bring about a settlement 'with a great partner' to hold what had been won.[46] Alluding to Mussolini's letter in January, and to his own reply a few days before the meeting, Hitler emphasized how British intransigence had forced him to conclude an alliance with Russia. But, although Stalin had deprived Bolshevism of its Jewish and international character and turned it into a 'slavic Moscowitism', Russia remained for Germany an 'absolutely foreign world'. 'For Germany only one partner came into question: Italy. Russia was only insurance cover.'[47] He ended his monologue by voicing his wish that Mussolini should bring Italy into the war in support of Germany at a moment of his own timing. In the few minutes left to him to speak, Mussolini – both overawed and enthused by Hitler – emphasized his keenness to join the war. Only the timing posed some problems. The Italian armed forces would not be ready for another four months or so. And Italy could not cope with fighting a long war. He would have to judge the right moment. After a quick snack, Mussolini and Ciano waved Hitler off from the platform as his Special Train set off back through the Tirol to Germany.[48] Mussolini was irritated that he had been able to say so little. Remarkably, he drew the conclusion from the meeting that Hitler was not preparing to launch a major land offensive.[49] Hitler was very satisfied with the outcome of the talks. Once more he was impressed by the Italian dictator – presumably, how well he had listened. 'Mussolini will go with us to the end,' was his assessment.[50] 'The Führer is not thinking at all of a rotten peace,' Goebbels noted, after Hitler's glowing account of the meeting with his Italian friend.[51]

Some sort of 'rotten peace' seems, however, to have been in Hitler's mind when he talked a month later about his plans for dealing with Britain. 'The Führer intends to deliver [England] a k.o. blow,' Goebbels recorded. 'Even so, he would make peace today. Condition: England out of Europe and our colonies back to us, rounded off (*abgerundet*). We'll see. He doesn't want at all to annihilate England, nor destroy its Empire. But we must have calm (*Ruhe*).' He went on to speak of building up Norway to a fortress comparable to Singapore, still regarded as unconquerable, which would deter Britain from contemplating a new war. It was good, he argued, that Italy had not joined the war the previous September. England would then have pulled back from the conflict, only to begin again in three to five years time, under more favourable circumstances. He drew the conclusion: 'If at all, then now.' Drawing on the lessons of the Scandinavian campaign, he underlined the crucial importance of air-power. The Luftwaffe had revolutionized warfare. 'And there we are in front,' he claimed. Germany might have fought the war with a completely misplaced naval programme. But the great ships were no longer a match for air-power. That lesson had been learnt. Whatever Hitler's stated preference for a peace to leave Britain as Germany's junior partner, sedated and quiescent, its dominance destroyed even if its Empire were to be nominally left intact – and it would be as well not to overrate his professed admiration of the Empire[52] – he was certain that Britain would only be forced to the conference table through the isolation left by the devastating military defeat he intended to inflict on France. And the sooner that took place, the better. 'The Führer presses for action as rapidly as possible,' commented Goebbels. 'We can't and won't wait for long.'[53]

Four days later, Hitler talked again of his plans. France had to be smashed, leaving England without a foot on the Continent, and powerless. He saw the crushing of France as 'an act of historical justice'. But Britain needed its overseas possessions and should not lose them. 'England can have peace if it keeps out of Europe and gives us back our colonies and a bit more besides. But that's only possible if it has already received a k.o. blow.' Fate would now have to take its course. The western offensive was only a matter of weather, and the most opportune moment.[54]

By early May, the British and French were anticipating that the German western offensive could begin at any time.[55] The intention to attack in the first week of May had, in fact, been revised in the light of events in Scandinavia. But it was finally set for 10 May.[56] Hitler was confident. To those who saw him at close quarters, he appeared calm and optimistic, as if the doubts of previous months had passed, and he was now letting events take their course. He thought that France would capitulate after around six weeks, and that England would then pull out of a war which, to continue, would mean losing its Empire – something wholly unimaginable.[57] The balance of military forces was roughly even.[58] What Hitler had not been fully informed about was the critical state of Germany's raw-material reserves: enough rubber for six months, enough fuel for only four months. Booty from the western campaign would prove crucial in securing the material base for continuing the war.[59]

The level of secrecy maintained even in Hitler's closest entourage in the days leading up to the offensive was profound. When his special armoured train, code-named *Amerika*, pulled out of a small, secluded station on the outskirts of Berlin on the evening of 9 May, his press chief, Otto Dietrich, thought he was *en route* to visit shipworks in Hamburg, and Hitler's secretaries thought they were setting out for Denmark and Norway to visit the troops. After midnight, the train quietly switched in the vicinity of Hanover from the northbound tracks and turned westward. Even then, the destination was not disclosed. But by now there was no longer any doubt of the purpose of the journey. Hitler was in excellent spirits throughout. Dawn was breaking when they got down from the train at a little station in the Eifel. It was near Euskirchen – though there was no station place-name to reveal this since all place-name signs in the area had been removed and replaced by yellow military indicators. Cars were waiting to drive the company through hilly, wooded countryside to their new temporary home: the Führer Headquarters near Münstereifel that had been given the name Felsennest (Rock Eyrie). The accommodation was cramped and simple. Apart from Hitler himself, only Keitel, Schaub, and a manservant had rooms in the first bunker. Jodl, Dr Brandt, Schmundt, Below, Puttkamer, and Keitel's adjutant were in a second. The rest had to be accommodated in the nearby village. The woods around were filled with the springtime twittering of birds. But as his staff gathered in front of Hitler's bunker the peaceful sounds of the countryside in spring were broken by the distant rumble of shellfire. Hitler pointed to the West. 'Gentlemen, the offensive against the western powers has just started,' he declared.[60]

II

That offensive proceeded with a breathtaking pace that stunned the world. Even Hitler and his military leaders scarcely dared hope for such a scale of early successes.[61] On the northern flank, the Dutch surrender followed within five days, the Queen and government fleeing to exile in England.

Before that, the terror-bombing, Guernica-style, of Rotterdam's old town had brought death and devastation from the skies. It was the trademark of the new type of warfare. Warsaw civilians had suffered it first; the people of British cities would soon come to dread it; and, later in the war, German citizens themselves would be exposed to its full horror. Belgian neutrality, for the second time in under thirty years, was breached along with that of the Dutch. On 18 May the Belgian army surrendered unconditionally, leaving King Leopold in effect a prisoner with the government in exile. Meanwhile, the 'sickle cut plan' was proving a brilliant and decisive success. Aided by the strategic and operational ineptitude of the French military command, German armoured units were able to sweep through the Ardennes, through Luxemburg and southern Belgium into northern France, breaking the thin line of French defence, and crossing the Meuse already on 13 May. Within ten days of the launching of the offensive, by the night of 20–21 May, the advance had covered 150 miles and reached the Channel coast. The 'sickle cut' had worked. The Allied forces had been cut in two; vast numbers were now squeezed between the coast and the oncoming German divisions. On 26 May the War Office in London bowed to what had become increasingly inevitable, and ordered the evacuation of the British Expeditionary Force, the bulk of it by then fighting a desperate rearguard action just east of Dunkirk, the last remaining Channel port in Allied hands. The next days would see almost 340,000 British and French soldiers – the vast proportion of the Allied troops still in combat in north-west France – carried to safety across the Channel in an improvised armada of small boats while the Luftwaffe pounded the harbour and beaches of the port.[62]

The evacuation had been greatly helped by Hitler's decision, at 11.42a.m. on 24 May, to halt the German advance with the spearhead a mere fifteen miles or so from Dunkirk. Post-war suggestions that Hitler was deliberately allowing the British troops to get away as an act of generosity to encourage Britain to come to the peace table with its armies intact are far-fetched.[63] Hitler himself was alleged to have told his entourage a fortnight or so later that 'the army is the backbone of England and the Empire. If we smash the invasion corps, the Empire is doomed. Since we neither want to nor can inherit it, we must leave it the chance. My generals haven't grasped that.'[64] Such sentiments, if they were indeed expressed in those terms, were no more than a self-justification for a military mistake. For the decision not to move on Dunkirk was taken for military reasons, and on military advice. According to his Luftwaffe adjutant, Nicolaus von Below, 'the English army had no significance for him' at Dunkirk.[65]

Hitler had flown that morning, 24 May, to Charleville, almost 100 miles east of the Channel, to visit the headquarters of Colonel-General Gerd von Rundstedt, commander of Army Group A, which had made the remarkable advance in the 'sickle movement' along the southern flank. When Hitler arrived at half-past eleven, Rundstedt gave him a report on the situation. The suggestion to hold back the motorized units came not from Hitler, but from Rundstedt, one of his most trusted generals. Hitler agreed, adding that the tanks had to be conserved for the coming operations in the south and that a further advance would restrict the scope for action of the Luftwaffe.[66] Hitler was keen to press on with the attack to the south without the delay that he thought would come about if they took a few days dealing with the surrounded allied troops in Dunkirk.[67] When Brauchitsch arrived next morning, the 25th, wanting to advance the tanks on to the plains, Hitler opposed him, arguing that the numerous canals criss-crossing Flanders made it an unsuitable terrain for tanks.[68] But he left the decision to Rundstedt, who rejected the suggestion because of the need to have the tanks recover for the operations to come in the south.[69] Halder, as well as Brauchitsch, was dismayed.[70] They would have to come to terms with a Supreme Commander of the Wehrmacht who intervened directly in the direction of operations.[71] But there was no magnanimity in the decision to hold back the tanks. As we have seen, Hitler wanted to strike Britain a knock-out blow to force her to accept peace-terms. He had no interest in allowing the British troops to escape captivity or destruction. He had been persuaded by Göring to let the Luftwaffe finish off the encircled enemy.[72] He thought few of the British would escape.[73]

In fact, the Luftwaffe could not deliver on Göring's promises. Despite its claims of success, bad weather and the Royal Air Force contrived to prevent the easy pickings Göring had imagined. Dunkirk did nothing to enhance the Luftwaffe's prestige.[74] Within two days, Hitler realized that the halt order had been an error. On 26 May, he reversed his decision and finally ordered the advance on Dunkirk to prevent further evacuations.[75] Few of the encircled troops had got away by then.[76] But the delay of forty-eight hours proved vital in enabling the British to orchestrate the extraordinary retreat – a masterpiece of improvisation accompanied by much good luck – over the next days.

In military terms Dunkirk seemed, as one stunning success followed another, of secondary importance to Germany. It amounted in reality to a massive defeat for Britain. But that the troops were brought back under such conditions to fight again another day was converted by the new British

Prime Minister Churchill (who had come into office on the very day that the western offensive had begun), and by popular myth, into a symbol of the British fighting spirit – the archetypal triumph in adversity. As such, the great setback at Dunkirk provided a boost to British morale at one of the lowest points in the nation's long history. In another way, too, Dunkirk was fateful. If the British Expeditionary Force had been lost, it is almost inconceivable that Churchill would have survived the growing pressure from those powerful forces within Britain that were ready to seek terms with Hitler.[77]

Towards the end of the first week in June, Hitler moved his headquarters to Bruly-le-Pêche, not far from Brussels.[78] The second stage of the German offensive was beginning. The French lines were rapidly overwhelmed. While the French had more guns and tanks than the Germans, they were hopelessly outmatched in air-power. Not just that: French weaponry and tactics were outdated, not attuned to the demands of modern, mechanized warfare. And, just as important, the French military leadership conveyed their sense of defeatism to the rank and file. Discipline collapsed along with morale. Taking their lead from their fighting men, civilians fled from the big cities in their thousands. Some looked to astrology. The faithful placed their trust in prayer and the intercession of St Génevieve. Neither would be enough.[79]

On 14 June German troops penetrated the Maginot Line south of Saarbrücken. That same day, less than five weeks since the launch of the western offensive, their comrades entered Paris.[80] A generation earlier, the fathers and uncles of these soldiers had fought for four years and not reached Paris. Now, the German troops had achieved it in a little over four weeks. The disparity in casualty figures mirrored the magnitude of the victory. Allied losses were reckoned at 90,000 dead, 200,000 wounded, and 1.9 million captured or missing. German dead numbered almost 30,000, total casualties just under 165,000.[81]

It was no wonder that Hitler felt on top of the world, slapping his thigh for joy – his usual expression of exultation – and laughing in relief, when he was brought the news at Bruly-le-Pêche on 17 June that Marshal Pétain's new French government had sued for peace.[82] The end of the war seemed imminent. Britain would now surely give in. Total victory, Hitler imagined, was within his grasp.

Mussolini had brought Italy into the war a week earlier, hoping to cash in on the action just before it was all over, in time to win rich pickings and bask in the glory of a cheap victory.[83] Hitler took no pleasure in greeting his new companion-in-arms when he flew to Munich to meet him on 18 June to discuss the French armistice request.[84] He wanted lenient terms for the French, and swiftly dispelled Mussolini's hopes of getting his hands on part of the French fleet. Hitler was anxious to avoid the French navy going over to the British – something which Churchill had already tried to engineer.[85] 'From all that he says it is clear that he wants to act quickly to end it,' recorded Ciano. 'Hitler is now the gambler who has made a big scoop and would like to get up from the table risking nothing more.'[86] Ribbentrop confirmed to Ciano that Hitler wanted peace with Britain in preference to war. Again the German Dictator stated that he had no wish to demolish the British Empire, something he claimed to regard as 'an important factor in world equilibrium'.[87] A hint of what he meant by this last phrase can be gleaned from a remark a fortnight or so later to Goebbels, that, if the Empire were destroyed, its inheritance would fall not to Germany but to 'foreign great powers', by which he had the United States, Japan, and probably also the Soviet Union chiefly in mind.[88] What Hitler's apparent magnanimity about the Empire would amount to for Britain was clearly foreseen by Churchill. Britain would become, the British Prime Minister stated, 'a vassal state of the Hitler empire'. 'A pro-German government,' he wrote to Roosevelt on 15 June, 'would certainly be called into being to make peace and might present to a shattered or starving nation an almost irresistible case for entire submission to the Nazi will.'[89]

Having won his great victory without any help from the Italians, Hitler was determined that the embarrassed and disappointed Mussolini, now forced to swallow his role as junior partner in the Axis, should not participate in the armistice negotiations with the French.[90] Already on 20 May, when German tanks had reached the French coast, Hitler had specified that the peace negotiations with France, at which the return of former German territory would be demanded, would be staged in the Forest of Compiègne, where the armistice of 1918 had taken place.[91] He now gave orders to retrieve Marshal Foch's railway carriage, preserved as a museum piece, in which the German generals had signed the ceasefire, and have it brought to the forest clearing. That defeat, and its consequences, had permanently seared Hitler's consciousness. It would now be erased by repaying the humiliation. At quarter past three on the afternoon of 21 June, Hitler, accompanied by Göring, Raeder, Brauchitsch, Keitel, Ribbentrop, and Heß, viewed the memorial recording the victory over the 'criminal arrogance of the German Reich', then took his place in the carriage, greeting in silence the French delegation. For ten minutes, he listened, again without a word though, as he later recounted, gripped by the feeling of revenge for the humiliation of

November 1918.[92] Keitel read out the preamble to the armistice terms. Hitler then left to return to his headquarters. The symbolic purging of the old debt was completed.[93] 'The disgrace is now extinguished. It's a feeling of being born again,' reported Goebbels after Hitler had told him of the dramatic events late that night on the telephone.[94]

France was to be divided – the north and western seaboard under German occupation, the centre and south to be left as a puppet state, headed by Pétain, with its seat of government at Vichy.[95] Following the signing of the Italian–French armistice on 24 June, all fighting was declared to have ceased at 1.35a.m. next morning. Hitler proclaimed the end of the war in the west and the 'most glorious victory of all time'. He ordered bells to be rung in the Reich for a week, and flags to be flown for ten days.[96] As the moment for the official conclusion of hostilities drew near, Hitler, sitting at the wooden table in his field headquarters, ordered the lights put out and the windows opened in order to hear, in the darkness, the trumpeter outside mark the historic moment.[97]

He spent part of the next days sightseeing. Max Amann (head of the Party's publishing concerns) and Ernst Schmidt, two comrades from the First World War, joined his regular entourage for a nostalgic tour of the battlefields in Flanders, revisiting the places where they had been stationed.[98] Then, on 28 June, before most Parisians were awake, Hitler paid his one and only visit to the occupied French capital.[99] It lasted no more than three hours. And its purpose was cultural, not military. Accompanied by the architects Hermann Giesler and Albert Speer, and his favourite sculptor, Arno Breker, Hitler landed at Le Bourget airport at, for him, the extraordinarily early hour of half-past five in the morning. The whistlestop sightseeing tour began at L'Opéra. All the lights were ablaze, as if for an evening gala performance, as the three large Mercedes pulled up. A white-haired French guide, deferential but reserved, took the small group through the empty building. Hitler was thrilled by its beauty. He had doubtless been reading up on the descriptions of the opera house during wakeful hours on the previous nights, and delighted in showing off his detailed knowledge. The guide refused the 50-Mark tip that Hitler had his adjutant attempt to proffer.[100] The tourists moved on. They drove past La Madeleine, whose classical form impressed Hitler, up the Champs Elysées, stopped at the Tomb of the Unknown Soldier below the Arc de Triomphe, viewed the Eiffel Tower, and looked in silence on the tomb of Napoleon in Les Invalides. Hitler admired the dimensions of the Panthéon, but found its interior (as he later recalled) 'a terrible disappointment',[101] and seemed indifferent to the medieval wonders of Paris, like the Sainte Chapelle. The tour ended, curiously, at the nineteenth-century testament to Catholic piety, the church of Sacré-Coeur. With a last look over the city from the heights of Montmartre, Hitler was gone. By mid-morning he was back in his field headquarters. Seeing Paris, he told Speer, had been the dream of his life.[102] But to Goebbels, he said he had found a lot of Paris very disappointing.[103] He had considered destroying it. However, he remarked, according to Speer, 'when we're finished in Berlin, Paris will only be a shadow. Why should we destroy it?'[104]

On 2 July Goebbels visited the new Führer Headquarters in the Black Forest to discuss arrangements for Hitler's triumphal return to Berlin and plans for a Reichstag speech directed at another 'peace offer' to Britain. The return was scheduled for the 6th, a Saturday, the speech for the Monday following. The speech would be generously framed, a last chance for England. He was doubtful that it would be well received. Churchill, he knew, would not accept the bait. But he had some hopes, though not strong, in others who were known to be making overtures aimed at peace. If London did not accept the terms, Goebbels noted menacingly, then it had only itself to blame for the consequences. 'They will be terrible,' he added.[105]

The reception awaiting Hitler in Berlin when his train pulled into the Anhalter-Bahnhof at three o'clock on 6 July was astonishing. It surpassed even the homecomings after the great pre-war triumphs like the Anschluß. Many in the crowds had been standing for six hours, as the dull morning gave way to the brilliant sunshine of the afternoon. The streets were strewn with flowers all the way from the station to the Reich Chancellery. Hundreds of thousands cheered themselves hoarse. Hitler, lauded by Keitel as 'the greatest warlord of all time', was called out time after time on to the balcony to soak up the wild adulation of the masses.[106] 'If an increase in feeling for Adolf Hitler is still possible, it had become reality with the day of the return to Berlin,' commented one report from the provinces.[107] In the face of such 'greatness', ran another, 'all pettiness and grumbling are silenced'.[108] Even opponents of the regime found it hard to resist the victory mood. Workers in the armaments factories pressed to be allowed to join the army. People thought final victory was around the corner. Only Britain stood in the way. For perhaps the only time during the Third Reich there was genuine war-fever among the population. Incited by incessant propaganda, hatred of Britain was now widespread. People were now thirsting to see the high-and-mighty long-standing rival finally brought to its knees.[109] But mingling with the aggression were still feelings of fear and anxiety.[110]

Whether triumphalist, or fearful, the wish to bring the war to a speedy end was almost universal.

Hitler had meanwhile changed his mind about delivering his Reichstag speech on the Monday. On 3 July British ships had sunk a number of French warships moored at the naval base of Mers-el-Kébir, near Oran, in French Algeria, killing 1,250 French sailors in the process. Churchill's move, a show of British determination, was to prevent the battle-fleet of his former allies falling into Hitler's hands.[111] For Hitler, this brought a new situation. He wanted to await developments. He was uncertain whether he ought to go ahead and appeal to England.[112] When Ciano met him the day after Hitler had returned to Berlin, the Italian Foreign Minister found him 'rather inclined to continue the struggle and to unleash a storm of wrath and of steel upon the British'. However, Ciano added, 'the final decision has not been reached, and it is for this reason that he is delaying his speech, of which, as he himself puts it, he wants to weigh every word.'[113] He was to postpone his speech three times – an indication of his uncertainty about how to proceed at this crucial time – before finally scheduling it for the 19th.[114] 'Despite everything the Führer still has a very positive attitude towards England,' remarked Goebbels. 'He is still not ready for the final blow. He wants to think over his speech again in peace and for that reason go to the Obersalzberg.' If London should refuse the last offer, then Britain would be 'immediately following dealt an annihilatory blow. The English apparently have no idea what then awaits them.'[115]

While he was at the Berghof, Hitler had talks with his military leaders about a possible invasion of Britain, should his 'peace offer' be rejected. At these discussions, an invasion was still seen as a last choice rather than first option. Raeder, reporting on a study that the naval leadership had been conducting since the previous November, had on his own initiative already as early as 21 May, during the early stages of the western offensive, raised with Hitler the possibility of a landing.[116] They had spoken again on 20 June about it, and Hitler had briefly also discussed the matter with Brauchitsch.[117] The Wehrmacht had officially learned on 2 July of Hitler's decision that under certain conditions a landing in Britain could be undertaken.[118] Raeder had advised Hitler in June that a naval landing could only take place once the Luftwaffe had secured air superiority over southern England.[119] He repeated this precondition when he met Hitler on 11 July on the Obersalzberg, advocating 'concentrated bombing' to begin forthwith. But naval ambitions went far beyond a presumed British surrender, thus obviating the need for what Raeder, as well as Hitler, saw as the risky venture of invading

Britain. Germany would need a big navy to defend its colonial empire, in particular against the looming threat of the United States.[120] Taking the opportunity to push the interests of the navy, Raeder held out, therefore, the prospect of building up a great battleship fleet to combat any potential Anglo-American naval alliance.[121] The next day Jodl outlined for Hitler initial thoughts on operational plans for a landing.[122] On Saturday, 13 July, it was Halder's turn to travel to the Berghof to report on operational plans.[123] But a landing was to be a last resort. 'The Führer is greatly puzzled by England's persisting unwillingness to make peace,' Halder noted. 'He sees the answer (as we do) in England's hope in Russia and therefore counts on having to compel her by main force to agree to peace. Actually that is much against his grain. The reason is that a military defeat of England will bring about the disintegration of the British Empire.' As Halder recorded, Hitler reiterated what he had told Goebbels and others. 'This would not be of any benefit to Germany. German blood would be shed to accomplish something that would benefit only Japan, the United States, and others.'[124]

The talk was only of England at this time. Hitler regretted that he had not done more to 'sign up' (*angeheuert*) the Duke of Windsor while he had still been King. He wondered how useful Sir Oswald Mosley – the leader of the 'Blackshirts', the British Union of Fascists – might be.[125] He remained uncertain how to act. 'It's my impression that F[ührer] is still unsure and doesn't know what he should do and how he should do it,' noted army adjutant Gerhard Engel, wondering whether Hitler would indeed give his Reichstag speech.[126] A brief trip out from the Berghof to the steelworks in Linz and tank factory at Wels saw him pressing for expansion. Whether or not the British should come to terms, German armaments were intended for use again before long.[127]

On 16 July Hitler then signed 'Directive No.16 for Preparations of a Landing Operation against England'. The preamble ran: 'Since England, in spite of its militarily hopeless situation, still gives no recognizable signs of readiness to come to terms, I have determined to prepare a landing operation against England and, if need be, to carry it out. The aim of this operation is to exclude the English motherland as a basis for the continuation of the war against Germany, and, if it should be necessary, to occupy it completely.'[128] Operational plans followed. But the qualifications in the preamble – 'if need be', 'if necessary' – indicated Hitler's half-heartedness.

This conveyed itself to his army leaders. Rundstedt, Commander-in-Chief in the West, simply did not take 'Sealion' seriously – a feeling endorsed by Göring's report of Hitler telling him privately that he did not intend to carry out the operation. He never even bothered to attend the amphibious landing exercises. To him and all who studied them, given the strength of the British navy, the logistic difficulties seemed insuperable.[129]

If the British would only see sense, thought Hitler, it would be far more desirable than an invasion. After signing the directive, he fixed his Reichstag speech for the evening of Friday, 19 July, in the Kroll Opera House.[130]

The Reichstag had a military appearance that evening. Six seats, of deputies who had fallen in the western campaign, had laurel wreaths placed on them. In the front row were the gold-braided top brass of the military, their chests heaving with medals and decorations, many preening themselves on their new promotions to Field-Marshals and Colonel-Generals.[131] (Hitler had a cynical view about promoting his military leaders. Through acts of generosity, as in ancient times, they would be bound all the more, whatever their political views, to their oaths of loyalty, and to him as the bestower of such gifts. He intended their salaries to be tax-free, and would not be miserly with donations of landed estates once the war was finally won.[132] This altered nothing of his view that the army leadership – Brauchitsch and Halder in particular – had been found seriously wanting once more, and that his own judgement had again been proved right in the western campaign.[133]) Hitler was in impressive form, speaking more quietly and less hysterically than was often the case. William Shirer, watching from the gallery, admired the performance. 'The Hitler we saw in the Reichstag tonight was the conqueror, and conscious of it, and yet so wonderful an actor, so magnificent a handler of the German mind, that he mixed superbly the full confidence of the conqueror with the humbleness which always goes down so well with the masses when they know a man is on top . . . His oratorical form was at its best . . . I've often admired the way he uses his hands, which are somewhat feminine and quite artistic. Tonight he used those hands beautifully, seemed to express himself almost as much with his hands – and the sway of his body – as he did with his words and the use of his voice.'[134]

The point of his speech, as he told Goebbels earlier that day, was to make Britain a brief but imprecise offer, indicating that it was the last word, and leaving the choice to London.[135] A large part of the speech, which lasted no less than two and a quarter hours, was spent describing the course of the war, praising the military achievements of the commanders, and listing their promotions. As he came to the names of the twelve generals who were to be made Field-Marshals, Hitler saluted each of them. From their places in the balcony, they stood to attention and returned the salute.[136] Special mention was made of Göring, now elevated to Reich Marshal. Göring was

like a child with a new toy when Hitler gave him the accompanying insignia.[137] Hitler then emphasized the strength of Germany's position. Only in
the last few minutes of his speech did he reach the point that everyone was
waiting for: his 'appeal to reason, also in England'.[138] The 'appeal' came
and went – in those words, and little besides. There was the usual accusation
levelled at Churchill as the warmonger. There was the threat that Britain,
and the British Empire, would be destroyed. There was a hypocritical
expression of regret for the victims of continued war. And there was the
victor's 'appeal to reason'. That was all.[139] It was little wonder that the
reaction, even among those around Hitler, was one of disappointment –
especially when the British categorical rejection of the 'offer' was announced
within the hour.[140]

Hitler had misjudged the mood in Britain. And his speech had not been
tuned to offer anything that might tempt the opponents of Churchill, who
could have formed a peace-lobby.[141] Ciano, who met Hitler the day after
the speech, was told that British reactions had ruled out any possibility of
an understanding being reached. Hitler said he was preparing to strike at
Britain, whose resistance would collapse under the first blows.[142] This was
meant for the Italians, but indirectly – through the known leaks – for British
ears, to help concentrate their minds. To Goebbels, Hitler had a different
line. He still did not want to accept England's answer at face-value. 'He
thinks of still waiting a bit.'[143]

He left the matter open when he met the Commanders-in-Chief of the
Wehrmacht on 21 July.[144] 'No clear picture on what is happening in England,'
Brauchitsch recorded Hitler as saying, when he reported back to Halder
next day. 'Preparations for a decision by arms must be completed as quickly
as possible.' Hitler would not allow the military initiative to be lost. But he
was evidently still hoping for a diplomatic solution. 'Crossing of Channel
appears very hazardous to the Führer. On that account, invasion is to be
undertaken only if no other way is left to bring terms with England,' Halder
reported. 'England's position is hopeless. The war is won by us,' Hitler stated.

But Britain still put her hopes in America, and in Russia. There was the
possibility, said Hitler, referring to rumours of crisis in London, that a
cabinet including Lloyd George, Chamberlain, and Halifax might come to
power and seek peace terms.[145] But, failing that, Britain would have to be
reduced by an air-offensive combined with intensified submarine warfare to
the state, by mid-September, when an invasion could be carried out. Hitler
would decide within days, after hearing Raeder's report in mid-week on
naval operational logistics, whether the invasion would be carried out by

autumn. Otherwise, it would be before the following May. The final decision on the intensity of submarine and air attacks would be left until the beginning of August. There was the possibility that the invasion might begin as early as 25 August.

Hitler turned finally to the issue which had already started to bother him: the position of Russia. Stalin, he pointed out, had his own agenda. He was flirting with Britain to keep her in the war, to tie down Germany, and to exploit the situation to undertake his own expansionist policy. There were no indications of any Russian aggression towards Germany. 'But,' went on Hitler, 'our attention must be turned to tackling the Russian problem and prepare planning.' It would take four to six weeks to assemble the German military force. Its object would be 'to crush the Russian army or at least take as much Russian territory as is necessary to bar enemy air raids on Berlin and Silesian industries'. He also mentioned the need to protect the Romanian oil-fields. Eighty to 100 divisions would be required. He contemplated attacking Russia that very autumn, to relieve the pressure of the air war on Britain.[146] Compared with what had been achieved in the West, Hitler had remarked to Jodl and Keitel already at the time of the French capitulation 'a campaign against Russia would be child's play (*Sandkastenspiel*)'.[147]

It was an astonishing prospect that Hitler held out to his army leaders. He was, of course, not yet committing himself to anything. But the two-front war which had always been anathema was now being entertained. Paradoxically, having advocated since the 1920s a showdown with the Soviet Union to destroy Bolshevism and win '*Lebensraum*', Hitler had now come back to the idea of a war against Russia for strategic reasons: to force his erstwhile would-be friend, Britain, now stubbornly holding out against the odds, to terms. The ideological aim of smashing Bolshevism, though apparently invoked by Hitler as part of his reasoning, was at this point secondary to the strategic need to get Britain out of the war.[148] It was a sign of the difficulties that Hitler had manoeuvred himself into. Britain would not play his game. But the military lesson he kept saying she would have to be taught, and which the German public now awaited, would be, he knew, a hazardous affair. So he was now moving to a step he – and most of his generals did not disagree – thought less dangerous: an attack on the Soviet Union.

In fact, the army command, worried about the build-up of Soviet troops in southern Russia in connection with Stalin's increasing pressure on the Balkan states, had already, in mid-June, added a further nine motorized divisions to the fifteen divisions previously designated for transfer to the east.[149] And on 3 July Halder, without any orders from Hitler but following indications evidently passed on to him by Weizsäcker, in the Foreign Office, showed himself ready to anticipate the change in direction, to 'work towards the Führer', when he deemed it appropriate to have the possibilities of a campaign against the Soviet Union tested. The Chief of Staff, ahead of Hitler at this point, raised with his operational planners 'the requirements of a military intervention which will compel Russia to recognize Germany's dominant position in Europe'.[150]

Hitler was still avoiding a final decision on Britain.[151] But it was with the impression that Lord Halifax's official spurning of his 'peace offer' in a broadcast speech on the evening of 22 July amounted to 'England's final rejection' that he left, for what was to prove the last time, for Bayreuth, to see next day a performance of *Götterdämmerung*. 'The die is cast,' wrote Goebbels. 'We're tuning press and radio to a fight.'[152] In fact, the die had not been finally cast. Hitler remained unsure how to proceed.

He had long since convinced himself of what German propaganda was trumpeting. It was he who wanted peace. Churchill, backed by the 'Jewish plutocracy', was the warmonger – the obstacle to the triumph. While in Bayreuth, Hitler saw the friend of his youth days, August Kubizek, for the last time. Hitler told Kubizek, as gullible as ever, that the war had hindered all his great plans for rebuilding Germany. 'I did not become Chancellor of the Great German Reich in order to wage war,' he said. Kubizek believed him.[153] Probably Hitler believed himself.

He went from Bayreuth to the Obersalzberg. While he was there, the army leadership learnt from Raeder that the navy could not be ready for operations against England before 15 September. The earliest date for an invasion, depending on the moon and tides, was the 26th of that month. If that date proved impossible, the invasion would have to be put off until the following May.[154] Brauchitsch was sceptical that the navy could provide the basis for an invasion in the autumn. (In fact, the navy had concluded that it was highly inadvisable to attempt to invade at any point that year, and was highly sceptical about the prospects of an invasion at any time.[155]) Halder agreed with Brauchitsch in eliminating the notion of an operation during bad weather. But they foresaw disadvantages, military and political, in a postponement to the following year. They considered possibilities of weakening Britain's overseas position through attacks on Gibraltar, Haifa, and Suez, support for the Italians in Egypt, and inciting the Russians to move on the Persian Gulf. An attack on Russia was rejected in favour of the maintenance of friendly relations.[156]

Hitler, meantime, had been privately consulting Jodl. On 29 July he asked the Chief of the Wehrmacht Directional Staff about deploying the army in the east, and whether it might be possible to attack and defeat Russia that very autumn. Jodl totally ruled it out on practical grounds. In that case, Hitler said, absolute confidence was needed. Feasibility studies were to be undertaken, but knowledge confined to only a few staff officers. Remarkably, in fact, the Wehrmacht had not waited for Hitler's order. 'The army,' Jodl was later to remark, 'had already learnt of the Führer's intentions at the stage when these were still being weighed up. An operational plan was therefore drawn up even before the order for this was given.' And already in July, as he later put it 'on his own initiative (*aus eigenem Antrieb)*', Major-General Bernhard von Loßberg, from Jodl's 'National Defence Department' (*Abteilung Landesverteidigung*), had begun work on an 'operational study for a Russian campaign (*an die Bearbeitung einer Operationsstudie für einen Rußlandfeldzug*)'.[157] The draft plan was at this stage merely intended to be held in readiness for the point at which it might be needed. Hitler's discussion with Jodl indicated that this point had arrived.

Loßberg was among the four members of Jodl's staff, headed by Warlimont, sitting in the restaurant car of the special train *Atlas*, in the station at Bad Reichenhall, when he came down from the Berghof to report on his discussion with Hitler.[158] According to Warlimont, the consternation at what they heard – meaning the dreaded war on two fronts – gave rise to an hour of bitter argument. Jodl countered by stating Hitler's opinion that it was better to have the inevitable war against Bolshevism now, with German power at its height, than later; and that by autumn 1941 victory in the East would have brought the Luftwaffe to its peak for deployment against Britain.[159] Whatever the objections – it is impossible to know whether Warlimont was exaggerating them in his post-war account – the feasibility studies under the code-name '*Aufbau-Ost*' (Build-Up in the East) were now undertaken with a greater sense of urgency.[160]

Two days later, on 31 July, Hitler met his military leaders at the Berghof. Raeder repeated the conclusion his naval planners had reached that the earliest date for an invasion of Britain could be no earlier than 15 September, and favoured postponing it until the following May. Hitler wanted to keep his options open. Things would become difficult with the passing of time. Air attacks should begin straight away. They would determine Germany's relative strength. 'If results of air warfare are unsatisfactory, invasion preparations will be stopped. If we have the impression that the English are crushed and that effects will soon begin to tell, we shall proceed to the attack,' he stated. He remained sceptical about an invasion. The risks were high; so, however, was the prize, he added. But he was already thinking of the next step. What if no invasion took place? He returned to the hopes Britain placed in the USA and in Russia. If Russia were to be eliminated, then America, too, would be lost for Britain because of the increase in Japan's power in the Far East. Russia was 'the factor on which England is relying the most'. The British had been 'completely down'. Now they had revived. Russia had been shaken by events in the West. The British were now clutching on, hoping for a change in the situation during the next few months.

He moved to his momentous conclusion: remove Russia from the equation. Halder's notes retained Hitler's emphasis. '*With Russia smashed, England's last hope would be shattered.* Germany then will be master of Europe and the Balkans. *Decision: Russia's destruction must therefore be made a part of this struggle. Spring 1941. The sooner Russia is crushed the better.* Attack achieves its purpose only if Russian state can be shattered to its roots with one blow. Holding part of the country alone will not do. Standing still for the following winter would be perilous. So it is better to wait a little longer, but with the resolute determination to eliminate Russia ... If we start in May 1941, we would have five months to finish the job.'[161]

Unlike the anxious reactions on the occasions in 1938 and 1939 when the generals had feared war with Britain, there is no indication that they were horror-struck at what they heard. (As we have noted, Halder, gleaning what was in the air, had anticipated Hitler in broaching, at the beginning of the month, the possibility of military intervention to force the Russians to recognize German dominance.)[162] The fateful underestimation of the Russian military potential was something Hitler shared with his commanders. Intelligence on the Soviet army was poor. But the underestimation was not solely the result of poor intelligence. Airs of disdain for Slavs mingled easily with contempt for what Bolshevism had managed to achieve. Contact with Soviet generals in the partition of Poland had not impressed the Germans. The dismal showing of the Red Army in Finland (where the inadequately equipped Finns had inflicted unexpected and heavy losses on the Soviets in the early stages of the 'Winter War' of 1939–40) had done nothing to improve its image in their eyes. Not least, there was the apparent madness which had prompted Stalin to destroy his own officer corps. Whereas an attack on the British Isles remained a perilous undertaking, an assault on the Soviet Union raised no great alarm. A true 'lightning war' could be expected here.[163]

The day after the meeting on the Berghof, Hitler signed Directive No.17, intensifying the air-war and sea-war against Britain as the basis for her 'final subjugation'. He explicitly – underscoring the sentence in the Directive – reserved for himself a decision on the use of terror bombing.[164] The offensive was set to begin four days later, but was postponed until the 8th. It was again postponed on account of the weather conditions until the 13th.[165] From then on, the German fighters sought to sweep the Royal Air Force from the skies. Wave after wave of attacks on the airfields of southern England was launched. Spitfires, Hurricanes and Messerschmitts wheeled, arched, dived, and strafed each other in the dramatic and heroic dogfights on which Britain's survival at this point depended. The early optimistic results announced in Berlin soon proved highly misleading.[166] The task was beyond the Luftwaffe. At first by the skin of their teeth the young British pilots held out, then gradually won the ascendancy. Despite Hitler's orders that he alone was to decide on terror-bombing, 100 planes of the Luftwaffe acting, it seems, under a loosely worded directive from Göring issued on 2 August, had attacked London's East End on the night of 24 August. As retaliation, the RAF carried out the first British bombing raids on Berlin the following night.[167] Ineffective though they were, they came as a shock to the people of Berlin. Göring had once joked that should British planes ever reach Germany, his name was not Hermann Göring, but Hermann Meier. From now on, caustic Berlin tongues dubbed him 'Herr Meier'.[168]

Hitler regarded the bombing of Berlin as a disgrace.[169] As usual, his reaction was to threaten massive retaliation. 'We'll wipe out their cities! We'll put an end to the work of these night pirates,'[170] he fumed at a speech in the Sportpalast on 4 September. He spoke with Göring about undertaking the revenge. From 7 September the nightly bombing of London began.[171] It was the turn of the citizens of Britain's capital to experience night after night the terror from the skies. The shift to terror-bombing marked a move away from the idea of the landing which Hitler had never whole-heartedly favoured. Persuaded by Göring, he now thought for a while that Britain could be bombed to the conference-table without German troops having to undertake the perilous landing.[172] But, dreadful though the 'Blitz' was, the Luftwaffe was simply not powerful enough to bomb Britain to submission. The chief of the Luftwaffe's Operational Staff (Luftwaffenführungstab), General Otto Hoffmann von Waldau, stated almost a month after the high-point of the 'Battle of Britain' that an air-fleet four times the size would have been needed to force Britain to its knees.[173]

Between 10 and 13 September there were signs that Hitler had gone utterly cold on the idea of a landing.[174] On 14 September he then told his commanders that the conditions for 'Operation Sealion' – the operational plan to attack Great Britain – had not been attained. The military chiefs themselves did not believe that a landing in England at that stage could be successfully carried out.[175] 'I had the impression at this discussion,' wrote Nicolaus von Below many years later, 'that Hitler had given up hope of a successful invasion of England the following spring. In autumn 1940 the great unknown, the fairly improvised crossing over the sea, frightened him. He was unsure.'[176]

Meanwhile, the dogfights over the Channel intensified during the first fortnight in September, reaching a climacteric on Sunday, the 15th. The Wehrmacht admitted 182 planes lost in that fortnight, forty-three on the 15th alone.[177] The horrors of the 'Blitz' would continue for months to be inflicted upon British cities – among the worst devastation the bombing of Coventry on the night of 14 November, as the German onslaught switched to the industrial belt of the Midlands to strike at more manageable targets than London.[178] But the 'Battle of Britain' was over. Hitler had never been convinced that the German air-offensive would successfully lay the basis for the invasion of which he was in any case so sceptical. On 17 September he ordered the indefinite postponement – though, for psychological reasons, not the cancellation – of 'Operation Sealion'.[179]

The peace-overtures had failed. The battle for the skies had failed. Meanwhile, on 3 September the grant of fifty destroyers to Britain by the USA – a deal which Roosevelt had eventually pushed through, initially against much opposition from the isolationists – was, despite the limited use of the elderly warships, the plainest indication to date that Britain might in the foreseeable future be able to reckon with the still dormant military might of the USA.[180] It was increasingly urgent to get Britain out of the war. Hitler's options were, in autumn 1940, still not closed off. There was the possibility of forcing Britain to come to terms through a strategy of attacks on her Mediterranean and Near Eastern strongholds. But once that option also faded Hitler was left with only one possibility: the one that was in his view not only strategically indispensable but embodied one of his most long-standing ideological obsessions. This point would not finally be reached until December 1940. By then it would be time to prepare for the crusade against Bolshevism.

III

Hitler did not have the power to bring the war to the conclusion he wanted. And, within Germany, he was powerless to prevent the governance of the Reich from slipping increasingly out of control. The tendencies already plainly evident before the war – unresolved Party-State dualism, unclear or overlapping spheres of competence, proliferation of *ad hoc* establishment of improvised 'special authorities' (*Sonderbehörden*) empowered to handle specific policy areas, administrative anarchy – were now sharply magnified. It was not that Hitler was a 'weak dictator'.[181] His power was recognized and acknowledged on all fronts. Nothing of significance was undertaken in contradiction to his known wishes. His popular support was immense. Opponents were demoralized and without hope. There was no conceivable challenge that could be mounted. The slippage from control did not mean a decline in Hitler's authority. But it did mean that the very nature of that authority had built into it the erosion and undermining of regular patterns of government and, at the same time, the inability to keep in view all aspects of rule of an increasingly expanding and complex Reich. Even someone more able, energetic, and industrious when it came to administration than Hitler could not have done it. And during the first months of the war, as we have seen, Hitler was for lengthy stretches away from Berlin and overwhelmingly preoccupied with military events. It was impossible for him to stay completely in touch with and be competently involved in the running of the Reich. But in the absence of any organ of collective government to replace the cabinet, which had not met since February 1938, or any genuine delegation of powers (which Hitler constantly shied away from, seeing it as a potentially dangerous dilution of his authority), the disintegration of anything resembling a coherent 'system' of administration inevitably accelerated. Far from diminishing Hitler's power, the continued erosion of any semblance of collective government actually enhanced it. Since, however, this disintegration went hand in hand – part cause, part effect – with the Darwinian struggle carried out through recourse to Hitler's ideological goals, the radicalization entailed in the process of 'working towards the Führer' equally inevitably accelerated.[182]

Little systematic planning for the practicalities of Reich government during a war had been carried out before the invasion of Poland in September 1939. As usual, much was improvised.[183] Arising as a type of 'standing committee' from the Reich Defence Council (Reichsverteidigungsrat), established in 1938 (which had met on only two occasions, each time to hear lengthy speeches by Göring), a Ministerial Council for the Defence of the Reich (Ministerrat für die Reichsverteidigung) was set up at the end of August 1939. This seems to have been Göring's idea, on the look-out, as always, for power aggrandizement. Hitler, for his part, was ready to make what amounted in practice to no great concession of power in order to offload some of his own administrative burden and speedily push through legislation necessary for the war effort. Not least, by pandering to the vanity of his designated successor and compensating him at the same time for his known objections to the war with Britain, he could at the same time deepen Göring's sense of loyalty and thereby invest in a small insurance policy. No preparations had been made for such a body when Hitler gave out verbal instructions, which civil servants from the Reich Chancellery turned into a decree within a couple of hours. The head of the glaringly pointless Constitutional Department (Verfassungsabteilung) in the Reich Ministry of the Interior learnt of the existence of the new body from the newspapers. No one in his Department had been consulted.

The six permanent members of the Ministerial Council comprised Göring (as chairman), Frick (as Plenipotentiary for Administration), Funk (Pleni-potentiary for the Economy), Lammers (head of the Reich Chancellery), Keitel (head of the High Command of the Wehrmacht), and Heß (Hitler's deputy as leader of the Party). The Council was given the right to promulgate decrees on internal matters with the power of law. But it was not intended to be a 'War Cabinet'. Neither the Foreign nor Propaganda Ministers were members. In the main the decrees were signed by Göring, Frick, and Lammers, but did not have to go to Hitler, as conventional laws did. Hitler was nevertheless careful to place restrictions on the Council which protected his own rights to overrule it if necessary. His own powers were delegated to, not replaced by, the Council.

In practice, the Council met only on a handful of occasions, for the last time in mid-November 1939. Most of the decrees it promulgated concerned relatively routine administrative and economic matters, and were brought about by the circulation of draft legislation rather than by collective deliber-ation. The number of ministerial representatives demanding a presence soon turned the few Council meetings that did take place into large and unwieldy affairs – precisely what it had been the intention to avoid. Göring himself lost interest. Hitler was quite happy to see the new body wither on the vine. An attempt to speed up the legislative process through a 'Three-Man Collective' (Dreierkollegium) of Frick, Funk, and Keitel proved no more successful. In fact, the triad never met a single time. Draft legislation was merely cleared with the other two agencies. And overlaps or clashes in competence were never resolved.

The half-hearted attempt to resurrect some form of collective government had not got off the ground. Partly, Göring's own autocratic style, combined with an administrative incompetence arising from his belief that 'will' was all that mattered, meant that any collective body under his command was certain to atrophy. His own contempt for bureaucracy meant that, like Hitler, he rode roughshod over it, favouring the elimination during the war of all legislation not absolutely necessary for the defence of the Reich.[184] Even more important, Hitler's own sharp antennae towards any restriction on his power, any limitation to the principles of his untrammelled personalized rule, vitiated from the outset the possibility of a true delegation of the head of government's role to Göring and erection of a genuine 'war cabinet'. Such was Hitler's sensitivity to anything which might impose limits on his own freedom of action, or constitute a possible internal threat to his position, that he would block Lammers's feeble attempts to reinstate cabinet meetings in 1942, and even refuse permission for ministers to gather occasionally for an evening around a beer table.[185]

Hitler was now largely removed from the day-to-day running of the Reich. But no individual, let alone any collective body, had filled the vacuum. The administrative disorder could only grow.

Ministers, or their State Secretaries, met from time to time in *Chefbesprechungen* (discussions of departmental heads) to try to resolve intractable conflicts or hammer out some compromise through horse-trading. But such meetings were no substitute for governmental coordination through a cabinet. And as the war progressed they turned more and more into mass assemblies, deflecting from any possible purpose that might have been served through bargaining to balance ministerial interests.[186] In any case, powerful ministers like Goebbels, with privileged access to Hitler, had little need of such a body. If their interests were not met they could take the matter to the top and usually obtain the authorization they wanted. The empire-building of Goebbels's Propaganda Ministry, along with the power-ambitions of the 'Special Authorities' like Göring's Four-Year Plan Organization, Ley's commissariat for housing, or Himmler's SS, ensured that conflict was both endemic and inimical to any sense of coordinated government.[187]

Other than for the privileged, the only link between government ministers and Hitler was through Lammers. Hitler insisted, soon after the start of the war, that he only be approached on any issue needing resolution once all heads of government departments had made their positions clear. With the exception of purely military matters, issues were to be presented to Hitler only by Lammers.[188] Any dispute was, therefore, contained at a level below Hitler. And, from his Olympian heights, he was able to side with the victors of the Darwinian struggle. It was less part of a carefully conceived 'divide-and-rule' strategy, than a necessary and inevitable consequence of protecting his leadership position from being dragged into the mire of the conflicts which his form of leadership – and the ideological dynamism which it incorporated – had inexorably spawned.[189]

The ideological drive of National Socialism was inextricable from the endemic conflict within the regime. Without this ideological drive, embodied in Hitler's 'mission' (as perceived by his more fanatical followers), the break-up of government into the near anarchy of competing fiefdoms and internecine rivalries is inexplicable. Other fascist-style regimes, including Mussolini's, did not show anything like the same pronounced tendencies towards governmental disintegration. The 'cumulative radicalization' in the Third Reich had its driving-force in the 'vision' of racial purification and empire represented by Hitler.[190] The beginning of the war, as we have already seen in the context of the lurch into outright barbarism in Poland and the launching of the 'euthanasia action' within Germany, had sharply intensified Hitler's own commitment to the fulfilment of long-standing ideological goals.[191] But internal radicalization went beyond Hitler's personal involvement. 'Working towards' his 'vision' was the key to success in the internal war of the regime.

Those 'working towards the Führer' in a quite literal sense were above all to be found in the Party and its main affiliations, especially the SS. The Party – a bureaucratic organization whose inner coherence was destroyed by its own non-bureaucratic aims of 'leadership' in the interests of long-term ideological goals – found itself in the war with extended and new tasks, mainly revolving around propaganda, control, and mobilization. The handing over to the Gauleiter, in their new capacity as Reich Defence Commissars, of extensive powers over civil administration at the regional level was one significant step in this direction.[192] The aim was to galvanize the civil administration and mobilize the population with the same spirit that had characterized the Party itself in its 'time of struggle'. The consequence was, however, a further inpenetrable level of administrative overlap, confusion, conflict, and chaos.

Hitler was keen to preserve his base of loyalty among the Gauleiter.

Especially the senior figures among them were still given privileged access. And from time to time meetings of Reichsleiter and Gauleiter were addressed by Hitler, naturally to sustain loyalty among some of the most trusted 'Old Fighters' and to convey guidelines for action, which then often fed into the state bureaucracy.[193] But the meetings were scarcely more than morale-boosting pep-talks. There was no formal discussion. And, as with his government ministers, Hitler was keen to avoid meetings which were not orchestrated from above. According to Baldur von Schirach, appointed in summer 1940 as Gauleiter of Vienna, Hitler regarded any unofficial meeting of more than three Gauleiter as a conspiracy.[194]

At the top of the Party, Heß's control over the Gauleiter was no greater than it had been before the war.[195] His office continued to have no more than a sporadic influence on policy, but did not cease in its attempts to exert pressure on the state in areas, such as racial questions, which were central to National Socialist ideology.[196] During 1940 such questions had reached nowhere near the intensity they would develop over the next year and a half. Bormann's takeover of the *de facto* leadership of the Party from May 1941, and the launch of the Russian campaign the following month, would take the Party's interference and scope for intervention in shaping the direction of policy on to a new plane. But the internal contradictions and incoherence would remain. They were beyond any individual, however powerful, to resolve. They were intrinsic to the very nature of the Party and the aims of the Leader it was striving to serve.

The greatest scope for the Party was in the occupied territories. We noted in the previous chapter the wide powers that Hitler bestowed upon Gauleiter Forster and Greiser in the incorporated areas of Poland. Building on the model already developed in Austria and the Sudetenland, the Party leaders were at the same time heads of the civil administration in their capacity as Reich Governors. This afforded the Party a far more decisive input in such areas than in the 'Old Reich'.[197] Hitler expressly emphasized in September 1940 that his Gauleiter in the east were 'alone responsible for carrying out the tasks required of them', and were not to be hemmed in by legal restrictions as in the Reich itself.[198] After the western offensive, the same special status was granted to the Chiefs of the Civilian Administration in Alsace, Lorraine, and Luxemburg. But the ambitions of Gauleiter Josef Bürckel to head a new Reichsgau Westmark through the addition of Lorraine (where he was Chief of Civilian Administration) to his Party Gau Saar-Palatinate were unfulfilled. His powers as Party boss in his Gau continued to exist side by side (and frequently conflicting) with those of the civil authorities in Lorraine.[199]

Even in the East, where the Party–State dualism appeared resolved, there was no lessening of power struggles and organizational conflict.[200] Here, any tension between government ministries in the Reich and Hitler's appointees to run the occupied territories could only have one outcome. But the Party bosses, and Hans Frank as Governor General, had to reckon with the near-unconfined power of the SS running alongside their own fiefdoms. Arthur Greiser, Reich Governor of the Wartheland, was on good terms with Himmler, as he was with the Higher SS and Police Leader in Posen, Wilhelm Koppe. A member of the SS himself, Greiser was fully committed to the most radical lines of 'ethnic struggle' advanced by Himmler (for whom, in his new capacity as Reich Commissioner for the Consolidation of Germandom, presiding over the brutal resettlement programme in the East, the 'War- thegau' was the most important province). The conflicts in Greiser's area were, therefore, minimal. In the neighbouring Gau of Danzig–Westprussia Albert Forster, no less keen than Greiser in his backing for Hitler's racial programme, was less compliant in his relations with Göring, Goebbels, Bormann, and, not least the Reichsführer-SS (of whom he is reported to have said: 'If I had a face like Himmler, I wouldn't speak of race at all').[201] And in the General Government, Hans Frank had increasing difficulties with the SS, especially the Higher SS and Police Leader there, Wilhelm Krüger, who could in the early years of the occupation always count upon the superior backing of Himmler, and, through him if necessary, Hitler himself.[202]

The clashes in the occupied territories of Poland, as the cases of Forster and Frank illustrate, were not about conflicting ideological aims. However bitter the rivalries, all those involved could have recourse to the 'wishes of the Führer', and claim they were working towards the fulfilment of his 'vision'. At stake were not aims, but methods – and, above all, realms of power. The very nature of the loose mandate given to Hitler's paladins, the scope they were given to build and extend their own empires, and the unclarity of the divisions of competence, guaranteed continued struggle and institutional anarchy. At the same time, it ensured the unfolding of ceaseless energy to drive on the ideological radicalization. Governmental disorder and 'cumulative radicalization' were two sides of the same coin.

IV

Radicalization of the National Socialist 'programme', vague as it was, could not possibly subside. The ways different power-groups and important individuals in positions of influence interpreted the ideological imperative represented by Hitler saw to it that the dream of the new society to be created through war, struggle, conquest, and racial purification was kept in full view. At the grass-roots level, banal – though for the individuals concerned certainly not unimportant – material considerations like the chronic housing shortage, the growing scarcity and increasing cost of consumer goods, or an acute shortage of farm labourers could produce resentments easily channelled towards disparaged minorities and fuelled by petty greed at the prospect of acquiring goods or property belonging to Jews. The flames of such social antagonisms were fanned by the hate-filled messages of propaganda. The mentalities that were fostered offered an open door to the fanaticism of the believers. The internal competition built into the regime ensured that the radical drive was not only sustained, but intensified as fresh opportunities were provided by the war. And as victory seemed imminent, new breathtaking vistas for rooting out racial enemies, displacing inferior populations, and building the 'brave new world' opened up.

With scarcely any direct involvement by Hitler, racial policy unfolded its own dynamic. Within the Reich, pressures to rid Germany of its Jews once and for all increased. In the asylums, the killing of the mentally sick inmates was in full swing. And the security mania of the nation at war, threatened by enemies on all sides and within, coupled with the heightened demands for national unity, encouraged the search for new 'outsider' target groups. 'Foreign workers', especially those from Poland, were in the front line of the intensified persecution.[203]

However, the real crucible was Poland. Here, racial megalomania had *carte blanche*. But it was precisely the absence of any systematic planning in the free-for-all of unlimited power that produced the unforeseen logistical problems and administrative cul-de-sacs of 'ethnic cleansing' which in turn evoked ever more radical, genocidal approaches.

Those who enjoyed positions of power and influence saw the occupation of Poland as an opportunity to 'solve the Jewish Question' – despite the fact that now more Jews than ever had fallen within the clutches of the Third Reich. For the SS, entirely new perspectives had emerged. Among Party leaders, all the Gauleiter wanted to be rid of 'their' Jews and now saw possibilities of doing so. These were starting points. At the same time, for those ruling the parts of former Poland which had been incorporated into the Reich, the expulsion of the Jews from their territories was only part of the wider aim of Germanization, to be achieved as rapidly as possible. This meant also tackling the 'Polish Question', removing thousands of Poles to make room for ethnic Germans from the Baltic and other areas, classifying the 'better elements' as German, and reducing the rest to uneducated helots available to serve the German masters. 'Ethnic cleansing' to produce the required Germanization through resettlement was intrinsically connected with the radicalization of thinking on the 'Jewish Question'.[204]

Beginning only days after the German invasion of Poland, Security Police and Party leaders in Prague, Vienna, and Kattowitz – seizing on the notions expounded by Heydrich of a 'Jewish reservation' to be set up east of Crakow – saw the chance of deporting the Jews from their areas.[205] Eichmann's own initiative and ambition appear to have triggered the hopes of immediate expulsion of the Jews.[206] The Chief of the Reich Criminal Police, Arthur Nebe, asked Eichmann around the same time, in mid-October 1939, when he could send Berlin's Gypsies into the reservation. Between 18 and 26 October Eichmann organized the transport of several thousands of Jews from Vienna, Kattowitz, and Moravia to the Nisko district, south of Lublin. Gypsies from Vienna were also included in the deportation. At the same time, the resettlement of the Baltic Germans began.[207] Within days of the Nisko transports beginning, the lack of provision for the deported Jews in Poland, creating chaotic circumstances following their arrival, led to their abrupt halt.[208] But it was a foretaste of the greater deportations to come.

At the end of the month, in his new capacity as Reich Commissar for the Consolidation of Germandom, Himmler ordered all Jews to be cleared out of the incorporated territories. The deportation of around 550,000 Jews was envisaged. On top of that came several hundred thousand of the 'especially hostile Polish population', making a figure of about a million persons in all.[209] From the largest of the areas designated for deportations and the resettlement of ethnic Germans, the Warthegau, it proved impossible to match the numbers initially charted for deportation, or the speed at which their removal had been foreseen. Even so, 128,011 Poles and Jews were forcibly deported under horrifying conditions by spring 1940.[210] Sadistic SS men would arrive at night, clear entire tenement blocks, and load up the inhabitants – subjected to every form of bestial humiliation – on to open lorries, despite the intense cold, to be taken to holding camps, from where they were herded into unheated and massively overcrowded cattle-trucks and sent south, without possessions and often without food or water. Deaths were frequent on the journeys. Those who survived often suffered from frostbite or other legacies of their terrible ordeal.[211] The deportees were sent to the General Government, seen in the annexed territories as a type of dumping-ground for undesirables. But the Governor General, Hans Frank, was no keener on having Jews in his area than were the Gauleiter of the incorporated regions. He envisaged them rotting in a reservation, but outside his own territory. In November 1939 Frank had plainly laid down the intentions for his own province. It was a pleasure, he stated, finally to be able physically to tackle the Jewish race: 'The more who die, the better ... The Jews should see that we have arrived. We want to have a half to three-quarters of all Jews put east of the Vistula. We'll suppress these Jews everywhere we can. The whole business is at stake here. The Jews out of the Reich, Vienna, from everywhere. We've no use for Jews in the Reich.'[212]

Around the same time that Frank was voicing such sentiments, the Reich Governor of the Wartheland, Arthur Greiser, speaking of encountering in Lodz 'figures who can scarcely be credited with the designation "person" (*Gestalten ... denen man kaum noch den Namen "Mensch" zubilligen kann*)', was letting it be known that the 'Jewish Question' was as good as solved.[213] However, by early 1940, his hopes (and those of Wilhelm Koppe, police chief of the Warthegau) of the quick expulsion of the Jews into the General Government were already proving vain ones. Hans Frank and his subordinates were starting to raise objections at the numbers of Jews they were being forced to take in, without any clear planning for what was to become of them, and with their own hopes of sending them on further to a reservation – an idea meanwhile abandoned – now vanished.[214] Frank was able to win the support of Göring, whose own interest was in preventing the loss of manpower useful for the war effort. Göring's strong criticism of the 'wild resettlement' at a meeting on 12 February ran counter to Himmler's demands for room for hundreds of thousands of ethnic Germans, already moved from their original homes. The very next day, Jews from Stettin were deported to the Lublin area to make way for Baltic Germans 'with sea-faring jobs'.[215] The police chief of the Lublin district, Odilo Globocnik, suggested that if the Jews coming to the General Government could not feed themselves, or be fed by other Jews, they should be left to starve.[216] On 24 March, at Frank's bidding, Göring felt compelled to ban all 'evacuation' into the General Government 'until further notice'.[217] Greiser was told that his request to deport the Warthegau's Jews would have to be deferred until August.[218] From 1 May 1940 the huge ghetto at Lodz, containing 163,177 persons, initially established only as a temporary measure until the War-thegau's Jews could be pushed over the border into the General Government, was sealed off from the rest of the city.[219] Mortalities from disease and starvation started to rocket during the summer.[220] At a meeting in Cracow on 31 July, Greiser was told by Frank in no uncertain terms of Himmler's assurance, under instructions by Hitler, that no more Jews were to be deported to the General Government.[221] And on 6 November 1940 Frank informed Greiser by telegram that there were to be no further deportations into the General Government before the end of the war. Himmler was aware of this. Any transports would be turned back.[222] The solution which to Greiser had seemed so close to hand a year earlier was indefinitely blocked.

As one door closed, another opened – or, for a brief moment, appeared to open. At the meeting in Cracow at the end of July, Greiser mentioned a new possibility that had emerged. He had heard personally from Himmler, he reported, 'that the intention now exists to shove the Jews overseas into specific areas'. He wanted early clarification.[223]

Already in 1937, as we noted in an earlier chapter, the SD had toyed with the idea of resettling Jews in an inhospitable part of the world. The barren stretches of Ecuador were one of the possibilities mentioned.[224] In the years 1938–40 the island of Madagascar, a French colony off the African coast, came to be talked of as a likely venue – an idea apparently first mooted by the orientalist scholar and antisemite Paul de Lagarde in 1885 and popularized in racist circles in the 1920s by Henry Hamilton Beamish, son of a British rear-admiral of Irish descent and founder in 1919 of an antisemitic organiz-ation entitled 'The Britons'.[225] Streicher, Göring, Rosenberg, Ribbentrop, and even Hjalmar Schacht had referred to this eventuality.[226] Streicher had aired the idea on occasion in the *Stürmer*. He was able to pick up on known pre-war discussions of the Polish authorities with the British and French about the possible transportation of large numbers of Jews to Madagascar.[227] Hitler himself had approved of the idea of a Jewish reservation in Mada-gascar in conversation with Göring in November 1938.[228] With the prospect looming larger in the spring of 1940 of regaining colonial territories in the near future (and acquiring some which had not previously belonged to Germany), Madagascar now began to be evoked as a distinct policy option rather than a distant vision.[229]

It seems to have been Himmler, perhaps testing the waters, who at this point first broached in the highest circles the idea of deporting the Jews to an African colony, though he did not refer specifically to Madagascar. In the middle of May, after a visit to Poland, the Reichsführer-SS produced a six-page memorandum entitled 'Some Thoughts on the Treatment of the Alien Population in the East', detailing brutal plans for racial selection in Poland, involving the removal of children of good racial stock to Germany and the suppression of ethnic identity among the rest through deprivation of all but the most elementary training in reading and writing to educate them to serve the German ruling class. 'As horrible and tragic as every individual case might be,' Himmler wrote, 'if the Bolshevik method of the physical eradication (*Ausrottung*) of a people is rejected from inner conviction as un-German and impossible, this is still the mildest and best method.'[230] The 'Polish' not 'Jewish Question' was the subject of the memorandum (which Hitler read and explicitly approved on 25 May, during the lull in the western campaign while the tanks were halted just outside Dunkirk, with instructions that it be circulated only to key individuals).[231] Only in one brief passage did Himmler mention what he envisaged would happen to the Jews. 'The term "Jew",' he wrote, 'I hope to see completely extinguished through the possibility of a large-scale emigration of all Jews to Africa or to some other colony.'[232]

Sensing what was in the wind, the newly appointed, highly ambitious head of the Foreign Ministry's 'Jewish Desk' (*Judenreferat*), Franz Rademacher, prepared a lengthy internal memorandum on 3 June putting forward, as a war aim, three options: removing all Jews from Europe; deporting western European Jews, for example, to Madagascar while leaving eastern Jews in the Lublin district as hostages to keep America paralysed in its fight against Germany (presuming the influence of American Jewry would in these circumstances deter the USA from entering the war); or establishing a Jewish national home in Palestine – a solution he did not favour.[233] This was the first time that Madagascar had been explicitly mentioned in a policy document as a possible 'solution to the Jewish Question'.[234] It was a product of Rademacher's initiative, rather than a result of instructions from above.[235] With the backing of Ribbentrop (who had probably himself gained the approval of Hitler and Himmler), Rademacher set to work to put detail on his proposal to resettle all Europe's Jews on the island of Madagascar, seeing them as under German mandate but Jewish administration.[236] Heydrich, presumably alerted by Himmler at the first opportunity, was, however, not prepared to concede control over such a vital issue to the Foreign Ministry. On 24 June he made plain to Ribbentrop that responsibility for handling the 'Jewish Question' was his, under the commission given to him by Göring in January 1939. Emigration was no longer the answer. 'A territorial final solution (*territoriale Endlösung*) will therefore be necessary.' He sought inclusion in all discussions 'which concern themselves with the final solution (*Endlösung*) of the Jewish question' – the first time, it seems, the precise words 'final solution' were used, and at this point plainly in the context of territorial resettlement.[237] By mid-August Eichmann and his right-hand man Theo Dannecker had devised in some detail – their memorandum was fourteen pages long – plans to put 4 million Jews on Madagascar. The SD's plan envisaged no semblance of Jewish autonomous administration. The Jews would exist under strict SS control.[238]

Soon after Rademacher had submitted his original proposal, in early June, the Madagascar idea had evidently been taken to Hitler, presumably by Ribbentrop. According to Paul Schmidt, Hitler had said to Mussolini during the meeting in Munich just following the French announcement of their readiness for an armistice that 'an Israelite state could be erected on Madagascar'.[239] Ribbentrop had told Ciano at the same time 'that it is the Führer's intention to create a free Jewish state in Madagascar to which he will compulsorily send the many millions of Jews who live on the territory of the old Reich as well as on the territories recently conquered'.[240] Two days after his meeting with Mussolini, Hitler again mentioned Madagascar to Grand Admiral Raeder.[241] On 8 July he returned to the topic during discussions with Hans Frank about the situation in the General Government. Frank told his colleagues on 12 July of the important decision of the Führer, supporting his own proposal, that no further Jewish transports should be sent to the General Government. 'In general political terms I would like to add,' remarked Frank, 'that it is planned within the shortest time imaginable following the conclusion of peace to transport the entire Jewish tribe (*Juden-sippschaft*) in the German Reich, in the General Government, and in the Protectorate to an African or American colony. One is thinking of Madagascar . . .' Since he had managed to have the General Government included in the plans, it would amount 'here too to a colossal relief in the foreseeable future'.[242] At the beginning of August, Hitler mentioned to the German Ambassador Otto Abetz in Paris 'that he intended to evacuate all the Jews from Europe after the war', which, of course, he thought would soon be over.[243] And in the middle of August, reporting on a conversation with Hitler, Goebbels noted: 'We want later to transport the Jews to Madagascar.'[244]

Already by this time the Madagascar plan had had its brief heyday. Putting it into effect would have depended not only on forcing the French to hand over their colony – a relatively simple matter – but on attaining control over the seas through the defeat of the British navy. With the continuation of the war the plan fell by the end of the year into abeyance and was never resurrected. But through the summer, for three months or so, the idea was taken seriously by all the top Nazi leadership, including Hitler himself.

Hitler's rapid endorsement of such an ill-thought-out and impracticable scheme reflected his superficial involvement in anti-Jewish policy during 1940. His main interests that year were plainly elsewhere, in the direction of war strategy. For the time being at least, the 'Jewish Question' was a secondary matter for him. His comments on the Jews usually followed promptings by others – such as Himmler, Frank, Ribbentrop, or Goebbels, all with direct interests in anti-Jewish policy. Similarly, his decisions, as with the blocking of the transport of Jews to the General Government, were largely reactive and, as in this case, giving the highest approval to a policy that had already been introduced. Hitler's visceral detestation of the Jews was undiminished. His keen intervention in the shaping of Goebbels's horrific 'documentary' *The Eternal Jew* was one indicator of this.[245] His central belief that the war would bring the solution to the 'problem' was, of course, unaltered. Goebbels reported the menacing remark after a discussion with Hitler at the beginning of June that 'we'll quickly be finished with the Jews after the war'.[246] But at the time there are no indications that Hitler had anything other than the vague Madagascar notion in mind.

However, the broad mandate to 'solve the Jewish Question' associated with Hitler's 'mission', coupled with the blockages in doing so in occupied Poland, sufficed. Others were more active than Hitler himself. To Goebbels, Hitler gave merely the assurance that the Jews were earmarked to leave Berlin, without approving any immediate action.[247] Some had more luck with their demands. As in the east, the Gauleiter given responsibilities in the newly occupied areas in the west were keen to exploit their position to get rid of the Jews from their Gaue. In July Robert Wagner, Gauleiter of Baden and now in charge of Alsace, and Josef Bürckel, Gauleiter of the Saar-Palatinate and Chief of the Civil Administration in Lorraine, both pressed Hitler to allow the expulsion *westwards* into Vichy France of the Jews from their domains. Hitler gave his approval. Some 3,000 Jews were deported that month from Alsace into the unoccupied zone of France.[248] In October, following a further meeting with the two Gauleiter, a total of 6,504 Jews were sent to France in nine trainloads, without any prior consultation with the French authorities. Bureaucrats gave meticulous detail to the police who were to round up the Jews, reminding them to turn off water and gas in the homes, hand over pets (against a receipt) to local government or Party officials, and label the keys to the apartments being vacated. Jews were allowed to take a suitcase of clothes, food for a few days, and 100 Reich Marks per person with them. Their property was confiscated. They had to be ready to leave within two hours. Some were forced out within quarter of an hour. A number committed suicide. Jews who were bedridden were loaded on to the trains on stretchers. The oldest Jew deported was a ninety-seven-year-old man from Karlsruhe. The police accompanied the transports, which were carried out in agreement with the Wehrmacht (even down to Wehrmacht vehicles being used to carry Jews from outlying districts to the 'collecting places'). After a horrifying journey lasting several days, the Jews were herded into camps in southern France at the foot of the Pyrenees. Neither food nor provisions were minimally adequate for the largely elderly deportees. The French authorities, the report on the deportations concluded, appeared to have in mind their further deportation to Madagascar as soon as the sea-passage was secure.[249]

Above all, the running in radicalizing anti-Jewish policy was made by the SS and Security Police leadership. While Hitler at this time paid relatively little attention to the 'Jewish Question' when not faced with a particular issue that one of his underlings had raised, Himmler and Heydrich were heavily engaged in planning the 'new order', especially in eastern Europe. By the autumn the Madagascar Plan was a dead letter – even though Eichmann was still waiting for a decision from Heydrich as late as December.[250] But by then Hitler's decision, taken under the impact of the failure to end the war in the West, to prepare for the invasion of the Soviet Union opened up new prospects again in the East for a 'solution' to the 'Jewish Question'. Once more, policy in the General Government was reversed. Hans Frank, who had been expecting in the summer to have the Jews from his area shipped to Madagascar, was now told that they had to stay. Emigration from the General Government was banned.[251] The brutal forced-labour conditions and ghettoization were already highly attritional. Jews were in practice often being worked to death.[252] An overtly genocidal mentality was already evident. Heydrich suggested starting an epidemic in the newly sealed Warsaw ghetto in autumn 1940 in order to exterminate the Jews there through such means.[253] It was into an area in which this mentality prevailed that Frank, so Hitler told him in December, had to be prepared to take more Jews.[254]

With Hitler playing little active role, but providing blanket approval, conditions and mentalities had been created in the occupied territories of former Poland in which full-scale genocide was only one step away.

Anti-Jewish policy had not followed a clear or straight line throughout 1940. But, particularly within the SS and Security Police leadership, the thinking and planning had moved in an implicitly genocidal direction. Hitler had responded to the vagaries of policy rather than providing clear direction. But his broad remit to 'remove' the Jews, and his 'prophecy' that the war would bring a solution to the 'Jewish Question', were enough. Paradoxically, the turn to preparations for war in the East had not emanated directly out of Hitler's twenty-year-old ideological obsession with 'Jewish-Bolshevism', but from the strategic consideration of forcing Britain to yield to German demands. But once the preparations for invading the USSR began to take concrete shape, in the spring of 1941, the ideological essence of the coming showdown with 'Jewish-Bolshevism' became central. By a circuitous route, rather than following a straight line, Hitler was returning to the core of his *Weltanschauung* – now no longer just verbiage, but taking the form of concrete policy steps that would take Germany into all-out genocide.

V

Before Hitler signed the directive in December 1940 to prepare what would rapidly be shaped into a 'war of annihilation' against the Soviet Union, there was a hiatus in which the immediate future direction of the war remained uncertain. Hitler was ready, during this phase that stretched from September to December 1940, to explore different possibilities of prising Britain out of the conflict before the Americans could enter it. Out of the failure of the 'peripheral strategy', a term hinted at by Jodl at the end of July,[255] which at no stage gained Hitler's full enthusiasm, the hardening of the intention to invade the Soviet Union, first mooted in July, emerged until, on 18 December, it was embodied in a war directive.

With the invasion of Russia in the autumn of 1940, as initially proposed by Hitler, excluded on practical grounds by Jodl, other ways of retaining the strategic initiative had to be sought. Hitler was open to a number of suggestions. Ribbentrop was able to resurrect the idea he had promoted before the war, of an anti-British bloc of Germany, Italy, Japan, and the Soviet Union. The new situation in the wake of the German victories in western Europe now also offered the prospect of extending the anti-British front through gaining the active cooperation of Spain and Vichy France in the Mediterranean zone, together with a number of satellite states in south-eastern Europe.[256] For Japan, the overrunning of the Netherlands and defeat of France, together with the serious weakening of Britain, offered a clear invitation to imperialist expansion in south-eastern Asia. The Dutch East Indies and French Indo-China provided irresistible temptation, with the lure of the British possessions – including Singapore, British Borneo, Burma, and beyond that India itself – as an eventual further prize. Japan's interests in expanding to the south made her willing now to ease the long-standing tensions in relations with the Soviet Union. At the same time, Japan was keen to improve relations with Germany, soured since the Hitler–Stalin Pact, in order to have a free hand in south-eastern Asia, unimpeded by potential German ambitions towards Indo-China and the Dutch East Indies. Already in May, Ribbentrop assured the Japanese of Germany's lack of interest in these territories. Hitler at this time opposed any formal alliance with Japan, or granting of a free hand in south-eastern Asia. Only in late summer, persuaded that Britain would not accept his 'offer', and concerned that America could soon enter the war (a step appearing closer since the news of the destroyer deal with Britain), did Hitler reverse this position.[257] The negotiations that began in late August led to the signing of the Tripartite Pact on 27 September 1940, under which Germany, Italy, and Japan agreed to assist each other in the event of one of the signatories being attacked by an external power not involved in the European or Sino-Japanese conflicts – meaning, of course, the United States.[258]

Raeder, too, was able to take advantage of Hitler's uncertainty in the late summer and autumn of 1940. In September the Commander-in-Chief of the navy put forward two memoranda strongly advocating a strategy directed at destroying Britain's strength in the Mediterranean and Near East. Raeder's aim was transparent enough: he wanted the bigger, more powerful navy that such a strategy would demand. For Hitler, the frontal assault on British possessions, providing the basis for further attacks on the British Empire, amounted to a reversal of his own long-held strategy.[259] Even so, keeping his options open for the time being on the best way to eliminate Britain from the war and deter the Americans from entering the conflict, Hitler was not discouraging to Raeder's ambitious proposal – aimed squarely against Great Britain – to seize control (with Spanish assistance) of Gibraltar and then the Suez Canal, before pushing through Palestine and Syria to the Turkish border. Bases in Dakar, Casablanca, and the Azores would strengthen Germany's hand in the Atlantic. Dominance of the Mediterranean would, in Raeder's grandiose vision, rob the British of their key strategic centre and force them out of the Near East. At the same time, it would secure Italian sway in East Africa (allowing Italy to fight at sea in the Indian Ocean), and block the possibility of the Americans acquiring bases in North-West Africa prior to entering the war. With Britain by this time compelled to sue for terms, Germany would be in such a strong position that she would have nothing to fear from the USA. Raeder even pandered to what he evidently knew to be Hitler's instinctive predilection for an attack on the Soviet Union. With Turkey 'in our power', the threat of the Soviet Union would be diminished. It would be 'questionable whether then moving against the Russians from the north would still be necessary', he concluded.[260]

Hitler did not demur. He remarked that after the conclusion of the alliance with Japan he wanted to carry out talks with Mussolini and perhaps with Franco before deciding whether it was more advantageous to work with France or Spain. He thought it more likely that the choice would fall on France, since Spain would demand a good deal, notably French Morocco, but offer little.[261] So it proved.

Franco had opportunistically looked to join the Axis in mid-June, counting on spoils in a war about to be won (as it seemed). He wanted Gibraltar, French Morocco, and Oran, the former Spanish province currently in French Algeria. There was at the time every reason for Hitler to avoid acting on proposals that could have jeopardized the armistice. In September, a diplomatic balancing-act to ensure the support for the Mediterranean strategy of France, Spain, and Italy now appeared desirable and timely. Ribbentrop and Ramón Serrano Suñer, Franco's brother-in-law and personal emissary, soon to be the Spanish Foreign Minister, met in Berlin on 16 September. Serrano, pro-Axis but a proud nationalist and pedantic lawyer as well as a devout Catholic, detested Ribbentrop, tactless and arrogant as usual, from the moment he saw him. Serrano rejected the request for the grant of one of the Canary isles as a German base, was non-committal about further proposals, and repeated Franco's shopping-list of demands made the previous June. Hitler was prepared to grant French Morocco if Germany could have bases and mining rights in the colony. Franco was having none of that. Serrano repeated the high Spanish price for entering the war. All that was forthcoming was an offer by Franco to meet Hitler on the Spanish border in October.[262]

Before that, on 4 October, Hitler met Mussolini again – as in March, at the Brenner. Ribbentrop, feeling unwell and uncharacteristically quiet, and Ciano were also present. Hitler attributed the British prolongation of the war, despite extensive German bombing, to the hope of American intervention and Russian aid. He thought the Tripartite Pact had reduced the risk of the former, and that the German troops moved to the eastern border were a deterrent to Stalin. Hitler raised the question of Spanish intervention, outlining Franco's demands. He indicated Germany's need for a base in Morocco, before attaining her own colonies in western Africa. Conceding the territorial demands of Franco (apart from Gibraltar), he went on, might provoke English occupation of the Canaries and the adhesion of North Africa to the Gaullist movement. Natural enemy of the Axis though she was, he did not rule out the possibility of gaining France for the anti-British coalition. Mussolini agreed on the stance to be taken towards Spain, reaffirming Italian demands of France to cede Nice, Corsica, Tunis, and Djibouti – claims in effect placed in cold storage at the armistice.[263] Ciano drew the conclusions from the meeting that the proposed landing in Britain would not take place, that the aim was now to win over France to the anti-British coalition, since Britain was proving more difficult to defeat than anticipated, and that the Mediterranean sector had, to Italy's advantage, won greater significance. Hitler, in Ciano's view, had also shown himself once more extremely anti-Bolshevik.[264]

The meeting had been cordial. But eight days later Mussolini's patience was stretched once more when he heard, without prior warning, that a German military commission had been dispatched to Bucharest and that the Germans were taking over the defence of the Romanian oil-fields. Mussolini's retaliation was to order the invasion of Greece for the end of the month, to present Hitler this time with a *fait accompli*.[265] Hitler had warned against such a venture on numerous occasions.[266]

On 20 October Hitler, accompanied by Ribbentrop, set out in his Special Train for southern France, bound first of all for a meeting, two days later, with Pierre Laval, Pétain's deputy and foreign minister in the Vichy regime. This proved encouraging. Laval, full of unctuous humility, opened up the prospect of close French collaboration with Germany, hoping for France's reward through retention of its African possessions and release from heavy reparations – both at the expense of Great Britain – once a peace-settlement could be concluded. Hitler did not seek firm details. Leaving no doubt that some African possessions would fall to Germany after the war, he was content to offer the inducement that the ease of terms for France would depend on the extent of French cooperation and rapidity with which the defeat of Britain could be attained. He extended an invitation to talks to Marshal Pétain, which Laval swiftly agreed to arrange.[267]

Hitler's train travelled on to Hendaye, on the Spanish border, for the meeting with the Caudillo on the 23rd. From Hitler's point of view, the meeting was purely exploratory. The next day, as arranged with Laval, he would be talking with Pétain in the same vein. The repulsing by Vichy forces of a British–Gaullist landing at Dakar, the French West African port, a month earlier, and attempt to seize West Africa encouraged the already existing inclination of Hitler and Ribbentrop towards France over Spain if the respective interests of the two could not be reconciled.[268] Hitler knew that his military chiefs were opposed to attempts to bring Spain into the war, and that Weizsäcker had also strongly advised that there was 'no practical worth' in Spain joining the Axis.[269] From Franco's angle, the aim was not to keep Spain out of the war but to make maximum gains from her entry.[270]

The meeting at the border station in Hendaye began behind schedule. Franco's rickety train, despite travelling only a short distance, was late arriving.[271] While they waited, Hitler and Ribbentrop walked up and down the platform, talking about how to handle the meeting. Hitler said he was unwilling to put in writing any territorial concessions to the Spaniards from French possessions. Given 'Latin garrulousness' the French would be sure to hear of them. In any case, went on Hitler, he could not expect the French to give up any of their possessions to the Spaniards, quite apart from the fact that the French Empire would then go over *en bloc* to General Charles de Gaulle (the leader of 'Free France', exiled in London), when the next day he was going to attempt to persuade Pétain to commit the French to active involvement in the conflict with Britain.[272] This meant, in effect, that Hitler had little or nothing to offer Franco, who wanted a great deal. The contours were set for the difficult meeting to follow.

It took place in the salon of Hitler's train.[273] Franco – little, fat, swarthy in complexion, his droning sing-song voice reminiscent, it was later said, of that of an Islamic prayer-caller – opened by stating his pleasure at the opportunity to meet the Führer and thanked him for all that Germany had done for Spain. Close bonds between the countries had been established during the Civil War, and he hoped they would continue. Spain would gladly fight on the side of Germany during the current war. However, the economic difficulties of the country ruled this out. Unmistakably and disappointingly to Spanish ears, however, Hitler spent much of his rambling address dampening down any hopes Franco might have had of major territorial gains at minimal cost. He began by outlining German military strength. He then pointed to the major problem: the danger of the French colonies going over to de Gaulle and the Allies and of Britain and America occupying the Atlantic islands – the Azores and Canaries – off the African coast. It was necessary, he continued, to bring the war to a speedy end. As long as the fight against Britain went on, Germany needed France as a base and to take up a clear position against England. His wish, Hitler said, was to construct 'a very big front against England'. But 'Spanish wishes and French hopes were hindrances' to this. He then went on – doubtless to Franco's irritation – largely to talk of his interest in reaching an arrangement with the French. He was prepared to offer France favourable terms and compensate her in a final peace settlement for territorial losses in Africa in return for support to bring the war to a speedy end. It became ever plainer, however, that he had little concrete to offer Spain. He proposed an alliance, with Spanish entry into the war in January 1941, to be rewarded by Gibraltar. But it was evident that none of the colonial territory in north Africa, coveted by Franco, was earmarked for Spain in Hitler's thinking.[274] The Spanish dictator said nothing for a while. Then he unfolded his list of exorbitant demands for foodstuffs and armaments. He added for good measure that in his view the German expectations of an early end to the war – Hitler had begun by claiming that militarily the war was as good as won – were exaggerated, and that the British government and fleet, backed by the USA, would continue the conflict from Canada. At one point, Hitler's irritation was so great that he got up from the table, stating that there was no point in continuing. But he calmed down and carried on. The talks produced, however, no more than an empty agreement, leaving the Spanish to decide when, if ever, they would join the Axis. Hitler was heard to mutter, as he left the meeting: 'There's nothing to be done with this chap (*Mit diesem Kerle ist nichts zu machen.*)'[275] Franco's comment to his foreign minister was: 'These people are intolerable. They want us to come into the war in exchange for nothing.'[276]

Ribbentrop was in a rage at the 'ungrateful coward Franco' when he flew the next day to Bordeaux, *en route* to the meeting with Pétain.[277] At Florence a few days later, Hitler told Mussolini that he 'would prefer to have three or four teeth taken out' than go through another nine hours' discussion with Franco – 'a brave spirit', he said, but not cut out to be a politician or organizer.[278] More privately, he raged about 'Jesuit swine' and 'misplaced Spanish pride'.[279]

The discussions with Pétain and Laval in Montoire on 24 October were no more fruitful. After the opening diplomatic niceties, Hitler, as he had done with Franco, underlined German military strength, the weakness of Britain's position, and his keenness to bring the war to an early end. He sought France's cooperation in the 'community' of countries he was in the process of organizing against Britain. The aged leader of Vichy France was non-committal and unspecific. He assured Hitler that everything would be done to sustain the security of French colonial territories in Africa (following the attempt on Dakar). He could confirm the principle of French collaboration with Germany, which Laval had agreed at his meeting with Hitler two days earlier, but could not enter into detail and needed to consult his government before undertaking a binding arrangement. Laval added that Pétain would need to summon the National Assembly – something he would be loath to do – before any declaration of war on Britain. Both Pétain and Laval hinted that the extent of French cooperation hinged on generous treatment by Germany and the acquisition of colonial territory after a final peace. Hitler had offered Pétain nothing specific. He had in return received no precise assurances of active French support, either in the fight against Britain or in steps to regain the territory lost in French Equatorial Africa to the 'Free French' of de Gaulle, allied with Britain.[280] The outcome was therefore inconsequential.[281]

Hitler professed himself content at the end of the meeting, and afterwards said he had been impressed by Pétain.[282] But coming on top of the strained discussion with Franco, and the greater significance thus falling on France's role in the Mediterranean, it was not surprising that Hitler and Ribbentrop travelled back to Germany with a sense of disappointment at the hesitancy of the French.[283] It was a slow journey, during which Hitler, dispirited and convinced that his initial instincts had been right, told Keitel and Jodl that he wanted to move against Russia during the summer of 1941.[284]

On crossing the German border Hitler received news that did nothing to improve his mood. He was informed that the Italians were about to invade Greece. He was furious at the stupidity of such a military action to take place in the autumn rains and winter snows of the Balkan hills.[285]

However, during the meeting of the two dictators and their foreign ministers in Florence on 28 October – essentially a report on the negotiations with Franco and Pétain – Hitler contained his feelings about the Italian Greek adventure, and the meeting passed in harmony.[286] Hitler spoke of the mutual distrust between himself and Stalin. However, he said, Molotov would shortly be coming to Berlin. (Ribbentrop had earlier that month persuaded Hitler to invite the Soviet Commissar for Foreign Affairs for talks.) It was his intention, he added, to steer Russian energies towards India. This remarkable idea was Ribbentrop's – part of his scheme to establish spheres of influence for Germany, Italy, Japan, and Russia (the powers forming his intended European–Asiatic Bloc to 'stretch from Japan to Spain').[287] It was an idea with a very short lifetime.

Briefing his military leaders in early November on his negotiations with Franco and Pétain, Hitler had referred to Russia as 'the entire problem of Europe' and said 'everything must be done to be ready for the great show-down'. But the meeting with his top brass showed that decisions on the prosecution of the war, whether it should be in the east or the west, were still open. Hitler had seemed to his army adjutant Major Engel, attending the meeting, 'visibly depressed', conveying the 'impression that at the moment he does not know how things should proceed'.[288] Molotov's visit in all prob-ability finally convinced Hitler that the only way forward left to him was the one which he had, since the summer, come to favour on strategic grounds, and to which he was in any case ideologically inclined: an attack on the Soviet Union.

Relations with the Soviet Union were already deteriorating seriously by the time Molotov had been invited to Berlin. Soviet designs on parts of Romania (which had been forced earlier in the summer to cede Bessarabia and northern Bukowina) and on Finland (effectively a Soviet satellite follow-ing defeat in the recent war) had prompted direct German involvement in these areas. Anxious about the Ploesti oilfields, Hitler had agreed in Sep-tember to General Antonescu's request to send a German military mission comprising a number of armoured divisions and air-force units to Romania, on the face of it to reorganize the Romanian army. Russian protests that the German guarantees of Romania's frontiers violated the 1939 pact were dismissed. In late November Romania came fully within the German orbit when she joined the Tripartite Pact. The German stance on Finland had altered at the end of July – the time that an attack on the Soviet Union had first been mooted. Arms deliveries were made and agreements allowing German troops passage to Norway were signed, again despite Soviet pro-tests. Meanwhile, the number of German divisions on the eastern front had been increased to counter the military build-up along the southern borders of the Soviet Union.[289]

Undaunted by the growing difficulties in German–Soviet relations, Rib-bentrop impressed upon the more sceptical Hitler the opportunities to build the anti-British continental bloc through including the Soviet Union, too, in the Tripartite Pact. Hitler indicated that he was prepared to see what came of the idea. But on the very day that talks with Molotov began, he put out a directive that, irrespective of the outcome, 'all already orally ordered preparations for the east [were] to be continued'.[290]

The invitation to Molotov had been sent on 13 October – before the fruitless soundings of Franco and Pétain were made.[291] On the morning of 12 November Molotov and his entourage arrived in Berlin. Weizsäcker thought the shabbily dressed Russians looked like extras in a gangster film.[292] The hammer and sickle on Soviet flags fluttering alongside swastika banners provided an extraordinary spectacle in the Reich's capital. But the Internationale was not played, apparently to avoid the possibility of Berliners, still familiar with the words, joining in. The negotiations, in Ribbentrop's study in the lavishly redesigned old Reich President's Palace, went badly from the start. Molotov, cold eyes alert behind a wire pince-nez, an occasional icy smile flitting across his chess-player's face, reminded Paul Schmidt – there to keep a written record of the discussions – of his old mathematics teacher. His pointed, precise remarks and questions posed a stark contrast to Ribbentrop's pompous, long-winded statements. He let Ribbentrop's initial comments, that Britain was already defeated, pass without comment. And he made little response to the German Foreign Minister's strong hints in the opening exchanges that the Soviet Union should direct her territorial interests towards the Persian Gulf, the Middle East, and India (plainly indicated, but not mentioned by name). But when Hitler joined the talks for the afternoon session, and provided his usual grand sweep of strategic interests, Molotov unleashed a hail of precise questions about Finland, the Balkans, the Tripartite Pact, and the proposed spheres of influence in Asia, catching the German leader off guard. Hitler was visibly discomfited, and sought a convenient adjournment.

Molotov had not finished. He began the next day where he had left off the previous afternoon. He did not respond to Hitler's suggestion to look to the south, and to the spoils of the British Empire. He was more interested, he said, in matters of more obvious European significance. He pressed Hitler on German interests in Finland, which he saw as contravening the 1939 Pact, and on the border guarantee given to Romania and the military mission sent there. Molotov asked how Germany would react were the Soviet Union to act in the same way towards Bulgaria. Hitler could only reply, unconvincingly, that he would have to consult Mussolini. Molotov indicated Soviet interest in Turkey, giving security in the Dardanelles and an outlet to the Aegean.

Symbolizing the fiasco of the two-day negotiations, the closing banquet in the Soviet Embassy ended in disarray under the wail of air-raid sirens. In his private bunker, Ribbentrop – showing once more his unerring instinct for clumsiness – pulled a draft agreement from his pocket and made one last vain attempt to persuade Molotov to concur in a four-power division of a large proportion of the globe. Molotov coldly reasserted Soviet interest in the Balkans and the Baltic, not the Indian Ocean.[293] The questions that interested the Soviet Union, went on Molotov, somewhat more expansively than during the actual negotiations, were not only Turkey and Bulgaria, and the fate of Romania and Hungary, but also Axis intentions in Yugoslavia, Greece, and Poland. The Soviet government also wanted to know about the German stance on Swedish neutrality. Then there was the question of outlets to the Baltic.[294] Later in the month, Molotov told the German Ambassador in Moscow, Graf von der Schulenburg, that Soviet terms for agreeing to a four-power pact included the withdrawal of German troops from Finland, recognition of Bulgaria as within the Russian sphere of influence, the granting of bases in Turkey, acceptance of Soviet expansion towards the Persian Gulf, and the cession by Japan of southern Sakhalin.[295]

Molotov listed these terms on 26 November.[296] Hitler did not need to wait so long. He viewed the talks in Berlin, he had told his army adjutant Major Engel before Molotov came to the Reich capital, as a test of whether Germany and the Soviet Union would stand 'back to back or breast to breast'.[297] The results of the 'test' were now plain, in Hitler's eyes. The two-day negotiations with Molotov had sufficed to show that irreconcilable territorial interests of Germany and the Soviet Union meant inevitable clashes in the near future. Hitler told Engel that he had in any case expected nothing from Molotov's visit. 'The talks had shown where the Russian plans were heading. M[olotov] had let the cat out of the bag. He (F[ührer]) was really relieved. It would not even remain a marriage of convenience. Letting the Russians into Europe meant the end of central Europe. The Balkans and Finland were also dangerous flanks.'[298]

Hitler's conviction, hardening since the summer, was confirmed: the strike against the Soviet Union had to take place in 1941. Some time in the autumn, probably following Molotov's visit, he sent his adjutants to search out a suitable location for field headquarters in the east. They recommended a spot in East Prussia, near Rastenburg, and he gave Todt orders to begin construction and have the headquarters completed by April.[299] On 3 December he congratulated Field-Marshal Fedor von Bock on his sixtieth birthday and told him that the 'Eastern Question is becoming acute'. He spoke of rumoured links between Russia and America, and Russia and England. To await developments was dangerous. But if the Russians were eliminated from the equation, British hopes of defeating Germany on the Continent would vanish, and Japanese freedom from worries about a Soviet attack from the rear meant American intervention would be made more difficult.[300]

Two days later, on 5 December, he reviewed the objectives of the planned attack on the Soviet Union with Brauchitsch and Halder. Soviet ambitions in the Balkans, he declared, were a source of potential problems for the Axis. 'The decision concerning hegemony in Europe will come in the battle against Russia,' he added. 'The Russian is inferior. The army lacks leadership.' The German advantage in terms of leadership, *matériel*, and troops would be at its greatest in the spring. 'When the Russian army is battered once,' continued Hitler, in his crass underestimation of Soviet forces, 'the final disaster is unavoidable.' The aim of the campaign, he stated, was the 'crushing of Russian manpower'. The key strikes were to be on the northern and southern flanks. Moscow, he commented, was 'of no great importance'. Preparations for the campaign were to be advanced in full force. The operation was expected to take place at the end of May.[301] Halder reported Hitler's thoughts to a meeting of military leaders on 13 December. The campaign, he told them, would involve the launching of 130–140 divisions against the Soviet Union by spring 1941.[302] There was no indication that Brauchitsch, Halder, or their subordinate commanders raised objections to Hitler's analysis. On 17 December Hitler summarized his strategy for Jodl by emphasizing 'that we must solve all continental European problems in 1941 since the USA would be in a position to intervene from 1942 onwards'.[303]

The following day, 18 December 1940, Hitler's war directive No.21 began: 'The German Wehrmacht must be prepared, also before the ending of the war against England, to *crush (niederzuwerfen) Soviet Russia in a rapid campaign.*'[304]

The operation had been code-named 'Otto' by the General Staff. It had been referred to as 'Fritz' by the Wehrmacht operational staff, and the draft directive No.21 laid before Jodl on 12 December had carried that name. When Jodl presented it to him five days later, Hitler changed the code-name to the more imperious 'Barbarossa' – an allusion to the mighty twelfth-century emperor, ruler of Germany's first Reich, who had dominated central Europe and led a crusade against the Infidel.[305] Hitler was now ready to plan his own crusade, against Bolshevism.

On 8–9 January 1941 Hitler held discussions at the Berghof with his military leaders. On the reasons for deciding to attack the Soviet Union, Hitler reiterated arguments he had been deploying since the previous summer. Partly, the argument rested on an understanding of Soviet intentions, sharpened since Molotov's visit. Stalin was shrewd, said Hitler, and would increasingly exploit Germany's difficulties. But the crux of his case was, as ever, the need to pull away what he saw as a vital prop to British interests. 'The possibility of a Russian intervention in the war was sustaining the English,' he went on. 'They would only give up the contest if this last continental hope were demolished.' He did not think 'the English were crazy (*sinnlos toll*). If they saw no further chance of winning the war, they would stop fighting, since losing it would mean they no longer had the power to hold together the Empire. Were they able to hold out, could put together forty to fifty divisions, and the USA and Russia were to help them, a very difficult situation for Germany would arise. That must not happen. Up to now he had acted on the principle of always smashing the most important enemy positions to advance a step. Therefore Russia must now be smashed. Either the English would then give in, or Germany would continue the fight against England in more favourable circumstances. The smashing of Russia would also allow Japan to turn with all its might against the USA,' hindering American intervention. He pointed to further advantages for Germany. The army in the east could be substantially reduced in size, allowing greater deployment of the armaments industry for the navy and Luftwaffe. 'Germany would then be unassailable. The gigantic territory of Russia contained immeasurable riches. Germany had to dominate it economically and politically, though not annex it. It would then preside over all possibilities of waging the struggle against continents in future. It could then not be defeated by anyone. If the operation were carried through,' Hitler concluded, 'Europe would hold its breath.'[306] If the generals listening had any reservations, they did not voice them.[307]

A little over a month later, Hitler added one further revealing argument – characteristically underlining the psychological aspect of mobilization. 'A conflict is inevitable. Once England is finished, he would not be able to rouse the German people to a fight against Russia; consequently Russia would have to be disposed of first.'[308]

During 1940 the twin obsessions of Hitler – 'removing the Jews', and '*Lebensraum*' – had come gradually into sharp focus. The development was scarcely accidental. But it had, even so, been in many respects an indirect process. The radicalization of anti-Jewish policy had largely been pushed along by the leadership of the Security Police, for the most part without specific involvement of Hitler (though certainly with his approval), until in Poland genocidal mentalities in near-genocidal conditions had acquired their own momentum. In the crucial area of war strategy, where his own active involvement was unquestionably crucial, Hitler's old obsession about 'living space' had returned via the difficulties he encountered in trying to force Britain out of the conflict. Now, in the first half of 1941, the practical preparations for the showdown that Hitler had always wanted could be made. In these months the twin obsessions would merge into each other. The decisive steps into genocidal war were about to be taken.

8

DESIGNING A 'WAR OF ANNIHILATION'

'The forthcoming campaign is more than just an armed conflict; it will lead, too, to a showdown of two different ideologies ... The Jewish-Bolshevik intelligentsia, the "oppressor" of the people up to now, must be eliminated.'

Operational guidelines for 'Barbarossa', 3 March 1941

'We must forget the concept of comradeship between soldiers. A Communist is no comrade before or after the battle. This is a war of annihilation.'

Hitler, addressing senior officers, 30 March 1941

'Whether right or wrong, we must win ... And when we have won, who will ask us about the method?'

Hitler, speaking to Goebbels, 16 June 1941

With the decision to invade the Soviet Union, confirmed in the directive of 18 December 1940, Hitler had closed off his strategic options. In his anxiety not to concede the initiative in the war, he had shifted the entire focus of the German war effort to the aim of inflicting comprehensive military defeat on the Soviet Union – and obliterating it as a political entity – within a matter of months. He was backed by his military leaders, who, even if some had private reservations, at no point raised serious objections to his proposed course of action. In retrospect, it seems sheer idiocy. At the time, Hitler's generals did not for the most part demur because they, like he, grossly underestimated Soviet military strength and capacity. Remarkable though it seems from a later perspective, the real anxiety from their point of view was directed not towards the Soviet Union but towards Great Britain – backed by its world empire and, it seemed increasingly likely, in due course by the untold resources of the USA. The gamble, which most military advisers – Admiral Raeder was an exception, Göring's early reservations were soon dispelled[1] – acceded to, rested on knocking out the USSR within a matter of four or five months to attain hegemony in Europe. Britain, her hand forced by Japanese action against Imperial territory in south-eastern Asia, would then have no choice but to come to terms. America, confronted in the Pacific by Japan, would keep out of the European arena. Germany would have won the war. Domination throughout Europe would be hers. Subsequent, and ultimately inevitable, confrontation with the USA could be contemplated from a position of strength.

Hitler had committed himself to action from which there was no turning back. Did he have a real choice? Grand-Admiral Raeder thought so. Some of the generals thought so. Ribbentrop thought so. Hitler himself, however, had only flirted in autumn 1940 with the 'peripheral strategy'. Having mooted immediately after the victory in the West a campaign against the Soviet Union, the war he had for long advocated as the ultimate necessity, he became increasingly wedded to the idea. The attempt to erode British strength in the Mediterranean through balancing the interests of Italy, Spain, and Vichy France was abandoned at the first sign of self-evident difficulties. Probably, Hitler's best strategy in autumn 1940 would have been to sit tight and await developments. Japan was playing her own game. As spring 1941 would show, she was willing to look to a rapprochement with the Soviet Union in order to have a free hand to the south. Direct conflict with Britain and the USA, as Japanese territorial ambitions insatiably grew, was almost inevitable. Had Hitler waited, the difficulties for both countries would without doubt have mounted sharply in the Pacific and the Far East. The Soviet Union and Germany, as Molotov's visit had demonstrated, faced undoubted clashes in Scandinavia and in the Balkans. Russian expansionist aims conflicted directly with German interests in these regions. But the USSR posed no direct threat to Germany at this time. Himmler, probably echoing Hitler's own views, had expressly rejected the notion of such a threat at a speech to Party functionaries around the time of Molotov's visit to Berlin in November 1940. Russia, he stated, was 'militarily harmless (*militärisch ungefährlich*)'. With a poor officer corps and badly equipped and trained, the Russian army 'cannot pose any danger to us at all (*Sie kann uns überhaupt nicht gefährlich werden*)'.[2] Had the will been there to co-exist and carve up continental Europe between them – effectively the basis of Ribbentrop's thinking – it is hard to see which power could have prevented it, given the global commitments of Britain and the threat posed by Japan in the Pacific. But none of these scenarios fitted Hitler's mentality – nor, ultimately, that of his military and Party leaders. From Hitler's perspective, Germany could not afford to wait. Russia posed, in his eyes, a threat which could only mount in the following year or so. An immediate German strike would both remove that threat, and destroy the British hopes that hinged on American intervention. On the other hand, to lose the initiative meant, from Hitler's point of view, to put himself and Germany in a strait-jacket that could only tighten. The war would then be lost. Germany's chance would have gone. And such was the international enmity towards Germany which he and the National Socialist regime had prompted that any concessions from weakness would most likely mean the demise of his regime and his own ousting from power.

Moreover, to refrain from the bold move, to remain passive, would be –

as seen by Hitler – to forfeit the psychological impetus that the war had built up. Sustaining the dynamism of the National Socialist Movement required the continuation of expansion, the conquest of new territories, the setting of new goals, the relentless pursuit of the millennium. The vision could not be limited; the quest could not be permanently halted through conventional territorial settlements that would leave – in Hitler's eyes and those of his followers – the grail of a new society built upon racial purity and racial domination still unattained. If Nazism were to sustain and reinvigorate itself, were not to lose its ideological edge, the war had to continue. There could be no subsiding into sterility – a point which Hitler had emphasized as long ago as the Hoßbach meeting in November 1937.[3]

Such considerations predominated in Hitler's mind. But there were, too, economic pressures, of which he was far from unaware. Germany had since 1939 become increasingly dependent upon the vast supplies of raw materials coming from the USSR. Under an agreement signed in January 1941, improving on that of February 1940, the Russians promised delivery of 2½ million tons of grain and 1 million tons of oil by May 1942, in return for German capital goods – in increasingly high demand in the war effort – whose delivery was scheduled to start in the summer of 1941. Problems in German supplies, given its overstretched war economy, were already causing tensions and difficulties in summer 1940. The economic problems in Germany were foreseen by planning experts as mounting in 1941. The dependence on Russia – anathema to all who put their faith in variants of autarkic policies resting on economic hegemony in Europe (*Großraumwirtschaft*) – was accordingly set to grow, not diminish. The Soviet threat to the Ploesti oil-fields in Romania posed real danger to the Axis war effort. Not for nothing did Hitler use this as an argument in remarking that the Russian air-force could turn these oil-fields into 'an expanse of smoking ruins . . . and the life of the Axis depends on those oil-fields'.[4]

Economic, military, strategic, and ideological motives were not separable in Hitler's thinking on the Soviet Union. They blended together, and were used by him with different strength at different times in persuading those in his company of the correctness and inevitability of his course of action. The cement holding them in place was, as it had been for nearly two decades, doubtless the imperative to destroy once and for all 'Jewish Bolshevism' – an aim which would at the same time provide the necessary security in 'living-space' and give Germany political and military dominance over the continent of Europe. But it was not until March 1941 that Hitler began to emphasize the overriding ideological objective of 'Operation Barbarossa'.

For Heydrich and Himmler, the chance to push for such an objective had already been recognized by that time.[5]

In the event, Hitler's attempt to avoid being pinioned in a strait-jacket through retaining the strategic initiative – the gamble of 'Operation Barbarossa' – would lead, by the end of 1941, as the German war effort met with setback and crisis, the war in the East dragged on into the infinite future, and the Americans finally entered the arena, to precisely the vice setting around Germany that Hitler had wanted to avoid. A way out would now be difficult, if not impossible. The chips were down. And, by that time, the death camps were commencing operations. Victory or total destruction were emerging as the only options left. Hitler's 'all-or-nothing' mentality had enveloped the German state and shaped the alternatives for its future. But by the end of 1941, though military fortune would fluctuate in a war that still had long to run, the odds would already be stacked in favour of destruction, not victory.

I

Between January and March 1941 the operational plans for 'Barbarossa' were put in place and approved by Hitler. Despite his show of confidence, he was inwardly less certain. On the very day that the directive for the attack on the Soviet Union was issued to the commanders-in-chief of the Wehrmacht, 18 December 1940, Major Engel had told Brauchitsch (who was still unclear whether Hitler was bluffing about invading the USSR) that the Führer was unsure how things would go. He was distrustful of his own military leaders, uncertain about the strength of the Russians, and disappointed in the intransigence of the British.[6] Hitler's lack of confidence in the operational planning of the army leadership was not fully assuaged in the first months of 1941. His intervention in the planning stage brought early friction with Halder, and led by mid-March to amendments of some significance in the detailed directives for the invasion.[7]

Already by the beginning of February, Hitler had been made aware of doubts – at any rate a mood less than enthusiastic – among some of the army leaders about the prospects of success in the coming campaign. General Thomas had presented to the Army High Command a devastating overview of deficiencies in supplies.[8] Halder had noted in his diary on 28 January the gist of his discussion with Brauchitsch early that afternoon about 'Barbarossa': 'The "purpose" ('Sinn') is not clear. We do not hit the English that way. Our economic potential will not be substantially improved. Risk in the west must not be underestimated. It is possible that Italy might collapse after the loss of her colonies, and we get a southern front in Spain, Italy, and Greece. If we are then tied up in Russia, a bad situation will be made worse.'[9] Misgivings were voiced by the three army group commanders, Field-Marshals von Leeb, von Bock, and von Rundstedt, when they lunched with Brauchitsch and Halder on 31 January.[10] Brauchitsch, as usual, was reluctant to voice any concern to Hitler. Bock, however, tentatively did so on 1 February. He thought the German army 'would defeat the Russians if they stood and fought'. But he doubted whether it would be possible to force them to accept peace-terms. Hitler was dismissive. The loss of Leningrad, Moscow, and the Ukraine would compel the Russians to give up the fight. If not, the Germans would press on beyond Moscow to Ekaterinburg. War production, Hitler went on, was equal to any demands. There was an abundance of material. The economy was thriving. The armed forces had more manpower than was available at the start of the war. Bock did not feel it even worth suggesting that it was still possible to back away from the conflict. 'I will fight,' Hitler stated. 'I am convinced that our attack will sweep over them like a hailstorm.'[11]

Halder pulled his punches at a conference with Hitler on 3 February. He brought up supply difficulties, but pointed to methods by which they could be overcome, and played down the risks that he had been emphasizing only days earlier. The army leaders accepted Hitler's emphasis on giving priority to the capture of Leningrad and the Baltic coast over Moscow. But they neglected to work out in sufficient detail the consequences of such a strategy.[12] Hitler was informed of the numerical superiority of the Russian troops and tanks. But he thought little of their quality. Everything depended upon rapid victories in the first days, and the securing of the Baltic and the southern flank as far as Rostow. Moscow, as he had repeatedly stressed, could wait. According to Below, Brauchitsch and Halder 'accepted Hitler's directives to wage war against Russia without a single word of objection or opposition'.[13]

In the days that followed the meeting, General Thomas produced further bleak prognoses of the economic situation. Fuel for vehicles sufficed for two months, aircraft fuel till autumn, rubber production until the end of March. Thomas asked Keitel to pass on his report to Hitler. Keitel told him that the Führer would not permit himself to be influenced by economic difficulties. Probably, the report never even reached Hitler. In any case, if Thomas was trying through presentation of dire economic realities to deter Hitler, his method was guaranteed to backfire. A further report demonstrated that if quick victories were attained, and the Caucasus oil-fields acquired, Germany could gain 75 per cent of the materials feeding the Soviet war industry. Such a prognosis could only serve as encouragement to Hitler and to other Nazi leaders.[14]

Hitler remained worried about a number of aspects of the OKH's planning. He was concerned that the army leadership was underestimating the dangers from Soviet strikes at the German flanks from the Pripet Marsh, and called in February for a detailed study to allow him to draw his own conclusions.[15] In mid-March, he contradicted the General Staff's conclusions, asserting – rightly, as things turned out – that the Pripet Marsh was no hindrance to army movement. He also thought the existing plan would leave the German forces overstretched, and too dependent upon what he regarded as the dubious strength of the Romanian, Hungarian, and Slovak divisions – the last of these dismissed merely on the grounds that they were Slavs – on the southern front. He ordered, therefore, the alteration from a two-pronged advance of Army Group South to a single thrust towards Kiev and down the Dnieper. Finally, he repeated his insistence that the crucial objective had to be to secure Leningrad and the Baltic, not push on to Moscow which, at a meeting with his military leaders on 17 March, he declared was 'completely immaterial' ('*Moskau völlig gleichgültig!*').[16] At this conference, these alterations to the original operational plan were accepted by Brauchitsch and Halder without demur.[17] With that, the military framework for the invasion was in all its essentials finalized.

II

While the preparations for the great offensive were taking shape, however, Hitler was preoccupied with the dangerous situation that Mussolini's ill-conceived invasion of Greece the previous October had produced in the Balkans, and with remedying the consequence of Italian military incompetence in North Africa.

He did everything possible to avoid discomfiting Mussolini when the Italian dictator, embarrassed by the military setbacks in Albania and North Africa (where greatly outnumbered British troops had early in the month captured the Italian stronghold of Bardia), arrived at the small station of Puch, near Salzburg, on 19 January for two days of talks at the Berghof.

Hitler and his military leaders were waiting on the platform in the snow.[18]

The talks began without delay. There was no hint of a mention of Italian military reversals. Discussion focused mainly on the Balkans, and on a renewed attempt, through personal persuasion by the Duce, to bring about Spanish intervention in the war and agreement to a German assault on Gibraltar.[19] Reporting to Ciano on his private talks, Mussolini said 'he found a very anti-Russian Hitler, loyal to us, and not too definite on what he intends to do in the future against Great Britain'. A landing was ruled out. The difficulty of such an operation contained an unacceptable risk of failure, after which Britain 'would know that Germany holds only an empty pistol'.[20]

On the afternoon of 20 January, Hitler spoke for about two hours in the presence of military experts on the approaching German intervention in Greece. 'He dealt with the question primarily from a technical point of view,' Ciano recorded, 'relating it to the general political situation. I must admit that he does this with unusual mastery. Our military experts are impressed.'[21] Though the 'very anti-Russian Hitler' that Mussolini saw pointed to the future dangers from the Soviet Union after Stalin's death, when the Jews, at present pushed out of the leadership, could take over again, and when Russian air-power could destroy the Romanian oil-fields, he gave not the slightest inkling that at that very time he was preparing to attack in the East.[22] As usual, the Italians would be kept in the dark until the last minute.

Mussolini returned from the talks 'elated' (as Ciano remarked) 'as he always is after a meeting with Hitler'.[23] It was as well the Duce left when he did. Had he stayed two days longer his growing sense of inferiority towards his senior Axis partner would have been sharpened still further by the disastrous news for his Fascist regime that now Tobruk had fallen to the British.[24]

Popular contempt in Germany for the Italian war effort was matched by the growing disdain of the Nazi leaders for their Fascist counterparts.[25] 'Mussolini has lost a great deal of prestige,' remarked Goebbels towards the end of January 1941, seeing the Duce's position weakened through the military débâcle in North Africa.[26] Whatever the doubts, and his own criticisms of the Italians, Hitler had no option but to stick with his Axis partner.[27]

In all, during the calamitous month of January the fighting in Libya had seen some 130,000 Italians captured by the British.[28] The likelihood of a complete rout for the Italians in North Africa had to be faced. By 6 February, Hitler was briefing the general he had selected to stop the British advance and hold Tripolitania for the Axis.[29] This was Erwin Rommel, who, with a combination of tactical brilliance and bluff, would throughout the second half of 1941 and most of 1942 turn the tables on the British and keep them at bay in North Africa.

Hitler's hopes of a vital strategic gain in the Mediterranean – notably affecting the situation in North Africa – by the acquisition of Gibraltar were, however, to be dashed again by the obstinacy of General Franco. Already at the end of January, Hitler had been informed by Jodl that 'Operation Felix' – the planned assault on Gibraltar – would have to be shelved, since the earliest it could now take place would be in mid-April. The troops and weapons would by then be needed for 'Barbarossa', at that time scheduled for a possible start only a month later.[30] Hitler still hoped that Mussolini, at his meeting on 12 February with Franco, might persuade the Caudillo to enter the war. The day before the meeting, Hitler sent Franco a personal letter, exhorting him to join forces with the Axis powers and to recognize 'that in such difficult times not so much wise foresight as a bold heart can rescue the nations'.[31] Franco was unimpressed. He repeated Spanish demands on Morocco, as well as Gibraltar. And he put forward in addition, as a price for Spain's entering the war at some indeterminate date, such extortionate demands for grain supplies – saying the 100,000 tons already promised by the Germans were sufficient for only twenty days – that there was no possibility they would be met.[32] Spain, as before, had to be left out of the equation.

III

Hitler confirmed the 'dreadful conditions' in Spain which Goebbels reported to him the day after his big speech in the Sportpalast on 30 January 1941, to mark the eighth anniversary of his appointment as Chancellor.[33] The Propaganda Minister found Hitler in high spirits, confident that Germany held the strategic initiative, convinced of victory, revitalized as always by the wild enthusiasm – like a drug to him – of the vast crowd of raucous admirers packed into the Sportpalast. 'I've seldom seen him like this in recent times,' Goebbels remarked.[34] 'The Führer always impresses me afresh,' he added. 'He is a true Leader, an inexhaustible giver of strength.'[35]

In his speech, Hitler had concentrated almost exclusively on attacking Britain. He did not devote a single syllable to Russia; nor did he mention the Soviet Union again in any public speech before 22 June 1941, the day of the invasion.[36] When speaking to Goebbels the following day, however, Hitler did refer to a report on Russia compiled on the basis of seven years' experience of the country by the son of the former prominent KPD member Ernst Torgler. 'Horrible!' commented Goebbels (presumably echoing Hitler's sentiments in recording the gist of their conversation). 'Everything confirmed what we suspected, believed, and also said.' Goebbels reinforced such impressions on the basis of a report on the situation in Moscow which he himself had received from a leading figure in his Ministry.[37]

One other aspect of Hitler's speech on 30 January was noteworthy. For the first time since the beginning of the war, he reiterated his threat 'that, if the rest of the world should be plunged into a general war through Jewry, the whole of Jewry will have played out its role in Europe!' 'They can still laugh today about it,' he added, menacingly, 'just like they used to laugh at my prophecies. The coming months and years will prove that here, too, I've seen things correctly.'[38] Hitler had made this threat, in similar tones, in his Reichstag speech of 30 January 1939. In repeating it now, he claimed to recall making his 'prophecy' in his speech to the Reichstag at the outbreak of war. But, in fact, he had not mentioned the Jews in his Reichstag speech on 1 September, the day of the invasion of Poland. He would make the same mistake in dating on several other occasions in the following two years.[39] It was an indication, subconscious or more probably intentional, that he directly associated the war with the destruction of the Jews.

Why did he repeat the threat at this juncture? There was no obvious contextual need for it. He had referred earlier in the speech to 'a certain Jewish-international capitalist clique', but otherwise had not played the antisemitic tune.[40] Probably the repeated 'prophecy' was intended, as was the original in January 1939, as a threat to what Hitler always regarded as a Jewish-run 'plutocracy' in Britain and the USA. It was a repeat of the blackmail ploy that he held the Jews in his power as hostages.

But within the few weeks immediately prior to his speech, Hitler had had the fate of the Jews on his mind, commissioning Heydrich at this point with the task of developing a new plan, replacing the defunct Madagascar scheme, to deport the Jews from the German sphere of domination.[41] His repeated 'prophecy' was presumably a veiled hint at such an intention, vague though any plan still was at this stage.

Perhaps Hitler had harboured his 'prophecy' in the recesses of his mind since he had originally made it. Perhaps one of his underlings had reminded him of it. But, most probably, it was the inclusion of the extract from his speech in the propaganda film *Der ewige Jude*, which had gone on public release in November 1940, that had stirred Hitler's memory of his earlier comment.[42] Whatever had done so, the repeat of the 'prophecy' at this point was ominous. Though he was uncertain precisely *how* the war would bring about the destruction of European Jewry, he was sure that this would be the outcome. And this was only a matter of months before the war against the arch-enemy of 'Jewish-Bolshevism' was to be launched. The idea of the war to destroy the Jews once and for all was beginning to take concrete shape in Hitler's mind.

According to the account – post-war recollections, resting partly on earlier, lost notes in diary form – of his army adjutant Gerhard Engel, Hitler discussed the 'Jewish Question' soon after his speech, on 2 February, with a group of his intimates.[43] Keitel, Bormann, Ley, Speer, and Ribbentrop's right-hand man and liaison officer Walther Hewel were present. Ley brought up the topic of the Jews. This was the trigger for Hitler to expound at length on his thoughts. He envisaged the war accelerating a solution. But it also created additional difficulties. Originally, it had lain within his reach 'to break the Jewish power at most in Germany'. He had thought at one time, he said, with the assistance of the British of deporting the half a million German Jews to Palestine or Egypt. But that idea had been blocked by diplomatic objections. Now it had to be the aim 'to exclude Jewish influence in the entire area of power of the Axis'. In some countries, like Poland and Slovakia, the Germans themselves could bring that about. In France, it had become more complicated following the armistice, and was especially important there. He spoke of approaching France and demanding the island of Madagascar to accommodate Jewish resettlement. When an evidently incredulous Bormann – aware, no doubt, that the Madagascar Plan had by now been long since shelved by the Foreign Ministry and, more importantly, by the Reich Security Head Office – asked how this could be done during the war, Hitler replied vaguely that he would like to make the whole 'Strength through Joy' fleet available for the task, but feared its exposure to enemy submarines. Then, in somewhat contradictory fashion, he added: 'He was now thinking about something else, not exactly more friendly.'[44]

This cryptic comment (assuming that Engels's account is an accurate representation of what Hitler had said) was, it can reasonably be speculated, a hint that the defeat of the Soviet Union, anticipated to take only a few months, would open up the prospect of wholesale deportation of the Jews to the newly conquered lands in the east – and forced labour under barbarous conditions in the Pripet marshlands (stretching towards White Russia in what were formerly eastern parts of Poland) and in the frozen, arctic wastes in the north of the Soviet Union. Such ideas were being given their first airing around this time by Himmler, Heydrich, and Eichmann.[45] They would not have hesitated in putting their ideas to Hitler. The thinking was now moving way beyond what had been contemplated under the Madagascar Plan, inhumane though that itself had been. In such an inhospitable climate as that now envisaged, the fate of the Jews would be sealed. Within a few years most of them would starve, freeze, or be worked to death.[46] The idea of a comprehensive territorial solution to the 'Jewish problem' had by now become effectively synonymous with genocide.

Hitler had been under continued pressure from Nazi leaders to deport the Jews from their own territories, with, now as before, the General Government seen as the favoured 'dumping ground'. Among the most persistent was the Gauleiter of Vienna, and former Hitler Youth Leader, Baldur von Schirach, who had been pressing hard since the previous summer to relieve the chronic housing problems of Vienna by 'evacuating' the city's 60,000 Jews to the General Government. Hitler had finally agreed to this in December 1940. The plans were fully prepared by the beginning of February 1941.[47] Fresh from his visit to Vienna in March, on the third anniversary of the Anschluß, Hitler discussed with Hans Frank and Goebbels the imminent removal of the Jews from Vienna. Goebbels, anxious to be rid of the Jews from Berlin, was placated with an indication that the Reich capital would be next. 'Later, they must sometime get out of Europe altogether,' the Propaganda Minister added.[48]

Despite the problems which had arisen in 1940 about the transfer of Jews and Poles into the General Government, Heydrich (partly under pressure from the Wehrmacht, which needed land for troop exercises) had approved in January 1941 a new plan to expel 771,000 Poles together with the 60,000 Jews from Vienna (bowing to the demands for deportation from Schirach, backed by Hitler) into Hans Frank's domain to make room for the settlement of ethnic Germans.[49] A major driving-force behind the urgency of the ambitious new resettlement programme was the need to accommodate (and incorporate in the work-force) ethnic Germans who had been brought to Poland from Lithuania, Bessarabia, Bukovina and elsewhere in eastern Europe and since then miserably housed in transit camps. Frank's subordinates were dismayed at having to cope with a massive new influx of 'undesirables'.[50] In the event, however, inevitable logistical complications of the new plan soon revealed it as a grandiose exercise in inhumane lunacy. By mid-March the programme had ground to a halt. Only around 25,000 people had been deported into the General Government. And only some 5,000, mainly elderly, Jews had been removed from Vienna.[51] There was still no prospect, within the confines of the territory currently under German control, of attaining either the comprehensive resettlement programme that Himmler was striving for, or, within that programme, solving what seemed to be becoming a more and more intractable problem: removing the Jews.

From comments made by Eichmann's associate, Theodor Dannecker, and, subsequently, by Eichmann himself, it was around the turn of the year 1940–41 that Heydrich gained approval from Hitler – whether through the intercession of Göring or of Himmler is not clear – for his proposal for the 'final evacuation' of German Jews to the General Government.[52] On 21 January Dannecker noted: 'In accordance with the will of the Führer, the Jewish question within the part of Europe ruled or controlled by Germany is after the war to be subjected to a final solution (*einer endgültigen Lösung*).' To this end, Heydrich had obtained from Hitler, via Himmler or Göring, the 'commission to put forward a final solution project (*Endlösungsprojektes*)'.[53] Plainly, at this stage, this was still envisaged as a territorial solution – a replacement for the aborted Madagascar Plan. Eichmann had in mind a figure of around 5.8 million persons.[54]

Two months later, Eichmann told representatives of the Propaganda Ministry that Heydrich 'had been commissioned with the final evacuation of the Jews (*endgültigen Judenevakuierung*)' and had put forward a proposal to that effect some eight to ten weeks earlier. The proposal had, however, not been accepted 'because the General Government was not in a position at that time to absorb a single Jew or a Pole'.[55] When, on 17 March, Hans Frank visited Berlin to speak privately with Hitler about the General Government – presumably raising the difficulties he was encountering with Heydrich's new deportation scheme – he was reassured, in what amounted to a reversal of previous policy, that the General Government would be the first territory to be made free of Jews.[56] But only three days after this meeting, Eichmann was still talking of Heydrich presiding over the 'final evacuation of the Jews' *into* the General Government.[57] Evidently (at least that was the line that Eichmann was holding to), Heydrich still at this point had his sights set on the General Government as offering the basis for a territorial solution. Frank was refusing to contemplate this. And Hitler had now opened up to him the prospect of his territory being the first to be rid of its Jews. Perhaps this was said simply to placate Frank. But in the light of the ideas already taking shape for a comprehensive new territorial solution in the lands soon to be conquered (it was presumed) of the Soviet Union, it was almost certainly a further indicator that Hitler was now envisaging a new option for a radical solution to the 'Jewish problem' once the war was over by mass deportation to the East.

Heydrich and his boss Himmler were certainly anxious to press home the opportunity to expand their own power-base on a grand scale by exploiting the new potential about to open up in the East. Himmler had lost no time in acquainting himself with Hitler's thinking and, no doubt, taking the chance to advance his own suggestions. On the very evening of the signing of the military directive for 'Operation Barbarossa' on 18 December, he had made his way to the Reich Chancellery for a meeting with Hitler. No record of what was discussed survives. But it is hard to imagine that Himmler did not raise the issue of new tasks for the SS which would be necessary in the coming showdown with 'Jewish-Bolshevism'.[58] It was a matter of no more at this point than obtaining Hitler's broad authority for plans still to be worked out.

Himmler and Heydrich were to be kept busy over the next weeks in plotting their new empire. Himmler informed a select group of SS leaders in January that there would have to be a reduction of some 30 million in the Slav population in the East.[59] The Reich Security Head Office commissioned the same month preparations for extensive police action.[60] By early February Heydrich had already carried out preliminary negotiations with Brauchitsch about using units of the Security Police alongside the army for 'special tasks'. No major difficulties were envisaged.[61]

IV

What such 'special tasks' might imply became increasingly clear to a wider circle of those initiated into the thinking for 'Barbarossa' during February and March. On 26 February General Georg Thomas, the Wehrmacht's economics expert, learned from Göring that an early objective during the occupation of the Soviet Union was 'quickly to finish off (*erledigen*) the Bolshevik leaders'.[62] A week later, on 3 March, Jodl's comments on the draft of operational directions for 'Barbarossa' which had been routinely sent to him made this explicit: 'all Bolshevist leaders or commissars must be liquidated forthwith'. Jodl had altered the draft somewhat before showing it to Hitler.[63] He now summarized Hitler's directions for the 'final version'. These made plain that 'the forthcoming campaign is more than just an armed conflict; it will lead, too, to a showdown between two different ideologies . . . The socialist ideal can no longer be wiped out in the Russia of today. From the internal point of view the formation of new states and governments must inevitably be based on this principle. The Jewish-Bolshevik intelligentsia, as the "oppressor" of the people up to now, must be eliminated.' The task involved, the directions went on, was 'so difficult that it cannot be entrusted to the army'.[64] Jodl had the draft retyped in double-spacing to allow Hitler to make further alterations. When the redrafted version was finally signed by Keitel on 13 March, it specified that 'the Reichsführer-SS has been given by the Führer certain special tasks within the operations zone of the army', though there was now no direct mention of the liquidation of the 'Bolshevik-Jewish intelligentsia' or the 'Bolshevik leaders and commissars'.[65]

Even so, the troops were to be directly instructed about the need to deal mercilessly with the political commissars and Jews they encountered. When he met Göring on 26 March, to deal with a number of issues related to the activities of the police in the eastern campaign, Heydrich was told that the army ought to have a three- to four-page set of directions 'about the danger of the GPU-Organization, the political commissars, Jews etc., so that they would know whom in practice they had to put up against the wall'.[66] Göring went on to emphasize to Heydrich that the powers of the Wehrmacht would be limited in the east, and that Himmler would be left a great deal of independent authority. Heydrich laid before Göring his draft proposals for the 'solution of the Jewish Question', which the Reich Marshal approved with minor amendments. These evidently foresaw the territorial solution, which had been conceived around the turn of the year, and already been approved by Himmler and Hitler, of deportation of all the European Jews into the wastelands of the Soviet Union, where they would perish.[67]

During the first three months of 1941, then, the ideological objectives of the attack on the Soviet Union had come sharply into prominence, and had largely been clarified. Most active in pressing forward the initiative had been Reinhard Heydrich, alongside his nominal boss Himmler.[68] Göring, the heads of the Four-Year Plan Organization, and the High Command of the Wehrmacht had also been deeply implicated. Hitler had authorized more than initiated. His precise role, as so often, is hidden in the shadows. But he had little need to move into the foreground. His radical views on 'Jewish-Bolshevism' were known to all. The different policy-objectives of the varying – and usually competing – power-groups in the regime's leadership could be reconciled by accepting the most radical proposals, from Heydrich and Himmler, on the treatment of the arch-enemy in the East. This, in any case, complied with Hitler's own ideological impulses. He set the tone once more, therefore, for the barbarism while others preoccupied themselves with its mechanics. And, in the context of the imminent showdown, the barbarism was now adopting forms and dimensions never previously encountered, even in the experimental training-ground of occupied Poland.

By mid-March, discussions between the Security Police and army leadership about the treatment of political commissars were, as we have already noted, well advanced. Here, too, in the fateful advance into the regime's planned murderous policy in the Soviet Union, the army leaders were complicitous. On 17 March, Halder noted comments made that day by Hitler: 'The intelligentsia put in by Stalin must be exterminated. The controlling machinery of the Russian Empire must be smashed. In Great Russia force must be used in its most brutal form.'[69] Hitler said nothing here of any wider policy of 'ethnic cleansing'. But the army leadership had two years earlier accepted the policy of annihilating the Polish ruling class. Given the depth of its prevalent anti-Bolshevism, it would have no difficulty in accepting the need for the liquidation of the Bolshevik intelligentsia.[70] By 26 March, a secret army order laid down, if in bland terms, the basis of the agreement with the Security Police authorizing 'executive measures affecting the civilian population'.[71] The following day, the Commander-in-Chief of the army, Field-Marshal von Brauchitsch, announced to his commanders of the eastern army: 'The troops must be clear that the struggle will be carried out from race to race (*von Rasse zu Rasse*), and proceed with necessary severity.'[72]

The army was, therefore, already in good measure supportive of the strategic aim and the ideological objective of ruthlessly uprooting and destroying the 'Jewish-Bolshevik' base of the Soviet regime when, on 30 March, in a speech in the Reich Chancellery to over 200 senior officers lasting almost two and a half hours, Hitler stated with unmistakable clarity his views of the coming war with the Bolshevik arch-foe, and what he expected of his army. This was not the time for talk of strategy and tactics. It was to outline to generals in whom he still had little confidence the nature of the conflict that they were entering. He rehearsed once more his familiar arguments. England's hopes had been placed in the United States and Russia. The Russian problem had to be settled without delay. This was the key to Germany's accomplishment of its other tasks. Manpower and *matériel* would then be at her disposal. In Russia, the aim had to be to crush the armed forces and break up the state. Hitler repeated his disparaging comments about Russian armaments – numerically superior but in quality poor. His confidence was undimmed. The Russians, he stated, would collapse under the combined onslaught of German tanks and planes. Once the military tasks had been achieved, no more than about sixty divisions would be needed in the east, releasing the rest for action elsewhere.

He went on to the most striking part of his speech – the ideological aims of the war. He was forthright: 'Clash of two ideologies. Crushing denunciation of Bolshevism, identified with a social criminality. Communism is an enormous danger for our future. We must forget the concept of comradeship between soldiers. A Communist is no comrade before or after the battle. This is a war of annihilation. If we do not grasp this, we shall still beat the enemy, but thirty years later we shall again have to fight the Communist foe. We do not wage war to preserve the enemy.' He went on to stipulate the 'extermination of the Bolshevist commissars and of the Communist intelligentsia'. 'We must fight against the poison of disintegration,' he continued. 'This is no job for military courts. The individual troop commanders must know the issues at stake. They must be the leaders in this fight' . . . 'Commissars and GPU men,' he declared, 'are criminals and must be dealt with as such.' The war would be very different to that in the West. 'In the East, harshness today means lenience in the future.' Commanders had to overcome any personal scruples.[73]

Brauchitsch claimed after the war that he had been surrounded by outraged generals when Hitler had finished speaking.[74] Had this been the case, it would merely have prompted the question why they (or Brauchitsch on their behalf) did not express their outrage to Hitler. However, General Warlimont, who was present, recalled 'that none of those present availed themselves of the opportunity even to mention the demands made by Hitler during the morning'.[75] When serving as a witness in a trial sixteen years after the end of the war, Warlimont, explaining the silence of the generals, declared that some had been persuaded by Hitler that Soviet Commissars were not soldiers but 'criminal villains (*kriminelle Verbrecher*)'. Others – himself included – had, he claimed, followed the officers' traditional view that as Head of State and Supreme Commander of the Wehrmacht Hitler 'could do nothing unlawful'.[76]

The day after Hitler's speech to the generals, 31 March 1941, the order was given to prepare, in accordance with the intended conduct of the coming campaign, as he had outlined it, guidelines for the 'treatment of political functionaries (*Hoheitsträger*)'. Exactly how this order was given, and by whom, is unclear. Halder presumed, when questioned after the war, that it came from Keitel.

'When one has seen how, dozens of times, Hitler's most casual observation would bring the over-zealous Field Marshal running to the telephone to let loose all hell, one can easily imagine how a random remark of the dictator's would worry Keitel into believing that it was his duty on this occasion to give factual expression to the will of the Führer even before the beginning of hostilities. Then he or one of his subordinates would have telephoned OKH and asked how matters stood. If OKH had in fact been asked such a question, they would naturally have regarded it as a prod in the rear and would have got moving at once.'[77] Whether there had been a direct command by Hitler, or whether – as Halder presumed – Keitel had once more been 'working towards the Führer', the guidelines initiated at the end of March found their way by 12 May into a formal edict.[78] For the first time, they laid down in writing explicit orders for the liquidation of functionaries of the Soviet system. The reasoning given was that 'political functionaries and leaders (commissars)' represented a danger since they 'had clearly proved through their previous subversive and seditious work that they reject all European culture, civilization, constitution, and order. They are therefore to be eliminated.'[79]

This formed part of a set of orders for the conduct of the war in the East (following from the framework for the war which Hitler had defined in his speech of 30 March) that were given out by the High Commands of the Army and Wehrmacht in May and June. Their inspiration was Hitler. That is beyond question. But they were put into operative form by leading officers (and their legal advisers), all avidly striving to implement his wishes.[80]

The first draft of Hitler's decree of 13 May 1941, the so-called 'Barbarossa-Decree', defining the application of military law in the arena of Operation Barbarossa, was formulated by the legal branch of the Wehrmacht High Command.[81] The order removed punishable acts committed by enemy civilians from the jurisdiction of military courts. Guerrilla fighters were to be peremptorily shot. Collective reprisals against whole village communities were ordered in cases where individual perpetrators could not be rapidly identified. Actions by members of the Wehrmacht against civilians would not be automatically subject to disciplinary measures, even if normally coming under the heading of a crime.[82]

The 'Commissar Order' itself, dated 6 June, followed on directly from this earlier order. Its formulation was instigated by the Army High Command.[83] The 'Instructions on the Treatment of Political Commissars' began: 'In the struggle against Bolshevism, we must *not* assume that the enemy's conduct will be based on principles of humanity or of international law. In particular, hate-inspired, cruel, and inhumane treatment of prisoners can be expected on the part of *all grades of political commissars*, who are the real leaders of resistance . . . To show consideration to these elements during this struggle, or to act in accordance with international rules of war, is wrong and endangers both our own security and the rapid pacification of conquered territory . . . Political commissars have initiated barbaric, Asiatic methods of warfare. Consequently, they will be dealt with *immediately* and with maximum severity. As a matter of principle, they will be shot at once, whether captured *during operations or otherwise showing resistance.*[84]

The ready compliance of leading officers with the guidelines established by Hitler for the criminal conduct of the war in the East was unsurprising. It had followed the gradual erosion of the traditional position of power of the armed forces' – especially the army's – leadership since 1933. Milestones on the way had been the Röhm affair of 1934 (when the SA's leaders had been liquidated, in no small measure to placate the army) and, especially, the Blomberg–Fritsch crisis of 1938. The great victory in the West in 1940 had silenced the doubters, underlining the rapidly growing inferiority complex of the armed forces' leadership towards Hitler. The subordination of the army to a Leader whose political programme had for long served its own ends had turned inexorably into subservience to a Leader whose high-risk gambles were courting disaster and whose ideological goals were implicating the army in outright criminality.

Not that this can be seen as the imposition of Hitler's will on a reluctant army. In part, the army leadership's rapid compliance in translating Hitler's ideological imperatives into operative decrees was in order to demonstrate its political reliability and avoid losing ground to the SS, as had happened during the Polish campaign.[85] But the grounds for the eager compliance went further than this. In the descent into barbarity the experience in Poland had been a vital element. Eighteen months' involvement in the brutal subjugation of the Poles – even if the worst atrocities were perpetrated by the SS, the sense of disgust at these had been considerable, and a few generals had been bold enough to protest about them – had helped prepare the ground for the readiness to collaborate in the premeditated barbarism of an altogether different order built into 'Operation Barbarossa'.

As the full barbarity of the Commissar Order became more widely known to officers in the weeks immediately prior to the campaign, there were, here too, honourable exceptions. Leading officers from Army Group B (to become Army Group Centre), General Hans von Salmuth and Lieutenant-Colonel Henning von Tresckow (later a driving-force in plans to kill Hitler), for example, let it be known confidentially that they would look for ways of persuading their divisional commanders to ignore the order. Tresckow commented: 'If international law is to be broken, then the Russians, not we, should do it first.'[86] As the remark indicates, that the Commissar Order was a breach of international law was plainly recognized.[87] Field-Marshal Fedor von Bock, Commander of Army Group Centre, rejected the shooting of partisans and civilian suspects as incompatible with army discipline, and used this as a reason to ignore the implementation of the Commissar Order.[88]

But, as Warlimont's post-war comments acknowledged, at least part of the officer corps believed Hitler was right that the Soviet Commissars were 'criminals' and should not be treated as 'soldiers' in the way that the enemy on the western front had been treated. Colonel-General Georg von Küchler, Commander of the 18th Army, for instance, told his divisional commanders on 25 April that peace in Europe could only be attained for any length of time through Germany presiding over territory that secured its food-supply, and that of other states. Without a showdown with the Soviet Union, this was unimaginable. In terms scarcely different from those of Hitler himself, he went on: 'A deep chasm separates us ideologically and racially from Russia. Russia is from the very extent of land it occupies an Asiatic state . . . The aim has to be, to annihilate the European Russia, to dissolve the Russian European state . . . The political commissars and GPU people are criminals. These are the people who tyrannize the population . . . They are to be put on the spot before a field court and sentenced on the basis of the testimony of the inhabitants . . . This will save us German blood and we will advance faster.'[89] Even more categorical was the operational order for Panzer Group 4, issued by Colonel-General Erich Hoepner (who three years later would be executed for his part in the plot to kill Hitler) on 2 May – still before the formulation of the Commissar Order: 'The war against the Soviet Union is a fundamental sector of the struggle for existence of the German people. It is the old struggle of the Germanic people against Slavdom, the defence of European culture against Moscovite-Asiatic inundation, the repulse of Jewish Bolshevism. This struggle has to have as its aim the smashing of present-day Russia and must consequently be carried out with unprecedented severity. Every military action must in conception and execution be led by the iron will mercilessly and totally to annihilate the enemy. In particular, there is to be no sparing the upholders of the current Russian-Bolshevik system.'[90]

The complicity of Küchler, Hoepner, and numerous other generals was built into the way they had been brought up and educated, into the way they thought. The ideological overlap with the Nazi leadership was considerable, and is undeniable. There was support for the creation of an eastern empire. Contempt for Slavs was deeply ingrained. The hatred of Bolshevism was rife throughout the officer corps.[91] Antisemitism – though seldom of the outrightly Hitlerian variety – was also widespread. Together, they blended as the ideological yeast whose fermentation now easily converted the generals into accessories to mass murder in the forthcoming eastern campaign.[92]

V

In the last week of March, three days before he defined the character of 'Operation Barbarossa' to his generals, Hitler received some highly unwelcome news with consequences for the planning of the eastern campaign. He was told of the military coup in Belgrade that had toppled the government of Prime Minister Cvetkovic and overthrown the regent, Prince Paul, in favour of his nephew, the seventeen-year-old King Peter II. Only two days earlier, in a lavish ceremony on the morning of 25 March in Hitler's presence in the palatial surrounds of Schloß Belvedere in Vienna, Cvetkovic had signed Yugoslavia's adherence to the Tripartite Pact, finally – following much pressure – committing his country to the side of the Axis. Hitler regarded this as 'of extreme importance in connection with the future German military operations in Greece'.[93] Such an operation would have been risky, he told Ciano, if Yugoslavia's stance had been questionable, with the lengthy communications line only some twenty kilometres from the Yugoslav border inside Bulgarian territory.[94] He was much relieved, therefore, although, he noted, 'internal relations in Yugoslavia could despite everything develop in more complicated fashion'.[95] Whatever his forebodings, Keitel found him a few hours after the signing visibly relieved, 'happy that no more unpleasant surprises were to be expected in the Balkans'.[96] It took less than forty-eight hours to shatter this optimism. The fabric of the Balkan strategy, carefully knitted together over several months, had been torn apart.

This strategy had aimed at binding the Balkan states, already closely interlinked economically with the Reich, ever more tightly to Germany. Keeping the area out of the war would have enabled Germany to gain maximum economic benefit to serve its military interests elsewhere.[97] The initial thrust was anti-British, but since Molotov's visit to Berlin German policy in the Balkans had developed an increasingly anti-Soviet tendency.[98]

Mussolini's reckless invasion of Greece the previous October had then brought a major revision of objectives. The threat posed by British military intervention in Greece could not be overlooked. The Soviet Union could not be attacked as long as danger from the south was so self-evident. By 12 November Hitler had issued Directive No. 18, ordering the army to make preparations to occupy from Bulgaria the Greek mainland north of the Aegean should it become necessary, to enable the Luftwaffe to attack any British air-bases threatening the Romanian oil-fields.[99] Neither the Luftwaffe nor navy leadership were satisfied with this, and pressed for the occupation of the whole of Greece and the Peloponnese. By the end of November, the Wehrmacht operational staff agreed.[100] Hitler's Directive No.20 of 13 December 1940 for 'Operation Marita' still spoke of the occupation of the Aegean north coast, but now held out the possibility of occupying the whole of the Greek mainland, 'should this be necessary'.[101] The intention was to have most of the troops engaged available 'for new deployment' as quickly as possible.[102]

With the directive for 'Barbarossa' following a few days later, it was obvious what 'new deployment' meant. The timing was tight. Hitler had told Ciano in November that Germany could not intervene in the Balkans before the spring.[103] 'Barbarossa' was scheduled to begin in May. When unusually bad weather delayed the complex preparations for 'Marita', the timing problems became more acute. And once Hitler finally decided in March – following earlier military advice, as we have seen – that the operation had to drive the British from the entire Greek mainland and occupy it, the campaign had to be both longer and more extensive than originally anticipated.[104] It was this which caused Hitler, in opposition to the strongly expressed views of the Army High Command, to reduce the size of the force initially earmarked for the southern flank in 'Barbarossa'.[105]

In the intervening months, strenuous efforts had been made on the diplomatic front to secure the allegiance of the Balkan states. Hungary, Romania, and Slovakia had joined the Tripartite Pact in November 1940.[106] Bulgaria, actively courted by Hitler since the previous autumn, finally committed itself to the Axis on 1 March.[107] The last piece in the jigsaw was the hardest to fit in: Yugoslavia. Its geographical position alone made it vital to the success of an attack on Greece. Here, too, therefore, beginning in November, every attempt was made to bring about a formal commitment to the Tripartite Pact. The promise of the Aegean port of Salonika offered some temptation.[108] The threat of German occupation – the stick, as always, alongside the carrot – provided for further concentration of minds. But it was plain that, among the people of Yugoslavia, allegiance to the Axis would not be a popular step. Hitler and Ribbentrop put Prince Paul under heavy pressure when he visited Berlin on 4 March. Despite the fear of internal unrest, which the Regent emphasized, Prince Paul's visit paved the way for the eventual signing of the Tripartite Pact on 25 March. Hitler was prepared to accept the terms which the Yugoslav government stipulated: a guarantee of the country's territorial integrity; no through-passage for German troops; no military support for the invasion of Greece; no future requests for military support; and backing for the claim to Salonika.[109] But within hours of Prime Minister Cvetkovic and Foreign Minister Cincar-Markovic signing the Pact in Vienna, high-ranking Serbian officers, who had long resented Croat influence in the government, staged their coup.[110]

Hitler was given the news on the morning of the 27th. He was outraged. He summoned Keitel and Jodl straight away. He would never accept this, he shouted, waving the telegram from Belgrade. He had been betrayed in the most disgraceful fashion and would smash Yugoslavia whatever the new government promised.[111] 'The Führer does not let himself be messed around in these matters,' noted Goebbels a day or two later.[112] Hitler had also immediately sent for the heads of the Luftwaffe and army – Göring and Brauchitsch – together with Foreign Minister Ribbentrop. As usual putting a favourable complexion on unwelcome events, he now emphasized the good fortune that the coup had taken place when it had done, and not after 'Barbarossa' had already begun.[113] As it was, there was still just about time to settle the Balkan issue.[114] But there was now great urgency. Halder had also been peremptorily summoned from Zossen. Hitler asked him forthwith how long he needed to prepare an attack on Yugoslavia. Halder provided on the spot the rudiments of an invasion-plan, which he had devised in the car on the way from Zossen.[115]

By one o'clock, Hitler was addressing a sizeable gathering of officers from the army and Luftwaffe.[116] 'Führer is determined,' ran the report of the Wehrmacht Operations Staff, '. . . to make all preparations to smash Yugo-slavia militarily and as a state-form.' Speed was of the essence. It was important to carry out the attack 'with merciless harshness' in a 'lightning operation'. This would have the effect of deterring the Turks and offering advantages for the subsequent campaign against Greece. The Croats would back Germany and be rewarded with their autonomy. The Italians, Hun-garians, and Bulgarians would have territorial gains at Yugoslavia's expense in return for their support. The beginning of 'Operation Barbarossa', Hitler added, would have to be postponed for up to four weeks.[117] There was no discussion.[118] He ordered preparations to begin immediately. The army and Luftwaffe were to indicate their intended tactics by the evening.

Jodl summarized Hitler's objectives in the military directive for the attack that went out the same day.[119] The plans for the invasion of Greece and the build-up to 'Barbarossa' were fully revised at breakneck speed to allow for the preliminary assault on Yugoslavia. Hitler gave no sign of acknowledgement of the work of his General Staff.[120] The operation was eventually scheduled to begin in the early hours of 6 April.[121] 'But that is now only a small beginning,' noted Goebbels. 'The problem of Yugoslavia will not take up too much time . . . The big operation then comes later: against R.'[122]

The Yugoslav crisis had caused Hitler's meeting with the hawkish Japanese Foreign Minister, Yosuke Matsuoka, to be put back a few hours. It also necessitated Ribbentrop being called away from the preliminary talks with his Japanese counterpart to attend Hitler's briefing.[123] Matsuoka's visit to Berlin was accompanied by enormous pomp and circumstance. Every effort was made to impress the important guest. As usual on state visits, cheering crowds had been organized – this time waving the little Japanese paper flags that had been handed out in their thousands. The diminutive Matsuoka, invariably dwarfed by lanky SS men around him, occasionally acknowledged the crowd's applause with a wave of his top-hat.[124]

Hitler placed great store on the visit. His hope – encouraged by Raeder and Ribbentrop – was to persuade the Japanese to attack Singapore without delay.[125] With 'Barbarossa' imminent, this would tie up the British in the Far East. The loss of Singapore would be a catastrophic blow for the still undefeated Britain. This in turn, it was thought in Berlin, would serve to keep America out of the war.[126] And any possible rapprochement between Japan and the USA, worrying signs of which were mounting, would be ended at one fell swoop.[127] Hitler sought no military assistance from Japan in the forthcoming war against the Soviet Union. In fact, he was not prepared to divulge anything of 'Barbarossa' – though in his talks with Matsuoka earlier that morning Ribbentrop had indicated a deterioration in Soviet–German relations and strongly hinted at the possibility that Hitler might attack the Soviet Union at some point.[128]

Hitler outlined for Matsuoka the military successes and position of the Axis powers. On all fronts they were in command. Britain had lost the war, and it was only a question of whether she would recognize this. Britain's two hopes, he went on, again singing the old refrain, were American aid and the Soviet Union. The former would play no significant part before

1942. And Germany had available 160 to 180 divisions which he would not hesitate to use against the Soviet Union if need be – though he added that he did not believe the danger would materialize. Japan, he implied, need have no fear of attack from the Soviet Union in the event of her moving against Singapore: 150 German divisions – Hitler more than doubled the actual number – were standing on the border with Russia.[129] No time could be more favourable, therefore, for the Japanese to act.[130]

Hitler had deployed his full rhetorical repertoire. But he was sorely disappointed at Matsuoka's reply. An attack on Singapore was, the Japanese Foreign Minister declared, merely a matter of time, and in his opinion could not come soon enough. But he did not rule Japan, and his views had not so far prevailed against weighty opposition. 'At the present moment,' he stated, 'he could not under these circumstances enter on behalf of his Japanese Empire into any commitment to act.'[131]

Hitler was going to get nothing out of Matsuoka, whom he later described as 'combining the hypocrisy of an American Bible missionary with the cunning of a Japanese Asiatic'.[132] It was clear: Hitler had to reckon without any Japanese military intervention for the foreseeable future. He continued to see this as a vital step in the global context. As Ciano noted, a few weeks later, 'Hitler still considers the Japanese card as extremely important in order, in the first place, to threaten and eventually counterbalance completely any American action.'[133] When Matsuoka returned briefly to Berlin in early April to report on his meeting with Mussolini, Hitler was prepared to give him every encouragement. He acceded to the request for technical assistance in submarine construction. He then made an unsolicited offer. Should Japan 'get into' conflict with the United States, Germany would immediately 'draw the consequences'. America would seek to pick off her enemies one by one. 'Therefore Germany would,' Hitler said, 'intervene immediately in case of a conflict Japan–America, for the strength of the three Pact powers was their common action. Their weakness would be in letting themselves be defeated singly.'[134] It was the thinking that would take Germany into war against the United States later in the year following the Japanese attack on Pearl Harbor. Meanwhile, the Soviet–Japanese neutrality pact which Matsuoka negotiated with Stalin on his way back through Moscow – ensuring that Japan would not be dragged into a conflict between Germany and the Soviet Union, and securing her northern flank in the event of expansion in south-east Asia – came as an unpleasant surprise to Hitler.[135]

While Matsuoka was in Berlin, preparations for 'Marita' were already furiously taking shape. Within little over a week they were ready. 'Operation Marita' was now set to begin at 5.20a.m. on Sunday morning, 6 April. The tension in the Propaganda Ministry and other agencies of the regime was feverish. Goebbels had already devised, with Hitler's approval, the radio fanfares for the Balkan campaign, taken from the opening of 'Prinz Eugen'.[136] At 1a.m., feeling the tension himself and about to snatch a few hours' sleep, he was summoned to the Führer. Hitler outlined the attack. He reckoned the campaign could take two months. Goebbels thought less. Hitler referred to the Friendship Treaty which the Soviet Union had signed with Yugoslavia only the day before.[137] He had no fear of Russia. He had taken sufficient precautions. If Russia wanted to attack, then the sooner the better. If Germany were not to act now, the whole of the Balkans and Turkey would be inflamed. That had to be prevented. The war against the Serbs would be carried out 'without mercy'.

The time seemed to drag. Goebbels drank tea with Hitler and, as a diversion, they talked about matters other than the war. Hitler turned to one of his favourite topics: making Linz into a cultural capital greater than Vienna. Goebbels said he would help as far as possible, in the first instance by setting up film studios there.[138] Another hour passed. Then 5.20a.m. came. The attack had started. Hitler felt he could now go to bed.[139]

Shortly afterwards, Goebbels read out on the radio the proclamation Hitler had dictated.[140] By then, hundreds of Luftwaffe bombers were turning Belgrade into a heap of smoking ruins. Hitler justified the action to the German people as retaliation against a 'Serbian criminal clique' in Belgrade which, in the pay of the British Secret Service, was attempting, as in 1914, to spread the war in the Balkans. The German troops would end their action once the 'Belgrade conspirators' had been overthrown and the last British soldiers had been forced out of the region.[141] What could, of course, not be revealed was that the invasion of Yugoslavia would, in at least one important respect, be a trial-run for 'Barbarossa'. Hitler had spoken privately about the campaign being 'merciless (*ohne Gnade*)'.[142] On 2 April, Chief of Staff General Halder – presumably acceding to a request from Heydrich – added two new target-groups alongside 'Emigrants, Saboteurs, Terrorists' to be dealt with by the Security Police and SD in the Balkan campaign: Communists and Jews.[143]

With the campaign in its early stages, Hitler left Berlin on the evening of 10 April, *en route* for his improvised field headquarters. These were located in his Special Train *Amerika*, stationed at the entrance to a tunnel beneath the Alps on a single-track section of the line from Vienna to Graz, in a wooded area near Mönichkirchen. The Wehrmacht Operational Staff, apart from Hitler's closest advisers, were accommodated in a nearby inn. The tunnel was to offer protection in the event of danger from the air.[144] The day before he left Berlin, Hitler had experienced the worst British air-raid yet over the Reich capital. Some of the historic buildings on Unter den Linden – including the State Opera House, the University, the State Library, and the Crown Prince's Palace – were damaged. Hitler was furious with Göring at the failure of the Luftwaffe. He immediately commissioned Speer with the rebuilding of the Opera House.[145]

Hitler remained in his secluded, heavily guarded field headquarters for a fortnight. He was visited there by King Boris of Bulgaria, Admiral Horthy, the regent of Hungary, and Count Ciano – vultures gathering at the corpse of Yugoslavia.[146] His fifty-second birthday on 20 April was bizarrely celebrated with a concert in front of the Special Train, after Göring had eulogized the Führer's genius as a military commander, and Hitler had shaken the hand of each of his armed forces' chiefs.[147] While there Hitler heard the news of the capitulation of both Yugoslavia and Greece.[148]

After overcoming some early tenacious resistance, the dual campaign against Yugoslavia and Greece had made unexpectedly rapid progress.[149] In fact, German operational planning had grossly overestimated the weak enemy forces. Of the twenty-nine German divisions engaged in the Balkans, only ten were in action for more than six days.[150] On 10 April Agram was reached, and an independent Croatian State proclaimed, resting on the slaughterous anti-Serb Ustasha Movement. Two days later Belgrade was reached. On 17 April the Yugoslav army surrendered unconditionally. Around 344,000 men entered German captivity. Losses on the victors' side were a mere 151 dead with 392 wounded and fifteen missing.[151]

In contrast to the punitive attack on Yugoslavia, Hitler's interest in the conquest of Greece was purely strategic. He forbade the bombing of Athens, and regretted having to fight against the Greeks. If the British had not intervened there (sending troops in early March to assist the Greek struggle against Mussolini's forces), he would never have had to hasten to the help of the Italians, he told Goebbels.[152] Meanwhile, the German 12th Army had rapidly advanced over Yugoslav territory on Salonika, which fell on 9 April. The bulk of the Greek forces capitulated on 21 April. A brief diplomatic farce followed. The blow to Mussolini's prestige demanded that the surrender to the Germans, which had in fact already taken place, be accompanied by a surrender to the Italians. To avoid alienating Mussolini, Hitler was forced to comply. The agreement signed by General List was disowned. Jodl was sent to Salonika with a new armistice. This time the Italians were party to it. This was finally signed, amid Greek protests, on 23 April.[153] Greeks taken prisoner numbered 218,000, British 12,000, against 100 dead and 3,500 wounded or missing on the German side. In a minor 'Dunkirk', the British managed to evacuate 50,000 men – around four-fifths of their Expeditionary Force, which had to leave behind or destroy its heavy equipment.[154] The whole campaign had been completed in under a month.[155]

A follow-up operation to take Crete by landing parachutists was, while he was in Mönichkirchen, somewhat unenthusiastically conceded by Hitler under pressure from Göring, himself being pushed by the commander of the parachutist division, General Kurt Student.[156] By the end of May, this too had proved successful. But it had been hazardous. And the German losses of 2,071 dead, 2,594 wounded, and 1,888 missing from a deployment of around 22,000 men were far higher than in the entire Balkan campaign. 'Operation Mercury' – the attack on Crete – convinced Hitler that mass paratroop landings had had their day. He did not contemplate using them in the assault the following year on Malta.[157] Potentially, the occupation of Crete offered the prospect of intensified assault on the British position in the Middle East. Naval High Command tried to persuade Hitler of this.[158] But his eyes were now turned only in one direction: towards the East.

On 28 April, Hitler had arrived back in Berlin – for the last time the warlord returning in triumph from a lightning victory achieved at minimal cost. Though people in Germany responded in more muted fashion than they had done to the remarkable victories in the West, the Balkan campaign appeared to prove once again that their Leader was a military strategist of genius. His popularity was undiminished. But there were clouds on the horizon. People in their vast majority wanted, as they had done all along, peace: victorious peace, of course, but above all, peace. Their ears pricked up when Hitler spoke of 'a hard year of struggle ahead of us' and, in his triumphant report to the Reichstag on the Balkan campaign on 4 May, of providing even better weapons for German soldiers 'next year'. Their worries were magnified by disturbing rumours of a deterioration in relations with the Soviet Union and of troops assembling on the eastern borders of the Reich.[159]

What the mass of the people had, of course, no inkling of was that Hitler had already put out the directive to prepare 'Operation Barbarossa' – the invasion of the Soviet Union – almost five months earlier. That directive, of 18 December, had laid down that preparations requiring longer than eight weeks should be completed by 15 May.[160] But it had not stipulated a date for the actual attack. (In one of the military conferences preceding the directive, on 5 December, Hitler had envisaged the end of May as the time to strike. But, so far in advance of a campaign which would be dependent upon weather conditions for the vital initial advantage, this was no more than a date to aim at.[161]) In his speech to military leaders on 27 March, immediately following news of the Yugoslav coup, Hitler had spoken of a delay of up to four weeks as a consequence of the need to take action in the Balkans.[162] Back in Berlin after his stay in Mönichkirchen, he lost no time – assured by Halder of transport availability to take the troops to the East – in arranging a new date for the start of 'Barbarossa' with Jodl: 22 June.[163]

Towards the end of the war, casting round for scapegoats, Hitler looked back on the fateful delay as decisive in the failure of the Russian campaign. 'If we had attacked Russia already from 15 May onwards,' he claimed, '. . . we would have been in a position to conclude the eastern campaign before the onset of winter.'[164] This was simplistic in the extreme – as well as exaggerating the inroads made by the Balkan campaign on the timing of 'Barbarossa'.[165] Weather conditions in an unusually wet spring in central Europe would almost certainly have ruled out a major attack before June – perhaps even mid-June.[166] Moreover, the major wear and tear on the German divisions engaged on the Balkan campaign came less from the belated inclusion of Yugoslavia than from the invasion of Greece – planned over many months in conjunction with the planning for 'Barbarossa'.[167] What did disadvantage the opening of 'Barbarossa' was the need for the redeployment at breakneck speed of divisions that had pushed on as far as southern Greece and now, without recovery time, had rapidly to be transported to their eastern positions.[168] In addition, the damage caused to tanks by rutted and pot-holed roads in the Balkan hills required a huge effort to equip them again for the eastern campaign, and probably contributed to the high rate of mechanical failure during the invasion of Russia.[169] Probably the most serious effect of the Balkan campaign on planning for 'Barbarossa' was the reduction of German forces on the southern flank, to the south of the Pripet Marshes.[170] But we have already seen that Hitler took the decision to that effect on 17 March, before the coup in Yugoslavia.

The weaknesses of the plan to invade the Soviet Union could not be laid at the door of the Italians, for their failure in Greece, or the Yugoslavs, for what Hitler saw as their treachery. The calamity, as it emerged, of 'Barbarossa' was located squarely in the nature of German war aims and ambitions. These were by no means solely a product of Hitler's ideological obsessiveness, megalomania, and indomitable willpower. Certainly, he had provided the driving-force. But he had met no resistance to speak of in the higher echelons of the regime. The army, in particular, had fully supported him in the turn to the East. And if Hitler's underestimation of Soviet military power was crass, it was an underestimation shared with his military leaders, who had lost none of their confidence that the war in the Soviet Union would be over long before winter.

VI

Meanwhile, Hitler was once more forced by events outside his control, this time close to home, to divert his attention from 'Barbarossa'.

When he stepped down from the rostrum at the end of his speech to Reichstag deputies on 4 May, he took his place, as usual, next to the Deputy Leader of the Party, his most slavishly subservient follower, Rudolf Heß.[171] Only a few days later, while Hitler was on the Obersalzberg, the astonishing news came through that his Deputy had taken a Messerschmitt 110 from Augsburg, flown off on his own *en route* for Britain, and disappeared. The news struck the Berghof like a bombshell.[172] The first wish was that he was dead. 'It's to be hoped he's crashed into the sea,' Hitler was heard to say.[173] Then came the announcement from London – by then not unexpected – that Heß had landed in Scotland and been taken captive. With the Russian campaign looming, Hitler was now faced with a domestic crisis. More important still: Heß had provided the British with a gift for propaganda or intelligence purposes. In fact, the decision was soon taken in the British cabinet to ignore the obvious propaganda opportunity in order to put pressure on Stalin at a critical juncture.[174]

On the afternoon of Saturday, 10 May, Heß had said goodbye to his wife, Ilse, and young son, Wolf Rüdiger, saying he would be back by Monday evening. From Munich he had travelled in his Mercedes to the Messerschmitt works in Augsburg. There, he changed into a fur-lined flying suit and Luftwaffe captain's jacket. (His alias on his mission was to be Hauptmann Alfred Horn.) Shortly before 6p.m. on a clear, sunlit evening, his Messer-schmitt 110 taxied on to the runway and took off. Shortly after 11p.m., after navigating himself through Germany, across the North Sea, and over the Scottish Lowlands, Heß wriggled out of the cockpit, abandoning his plane not far from Glasgow, and parachuted – something he had never practised – to the ground, injuring his leg as he left the plane.

Air defence had picked up the flight path, and observers had seen the plane's occupant bale out before it exploded in flames. A local Scottish farmhand, Donald McLean, was, however, first on the scene. He quickly established that the parachutist, struggling to get out of his harness, was unarmed. Asked whether he was British or German, Heß replied that he was German; his name was Hauptmann Alfred Horn, and he had an important message to give to the Duke of Hamilton. Another local man, the elderly William Craig, had by this time arrived on the scene. While Craig went off to summon assistance, the limping Heß was escorted back to the cottage where McLean lived with his wife and mother, and offered a cup of tea (which he declined in favour of water). Within a short time, a few members of the local Home Guard, already heading for the farm after seeing a parachutist come down near by, entered the cottage. Smelling of whisky and prodding their prisoner with an old First World War pistol, they bundled him into a car and drove him to Home Guard headquarters – a scout-hut in the next village. Police and more Home Guard officers, curious about the German captive as word spread, soon turned up. They were followed a little later by Major Graham Donald, Assistant Group Officer of the Royal Observer Corps, who had seen the course of Heß's plane charted on his maps before it had disappeared from trace. The prisoner, by now – well after midnight, an hour and a half or more after landing – tired and probably becoming increasingly agitated about the prospects of fulfilling his 'mission', impressed upon Donald that he had a vital secret message for the Duke of Hamilton. Donald undertook to contact the Duke. But he was not deceived by 'Hauptmann Horn'; he said he would tell the Duke of Hamilton that he had Rudolf Heß in his custody. The Duke had by then, in fact, already been informed that a captured German pilot was demanding to speak to him, though he had not been until Donald's telephone call aware of the apparent true identity of the pilot. Even now, when told who urgently awaited his presence, the Duke showed remarkably little inclination to put himself out that night to come and see the prisoner of such high rank who was claiming to have brought him a vitally important message.[175]

The Duke, a wing-commander in the RAF, did eventually arrive from his base to talk to the German captive by mid-morning on 11 May. The discussion was inconsequential, but convinced Hamilton that he was indeed face to face with Heß. By the evening he had flown south, summoned to report to Churchill at Ditchley Park in Oxfordshire, a palatial eighteenth-century residence in magnificent grounds, frequently used by the British Prime Minister as a weekend headquarters. Churchill was in the midst of a dinner party. A film, the hilarious *The Marx Brothers Go West*, had been arranged for the evening. Churchill was glad of the diversion from the gloomy news coming in of the damage wrought by a heavy air-raid on London the previous night. 'Now, come and tell us this funny story of yours,' Churchill joked to Hamilton, as he entered the dining-room. Hamilton suggested the story would be better told in private. The other guests, apart from the Secretary of State for Air, Sir Archibald Sinclair, withdrew. Hamilton then described what had happened. But a full debriefing had to wait until after midnight. 'Hess or no Hess,' Churchill announced, 'I am going to see the Marx Brothers.'[176]

By the following day, Monday 12 May, the professionals from the Foreign Office were involved. It was decided to send Ivone Kirkpatrick, from 1933 to 1938 First Secretary at the British Embassy in Berlin and a strong opponent of Appeasement, to interrogate Heß. Kirkpatrick and Hamilton left to fly to Scotland in the early evening. It was after midnight by the time they arrived at Buchanan Castle, near Loch Lomond, to confront the prisoner.[177]

The first Hitler knew of Heß's disappearance was in the late morning of Sunday, 11 May, when Karl-Heinz Pintsch, one of the Deputy Führer's adjutants, turned up at the Berghof. He was carrying an envelope containing a letter which Heß had given him shortly before taking off, entrusting him to deliver it personally to Hitler. With some difficulty, Pintsch managed to make plain to Hitler's adjutants that it was a matter of the utmost urgency, and that he had to speak personally to the Führer.[178] When Hitler read Heß's letter, the colour drained from his face.[179] Albert Speer, busying himself with architectural sketches at the time, suddenly heard an 'almost animal-like scream'. Then Hitler bellowed, 'Bormann immediately! Where is Bormann?!'[180]

In his letter, Heß had outlined his motives for flying to meet the Duke of Hamilton, and aspects of a plan for peace between Germany and Britain to be put before 'Barbarossa' was launched. He claimed he had made three previous attempts to reach Scotland, but had been forced to abort them because of mechanical problems with the aircraft.[181] His aim was to bring about, through his own person, the realization of Hitler's long-standing idea of friendship with Britain which the Führer himself, despite all efforts, had not succeeded in achieving. If the Führer were not in agreement, then he could have him declared insane.[182]

Göring – residing at the time in his castle at Veldenstein near Nuremberg – was telephoned straight away. Hitler was in no mood for small-talk. 'Göring, get here immediately,' he barked into the telephone. 'Something

dreadful has happened.' Ribbentrop was also summoned.[183] Hitler, meanwhile, had ordered Pintsch, the hapless bearer of ill tidings, and Heß's other
adjutant, Alfred Leitgen, arrested, and spent his time marching up and down
the hall in a rage.[184] The mood in the Berghof was one of high tension and
speculation.[185] Amid the turmoil, Hitler was clear-sighted enough to act
quickly to rule out any possible power-vacuum in the Party leadership arising
from Heß's defection. That very day, he issued a terse edict stipulating that
the former office of the Deputy Leader would now be termed the Party
Chancellery, and be subordinated to him personally. It would be led, as
before, by Party Comrade Martin Bormann.[186] It was reminiscent of the way
Hitler had dealt with the Gregor Strasser crisis of 1932 by – at least nominally
– taking the reins into his own hands.[187] In practice, making Bormann the
chief of the Party's central office would provide from now on a level of
interventionist zeal by the Party, increasingly imposing its ideologically
driven activism on the regime's administration, on a scale which had never
been witnessed under Heß.[188]

Accompanied by General Ernst Udet, Göring arrived during the evening.
Hitler repeated the hope that Heß had crashed. He asked Göring and Udet
whether it was probable that Heß would manage to reach his flight-target
near Glasgow. They thought it could be ruled out. In their view, Heß did
not have sufficient mastery of the technical equipment. Hitler disagreed. At
that, Ribbentrop was dispatched to Rome to prevent any potential rift in
the Axis. The news from London could break at any time. It was vital to
obviate any presumption by Mussolini that Germany was attempting to
arrange a separate peace with Britain.[189]

Hitler was furious to learn that Heß, despite being banned from flying,
had prepared his plans in minute detail. He persuaded himself – taking his
lead from what Heß himself in his letter had suggested – that the Deputy
Führer was indeed suffering from mental delusion, and insisted on making
his 'madness' the centre-point of the extremely awkward communiqué
which had to be put out to the German people.[190] Since there was still
nothing from Britain, but some sort of official announcement from Berlin
was thought to be unavoidable, it was suggested that the Deputy Führer
had probably crashed *en route*. There was still no word of Heß's whereabouts when the communiqué was broadcast at 8p.m. that evening. The
communiqué mentioned the letter which had been left behind, showing 'in
its confusion unfortunately the traces of a mental derangement', giving
rise to fears that he had been the 'victim of hallucinations'. 'Under these
circumstances,' the communiqué ended, it had to be presumed that 'Party

Comrade Heß had somewhere on his journey crashed, that is, met with an accident'.[191]

Goebbels, overlooked in the first round of Hitler's consultations, had by then also been summoned to the Obersalzberg. 'The Führer is completely crushed,' the Propaganda Minister noted in his diary. 'What a spectacle for the world: a mentally-deranged second man after the Führer.'[192] The following day, on reaching the Berghof, he was shown the letters left by Heß. 'A muddle-headed shambles, schoolboy dilettantism,' was his verdict on Heß's intention to work through the Duke of Hamilton to bring down Churchill and attain peace-terms. 'That Churchill would immediately have him arrested hadn't, unfortunately, occurred to him.' The letters, he claimed, were full of 'half-baked occultism'. He pointed to Heß's belief in horoscopes. 'A thoroughly pathological business,' he concluded.[193] Meanwhile, early on 13 May, the BBC in London had brought the official announcement that Heß indeed found himself in British captivity.

The first German communiqué composed by Hitler the previous day would plainly no longer suffice. The new communiqué of 13 May acknowledged Heß's flight to Scotland, and capture. It emphasized his physical illness – he had suffered from a gall-bladder complaint – stretching back years, which had put him in the hands of mesmerists, astrologists, and the like, bringing about 'a mental confusion' that had led to the present action. It also held open the possibility that he had been entrapped by the British Secret Service. Affected by delusions, he had undertaken the action of an idealist without any notion of the consequences. His action, the communiqué ended, would alter nothing in the struggle against Britain.[194]

The two communiqués, forced ultimately to concede that the Deputy Führer had flown to the enemy, and attributing the action to his mental state, bore all the hallmarks of a hasty and ill-judged attempt to play down the enormity of the scandal. Remarkably, Goebbels had not been informed of what had happened until the evening of 12 May.[195] Hitler had not turned to him for propaganda advice on how to present the débâcle, but had relied instead at first on Otto Dietrich, the Press Chief. Goebbels was highly critical from the outset about the 'mental illness' explanation. None of the Reichsleiter and Gauleiter who inundated him with telephone calls about the position, he wrote, believed the 'madness' story. 'It sounds so absurd that it could be taken for a mystification,' he frankly admitted.[196] His own preference would have been to say nothing until forced to do so, then to suggest that Heß, as had been claimed of Gregor Strasser in 1932, had 'evidently lost his nerve' at the last minute.[197] This way, weakness rather

than insanity could have been blamed. It would have been an easier interpretation to defend.[198] As it was, a real difficulty had to be faced: how to explain
that a man recognized for many years as mentally unbalanced had been left
in such an important position in the running of the Reich. 'It's rightly asked
how such an idiot could be the second man after the Führer,' Goebbels
remarked.[199]

SD reports and other soundings of popular reactions told Goebbels of
the damaging impact on the morale of the people.[200] For the Nazi Party's
standing, the fall-out from the Heß affair was disastrous. Hefty and sustained criticism of the Party and its representatives had been widespread
even during the victorious summer of 1940. Alongside the adulation for the
Führer and the eulogies for the Wehrmacht went feelings that the Party and
its representatives had perhaps once served some purpose, but were by now
superfluous. Many thought the Party functionaries were corrupt, interfering,
and self-serving – feathering their own nest at home, shirking, and draft-
dodging while the indomitable Führer and his brave soldiers were at the
front, facing the enemy. As before the war, the corruption, high-handedness,
loose living, and other personal failings of the jumped-up 'tin-pot gods
(Nebengötter)' were the subject of extensive condemnation. The popular
distaste was much in evidence in the months before the Heß scandal. It was,
then, scarcely surprising that, alongside the deep shock and dismay felt by
Party members and loyal supporters, Heß's defection now evoked a wave
of massive criticism cascading down on the heads of the Party hacks.[201]

A sense of the popular feeling could be grasped from the innumerable
wild rumours that sprouted overnight in all parts of the Reich in what one
government official dubbed 'the month of rumours'.[202] It was, for instance,
rumoured that Himmler and Ley had fled abroad, that the Gauleiter of
Upper Bavaria, Adolf Wagner, had been caught on the border trying to
export into Switzerland 22 million Reich Marks robbed from monasteries,
and that Alfred Rosenberg, Julius Streicher, Count Helldorf (the Police
Chief of Berlin), and Walther Darré (the Blut und Boden guru) had been
shot for their involvement in Heß's 'treason'.[203] Of course, none of the
rumours was true. But their existence – and negative rumour was an
important mode of criticism in the police state – graphically highlights the
low popular esteem of leading Party representatives. Goebbels felt the blow
to prestige so deeply that he wanted to avoid being seen in public. 'It's like
an awful dream,' he remarked. 'The Party will have to chew on it for a long
time.'[204] The only solution from his point of view was to batten down the
hatches and let the hurricane blow itself out. Soon he was commenting that

the issue was losing its dramatic effect.[205] It was turning into a nine-days' wonder.

Hitler himself was occasionally caught in the line of fire of criticism. One popular joke doing the rounds at the time had Heß summoned before Churchill. The British Prime Minister, bulldog expression on his face, cigar in his mouth, was supposed to have said: 'So you're the madman are you?' 'Oh, no,' Heß replied, 'only his Deputy.'[206] But, generally, the contrast between the scarcely diluted contempt for the Party functionaries and the massive popularity of Hitler himself, embodying all that was seen to be positive in National Socialism, was stark. Much sympathy was voiced for the Führer who now had this, on top of all his other worries, to contend with. As ever, it was presumed that, while he was working tirelessly on behalf of the nation, he was kept in the dark, let down, or betrayed by some of his most trusted chieftains.[207]

This key element of the 'Führer myth' was one that Hitler himself played to when, on 13 May, he addressed a rapidly arranged meeting of the Reichsleiter and Gauleiter at the Berghof. There was an air of tension when Göring and Bormann, both grim-faced, entered the hall before Hitler made his appearance. Bormann read out Heß's final letter to Hitler. The feeling of shock and anger among those listening was palpable. Then Hitler came into the room. Much as in the last great crisis within the Party leadership, in December 1932, he played masterfully on the theme of loyalty and betrayal.[208] Heß had betrayed him, he stated. He appealed to the loyalty of his most trusted 'old fighters'. He declared that Heß had acted without his knowledge, was mentally ill, and had put the Reich in an impossible position with regard to its Axis partners. He had sent Ribbentrop to Rome to placate the Duce. He stressed once more Heß's long-standing odd behaviour (his dealings with astrologists and the like). He castigated the former Deputy Führer's opposition to his own orders in continuing to practise flying. Heß, he said, had arranged for a specially adapted Messerschmitt to be fitted out, and had had regular weather charts for the North Sea sent to him for months. A few days before Heß's defection, he went on, the Deputy Führer had come to see him and asked him pointedly whether he still stood to the programme of cooperation with England that he had laid out in *Mein Kampf*. Hitler said he had, of course, reaffirmed this position.

When he had finished speaking, Hitler leaned against the big table near the window. According to one account, he was 'in tears and looked ten years older'.[209] 'I have never seen the Führer so deeply shocked,' Hans Frank told a gathering of his subordinates in the General Government a few days later.[210] As he stood near the window, gradually all the sixty or seventy persons present rose from their chairs and gathered round him in a semicircle. No one spoke a word.[211] Then Göring provided an effusive statement of the devotion of all present. The intense anger was reserved only for Heß.[212] The 'core' following had once more rallied around their Leader, as in the 'time of struggle', at a moment of crisis. The regime had suffered a massive jolt; but the Party leadership, its backbone, was still holding together.

At least one of those present, Gauleiter Ernst Wilhelm Bohle of the *Auslandsorganisation* (Foreign Countries' Organization), thought – or so he asserted after the war – that Heß had acted with Hitler's full knowledge and encouragement.[213] Some other contemporaries, notably General Karl Heinrich Bodenschatz, Göring's adjutant, who was present at the Berghof when the news was broken to Hitler, also remained convinced of his involvement. Their voices have sometimes carried weight down the ages. However, there is not a shred of compelling and sustainable evidence to support the case.[214]

All who saw Hitler in the days after the news of Heß's defection broke registered his profound shock, dismay, and anger at what he saw as betrayal. This has sometimes been interpreted, as it was also by a number of contemporaries, as clever acting on Hitler's part, concealing a plot which only he and Heß knew about.[215] Hitler was indeed capable, as we have noted on more than one occasion, of putting on a theatrical performance. But if this was acting, it was of Hollywood-Oscar calibre.

That the Deputy Führer had been captured in Britain was something that shook the regime to its foundations. As Goebbels sarcastically pointed out, it never appears to have occurred to Heß that this could be the outcome of his 'mission'. It is hard to imagine that it would not have crossed Hitler's mind, had he been engaged in a plot. But it would have been entirely out of character for Hitler to have involved himself in such a hare-brained scheme. His own acute sensitivity towards any potential threat to his own prestige, towards being made to look foolish in the eyes of his people and the outside world, would itself have been sufficient to have ruled out the notion of sending Heß on a one-man peace-mission to Britain. But, in any case, there was every reason, from his own point of view, *not* to have become involved and to have most categorically prohibited what Heß had in mind.

Certainly, Hitler was a gambler. But he invariably weighed the odds and took what seemed to him calculable risks. He was always highly nervous, even hesitant, before any attempted coup. In this instance, his behaviour was unremarkable in the days building up to the Heß drama. The chances of the Heß flight succeeding – even if, for which there is no evidence, there had been enticement from the British Secret Service – were so remote that Hitler would not conceivably have entertained the prospect.[216] And had he done so, it is hard to believe that he would have settled on Heß as his emissary. Heß had not been party to the planning of 'Barbarossa'. He had been little in Hitler's presence over the previous months. His competence was confined strictly to Party matters. He had no experience in foreign affairs. And he had never been entrusted previously with any delicate diplomatic negotiations.[217]

In any case, Hitler's motive for contemplating a secret mission such as Heß attempted to carry out would be difficult to grasp. For months Hitler had been single-mindedly preparing to attack and destroy the Soviet Union precisely in order to force Britain out of the war. He and his generals were confident that the Soviet Union would be comprehensively defeated by the autumn. The timetable for the attack left no room for manoeuvre. The last thing Hitler wanted was any hold-up through diplomatic complications arising from the intercession by Heß a few weeks before the invasion was to be launched. Had 'Barbarossa' not taken place before the end of June, it would have had to be postponed to the following year. For Hitler, this would have been unthinkable. He was well aware that there were those in the British establishment who would still prefer to sue for peace. He expected them to do so *after*, not *before*, 'Barbarossa'.

Rudolf Heß at no time, whether during his interrogations after landing in Scotland, in discussions with his fellow-captives while awaiting trial in Nuremberg, or during his long internment in Spandau, implicated Hitler. His story never wavered from the one he gave to Ivone Kirkpatrick at his first interrogation on 13 May 1941. 'He had come here,' so Kirkpatrick summed up in his report, 'without the knowledge of Hitler in order to convince responsible persons that since England could not win the war, the wisest course was to make peace now. From a long and intimate knowledge of the Führer, which had begun eighteen years ago in the fortress of Landsberg, he could give his word of honour that the Führer had never entertained any designs against the British Empire. Nor had he ever aspired to world domination. He believed that Germany's sphere of interest was in Europe and that any dissipation of Germany's strength beyond Europe's frontiers would be a weakness and would carry with it the seeds of Germany's destruction.' He admitted, when pressed by Kirkpatrick on whether Russia was to be seen as part of Europe or Asia, that Germany had some demands on Russia, but denied that Hitler was planning to attack the Soviet Union.[218]

Heß's British interlocutors rapidly reached the conclusion that he had nothing to offer which went beyond Hitler's public statements, notably his 'peace appeal' before the Reichstag on 19 July 1940. Kirkpatrick concluded his report: 'Heß does not seem . . . to be in the near counsels of the German government as regards operations; and he is not likely to possess more secret information than he could glean in the course of conversations with Hitler and others.'[219] If, in the light of this, Heß was following out orders from Hitler himself, he would have had to be as supreme an actor – and to have continued to be so for the next four decades – as was, reputedly, the Leader he so revered. But, then, to what end? He said nothing that Hitler had not publicly on a number of occasions stated himself.[220] He brought no new negotiating position. It was as if he presumed that the mere fact of the Deputy Führer voluntarily – through an act involving personal courage – putting himself in the hands of the enemy was enough to have made the British government see the good will of the Führer, the earnest intentions behind his aim of cooperation with Britain against Bolshevism, and the need to overthrow the Churchill 'war-faction' and settle amicably.[221] The naïvety of such thinking points heavily in the direction of an attempt inspired by no one but the idealistic, other-worldly, and muddle-headed Heß.

His own motives were not more mysterious or profound than they appeared. Heß had seen over a number of years, but especially since the war had begun, his access to Hitler strongly reduced. His nominal subordinate, Martin Bormann, had in effect been usurping his position, always in the Führer's company, always able to put in a word here or there, always able to translate his wishes into action. A spectacular action to accomplish what the Führer had been striving for over many years would transform his status overnight, turning 'Fräulein Anna', as he was disparagingly dubbed by some in the Party, into a national hero.[222]

Heß had remained highly influenced by Karl Haushofer – his former teacher and the leading exponent of geopolitical theories which had influenced the formation of Hitler's ideas of *Lebensraum* – and his son Albrecht (who later became closely involved with resistance groups). Their views had reinforced his belief that everything must be done to prevent the undermining of the 'mission' that Hitler had laid out almost two decades earlier: the attack on Bolshevism *together with*, not in opposition to, Great Britain. Albrecht Haushofer had made several attempts to contact the Duke of Hamilton – a prominent member of the Anglo-German Society known to have sympathized with notions of close and peaceful cooperation between Britain and Germany – before the Heß escapade, but had received no replies to his letters. Hamilton himself strenuously denied, with justification it seems, receiving the letters, and also denied Heß's claim to have met him at the Berlin Olympics in 1936.[223]

By August 1940, when he began to plan his own intervention, Heß was deeply disappointed in the British response to the 'peace-terms' that Hitler had offered. He was aware, too, that Hitler was by this time thinking of attacking the Soviet Union even before Britain was willing to 'see sense' and agree to terms. The original strategy lay thus in tatters. Heß saw his role as that of the Führer's most faithful paladin, now destined to restore through his personal intervention the opportunity to save Europe from Bolshevism – a unique chance wantonly cast away by Churchill's 'warmongering' clique which had taken over the British government. Heß acted without Hitler's knowledge, but in deep (if confused) belief that he was carrying out his wishes.

Heß now became an unwitting pawn in the moves by British intelligence to bluff Stalin. Churchill was reluctantly dissuaded by Anthony Eden and Alexander Cadogan, Permanent Under-Secretary at the Foreign Office, from his initial instinct to make maximum propaganda capital out of Heß's capture – something Hitler and Goebbels both expected and feared.[224] Prompted by a report from Sir Stafford Cripps, the British Ambassador to Moscow, that Heß's flight to Scotland had newly inflamed the old paranoia in the Soviet leadership of a peace arranged between Britain and Germany at Russia's cost, Eden and Cadogan devised a more subtle ploy, aimed at strengthening Soviet resistance to Hitler. The absence of anything more than the most terse public statement about Heß's capture was part of the idea.[225]

By the beginning of June, thanks to the code-breaker 'Ultra', which since mid-1940 had enabled the decrypting of German military intelligence cyphers, the British cabinet was aware that Hitler would strike against the Soviet Union during the second half of the month.[226] The British had also been tipped off, indirectly, through a leak passed on via Dahlerus, by no less a person than Göring – concerned, as Heß was, to avoid a two-front war.[227] Anxious to wean the Soviet Union away from Germany, Churchill was among a number of those who had let Stalin know as early as April to expect a German attack.[228]

The aim of Eden, Cadogan, and Lord Beaverbrook was now to exploit Heß's capture by sowing further doubts in Stalin's mind about whether

Britain was about to strike a deal with Hitler, based upon peace proposals advanced by the former Deputy Führer, while at the same time, through warnings of German intentions, leaving the door open to a *rapprochement* between Britain and the Soviet Union. The threat of a compromise peace, it was reasoned, might strengthen Moscow's fears of isolation to the extent that the Red Army could launch a preventive attack on the Wehrmacht. At the same time, supplying Stalin with information about German plans could encourage him to seek contact with Britain. Either way, British interests would be well served. Stalin was, therefore, sent deliberately conflicting signals of British intentions. Under the pressure they were attempting subtly to exert, the British Secret Service envisaged a third – the most likely – reaction by Stalin: adopting a wait-and-see stance.[229]

Predictably, Stalin indeed followed the third option. He brushed away warnings, confident that Hitler would not risk a two-front war. Heß's defection bolstered this confidence, since Stalin presumed the Deputy Führer had been commissioned by Hitler to put out peace feelers, and that only a few weeks remained available if an attack were to be launched. The silence from London about Heß together with rumours that Britain might be ready to pull out of the war, aligned with the warnings of an imminent attack by Hitler on Russia, further reinforced the presumption of a serious split within the British government. From Stalin's point of view, this meant the likelihood of delay, thereby hindering agreement with Germany, and blocking the chances of a German attack while there was still time that year.[230]

However, Stalin tried to keep his options open – just in case. On the day that the capture of Heß was announced in London, 13 May, Stalin had four additional armies moved into the western border area of the Soviet Union. A further twenty-five divisions followed early in June, when rumours of Berlin and London agreeing a separate peace were rife.[231] By the time 'Barbarossa' came to be launched, large Russian tank divisions were ranged in forward positions in an arc around Bialystok and Lemberg. They were intended to be in a position to convert readily into an attack-force should, against Stalin's expectations, a separate peace be speedily agreed between Britain and Germany.[232]

Stalin had seen in Heß's flight to Britain a rationality, as part of Hitler's planned strategy, which was not there. He had been encouraged in this by British policy. What the Soviet dictator could not contemplate was, unfortunately for him and his country, the real position: that Hitler had had nothing to do with the absurd Heß adventure; that he had no desire at this point to enter into negotiations with Britain; and that he was fixated upon a 'war of annihilation' to destroy the Soviet Union, aimed at leaving Britain then with no choice but to seek terms.

VII

By the middle of May, after a week preoccupied by the Heß affair, Hitler could begin to turn his attention back to this imminent showdown. The directive he signed on 23 May, supporting the pro-Axis regime in Iraq (which had come to power following a military coup at the beginning of April, had refused to allow British troop movements in the country, and had sent Iraqi troops to surround a British air-base) had little more than nominal significance. A small number of German aeroplanes, carrying troops, had already flown to Iraq in mid-May. They could do little to help the weak Iraqi army fend off the invading British relief forces, which ultimately re-established a pro-British administration. In any case, Hitler's directive made plain that a decision on any German attempt to undermine the British position in the eastern Mediterranean and the Persian Gulf would only follow 'Barbarossa'.[233]

The end of what had been a troubled month for Hitler brought further gloom to the Berghof with the news on 27 May of the loss of the powerful pocket-battleship *Bismarck*, sunk in the Atlantic after a fierce battle with British warships and planes. Some 2,300 sailors went down with the ship.[234] Hitler did not brood on the human loss. His fury was directed at the naval leadership for unnecessarily exposing the vessel to enemy attack – a huge risk, he had thought, for potentially little gain.[235]

Meanwhile, the ideological preparations for 'Barbarossa' were now rapidly taking concrete shape. Hitler needed to do nothing more in this regard. He had laid down the guidelines in March. These sufficed, we saw earlier, for the High Commands of the Wehrmacht and the Army to convert them in May and early June into the series of orders to liquidate the Soviet Political Commissars and offer a 'shooting licence'[236] against the Russian civilian population outside the jurisdiction of military courts for German soldiers.[237] It was during May, too, that Heydrich assembled the four *Einsatzgruppen* ('task groups') which would accompany the army into the Soviet Union. Each of the *Einsatzgruppen* comprised between 600 and 1,000 men (drawn largely from varying branches of the police organization, augmented by the Waffen-SS) and was divided into four or five *Einsatzkommandos* ('task forces') or *Sonderkommandos* ('special forces').[238] The middle-ranking commanders for the most part had an educated background. Highly qualified academics, civil servants, lawyers, a Protestant pastor, and even an opera singer, were among them.[239] The top leadership was drawn almost exclusively from the Security Police and SD.[240] Like the leaders of the Reich Security Head Office, they were in the main well-educated men, of the generation, just too young to have fought in the First World War, that had sucked in *völkisch* ideals in German universities during the 1920s.[241] During the second half of May, the 3,000 or so men selected for the *Einsatzgruppen* gathered in Pretzsch, north-east of Leipzig, where the Border Police School served as their base for the ideological training that would last until the launch of 'Barbarossa'.[242] Heydrich addressed them on a number of occasions. He avoided narrow precision in describing their target-groups when they entered the Soviet Union. But his meaning was, nevertheless, plain. He mentioned that Jewry was the source of Bolshevism in the East and had to be eradicated in accordance with the Führer's aims. And he told them that Communist functionaries and activists, Jews, Gypsies, saboteurs, and agents endangered the security of the troops and were to be executed forthwith.[243] By 22 June the genocidal whirlwind was ready to blow.

'Operation Barbarossa rolls on further,' recorded Goebbels in his diary on 31 May. 'Now the first big wave of camouflage goes into action. The entire state and military apparatus is being mobilized. Only a few people are informed about the true background.' Apart from Goebbels and Ribbentrop, ministers of government departments were kept in the dark. Goebbels's own ministry had to play up the theme of invasion of Britain. Fourteen army divisions were to be moved westwards to give some semblance of reality to the charade.[244]

As part of the subterfuge that action was to be expected *in the West* while preparations for 'Barbarossa' were moving into top gear, Hitler hurriedly arranged another meeting with Mussolini on the Brenner Pass for 2 June.[245] It was little wonder that the Duce could not understand the reason for the hastily devised talks.[246] Hitler's closest Axis partner was unwittingly playing his part in an elaborate game of bluff.

Hitler did not mention a word of 'Barbarossa' to his Italian friends. He claimed on the return journey to have dropped a hint.[247] But, if so, it completely passed Mussolini by. The two dictators talked alone for almost two hours, before being joined by their Foreign Ministers. Hitler had wept, Mussolini reported, when he spoke about Heß.[248] If so, he was weeping about the political damage the former Deputy Führer had done. There were no personal lamentations for the loss of one of his most loyal devotees over so many years.[249] Ciano and Ribbentrop were meanwhile reviewing relations with a number of countries and the general state of the war. 'Rumours in circulation on the beginning operations against Russia in the near future,' remarked Ribbentrop, 'are to be considered devoid of foundation, at least excessively premature.' He conveyed the impression that the German build-up of troops was solely in response to the Soviet military concentration on the German frontier, and that any action by the Reich would only follow an attempted attack by the Red Army.[250]

Hitler had evidently, to Mussolini's irritation, monopolized their private 'discussion'. He now proceeded to do the same in the presence of the Foreign Ministers. His rambling *tour d'horizon* was practically devoid of any genuine substance that might have warranted an urgent meeting.[251] The Italians, worried that the purpose of the meeting was to force concessions on them to the advantage of France, were glad to learn that relations between Germany and France were unchanged.[252] Hitler, his views as always amplified by Ribbentrop, described what he saw as an increasingly critical situation in Britain, speculating on Lloyd George as Churchill's likely successor and a much more amenable policy towards peace with the Axis as a consequence. He ruled out an invasion of Cyprus, which Mussolini had encouraged. Finally, turning to the 'Jewish Question', Hitler declared that 'all Jews must get out of Europe altogether after the war', and mentioned Madagascar – a project definitively discarded over six months earlier – as a possible solution.[253] The Soviet Union was noticeable for its absence in the discourse.[254]

The published communiqué simply stated that the Führer and Duce had held friendly discussions lasting several hours on the political situation.[255] The deception had been successful. Ciano's general impression was 'that for the moment Hitler has no precise plan of action'. Mussolini, too, so Ciano remarked, was 'convinced that a compromise peace would be received by the Germans with the greatest enthusiasm. "They are now sick of victories . . ."'[256]

When he met the Japanese ambassador Oshima the day after his talks with Mussolini, Hitler dropped a broad hint – which was correctly understood – that conflict with the Soviet Union in the near future was unavoidable.[257] But the only foreign statesman to whom he was prepared to divulge more than hints was the Romanian leader General Antonescu, when Hitler met him in Munich on 12 June.[258] Antonescu had to be put broadly in the picture.

After all, Hitler was relying on Romanian troops for support on the southern flank. Antonescu was more than happy to comply. He volunteered his forces without Hitler having to ask. When 22 June arrived, he would proclaim to his people a 'holy war' against the Soviet Union.[259] The bait of recovering Bessarabia and North Bukowina, together with the acquisition of parts of the Ukraine, was sufficiently tempting to the Romanian dictator.[260] Even to Antonescu, a few days before 'Barbarossa', Hitler betrayed as little as possible. His explanation for the coming showdown with the Soviet Union was couched entirely in terms of a necessary defensive reaction to counter the military menace posed to Germany and Europe through Stalin's expansionism. He mentioned no date. Antonescu divined, however, that one was imminent.[261] The Romanian leader agreed that a conflict with Russia could not be delayed. The Soviet army would not offer strong resistance, he thought, and the people wanted their liberation. The Romanian people were thirsting for their revenge for the injustices they had suffered at the hands of the Russians. Comparisons with Napoleon were out of place, he said, given the motorization of modern warfare. Hitler rejoined 'that the aim of the action did not consist of allowing the Russian armies to retreat into their vast land, but that the armies had to be annihilated (*vernichtet*)'.[262]

On 14 June Hitler held his last major military conference before the start of 'Barbarossa'. The generals arrived at staggered times at the Reich Chancellery to allay suspicion that something major was afoot. Hitler sought an account from each army commander of planned operations in the respective theatres during the first days of the invasion. For the most part he listened without interruption. The picture he gleaned was one of numerical advantage, but qualitative inferiority, of the Red Army. The outlook was, therefore, positive. After lunch, Hitler spoke for about an hour.[263] He went over the reasons for attacking Russia. Once again, he avowed his confidence that the collapse of the Soviet Union would induce Britain to come to terms.[264] Hitler emphasized that the war was a war against Bolshevism. The Russians would fight hard and put up tough resistance. Heavy air-raids had to be expected. But the Luftwaffe would attain quick successes and smooth the advance of the land forces. The worst of the fighting would be over in about six weeks. But every soldier had to know what he was fighting for: the destruction of Bolshevism. If the war were to be lost, then Europe would be bolshevized.[265] Most of the generals had concerns about opening up the two-front war, the avoidance of which had been a premiss of military planning. But they did not voice any objections. Brauchitsch and Halder did not speak a word.[266]

Two days later Hitler summoned Goebbels to the Reich Chancellery – he was told to enter through a back door in order not to raise suspicions – to explain the situation. Hitler looked well, thought Goebbels, despite living in an extraordinary state of tension, as invariably was the case before major 'actions'. Hitler told Goebbels that once the 'action' had started, he would become calm, as had been the case on numerous earlier occasions.[267] He greeted his Propaganda Minister warmly. Then he gave him an account of developments. The Greek campaign had taken its toll of *matériel*, so that the military build-up had been somewhat delayed. But it would be completed now within a week, and the attack on Russia would then immediately commence. It was good that the weather was so poor, Hitler remarked, and that the harvest in the Ukraine had not yet ripened. As a result, they could hope to gain most of it. The attack would be the most massive history had ever seen. There would be no repeat of Napoleon (a comment perhaps betraying precisely those subconscious fears of history indeed repeating itself). The Russians had around 180–200 divisions, about as many as the Germans, he said, though there was no comparison in quality. And the fact that they were massed on the Reich borders was a great advantage. 'They would be smoothly rolled up.' Hitler thought 'the action' would take about four months. Goebbels estimated even less time would be needed: 'Bolshevism will collapse like a house of cards,' he thought. Hitler had by this time convinced himself of the preventive war theory he had con- cocted. 'We have to act,' Goebbels recounted. 'Moscow wants to keep out of the war till Europe is exhausted and sucked of its life-blood. Then Stalin would like to act, to bolshevize Europe, and bring in his form of rule.' The German action would put a stop to this. No geographical limits were put on 'the action'. The fight would continue until Russian power had ceased to exist.

Goebbels continued his summary of Hitler's argument – that the defeat of Russia would free some 150 divisions and massive resources for the conflict with Britain. 'The thrust (*Tendenz*) of the entire campaign is clear,' wrote Goebbels: 'Bolshevism must fall and England will have its last conceiv- able continental weapon knocked out of its hand.' 'The Bolshevik poison must be removed from Europe.' All true Nazis, he added, would rejoice to see the day that 'genuine socialism' took the place of 'Jewish Bolshevism' in Russia. The Pact of 1939 – 'a stain on our badge of honour' – would be washed away. 'That which we have spent our lives fighting, we will now annihilate.' He conveyed this thought to Hitler, who said: 'Whether right or wrong, we must win. That is the only way. And it is morally right and necessary. And when we have won, who will ask us about the method? In any case, we have chalked up so much that we have to win, otherwise our entire people – and in first place we ourselves, with all that is dear to us – will be wiped out.'

Hitler asked Goebbels about public opinion. The Propaganda Minister replied that people believed that relations with the Soviet Union were still sound, but would be behind the regime 'when we call on them'. He pointed out that the veil of secrecy had meant an entirely different approach to that previously deployed. Pamphlets were now being produced *en masse* by printers and packers who were confined to the Propaganda Ministry until the invasion took place. In fact, Goebbels was less in touch with opinion than he imagined. Given the extent of the military build-up in the eastern provinces of the Reich, it was hardly surprising that rumours had been rife for weeks about an imminent conflict with Russia.[268] Even so, the concealment was broadly successful. According to one internal report, 'the concentration of numerous troops in the eastern areas had allowed speculation to arise that significant events were afoot there, but nevertheless probably the overwhelming proportion of the German people did not think of any warlike confrontation with the Soviet Union'.[269]

Goebbels himself, after his meeting with Hitler on 18 June, had been driven out of the back gate of the Reich Chancellery and through the city, 'where people are harmlessly walking about in the rain. Happy people,' he wrote, 'who know nothing of all our concerns and live for the day.'[270]

By 18 June, 200,000 pamphlets had been printed for distribution to the troops.[271] On 21 June Hitler dictated the proclamation to the German people to be read out the next day.[272] Hitler was by this time looking over-tired, and was in a highly nervous state, pacing up and down, apprehensive, involving himself in the minutiae of propaganda such as the fanfares that were to be played over the radio to announce German victories.[273] Goebbels was called to see him in the evening. They discussed the proclamation, to which Goebbels added a few suggestions. They marched up and down his rooms for three hours. They tried out the new fanfares for an hour. Hitler gradually relaxed somewhat. 'The Führer is freed from a nightmare the closer the decision comes,' noted Goebbels. 'It's always so with him.' Once more Goebbels returned to the inner necessity of the coming conflict, of which Hitler had convinced himself: 'There is nothing for it than to attack,' he wrote, summing up Hitler's thoughts. 'This cancerous growth has to be burned out. Stalin will fall.' Since July the previous year, Hitler indicated, he had worked on the preparations for what was about to take place. Now the moment had arrived. Everything had been done which could have been done. 'The fortune of war must now decide.' At 2.30a.m., Hitler finally decided it was time to snatch a few hours' sleep.[274] 'Barbarossa' was due to begin within the next hour.[275]

Goebbels was too nervous to follow his example. At 5.30a.m., just over two hours after the German guns had opened fire on all borders, the new Liszt fanfares sounded over German radios. Goebbels read out Hitler's proclamation.[276] It amounted to a lengthy pseudo-historical justification for German preventive action. The Jewish-Bolshevik rulers in Moscow had sought for two decades to destroy not only Germany, but the whole of Europe. Hitler had been forced, he claimed, through British encirclement policy to take the bitter step of entering the 1939 Pact.[277] But since then the Soviet threat had magnified. At present there were 160 Russian divisions massed on the German borders. 'The hour has now therefore arrived,' Hitler declared, 'to counter this conspiracy of the Jewish-Anglo-Saxon warmongers and the equally Jewish rulers of the Bolshevik headquarters in Moscow.'[278] A slightly amended proclamation went out to the soldiers swarming over the border and marching into Russia.[279]

On 21 June, Hitler had at last composed a letter to his chief ally, Benito Mussolini, belatedly explaining and justifying his reasons for attacking the Soviet Union. The letter was delivered to Ciano at 3a.m. next morning, just as the attack was about to begin. Ciano had to disturb Mussolini to convey the news to him – greatly to the annoyance of the Italian dictator, who complained that the Germans told him nothing then broke his sleep to announce a *fait accompli*.[280] Once more, the same arguments, all resting on the need to undertake a preventive strike, were rehearsed. Characteristically, Hitler underlined the dangers of waiting. Time, as always, was not on Germany's side. The Soviet Union would be stronger in a year's time, England – pinning its hopes on the USSR – would be even less ready for peace, and by then the mass delivery of material from the USA would be coming available. His conclusion was typical: 'Whatever may now come, Duce, our situation cannot become worse as a result of this step; it can only improve.' Hitler ended his letter with sentences which, as with his comments to Goebbels, give insight into his mentality on the eve of the titanic contest: 'In conclusion, let me say one more thing, Duce. Since I struggled through to this decision, I again feel spiritually free. The partnership with the Soviet Union, in spite of the complete sincerity of the efforts to bring about a final conciliation, was nevertheless often very irksome to me, for in some way or other it seemed to me to be a break with my whole origin, my concepts, and my former obligations. I am happy now to be relieved of these mental agonies.'[281]

The most destructive and barbaric war in the history of mankind was beginning. It was the war that Hitler had wanted since the 1920s – the war against Bolshevism. It was the showdown. He had come to it by a round-about route. But, finally, Hitler's war was there: a reality.

For almost a year this war had been consciously worked towards and prepared by the German leadership. Hitler's inability to bring Britain to the conference table had provided the spur to contemplate the bold move of a strike in the East even while the contest in the West remained unsettled. The perceived shortage of time, given the looming threat of the USA and the near-certainty of at least indirect involvement in the war through massive supplies of material if the war dragged into a further year, was the driving-force. The need to secure unlimited sources of raw materials from Soviet territory and to ensure that there would be no interruption to oil supplies from Romania was an additional central motive. Ideological considerations – the need to eradicate Bolshevism once and for all – deeply embedded in Hitler's psyche for almost two decades, had not been the primary determinant of the timing of the showdown. But they gave it its indelible colouring, its sense not just of war, but of crusade.

Had Britain been ready to come to terms, the war against the Soviet Union would nonetheless have still gone ahead at some point – in the conditions Hitler had always hoped for. Hitler had sought the conflict. He was the main author of a war which had been a central element in his thinking for almost two decades. But when it came actually to planning, not just imagining, the showdown, the Wehrmacht leadership, including the leaders of the army, the key branch of the armed forces as regards the war in the east, had gone along with every step. They had let Hitler dictate the course of events. At no point had they seriously attempted to discourage him. On the contrary, the combination of anti-Bolshevism and gross under-estimation of Soviet military capabilities had prompted army chiefs to be no less optimistic than Hitler himself about the ease with which the USSR would be defeated.

If the initial aims had been forged by strategic consideration, the ideological input had not been long in coming. Himmler and Heydrich, rapidly spotting a chance to extend their own empire and to create an entire new vast area for their racial experiments, had no difficulty in exploiting Hitler's long-established paranoia about 'Jewish-Bolshevism' to advance new schemes for solving 'the Jewish problem'. By March, Hitler had laid down the parameters of a genocidal war which willing agents in the Wehrmacht as well as the SS leadership were only too ready to translate into firm guidelines for action.

The war in the East, which would decide the future of the Continent of Europe, was indeed Hitler's war. But it was more than that. It was not inflicted by a tyrannical dictator on an unwilling country. It was acceded to, even welcomed (if in different measure and for different reasons), by all sections of the German élite, non-Nazi as well as Nazi. Large sections of the ordinary German population, too, including the millions who would fight in lowly ranks in the army, would – once they had got over their initial shock – go along with the meaning Nazi propaganda imparted to the conflict, that of a 'crusade against Bolshevism'. The more ideologically committed pro-Nazis would entirely swallow the interpretation of the war as a preventive one to avoid the destruction of western culture by the Bolshevik hordes. They fervently believed that Europe would never be liberated before 'Jewish-Bolshevism' was utterly and completely rooted out. The path to the Holocaust, intertwined with the showdown with Bolshevism, was prefigured in such notions. The legacy of over two decades of deeply rooted, often fanatically held, feelings of hatred towards Bolshevism, fully interlaced with antisemitism, was about to be revealed in its full ferocity.

9

SHOWDOWN

'It is thus probably no overstatement to say that the Russian campaign has been won in the space of two weeks.'

General Halder, 3 July 1941

'The whole situation makes it increasingly plain that we have underestimated the Russian colossus.'

General Halder, 11 August 1941

'What India was for England, the eastern territory will be for us.'

Hitler, speaking privately in the Führer Headquarters, August 1941

At dawn on 22 June over 3 million German troops advanced over the borders and into Soviet territory. By a quirk of history, as Goebbels noted somewhat uneasily, it was exactly the same date on which Napoleon's Grand Army had marched on Russia 129 years earlier.[1] The modern invaders deployed over 3,600 tanks, 600,000 motorized vehicles (including armoured cars), 7,000 artillery pieces, and 2,500 aircraft. Not all their transport was mechanized; as in Napoleon's day, they also made use of horses – 625,000 of them. Facing the invading armies, arrayed on the western frontiers of the USSR, were nearly 3 million Soviet soldiers, backed by a number of tanks now estimated to have been as many as 14–15,000 (almost 2,000 of them the most modern designs), over 34,000 artillery pieces, and 8–9,000 fighter-planes.[2] The scale of the titanic clash now beginning, which would chiefly determine the outcome of the Second World War and, beyond that, the shape of Europe for nearly half a century, almost defies the imagination.

I

Despite the numerical advantage in weaponry of the defending Soviet armies, the early stages of the attack appeared to endorse all the optimism of Hitler and his General Staff about the inferiority of their Bolshevik enemies and the speed with which complete victory could be attained. The three-pronged attack led by Field Marshals Wilhelm Ritter von Leeb in the north, Fedor von Bock in the centre, and Gerd von Rundstedt in the south initially made astonishing advances. By the end of the first week of July Lithuania and Latvia were in German hands. Leeb's advance in the north, with Leningrad as the target, had reached as far as Ostrov. Army Group Centre had pushed even farther. Much of White Russia had been taken. Minsk was encircled. Bock's advancing armies already had the city of Smolensk in their sights. Further south, by mid-July Rundstedt's troops had captured Zitomir and Berdicev.[3]

The Soviet calamity was immense – and avoidable. Even as the German tanks were rolling forwards, Stalin still thought Hitler was bluffing, that he would not dare attack the Soviet Union until he had finished with Britain. Stalin had been well informed on the German military build-up and the growing menace of invasion. He had anticipated some German territorial demands but was confident that, if necessary, negotiations could stave off an attack in 1941 at least. By the following year, the Soviet Union would be more prepared. Though two of the top-ranking Soviet generals, Marshal Semyon Timoshenko and General Georgi Zhukov, had put forward a plan on 15 May for a pre-emptive strike against Germany, Stalin had dismissed such a notion out of hand, fearing it would provoke the attack he wanted to avoid. There were no plans to invade Germany. A preventive war against an imminent Soviet invasion of the Reich was a Nazi propaganda legend.[4] So convinced was Stalin of the correctness of his own diagnosis of the situation that he had chosen to ignore a veritable flood of intelligence reports warning of the imminent danger, some even predicting the precise date of the invasion.[5] Once the attack took place, Stalin fell for days into a state of near mental collapse and deep depression. Amid violent mood-swings, one of his first actions was to hurl abuse at his military leaders and sack some of his top commanders.[6]

Stalin's bungling interference and military incompetence had combined with the fear and servility of his generals and the limitations of the inflexible Soviet strategic concept to rule out undertaking the necessary precautions to create defensive dispositions and fight a rearguard action. Instead, whole armies were left in exposed positions, easy prey for the pincer movements of the rapidly advancing panzer armies.[7] In a whole series of huge encircle-ments, the Red Army suffered staggering losses of men and equipment. By the autumn, some 3 million soldiers had trudged in long, dismal columns into German captivity. A high proportion would suffer terrible inhumanity in the hands of their captors, and not return.[8] Roughly the same number had by then been wounded or killed.[9] The barbaric character of the conflict, evident from its first day, had been determined, as we have seen, by the German plans for a 'war of annihilation' that had taken shape since March. Soviet captives were not be treated as soldierly comrades, Geneva conventions were regarded as non-applicable, political commissars – a category interpreted in the widest sense – were peremptorily shot, the civilian population subjected to the cruellest reprisals.[10] Atrocities were not confined to the actions of the Wehrmacht. On the Soviet side, Stalin recovered sufficiently from his trauma at the invasion to proclaim that the conflict was no ordinary war, but a 'great patriotic war' against the invaders. It was necessary, he declared, to form partisan groups to organize 'merciless battle'.[11] Mutual fear of capture fed rapidly and directly into the spiralling barbarization on the eastern front. But it did not cause the barbarization in the first place. The driving-force was the Nazi ideological drive to extirpate 'Jewish-Bolshevism'. Hitler's response in private to Stalin's speech was revealing. The declaration of partisan war, he remarked, had the advantage of allowing the extermination of anyone who got in the way.[12] The wide interpretation of 'partisans' by the Security Police ensured that Jews were particularly prominent among the increasing numbers liquidated.

Already on the first day of the invasion reports began reaching Berlin of up to 1,000 Soviet planes destroyed and Brest-Litowsk taken by the advancing troops. 'We'll soon pull it off,' wrote Goebbels in his diary. He immediately added: 'We must soon pull it off. Among the people there's a somewhat depressed mood. The people want peace ... Every new theatre of war causes concern and worry.'[13]

The main author of the most deadly clash of the century, which in almost four years of its duration would produce an unimaginable harvest of sorrow for families throughout central and eastern Europe and a level of destruction never experienced in human history, left Berlin around midday on 23 June. Hitler was setting out with his entourage for his new field headquarters, chosen for him the previous autumn, near Rastenburg in East Prussia.[14] The presumption was, as it had been in earlier campaigns, that he would be there a few weeks, make a tour of newly conquered areas, then return to Berlin. This was only one of his miscalculations. The 'Wolf's Lair' (*Wolfsschanze*) near Rastenburg was to be his home in the main for the next three and a half years. He would finally leave it a broken man in a broken country.

The Wolf's Lair – another play on Hitler's favourite pseudonym from the 1920s, when he liked to call himself 'Wolf' (allegedly the meaning of 'Adolf', and implying strength) – was hidden away in the gloomy Masurian woods, about eight kilometres from the small town of Rastenburg.[15] Hitler and his accompaniment arrived there late in the evening of 23 June. The new surroundings were not greatly welcoming. The centre-point consisted of ten bunkers, erected over the winter, camouflaged and in parts protected against air-raids by two metres thickness of concrete. Hitler's bunker was at the northern end of the complex. All its windows faced north so that he could avoid the sun streaming in. There were rooms big enough for military conferences in Hitler's and Keitel's bunkers, and a barracks with a dining-hall for around twenty people. Another complex – known as HQ Area 2 – a little distance away, surrounded by barbed wire and hardly visible from the road, housed the Wehrmacht Operations Staff under Warlimont. The army headquarters, where Brauchitsch and Halder were based, were situated a few kilometres to the north-east. Göring – designated by Hitler on 29 June to be his successor in the event of his death – and the Luftwaffe staff stayed in their special trains.[16]

Hitler's part of the Führer Headquarters, known as 'Security Zone One', swiftly developed its own daily rhythm. The central event was the 'situation discussion' at noon in the bunker shared by Keitel and Jodl. This frequently ran on as long as two hours. Brauchitsch, Halder, and Colonel Adolf Heusinger, chief of the army's Operations Department, attended once or twice a week. The briefing was followed by a lengthy lunch, beginning in these days for the most part punctually at 2p.m., Hitler confining himself as always strictly to a non-meat diet. Any audiences that he had on non-military matters were arranged for the afternoons. Around 5p.m. he would call in his secretaries for coffee. A special word of praise was bestowed on the one who could eat most cakes. The second military briefing, given by Jodl, followed at 6p.m. The evening meal took place at 7.30p.m., often lasting two hours. Afterwards there were films. The final part of the routine was the gathering of secretaries, adjutants, and guests for tea, to the accompaniment of Hitler's late-night monologues.[17] Those who could snatched a nap some time during the afternoon so they could keep their eyes open in the early hours.[18] Sometimes, it was daylight by the time the nocturnal discussions came to an end.[19]

Hitler always sat in the same place at meals, with his back to the window, flanked by Press Chief Dietrich and Jodl, with Keitel, Bormann, and Bodenschatz opposite him. Generals, staff officers, adjutants, Hitler's doctors, and any guests visiting the Führer Headquarters made up the rest of the complement.[20] The atmosphere was good in these early days, and not too formal. The mood at this time was still generally optimistic.[21] Life in the FHQ had not yet reached the stage where it could be described by Jodl as half-way 'between a monastery and a concentration camp'.[22]

Two of Hitler's secretaries, Christa Schroeder and Gerda Daranowski, had also accompanied him to his field headquarters. Christa Schroeder described their life there to a friend, one week after arriving. Their living quarters were very simple. The sleeping section of their bunker was no larger than a compartment in a railway carriage. They had a toilet, a mirror, and a radio, but not much else. There were shower rooms, but without hot water in the early weeks. They had as good as nothing to do. Sleeping, eating, drinking, and chatting filled up most of their day. Some of the men in the otherwise entirely male company of the FHQ soon started to complain that the presence of Hitler's two under-employed secretaries in the military complex was quite superfluous.[23] Much of the secretaries' energy was spent trying to swat away a constant plague of midges. Hitler complained that his advisers who had picked the spot had chosen 'the most swampy, midge-infested, and climatically unfavourable area for him', and joked that he would have to send in the Luftwaffe on the midge-hunt.[24] 'The chief', as those in his daily company called him, was generally in a good mood during the first part of the Russian campaign. He enjoyed light banter with his secretaries. When Christa Schroeder could not find her torch one night, as she emerged into the dark compound, Hitler remarked that she should not think he had stolen it. 'I'm a country (*Ländledieb*) thief, not a lamp (*Lämpledieb*) thief,' he quipped.[25]

How monochrome life in the confines of the Führer Headquarters rapidly became for Hitler's secretaries was indicated in Christa Schroeder's comments in a letter to a friend at the end of August: 'We are permanently cut off from the world wherever we are – in Berlin, on the Mountain [at the Berghof], or on travels. It's always the same limited group of people, always the same routine inside the fence.' The danger was, she went on, 'of losing contact with the real world'. Only the common life of the Wolfsschanze's inhabitants, revolving around 'the Chief', held the group together, she wrote. But should Hitler be absent, things immediately fell apart.[26]

As in Berlin or at the Berghof, a word during meals on one of Hitler's favourite topics could easily trigger an hour-long monologue.[27] In these early days, he usually faced a big map of the Soviet Union pinned to the wall. At the drop of a hat, he would launch into yet another harangue about the danger that Bolshevism signified for Europe, and how to wait another year would have been too late. On one occasion, his secretaries heard Hitler, as he stood in front of a big map of Europe, point to the Russian capital and say: 'In four weeks we'll be in Moscow. Moscow will be razed to the ground.'[28] Everything had gone much better than could have been imagined, he remarked. They had been lucky that the Russians had placed their troops on the borders and not pulled the German armies deep into their country, which would have caused difficulties with supplies.[29] Two-thirds of the Bolshevik armed forces and five-sixths of the tanks and aircraft were destroyed or severely damaged, he told Goebbels, on the Propaganda Minister's first visit to Führer Headquarters on 8 July.[30] After assessing the military situation in detail with his Wehrmacht advisers, Goebbels noted, the Führer's conclusion was 'that the war in the East was in the main already won'.[31] There could be no notion of peace-terms with the Kremlin. (He would think differently about this only a month later.) Bolshevism would be wiped out and Russia broken up into its component parts, deprived of any intellectual, political, or economic centre. Japan would attack the Soviet Union from the east in a matter of weeks. He foresaw England's fall 'with a sleepwalker's certainty'. Whether he would take up any offer of a compromise peace from London he could not say.[32] On other occasions, even at this early stage, Hitler was less ebullient, betraying signs of uncertainty about the Soviet Union, about which, he said, they knew so little.[33]

News came in of 3,500 aircraft and over 1,000 Soviet tanks destroyed. But there was other news of fanatical fighting by Soviet soldiers who feared the worst if they surrendered. Hitler was to tell the Japanese Ambassador Oshima on 14 July that 'our enemies are not human beings any more, they are beasts'.[34] It was, then, doubtless echoing her 'chief' and the general atmosphere in FHQ when Christa Schroeder remarked to her friend that 'from all previous experience it can be said to be a fight against wild animals'.[35]

Hitler had permitted no Wehrmacht reports during the very first days of the campaign.[36] But Sunday, 29 June – a week after the attack had started – was, as Goebbels described it, 'the day of the special announcements'. Twelve of them altogether, each introduced by the 'Russian Fanfare' based on Liszt's 'Hungarian Rhapsody', were broadcast, beginning at 11 a.m. that morning.[37] Dominance in the air had been attained, the reports proclaimed. Grodno, Brest-Litowsk, Vilnius, Kowno, and Dünaburg were in German hands. Two Soviet armies were encircled at Bialystok. Minsk had been taken. The Russians had lost, it was announced, 2,233 tanks and 4,107 aircraft. Enormous quantities of *matériel* had been captured. Vast numbers of prisoners had been taken. But the popular reception in Germany was less enthusiastic than had been hoped. People rapidly tired of the special announcements, one after the other, and were sceptical about the propaganda. Instead of being excited, their senses were dulled. Goebbels was furious at the OKW's presentation, and vowed that it would never be repeated.[38]

The invasion of the Soviet Union, for which, as we have seen, there had in contrast to previous campaigns been of necessity no prior manipulation of popular opinion, was presented to the German public as a preventive war. This had been undertaken by the Führer, so Goebbels's directives to the press ran, to head off at the last minute the threat to the Reich and the entire western culture through the treachery of 'Jewish-Bolshevism'. At any moment the Bolsheviks had been planning to strike against the Reich and to overrun and destroy Europe. Only the Führer's bold action had prevented this.[39] More extraordinary than this propaganda lie is the fact that Hitler and Goebbels had convinced themselves of its truth.[40] Fully aware of its falseness, they had to play out a fiction even among themselves to justify the unprovoked decision to attack and utterly destroy the Soviet Union.

By the end of June the German encirclements at Bialystok and Minsk had produced the astonishing toll of 324,000 Red Army prisoners, 3,300 tanks, and 1,800 artillery pieces captured or destroyed. Little over a fortnight later the end of the battle for Smolensk doubled these figures.[41] Already by the second day of the campaign, German estimates put numbers of aircraft shot down or destroyed on the ground at 2,500. When Göring expressed doubts at the figures they were checked and found to be 200–300 below the actual total.[42] After a month of fighting, the figure for aircraft destroyed had reached 7,564.[43] By early July it was estimated that eighty-nine out of 164 Soviet divisions had been entirely or partially destroyed, and that only nine out of twenty-nine tank divisions of the Red Army were still fit for combat.[44]

The scale of underestimation of Soviet fighting potential would soon come as a severe shock. But in early July it was hardly surprising if the feeling in the German military leadership was that 'Barbarossa' was on course for complete victory, that the campaign would be over, as predicted, before the winter. On 3 July Halder summed up his verdict in words which would come to haunt him: 'It is thus probably no overstatement to say that the Russian campaign has been won in the space of two weeks.' He did at least have the foresight to acknowledge that this did not mean that it was over: 'The sheer geographical vastness of the country and the stubbornness of the resistance, which is carried on with all means, will claim our efforts for many more weeks to come.'[45]

II

The territorial gains brought about by the spectacular successes of the Wehrmacht in the first phase of 'Barbarossa' gave Hitler command over a greater extent of the European continent than any ruler since Napoleon. His power and might were at their peak. In his lunchtime or late-night monologues to his regular retinue in the Führer Headquarters, he revealed few, if any, signs of the wear and tear on his nerves which growing conflict with his army leaders and shifting fortunes at the front would cause during the coming weeks. His rambling, discursive outpourings were the purest expression of unbounded, megalomaniac power and breathtaking inhumanity. They were the face of the future in the vast new eastern empire, as he saw it.

'The beauty of the Crimea,' he rhapsodized late at night on 5 July 1941, would be made accessible to Germans through a motorway. It would be their version of the Italian or French riviera.[46] Every German, after the war, he remarked, had to have the chance with his 'People's Car' (*Volkswagen*) personally to see the conquered territories, since he would have 'to be ready if need be to fight for them'. The mistake of the pre-war era of limiting the colonial idea to the property of a few capitalists or companies could not be repeated. Roads would be more important in the future than the railways for passenger transport. Only through travel by road could a country be known, he asserted.[47]

He was asked whether it would be enough to stretch the conquests to the Urals. 'Initially', that would suffice, he replied. But Bolshevism had to be exterminated, and it would be necessary to carry out expeditions from there to eradicate any new centres that might develop. 'St Petersburg' – as he called Leningrad – 'was as a city incomparably more beautiful than Moscow.'[48] But its fate, he decided, was to be identical to that of the capital. 'An example was to be made here, and the city will disappear completely from the earth.' It was to be sealed off, bombarded, and starved out.[49] He imagined, too, that little would ultimately be left of Kiev. He saw the destruction of Soviet cities as the basis for lasting German power in the conquered territories.[50] No military power was to be tolerated within 300 kilometres east of the Urals.[51] 'The border between Europe and Asia,' he stated, 'is not the Urals but the place where the settlements of Germanic types of people stop and pure Slavdom begins. It is our task to push this border as far as possible to the east, and if necessary beyond the Urals.'[52]

Hitler thought the Russian people fit for nothing but hard work under coercion.[53] 'The Slavs,' he declared, 'were a rabbit-family (*Kaninchenfamilie*) who would never proceed beyond the family association if not forced to do so by a ruling class. Their natural and desired condition was one of general disorganization.'[54] 'The Ukrainians,' he remarked on another occasion, 'were every bit as idle, disorganized, and nihilistically asiatic as the Greater Russians.' To speak of any sort of work ethic was pointless. All they understood was 'the whip'. He admired Stalin's brutality. The Soviet dictator, he thought, was 'one of the greatest living human beings since, if only through the harshest compulsion, he had succeeded in welding a state out of this Slavic rabbit-family'.[55] He described 'the sly Caucasian' as 'one of the most extraordinary figures of world history', who scarcely ever left his office but could rule from there through a subservient bureaucracy.[56]

Hitler's model for domination and exploitation remained the British Empire. His inspiration for the future rule of his master-race was the Raj. He voiced his admiration on many occasions for the way such a small country as Great Britain had been able to establish its rule throughout the world in a huge colonial empire. British rule in India in particular showed what Germany could do in Russia. It must be possible to control the eastern territory with a quarter of a million men, he stated. With that number the British ruled 400 million Indians. Russia would always be dominated by German rulers. They must see to it that the masses were educated to do no more than read road signs, though a reasonable living standard for them was in the German interest.[57] The south of the Ukraine, in particular the Crimea, would be settled by German farmer-soldiers. He would have no worries at all about deporting the existing population somewhere or other to make room for them. The vision was of a latter-day feudal type of settlement: there would be a standing army of 1½–2 million men, providing some 30–40,000 every year for use each year when their twelve-year service was completed. If they were sons of farmers, they would be given a farmstead, fully equipped, by the Reich in return for their twelve years of military service. They would also be provided with weapons. The only condition was that they must marry country- not town-girls.[58] German peasants would live in beautiful settlements, linked by good roads to the nearest town. Beyond this would be 'the other world' where the Russians lived under German subjugation. Should there be a revolution, 'all we need to do is drop a few bombs on their cities and the business will be over'.[59] After ten years, he foresaw, there would be a German élite, to be counted on when there were new tasks to be undertaken. 'A new type of man will come to the fore, real master-types, who of course can't be used in the west: viceroys.'[60]

German administrators would be housed in splendid buildings; the governors would live in 'palaces'.[61]

His musings on the prospect of a German equivalent of India continued on three successive days and nights from 8–11 August. India had given the English pride. The vast spaces had obliged them to rule millions with only a few men. 'What India was for England, the eastern territory will be for us,' he declared.[62]

For Hitler, India was the heart of an empire that had brought Britain not only power, but prosperity. Ruthless economic exploitation had always been central to his dream of the German empire in the east. Now, it seemed, that dream would soon become reality. 'The Ukraine and then the Volga basin will one day be the granaries of Europe,' he foresaw. 'And we'll also provide Europe with iron. If Sweden won't supply it one of these days, good, then we'll take it from the east.[63] Belgian industry can exchange its products – cheap consumer wares – for corn from these areas. From Thuringia and the Harz mountains, for example, we can remove our poor working-class families to give them big stretches of land (*große Räume*).'[64] 'We'll be an exporter of corn for all in Europe who need it,' he went on, a month later. 'In the Crimea we will have citrus fruits, rubber plants (with 40,000 hectares we'll make ourselves independent), and cotton. The Pripet marches will give us reeds. We will deliver to the Ukrainians head-scarves, glass chains as jewellery, and whatever else colonial peoples like. We Germans – that's the main thing – must form a closed community like a fortress. The lowest stable-lad must be superior to any of the natives . . .'[65]

Autarky, in Hitler's thinking, was the basis of security. And the conquest of the east, as he had repeatedly stated in the mid-1920s, would now offer Germany that security. 'The struggle for hegemony in the world will be decided for Europe through the occupation of the Russian space,' he told his entourage in mid-September. 'This makes Europe the firmest place in the world against the threat of blockade.'[66] He returned to the theme a few days later. 'As soon as I recognize a raw material as important for the war, I put every effort into making us independent in it. Iron, coal, oil, corn, livestock, wood – we must have them at our disposal . . . Today I can say: Europe is self-sufficient, as long as we just prevent another mammoth state existing which could utilize European civilization to mobilize Asia against us.' He compared, as he had frequently done many years earlier, the benefits of autarky with the international market economy and the mistakes, as he saw them, made by Britain and America through their dependence upon exports and overseas markets, bringing cut-throat competition, corresponding high tariffs and production costs, and unemployment. Britain had increased unemployment and impoverished its working class by the error of industrializing India, he continued. Germany was not tied to exports, and this had meant that it was the only country without unemployment. 'The country that we are now opening up is for us only a raw-material source and marketing area, not a field for industrial production ... We won't need any more to look for an active (*aufnahmefähigen*) market in the Far East. Here is our market. We simply need to secure it. We'll deliver cotton goods, cooking-pots, all simple articles for satisfying the demand for the necessities of life. We won't be able to produce anything like so much as can be marketed here. I see there great possibilities for the build-up of a strong Reich, a true world-power ... For the next few hundred years we will have a field of activity without equal.'[67]

Hitler was blunt about his justification for conquering this territory: might was right. A culturally superior people, deprived of 'living space', needed no further justification.[68] It was for him, as always, a matter of the 'laws of nature'. 'If I harm the Russians now, then for the reason that they would otherwise harm me,' he declared. 'The dear God, once again, makes it like that. He suddenly casts the masses of humanity on to the earth and each one has to look after himself and how he gets through. One person takes something away from the other. And at the end you can only say that the stronger wins. That is after all the most sensible order of things.'[69]

There would be no end of the struggle in the east, that was clear, even after a German victory. Hitler spoke of building an 'Eastern Wall' along the Urals as a barrier against sudden inroads from the 'dangerous human reservoir' in Asia. It would be no conventional fortification, but a live wall built of the soldier-farmers who would form the new eastern settlers. 'A permanent border struggle in the east will produce a solid stock and prevent us from sinking back into the softness of a state system based purely on Europe.'[70] War was for Hitler the essence of human activity. 'What meeting a man means for a girl,' he declared, 'war meant for him.'[71] He referred back frequently in these weeks to his own experiences in the First World War, probably the most formative of his life. Looking at the newsreel of the 'Battle of Kiev', he was completely gripped by 'a heroic epic such as there had never previously been'. He immediately then added (in flat contradiction) that it had been like that in what he always called 'the World War', but that nobody had been able to record it in the same way for posterity. 'I'm immensely happy to have experienced the war in this way,' he added.[72] If he could wish the German people one thing, he remarked on another occasion, it would be to have a war every fifteen to twenty years. If reproached for the loss of 200,000 lives, he would reply that he had enlarged the German nation by 2½ million, and felt justified in demanding the sacrifice of the lives of a tenth. 'Life is horrible (*grausam*). Coming into being, existing, and passing away, there's always a killing (*ein Töten*). Everything that is born must later die. Whether it's through illness, accident, or war, that remains the same.'[73]

Hitler's notions of a social 'new order' have to be placed in this setting of conquest, ruthless exploitation, the right of the powerful, racial dominance, and more or less permanent war in a world where life was cheap and readily expendable. His ideas often had their roots in the resentment that still smouldered at the way his own 'talents' had been left unrecognized or the disadvantages of his own social status compared with the privileges of the high-born and well-to-do. Thus he advocated free education, funded by the state, for all talented youngsters. Workers would have annual holidays and could expect once or twice in their lives to go on a sea-cruise.[74] He criticized the distinctions between different classes of passengers on such cruise ships. And he approved of the introduction of the same food for both officers and men in the army.[75] Hitler might appear to have been promoting ideas of a modern, mobile, classless society, abolishing privilege and resting solely upon achievement. But the central tenet remained race, to which all else was subordinated. Thus, in the east, he said, all Germans would travel in the upholstered first- or second-class railway carriages – to separate them from the native population.[76] It was a social vision which could have obvious attractions for many members of the would-be master-race. The image was of a cornucopia of wealth flowing into the Reich from the east. The Reich would be linked to the new frontiers by motorways cutting through the endless steppes and the enormous Russian spaces. Prosperity and power would be secured through the new breed of supermen who lorded it over the downtrodden Slav masses.

The vision, to those who heard Hitler describe it, appeared excitingly modern: a break with traditional class- and status-bound hierarchies to a society where talent had its reward and there was prosperity for all – for all Germans, that is. Indeed, elements of Hitler's thinking were unquestionably modern.[77] He looked, for instance, to the benefits of modern technology, envisaging steam-heated greenhouses giving German cities a regular supply of fresh fruit and vegetables all through the winter.[78] He looked, too, to modern transport to open up the east. While the bounty of the east pouring into Germany would be brought by train, the car for Hitler was the vital transport means of the future.[79] But for all its apparent modernity, the social vision was in essence atavistic. The colonial conquests of the nineteenth century provided its inspiration. What Hitler was offering was a modernized version of old-fashioned imperialist conquest, now translated to the ethnically mixed terrain of eastern Europe where the Slavs would provide the German equivalent of the conquered native populations of India and Africa in the British Empire.

By mid-July, the key steps had been taken to translate the horrendous vision into reality. At an important five-hour meeting in the Führer Headquarters on 16 July attended by Göring, Rosenberg, Lammers, Keitel, and Bormann, Hitler established the basic guidelines of policy and practical arrangements for administering and exploiting the new conquests. Once more, the underlying premiss was the social-Darwinist justification that the strong deserved to inherit the earth. But the sense that what they were doing was morally objectionable nevertheless ran through Hitler's opening comments, as reported by Bormann. 'The motivation of our steps in the eyes of the world must be directed by tactical viewpoints. We must proceed here exactly as in the cases of Norway, Denmark, Holland, and Belgium. In these cases, too, we had said nothing about our intentions and we will sensibly continue not to do so,' Bormann recorded. 'We will then again emphasize that we were compelled to occupy an area to bring order, and to impose security. In the interest of the native population we had to see to providing calm, food, transport etc. etc. Therefore our settlement. It should then not be recognizable that a final settlement is beginning! All necessary measures – shooting, deportation etc. – we will and can do anyway. We don't want to make premature and unnecessary enemies. We will simply act, therefore, as if we wish to carry out a mandate. But it must be clear to us that we will never again leave these territories,' Hitler's blunt statement continued. 'Accordingly, it is a matter of: 1. doing nothing to hinder the final settlement but rather preparing this in secret; 2. emphasizing that we are the liberators . . . Basically, it's a matter of dividing up the giant cake so that we can first rule it, secondly administer it, and thirdly exploit it. The Russians have now given out the order for a partisan war behind our front. This partisan war again has its advantage: it gives us the possibility of exterminating anything opposing us. As a basic principle: the construction of a military power west of the Urals must never again be possible, even if as a consequence we have to wage war for a hundred years.'[80]

Hitler proceeded to make appointments to the key positions in the occupied east. Rosenberg was confirmed next day as head of what appeared on the surface to be the all-powerful Reich Ministry for the Occupied Eastern Territories.[81] But nothing was as it seemed in the Third Reich. Rosenberg's authority, as Hitler's decree made clear, did not touch the respective spheres of competence of the army, Göring's Four-Year Plan organization, and the SS. The big guns, in other words, were outside Rosenberg's control. More than that, Rosenberg's own conception of winning certain nationalities as allies, under German tutelage, against Greater Russia – notions which he and his staff had been working on since the spring – fell foul of Himmler's policy of maximum repression and brutal resettlement and Göring's aims of total economic exploitation. Himmler was within weeks in receipt of plans for deporting in the coming twenty-five years or so over 30 million people into far more inhospitable climes further eastward. Göring was envisaging the starvation in Russia of 20–30 million persons – a prospect advanced even before the German invasion by the Agricultural Group of the Economic Staff for the East.[82] All three – Rosenberg, Himmler, and Göring – could find a common denominator in Hitler's goal of destroying Bolshevism and acquiring 'living space'. But beyond that minimum, Rosenberg's concept – no less ruthless, but more pragmatic – had no chance when opposed to the contrary idea, backed, as we have seen, by Hitler's own vision, of absolute rapaciousness and repression.[83]

Opposing Rosenberg's wishes, Hitler had yielded in the conference of 16 July to the suggestion of Göring, backed by Bormann, that the – even by Nazi standards – extraordinarily brutal and independent-minded Erich Koch, Gauleiter of East Prussia, should be made Reich Commissar of the key territory of the Ukraine.[84] Koch, like Hitler, but in contrast to Rosenberg, rejected any idea of a Ukrainian buffer-state. His view was that from the very beginning it was necessary 'to be hard and brutal'. He was held in favour in Führer Headquarters. Everyone there thought he was the most suitable person to carry out the requirements in the Ukraine. It was seen as a compliment when they called him the 'second Stalin'.[85]

In contrast to the tyrant, Koch, who continued to prefer his old East Prussian domain to his new fiefdom, Hinrich Lohse, appointed as Reich Commissar in the Baltic, now renamed the Ostland, made himself a subject of ridicule among the German occupying forces in his own territory with his fanatical and often petty bureaucratization, unleashed in torrents of decrees and directives. For all that, he was weak in the face of the power of the SS, and other competing agencies.[86] Similarly, Wilhelm Kube, appointed at the suggestion of Göring and Rosenberg as General Commissar in Belorussia, proved not only corrupt and incompetent on a grandiose scale, but another weak petty dictator in his province, his instructions often ignored by his own subordinates, and forced repeatedly to yield to the superior power of the SS.[87]

The course was set, therefore, for a 'New Order' in the east which belied the very name. Nothing resembled order. Everything resembled the war of all against all, built into the Nazi system in the Reich itself, massively extended in occupied Poland, and now taken to its logical dénouement in the conquered lands of the Soviet Union.

III

In fact, despite the extraordinary gains made by the advancing Wehrmacht, July would bring recognition that the operational plan of 'Barbarossa' had failed. And for all the air of confidence that Hitler displayed to his entourage in the Wolf's Lair, these weeks also produced early indications of the tensions and conflicts in military leadership and decision-making that would continue to bedevil the German war effort. Hitler intervened in tactical matters from the outset. As early as 24 June he had told Brauchitsch of his worries that the encirclement at Bialystok was not tight enough.[88] The following day he was expressing concern that Army Groups Centre and South were operating too far in depth. Halder dismissed the worry. 'The old refrain!' he wrote in his diary. 'But that is not going to change anything in our plans.'[89] On 27, 29, and 30 June and again on 2 and 3 July Halder recorded worried queries or interventions by Hitler in tactical deployments of troops.[90] 'Again the whole place is in a state of jitters,' Halder remarked about FHQ on 3 July, 'because the Führer is afraid that the wedge of Army Group South now advancing eastward might be threatened by flank attacks from north and south.' Halder admitted that in tactical terms the fear was not unwarranted. But he resented the interference. 'What is lacking on top level,' he confided to his diary notes, 'is that confidence in the executive commands which is one of the most essential features of our command organization, and that is so because it fails to grasp the coordinating force that comes from the common schooling and education of our Leader Corps.'[91]

Halder's irritation at Hitler's interference was understandable. But the errors and misjudgements, even in the first, seemingly so successful, phase of 'Barbarossa', were as much those of the professionals in Army High Command as of the former First World War corporal who now thought he was the greatest warlord of all time.

The mounting conflict with Hitler revolved around the implementation of the 'Barbarossa' strategic plan that had been laid down the previous December in Directive 21. This in turn had emanated from the feasibility studies carried out during the summer by military strategists. Planning had, in fact, been initiated as we noted, by Halder on 3 July 1940 almost a month *before* Hitler gave the verbal orders on the 31st to prepare a spring campaign in the East.[92] Feasibility studies followed, the most important, produced at the beginning of August 1940, by General Erich Marcks, Chief of Staff of the 18th Army. War games were carried out at Army Headquarters to test the studies. Army High Command had favoured at this point, based especially on the 'Marcks Plan', making Moscow the key objective. Hitler's own, different, conception was not dissimilar in a number of essentials from the independent strategic study prepared for the Wehrmacht Operational Staff by Lieutenant-Colonel Bernhard Loßberg in September 1940, though it differed from this, too, on the crucial question of Moscow.[93]

The emphasis in Hitler's 'Barbarossa Directive' in December, and in all subsequent strategic planning, had been on the thrusts to the north, to take Leningrad and secure the Baltic, with a further thrust to the south, to take the Ukraine.[94] Even if unenthusiastically, the Army General Staff had accepted the significant alteration of what it had originally envisaged. According to this amended plan, Army Group Centre was to advance as far as Smolensk before swinging to the north to meet up with Leeb's armies for the assault on Leningrad. The taking of Moscow figured in the agreed plan of 'Barbarossa' only once the occupation of Leningrad and Kronstadt had been completed.[95]

Already on 29 June Hitler was worried that Bock's Army Group Centre, where the advance was especially spectacular, would overreach itself.[96] On 4 July he claimed that he faced the most difficult decision of the campaign: whether to hold to the original 'Barbarossa' plan, amend it to provide for a deep thrust towards the Caucasus (in which Rundstedt would be assisted by some of Army Group Centre's panzer forces), or retain the panzer concentration in the centre and push forward to Moscow.[97] The decision he reached by 8 July was the one wanted by Halder: to press forward the offensive of Army Group Centre with the aim of destroying the mass of the enemy forces west of Moscow.[98] The amended strategy now discarded Army Group Centre's turn towards Leningrad, built into the original 'Barbarossa' plan.[99] The 'ideal solution', Hitler accepted, would be to leave Leeb's Army Group North to attain its objectives by its own means.[100] However, Hitler was even now by no means reconciled to the priority of capturing Moscow – in his eyes, as he said, 'merely a geographical idea'.[101]

The conflict with Army High Command, supported by Army Group Centre, about concentration on the taking of Moscow as the objective, continued over the next weeks. Hitler pressed, in revised operational form, for priority to be given to the capture of Leningrad, and now included in the south the drive to the industrial area of Kharkhov and into the Caucasus, to be reached before the onset of winter. At the same time, his 'Supplement to Directive No.33', dated 23 July, indicated that Army Group Centre would destroy the enemy between Smolensk and Moscow by its infantry divisions alone, and would then 'take Moscow into occupation'.[102]

By late July Halder had changed his tune about the certainty and speed of victory. Early in the month he had told Hitler that only forty-six of the known 164 Soviet divisions were still capable of combat. This had been in all probability an overestimation of the extent of destruction; it was certainly a rash underestimation of the enemy's ability to replenish its forces. On 23 July he revised the figure to a total of ninety-three divisions. The enemy had been 'decisively weakened', but by no means 'finally smashed', he concluded. As a consequence, since the Soviet reserves of manpower were now seen to be inexhaustible, Halder argued even more forcefully that the aim of further operations had to be the destruction of the areas of armaments production around Moscow.[103]

As the strength of Soviet defences was being revised, the toll on the German army and Luftwaffe also had to be taken into account. Air-crews were showing signs of exhaustion; their planes could not be maintained fast enough. By the end of July only 1,045 aircraft were serviceable. Air-raids on Moscow demanded by Hitler were of little effect because so few planes were available. Most of the seventy-five raids on the Soviet capital carried out over the next months were undertaken by small numbers of bombers, scarcely able to make a pinprick in Soviet armaments production.[104] The infantry were even more in need of rest. They had been marching, and engaged in fierce fighting, for over a month without a break. The original operational plan had foreseen a break for recuperation after twenty days. But the troops had received no rest by the fortieth day, and the first phase of the campaign was not over.[105] By this time, casualties (wounded, missing, and dead) had reached 213,301 officers and men.[106] Moreover, despite miracles worked by Quartermaster-General Eduard Wagner's organization, transport problems on roads often unfit even in midsummer for mechanized transport brought immeasurable problems of maintaining supply-lines of fuel, equipment, and provisions to the rapidly advancing army. Supplies for Army Group Centre required twenty-five goods trains a day. But despite working round the clock to convert the railway lines to a German gauge, only eight to fifteen trains a day were reaching the front line in late July and early August.[107]

It was becoming obvious already by the end of July that the revised 'Barbarossa' operational plan as laid down in Hitler's Supplement to Directive No.33 could not be carried out before winter descended.[108] Hitler interpreted this as demanding panzer support from Army Group Centre for the assault on Leningrad. Moscow could wait. Halder took the diametrically opposite view. Making Moscow the objective would ensure that the Soviets committed the bulk of their forces to its defence. Taking the city, including its communications system and industries, would split the Soviet Union and render resistance more difficult. The implication was that the capture of the capital would bring about the fall of the Soviet system, and the end of the eastern war.[109] If the attack on Moscow were not pushed through with all speed, the enemy would bring the offensive to a halt before winter, then regroup. The military aim of the war against the Soviet Union would have failed.[110]

Hitler was still adamant that capturing the industrial region of Kharkhov and the Donets Basin and cutting off Soviet oil supplies would undermine resistance more than the fall of Moscow.[111] But he was wavering. At this point, even Jodl and the Wehrmacht Operations Staff had been converted to the need to attack Moscow.[112] Citing the arrival of strong enemy reinforcements facing and flanking Army Group Centre, Hitler now, on 30 July, cancelled the Supplement to Directive No.33.[113] Halder was momentarily ecstatic. 'This decision frees every thinking soldier of the horrible vision obsessing us these last few days, since the Führer's obstinacy made the final bogging down of the eastern campaign appear imminent.'[114] But when Directive No.34 was issued the same day it offered Halder little comfort. Army Group Centre was to recuperate for the next attack; in the north the assault on Leningrad was to continue; and Army Group South was to destroy the enemy forces west of the Dnieper and in the vicinity of Kiev.[115] The real decision – for or against the drive to Moscow – had effectively just been postponed for a while.[116]

In early August Hitler remained wedded to Leningrad as the priority. He reckoned this would be cut off by 20 August, and then troops and aircraft could be redeployed by Army Group Centre. The second priority for Hitler was, as before, 'the south of Russia, especially the Donets region', which formed the 'entire basis of the Russian economy'. Moscow was a clear third on his priority-list. He recognized that in this order of priorities the capital could not be taken before winter. Halder tried unavailingly to get Brau-chitsch to obtain a clear decision on whether to put everything into delivering the enemy a fatal blow at Moscow or taking the Ukraine and the Caucasus for economic reasons. He persuaded Jodl to intervene with Hitler to con-vince him that the objectives of Moscow *and* the Ukraine had to be met.[117]

By now, Halder was realizing the magnitude of the task facing the Wehrmacht. 'The whole situation makes it increasingly plain that we have underestimated the Russian colossus,' he wrote on 11 August. 'At the outset of the war, we reckoned with about 200 enemy divisions. Now we have already counted 360. These divisions indeed are not armed and equipped according to our standards, and their tactical leadership is often poor. But there they are, and if we smash a dozen of them, the Russians simply put up another dozen . . . And so our troops, sprawled over an immense front line, without any depth, are subjected to the incessant attacks of the enemy.'[118]

In his Supplement to Directive No.34, issued on 12 August, Hitler for the first time stated categorically that once the threats from the flanks were eliminated and the panzer groups were refreshed the attack on the enemy forces massed for the protection of Moscow was to be prosecuted. The aim was 'the removal from the enemy before winter of the entire state, armaments, and communications centre around Moscow', ran the direc-tive.[119] Three days later, however, Hitler intervened once more in the tactical dispositions by ordering panzer forces from the northern flank of Army Group Centre to help Army Group North resist a strong Soviet counter-attack.[120]

His concession, if heavily qualified, on Moscow, then – in effect – rapid negation of the decision, may have been affected by the severe attack of dysentery from which he was suffering in the first half of August. Despite mounting hypochondria, he had, in fact, over the past years enjoyed remark-ably good health – perhaps surprisingly so, given his eating habits and lifestyle. But he had now been laid low at a vital time. Goebbels found him still unwell and 'very irritable', though on the mend, when he visited FHQ on 18 August. The weeks of tension, and the unexpected military difficulties of the past month – 'a distinctly bad time' – had taken their toll, the Propaganda Minister thought.[121] In fact, electrocardiograms taken at the time indicated that Hitler had rapidly progressive coronary sclerosis. Morell's discussion of the results of the tests could have done little to lift Hitler's mood, or to lessen his hypochondria.[122]

Probably Hitler's ill-health in August, at a time when he was stunned by the recognition of the gross underestimation by German intelligence of the true level of Soviet forces, temporarily weakened his resolve to continue the war in the east. Goebbels was plainly astonished, on his visit to FHQ on 18 August, to hear Hitler entertain thoughts of accepting peace terms from Stalin and even stating that Bolshevism, without the Red Army, would be no danger to Germany.[123] (Stalin, in fact, appears briefly to have contemplated moves to come to terms, involving large-scale surrender of Soviet territory, in late July.)[124] In a pessimistic state of mind about an early and comprehensive victory in the east, Hitler was clutching at straws: perhaps Stalin would sue for peace; maybe Churchill would be brought down; quite suddenly peace might break out. The turnabout could come as quickly as it had done in January 1933, he suggested (and would do so on other occasions down to 1945), when, without prospects at the start of the month, the National Socialists had within a matter of weeks found themselves in power.[125]

Halder's own nerves were by this point also frayed. He now thought the time had come to confront Hitler once and for all with the imperative need to destroy the enemy forces around Moscow. On 18 August Brauchitsch sent Halder's memorandum on to Hitler. It argued that Army Groups North and South would have to attain their objectives from within their own resources, but that the main effort must be the immediate offensive against Moscow, since Army Group Centre would be unable to continue its operations after October on account of weather conditions.[126]

Halder's memorandum had been prepared by Colonel Heusinger, the army's Chief of Operations Department. Two days after its submission, Heusinger discussed the memorandum with Jodl. Hitler's closest military adviser suggested psychological motives behind the dictator's strategic choices. Heusinger recalled Jodl saying that Hitler had 'an instinctive aversion to treading the same path as Napoleon. Moscow gives him a sinister feeling (*etwas Unheimliches*).' When Heusinger reaffirmed the need to defeat the enemy forces at Moscow, Jodl replied: 'That's what you *say*. Now I will tell you what the Führer's answer will be: There is at the moment a much better possibility of beating the Russian forces. Their main grouping is now east of Kiev.' Heusinger pressed Jodl to support the memorandum. Jodl finally remarked: 'I will do what I can. But you must admit that the Führer's reasons are well thought out and cannot be pushed aside just like that. We must not try to compel him to do something which goes against his inner convictions. His intuition has generally been right. You can't deny that!'[127] The Führer myth still prevailed – and among those closest to Hitler.

Predictably, Hitler's reply was not long in coming – and was a devastating riposte to Army High Command. On 21 August, Army High Command was told that Hitler rejected its proposals as out of line with his intentions. Instead, he ordered: 'The principal object that must be achieved yet before the onset of winter is not the capture of Moscow, but rather, in the South, the occupation of the Crimea and the industrial and coal region of the Donets, together with isolation of the Russian oil regions in the Caucasus and, in the North, the encirclement of Leningrad and junction with the Finns.' The immediate key step was the encirclement and destruction of the exposed Soviet Fifth Army in the region of Kiev through a pincer movement from Army Groups Centre and South. This would open the path for Army Group South to advance south-eastwards towards Rostov and Kharkhov. The capture of the Crimea, Hitler added, was 'of paramount importance for safeguarding our oil supply from Romania'. All means had to be deployed, therefore, to cross the Dnieper quickly to reach the Crimea before the enemy could call up new forces.[128]

Hitler developed his arguments the following day in a 'Study' blaming Army High Command for failing to carry out his operational plan, reaffirming the necessity of shifting the main weight of the attack to the north and south, and relegating Moscow to a secondary target. Brauchitsch was accused of lack of leadership in allowing himself to be swayed by the special interests of the individual army groups. And particularly wounding was the praise, in contrast, handed out to Göring's firm leadership of the Luftwaffe.[129]

In this 'Study' of 22 August, Hitler rehearsed once more the objective of eliminating the Soviet Union as a continental ally of Britain, thereby removing from Britain hope of changing the course of events in Europe. This objective, he claimed, could only be attained through annihilation of Soviet forces and the occupation or destruction of the economic basis for continuing the war, with special emphasis on sources of raw materials. He reasserted the need to concentrate on destroying the Soviet position in the Baltic and on occupying the Ukraine and Black Sea region, which were vital in terms of raw materials for the Soviet war economy. He also underlined the need to protect German oil supplies in Romania. Army High Command was to blame for ignoring his orders to press home the advance on Leningrad. He insisted that the three divisions from Army Group Centre, intended from the beginning of the campaign to assist the numerically weaker Army Group North, should be rapidly supplied, and that the objective of capturing Leningrad would then be met. Once this was done, the motorized units supplied by Army Group Centre could be used to concentrate on their sole remaining objective, the advance on Moscow. In the south, too, there was to be no diversion from original plans to move on Moscow. Once the destruction of the Soviet forces east and west of Kiev which threatened the flank of Army Group Centre was accomplished, he argued, the advance on Moscow would be significantly eased. He rejected, therefore, the Army High Command's proposals for the further conduct of operations.[130]

In the privacy of his diary notes, Halder could not contain himself. 'I regard the situation created by the Führer's interference unendurable for the OKH,' he wrote. 'No other but the Führer himself is to blame for the zigzag course caused by his successive orders.' The treatment of Brauchitsch, Halder went on, was 'absolutely outrageous'. Halder had proposed to the Commander-in-Chief that both should offer their resignation. But Brauchitsch had refused such a step 'on the grounds that the resignations would not be accepted and so nothing would be changed'.[131]

Deeply upset, Halder flew next day to Army Group Centre headquarters. The assembled commanders predictably backed his preference for resuming the offensive on Moscow. They were agreed that to move on Kiev would mean a winter campaign. Field-Marshal von Bock suggested that General Heinz Guderian, one of Hitler's favourite commanders, and particularly outspoken at the meeting, should accompany Halder to Führer Headquarters in an attempt to persuade the dictator to change his mind and agree to Army High Command's plan.

It was getting dark as Halder and Guderian arrived in East Prussia. According to Guderian's later account – naturally aimed at reflecting himself in the best light – Brauchitsch forbade him to raise the question of Moscow. The southern operation had been ordered, the Army Commander-in-Chief declared, so the problem was merely one of how to carry it out. Discussion was pointless. Neither Brauchitsch nor Halder accompanied Guderian when he went in to see Hitler, who was flanked by a large entourage including Keitel, Jodl, and Schmundt. Hitler himself raised the issue of Moscow, according to Guderian, and then, without interruption, let him unfold the arguments for making the advance on the Russian capital the priority. When Guderian had finished, Hitler started. Keeping his temper, he put the alternative case. The raw materials and agricultural base of the Ukraine were vital for the continuation of the war, he stated. The Crimea had to be neutralized to rule out attacks on the Romanian oil-fields from Soviet aircraft-carriers. 'My generals know nothing about the economic aspects of war,' Guderian heard him say for the first time. Hitler was adamant. He had already given strict orders for an attack on Kiev as the immediate strategic objective. Action had to be carried out with that in mind. All those present nodded at every sentence that Hitler spoke. The OKW representatives were entirely behind him. Guderian felt isolated. He avoided all further argument. He took the view, so he remarked much later, that since the decision to attack the Ukraine was confirmed, it was now his task to ensure that it was carried out as effectively as possible to ensure victory before the autumn rains.

When he reported to Halder next day, 24 August, the Chief of the Army General Staff fell into a rage at Guderian's complete volte-face on being confronted by Hitler at first hand.[132] Halder's dismay was all the greater since Guderian, whom he had considered as a possible future Army Commander-in-Chief, had been among the most vehement critics of Hitler during the meeting at Army Group Centre Headquarters the previous day.[133] Bock shared Halder's contempt for the way the outspoken and forthright Guderian had caved in under Hitler's pressure.[134] In reality, whatever the opprobrium now heaped on him by his superiors, there had been little prospect of Guderian changing Hitler's mind.[135] At any rate, the die was cast. The great battle for Kiev and mastery of the Ukraine was about to begin.

By the time the 'Battle of Kiev' was over on 25 September – the city of Kiev itself had fallen six days earlier – the Soviet south-west front was totally destroyed. Hitler's insistence on sending Guderian's Panzer Group south to bring about the encirclement had led to an extraordinary victory. An astonishing number of Soviet prisoners – around 665,000 – were taken. The enormous booty captured included 884 tanks and 3,018 artillery pieces.[136] The victory paved the way for Rundstedt to go on to occupy the Ukraine, much of the Crimea, and the Donets Basin, with further huge losses of men and material for the Red Army.[137] In the light of the immense scale of the Soviet losses in the three months since the beginning of 'Barbarossa', the German military leadership now concluded that the thrust to Moscow – given the name 'Operation Typhoon' – could still succeed despite starting so late in the year.[138]

It was scarcely any wonder, basking in the glow of the great victory at Kiev, that Hitler was in ebullient mood when Goebbels spoke alone with him in the Führer Headquarters on 23 September. Hitler's reported comments afford a notable insight into his thinking at this juncture. After bitterly complaining about the difficulties in getting his way with the 'experts' in the General Staff, Hitler expressed the view that the defeats imposed on the Red Army in the Ukraine marked the breakthrough. 'The spell is broken,' Goebbels recorded. Things would now unfold quickly on other parts of the front. New great victories could be expected in the next three to four weeks. By mid-October, the Bolsheviks would be in full retreat. The next thrust was towards Kharkov, which would be reached within days, then to Stalingrad and the Don. Once this industrial area was in German hands, and the Bolsheviks were cut off from their coal supplies and the basis of their armaments production, the war was lost for them.

Leningrad, birthplace of Bolshevism, Hitler repeated, would be destroyed street by street and razed to the ground. Its 5 million population could not be fed.[139] The plough would one day once more pass over the site of the city. Bolshevism began in hunger, blood, and tears. It would end the same way. Asia's entry-gate to Europe would be closed, the Asiatics forced back to where they belonged. A similar fate to Leningrad, he reiterated, might also befall Moscow. The attack on the capital would follow the capture of the industrial basin. The operation to surround the city should be completed by 15 October. And once German troops reached the Caucasus Stalin was lost. Hitler was sure that in such a situation, Japan would not miss the opportunity to make gains in the east of the Soviet Union. What then happened would be up to Stalin. He might capitulate. Or he might seek a 'special peace', which Hitler would naturally take up. With its military power broken, Bolshevism would represent no further danger. It could be driven back to Asia. It might retain extra-European imperialist ambitions, but that could be a matter of indifference to Germany.

He returned to a familiar theme. With the defeat of Bolshevism, England would have lost its last hope on the Continent. Its last chance of victory would disappear. And the increasing successes by U-boats in the Atlantic which would follow in the next weeks would put further pressure on a Churchill who was betraying signs of nervous strain.[140] Hitler did not rule out Britain removing Churchill in order to seek peace. Hitler's terms would be as they always were: he was prepared to leave the Empire alone, but Britain would have to get out of Europe. The British would probably grant Germany a free hand in the east, but try to retain hegemony in western Europe. That, he would not allow. 'England had always felt itself to be an insular power. It is alien to Europe, or even hostile to Europe. It has no future in Europe.'[141]

All in all, the prospects at this point, in Hitler's eyes, were rosy. One remark indicated, however, that an early end to the conflict was not in sight. Hitler told Goebbels in passing – his assumption would soon prove disastrously misplaced – that all necessary precautions had been made for wintering the troops in the east.[142]

By this time, in fact, Hitler and the Wehrmacht leaders had already arrived at the conclusion that the war in the East would not be over in 1941. The collapse of the Soviet Union, declared an OKW memorandum of 27 August, approved by Hitler, was the next and decisive war aim. But, the memorandum ran, 'if it proves impossible to realize this objective completely during 1941, the continuation of the eastern campaign has top priority for 1942'.[143] The military successes over the summer had been remarkable. But the aim of the quick knock-out blow at the heart of the 'Barbarossa' plan had not been realized. In spite of their vast losses, the Soviet forces had been far from comprehensively destroyed. They continued to be replenished from an apparently limitless reservoir of men and resources, and to fight tooth and nail in the proclaimed 'Great Patriotic War' against the aggressor. German losses were themselves not negligible. Already before the 'Battle of Kiev', casualties numbered almost 400,000, or over 11 per cent of the eastern army.[144] Replacements were becoming more difficult to find. By the end of September, half of the tanks were out of action or in different stages of repair.[145] And by now the autumn rains were already beginning to turn the roads into impassable quagmires. Whatever the successes of the summer, objective grounds for continued optimism had to be strongly qualified. The drive to Moscow that began on 2 October, seeking the decisive victory before the onset of winter, rested on hope more than expectation. It was a desperate last attempt to force the conclusive defeat of the Soviet Union before winter. It amounted to an improvisation marking the failure of the original 'Barbarossa' plan rather than its crowning glory.[146]

Hitler's own responsibility for the difficulties now faced by the German army is evident. Whereas Stalin learnt from the calamities of 1941 and came to leave military matters increasingly to the experts,[147] Hitler's interference in tactical detail as well as grand strategy, arising from his chronic and intensifying distrust of the Army High Command, was, as Halder's difficulties indicated, intensely damaging. The tenacity and stubbornness with which he refused to concede the priority of an attack on Moscow, even when for a while, at the end of July, not just the army leadership but his own closest military adviser, Jodl, had accepted the argument, was quite remarkable. After the glorious victories of 1940, Hitler believed his own military judgement was superior to that of any of his generals. His contempt for Brauchitsch and Halder was reinforced on every occasion that their views on tactics differed from his. Conversely, the weeks of conflict, and the bewildering way in July and August in which directives were arrived at, then amended, undermined the confidence in Hitler not just of the hopelessly supine Brauchitsch and of Halder's Army General Staff, but also of the field commanders.

But the problem was not one-sided. Certainly, as we have seen, the invasion of the Soviet Union was Hitler's own idea – and that at the height of the triumph in summer 1940. But far from dismissing the idea as illusory, vainglorious, or risky to a degree that courted outright disaster, the army's feasibility studies that summer had underwritten the proposition. The tension between the conflicting conceptions of the eastern campaign was still inwardly unresolved as far as Halder was concerned when Hitler's Directive No.21 was issued on 18 December 1940, indicating Moscow as a secondary rather than primary objective. The conflict of the coming summer months was prefigured in this unresolved contradiction even before the campaign had started. If reluctantly, Army High Command had apparently accepted the alternative strategy which Hitler favoured. Strategic planning of the attack in subsequent months followed from this premiss.

The strategy of first gaining control over the Baltic and cutting off essential Soviet economic heartlands in the south, while at the same time protecting German oil supplies in Romania, before attacking Moscow was not in itself senseless. And the fear that a frontal assault on Moscow would simply drive back instead of enveloping Soviet forces was a real one. Army High Command's preference to deviate from the plan of 'Barbarossa' once the campaign was under way was not a self-evident improvement. The reversion to Halder's originally preferred strategy was tempting because Army Group Centre had advanced faster and more spectacularly than anticipated, and was pressing hard to be allowed to continue and, as it thought, finish the job by taking Moscow. But even more it now followed from the realization that the army's intelligence on Soviet military strength had been woeful. The attack on Moscow, though favoured in the OKH's thinking from an early stage, had in fact come to be a substitute for the 'Barbarossa' plan, which had gone massively awry not simply because of Hitler's interference, but also because of the inadequacy and failures of the army leadership.

Since Hitler had placed the key men, Brauchitsch and Halder, in their posts, he must take a good deal of the blame for their failings. But as Commander in Chief of the Army, Brauchitsch was hopelessly weak and ineffectual. His contribution to strategic planning appears to have been minimal. Torn between pressures from his field commanders and bullying from Hitler, he offered a black hole where clear-sighted and determined military leadership was essential. Long before the crisis which would ultimately bring his removal from office, Brauchitsch was a broken reed. The contempt with which Hitler treated him was not without justification.

Halder, partly though his own post-war apologetics and his flirtations (though they came to nothing) with groups opposed to Hitler, has been more generously viewed by posterity. As Chief of the General Staff, responsibility for the planning of army operations was his. The chequered relations with the High Command of the Wehrmacht, in large measure Hitler's own mouthpiece, of course gravely weakened Halder's position. But the Chief of the General Staff failed to highlight difficulties in the original 'Barbarossa' plan. The northward swing of Army Group Centre forces was not fully worked out. The problems that motorized forces would face in the terrain between Leningrad and Moscow were not taken into account. Halder was lukewarm from the outset about the concentration on the Baltic and would have preferred the frontal assault on Moscow. But instead of being settled beforehand, the dispute, as we have noted, was left to fester once the campaign was under way.[148]

Moreover, the all-out attack on Moscow that Halder – and Commander of Army Group Centre Bock – were urging, would itself have been a highly risky venture. It would then almost certainly have been impossible to eliminate the large Soviet forces on the flanks (as happened in the 'Battle of Kiev'). And the Russians were expecting the attack on the capital. Had the Wehrmacht reached the city, in the absence of a Luftwaffe capable of razing Moscow to the ground (as Hitler wanted), the result would probably have been a preview of what was eventually to happen at Stalingrad. And even had the city been captured, the war would not have been won. A Soviet psychological, political, economic, and military collapse as a consequence would have been unlikely.[149]

Whatever the speculation on this, that the eastern campaign was blown off course already by late summer of 1941 cannot solely, or even mainly, be put down to Hitler's meddling in matters which should have been left to the military professionals. The implication, encountered in some post-war memoirs, that, left to their own devices, the military would have won the war in the east for Germany was both a self-defensive and an arrogant claim. The escalating problems of 'Barbarossa' were ultimately a consequence of the calamitous miscalculation that the Soviet Union would collapse like a pack of cards in the wake of a *Blitzkrieg* resting on some highly optimistic assumptions, gross underestimation of the enemy, and extremely limited resources.[150] This was Hitler's miscalculation. But it was shared by his military planners.

IV

While the tumultuous developments on the eastern front unfolded, the Reich was gradually turning into a Führer state with an absentee Führer. During the summer of 1940, Hitler had been away at his headquarters on the western front for approaching two months.[151] It had been no more than an interlude. But once the eastern campaign had started, and especially once it was realized that this was to be no repeated rapid military triumph, his absence became prolonged and then, in effect, permanent. Whereas Churchill was concerned to speak to the British people and let himself be seen as often as was practicable, Hitler practically disappeared from the public eye. During the remaining months of 1941, and with the popular mood in the Reich far from buoyant, he scarcely left his field headquarters to appear in public in Germany. Pressed by Goebbels to give a speech to rouse sagging morale, he deigned to spend six hours in Berlin on 3 October. A month later, on 8 November, he travelled to Munich, gave his customary address to the 'Old Fighters' of the Movement to commemorate the Putsch, spoke next day to the Reichs- and Gauleiter, and left immediately for the Wolf's Lair. And he attended on 21 November the funeral in Berlin of General Ernst Udet (the First World War flying-ace in charge of air armaments who had committed suicide after Göring had made him the scapegoat for the Luftwaffe's failures on the eastern front), returning six days later for the ceremony prolonging the Anti-Comintern Pact and using the occasion to receive a number of foreign dignitaries before departing again for his field headquarters in East Prussia after a stay of two days.[152]

Otherwise the German people saw him only in occasional newsreel clips, usually in the company of his generals. His continued absence in 1941 was the start of a process which, as the war progressed and final victory became a mirage, would transform the most notable populist leader of the twentieth century, the masterly demagogue whose power base had rested in no small measure on his unrivalled ability to play on the expectations and resentments of the people, into a remote and distant figure.

Hitler's increasing detachment meant an inevitable acceleration of the existing, strongly developed tendency towards the disintegration of any semblance of coordinated administration of the Reich. The stark figures for governmental legislation provide an indicator. Out of 445 pieces of legislation in 1941, only seventy-two laws, published Führer decrees, and ministerial decrees represented any semblance of inter-ministerial policy

formation. The remaining 373 decrees were produced by individual ministries without wider consultation.[153]

Bormann's appointment as head of the newly designated Party Chancellery in May 1941 accentuated rather than checked the trend. His proximity
to Hitler, bureaucratic energy, ideological commitment, and ruthless drive
certainly gave the Party new impetus and scope for intervention, after years
of leadership by the weak and ineffectual Rudolf Heß. Bormann saw his
role, in belonging 'to the closest staff of the Führer', as channelling selected
information to Hitler and 'continually informing the Reichsleiter, Gauleiter,
and heads of organizations of the decisions and opinions of the Führer'.[154]
Though, under the influence of events in the east, Bormann's leadership of
the Party now accentuated the ideological tone and radicalization of policy
on the home front, it brought no coordination of government. On the
contrary: the consequence in practice was to intensify still further intergovernmental conflict and heighten the unresolvable tension built into the
Nazi regime between the demands of bureaucratic administration and
the anti-bureaucratic pressures of an ideologically driven leadership of the
regime.[155]

Hitler's role remained, of course, pivotal. He was, as ever, the linchpin
of the system (if 'system' is an appropriate term for such an administrative
free-for-all) and the fount of ideological legitimation. He was also kept
informed, though in unsystematic and ill-balanced ways, of, frequently,
quite trivial as well as more important issues. But the insistence on retaining
all the overriding controls of every significant sphere of rule in his own
hands, coupled with his physical absence from the centre of government,
almost total preoccupation with the war effort, and complete distaste for
bureaucratic methods, meant an inescapable fragmentation of the machinery
of government and, accompanying it, an ever-intensifying radicalization of
the regime.

Hitler's ultimate gamble of war in the east to destroy Bolshevism with
one swift knock-out blow was also to put his own popularity at risk, and
with that the very focus of the regime's support. Hitler's immense popularity
had been attained during the 1930s through successes, beyond all else
through 'victories without bloodshed' that had brought territorial expansion
and returned national pride and strength to a humiliated country. Once war
had begun in 1939, the victories were quick, spectacular and, if not 'without
bloodshed', then nevertheless relatively painless for the German people. But
to retain the heights of popularity reached after the stunning victory over
France in 1940, Hitler needed to bring final victory. That had so far eluded

him. Sensitive as he was to the fickleness of popular support, and never forgetting how collapsing morale had given way to revolutionary fervour in 1917–18, he knew how much rested on the rapid and complete crushing of the Soviet Union. Victory in the east would produce the material base of lasting power and prosperity – endless bounty from the riches of the new territories to improve living standards at home, and limitless opportunities for upward mobility, wealth, and domination. Failure to deliver the knock-out blow would, by contrast, endanger the regime. It meant prolonged war – in its wake, increasing sacrifice and privation, suffering and misery, and with that in due course the conditions in which the regime's popularity and his own unique authority could be undermined.

Though Nazi loyalists welcomed the showdown with the arch-enemy, following the uneasy period of what they saw as an artificial and purely tactical pact, the initial reactions of the German people to the beginning of 'Barbarossa', unprepared as they were for the extension of the war in the east, were for the most part anxiety and dismay.[156] As we have already noted, the first 'special announcements' of the remarkable advance and military successes of the Wehrmacht had, as Goebbels realized, far from their desired effect. As the triumphalist communiqués of the Wehrmacht High Command continued to blare out of their radios, one bulletin after another reporting yet a further grandiose victory, proclaiming the total defeat or annihilation of the enemy, and announcing Stalin's deployment of his last reserves, hopes were raised of an early end to the conflict. (They were encouraged by the tone of propaganda: Goebbels had told media representatives on 22 June that the war in the east would be over within eight weeks.[157]) Ardent Nazis were naturally jubilant, outright opponents depressed. But the deep anxieties and hopes of an early peace – a victorious one if at all possible, but above all an end to war – among the mass of the population could not for long be banished. And, however great the reported victories of the Wehrmacht were, no end seemed in sight. As the summer wore on, it was obvious that Stalin had far from used up his last reserves. Scepticism in the reports started to mount. Moreover, accounts of hard fighting, fierce resistance by the Red Army, and, especially, of 'horrible bestialities' and the 'inhumane way of fighting of the Bolsheviks' and 'criminal types' in the 'Jewish state', not unnaturally increased the worries, whatever the scale of the victories, of those with fathers, brothers, sons, and husbands at the front.[158]

A young soldier, just married and home on leave, left an indication in his diary of the mood after only two weeks of fighting when he attended a

Sunday morning service in his church: 'There were read out – in a quite matter-of-fact way – the name, year of birth, date and place of death of the dead and fallen, and precisely these cold facts had a doubly moving effect. The widows sobbed throughout the church . . .'[159] But such observations did not prevent approval of Nazi aims. The same soldier noted, a few days later, his approval of the antisemitic films *Jud Süß* and *Die Rothschilds*, remarking on how the Jewish banking family had been able through their money to determine the politics of Europe. And when, in early August, he watched newsreels of the fighting in the east, he commented on the 'demonic' manner of fighting of the Red Army – contemptuous of 'all rules of civility and humanity', 'truly Russian-Asiatic', as he put it.[160]

Attitudes towards the war – and the need to fight it – were divided. In stark contrast with the views of this soldier, the wishes of a farming community in northern Franconia, according to the outspoken report of the local Landrat, could scarcely have been more distant from the ideological aims of the Nazi leadership. There was in his area, he wrote, 'not the least understanding for the realization of plans for world domination . . . Overworked and exhausted men and women do not see why the war must be carried still further into Asia and Africa.'[161] At the end of August, the same Landrat wrote: 'I have only the one wish, that one of the officials in Berlin or Munich . . . should be in my office some time when, for example, a worn-out old peasant beseechingly requests allocation of labourers or other assistance, and as proof of his need shows two letters, in one of which the company commander of the elder son answers that leave for the harvest cannot be granted, and in the other of which the company commander of the younger son informs of his heroic death in an encounter near Propoiszk.'[162]

From the point of view of most ordinary Germans, the 'good times', as they remembered them from the 1930s, were over. Conditions of daily life were deteriorating sharply. The cause of this was, they saw, the war. What was needed was an end to war and return to 'normality', not yet another – unnecessary, as many people thought – extension of the conflict, and now against the most implacable and dangerous enemy. Daily concerns dominated the mood, alongside fears for loved ones at the front. Reports from cities highlighted the 'catastrophic state of provisions' and anger at food shortages and high prices. Industrial workers were becoming increasingly alienated by working conditions and wage levels. The 'little man' was again the stupid one, the SD from Stuttgart reported as a commonly held view. He was having to work hard at great sacrifice, as had always been the case, to benefit the 'big noises (*Bonzen*), plutocrats, toffee-nosed (*Standesdünkel*),

and war-profiteers'. 'What does national community mean here?' was plain-
tively asked.[163] In the Alpine reaches of southern Bavaria, the mood was
'bad and tired of war', dominated by the 'constantly mounting great and
small worries of everyday life', and – it was somewhat theatrically claimed
– comparable with that of 1917.[164]

On top of this came new worries. It was while the ferocious warfare was
raging on the eastern front that, within the Reich, the Nazi regime's renewed
assault on Christianity, which had begun in early 1941, reached its climax.
At the same time, the disturbing rumours – which over the previous year
had spread like wildfire – about the killing of mentally sick patients taking
place in asylums were causing intensified disquiet. Elimination of 'life not
worth living' had an increasingly threatening ring to it, potentially for every
family, as psychologically scarred as well as physically badly injured young
soldiers in ever larger numbers were brought back from the front and housed
in hospitals, sanatoria, and asylums throughout the Reich.

Despite Hitler's own repeatedly expressed wish for calm in relations with
the Churches as long as the war lasted – the reckoning with Christianity, in
his view, had to wait for the final victory – a wave of anti-Church agitation,
accompanied by an array of new measures, had taken place during the first
half of 1941. The activism appears in the main to have come from below,
as anti-Church radicals exploited wartime needs to try to break the vexing
hold – strengthened by the anxieties of the war itself – which the Churches
continued to have on the population. But it certainly had encouragement
from above, particularly through Bormann and the Party Chancellery. In a
confidential circular to all Gauleiter in June 1941, Bormann had expressly
declared that Christianity and National Socialism were incompatible. The
Party must struggle, therefore, to break the Church's power and influence.[165]
Whether this represented Hitler's wishes, given his essential stance on
relations with the Churches during the war, is extremely doubtful. On the
other hand, Bormann never acted directly contrary to what Hitler wanted.
Most probably, he misinterpreted on this occasion Hitler's repeated rantings
about the malevolent influence of Christianity and sent the wrong signals
to Party activists.[166]

By the time Bormann wrote his circular, antagonism among churchgoers
had already intensified through bans on Church publications, the replacement of Catholic nuns by 'brown sisters' from the Nazi welfare organization
(the Nationalsozialistische Volkswohlfahrt, or NSV), the shifting of celebrations of feast days from weekdays to the nearest Sunday, and attempts to
abolish school prayers. Rumours spread that baptism of children would

soon no longer be allowed, and that priests would be turned out of their presbyteries. In some localities, the closure of monasteries, eviction of the monks, and sequestration of monastic property to accommodate refugees or provide space for Party offices caused immense anger.[167]

A highpoint of popular unrest provoked by Nazi attacks on the Church occurred in predominantly Catholic Bavaria in the summer of 1941. The Gauleiter of the 'Traditional Gau' of Munich and Upper Bavaria, one of Hitler's oldest allies, Adolf Wagner, acting in his capacity as Education Minister, had ordered in April the removal of crucifixes from Bavarian schoolrooms. Whether, as was later claimed, he was trying 'to give visible effect to the teaching handed down by Reichsleiter Bormann, that National Socialism and Christianity are irreconcilable opposites', or whether he was acting on his own initiative cannot be established.[168] Wagner's order went out several weeks before Bormann's circular, which cannot, therefore, have provoked the 'action'. But Wagner probably read the signals coming from Party headquarters earlier in the year and acted – without apparently any consultation in Bavaria itself – to give direct meaning to the anti-Church drive in his own province, where the power of Catholicism was a thorn in the side of the Party, by attacking the very symbol of Christianity itself.

The result, in any case, was to stir up a torrent of embittered protest, articulated above all by mothers of schoolchildren. Their letters to loved ones at the front were read by soldiers incredulous at what the 'Bolsheviks in the homeland' were doing, and threatened to have a damaging effect on the troops' morale. Mass meetings in village halls, refusal to send children to school, collection of signatures on petitions, and public demonstrations by angry mothers meant that the matter could not be ignored. One petition, accompanied by a signed list containing 2,331 names, ran: 'The sons of our town stand in the east in the struggle against Bolshevism. Many are giving their lives in the cause. We cannot understand that particularly in this hard time people want to take the cross out of the schools.'[169] Wagner was forced to revoke his earlier order. But things had become so chaotic that Party functionaries in some areas only then started actually removing the cruci-fixes. It was autumn before the heat generated wholly unnecessarily by the issue gradually subsided. The damage done to the standing of the Party in such regions was immeasurable and irreparable.[170]

Hitler did not escape the wrath of Bavarian Catholics. Farmers in some areas removed his picture from their houses. 'Rather Wilhelm by the grace of God than the idiot of Berchtesgaden (*Lieber Wilhelm von Gottes Gnaden als den Depp von Berchtesgaden*)' was a sentiment registered in Munich.[171]

But the Führer myth – of his ignorance of actions carried out behind his back by his underlings – was still strong, if not wholly unscathed. 'The Führer doesn't want this, and certainly knows nothing of this removal of the crosses,' shouted one woman during a demonstration.[172] 'You wear brown shirts on top, but inside you're Bolsheviks and Jews. Otherwise you wouldn't be able to carry on behind the Führer's back,' ran an anonymous letter traced to a woman in the Berchtesgaden area.[173] As such remarks indicate, the strength of feeling on the Crucifix issue was entirely compatible with support for Hitler, and for the 'crusade against godless Bolshevism', which Catholic Bishops themselves had applauded.[174] But the Crucifix issue, though confined to one part of Germany, had cast momentary light on the increasing fragility of backing for Party and regime as the inevitable radicalization and lack of coordinated, pragmatic policy intensified. Aggression turned outwards, as long as it was painless and successful, was largely unobjectionable, it seems. But as soon as aggression was directed inwards, at widely held traditional belief systems as opposed to unloved but harmless minorities, it was a different matter altogether. The 'total claim' made by Nazism, its intolerance towards any institutional framework the Movement did not control, and the inbuilt 'cumulative radicalization' of the system meant, therefore, an inexorable trend towards greater, not less, social conflict.[175]

This now emerged in an issue at the very heart of the regime's ideology as, in midsummer 1941, serious disquiet over the 'euthanasia action' came out into the open. All too credible rumours about the killing of asylum patients had been circulating since summer 1940. Taking place in selected asylums within Germany, in close reach of major centres of population, it had been impossible to keep the 'action' as close a secret as had been intended. Those in the immediate vicinity saw the grey buses arrive, the patients unload and enter the asylum, the crematorium chimneys continually smoking.[176] Occasionally, as at Absberg in Franconia in February 1941, there had been public demonstrations of sympathy for the victims as they were loaded on to the buses to take them to what everyone knew was a certain death.[177] The secrecy, and absence of any public statement, let alone law, authorizing what was known to be happening, stoked the fires of alarm. Protest letters landed in the Reich Chancellery and the Reich Justice Ministry. Some were even from dyed-in-the-wool National Socialists.[178] Others, on occasion not mincing words, were from prominent churchmen.[179] But the churchmen up to this point had kept their protests confidential. On 7 July a pastoral letter from German bishops was read out in Catholic churches, declaring that it was wrong to kill except in war or for self-defence.[180] But this veiled attempt to criticize the 'euthanasia action' left no obvious mark. The death-mills stayed working.

Then, on 3 August 1941, Bishop Clemens August Graf von Galen, the Catholic Bishop of Münster in Westphalia, referring to the pastoral letter, in a most courageous sermon in the St Lamberti Church in Münster, openly denounced in plain terms what was happening. Galen, deeply conservative, anti-liberal, and anti-socialist, had been thought in some Church circles in the 1930s even to be a Nazi sympathizer.[181] In June 1941, like some other Catholic bishops, he had welcomed the attack on the Soviet Union and offered his prayers for the 'successful defence against the Bolshevik threat to our people'.[182] But by July, as Münster suffered under a hail of British bombs, he delivered a series of sermons denouncing in the most forthright terms the Gestapo's suppression of religious orders in the city.[183]

On 14 July, a day after a sermon attacking the closure of the monasteries, Galen sent a telegram to the Reich Chancellery requesting Hitler to defend the people against the Gestapo. The following Sunday, 20 July, he read out the telegram in church. Two days later he wrote to Lammers with what could only be seen as a criticism of Hitler and his state. The Führer's involvement with foreign and military matters was such, Galen remarked, that he was not in a position to deal with all the petitions and complaints sent to him. 'Adolf Hitler is not a divine being, raised above every natural limitation, who is able to keep an eye on and direct everything at the same time. However, when as a result of this overloading with work of the responsible leader . . . the Gestapo shatters unrestrained the home front . . . then I know (I am called upon) . . . to raise my voice loudly.'[184]

Popular unrest at the closing of the monasteries was also brought to Hitler's attention by Lammers on 29 July while a protest by Bishop Franz Rudolf Bornewasser of Trier was being discussed. It seems likely that Galen's telegram, and the contents of his letter to Lammers, were referred to Hitler at the same time. Bishop Bornewasser's confidential protest had already linked the unrest over the closing of monasteries to the disquiet about the killing of 'unworthy life'. Galen now did the same – but in public. His fury over the dissolution of the monasteries lit the fuse for his open assault on the Nazi 'euthanasia programme'.[185]

In his sermon on 3 August, Bishop Galen again pilloried the Gestapo for its attacks on Catholic religious orders. Then he came to the 'euthanasia action'. 'There is a general suspicion verging on certainty,' the Bishop stated, 'that these numerous deaths of mentally ill people do not occur of themselves but are deliberately brought about, that the doctrine is being followed, according to which one may destroy so-called "worthless life", that is kill innocent people if one considers that their lives are of no further value for the nation and the state.' In emotional terms, Galen pointed out the implications. People who had become invalids through labour and war, and the soldier risking his life at the front, would all be at risk. 'Some commission can put us on the list of the "unproductive", who in their opinion have become worthless life. And no police force will protect us and no court will investigate our murder and give the murderer the punishment he deserves. Who will be able to trust his doctor any more? He may report his patient as "unproductive" and receive instructions to kill him. It is impossible to imagine the degree of moral depravity, of general mistrust that would then spread even through families if this dreadful doctrine is tolerated, accepted, and followed.'[186]

Even before Galen delivered his sermon, Hitler had been sufficiently concerned about morale and popular unrest at such a critical juncture of the war that he had issued orders to Gauleiter to cease until further notice all seizures of Church and monastic property. Under no circumstances were independent actions by Gauleiter permissible. Similar instructions went to the Gestapo.[187] According to Papen, Hitler attributed all the blame to the hotheads in the Party. He had told Bormann that the 'nonsense' had to stop, and that he would tolerate no conflict, given the internal situation.[188] It was simply a tactical move. Hitler sympathized with the radicals, but acted pragmatically.[189] As his comments a few months later made plain, he fully approved of the closure of the monasteries.[190] Only the need for peace in relations with the Churches to avoid deteriorating morale on the home front determined his stance. Events in the Warthegau (where by 1941 94 per cent of churches and chapels in the Posen-Gnesen diocese were closed, 11 per cent of the clergy murdered, and most of the remainder thrust into prisons and concentration camps) showed the face of the future.[191] A victorious end to the war would unquestionably have brought a renewed, even more savage onslaught on the Churches. But in the context of such widespread unrest, Hitler had to take seriously the impact of Galen's sermon on the killing of asylum patients, a copy of which had been brought to him by Lammers.[192] Moreover, with that sermon, reproduced in thousands of clandestine copies and circulated from hand to hand, the secrecy surrounding the 'euthanasia action' had been broken.[193]

The Nazi leadership realized that it was helpless in the circumstances to take strong action against Galen. It was suggested to Bormann that Galen should be hanged. Bormann answered that, while the death penalty was certainly warranted, 'considering the war circumstances the Führer would scarcely decree this measure'. Goebbels acknowledged that if anything were undertaken against the Bishop, support from the population of Münster and Westphalia could be written off during the war.[194] He hoped that a favourable turn in the eastern campaign would provide the opportunity to deal with him.[195] Not surprisingly, since he was aware of Hitler's concern about the decline in morale in the wake of the Church conflict, Goebbels spoke against arousing public discussion over 'euthanasia' at precisely that time. 'Such a debate,' noted Goebbels, 'would only inflame feelings anew. In a critical period of the war, that is extraordinarily inexpedient. All inflammatory matters should be kept away from the people at present. People are so occupied with the problems of the war that other problems only arouse and irritate them.'[196] Goebbels's comments on popular opinion during his visit to Führer Headquarters on 18 August must have reinforced Hitler's view that the time had come to calm the unrest at home. On 24 August, Hitler stopped the T4 'euthanasia action' as secretly as he had started it two years earlier.[197]

On the very same day, Hitler, through an internal Party circular, ordered replacement buildings for damaged hospitals in areas threatened by bombing raids to be constructed. The barrack-like prefabricated constructions were to be attached to asylums and nursing homes, which were to have their existing patients relocated in order to make room for air-raid victims. The costs of the removal of the patients were to be borne by the 'Community Patients Transport Service' – precisely the same organization, run by the Chancellery of the Führer, whose buses had carried the asylum inmates to their deaths in the 'euthanasia' centres. Specifically acknowledging the disquiet which this would cause, the order – signed by none other than Hitler's doctor, Karl Brandt, who along with Bouhler had been authorized in autumn 1939 to carry out the 'euthanasia action' – stated that relatives would be informed in advance about the destination of the patients, and would be able to visit them there. The press would undertake a propaganda campaign to explain what was happening and prevent rumours spreading.[198]

In his sermon of 3 August, Bishop Galen had cleverly brought the 'euthanasia action' into connection with the bombing-raids on Münster, which he hinted were a 'punishment of God' for the offences against the Commandment 'Thou shalt not kill.' Galen's sermon had linked the three areas – attacks on the Church, 'euthanasia', and bombing-raids on German cities – in which alienation of the population from the regime, and the consequent threat to morale, was greatest. The population of the industrial belt of Westphalia were bearing the brunt of the raids. As SD reports pointed out, morale in the area was suffering accordingly. At the same time the attacks on the monasteries and religious orders in the area had reached their high point. And this was at precisely the juncture when the patients from the Westphalian asylums were being deported to the 'euthanasia' killing-centres. Any attempt to provide emergency hospitals for the victims of the air-raids, to combat the effect on morale, had to make use of the spare capacity of the asylums. But this could only be attained by removing the patients. And this would immediately give rise to further unrest. It was in the grip of this strait-jacket that Hitler bowed to the pressure created by Galen's protest. His pragmatic solution, it seems, was to halt the T4 'Action' in order to be able to offer the hospital care for air-raid victims, and the accompanying assurances necessary to calm the unrest in Westphalia and restore morale.[199]

By the time of Hitler's 'halt order', the T4 'euthanasia action' had already killed more than the 70,000 victims foreseen at the outset of the 'programme'.[200] Bouhler had in fact boasted to Goebbels as early as January 1941 that 40,000 mentally sick patients had already been liquidated, and that there were another 60,000 still to be dealt with.[201] By the end of 1941, the number gassed, starved to death, or poisoned with lethal injections was nearer 100,000 than 70,000.[202] The 'halt order' ended the 'euthanasia programme' neither completely nor permanently. Tens of thousands of concentration-camp prisoners, ill or incapable of work, were, after selection by doctors, to perish in existing, or newly established, 'euthanasia'-centres by 1945.[203] As for the T4 personnel: new tasks were rapidly found for them. The experts in gassing techniques were, within a few weeks, already being redeployed to start the planning in Poland of a far larger mass-killing 'programme': the extermination of Europe's Jews.

V

In his lengthy talk with Hitler on 23 September, Goebbels took the opportunity to describe the state of morale within Germany. Hitler, remarked the Propaganda Minister, was well aware of the 'serious psychological test (*Belastungsprobe*)' to which the German people had been subjected over the past weeks. After the notable slide in morale, Goebbels pressed Hitler, who had not appeared in public since the start of the Russian campaign and had last spoken to the German people on 4 May, following the victorious Balkan campaign, to come to Berlin to address the nation. Hitler agreed that the time was ripe, and asked Goebbels to prepare a mass meeting to open the Winter Aid campaign at the end of the following week.[204] The date of the speech was fixed for 3 October. Even on the day before, Goebbels had a struggle with Führer Headquarters to establish that Hitler would, indeed, be coming to Berlin to speak in the Sportpalast. Only in the evening did Hitler finally confirm his appearance. Goebbels was now at last able to make the preparations. That day, 2 October, 'Operation Typhoon', the great offensive against Moscow, had been launched.[205] The early news from the front was good. The scene for the speech could not have been better, thought Goebbels. He hoped the Führer would be in good form. 'The impression of his address in Germany and in the entire world will then, after a six-month period of silence, be an immense one.'[206]

In his proclamation to the soldiers on the Eastern Front at the start of 'Operation Typhoon', Hitler described Bolshevism as essentially similar to the worst kind of capitalism in the poverty it produced, stressing that 'the bearers of this system are also in both cases the same: Jews and only Jews!'[207] Now was the last push before winter to deliver the enemy 'the deadly thrust'.[208] Similar sentiments were to dominate his address to the nation.

Around 1p.m. next day, Hitler's train pulled into Berlin. Goebbels was immediately summoned to the Reich Chancellery. He found Hitler looking well and full of optimism. In the privacy of Hitler's room, he was given an overview of the situation at the front. The advance was proceeding better than expected. Big successes were being attained. 'The Führer is convinced,' commented Goebbels, 'that if the weather stays moderately favourable the Soviet army will be essentially smashed within fourteen days.'[209] Through the proclamation, every soldier knew what was at stake: annihilating the Bolshevik army before the onset of winter; or getting stuck half-way and having to put off the decision until the following year. Hitler was of the opinion that the worst of the war would be over if the attack succeeded: 'for what will we gain in new armaments and economic potential from the industrial areas lying before us! We have already conquered so many sources of oil that the oil which the Soviet Union had promised to us on the basis of earlier economic treaties now flows to us from our own production.'[210] The USA were in no position to affect the course of the war. Once Germany had the decisive Russian agricultural and industrial areas in its possession, 'we will be fairly independent and can cut off the English imports through our U-Boats and Luftwaffe'.[211] Hitler was in no mood for compromises. He thought it necessary to come to a clear decision with Britain, since otherwise the 'bloody showdown would have to be repeated in a few years'. He did not think it likely that Stalin would capitulate, though he could not rule it out.[212] He also thought the 'London plutocracy' would continue to wage tough resistance. But his view was 'that everything that happens is on the whole the product of fate'. It was good, in retrospect, that none of the peace feelers since 1939 involving Poland, France, and Britain had come to anything. 'The most cardinal problems would then have still remained unsolved, and would doubtless sooner or later have again led to war. Another military force besides ours must never exist in Europe.'[213]

Cheering crowds, which the Party never had any trouble in mobilizing, lined the streets as Hitler was driven in the afternoon to the Sportpalast. A rapturous reception awaited him in the cavernous hall.[214] Goebbels compared it with the mass meetings in the run-up to power.[215] The first part of Hitler's speech was spent in blaming the war on Britain's warmongering clique, backed by international Jewry.[216] He went on to justify the attack on the Soviet Union as preventive. He said German precautions had been incomplete on only one thing: 'We had no idea how gigantic the preparations of this enemy were against Germany and Europe, and how immense the danger was, how by a hair's breadth we have escaped the annihilation not only of Germany, but of the whole of Europe.' He described the threat as 'a second Mongol storm of a new Gengis Khan'. But, he claimed, at last coming out with the words that his audience were anxious to hear: 'I can say today that this enemy is already broken and will not rise up again.'[217]

He went on, to the delight of his audience, to pour scorn on British propaganda and heap praise both on the Wehrmacht and on the efforts of the home front. Almost every sentence towards the end was interrupted by storms of applause. Hitler, despite the lengthy break, had not lost his touch. The audience in the Sportpalast rose as one in an ecstatic ovation at the end.[218] Hitler was thrilled with his reception. The mood, he said, was just as it had been in the 'time of struggle' before 1933. And the cheering of the ordinary Berliners in the streets had 'not for a long time been so great and genuine'.[219] But he was in a hurry to get away. He was driven straight back to the station. By 7p.m., a mere six hours after he had arrived, he was on his way back to his headquarters in East Prussia.[220]

Goebbels had been with Hitler on the way to the station as the latest news came in from the front. The advance was going even better than expected.[221] The Führer had taken all factors into account, commented Goebbels. Realistically assessing all circumstances, he had reached the conclusion 'that victory can no longer be taken from us'.[222] Only the weather gave rise to concern. 'If the weather stays as it is at present,' the Propaganda Minister wrote, 'then we might hope that our wishes will be fulfilled.'[223]

The Russian weather was, however, predictable. It would, all too soon, turn wet. Within weeks, the rains would give way to arctic conditions. However optimistic Hitler appeared to be, his military leaders knew they were up against time.[224]

The early stages of the advance could, nonetheless, scarcely have gone better. Halder purred, soon after its start, that Operation Typhoon was 'making pleasing progress' and pursuing 'an absolutely classical course'.[225] The German army had thrown seventy-eight divisions, comprising almost 2 million men, and nearly 2,000 tanks, supported by a large proportion of the Luftwaffe, against Marshal Timoshenko's forces.[226] Once more, the Wehrmacht seemed invincible. Once more, vast numbers of prisoners – 673,000 of them – fell into German hands, along with immeasurable amounts of booty, this time in the great encirclements of the double battle of Brjansk and Viaz'ma in the first half of October.[227] It was hardly any wonder that the mood in the Führer Headquarters and among the military leadership was buoyant. Jodl thought the victory at Viaz'ma the most decisive day of the Russian war, comparable with Königgrätz.[228] Quartermaster Eduard Wagner imagined the Soviet Union to be on the verge of collapse. In a letter to his wife on 5 October, he wrote: 'At present the Moscow operation is under way. We have the impression that the last great collapse is imminent . . . Operational aims are set that would once have made one's hair stand on end. Eastwards of Moscow! Then, I estimate, the war will be largely over and perhaps there will then indeed be the collapse of the system. That'll take us on a good stretch in the war against England. Over and again, I'm amazed at the Führer's military judgement. He is intervening this time, one could say decisively, in the course of the operations, and up to now he has always been right.'[229]

On the evening of 8 October, Hitler spoke of the decisive turn in the military situation over the previous three days. Werner Koeppen, Rosenberg's liaison at Führer Headquarters, reported to his boss that 'the Russian army can essentially be seen as annihilated'.[230] Hitler's view – he would soon have to revise it drastically – was that Bolshevism was heading for ruin through lack of tank defences. [231] 'The rapid collapse of Russia would have a disastrous impact on England,' he asserted. Churchill had placed all his hopes in the Russian war-machine. 'Now that too is past.'[232]

Hitler had been in an unusually good mood at the meal table on the evening of 4 October, having just returned from a visit to Army High Command's headquarters to congratulate Brauchitsch on his sixtieth birthday. Not for the first time, he gazed into the future in the 'German East'. Within the next half-century, he foresaw 5 million farms settled there by former soldiers who would hold down the Continent through military force. He placed no value in colonies, he said, and could quickly come to terms with England on that score. Germany needed only a little colonial territory for coffee and tea plantations. Everything else it could produce on the Continent. Cameroon and a part of French Equatorial Africa or the Belgian Congo would suffice for Germany's needs. 'Our Mississippi must be the Volga, not the Niger,' he concluded.[233]

Next evening, after Himmler had regaled those round the dinner table with his impressions of Kiev, and how 80–90 per cent of the impoverished population there could be 'dispensed with', Hitler came round to the subject of German dialects. It started with his dislike of the Saxon accent and spread to a rejection of all German dialects. They made the learning of German for foreigners more difficult. And German now had to be made into the general form of communication in Europe.[234]

Hitler was still in expansive frame of mind when Reich Economics Minister Walther Funk visited him on 13 October. The eastern territories would mean the end of unemployment in Europe, he claimed. He envisaged river links from the Don and the Dnieper between the Black Sea and the Danube, bringing oil and grain to Germany. 'Europe – and not America – will be the land of unlimited possibilities.'[235]

Four days later, the presence of Fritz Todt prompted Hitler to an even more grandiose vision of new roads stretching through the conquered territories. Motorways would now run not just to the Crimea, but to the Caucasus, as well as more northerly areas. German cities would be established as administrative centres on the river crossings. Three million prisoners-of-war would be available to supply the labour for the next twenty years. German farmsteads would line the roads. 'The monotonous Asiatic-like steppe would soon offer a totally different appearance.' He now spoke of 10 million Germans, as well as settlers from Scandinavia, Holland, Flanders, and even America putting down roots there. The Slav population would 'have to vegetate further in their own dirt away from the big roads'. Knowing how to read the road-signs would be quite sufficient education. Those eating German bread today, he said, did not get worked up about the regaining of the East Elbian granaries with the sword in the twelfth century. 'Here in the east a similar process will repeat itself for a second time as in the conquest of America.' Hitler wished he were ten to fifteen years younger to experience what was going to happen.[236]

But by this time weather conditions alone meant the chances of Hitler's vision ever materializing were sharply diminishing. The weather was already bad. By mid-October, military operations had stalled as heavy rains swept over the front. Units were stranded. The vehicles of Army Group Centre were bogged down on impassable roads. Away from the choked roads, nothing could move. 'The Russians are impeding us far less than the wet and the mud,' commented Field-Marshal Bock.[237] Everywhere, it was a 'struggle with the mud'.[238] On top of that, there were serious shortages of fuel and munitions.[239]

There was also, not before time, concern now about winter provisions for the troops. Hitler directly asked Quartermaster-General Wagner, on a visit to Führer Headquarters, about this on 26 October. Wagner promised that Army Groups North and South would have a half of their necessary provisions by the end of the month but Army Group Centre, the largest of the three, would only have a third. Supplying the south was especially difficult since the Soviets had destroyed part of the railway track along the Sea of Azov.[240] A few days later, on 1 November, Hitler paid a visit to the headquarters of the Army High Command to look at the exhibition of winter clothing which Wagner had assembled. Once more the Quarter-master-General assured Hitler that provision of the troops with sufficient clothing was in hand. Hitler accepted the assurance.[241] When Wagner spoke to Goebbels, he gave the Propaganda Minister the impression that 'everything had been thought of and nothing forgotten'.[242]

In fact, Wagner appears to have become seriously concerned by this vital matter only with the rapid deterioration of the weather in mid-October, while Halder had been aware as early as August that the problem of transport of winter clothing and equipment to the eastern front could only be solved by the defeat of the Red Army before the worst of the weather set in.[243] Brauchitsch was still claiming, when he had lengthy talks with Goebbels on 1 November, that an advance to Stalingrad was possible before the snows arrived and that by the time the troops took up their winter quarters Moscow would be cut off.[244] By now this was wild optimism. Brauchitsch was forced to acknowledge the existing weather problems, the impassable roads, transport difficulties, and the concern about the winter provisioning of the troops.[245] In truth, whatever the unrealism of the Army and Wehrmacht High Commands about what was attainable in their view before the depths of winter, the last two weeks of October had had a highly sobering effect on the front-line commanders and the initial exaggerated hopes of the success of 'Operation Typhoon'.[246] By the end of the month the offensive of Army Group Centre's exhausted troops had ground temporarily to a halt.[247]

The impression which Hitler gave, however, in his traditional speech to the Party's old guard, assembled in the Löwenbräukeller in Munich on the late afternoon of 8 November, the anniversary of the 1923 Putsch, was quite different.[248] The speech was intended primarily for domestic consumption.[249] It aimed to boost morale, and to rally round the oldest and most loyal members of Hitler's retinue after the difficult months of summer and autumn. Hitler paraded once more before his audience the victories in earlier campaigns and why he had felt compelled to attack the Soviet Union. He went on to describe the scale of the Soviet losses. 'My Party Comrades,' he declared, 'no army in the world, including the Russian, recovers from those.'[250] 'Never before,' he went on, 'has a giant empire been smashed and struck down in a shorter time than Soviet Russia.'[251] He remarked on enemy claims that the war would last into 1942. 'It can last as long as it wants,' he retorted. 'The last battalion in this field will be a German one.'[252] Despite the triumphalism, it was the strongest hint yet that the war was far from over.

The next day, after the usual ceremony at the 'Temples of Honour' of the Putsch 'heroes' on the Königsplatz in Munich, Hitler addressed his Reichsleiter and Gauleiter. The speech was in effect an appeal for uncon-ditional loyalty to the very backbone of the Party, Hitler's essential hardcore body of diehard support. His way of doing this, as usual, was a mixture of veiled threat and pathos. Those who stepped out of line, showed themselves weak, or conspired against him would be ruthlessly dealt with, was the first part of his message. He referred to the dismissal (in the previous year) of Josef Wagner from his position as Gauleiter of Westphalia-South and of Silesia. Wagner's pro-Catholic sympathies (and those of his wife) were declared incompatible with the post of a Gauleiter. He had actually been the victim of inner-party intrigues. But the last straw for Hitler had been a letter from Frau Wagner (apparently with her husband's backing), forbid-ding their daughter to marry a non-Christian SS-man. Hitler spoke darkly of the conspiratorial behaviour of Wagner and former SA chief Captain Franz Pfeffer von Salomon – now lodged in a concentration camp.[253] Both were said to have had close relations with Rudolf Heß. Hitler stressed what a blow for him the Heß affair had been, and how thankful he was that British propaganda had missed the opportunity to portray the Deputy Führer as his ambassador carrying a peace-offer. Germany would have lost its allies as a result, Hitler imagined – something which even now stopped the blood in the veins.

He moved to pathos. There could never be any thought of capitulation. He would continue the war until it finished in victory. 'And should a serious crisis afflict the Fatherland,' he said with no sense of an apparent contradiction, 'he would be seen with the last division.'[254] To ensure the morale of the population, he placed his entire trust in the Party and his Reichsleiter and Gauleiter, 'who must now place themselves around him as a solemnly sworn body (*festverschworenes Korps*)'.[255] The Soviet Union he saw as already defeated, though it was impossible to predict how long resistance would last. He hoped to reach the goals intended before winter within four weeks. Then the troops could take up their winter quarters.

He ended with an appeal to have confidence, and to rejoice in the opportunity to take part in a struggle to shape Europe's future. Germany was in a position to counter the greatest efforts of the United States. And what the overthrow of the Soviet Union signified could still not be fully grasped. It would give Germany land of limitless horizons. 'This land, which we have conquered with the blood of German sons, will never be surrendered. Some time later millions of German peasant families will be settled here in order to carry the thrust of the Reich far to the east.'[256]

Shortly after his speech, Hitler was again on his way back to East Prussia, arriving back in the Wolf's Lair on the evening of the next day.[257] In the east, by this time, the snow was falling. Torrential rain had given way to ice and temperatures well below zero Fahrenheit. Even tanks were often unable to cope with ice-covered slopes. For the men, conditions were worsening by the day. There was already an acute shortage of warm clothing to protect them. Severe cases of frostbite were becoming widespread. The combat-strength of the infantry had sunk drastically.[258] Army Group Centre alone had lost by this time approaching 300,000 men, with replacements of little more than half that number available.[259]

It was at this point, on 13 November, that, at a top-level conference of Army Group Centre, in a temperature of −8 degrees Fahrenheit, Guderian's panzer army, as part of the orders for the renewed offensive, was assigned the objective of cutting off Moscow from its eastward communications by taking Gorki, 250 miles to the *east* of the Soviet capital.[260] The astonishing lack of realism in the army's orders derived from the perverse obstinacy with which the General Staff continued to persist in the view that the Red Army was on the point of collapse, and was greatly inferior to the Wehrmacht in fighting-power and leadership. Such views, despite all the evidence to the contrary, still prevailing with Halder (and, indeed, largely shared by the Commander-in-Chief of Army Group Centre, Bock), underlay the memorandum, presented by the General Staff on 7 November, for the second offensive.[261] The hopelessly optimistic goals laid down – the occupation of Maykop (a main source of oil from the Caucasus), Stalingrad, and Gorki were on the wish-list – were the work of Halder and his staff. There was no pressure by Hitler on Halder. In fact, quite the reverse: Halder pressed for acceptance of his operational goals. These corresponded in good measure with goals Hitler had foreseen as attainable only in the following year.[262] Had Hitler been more assertive at this stage in rejecting Halder's proposals, the disasters of the coming weeks might have been avoided. As it was, Hitler's uncertainty, hesitancy, and lack of clarity allowed Army High Command the scope for catastrophic errors of judgement.[263]

The opposition which Halder's plans encountered at the conference on 13 November then resulted in a restriction of the goals to a direct assault on Moscow. This was pushed through in full recognition of the insoluble logistical problems and immense dangers of an advance in near-arctic conditions without any possibility of securing supplies. Even the goal was not clear. The breach of Soviet communications to the east could not possibly be attained. Forward positions in the vicinity of Moscow were utterly exposed. Only the capture of the city itself, bringing – it was presumed – the collapse and capitulation of the Soviet regime and the end of the war, could justify the risk.[264] But with insufficient air-power to bomb the city into submission before the ground-troops arrived, entry into Moscow would have meant street-by-street fighting. With the forces available, and in the prevailing conditions, it is difficult to see how the German army could have proved victorious.

Nevertheless, in mid-November the drive on Moscow recommenced. Hitler was by now distinctly uneasy about the new offensive. On the evening of 25 November he expressed, according to the recollection of his Army Adjutant, Major Gerhard Engel, his 'great concern about the Russian winter and weather'. 'We started a month too late,' he went on, returning once more to the strategy he had always favoured. 'The ideal solution would be the fall of Leningrad, capture of the southern area, and then, in that event, a pincer attack on Moscow from south and north together with frontal assault. Then there would be the prospect of an eastern wall with military bases.' Hitler ended, characteristically, by remarking that time was 'his greatest nightmare'.[265]

A few days earlier, Hitler had been more outwardly optimistic in a three-hour conversation with Goebbels. The Propaganda Minister remarked on how well Hitler was looking – almost unscathed from the pressures of the war, he thought. At first the discussion ranged over the situation in North Africa, where Hitler was more pessimistic than Army High Command about holding the position, given the inability to transport sufficient troops and material to that front. He foresaw setbacks there, and advised Goebbels not to raise expectations of military success. But his eyes were so fixed on the east, Goebbels recorded, that he regarded events in North Africa as no more than 'peripheral', and unable to affect events on the Continent itself.[266] Hitler then turned to the eastern campaign. Once more he repeated his intention of destroying Leningrad and Moscow. 'If the weather stays favourable, he still wants to make the attempt to encircle Moscow and thereby abandon it to hunger and devastation.'[267]

Whether an advance to the Caucasus would prove successful depended on the weather. But the improvement in weather and road conditions – on the frozen surfaces, instead of mud – had at least allowed motorized units to operate again. The supplies problems were serious. But he remained confident that the troops would master the situation. Goebbels asked him if he still believed in victory. Typically, he answered that 'if he had believed in victory in 1918 when he lay without help as a half-blinded corporal in a Pomeranian military hospital, why should he not now believe in our victory when he controlled the strongest armed forces in the world and almost the whole of Europe was prostrate at his feet?' He played down the difficulties; they occurred in every war. 'World history was not made by weather,' he added.[268]

Three days later, Goebbels was telephoned from FHQ and told to be cautious in his propaganda about the exhibition of winter clothing for the troops. It was proving scarcely possible to transport the provisions to the front. In these circumstances, such an exhibition at home could stir up 'bad blood'.[269] The caution was justified. Within weeks, the start of an emergency winter-clothing collection in Germany would give the most obvious sign that propaganda reassurance about provisions for the troops had been misplaced. It pointed unmistakably to a serious failure in planning.[270]

On 29 November, with Hitler once again briefly in Berlin, Goebbels had a further chance to speak with him at length. Hitler appeared full of optimism and confidence, brimming with energy, in excellent health.[271] He professed still to be positive, despite the reversal in Rostov, where General Ewald von Kleist's panzer army had been forced back the previous day after initially taking the city.[272] Hitler now intended to withdraw sufficiently far from the city to allow massive air-raids which would bomb it to oblivion as a 'bloody example'. The Führer had never favoured, wrote Goebbels, taking any of the Soviet major cities. There were no practical advantages in it, and it simply left the problem of feeding the women and children. There was no doubt, Hitler went on, that the enemy had lost most of their great armaments centres. That, he claimed, had been the aim of the war, and had been largely achieved. He hoped to advance further on Moscow. But he acknowledged that a great encirclement was impossible at present. The weather uncertainty meant any attempt to advance a further 200 kilometres to the east, without secure supplies, would be madness. The front-line troops would be cut off and would have to be withdrawn with a great loss of prestige which, at the current time, could not be afforded. So the offensive had to take place on a smaller scale.[273] Hitler still expected Moscow to fall. When it did, there would be little left of it but ruins. In the following year, there would be an expansion of the offensive to the Caucasus to gain possession of Soviet oil supplies – or at least deny them to the Bolsheviks. The Crimea would be turned into a huge German settlement area for the best ethnic types, to be incorporated into the Reich territory as a Gau – named the 'Ostrogoth Gau' (*Ostgotengau*) as a reminder of the oldest Germanic traditions and the very origins of Germandom.[274]

Hitler was evidently by this time in his element, and allowing Goebbels a sight of the vision of German prosperity based on colonization and exploitation of the east that he had expounded many times to his entourage in the Wolf's Lair. He returned, as always, to the threat from the west. It was only a matter of when London would recognize the 'hopeless position of the plutocracies'.[275] He expressed confidence – in contrast to some of his comments only a few days later – that the troops were being provided with winter equipment. Once that was the case, the weather would determine how far the advance would go. 'What cannot be achieved now, will be achieved in the coming summer,' were Hitler's sentiments, according to Goebbels's notes. 'In any event, the Bolsheviks were to be driven back to Asia. European Russia must be won for Europe.' Hitler saw 1942 as difficult, but a far better situation developing in 1943. Foodstuffs and raw materials were now available from the occupied European parts of the Soviet Union. Once the exploitation of the area was properly organized, 'our victory can no longer be endangered'.[276]

Hitler's show of optimism was put on to delude Goebbels – or himself. On the very same day that he spoke with the Propaganda Minister, he was told by Walter Rohland – in charge of tank production and just back from a visit to the front – in the presence of Keitel, Jodl, Brauchitsch, Leeb, and other military leaders, of the superiority of the Soviet panzer production. Rohland also warned, in the light of his own experience gleaned from a trip to the USA in 1930, of the immense armaments potential which would be ranged against Germany should America enter the war. The war would then be lost for Germany.[277] Fritz Todt, one of Hitler's most trusted and gifted ministers, who had arranged the meeting about armaments, followed up Rohland's comments with a statement on German armaments production. Whether in the meeting, or more privately afterwards, Todt added: 'This war can no longer be won militarily.' Hitler listened without interruption, then asked: 'How, then, should I end this war?' Todt replied that the war could only be concluded politically. Hitler retorted: 'I can scarcely still see a way of coming politically to an end.'[278]

As Hitler was returning to East Prussia on the evening of 29 November, the news coming in from the front was not good.[279] Over the next days things were to worsen markedly.

Immediately on his return to the Wolf's Lair, Hitler fell into 'a state of extreme agitation' about the position of Kleist's panzer army, thrown back from Rostov. Kleist wanted to move back to a secure defensive position at the mouth of the Bakhmut river. Hitler forbade this and demanded the retreat be halted further east. Brauchitsch was summoned to Führer Headquarters and subjected to a torrent of abuse. Browbeaten, the Commander-in-Chief, an ill and severely depressed man, passed on the order to the Commander of Army Group South, Field-Marshal von Rundstedt. The reply came from Rundstedt, evidently not realizing that the order had come from Hitler himself, that he could not obey it, and that either the order must be changed or he be relieved of his post.[280] This reply was passed directly to Hitler. In the early hours of the following morning, Rundstedt, one of Hitler's most outstanding and loyal generals, was sacked – the scapegoat for the setback at Rostov – and the command given to Field-Marshal Walter von Reichenau.[281] Later that day, Reichenau telephoned to say the enemy had broken through the line ordered by Hitler and requested permission to retreat to the line Rundstedt had demanded. Hitler concurred.[282]

On 2 December, Hitler flew south to view Kleist's position for himself. He was put fully in the picture about the reports, which he had not seen, from the Army Group prior to the attack on Rostov. The outcome had been accurately forecast. He exonerated the Army Group and the panzer army from blame. But he did not reinstate Rundstedt.[283] That would have amounted to a public acceptance of his own error.

By that same date, 2 December, German troops, despite the atrocious weather, had advanced almost to Moscow. Reconnaissance troops reached a point only some twelve miles from the city centre.[284] But the offensive had become hopeless. In intense cold – the temperature outside Moscow on 4 December had dropped to −32 degrees Fahrenheit – and without adequate support, Guderian decided on the evening of 5 December to pull back his troops to more secure defensive positions. Hoepner's 4th Panzer Army and Reinhardt's 3rd, some twenty miles north of the Kremlin, were forced to do the same.[285] On 5 December, the same day that the German offensive irredeemably broke down, the Soviet counter-attack began. By the following day, 100 divisions along a 200-mile stretch of the front fell upon the exhausted soldiers of Army Group Centre.[286]

VI

Amid the deepening gloom in the Führer Headquarters over events in the east, the best news Hitler could have wished for arrived. Reports came in during the evening of Sunday, 7 December that the Japanese had attacked the American fleet anchored at Pearl Harbor in Hawaii.[287] Early accounts indicated that two battleships and an aircraft carrier had been sunk, and four others and four cruisers severely damaged.[288] The following morning President Roosevelt received the backing of the US Congress to declare war on Japan.[289] Winston Churchill, overjoyed now to have the Americans 'in the same boat' (as Roosevelt had put it to him), had no difficulty in obtaining authorization from the War Cabinet for an immediate British declaration of war.[290]

Hitler thought he had good reason to be delighted. 'We can't lose the war at all,' he exclaimed. 'We now have an ally which has never been conquered in 3,000 years.'[291]

This rash assumption was predicated on the view which Hitler had long held: that Japan's intervention would both tie the United States down in the Pacific theatre, and seriously weaken Britain through an assault on its possessions in the Far East.[292] Goebbels echoed the expectations: 'Through the outbreak of war between Japan and the USA, a complete shift in the general world picture has taken place. The United States will scarcely now be in a position to transport worthwhile material to England let alone the Soviet Union.'[293]

Relations between Japan and the USA had been sharply deteriorating throughout the autumn. With the collapse of any *rapprochement* by mid-October over the loosening of the economic sanctions which were biting hard in Japan, the government of Prince Konoye had resigned and been replaced by an administration headed by General Tojo.[294] Since then, the hardliners and warmongers in the military had been increasingly in the ascendant. Early in November they had fixed a deadline for agreement with the Americans. If none could be reached, they had stipulated, there would be war.[295] Though kept in the dark about details, the German Ambassador in Tokyo, General Eugen Ott, informed Berlin early in November of his impressions that war between Japan and the USA and Britain was likely. He had also learned that the Japanese administration was about to ask for an assurance that Germany would go to Japan's aid in the event of her becoming engaged in war with the USA.[296] Such information doubtless lay behind Hitler's optimism, when speaking to Goebbels in the middle of the month, that Japan would 'actively enter the war in the foreseeable future'.[297]

The Japanese leadership had, in fact, taken the decision on 12 November that, should war with the USA become inevitable, an attempt would be made to reach agreement with Germany on participation in the war against America, and on a commitment to avoid a separate peace. Any insistence by Germany on Japan's involvement in the war against the Soviet Union would be met with the response that Japan did not intend to intervene for the time being. Should Germany then delay her entry into the war against the USA, this would have to be taken on board.[298]

On 21 November Ribbentrop had laid down the Reich's policy to Ott: Berlin regarded it as self-evident that if either country, Germany or Japan, found itself at war with the USA, the other country would not sign a separate peace.[299] Two days later, General Okamoto, the head of the section of the Japanese General Staff dealing with foreign armies, went a stage further. He asked Ambassador Ott whether Germany would regard itself as at war with the USA if Japan were to open hostilities.[300] There is no record of Ribbentrop's replying to Ott's telegram, which arrived on 24 November. But when he met Ambassador Oshima in Berlin on the evening of 28 November, Ribbentrop assured him that Germany would come to Japan's aid if she were to be at war with the USA. And there was no possibility of a separate peace between Germany and the USA under any circumstances. The Führer was determined on this point.[301]

For the Japanese, little depended on the agreement with Germany. Already two days before Ribbentrop met Oshima, Japanese air and naval forces had set out for Hawaii. And on 1 December, the order had been given to attack on the 7th.[302]

Ribbentrop's assurances were fully in line with Hitler's remarks during Matsuoka's visit to Berlin in the spring, that Germany would immediately draw the consequences should Japan get into conflict with the USA.[303] But at this point, before entering any formal agreement with the Japanese, Ribbentrop evidently deemed it necessary to consult Hitler. He told Oshima this on the evening of 1 December.[304] The next day, Hitler flew, as we have seen, to visit Army Group South following the setback at Rostov. Bad weather forced him to stay overnight in Poltava on the way back, where he was apparently cut off from communications. He was able to return to his headquarters only on 4 December.[305] Ribbentrop reached him there and gained approval for what amounted to a new tripartite pact – which the German Foreign Minister rapidly agreed with Ciano – stipulating that should war break out between any one of the partners and the USA, the other two states would immediately regard themselves as also at war with America.[306] Already before Pearl Harbor, therefore, Germany had effectively committed itself to war with the USA should Japan – as now seemed inevitable – become involved in hostilities.

The agreement, which had inserted the mutual pledge and not just left a one-sided commitment, was still unsigned when the Japanese attacked Pearl Harbor. This unprovoked Japanese aggression gave Hitler what he wanted without having already committed himself formally to any action from the German side. However, he was keen to have a revised agreement – completed on 11 December, and now stipulating only an obligation not to conclude an armistice or peace treaty with the USA without mutual consent – for propaganda reasons: to include in his big speech to the Reichstag that afternoon.[307]

The idea of a speech to the Reichstag in mid-December, giving an account of the war-year 1941, had been in Hitler's mind for some weeks. He had spoken to Goebbels about it as early as 21 November.[308] Immediately following Pearl Harbor, he decided to make a declaration of war on the USA the high-point of his long-planned speech. As soon as he heard the news of the Japanese attack, he telephoned Goebbels, expressing his delight, and ordering the summoning of the Reichstag for Wednesday, 10 December, 'to make the German stance clear'. Goebbels commented: 'We will, on the basis of the Tripartite Pact, probably not avoid a declaration of war on the United States. But that's now not so bad. We're now to a certain extent protected on the flanks. The United States will no longer be so rashly able to provide England with aircraft, weapons, and transport-space, since it can be presumed that they will need all that for their own war with Japan.'[309]

From a propaganda point of view, the Japanese attack at Pearl Harbor was most timely for Hitler. Given the crisis on the eastern front, he had little of a positive nature to include in a progress-report to the German people. No further mention had, in fact, been made of a speech to the Reichstag since he had himself originally raised the prospect weeks earlier. With nothing but setbacks and a prolonged war, contrary to all promises, to account for, he would almost certainly have wished to avoid a speech. But now the Japanese attack gave him a positive angle. On 8 December, Ribbentrop told Ambassador Oshima that the Führer was contemplating the best way, from the psychological point of view, of declaring war on the United States.[310] Since he wanted time to prepare carefully such an important speech, Hitler had the assembling of the Reichstag postponed from 10 December, the date he had originally stipulated, to the next day, despite Japanese pressure for an earlier date.[311] At least, Goebbels remarked, the time of the speech, three o'clock in the afternoon, though scarcely good for the German public, would allow the Japanese and Americans to hear it.[312]

On the morning of 9 December, Hitler's train pulled in at the Anhalter Bahnhof in Berlin.[313] He told Goebbels, who saw him at midday, of his suprise and initial incredulity at the attack on Pearl Harbor, though he had always expected that Japan would be forced to act before long if she did not want to give up her claim to world-power status.[314] 'The Führer is beaming again with optimism and confidence in victory,' Goebbels remarked. 'It is good, after so many days when we've had to digest unpleasant news, to come into direct contact with him again.'[315] Hitler still had to prepare his speech. He gave Goebbels a résumé of what he intended to say.[316] But when Goebbels saw him again the following lunchtime, 10 December, Hitler had still found no time, he said, to begin work on the speech.[317]

That Germany *would* declare war on the USA was, as we have seen, a matter of course. No agreement with the Japanese compelled it.[318] But Hitler did not hesitate. A formal declaration might have to wait until the Reichstag could be summoned. But at the earliest opportunity, on the night of 8–9 December, he had already given the order to U-boats to sink American ships.[319] A formal declaration of war was necessary to ensure as far as possible – in accordance with the agreement of 11 December – that Japan would remain in the war.[320] And it was also important, from Hitler's point of view, to retain the initiative, and not let this pass to the United States.

Certain, as he had been for many months, that Roosevelt was just looking for the chance to intervene in the European conflict, Hitler thought that his declaration was merely anticipating the inevitable and, in any case, formalizing what was in effect already the situation. Not least, for the German public, it was important to demonstrate that he still controlled events. To await a certain declaration of war from America would, from Hitler's standpoint, have been a sign of weakness.[321] Prestige and propaganda, as always, were never far from the centre of Hitler's considerations. 'A great power doesn't let itself have war declared on it, it declares war itself,' Ribbentrop – doubtless echoing Hitler's sentiments – told Weizsäcker.[322]

Hitler's speech on the afternoon of Thursday, 11 December, lasted one and a half hours.[323] It was not one of his best. The first half consisted of no more than the lengthy, triumphalist report on the progress of the war which Hitler had intended to provide long before the events of Pearl Harbor. There was some surprise at the figure of 160,000 German dead which Hitler gave; a far higher figure had been presumed.[324] (The figure matched, in fact, those available to the army leadership, though Hitler omitted to mention that total German losses, including wounded and more than 35,000 missing, were by this time over 750,000 men.)[325] The rest of the speech was largely taken up with a long-drawn-out, sustained attack on Roosevelt. Hitler built up the image of a President, backed by the 'entire satanic insidiousness' of the Jews, set on war and the destruction of Germany.[326] Eventually he came to the climax of his speech: the provocations – up to now unanswered – had finally forced Germany and Italy to act. He read out a version of the statement he had had given to the American Chargé d'Affaires that afternoon, with a formal declaration of war on the USA. He then read out the new agreement, signed that very day, committing Germany, Italy, and Japan to rejecting a unilateral armistice or peace with Britain or the USA.[327]

In Goebbels's view, Hitler's speech had had a 'fantastic' effect on the German people, to whom the declaration of war had come neither as a surprise, nor a shock.[328] In reality, the speech had been able to do little to raise morale which, given the certain extension of the war into the indefinite future, and now the opening of aggression against a further powerful adversary, had sunk to its lowest point since the conflict began.[329]

Goebbels was, in fact, not blind to the poor state of morale.[330] Hitler, for his part, had the capacity, as always, to convince not only himself, but those in his presence, that things were less bad than they seemed. Not only did he see Japan's entry into the war as a turning-point. He also continued to convey optimism about the eastern front, despite the depressing situation there. 'The Führer doesn't take too tragically the events in the theatre of the eastern campaign,' Goebbels recorded, after he had spoken to Hitler on 9 December.[331] Weather and supplies problems had compelled a need, already present, for a break to build up strength and resources for a spring offensive against the Soviet Union – in the south at the end of April, and in the centre in mid-May. This would be so carefully prepared that it would quickly lead to victory. By then the army would be completely ready, and would not have to tap its last reserves.

Hitler's ability to put a positive gloss even on a major setback allowed him even to see the onset of the bad weather in the east in the autumn as an advantage. Had the rainy weather not arrived when it did, he said, German troops would have pushed so far forward that the supplies problem could not have been solved. This showed 'how good fate is to us and how it prevents us through its own intervention from mistakes which without that we would doubtless have made'.[332] He acknowledged how necessary it had been to call off the offensive in order to give time for the exhausted troops to recuperate. And he admitted that there were at present no sufficient weapons to counter the heavy Russian panzers. Where they kept producing them from was a mystery, but 'currently the most serious concern of the front'. 'The Bolsheviks,' he went on, 'are for the most part comparable with animals; but animals, too, are sometimes unyielding (*standhaft*), and since the Soviet Union needs take no consideration of its own people, it is in a certain way superior to us.'[333] But Hitler concluded that the recent setbacks were only temporary ones, and that Germany's position, especially after the entry of the Japanese into the war, was so favourable that 'the conclusion of this mighty continental struggle was not in doubt'.[334]

The following day, Hitler was at least somewhat more realistic. He conceded that the situation in the east was 'at the moment not very good', and agreed with Goebbels's wishes to prepare the people for unavoidable setbacks through propaganda more attuned to the realism of the harshness of war and the sacrifices it demanded. Hitler and Goebbels evidently discussed the catastrophic lack of winter clothing for the troops, and the effect this was having on morale.[335] Goebbels was well aware from the bitter criticism in countless soldiers' letters to their loved ones of how bad the impact of the supplies crisis was on morale, both at the front and at home.[336] But Hitler's eyes were already set on the big spring offensive in 1942.[337] And, as always when faced with setbacks, he pointed to the 'struggle for power', and how difficulties had at that time been overcome.[338]

The need to boost morale, in the first instance among those he held responsible for upholding it on the home front, undoubtedly lay behind Hitler's address – the second in little over a month – to his Gauleiter on the afternoon of 12 December.

He began with the consequences of Pearl Harbor. If Japan had not entered the war, he would have at some point had to declare war on the USA. 'Now the East-Asia conflict falls to us like a present in the lap,' Goebbels reported him saying. The pyschological significance should not be underrated. Without the conflict between Japan and the USA, a declaration of war on the Americans would have been difficult to accept by the German people. As it was, it was taken as a matter of course. The extension to the conflict also had positive consequences for the U-boat war in the Atlantic. Freed of restraint, he expected the tonnage sunk now to increase greatly – and this would probably be decisive in winning the war. Aware of objections that the alliance with the Japanese stood opposed to 'the interests of the white man in East Asia', Hitler was frank, forthright, and pragmatic: 'Interests of the white race must at present give place to the interests of the German people. We are fighting for our life. What use is a fine theory if the basis of life (*Lebensboden*) is taken away? . . . In a life-and-death struggle, all means available to a people are right. We would ally ourselves with anyone if we could weaken the Anglo-Saxon position.'[339]

He turned to the war in the east. Both tone and content were much as they had been with Goebbels in private. He acknowledged that the troops had had for the time being to be pulled back to a defensible line, but, given the supplies problems, saw this as far better than standing some 300 kilometres further east. The troops were now being saved for the coming spring and summer offensive. A new panzer army in preparation within Germany would be ready by then. He also alluded to the difficulties in defending against the Russian tanks, but pointed out that a new anti-tank gun was well in preparation. He viewed the general situation very favourably. The North African campaign, he misleadingly stated, was well provided for, and an Allied landing on the Continent for the time being out of the question. The difficulties faced at present were determined by the elements (*naturbedingt*).[340]

It was his firm intention, he declared, in the following year to finish off (*erledigen*) Soviet Russia at least as far as the Urals. 'Then it would perhaps be possible to reach a point of stabilization in Europe through a sort of half-peace', by which he appeared to mean that Europe would exist as a self-sufficient, heavily armed fortress, leaving the remaining belligerent powers to fight it out in other theatres of war. An attack on the European

Continent, he claimed, would then be much less possible than at present. And given the progress made in German anti-aircraft weapons, he was 'extraordinarily sceptical' about the impact, which, he thought, would become ever more limited, of British air-raids. If this turned out to be the case, he claimed, Britain would be in a quandary.[341]

He outlined his vision of the future. His National Socialist conviction, he said, had become even stronger during the war. It was essential after the war was over to undertake a huge social programme embracing workers and farmers. The German people had deserved this. And it would provide – always the political reasoning behind the aim of material improvement – the 'most secure basis of our state system (*unseres staatlichen Gefüges*)'. The enormous housing programme he had in mind would, he stated openly, be made possible through cheap labour – through depressing wages. The work would be done by the forced labour of the defeated peoples. He pointed out that the prisoners-of-war were now being fully employed in the war economy. This was as it should be, he stated, and had been the case in antiquity, giving rise in the first place to slave labour. German war debts would doubtless be 200–300 billion Marks. These had to be covered through the work 'in the main of the people who had lost the war'. The cheap labour would allow houses to be built and sold at a substantial profit which would go towards paying off the war-debts within ten to fifteen years.[342]

Hitler put forward once more his vision of the east as Germany's 'future India', which would become within three or four generations 'absolutely German'.[343] There would, he made clear, be no place in this utopia for the Christian Churches. After the trouble of the summer, he had to take a line which both appeased the Party hotheads but also restrained their instincts. For the time being, he ordered slow progression in the 'Church Question'. 'But it is clear,' noted Goebbels, himself numbering among the most aggressive anti-Church radicals, 'that after the war it has to find a general solution ... There is, namely, an insoluble opposition between the Christian and a Germanic-heroic world-view.'[344]

Pressing engagements in Berlin – particularly the audience next day with Ambassador Oshima to award him the Great Golden Cross of the Order of the German Eagle – prevented Hitler from returning that evening, as he had intended, to the Wolf's Lair.[345] When he eventually reached his headquarters again, in the morning of 16 December, it was back to a reality starkly different from the rosy picture he had painted to his Gauleiter.[346] A potentially catastrophic military crisis was unfolding.

VII

Already before Hitler had left for Berlin, Field-Marshal von Bock had outlined the weakness of his Army Group against a concentrated attack, and stated the danger of serious defeat if no reserves were sent.[347] Then, while Hitler was in the Reich capital, as the Soviet counter-offensive penetrated German lines, driving a dangerous wedge between the 2nd and 4th Armies, Guderian reported the desperate position of his troops and a serious 'crisis in confidence' of the field commands.[348] After Schmundt had been sent to Army Group Centre on 14 December to discuss the situation at first hand, Hitler responded immediately, neither awaiting the report from Brauchitsch, who had accompanied Schmundt, nor involving Halder.[349] Colonel-General Friedrich Fromm, Commander of the Reserve Army, was summoned and asked for a report on the divisions that could be sent straight away to the eastern front. Göring and the head of the Wehrmacht transport, Lieutenant-General Rudolf Gercke, were told to arrange the transport.[350] Four and a half divisions of reserves, assembled throughout Germany at breakneck speed, were rushed to the haemorrhaging front. Another nine divisions were drummed up from the western front and the Balkans.[351] On 15 December Jodl passed on to Halder Hitler's order that there must be no retreat where the front could possibly be held. But where the position was untenable, and once preparations for an orderly withdrawal had been made, retreat to a more defensible line was permitted.[252] This matched the recommendations of Bock and of the man who would soon replace him as Commander of Army Group Centre, at this time still commanding the 4th Army, Field-Marshal Günther von Kluge.[353] That evening, Brauchitsch, deeply depressed, told Halder that he saw no way out for the army from its current position.[354] Hitler had by this time long since ceased listening to his broken Army Commander-in-Chief – by now, as Halder put it, 'scarcely any longer even a postman (kaum mehr Briefträger)' – and was dealing directly with his Army Group Commanders.[355]

Bock had, in fact, already recommended to Brauchitsch on 13 December that Hitler should make a decision on whether the Army Group Centre should stand fast and fight its ground, or retreat. In either eventuality, Bock had openly stated, there was the danger that the Army Group would collapse 'in ruins (in Trümmer)'. Bock advanced no firm recommendation. But he indicated the disadvantages of retreat: the discipline of the troops might give way, and the order to stand-fast at the new line be disobeyed.[356] The implication was plain. The retreat might turn into a rout. Bock's evaluation of the situation, remarkably, had not been passed on to Hitler at the time. He only received it on 16 December, when Bock told Schmundt what he had reported to Brauchitsch three days earlier.[357]

That night, Guderian, who two days earlier had struggled through a blizzard for twenty-two hours to meet Brauchitsch at Roslavl and put his case for a withdrawal, was telephoned on a crackly line by Hitler: there was to be no withdrawal; the line was to be held; replacements would be sent.[358] Army Group North was told the same day, 16 December, that it had to defend the front to the last man. Army Group South had also to hold the front and would be sent reserves from the Crimea after the imminent fall of Sevastopol. Army Group Centre was informed that extensive withdrawals could not be countenanced because of the wholesale loss of heavy weapons which would ensue. 'With personal commitment of the Commander, subordinate commanders, and officers, the troops were to be compelled to fanatical resistance in their positions without respect for the enemy breaking through on the flanks or rear.'[359]

Hitler's decision that there should be no retreat, conveyed to Brauchitsch and Halder in the night of 16–17 December, was his own. But it seems to have taken Bock's assessment as the justification for the high-risk tactic of no-retreat. His order stated: 'There can be no question of a withdrawal. Only in *some* places has there been deep penetration by the enemy. Setting up rear positions is fantasy. The front is suffering from one thing only: the enemy has more soldiers. It doesn't have more artillery. It's much worse than we are.'[360]

On 13 December, Field-Marshal von Bock had submitted to Brauchitsch his request to be relieved of his command, since, so he claimed, he had not overcome the consequences of his earlier illness.[361] Five days later, Hitler had Brauchitsch inform Bock that the request for leave was granted. Kluge took over the command of Army Group Centre.[362] On 19 December it was the turn – long overdue – of the Commander-in-Chief of the Army, Field-Marshal Walther von Brauchitsch, to depart.

Brauchitsch's sacking had been on the cards for some time. Hitler's military adjutants had been speculating over his replacement since mid-November.[363] His health had for weeks been very poor. He had suffered a serious heart attack in mid-November.[364] At the beginning of December, his health, Halder noted, was 'again giving cause for concern' under the pressure of constant worrying.[365] Hitler spoke of him even in November as 'a totally sick man, at the end of his tether'.[366] Squeezed in the conflict between Hitler and Halder, Brauchitsch's position was indeed unenviable. But his own feebleness had contributed markedly to his misery. Constantly trying to balance demands from his Army Group Commanders and from Halder with the need to please Hitler, his weakness and compliance had left him ever more exposed in the gathering crisis to a Leader who from the start lacked confidence in his army leadership and was determined to intervene in tactical dispositions. It was recognized by those who saw the way Hitler treated him that Brauchitsch was no longer up to the job.[367] Brauchitsch, for his part, was anxious to resign, and tried to do so immediately following the start of the Soviet counter-offensive in the first week of December. He thought of Kluge or Manstein as possible successors.[368]

Hitler disingenuously told Schmundt at the time (and commented along similar lines to his Luftwaffe adjutant, Nicolaus von Below, two days later) that he was clueless about a replacement. Schmundt had for some time favoured Hitler himself taking over as head of the army, to restore confidence, and now put this to him. Hitler said he would think about it.[369] According to Below, it was in the night of 16–17 December that Hitler finally decided to take on the supreme command of the army himself. At the height of the crisis which culminated in the 'stand-fast' order, Brauchitsch had shown himself in Hitler's eyes to be once and for all dispensable.[370] The names of Manstein and Kesselring were thrown momentarily into the ring. But Hitler did not like Manstein, brilliant commander though he was. And Field-Marshal Albert Kesselring, known as a tough and capable organizer, and an eternal optimist, was earmarked for command of the Luftwaffe in the Mediterranean (and, perhaps, was in addition thought to be too much in Göring's pocket).[371] In any case, Hitler had convinced himself by this time that being in charge of the army was no more than a 'little matter of operational command' that 'anyone can do'.[372] Halder, who, it might have been imagined, would have had most to lose by the change-over, in fact appears to have welcomed it. He seems momentarily to have deluded himself that through this move, taking him directly into Hitler's presence in decision-making, he might expand his own influence to matters concerning the entire Wehrmacht. Keitel put an early stop to any such pretensions, ensuring that, as before, Halder's responsibilities were confined to strictly army concerns and that he himself took over all non-operational tasks which had previously pertained to the OKH.[373]

Hitler's takeover of the supreme command of the army was formally announced on 19 December.[374] In one sense, since Brauchitsch had been increasingly bypassed during the deepening crisis, the change was less fundamental than it appeared. But it meant, nevertheless, that Hitler was now taking over direct responsibility for tactics, as well as grand strategy. No other head of a belligerent state – not even Stalin, who after the early débâcle, pulled back somewhat from direct intervention in army tactics – was so closely involved in the minutiae of military affairs. Hitler was absurdly overloading himself still further. And his takeover of direct command of the army would deprive him, in the eyes of the German public, of scapegoats for future military disasters.[375]

Immediately on the heels of the announcement of Brauchitsch's resignation came an even plainer sign of crisis in the east. On 20 December, Hitler published an appeal to the German people to send warm winter clothing for the troops in the east.[376] Goebbels listed all the items of clothes to be handed in during a lengthy radio broadcast that evening.[377] The population responded with shock and anger – astonished and bitter that the leadership had not made proper provision for the basic necessities of their loved ones fighting at the front and exposed to a merciless, polar winter.[378]

Also on the day after Brauchitsch's dismissal, Hitler sent a strongly-worded directive to Army Group Centre, reaffirming the order issued four days earlier to hold position and fight to the last man. 'The fanatical will to defend the ground on which the troops are standing,' ran the directive, 'must be injected into the troops with every possible means, even the toughest ... Where this will is not fully present the front will begin to crumble (*ins Wanken geraten*) without any prospect of stabilizing it once more in a prepared position. For, every officer and man must be clear that the withdrawal of the troops will expose them to the dangers of the Russian winter far more than staying in position, however inadequately equipped it may be. That is quite apart from the considerable, unavoidable material losses which must occur in a withdrawal ... Talk of Napoleon's retreat is threatening to become reality. Thus, there must only be a withdrawal where there is a prepared position further in the rear ... But if troops have to leave a position without being offered an equivalent substitute, then a crisis of confidence in the leadership threatens to develop from every retreat.' Where a systematic withdrawal was to take place, Hitler ordered the most brutal scorched-earth policy. 'Every piece of territory which is forced to be left to the enemy must be made unusable for him as far as possible. Every place of inhabitation must be burnt down and destroyed without consideration for the population, to deprive the enemy of all possibility of shelter.' He concluded with an appeal to the force of will and to a sense of superiority which must not be lost. There was, he declared, 'no reason that the troops should lose their sense of superiority, constantly proven up to now, over this enemy. On the contrary, it will depend on strengthening everywhere the justified self-confidence and on possessing the will to cope with this enemy and the difficulties conditioned by the weather until sufficient reinforcements have arrived and the front is thereby finally secured.'[379]

One commander, more unwilling than most to accept Hitler's 'Halt Order' lying down, was the panzer hero Guderian. Through Schmundt, Guderian had a direct line to Hitler.[380] He made use of it to arrange a special meeting at Führer Headquarters where he could put his case for withdrawal openly to Hitler. Guderian had his own way in dealing with military orders which he found unacceptable. With Bock's connivance, he had tacitly ignored or bypassed early orders, usually by acting first and notifying later. But with Bock's replacement by Kluge, that changed. Guderian and Kluge did not get on. Hitler was well informed of Guderian's 'unorthodoxy'. It is perhaps suprising, then, that he was still prepared to grant the tank commander an audience, lasting five hours, on 20 December, and allow him to put his case at length.[381]

All Hitler's military entourage were present. Guderian informed him of the state of the 2nd Panzer Army and 2nd Army, and his intention of retreating. Hitler expressly forbade this. But Guderian was not telling the whole story. The retreat, for which he had presumed to receive authorization from Brauchitsch six days earlier, was already under way. Hitler was unremitting. He said that the troops should dig in where they stood and hold every square yard of land. Guderian pointed out that the earth was frozen to a depth of five feet. Hitler rejoined that they would then have to blast craters with howitzers, as had been done in Flanders during the First World War. Guderian quietly pointed out that ground conditions in Flanders and Russia in midwinter were scarcely comparable. Hitler insisted on his order. Guderian objected that the loss of life would be enormous, Hitler pointed to the 'sacrifice' of Frederick the Great's men. 'Do you think Frederick the Great's grenadiers were anxious to die?' Hitler retorted. 'They wanted to live, too, but the king was right in asking them to sacrifice themselves. I believe that I, too, am entitled to ask any German soldier to lay down his life.' He thought Guderian was too close to the suffering of his troops, and had too much pity for them. 'You should stand back more,' he suggested. 'Believe me, things appear clearer when examined at longer range.'[382]

Guderian returned to the front empty-handed. Within days, Kluge had requested the tank commander's removal, and on 26 December, Guderian was informed of his dismissal.[383] He was far from the last of the top-line generals to fall from grace during the winter crisis. Within the following three weeks Generals Helmuth Förster, Hans Graf von Sponeck, Erich Hoepner, and Adolf Strauß were sacked, Field-Marshal von Leeb was relieved of his command of Army Group North, and Field-Marshal von Reichenau died of a stroke. Sponeck was sentenced to death – subsequently commuted – for withdrawing his troops from the Kerch peninsula on the Crimean front. Hoepner, also for retreating, was summarily expelled from the army with loss of all his pension rights.[384] By the time that the crisis was overcome, in spring, numerous subordinate commanders had also been replaced.[385]

The crisis lasted into January. On New Year's Eve, while the newly acquired gramophone blared out *Lieder* by Richard Strauß and, of course, the inevitable Wagner, and the inhabitants of the Führer Headquarters got tipsier and merrier, Hitler spent three hours on the telephone to Kluge, insisting that the front be held.[386] When he was eventually finished, he summoned his secretaries for tea in the middle of the night. Their good spirits soon evaporated. Hitler swiftly dampened the mood by nodding off to sleep. The merry-making palled. His entourage, coming in to congratulate him, removed their smiles and put on serious faces. It was so dreadful that Christa Schroeder went back to her room and burst into tears. She found the remedy in returning to the mess and joining a few of the young officers there in singing sea-shanties to the accompaniment of copious amounts of alcohol.[387]

It was mid-January before Hitler was prepared to concede the tactical withdrawal for which Kluge had been pleading.[388] By the end of the month, the worst was over. The eastern front, at enormous cost, had been stabilized. Hitler claimed full credit for this. It was, in his eyes, once more a 'triumph of the will'. Looking back, a few months later, he blamed the winter crisis on an almost complete failure of leadership in the army. One general had come to him, he said, wanting to retreat. He had asked the general whether he really thought it would be less cold fifty kilometres to the rear. He had also asked whether the retreat would only stop at the borders of the Reich. On hearing that it might indeed be necessary to withdraw so far, he immediately dismissed the general, he said, telling him to get back to Germany as quickly as possible. He would himself take over the leadership of the army, and it would stay where it was. It was plain to him, he went on, that a retreat would have meant 'the fate of Napoleon'. He had ruled out any retreat at all. 'And I pulled it off! That we overcame this winter and are today in the position again to proceed victoriously . . . is solely attributable to the bravery of the soldiers at the front and my firm will to hold out, cost what it may.'[389]

Salvation through the Führer's genius was, of course, the line adopted (and believed) by Goebbels and other Nazi leaders.[390] Their public statements combined pure faith and impure propaganda. But despite Halder's outright condemnation – after the war – of Hitler's 'Halt Order', not all military experts were so ready to interpret it as a catastrophic mistake. Kluge's Chief of Staff, General Guenther Blumentritt, for instance, was prepared to acknowledge that the determination to stand fast was both correct and decisive in avoiding a much bigger disaster than actually occurred.[391]

Hitler's early recognition of the dangers of a full-scale collapse of the front, and the utterly ruthless determination with which he resisted demands to retreat, probably did play a part in avoiding a calamity of Napoleonic proportions.[392] But, had he been less inflexible, and paid greater heed to some of the advice coming from his field commanders, the likelihood is that the same end could have been achieved with far smaller loss of life. Moreover, stabilization was finally achieved only after he had relaxed the 'Halt Order' and agreed to a tactical withdrawal to form a new front line.[393]

The strains of the winter crisis had left their mark on Hitler. He was now showing unmistakable signs of physical wear and tear. Goebbels was shocked when he saw him in March. Hitler looked grey, and much aged. He admitted to his Propaganda Minister that he had for some time felt ill and often faint. The winter, he acknowledged, had also affected him psychologically.[394] But he appeared to have withstood the worst. His confidence was, certainly to all outward appearances, undiminished. Hints, given in the autumn, of doubts at the outcome of the war, were no longer heard.[395] He told his entourage in the Führer Headquarters that the entry of Japan had been a turning-point in history, which would denote 'the loss of a whole continent' – regrettable, because the loss would be that of the 'white race'.[396] The British would not be able to prevail against Japan once Singapore had been lost.[397] The question would then be whether Britain could hold on to India. He was sure that, offered the chance of keeping India (and preventing the complete disintegration of the Empire) while abandoning Europe to Germany, almost the entire British population would be in favour.[398]

Against what had seemed in the depths of the winter crisis almost insuperable odds, Germany was ready by spring to launch another offensive in the east. The war still had a long way to go.[399] Certainly, the balance of forces at this juncture was by no means one-sided. And the course of events would undergo many vagaries before defeat for Germany appeared inexorable. But the winter of 1941–2 can nevertheless, in retrospect, be seen to be not merely a turning-point, but the beginning of the end.[400]

The aim advanced by Hitler since the summer of 1940, with the backing of his military strategists, had been to force Britain to come to terms and keep America out of the war through inflicting a swift and comprehensive defeat upon the Soviet Union. By the end of 1941, Germany had failed to defeat the Soviet Union and was now embroiled in a long, enormously bitter and costly, war in the east. Britain had not only been uninterested in coming to terms, but was now fighting alongside the USA and, since concluding a mutual assistance agreement in Moscow on 12 July 1941, allied – whatever the continuing frictions – with the Soviet Union.[401] Not least, Germany was now at war with America. Whatever Hitler's contempt, he knew no ways of defeating the USA.[402] And if final victory over the Soviet Union could not rapidly be achieved, America's mighty resources would soon weigh in the contest. Hitler now had to place his hopes in the Japanese, who might seriously weaken the British and lock the USA into conflict in the Pacific. But he could no longer depend upon the power of German arms alone. Germany no longer held the initiative. He had always predicted that time was running against Germany in its bid for supremacy. His own actions more than those of anyone else had ensured that this was indeed now proving to be the case. Though it would not become fully plain for some months, Hitler's gamble, on which he had staked nothing less than the future of the nation, had disastrously failed.

10

FULFILLING THE 'PROPHECY'

'I already stated on 1 September 1939 in the German Reichstag – and I refrain from over-hasty prophecies – that this war will not come to an end as the Jews imagine, with the extermination of the European–Aryan peoples, but that the result of this war will be the annihilation of Jewry. For the first time the old Jewish law will now be applied: an eye for an eye, a tooth for a tooth.'

Hitler, speaking in the Sportpalast,
Berlin, 30 January 1942

'A judgement is being carried out on the Jews which is barbaric, but fully deserved. The prophecy which the Führer gave them along the way for bringing about a new world war is beginning to become true in the most terrible fashion . . . Here, too, the Führer is the unswerving champion and spokesman of a radical solution.'

Goebbels, diary entry, 27 March 1942

It was no accident that the war in the east led to genocide. The ideological objective of eradicating 'Jewish-Bolshevism' was central, not peripheral, to what had been deliberately designed as a 'war of annihilation'. It was inseparably bound up with the military campaign. With the murderous onslaught of the Einsatzgruppen, backed by the Wehrmacht, launched in the first days of the invasion, the genocidal character of the conflict was already established. It would rapidly develop into an all-out genocidal programme, the like of which the world had never seen.

Hitler spoke a good deal during the summer and autumn of 1941 to his close entourage in the most brutal terms imaginable about his ideological aims in crushing the Soviet Union. During the same months, he also spoke on numerous occasions in his monologues in the Führer Headquarters – though invariably in barbaric generalizations – about the Jews. These were the months in which, out of the contradictions and lack of clarity of anti-Jewish policy, a programme to kill all the Jews in Nazi-occupied Europe began to take concrete shape.

In contrast to military affairs, where his repeated interference reflected his constant preoccupation with tactical minutiae and his distrust of the army professionals, Hitler's involvement in ideological matters was less frequent and less direct. Hitler had laid down the guidelines in March 1941. He needed to do little more. Self-combustion would see to it that, once lit, the genocidal fires would rage into a mighty conflagration amid the barbarism of the war to destroy 'Jewish-Bolshevism'. When it came to ideological aims, in contrast to military matters, Hitler had no need to worry that the 'professionals' would let him down. He could rest assured that Himmler and Heydrich, above all, would leave no stone unturned in eliminating the ideological enemy once and for all. And he could be equally certain that they would find willing helpers at all levels among the masters of the new *Imperium* in the east, whether these belonged to the Party, the police, or the civilian bureaucracy.

Just as, from autumn 1939 onwards until his 'halt order' of August 1941, he had seen no need to involve himself in the 'euthanasia action' any further, once he had authorized its commencement, so now he would see no cause to participate in the daily business of the dirty work of genocide. That was neither his style, nor his inclination.[1] Organization, planning, and execution could confidently be left to others. There was no shortage of those keen to 'carry out practical work for our Führer'.[2] It was sufficient that his authorization for the major steps was provided; and that he could take for granted that, with regard to the 'Jewish Question', his 'prophecy' of 1939 was being fulfilled.

I

On the eve of 'Barbarossa', Hitler had assured Hans Frank that the Jews would be 'removed' from the General Government 'in the foreseeable future'. Frank's province could therefore be regarded merely as a type of 'transit camp' (*Durchgangslager*).[3] Frank registered the pleasure at being able to 'get rid' of the Jews from the General Government, and remarked that Jewry was 'gradually perishing' in Poland. 'The Führer had indeed prophesied that for the Jews,' commented Goebbels.[4] From early in the year the intention had been, as we have already noted, to deport the Jews from Frank's domain to the east, following the victory over the Soviet Union – expected by the autumn.[5] The Jews from Poland, then from the rest of Europe, would be wiped out in the east within a few years by starvation and being worked to death in the icy wastes of an arctic climate. For those incapable of work, the intended fate, if not spelled out, was not difficult to imagine.

The 5–6 million Jews of the USSR were included in the wholesale resettlement scheme for the racial reordering of eastern Europe, the 'General Plan for the East' which Himmler, two days after the launch of 'Barbarossa', had commissioned his settlement planners to prepare. The Plan envisaged the deportation over the subsequent thirty years of 31 million persons, mainly Slavs, beyond the Urals and into western Siberia.[6] Without doubt, the Jews would have been the first ethnic group to perish in a territorial solution which, for them, was tantamount to their death warrant. What was intended was in itself plainly genocidal. The 'territorial solution' could, therefore, be seen as a type of intended 'final solution'. But shooting or gassing to death all the Jews of Europe – the full-scale industrialized killing programme that evolved over the following months into what would then be a differently defined 'final solution' – was at this stage not in mind.

Reinhard Heydrich had already in March received the green light from Hitler to send the Einsatzgruppen into the Soviet Union in the wake of the Wehrmacht to 'pacify' the conquered areas by eradicating 'subversive elements'. Hitler had specified in March that 'the Bolshevist-Jewish intelligentsia must be eliminated'.[7] Heydrich had been more than ready to apply a most liberal interpretation to this mandate in his briefings to the Einsatzgruppen in Pretzsch and Berlin in the weeks before the campaign.

According to a letter which Heydrich sent on 2 July to the four newly appointed Higher SS and Police Leaders for the conquered areas of the Soviet Union, the Einsatzgruppen had been instructed to liquidate, alongside Communist functionaries and an array of 'extremist elements', 'all Jews in the service of the Party and state'.[8] Heydrich's verbal briefings must have made clear that the widest interpretation was to be placed on such an instruction.

From the beginning, the killings were far from confined to Jews who were Communist Party or State functionaries. Already on 3 July, for instance, the chief of the Einsatzkommando in Luzk in eastern Poland had some 1,160 Jewish men shot. He said he wanted to put his stamp on the town.[9] In Kaunas (Kowno) in Lithuania as many as 2,514 Jews were shot on 6 July.[10] Shootings were carried out by Einsatzkommando 3, based in this area, on twenty days in July. Of the 'executions', totalling 4,400 (according to a meticulous listing), the vast majority were Jews.[11] But the briefings had evidently not been unambiguous.[12] They were capable of being interpreted in different ways. Whereas Einsatzgruppe A, in the Baltic, was almost unconstrained in its killing, Einsatzgruppe B in White Russia initially targeted, in the main, the Jewish 'intelligentsia', while Einsatzgruppe C spoke of working the Jews to death in reclaiming the Pripet Marshes.[13] While some Einsatzkommandos were slaughtering Jews more or less indiscriminately, one killer squad in Chotin on the Dnjestr confined its murderous action in early July to Communist and Jewish 'intellectuals' (apart from doctors).[14]

In the Baltic, the butchery of Einsatzgruppe A was especially ferocious. The first massacre of Jews took place on 24 June, only two days after the beginning of 'Barbarossa', in the small Lithuanian township of Gargzdai, lying just behind the border. Men from the Security Police and a police unit from Memel shot dead 201 Jews that afternoon. By 18 July, the killing squads had claimed 3,300 victims; by August the death-toll had reached between 10,000 and 12,000 mainly male Jews together with Communists.[15]

The killing units were assisted in the early stages by Lithuanian nationalists who were prompted into savage pogroms against the Jews.[16] In Kowno, Jews were clubbed to death one by one by a local enthusiast while crowds of onlookers – women holding their children up to see – clapped and cheered. One eyewitness recalled that around forty-five to fifty Jews were killed in this way within three-quarters of an hour. When the butcher had finished his slaughter, he climbed on to the heap of corpses and played the Lithuanian national anthem on an accordion. German soldiers stood by impassively, some of them taking photographs.[17] The Wehrmacht commander in the area, General-Colonel Ernst Busch, took the view, on hearing reports of the atrocities, that it was a matter of internal Lithuanian disputes, and that he had no authority to intervene. It was seen as exclusively a matter for the security police.[18]

Hitler was keen to keep abreast of the killing operations in the Soviet Union. On 1 August SS-Brigadeführer Heinrich Müller, head of the Gestapo, had passed an encyphered message to the commanders of the four Einsatzgruppen: 'Continual reports from here on the work of the Einsatzgruppen in the east are to be presented to the Führer.'[19]

Goebbels registered his satisfaction, when he received a detailed report in mid-August, at the information that 'vengeance was being wreaked on the Jews in the big towns' of the Baltic, and that they were 'being slain in their masses on the streets by the self-protection organizations'. He connected the killing directly with Hitler's 'prophecy' of January 1939. 'What the Führer prophesied is now taking place,' he wrote, 'that if Jewry succeeded in provoking another war, it would lose its existence.'[20] Three months later, when he visited Vilnius, Goebbels spoke again of the 'horrible (grauenhaft)' 'revenge' of the local population against the Jews, who had been 'shot down in their thousands' and were still being 'executed' by the hundred. The rest had been impressed into ghettos and worked for the benefit of the local economy. The ghetto inhabitants, he commented, were 'vile figures (scheuß-liche Gestalten)'. He described the Jews as 'the lice of civilized mankind. They had to be somehow eradicated (ausrotten), otherwise they would always again play their torturing (peinigende) and burdensome role. The only way to cope with them is to treat them with the necessary brutality. If you spare them, you'll later be their victim.'[21]

35. Hitler bids farewell to Franco following their talks at Hendaye, on the borders of France and Spain, on 23 October 1940. The smiles concealed the dissatisfaction felt by each of the dictators at the outcome of the talks.

36. Hitler meets the French head of state, Marshal Pétain, at Montoire on 24 October 1940 for talks which produced little tangible result.

37. Ribbentrop talking to Molotov, the Soviet Foreign Minister, at a reception in the Hotel Kaiserhof during the latter's visit to Berlin, 12–14 November 1940. The tough talks with Molotov confirmed to Hitler that he was right to plan for an attack on the Soviet Union in 1941.

38. Hitler and the Japanese Foreign Minister, Matsuoka, in the Reich Chancellery in Berlin on 27 March 1941. Foreign Ministry official and interpreter Dr Paul Schmidt, who compiled the record of the meeting, is on the left. Matsuoka remained non-committal about Japanese intentions. Hitler had earlier that day given directions to his military leaders about the invasion of Yugoslavia.

39. Hitler at his headquarters at Mönichkirchen near Graz in mid-April 1941, during the Balkan campaign, talking to General Alfred Jodl (*left*), head of the Wehrmacht Operations Staff. Nicolaus von Below, his Luftwaffe adjutant, is behind Hitler.

40. A thoughtful Hitler, accompanied by head of the Wehrmacht High Command Field-Marshal Wilhelm Keitel, travelling by train on 30 June 1941 to the headquarters of Army High Command in Angerburg, not far from his own new Führer Headquarters at the Wolf's Lair, near Rastenburg, in East Prussia.

41. An Anti-Bolshevik Poster: 'Europe's victory is Your Prosperity'. With Britain destroyed, the mailed fist of Nazi Germany smashes Stalin's Bolshevism.

42. Field-Marshal Walther von Brauchitsch (*right*), the weak Commander-in-Chief of the Army between February 1938 and his dismissal in December 1941, in a briefing with General Franz Halder, Chief of the General Staff from 1938 to 1942.

43. Field-Marshal Keitel discussing military matters with Hitler at the Wolf's Lair soon after the invasion of the Soviet Union.

44. Reichsführer-SS and Chief of the German Police Heinrich Himmler (*left*) alongside his right-hand man SS-Obergruppenführer Reinhard Heydrich, head of the Reich Security Head Office. With Hitler's authorization, the steps were taken under their aegis in 1941–2 to implement the 'Final Solution of the Jewish Question'.

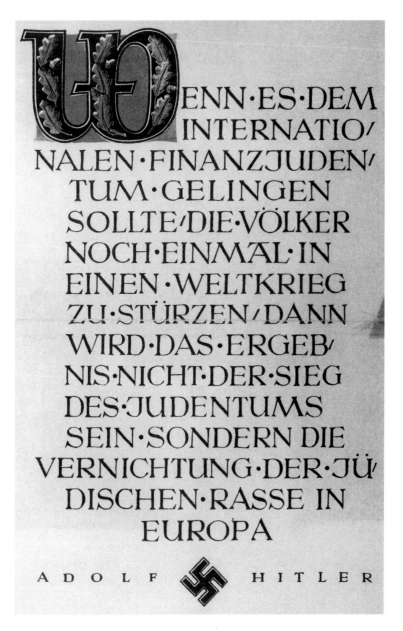

45. *'Should the international Jewish financiers succeed once again in plunging the nations into a world war, the result will be not the victory of Jews but the annihilation of the Jewish race in Europe' – Adolf Hitler.* The 'prophecy' that Hitler had announced to the Reichstag on 30 January 1939. The poster was produced in September 1941 as a 'Slogan of the week' by the central office of the Nazi Party's Propaganda Department and distributed to Party branches throughout the Reich.

46. (*top*) Hitler salutes the coffin of Reinhard Heydrich, who had been assassinated by Czech patriots flown in from Britain, at the state funeral of the Security Police Chief in the Mosaic Salon of the New Reich Chancellery in Berlin on 9 June 1942.

47. (*inset*) Hitler comforts Heydrich's sons at the state funeral. Privately, he was critical of Heydrich's carelessness in regard to his own security. Other Nazi leaders in the photo are, *left to right*: Kurt Daluege (head of the Ordnungspolizei); Bernhard Rust (Reich Minister for Education); Alfred Rosenberg (Reich Minister for the Occupied Eastern Territories); Viktor Lutze (SA Chief of Staff); Baldur von Schirach (Reich Governor and Gauleiter of Vienna); Robert Ley (Nazi Party Organization Leader and head of the German Labour Front); Himmler; Wilhelm Frick (Reich Minister of the Interior); and Göring.

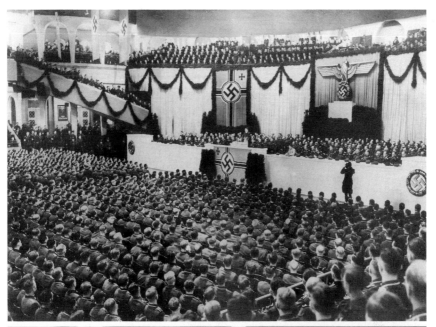

48. (*top*) Hitler addresses 12,000 officers and officer-candidates in the Sportpalast in Berlin on 28 September 1942.

49. Some of the assembled young officers cheering Hitler at the meeting.

50. (*left*) Field-Marshal Fedor von Bock in 1942, as Commander-in-Chief of Army Group South. During the second half of 1941 he had commanded Army Group Centre, which had spearheaded the thrust to Moscow. Though increasingly critical of Hitler's military leadership, he remained a loyalist.

51. (*right*) Field-Marshal Erich von Manstein, possibly Hitler's most gifted military commander. Despite his growing differences with Hitler, he refused to join the conspiracy against him, stating: 'Prussian field-marshals do not mutiny.'

52. (*below*) Hitler speaking on 'Heroes' Memorial Day', 15 March 1942, in the Ehrenhof ('courtyard of honour') of the Arsenal on Unter den Linden in Berlin.

53. The Eastern Front, July 1942. Motorized troops drive away from a blazing Russian village they have destroyed.

54. (*left*) Hitler's 'clients': entertaining the heads of satellite states. Hitler greets the Croatian head of state, Dr Ante Pavelic, in the Wolf's Lair on 29 April 1943.

55. (*below*) Hitler on his way to discussions with the Romanian leader, Marshal Antonescu (*centre*), at Führer Headquarters on 13 February 1942. Hitler's interpreter Paul Schmitt is on the left.

56. Hitler greets King Boris III of Bulgaria in the Wolf's Lair on March 1942. Little over a week after a subsequent tense visit, on 15 August 1943, King Boris died suddenly of a heart attack, giving rise to rumours abroad that Hitler had had him poisoned.

57. (*left*) The turn of the Slovakian President, Monsignor Dr Josef Tiso, to visit Hitler on 23 April 1943 at the restored baroque palace of Klessheim, near Salzburg.

58. (*right*) Hitler greets the Finnish leader Marshal Mannerheim at the Wolf's Lair on 27 June 1942. Keitel is in the background.

59. Admiral Horthy, Hungarian head of state, speaks with (*left to right*) Ribbentrop, Keitel, and Martin Bormann during a visit to the Wolf's Lair on 8–10 September 1941. Later visits, as the fortunes of war deteriorated, proved less harmonious than this one.

60. (*top*) The Over-extended Front. By 1942 demands for men and equipment across a vast range of fronts and conditions had generated just the strategic incoherence Hitler had always feared. Norway: A 'Do 24' seaplane is deposited on land by the crane of a salvage vessel, to be towed to a repair hangar.

61. (*centre*) The Over-extended Front. Leningrad: A huge cannon, mounted on a train, fires on the besieged city. The gun weighed 145 tons, had a barrel 16.4 metres long, and had a range of 46.6 kilometres.

62. (*bottom*) The Over-extended Front. Libya: German tanks rolling along the front in Cyrenaica.

63. The Over-extended Front. Bosnia: An expedition to hunt down partisans.

64. An exhausted German soldier on the Eastern Front.

and the connections between the Jews and the partisan movement. The participants took away from their 'orientation course' the plain message to serve as the guideline for future 'pacification' policy: 'Where there's a partisan, there's a Jew, and where there's a Jew, there's a partisan.'[31]

Such voices were influential. There were, however, others.[32] Some commanders insisted on rigorous separation of the Wehrmacht from the actions of the Security Police. One of these, General Karl von Roques, put out an order at the end of July prohibiting any participation by his men in pogroms on the grounds that it was 'unsoldierly' and would seriously damage the standing of the Wehrmacht.[33] However, his order was ineffective. Cases continued to occur in which 'soldiers and also officers had independently undertaken shootings of Jews or participated in them'. In September, he was forced to issue another order, in which he repeated that 'executive measures', especially against Jews, were solely the province of the Higher SS and Police Leader, and any unauthorized shootings by individual soldiers, or participation in 'executive measures' of the SS and police would be treated as disobedience and subjected to disciplinary action.[34]

From letters home from the front, it is plain that many ordinary German soldiers needed little persuasion that the merciless onslaught on the Jews was justified. Subjected for years to incessant indoctrination at school and in the Hitler Youth about the Jews, and inundated since the beginning of 'Barbarossa' with propaganda about the horrors of 'Jewish-Bolshevism', on the march into Russia they frequently looked to confirm their prejudices.[35] One soldier, writing home in July, remarked on his shock at 'evidence of Jewish, Bolshevik atrocities, the likes of which I have hardly believed possible', and promised that he and his comrades were taking revenge.[36] Another wrote, also in July: 'Everyone, even the last doubter, knows today that the battle against these subhumans, who've been whipped into a frenzy by the Jews, was not only necessary but came in the nick of time. Our Führer has saved Europe from certain chaos.'[37] Given such a mentality, it was not surprising that many Wehrmacht units were themselves involved in the shooting of Jews and other atrocities from the earliest phase of 'Barbarossa'.[38]

In the early weeks of 'Barbarossa', the 'actions' undertaken by the Einsatzgruppen and their sub-units mainly targeted male Jews. The killing, though horrifying, was on nothing like the scale that it reached from August onwards. One particularly murderous Einsatzkommando in Lithuania, for example, killed *nine* times as many Jews in August and *fourteen* times as many in September as it had done in July.[39] What was regarded as a large-scale 'action' in the first weeks had usually involved the shooting of hundreds of Jews, in rare instances more than 1,000. But by the beginning of October Einsatzkommando 4a, attached to Einsatzgruppe C in the Ukraine, could report with cold precision: 'In retaliation for the arson in Kiev, all Jews were arrested and on 29 and 30.9 a total of 33,771 Jews were executed.'[40] This was the notorious massacre at Babi-Yar, outside Kiev. The Jews – many of them women, children, and old people – had been rounded up in retaliation for a series of explosions in the city, killing some hundreds of German soldiers, a few days earlier, just before Kiev had fallen to the Wehrmacht. They were marched in small groups to the outskirts of the city, forced to undress, then to stand on a mound above the ravine of Babi-Yar. As the repeated salvoes of the killing-squads rang out, the lifeless bodies of the victims fell on to the growing mound of corpses below them.[41]

Women and children – seen as possible 'avengers' of the future – were now, following verbal instructions passed down the line by Himmler then by the commanders of the various killer squads during August, generally included in the massacres.[42] Thus, Einsatzkommando 3 shot 135 women among 4,239 Jews 'executed' during July, but 26,243 women and 15,112 children in the total of 56,459 Jews murdered during September 1941.[43] Taking the four Einsatzgruppen and their sub-units together, the Jews killed before mid-August numbered around 50,000 – a massive increase on the scale of the murders in Poland, but only a tenth of the estimated half a million who would perish in the next four months.[44]

The huge increase in number of victims demanded different killing techniques. At first, a semblance of martial law and 'execution' by firing-squad was preserved. But after a few weeks, the killers took turns with a submachine-gun, mowing down their naked victims as they knelt at the edge of a pit. The killing had rapidly moved 'from military procedure to mass butchery'.[45]

Some Einsatzgruppen leaders claimed after the war that Heydrich had conveyed to them in his briefings the Führer's order to exterminate the Jews in the Soviet Union.[46] But the actual variation in the scale of the killing operations in the first weeks, and the sharp escalation from around August onwards, strongly suggests that, in fact, no general mandate to exterminate Soviet Jewry in its entirety had been issued before 'Barbarossa' began.[47] The number of men – around 3,000 in all, the core drawn heavily from the Gestapo, criminal police, regular police (*Ordnungspolizei*), and SD – initially engaged in the Einsatzgruppen actions would, in any case, have been incapable of implementing a full-scale genocidal programme, and could scarcely have been assembled with one in mind.[48] The sharp increase in their numbers through supplementary police battalions began in late July. By the end of the year, there were *eleven* times as many members of the killing units as had been present at the start of 'Barbarossa'.[49]

On 15 August, immediately after witnessing that morning an 'execution' of Jews near Minsk which made him feel sick, Himmler had told his men that he and Hitler would answer to history for the necessary extermination of Jews as 'the carriers of world Bolshevism'.[50] It was during his visits to the killing units in the east that month that Himmler, as we have seen, instructed them to widen the slaughter, now to include women and children.[51] Had he received explicit new authorization from Hitler? Or did he presume that the Führer's existing mandate sufficed for the massive extension of the killing operations?

What passed between the two men during the five days, from 15 to 20 July, that Himmler was staying in the Führer Headquarters is not known.[52] But while in FHQ, Himmler had received minutes of the important meeting that Hitler had had on the 16th with Göring, Bormann, Lammers, Keitel, and Rosenberg. At the meeting, as we have already noted, Hitler had stated that Germany would never leave the conquered territories. All measures necessary for a final settlement, such as shooting and deportation, ought to be taken. He had made the telling remarks that the partisan war proclaimed by Stalin provided 'the possibility of exterminating anything opposing us (*die Möglichkeit auzurotten, was sich gegen uns stellt*)' and that pacification of the conquered territory could best be achieved by shooting dead anyone 'who even looked askance (*daß man jeden, der nur schief schaut, totsch-ieße*)'.[53] A day later, Hitler issued a decree giving Himmler responsibility for security in the newly established civilian regions of German rule in the east. Effectively, this placed the 'Jewish Question' as part of a wider policing remit directly in Himmler's hands.[54]

Within a week, Himmler had increased the 'policing' operations behind the front line in the east by 11,000 men, the start of the far bigger build-up that was to follow.[55] Most probably, catching Hitler's mood at the time, Himmler had pointed out the insufficiency of the forces currently available to him for the 'pacification' of the east, then requested, and been granted, the authority to increase the force to an appropriate level. That the Jews, as had been the case from the beginning of the campaign, were viewed as the prime target group to be exterminated – under the pretext of offering the most dangerous opposition to the occupation – would have meant that no specific mandate about their treatment within the general 'pacification' remit was necessary. In dealing with the Jews in the east as he saw fit, Himmler could take it for granted that he was 'working towards the Führer'.

II

Hitler's own comments about the Jews around this time would certainly have assured Himmler of this. In the twilight hours before dawn on 10 July, Hitler had remarked: '"I feel like the Robert Koch of politics. He found the bacillus of tuberculosis and through that showed medical scholarship new ways. I discovered the Jews as the bacillus and ferment of all social decomposition. Their ferment. And I have proved one thing: that a state can live without Jews; that the economy, culture, art, etc. etc. can exist without Jews and indeed better. That is the worst blow I have dealt the Jews."'[56]

He retained his biological terminology when speaking – with remarkable openness – to the Defence Minister of the newly-created brutally racist state of Slovakia, Marshal Sladko Kvaternik, on 22 July. He had begun with a revealing illogicality: not he, but Stalin, would this time meet with the fate of Napoleon. It was not the first time he had made a remark which hinted at a deep-lying uncertainty about his decision to invade Russia.[57] In the first weeks of the 'war of annihilation' that he had unleashed, Hitler's genocidal mentality was surfacing. As in his discussions with the Japanese Ambassador Oshima a week earlier, Hitler went on to describe the Russian people as 'bestial'. In advising Kvaternik to intervene at home with an iron fist against 'criminals and anti-social elements', Hitler declared that there was only one thing to be done with them: 'annihilate (vernichten) them!' It was necessary to 'do away with (beseitigen) them' or, if they were not dangerous, to lock them in concentration camps from which they must never be let out.[58] Towards the end of the talks, Hitler turned to the Jews. He called them 'the scourge of mankind'. 'Jewish commissars' had wielded brutal power in the Baltic, he stated. And now the Lithuanians, Estonians, and Latvians were taking 'bloody revenge' against them. He went on: 'If the Jews had free rein as in the Soviet paradise, they would put the most insane plans into effect. Thus Russia has become a plague-centre (Pestherd) for mankind . . . For if only one state tolerates a Jewish family among it, this would provide the core bacillus (Bazillenherd) for a new decomposition. If there were no more Jews in Europe, the unity of the European states would be no longer disturbed. Where the Jews are sent to, whether to Siberia or Madagascar, is immaterial.'[59]

The frame of mind was overtly genocidal. The reference to Madagascar was meaningless. It had been ruled out as an option months earlier. But Siberia, which had in the interim come into favour, would itself have meant genocide of a kind. It was in such a frame of mind that Hitler had agreed to the big increase in the number of police units in the east, and presumably given Himmler *carte blanche* to operate as he should see fit in 'cleansing' the conquered eastern territories of Jews. And, from his comments to Kvaternik, Hitler was plainly contemplating a 'solution to the Jewish Question' not just in the Soviet Union, but throughout the whole of Europe.

No decision for the 'Final Solution' – meaning the physical extermination of the Jews throughout Europe – had yet been taken. But genocide was in the air. In the Warthegau, the biggest of the annexed areas of Poland, the Nazi authorities were still divided in July 1941 about what to do with the Jews whom they had been unable to deport to the General Government. One idea was to concentrate them in one huge camp which could easily be policed, near to the centre of coal production, and gain maximum economic benefit from their ruthless exploitation. But there was the question of what to do about those Jews incapable of working.

A memorandum sent on 16 July 1941 to Eichmann, at Reich Security Head Office, by the head of the SD in Posen, SS-Sturmbannführer Rolf-Heinz Höppner, struck an ominous note. 'There is the danger this winter,' his cynical report to Eichmann read, 'that the Jews can no longer all be fed. It is to be seriously considered whether the most humane solution might not be to finish off those Jews not capable of labour by some sort of fast-working preparation.' Asking for Eichmann's opinion, Höppner concluded: 'The things sound in part fantastic, but would in my view be quite capable of implementation.'[60]

On the last day of the month, Heydrich had Eichmann draft a written authorization from Göring – nominally in charge of anti-Jewish policy since January 1939 – to prepare 'a complete solution (*Gesamtlösung*) of the Jewish question in the German sphere of influence in Europe'.[61] The mandate was framed as a supplement to the task accorded to Heydrich on 24 January 1939, to solve the 'Jewish problem' through 'emigration' and 'evacuation'. Heydrich was now commissioned to produce an overall plan dealing with the organizational, technical, and material measures necessary.[62] This written mandate was an extension of the verbal one which he had already received from Göring no later than March.[63] It enhanced his authority in dealings with state authorities, and laid down a marker for his control over the 'final solution' once victory in the east – presumed imminent – had been won.[64] Hitler did not need to be consulted.[65]

The dragnet was closing on the Jews of Europe. But Heydrich's mandate was not the signal to set up death camps in Poland. The aim at this point was still a territorial solution – to remove the Jews to the east.[66] Within the next few months, recognition that the great gamble of the rapid knockout victory in the east had failed would irrevocably alter that aim.

III

With victory apparently within Germany's grasp, pressures to intensify the discrimination against the Jews and to have them deported from the Reich were building up.[67] The growing privations of the war allowed Party activists to turn daily grievances and resentment against the Jews. The SD in Bielefeld reported, for instance, in August 1941 that strong feeling about the 'provocative behaviour of Jews (*das provozierende Verhalten der Juden*)' had brought a ban on Jews attending the weekly markets 'in order to avoid acts of violence' (*um Tätlichkeiten zu vermeiden*)'. In addition, there had been general approval, so it was alleged, for an announcement in the local newspapers that Jews would receive no compensation for damage suffered as a result of the war. It was also keenly felt, it was asserted, that Jews should only be served in shops once German customers had had their turn. The threat of resort to self-help and use of force against Jews if nothing was done hung in the air. Ominously, it was nonetheless claimed that these measures would not be enough to satisfy the population. Demands were growing for the introduction of some compulsory mark of identification such as had been worn by Jews in the General Government since the start of the war, in order to prevent Jews avoiding the restrictions imposed on them.[68]

Evidently, Party fanatics were at work – successfully, so it seems – in stirring up opinion against the Jews. The pressure from below was music to the ears of Party and police leaders like Goebbels and Heydrich anxious for their own reasons to step up discrimination against the Jews and remove them altogether from Germany as soon as possible. It did not take long for it to be fed through Goebbels to Hitler himself.

An identification mark for Jews was something Hitler had turned down when it had been demanded in the aftermath of 'Crystal Night'. He had not thought it expedient at the time. But he was now to be subjected to renewed pressure to change his mind. By mid-August, Goebbels had convinced himself that the 'Jewish Question' in Berlin had again become 'acute'. He claimed soldiers on leave could not understand how Jews in Berlin could still have 'aryan' servants and big apartments. Jews were undermining morale through comments in queues or on public transport. He thought it necessary, therefore, that they should wear a badge so that they could be immediately recognized.[69]

Three days later a hastily summoned meeting at the Ministry of Propaganda, filled with Party hacks, attempted to persuade representatives from other ministries of the need to introduce identification for the Jews. Eichmann, the RSHA representative, reported that Heydrich had already put a proposal to this effect to Göring a short while earlier. Göring had sent it back, saying the Führer had to decide. On this, Heydrich had reformulated his proposal, which would be sent to Bormann, for him to speak to Hitler about it.[70] The view from the Propaganda Ministry embroidered upon the remarks Goebbels had entrusted to his diary a few days earlier. The Jews of Berlin, it was alleged, were a 'centre of agitation', occupying much-needed apartments. Among other things, they were responsible, through their hoarding of food, even for the shortage of strawberries in the capital. Soldiers on leave from the east could not comprehend that Jews were still allowed such licence. Most of the Jews were not in employment. These should be 'carted off' to Russia (*nach Rußland abkarren*). 'It would be best to kill them altogether (*am besten wäre es, diese überhaupt totzuschlagen*).'[71] On the question of 'evacuation of the Jews from the Old Reich', Eichmann commented that Heydrich had put a proposal to the Führer, but that this had been refused, and that the Security Police Chief was now working on an amended proposal for the partial 'evacuation' of Jews from major cities.[72] Given the alleged urgency of the need to protect the mood of the front soldiers, Goebbels, it was announced, intended to seek an audience with the Führer at the earliest opportunity.[73]

This was the purpose of the Propaganda Minister's visit to FHQ on 18 August. He encountered a Hitler recovering from illness, in the middle of a running conflict with his army leaders, in a state of nervous tension, and highly irritable.[74] In this condition, Hitler was doubtless all the more open to radical suggestions. Eventually raising the 'Jewish problem', Goebbels undoubtedly repeated the allegations about Jews damaging morale, especially that of front soldiers. He was pushing at an open door. Hitler must have been reminded of the poor morale which had so disgusted him in Berlin and Munich towards the end of the First World War, for which he (and many others) had blamed the Jews. He granted Goebbels what the Propaganda Minister had come for: permission to force the Jews to wear a badge of identification. According to Goebbels, Hitler expressed his conviction that his Reichstag 'prophecy' – that 'if Jewry succeeded in again provoking a world war, it would end in the destruction of the Jews' – was coming about with a 'certainty to be thought almost uncanny'. The Jews in the east were having to pay the bill, noted Goebbels. Jewry was an alien body among cultural nations. 'At any rate the Jews will not have much cause to laugh in a coming world,' Goebbels reported him as saying.[75]

Next day, Goebbels wrote that he would now become immediately active in the 'Jewish Question', since the Führer had given him permission to introduce a large yellow Star of David to be worn by every Jew. Once the Jews wore this badge, Goebbels was certain they would rapidly disappear from view in public places. 'If it's for the moment not yet possible to make Berlin into a Jew-free city, the Jews must at least no longer appear in public,' he remarked. 'But beyond that, the Führer has granted me permission to deport the Jews from Berlin to the east as soon as the eastern campaign is over.' Jews, he added, spoiled not just the appearance but the mood of the city. Forcing them to wear a badge would be an improvement. But, he wrote, 'you can only stop it altogether by doing away with them. We have to tackle the problem without any sentimentality.'[76]

On 1 September, a police decree stipulated that all Jews over the age of six had to wear the Star of David. A week later, preparing the population for its introduction, Goebbels ensured that the party Propaganda Department put out a special broadsheet, with massive circulation, in its publication *Wochensprüche* (Weekly Maxims), emblazoned with Hitler's 'prophecy'.[77]

According to SD reports – echoing in the main no doubt hardline feelings in Party circles – the introduction of the Yellow Star met with general approval but, in the eyes of some, did not go far enough, and needed to be extended to *Mischlinge* as well as full Jews. Some said the Yellow Star should also be worn on the back.[78] Not all ordinary Germans responded in the same way as the Party radicals. There were also numerous indications of distaste and disapproval for the introduction of the Yellow Star, along with sympathy for the victims. According to the diary entry of one woman in Berlin, who had a strong antipathy to the regime, 'the mass of the people is not pleased at this new decree. Almost all who come across us are ashamed as we are.'[79] The Dresden intellectual Victor Klemperer, depressed and fearful at venturing out of doors once the Star of David singled him out, encountered indirect words of comfort from a tram-driver. On another occasion a driver, thumping his fist on his control-panel, exclaimed to Klemperer's wife: 'Such a mean trick! (*Solch eine Gemeinheit!*)'[80] Inge Deutschkron, then a young woman living in Berlin, emphasized like Klemperer the devastating discriminatory isolation of the Yellow Star, but recalled some small acts of kindness and a mixture of attitudes: 'There were people who looked at me with hate; there were others whose glances betrayed sympathy; and others again looked away spontaneously.'[81] It is impossible to be certain which was the more typical response.[82] Open support for Jews was at any rate dangerous. Goebbels castigated those who felt any sympathy for their plight, threatening them with incarceration in a concentration camp. He turned up his antisemitic invective to an even higher volume.[83] Whatever the level of sympathy, it could carry no weight beside the shrill clamour of the radicals, whose demands – voiced most notably by the Reich Minister of Propaganda – were targeted ever more at removal of the Jews altogether. As Goebbels had recognized, deportation had to wait. But the pressure for it would not let up.

On 22 August, SS-Sturmbannführer Carltheo Zeitschel, Legation Counsellor at the German Embassy in Paris, produced a memorandum for the Ambassador, Otto Abetz, suggesting that the newly occupied areas of the east offered the possibility of 'an ultimate (endgültigen) satisfactory solution' to the 'Jewish problem'. He recommended deporting the Jews from all over Europe into 'a special territory' to be sealed off for them. Transport, he thought, would not pose insuperable problems – Jews from the General Government, he even indicated, could go by road in their own vehicles – and could be implemented even during the war. He advocated putting his suggestion to Ribbentrop, Rosenberg, and Himmler, as well as to Göring who, he thought, was particularly open to ideas on the 'Jewish problem' and, after his experience in the eastern campaign, would probably offer strong support. If these suggestions were taken up, argued Zeitschel, 'we could then have Europe Jew-free in the shortest time'.[84]

Much of the pressure for deportation came from the Security Police. Not surprisingly, the Security Police in the Warthegau, where the Nazi authorities had been trying in vain since autumn 1939 to expel the Jews from the province, were in the front ranks. It must have been towards the end of August that Eichmann asked the SD chief in Posen, SS-Sturmbannführer Rolf-Heinz Höppner – the self-same Höppner who had written to him in July suggesting the possible liquidation of Jews in his area who were incapable of working during the coming winter through a 'fast-working preparation' – for his views on resettlement policy and its administration.

Höppner's fifteen-page memorandum, sent to Eichmann on 3 September, was not concerned solely, or even mainly, with deporting Jews, but the 'Jewish problem' formed nevertheless part of his overview of the potential for extensive resettlement on racial lines. His views corresponded closely with the ideas worked out under the General Plan for the East (*Generalplan Ost*). He envisaged deportations once the war was over 'out of German settlement space' of the 'undesirable sections of the population' from the Great German Reich and of peoples from eastern and south-eastern Europe deemed racially unfit for Germanization. He specifically included 'the ultimate (*endgültige*) solution of the Jewish Question', not just in Germany but also in all states under German influence, in his suggestions. The areas he had in mind for the vast number of deportees were the 'large spaces in the current Soviet Union'. He added that it would be pure speculation (*Phantasterei*) to consider the organization of these territories 'since first the basic decisions have to be taken'. It was essential, however, he stated, that there should be complete clarity from the outset about the fate of the 'undesirables', 'whether the aim is to establish for them permanently a certain form of existence, or whether they should be completely wiped out (*ausgemerzt*)'.[85]

Höppner, aware of thinking in the upper echelons of the SD, was plainly open to ideas of killing Jews. He himself, after all, had expressed such an idea some weeks earlier. But in early September he was evidently not aware of any decision to exterminate the Jews of Europe. As far as he was concerned, the goal was still their expulsion to the available 'spaces' in the dismantled Soviet Union once the war was over.

IV

Despite the mounting pressure for deportation, however, removal of the Jews to the east was at this point still blocked. When the German authorities in Serbia tried in mid-September to have 8,000 Jews deported to Russia, they received a peremptory reply from Eichmann. Not even the Jews from Germany could be sent there. He proposed shooting them.[86]

Any decision to allow the deportation of the Jews of Europe to the east could only be taken by Hitler. He had rejected Heydrich's proposal to deport them only a few weeks earlier. Without Hitler's approval, Heydrich had been powerless to act. Hitler was even now, in September, unwilling to take this step, though the pressure was mounting. Why Hitler resisted the pressure up to this point can only be surmised. He had, of course, presumed that deportations and a final settlement of the 'Jewish Question' would follow upon the victorious end of a war expected to last four or five months. But by this time, Hitler was well aware that this expectation had been an illusion. The old 'hostage' idea probably still played its part. In his warped understanding, holding Jews in his possession offered a bargaining counter with the 'Jewish-run' western 'plutocracies', especially the USA. But there were more practical considerations. Where were the Jews to be sent? The areas currently under German occupation were intended for 'ethnic cleansing', not as a Jewish reservation. Soviet Jews were now being slaughtered there in thousands. But how to deal with an influx of millions more Jews from all over Europe into the area posed problems of an altogether different order. Mass starvation – the fate to which Hitler was prepared to condemn the citizens of Leningrad and Moscow – still required an area to be made available for the Jews to be settled until they starved to death. This had to be in territory intended for the 'export', not 'import', of 'undesirables'. Alternatively, it could only be in the battle-zone itself, or at least in its rear. But this was simply an impracticality; moreover, the Einsatzgruppen had been deployed to wipe out tens of thousands of Jews precisely in such areas; and from Hitler's perspective it would have meant moving the most potent racial enemy to the place where it was most dangerous.

So, as long as the war in the east raged, Hitler must have reasoned, the expulsion of the Jews to perish in the barren wastes to be acquired from the Soviet Union simply had to wait. And if deporting Jews to Russia to be shot like the Soviet Jews was contemplated, the practical problems – even with the greatly increased manpower available – of undertaking a wholesale extermination programme through mass shootings effectively ruled out this option, at any rate as a short-term solution. Then there was the question of transport. Not enough trains were available to get supplies to the front line. That was more urgent than shipping Jews to the east. Once the war was over, the trains assigned to bring troops back from the east, along with millions of tons of grain and crate-loads of booty, could easily be used on the outward journey to carry Jews to their fate.[87]

Suddenly, in mid-September, Hitler changed his mind. There was no overt indication of the reason. But in August, Stalin had ordered the deportation of the Volga Germans – Soviet citizens of German descent who had settled in the eighteenth century along the reaches of the Volga river. At the end of the month the entire population of the region – more than 600,000 people – were forcibly uprooted and deported in cattle waggons under horrific conditions, allegedly as 'wreckers and spies', to western Siberia and northern Kazakhstan. In all, little short of a million Volga Germans fell victim to the deportations.[88] It was the first of Stalin's terrible moves to destroy the nationalities in the south of the Soviet Union. The news of the savage deportations had become known in Germany in early September.[89] Goebbels had hinted that they could prompt a radical reaction.[90] It was not long in coming. Alfred Rosenberg, the recently appointed Reich Minister for the Occupied Eastern Territories, lost little time in advocating 'the deportation (*Verschickung*) of all the Jews of central Europe' to the east in retaliation. His liaison at Army Headquarters, Otto Bräutigam, was instructed by Rosenberg on 14 September to obtain Hitler's approval for the proposal. Bräutigam eventually succeeded in attracting the interest of Hitler's chief Wehrmacht adjutant, Rudolf Schmundt, who recognized it as 'a very important and urgent matter' which would be of great interest to Hitler.[91]

Revenge and reprisal invariably played a large part in Hitler's motivation. But at first he hesitated. His immediate response was to refer the matter to the Foreign Office. Ribbentrop was initially non-committal. He wanted to discuss it personally with Hitler.[92] Werner Koeppen, Rosenberg's liaison officer at FHQ, noted: 'The Führer has so far still made no decision in the question of taking reprisals against the German Jews on account of the treatment of the Volga Germans.' He was said to be contemplating making this move in the event of the United States entering the war.[93]

The remark gives a clue to Hitler's thinking. He had continued to hold to the 'hostage' notion – embodied in his 1939 'prophecy' and aimed at deterring the USA from entering the war through the threat of what would then happen to the Jews of Europe. In August, Roosevelt and Churchill had met for talks on warships off the coast of Newfoundland and in the 'Atlantic Charter' proclaimed their common principles of free and peaceful coexistence of nations in a post-Nazi world.[94] Roosevelt had also declared on 11 September that the US navy would shoot on sight at Axis warships in waters essential for American defence. It seemed increasingly a matter of time before the United States became fully involved in hostilities as an ally of Britain. The deportation of the Jews at this juncture, prompted by the Soviet deportations of the Volga Germans, was Hitler's stark reminder to the Americans of his prophecy: that European Jews would pay the price should the USA enter the war.[95]

With such thoughts in mind, Hitler was now ready to accept the case put by Heydrich and Himmler, reflecting demands and suggestions reaching them from their own underlings, and from the Gauleiter of the big cities, that it was urgently necessary to put the longstanding plans for a comprehensive 'solution to the Jewish Question' into action, and that deportation to the east was indeed feasible despite the unfinished war there. Why he was now prepared to bend to such arguments also lay partly, no doubt, in his acceptance that an early end to the Russian campaign was not in sight. It was, in fact, precisely the juncture at which he acknowledged that the war in the east would stretch into 1942.[96] Tackling the 'final solution of the Jewish Question', he would have acknowledged, could not wait that long. If victory over Bolshevism had to be delayed, he must have concluded, the time of reckoning with his most powerful adversary, the Jews, should be postponed no longer. They had brought about the war; they would now see his 'prophecy' fulfilled.

It would have been remarkable, when Himmler lunched with Hitler at the 'Wolf's Lair' on 16 September, had the deportation issue not been raised.[97] Almost certainly, the Reichsführer-SS pressed for the Reich's Jews to be deported. The following day, Ribbentrop met Hitler to discuss the Rosenberg proposal. That evening, 17 September, Himmler paid the Foreign Minister a visit.[98] By then, Hitler must have agreed to the suggestions to start deporting German, Austrian, and Czech Jews to the east. Himmler evidently left with the authorization. He gave notification of the decision next day.

Again, the Warthegau played a direct part in events. On 18 September, Arthur Greiser, Reich Governor and Gauleiter of the Warthegau, received a letter from Himmler. 'The Führer wishes,' ran the missive, 'that the Old Reich and the Protectorate [Bohemia and Moravia] are emptied and freed of Jews from the west to the east as soon as possible.' Himmler told Greiser that it was his intention to deport the Jews first into the Polish territories which had come to the Reich two years earlier, then 'next spring to expel them still further to the east'. With this in mind, he was sending 60,000 Jews to the Lodz ghetto, in Greiser's province, for the winter.[99]

Around the middle of September, then, Hitler had bowed to the pressure to deport the German and Czech Jews to the east, some of them via a temporary stay in Lodz (where the ghetto was already known to be seriously overcrowded). It was the trigger to a crucial new phase in the gradual emergence of a comprehensive programme for genocide. Initiatives would tumble out, one after the other, during the next few months in widening the scope of the killing.

The decision to begin deporting the German, Austrian, and Czech Jews to the east, while the war was still raging, was a fateful one. It brought 'the final solution of the Jewish question' throughout the whole of Europe a massive step closer. We can only speculate on how it was arrived at, only surmise the course of the conversation between Hitler and Himmler during or after lunch on 16 September.

It would have stayed, almost certainly, at the level of terrible generalities. A start in the full-scale resettlement programme, and, in particular, in implementing Heydrich's plan for a 'total solution of the Jewish Question', Himmler perhaps argued, could be made by transporting the Reich and Protectorate Jews to the east. This would be a deserved retaliation for the Soviet deportation of the Volga Germans. It would meet the wishes of the Party. It would address the complaints of the Gauleiter by relieving the housing problems of the big cities. And it would – an argument sure to impress Hitler – prevent the seditious undermining of morale by Jews spreading disaffection on the home front. Space for the deported Jews, Himmler perhaps continued, could be found for the time being in abandoned Soviet labour camps. There, they could be put to work until they perished. Any 'dangerous elements' could be liquidated immediately, along with those Jews incapable of working. Perhaps acknowledging transport difficulties, Himmler would have accepted that many of the Jews could only in the first instance be sent as far as Poland, before further dispatch to Russia the following spring or summer when, it was presumed, the war there would finally be over. It is unlikely that details were discussed.

However, even when it was agreed that the Reich Jews should be deported in stages, there remained the question of what to do with the millions of Jews in eastern Europe, particularly in Poland. Hans Frank had been promised the speedy removal of the Jews from the General Government. Arthur Greiser was desperate to deport the Jews from the Warthegau. If Himmler raised these issues, he was probably given the green light to 'solve the problem' as best he could, within Poland itself, making a start on the Jews who were unable to work.

The question of the consumption of scarce food resources was a crucial consideration, a vital element in the gathering whirlwind of extermination.[100] Feeding 'burdensome existences (*Ballastexistenzen*)' had been a central part of the thinking behind the 'euthanasia action' in the Reich itself. In the east, the inhumanity towards the subjugated and despised 'inferior peoples' meant that the most brutal stance imaginable was adopted on this issue. As the war expanded, and the problems of ensuring food supplies mounted, civilian and military authorities pressed all the harder for savings to be made at the cost of political, ideological, and racial enemies – above all, the Jews. Hitler's own views would have made him open to any suggestion by Himmler that Jews who could not work – the elderly, the infirm, children, for example – should be liquidated.[101] In these very days, Hitler was telling Goebbels that it was necessary for Leningrad to 'disappear completely'. It would be impossible, even on taking it, to feed its 5 million population. Where would the food supplies and transport for them come from? he asked. The town where Bolshevism began would be razed to the ground – a 'hard but justifiable nemesis of history', as Goebbels put it.[102] Hitler's conclusion about the necessary fate of the Jews about this time was no milder.

Hitler's agreement to the deportation of the German Jews was not tantamount to a decision for the 'Final Solution'.[103] It is doubtful whether a single, comprehensive decision of such a kind was ever made. But Hitler's authorization of the deportations opened the door widely to a whole range of new initiatives from numerous local and regional Nazi leaders who seized on the opportunity now to rid themselves of their own 'Jewish problem', to start killing Jews in their own areas. There was a perceptible quickening of the genocidal tempo over the next few weeks. The speed and scale of the escalation in killing point to an authorization by Hitler to liquidate the hundreds of thousands of Jews in various parts of the east who were incapable of work.[104] But there was as yet no coordinated, comprehensive programme of total genocide. This would still take some months to emerge.

V

Within a few days of the decision to deport the Reich Jews, Goebbels was back at FHQ, seizing the opportunity to press once more for the removal of the Jews from Berlin. Before his audience with Hitler, he had the chance to speak with Reinhard Heydrich. Himmler, Neurath, and a number of other leading figures were also in the Wolf's Lair. The occasion for the assembly of notables was Hitler's decision to 'retire' Neurath as Reich Protector in Prague, following intrigues against him by radicals within the Nazi administration in the former Czech capital, able to exploit reports of a mounting incidence of strikes and sabotage. Levels of repression had been relatively constrained under Neurath.[105] But the growing disturbances now prompted Hitler to put in a hard man, Security Police Chief Heydrich – nominally as Deputy Reich Protector – with a mandate to crush with an iron fist all forms of resistance.

Goebbels lost no time in reminding Heydrich of his wish to 'evacuate' the Jews from Berlin as soon as possible. Heydrich evidently told the Propaganda Minister that this would be the case 'as soon as we have reached a clarification of the military question in the east. They [the Jews] should all in the end be transported into the camps established by the Bolsheviks.

These camps had been set up by the Jews. What was more fitting, then, than that they should now also be populated by the Jews.'[106]

During his two-hour meeting alone with Hitler, Goebbels had no trouble in eliciting the assurance he wanted, that Berlin would soon be rid of its Jews. 'The Führer is of the opinion,' Goebbels noted down next day, 'that the Jews have eventually to be removed from the whole of Germany. The first cities to be made Jew-free are Berlin, Vienna, and Prague. Berlin is first in the queue, and I have the hope that we'll succeed in the course of this year in transporting a substantial portion of the Berlin Jews away to the east.'[107]

He was in the event to be left less than wholly satisfied. He noted towards the end of October that a beginning had been made with deporting Berlin's Jews. Several thousand had been sent in the first place to Litzmannstadt (as Lodz was now officially called).[108] But he was soon complaining about obstacles to their rapid 'evacuation'.[109] And in November he learnt from Heydrich that the deportations had raised more difficulties than foreseen.[110]

Goebbels kept up the pressure with a hate-filled tirade in *Das Reich* – a 'quality' newspaper reaching over 1½ million homes – on 16 November, entitled 'The Jews are Guilty'. He explicitly cited Hitler's 'prophecy' of the 'annihilation of the Jewish race in Europe', stating: 'We are experiencing right now the fulfilment of this prophecy.' The fate of the Jews, he declared, was 'hard, but more than justified', and any sympathy or regret was entirely misplaced.[111] Goebbels ordered the widest circulation of the article to the troops on the eastern front.[112] At home, the article was said by the SD to have 'found a strong echo' in the population, though there had been criticism from churchgoers.[113] Goebbels was pleased with the positive response in Party circles. The article provided, he said, 'compelling arguments' for the 'little Party member' to use 'in his daily struggle'.[114]

The Propaganda Minister again raised the deportation of Berlin's Jews with Hitler during their three-hour discussion a few days later, on 21 November. Hitler, as usual, was easily able to assuage Goebbels. He told him he agreed with his views on the 'Jewish Question'. He wanted an 'energetic policy' against the Jews – but one which would not 'cause unnecessary difficulties'. The 'evacuation of the Jews' had to take place city by city, and it was still uncertain when Berlin's turn would come. When the time arrived, the 'evacuation' should be concluded as quickly as possible.[115]

Once again, as had repeatedly been the case with Frank in Cracow and Schirach in Vienna, Hitler had raised hopes which encouraged pressure for radical action from his subordinates. That the hopes could be fulfilled less easily than anticipated then simply fanned the flames, encouraging the frantic quest for an ultimate solution to the problem which nothing but the Nazis' own ideological fanaticism had created in the first place.[116]

Both Himmler and Heydrich were still speaking in October of deporting the Jews to the east; Riga, Reval, and Minsk were all mentioned. Plans were set in train for extermination camps in Riga and, it seems, in Mogilew, some 130 miles east of Minsk. Transport difficulties and continued partisan warfare eventually caused their abandonment.[117] But, prompted by the murderous initiatives being undertaken by their minions who had rapidly realized that they were being shown a green light and lost no time in preparing to set localized genocides in motion, the attention of the SS leaders was starting to switch to Poland, which posed fewer logistical difficulties, as an area in which a 'final solution of the Jewish Question' could take place.[118]

The use of poison gas had already been contemplated before the deport-ation order was granted. More efficient, less public, and – with characteristic Nazi cynicism – less stressful (for the murderers, that is) ways of killing than mass shootings were required. The use of gas-vans, already deployed in East Prussia in 1940 to kill 'euthanasia' victims, offered one alternative though, it soon proved, had its own drawbacks.[119] Other methods, involving stationary killing installations, were considered. At the beginning of Sep-tember, several hundred Russian prisoners-of-war were gassed in Auschwitz, then a concentration camp mainly for Poles, as an experiment in connection with a large crematorium that had been ordered in October from the Erfurt firm of J.A. Topf and Sons. The poison-gas Zyklon-B was used for the first time on the Soviet prisoners; it would by summer 1942 be in regular use for exterminating the Jews of Europe, ferried by the train-load to the huge killing factory of Auschwitz-Birkenau.[120]

Once the decision to deport the Reich Jews to the east had been taken, things began to move rapidly. Heydrich told Gauleiter Alfred Meyer, State Secretary in Rosenberg's Ministry for the Occupied Eastern Territories, on 4 October that attempts by industry to claim Jews as part of their workforce 'would vitiate the plan of a total evacuation (*Aussiedlung*) of the Jews from the territories occupied by us'.[121] Later that month, following a visit to Berlin by the Lublin Police Chief, SS-Brigadeführer Odilo Globocnik, evidently aimed at instigating the extermination of the Jews in his district, Polish labourers were commandeered by the SS to construct a camp at Belzec in eastern Poland. Experts on gassing techniques used on patients in the 'euthanasia action' followed a few weeks later, now redeployed in Poland to advise on the gas chambers being erected at Belzec.[122] Initially, the aim was to use Belzec, whose murderous capacity was in the early months relatively small, for the gassing of Jews from the Lublin area who were incapable of work.[123] Only gradually did the liquidation of *all* Polish Jews become clarified as the goal – embodied in what, with the addition of two other camps, Sobibor and Treblinka, in spring 1942, came eventually to be known as 'Aktion Reinhardt'.[124]

In the autumn, too, Eichmann was sent to Auschwitz for discussions with Rudolf Höß, the commandant there, about gassing installations.[125] Mass-killing operations at Belzec began in the spring of 1942, in Auschwitz in the summer. They had been preceded by developments in the Warthegau. There, the first of twenty transports in autumn 1941 bringing German Jews to Lodz had arrived on 16 October. The authorities in Lodz had at first objected vehemently to the order in September to take in more Jews. Himmler was implacable. He sharply reprimanded the Government President of Lodz, Friedrich Uebelhoer, himself the bearer of an honorary SS rank. But alongside the reprimand, the Lodz authorities had evidently been assuaged by being told that those Jews incapable of working would soon be liquidated. Mass killings by shooting and gassing (in gas-vans) were already taking place in the autumn weeks. At the same time, Herbert Lange, head of a Special Command which had earlier been deployed at Soldau in East Prussia to gas the inmates of mental asylums, began looking for a suitable location to set up operations for the systematic extermination of the Jews of the Warthegau.[126]

At some point, Gauleiter Greiser asked – and was given – Himmler's permission to liquidate 100,000 Jews in his area.[127] There is no direct indication that Greiser's request went beyond Himmler. It would, of course, not have been necessary to take the request further, had it been known that Hitler had already accorded his general authorization for the mass killing of Jews in Poland. That Hitler's approval, however broad, was essential can be read out of a further initiative coming from the head of government in the Warthegau. When, some months later, Wilhelm Koppe, Higher SS and Police Chief in the Warthegau, wrote to Himmler in support of Greiser's request to extend the killing to 30,000 Poles suffering from incurable tuberculosis, the answer given by the Reichsführer's personal adjutant, SS-Sturmbannführer Rudolf Brandt, was that 'the last decision in this matter must be taken by the Führer'.[128] Greiser's own revealing comment on the need to consult Hitler was: 'I myself do not believe that the Führer needs to be asked again in this matter, especially since at our last discussion with regard to the Jews he told me that I could proceed with these according to my own judgement.'[129] Such a response would indeed have been typical of Hitler's approach. But the episode does suggest that, if it were necessary to have Hitler's approval for the extermination of 30,000 Poles with incurable tuberculosis, it would have been essential to have had at least his blanket authorization for the killing of 100,000 Jews. When exactly Greiser spoke to Hitler directly about the Jews in his area cannot be precisely determined. The most likely date was before the decision was taken to exterminate the 100,000 Jews referred to in the initial correspondence with Himmler. Whether Hitler was consulted on the precise developments or not, his overall approval was evidently necessary. By the first week of December 1941, Chelmno, a gas-van station in the south of the Warthegau, had become the first extermination unit to commence operations.[130]

The Warthegau was not the only area scheduled to receive the deportees. Shortly before the killing in Chelmno commenced, the first transports of German Jews had arrived in the Baltic. The initial intention was to send them to Riga, to be placed in a concentration camp outside the city prior to further deportation eastwards. Hitler had approved proposals from the local commander of the Security Police, SS-Sturmbannführer Dr Otto Lange, to set up the concentration camp. Lange had, however, proposed erecting a camp for Latvian Jews. This was turned, in accordance with a 'wish' of the Führer, into the construction of a 'big concentration camp' for Jews from Germany and the Protectorate. Some 25,000 were expected to be interned there, en route, it was said, for an eventual destination 'farther east'.[131] Some Nazi leaders, at least, were well aware by now what deportation to the east meant. When Goebbels, still pressing to have the Jews of Berlin deported as quickly as possible, referred in mid-December to the deportation of Jews from the occupied part of France to the east, he said it was 'in many cases synonymous with the death penalty'.[132]

By the time the first Jews were due to arrive in Riga from the Reich, the building of the camp had scarcely begun. An improvised solution had to be found. Instead of heading for Riga, the trains were diverted to Kowno in Lithuania. Between 25 and 29 November, terrified and exhausted Jews were taken from five trains arriving in Kowno from Berlin, Frankfurt, Munich, Vienna, and Breslau and, without any selection on grounds of ability to work, promptly taken out and shot by members of the locally based Einsatzkommando. The same fate awaited 1,000 German Jews who then did arrive in Riga on 30 November. They were simply taken straight out into the forest and shot, along with some 14,000 Latvian Jews from the Riga ghetto.

Himmler had earlier in the month told the police chief in the area, Friedrich Jeckeln, 'that all the Jews in the *Ostland* down to the very last one must be exterminated (*vernichtet*)'.[133]

However certain Jeckeln was of his murderous mandate, other Nazi leaders in the east still had their doubts. Hinrich Lohse, Reich Commissar for the Eastern Region (*Ostland*), and Wilhelm Kube, General Commissar for Belorussia (*Weißruthenien*), were among those who were less sure that Reich Jews were meant to be included in the mass shootings and indiscriminately slaughtered together with the Jews from the east. They now sought urgent clarification from the Reich Ministry for the Occupied Eastern Territories and from Reich Security Head Office. Lohse, pressed by the Wehrmacht to retain Jewish skilled workers, wanted guidance on whether or not economic criteria were relevant in determining whether Jews were to be liquidated. In Minsk, where 12,000 Jews from the local ghetto had been shot by the Security Police to make way for an influx of German Jews, Kube protested that 'people coming from our own cultural sphere' should be differently treated than the 'native brutish hordes (*bodenständigen vertierten Horden*)'.[134] He wanted to know whether exceptions were to be made for part-Jews (*Mischlinge*), Jews with war decorations, or Jews with 'aryan' partners. Other protests and queries, reflecting both unease and lack of clarity over the intended fate of the Jews from the Reich, reached the Ostministerium and RSHA. These prompted Himmler to intervene on 30 November to try to prohibit the liquidation of the train-load of 1,000 German Jews – many of them elderly, some bearers of the Iron Cross First Class – sent to Riga. His telephone-call came too late. By then the Jews had already been slaughtered by Jeckeln's killing-squads.[135]

The previous day, 29 November, Heydrich had sent out invitations to several State Secretaries and to selected SS representatives to a conference to take place close to the Wannsee, a beautiful lake on the western rim of Berlin, on 9 December. Heydrich wanted to inculcate relevant government ministries in the RSHA's plans to deport to the east all the Jews within Germany's grasp throughout Europe.[136] In addition, he was keen to ensure, in line with the commission he had requested and been granted at the end of July, that his primacy in orchestrating the deportations was recognized by all parties involved.[137] On 8 December, the day before the conference was scheduled to take place, Heydrich had it postponed to 20 January 1942.

The postponement was caused by the dramatic events unfolding in the Pacific and in eastern Europe. The Japanese attack on Pearl Harbor on 7 December would, as Heydrich knew, bring within days a German declaration of war on the USA. With that, the European war would become a world war. Meanwhile, the opening of the first major counter-offensive by the Red Army on 5 December had blocked for the forseeable future any prospect of mass deportations into Soviet territory.[138] Both developments carried important consequences for the deportation programme. Their impact soon became evident.

Plans to bring about a 'final solution' to the 'Jewish Question' were about to enter a new phase – one more murderous than ever.

VI

Hitler's responsibility for the genocide against the Jews cannot be questioned. Yet for all his public tirades against the Jews, offering the strongest incitement to ever more radical onslaughts of extreme violence, and for all his dark hints that his 'prophecy' was being fulfilled, he was consistently keen to conceal the traces of his involvement in the murder of the Jews. Perhaps even at the height of his own power he feared theirs, and the possibility one day of their 'revenge'. Perhaps, sensing that the German people were not ready to learn the deadly secret, he was determined – his own general inclination to secrecy was, as always, a marked one – not to speak of it other than in horrific, but imprecise, terms. Whatever the reasons, he could never have delivered the sort of speech which, notoriously, Himmler would give in Posen two years later when he described what it was like to see 1,000 corpses lying side by side and spoke openly of 'the extermination (*Ausrottung*) of the Jewish people' as a 'glorious page in our history that has never been written and is never to be written'.[139] Even in his inner circle Hitler could never bring himself to speak with outright frankness about the killing of the Jews. Full knowledge of their murder was evidently not to be touched upon directly in his presence, even among the close band of criminal conspirators.

Even so, compared with the first years of the war when he had neither in public nor – to go from Goebbels's diary accounts – in private made much mention of the Jews, Hitler did now, in the months when their fate was being determined, refer to them on numerous occasions. Invariably, whether in public speeches or during comments in his late-night monologues in his East Prussian headquarters, his remarks were confined to generalities – but with the occasional menacing allusion to what was happening.

At lunch on 6 October, conversation focused mainly on eliminating Czech resistance following Heydrich's appointment on 27 September as Deputy Reich Protector. Hitler spoke of ways 'to make the Czechs small'. Shooting ten hostages for every act of sabotage where the perpetrator could not be found was one method. Another – as usual, the carrot as well as the stick – was to improve food-rations in factories where there was no case of sabotage. His third means was the deportation of the Jews. He was speaking about three weeks after he had agreed to their deportation from the Reich and the Protectorate. His comments reveal at least one of the reasons why he agreed to deport them: he continued to believe in the Jews as dangerous 'fifth-columnists', spreading sedition among the population. It was exactly what he had thought of the role of the Jews in Germany during the First World War. 'All Jews must be removed from the Protectorate,' he declared around the lunch-table, 'and not just into the General Government, but straight away further to the east. This is at present not practical merely because of the great demand of the military for means of transport. Along with the Protectorate's Jews, all the Jews from Berlin and Vienna should disappear at the same time. The Jews are everywhere the pipeline through which all enemy news rushes with the speed of wind into all branches of the population.'[140]

On 21 October, a month after the deportation order, as part of a diatribe comparing 'Jewish Christianity' with 'Jewish Bolshevism', he compared the fall of Rome with latter-day Bolshevization through the Jews. 'If we eradicate (*ausrotten*) this plague,' he concluded, 'we will be carrying out a good deed for mankind, of the significance of which our men out there can have no conception.'[141] Four days later his guests were Himmler (a frequent visitor to the Wolf's Lair during these weeks) and Heydrich.[142] The conversation again revolved mainly around the connections of Jewry and Christianity.[143] Hitler reminded his guests and his regular entourage of his 'prophecy'. 'This criminal race has the two million dead of the World War on its conscience,' he went on, and 'now again hundreds of thousands. Don't anyone tell me we can't send them into the marshes (*Morast*)! Who bothers, then, about our people? It's good when the horror (*der Schrecken*) precedes us that we are exterminating Jewry. The attempt to found a Jewish state will be a failure.'[144] These notes of Hitler's rantings were disjointed. But, although lacking coherence, they point to his knowledge of the attempts – eventually given up – in the summer to drown Jewish women by driving them into the Pripet marshes.[145] Hitler's allocation of guilt for the dead of the First World War and the current war to the Jews, and the recourse once more to his 'prophecy', underline his certainty that the destruction of Jewry was imminent. But, other than the reference to the efficacy of rumours of extermination, there was no suggestion of the looming 'Final Solution'. With Himmler and Heydrich as his guests, it was scarcely necessary to dissemble. However, no significance ought to be attached to the absence of any reference.[146] By mid-October the consequences flowing from the deportation order of the previous month had still to merge into the full genocidal programme.

On the evening of 5 November, remarks about the 'racial inferiority' of the English lower class led Hitler once more into a monologue about the Jews. As usual, he linked it to the war. This was the 'most idiotic war' that the British had ever begun, he ranted, and would lead in defeat to an outbreak of antisemitism in Britain which would be without parallel. The end of the war, he proclaimed, would bring 'the fall of the Jew'.[147] He then unleashed an extraordinary verbal assault on the lack of ability and creativity of Jews in every walk of life but one: lying and cheating. The Jew's 'entire building will collapse if he is refused a following,' he went on. 'In one moment, it's all over. I've always said the Jews are the most stupid devils that exist. They don't have a true musician, thinker, no art, nothing, absolutely nothing. They are liars, forgers, deceivers. They've only got anywhere through the simple-mindedness of those around them. If the Jew were not washed by the Aryan, he wouldn't be able to see out of his eyes for filth. We can live without the Jews. But they can't live without us.'[148]

The links, as he saw them, between the Jews and the war that they had allegedly inspired, now also, after years in which he had scarcely mentioned the Jews, found a prominent place in his public speeches. But, whatever the rhetorical flourishes, whatever the propaganda motive in appealing to the antisemitic instincts of his hard-core supporters in the Party, there cannot be the slightest doubt, on the basis of his private comments, that Hitler believed in what he said.

In his speech to the 'Old Guard' of veterans of the Putsch, on 8 November 1941, Hitler pressed home the theme of Jewish guilt for the war. Despite the victories of the previous year, he stated, he had still worried because of his recognition that behind the war stood 'the international Jew'. They had poisoned the peoples through their control of the press, radio, film, and theatre; they had made sure that rearmament and war would benefit their business and financial interests; he had come to know the Jews as the instigators of world conflagration. England, under Jewish influence, had been the driving-force of the 'world-coalition against the German people'. But it had been inevitable that the Soviet Union, 'the greatest servant of

Jewry', would one day confront the Reich. Since then it had become plain that the Soviet state was dominated by Jewish commissars. Stalin, too, was no more than 'an instrument in the hand of this almighty Jewry'. Behind him stood 'all those Jews who in thousandfold ramification lead this powerful empire'. This 'insight', Hitler suggested, had weighed heavily upon him, and compelled him to face the danger from the east.[149]

Hitler returned to the alleged 'destructive character' of the Jews when talking again to his usual captive audience in the Wolf's Lair in the small hours of 1–2 December. Again, there was a hint, but no more than that, of what Hitler saw as the natural justice being meted out to the Jews: 'he who destroys life, exposes himself to death. And nothing other than this is happening to them' – to the Jews.[150] The gas-vans of Chelmno would start killing the Jews of the Warthegau in those very days.[151] In Hitler's warped mentality, such killing was natural revenge for the destruction caused by the Jews – above all in the war which he saw as their work. His 'prophecy' motif was evidently never far from his mind in these weeks as the winter crisis was unfolding in the east. It would be at the forefront of his thoughts in the wake of Pearl Harbor. With his declaration of war on the USA on 11 December, Germany was now engaged in a 'world war' – a term used up to then almost exclusively for the devastation of 1914–18. In his Reichstag speech of 30 January 1939, he had 'prophesied' that the destruction of the Jews would be the consequence of a new world war. That war, in his view, had now arrived.

On 12 December, the day after he had announced Germany's declaration of war on the USA, Hitler addressed the Reichsleiter and Gauleiter – an audience of around fifty persons – in his rooms in the Reich Chancellery. Much of his talk ranged over the consequences of Pearl Harbor, the war in the east, and the glorious future awaiting Germany after final victory. He also spoke of the Jews. And once more he evoked his 'prophecy'.

'With regard to the Jewish Question,' Goebbels recorded, summarizing Hitler's comments, 'the Führer is determined to make a clear sweep of it (*reinen Tisch zu machen*). He prophesied that, if they brought about another world war, they would experience their annihilation (*Vernichtung*). That was no empty talk (*keine Phrase*). The world war is there. The annihilation of Jewry must be the necessary consequence. This question is to be viewed without any sentimentality. We're not there to have sympathy with the Jews, but only sympathy with our German people. If the German people has again now sacrificed around 160,000 dead in the eastern campaign, the originators of this bloody conflict will have to pay for it with their own lives.'[152]

The tone was more menacing and vengeful than ever. The original 'prophecy' had been a warning. Despite the warning, the Jews – in Hitler's view – had unleashed the world war. They would now pay the price.

Hitler still had his 'prophecy' in mind when he spoke privately to Alfred Rosenberg, Reich Minister for the Eastern Territories, on 14 December, two days after his address to the Gauleiter. Referring to the text of a forthcoming speech, on which he wanted Hitler's advice, Rosenberg remarked that his 'standpoint was not to speak of the extermination (*Ausrottung*) of Jewry. The Führer approved this stance and said they had burdened us with the war and brought about the destruction so it was no wonder if they would be the first to feel the consequences.'[153]

The party chieftains who had heard Hitler speak on 12 December in the dramatic context of war now against the USA and unfolding crisis on the eastern front understood the message. No order or directive was necessary. They readily grasped that the time of reckoning had come. On 16 December, Hans Frank reported back to leading figures in the administration of the General Government. 'As regards the Jews,' he began, 'I'll tell you quite openly: an end has to be made one way or another.' He referred explicitly to Hitler's 'prophecy' about their destruction in the event of another world war. He repeated Hitler's expression in his address to the Gauleiter that sympathy with the Jews would be wholly misplaced. The war would prove to be only a partial success should the Jews in Europe survive it, Frank went on. 'I will therefore proceed in principle regarding the Jews that they will disappear. They must go,' he declared. He said he was still negotiating about deporting them to the east. He referred to the rescheduled Wannsee Conference in January, where the issue of deportation would be discussed. 'At any event,' he commented, 'a great Jewish migration will commence.' 'But,' he asked: 'what is to happen to the Jews? Do you believe they'll be accommodated in village settlements in the *Ostland*? They said to us in Berlin: why are you giving us all this trouble? We can't do anything with them in the *Ostland* or in the Reich Commissariat [Ukraine] either. Liquidate them yourselves! . . . We must destroy (*vernichten*) the Jews wherever we find them and wherever it is possible to do so . . .' A programme for bringing this about was evidently, however, still unknown to Frank. He did not know how it was to happen. 'The Jews are also extraordinarily harmful to us through their gluttony,' he continued. 'We have in the General Government an estimated 2.5 million – perhaps with those closely related to Jews and what goes with it, now 3.5 million Jews. We can't shoot these 3.5 million Jews, we can't poison them, but we must be able to take steps leading somehow to a success in extermination (*Vernichtungserfolg*) . . .'[154]

The 'Final Solution' – meaning the physical extermination of the Jews of Europe – was still emerging. The ideology of total annihilation was now taking over from any lingering economic rationale of working the Jews to death. 'Economic considerations should remain fundamentally out of consideration in dealing with the problem' was the answer finally given on 18 December to Lohse's inquiry about using skilled Jewish workers from the Baltic in the armaments industry.[155] On the same day, in a private discussion with Himmler, Hitler confirmed that in the east the partisan war, which had expanded sharply in the autumn, provided a useful framework for destroying the Jews. They were 'to be exterminated as partisans (*Als Partisanen auszurotten*)', Himmler noted as the outcome of their discussion.[156] The separate strands of genocide were rapidly being pulled together.

On 20 January 1942, the conference on the 'final solution', postponed from 9 December, eventually took place in a large villa by the Wannsee. Alongside representatives from the Reich ministries of the Interior, Justice, and Eastern Territories, the Foreign Office, from the office of the Four-Year Plan, and from the General Government, sat Gestapo chief SS-Gruppenführer Heinrich Müller, the commanders of the Security Police in the General Government and Latvia, Karl Schoengarth and Otto Lange, together with Adolf Eichmann (the RSHA's deportation expert, who had the task of producing a written record of the meeting).[157]

Heydrich opened the meeting by recapitulating that Göring had given him responsibility – a reference to the mandate of the previous July – for preparing 'the final solution of the European Jewish question'. The meeting aimed to clarify and coordinate organizational arrangements. (Later in the meeting an inconclusive attempt was made to define the status of part-Jews (*Mischlinge*) in the framework of deportation plans.)[158] Heydrich surveyed the course of anti-Jewish policy, then declared that 'the evacuation of the Jews to the east has now emerged, with the prior permission of the Führer, as a further possible solution instead of emigration'. He spoke of gathering 'practical experience' in the process for 'the coming final solution of the Jewish question', which would embrace as many as 11 million Jews across Europe (stretching, outside German current territorial control, as far as Britain and Ireland, Switzerland, Spain, Turkey, and French north African colonies). In the gigantic deportation programme, the German-occupied territories would be combed from west to east. The deported Jews would be put to work in large labour gangs. Many – perhaps most – would die in the process. The particularly strong and hardy types who survived would have 'to be dealt with accordingly'.

Though there was, as Eichmann later testified, explicit talk at the conference – not reflected in the minutes – of 'killing and eliminating and exterminating (*Töten und Eliminieren und Vernichten*)',[159] Heydrich was not orchestrating an existing and finalized programme of mass extermination in death-camps. But the Wannsee Conference was a key stepping-stone on the path to that terrible genocidal finality. A deportation programme aimed at the annihilation of the Jews through forced labour and starvation in occupied Soviet territory following the end of a victorious war was rapidly giving way to the realization that the Jews would have to be systematically destroyed before the war ended – and that the main locus of their destruction would no longer be the Soviet Union, but the territory of the General Government.[160]

That the General Government should become the first area to implement the 'Final Solution' was directly requested at the conference by its representative, State Secretary Josef Bühler. He wanted the 2½ million Jews in his area – most of them incapable of work, he stressed – 'removed' as quickly as possible. The authorities in the area would do all they could to help expedite the process.[161] Bühler's hopes would be fulfilled over the next months. The regionalized killing in the districts of Lublin and Galicia was extended by spring to the whole of the General Government, as the deportation-trains began to ferry their human cargo to the extermination camps of Belzec, Sobibor, and Treblinka. By this time, a comprehensive programme of systematic annihilation of the Jews embracing the whole of German-occupied Europe was rapidly taking shape. By early June a programme had been constructed for the deportation of Jews from western Europe.[162] The transports from the west began in July. Most left for the largest of the extermination camps by this time in operation, Auschwitz-Birkenau in the annexed territory of Upper Silesia. The 'final solution' was under way. The industrialized mass murder would now continued unabated. By the end of 1942, according to the SS's own calculations, 4 million Jews were already dead.[163]

Hitler had not been involved in the Wannsee Conference. Probably he knew it was taking place; but even this is not certain. There was no need for his involvement. He had signalled yet again in unmistakable terms in December 1941 what the fate of the Jews should be now that Germany was embroiled in another world war. By then, local and regional killing initiatives had already developed their own momentum. Heydrich was more than happy to use Hitler's blanket authorization of deportations to the east now to expand the killing operations into an overall programme of Europe-wide genocide.

On 30 January 1942, the ninth anniversary of the 'seizure of power', Hitler addressed a packed Sportpalast. As he had been doing privately over the past weeks, he invoked once more – how often he repeated the emphasis in these months is striking – his 'prophecy' of 30 January 1939. As always, he wrongly dated it to the day of the outbreak of war with the attack on Poland. 'We are clear,' he declared, 'that the war can only end either with the extermination of the aryan peoples or the disappearance of Jewry from Europe.' He went on: 'I already stated on 1 September 1939 in the German Reichstag – and I refrain from over-hasty prophecies – that this war will not come to an end as the Jews imagine, with the extermination of the European-Aryan peoples (*nämlich daß die europäisch-arischen Völker aus-gerottet werden*), but that the result of this war will be the annihilation (*Vernichtung*) of Jewry. For the first time the old Jewish law will now be applied: an eye for an eye, a tooth for a tooth . . . And the hour will come when the most evil world-enemy of all time will have played out its role, at least for a thousand years.'[164]

The message was not lost on his audience. The SD – no doubt picking up comments made above all by avid Nazi supporters – reported that his words had been 'interpreted to mean that the Führer's battle against the Jews would be followed through to the end with merciless consistency, and that very soon the last Jew would disappear from European soil'.[165]

VII

When Goebbels spoke to Hitler in March, the death-mills of Belzec had commenced their grisly operations.[166] As regards the 'Jewish Question', Hitler remained 'pitiless', the Propaganda Minister recorded. 'The Jews must get out of Europe, if need be through use of the most brutal means,' was his view.[167]

A week later, Goebbels left no doubt what 'the most brutal means' implied. 'From the General Government, beginning with Lublin, the Jews are now being deported to the east. A fairly barbaric procedure, not to be described in any greater detail, is being used here, and not much more remains of the Jews themselves. In general, it can probably be established that 60 per cent of them must be liquidated, while only 40 per cent can be put to work ... A judgement is being carried out on the Jews which is barbaric, but fully deserved. The prophecy which the Führer gave them along the way for bringing about a new world war is beginning to become true in the most terrible fashion. No sentimentality can be allowed to prevail in these things. If we didn't fend them off, the Jews would annihilate (*vernichten*) us. It's a life-and-death struggle between the aryan race and the Jewish bacillus. No other government and no other regime could produce the strength to solve this question generally. Here, too, the Führer is the unswerving champion and spokesman of a radical solution . . .'[168]

Goebbels himself had played no small part over the years in pushing for a 'radical solution'. He had been one of the most important and high-placed of the Party activists pressing Hitler on numerous occasions to take radical action on the 'Jewish Question'. The Security Police – Heydrich's role was, if anything, probably more important even than Himmler's – had been instrumental in gradually converting an ideological imperative into an extermination plan. Many others, at different levels of the regime, had contributed in greater or lesser measure to the continuing and untrammelled process of radicalization. Complicity was massive, from the Wehrmacht leadership and captains of industry down to Party hacks, bureaucratic minions, and ordinary Germans hoping for their own material advantage through the persecution then deportation of a helpless, but unloved, minority which had been deemed to be the inexorable enemy of the new 'people's community'.

But Goebbels knew what he was talking about in singling out Hitler's role. This had often been indirect, rather than overt. It had consisted of authorizing more than directing. And the hate-filled tirades, though without equal in their depth of inhumanity, remained at a level of generalities. Nevertheless, there can be no doubt about it: Hitler's role had been decisive and indispensable in the road to the 'Final Solution'. Had he not come to power in 1933 and a national-conservative government, perhaps a military dictatorship, had gained power instead, discriminatory legislation against Jews would in all probability still have been introduced in Germany. But without Hitler, and the unique regime he headed, the creation of a programme to bring about the physical extermination of the Jews of Europe would have been unthinkable.

11

LAST BIG THROW OF THE DICE

'If I don't get the oil of Maykop and Grozny, then I must finish this war.'   *Hitler, spring 1942*

'Overall picture: have we extended the risk too far?'
                    General Halder, 15 August 1942

'You can be sure,' he added, 'that nobody will get us away from this place again!'
         Hitler, speaking of Stalingrad, 30 September 1942

'How can someone be so cowardly? I don't understand it. So many people have to die. Then such a man goes and besmirches in the last minute the heroism of so many others.'   *Hitler, on 1 February 1943 on hearing of the surrender of Field-Marshal Paulus at Stalingrad*

Snow still lay on the ground at the Wolf's Lair. An icy wind gave no respite from the cold. But, at the end of February 1942, there were the first signs that spring was not far away.[1] Hitler could not wait for the awful winter to pass.[2] He felt he had been let down by his military leaders, his logistical planners, his transport organizers; that his army commanders had been faint-hearts, not tough enough when faced with crisis; that his own strength of will and determination had alone staved off catastrophe. Every crisis in his own mind amounted to a contest of will. The winter crisis had been no different. Coming through it had been yet another 'triumph of the will', comparable as he saw it with winning power against the odds in 1933. That the gamble of knocking out the Soviet Union within a few months had been absurd, or that the overall strategy of 'Barbarossa' had been flawed from the outset, never entered his head; nor that his own constant interference had compounded the problems of military command. The winter crisis had sharpened his sense, never far from the surface, that he had to struggle not just against external enemies, but against those who were inadequate, incapable, or even disloyal, in his own ranks. But the crisis had been surmounted. His leadership, he believed, had saved his army from the fate of Napoleon's troops. They had survived the Russian winter. This in itself was a psychological blow to the enemy, which had also suffered grievously. It was necessary now to attack again as soon as possible; to destroy this mortally weakened enemy in one final great heave. This was how his thoughts ran. In the insomniac nights in his bunker, he was not just wanting to erase the memories of the crisis-ridden cold, dark months. He could hardly wait for the new offensive in the east to start – the push to the Caucasus, Leningrad, and Moscow, which would wrestle back the initiative once more.[3] It would be a colossal gamble. Should it fail, the consequences would be unthinkable.

For those in the Führer Headquarters not preoccupied with military planning, life was dull and monotonous. Hitler's secretaries would go for a daily walk to the next village and back. Otherwise, they whiled away the hours. Chatting, a film in the evenings, and the obligatory gathering each afternoon in the Tea House and late at night again for tea made up the day. 'Since the tea-party always consists of the same people, there is no stimulation from outside, and nobody experiences anything on a personal level,' Christa Schroeder wrote to a friend in February 1942, 'the conversation is often apathetic and tedious, wearying, and irksome. Talk always runs along the same lines.' Hitler's monologues – outlining his expansive vision of the world – were reserved for lunch or the twilight hours. At the afternoon tea-gatherings, politics were never discussed. Anything connected with the war was taboo. There was nothing but small-talk. Those present either had no independent views, or kept them to themselves. Hitler's presence dominated. But it seldom now did much to animate. He was invariably tired, but found it hard to sleep. His insomnia made him reluctant to go to bed. His entourage often wished he would do so. The tedium for those around him seemed at times incessant. Occasionally, it was relieved in the evenings by listening to records – Beethoven symphonies, selections from Wagner, or Hugo Wolf's *Lieder*. Hitler would listen with closed eyes. But he always wanted the same records. His entourage knew the numbers off by heart. He would call out: '*Aida*, last act,' and someone would shout to one of the manservants: 'Number hundred-and-something.'[4]

The war was all that mattered to Hitler. Yet, cocooned in the strange world of the Wolf's Lair, he was increasingly severed from its realities, both at the front and at home. Detachment ruled out all vestiges of humanity. Even towards those in his own entourage who had been with him for many years, there was nothing resembling real affection, let alone friendship; genuine fondness was reserved only for his young Alsatian.[5] He had described the human being the previous autumn as no more than 'a ridiculous "cosmic bacterium" (*eine lächerliche "Weltraumbakterie"*)'.[6] Human life and suffering was, thus, of no consequence to him. He never visited a field-hospital, nor the homeless after bomb-raids. He saw no massacres, went near no concentration camp, viewed no compound of starving prisoners-of-war. His enemies were in his eyes like vermin to be stamped out. But his profound contempt for human existence extended to his own people. Decisions costing the lives of tens of thousands of his soldiers were made –

perhaps it was only thus possible to make them – without consideration for any human plight. As he had told Guderian during the winter crisis, feelings of sympathy and pity for the suffering of his soldiers had to be shut out.[7] For Hitler, the hundreds of thousands of dead and maimed were merely an abstraction, the suffering a necessary and justified sacrifice in the 'heroic struggle' for the survival of the people.

Among ordinary soldiers, amid the brutality and barbarization, less heroic views of war could be encountered. One soldier on the eastern front who, in peacetime, had attended the Party rallies at Nuremberg, mourned the death of a comrade at the end of January. 'Why must it always be: sacrifice, struggle, victory, death!' he lamented. 'Is the heroic death then the ideal of this globe?.'[8] A young recruit from Cologne, by no means opposed to the regime, wrote in his diary a few weeks later, while in training in East Prussia before being sent to the eastern front: 'I'm convinced that, if I knew that all this really had a meaning, I could and would voluntarily achieve much more. But for what? I ask myself. For what and for whom must we perish? For what and for whom be a slave? For what starve, freeze, and then finally croak? For what? For what? A thousand questions – no answer.'[9]

The ties which had bound a high proportion of the German population to Hitler since 1933 were starting to loosen. SD reports from early 1942 still declared that people craved shots of Hitler in the newsreels. 'A smile of the Führer. His look itself gives us strength and courage again.' Such effusions were mentioned as commonplace remarks.[10] But Hitler was becoming a remote figure, a distant warlord. His image had to be refashioned by Goebbels to match the change which the Russian campaign had brought about. The première of his lavish new film, *The Great King*, in early 1942 allowed Goebbels to stylize Hitler by association as a latter-day Frederick the Great, isolated in his majesty, conducting a heroic struggle for his people against mighty enemies and ultimately overcoming crisis and calamity to emerge triumphant.[11] It was a portrayal which increasingly matched Hitler's self-image during the last years of the war.[12]

But the changed image could do nothing to alter reality: the German people's bonds with Hitler were to weaken immeasurably as victories turned into defeats, advances into retreats, expansion into contraction, as the death-toll mounted catastrophically, allies deserted, and the war came to be widely recognized as leading to inevitable disaster. And as the war turned inexorably against Germany, Hitler cast around all the more for scapegoats.

I

An early complication in 1942 arose with the loss of his armaments minister, Dr Fritz Todt, in a fatal air-crash on the morning of 8 February, soon after taking off from the airfield at the Führer Headquarters.

Todt had masterminded the building of the motorways and the Westwall for Hitler.[13] In March 1940 he had been been given the task, as a Reich Minister, of coordinating the production of weapons and munitions.[14] Yet a further major office had come his way in July 1941 with the centralization in his hands of control over energy and waterways.[15] In the second half of the year, as the first signs of serious labour shortage in German industry became evident, Todt was commissioned with organizing the mass deployment within Germany of Soviet prisoners-of-war and civilian forced labourers.[16] The accumulation of offices pivotal to the war economy was an indication of Hitler's high esteem for Todt. This was reciprocated. Todt was a convinced National Socialist. But by late 1941, fully aware of the massive armaments potential of the USA and appalled at the logistical incompetence of the Wehrmacht's economic planning during the eastern campaign, he had become deeply pessimistic, certain that the war could not be won.[17]

His public statements naturally betrayed none of his private doubts. And during December and January, he had taken the vital steps in conjunction with industry in drastically rationalizing and concentrating armaments production. Hitler, who had been made aware of the gross inefficiencies in the production of weaponry and was anxious to maximize the turn-out of armaments during 1942, backed the changes.[18] The decisive alteration was to give greater scope and incentive to industry to improve its own efficiency as well as freeing armaments production from intervention from the military and Four-Year Plan Organization and some of the stifling bureaucratic controls which had been imposed on it.[19] At the same time, the priorities that had been accorded the Luftwaffe and navy, when it was presumed the war in the east would easily and quickly be won, were reversed to favour the army.[20]

On the morning of 7 February, Todt flew to Rastenburg to put to Hitler proposals which had arisen from his meeting a few days earlier with representatives of the armaments industries.[21] What else transpired during his meeting with Hitler that afternoon is not known. No one else was present, and no notes or minutes were made. Later speculation that Todt demanded more extensive powers than Hitler was prepared to grant him, threatened resignation, or expounded defeatist views on the war rested on guesswork and some unreliable evidence.[22] But the meeting was plainly anything but harmonious. In depressed mood, and after a restless night, Todt left next morning to head for Munich in a twin-engined Heinkel 111. His own plane, a Junkers 52, was currently under repair, and he had borrowed the Heinkel – the personal plane of Field-Marshal Sperrle – from the Luftwaffe. It was flown by Todt's usual pilot, who took it on a brief test-flight shortly before take-off.[23]

Shortly after leaving the runway, the plane turned abruptly, headed to land again, burst into flames, and crashed. The bodies of Todt and four others on board were yanked with long poles from the burning wreckage. An official inquiry ruled out sabotage.[24] But suspicion was never fully allayed.[25] What caused the crash remained a mystery. Hitler, according to witnesses who saw him at close quarters, was deeply moved by the loss of Todt, whom, it was said, he still greatly admired and needed for the war economy.[26] Even if, as was later often claimed, the breach between him and Todt had become irreparable on account of the Armaments Minister's forcefully expressed conviction that the war could not be won, it is not altogether obvious why Hitler would have been so desperate as to resort to having Todt killed in an arranged air-crash at his own headquarters in circumstances guaranteed to prompt suspicion. Had he been insistent upon dispensing with Todt's services, 'retirement' on ill-health grounds would have offered a simpler solution. The only obvious beneficiary from Todt's demise was the successor Hitler now appointed with remarkable haste: his highly ambitious court architect, Albert Speer. But Speer's relationship with Todt had been excellent. And the only 'evidence' later used to hint at any involvement by Speer was his presence in the Führer Headquarters at the time of the crash and his rejection, a few hours before the planned departure, of an offer of a lift in Todt's aeroplane.[27] Whatever the cause of the crash that killed Todt – and the speed with which Hitler had the investigation hushed up naturally fuelled suspicion – it brought Albert Speer, till then in the second rank of Nazi leaders and known only as Hitler's court-architect and a personal favourite of the Führer, into the foreground.

Speer's meteoric rise in the 1930s had rested on shrewd exploitation of the would-be architect Hitler's building mania, coupled with his own driving ambition and undoubted organizational talent. Hitler liked Speer. 'He is an artist and has a spirit akin to mine,' he said. 'He is a building-person like me, intelligent, modest, and not an obstinate military-head.'[28] Speer later remarked that he was the nearest Hitler came to having a friend.[29] Now, Speer was in exactly the right place – close to Hitler – when a successor to Todt was needed. Six hours after the Reich Minister's sudden death, Speer was appointed to replace him in all his offices.[30] The appointment came as a surprise to many – including, if we are to take his own version of accounts at face value, Speer himself.[31] But Speer was certainly anticipating succeeding Todt in construction work – and possibly more.[32] At any rate, he lost no time in using Hitler's authority to establish for himself more extensive powers than Todt had ever enjoyed.[33] Speer would soon enough have to battle his way through the jungle of rivalries and intrigues which constituted the governance of the Third Reich. But once Hitler, the day after returning to Berlin for Todt's state funeral on 12 February (at which he himself delivered the oration as his eyes welled with, perhaps crocodile, tears),[34] had publicly backed Speer's supremacy in armaments production in a speech to leaders of the armaments industries, the new minister, still not quite thirty-eight years of age, found that 'I could do within the widest limits practically what I wanted'.[35] Building on the changes his predecessor had initiated, adding his own organizational flair and ruthless drive, and drawing on his favoured standing with Hitler, Speer proved an inspired choice. Over the next two years, despite intensified Allied bombing and the fortunes of war ebbing strongly away from Germany, he presided over a doubling of armaments output.[36]

Hitler was full of confidence when Goebbels had the chance to speak at length with him during his stay in Berlin following Todt's funeral. After the travails of the winter, the Dictator had reason to feel as if the corner was turned. During the very days that he was in Berlin the British were suffering two mighty blows to their prestige. Three German battleships, *Gneisenau*, *Scharnhorst*, and *Prinz Eugen*, had steamed out of Brest and, under the very noses of the British, passed through the English Channel with minimal damage, heading for safer moorings at Wilhelmshaven and Kiel. Hitler could scarcely contain his delight.[37] At the same time, the news was coming in from the Far East of the imminent fall of Singapore. Hitler expressed his admiration for the Japanese.[38] But it was tinged with a feeling that the British were losing their Empire when they could have accepted his 'offer' and fought alongside instead of against Germany. 'This is wonderful, though perhaps also sad, news,' he had said to the Romanian leader Antonescu a few days earlier.[39] He told Ribbentrop not to overdo the pronouncements on the fall of Singapore. 'We've got to think in centuries,' he apparently said. 'One day the showdown with the yellow race will come.'[40] Goebbels

LAST BIG THROW OF THE DICE 505

noted a degree of resignation that the Japanese advances meant 'the driving-back of the white man' in the Far East.[41] But, despite his racial prejudices, Hitler took a pragmatic view. 'I'm accused of sympathizing with the Japanese,' his secretary recalled him saying. 'What does sympathizing mean? The Japanese are yellow-skinned and slit-eyed. But they are fighting against the Americans and English, and so are useful to Germany.'[42] His enemy's enemy was his friend, in other words.

Most of all, Hitler was content about the prospects in the East. The problems of winter had been overcome, and important lessons learned. 'Troops who can cope with such a winter are unbeatable,' Goebbels noted. Now the great thaw had set in. 'The Führer is planning a few very hard and crushing offensive thrusts, which are already in good measure prepared and will doubtless lead gradually to the smashing of Bolshevism.'[43] Hitler conveyed the same enthusiasm in a morale-boosting speech to almost 10,000 trainee officers in the Sportpalast on 15 February. The world had been opposed to Frederick the Great and Bismarck. 'Today, I have the honour to be this enemy,' he declared, 'because I am attempting to create a world power out of the German Reich.' He was proud beyond measure that Providence had given him the opportunity to lead the 'inevitable struggle'. *They* should be proud to be part of such momentous events.[44] They gave him a rapturous reception. He left the huge hall with storms of applause and wild cheering ringing in his ears.[45] He returned to his headquarters assured as ever that, whatever his problems with the High Command, he had the total backing of his young officers and men. For their part, enthused by Hitler's rhetoric, the newly commissioned officers had little real awareness of what awaited them on active service in the east.

II

On 15 March, Hitler was back again in Berlin. The serious losses over the winter made it essential that he attend the midday ceremony on Heroes' Memorial Day. Only at the end of his speech did Hitler come to the commemoration of the dead. For the most part he offered no more than his usual regurgitation of the responsibility of the 'Jewish-capitalist world conspirators' for the war and heroization of the struggle – aimed, he asserted, at a lasting peace.[46] He portrayed the previous months as a struggle above all against the elements in a winter the like of which had not been seen for almost a century and a half.[47] 'But one thing we know today,' he declared.

'The Bolshevik hordes, which were unable to defeat the German soldiers and their allies this winter, will be beaten by us into annihilation this coming summer.'[48]

Many people were too concerned about the rumoured reductions in food rations to pay much attention to the speech.[49] Goebbels was well aware that food supplies had reached a critical point and that it would need a 'work of art' to put across to the people the reasons for the reductions.[50] He acknowledged that the cuts would lead to a 'crisis in the internal mood'.[51] Hitler, in full recognition of the sensitivity of the situation, had summoned the Propaganda Minister to his headquarters to discuss the issue before ration-cuts were announced.[52] Goebbels had so many problems to bring to Hitler's attention that he scarcely knew where he should begin.[53] His view was that the deterioration in morale at home demanded tough measures to counter it. People would understand the hardships of war if they fell equally on all the population. But as it was – Goebbels's own class resentments came strongly into play – the better-off were able through the black market and 'connections' to avoid serious deprivations. Göring had signed a law banning the black market. But its severity had been reduced through the intervention of the Economics Minister. Goebbels was determined to take the matter to the Führer, and hoped for the support of Bormann and the Party in getting Hitler to intervene to back more radical measures.[54]

On his return to Berlin on 18 March after some days away in the 'Ostmark' and Bavaria, Goebbels had been appalled at a 'scandalous scene' in the station where soldiers travelling to the eastern front were having to stand in the corridors of trains 'while fine ladies, returning sunburnt from holiday, naturally had their sleeping-compartments'. What was needed, he claimed, was a law under which 'all offences against known National Socialist principles of leadership of the people in war will be punished with corresponding retribution'.[55] That, too, he was going to put before Hitler during his visit to the Führer Headquarters. But Goebbels felt that, as things were, a radical approach to the law, necessary in total war, was being sabotaged by representatives of the formal legal system. He approved of Bormann's demands for tougher sentences for black-marketeering.[56] And he took it upon himself to press Hitler to change the leadership of the Justice Ministry, which since Gürtner's death the previous year had been run by the State Secretary, Franz Schlegelberger. 'The bourgeois elements still dominate there,' he commented, 'and since the heavens are high and the Führer far away, it's extraordinarily difficult to succeed against these stubborn and listlessly working authorities.'[57] It was in this mood – determined to persuade

Hitler to support radical measures, attack privilege, and castigate the state bureaucracy (above all judges and lawyers) – that Goebbels arrived at the Wolf's Lair on the ice-cold morning of 19 March.[58]

He met a Hitler showing clear signs of the strain he had been under during the past months, in a state of mind that left him more than open to Goebbels's radical suggestions. He needed no instruction about the mood in Germany, and the impact the reduction in food rations would have.[59] Lack of transport prevented food being brought from the Ukraine, he complained. The Transport Ministry was blamed for the shortage of locomotives. He was determined to take tough measures. Goebbels then lost no time in berating the 'failure' of the judicial system. Hitler did not demur. Here, too, he was determined to proceed with 'the toughest measures'. Goebbels paraded before Hitler his suggestion for a new comprehensive law to punish offenders against the 'principles of National Socialist leadership of the people'. He wanted the Reich Ministry of Justice placed in new hands, and pressed for Otto Thierack, 'a real National Socialist', an SA-Gruppenführer, and currently President of the notorious People's Court (*Volksgerichtshof*) – responsible for dealing with cases of treason and other serious offences against the regime – to take the place left by Gürtner.[60] Five months later, Hitler would make the appointment that Goebbels had wanted, and, in Thierack's hands, the capitulation of the judicial system to the police state would become complete.[61]

For now, Hitler placated Goebbels with a suggestion to prepare the ground for a radical assault on social privilege by recalling the Reichstag and having it bestow upon him 'a special plenipotentiary power' so that 'the evil-doers know that he is covered in every way by the people's community'. Given the powers which Hitler already possessed, the motive was purely populist. An attack on the civil servants and judges, and upon the privileged in society – or, as Hitler put it, 'saboteurs' and 'neglecters of duty in public functions' – could not fail to be popular with the masses. Up to this point, judges could not be dismissed – not even by the Führer. There were limits, too, to his rights of intervention in the military sphere. The case of Colonel-General Erich Hoepner still rankled deeply. Hitler had sacked Hoepner in January and dismissed him from the army in disgrace for retreating in disobedience to his 'Halt Order'. Hoepner had then instituted a law-suit against the Reich over the loss of his pension rights – and won. With Hitler's new powers, this could never happen again. Examples could be set in the military and civilian sector to serve as deterrents to others and 'clear the air'.[62]

'In such a mood,' wrote Goebbels the next day, 'my suggestions for the radicalization of our war-leadership naturally had an absolutely positive effect on the Führer. I only need to touch a topic and I have already got my way. Everything that I put forward individually is accepted piece for piece by the Führer without contradiction.'[63]

The encouragement of Hitler to back the radicalization of the home-front continued after Goebbels's return from the Wolf's Lair. Apart from the Propaganda Minister, it came in particular from Bormann and Himmler. On 26 March, the SD reported on a 'crisis of confidence' resulting from the failure of the state to take a tough enough stance against black-marketeers and their corrupt customers among the well-placed and privileged. Himmler, it seems, had directly prompted the report; Bormann made Hitler aware of it. Three days later, Goebbels castigated black-marketeering in *Das Reich*, publicizing two instances of the death-penalty being imposed on profiteers.[64]

It was on this same evening, that of 29 March, Hitler treated his small audience in the Wolf's Lair to a prolonged diatribe on lawyers and the deficiencies of the legal system, concluding that 'every jurist must be defective by nature, or would become so in time'.[65]

This was only a few days after he had personally intervened in a blind rage with acting Justice Minister Schlegelberger and, when he proved dilatory, with the more eagerly compliant Roland Freisler (later the infamous President of the People's Court as successor to Thierack but at this time Second State Secretary in the Justice Ministry), to insist on the death penalty for a man named Ewald Schlitt. This was on no more solid basis than the reading of a sensationalized account in a Berlin evening paper of how an Oldenburg court had sentenced Schlitt to only five years in a penitentiary for a horrific physical assault – according to the newspaper account – that had led to the death of his wife in an asylum. The court had been lenient because it took the view that Schlitt had been temporarily deranged. Schlegelberger lacked the courage to present the case fully to Hitler, and to defend the judges at the same time. Instead, he promised to improve the severity of sentencing. Freisler had no compunction in meeting Hitler's wishes. The original sentence was overturned. In a new hearing, Schlitt was duly sentenced to death, and guillotined on 2 April.[66]

Hitler had been so enraged by what he had read on the Schlitt case – which matched all his prejudices about lawyers and fell precisely at the time when the judicial system was being made the scapegoat for the difficulties on the home front – that he had privately threatened, should other 'excessively lenient' sentences be produced, 'to send the Justice Ministry to the devil through a Reichstag law'.[67] As it was, the Schlitt case was brought into service as a pretext to demand from the Reichstag absolute powers over the law itself.

Hitler rang Goebbels on 23 April to tell him that he had now decided to deliver the speech to the Reichstag he had for long had in mind. Goebbels undertook to make the necessary arrangements to summon the Reichstag for 3p.m. on Sunday, 26 April.[68]

Goebbels went round to the Reich Chancellery for lunch shortly after Hitler's arrival in Berlin at midday on the 25th. He found him looking well and feeling in good form, though in a particularly sour mood at the failure of air-defences to protect the Heinkel works in Rostock from damage in a bombing raid, following the opening of the British bombing offensive with a devastating attack on Lübeck at the end of March.[69] Hitler extended his criticism from the Luftwaffe to the lack of initiative of the 'unmodern' navy and its lack of any 'leadership of stature'.[70] But, as regards the eastern front, he was confident that the lessons of the winter had been learned and full of optimism about the coming offensive, now in an advanced stage of preparation. Reports had been handed to him detailing starvation and cannibalism among the army and civilian population of the Soviet Union, and the abysmal level of equipment of the Red Army's soldiers.[71] It seemed – something he would persistently claim throughout 1942 – that the Soviet Union was almost on its last legs. Goebbels was clearly less certain that Germany would attain decisive successes in the summer. And Hitler himself gave an indication that total victory in the east would not be attained in 1942, speaking of building a more solid line of defence in the coming winter, when supplies for the German troops would no longer pose a problem.[72]

He soon launched into one of his favourite obsessions – vegetarianism. Much of the remainder of the 'discussion' consisted of a lecture on the dangers of meat-eating.[73] In the war, Hitler remarked, there was little to be done about upturning eating methods. But he intended to see to the problem once the war was over. Similarly with the question of the Christian Churches – one of Goebbels's pet themes, which he brought up once more: it was necessary for the time being, commented Hitler, not to react to the 'seditious' actions of the clergy; 'the showdown' would be saved for a 'more advantageous situation after the war' when he would have to come as the 'avenger'.[74]

In a shortened lunch next day, just before Hitler's Reichstag speech, a good deal of the talk revolved around the devastation of Rostock in a renewed British raid – the heaviest so far. Much of the housing in the centre of the Baltic harbour-town had been destroyed. But the Heinkel factory had lost only an estimated 10 per cent of its productive capacity.[75] German retaliation to British raids had consisted of attacks on Exeter and Bath. Goebbels favoured the complete devastation of English 'cultural centres'.[76] Hitler, furious at the new attack on Rostock, agreed, according to Goebbels's account. Terror had to be answered with terror. English 'cultural centres', seaside resorts, and 'bourgeois towns' would be razed to the ground. The psychological impact of this – and that was the key thing – would be far greater than that achieved through mostly unsuccessful attempts to hit armaments factories. German bombing would now begin in a big way. He had already given out the directive to prepare a lengthy plan of attack on such lines.[77]

Goebbels raised – during the midday meal, not in private discussion – the 'Jewish Question' once more. By this time some if not all of the slaughterhouses in Poland were in operation. Hitler's remarks remained, as always, menacingly unspecific. He briefly restated, according to Goebbels, his 'pitiless (*unerbittlich*)' stance: 'he wants to drive the Jews absolutely out of Europe'. The Propaganda Minister knew, as did other 'insiders', what this meant. He had, after all, referred to the liquidation of the Jews in unmistakable terms in his own diary entry only a month earlier.[78] The 'hardest punishment' that could be inflicted on the Jews was 'still too mild', he now added.[79]

Why Hitler had chosen this moment to summon the Reichstag was the subject of much speculation and rumour among the mass of the population. But the background to it and the coming assault on the judicial system remained closely guarded secrets.[80] What turned out to be the last ever session of the Great German Reichstag began punctually at 3p.m. that afternoon. Hitler spoke for little over an hour. He was nervous at the beginning, starting hesitantly, then speaking so fast that parts of his speech were scarcely intelligible.[81] Much of it was taken up with the usual long-winded account of the background to the war. This was followed by a description of the struggle through the previous winter – with a strong hint that the war would not be over before a new winter had to be faced.[82] He then came to the centrepoint of his address. He implied that transport, administration, and justice had been found lacking. There was a side-swipe (without naming names) at General Hoepner: 'no one can stand on their well-earned rights', but had to know 'that today there are only duties'. He requested from the Reichstag, therefore, 'the express confirmation that I possess the legal right to hold each one to fulfilment of his duties' with rights to dismiss from office without respect to 'acquired rights'. Using the Schlitt case as his example, he launched into a savage attack on the failings of the judiciary. From now on, he said, he would intervene in such cases and dismiss judges 'who visibly fail to recognize the demands of the hour'.[83]

As soon as Hitler had finished speaking, Göring read out the 'Resolution (*Beschluß*)' of the Reichstag. This unusual form of decree – a proposal by the Reichstag President for approval by the members of the Reichstag – had been suggested, then composed, by Lammers at breakneck speed before the session in order to obviate any constitutional problems but also to underline the formal granting by the popular assembly of such far-reaching powers to Hitler.[84] According to the 'Resolution', Hitler was empowered 'without being bound to existing legal precepts', in his capacity as 'Leader of the Nation, Supreme Commander of the Wehrmacht, Head of Government and supreme occupant of executive power, as supreme law-lord (*oberster Gerichtsherr*) and as Leader of the Party' (the last an addition specifically inserted by Lammers), to remove from office and punish anyone, of whatever status, failing to carry out his duty, without respect to pensionable rights, and without any stipulated formal proceedings.[85]

Naturally, the 'Resolution' was unanimously approved.[86] The last shreds of constitutionality had been torn apart. Hitler now *was* the law.

Many people were surprised that Hitler needed any extension of his powers. They wondered what had gone on that had prompted his scathing attacks on the internal administration. Disappointment was soon registered that no immediate actions appeared to follow his strong words.[87] Lawyers, judges, and civil servants were not unnaturally dismayed by the assault on their professions and standing. What had caused it was in their eyes a mystery. The Führer had evidently, they thought, been crassly misinformed.[88] The consequences were, however, unmistakable. As the head of the judiciary in Dresden pointed out, with the ending of all judicial autonomy Germany had now become a 'true Führer state'.[89]

Hitler could ignore the predictable lamentations from judges and lawyers who, with few exceptions, would nevertheless continue to comply with everything demanded of them. In futile attempts to defend status and authority, they would more readily than ever bend over backwards to accommodate every inhumane initiative, thereby undermining precisely what they hoped to preserve – a state based upon the rule of law, however harsh, and the power of the judiciary to interpret and impose that law. Hitler's populist instincts had not deserted him. Less elevated sections of the population enthused over his assault on rank and privilege.[90] This had successfully allowed him to divert attention from more fundamental questions about the failures of the previous winter and to provide a much-needed morale-booster through easy attacks on cheap targets.

After his speech, Hitler, warmed by the euphoria in the Reichstag, the enthusiasm of the crowds lining the streets back to the Reich Chancellery, and the fawning congratulations of his entourage, could relax, look forward to a break in his alpine retreat, and unfold his plans for the great refashioning of Linz into '*the* city on the Danube', a cultural metropolis to outshine Vienna.[91]

For the mass of the German people, only the prospect of the peace that final victory would bring could sustain morale for any length of time. Many 'despondent souls', ran one Party report on the popular mood, were 'struck only by one part of the Führer's speech: where he spoke of the preparations for the winter campaign of 1942-43. The more the homeland has become aware of the cruelty and hardship of the winter struggle in the east, the more the longing for an end to it has increased. But now the end is still not in sight. Many wives and mothers are suffering as a result.'[92] The hopes briefly raised by the successes of the summer offensive would rapidly give way to despair in the calamities that the coming autumn and winter would bring.

III

Hours after his Reichstag speech, Hitler left for Munich, *en route* to the Berghof and a meeting with Mussolini. He was in expansive mood next lunchtime at his favourite Munich restaurant, the Osteria.[93] He held forth to Hermann Giesler, one of his favoured architects, and his companion-in-arms from the old days of the Party's early struggles in Munich, Hermann Esser, on his plans for double-decker express trains to run at 200 kilometres an hour on four-metre-wide tracks between Upper Silesia and the Donets Basin. Naturally, there would be difficulties in bringing about this rail programme, he admitted, but one should not be put off by them.[94] Two days later, at a snow-covered Berghof with Eva Braun acting as hostess, he was regaling his supper guests with complaints about the lack of top Wagnerian tenors in Germany, and the deficiencies of leading conductors Bruno Walter and Hans Knappertsbusch. Walter, a Jew who had become renowned as the director of the Bavarian State Opera and Leipziger Gewandhaus before being forced out by the Nazis in 1933 and emigrating to America, was an 'absolute nonentity', claimed Hitler, who had ruined the orchestra of the

Vienna State Opera to the extent that it was capable only of playing 'beer music'. Although Walter's arch-rival Knappertsbusch, tall, blond, blue-eyed, had the appearance of a model 'aryan' male, listening to him conduct an opera was 'a punishment' to Hitler's mind, as the orchestra drowned out the singing and the conductor performed such gyrations that it was painful to look at him. Only Wilhelm Furtwängler, who had turned the Berlin Philharmonic into such an outstanding, magnificent orchestra, one of the regime's most important cultural ambassadors, and acknowledged maestro in conducting the Führer's own favourite Beethoven, Brahms, Bruckner, and Wagner, met with his unqualified approval.[95]

Between monologues, he had had 'discussions' with Mussolini in the baroque Klessheim Castle, once a residence of the Prince Bishops of Salzburg, now luxuriously refurbished with furniture and carpets removed from France to make a Nazi guest-house and conference-centre.[96] The atmosphere was cordial. Hitler looked tired to Ciano, and bearing the signs of the strains of the winter. His hair, Ciano noticed, was turning grey. Hitler's primary aim was to convey optimism to Mussolini about the war in the east.[97] Ribbentrop's message to Ciano, in their separate meeting, was no different: the 'genius of the Führer' had mastered the evils of the Russian winter; a coming offensive towards the Caucasus would deprive Russia of fuel, bring the conflict to an end, and force Britain to terms; British hopes from America amounted to 'a colossal bluff'.[98]

The talks continued the next day, now with military leaders present, at the Berghof. How much of a genuine discussion there was is plain from Ciano's description: 'Hitler talks, talks, talks, talks,' non-stop for an hour and forty minutes. Mussolini, used himself to dominating all conversation, had to suffer in silence, occasionally casting a surreptitious glance at his watch. Ciano switched off and thought of other things. Keitel yawned and struggled to keep awake. Jodl did not manage it: 'after an epic struggle', he finally fell asleep on a sofa.[99] Mussolini, overawed as always by Hitler, was, apparently, satisfied with the meetings.[100]

In reality, they had no concrete results. Hitler had, as usual, begun with a rosy-hued account of the war in the east, giving the impression that Soviet industrial capacity had fallen sharply and that the military calibre of the Red Army had also diminished. He drew the conclusion, typically, that 'it can therefore in no way become worse, but only better'.[101] He repeated his assumption that if Russia were defeated, Britain's hopes would have gone. But he went on to indicate the dangers of a British landing in the west, or in North Africa. With either eventuality in mind, there was need, he urged, for great caution in dealing with France, whose collaboration was merely opportunistic. In North Africa, it had to be reckoned that the French colonies would support an Allied invasion. The Axis powers had therefore to be ready, he stressed to Mussolini, to seize unoccupied France at any critical moment. Hitler was half-hearted about the Italians' plans for an early assault on Malta. As far as the Mediterranean was concerned, his own priority was to provide what limited support he could to Rommel's forthcoming North African offensive, soon to be launched. This had to precede an attack on Malta.[102] His eyes were, however, on the east. That is where the war on land would be decided, he declared.[103]

Back at the Berghof, after the Italian party had left, Hitler told his lunchtime ensemble how impressed he had been by Hermann Giesler's spacious refurbishment of Klessheim. 'Generous ideas' about spaciousness needed to be incorporated by architects into town-planning in Germany. Then the higgledy-piggledy housing complexes of Zwickau, Gelsenkirchen, Bitterfeld and other towns 'without any culture' could be avoided. 'It was, therefore, his firm resolution,' he was recorded as stating, 'to see to it that a bit of culture comes even into the smallest town and that as a result the appearance of our towns slowly reaches an ever-higher level.'[104]

A week later, on 8 May, the Wehrmacht began its planned spring offensive. The first targets for Manstein's 11th Army, as laid down in Hitler's directive of 5 April, were the Kerch peninsula and Sevastopol in the Crimea.[105] The directive stipulated the drive on the Caucasus, to capture the oil-fields and occupy the mountain passes that opened the route to the Persian Gulf, as the main goal of the summer offensive to follow, codenamed 'Blue'. The removal of the basis of the Soviet war-economy and the destruction of remaining military forces – thought catastrophically weakened over the winter – would, it was presumed, bring victory in the east. There, Hitler had reasserted in planning the summer operations, the war would be decided.[106] The key factor was no longer 'living space', but oil. 'If I don't get the oil of Maykop and Grozny,' Hitler admitted, 'then I must finish (*liquidieren*) this war.'[107]

The Wehrmacht and Army High Commands did not contradict the strategic priority. In any case, they had no better alternative to recommend. And the lack of a coordinated command structure meant, as before, competition for Hitler's approval – a military version of 'working towards the Führer'.[108] It was not a matter of Hitler imposing a dictat on his military leaders. Despite his full recognition of the gravity of the German losses over the winter, Halder entirely backed the decision for an all-out offensive to destroy the basis of the Soviet economy.[109] The April directive for 'Blue' bore his clear imprint.[110] And despite the magnitude of their miscalculation the previous year, operational planners, fed by highly flawed intelligence, far from working on the basis of a 'worst-case-scenario', backed the optimism about the military and economic weakness of the Soviet Union.[111]

Whatever the presumptions of Soviet losses – on which German intelligence remained woefully weak – the Wehrmacht's own strength, as Halder knew only too well, had been drastically weakened. Over a million of the 3.2 million men who had attacked the Soviet Union on 22 June 1941 were by now dead, captured, or missing.[112] At the end of March, only 5 per cent of army divisions were fully operational.[113] The figures that Halder gave Hitler on 21 April were chilling in the extreme. Some 900,000 men had been lost since the autumn, only 50 per cent replaced (including the call-up of all available twenty-year-olds, and serious inroads into the labour-force at home). Only around 10 per cent of the vehicles lost had been replaced (though most of the losses of tracked vehicles could be made good). Losses of weapons were also massive. At the beginning of the spring offensive, the eastern front was short of around 625,000 men.[114] Given such massive shortages, everything was poured into bolstering the southern offensive in the Soviet Union. Of the sixty-eight divisions established on this part of the front, forty-eight had been entirely, and seventeen at least partly, reconstituted.[115]

Poor Soviet intelligence meant the Red Army was again unprepared for the German assault when it came.[116] By 19 May, the Kerch offensive was largely over, with the capture of 150,000 prisoners and a great deal of booty. A heavy Soviet counter on Kharkhov had been, if with difficulty, successfully fended off.[117] By the end of May, the battle at Kharkhov had also resulted in a notable victory, with three Soviet armies destroyed, and over 200,000 men and a huge quantity of booty captured.[118] This was in no small measure owing to Hitler's refusal, fully endorsed by Halder, to allow Field-Marshal Bock, since mid-January Commander of Army Group South, to break off the planned offensive and take up a defensive position.[119]

Hitler had reason to feel pleased with himself when he spoke for two hours behind closed doors in the Reich Chancellery to the Reichsleiter and Gauleiter on the afternoon of 23 May. He had come to Berlin for the funeral of Carl Röver, Gauleiter of Weser-Ems, which had taken place the previous day.[120] After a difficult period, also on the home front, he evidently could not miss the opportunity to bolster the solidarity and loyalty of his long-standing Party stalwarts, a vital part of his power-base. And in such company, he was prepared to speak with some candour about his aims.

One of these was the Party's own work. The death of such a valued comrade as Röver was an indication that successors for Party leaders of his generation, now aged between forty-five and sixty years old (the dead Gauleiter had been born in 1889), needed to be cultivated. But they would not be able to tackle problems which the 'sworn community' of the original Party leadership had eschewed. It was his usual fixation with the question of time and mortality. They had been destined (*ausersehen*) to solve the problems which the National Socialist revolution had brought to the fore. Nothing must be put off. However inconvenient, the issues must be successfully solved. He hoped himself to survive the war. He was convinced that no one else would be able to master its difficulties.[121]

Hitler turned to the war in the east. He described the winter crisis, castigating the failings of the leaders of the Wehrmacht, the organizers of transport, the judiciary, and the civil service.[122] Japan's intervention had been a blessing, at a time when Germany was facing catastrophe. Some established army leaders had lost their nerve in this situation. He alone – this was the gist of his remarks – had, through his unyielding refusal of requests to retreat, prevented 'a Napoleonic débâcle'.[123] He had praise for the Waffen-SS in the east, and for the Party as the backbone of the home front, the counter to doubts and pessimism.[124] He was determined, after their 'insidious' behaviour during the winter, he said, doubtless playing here on the many complaints fed to him by Goebbels and the other Gauleiter, to destroy the Christian Churches after the war.[125] A revolution against the regime would never occur, he declared, if rebellious elements were dealt with in time. He had given Himmler express orders, should there be a danger of the Reich 'sinking into chaos', to 'shoot the criminals in all concentration camps'.[126]

Hitler said he recognized in Stalin a 'man of stature who towered above the democratic figures of the Anglo-Saxon powers'. He naturally knew, Goebbels reported him as saying, 'that the Jews are determined under all circumstances to bring this war to victory for them, since they know that defeat also means for them personal liquidation'. It was a more forthright version of his 'prophecy' – on this occasion unmistakably and explicitly linking it, in Goebbels's understanding of what was intended, with the physical liquidation of the Jews.[127]

Hitler emphasized that the war in the east was not comparable with any war in the past. It was not a simple matter of victory or defeat, but of 'triumph or destruction (*Triumph oder Untergang*)'. He was aware of the enormous capacity of the American armaments programme. But the scale of output claimed by Roosevelt 'could in no way be right'. And he had good information on the scale of Japanese naval construction. He reckoned on serious losses for the American navy when it clashed with the Japanese fleet.[128] He took the view 'that in the past winter we have won the war'. Preparations were now in place to launch the offensive in the south of the Soviet Union to cut off the enemy's oil supplies. He was determined to finish off the Soviets in the coming summer.[129]

He looked to the future. His vision was very familiar to those who had been his lunch or supper guests in the Wolf's Lair. Hitler was frank about his imperialist aims. The Reich would massively extend its land in the east, gaining coal, grain, oil, and above all national security. In the west, too, the Reich would have to be strengthened. The French would 'have to bleed for that'. But there it was a strategic, not an ethnic, question. 'We must solve the ethnic (*völkischen*) questions in the east.' Once the territory needed for the consolidation of Europe was in German hands, it was his intention to build a gigantic fortification, like the *limes* of Roman times, to separate Asia from Europe. He went on with his vision of a countryside settled by farmer-soldiers, building up a population of 250 million within seventy or eighty years. Then Germany would be safe against all future threats. It should not be difficult, he claimed, to preserve the ethnic-German (*völkisch*) character of the conquered territories. 'That would also be the actual meaning of this war. For the serious sacrifice of blood could only be justified through later generations gaining from it the blessing of waving cornfields.' Nice though it would be to acquire a few colonies to provide rubber or coffee, 'our colonial territory is in the east. There are to be found fertile black earth and iron, the bases of our future wealth.' He ended his vision of the future with the vaguest notion of what he understood as a social revolution. The National Socialist Movement, he said, had to make sure that the war did not end in a capitalist victory, but in a victory of the people. A new society would have to be constructed out of the victory, one resting not on money, status, or name, but on courage and test of character (*Bewährung*). He was confident that victory would be Germany's. Once the 'business in the east' was finished – in the summer, it was to be hoped – 'then the war is practically won for us. Then we will be in the position of conducting a large-scale pirate-war against the Anglo-Saxon powers, which in the long run they will not be able to withstand.'[130]

Little over a week later, Hitler was back in Berlin again, this time to address around 10,000 young officers in the Sportpalast on 30 May. Naturally, he struck a different tone. But essentially it offered the same images of the dire spectre of a Bolshevik victory and the power and prosperity of imperialist conquest. Kerch and Kharkov were, he told them, merely the 'prelude' to what was to follow in the summer. Germany would – and must – succeed, he declared. If the enemy proved victorious, then 'our German people would be exterminated (*ausgerottet*). Asiatic barbarity would plant itself in Europe. The German woman would be fair game for these beasts. The intelligentsia would be slaughtered. Whatever gives us the characteristic features of a higher form of mankind would be exterminated and annihilated (*vernichtet*).' Victory for the Reich, on the other hand, and the acquisition of 'living-space', would give future generations grain, iron, coal, oil, flax, rubber, and wood in abundance.[131]

Hitler had been in ebullient mood when Goebbels saw him at lunchtime in the Reich Chancellery on the day before his speech to the officers. With the advance to the Caucasus, he told his Propaganda Minister, 'we'll be pressing the Soviet system so to say on its Adam's Apple.'[132] He thought the new Soviet losses at Kerch and Kharkov were not reparable; Stalin was reaching the end of his resources; there were major difficulties with food-supplies in the Soviet Union; morale there was poor.[133] He had concrete plans for the extension of the Reich borders also in the West. He took it as a matter of course that Belgium, with its ancient Germanic provinces of Flanders and Brabant, would be split into German *Reichsgaue*. So would, whatever the views of Dutch National Socialist leader Anton Mussert, the Netherlands.[134]

Two days earlier, on 27 May, one of Hitler's most important henchmen, Reinhard Heydrich, Chief of the Security Police and since the previous autumn Deputy Protector of Bohemia and Moravia, had been fatally wounded in an assassination attempt carried out by patriotic Czech exiles who had been flown from London – with the aid of the British subversive warfare agency, the Special Operations Executive (SOE) – and parachuted into the vicinity of Prague. Heydrich's own security had become lax. That morning, he left his palatial residence at Panenske Brezany, around twelve miles from Prague, to drive to his headquarters at the Hradcany Castle in the capital without bodyguard, in an open Mercedes, alone with his chauffeur. He always took the same route. The two assassins, and their comrade who would serve as the look-out, had observed him regularly. Heydrich was a little late leaving that morning. It was just after 10.30a.m. when the look-out flashed the signal by mirror that his car was approaching the hairpin bend where it would be forced to slow down, and where the attempt would be made. As the car slowed, the first Czech agent, Josef Gabcik, stepped out, pulled a sten-gun from under his coat, and pressed the trigger. The gun jammed. But Gabcik's companion, Jan Kubis, ran towards the car and lobbed his grenade at it. The bomb hit the back wheel and exploded. Heydrich, injured in the blast, tried to pursue his assailant, before collapsing. Kubis, also wounded by the explosion, escaped on a bicycle. Gabcik disappeared on a crowded tram after shooting Heydrich's chauffeur in both legs. The look-out walked away quietly. By the wrecked Mercedes, one of the most powerful men in Hitler's Reich lay mortally injured.[135]

Hitler always favoured brutal reprisals. There could be no doubt that the attack on one of the key representatives of his power would provoke a ferocious response.

The assassins themselves were betrayed, for a large money reward, by another Czech SOE agent. Eventually trapped by the SS, they committed suicide after engaging in a gun-battle. But their deaths contributed little towards satiating the Nazi blood-lust. To this end, over 1,300 Czechs, some 200 of them women, were eventually rounded up by the SS and executed. On 10 June the entire village of Lidice – the name had been found on a Czech SOE agent arrested earlier – was to be destroyed, the male inhabitants shot, the women taken to Ravensbrück concentration camp, the children removed.[136]

Hitler's mood was ripe for Goebbels to bring up once more the question of the deportation of Berlin's remaining Jews. The involvement of a number of young Jews (associated with a Communist-linked resistance group led by Herbert Baum) in the arson attempt at the anti-Bolshevik exhibition 'The Soviet Paradise' in Berlin's Lustgarten on 18 May enabled the Propaganda Minister to emphasize the security dangers if the 40,000 or so Jews he reckoned were still in the Reich capital were not deported.[137] He had been doing his best, he had noted a day earlier, to have as many Jews as possible from his domain 'shipped off to the east'.[138] Goebbels now pleaded for 'a more radical Jewish policy' and, he said, 'I push at an open door with the Führer,' who told Speer to find replacements for the Jews in the armaments industry with 'foreign workers' as soon as possible.[139]

Talk moved to the dangers of possible internal revolt in the event of a critical situation in the war, something Hitler had touched upon in his speech to the Gauleiter a few days earlier.[140] If the danger became acute, he now repeated, the prisons 'would be emptied through liquidations' to prevent the possibility of the gates being opened to let the 'revolting mob' loose on the people.[141] But in contrast to 1917 there was nothing to fear from the German workers, remarked Hitler. All German workers desired victory. They had most to lose by defeat and would not contemplate stabbing him in the back. 'The Germans take part in subversive movements only when the Jews lure them into it,' Goebbels had Hitler saying. 'Therefore one must liquidate the Jewish danger, cost what it takes.' West-European civilization only provided a façade of assimilation. Back in the ghetto, Jews soon returned to type. But there were elements among them who operated 'with dangerous brutality and thirst for revenge (Rachsucht)'. 'Therefore,' recorded Goebbels, 'the Führer does not wish at all that the Jews be evacuated to Siberia. There, under the hardest living conditions, they would doubtless again represent a vigorous element. He would most like to see them resettled in Central Africa. There they would live in a climate that would certainly not make them strong and capable of resistence. At any rate, it is the aim of the Führer to make Western Europe entirely free of Jews. Here they can no longer have any home.'[142]

Did such remarks mean that Hitler was unaware that the 'Final Solution' was under way, that Jews had already been slaughtered in their thousands in Russia and were now being murdered by poison gas in industrialized mass-killing centres already operating in Chelmno, Belzec, Sobibor, and Auschwitz-Birkenau (with Treblinka and Maidanek soon to follow)? That seems inconceivable, even if he did not need to be informed of the fine detail of what was taking place, or for that matter of the very names of the extermination camps. As we have noted, reports of the slaughter by the Einsatzgruppen in the USSR had been requested to be sent to Hitler on a regular basis. In December 1941, he had explicitly affirmed to Himmler that Jews – meaning, certainly, those in the east – were to be 'exterminated as partisans'. And in March 1942, Goebbels had referred to Hitler as the inspiration behind the most 'radical solution' of the 'Jewish question', in referring to the liquidation of the Jews from the Lublin district.

On 9 April 1942, a time when the deportations from western European countries to the gas-chambers of Poland were also getting under way, Hans Frank told his underlings in the General Government that orders for the liquidation of the Jews came 'from higher authority'.[143] Himmler himself was to claim explicitly in an internal, top-secret, letter to SS-Obergruppenführer Gottlob Berger, Chief of the SS Main Office, on 28 July 1942, that he was operating directly under Hitler's authority: 'The occupied Eastern territories are being made free of Jews. The Führer has placed the implementation of this very difficult order on my shoulders.'[144]

How much detail Hitler asked for, or was given, cannot be known. But, one indication at the very least, that he was aware of the slaughter of huge numbers of Jews, is provided by a report which Himmler had drawn up for him at the end of 1942 providing statistics on Jews 'executed' in southern Russia on account of alleged connection with 'bandit' activity. Having ordered in mid-December that partisan 'bands' were to be combated 'by the most brutal means (*mit den allerbrutalsten Mitteln*)', also to be used against women and children, Hitler was presented by Himmler with statistics for southern Russia and the Ukraine on the number of 'bandits' liquidated in the three months of September, October, and November 1942. The figures for those helping the 'bands' or under suspicion of being connected with them listed 363,211 'Jews executed'. The connection with subversive activity was an obvious sham. Others in the same category 'executed' totalled 'only' 14,257.[145]

Four months after this, in April 1943, Himmler would have an abbreviated statistical report on 'the Final Solution of the Jewish Question' sent to Hitler. Aware of the taboo in Hitler's entourage on explicit reference to the mass killing of the Jews, Himmler had the statistical report presented in camouflage language. The fiction had to be maintained. Himmler ordered the term 'Special Treatment' (itself a euphemism for killing) deleted from the shortened version to be sent to Hitler. His statistician, Dr Richard Korherr, was ordered simply to refer to the 'transport of Jews'. There was reference to Jews being 'sluiced through' unnamed camps. The camouflage-language was there to serve a specific purpose. Hitler would understand what it meant, and recognize the Reichsführer-SS's 'achievement'.[146]

When he spoke at lunchtime on 29 May 1942 to Goebbels and to his other guests at his meal-table about his preference for the 'evacuation' of the Jews to Central Africa, Hitler was sustaining the fiction which had to be upheld even in his 'court circle' that the Jews were being resettled and put to work in the east.[147] Goebbels himself, in his diary entry, went along with the fiction, though he knew only too well – as an earlier explicit entry in his diary indicates – what was happening to the Jews in Poland.[148] Hitler, as we noted in the previous chapter, had spoken in early 1941 of deporting the Jews to the east. The Madagascar Plan, if he had ever taken it seriously, had by then been abandoned for some time. In September 1941 he had authorized the deportation of the Jews to the east. Speaking now of sending the Jews to central Africa, when only a fortnight earlier he had once more indicated how little interest he had in overseas colonies and when, at this juncture, there was no prospect of attaining territory there, amounted to no more than a fig-leaf to cover what he knew was actually happening.[149] Hitler had by now internalized his authorization of the killing of the Jews. It was typical of his way of dealing with the 'Final Solution' that he spoke of it either by repeating what he knew had long since ceased to be the case; or by alluding to the removal of Jews from Europe (often in the context of his 'prophecy') at some distant point in the future.

Hitler's preoccupation with secrecy remained intense. Nowhere is there an explicit indication, even in discussions with adjutants or secretaries, of his knowledge of the extermination of the Jews.[150] The subject was probably mentioned, if at all, only privately to Himmler and in general terms (as in their discussion on 18 December 1941), and otherwise darkly hinted at in camouflaged remarks, whose meanings were perfectly well understood by those aware of what was happening. Himmler adopted the same strategy.[151]

Why was Hitler so anxious to maintain the fiction of resettlement, and uphold the 'terrible secret' even among his inner circle? A partial explanation is doubtless to be found in Hitler's acute personal inclination to extreme secrecy which he translated into a general mode of rule, as laid down in his 'Basic Order' of January 1940, that information should only be available on a 'need-to-know' basis.[152] Knowledge of extermination could provide a propaganda gift to enemies, and perhaps stir up unrest and internal difficulties in the occupied territories, particularly in western Europe.[153] And as regards public opinion in the Reich itself, the Nazi leadership believed that the German people were not ready for the gross inhumanity of the extermination of the Jews.[154] Hitler had agreed with Rosenberg in mid-December 1941, directly following the declaration of war on the USA, that it would be inappropriate to speak of extermination in public.[155] Late in 1942, Bormann was keen to quell rumours circulating about the 'Final Solution' in the east.[156] Himmler would later, speaking to SS leaders, refer to it as 'a never to be written glorious page of our history'.[157] Evidently, it was a secret to be carried to the grave.

In his public statements referring to his 1939 'prophecy', Hitler could now lay claim to his place in 'the glorious secret of our history' while still detaching himself from the sordid and horrific realities of mass killing.[158] Beyond that, a further incentive to secrecy was that Hitler wanted no bureaucratic and legal interference. He had experienced this in the 'euthanasia action', necessitating his unique written authorization, and the problems which subsequently arose from it. His tirades about the judicial system and bureaucracy in the spring of 1942 were a further indicator of his sensitivity towards such interference. To avoid any legalistic meddling, Himmler explicitly refused in the summer of 1942 to entertain attempts to define 'a Jew'.[159]

In addition, there was probably, however, a deep psychological underlay to Hitler's obsessive secretiveness about the fate of the Jews. The Third Reich was mighty, but even now perhaps, so his warped thinking must have run, not so mighty as the power of the Jews – the 'world conspiracy' in which he still fervently believed. He still had no means of tackling the Jews whom he believed to be behind the war with Britain and, above all, with the USA. Whatever his public optimism, there is the occasional veiled hint that he entertained the thought, in the darkness of his insomniac nights, that he might lose the war, that his enemies might prevail.[160] Some ordinary Germans, swallowing Nazi propaganda and betraying their ingrained prejudices, voiced their worries by the middle of the war of the 'revenge of the Jews' if Germany were to lose its struggle.[161] It seems hardly conceivable that Hitler did not also entertain such a concern in the recesses of his mind. Withholding his knowledge of the 'Final Solution', even from his close associates, would ensure that such information could not reach his archenemies.

IV

Manstein's difficulties in taking Sevastopol held up the start of 'Operation Blue' – the push to the Caucasus – until the end of June.[162] But at this point, Hitler need have no doubts that the war was going well. In the Atlantic, the U-boats had met with unprecedented success. In the first six months of 1942, they had sunk almost a third more shipping tonnage than during the whole of 1941, and far fewer U-boats had been lost in the process.[163] And on the evening of 21 June came the stunning news that Rommel had taken Tobruk. Through brilliant tactical manoeuvring during the previous three weeks, Rommel had outwitted the ineffectively led and poorly equipped British 8th Army and was then able to inflict a serious defeat on the Allied cause by seizing the stronghold of Tobruk, on the Libyan coast, capturing 33,000 British and Allied prisoners-of-war (many of them South African) and a huge amount of booty.[164] It was a spectacular German victory and a disaster for the British. The doorway to German dominance of Egypt was wide open. All at once there was a glimmering prospect in view of an enormous pincer of Rommel's troops pushing eastwards through Egypt and the Caucasus army sweeping down through the Middle East linking forces to wipe out the British presence in this crucial region.[165] Hitler, overjoyed, immediately promoted Rommel to Field-Marshal. Italian hopes of German support for an invasion of Malta were now finally shelved until later in the year. Hitler backed instead Rommel's plans to advance to the Nile. Within days, German troops were in striking distance of Alexandria.[166]

One dark cloud on an otherwise sunny horizon was, however, the damage being caused to towns in western Germany by British bombing raids. On 30 May, Hitler had said that he did not think much of the RAF's threats of heavy air-raids. Precautions, he claimed, had been taken. The Luftwaffe had so many squadrons stationed in the west that destruction from the air would be doubly repaid.[167] That very night, the city centre of Cologne was devastated by the first 1,000-bomber raid. The Luftwaffe's own claims that only seventy British bombers were involved, of which forty-four had been shot down, were regarded even by the Nazi leadership as absurd. Hitler believed the more realistic reports from the Party regional office in Cologne. Goebbels had himself telephoned Führer Headquarters to give an estimate of 250–300 bombers taking part.[168] Hitler was enraged at the failure of the Luftwaffe to defend the Reich, blaming Göring personally for neglecting the construction of sufficient flak installations.[169]

Despite the bombing of Cologne, the military situation put Hitler and his entourage in excellent mood in early June. On the first day of the month Hitler was flown in his 'Führer Machine' – a spacious, four-engined Focke-Wulff, with simple interior and few special features other than a writing desk in front of his own seat – to Army Group South's headquarters at Poltava to discuss with Field-Marshal Bock the timing and tactics of the coming offensive. Apart from Manstein, all the commanders were present as Hitler agreed to Bock's proposal to delay the start of 'Operation Blue' for some days in order to take full advantage of the victory at Kharkov to destroy Soviet forces in adjacent areas. Hitler informed the commanders that the outcome of 'Blue' would be decisive for the war.[170] Back in the Wolf's Lair, he told his lunchtime gathering next day that the number of blue-eyed, blonde women he had seen in Poltava had slightly shaken his racial views.[171] He had been astonished at how well-fed and -clothed the people of the area were. There could be no talk there of famine.[172]

On 4 June, Hitler paid a surprise visit – it had been arranged only the previous day – to Finland. Officially, the visit was to mark the seventy-fifth birthday of the Finnish military hero, Marshal Baron Carl Gustaf von Mannerheim, supreme commander of the Finnish armed forces. How pleased Mannerheim was to have his birthday party hijacked by Hitler can only be surmised. But the Finns had little choice other than to comply. Despite their growing unease at the alliance with Germany, which they had entered into prior to 'Barbarossa' in the expectation of a swift and comprehensive victory of the Wehrmacht,[173] no current alternative to German tutelage was available. For Hitler, some sense of the significance he attached to the meeting can be judged from the fact that, apart from a number of trips to Italy and his meetings in southern France with Pétain and Franco in 1940, it was the only time he had travelled to an area outside direct German control.[174]

The aim of the informal visit was to bolster Finnish solidarity with Germany through underlining for Mannerheim – a veteran of struggles with the Red Army – the immensity of the threat of Bolshevism. The Finns would at the same time be warned about any possible considerations of leaving German 'protection' and putting out feelers to the Soviet Union. In addition, the visit would head off any possible ties of Finland with the western Allies.[175]

The meeting took place in Mannerheim's special train in the middle of woods near the air-field at Immola.[176] First came the ceremonials – Hitler presented Mannerheim with the Great Golden Cross of the German Order of the Eagle – followed by lunch. Then the main participants withdrew for a confidential meeting. For an hour and a half, Hitler ran through his usual account of the war for his almost entirely silent small audience of Mannerheim, State President Risto Ryti, and Keitel. Shorn of its usual hectoring and guttural tone, his Austrian accent helped to make his rhetoric on the tape-recorded first eleven minutes – a unique survival of political comments recorded without Hitler's knowledge – sound more lively and engaged than a written précis might make it appear.[177] His main concern was to emphasize the growing danger from the Soviet Union – far greater than had been imagined even at the start of 'Barbarossa' – and the inevitability of the conflict. He underscored the consistency of German policy.[178] Of course, he held to the version that Germany had been forced to act through a preventive war to head off imminent Soviet aggression.[179] Hitler's monologue amounted by that point to no more than a broad survey of the war. He had no intention of entering into any discussion of future military plans. He never once, for instance, mentioned the coming offensive. The Finns were only informed of that one day before it began, during Mannerheim's return visit.[180]

The meeting had no concrete results. That was not its aim. For now, Hitler had reassured himself that he had the Finns' continued support. He was well satisfied with the visit.[181] For their part, the Finns maintained their superficially good relations with Germany, while keeping a watchful eye on events. The course of the war over the next six months conveyed its own clear message to them to begin looking for alternative loyalties.[182]

While Hitler was *en route* to Finland, news came through from Prague that Reinhard Heydrich had died of the wounds he had suffered in the attack on 27 May.[183] Back in his headquarters, Hitler put it down to 'stupidity or pure dimwittedness (*reinen Stumpfsinn*)' that 'such an irreplaceable man as Heydrich should expose himself to the danger' of assassins, by driving without adequate bodyguard in an open-top car, and insisted that Nazi leaders comply with proper security precautions.[184] Hitler was in reflective mood at the state funeral in Berlin on 9 June. So soon after the loss of Todt, it seemed to him – and, in fact, was not far from the truth – as if the Party and state leadership only assembled for state funerals.[185] He spent time in the evening reminiscing with Goebbels about the early days of the Party, how hard it had been to book a hall in Munich, the difficulties in filling the Circus Krone, his relief at speaking for the first time in the Sportpalast to an audience that neither smoked nor drank, and paid attention. 'The Führer is very happy in these memories,' remarked Goebbels. 'He lives from the past, which seems to him like a lost paradise.'[186]

V

'Operation Blue', the great summer offensive in the south, began on 28 June.[187] A week earlier, a German plane carrying operational plans for 'Blue' had crashed behind enemy lines.[188] Stalin thought it was deliberate disinformation and ignored it, as he did warnings from Britain.[189] The offensive, carried out by five armies in two groups against the weakest part of the Soviet front, between Kursk in the north and Taganrog on the Sea of Azov in the south, was able – as 'Barbarossa' had done the previous year – to use the element of surprise to make impressive early gains.[190] Meanwhile, on 1 July, finally, the fall of Sevastopol brought immediate promotion to Field-Marshal for Manstein.[191]

After the initial break through the Russian lines, the rapid advance on Voronezh ended in the capture of the city on 6 July. This brought, however, the first confrontation of the new campaign between Hitler and his generals. Voronezh itself was an unimportant target. But a Soviet counter-attack had tied down two armoured divisions in the city for two days. This slowed the south-eastern advance along the Don and allowed enemy forces to escape. Hitler was enraged that Bock had ignored his instructions that the advance of the panzer divisions was to proceed without any hold-ups to the Volga in order to allow maximum destruction of the Soviet forces. In fact, when he had flown to Bock's headquarters at Poltava on 3 July, Hitler had been far less dogmatic and clear in face-to-face discussion with the field-marshal than he was in the map-room of the Wolf's Lair.[192] But that did not save Bock. Hitler said he was not going to have his plans spoiled by field-marshals as they had been in autumn 1941. Bock was dismissed and replaced by Colonel-General Freiherr Maximilian von Weichs.[193]

To be closer to the southern front, Hitler moved his headquarters on 16 July to a new location, given the name 'Werwolf', near Vinnitsa in the Ukraine.[194] Sixteen planes, their engines already whirring, waited on the runway at the Wolf's Lair that day for Hitler and his entourage to take them on a three-hour flight to their new surrounds. After a car-ride along rutted roads, they finally arrived at the damp, mosquito-infested huts that were to be their homes for the next three and a half months.[195] Even the Wolf's Lair began to seem idyllic. At the 'Werwolf', the days were stiflingly hot, the nights, even in high summer, distinctly chilly. The mosquitoes were an even greater plague than they had been in East Prussia. Everyone had to take each day a bitter-tasting medicine called Atibrin as a precaution against malaria. Halder was pleased enough with the layout of the new head-quarters. Hitler's secretaries were less happy with their cramped quarters. As at Rastenburg, they had little to do and were bored. A visit to a local abattoir and meat-processing plant, collective farm, or decrepit theatre in the nearby town was, apart from watching old films, the closest thing to escapism.[196] For Hitler, the daily routine was unchanged from that in the Wolf's Lair. At meals – his own often consisted of no more than a plate of vegetables with apples to follow – he could still appear open, relaxed, engaged.[197] As always, he monopolized dinner-table topics of conversation on a wide variety of topics that touched on his interests or obsessions. These included the evils of smoking, the construction of a motorway system throughout the eastern territories, the deficiencies of the legal system, the achievements of Stalin as a latter-day Ghengis Khan, keeping the standard of living low among the subjugated peoples, the need to remove the last Jews from German cities, and the promotion of private initiative rather than a state-controlled economy.[198]

Away from the supper soliloquies, however, tension mounted once more between Hitler and his military leaders. The military advance continued to make ground. But the numbers of Soviet prisoners captured steadily diminished. This was endlessly discussed at FHQ.[199] Hitler's military advisers were worried. They took it that the Soviets were pulling back their forces in preparation for a big counter-offensive, probably on the Volga, in the Stalingrad region.[200] Halder had warned as early as 12 July of concern at the front that the enemy, recognizing German envelopment tactics, was avoiding direct fight and withdrawing to the south.[201] Hitler's view was, however, that the Red Army was close to the end of its tether. He pressed all the more for a speedy advance.[202]

His impulsive, though sometimes – as the Voronezh episode had shown – unclear or ambiguous command-style caused constant difficulties for the operational planners. But the essential problem was more far-reaching. Hitler felt compelled by two imperatives: time, and material resources. The offensive had to be completed before the might of Allied resources came fully into play. And possession of the Caucasian oil-fields would, in his view, both be decisive in bringing the war in the east to a successful conclusion, and provide the necessary platform to continue a lengthy war against the Anglo-Saxon powers.[203] If this oil were not gained, Hitler had said, the war would be lost for Germany within three months.[204] Following his own logic, Hitler had, therefore, no choice but to stake everything on the ambitious strike to the Caucasus in a victorious summer offensive.[205] Even if some sceptical voices could be heard, Halder and the professionals in Army High Command had favoured the offensive. But the gap, already opened up the previous summer, between them and the dictator was rapidly widening. What Hitler saw as the negativity, pessimism, and timidity of Army High Command's traditional approaches drove him into paroxysms of rage. Army planners for their part had cold feet about what increasingly seemed to them a reckless gamble carried out by dilettante methods, more and more likely to end in disaster. But they could not now pull out of the strategy which they had been party to implementing. A catastrophe at Stalingrad was the heavy price that would soon be paid. The German war effort had set in train its own self-destructive dynamic.

The risk of military disaster was seriously magnified by Hitler's Directive No.45 of 23 July 1942. Thereafter, a calamity was waiting to happen. Unlike the April directive, in which Halder's hand had been visible, this directive rested squarely on a decision by Hitler, which the General Staff had sought to prevent.[206] The directive for the continuation of 'Blue', now renamed 'Operation Braunschweig', began with a worryingly unrealistic claim: 'In a campaign of little more than three weeks, the broad goals set for the southern flank of the eastern front have been essentially achieved. Only weak enemy forces of the Timoshenko armies have succeeded in escaping envelopment and reaching the southern bank of the Don. We have to reckon with their reinforcement from the Caucasus area.'[207]

Earlier in the month, Hitler had divided Army Group South into a northern sector (Army Group B, originally under Field-Marshal von Bock, then, after his sacking, under Colonel-General Freiherr von Weichs) and a southern sector (Army Group A, under Field-Marshal Wilhelm List).[208] The original intention, under his Directive No.41 of 5 April, had been to advance on the Caucasus *following* the encirclement and destruction of Soviet forces in the vicinity of Stalingrad. This was now altered to allow attacks on the Caucasus and Stalingrad (including the taking of the city itself) to proceed *simultaneously*. List's stronger Army Group A was left to destroy enemy forces in the Rostov area, then conquer the whole of the Caucasus region alone. This was to include the eastern coast of the Black Sea, crossing the Kuban and occupying the heights around the oil-fields of Maykop, controlling the almost impenetrable Caucasian mountain passes, and driving south-eastwards to take the oil-rich region around Grozny, then Baku, far to the south on the Caspian Sea. The attack on Stalingrad was left to the weaker Army Group B, which was expected thereafter to press on along the lower Volga to Astrakhan on the Caspian.[209] The strategy was sheer lunacy.

Only the most incautiously optimistic assessment of the weakness of the Soviet forces could have justified the scale of the risk involved. But Hitler took precisely such a view of enemy strength. Moreover, he was as always temperamentally predisposed to a risk-all strategy, with alternatives dismissed out of hand and boats burned to leave no fall-back position. As always, his self-justification could be bolstered by the dogmatic view that there was no alternative. Halder, aware of more realistic appraisals of Soviet strength, and the build-up of forces in the Stalingrad area, but unable to exert any influence upon Hitler, was by now both seriously concerned and frustrated at his own impotence.[210] On 23 July, the day that Hitler issued his Directive No.45, Halder had written in his diary: 'This chronic tendency to underrate enemy capabilities is gradually assuming grotesque proportions and develops into a positive danger. The situation is getting more and more intolerable. There is no room for any serious work. This so-called leadership is characterized by a pathological reacting to the impressions of the moment and a total lack of any understanding of the command machinery and its possibilities.'[211] On 15 August, Halder's notes for his situation report began: 'Overall picture: have we extended the risk too far?'[212] The question was well warranted. But the insight had come rather late in the day.

By mid-August, Army Group A had swept some 350 miles to the south, over the north Caucasian plain. It was now far separated from Army Group B, with a lengthy exposed flank, and formidable logistical problems of ensuring supplies.[213] Its advance now slowed markedly in the wooded foothills of the northern Caucasus.[214] Maykop was taken, but the oil-refineries were left in ruins, systematically and expertly destroyed by the retreating Soviet forces.[215] The impetus had by now been lost. Hitler showed little sense of realism when he spoke privately to Goebbels on 19 August. Operations in the Caucasus, he said, were going extremely well. He wanted to take possession of the oil-wells of Maykop, Grozny, and Baku during the summer, securing Germany's oil supplies and destroying those of the Soviet Union. Once the Soviet border had been reached, the breakthrough into the Near East would follow, occupying Asia Minor and overrunning Iraq, Iran, and Palestine, to cut off Britain's oil supplies. Within two or three days, he wanted to commence the big assault on Stalingrad. He intended to destroy the city completely, leaving no stone on top of another. It was both psychologically and militarily necessary. The forces deployed were reckoned to be sufficient to capture the city within eight days.[216]

These were scarcely signs of waning self-confidence.[217] But his over-reaction, two days later, when news reached him that mountain troops had placed the German flag on the Elbrus, highest mountain of the Caucasus range at 5,630 metres, suggests that his self-confidence was a front, perhaps above all for himself. Beneath the façade, his nerves were edgy, his anxiety about the offensive growing. The troops presumably thought he would be pleased. In fact, he was furious at what he saw as a pointless mountaineering feat devoid of military purpose.[218] Speer later wrote that he had seldom seen him so enraged, fuming for days at 'these mad mountaineers' who deserved to be put before a military court. In the middle of a war, he ranted, their idiotic ambition had driven them to climb an idiotic peak, when he had ordered everything to be concentrated on the taking of Suchum. It was in truth a minor escapade. But from Hitler's near-hysterical over-reaction it seemed, Speer recalled, as if they had ruined his entire operational plan.[219]

The last significant successes of Army Group B, meanwhile, had been in encircling and destroying two Russian armies south-west of Kalac, on the Don due west of Stalingrad, on 8 August.[220] Advancing in punishing heat and hindered through chronic fuel shortage, on 23 August, the 6th Army, under General Friedrich Paulus, succeeded in reaching the Volga, north of Stalingrad.[221] Amid heavy Soviet defences, the advance ground rapidly to a halt. The summer offensive had, as it turned out, run its course in less than two months.[222] As early as 26 August Halder was noting: 'Near Stalingrad, serious tension on account of superior counter-attacks of the enemy. Our divisions are no longer very strong. The command is heavily under nervous strain.'[223] The 6th Army was, however, able to consolidate its position. Over the next weeks, it even gained the advantage. But the nightmare of Stalingrad was only just beginning.

While the southern part of the massively extended front was running out of steam, with the 6th Army now bogged down at Stalingrad and List's Army Group A stalled in the Caucasus, Kluge's Army Group Centre had encountered a damaging setback, suffering horrendous casualties in an ill-fated attempt ordered by Hitler to wipe out Russian forces at Sukhinichi, 150 miles west of Moscow, from where it was hoped to establish the basis for a renewed drive on the capital. Kluge, on a visit to 'Werwolf' on 7 August, had asked Hitler to remove two armoured divisions from the offensive at Sukhinichi to deploy them against a threatening Soviet counter-attack in the Rzhev area. Hitler had refused, insisting that they be retained for the Sukhinichi offensive. Kluge had marched out saying 'You, my Führer, therefore assume responsibility for this.'[224]

And in the north, by the end of August expectations of launching an assault and finally taking the hunger-torn city of Leningrad had been mass-ively dented through the Soviet counter-offensive south of Lake Lagoda. Manstein's 11th Army had been brought up from the southern front to lead the planned final assault on Leningrad in September in the 'Northern Lights' offensive. Instead it found itself engaged in fending off the Soviet strike. There was no possibility of capturing Leningrad and razing it to the ground. The last chance of that had gone.[225] Hitler's outward show of confidence in victory could not altogether conceal his mounting inner anxiety. His temper was on a short fuse. Outbursts of rage became more common.[226] He cast around as always for scapegoats for the rapidly deteriorating military situation in the east. It did not take him long to find them.

Relations with Halder had already reached rock-bottom. On 24 August, the worsening situation at Rzhev had prompted the Chief of the General Staff to urge Hitler to allow a retreat of the 9th Army to a more defensible shorter line. In front of all those assembled at the midday conference, Hitler rounded on Halder. 'You always come here with the same proposal, that of withdrawal,' he raged. 'I demand from the leadership the same toughness as from the front-soldiers.' Halder, deeply insulted, shouted back: 'I have the toughness, my Führer. But out there brave musketeers and lieutenants are falling in thousands and thousands as useless sacrifice in a hopeless situation simply because their commanders are not allowed to make the only reasonable decision and have their hands tied behind their backs.'[227] Hitler stared at Halder. 'What can you, who sat in the same chair (*Drehschemel*) in the First World War, too, tell me about the troops, Herr Halder, you, who don't even wear the black insignia of the wounded?'[228] Appalled, and embarrassed, the onlookers dispersed. Hitler tried to smooth Halder's ruffled feathers that evening. But it was plain to all who witnessed the scene that the Chief of Staff's days were numbered.[229]

Even Hitler's military right hand, the loyal and devoted Jodl, was now made to feel the full impact of his wrath. On 5 September List had asked for Jodl to be been sent to Army Group A headquarters at Stalino, north of the Sea of Azov, to discuss the further deployment of the 39th Mountain Corps.[230] The visit took place two days later. From Hitler's point of view, the purpose was to urge List to accelerate the advance on the largely stalled Caucasus front. Hitler's patience at the lack of progress had been extremely thin for some time. But far from bringing back positive news, Jodl returned that evening with a devastating account of conditions. It was no longer possible to force the Soviets back over the mountain passes. The most that could be achieved, with greater mobility and maximum concentration of forces, was a last attempt to reach Grozny and the Caspian Sea. Hitler grew more angry with every sentence. He lashed out at the 'lack of initiative' of the army leadership; and now for the first time attacked Jodl, the messenger bearing bad news.[231] It was the worst crisis in relations between Hitler and his military leaders since the previous August.[232] Hitler was in a towering rage. But Jodl stood his ground. It turned into a shouting-match.[233] Jodl fully backed List's assessment of the position. Hitler exploded. He accused Jodl of betraying his orders, being talked round by List, and taking sides with the Army Group. He had not sent him to the Caucasus, he said, to have him bring back doubts among the troops.[234] Jodl retorted that List was faithfully adhering to the orders Hitler himself had given.[235] Beside himself with rage, Hitler said his words were being twisted. Things would have to be different. He would have to ensure that he could not be deliberately misinterpreted in future.[236] Like a prima donna in a pique, Hitler stormed out, refusing to shake hands (as he invariably had done at the end of their meetings) with Jodl and Keitel.[237] Evidently depressed as well as angry, he said to his Wehrmacht adjutant Schmundt that night, 'I'll be glad when I can take off this detestable uniform and trample on it.'[238] He saw no end to the war in Russia since none of the aims of summer 1942 had been realized. The anxiety about the forthcoming winter was dreadful, he said. 'But on the other hand,' noted Army Adjutant Engel, 'he will retreat nowhere.'[239]

Hitler now shut himself up in his darkened hut during the days. He refused to appear for the communal meals. The military briefings, with as few present as possible, took place in a glacial atmosphere in his own hut, not in the headquarters of the Wehrmacht staff. And he refused to shake hands with anyone. Within forty-eight hours, a group of shorthand typists, practised stenographers from the Reichstag (where the need for active stenographers was by now hardly pressing), arrived at FHQ. Hitler had insisted upon a record of all military briefings being taken so that he could not again be misinterpreted.[240]

The day after the confrontation with Jodl, Hitler dismissed List. Demonstrating his distrust of his generals, he himself for the time being took over the command of Army Group A. He was now commander of the armed forces, of one branch of those armed forces, and of one group of that branch. At the same time, Keitel was deputed to tell Halder that he would soon be relieved of his post. Keitel himself and Jodl were also rumoured to be slated for dismissal.[241] Jodl admitted privately that he had been at fault in trying to point out to a dictator where he had gone wrong. This, Jodl said, could only shake his self-confidence – the basis of his personality and actions. Jodl added that whoever his own replacement might be, he could not be more of a staunch National Socialist than he himself was.[242]

In the event, the worsening conditions at Stalingrad and in the Mediterranean prevented the intended replacement of Jodl by Paulus and Keitel by Kesselring.[243] But there was no saving Halder. Hitler complained bitterly to Below that Halder had no comprehension of the difficulties at the front and was devoid of ideas for solutions. He coldly viewed the situation only from maps and had 'completely wrong notions' about the way things were going.[244] Hitler pondered Schmundt's advice to replace Halder by Major-General Kurt Zeitzler, a very different type of character – a small bald-headed, ambitious, dynamic forty-seven-year-old, firm believer in the Führer, who had been put in by Hitler in April to shake up the army in the west and, as Rundstedt's chief of staff, to build up coastal defences.[245] Göring, too, encouraged Hitler to get rid of Halder.[246]

That point was reached on 24 September. A surprised Zeitzler had by then been summoned to FHQ and told by Hitler of his promotion to full General of the Infantry and of his new responsibilities.[247] After what was to be his last military briefing, Halder was, without ceremony, relieved of his post. His nerves, Hitler told him, were gone, and his own nerves also strained. It was necessary for Halder to go, and for the General Staff to be educated to believe fanatically in 'the idea'. Hitler, Halder noted in his final diary entry, was determined to enforce his will, also in the army.[248]

The traditional General Staff, for long such a powerful force, its Chief now discarded like a spent cartridge, had arrived at its symbolic final point of capitulation to the forces to which it had wedded itself in 1933. Zeitzler began the new regime by demanding from the members of the General Staff belief in the Führer.[249] He himself would soon realize that this alone would not be enough.

VI

The battle for Stalingrad was by now looming. Both sides were aware how critical it would be. The German leadership remained optimistic.

Hitler's plans for the massively over-populated city on the Volga were similar to the annihilatory intentions he had held about Leningrad and Moscow. 'The Führer orders that on entry into the city the entire male population should be done away with (*beseitigt*),' the Wehrmacht High Command recorded, 'since Stalingrad, with its thoroughly Communist population of a million, is especially dangerous.'[250] Halder noted simply, without additional comment: 'Stalingrad: male population to be destroyed (*vernichtet*), female to be deported'.[251]

When he visited FHQ on 11 September, General von Weichs, Commander of Army Group B, had told Hitler he was confident that the attack on the inner city of Stalingrad could begin almost immediately and be completed within ten days.[252] Indeed, the early signs were that the fall of the city would not be long delayed. But by the second half of September, the contest for Stalingrad had already turned into a battle of scarcely imaginable intensity and ferocity. The fighting was taking place often at point-blank range, street by street, house by house. German and Soviet troops were almost literally at each other's throats. The final taking of what had rapidly become little more than a shell of smoking ruins, it was coming to be realized, could take weeks, even months.[253]

Elsewhere, too, the news was less than encouraging. Rommel's offensive at El Alamein in the direction of the Suez Canal had to be broken off already on 2 September, only three days after it had begun. Rommel remained confident, both publicly and in private, over the next weeks, though he reported on the serious problems with shortages of weapons and equipment when he saw Hitler on 1 October to receive his Field-Marshal's baton.[254] In reality, however, the withdrawal of 2 September would turn out to be the beginning of the end for the Axis in North Africa.[255] Its morale revitalized under a new commander, General Bernard Montgomery, and its lost, out-of-date armour replaced by new Sherman tanks, the 8th Army would by autumn prove more than a match for Rommel's limited forces.[256]

In the Reich itself, the British nightly raids had intensified. Munich, Bremen, Düsseldorf, and Duisburg were among the cities that now suffered serious destruction.[257] Hitler said he was glad his own apartment in Munich had been badly damaged; he would not have liked it spared – obviously it would not have looked good – if the rest of the city had been attacked. He thought the raid might have a salutary effect in waking up the population of Munich to the realities of the war.[258] Air-raids had another good side, he had told Goebbels in mid-August: the enemy had 'taken work from us' in destroying buildings that would in any case have had to be torn down to allow the improved post-war town planning.[259] Such remarks scarcely betrayed much feeling for the suffering of ordinary people in the raids. For these, the wail of the sirens, disturbed nights in air-raid shelters, and rumours – exaggerated or not – of the horrors in other cities tore at the nerves. And the helplessness of the Luftwaffe to defend their cities shook people's confidence in the leadership.[260] Hitler felt his own impotence to respond as he would have liked: by revenge through even greater destruction of British cities. But there was a shortage of German bombers. The Heinkel 177 had, as Hitler had long predicted, proved unsuccessful, with repeated engine failures preventing its active use. And the Junkers 88 could not be produced in sufficient numbers, since priority had to be accorded to fighters. Powerless to do much against the mounting threat from the skies, Hitler said he trusted Göring's assurances that things would soon be improved in the Luftwaffe.[261]

At the end of September, Hitler flew back to Berlin. He had promised Goebbels to use the opening of the Winter Aid campaign to address the nation during the second half of September.[262] Once more, it was important to sustain morale at a vital time.

He looked well when Goebbels saw him at a late lunch on 28 September, after speaking to 12,000 young officers in the Sportpalast. He was more optimistic than Goebbels had imagined he would be about Stalingrad. The city would soon be taken, Hitler claimed. Then the advance on the Caucasus could proceed again, even during the winter. Goebbels did not share the optimism.[263] It was as if Hitler felt unable to deviate, even in private, from the fiction that all was going well in the eastern campaign. His Luftwaffe adjutant, Below, thought Hitler was by now starting to deceive himself about the realities of the situation.[264]

Next day, Hitler spoke to a small group of generals, along with Göring and Speer, about the dangers of an invasion in the west. Fiasco though it had been, the attempted landing of Canadian troops in Dieppe in mid-August had been a new reminder of the threat. But by the spring, when the new Atlantic Wall with its 15,000 bunkers was constructed, the Reich would be immune, he claimed.[265]

Hitler's Sportpalast speech on 30 September combined a glorification of German military achievements with a sarcastic, mocking attack on Churchill and Roosevelt.[266] This was nothing new, though the hand-picked Sportpalast audience lapped it up. They, and the wider audience listening to the broadcast of the speech, took especial note when Hitler suggested that, after the perils of the last winter had been surmounted, the worst was now behind them, and the economic benefits of the occupied territories would soon be flowing to Germany to improve the standard of living.[267] He went on to repeat his prophecy about the Jews – by now a regular weapon in his rhetorical armoury – in the most menacing phrases he had so far used: 'The Jews used to laugh, in Germany too, about my prophecies. I don't know if they're still laughing today, or whether the laughter has already gone out of them. But I, too, can now only offer the assurance: the laughter will go out of them everywhere. And I will also be right in my prophecies.'[268] But the speech was most notable of all for his assurances about the battle for Stalingrad. The metropolis on the Volga, bearing the Soviet leader's name, was being stormed, he declared, and would be taken. 'You can be sure,' he added, 'that nobody will get us away from this place again!'[269]

His public display of optimism was unbounded, even in a more confined forum, when he addressed the Reichs- and Gauleiter for almost three hours the following afternoon. He felt at ease, he told the gathering, in the company of his most long-standing Party comrades.[270] 'The Gauleiter,' he had told Goebbels in mid-August, 'never cheat me' – unlike, he had said, his generals. 'They are my most loyal and reliable colleagues. If I lost trust in them I wouldn't know whom to trust.'[271] He outlined the plans to thrust to the Caucasus, to cut the Soviet Union off from its oil. He said he had wanted to undertake that the previous year, but Brauchitsch had pushed the campaign in a completely different direction, towards Moscow 'which is relatively uninteresting for us'. But he was certain that Germany would now gain possession of the oil-fields of Grozny, while a first priority was to get those oil-wells captured in a ruined state in Maykop flowing again. 'The capture of Stalingrad,' recorded Goebbels, 'is for him an established fact,' even if it could still take a little time. Once that was attained, Astrakhan would be the next target, then the destruction by the Luftwaffe of the key Soviet oil-fields of Baku. Thereafter, as he had already told Goebbels several weeks earlier (when he had spoken of overrunning Iraq, Iran, and Palestine), his sights were set on the British oil supplies from Mesopotamia and the Middle East.[272] Surveying the position of his enemies, Hitler came to the remarkable conclusion that 'the war was practically lost for the opposing side, no matter how long it was in a position to carry it on'. Only an internal upheaval in Germany could snatch victory for the enemy. It was the Party's job to see that that could never happen. He had effusive praise for the Party's work. The longer the war went on, commented Goebbels, the closer the Führer came to the Party.[273]

Hitler's absurd optimism at the beginning of October scarcely accorded with the growing anxieties of his military advisers about the situation in Stalingrad. Winter was now no longer far off. Paulus, Weichs, Jodl, and Zeitzler all favoured pulling back from a target which, largely in ruins, had by now lost all significance as a communications and armaments centre, and taking up more secure winter positions. The only alternative was to pour in heavy reinforcements.[274] Hitler's view – he had said so to Goebbels in mid-August – was that this time winter had been so well prepared for that the soldiers in the east would be living better than most of them had done in peacetime.[275]

On 6 October, after Paulus had reported a temporary halt to the attack because his troops were exhausted, Hitler ordered the 'complete capture' of Stalingrad as the key objective of Army Group B.[276] There might indeed have been something to be said for choosing the protection of even a ruined city to the open, exposed steppes over the winter had the supplies situation been as favourable as Hitler evidently imagined it to be, had the supply lines been secure, and had the threat of a Soviet counter-offensive been less large. However, the indicators are that only insufficient winter provision for the 6th Army had been made. Supply-lines were now overstretched on an enormously long front, and far from secure on the northern flank. And intelligence was coming in of big concentrations of Soviet troops which might pose real danger to the position of the 6th Army. Withdrawal was the sensible option.[277]

Hitler would not hear of it. At the beginning of October, Zeitzler and Jodl heard him for the first time, in outrightly rejecting their advice about the danger of being bogged down in house-to-house fighting with heavy losses, stress that the capture of the city was necessary not just for operational, but for 'psychological' reasons: to show the world the continued strength of German arms, and to boost the morale of the Axis allies.[278] More than ever contemptuous of generals and military advisers who lacked the necessary strength of will, and convinced that he alone had prevented an ignominious full-scale retreat through his unbending insistence on standing fast the previous winter, he now refused to countenance any suggestion of withdrawal from Stalingrad. But his 'halt order' of the previous winter had had tactical merit. This time, it had none. Fear of loss of face had taken over from military reasoning. Hitler's all too public statements in the Sportpalast and then to his Gauleiter had meant that taking Stalingrad had become a matter of prestige.[279] And, though he claimed the fact that the city bore Stalin's name was of no significance,[280] retreat from precisely this city would clearly compound the loss of prestige.

In the meantime, Hitler was starting to acknowledge mounting concern among his military advisers about the build-up of Soviet forces on the northern banks of the Don – the weakest section of the front, where the Wehrmacht was dependent on the resolution of its allied armies – the Romanians, Hungarians, and Italians.[281]

The situation in North Africa was by this time also critical. Montgomery's 8th Army had begun its big offensive at El Alamein on 23 October. Rommel had quickly been sent back from sick-leave to hold together the defence of the Axis forces and prevent a breakthrough. Hitler's initial confidence that Rommel would hold his ground had rapidly evaporated. Lacking fuel and munitions, and facing a numerically far superior enemy, Rommel was unable to prevent Montgomery's tanks penetrating the German front in the renewed massive onslaught that had begun on 2 November. The following day, Hitler sent a telegram in response to Rommel's depressing account of the position and prospects of his troops. 'In the situation in which you find yourself,' ran his message to Rommel, 'there can be no other thought than to stick it out, not to yield a step, and to throw every weapon and available fighter into the battle.' Everything would be done to send reinforcements. 'It would not be the first time in history that the stronger will triumphed over stronger enemy battalions. But you can show your troops no other way than victory or death.'[282] Rommel had not waited for Hitler's reply. Anticipating what it would be, he had ordered a retreat hours before it arrived. Generals had been peremptorily dismissed for such insubordination during the winter crisis at the beginning of the year. Rommel's standing with the German people – only weeks earlier, he had been fêted as a military hero – was all that now saved him from the same ignominy.[283]

By 7 November, when Hitler travelled to Munich to give his traditional address in the Löwenbräukeller to the marchers in the 1923 Putsch, the news from the Mediterranean had dramatically worsened. *En route* from Berlin to Munich,[284] his special train was halted at a small station in the Thuringian Forest for him to receive a message from the Foreign Office: the Allied armada assembled at Gibraltar, which had for days given rise to speculation about a probable landing in Libya, was disembarking in Algiers and Oran.[285] It would bring the first commitment of American ground-troops to the war in Europe.[286]

Hitler immediately gave orders for the defence of Tunis. But the landing had caught him and his military advisers off-guard. And Oran was out of reach of German bombers, which gave rise to a new torrent of rage at the incompetence of the Luftwaffe's lack of planning.[287] Further down the track, at Bamberg, Ribbentrop joined the train. He pleaded with Hitler to let him put out peace feelers to Stalin via the Soviet embassy in Stockholm with an offer of far-reaching concessions in the east. Hitler brusquely dismissed the suggestion: a moment of weakness was not the time for negotiations with an enemy.[288] In his speech to the Party's 'Old Guard' on the evening of 8 November, Hitler then publicly ruled out any prospect of a negotiated peace. With reference to his earlier 'peace offers', he declared: 'From now on there will no more offer of peace.'[289]

It was hardly the atmosphere which Hitler would have chosen for a big speech. Not only had he nothing positive to report; the speech had to take place in the midst of a military crisis. Goebbels even had difficulty in pinning down exactly when the speech should start. Hitler needed time after his arrival in Munich to orientate himself on the Allied landing in North Africa and decide what to do.[290] He was still uncertain when he arrived in the Brown House at 4p.m. He discussed the position of France and Italy with Goebbels, Himmler, Ribbentrop, and Keitel. Telephone calls were made to Paris, Rome, and Vichy. No decision could be arrived at in the brief time before the speech, which had been put back from its scheduled time to begin, eventually, at 6p.m.[291]

According to Goebbels, the news on the radio of the Allied landing in Africa had 'electrified' the Party gathering. 'Everyone knows that, if things are pushed down a certain path, we are standing at a turning-point of the war.'[292] But if the Party's 'Old Fighters' expected any enlightenment from Hitler on the situation, they were to be disappointed. The usual verbal assaults on Allied leaders and blustering parallels with the internal situation before the 'seizure of power' were all he had to offer. Refusal to compromise, the will to fight, determination to overcome the enemy, the lack of any alternative to complete success, and the certainty of final victory in a war for the very existence of the German people formed the basis of the message. Unlike the Kaiser, who had capitulated in the First World War at 'quarter to twelve', he ended, so he stated, 'in principle always at five past twelve'.[293] He again held out the prospect of imminent victory in Stalingrad. 'I wanted to take it and, you know, we are modest: we have it. There are only a few tiny places there.' If it was still taking a little time, it was because he wanted to avoid a second Verdun. He did not touch upon the Allied landings in North Africa. And the retreat forced upon Rommel's Afrika Korps by the British 8th Army was passed over in a single sentence: 'If they say they advanced somewhere in the desert; they've already advanced a few times and have had to pull back again.'[294]

For the fourth and last time in the year, Hitler invoked his 'prophecy' about the Jews. At that point in his big speech, he had just ruled out compromise and any peace-offer with external enemies. He referred to his earlier stance towards the enemy within. It had been impossible to come to any understanding with them (so Hitler now said, though at the time he had made a point of not seeking one). They had wanted force; and got it. 'And these internal enemies, they have been eliminated (*beseitigt*),' he said. Then he came to the Jews. 'Another power too, which was once very present in Germany, has meanwhile learnt that National Socialist prophecies are not empty talk. That is the main power which we have to thank for all the misfortune: international Jewry. You will still remember the meeting of the Reichstag in which I declared: If Jewry somehow thinks it can bring about an international world war to exterminate European races, then the result will be not the extermination of the European races but the extermination (*Ausrottung*) of Jewry in Europe. I've always been laughed at as a prophet. Of those who laughed then, countless ones are no longer laughing today. And those who are still laughing, will also perhaps not be doing so before long (*in einiger Zeit*).'[295]

The speech was not one of Hitler's best. He had been a compelling speaker when he had been able to twist reality in plausible fashion for his audience. But now, he was ignoring unpalatable facts, or turning them on their head. The gap between rhetoric and reality had become too wide. To most Germans, as SD reports were making apparent, Hitler's speeches could no longer have more than a superficial impact. Even those momentarily roused by his verbal show of defiance were quickly overwhelmed once more by the concerns of everyday existence – food supplies, labour shortages, work conditions, worries about loved ones at the front, air-raids. And the news of the Allied landing in North Africa cast a deep pall of gloom about mighty forces stacked against Germany in a war whose end seemed even farther away than ever. This came on top of growing unease, whatever Hitler had said, about Stalingrad. Criticism of the German leadership for embroiling people in such a war was now more commonplace (if necessarily for the most part carefully couched), and often implicitly included Hitler – no longer detached, as he used to be, from the negative side of the regime. Hitler's popularity had sagged. Rumours that he was physically or mentally ill, had suffered a nervous breakdown, had to be permanently attended by doctors, and fell into such frenzies of rage that he resorted to biting the carpet, had become widespread since the summer of 1942.[296] The implication that the German leader and his regime were out of control was uncomfortably close to the truth.

But Hitler's key audience had, primarily, been not the millions glued to their radio-sets, but his oldest Party loyalists inside the hall.[297] It was essential to reinforce this backbone of Hitler's personal power, and of the will to hold together the home front. Here, among this audience, Hitler could still tap much of the enthusiasm, commitment, and fanaticism of old.[298] He knew the chords to play. The music was a familiar tune. But everyone there must have recognized – and in some measure shared – a sense of self-deception in the lyrics.

He stayed in the company of his Gauleiter, his most trusted paladins, until three in the morning. Every conceivable topic was discussed. Hitler held forth, among other things, on his theory that cancer was caused by smoking. Only the war was not touched upon. That was perhaps for the best in the circumstances, commented Goebbels.[299]

Hitler's real concern that evening was the reaction of the French to the events in North Africa; the Ministerial Council was meeting in Vichy at that very time. He initially told Ambassador Abetz to press the Vichy regime to declare war on the British and Americans. But, realizing that the French would play for time, when time was of the essence, he was then forced to soften his demands and not insist upon a formal declaration of war. The telephone wires between Munich, Vichy, and Rome were buzzing all evening, but no conclusive steps were agreed. At that point, Hitler decided upon a meeting in Munich with Laval and Mussolini. By then, news was coming in that the initial resistance was crumbling in French North Africa.[300] The landing had been secured.

By the time Ciano arrived in Munich – Mussolini felt unwell and declined to go – Hitler had heard that General Henri Giraud had put himself at the service of the Allies and been smuggled out of France and transported to North Africa. Commander of the French 7th Army before the débâcle of 1940 and imprisoned since that time, Giraud had escaped captivity and fled to unoccupied France earlier in the year. The danger was that he would now provide a figurehead for French resistance in North Africa and a focus of support for the Allies. Suspicion, which soon proved justified, was also mounting by the hour that Admiral Jean François Darlan, too, head of the French armed forces, was preparing to change sides. The Americans had won Darlan over just before the 'Torch' landings with an offer to recognize him as head of the French government. Inevitable conflict with the British, who favoured de Gaulle, was to be obviated when a young French monarchist assassinated Darlan just before Christmas.[301]

Hitler, as we noted, had stressed the need to be ready to occupy southern France in his talks with Mussolini at the end of April. The concern about Giraud and Darlan now meant that any thought of concessions to the French had been dissipated. When Ciano met Hitler on the evening of 9 November – Laval was travelling by car and expected only during the night – he had made up his mind. Laval's input would be irrelevant. Hitler would not 'modify his already definite point of view: the total occupation of France, landing in Corsica, a bridgehead in Tunisia'.[302] When he eventually arrived, Laval, looking like a minor French provincial worthy, out of place among the military top brass and trying to pass pleasantries about his long journey, was treated with scarcely more than contempt. Hitler demanded landing points in Tunisia. Laval tried to wring concessions from Italy. Hitler refused to waste time on such deliberations. Laval, anxious to avoid responsibility for yielding territory to the Axis, suggested he should be faced with a *fait accompli*. He apparently had not realized that this was precisely what was intended.

While Laval was in the next room having a smoke, Hitler gave the order to occupy the remainder of France next day – 11 November, and the anniversary of the Armistice of 1918. Laval was to be informed next morning.[303] In a letter to Marshal Pétain and a proclamation to the French people on 11 November, Hitler justified the occupation through the necessity to defend the coast of southern France and Corsica against Allied invasion from the new base in North Africa.[304] That morning, German troops occupied southern France without military resistance, in accordance with the plans for 'Operation Anton' which had been laid down in May.[305]

At the Berghof for a few days, Hitler's mask of ebullience slipped a little. Below found him deeply worried about the Anglo-American actions. He was also concerned about supplies difficulties in the Mediterranean, which British submarines had intensified. His trust in the Italians had disappeared. He was sure that they were leaking intelligence about the movement of German supply ships to the British. The deficiencies of the Luftwaffe also preoccupied him. Göring, Below heard, was not on top of things. Hitler preferred to deal with the Luftwaffe Chief of Staff Hans Jeschonnek about detailed matters. Defence of the Reich depended too much on planes that were in the wrong place, or prevented from flying through bad weather. More flak artillery was needed in the vicinity of German cities. As regards the eastern front, he was hoping for 'no new surprises', but feared a large-scale Soviet offensive was imminent.[306]

VII

On 19 November, Zeitzler told Hitler that the Soviet offensive had begun. Immediately, the Soviet forces to the north-west and west of Stalingrad broke through the weak part of the front held by the Romanian 4th Army. General Ferdinand Heim's 48th Panzer Corps was sent in, but failed to heal the breach. Furious, Hitler dismissed Heim. He later ordered him to be sentenced to death – a sentence not carried out only through the intervention of Schmundt.[307] The next day the Red Army's 'Stalingrad Front' broke through the divisions of the Romanian 4th Army south of the city and met up on 22 November with the Soviet forces that had penetrated from north and west. With that, the 220,000 men of the 6th Army were completely encircled.[308]

Hitler had decided to return to the Wolf's Lair that evening. His train journey back from Berchtesgaden to East Prussia took over twenty hours, owing to repeated lengthy stops to telephone Zeitzler. The new Chief of the General Staff insisted on permission being granted to the 6th Army to fight their way out of Stalingrad. Hitler did not give an inch.[309] Already on 21 November he had sent an order to Paulus: '6th Army to hold, despite danger of temporary encirclement.'[310] On the evening of 22 November, he ordered: 'The army is temporarily encircled by Russian forces. I know the 6th Army and its Commander-in-Chief and know that it will conduct itself bravely in this difficult situation. The 6th Army must know that I am doing everything to help it and to relieve it.'[311] He thought the position could be remedied. Relief could be organized to enable a break-out. But this could not be done overnight. A plan was hastily devised to deploy Colonel-General Hermann

Hoth's 4th Panzer Army, south-west of Stalingrad, to prepare an attack to relieve the 6th Army. But it would take about ten days before it could be attempted. In the meantime, Paulus had to hold out, while the troops were supplied by air-lift. It was a major, and highly risky operation. But Göring assured Hitler that it could be done. Jeschonnek did not contradict him. Zeitzler, however, vehemently disagreed. And from within the Luftwaffe itself, Colonel-General Wolfram Freiherr von Richthofen, who normally had Hitler's ear, raised the gravest doubts both on grounds of the weather (with temperatures already plummeting, icy mists, and freezing rain icing up the wings of the planes) and of the numbers of available aircraft. Hitler chose to believe Göring.[312]

Hitler's decision to air-lift supplies to the 6th Army until relief arrived was taken on 23 November. By then he had heard from Paulus that stores of food and equipment were perilously low and certainly insufficient for a defence of the position. Paulus sought permission to attempt to break out. Weichs, Commander-in-Chief of Army Group B, and Chief of the General Staff Zeitzler also fully backed this as the only realistic option.[313] Zeitzler, evidently acting on the basis of a remarkable misunderstanding, actually informed Weichs at 2a.m. on 24 November that he had 'persuaded the Führer that a break-out was the only possibility of saving the army'. Within four hours the General Staff had to transmit exactly the opposite decision by Hitler: the 6th Army had to stand fast and would be supplied from the air until relief could arrive.[314] The fate of almost quarter of a million men was sealed with this order.

Hitler was not totally isolated in military support for his decision. Field-Marshal von Manstein had arrived that morning, 24 November, at Army Group B headquarters to take command, as ordered by Hitler three days earlier, of a new Army Group Don (which included the trapped 6th Army). The main objective was to shore up the weakened front south and west of Stalingrad, to secure the lines to Army Group A in the Caucasus. He also took command of General Hoth's attempt to relieve the 6th Army.[315] But in contrast to Paulus, Weichs, and Zeitzler, Manstein did not approve an attempt to break out before reinforcements arrived, and took an optimistic view of the chances of an air-lift. Manstein was one of Hitler's most trusted generals. His assessment can only have strengthened Hitler's own judgement.[316]

By mid-December, Manstein had changed his view diametrically. Richthofen had persuaded him that, in the atrocious weather conditions, an adequate air-lift was impossible. Even if the weather relented, air supplies could not be sustained for any length of time.[317] Manstein now pressed on numerous occasions for a decision to allow the 6th Army to break out.[318] But by then the chances of a break-out had grossly diminished; in fact, once Hoth's relief attempt was held up in heavy fighting some fifty kilometres from Stalingrad and some days later finally forced back, they rapidly became non-existent.[319] On 19 December, Hitler once more rejected all pleas to consider a break-out. Military information in any case now indicated that the 6th Army, greatly weakened and surrounded by mighty Soviet forces, would be able to advance a maximum of thirty kilometres to the south-west – not far enough to meet up with Hoth's relief Panzer army.[320] On 21 December, Manstein asked Zeitzler for a final decision on whether the 6th Army should attempt to break out as long as it could still link with the 57th Panzer Corps, or whether the Commander-in-Chief of the Luftwaffe could guarantee air-supplies over a lengthy period of time. Zeitzler cabled back that Göring was confident that the Luftwaffe could supply the 6th Army, though Jeschonnek was by now of a different opinion. Hitler allowed an inquiry of the 6th Army Command about the distance it could expect to advance towards the south if the other fronts could be held. The reply came that there was fuel for twenty kilometres, and that it would be unable to hold position for long. Hoth's army was still fifty-four kilometres away.[321] Still no decision was taken. 'It's as if the Führer is no longer capable [of taking one],' noted the OKW's war-diarist Helmuth Greiner.[322]

6th Army Command itself described the tactic of a mass break-out without relief from the outside – 'Operation Thunderclap' – as 'a catastrophe-solution' ('Katastrophenlösung').[323] That evening, Hitler dismissed the idea: Paulus only had fuel for a short distance; there was no possibility of breaking out.[324] Two days later, on 23 December, Manstein had to remove units from Hoth's 4th Panzer Army to hold the crumbling left flank of his Army Group. With that, Hoth had to pull back his weakened forces. The attempt to break the siege of Stalingrad had failed.[325] The 6th Army was doomed.

Paulus still sought permission to break out. But by Christmas Eve, Manstein had given up trying to persuade Hitler to give approval to what by this time could only be seen as a move of sheer desperation, without hope of success. The main priority was now to hold the left flank to prevent an even worse catastrophe.[326] This was essential to enable the retreat of Army Group A from the Caucasus.[327] Zeitzler had put the urgency of this retreat to Hitler on the evening of 27 December. Hitler had reluctantly agreed, then later changed his mind. It was too late. Zeitzler had telephoned through Hitler's initial approval. The retreat from the Caucasus was under way.[328] Stalingrad had become a lesser priority.[329]

Preoccupied though he was with the eastern front, and in particular with the now inevitable catastrophe in Stalingrad, Hitler could not afford to neglect what was happening in North Africa. And he was increasingly worried about the resolve of his Italian allies.

Montgomery had forced Rommel's Afrika Corps into headlong retreat, and would drive the German and Italian army out of Libya altogether during January 1943.[330] Encouraged by Göring, Hitler was now convinced that Rommel had lost his nerve.[331] But at least the 50,000 German and 18,000 Italian troops rushed to Tunis in November and December had seriously held up the Allies, preventing their rapid domination of North Africa and ruling out an early assault on the European continent itself.[332] Even so, Hitler knew the Italians were wobbling. Göring's visit to Rome at the end of November had confirmed that.[333] Their commitment to the war was by now in serious doubt.[334] And when Ciano and Marshal Count Ugo Cavalero, the head of the Italian armed forces, arrived at the Wolf's Lair on 18 December for three days of talks, it was in the immediate wake of the catastrophic collapse of the Italian 8th Army, overwhelmed during the previous two days by the Soviet offensive on the middle stretches of the Don. Hitler concealed his fury and dismay at what he saw as the military weakness of his Axis partner, alluding only in a single sentence to the Italian setbacks. His chief interest in the talks was in pressing upon the Italians the urgent need to intensify efforts – through greater sacrifices from the civilian population – to ensure sufficient transport for vital supplies to the forces in North Africa, emphasizing that this was 'decisive for the war'. From the Italian point of view, the central concern was to suggest to Hitler that the time had come to end the war in the east and seek a settlement with the Soviet Union.[335]

It was the first time a summit with the Italians had taken place in East Prussia. Ciano referred to 'the sadness of that damp forest and boredom of collective living in the Command barracks'. 'There isn't a spot of colour,' he continued, 'not one vivid note. Waiting-rooms filled with people smoking, eating, chatting. Kitchen odour, smell of uniforms, of boots.'[336] The talks produced little that was constructive for either side. When Ciano put Musso-lini's case for Germany coming to terms with the Soviet Union in order to put maximum effort into defence against the western powers, Hitler was dismissive. Were he to do that, he replied, he would be forced within a short time to fight a reinvigorated Soviet Union once more.[337] The Italian guests were non-committal towards Hitler's exhortations to override all civilian considerations in favour of supplies for North Africa.[338]

For the German people, quite especially for the many German families with loved ones in the 6th Army, Christmas 1942 was a depressing festival. A radio broadcast linking troops on all the fighting fronts, including Stalingrad, brought tears to the eyes of many a family gathered around the Christmas tree back home, as the men at the 'front on the Volga' joined their comrades in singing 'Silent Night'. The listeners at home did not know the link-up was a fake.[339] Nor did they know that 1,280 German soldiers died at Stalingrad on that Christmas Day in 1942.[340] They were, however, aware by then of an ominous fate hanging over the 6th Army.

The triumphalist propaganda of September and October, suggesting that victory at Stalingrad was just around the corner, had given way in the weeks following the Soviet counter-offensive to little more than ominous silence. Indications of hard fighting were sufficient, however, to make plain that things were not going to plan. Rumours of the encirclement of the 6th Army – passed on through despairing letters from the soldiers entrapped there – swiftly spread.[341] It soon became evident that the rumours were no less than the truth. As the sombre mood at home deepened by the day, the terrible struggle in the streets of Stalingrad headed towards its inexorable dénouement.

Last letters home confirmed the worst fears. 'Please don't be sad and weep for me, when you receive this, my last letter,' wrote one captain to his wife in mid-January. 'I'm standing here in an icy storm in a hopeless position in the city of fate, Stalingrad. Encircled for months, we will tomorrow begin the last fight, man against man.'[342] Another soldier compared the miserable reality of death in Stalingrad with the imagery of heroism: 'They're falling like flies, and no one bothers and buries them. Without arms and legs and without eyes, with stomachs ripped open, they lie around everywhere.'[343] 'We're completely alone, without help from outside,' ran another last letter home. 'Hitler has left us in the lurch. This letter is going off while the airfield is still in our possession. We're in the north of the city. The men of my battery guess it, too, but don't know it as certainly as I do. This, then, is what the end looks like.'[344] Some clutched vainly, even now, to final strands of belief in Hitler. 'The Führer solidly promised to get us out of here. That's been read out to us and we firmly believed it. I still believe it today, because I have to believe in something . . . I have believed my entire life, or at least eight years of it, always in the Führer and his word. It's horrible how they're in doubt here, and shameful to hear words spoken that you can't contradict because they're in line with the facts.'[345] Such sentiments were by this time rare indeed among those fighting, suffering, and dying in the hell-hole of

Stalingrad. Far more typical was the wretchedness expressed in the last letter of another despairing soldier: 'I love you, and you love me, and so you should know the truth. It is in this letter. The truth is the knowledge of the hardest struggle in a hopeless situation. Misery, hunger, cold, resignation, doubt, despair, and horrible dying . . . I'm not cowardly, just sad that I can give no greater proof of my bravery than to die for such pointlessness, not to say crime . . . Don't be so quick to forget me.'[346]

A series of letters from senior officers in the 6th Army, describing their plight in graphic detail, were received by Hitler's Luftwaffe Adjutant, Nicolaus von Below. He showed them to Hitler, reading out key passages. Hitler listened without comment, except once commenting inscrutably that 'the fate of the 6th Army left for all of us a deep duty in the fight for the freedom of the our people'.[347] Below had the impression that Hitler realized by this time that victory in a two-front war against the Russians and the Americans could not be won. But Hitler betrayed no outward sign of weakening. He felt obliged to maintain the charade, even in his inner circle, that the war *would* be won – and he was able still to convey his optimism to those around him. What he really thought, no one knew.[348]

After Paulus had rejected a call to surrender, the final Soviet attack to destroy the 6th Army began on 10 January. An emissary to the Wolf's Lair, seeking permission for Paulus to have freedom of action to bring an end to the carnage went unheeded by Hitler. On 15 January, he commissioned Field-Marshal Erhard Milch, the Luftwaffe's armaments supremo and mastermind of all its transportation organization, with flying 300 tons of supplies a day to the besieged army. It was pure fantasy – though partly based on the inaccurate information that Zeitzler complained about on more than one occasion. Snow and ice on the runways in sub-arctic temperatures often prevented take-offs and landings. In any case, on 22 January the last airstrip in the vicinity of Stalingrad was lost. Supplies could now only be dropped from the air. The remaining frozen, half-starved troops, under constant heavy fire, were often unable to salvage them.[349]

By this time, the German people were already being prepared for the worst. After a long period of silence, the Wehrmacht report on 16 January had spoken in ominous terms of a 'heroically courageous defensive struggle against the enemy attacking from all sides'.[350] After Goebbels had visited the Wolf's Lair on 22 January, and obtained Hitler's backing for a radicalization of the home front in a drive for 'total war', the press was immediately instructed to speak of 'the great and stirring heroic sacrifice which the troops encircled at Stalingrad are offering the German nation'. This was now to be brought into the direct context of mobilizing the population for 'total war'.[351]

Hitler had bluntly described the plight of the 6th Army to Goebbels at their meeting. There was scarcely a hope of rescuing the troops. It was a 'heroic drama of German history'.[352] News came in as they talked, outlining the rapidly deteriorating situation. Hitler was said by Goebbels to have been 'deeply shaken'.[353] But he did not consider attaching any blame to himself. He complained bitterly about the Luftwaffe, which had not kept its promises about levels of supplies.[354] Schmundt separately told Goebbels that these had been illusory. Göring's staff had given him the optimistic picture they presumed he wanted, and he had passed this on to the Führer.[355] It was a problem that afflicted the entire dictatorship – up to and including Hitler himself. Only positive messages were acceptable. Pessimism (which usually meant realism) was a sign of failure. Distortions of the truth were built into the communications system of the Third Reich at every level – most of all in the top echelons of the regime.

Even more than he felt let down by his own Luftwaffe, Hitler voiced utter contempt for the failure of the German allies to hold the line against the Soviet counter-attack. The Romanians were bad, the Italians worse, and worst of all were the Hungarians.[356] The catastrophe would not have occurred had the entire eastern front been controlled by German units, as he had wanted. The German bakers' and baggage-formations, he fumed, had performed better than the élite Italian, Romanian, and Hungarian divisions. But he did not think the Axis partners were ready to desert. Italy would 'like to dance out of line'; though as long as Mussolini was there, this could be ruled out. The Duce was clever enough to know that it would mean the end of Fascism, and his own end. Romania was essential to Germany for its oil, Hitler said. He had made it plain to the Romanians what would come their way should they attempt anything stupid.[357]

Hitler still hoped – at least that is what he told Goebbels – that parts of the 6th Army could hold out until they could be relieved.[358] In fact, he knew better than anyone that there was not the slightest chance of it. The 6th Army was on its last legs. On 22 January, the very day that Goebbels had had his talks with Hitler at FHQ, Paulus had requested permission to surrender. Hitler rejected it. He then rejected a similar plea from Manstein to allow the 6th Army's surrender. As a point of honour, he stated, there could be no question of capitulation. In the evening, he telegraphed the 6th Army to say that through its struggle it had made an historic contribution in the greatest struggle in German history.[359] The army was to stand fast 'to the last soldier and the last bullet'.[360]

Since 23 January the 6th Army had been beginning to break up. It was split in two as Soviet troops cutting through from the south and the west of the city joined forces. By 26 January the division of the 6th Army was complete.[361] One section raised the white flag on the 29th. The same day, Paulus sent Hitler a telegram of congratulations on the tenth anniversary of his takeover of power on the 30th.[362]

The 'celebrations' in Germany for the anniversary of Hitler's day of triumph in January 1933 were in a low key. All bunting was banned.[363] Hitler did not give his usual speech. He remained in his headquarters and left it to Goebbels to read out his proclamation.[364] A single sentence referred to Stalingrad: 'The heroic struggle of our soldiers on the Volga should be a warning for everybody to do the utmost for the struggle for Germany's freedom and the future of our people, and thus in a wider sense for the maintenance of our entire continent.'[365] In Stalingrad itself, the end was approaching. Feelers were put out by the remnants of the 6th Army to the Soviets that very evening, 30 January 1943, for a surrender. Negotiations took place next day.[366] On that day, the announcement was made that Paulus had been promoted to Field-Marshal.[367] He was expected to end the struggle with a hero's death. In the evening, he surrendered.[368] Two days later, on 2 February, the northern sector of the surrounded troops also gave in. The battle of Stalingrad was over. Around 100,000 men from twenty-one German and two Romanian divisions had fallen in battle. A further 113,000 German and Romanian soldiers were taken prisoner. Only a few thousand would survive their captivity.[369]

VIII

Hitler made no mention of the human tragedy when he met his military leaders at the midday conference on 1 February. What concerned him was the prestige lost through Paulus's surrender. He found it impossible to comprehend, and impossible to forgive. 'Here a man can look on while 50–60,000 of his soldiers die and defend themselves bravely to the last. How can he give himself up to the Bolsheviks?' he asked, nearly speechless with anger at what he saw as a betrayal.[370] He could have no respect for an officer who chose captivity to shooting himself.[371] 'How easy it is to do something like that. The pistol – that's simple. What sort of cowardice does it take to pull back from it?'[372] 'No one else is being made field-marshal in this war,' he avowed (though he did not keep to his word).[373] He was certain – it proved an accurate presumption – that, in Soviet hands, Paulus and the other captured generals would within no time be promoting anti-German propaganda. Drawing on horror-stories of tortures in Russian prisons that had circulated in the *völkisch* press since the early 1920s, he said: 'They'll lock them up in the rat-cellar, and two days later they'll have them so softened-up (*mürbe*) that they'll talk straight away . . . They'll now come into the Lubljanka, and there they'll be eaten by rats. How can someone be so cowardly? I don't understand it. So many people have to die. Then such a man goes and besmirches in the last minute the heroism of so many others. He could release himself from all misery and enter eternity, national immortality, and he prefers to go to Moscow. How can there be a choice? That's crazy.'[374]

For the German people, Paulus's missed chance to gain immortality was scarcely a central concern. Their thoughts, when they heard the dreaded announcement – false to the last – on 3 February that the officers and soldiers of the 6th Army had fought to the final shot and 'died so that Germany might live', were of the human tragedy and the scale of the military disaster.[375] The 'heroic sacrifice' was no consolation to bereft relatives and friends.[376] The women of Nuremberg were among those with many husbands, fathers, sons, or brothers in the 6th Army. As the news broke on 3 February they tore copies of newspapers out of the hands of sellers, shouting and wailing, beside themselves with grief. Men hurled abuse at the Nazi leadership. 'Hitler has lied to us for three months,' people raged. Gestapo men mingled in the crowds. But none of them intervened to arrest individuals from the distraught and angry crowds. It was rumoured that they had been instructed to hold back.[377]

The SD reported that the whole nation was 'deeply shaken' by the fate of the 6th Army. There was deep depression, and widespread anger that Stalingrad had not been evacuated or relieved while there was still time. People asked how such optimistic reports had been possible only a short time earlier. They were critical of the underestimation – as in the previous winter – of the Soviet forces. Many now thought the war could not be won, and were anxiously contemplating the consequences of defeat.[378]

Hitler had until Stalingrad been largely exempted from whatever criticisms people had of the regime. That now altered sharply.[379] His responsibility for the débâcle was evident. 'For the first time,' as Ulrich von Hassell noted, 'the critical murmurings relate directly to him. To this extent there is a genuine leadership crisis . . . The sacrifice of most precious blood for the sake of pointless or criminal prestige is again plain to see.'[380] People had expected Hitler to give an explanation in his speech on 30 January.[381] His obvious reluctance to speak to the nation only heightened the criticism. The regime's opponents were encouraged. Graffiti chalked on walls attacking Hitler, 'the Stalingrad Murderer', were a sign that underground resistance was not extinct.[382] Appalled at what had happened, a number of army officers and highly-placed civil servants revived conspiratorial plans largely dormant since 1938–9.[383]

In Munich, a group of students, together with one of their professors, whose idealism and mounting detestation of the criminal inhumanity of the regime had led them the previous year to form the 'White Rose' opposition-group, now openly displayed their attack on Hitler. The medical students Alexander Schmorell and Hans Scholl had formed the initial driving-force, and had soon been joined by Christoph Probst, Sophie Scholl (Hans's sister), Willi Graf, and Kurt Huber, Professor of Philosophy at Munich University, whose critical attitude to the regime had influenced them in lectures and discussions. All the students came from conservative, middle-class backgrounds. All were fired by Christian beliefs and humanistic idealism. The horrors on the eastern front, experienced for a short time at first hand when Graf, Schmorell, and Hans Scholl were called up, converted the lofty idealism into an explicit, political message. 'Fellow Students!' ran their final manifesto (composed by Professor Huber), distributed in Munich University on 18 February. 'The nation is deeply shaken by the destruction of the men of Stalingrad. The genial strategy of the World War [I] corporal has senselessly and irresponsibly driven (*gehetzt*) three hundred and thirty thousand German men to death and ruin. Führer, we thank you!'[384]

It was a highly courageous show of defiance. But it was suicidal. Hans and Sophie Scholl were denounced by a porter at the university (who was subsequently applauded by pro-Nazi students for his action), and quickly arrested by the Gestapo. Christoph Probst was picked up soon afterwards. Their trial before the 'People's Court', presided over by Roland Freisler, took place within four days. The verdict – the death-sentence – was a foregone conclusion. All three were guillotined the same afternoon. Willi Graf, Kurt Huber, and Alexander Schmorell suffered the same fate some months later. Other students on the fringe of the movement were sentenced to long terms of imprisonment.[385]

The regime had been badly stung. But it was not at the point of collapse. It would lash back without scruple and with utter viciousness at the slightest hint of opposition. The level of brutality towards its own population was about to rise sharply as external adversity mounted.

If Hitler felt any personal remorse for Stalingrad or human sympathy for the dead of the 6th Army and their relatives, he did not let it show. Those in his close proximity could detect the signs of nervous strain.[386] He hinted privately at his worry that his health would not stand up to the pressure.[387] His secretaries had to put up with even longer nocturnal monologues as his insomnia developed chronic proportions. The topics were much the same as ever: his youth in Vienna, the 'time of struggle', the history of mankind, the nature of the cosmos. There was no relief from the boredom for his secretaries, who by now knew his outpourings on all topics more or less off by heart. There were not even any longer the occasional evenings listening to records to break up the tedium. Hitler, as he had told Goebbels some weeks earlier, now no longer wanted to listen to music.[388] Talking was like a drug for him. He told one of his doctors two years later that he had to talk – about more or less anything other than military issues – to divert him from sleepless nights pondering troop dispositions and seeing in his mind where every division was at Stalingrad.[389] As Below guessed, the bad news from the North African as well as from the eastern front must have led to serious doubts, in the privacy of his own room in the bunker of his head-quarters, about whether the war could still be won.[390] But outwardly, even among his entourage at the Wolf's Lair, he had to sustain the façade of invincibility. No crack could be allowed to show. Hitler remained true to his creed of will and strength. A hint of weakness, in his thinking, was a gift to enemies and subversives. A crevice of demoralization would then swiftly widen to a chasm. The military, and above all else the Party, leaders must, therefore, never be allowed a glimmer of any wavering in his own resolution.

There was not a trace of demoralization, depression, or uncertainty when he spoke to the Reichs- and Gauleiter for almost two hours at his headquarters on 7 February.[391] He told them at the very beginning of his address that he believed in victory more than ever. Then he described what Goebbels referred to as 'the catastrophe on the eastern front'.[392] Hitler did not look close to home for the failings. While he said he naturally accepted full responsibility for the events of the winter,[393] he left no doubt where in his view the real fault lay. From the beginning of his political career – indeed, from what is known of his earliest remarks on politics – he had cast around for scapegoats. The trait was too embedded in his psyche for him to stray from it now that, for the first time, an unmitigated national disaster had to be explained. Addressing the Party leadership, as in his private discussion with Goebbels a fortnight or so earlier, he once more placed the blame for the disaster at Stalingrad squarely on the 'complete failure' of

Germany's allies – the Romanians, Italians, and Hungarians – whose fighting powers met with his 'absolute contempt'.[394] The consequence of the collapse of Germany's allies in the defensive front had been to endanger the Caucasus army. This had necessitated the 'extraordinarily difficult order, involving much sacrifice', that the 6th Army should stand fast and bind in the Red Army 'to prevent the catastrophe gripping the entire eastern front'. Dreadful weather conditions, he said, had prevented it being supplied from the air, as had been presumed possible. Hitler took the view that the crisis, in broad terms, could be taken to be mastered. 'The Caucasus army had been saved through the sacrifice of the 6th Army in Stalingrad.'[395]

Not just the search for scapegoats, but the feeling of treachery and betrayal was entrenched in Hitler's thinking. Another strand of his explanation for the disaster at Stalingrad was the prospect of imminent French betrayal, forcing him to retain several divisions, especially SS-divisions, in the west when they were desperately needed in the east.[396] But Hitler had the extraordinary capacity, as his Luftwaffe adjutant Below noted, of turning negative into positive, and convincing his audience of this.[397] A landing by the Allies in France would have been far more dangerous, he claimed, than that which had taken place in North Africa and had been checked through the occupation of Tunis.[398] He saw grounds for optimism, too, in the success of the U-boats, and in Speer's armaments programme enabling better flak defence against air-raids together with full-scale production by the summer of the Tiger tank.[399]

Much of the rest of Hitler's address was on the 'psychology' of war. Goebbels had shrewdly played on Hitler's instincts in demanding the radicalization of the 'home front' and the move to 'total war'. The urgings of the Propaganda Minister found their echo in Hitler's rallying-call to his Gauleiter. The crisis was more of a psychological than a material one, he declared, and must therefore be overcome by 'psychological means'. It was the Party's task to achieve this. The Gauleiter should remember the 'time of struggle'. Radical measures were now needed. Austerity, sacrifice, and the end of any privileges for certain sectors of society was the order of the day. The setbacks but eventual triumph of Frederick the Great – the implied comparison with Hitler's own leadership was plain – were invoked.[400] The setbacks now being faced – solely the fault of Germany's allies – even had their own psychological advantages. Propaganda and the Party's agitation could awaken people to the fact that they had stark alternatives: becoming master of Europe, or undergoing 'a total liquidation and extermination'.[401]

Hitler pointed out one advantage which, he claimed, the Allies possessed:

that they were sustained by international Jewry. The consequence, Goebbels reported Hitler as saying, was 'that we have to eliminate Jewry not only from Reich territory but from the whole of Europe'. Goebbels noted approvingly that Hitler had again adopted his own viewpoint, and that within the foreseeable future there would be no more Jews in Berlin. 'The ruthlessness towards Jewry which [Hitler] impresses on all Gauleiter,' Goebbels added, 'has long since been the political order of the day in Berlin.'[402]

Hitler categorically ruled out, as he always had done, any possibility of capitulation.[403] He stated that any collapse of the German Reich was out of the question. But his further remarks betrayed the fact that he was contemplating precisely that. The event of such a collapse 'would represent the ending of his life', he declared. It was plain who, in such an eventuality, the scapegoats would be: the German people themselves. 'Such a collapse could only be caused through the weakness of the people,' Goebbels recorded Hitler as saying. 'But if the German people turned out to be weak, they would deserve nothing else than to be extinguished by a stronger people; then one could have no sympathy for them.'[404] The sentiment would stay with him to the end.

To the Party leadership, the backbone of his support, Hitler could speak in this way. The Gauleiter could be rallied by such rhetoric. They were after all fanatics as Hitler himself was. They were part of his 'sworn community'. The responsibility of the Party for the radicalization of the 'home front' was music to their ears. In any case, whatever private doubts (if any) they harboured, they had no choice but to stick with Hitler. They had burnt their boats with him. He was the sole guarantor of their power.

The German people were less easily placated than Hitler's immediate viceroys. When he spoke in Berlin to the nation for the first time since Stalingrad, on the occasion (which this year, of all years, he could not possibly avoid) of Heroes' Memorial Day on 21 March 1943, his speech gave rise to greater criticism than any Hitler speech since he had become Chancellor.[405]

The speech was one of Hitler's shortest. Goebbels was pleased that it was only fifteen pages long; it lessened the chances of being interrupted by the British air-raid that was feared and predicted.[406] Hitler told Goebbels that he wanted to use the speech for another fierce attack on Bolshevism. He felt like an old propagandist, he said: propaganda meant repetition.[407] Perhaps it was the anxiety, as Goebbels had hinted, about a possible air-raid which made Hitler race through his speech in such a rapid and dreary monotone. Whatever the reason, the routine assault on Bolshevism and on Jewry as the force behind the 'merciless war' could stir little enthusiasm. Disappointment was profound. Rumours revived about Hitler's poor health – along with others that it had been a substitute who had spoken, while the real Führer was under house-arrest on the Obersalzberg suffering from a mental breakdown after Stalingrad. Extraordinary was the fact that Hitler never even directly mentioned Stalingrad in a ceremony meant to be devoted to the memory of the fallen and at a time where the trauma was undiminished. And his passing reference, at the end of his speech, to a figure of 542,000 German dead in the war was presumed to be far too low and received with rank incredulity.[408]

Reactions to the speech were a clear indicator that the German people's bonds with Hitler were dissolving. This was no overnight phenomenon. But Stalingrad was the point at which the signs became unmistakable. There was no rebellion in the air; Hitler was right about that. The mood was sullenly depressed, anxious about the present, fearful of the future, above all else weary of the war; but not rebellious. To all but the few who had served the regime from the inside, had contacts in high places with recourse to the power of the military, and were now actively conspiring to bring about Hitler's downfall, thoughts of overthrowing the regime could scarcely be entertained. The regime was far too strong, its capacity for repression far too great, its readiness to strike down all opposition far too evident (and becoming even more so as positive support waned and loyalties weakened). The reserves of hard-core Nazi support were still substantial. They could be found especially – though here, too, there were unmistakable signs of erosion – among members of a younger generation that had swallowed Nazi ideals in school, among many ordinary front soldiers desperately clinging to a ray of hope, and, naturally, most of all among Party activists who had combined fervent belief with careerism.[409] Fanatical devotees of the Führer cult, who had not wavered in their adulation of Hitler, or who were implicated in the crimes against humanity which he had inspired, remained in control of the home front, itching to resort to any measures, however ruthless, to shore up the regime's foundations. For the bulk of the population, there was no alternative to struggling on.

In this, at least, the dictator and the people he led were at one. Hitler, as more and more ordinary citizens now recognized, had closed off all avenues that might have brought compromise peace. The earlier victories were increasingly seen in a different light. There was no end in sight. But it now seemed clear to growing numbers of ordinary citizens that Hitler had taken them into a war which could only end in destruction, defeat, and disaster. There was still far to go, but over the next months the miseries of war would rebound in ever greater ferocity on the population of Germany itself. What was revealed after Stalingrad would become over those months ever clearer: for all the lingering strength of support, the German people's love affair with Hitler was at an end. Only the bitter process of divorce remained.

12

BELEAGUERED

'We have not only a "leadership crisis", but strictly speaking a "Leader crisis"!'

Speer, recalling Goebbels's assessment in late February 1943

'Germany and its allies were in the same boat on a stormy sea. It was obvious that in this situation anyone wanting to get off would drown immediately.'

Hitler, speaking to Admiral Horthy of Hungary, April 1943

'Herr Feldmarschall: we are not master here of our own decisions.'

Hitler to Field-Marshal von Kluge, 26 July 1943, after the fall of Mussolini the previous day

'A glorious page in our history, and one that has never been written and never can be written ... We had the moral right, we had the duty to our people, to destroy this people which wanted to destroy us.'

Himmler, speaking to SS leaders in Posen about the 'Final Solution of the Jewish Question', 4 October 1943

'The English claim that the German people have lost their trust in the Führer,' Goebbels declared. It was the opening to the fifth of his ten rhetorical questions towards the end of his two-hour speech proclaiming 'total war' on the evening of 18 February 1943. The hand-picked audience in Berlin's Sportpalast rose as one man to denounce such an outrageous allegation. A chorus of voices arose: 'Führer command, we will obey.' The tumult lasted for what seemed an age. Orchestrating the frenzied mood to perfection, the propaganda maestro eventually broke in to ask: 'Is your trust in the Führer greater, more faithful, and more unshakeable than ever? Is your readiness to follow him in all his ways and to do everything necessary to bring the war to a triumphant end absolute and unrestricted?' Fourteen thousand voices hysterically cried out in unison the answer invited by Goebbels in his bid to quell doubters at home and to relay to the outside world the futility of any hope of inner collapse in Germany. Goebbels ended his morale-boosting peroration – which had been interrupted more than 200 times by clapping, cheering, shouts of approbation, or thunderous applause – with the words of Theodor Körner, the patriotic poet from the time of Prussia's struggle against Napoleon: 'Now people, arise – and storm burst forth!' The great hall erupted. Amid the wild cheering the national anthem 'Deutschland, Deutschland über alles' and the Party's 'Horst-Wessel-Lied' rang out. The spectacle ended with cries of 'the great German Leader Adolf Hitler, Sieg Heil, Sieg Heil.'[1]

The speech was intended to demonstrate the complete solidarity of people and leader, conveying Germany's utter determination to carry on, and even intensify, the fight until victory was attained.[2] But the solidarity, despite the impression temporarily left by Goebbels's publicity spectacular, was by this time shrinking fast, the belief in Hitler among the mass of the population seriously undermined. What Goebbels did, in fact, was to solicit from his audience 'a kind of plebiscitary "Ja" to self-destruction'[3] in a war which Germany could by now neither win nor end through a negotiated peace.

The dwindling hopes of victory had already turned, for those with any sense of realism, into the near certainty of ultimate defeat. Over the next months, the German people, the Nazi regime, and its Leader would become ever more beleaguered. Friends and allies would desert, territorial gains crumble, ever-intensifying air-raids lay waste German cities, the insurmountable Allied superiority of manpower and weaponry manifest itself ever more plainly, and indications at home begin to multiply that, whatever Goebbels's rhetoric might suggest, loyalties towards the regime, and even towards Hitler personally, had become severely weakened. Nevertheless, the defiance and resolve evoked in Goebbels's Sportpalast speech, shored up by new levels of draconian repression as support for the regime dwindled, helped to rule out any prospect of collapse on the home front. This in turn would drag out the demise of the regime for a further two years, ensuring that death and devastation were to be maximized during a prolonged backs-to-the-wall struggle against increasingly impossible odds.

In the spirit he was attempting to evince through his Sportpalast speech, Goebbels was at one with Hitler. Goebbels's advocacy of the need to instil the fanatical will to victory in the entire people and to mobilize the home front psychologically into accepting the most radical measures in an all-out struggle for the nation's survival had met with Hitler's approval on a number of occasions during the previous months. Whether, as he usually did, the Propaganda Minister had shown the text of his speech to Hitler in advance of the Sportpalast meeting is not altogether clear.[4] Hitler was visiting his field headquarters in the Ukraine at the time of the speech. Communication with him, Goebbels remarked, was difficult but, he felt, in any case unnecessary since the main propaganda lines had already been established.[5] Though he did not listen to the broadcast, Hitler immediately asked for the text to be sent to him and praised it shortly afterwards to Goebbels in glowing terms. There was, indeed, nothing in the speech to which Hitler might have taken exception.[6]

However, Goebbels's hopes that the speech would bring him Hitler's authorization to concentrate the direction of 'total war' in his own hands were swiftly dashed. The Propaganda Minister had long pressed for practical measures to radicalize the war effort. His own approach concentrated, of course, predominantly on psychological mobilization. Others, prominent

among them Speer and the Wehrmacht leadership, focused their attention
more squarely on the manpower needs of the armed forces and armaments
industry, and the problem of how to squeeze out remaining reserves of
labour. What they understood by 'total war' included the deployment of
still unused female labour in industrial production, which they knew their
enemies had accomplished. Hitler, shored up by Göring, had, however,
resisted imposing increased hardship and material sacrifice on the civilian
population. He was conscious as ever of the collapse of morale on the home
front during the First World War, certain that this had undermined the
military effort and paved the way for revolution.[7] His anxiety about the
impact on morale of their men-folk at the front, coupled with his traditionalist views about the domestic role of women, had led him to oppose the
conscription of female labour to work in the hard-pressed armaments
industries.[8] Nevertheless, during the Stalingrad crisis he had finally conceded
the aim of the complete mobilization of all conceivable labour and resources
of the home front, and some initial measures had been introduced.[9]

Goebbels had, however, miscalculated. Direction of the 'total war' effort
largely bypassed him. His ambitions to take control of the home front
were ignored. The move to 'total war' extended far more widely than
psychological mobilization, where he was an unrivalled master. 'Behind the
throne', at the level below Hitler, the move unleashed new power games as
his chieftains – prominent among them (besides Goebbels himself) Göring,
Speer, Robert Ley (boss of the German Labour Front), Fritz Sauckel (Plenipotentiary for Labour Deployment), and not least Bormann – jockeyed for
position to occupy the new spheres of control that were opening up.[10] Unable
to adjudicate in any rational or systematic fashion in the inevitable conflicts
arising from overlapping and sometimes contradictory spheres of competence, but careful as always to protect his own power, Hitler never allowed
Goebbels the authority the latter craved on the home front. The 'total war'
effort juddered on to partial successes in individual areas. But the absence
of strong, consistent leadership from the top on the home front produced
what Goebbels lamented as 'a complete lack of direction in German domestic
policy'.[11] It axiomatically ruled out coherent, well-organized, and clearly
coordinated planning – and with that any illusions that the Propaganda
Minister might have had that he would be given a free hand in domestic
affairs. When, eventually, Hitler did become prepared to appoint Goebbels
'Plenipotentiary for Total War Deployment', on 20 July 1944, it was very
late in the day and, in any case, even then the powers granted were heavily
circumscribed.[12]

The results of Goebbels's big speech, therefore, in terms of his own ambitions to take control of the 'total war' effort, were disappointing. For all its bombast, the Sportpalast spectacular had little lasting effect. Goebbels was soon to learn anew the lesson that, mighty though he was, he remained only one player in the power-games to try to secure the backing of Hitler's unqualified authority. He would also rapidly realize again, in the aftermath of the speech, that although the dictator's own authority was undiminished, his physical absence, preoccupation with military matters, and sporadic, semi-detached involvement in the day-to-day governance of the Reich meant that he was more than ever exposed to the influence of those in his presence – 'the entire baggage of court-idiots and irresponsible agitators'[13] – incapable of reconciling or overriding the competing interests of his feuding barons. Even had he been willing, therefore, he was completely unable to impose clear strands of authority to combat the already advanced signs of disintegration in government and administration.

For Hitler, the months after Stalingrad intensified the familiar, ingrained character-traits. The façade of often absurd optimism remained largely intact, even among his inner circle. The show of indomitable will continued. The flights of fantasy, detached from reality, took on new dimensions. But the mask slipped from time to time in remarks revealing deep depression and fatalism. It was fleeting recognition of what he already inwardly acknowledged: he had lost the initiative for ever. The recognition invariably brought new torrents of rage, lashing any who might bear the brunt of the blame – most of all, as ever, his military leaders. They were all liars, disloyal, opposed to National Socialism, reactionaries, and lacking in any cultural appreciation, he ranted. He yearned to have nothing more to do with them.[14] Ultimately, he would blame the German people themselves, whom he would see as too weak to survive and unworthy of him in the great struggle. As setback followed setback, so the beleaguered Führer resorted ever more readily to the search for ruthless revenge and retaliation, both on his external enemies – behind whom, as always, he saw the demonic figure of the Jew – and on any within who might dare to show defeatism, let alone 'betray' him. There were no personal influences that might have moderated his fundamental inhumanity. The man who had been idolized by millions was friendless – apart from (as he himself commented) Eva Braun and his dog, Blondi.[15]

The war, and the hatreds Hitler had invested in it, consumed him ever more. The musical evenings had stopped after Stalingrad.[16] He ate on his own a good deal of the time, to avoid having to converse with his generals.

Outside the war and his buildings mania, he could rouse little interest. He told Goebbels how he longed to be able to go to the theatre or see cinema again, to be among people as he used to be, to enjoy life once more when the war was ended.[17] This was mere nostalgia in the midst of a war of which, though he failed to see it, he was the main author, and which had been at the centre of his thoughts for two decades. He was by now in many respects an empty, burnt-out shell of an individual. But his resilience and strength of will remained extraordinary. And in the strangely shapeless regime over which he presided, his power was still immense, unrestricted, and uncontested.

As the war that Hitler had unleashed 'came home to the Reich', the dictator – now rapidly ageing, becoming increasingly a physical wreck, and showing pronounced signs of intense nervous strain – distanced himself ever more from his people. It was as if he could not face them now that there were no more triumphs to report, and he had to take the responsibility for the mounting losses and misery. Even before the Stalingrad calamity, in early November 1942, when his train had by chance stopped directly alongside a troop train returning from the east carrying dejected-looking, battle-weary soldiers, his only reaction had been to ask one of his manservants to pull down the blinds.[18] As Germany's war fortunes plummeted between 1943 and 1945, the former corporal from an earlier great war never sought to experience at first hand the feelings of ordinary soldiers.

The number of big public speeches he delivered constituted a plain indicator of the widening gulf between Führer and people. In 1940 Hitler had given nine big public addresses, in 1941 seven, in 1942 five. In 1943 he gave only two (apart from a radio broadcast on 10 September) – on 'Heroes' Memorial Day' on 21 March, and to the Old Guard in the Löwenbräukeller in Munich, as usual, on 8 November.[19] The bulk of his time was spent well away from the government ministries in Berlin's Wilhelmstraße – and well away from the German people – at his field headquarters, or at his mountain eyrie above Berchtesgaden. He spent no more than a few days in Berlin – mainly in May – during the whole of 1943. For some three months in all he was at the Berghof. During the rest of the time he was cooped up in his headquarters in East Prussia, leaving aside a number of short visits to the Ukraine.[20]

Goebbels lamented in July 1943 the way Hitler had cut himself off from the masses. These, commented the Propaganda Minister, had provided the acclaim on which his unique authority had rested. He had given them the belief and trust that had been the focal point of the regime's support. But now, in Goebbels's eyes, that relationship was seriously endangered – and with it the stability of the regime. He pointed to the large number and critical tone of the letters – half of them anonymous – arriving at the Propaganda Ministry. 'Above all, the question is again and again raised in these letters,' he went on, 'why the Führer never visits the areas which have suffered from air-raids, why Göring never shows himself, but especially why the Führer does not even speak to the German people to explain the current situation. I regard it as most necessary that the Führer does that, despite his burden through the events in the military sector. One can't neglect the people too long. Ultimately, they are the heart of our war effort. If the people were once to lose their strength of resistance and belief in the German leadership, then the most serious leadership crisis which ever faced us would have been created.'[21]

I

The move to 'total war', introduced during the Stalingrad crisis, provided the final demonstration that no semblance of collective government and rational decision-making within the Reich was compatible with Hitler's personal rule.

The drive to mobilize all remaining reserves from the home front – what came to be proclaimed as 'total war' – had its roots in the need to plug the huge gap in military manpower left by the high losses suffered by the Wehrmacht during the first months of 'Barbarossa'. As early as December 1941, Keitel had demanded a weeding out of superfluous personnel from the bureaucracies of government ministries, the economy, and the Wehrmacht itself.[22] This had led to attempts to release personnel for the army by simplifying the extraordinarily unwieldy and cumbersome governmental administration. The proliferation of 'special authorities' alongside government ministries and the Party-State dualism – direct products of the Führer state – alongside the new administrative tasks created by the demands of the war had led to a colossal expansion of bureaucracy, churning out hundreds of regulations, decrees, and ordinances. The amount of red tape involved was suffocating. There was huge resentment at what was dubbed a 'paper war'.

Hitler's tirades against government bureaucracy were well known to all those who came into contact with him. His scorn for legally minded administrators knew no bounds. He took the view that their number could

be cut by two-thirds.[23] So there was no difficulty in pandering to his prejudices. It was easy to gain his support for the action to reduce bureaucracy.
To implement any such measures was a different matter. Hitler's own stance
was in practice often hesitant, contradictory, and ultimately, in the main,
conservative. And despite Hitler's backing, attempts to cut the personnel of
government offices rapidly ran up against powerful vested interests. The
results were predictably meagre.[24] The manpower demands of the front
inevitably, however, forced renewed efforts to squeeze out any surplus
personnel back home. In the autumn of 1942, Hitler had commissioned
General Walter von Unruh, who had earlier been relatively successful in
freeing personnel from military and civilian bureaucracies in the eastern
occupied territories, to sift through the civil administration and even the
armaments economy.[25] But this, too, had produced little as government
ministers successfully fended off the worst inroads into their personnel. And
when General von Unruh attempted to claw back some of those engaged on
the Führer's grandiose building projects (including sixty-eight men aged
thirty-five or under employed in the planning office for the intended
rebuilding of much of the centre of Munich), Hitler predictably decided that
they could not be released.[26]

Before the failure of Unruh's efforts had become clear, Hitler had, at
Christmas 1942, given the orders for more radical measures to raise manpower for the front and the armaments industries. Martin Bormann was
commissioned to undertake the coordination of the efforts, in collaboration
with Head of the Reich Chancellery Hans-Heinrich Lammers.[27] Goebbels
and Sauckel were immediately informed. The aim was to close down all
businesses whose trade was in 'luxury' items or was otherwise not necessary
for the war effort, and to redeploy the personnel in the army or in arms
production. Women were to be subject to conscription for work. Releasing
men for front-service was impossible, it was agreed, unless women could
replace them in a variety of forms of work. According to the Propaganda
Ministry, the number of women working had dropped by some 147,000
since the start of the war.[28] And of 8.6 million women in employment at the
end of 1942, only 968,000 worked in armaments.[29] In the spring of 1942,
Hitler had rejected outright the conscription of women to work in war
industries. Industrialists had been pressing for this, and Speer had taken up
their demand. But Sauckel, jealously guarding his own province and claiming
responsibility for labour deployment was his alone, had held Speer at bay,
backed by Göring and calling upon the support of the Führer. Probably, as
Speer suggests, Sauckel had therefore solicited Hitler's rejection of female

conscription.[30] According to Sauckel's version, Hitler's reasons had been ideological.[31] The birth-rate of the nation would be threatened and as a consequence Germany's racial strength undermined. He also thought that women would be exposed to moral danger.[32]

But by early 1943, the labour situation had worsened to the extent that Hitler was compelled to concede that the conscription of women could no longer be avoided. Even the forced labour of, by this time, approaching 6 million foreign workers and prisoners-of-war could not compensate for the 11 million or so men who had been called up to the Wehrmacht.[33] The most he could do to limit what he regarded as a move likely to damage morale was to raise the age of eligibility from sixteen years, as agreed by the government ministers involved, to seventeen.[34] In an unpublished Führer Decree of 13 January 1943, women between seventeen and fifty years old were ordered to report for deployment in the war effort.[35] There was little enthusiasm among those affected. Women made use of the exemption criteria – including responsibility for children, and employment in agriculture or the civil service – and any personal connections to avoid duty where they could. Where that was impossible, they headed in the main for light desk jobs, leaving the armaments industries still short of women employees.[36]

Even before Hitler signed the decree, the wrangling over spheres of competence had begun in earnest. In order to retain a firm grip on the 'total war' measures and prevent the dissipation of centralized control, Lammers, backed by the leading civil servants in the Reich Chancellery, Leo Killy and Friedrich Wilhelm Kritzinger, suggested to Hitler that all measures should be taken 'under the authority of the Führer', and that a special body be set up to handle them. The idea was to create a type of small 'war cabinet'; the 'Ministerial Council for the Defence of the Reich', as we noted in an earlier chapter, had potentially constituted such, but had never functioned as one in practice, and had long fallen into desuetude. Lammers thought the most appropriate arrangement would be for the heads of the three main executive arms of the Führer's authority – the High Command of the Wehrmacht, the Reich Chancellery, and the Party Chancellery – to act in close collaboration, meeting frequently, keeping regular contact with Hitler himself, and standing above the particularist interests of individual ministries. Hitler agreed. He evidently saw no possible threat to his position from such an arrangement. On the contrary: the three persons involved – Keitel, Lammers, and Bormann – could be guaranteed to uphold his own interests at the expense of any possible over-mighty subjects. An indication that this was, indeed, Hitler's thinking was the exclusion of Göring, Goebbels, and Speer from the coordinating body – soon known as the 'Committee of Three' (*Drei-erausschuß*).[37] This was to last until the autumn before withering away – a further casualty of Hitler's refusal to concede any actual power that might conflict with his authority as Führer, and of his unsystematic, dilettante style of rule.

From the very outset, the Committee was only empowered to issue enabling ordinances in accordance with the general guidelines he had laid down. It was given no autonomy.[38] Hitler reserved, as always, the final decision on anything of significance to himself. It was an exaggeration when Speer later claimed that it had been the intention of the three members of the Committee to control Hitler's power.[39] The loyalty of all three, and their subservience to Hitler's will, was beyond question. They did nothing in practice which might have conflicted with Hitler's wishes. And, though Speer emphasized Bormann's plans to use the Committee to further his own power-ambitions, the head of the Party Chancellery seems to have been largely content in practice to leave the bulk of the routine business to Lammers – hardly a man aiming to take over the Reich.[40]

The 'Committee of Three' had, in all, eleven formal meetings between January and August 1943. The heads of government departments were invited, but the meetings did not amount, as Speer later claimed, to a revival of the cabinet.[41] The Committee, for all its potential for aggrandizement of power as a body operating in close proximity to the Führer, rapidly ran up against deeply ingrained vested interests both in government ministries and in Party regional offices concerned to hold on to their personnel and to their spheres of competence which might have been threatened in any move to centralize and simplify the regime's tangled lines of administration.[42] It had little chance of breaking down the fiefdoms on which Nazi rule rested, and soon revealed that any hopes of bringing any order to the Third Reich's endemic administrative chaos were utterly illusory.

Nevertheless, Hitler's mightiest subjects were determined to do everything they could to sabotage a development which they saw as inimical to their own power-positions – and from which they had been excluded. The first notions of a challenge to the role of the 'Committee of Three' were intimated during the reception in Goebbels's residence following his 'total war' speech on 18 February. Nine days later, Funk, Ley, and Speer met again over cognac and tea in Goebbels's stately apartments – gloomy now that the light-bulbs had been removed to comply with the new 'total war' demands – to see what could be done.[43] Soon afterwards, at the beginning of March, Goebbels travelled from Berlin down to Berchtesgaden to plot with Göring a way of sidelining the Committee. Speer had already sounded him out.[44] In talks lasting five hours at Göring's palatial villa on the Obersalzberg, partly with Speer present, the Reich Marshal, dressed in 'somewhat baroque clothes',[45] was quickly won over.

The 'Committee of Three', which he scornfully labelled 'the three kings',[46] was a worry to him too. He detested Lammers as a 'super bureaucrat' who wanted to put the Reich leadership back in the hands of the government officials. Hitler, thought Göring, had not seen through Lammers. It was necessary to open the Führer's eyes. Bormann was, of course, following his own ambitious ends. Keitel was a complete nonentity.[47] Former differences between Göring and Goebbels were waved aside. Göring's considerable ego had been much deflated through losing favour with Hitler on account of the Luftwaffe's failure to prevent the bombing of German cities. Goebbels flattered him, and at the same time reproached him for allowing the Ministerial Council for the Defence of the Reich to fall into disuse. The Propaganda Minister's plan – actually it had initally been suggested by Speer[48] – was to revive the Ministerial Council, under Göring's chairmanship, and to give it the membership to turn it into an effective body to rule the Reich, leaving Hitler free to concentrate on the direction of military affairs. Goebbels spoke of 'the total lack of a clear leadership in domestic and foreign policy'.[49] Göring said that the Führer seemed to him to have aged fifteen years since the start of the war. He had shut himself off too much, and had a mentally and physically unhealthy lifestyle. But there was probably nothing to be done about that.[50]

Goebbels couched his arguments in terms of loyalty to Hitler, and the need to relieve him of oppressive burdens to free him for military leadership. Hitler's depressed mood – he had indicated from time to time that death held no fears for him – was, said Goebbels, understandable; all the more reason, then, for his 'closest friends' to form 'a solid phalanx around his person'. He reminded Göring of what threatened if the war were lost: 'Above all as regards the Jewish Question, we are in it so deeply that there is no getting out any longer. And that's good. A Movement and a people that have burnt their boats fight, from experience, with fewer constraints than those that still have a chance of retreat.'[51] The Party needed revitalizing.[52] And if Göring could now reactivate the Ministerial Council and put it in the hands of Hitler's most loyal followers, argued Goebbels, the Führer would surely be in agreement.[53]

Goebbels suggested that he and Göring approach the appropriate persons. But none of these should be initiated into the actual intention of sidelining the 'Committee of Three' and transferring authority to the Ministerial Council. They would choose their moment to put the proposition to Hitler himself. This would, they knew, not be easy, despite Goebbels's repeated protestations that the Führer would be happy about the idea. Goebbels and Speer undertook to work on Hitler in the interim. Göring and Goebbels would meet again in a fortnight. They did not doubt that they would swiftly master the problem of 'the three kings'.[54]

The problem, however, especially as Goebbels saw it, went beyond the 'Committee of Three': it was a problem of Hitler himself. Naturally, Goebbels's own ambitions to take over the direction of the home front – to instil a revolutionary drive into the 'total war' effort – played an important part in his scheming. But there was more to it than that. The war had to be won. The prospect of losing it did not bear thinking about. To rescue the war effort, stronger leadership at home was needed. Goebbels remained utterly loyal to the person he had for years regarded as an almost deified father-figure. But he saw in Hitler's leadership style – his absence from Berlin, his detachment from the people, his almost total preoccupation with military matters, and, above all, his increasing reliance on Bormann for everything concerning domestic matters – a fundamental weakness in the governance of the Reich. A consummate politician himself, Goebbels could scarcely understand how Hitler could neglect politics for the subordinate matter of military command.[55]

In his diary, Goebbels complained of a 'leadership crisis'. He thought the problems among the subordinate leaders were so grave that the Führer ought to sweep through them with an iron broom.[56] 'Look at the Minister of the Interior,' he fumed. 'At 67 years of age, he [Frick] spends three quarters of the entire year at the Chiemsee' – the biggest of the beautiful Bavarian lakes, some sixty miles south-east of Munich – 'instead of carrying out his duties in Berlin. Göring is to be found at Karinhall, Bouhler in Nußdorf,' their country houses. 'The entire Reich and Party leadership is on holiday.' The Führer carried, indeed, a crushing burden through the war. But that was because he would take no decisions to alter the personnel so that he would not need bothering with every trivial matter.[57] Goebbels thought – though he expressed it discreetly – that Hitler was too weak to do anything. 'When a matter is put to him from the most varied sides,' he wrote, 'the Führer is sometimes somewhat vacillating (*schwankend*) in his decisions. He also doesn't always react correctly to people. A bit of help is needed there.'[58]

When he had spoken privately in his residence to Speer, Funk, and Ley just over a week after his 'total war' speech, he had gone further. According to Speer's later account, Goebbels had said on that occasion: 'We have not only a "leadership crisis", but strictly speaking a "Leader crisis"!' The others agreed with him. 'We are sitting here in Berlin. Hitler does not hear what we have to say about the situation. I can't influence him politically,' Goebbels bemoaned. 'I can't even report to him about the most urgent measures in my area. Everything goes through Bormann. Hitler must be persuaded to come more often to Berlin.' Goebbels added that Hitler had lost his grip on domestic politics, which Bormann controlled by conveying the impression to the Führer that he still held the reins tightly in his grasp.[59] With Bormann given the title, on 12 April, of 'Secretary of the Führer', the sense, acutely felt by Goebbels, that the Party Chancellery chief was 'managing' Hitler was even further enhanced.[60]

Goebbels and Speer might lament that Hitler's hold on domestic affairs had weakened. But when they saw him in early March, intending to put their proposition to him that Göring should head a revamped Ministerial Council for the Defence of the Reich to direct the home front, it was they who proved weak. Speer had flown to Hitler's headquarters, temporarily moved back to Vinnitsa in the Ukraine, on 5 March to pave the way for a visit by Goebbels. The Propaganda Minister arrived in Vinnitsa three days later. Straight away, Speer urged caution. The continued, almost unhindered, bombing raids on German towns had left Hitler in a foul mood towards Göring and the inadequacies of the Luftwaffe. It was hardly a propitious moment to broach the subject of reinstating the Reich Marshal to the central role in the direction of domestic affairs. Goebbels thought nonetheless that they had to make the attempt.[61]

At their first meeting, over lunch, Hitler, looking tired but otherwise well, and more lively than of late, launched as usual into a bitter onslaught on the generals who, he claimed, were cheating him wherever they could do so.[62] He carried on in the same vein during a private four-hour discussion alone with Goebbels that afternoon. He was furious at Göring, and at the entire Luftwaffe leadership with the exception of the Chief of the General Staff Hans Jeschonnek. Characteristically, Hitler thought the best way of preventing German cities being reduced to heaps of rubble was by responding with 'terror from our side'.[63] Despite his insistence to Speer that they had to go ahead with their proposal, Goebbels evidently concluded during his discussion with Hitler that it would be fruitless to do so. 'In view of the general mood,' he noted, 'I regard it as inopportune to put to the Führer the question of Göring's political leadership; it's at present an unsuitable moment. We must defer the business until somewhat later.'[64] Any hope of raising the matter, even obliquely, when Goebbels and Speer sat with Hitler by the fireside until late in the night was dashed when news came in of a heavy air-raid on Nuremberg. Hitler fell into a towering rage about Göring and the Luftwaffe leadership. Speer and Goebbels, calming Hitler only with difficulty, postponed their plans. They were never resurrected.[65]

Goebbels and Speer had failed at the first hurdle. Face to face with Hitler, they felt unable to confront him. Hitler's fury over Göring was enough to veto even the prospect of any rational discussion about restructuring Reich government. But the problem went further. Goebbels and Speer, blaming distraction through the command of military strategy and Bormann's deviousness, thought that Hitler was unable or unprepared to sweep through the jungle of conflicting authorities and radicalize the home front as they wanted him to. In this, they were holding to the illusion that the regime was reformable, but that Hitler was unwilling to reform it. What they did not fully grasp was that the shapeless 'system' of governance that had emerged was both the inexorable product of Hitler's personalized rule and the guarantee of his power.

In a modern state, necessarily resting on bureaucracy and dependent upon system and regulated procedure, centring all spheres of power in the hands of one man – whose leadership style was utterly unbureaucratic and whose approach to rule was completely unsystematic, resting as it did on a combination of force and propaganda – could only produce administrative chaos amid a morass of competing authorities. But this same organizational incoherence was the very safeguard of Hitler's power, since every strand of authority was dependent on him. Changing the 'system' without changing its focal point was impossible. Hitler was incapable of reforming his Reich; nor, in any case, could he have any interest in doing so. He continued, as ever, to intervene wilfully and arbitrarily in a wide array of matters, often of a trivial nature, undermining as he did so any semblance of governmental order or rationality.

Goebbels and Speer did not immediately give up their efforts. Together with Ley and Funk, they met Göring for three hours on 17 March, going over much of the same ground that they had covered when they had met the Reich Marshal earlier in the month in Berchtesgaden. The upshot was no more than an agreement that Göring would propose to the Führer in the near future that he 'activate somewhat the German leadership at home' by resurrecting the Ministerial Council and adding to it Speer, Ley, Himmler, and Goebbels. The Propaganda Minister even manipulated Göring into accepting him as his deputy in the running of the intended weekly meetings.[66] Predictably, nothing came of it. During April, Göring was included by Lammers, with Hitler's approval, in two meetings of the 'Committee of Three', dealing with the application of the Führer Decree on Total War to the occupied territories. His antagonism to the Committee seems thereafter largely to have evaporated.[67] As so often, Göring's initial energy soon gave way to lethargy. In any case, his star had sunk so deep in the wake of further heavy air-raids that he must have realized how little realistic hope he had of gaining Hitler's backing for any new position of authority. A diplomatic illness – whether or not associated with his sizeable daily intake of narcotics is not known – came to his aid.[68] April ended with him prescribed bed-rest by his doctor.[69] As Speer was to comment laconically, it was only in Nuremberg, on trial for his life, that Göring came fully to life again.[70]

Goebbels was still talking as late as September of finding enough support to block Lammers's attempt (as the Propaganda Minister saw it) to arrogate authority to himself on the back of a Führer decree empowering him to review any disputes between ministers and decide whether they should be taken to Hitler.[71] But by that time, there was scant need of intrigue to stymie the 'Committee of Three'. It had already atrophied into insignificance.

Proposals to cut down on bureaucracy, simplify government adminis-tration, and save manpower were largely vitiated by Hitler himself. When faced with a decision on proposals to abolish a number of local government districts (*Landkreise*) and merge them with their neighbours, Hitler's anti-bureaucratic instincts gave way to cautious conservatism. The districts would stay as they were. The office of the *Landrat* (district prefect) was especially important during wartime, wrote Bormann – doubtless echoing Hitler – in a letter to Reich Minister of the Interior Wilhelm Frick on 15 June 1943. The wartime regulation of the economy (*Zwangsbewirtschaftung*) had greatly increased the public's need for access to the *Landrat*'s office. Any trace of popular unrest had to be avoided. And, in any case, the manpower savings would be small.[72]

Hitler saw the 'home front', as always, mainly in terms of morale and would rule out any measures that might weaken it. He similarly blocked, partly at Lammers's suggestion, attempts to simplify regional government and *Länder* administration.[73] Even plans to dissolve the Prussian Finance Ministry, where there was extensive and unnecessary duplication with the Reich Finance Ministry, came to nothing. Hitler said he could not decide on the matter without consulting Göring about it. Göring implied he preferred reduction to abolition. By June, Bormann was left isolated in pleading for the abolition of the Ministry. Lammers was able to garner support for its retention, without personnel reductions.[74]

Almost the only achievement of lasting effect by the 'Committee of Three' during its nine months or so in action was a moratorium on the creation of new civil service posts.[75] Its attempts to close down small businesses deemed unnecessary for the war effort came up with negligible results – and attained at a massive cost of alienation of those whose livelihood was threatened.[76] Reports from the SD reflected the antagonism felt as small traders faced ruin through their shops being shut and the public, denied consumer outlets and already limited leisure pursuits, were alienated through the closure of bars and restaurants.[77] One local SD report, from Bad Kissingen in Lower Franconia, summed up the mood: 'The regard for the NSDAP has been gravely damaged by the intervention of the Party in the business closures and labour deployment in the province. According to rumour, national comrades stricken by closures and by loss of relatives have pulled down and smashed pictures of the Führer in their homes.'[78]

The futility of the Committee's efforts and the hopeless irrationality of government in the Führer state were revealed in all their starkness by the deliberations, lasting six months in all at one of the most critical junctures of the war, about whether to ban horse-racing. Goebbels tried to instigate a ban following complaints (he claimed) from Berlin workers about racing taking place on Sundays while they had to work. He demanded a directive from Hitler. Bormann and Lammers persuaded the dictator that workers should not be denied one of the limited forms of entertainment still available. But after a visit by Goebbels to Führer Headquarters, Hitler changed his mind and favoured a ban. He was now belaboured by various interested parties. Lammers eventually passed on a ruling that specific named race-courses were to be kept open. The Reich Defence Commissars (all of them Gauleiter) in these areas had permission to ban any race-meetings if they thought the needs of morale demanded this. The rest of the racecourses – along with bookies' offices – were to be closed. Unsurprisingly, protests were immediately voiced by provincial Party bosses who felt their own areas were disadvantaged.

A dispute in Munich between Gauleiter Paul Giesler (brother of court-architect, Hermann) and the corrupt, roughneck city councillor Christian Weber, one of Hitler's longest-standing cronies, had to go as far as the Führer himself to find its resolution. Weber was a classical product of the Party's early days in Munich. A former pub-bouncer and beer-hall bruiser, he had been elevated in the Third Reich to a host of honorary offices in the 'capital city of the Movement', with an apartment in the *Residenz* formerly inhabited by the Kings of Bavaria. He was detested locally for the way he flaunted the wealth and power his favour with Hitler had brought him. Some scurrilously thought his advancement was to keep him from spilling unwelcome secrets about the Führer's lifestyle in the early years. But Hitler would have had other ways of handling such indirect blackmail. Weber had certainly rendered Hitler valuable service in the Munich street-fighting days. His rise to local riches and notoriety was simply a particularly colourful expression of the gross corruption that was an endemic feature of the Third Reich. But at any rate, as an 'Old Fighter' – literally – from the earliest times, and owner (among many other things, including a monopoly of the regional bus service) of the racecourse at Riem, Weber had to be placated.[79] So, however, did Giesler, Hitler's most important lieutenant in Bavaria, and a fanatical supporter of the 'total war' drive. Hitler's judgement-of-Solomon 'decision' was that racing should be banned at Riem (on the grounds that it could only be reached by car and bus, thus causing unnecessary petrol usage), but allowed in the city centre on the Theresienwiese.

Shortly afterwards he noticed a newspaper advertisement for horse-racing in Berlin and remarked to Bormann that Munich should not be disadvantaged against the Reich capital. Racing was again to be permitted in Riem. As the issue rumbled on, various authorities became involved. Lammers and Bormann exchanged letters. His opinion sought yet again, Hitler came up with the intriguing macro-economic reflection that betting absorbed surplus spending power. The Gauleiter continued their complaints. Finally, after six months of wrangling on an issue of such breathtaking triviality, Bormann and Lammers agreed, in accordance with 'an expression of will of the Führer', to permit horse-racing and bookmaking in general terms – but to leave the decision in each individual case to the respective Reich Defence Commissar.[80] Ultimately, therefore, no decision had been taken, other than to leave matters to the whim of the Party bosses.

Little could demonstrate more clearly the absurdity of the dictatorship's patterns of rule (or lack of them). Hitler's power was intact. His *imprimatur* had been sought on several occasions by all parties concerned. No one else could settle the matter. But nor, except by the ultimate retreat from a decision, could Hitler. His wavering, fluctuating interventions – often evidently following the advice of the last person to have spoken to him – dragged out the affair. But it was scarcely rational in the first place that a head of state and commander of the armed forces should be repeatedly bothered in the middle of a world war by various underlings involved in petty disputes over horse-racing. The problem was, here as in other instances: he had delegated no genuine authority to the 'Committee of Three'; they in turn had to call upon him at every point; and this was frequently necessary, as in the horse-racing case, because there was no central Reich body to reach sensibly agreed decisions and impose them as government policy. The failed experiment of the 'Committee of Three' showed conclusively that, however weak their structures, all forms of collective government were doomed by the need to protect the arbitrary 'will of the Führer'. But it was increasingly impossible for this 'will' to be exercised in ways conducive to the functioning of a modern state, let alone one operating under the crisis conditions of a major war. As a system of government, Hitler's dictatorship had no future.

I I

Matters at home were far from Hitler's primary concern in the spring and summer of 1943. He was, in fact, almost solely preoccupied with the course of the war. The strain of this had left its mark on him. Guderian, back in favour after a long absence, was struck at their first meeting, on 20 February 1943, by the change in Hitler's physical appearance since the last time he had seen him, back in mid-December 1941: 'In the intervening fourteen months he had aged greatly. His manner was less assured than it had been and his speech was hesitant; his left hand trembled.'[81]

When President Roosevelt, at the end of his meeting to discuss war strategy with Churchill and the Combined Chiefs of Staff at Casablanca in French Morocco between 14 and 24 January 1943, had – to the British Prime Minister's surprise – announced at a concluding press conference that the Allies would impose 'unconditional surrender' on their enemies, it had matched Hitler's Valhalla mentality entirely.[82] For him, the demand altered nothing. It merely added further confirmation that his uncompromising stance was right. As he told his Party leaders in early February, he felt liberated as a result from any attempts to persuade him to look for a negotiated peace settlement.[83] It had become, as he had always asserted it would, a clear matter of victory or destruction. Few, even of his closest followers, as Goebbels admitted, could still inwardly believe in the former. But compromises were ruled out. The road to destruction was opening up ever more plainly. For Hitler, closing off escape routes had distinct advantages. Fear of destruction was a strong motivator.

Some of Hitler's leading generals, most notably Manstein, had tried to persuade him immediately after Stalingrad that he should, if not give up the command of the army, at least appoint a supremo on the eastern front who had his trust. Manstein was the obvious candidate for the post of 'Supreme Commander in the East'. But Hitler was having none of it. He knew, he said, no commander whom he could trust to take such a command.[84] Probably, as Guderian suspected, Manstein was too independent and forthright in his views for Hitler. After the bitter conflicts over the previous months, he preferred the compliancy of a Keitel to the sharply couched counter-arguments of a Manstein.[85] It meant a further weakening of Germany's military potential. But Hitler's instinctive reaction to the disaster at Stalingrad was not to concede anything; he had to wrest back the initiative on the eastern front without delay.

Manstein's push to retake Kharkhov and reach the Donets by mid-March had been a much-needed success. Over 50,000 Soviet troops had perished.[86] It had suggested yet again to Hitler that Stalin's reserves must be drying up.[87] His confidence boosted, he returned in mid-March from Vinnitsa to the Wolf's Lair, as Warlimont put it, 'with the air of a victorious war-lord, clearly considering himself and *his* leadership primarily responsible for the favourable turn of events in the East which had temporarily ended the withdrawal after Stalingrad.'[88] When Goebbels saw him on 19 March, 'looking extraordinarily fresh and healthy', he was 'very happy that he has succeeded in again completely closing the front'.[89] Immediately, he wanted to go on the offensive. It was important to strike while the Red Army was still smarting from the reversal at Kharkhov. It was also necessary to send a signal to the German population, deeply embittered by Stalingrad, and to the Reich's allies, that any doubts in final victory were wholly misplaced.

At this point, the split in military planning between the army's General Staff, directly responsible for the eastern front, and the operations branch of Wehrmacht High Command (in charge of all other theatres) surfaced once more. The planners in the High Command of the Wehrmacht favoured a defensive ploy on all fronts to allow the gradual build-up and mobilization of resources throughout Europe for a later grand offensive. The Army High Command thought differently. It wanted a limited but early offensive. The danger of the defensive strategy, army leaders argued, was the need to commit extensive German forces to the eastern front as long as the Soviet Union posed a threat, thus weakening the defences, notably in the Mediterranean and in western Europe. Stabilizing the eastern front was, therefore, the first priority. A successful offensive was needed to achieve this. Chief of the Army General Staff Kurt Zeitzler had devised an operation involving the envelopment and destruction of a large number of Soviet divisions on a big salient west of Kursk, an important rail junction some 500 miles south of Moscow. Five Soviet armies were located within the westward bulge in the front, around 120 miles wide and 75 miles deep, left from the winter campaign of 1942–3. If victorious, the operation would gravely weaken the Soviet offensive potential.[90]

There was no question which strategy would appeal to Hitler. He swiftly supported the army's plan for a decisive strike on a greatly shortened front – about 150 kilometres compared with 2,000 kilometres in the 'Barbarossa' invasion of 1941. The limited scope of the operation reflected the reduction in German ambitions in the east since June 1941. Even so, a tactical victory through destruction of the Soviet bulge centred on Kursk would have been of great importance. It would, in all likelihood, have eliminated the prospect of any further Soviet offensive in 1943, thereby freeing German troops for redeployment in the increasingly threatening Mediterranean theatre. The order for what was to become 'Operation Citadel', issued on 13 March, foresaw a pincer attack by part of Manstein's Army Group from the south and Kluge's from the north, enveloping the Soviet troops in the bulge.[91] In his confirmation order of 15 April, Hitler declared: 'This attack is of decisive importance. It must be a quick and conclusive success. It must give us the initiative for this spring and summer . . . Every officer, every soldier must be convinced of the decisive importance of this attack. The victory of Kursk must shine like a beacon to the world.'[92] It was to do so. But hardly as Hitler had imagined.

'Citadel' was scheduled to begin in mid-May. But, as in the previous two years, significant delays set in which were damaging to the operation's success. These were not directly of Hitler's making. But they did again reveal the serious problems in the military command-structure and process of decision-making. They arose from disputes about timing among the leading generals involved. On 4 May, Hitler met them in Munich to discuss 'Citadel'.[93] Manstein and Kluge wanted to press ahead as soon as possible. This was the only chance of imposing serious losses on the enemy. Otherwise, they argued, it was better to call off the operation altogether. They were seriously worried about losing the advantage of surprise and about the build-up of Soviet forces should there be any postponement. The heavy defeat at Stalingrad and weakness of the southern flank deterred other generals from wishing to undertake a new large-scale offensive so quickly.[94] Colonel-General Walter Model – known as an especially tough and capable commander, which had helped make him one of Hitler's favourites, and detailed to lead the 9th Army's assault from the north – recommended a delay until reinforcements were available.[95] He picked up on the belief of Zeitzler, also high in favour with Hitler, that the heavy Tiger tank, just rolling off the production lines, and the new, lighter, Panther tank would provide Germany with the decisive breakthrough necessary to regaining the initiative.[96] Hitler had great hopes of both tanks. He gave Model his backing.

Manstein equivocated. Kluge now came out in favour of Zeitzler's plan. Guderian, supported by Speer, opposed it, pointing out that the known deficiencies of the Panther could not be ironed out before the offensive, and that, in any case, reserves should be spared for the priority of preparing to repel the inevitable invasion the following year in the west. When, a few days later, Guderian tried to persuade Hitler that an offensive that year in the east was unnecessary, he had the impression that the Führer was non-committal. Perhaps Hitler was indeed getting cold feet about the operation by this time. Or, perhaps, his show of half-heartedness was merely to avoid confrontation with Guderian.[97] As the weeks rolled by, with further delays, the deteriorating situation in North Africa gave Hitler cause for worry. Would he need to rush troops to the southern theatre who were tied up in 'Citadel'?[98]

At any rate, on 4 May, he postponed 'Citadel' until mid-June. It was then further postponed, eventually getting underway only in early July. Even by that date, fewer Tiger and Panther tanks were available than had been envisaged. And the Soviets, tipped off by British intelligence and by a source within the Wehrmacht High Command, had built up their defences and were ready and waiting.[99]

Meanwhile, the situation in North Africa was giving grounds for the gravest concern. Some of Hitler's closest military advisers, Jodl among them, had been quietly resigned to the complete loss of North Africa as early as December 1942.[100] Hitler himself had hinted at one point that he was contemplating the evacuation of German troops.[101] But no action had followed. He was much influenced by the views of the Commander-in-Chief South, Field-Marshal Kesselring, one of nature's optimists and, like most in high places in the Third Reich, compelled in any case to exude optimism whatever his true sentiments and however bleak the situation was in reality.[102] In dealings with Hitler – as with other top Nazi leaders whose mentality was attuned to his – it seldom paid to be a realist. Too easily, realism could be seen as defeatism. Hitler needed optimists to pander to him – yet another form of 'working towards the Führer'. In the military arena, this reinforced the chances of serious strategic blunders.

In March, buoyed by Manstein's success at Kharkhov, Hitler had declared that the holding of Tunis would be decisive for the outcome of the war. It was, therefore, a top priority.[103] With the refusal to contemplate any withdrawal, the next military disaster beckoned. When Below flew south at the end of the month to view the North African front and report back to Hitler, even Kesselring was unable to hide the fact that Tunis could not be held. Colonel-General Hans-Jürgen von Arnim, who had taken over the North African command from the exhausted and dispirited Rommel, was of the same opinion. Kesselring's staff were even more pessimistic: they saw no chance of successfully fending off an Allied crossing from Tunis to Sicily once – which they regarded as a certainty – North Africa had fallen. When Below reported back, Hitler said little. It seemed to his Luftwaffe adjutant that he had already written off North Africa and was inwardly preparing himself for the eventual defection of his Italian partners to the enemy.[104]

In early April, Hitler had spent the best part of four days at the restored baroque palace of Klessheim, near Salzburg, shoring up Mussolini's battered morale – half urging, half browbeating the Duce to keep up the fight, knowing how weakened he would be through the massive prestige blow soon to descend in North Africa. Worn down by the strain of war and depression, Mussolini, stepping down from his train with assistance, looked a 'broken old man' to Hitler.[105] The Duce also made a subdued impression on interpreter Dr Paul Schmidt as he pleaded forlornly for a compromise peace in the east in order to bolster defences in the west, ruling out the possibility of defeating the USSR.[106] Dismissing such a notion out of hand, Hitler reminded Mussolini of the threat that the fall of Tunis would pose for Fascism in Italy. He left him with the impression 'that there can be no other salvation for him than to achieve victory with us or to die'.[107] He exhorted him to do the utmost to use the Italian navy to provide supplies for the forces there. The remainder of the visit consisted largely of monologues by Hitler – including long digressions about Prussian history – aimed at stiffening Mussolini's resistance.[108] Hitler was subsequently satisfied that this had been achieved.[109]

The talks with Mussolini amounted to one of a series of meetings with his allies that Hitler conducted during April, while staying at the Berghof. King Boris of Bulgaria, Marshal Antonescu of Romania, Admiral Horthy of Hungary, Prime Minister Vidkun Quisling of Norway, President Tiso of Slovakia, 'Poglavnik' (Leader) Ante Pavelic of Croatia, and Prime Minister

Pierre Laval from Vichy France all visited the Berghof or Klessheim by the end of the month.[110] In each case, the purpose was to stiffen resolve – partly by cajoling, partly by scarcely veiled threats – and to keep faint-hearts or waverers tied to the Axis cause.

Hitler let Antonescu know that he was aware of tentative approaches made by Romanian ministers to the Allies. He posed, as usual, a stark choice of outright victory or 'complete destruction' in a fight to the end for 'living space' in the east. Part of Hitler's implicit argument, increasingly, in attempting to prevent support from seeping away was to play on complicity in the persecution of the Jews. His own paranoia about the responsibility of the Jews for the war and all its evils easily led into the suggestive threat that boats had been burned, there was no way out, and retribution in the event of a lost war would be terrible. The hint of this was implicit in his disapproval of Antonescu's treatment of the Jews as too mild, declaring that the more radical the measures the better it was when tackling the Jews.[111]

In his meetings with Horthy at Klessheim on 16–17 April, Hitler was more brusque. Horthy was berated for feelers to the enemy secretly put out by prominent Hungarian sources but tapped by German intelligence. He was told that 'Germany and its allies were in the same boat on a stormy sea. It was obvious that in this situation anyone wanting to get off would drown immediately.'[112] As he had done with Antonescu, though in far harsher terms, Hitler criticized what he saw as an over-mild policy towards the Jews. Horthy had mentioned that, despite tough measures, criminality and the black market were still flourishing in Hungary. Hitler replied that the Jews were to blame. Horthy asked what he was expected to do with the Jews. He had taken away their economic livelihood; he could scarcely have them all killed. Ribbentrop intervened at this point to say that the Jews must be 'annihilated (*vernichtet*)' or locked up in concentration camps. There was no other way. Hitler regaled Horthy with statistics aimed at showing the strength of former Jewish influence in Germany. He compared the 'German' city of Nuremberg with the neighbouring 'Jewish' town of Fürth.[113] Wherever Jews had been left to themselves, he said, they had produced only misery and dereliction. They were pure parasites. He put forward Poland as a model. There, things had been 'thoroughly cleaned up'. If Jews did not want to work 'then they would be shot. If they could not work, then they would have to rot (*verkommen*).' As so often, he deployed a favourite bacterial simile. 'They would have to be treated like tuberculosis bacilli from which a healthy body could become infected. This would not be cruel if it were considered that even innocent creatures, like hares and deer, had to be killed. Why should the beasts that want to bring us Bolshevism be spared?'[114]

Hitler's emphasis on the Jews as germ-bacilli, and as responsible for the war and the spread of Bolshevism, was of course nothing new. And his deep-seated belief in the demonic power still purportedly in the hands of the Jews as they were being decimated needs no underlining. But this was the first time that he had used the 'Jewish Question' in diplomatic discussions to put heads of state under pressure to introduce more draconian anti-Jewish measures. What prompted this?

He would have been particularly alerted to the 'Jewish Question' in April 1943. The previous month, he had finally agreed to have what was left of Berlin's Jewish community deported.[115] In April, he was sent the breakdown, already mentioned, prepared by the SS's statistician Richard Korherr of almost a million and a half Jews 'evacuated' and 'channelled through (durchgeschleust)' Polish camps.[116] From the middle of the month, he was increasingly frustrated by accounts of the battle raging in the Warsaw ghetto, where the Waffen-SS, sent in to raze it to the ground, were encountering desperate and brave resistance from the inhabitants.[117] Not least, only days before his meeting with Horthy, mass graves containing the remains of thousands of Polish officers, murdered in 1940 by the Soviet Security Police, the NKVD, had been discovered in the Katyn Forest, near Smolensk. Hitler immediately gave Goebbels permission to make maximum propaganda capital out of the issue.[118] He also instructed Goebbels to put the 'Jewish Question' at the forefront of propaganda. Goebbels seized upon the Katyn case as an excellent opportunity to do just this.[119]

Hitler's directive to Goebbels to amplify the propaganda treatment of the persecution of the Jews, and his explicit usage of the 'Jewish Question' in his meetings with foreign dignitaries, plainly indicate instrumental motives. He believed, as he always had done, unquestioningly in the propaganda value of antisemitism. He told his Gauleiter in early May that antisemitism, as propagated by the Party in earlier years, had once more to become the core message. He held out hopes of its spread in Britain. Antisemitic propaganda had, he said, to begin from the premiss that the Jews were the leaders of Bolshevism and prominent in western plutocracy. The Jews had to get out of Europe. This had constantly to be repeated in the political conflict built into the war.[120] In his meetings with Antonescu and Horthy, Hitler was speaking, as always, for effect. As we have noted, he hoped to bind his wavering Axis partners closer to the Reich through complicity in the persecution of the Jews. In the autumn, in speeches held in Posen, Himmler would use the 'Jewish Question' in similar, but even more explicit, fashion to hold the Nazi leadership ever more tightly together through their complicity in the mass murder of the Jews.

Though satisfied with the outcome of his talks with Antonescu, Hitler felt he had failed to make an impact on Horthy. Goebbels suspected that Hitler's harsh tone had not been helpful. The Hungarians, he remarked, recognized Germany's weak position and knew wars were not won simply with words.[121] Hitler told the Gauleiter that he had not succeeded in persuading Horthy of the need for tougher measures against the Jews. Horthy had put forward what Hitler described – only from his perspective could they be seen as such – as 'humanitarian counter-arguments'. Hitler naturally dismissed them. As Goebbels summarized it, Hitler said: 'Towards Jewry there can be no talk of humanity. Jewry must be cast down to the ground.'[122]

Earlier in the spring, Ribbentrop, picking up on fears expressed by Axis partners about their future under German domination, had put to Hitler loose notions of a future European federation.[123] How little ice this cut with the Dictator can be seen from his reactions to his April meetings with heads of state and government – particularly the unsatisfactory discussion with Horthy. He drew the consequence, he told the Gauleiter in early May, that the 'small-state rubbish (*Kleinstaatengerümpel*)' should be 'liquidated as soon as possible'. Europe must have a new form – but this could only be under German leadership. 'We live today,' he went on, 'in a world of destroying and being destroyed.' He expressed his certainty 'that the Reich will one day be master of the whole of Europe', paving the way for world domination. He hinted at the alternative. 'The Führer paints a shocking picture for the Reichs- and Gauleiter of the possibilities facing the Reich in the event of a German defeat. Such a defeat must therefore never find a place in our thoughts. We must regard it from the outset as impossible and determine to fight it to the last breath.'[124]

Speaking to Goebbels on 6 May in Berlin, where he had come to attend the state funeral of SA-Chief Viktor Lutze (who had been killed in a car accident), Hitler accepted that the situation in Tunis was 'fairly hopeless'. The inability to get supplies to the troops meant there was no way out. Goebbels summarized the way Hitler was thinking: 'When you think that 150,000 of our best young people are still in Tunis, you rapidly get an idea of the catastrophe threatening us there. It'll be on the scale of Stalingrad, and certainly also produce the harshest criticism among the German people.'[125] But when he spoke the next day to the Reichs- and Gauleiter,

Hitler never mentioned Tunis, making no reference at all to the latest news that Allied troops had penetrated as far as the outskirts of the city and that the harbour was already in British hands.[126]

Axis troops were, in fact, by then giving themselves up in droves. Within a week, on 13 May, almost a quarter of a million of them – the largest number taken so far by the Allies, around half of them German, the remainder Italian – surrendered. Only about 800 managed to escape.[127] North Africa was lost. The catastrophe left the Italian Axis partner reeling. For Mussolini, the writing was on the wall. But for Hitler, too, the defeat was nothing short of calamitous. One short step across the Straits of Sicily by the Allies would mean that the fortress of Europe was breached through its southern underbelly.

In the Atlantic, meanwhile, the battle was in reality lost, even if it took some months for this to become fully apparent. The resignation on 30 January 1943 as Commander-in-Chief of the Navy of Grand-Admiral Raeder, exponent of what Hitler had come to recognize as an outmoded naval strategy based upon a big surface battle fleet, and his replacement by Karl Dönitz, protagonist of the U-boat, had signalled an important shift in priorities.[128] Hitler told his Gauleiter on 7 May that the U-boat was the weapon to cut through the arteries of the enemy. This weapon was, in his view, at the very beginning of its development. He expected great things of it.[129] At the end of the month, he told Dönitz: 'There can be no question of easing up on the U-boat war. The Atlantic is my western approach (*Vorfeld*), and if I have to wage a defensive there, it's better than only being able to defend on the coast of Europe.' He immediately agreed to Dönitz's request to increase the construction rate of U-boats from thirty to forty a month.[130] But, in fact, that very month forty-one U-boats carrying 1,336 men had been lost in the Atlantic – the highest losses in any single month during the war – and the number of vessels in operation at any one time had already passed its peak. In the light of the losses, Dönitz ordered the U-boats away from the Atlantic convoy routes and moved them to south-west of the Azores.[131] The deciphering of German codes by British intelligence, using the 'Ultra' decoder, was allowing U-boat signals to be read. It was possible to know with some precision where the U-boats were operating. The use of long-range Liberators, equipped with radar, and able to cover 'the Atlantic Gap' – the 600-mile stretch of the ocean from Greenland to the Azores, previously out of range of aircraft flying from both British and American shores – was a second strand of the mounting Allied success against the U-boat menace.[132] The crucial supplies between North America and Britain, gravely imperilled over the previous two years, could flow with increasing security. Nothing could hinder the Reich's increasing disadvantage against the material might of the western Allies.

Hitler's greatest worry, once Tunis had fallen, was the condition of his longest-standing ally. Immediately after the fall of Tunis, the Wehrmacht High Command's Operations Staff had outlined – probably at Hitler's request – a scenario 'should Italy withdraw from the war'. It posited the likelihood of the Allies forcing their way on to the European continent through the unstable and weakly defended Balkans. Hitler, in part it seems misled by a false lead given by British intelligence, which had deliberately planted disinformation on a corpse left floating off the Spanish coast,[133] disagreed with his own staff and with Mussolini in thinking an Allied landing would be attempted not in Sicily, but in Sardinia. Contingency plans were made to move forces from both the western and eastern fronts to the Mediterranean, and to put Rommel – now largely restored to health – in command in Italy should an Italian collapse take place.[134]

By the time he heard a report on the situation in Italy in mid-May from Konstantin Alexander Freiherr von Neurath, son of the former Foreign Minister, and one-time Foreign Office liaison to Rommel's Afrika Korps, Hitler was deeply gloomy. He thought the monarchists and aristocracy had sabotaged the war-effort in Italy from the beginning. He blamed them for preventing an Italian declaration of solidarity with Germany in 1939. If such a declaration had been forthcoming, he asserted, the British would not have hastened to sign the Guarantee for Poland, the French would not have gone along in their wake, and the war would not have broken out.[135] He thought there was no longer the will in Italy to transport troops to Sicily to defend against an Allied landing. Whatever the Duce's personal strength of will – and Hitler continued to detach him from his savage criticism of the Italians – it was being sabotaged.[136]

There was a big question mark, he thought, over Mussolini's health – he had suffered from a stomach ulcer since September of the previous year – and his age, now approaching sixty, told against him. Hitler was sure that the reactionary forces associated with the King, Victor Emmanuel III – whose nominal powers as head of state had nevertheless still left him as the focus of a potential alternative source of loyalty – would triumph over the revolutionary forces of Fascism. A collapse had to be reckoned with.[137] Plans must be made to defend the Mediterranean without Italy.[138] How this was to be done with an offensive imminent in the east and no troops to spare, he did not say.

Hitler had intended around this time to move back to Vinnitsa. But the postponement of 'Citadel', the precarious situation in the Mediterranean, and problems with his own health made him decide suddenly to return from a short stay at the Wolf's Lair to the Obersalzberg.[139] He remained there until the end of June. During his weeks in the Bavarian Alps, the Ruhr district, Germany's industrial heartland, continued to suffer devastation from the skies. In May there had been spectacular attacks on the big dams that supplied the area's water. Had they been sustained, the damage done would have been incalculable. As it was, the dams could be repaired. Since the 'dam-buster' raids, the major cities of Duisburg, Düsseldorf, Bochum, Dortmund, and Wuppertal-Barmen had been laid waste in intensive night bombardment. The inadequacy of the air-defences was all too apparent. Hitler continued to vent his bile on Göring and the Luftwaffe.[140] But his own powerlessness to do anything about it was exposed. Goebbels at least showed his face, touring the bombed-out cities, speaking at a memorial service in his home town of Elberfeld, and at a big rally in Dortmund.[141] Hitler stayed in his alpine idyll. The Propaganda Minister thought a visit by the Führer pyschologically important for the population of the Ruhr. Though Goebbels had been impressed by the positive response he had encountered during his staged tour, more realistic impressions of morale provided in SD reports painted a different picture. Anger at the regime's failure to protect them was widespread. The 'Heil Hitler' greeting had almost disappeared. Hostile remarks about the regime, and about Hitler personally, were commonplace.[142]

Hitler promised Goebbels towards the end of June that he would pay an extended visit to the devastated area. It was to take place 'the next week, or the week after that'. Hitler knew only too well that this was out of the question. He had by then scheduled the beginning of 'Citadel' for the first week in July. And he expected the Allied landing off the Italian coast at any time. The human suffering of the Ruhr population had, ultimately, little meaning for him. 'As regrettable as the personal losses are,' he told Goebbels, 'they have unfortunately to be taken on board in the interest of a superior war-effort (*Kriegführung*).'[143]

While on the Obersalzberg, Hitler was chiefly preoccupied with the prospect of an imminent invasion by the Allies in the south, and the approaching 'Citadel' offensive in the east.

He still thought that the Allied landing would come in Sardinia. Sicily was in his view secure enough, and could be held. (Since most of the island's defenders were Italian, Hitler must have been either less confident than he seemed, or have amended his normally scathing assessment of the Italian armed forces.) He was determined not to retreat from Italy. There would be no withdrawal as far as the Po Valley, even were the Italians to pull out of the war. It was the first rule of the German conduct of war to fight away from the homeland. He thought the Italians more likely to give in bit by bit in deals with the enemy than to capitulate outright. His confidence in Mussolini had finally evaporated. It would be different, he thought, were the Duce still young and fit. But he was old and worn out. The royal family could not be trusted an inch. And – he added a characteristic last reflection – the Jews had not been done away with (*beseitigt*) in Italy, whereas in Germany (as Goebbels summarized) 'we can be very glad that we have followed a radical policy. There are no Jews behind us who could inherit from us.'[144]

As the war had turned remorselessly against Germany, the beleaguered Führer had reverted ever more to his obsession with Jewish responsibility for the conflagration. In his Manichean world-view, the fight to the finish between the forces of good and evil – the Aryan race and the Jews – was reaching its climax. There could be no relenting in the struggle to wipe out Jewry.

Little over a month earlier, Hitler had talked at length, prompted by Goebbels, about the 'Jewish Question'. The Propaganda Minister thought it one of the most interesting discussions he had ever had with the Führer.[145] Goebbels had been re-reading *The Protocols of the Elders of Zion* – the crude Russian forgery purporting to outline a Jewish conspiracy to rule the world – with an eye on its use in current propaganda. He raised the matter over lunch. Hitler thought antisemitic propaganda would play an important part in the war effort, particularly in its impact on the British. He was certain of the 'absolute authenticity' of the *Protocols*. The Jews, he thought, were not working to a fixed programme; they were following, as always, their 'racial instinct'.[146] The Jews were the same all over the world, Goebbels noted him as saying, whether in the ghettos of the east 'or in the bank palaces of the City [of London] or Wall Street', and would instinctively follow the same aims and use the same methods without the need to work them out together. The question could well be posed, he went on (according to Goebbels's summary of his comments), as to why there were Jews at all. It was the same question – again the familiar insect analogy – as why there were Colorado beetles (*Kartoffelkäfer*). His most basic belief – life as struggle – provided, as always, his answer. 'Nature is ruled by the law of struggle. There will always be parasitic forms of existence to accelerate the struggle and intensify the process of selection between the strong and the weak . . . In nature, life always works immediately against parasites; in the existence of peoples that is not exclusively the case. From that results the Jewish danger. So there is nothing else open to modern peoples than to exterminate the Jews (*Es bleibt also den modernen Völkern nichts anderes übrig, als die Juden auszurotten*).'[147]

The Jews would use all means to defend themselves against this 'gradual process of annihilation (*allmählichen Vernichtungsprozeß*)'. One of its methods was war.[148] It was the same warped vision embodied in Hitler's 'prophecy': Jews unleashing war, but bringing about their own destruction in the process. World Jewry, in Hitler's view, was on the verge of a historic downfall (*geschichtlichen Sturz*). This would take time. He was presumably alluding to Jews out of German reach, especially in the USA, when he commented that some decades would be needed 'to cast them out of their power. That is our historic mission, which cannot be held up, but only accelerated, by the war. World Jewry thinks it is on the verge of a world victory. This world victory will not come. Instead there will be a world downfall. The peoples who have earliest recognized and fought the Jew will instead accede to world domination.'[149]

Four days after this conversation, on 16 May, SS-Brigadeführer Jürgen Stroop telexed the news: 'The Jewish quarter of Warsaw is no more! The grand operation terminated at 20.15 hours when the Warsaw synagogue was blown up . . . The total number of Jews apprehended and destroyed, according to record, is 56,065 . . .'[150] A force of around 3,000 men, the vast majority from the SS, had used a tank, armoured vehicles, heavy machine-guns, and artillery to blow up and set fire to buildings which the Jews were fiercely defending and to combat the courageous resistance put up by the ghetto's inhabitants, armed with little more than pistols, grenades, and Molotov cocktails. The month-long ghetto uprising had exacerbated Hitler's mounting frustration with Hans Frank's inability to maintain order in the General Government amid increasing unrest caused by SS attempts to uproot and deport 108,000 Poles from the Zamosc district in the Lublin area in order to resettle it with Germans.[151] His long-standing readiness to link Jews with subversive or partisan actions made Hitler all the keener to hasten their destruction. After Himmler had discussed the matter with him on 19 June, he noted that 'the Führer declared, after my report (*Vortrag*), that the evacuation of the Jews, despite the unrest that would thereby still arise in the next 3 to 4 months, was to be radically carried out and had to be seen through'.[152]

Such discussions were always private. Hitler still did not speak of the fate of the Jews, except in the most generalized fashion, even among his inner circle. It was a topic which all in his company knew to avoid. To think of criticizing the treatment of the Jews was, of course, anathema. The only time the issue was raised occurred unexpectedly during the two-day visit to the Berghof in late June of Baldur von Schirach, Gauleiter of Vienna, and his wife, Henriette. The daughter of his photographer, Heinrich Hoffmann, Henriette had known Hitler since she was a child. She thought she could speak openly to him. Her husband had, however, fallen from favour somewhat, partly following Hitler's disapproval of the modern paintings on show in an art exhibition which Schirach had staged in Vienna earlier in the year.[153] Henriette told Baldur on the way to Berchtesgaden that she wanted to let Hitler know what she had witnessed recently in Amsterdam, where she had seen a group of Jewish women brutally herded together and deported. An SS man had offered her valuables taken from the Jews at a knock-down price. Her husband told her not to mention it. Hitler's reactions were unpredictable. And – a typical response at the time – in any case she could not change anything.[154]

Already during the first day of their visit, 23 June, Schirach had managed to prompt an angry riposte from Hitler with a suggestion that a different policy in the Ukraine might have paid dividends.[155] Next afternoon, Hitler was in an irritable mood during the statutory afternoon visit to the Tea House. The atmosphere was icy.[156] It remained tense in the evening, when they gathered around the fire in the hall of the Berghof. Henriette was sitting next to Hitler, nervously rubbing her hands, speaking quietly. All at once, Hitler jumped up, marched up and down the room, and fumed: 'That's all I need, you coming to me with this sentimental twaddle. What concern are these Jewish women to you?' The other guests did not know where to look. There was a protracted, embarrassed silence. The logs could be heard crackling in the fireplace.

When Goebbels arrived, he turned the scene to his advantage by playing on Hitler's aversion to Vienna. Hitler rounded on the hapless Schirach, praising the achievements of Berlin – Goebbels's domain, of course – and castigating his Gauleiter's work in Vienna. Beside himself with anger, Hitler said it was a mistake ever to have sent Schirach to Vienna at all, or to have taken the Viennese into the Reich. Schirach offered to resign. 'That's not for you to decide. You are staying where you are,' was Hitler's response. By then it was four in the morning. Bormann let it be known to the Schirachs that it would be best if they left. They did so without saying their goodbyes, and in high disgrace.[157]

The week before the Schirach incident, Hitler had finally decided to press ahead with the 'Citadel' offensive. His misgivings can only have been increased by Guderian's reports that the 'Panther' tank still had major weaknesses and was not ready for front-line action.[158] And in the middle of the month, he was presented with the OKW's recommendation that 'Citadel' should be cancelled. It was now running so late that there was an increasing chance that it would clash with the expected Allied offensive in the Mediterranean. Jodl, just back from leave, agreed that it was dangerous and foolhardy to commit troops to the east in the interests of, at best, a limited success when the chief danger at that time lay elsewhere. Again, the split between the OKW and army leadership came into play. Zeitzler, the army's Chief of the General Staff, objected to what he regarded as interference. Guderian suspected that Zeitzler's influence was decisive in persuading Hitler to go ahead.[159] At any rate, Hitler rejected the advice of the Wehrmacht's Operations Staff. Citadel's opening was scheduled for 3 July, then postponed one last time for two more days.[160]

Despite Guderian's warnings, Hitler confidently told Goebbels in late June that the Wehrmacht had not been so strong in the east since 1941, and that if they were to wait 'for a few more weeks yet' they would have the new 'Panthers' and a good number of the 'Tiger', 'the best tank in the world at present'. He had given up his plans for the Caucasus and Middle East. There could be no dreams of pushing ahead to the Urals. The unreliability of Germany's allies, especially the Italians, had forced this. If they had held out, the Caucasus would have been occupied and the loss of North Africa would then probably have been avoided. But Hitler thought the Soviet Union would one day collapse through starvation. The east remained for him the 'decisive front'.[161]

At the end of June, Hitler returned to the Wolf's Lair for the beginning of 'Citadel'. On 1 July, he addressed his commanders. He explained the delay partly by the need to await the panzer reinforcements which, he claimed, now offered for the first time superiority over the Soviets, and partly (if unconvincingly) by the danger of a successful Allied landing in the Mediterranean had the offensive come earlier. The decision to go ahead was determined, he stated, by the need to forestall a Soviet offensive later in the year. A military success would also have a salutary effect on Axis partners, and on morale at home.[162] Four days later, the last German offensive in the east was finally launched. It was the beginning of a disastrous month.

III

Bombardment from Soviet heavy artillery just before the offensive began gave a clear indication that the Red Army had been alerted to the timing of 'Citadel.'[163] At least 2,700 Soviet tanks had been brought in to defend Kursk. They faced a similar number of German tanks. The mightiest tank battle in history raged for over a week.[164] At first both Model and Manstein made good inroads, if with heavy losses. The Luftwaffe also had initial successes. But Guderian proved correct in his warnings of the deficiencies of the 'Panther'. Most broke down. Few remained in action after a week. Manstein's drive was hindered rather than helped by the tank in which such high hopes had been placed. The ninety Porsche 'Tiger' tanks deployed by Model also revealed major battlefield weaknesses. They had no machine-guns, so were ill-equipped for close-range fighting. They were unable, therefore, to neutralize the enemy.[165] In the middle of the month, the Soviets launched their own offensive against the German bulge around Orel to the north of the 'Citadel' battlefields, effectively to Model's rear. Though Manstein was still advancing, the northern part of the pincer was now endangered.

On 13 July, Hitler summoned Manstein and Kluge, the two Army Group Commanders, to assess the situation. Manstein was for continuing. Kluge stated that Model's army could not carry on. Reluctantly, Hitler brought 'Citadel' to a premature end.[166] The Soviet losses were greater. But 'Citadel' had signally failed in its objectives. Guderian summed up: 'By the failure of "Citadel" we had suffered a decisive defeat. The armoured formations, reformed and re-equipped with so much effort, had lost heavily both in men and in equipment and would now be unemployable for a long time to come.'[167] Warlimont's view was similar: 'Operation Citadel was more than a battle lost; it handed the Russians the initiative and we never recovered it again right up to the end of the war.'[168]

Equally dire events were unfolding in the Mediterranean. Overnight from 9–10 July, reports came in of an armada of ships carrying large Allied assault forces from North Africa to Sicily. A landing had been expected. Hitler, as we noted, had thought Sardinia the most likely destination. The precise timing now caught him unawares. The German troops in Sicily – only two divisions – were too few in number to hold the entire coast. Defence relied heavily upon Italian forces. Allied air superiority was soon all too evident. And alarming news came in of Italian soldiers casting away their weapons and fleeing. Though heavy fighting continued throughout

July, within two days it was plain that the Allied landing had been success-ful.[169] Kesselring reported on 13 July that Sicily 'could not be held with German forces alone'. Two days later, Jodl went further and declared that 'as far as can be foreseen Sicily cannot be held'.[170] A meeting with Mussolini was urgent. On 18 July Hitler left his East Prussian headquarters for the Berghof. Early the following day he flew to see Mussolini in Feltre, near Belluno, in northern Italy.[171] It was to prove the last time he set foot on Italian soil.

After landing at Treviso, Hitler and Mussolini travelled in the Duce's train to a station near Feltre, and then still had an hour's drive in open-top cars in the sweltering heat until they reached the villa chosen for the meeting, which began at noon. No sooner had Hitler begun to speak than news came in of a heavy air-raid on Rome, the first the city had suffered, causing panic among the population and encouraging the recognition that the Fascist regime was on the verge of collapse. Hitler spoke non-stop for two hours. Mussolini, tired and unwell, could not follow all that he was saying. The Duce's entourage understood little or nothing. In any case, the speech was devoid of substantive proposals. It amounted to no more than a battery of propaganda, aimed at bolstering the Duce's faltering morale and preventing Italy agreeing a separate peace. It was embarrassingly thin to some of those present. Hitler avoided putting the concrete proposals wanted by his military staff for a unified command structure of the Axis forces in Sicily. Mussolini disgusted his own military advisers by his feebleness. He commented sub-sequently that he had felt his own willpower ebbing away as Hitler spoke. After the speech Hitler spoke privately over lunch with Mussolini, telling him that Germany had improved U-boats in preparation along with secret weapons capable of razing London to the ground within a week. Then it was time for the tedious journey back to Treviso aerodrome. Hitler's generals thought the visit had been a wasted effort. Hitler himself – con-vinced still of the power of his own rhetoric – probably thought he had once more succeeded in stirring Mussolini's fighting spirits.[172] He was soon disabused. On the very evening after the Feltre talks, he was shown an intelligence report sent on by Himmler that a *coup d'état* was being planned to replace Mussolini by Marshal Pietro Badoglio.[173]

During the course of Saturday, 24 July, reports started to come in that the Fascist Grand Council had been summoned for the first time since early in the war. It looked as if the Fascist old guard were going to press Mussolini to lay down some of his accumulated offices of state in order to devote more energy to the war effort.[174] Probably, this is what Mussolini himself thought.

He may also have been looking for a pretext to break with Germany. Mussolini's ill-health perhaps combined with an over-confidence that he would ultimately have little difficulty in manipulating the Grand Council. Whatever the reasons, the way he responded to his increasingly strident critics at the meeting was strangely apathetic, dulled, and supine. The Council began its deliberations at 5p.m. that evening. These lasted in all for ten hours, culminating in an astonishing vote of nineteen to seven to request the King to seek a policy more capable of saving Italy from destruction.[175] Even then the Duce did not fully see the danger. He went to see the King – about whom he had far fewer doubts than did Hitler – later that morning, unaware of what was to befall him. During Mussolini's audience, the King abruptly interrupted him, announcing that, since the war appeared lost and army morale was collapsing, Marshal Badoglio would take over his offices as prime minister. As a stunned Duce left the royal chambers the police, who for weeks had had plans for his arrest, put them into effect. Mussolini was bundled into a waiting ambulance and, accompanied by several members of the *carabinieri*, driven off at speed to house arrest, temporarily on the Mediterranean island of Ponza. He was told the island had entertained some famous prisoners in the past – among them Nero's mother, a sixth-century Pope, and in later times a Grand Master of the Freemasons.[176]

While Hitler was holding his regular military briefing at midday on 25 July, what was filtering through from Rome still amounted to little more than rumours. Walther Hewel, Ribbentrop's liaison at FHQ, passed on the news that Roberto Farinacci, the radical Fascist boss of Cremona and former Party Secretary, had been behind the summoning of the Grand Council. Hitler remarked that Farinacci was lucky he had done it in Italy, not in Germany. He would have had him immediately picked up by Himmler. 'What'll come out of it, anyway?' he asked. 'Twaddle' was his own answer.[177] The meeting – and especially its outcome – can only have reinforced his satisfaction at never allowing a Nazi Party Senate to come into existence.

By the time of the evening military briefing in the Führer Headquarters, the sensational news from Italy had broken, though there was still not complete clarity. Almost the entire session was taken up with the implications. Since Italy had not pulled out of the war, plans to occupy the country in such an event – code-named 'Alarich' – could not be put into operation. But in a highly agitated mood, Hitler demanded immediate action to occupy Rome and depose the new regime. He denounced what had taken place as 'naked treachery', describing Badoglio as 'our grimmest enemy'.[178] He still had belief in Mussolini – so long as he was propped up by German arms.

Presuming the Duce still at liberty, he wanted him brought straight away to Germany. He was confident that in that event the situation could still be remedied. He fumed that he would send troops to Rome the next day to arrest the 'rabble' – the entire government, the King, the Crown Prince, Badoglio, the 'whole bunch'. In two or three days there would then be another coup.[179] He had Göring – 'ice-cold in the most serious crises', as he had repeatedly stated at midday, the Reich Marshal's failings as head of the Luftwaffe temporarily forgotten – telephoned and told him to come as quickly as he could to the Wolf's Lair.[180] Rommel was located in Salonika and summoned to present himself without delay. Hitler intended to put him in overall command in Italy.[181] He wanted Himmler contacted.[182] Goebbels, too, was telephoned and told to leave straight away for East Prussia. The situation, Goebbels acknowledged, was 'extraordinarily critical.'[183] Ribbentrop, still not recovered from a chest infection, was ordered up from Fuschl, his residence in the Salzkammergut near Salzburg.[184] Soon after midnight, Hitler met his military leaders for the third time in little over twelve hours, frantically improvising details of the evacuation from Sicily and the planned occupation of Rome, together with the seizure of the members of the new Italian government.[185]

At ten o'clock that morning, 26 July, Hitler met Goebbels and Göring, just arrived in FHQ. Ribbentrop joined them half an hour later. Goebbels had already been exchanging views on the situation with Himmler and Bormann. It was still only possible to guess at what had happened. But Goebbels was close to the mark in his own assumptions about how the coup had taken place. How a regime that had been in power for twenty-one years could be overthrown so quickly from within gave him pause for thought.[186] Could something similar take place closer to home? Hitler gave his own interpretation of the situation. He presumed that Mussolini had been forced out of power. Whether he was still alive was not known, but he would certainly be unfree. Hitler saw the forces of Italian freemasonry – banned by Mussolini but still at work behind the scenes – behind the plot. Ultimately, he claimed, the coup was directed at Germany since Badoglio would certainly come to an arrangement with the British and Americans to take Italy out of the war. The British would now look for the best moment for a landing in Italy – perhaps in Genoa in order to cut off German troops in the south. Military precautions to anticipate such a move had to be taken.

Hitler explained, too, his intention of transferring a parachute division, currently based in southern France, to Rome as part of the move to occupy the city. The King, Badoglio, and the members of the new government would be arrested and flown to Germany. Once they were in German hands, things would be different. Possibly Farinacci, who had escaped arrest by fleeing to the German embassy, and was now *en route* to FHQ, could be made head of a puppet government if Mussolini himself could not be rescued. Hitler saw the Vatican, too, as deeply implicated in the plot to oust Mussolini. In the military briefing just after midnight he had talked wildly of occupying the Vatican and 'getting out the whole lot of swine'.[187] Goebbels and Ribbentrop dissuaded him from such rash action, certain to have damaging international repercussions. Hitler still pressed for rapid action to capture the new Italian government. Rommel, who by then had also arrived in FHQ and was earmarked for supreme command in Italy, opposed the improvised, high-risk, panicky response. He favoured a carefully pre-pared action; but that would probably take some eight days to put into place.[188] The meeting ended with the way through the crisis still unclear.

By this time, reports were coming in of anti-fascist demonstrations on the streets of Rome. There were evident signs, too, of marked unease and uncertainty among the German population. Nazi supporters were shocked at Mussolini's overthrow. Illegal opposition groups saw a ray of hope. The notion that something similar could take place in Germany 'can be heard constantly', according to the SD's soundings of popular opinion: 'the idea that the form of government thought in the Reich to be unshakable could in Germany, too, suddenly be altered, is very widespread.'[189] Goebbels's propaganda machine faced problems. As Goebbels recognized, he could not tell the truth that 'it was a matter of a far-reaching organizational and ideological crisis of Fascism, perhaps even of its liquidation'. Knowledge of what was happening in Italy 'could in certain circumstances incite some subversive elements in Germany who perhaps believed they could contrive the same with us that Badoglio and company have contrived in Rome'. Hitler did not think there was much danger of that. But he commissioned Himmler just the same to suppress any indications with maximum ruth-lessness.[190]

The midday military conference was again taken up with the issue of moving troops to Italy to secure above all the north of the country, and with the hastily devised scheme to capture the Badoglio government.[191] Field-Marshal von Kluge, who had flown in from Army Group Centre – desperately trying to hold the Soviet offensive in the Orel bulge, to the north of Kursk – was abruptly told of the implications of the events in Italy for the eastern front. Hitler said he needed the crack Waffen-SS divisions currently assigned to Manstein in the south of the eastern front to be transferred immediately to Italy. That meant Kluge giving up some of his forces to reinforce Manstein's weakened front. Kluge forcefully pointed out, though to no avail, that this would make defence in the Orel region impossible. But the positions on the Dnieper being prepared for an orderly retreat by his troops to be taken up before winter were far from ready. What he was being asked to do, protested Kluge, was to undertake 'an absolutely overhasty evacuation'. 'Even so, Herr Feldmarshall: we are not master here of our own decisions,' rejoined Hitler.[192] Kluge was left with no choice.

Meanwhile, Farinacci had arrived. His description of what had happened and his criticism of Mussolini did not endear him to Hitler. Any idea of using him as the figurehead of a German-controlled regime was discarded.[193] Hitler spoke individually to his leading henchmen before, in need of a rest after a hectic twenty-four hours, retiring to his rooms to eat alone. He returned for a lengthy conference that evening, attended by thirty-five persons. But the matter was taken no further.[194] Next day, he was still determined to act without delay, 'whatever it might cost'. He preferred 'generous improvisation' to 'systematic work starting too late and allowing things in Italy to become too consolidated'. But Rommel was sceptical about the planned military operations.[195] So were Jodl and Kesselring.[196] Within a few days, Hitler was forced to concede that any notion of occupying Rome and sending in a raiding party to take the members of the Badoglio government and the Italian royal family captive was both precipitate and wholly impracticable.[197] The plans were called off. Hitler's attention focused now on discovering the whereabouts of the Duce and bringing him into German hands as soon as possible. In the meantime, he left for him in the possession of Kesselring a copy of the collected works of Nietzsche as a sixtieth birthday present. Evidently, he presumed that the Duce, once located, would have the time and inclination to reflect on the 'will to power'.[198]

With the Italian crisis still at its height, the disastrous month of July drew to a close amid the heaviest air-raids to date. Between 24 and 30 July, the Royal Air Force's Bomber Command, using the release of aluminium strips to blind German radar, unleashed 'Operation Gomorrha' – a series of devastating raids on Hamburg, outdoing in death and destruction anything previously experienced in the air-war. Waves of incendiaries whipped up horrific fire-storms, turning the city into a raging inferno, consuming everything and everybody in their path. People suffocated in their thousands in cellars or were burnt to cinders on the streets. An estimated 30,000 people lost their lives; over half a million were left homeless; twenty-four hospitals, fifty-eight churches, and 277 schools lay in ruins; over 50 per cent of the city was completely gutted.[199] As usual, Hitler revealed no sense of remorse at any human losses. He was chiefly concerned about the psychological impact. When he was given news that fifty German planes had mined the Humber estuary, he exploded: 'You can't tell the German people in this situation: that's mined; 50 planes have laid mines! That has no effect at all . . . You only break terror through terror! We have to have counter-attacks. Everything else is rubbish.'[200]

Hitler mistook the mood of a people with whom he had lost touch. What they wanted, in their vast majority, was less the retaliation that was Hitler's only thought than proper defence against the terror from the skies and – above all else – an end to the war that was costing them their homes and their lives. SD reports caught rumours of unrest which the police had had to suppress, and spoke – recalling 1918 – of a 'November mood' among the population.[201] Gauleiter Karl Kaufmann repeatedly requested Hitler to visit the ruins of Germany's second largest city. But the Führer would not even receive a party of those who had performed outstanding feats in the emergency services.[202] Goebbels pleaded for Hitler to speak on the radio, even for only a quarter of an hour. 'The Führer has not spoken to the public since Heroes' Memorial Day [21 March],' Goebbels added. 'He has disappeared somewhat into the clouds. That's not good for the practical war effort.' Hitler agreed to speak – probably later in the week.[203] Naturally, nothing came of it. That Hitler would not speak to the people was incomprehensible to Goebbels. 'At any rate, the unrest among the broad masses has grown to such an extent that only a word from the Führer himself can again clarify matters,' he ruminated. But Hitler adjudged the current situation 'as unsuitable as could be imagined'.[204] In any case, he remained, as he had been throughout the agony of Hamburg, more taken up with events in Italy.

Remarkably enough, despite the frenetic urgency of the crisis meetings following Mussolini's deposition, the major military decisions had, in fact, been postponed or were left unimplemented. The flurry of activity had produced little. The war council to which his acolytes had been summoned post haste from all over the Reich had left matters in the air. The spontaneous 'decisions' taken in the lengthy military briefings – amid outbursts of menacing invective towards the Badoglio 'clique' – came in the main to nothing, or were toned down in the light of calmer professional judgement. Badoglio's protestations that Italy's commitment to the war was unchanged meant that Germany had to move cautiously. Wiser counsels had prevailed over Hitler's impulsive urge to occupy Rome and depose the government. And though

Hitler had still rejected any evacuation of Sicily, insistent that the enemy should not set foot on the Italian mainland, Kesselring had taken steps to prepare the ground for what proved a brilliantly planned evacuation on the night of 11–12 August, catching the Allies by surprise and allowing 40,000 German and 62,000 Italian troops, with their equipment, to escape to safety. The last German troops in Sicily were finally given the order to undertake a fighting withdrawal to the mainland on 17 August.[205] The split command between Kesselring in the south and Rommel in the north of Italy had been left in place.[206] But as August drew on, suspicions mounted that it would not be long before the Italians defected. And at the end of the month, directives for action in the event of an Italian defection, in the drawer for months and now refashioned under the code-name 'Axis', were issued.[207]

Under the pressure of the events in Italy, Hitler had finally made one overdue move at home. For months, egged on by Goebbels, he had expressed his dissatisfaction with the Reich Minister of the Interior, Wilhelm Frick, whom he contemptuously regarded as 'old and worn-out'.[208] But he could think of no alternative. He continued to defer any decision until the toppling of Mussolini concentrated his mind, persuading him that the time had come to stiffen the grip on the home front and eliminate any prospect of poor morale turning into subversive action. The man he could depend upon to do this was close at hand.

On 20 August he appointed Reichsführer-SS Heinrich Himmler as the new Reich Minister of the Interior. The appointment amounted to Hitler's tacit recognition that his authority at home now rested on police repression, not the adulation of the masses he had once enjoyed.[209] To save face, as usual, Frick was allowed to remain a Reich Minister and 'kicked upstairs' – seemingly given an important new post, replacing Neurath (who had not functioned in the post since September 1941) as Reich Protector of Bohemia and Moravia. Even here, to ensure that Frick's powers remained nominal, State Secretary Karl Hermann Frank was given a new title of State Minister for Bohemia and Moravia and enhanced authority.[210]

On 3 September the first British troops crossed the Straits of Messina to Italy, landing at Reggio di Calabria. That same day, the Italians secretly signed their armistice with the Allies which became public knowledge five days later.[211]

On 8 September Hitler had flown for the second time within a fortnight to Army Group South's headquarters at Zaporozhye, on the lower Dnieper north of the Sea of Azov, to confer with Manstein about the increasingly critical situation on the southern flank of the eastern front. It was to be the last time he set foot on territory captured from the Soviet Union. A few days earlier, following Soviet breakthroughs, he had been forced to authorize withdrawal from the Donets Basin – so important for its rich coal deposits – and from the Kuban bridgehead over the Straits of Kerch, the gateway to the Crimea. Now the Red Army had breached the thin seam which had knitted together Kluge's and Manstein's Army Groups and was pouring through the gap. Retreat was the only possible course of action.[212]

Hitler found a tense atmosphere at the Wolf's Lair on his return. What he had long anticipated – despite reassuring noises to the contrary from Kesselring, and from the German Embassy in Rome – was reality. British and American newspapers had that morning, 8 September, carried reports that the capitulation of the Italian army was imminent. By the afternoon, the news was hardening. At 6p.m. that evening the stories were confirmed by the BBC in London.[213] Once again, Nazi leaders were summoned to Führer Headquarters for a crisis-meeting next day.[214] The unseasonably cold, wet weather provided a fitting backdrop.[215] Partly from spite, partly because he might know too much and prove dangerous, Hitler had Prince Philip of Hesse, the King of Italy's son-in-law, who had been at FHQ for some weeks, promptly arrested and deposited in Gestapo Headquarters in Königsberg.[216] The order had meanwhile been given to set 'Operation Axis' in motion. 'The Führer,' wrote Goebbels, 'is determined to make a *tabula rasa* in Italy.'[217]

The BBC's premature announcement gave the OKW's Operations Staff a head start. Sixteen German divisions had been moved to the Italian mainland by this time. The battle-hardened SS units withdrawn from the eastern front in late July and early August and troops withdrawn from Sicily, Corsica, and Sardinia were in position to take control in central Italy. By 10 September, Rome was in German hands. Italian troops were disarmed. Small pockets of resistance were ruthlessly put down; one division that held out until 22 September ended with 6,000 dead. Over 650,000 soldiers entered German captivity. Only the bulk of the small navy and ineffective air-force escaped and were given over to the Allies. Within a few days Italy was occupied by its former Axis partner.[218]

Hours after the Italian capitulation, the Allies had landed in the Gulf of Salerno, thirty miles or so south-east of Naples. The dogged German resistance they encountered for a week before reinforcements enabled them to break out of their threatened beachhead – linking forces with troops from Montgomery's 8th Army advancing northwards from Reggio di Calabria, and entering Naples on 1 October – was an indicator of what was in store for the Allies during the coming months as the Wehrmacht made them fight for every mile of their northward progression.

It was plain to the German leadership, however, that it would be even more difficult, in the new situation, for the armed forces to cope with the mounting pressures on both the eastern and the southern fronts.[219] Goebbels saw the need looming to seek peace with either the Soviet Union or the western Allies. He suggested the time had come to sound out Stalin. Ribbentrop took the same line. He had tentative feelers put out to see whether the Soviet dictator would bite.[220] But Hitler dismissed the idea. If anything, he said, he preferred to look for an arrangement with Britain – conceivably open to one. But, as always, he would not consider negotiating from a position of weakness. In the absence of the decisive military success he needed, which was receding ever more into the far distance, any hope of persuading him to consider an approach other than the remorseless continuation of the struggle was bound to be illusory.[221]

At least Goebbels, backed by Göring, successfully this time pleaded with Hitler to speak to the German people. To the last minute before recording the broadcast, on 10 September, Hitler showed his reluctance. He wanted to delay, to see how things turned out. Goebbels went through the text with him line by line. Eventually, he got the Führer to the microphone. The speech itself – largely confined to unstinting praise for Mussolini, condemnation of Badoglio and his supporters, the claim that the 'treachery' had been foreseen and every necessary step taken, and a call to maintain confidence and sustain the fight – had nothing of substance to offer, other than a hint at coming retaliation for the bombing of German cities.[222] But Goebbels was satisfied. Reports suggested the speech had gone down well, and helped revive morale.[223] He had, he said, achieved the main purpose of his visit to FHQ. He thought Hitler was relieved to get the speech off his chest after such a long time. And he wrung out of him a promise to speak soon in the Sportpalast to open the Winter Aid campaign. He thought he could give him back the taste for coming 'directly in contact with the people'.[224] Once more, he would be disappointed.

As far as the situation in Italy itself was concerned, Hitler was at this time resigned to losing any hold over the south of the country. His intention was to withdraw to the Apennines, long foreseen by the OKH Operations Staff as the favoured line of defence. However, he worried about the Allies advancing from Italy through the Balkans. By autumn, this concern was to persuade him to change his mind and defend Italy much further to the south. A consequence was to tie down forces desperately needed elsewhere.[225]

The Wehrmacht's rapid successes in taking hold of Italy so speedily provided some relief. Hitler's spirits then soared temporarily when the stunning news came through on the evening of 12 September that Mussolini, whose whereabouts had been recently discovered, had been freed from his captors in a ski hotel on the highest mountain in the Abruzzi through an extraordinarily daring raid by parachutists and SS-men carried in by glider and led by the Austrian SS-Hauptsturmführer Otto Skorzeny.[226] The euphoria did not last long. Hitler greeted the ex-Duce warmly when Mussolini, no longer the preening dictator but looking haggard and dressed soberly in a dark suit and black overcoat, was brought to Rastenburg on 14 September. But Mussolini, bereft of the trappings of power, was a broken man. The series of private talks they had left Hitler 'extraordinarily disappointed'.[227] Three days later, Mussolini was dispatched to Munich to begin forming his new regime.[228] By the end of September he had set up his reconstituted Fascist 'Repubblica di Salò' in northern Italy, a repressive, brutish police state run by a combination of cruelty, corruption, and thuggery – but operating unmistakably under the auspices of German masters.[229] The one-time bombastic dictator of Italy was now plainly no more than Hitler's tame puppet, and living on borrowed time.

As autumn progressed, the situation on the eastern front predictably worsened. Even in private in late September, speaking only to Goebbels (allowed to join the Führer's morning walk with his Alsatian, Blondi), Hitler had been remarkably optimistic. He was confident that the rapid withdrawal to the Dnieper would be successful and leave defences that would be impenetrable over the winter. The shortening of the front by some 350 kilometres would at the same time release troops for a floating reserve of thirty-four divisions, capable of being rushed at short notice to whichever front most needed them.[230]

Hitler's optimism was soon shown to be utterly misplaced. The redeployment of troops to Italy weakened the chances of staving off the Soviet offensive. And the failure to erect the 'eastern wall' of fortifications along the Dnieper during the two years that it had been in German hands now proved costly. The speed of the Soviet advance gave no opportunity to construct any solid defence line.[231] By the end of September the Red Army had been able to cross the Dnieper and establish important bridgeheads on the west banks of the great river. The German bridgehead at Zaporozhye was lost in early October. By then, the Wehrmacht had been pushed back about 150 miles along the southern front. German and Romanian troops were also cut off on the Crimea, which Hitler refused to evacuate fearing, as of old, the opportunities it would give for air-attacks on Romanian oil-fields, and concerned about the message it would send to Turkey and Bulgaria. By the end of the month, the Red Army had pushed so far over the big bend of the Dnieper in the south that any notion of the Germans holding their intended defensive line was purely fanciful. To the north, the largest Soviet city in German hands, Kiev, was recaptured on 5–6 November. Manstein wanted to make the attempt to retake it. For Hitler, the lower Dnieper and the Crimea were more important. Control of the lower Dnieper held the key to the protection of the manganese ores of Nikopol, vital for the German steel industry. And should the Red Army again control the Crimea, the Romanian oil-fields would once more be threatened from the air.[232] But, whatever Hitler's thirst for new military successes, the reality was that by the end of 1943, the limitless granaries of the Ukraine and the industrial heartlands of the northern Caucasus, seen by Hitler on so many occasions as vital to the war effort (as well as the source of future German prosperity in the 'New Order'), were irredeemably lost.[233]

IV

Not lost, however, was the war against the Jews – in Hitler's eyes, the authors of the entire world conflagration. As we noted, Hitler had agreed in June to Himmler's wish to complete the 'evacuation' of the Polish Jews. By autumn 1943, 'Aktion Reinhardt' was terminated: in the region of 1½ million Jews had been killed in the gas chambers of extermination camps at Belzec, Sobibor, and Treblinka in eastern Poland.[234] The SS leadership were now pressing hard for the extension of the 'Final Solution' to all remaining corners of the Nazi *imperium* – even those where the deportations were likely to have diplomatic repercussions. Among these were Denmark and Italy.

The Nazi authorities were well aware that any move against Danish Jews was likely to result in public protests and sour relations with the occupying power. There was little antisemitism in the land. The tiny Jewish minority was fully integrated into Danish society. An attack on the Jews would be seen widely as an assault on Danish citizens. Even so, the SS leadership decided in summer that the time was ripe. Werner Best, the Reich Plenipotentiary in Denmark, pressed for action to be taken. In September, Hitler complied with his request to have the Danish Jews deported, dismissing Ribbentrop's anxieties about a possible general strike and other civil disobedience. Though these did not materialize, the round-up of Danish Jews was a resounding failure. Several hundred – under ten per cent of the Jewish population – were captured and deported to Theresienstadt. Most escaped. Countless Danish citizens helped the overwhelming majority of their Jewish countrymen – in all 7,900 persons, including a few hundred non-Jewish marital partners – to flee across the Sound to safety in neutral Sweden in the most remarkable rescue action of the war.[235]

In October, Hitler accepted Ribbentrop's recommendation to have Rome's 8,000 Jews sent 'as hostages' to the Austrian concentration camp at Mauthausen. This followed moves by the Reich Security Head Office in Berlin, which wanted to deport them to Upper Italy to be 'liquidated'. Anticipating possible problems with the Vatican, Ribbentrop appears to have modified the SS's intentions in suggesting the deportation to Mauthausen. Again, the 'action' to round up the Jews misfired. Most of the Jewish community were able to avoid capture. Some were hidden by disgusted non-Jewish citizens. Thousands found shelter in Rome's convents and monasteries, or in the Vatican itself. In return, the Papacy was prepared to maintain public silence on the outrage. A strong and unequivocal protest from the Pontiff might well have deterred the German occupiers, unsure of the reactions, and prevented the deportations of the Jews they could lay their hands upon. The Germans were expecting such a protest. It never came. Despite Hitler's directive, following his Foreign Minister's advice, those Jews captured were not, in fact, sent to Mauthausen. Of the 1,259 Jews who fell into German hands, the majority were taken straight to Auschwitz.[236]

Hitler's compliance with SS demands to speed up and finish off the 'Final Solution' was unquestionably driven by his wish to complete the destruction of those he held responsible for the war. He wanted, now as before, to see the 'prophecy' he had declared in 1939 and repeatedly referred to, fulfilled. But, even more so than in the spring when he had encouraged Goebbels to turn up the volume of antisemitic propaganda, there was also the need, with backs to the wall, to hold together his closest followers in a sworn 'community of fate', bonded by their own knowledge of and implication in the extermination of the Jews.

On 4 October, Reichsführer-SS Heinrich Himmler spoke openly and frankly about the killing of the Jews to SS leaders gathered in the town hall in Posen, the capital of the Warthegau. He said he was 'referring to the Jewish evacuation programme, the extermination of the Jewish people'. It was, he went on, 'a glorious page in our history, and one that has never been written and never can be written. For we know how difficult we would have made it for ourselves if, on top of the bombing raids, the burdens and the deprivations of war, we still had Jews today in every town as secret saboteurs, agitators, and troublemakers. We would now probably have reached the 1916–17 stage when the Jews were still part of the body of the German people (*Volkskörper*).' The mentality was identical with Hitler's. 'We had the moral right, we had the duty to our people,' Himmler concluded, 'to destroy this people which wanted to destroy us . . . We do not want in the end, because we have exterminated a bacillus, to become ill through the bacillus and die.'[237] The vocabulary, too, was redolent of Hitler's own. Himmler did not refer to Hitler. There was no need to do so. The key point for the Reichsführer-SS was not to assign responsibility to a single person. The crucial purpose of his speech was to stress their joint responsibility, that they were all in it together.[238]

Two days later, in the same Golden Hall in Posen, Himmler addressed the Reichs- and Gauleiter of the Party. The theme was the same one. He gave, as Goebbels recorded, an 'unvarnished and candid picture' of the treatment of the Jews.[239] Himmler declared: 'We faced the question: what should we do with the women and children? I decided here too to find a completely clear solution. I did not regard myself as justified in exterminating the men – that is to say, to kill them or have them killed – and to allow the avengers in the shape of the children to grow up for our sons and grandchildren. The difficult decision had to be taken to have this people disappear from the earth.' Himmler seemed to be indicating that the extension of the killing to women and children had been his initiative. He immediately, however, associated himself and the SS with a 'commission' (*Auftrag*) – 'the most difficult which we have had so far.'[240] The Gauleiter, among them Goebbels who had spoken directly with Hitler on the subject so many times, would have had no difficulty in presuming whose authority lay behind the 'commission'. Again, the purpose of the remarkably frank disclosures on the taboo subject was plain. Himmler marked on a list those who had not attended his speech or noted its contents.[241]

Himmler's speeches, ensuring that his own subordinates and the Party leadership were fully in the picture about the extermination of the Jews, had been – there can be no doubt about it – carried out with Hitler's approval. The very next day after listening to Himmler, the Gauleiter were ordered to attend the Wolf's Lair to hear Hitler himself give an account of the state of the war. That the Führer would speak explicitly on the 'Final Solution' was axiomatically ruled out. But he could now take it for granted that they understood that there was no way out. Their knowledge underlined their complicity. Unusually, Goebbels made no diary entry that day. Only the published communiqué on the meeting survives. But it is not unenlightening. 'The entire German people know,' Hitler had told the Reichs- and Gauleiter, 'that it is a matter of whether they exist or do not exist. The bridges have been destroyed behind them. Only the way forward remains.'[242]

When (for the last time, as it turned out) Hitler addressed the Party's 'Old Guard' in Munich's Löwenbräukeller on the Putsch anniversary, 8 November, he was as defiant as ever.[243] According to SD reports, the speech, broadcast on the radio, went down well – though in the main only among Party fanatics and fervent believers. Their morale was again temporarily lifted, especially by the strong hints of imminent retaliation against Britain for the bombing terror – to be unleashed during the second half of November in five major raids on Berlin itself.[244] Few others could find in the empty bombast any consolation for lives of loved ones sacrificed in vain, homes destroyed, cities laid waste, hardship and misery, and a war which they recognized as to all intents and purposes lost.[245] But those careless enough to voice such sentiments had to reckon with swift retribution. Their fate had been expressly indicated in Hitler's speech. There would be no capitulation, no repeat of 1918, he had declared once again – the nightmare of that year indelibly imprinted on his psyche – and no undermining of the front by subversion at home. Any overheard subversive or defeatist remark, it was clear, would cost the person making it his or her head.[246]

By this time – though of course he made no hint of it in his speech – Hitler was anxious about a looming new grave military threat, one which, if not repulsed, would result in Germany's destruction: what he took to be the certainty of an invasion in the west during the coming year. 'The danger in the east remains,' ran his preamble to his Directive No.51 on 3 November, 'but a greater danger is looming in the west: the Anglo-Saxon landing! . . . If the enemy succeeds here in breaking through our defence on a broad front, the consequences within a short time are unforeseeable. Everything suggests that the enemy, at the latest in spring but perhaps even earlier, will move to attack the western front of Europe.'[247]

To his military advisers, on 20 December, he said he was certain that the invasion would take place some time after mid-February or early March. The next months would be spent in preparation for the coming great assault in the west. This, Hitler remarked, would 'decide the war'.[248]

13

HOPING FOR MIRACLES

'There are so many disagreements on the enemy side, that the coalition is bound to fall apart one day.'

Hitler, speaking to Field-Marshal von Manstein,
4 January 1944

'I wish these prognoses of the Führer were right. We've been so often disappointed recently that you feel some scepticism rising up within you.'

Goebbels, 4 March 1944

'The Führer did not know whether or when an invasion would occur, but the English had adopted measures which could only be maintained for 6–8 weeks and a serious crisis would break out in England if the invasion did not occur. He would then deploy new technical weapons which were effective within a radius of 250–300 kilometres and would transform London into a heap of ruins.'

Hitler, speaking to Mussolini, 22 April 1944

'If we repel the invasion, then the scene in the war will be completely transformed. The Führer reckons for certain with this. He has few worries that this couldn't succeed.'

Goebbels, 7 June 1944

I

'The year 1944 will make tough and severe demands of all Germans. The course of the war, in all its enormity, will reach its critical point during this year. We are fully confident that we will successfully surmount it.'[1] This, and the prospect of new cities rising resplendently after the war from the bombed-out ruins, was all Hitler had to offer readers of his New Year proclamation in 1944. Fewer than ever of them were able to share his confidence. For the embattled soldiers at the front, Hitler's message was no different. The military crisis of 1943 had been brought about, he told them, by sabotage and treachery by the French in North Africa and the Italians following the overthrow of Mussolini. But the greatest crisis in German history had been triumphantly mastered. However hard the fighting in the east had been, 'Bolshevism has not achieved its goal.' He glanced at the western Allies, and at the future: 'The plutocratic western world can undertake its threatened attempt at a landing where it wants: it will fail!'[2]

Since Germany had been forced on to the defensive, experiencing only setbacks, Hitler had not changed his tune. His stance had become immobilized, fossilized. In his view, the military disasters had been the consequence of betrayal, incompetence, disobedience of orders, and, above all, weakness. He conceded not a single error or misjudgement on his own part. No capitulation; no surrender; no retreat; no repeat of 1918; hold out at all costs, whatever the odds: this was the unchanging message. Alongside this went the belief – unshakeable (apart, perhaps, from his innermost thoughts and bouts of depression during sleepless nights) but an item of blind faith, not resting on reason – that the strength to hold out would eventually lead to a turning of the tide, and to Germany's final victory. In public, he expressed his unfounded optimism through references to the grace of Providence. As he put it to his soldiers on 1 January 1944, after overcoming the defensive period then returning to the attack to impose devastating blows on the enemy, 'Providence will bestow victory on the people that has done most to earn it.' His instinctive belief in reward for the strongest remained intact. 'If, therefore, Providence grants life as the prize to those who have fought and defended the most courageously, then our people will find mercy from the just arbiter who at all times gave victory to the most meritorious.'[3]

However hollow such sentiments sounded to men at the various fronts, suffering untold hardships, enduring hourly danger, often realizing they would never see their loved ones again, they were, for Hitler himself, far from mere cynical propaganda. He had to believe these ideas – and did, certainly down to the summer of 1944, if not longer. The references, in public and private, to 'Providence' and 'Fate' increased as his own control over the course of the war declined.[4] The views on the course of the war which he expressed to his generals, to other Nazi leaders (including private conversations with Goebbels), and to his immediate entourage gave no inkling that his own resolve was wavering, or that he had become in any way resigned to the prospect of defeat. If it was an act, then it was one brilliantly sustained, and remained substantially unchanged whatever the context or personnel involved. 'It is impressive, with what certainty the Führer believes in his mission,' noted Goebbels in his diary in early June 1944.[5] Others who saw Hitler frequently, in close proximity, and were less impressionable than Goebbels, thought the same.[6] Without the inner conviction, Hitler would have been unable to sway those around him, as he continued so often to do, to find new resolve. Without it, he would not have engaged so fanatically in bitter conflicts with his military leaders. Without it, he would have been incapable, not least, of sustaining in himself the capacity to continue, despite increasingly overwhelming odds.

The astonishing optimism did not give way, despite the mounting crises and calamities of the first half of 1944. But the self-deception involved was colossal. Hitler lived increasingly in a world of illusion, clutching as the year wore on ever more desperately at whatever straws he could find. The invasion, when it came, would be repulsed without doubt, he thought. He placed enormous hopes, too, in the devastating effect of the 'wonder-weapons'. When they failed to match expectations, he would remain convinced that the alliance against him was fragile and would soon fall apart, as had occurred in the Seven Years War two centuries earlier following the indomitable defence of one of his heroes, Frederick the Great. Even at the very end of a catastrophic year for Germany, he would not give up hope of this happening. He would still be hoping for miracles.

He had, however, no rational ways out of the inevitable catastrophe to offer those who, in better times, had lavished their adulation upon him. Albert Speer, in a pen-picture drawn immediately after the war, saw Hitler's earlier 'genius' at finding 'elegant' ways out of crises eroded by relentless overwork imposed on him by war's demands, undermining the intuition which had required the more spacious and leisured lifestyle suited to an artistic temperament. The change in work-patterns – turning himself, against his natural temperament, into an obsessive workaholic, preoccupied by detail, unable to relax, surrounded by an unchanging and uninspiring entourage – had brought in its train, thought Speer, enormous mental strain together with increased inflexibility and obstinacy in decisions which had closed off all but the route to disaster.[7]

It was certainly the case that Hitler's entire existence had been consumed by the prosecution of the war. The leisured times of the pre-war years were gone. The impatience with detail, detachment from day-to-day issues, preoccupation with grandiose architectural schemes, generous allocation of time for relaxation, listening to music, watching films, indulging in the indolence which had been a characteristic since his youth, had indeed given way to a punishing work-schedule in which Hitler brooded incessantly over the most detailed matters of military tactics, leaving little or no space for anything unconnected with the conduct of war in a routine essentially unchanged day in and day out. Nights with little sleep; rising late in the mornings; lengthy midday and early evening conferences, often extremely stressful, with his military leaders; a strict, spartan diet, and meals often taken alone in his room; no exercise beyond a brief daily walk with his Alsatian bitch, Blondi; the same surroundings, the same entourage; late-night monologues to try to wind down (at the expense of his bored entourage), reminiscing about his youth, the First World War, and the 'good old times' of the Nazi Party's rise to power; then, finally, another attempt to find sleep: such a routine – only marginally more relaxed when he was at the Berghof – could not but be in the long run harmful to health and was scarcely conducive to calm and considered, rational reflection.

All who saw him pointed out how Hitler had aged during the war.[8] He had once appeared vigorous, full of energy, to those around him. Now, his hair was greying fast, his eyes were bloodshot, he walked with a stoop, he had difficulty controlling a trembling left arm; for a man in his mid-fifties, he looked old.[9] Despite his mounting hypochondria, Hitler had in fact enjoyed extremely robust health during the 1930s. But his health had started to suffer notably from 1941 onwards. Even then he spent scarcely a day bedridden through illness. But the increased numbers of pills and injections provided every day by Dr Morell – ninety varieties in all during the war and twenty-eight different pills each day – could not prevent the physical deterioration.[10]

By 1944, Hitler was a sick man – at times during the year extremely unwell. Cardiograms, the first taken in 1941, had revealed a worsening heart condition.[11] And beyond the chronic stomach and intestinal problems that had increasingly come to plague him, Hitler had since 1942 developed symptoms, becoming more pronounced in 1944, which point with some medical certainty to the onset of Parkinson's Syndrome. Most notably, an uncontrollable trembling of the left arm, jerking in his left leg, and a shuffling gait, were unmistakable to those who saw him at close quarters.[12] But although the strains of the last phase of the war took their toll on him, there is no convincing evidence that his mental capacity was impaired.[13] Hitler's rages and violent mood-swings were inbuilt features of his character, their frequency in the final phase of the war a reflection of the stress from the rapidly deteriorating military conditions and his own inability to change them, bringing, as usual, wild lashings at his generals and any others on whom he could lay the blame that properly began at his own door.

In looking to the loss of 'genius' through pressures of overwork inappropriate to Hitler's alleged natural talent for improvisation, Speer was offering a naïve and misleading explanation of Germany's fate, ultimately personalizing it in the 'demonic' figure of Hitler.[14] The adoption of such a harmfully over-burdensome style of working was no chance development. It was the direct outcome of an extreme form of personalized rule which had already by the time war began seriously eroded the more formal and regular structures of government and military command that are essential in modern states. No other war leader – not Churchill, Roosevelt, or even Stalin – was so consumed by the task of running military affairs, so unable to delegate authority. The breakdown of governmental structures in Germany had gone yet further than their erosion in the Soviet state under Stalin's despotism. The reins of power were entirely held in Hitler's hands. He was still backed by major power bases. None existed – whatever the growing anxieties among the military, some leading industrialists, and a number of senior figures in the state bureaucracy about the road down which he was taking them – that could bypass the Führer. All vital measures, both in military and in domestic affairs, needed his authorization. There were no overriding coordinating bodies – no war cabinet, no politburo. But Hitler, forced entirely on to the defensive in running the war, was now often almost paralysed in his thinking, and often in his actions. And in matters relating to the 'home front', while refusing to concede an inch of his authority he was, as Goebbels interminably bemoaned, nevertheless incapable of more than sporadic, unsystematic intervention or prevaricating inaction.

Far more gifted individuals than Hitler would have been overstretched and incapable of coping with the scale and nature of the administrative problems involved in the conduct of a world war. Hitler's triumphs in foreign policy in the 1930s, then as war leader until 1941, had not arisen from his 'artistic genius' (as Speer saw it), but in the main from his unerring skill in exploiting the weaknesses and divisions of his opponents, and through the timing of actions carried out at breakneck speed. Not 'artistic genius', but the gambler's instinct when playing for high stakes with a good hand against weak opponents had served Hitler well in those earlier times. Those aggressive instincts worked as long as the initiative could be retained. But once the gamble had failed, and he was playing a losing hand in a long-drawn-out match with the odds becoming increasingly more hopeless, the instincts lost their effectiveness. Hitler's individual characteristics now fatefully merged, in conditions of mounting disaster, into the structural weaknesses of the dictatorship. His ever-increasing distrust of those around him, especially his generals, was one side of the coin. The other was his unbounded egomania which cholerically expressed itself – all the more pronounced as disasters started to accumulate – in the belief that no one else was competent or trustworthy, and that he alone could ensure victory. His takeover of the operational command of the army in the winter crisis of 1941 had been the most obvious manifestation of this disastrous syndrome.

Speer's explanation was even more deficient in ignoring the fact that Germany's catastrophic situation in 1944 was the direct consequence of the steps which Hitler – overwhelmingly supported by the most powerful forces within the country, and widely acclaimed by the masses – had taken in the years when his 'genius' (in Speer's perception) had been less constrained. Not changes in his work-style, but the direct result of a war he – and much of the military leadership – had wanted meant that Hitler could find no 'elegant' solution to the stranglehold increasingly imposed by the mighty coalition which German aggression had called into being. He was left, therefore, with no choice but to face the reality that the war was lost, or to hold fast to illusions.

Ever fewer Germans shared Hitler's undiminished fatalism about the outcome of the war. The dictator's rhetoric, so powerful in 'sunnier' periods, had lost its ability to sway the masses. Either they believed what he said; or they believed their own eyes and ears – gazing out over devastated cities, reading the ever-longer lists of fallen soldiers in the death-columns of the newspapers, hearing the sombre radio announcements (however they were dressed up) of further Soviet advances, seeing no sign that the fortunes of war were turning. Hitler sensed that he had lost the confidence of his people. The great orator no longer had his audience. With no triumphs to proclaim, he did not even want to speak to the German people any longer. The bonds between the Führer and the people had been a vital basis of the regime in earlier times. But now, the gulf between ruler and ruled had widened to a chasm.

During 1944 Hitler would distance himself from the German people still further than he had done in the previous two years. He was physically detached – cocooned for the most part in his field headquarters in East Prussia or in his mountain eyrie in Bavaria – and scarcely now visible, even in newsreels, for ordinary Germans.[15]

On not a single occasion during 1944 did he appear in public to deliver a speech. When, on 24 February, the anniversary of the proclamation of the Party Programme of 1920, he spoke in the Hofbräuhaus in Munich to the closed circle of the Party's 'Old Guard', he expressly refused Goebbels's exhortations to have the speech broadcast and no mention was made of the speech in the newspapers.[16] Twice, on 30 January 1944 and early on 21 July, he addressed the nation on the radio. Otherwise the German people did not hear directly from their Leader throughout 1944. Even his traditional address to the 'Old Fighters' of the Party on 8 November was read out by Himmler. For the masses, Hitler had become a largely invisible leader. He was out of sight and for most, probably, increasingly out of mind – except as an obstacle to the ending of the war.

The intensified level of repression during the last years of the war, along with the negative unity forged by fear of the victory of Bolshevism, went a long way towards ensuring that the threat of internal revolt, as had happened in 1918, never materialized. But, for all the continuing (and in some ways astonishing) reserves of strength of the Führer cult among outright Nazi supporters, Hitler had become for the overwhelming majority of Germans the chief hindrance to the ending of the war. Ordinary people might prefer, as they were reported to be saying, 'an end with horror' to 'a horror without end'.[17] But they had no obvious way of altering their fate. Only those who moved in the corridors of power had any possibility of removing Hitler. Some groups of officers, through conspiratorial links with certain highly-placed civil servants, were plotting precisely that. After a number of abortive attempts, their strike would come in July 1944. It would prove the last chance the Germans themselves had to put an end to the Nazi regime. The bitter rivalries of the subordinate leaders, the absence of any centralized forum (equivalent to the Fascist Grand Council in Italy) from which an internal coup could be launched, the shapelessness of the structures of Nazi rule yet the indispensability of Hitler's authority to every facet of that rule, and, not least, the fact that the regime's leaders had burnt their boats with the Dictator in the regime's genocide and other untold acts of inhumanity, ruled out any further possibility of overthrow. With that, the regime had only its own collective suicide in an inexorably lost war to contemplate. But like a mortally wounded wild beast at bay, it fought with the ferocity and ruthlessness that came from desperation. And its Leader, losing touch ever more with reality, hoping for miracles, kept tilting at windmills – ready in Wagnerian style in the event of ultimate apocalyptic catastrophe, and in line with his undiluted social-Darwinistic beliefs, to take his people down in flames with him if it proved incapable of producing the victory he had demanded.

II

Readiness for the invasion in the West, certain to come within the next few months, was the overriding preoccupation of Hitler and his military advisers in early 1944. They were sure that the critical phase directly following the invasion would decide the outcome of the war.[18] Hopes were invested in the fortifications swiftly being erected along the Atlantic coast in France, and in the new, powerful weapons of destruction that were under preparation and would help the Wehrmacht to inflict a resounding defeat on the invaders as soon as they set foot on continental soil. Forced back, with Britain reeling under devastating blows from weapons of untold might, against which there was no defence, the western Allies would realize that Germany could not be defeated; the 'unnatural' alliance with the Soviet Union would split apart; and, freed of the danger in the west, the German Reich could devote all its energies, perhaps now even with British and American backing following a separate peace agreement, to the task of repelling and defeating Bolshevism. So ran the optimistic currents of thought in Hitler's headquarters.

Meanwhile, developments on the eastern front – the key theatre of the war – were more than worrying enough to hold Hitler's attention. A new Soviet offensive in the south of the eastern front had begun on 24 December 1943, making rapid advances, and dampening an already dismal Christmas mood in the Führer Headquarters. Hitler spent New Year's Eve closeted in his rooms alone with Bormann.[19] He took part in no festivities. At least in the company of Martin Bormann, his loyal right hand in all Party matters, he was 'among his own'. In his daily military conferences, it was different. The tensions with his generals were palpable. Some loyalists around Hitler, such as Jodl, shared in some measure his optimism. Others were already more sceptical. According to Hitler's Luftwaffe adjutant, Nicolaus von Below, even the initially starry-eyed Chief of Staff Zeitzler by now did not believe a word Hitler said.[20] What Hitler really felt about the war, whether he harboured private doubts that conflicted with the optimism he voiced at all times, was even for those regularly in his close company impossible to deduce.[21]

Whatever his innermost thoughts, his outward stance was predictable. Retreat, whatever the tactical necessity or even advantage to be gained from it, was ruled out. When the retreat then inevitably did eventually take place, it was invariably under less favourable conditions than at the time that it had been initially proposed. 'Will' to hold out was, as always, the supreme value for Hitler. In the winter crisis of 1941, his refusal to sanction retreat had probably prevented headlong collapse. But since then the relentless Soviet advance, backed by superiority in weaponry and manpower, had forced the need for a defensive strategy which was foreign to Hitler's nature, and which required more than repeated emphasis on 'will' and fighting spirit. In late December, prompted by concern that the subversive propaganda put out in Moscow by the Soviet-backed '*Freies Deutschland*' ('Free Germany'),[22] aimed at undermining morale among the German troops, was indeed having such an effect, Hitler, prompted by Himmler and Bormann, had ordered the establishment of National Socialist Leadership Officers to instil the spirit of the Nazi movement within the Wehrmacht.[23] What was, in fact, required was greater military skill and tactical flexibility than the Commander-in-Chief of the Army himself could muster. In these circumstances, Hitler's obstinacy and interference in tactical matters posed ever greater difficulties for his field commanders.

Manstein encountered Hitler's inflexibility again when he flew on 4 January 1944 to Führer Headquarters to report on the rapidly deteriorating situation of Army Group South. Soviet forces, centred on the Dnieper bend, had made major advances. These now posed an ominous threat to the survival of the 4th Panzer Army (located in the region between Vinnitsa and Berichev). The breach of this position would open up a massive gap between Army Groups South and Centre, putting therefore the entire southern front in mortal peril. This demanded, in Manstein's view, the urgent transfer of forces northwards to counter the threat. This could only be done by evacuating the Dnieper bend, abandoning Nikopol (with its manganese supplies) and the Crimea, and drastically reducing the front to a length which could more easily be defended. Hitler refused point-blank to countenance such a proposal. Losing the Crimea, he argued, would prompt the defection of Turkey, together with Bulgaria and Romania. Reinforcements for the threatened northern wing could not be drawn from Army Group North, since that could well lead to the defection of Finland, loss of the Baltic, and lack of availability of vital Swedish ore. Forces could not be drawn from the west before the invasion had been repelled. 'There were so many disagreements on the enemy side,' Manstein recalled Hitler stating, 'that the coalition was bound to fall apart one day. To gain time was therefore a matter of paramount importance.' Manstein would simply have to hold out until reinforcements were available.[24]

When the military conference was over, Manstein asked to see Hitler privately, in the company only of Zeitzler, the Chief of the Army General Staff. Reluctantly (as usual when unsure of what was coming), Hitler agreed. Once the room had emptied, Manstein began. Hitler's demeanour, already cold, soon touched freezing-point. His eyes bored like gimlets into the field-marshal as Manstein stated that enemy superiority alone was not responsible for the plight of the army in the east, but that this was 'also due to the way in which we are led'.[25] Manstein, persevering undaunted despite the intimidating atmosphere, renewed the request he had put on two earlier occasions, that he himself should be appointed overall Commander-in-Chief for the eastern front with full independence of action within overall strategic objectives, in the way that Rundstedt in the west and Kesselring in Italy enjoyed similar authority. This would have meant the effective surrender by Hitler of his powers of command in the eastern theatre. He was having none of it. But his argument backfired. 'Even I cannot get the field-marshals to obey me!' he retorted. 'Do you imagine, for example, that they would obey you any more readily?' Manstein replied that his orders were never disobeyed. At this, Hitler, his anger under control though the insubordination plainly registered, closed the discussion.[26] Manstein had had the last word. But he returned to his headquarters empty-handed.

Not only had he no prospect of appointment as Commander-in-Chief in the eastern theatre; Manstein's outspoken views were by now prompting doubts in Hitler's mind about his suitability in command of Army Group South. Meanwhile, Hitler's orders for Manstein's troops were clear: there was to be no pulling back. Tenacious German defiance in the Dnieper bend and at Nikopol did in fact succeed in holding up the Soviet advance for the time being. But the loss of this territory, and of the Crimea itself, was a foregone conclusion, merely temporarily delayed.

Guderian, another of Hitler's one-time favourite commanders, fared no better than Manstein when he attempted, at a private audience in January, to persuade Hitler to simplify and unify military command by appointing a trusted general to a new position of Chief of the Wehrmacht General Staff. This, aimed at removing the damaging weakness at the heart of the Wehrmacht High Command, would have meant the dismissal of Keitel. Hitler rejected this out of hand. It would also have signified, as Hitler had no difficulty in recognizing, a diminution of his own powers within the military command. Like Manstein, Guderian had met an immovable obstacle. Like Manstein's, his recommendations of tactical retreats fell on stony ground. As he later summarized: 'So nothing was altered. Every square yard of ground continued to be fought for. Never once was a situation which had become hopeless put right by a timely withdrawal.'[27]

The level to which relations between Hitler and his senior generals — among them those who had been his most loyal and trusted commanders — had sunk was revealed by a flashpoint at the lengthy speech Hitler gave to 100 or so of his military leaders on 27 January.[28] After a simple lunch, during which the atmosphere was noticeably cool, Hitler offered little more (following the usual long-winded resort to the lessons of history, emphasis on 'struggle' as a natural law, and description of his own political awakening and build-up of the Party) than an exhortation to hold out. For this, indoctrination in the spirit of National Socialism was vital. Of one thing, he told them, they could be certain: 'that there could never be even the slightest thought of capitulation, whatever might happen'. The only point of substance in the lengthy address was the briefest of allusions to new weapons which were on the way, especially U-boats, from which he expected a complete reversal of fortunes in the war at sea.[29] At the high-point of his peroration, Hitler touched on the central purpose of his address. He spoke of his right to demand of his generals not simply loyalty, but fanatical support. Full of pathos, he declared: 'In the last instance, if I should ever be deserted as supreme Leader, I must have as the last defence (*Letztes*) around me the entire officer-corps who must stand with drawn swords rallied round me.'[30] A minor sensation then occurred: Hitler was interrupted – something which had never happened since the beerhalls of Munich – as Field-Marshal von Manstein exclaimed: 'And so it will be, *mein Führer*.'[31] Hitler was visibly taken aback, and lost the thread of what he was saying. He stared icily, uttered 'That's good. If that's the case, we can never lose this war, never, come what may. For the nation will then go into the war with the strength that is necessary. I note that very gladly, Field-Marshal von Manstein!' He quickly recovered, emphasizing the need, even so, for greater advances in the 'education' of the officer corps.[32] In a literal sense, Manstein's words could be seen to be not only harmless, but encouraging.[33] But, as Manstein himself indicated after the war, the implied meaning was more critical of Hitler. The interruption, the field-marshal later recalled, arose from a rush of blood as he sensed that Hitler had impugned the honour of himself and his fellow officers by implying that their loyalty might be in question.[34]

Hitler, for his part, saw in the interruption a reproach for his mistrust of his generals.[35] The meeting with Manstein three weeks earlier still rankled with him, as did a frank letter which the field-marshal had subsequently sent.[36] Within minutes of the interruption, Hitler had summoned Manstein to his presence. With Keitel in attendance, Hitler forbade Manstein to interrupt in future. 'You yourself would not tolerate such behaviour from your own subordinates,' he stated, adding, in a gratuitous insult, that Manstein's letter to him a few days earlier had presumably been to justify himself to posterity in his war diary. Needled at this, Manstein retorted: 'You must excuse me if I use an English expression in this connection, but all I can say to your interpretation of my motives is that I am a gentleman.' On this discordant note, the audience came to a close.[37] Manstein's days were plainly numbered.[38]

At noon three days later, the eleventh anniversary of the takeover of power, Hitler addressed the German people. As in the previous year, he did not travel to Berlin. In 1943, in the throes of the Stalingrad débâcle, Göring had spoken in his place. This time, he spoke himself, but confined himself to a relatively short radio address from his headquarters. As his voice crackled through the ether from the Wolf's Lair in East Prussia, the wailing sirens in Berlin announced the onset of another massive air-attack on the city. Symbolically – it might seem in retrospect – the Sportpalast, scene of many Nazi triumphs in the 'time of struggle' before 1933, and where so often since then tens of thousands of the Party faithful had gathered to hear Hitler's big speeches, was gutted that night in a hail of incendiaries.[39]

Hitler's radio broadcast could offer listeners nothing of what they yearned to hear: when the war would be over, when the devastation from the air would be ended. Instead, what they heard was no more than a rant (along the usual lines, accompanied by the normal savage vocabulary of 'Jewish bacteria') about the threat of Bolshevism. In the event of victory, he repeated, Bolshevism would eradicate Germany and overrun the rest of Europe – the aim of international Jewry which could be combated only by the National Socialist state, built up over the previous eleven years.[40] Not a word was said in consolation to those who had lost loved ones at the front, or about the human misery caused by the bomb-raids. Even Goebbels acknowledged that, in bypassing practically all the issues that preoccupied ordinary people, the speech had failed to make an impact.[41] Indeed, SD reports in the following days – full of references to war-weariness, anxiety over the eastern front and the bombing, and disbelief that the war could still be won – made no mention of reactions to the Führer's speech. It was a remarkable contrast with earlier years. His propaganda slogans were now falling on deaf ears. And his earlier promises of retaliation for the laying waste of German cities were flatly disbelieved as the mood plummeted following the latest bombing-raid on Berlin. Indirectly, judgement on the speech could be read into reported remarks such as: 'We don't want any tranquillizer pills. Tell us instead where Germany really stands'; or the comment of a Berlin worker, that only 'an idiot can tell me the war will be won'.[42]

III

Scepticism both about the capabilities of German air-defence to protect cities against the menace from the skies, and about the potential for launching retaliatory attacks on Britain was well justified. Göring's earlier popularity had long since evaporated totally among the mass of the public as his once much-vaunted Luftwaffe had shown itself utterly incapable of preventing the destruction of German towns and cities. Nor did the latest wave of raids, particularly the severe attack on Berlin, do much to improve the Reich Marshal's standing at Führer Headquarters. It took little to prompt Hitler to withering tirades against Göring's competence as Luftwaffe chief. In particular, Goebbels, who both as Gauleiter of Berlin and with new responsibilities for coordinating measures for civil defence in the air-war possibly had more first-hand experience than any other Nazi leader of the impact of the Allied bombing of German cities, lost no opportunity whenever he met

Hitler to vent his spleen on Göring.[43] But however violently he condemned what Goebbels described as 'Göring's total fiasco' in air-defence,[44] Hitler would not consider parting company with one of his longest-serving paladins. When Goebbels discussed the failure of the Luftwaffe with him at the beginning of March, Hitler even showed sympathy for the Reich Marshal's position. 'The Führer completely understands,' Goebbels recorded, 'that Göring is somewhat nervous in his present situation. But he thinks that we therefore have to help him all the more. He can for the moment stand no criticism. You have to tread very carefully to tell him this or that.'[45] On a subsequent occasion, when blame was attached to the Reich Marshal for the 'catastrophic inferiority' in the air, Goebbels reported that Hitler 'could do nothing about Göring because the authority of the Reich or the Party would thereby suffer the greatest damage.'[46] It would remain Hitler's position throughout the year.

A big hope of making a dent in Allied air superiority rested on the production of the jet-fighter, the Me262, which had been commissioned the previous May. Its speed of up to 800 kilometres per hour meant that it was capable of outflying any enemy aircraft. But when the aircraft designer Professor Willi Messerschmitt had told Hitler of its disproportionately heavy fuel consumption, it had led by September 1943 to its production priority being removed. This was restored only a vital quarter of a year later, on 7 January 1944, when Speer and Milch were summoned to Hitler's headquarters to be told, on the basis of English press reports, that British testing of jet-planes was almost complete. Hitler now demanded production on the Me262 to be stepped up immediately so that as many jets as possible could be put into service without delay. But valuable time had been lost. It was plain that the first machines would take months to produce. Whether Hitler was as clearly informed of this as Speer later claimed is questionable.[47] When Captain Hanna Reitsch, who had risen to become one of his star pilots, visited Hitler at the end of February to receive her Iron Cross, First Class, she proposed setting up a Kamikaze-squad along Japanese lines. Hitler refused, saying he expected great things in the near future from the early deployment of his jets. Reitsch pointed out that it would be months before this could happen. Hitler's Luftwaffe adjutant Nicolaus von Below reinforced the point later that evening. But Hitler was adamant that the Luftwaffe had informed him differently, and that the dates he had laid down would be met. No one had openly contradicted his demands, he stated.[48] Speer himself, according to Goebbels, was confident that the new jets would bring a radical change of fortunes in the air-war.[49]

Hitler's instincts, as always, veered towards attack as the best form of defence. He looked, as did – impatiently and more and more disbelievingly – large numbers of ordinary Germans, to the chance to launch devastating weapons of destruction against Great Britain, giving the British a taste of their own medicine and forcing the Allies to rethink their strategy in the air-war. Here, too, his illusions about the speed with which the 'wonder-weapons' could be made ready for deployment, and their likely impact on British war strategy, were shored up by the optimistic prognoses of his advisers.

Speer had persuaded Hitler as long ago as October 1942, after witnessing trials at Peenemünde earlier in the year, of the destructive potential of a long-range rocket, the A4 (later better known as the V2) able to enter the stratosphere *en route* to delivering its bombs – and unstoppable devastation – on England. Hitler had immediately ordered their mass-production on a huge scale. When Werner von Braun, the genius behind the construction, had explained some months later what the rocket was capable of, and shown him a colour-film of it in trials, Hitler's enthusiasm was unbounded. It was, he told Speer, 'the decisive weapon of the war', which would lift the burden on Germany when unleashed on the British. Production was to be advanced with all speed – if need be at the expense of tank production. By autumn 1943 it had already become plain that any expectation of early deployment was wildly optimistic.[50] But in February 1944, Speer was still indicating to Goebbels that the rocket programme could be ready by the end of April.[51] In the event, it would be September before the rockets were launched.[52]

The alternative project of the Luftwaffe, the 'Kirschkern' Programme, which produced what came to be known as the V1 flying-bombs, was more advanced. This, too, went back to 1942. And, like the A4 project, hopes of it were high and expectations of its production-rate optimistic. Production began in January 1944. Tests were highly encouraging.[53] Speer told Goebbels in early February it would be ready at the beginning of April.[54] Milch pictured for Hitler, a month later, total devastation in London in a wave of 1,500 flying-bombs over ten days, beginning on Hitler's birthday, 20 April, with the remainder to be dispatched the following month. Within three weeks of exposure to such bombing, he imagined, Britain would be on its knees.[55] Given the information he was being fed, Hitler's illusions become rather more explicable. Competition, in this case between the army's A4 project and the 'Kirschkern' Programme of the Luftwaffe, played its part. And 'working towards the Führer', striving – as the key to retaining power and position – to accomplish what it was known he would favour, to provide the miracle he wanted, and to accommodate his wishes, however unrealistic, still applied. Reluctance to convey bad or depressing news to him was the opposite side of the same coin. Together, the consequence was inbuilt, systemic, over-optimism – shoring up unrealizable hopes, inevitably leading to sour disillusionment.

IV

During February, Hitler, perusing the international press summarized for him as usual in the overview provided by his Press Chief Otto Dietrich, had seen a press notice from Stockholm stating that a general staff officer of the army had been designated to shoot him. SS-Standartenführer Johann Rattenhuber, responsible for Hitler's personal safety, was instructed to tighten security at the Wolf's Lair. All visitors were to be carefully screened; not least, briefcases were to be thoroughly searched. Hitler had reservations, however, about drawing security precautions too tightly.[56] In any case, within days the matter lost its urgency since he decided to leave the Wolf's Lair and move to the Berghof, near Berchtesgaden. The recent air-raids on Berlin and increasing allied air-supremacy meant that the prospect of a raid on Führer Headquarters could no longer be ruled out. It was essential, therefore, to strengthen the walls and roofs of the buildings. While workers from the Todt Organization were carrying out the extensive work, head-quarters would be transferred to Berchtesgaden.[57] On the evening of 22 February, having announced that he would be speaking to the 'Old Guard' in Munich on the 24th at the annual celebration of the announcement of the Party Programme in 1920, he left the Wolf's Lair in his special train and headed south.[58] He would not return from the Berghof until mid-July.

He had been unwell in the middle of the month. His intestinal problems were accompanied by a severe cold. The trembling in his left leg was noticeable.[59] He also complained of blurred vision in his right eye, diagnosed a fortnight later by an ophthalmic specialist as caused by minute blood-vessel haemorrhaging.[60] His health problems were by now chronic, and mount-ing.[61] But he was a good deal better by the time he arrived on 24 February in one of his old haunts, Munich's Hofbräuhaus, to deliver his big speech to a large gathering of fervent loyalists, the Party's 'Old Guard' as they called themselves.[62] In this company, Hitler was in his element. His good speaking-form returned. The old certitudes sufficed. He believed, the assembled fanatics heard, more firmly than ever in the victory that toughness in holding out would bring; retaliation was on its way in massive attacks on London; the allied invasion, when it came, would be swiftly repelled. His peroration reached culmination-point when he told his wildly enthusiastic audience, which interrupted constantly with rapturous applause, that the road from the promulgation of the Party Programme to the takeover of power had been far harder and more hopeless than that which the German people had to go down to attain victory.

He would go his way without compromise. He linked this to the 'Jewish Question': just as the Jews had been 'smashed down' in Germany, so they would be in the entire world. The Jews of England and America – held as always to blame for the war – could expect what had already happened to the Jews of Germany. It was a crude attack on the prime Nazi ideological target as compensation for the lack of any tangible military success. But it was exactly what this audience wanted to hear. They loved it.[63] Many of them were less enamoured with the evening after the speech, spent in a cold and damp air-raid shelter, fearing a heavy raid on Munich which did not materialize.[64] By then, Hitler had left Munich and headed for the Berghof – its alpine splendour now also affected by the danger from the air, covered by camouflage netting, its great hall dimly lit, connected with newly constructed passages to air-raid bunkers.[65]

At the beginning of March, Hitler summoned Goebbels to the Berghof. The immediate reason was the prospect of the imminent defection of Finland.[66] In fact, for the time being this proved a false alarm. Finland would eventually secede only six months later.[67] But the meeting with Goebbels on 3 March was, as usual, not confined to a specific issue, and prompted another *tour d'horizon* by Hitler, allowing a glimpse into his thinking at this juncture.

He told Goebbels that, in the light of the Finnish crisis, he was now determined to put an end to the continued 'treachery' in Hungary. The government would be deposed and arrested, the head of state Admiral Horthy placed under German 'protection', the troops disarmed, and a new regime installed. Then the Hungarian aristocracy and, especially, the Budapest Jews (who, naturally, were taken to be behind the problem) could be tackled. Weapons, manpower, oil, and foodstuffs to be confiscated from Hungary would all stand Germany in good stead. The whole issue would be dealt with as soon as possible.[68]

On the military situation, Hitler exuded confidence. He thought a shortened front in the east could be held. He wanted to turn to the offensive again in the summer. For this he would need forty divisions that would have to be drawn from the west following the successful repulsion of an invasion. Before that, the southern flank would have to be cleared up. He was concerned at the difficulties in breaking down the bridgehead at Anzio, on the west coast of Italy, where the Allies had landed some 70,000 mainly American troops in January but had failed to exploit the element of surprise and found themselves pinned down.[69] He blamed, as usual, his military leaders, in particular his commander in the area, Kesselring, and regretted giving him such unrestricted powers of command. It was, thought Hitler, another indication that 'he had to do everything himself'.[70]

On the invasion to be expected in all probability during the subsequent months, Hitler was 'absolutely certain' of Germany's chances. He outlined the strength of forces to repel it, emphasizing especially the quality of the SS-divisions that had been sent there. He also pointed to the superiority of Germany's weaponry, especially tanks, where the new 'Panther' and 'Tiger' tanks, if not available in adequate numbers as yet, were a great improvement on the older models. (Despite ever intensifying bombing raids, the dispersal of industrial plant under Speer had managed so far to sustain production.) Even in the air, Hitler reckoned Germany would be able to hold its own. It was rare for Goebbels to offer any hint of criticism of Hitler in his diary entries. But on this occasion the optimism seemed unfounded, even to the Propaganda Minister, who noted: 'I wish these prognoses of the Führer were right. We've been so often disappointed recently that you feel some scepticism rising up within you.'[71]

Hitler also expected a great deal from the 'retaliation', which he envisaged being launched in massive style in the second half of April, and from the new fire-power and radar being built into German fighters. He thought the back of the enemy's air-raids would be broken by the following winter, after which Germany could then 'again be active in the attack on England'.[72] Hitler needed little invitation to pour out his bile on his generals. It was easier for Stalin, he commented. He had had shot the sort of generals who were causing problems in Germany. But as regards the 'Jewish question', Germany was benefiting from its radical policy: 'the Jews can do us no more harm.'[73]

Within just over two weeks of Hitler's talk with Goebbels, Hungary had been invaded – the last German invasion of the war. The genesis of the decision to occupy Hungary reached back, in fact, as far as the defeat at Stalingrad. As we saw, Hitler had been scathing in his criticism of the Hungarian (and Romanian) divisions there. The Hungarians (along with the Romanians) had, for their part, begun tacitly to put out feelers to the Allies. Learning of these, Hitler had left Horthy and Antonescu in no doubt about the consequences of any treachery. He had been satisfied with Antonescu's declarations of loyalty, but continued to harbour serious doubts about the Hungarians. Following Italy's defection in September, he had in any case had operational plans – Margarethe I and Margarethe II – drawn up for the occupation of Hungary and Romania should the need arise to nip in the bud any looming dangers. A letter from Horthy on 12 February 1944 demanding the return of nine Hungarian divisions from the eastern front, needed, so he claimed, to defend the Carpathian border against a Soviet breakthrough, had set alarm-bells ringing. The urgency was all the greater because the Red Army was indeed advancing towards the Carpathians, which Hitler did not want to see defended only by the 'unreliable' Hungarians. More than that: German intelligence had learned that the Hungarians had attempted to make diplomatic overtures both to the western Allies and to the Soviet Union.[74]

From Hitler's point of view, in full concurrence with the opinion of his military leaders, it was high time to act. The order for Margarethe I was issued on 11 March. German troops only – drawn in part from the western front – were to be used; the original plan had foreseen the deployment, in addition, of Slovakian, Romanian, and Croat units.[75] The use of troops from their disliked neighbours to install a puppet government would have done little to encourage future Hungarian loyalty to Germany. In any case, at his meeting with Hitler in Klessheim on 26–8 February (at which he had once again, without the slightest prospect of success, suggested putting out peace-feelers to the west),[76] Antonescu had refused to allow Romanian participation in the occupation of Hungary unless accompanied by the immediate return of the substantial tracts of territory which Romania had been forced to concede to Hungary in 1940. In wanting to avoid any alienation of Hungarian support after the occupation, Hitler had been unable to agree to this.[77] He did, however, eventually concede, again going against the original intention, to the suggestion of Field-Marshal von Weichs that the Hungarian military should not be disarmed as long as Horthy was prepared to go along with the invasion and prevent any resistance.[78] And, in a further attempt to avoid unnecessarily provoking resistance by the Hungarians, Horthy was to be given the opportunity to 'invite' the Germans into his country, along the tried and tested methods used in Austria and Czechoslovakia in 1938 and 1939.[79]

Thinking he was coming to discuss the issues raised in his unanswered letter to Hitler of 12 February, in particular, troop withdrawals from the eastern front, the seventy-five-year-old Hungarian head of state arrived at Klessheim, together with his foreign minister, war minister, and chief of general staff, on the morning of 18 March. He had walked into a trap.

Hitler and Horthy conducted their talks in German, without interpreters present. Paul Schmidt, Hitler's interpreter, was waiting with his colleagues outside in the hall when, suddenly, the door to the room in the palace where the talks were being held was flung open and Admiral Horthy, red in the face, rushed out, followed hurriedly by a furious Hitler, who eventually managed to catch up with his discomfited guest to accompany him to his rooms, as protocol demanded, before disappearing in a rage for urgent discussions with Ribbentrop.[80]

The meeting with the Hungarian head of state had, indeed, been tempestuous. Hitler had at the outset accused the Hungarian government, on the basis of information from the German secret service, of negotiating with the Allies in an attempt to take Hungary out of the war. Holding fast, as ever, to his notion that the Jews were behind the war, and that, consequently, the continued existence of Jews in any country provided, in effect, a fifth-column subverting and endangering the war effort, Hitler was especially aggressive in accusing Horthy of allowing almost a million Jews to exist without any hindrance, which had to be seen from the German side as a threat to the eastern and Balkan fronts. Consequently, the German leadership, continued Hitler, had justified fears of a defection taking place, similar to that which had happened in Italy. He had, therefore, decided upon the military occupation of Hungary, and demanded Horthy's agreement to this in a signed joint declaration. Horthy refused to sign. The temperature in the meeting rose. Hitler declared that if Horthy did not sign, the occupation would simply take place without his approval. Any armed resistance would be crushed by Croatian, Slovakian, and Romanian as well as German troops. Horthy threatened to resign. Hitler said that in such an event he could not guarantee the safety of the Admiral's family. At this base blackmail, Horthy sprang to his feet, protesting: 'If everything here is already decided, there's no point in staying any longer. I'm leaving immediately,' and stormed out of the room.[81]

While Horthy was demanding to be taken to his special train, and Ribbentrop was berating Döme Sztojay, the Hungarian ambassador in Berlin, an air-raid alarm sounded. In fact, the 'air-raid' was merely a ruse, complete with smoke-screen covering of the palace at Klessheim, and alleged severance of telephone links with Budapest. This elaborate deceit was used to persuade Horthy to put aside thoughts of a premature departure and compel him to enter into renewed talks with Hitler. Ribbentrop let Schmidt know, in an aside, that if Horthy did not concur with German demands, he would not be returning with an honorary escort, but as a prisoner. The browbeating and chicanery, as usual, did the trick. When Horthy returned to his train that evening, it was in the accompaniment of Security Police chief Ernst Kaltenbrunner and Ribbentrop's emissary in Hungary, Edmund Veesenmayer, endowed with plenipotentiary powers to ensure that German interests were served. And this was only once Horthy had finally agreed to install a puppet regime, with Sztojay as prime minister, ready to do German bidding.[82]

Next day, 19 March 1944, Hungary was in German hands. Not only could extra raw materials and manpower immediately be exploited for the German war effort; but, as Hitler had told Goebbels a fortnight earlier, the 'Jewish question' could now be tackled in Hungary.[83]

With the German takeover in Budapest, Hungary's large and still intact Jewish community – some 750,000 persons – was doomed. The new masters of Hungary did not lose a minute. Eichmann's men entered Budapest with the German troops. Within days, 2,000 Jews had been rounded up. The first deportation – a train with over 3,000 Jewish men, women, and children packed in indescribable conditions into about forty cattle-wagons – left for Auschwitz a month later.[84] By early June, ninety-two trains had carried almost 300,000 Hungarian Jews to their deaths.[85] When Horthy halted the deportations a month later, triggering the events that would lead to his own deposition, 437,402 Hungarian Jews had been sent to the gas-chambers.[86]

V

On the day that German troops entered Hungary, a strange little ceremony took place at the Berghof.[87] The field-marshals, who had been summoned from different parts of the front, witnessed the presentation to Hitler by their senior, Rundstedt, of a declaration of their loyalty, which they had all signed. The signatures had all been collected, on a tour of the front, by Hitler's chief Wehrmacht adjutant, General Schmundt. The idea, characteristically, had come from Goebbels (though this was kept quiet, and not made known to Hitler).[88] It had been prompted by the anti-German subversive propaganda disseminated from Moscow by the captured General Walter von Seydlitz-Kurzbach and other officers who had fallen into Soviet hands at Stalingrad.[89] In reality, the effect of the Seydlitz propaganda was minimal. But these were nervous times for the Nazi leadership. Schmundt's main intention, in any case, was to remove Hitler's distrust towards his generals, and to improve the icy relations which had been so much in evidence at the January meeting interrupted by Manstein. It was, nevertheless, both remarkable in itself and a clear sign that all was not well, if in the midst of such a titanic conflict the senior military leaders should see fit to produce a signed declaration of loyalty to their supreme commander and head of state. Manstein, the last field-marshal to sign the document, certainly thought so. He felt the declaration to be quite superfluous from a soldier's point of view.[90] Hitler seemed moved by the occasion.[91] It was a rare moment of harmony in his dealings with his generals.

Normality was, however, soon to be resumed. Within a week, Manstein was back at the Berghof. The 1st Panzer Army, under General Hans Valentin Hube, was in imminent danger of encirclement by Soviet troops who had broken through from Tarnopol to the Dniester. Manstein insisted (against Hube's recommendation that his army seek safety by retreating to the south over the Dniester) on a breakthrough to the west, in order to build a new front in Galicia. For this, reinforcements to assist the 1st Panzer Army would be necessary. For these to be provided from some other part of the front, Hitler's agreement was necessary. Sharp exchanges took place between Manstein and Hitler at the midday military conference. But Hitler refused to concede to Manstein's request, and held the field-marshal personally responsible for the unfavourable position of his Army Group. Further deliberation was adjourned until the evening. Disgusted, Manstein told Schmundt that he wished to resign his command if his orders did not gain Hitler's approval.

When discussion continued at the evening conference, however, Hitler had, astonishingly, changed his mind. Who or what had persuaded him to do so, or whether he had simply brooded on the matter before altering his decision, is unclear. At any rate, he now offered Manstein the reinforcements he wanted, including an SS Panzer Corps to be taken away from the western front.[92] Manstein went away momentarily satisfied. But Hitler resented having concessions wrung from him – particularly after his initial refusal in front of a sizeable audience. And, from Hitler's point of view, Manstein had in previous weeks been both troublesome and ineffectual in command. Hitler's way of dealing with major military setbacks was invariably (apart from his kid-glove treatment of his old political ally, Göring, as Luftwaffe chief despite the disasters in the air-war) to blame the commander and to look for a replacement who would fire the fighting morale of the troops and shore up their will to continue. It was time for a parting of the ways with Manstein, as it was with another senior field-marshal, Kleist, who, two days after Manstein, had also paid a visit to the Berghof, requesting permission for Army Group A on the Black Sea coast to pull back from the Bug to the Dniester.[93]

On 30 March, Manstein and Kleist were picked up in Hitler's Condor aircraft and taken to the Berghof. Zeitzler told Manstein that after his last visit, Göring, Himmler, and probably Keitel had agitated against him. Zeitzler had himself offered to resign, an offer that had been summarily turned down.[94] Schmundt had seen to it that the dismissals of the two field-marshals were carried out with decorum, not with rancour.[95] They were replaced by Walter Model and Ferdinand Schörner, both tough generals and favourites of Hitler, whom he regarded as ideal for rousing the morale of the troops and instilling rigorous National Socialist fighting spirit in them. At the same time, the names of the army groups were altered to Army Group North Ukraine and Army Group South Ukraine. The Ukraine had, in fact, already been lost. The symbolic renaming was part of the aim of reviving morale by implying that it would soon be retaken.

Soon enough, it would become clear yet again that changes in personnel and nomenclature would not suffice. The new commanders were no more able to stop the relentless Soviet advance than Manstein and Kleist had been. On 2 April, Hitler issued an operational order which began: 'The Russian offensive on the south of the eastern front has passed its high-point. The Russians have used up and split up their forces. The time has come to bring the Russian advance finally to a halt.'[96] It was a vain hope. A crucial component of the new lines drawn up was the provision for the Crimea, to be held at all cost. It was an impossibility. Odessa, the port on the Black Sea which was vital to supply-lines for the Crimea, had been abandoned on 10 April. By early May, the entire Crimea was lost, with Hitler forced to agree in the night of 8–9 May to the evacuation of Sevastopol by sea. The vain struggle to hold on to the Crimea had cost over 60,000 German and Romanian lives.[97] When the Soviet spring offensive came to a halt, the Germans had been pushed back in some sectors by as much as 600 miles inside a year.[98]

Hitler was furious about the collapse in the Crimea when Goebbels had the opportunity – the first for a month – of a private discussion with him in Munich on 17 April, following the funeral of Adolf Wagner, his former trusted chieftain in the 'traditional Gau' of Munich and Upper Bavaria.

Events on the eastern front had moved much faster and developed more critically than could have been expected, Hitler remarked. Looking as always for scapegoats, he directed his fury at the commander in the Crimea, General Erwin Jaenecke, whom he saw as a defeatist, for too long thinking only of retreat. He spoke of a court-martial to establish the guilt of the military leadership on the Crimea (and ordered one at Jaenecke's dismissal, following the evacuation of Sevastopol in early May).[99] Hitler told Goebbels that he had brought the eastern front under control, and that, overall, the retreat had been stopped. 'That would be marvellous,' was Goebbels's all too justified sceptical remark in his diary. Already, Hitler was thinking of a new offensive. When it would take place could not be known. But in Hitler's eyes, it would follow directly upon the repelling of the invasion in the west. Turning to the western front, Hitler was full of praise for Rommel's work in building up the Atlantic defences. The invasion would certainly come, he said, and perhaps even within the next month. But Rommel had given him a binding promise that everything would be ready by 1 May. Hitler's own, at times seemingly absurd, optimism was certainly unrealistic. But it gained constant replenishment through the over-eagerness of his generals, as well as his party bosses, to say what they knew he wanted to hear. Self-deception, as well as deception, ran through the entire regime. Hitler was certain that the invasion would be repelled in grand style, and that this would lead to a crisis in Britain. Retaliation could then be let loose on a demoralized people, unleashing a shock of earthquake proportions.[100]

Goebbels was still concerned about Hitler's health. When they had last met, just over a month earlier at the Berghof, they had been entertained by some of Eva Braun's home movies from earlier years. Viewing the amateur films, it was plain how Hitler had aged and physically deteriorated during the war.[101] Goebbels suggested to him that he might speak to the German people on 1 May. He had not been well enough to speak on 'Heroes' Memorial Day' on 12 March, when Grand-Admiral Dönitz – one of the few military leaders whom Hitler greatly respected, and evidently a coming man – substituted for him.[102] Hitler told Goebbels (who remarked on his nervous strain, particularly about Hungary, over the past weeks) that he was sleeping only about three hours a night – an exaggeration, but the long-standing problems of insomnia had certainly worsened. He did show some apparent inclination to give a radio address on 1 May, but claimed his health was not up to giving a speech in public. He did not know whether he could manage it.[103]

It was an excuse. When, following his discussion with Goebbels, he gave a fiery pep-talk, unprepared and without notes, to his Party leaders, there was no hint of concern about whether he might break down part-way through his speech (in which he declared, among other confidence-boosting claims, that the Soviet advance also had its advantages in bringing home to all nations the seriousness of the threat).[104] But when speaking to the 'Old Guard', he was in trusted company. A speech, in the circumstances, to a mass audience when he was well aware of the slump in mood of the population was a different matter altogether.[105]

Hitler's birthday that year, his fifty-fifth, had the usual trappings and ceremonials. Goebbels had Berlin emblazoned with banners and a new slogan of resounding pathos: 'Our walls broke, but our hearts didn't.' The State Opera house on Unter den Linden was festively decorated for the usual celebration, attended by dignitaries from state, party, and Wehrmacht. Goebbels portrayed Hitler's historic achievements. The Berlin Philharmonia, conducted by Hans Knappertsbusch, played Beethoven's 'Eroica' Symphony.[106] But the mood among the Nazi faithful at such events was contrived. Goebbels was well aware from reports from the regional propaganda offices that the popular mood was 'very critical and sceptical', and that 'the depression in the broad masses' had reached 'worrying levels.'[107] Away from the set-piece propaganda, enthusiasm was sparser and more muted. Bavarian reports from rural areas mentioned that little bunting was to be seen. Where loved ones had not returned from the war, this was especially noticeable.[108] For such people, Goebbels's eulogy in the Party's main newspaper, the *Völkischer Beobachter*, stating that 'the German people had never looked up to its Führer so full of belief as in the days and hours that it became aware of the entire burden of this struggle for our life' sounded particularly hollow.[109]

Even at the Berghof, the mood was only superficially festive. Before the midday military briefing Hitler received the congratulations of all members of the household, and inspected all the presents arrayed in the dining-hall. Later there was to be a display of new prototype tanks on the Salzburg motorway, near Klessheim. But as soon as Chief of Staff Zeitzler appeared, it was business as usual as Hitler disappeared for discussions on the military situation.[110] Among the guests that day was General Hube, high in Hitler's esteem, who in recognition of his success in breaking through the Soviet encirclement with his 1st Panzer Army was promoted to Colonel-General. Hitler even had him in mind as a possible new army Commander-in-Chief. Late that night, Hitler gave his permission for Hube to depart for Berlin. The plane hit a tree on take-off, a wing broke off, and Hube was killed. It was almost a double tragedy for Hitler. Walther Hewel, Ribbentrop's liaison at Führer Headquarters and well-liked at the Berghof, escaped the crash with no more than concussion and severe bruising. The loss of such an outstanding general as Hube was a blow to Hitler. He even took the risk of flying to Berlin – Goebbels thought it madness, given Allied dominance of the skies – a few days later, making a rare visit to the capital to honour Hube at an elaborate state funeral.[111]

In the interim, on 22 April, Hitler had once more entertained Mussolini to a lengthy monologue at Klessheim, aimed at stiffening his backbone. He drove home the dangers facing Germany and its allies. He did not betray a trace of defeatism. 'The Führer did not know whether or when an invasion would occur,' the record of the meeting ran, 'but the English had adopted measures which could only be maintained for 6–8 weeks and a serious crisis would break out in England if the invasion did not occur. He would then deploy new technical weapons which were effective within a radius of 250–300 kilometres and would transform London into a heap of ruins.'[112] The wishful thinking was necessary – and not just to shore up the flagging morale of the Duce.

VI

A familiar face, not seen for some months, had returned to the Berghof in mid-April. Since being admitted to the Red Cross hospital at Hohenlychen, seventy miles north of Berlin, for a knee operation (accompanied by severe nervous strain), Albert Speer had been out of circulation. Hitler had seen him briefly in March, while Speer was convalescing for a short time at Klessheim, but the armaments minister had then left for Meran, in South Tyrol, to recover in the company of his family.[113]

An absent minister was an invitation, in the Third Reich, for others thirsting for power to step into the vacuum. Karl Otto Saur, the able head of the technical office in Speer's ministry, had taken the opportunity to exploit Hitler's favour in his boss's absence. When a Fighter Staff had been set up in March – linking Speer's ministry with the Luftwaffe to speed up and coordinate production of air-defence – Hitler placed it, against Speer's express wishes, in the hands of Saur.[114] And when, stung by the near-unhampered bombing of German cities, Hitler discovered that little progress had been made on the building of huge underground bomb-proof bunkers to protect fighter production against air-raids, Speer's other right-hand man, Xaver Dorsch, head of the central office of the massive construction apparatus, the Organization Todt (OT), spotted his chance. Göring, pressed by Hitler on the non-production of the bunkers, and keen to emerge from the opprobrium of the continued failure of air-defence, summoned Dorsch in mid-April and told him that the OT would have to build the bunkers without delay. Dorsch replied that he had no authority within the Reich itself; Speer had designated the OT only for work outside the Reich borders. But he was alert enough and sufficiently briefed on the purpose and potential of the meeting to produce plans for such a project in France. Göring reported back to Hitler. That evening, Dorsch was commissioned by Hitler with the sole responsibility for the building of the six immense bunkers within the Reich itself – thereby overriding Speer – accompanied by full authority to assure the work had top priority.

Dorsch had promised Hitler the completion of the bunkers by November. Speer knew this to be impossible.[115] But this bothered him less than the undermining of his own power-base. Speer had not reached his high position without an ability to take care of his own interests in the ruthless scheming and jockeying for position that went on around Hitler. He was not prepared to accept the undermining of his own authority without a fight. On 19 April, he wrote a long letter to Hitler complaining at the decisions he had taken and demanding the restoration of his own authority over Dorsch. He let it be known that he wished to resign should Hitler not accede to his wishes. Hitler's initial anger at the letter gave way to the more pragmatic consideration that he still needed Speer's organizational talents. He passed a message to Speer, via Erhard Milch, Luftwaffe armaments supremo, that he still held him in high esteem. On 24 April, Speer appeared at the Berghof. Hitler, formally attired, gloves in hand, came out to meet him, accompanying him like some foreign dignitary into the imposing hall. Speer, his vanity touched, was immediately impressed. Hitler went on to flatter Speer. He told him that he needed him to oversee all building works. He was in agreement with whatever Speer thought right in this area. Speer was won over. That evening, he was back in the Berghof 'family', making small-talk with Eva Braun and the others in the late-night session around the fire. Bormann suggested listening to some music. Records of music by Wagner, naturally, and Johann Strauß's *Die Fledermaus* were put on. Speer felt at home again.[116]

In Speer's absence, and despite the extensive damage from air-raids, Saur had in fact masterminded a remarkable increase in fighter-production – though with a corresponding decline in output of bombers. Delighted as he was with better prospects of air-defence, Hitler's instincts lay, as always, in aggression and regaining the initiative through bombing. The new chief of the Luftwaffe operations staff, Karl Koller, was, therefore, pushing at an open door when he presented Hitler with a report, in early May, pointing out the dangerous decline in production of bombers, and what was needed to sustain German dominance. Hitler promptly told Göring that the low targets for bomber-production were unacceptable. Göring passed the message to the Fighter Staff that there was to be a trebling of bomber production – alongside the massive increase in fighters to come off the production lines. Eager to please, as always, Göring had told Hitler of rapid progress in the production of the jet, the Me262, of which the Dictator had such high hopes.[117]

The previous autumn, having as we noted removed top priority from production of the Me262 because of its heavy fuel-consumption, Hitler had changed his mind. He had been led to believe – possibly it was a misunderstanding – by the designer, Professor Willi Messerschmitt, that the jet, once in service, could be used not as a fighter, but as a bomber to attack Britain and to play a decisive role in repelling the coming invasion, wreaking havoc on the beaches as Allied troops were disembarking. Göring, at least as unrealistic as his Leader in his expectations, promised the jet-bombers would be available by May.[118] At his meeting with Speer and Milch in January, when he demanded accelerated production of the jet, Hitler had stated, to the horror of the Luftwaffe's technical staff, that he wanted to deploy it as a bomber. Arguments to the contrary were of no avail.[119]

Now, on 23 May, in a meeting at the Berghof with Göring, Saur, and Milch about aircraft production, he heard mention of the Me262 as a fighter. He interrupted. He had presumed, he stated, that it was being built as a bomber. It transpired that his instructions of the previous autumn, unrealistic as they were, had been simply ignored. Hitler exploded in fury, ordering the Me262 – despite all technical objections levelled by the experts present – to be built exclusively as a bomber. Göring lost no time in passing the brickbats down the line to the Luftwaffe construction experts. But he had to tell Hitler that the major redesign needed for the plane would now delay production for five months.[120] Whether fuel would by that time be available for it was another matter. Heavy American air-raids on fuel plants in central and eastern Germany on 12 May, to be followed by even more destructive raids at the end of the month, along with Allied attacks, carried out from bases in Italy, on the Romanian oil-refineries near Ploesti, halved German fuel production. Nimbly taking advantage of Göring's latest embarrassment, Speer had no trouble in persuading Hitler to transfer to his ministry full control over aircraft production.[121]

Three days after the wrangle about the Me262, another, larger, gathering took place on the Obersalzberg. A sizeable number of generals and other senior officers, who had been participants in ideological training courses and were ready to return to the front, had been summoned to the Berghof to hear a speech by Hitler – one of several such speeches he gave between autumn 1943 and summer 1944.[122] They assembled on 26 May in the Platterhof, the big hotel adjacent to the Berghof on the site of the far more modest Pension Moritz, where Hitler had stayed in the 1920s. Two days earlier, they had been addressed by Reichsführer-SS Himmler, who had sought to strengthen their National Socialist commitment by emphasizing how the 'Jewish Question', a matter 'decisive for the internal security of the Reich and Europe', had been 'solved without compromise, according to command and rational understanding (*verstandesmäßiger Erkenntnis*).'[123] The 'Final Solution' was being used both to harden fighting morale – and to point out to the military commanders about to head for the front that they and the leaders of the regime were all in the same boat, all complicitous in the killing of the Jews. Hitler spoke to the officers that afternoon. His purpose, like Himmler's, was to cement their identity as a group with the ideals of National Socialism that he embodied.[124] And like Himmler, he would refer in unmistakable terms to what was happening to the Jews.

After a lengthy preamble outlining, as usual, how he came to his own political convictions and leadership of party and state, Hitler expounded the virtues of intolerance, based upon his social-Darwinistic principles, emphasizing that 'the whole of life is a perpetual intolerance', that there was 'no tolerance in nature' which 'destroys (*vernichtet*) everything incapable of life'.[125] He went on to stress the leadership qualities to be found only in the Nordic race, the forging of a new classless society under National Socialism, and the glorious future that would follow final victory. A central passage in the speech touched on the 'Final Solution'. Hitler spoke of the Jews as a 'foreign body' in the German people which, though not all had understood why he had to proceed 'so brutally and ruthlessly', it had been essential to expel.[126]

He came to the key point. 'In removing the Jews,' he went on, 'I eliminated in Germany the possibility of creating some sort of revolutionary core or nucleus. You could naturally say: Yes, but could you not have done it more simply – or not more simply, since everything else would have been more complicated – but more humanely? Gentlemen,' he continued, 'we are in a life-or-death struggle. If our opponents are victorious in this struggle, the German people would be eradicated (*ausgerottet*). Bolshevism would slaughter millions and millions and millions of our intellectuals. Anyone not dying through a shot in the neck would be deported. The children of the upper classes would be taken away and eliminated. This entire bestiality has been organized by the Jews.' He spoke of 40,000 women and children being burnt to death through the incendiaries dropped on Hamburg, adding: 'Don't expect anything else from me except the ruthless upholding of the national interest in the way which, in my view, will have the greatest effect and benefit for the German nation.' At this the officers burst into loud and lasting applause.

He continued: 'Here just as generally, humanity would amount to the greatest cruelty towards one's own people. If I already incur the Jews' hatred, I at least don't want to miss the advantages of such hatred.' Shouts of 'quite right' were heard from his audience. 'The advantage,' he went on, 'is that we possess a cleanly organized entity with which no one can interfere. Look in contrast at other states. We have gained insight into a state which took the opposite route: Hungary. The entire state undermined and corroded, Jews everywhere, even in the highest places Jews and more Jews, and the entire state covered, I have to say, by a seamless web of agents and spies who have desisted from striking only because they feared that a premature strike would draw us in, though they waited for this strike. I have intervened here too, and this problem will now also be solved.' He cited once again his 'prophecy' of 1939, that in the event of another war not the German nation but Jewry itself would be 'eradicated' (*ausgerottet*). The audience vigorously applauded.[127] Continuing, he underlined 'one sole principle, the maintenance of our race'. What served this principle, he said, was right; what detracted from it, wrong.[128] He concluded, again to storms of applause, by speaking of the 'mission' of the German people in Europe. As always, he posed stark alternatives: defeat in the war would mean 'the end of our people', victory 'the beginning of our domination over Europe'.[129]

VII

Whatever nervousness was felt at the Berghof in the early days of June about an invasion which was as good as certain to take place within the near future, there were few, if any, signs of it on the surface. To Hitler's Luftwaffe adjutant, Nicolaus von Below, it seemed almost like pre-war times on the Obersalzberg. Hitler would take Below's wife on one side when she was invited to lunch and talk about the children or her parents' farm. In the afternoon, Hitler would gather up his hat, his walking-stick, and his cape, and lead the statutory walk to the Tea House for coffee and cakes. In the evenings, around the fire he would find some relaxation in the inconsequential chat of his guests or would hold forth, as ever, on usual themes – great personalities of history, the future shape of Europe, carrying out the work of Providence in combating Jews and Bolsheviks, the influence of the churches, and, of course, architectural plans, along with the usual reminiscences of earlier years.[130] Even the news, on 3–4 June, that the Allies had taken Rome, with the German troops pulling back to the Apennines, was received calmly. For all its obvious strategic importance, Italy was, for Hitler, little more than a sideshow.[131] He would have little longer to wait for the main event.

Hitler seemed calm, and looked well compared with his condition in recent months, when Goebbels accompanied him to the Tea House on the afternoon of 5 June. Earlier, he had told the Propaganda Minister that the plans for retaliation were now so advanced that he would be ready to unleash 300–400 of the new pilotless flying-bombs on London within a few days.[132] (He had, in fact, given the order for a major air-attack on London, including use of these new weapons, on 16 May.)[133] He repeated how confident he was that the invasion, when it came, would be repulsed. Rommel, he said, was equally confident.[134] The field-marshal indeed appeared to have overcome much of his initial scepticism of the previous autumn, when Hitler had made him responsible for the Atlantic defences (though Goebbels thought the report by one of his underlings, following a visit to Rommel, 'to some extent alarming').[135] On 4 June Rommel had even left for a few days' leave with his family near Ulm. Other commanding officers in the west were equally unaware of the imminence of the invasion, though reconnaissance had provided telegraph warnings that very day of things stirring on the other side of the channel. Nothing of this was reported to OKW at Berchtesgaden or, even more astonishingly, to General Friedrich Dollmann's 7th Army directly on the invasion front.[136]

On their walk to the Tea House, Goebbels spotted no signs of depression or mental tiredness in Hitler. He was still unfolding plans for a future after the war. He ruled out any arrangement with Britain. He thought the country finished, and was determined, given half an opportunity, to impart the death-blow. The English plutocracy had planned, he went on, for war against Germany since 1936. Britain and Italy would eventually be made to pay for the war. Goebbels returned from the walk with fears for the course of the war should Hitler's health not hold up. The Propaganda Minister

entrusted one wish to his diary, following discussion of a number of personnel issues (not least, his long-standing criticisms of Göring and Ribbentrop):
that the Führer 'may become harder in his material and personnel decisions
than he actually is'.[137] Among such decisions, Goebbels was still hoping that
Hitler would provide him with full powers to introduce genuine 'total war'
measures – far more radical than those adopted so far – within Germany.
For this, the Propaganda Minister would still have to wait some weeks.

That evening, Goebbels was back at the Berghof. After the meal Hitler
and his entourage viewed the latest newsreel. The discussion moved to
films and the theatre. Eva Braun joined in with pointed criticism of some
productions. 'We sit then around the hearth until two o'clock at night,'
wrote Goebbels, 'exchange reminiscences, take pleasure in the many fine
days and weeks we have had together. The Führer inquires about this and
that. All in all, the mood is like the good old times.' A thunderstorm broke
as Goebbels left the Berghof. It was four hours since the first news started
to trickle in that the invasion would begin that night. Goebbels had been
disinclined to believe the tapping into enemy communications. But coming
down the Obersalzberg to his quarters in Berchtesgaden, the news was all
too plain; 'the decisive day of the war had begun.'[138]

Hitler went to bed not long after Goebbels had left, probably around
3a.m. When Speer arrived next morning, seven hours later, Hitler had still
not been wakened with the news of the invasion. In fact, it seems that the
initial scepticism at the Supreme Command of the Wehrmacht that this
indeed was the invasion had been finally dispelled only a little while earlier,
probably between 8.15 and 9.30a.m.[139] Influenced by German intelligence
reports,[140] Hitler had spoken a good deal in previous weeks that the invasion
would begin with a decoy attack to drag German troops away from the
actual landing-place. (In fact, Allied deception through the dropping of
dummy parachutists and other diversionary tactics did contribute to initial
German confusion about the location of the landing.[141]) His adjutants now
hesitated to waken him with mistaken information. According to Speer,
Hitler – who had earlier correctly envisaged that the landing would be on
the Normandy coast – was still suspicious at the lunchtime military conference that it was a diversionary tactic put across by enemy intelligence. Only
then did he agree – Jodl had earlier been opposed[142] – to the already
belated demand of the Commander-in-Chief in the West, Field-Marshal von
Rundstedt (who had expressed uncertainty in telegrams earlier that morning
about whether the landing was merely a decoy), to deploy two panzer
divisions held in reserve in the Paris area against the beachhead that was

rapidly being established over 100 miles away.[143] The delay was crucial. Had they moved by night, the panzer divisions might have made a difference. Their movements by day were hampered by heavy Allied air-attacks, and they suffered severe losses of men and material.[144]

At the first news of the invasion, Hitler had seemed relieved – as if, thought Goebbels, a great burden had fallen from his shoulders. What he had been expecting for months was now reality. It had taken place, he said, exactly where he had predicted it.[145] The poor weather, he added, was on Germany's side.[146] He exuded confidence, declaring that it was now possible to smash the enemy. He was 'absolutely certain' that the Allied troops, for whose quality he had no high regard, would be repulsed. 'If we repel the invasion,' Goebbels noted, 'then the scene in the war will be completely transformed. The Führer reckons for certain with this. He has few worries that this couldn't succeed.' No one among the Nazi leaders congregated in Klessheim to receive the new Hungarian premier Döme Sztojay dreamt of contradicting Hitler. Göring thought the battle as good as won. Ribbentrop was, as always, 'entirely on the Führer's side. He is also more than sure, without, like the Führer, being able to give reasons in detail for it,' wryly commented Goebbels – like Jodl, one of the quiet sceptics.[147] There were good grounds for scepticism. In fact, the delay in reaction on the German side had helped to ensure that by then the battle of the beaches was already as good as lost.

The vanguard of the huge Allied armada of almost 3,000 vessels approaching the Normandy coast had disgorged the first of its American troops on to Utah Beach, on the Cotentin peninsula, at 6.30a.m., meeting no notable resistance. Landings following shortly afterwards at the British and Canadian sites – Gold, Juno, and Sword Beaches – also went better than expected. Only the second American landing at Omaha Beach, encountering a good German infantry division which happened to be in a state of readiness and behind a particularly firm stretch of fortifications, ran into serious difficulties. Troops landing on the exposed beach were simply mown down. The casualty rate was massive. The advantage, other than in sheer numbers, lay plainly with the defenders. Omaha gave a horrifying taste of what the landings could have faced elsewhere had the German defence been properly prepared and waiting. But even at Omaha, after several torrid hours of terrible blood-letting, almost 35,000 American troops were finally able to push forward and gain a foothold on French soil. By the end of the day, around 156,000 Allied troops had landed, had forged contact with the 13,000 American parachutists dropped behind the flanks of the enemy lines several hours before the landings, and been able successfully to establish beachheads – including one sizeable stretch some thirty kilometres long and ten deep.[148]

What appears at times in retrospect to have been almost an inexorable triumph of 'Operation Overlord' could have turned out quite differently. Hitler's initial optimism had not, in fact, been altogether unfounded. He had presumed the Atlantic coast better fortified than was the case. Even so, the advantage ought in the decisive early stages to have lain with the defenders of the coast – as it did at Omaha. But the dilatory action was costly in the extreme. The divisions among the German commanders and lack of agreement on tactics between Rommel (who favoured close proximity of panzer divisions to the coast in the hope of immediately crushing an invading force) and General Leo Geyr von Schweppenburg, commander of Panzer Group West (wanting to hold the armour back until it was plain where it should be concentrated), had been a significant weakness in the German planning for the invasion.[149] Allied strategic decoys, as we have noted, also played a part in the early confusion of the German commanders on the invasion night itself. Not least, massive Allied air-superiority – compared with over 10,000 Allied sorties on D-Day, the Luftwaffe could manage to put in the air only eighty fighters based in Normandy[150] – gave the invading forces a huge advantage in the cover provided during the decisive early stages. Once the Allied troops were ashore and had established their beachheads, the key question was whether they could be reinforced better and faster than the Germans. Here, the fire-power from the air came into its own. The Allied planes could at one and the same time seriously hamper the German supply-lines, and help to ensure that reinforcements kept pouring in across the Normandy beaches.[151] By 12 June, the five Allied beachheads had been consolidated into a single front, and the German defenders, if slowly, were being pushed back. Meanwhile, American troops were already striking out across the Cotentin peninsula.[152] The road to the key port of Cherbourg was opening up.

Nazi leaders, for whom early optimism about repelling the invasion had within days evaporated, retained one big hope: the long-awaited 'miracle weapons'. Not only Hitler thought these would bring a change in war-fortunes.[153] More than fifty sites had been set up on the coast in the Pas de Calais from which the V1 flying-bombs – early cruise missiles powered by jet engines and difficult to shoot down – could be fired off in the direction of London. Hitler had reckoned with the devastating effect of a mass attack on the British capital by hundreds of the new weapons being fired simultaneously. The weapon had then been delayed by a series of production problems. Now Hitler pressed for action. But the launch-sites were not ready. Eventually, on 12 June, ten flying-bombs were catapulted off their ramps. Four crashed on take-off; only five reached London, causing minimal damage.[154] In fury, Hitler wanted to cancel production. But three days later, the sensational effect of the successful launch of 244 VIs on London persuaded him to change his mind.[155] He thought the new destructive force would quickly lead to the evacuation of London and disruption of the Allied war effort.[156]

The triumphalist tones of the Wehrmacht report on the launch of the V1, and of a number of newspaper articles, were equally fanciful, filling Goebbels – still anxious to shore up a mood of hold-out-at-all-costs instead of dangerous optimism – with dismay.[157] The impression had been created, noted the Propaganda Minister with consternation, that the war would be over within days. He was anxious to stop such illusions. The euphoria could quickly turn into blaming the government. He ordered the reports to be toned down, and exaggerated expectations to be dampened – persuading Hitler that his own instructions to the press, guaranteed to foster the euphoric mood, follow the new guidelines.[158]

The continued advance of the Allies, but also what seemed the new prospects offered by the V1, prompted Hitler to fly in the evening of 16 June from Berchtesgaden together with Keitel and Jodl and the rest of his staff to the western front to discuss the situation with his regional commanders, Rundstedt and Rommel. He wanted to boost their wavering morale by underlining the strengths of the V1, while at the same time stressing the imperative need to defend the port of Cherbourg.[159] After their four Focke-Wulf Condors had landed in Metz, Hitler and his entourage drove in the early hours of the next morning in an armour-plated car to Margival, north of Soissons, where the old Führer Headquarters built in 1940 had been installed, at great expense, with new communications equipment and massively reinforced. The talks that morning took place in a nearby bomb-proof railway-tunnel.[160]

Hitler, looking pale and tired, sitting hunched on a stool, fiddled nervously with his glasses and played with coloured pencils while addressing his generals, who had to remain standing.[161] Rundstedt reported on the developments of the previous ten days, concluding that it was now impossible to expel the Allies from France.[162] Hitler bitterly laid the blame at the door of the local commanders. Rommel countered by pointing to the hopelessness of the struggle against such massive superior force of the Allies. Hitler turned to the V1 – a weapon, he said, to decide the war and make the English anxious for peace. Impressed by what they had heard, the field-marshals asked for the Vı to be used against Allied beachheads, only to be told by General Erich Heinemann, the commander responsible for the launch of the flying-bomb, that the weapon was not precise enough in its targeting to allow this. Hitler promised them, however, that they would soon have jet-fighters at their disposal to gain control of the skies. As he himself knew, however, these had, in fact, only just gone into production.[163]

After lunch (taken in a bunker because of the danger of air-attacks), Hitler spoke alone with Rommel. The discussion was heated at times. The field-marshal painted a bleak picture of the prospects. The western front could not be held for much longer, he stated, beseeching Hitler to seek a political solution. 'Pay attention to your invasion front, not to the continuation of the war,' was the blunt reply he received.[164] Hitler waited no longer, and flew back to Salzburg that afternoon. At the Berghof that evening, dissatisfied at the day's proceedings, Hitler remarked to his entourage that Rommel had lost his nerve and become a pessimist. 'Only optimists can pull anything off today,' he added.[165]

The following day, 18 June, the Americans reached the western coast of the Cotentin peninsula, effectively cutting off the peninsula and the port of Cherbourg from reinforcements for the Wehrmacht. 'They're stating quite specifically that they have got through. Are they through or not?' asked Hitler at the evening military conference. 'Yes indeed, they're through,' was Jodl's answer.[166]

Eight days later, the German garrison in Cherbourg surrendered. With this port in their possession (even if it took nearly a month to repair German destruction and make use of the harbour), and almost total control of the skies, the Allies had few further worries about their own reinforcements. Advance against tenacious defence was painfully slow. But the invasion had been a success. Any prospect of forcing the Allied troops, arriving in ever greater numbers, back into the sea had long since dissolved.[167] Hitler was furious that the Allies had gained the initiative. He was left now with little more than the hope that the Alliance would split.[168]

When Goebbels saw him for a three-hour private discussion on 21 June, he remained resistant, however, to suggestions that the time had come to take drastic steps, finally, to introduce the 'total war' that the Propaganda Minister had advocated for so long. Goebbels had used one of his best contacts at Führer Headquarters, Wehrmacht adjutant General Schmundt, to engineer his visit and prepare the ground for his proposals.[169] On arrival at the Berghof, Goebbels heard a report by Schmundt and Julius Schaub, the general factotum, of Hitler's visit to the western front, and of his decision, in the light of the situation there, to remove two panzer divisions from the east. While they talked, news came in of the heaviest daytime raids yet on Berlin – destroying many of the main representative and government buildings in the centre of the city. Göring's popularity had, unsurprisingly, sunk to an all-time low on the Obersalzberg, with Hitler raging about the Reich Marshal's incompetence. Goebbels also had a chance to speak to Speer, who told him of the precarious situation following the American raids on the fuel plants. By August, fuel for tanks and planes would be in short supply. Drastic measures were needed to contain consumption in the civilian sector. Having seen Salzburg, on his arrival there, looking as it had done in peacetime, Goebbels's instincts to press for new powers to take control over the revitalization of the 'total war' effort and the mobilization of remaining forces on the home front were sharpened still further.[170]

After lunch, sitting together in the great hall of the Berghof, with its huge window opening out to a breathtaking panorama of the Alps, Goebbels fully expounded his argument. He expressed his doubts about groundless optimism, 'not to say illusions', about the war. 'Total war' had remained a mere slogan. The crisis had to be recognized before it could be overcome. A thorough reform of the Wehrmacht was urgently necessary. Göring, he had observed (here came the usual attacks on the Reich Marshal), lived in a complete fantasy world. The Propaganda Minister extended his attack to the remainder of the top military leadership. The Führer needed a Scharnhorst and a Gneisenau – the Prussian military heroes who had created the army that repelled Napoleon – not a Keitel and a Fromm (commander of the Reserve Army), he declared. Goebbels promised that he could raise a million soldiers through a rigorous reorganization of the Wehrmacht and draconian measures in the civilian sphere. The people expected and wanted tough measures. Germany was close to being plunged into a crisis which could remove any possibility of taking such measures with any prospect of success. It was necessary to act with realism, wholly detached from any defeatism, and to act now.[171]

Characteristically, Hitler began his wordy reply with a potted history of the Wehrmacht. He accepted that there were some weaknesses in the organization of the Wehrmacht, and that few of its leaders were National Socialists. But to dispense with them during the war would be a nonsense (Unding), since there were no replacements. He defended Keitel and Fromm. The overblown organization of the Wehrmacht had been necessary for the occupation of the huge areas of the east that had been conquered. Though these had now largely been lost, a reorganization could not take place overnight. Hitler was bitter at the 'absolute failure' of the Luftwaffe, which he laid at Göring's door. His own wishes had been ignored by Luftwaffe technical experts. Reform in the Luftwaffe was needed, and had already been started. He could not rely upon his generals, who had 'swindled' him the whole time. The war had not produced a single genius among them.

Despite his criticisms, his answer could offer Goebbels little encouragement. All in all, Hitler concluded, the time was not ripe for the extraordinary measures the Propaganda Minister wanted. Despite Goebbels's pleas, he wanted to proceed for the time being with the tried and tested methods. He thought that they would come through the present crises with such methods. If more serious crises took place – among them, entry of Turkey on the Allied side, the collapse of Finland, inability (which he acknowledged as a possibility) to hold the eastern front, or failure to break the bridgeheads in the west – then he would be ready to take 'completely abnormal measures'. Goebbels summed up: 'The Führer does not regard the crisis as sufficiently serious and compelling that it could persuade him to pull out all the stops.'[172] Hitler told Goebbels that the instant he felt the need to resort to 'final measures', he would bestow the appropriate powers on the Propaganda Minister. But 'for the time being he wanted to proceed along the evolutionary, not revolutionary, way'. Goebbels went away empty-handed, leaving what he regarded as one of the most serious meetings he had had with Hitler sorely disappointed.[173]

Goebbels was evidently dubious about Hitler's continued positive gloss on military prospects. He doubted, correctly, the reassurances that it ought to be possible to hold Cherbourg until the two new divisions from the east could arrive; and Hitler's view that a massive panzer attack could then destroy the Allied bridgehead. On the 'wonder-weapons', however, the Führer's expectations seemed realistic enough to the Propaganda Minister. Hitler did not, thought the Propaganda Minister, over-estimate the impact of the V1 (short for *Vergeltungswaffe-1* – 'Retaliation Weapon 1'), as Goebbels had now dubbed the flying-bomb. But he hoped to have the A4 rocket (later renamed the V2) ready for launching by August, and looked to its destructive power to help decide the war. Hitler ruled out once again any prospect of an 'arrangement' with Britain, but was less inclined – so Goebbels inferred – to dismiss the possibility at some point of coming to terms with the Soviet Union. This could not be entertained given the present military situation, though a significant shift in fortunes in the Far East might alter the position. As Goebbels realized, however, this was entering the realm of vague musings.[174]

If Hitler had been unnerved at all by what he had heard from his commanders in the west during his short and turbulent visit a few days earlier, he had shown not the slightest trace of it during his private discussion with Goebbels. And when, the next afternoon, he again addressed his generals – adumbrating once more his belief in the survival of the fittest, emphasizing that no internal revolution was possible since the Jews were 'gone' and that he would mercilessly wipe out the slightest hint of internal subversion, stressing that to give in always meant 'destruction . . . in the long run complete destruction', that the current struggle was for Germany's very existence, and, underlining his unshaken belief that he had been called by Providence, that the dangers would be surmounted, that 'this new state will never capitulate' – he again performed to perfection the role of Führer, with no hint of weakness or doubt.[175] He could still enthuse his audience – at least momentarily.[176]

That same day, 22 June 1944, exactly three years since the beginning of Operation Barbarossa, the Red Army launched its new big offensive in the east. Hitler had predicted that Stalin would not be able to resist the appeal of launching his offensive on that day.[177] The main thrust of the massive Soviet offensive – the biggest undertaken, deploying almost 2½ million men and over 5,000 tanks, backed by 5,300 planes, and given by Stalin the code-name 'Bagration' after a military hero in the destruction of Napoleon's Grand Army in 1812 – was aimed at the Wehrmacht's Army Group Centre.[178] Based on fatally flawed intelligence relayed to Chief of Staff Zeitzler by the head of the eastern military intelligence service, Reinhard Gehlen, German preparations had, in fact, anticipated an offensive on the southern part of the front, where all the reserves and the bulk of the panzer divisions had been concentrated. Army Group Centre had been left with a meagre thirty-eight divisions, comprizing only half as many men and a fifth of the number of tanks as the Red Army had, in a section of the front stretching over some 800 miles.[179] Only belatedly, it appears, did the realization dawn, against the continued advice of Chief of the General Staff Zeitzler, that the offensive was likely to come against Army Group Centre.[180] But when Field-Marshal Ernst Busch, Commander-in-Chief of Army Group Centre, recommended shortening the front to more defensible limits, Hitler contemptuously asked whether he too was one of those generals 'who always looked to the rear'.[181]

The relatively mild beginnings of the offensive then misled Hitler's military advisers into thinking initially that it was a decoy.[182] However, the initial opening was sufficient to breach the German defences around Vitebsk.

Suddenly, the first big wave of tanks swept through the gap. Others rapidly followed. Bombing and heavy artillery attacks accompanied the assault. Busch appealed to Hitler to abandon the 'fortified places' (*Feste Plätze*) in Vitebsk, Orsha, Mogilev, and Bobruisk, which had been established in the spring in a vain attempt to create a set of key defensive strongholds – fortresses to be held come what may under the command of selected tough generals.[183]

Hitler's answer could have been taken as read. The 'fortified places' were to be held at all costs; every square metre of land was to be defended.[184] Busch, one of Hitler's fervent admirers among the generals, accepted the order without demur. He sought to carry it out unquestioningly as a demonstration of his loyalty. The consequences were predictable. The Red Army swept around the strongholds, and the German not Soviet divisions were tied down, then encircled and finally destroyed by the forces following in the wake of the advance troops.[185] The Wehrmacht divisions lost through such a disastrous tactical error would have been vital in defending other parts of the front.[186]

Within two days of the start of the offensive, the 3rd Panzer Army in Vitebsk had been cut off, followed a further two days later by the encirclement of the 9th Army near Bobruisk. By the first days of July, the 4th Army faced the same fate near Minsk. Reinforcements drawn from the southern part of the front could not prevent its destruction. By the time the offensive through the centre slowed by mid-July, the Soviet breakthrough had advanced well over 200 miles, driven a gap 100 miles wide through the front, and was within striking range of Warsaw. Army Group Centre had by then lost twenty-eight divisions with 350,000 men in a catastrophe even greater than that at Stalingrad. By this time, devastating offensives in the Baltic and in the south were gathering momentum.[187] The next months would bring even worse calamities and, together with the unstoppable advance of the Allies in the west, would usher in the final phase of the war.

VIII

Hitler's response to the military disasters of the early summer was characteristic: he blamed others, and sacked his commanders. Whatever Hitler's capabilities as a military strategist had been, they had paid dividends only while Germany held the whip-hand and lightning offensives had been possible. Once – irrevocably after the failure of 'Citadel' in summer 1943 –

a defensive strategy had become the only one available, Hitler's inadequacies as supreme German warlord were fully exposed. As the records of the military conferences with his advisers indicate, it was not that he was wholly devoid of tactical knowledge, despite his lack of formal training. Nor was it the case, as was sometimes adumbrated in post-war apologetics of German generals, that professionals who knew better were invariably forced into compliance with the lunatic orders of an amateur military bungler. As the verbatim notes of the conferences show, Hitler's tactics were frequently neither inherently absurd, nor did they usually stand in crass contradiction to the military advice he was receiving.

Even so: at points of crisis, the tensions and conflicts invariably surfaced. And by 1944, the individual military crises were accumulating into one almighty, life-or-death crisis for the regime itself. Hitler's political adroitness was by this time long gone. He dismissed out of hand all contemplation of a possible attempt to reach a political solution. Bridges had been burnt (as he had indicated on several occasions); there was no way back. And, since he refused any notion of negotiating from a position other than one of strength, from which all his earlier successes had derived, there was in any case no opportunity to seek a peace settlement. The gambling instinct which had stood Hitler in such good stead down to 1941 had long since lost its effectiveness in what had become a backs-to-the-wall struggle. But the worse the situation became, the more disastrously self-destructive became Hitler's other overriding and irrational instinct – that 'will' alone would triumph over all adversity, even grossly disparate levels of manpower and weaponry. As we have seen, he was wont, on occasion, to compare – absurdly – the adversity he had often faced in his rise to power with the current adversity in the throes of a world war. In a sense, his own invariable resort – all the more, the worse the crisis became – to a simple belief in 'triumph of the will' as the way out was indeed a replication of his attitude at critical junctures during the 'time of struggle' (such as the Party Leadership crisis of July 1921 or the crisis surrounding Gregor Strasser in December 1932). The innate self-destructive tendency which had been implicit in his all-or-nothing stance at such times now conveyed itself, catastrophically, to military leadership.

It was inevitable that seasoned military strategists and battle-hardened generals, schooled in more subtle forms of tactical command, would clash with him – often stridently – when their reading of the options available was so diametrically at variance with those of their supreme commander, and where the orders he emitted seemed to them so plainly militarily suicidal.

They were also, however, schooled in obedience to orders of a superior; and Hitler was head of state, head of the armed forces, and since 1941 – disastrously – commander-in-chief (responsible for tactical decisions) of the army. Refusal to obey was not only an act of military insubordination; it was a treasonable act of political resistance.

Few were prepared to go down that route. But loyalty even to the extent of belief in the Führer's mission was no safeguard against dismissal if near-impossible demands were not met. In accordance with his warped logic, where 'will' had not triumphed, however fraught the circumstances, Hitler blamed the weakness or inadequacy of the commander. Another commander with a superior attitude, he presumed, would bring a different result – however objectively unfavourable the actual position. The commander of Army Group Centre, Field-Marshal Busch, a Hitler loyalist, correspondingly paid the price for the 'failure' of Army Group Centre during the onset of the Soviet offensive. He was dismissed by Hitler on 28 June, and replaced by one of his favourite commanders, the tough and energetic newly-promoted Field-Marshal Walter Model (who at the same time retained his command of Army Group North Ukraine) – dubbed by some, given the frequency with which he was charged with tackling a crisis, 'Hitler's fireman'.[188]

Within days, there was a change of command, too, in the west. Reports to the Supreme Command of the Wehrmacht submitted by the Commander-in-Chief, Field-Marshal von Rundstedt, and the Commander of Panzer Group West, General Geyr von Schweppenburg, had drawn a pessimistic picture of the prospects of holding the lines against enemy inroads in France. Jodl played to Hitler's sentiments by noting that this meant the first step towards the evacuation of France. The report had followed similarly realistic assessments of the situation on the western front delivered by Rundstedt and Rommel at the Berghof two days earlier, on 29 June.[189] On 3 July, Rundstedt received a handwritten notice of his dismissal from Hitler. Officially, he had been replaced on grounds of health.[190] The sacking of Geyr and Field-Marshal Hugo Sperrle, who had been responsible for air-defences in the West, also followed. Rundstedt's replacement, Kluge, at that time high in Hitler's esteem, arrived in France, as Guderian later put it, 'still filled with the optimism that prevailed at Supreme Headquarters'.[191] He soon learnt differently.

Another military leader who fell irredeemably from grace at this time was Chief of the General Staff Kurt Zeitzler. When appointed as replacement to Halder in September 1942, Zeitzler had impressed Hitler with his drive, energy, and fighting spirit – the type of military leader he wanted. The relationship had palled visibly since the spring of 1944, when Hitler had pinned a major part of the blame for the loss of the Crimea on Zeitzler. By May, Zeitzler was indicating his wish to resign. The Chief of Staff's strong backing at the end of June for withdrawing the threatened Army Group North in the Baltic to a more defensible line, and his pessimism about the situation on the western front amounted to the last straw. Zeitzler could no longer see the rationale of Hitler's tactics; Hitler was contemptuous of what he saw as the defeatism of Zeitzler and the General Staff. At the end of his tether following furious rows with Hitler, Zeitzler simply disappeared from the Berghof on 1 July. He had suffered a nervous breakdown. Hitler never spoke to him again. He would have Zeitzler dismissed from the Wehrmacht in January 1945, refusing him the right to wear uniform. Until his replacement, Guderian, was appointed on 21 July, the army was effectively without a Chief of the General Staff.[192]

The Soviet advance had left the Red Army, in the northern sector of the front, poised not far from Vilna in Lithuania. Already, the borders of East Prussia were in their sights. On 9 July, Hitler flew with Keitel, Dönitz, Himmler, and Luftwaffe Chief of Staff General Günther Korten back to his old headquarters near Rastenburg in East Prussia. Field-Marshal Model and General Johannes Frießner, recently appointed as commander of Army Group North in place of General Georg Lindemann, joined them from the eastern front. The discussions ranged mainly over plans for the urgent creation of a number of new divisions to shore up the eastern front and protect any inroads into East Prussia. Model and Frießner sounded optimistic. Hitler, too, thought his Luftwaffe adjutant, Below, also remained positive about developments on the eastern front. Hitler flew back to the Berghof that afternoon.[193] He had already hinted that, in the light of the situation in the east, he would have to move his headquarters back to East Prussia, even though the fortifications of his accommodation there were still incomplete. Reading between the lines of one or two comments, Below gained the impression, he later wrote, that during what were to prove Hitler's last days at the Berghof, before he left on 14 July for the Wolf's Lair, never to return, he was no longer under any illusions about the outcome of the war. Even so, any hints of pessimism were more than countered by repeated stress on continuing the war, the impact of the new weapons, and ultimate victory. Once more, it was plain to Below that Hitler would never capitulate.[194] There would be no repeat of 1918. Hitler's political 'mission' had been based from the outset on that premise. The entire Reich would go down in flames first.

Hitler had lived amid the relative tranquillity of the Obersalzberg for almost four months. The regular entourage at the Berghof had dwindled somewhat in that time. And in the days before departure there had been few guests to enliven proceedings. Hitler himself had seemingly become more reserved. On the last evening, perhaps sensing he would not see the Berghof again, he had paused in front of the pictures hanging in the great hall. Then he had kissed the hand of Below's wife and Frau Brandt, the wife of one of his doctors, bidding them farewell.[195] Next morning, 14 July, he flew back to East Prussia, returning to a Wolf's Lair now heavily reinforced and scarcely recognizable from its appearance when first set up in 1941. He arrived in the late morning. At one o'clock he was running the military conference there as if he had never been away. He was more stooping in his gait than earlier. But his continued strength of will, despite the massive setbacks, continued to impress the admiring Below.[196] For others, this strength of will – or obstinate refusal to face reality – was precisely what was preventing an end to the war and dragging Germany to inevitable catastrophe. They were determined to act before it was too late – to save what was left of the Reich, lay the foundations of a future without Hitler, and show the outside world that there was 'another Germany' beyond the forces of Nazism.

Among the conferences held during the last days at the Berghof were two, on 6 and 11 July, related to the mobilization of the 'home army' (*Heimatheer*). They were attended by a young officer with a patch over one eye, a shortened right arm, and two fingers missing from his left hand – all the consequence of serious injuries suffered during the African campaign.[197] The officer, Colonel Claus Schenk Graf von Stauffenberg, chief of staff since 1 July of Colonel-General Friedrich Fromm, Commander-in-Chief of the reserve army, was present, a day after Hitler's arrival at the Wolf's Lair, at a further conference about strengthening the home army.[198]

The question of creating new divisions from the home army was once more on the agenda for the military conference on 20 July. Again, Stauffenberg was ordered to be present.

This time, he planted a time-bomb, carried in his briefcase, under the oaken table in the centre of the wooden barracks where Hitler was holding the conference. Hitler began the briefing, half an hour earlier than usual, at 12.30p.m. Fifteen minutes later the bomb exploded.[199]

14

LUCK OF THE DEVIL

'It's not a matter any more of the practical aim, but of showing the world and history that the German resistance movement at risk of life has dared the decisive stroke. Everything else is a matter of indifference alongside that.'

Major-General Henning von Tresckow, June 1944

'It is now time that something was done. But the man who has the courage to do something must do it in the knowledge that he will go down in German history as a traitor. If he does not do it, however, he will be a traitor to his own conscience.'

Colonel Claus Schenk Graf von Stauffenberg, July 1944

'A tiny clique of ambitious, unconscionable, and at the same time criminal, stupid officers has forged a plot to eliminate me and at the same time to eradicate with me the staff practically of the German armed forces' leadership.'

Hitler, 21 July 1944

Stauffenberg's attempt to kill Hitler on 20 July 1944 had a lengthy prehistory.[1] The complex strands of this prehistory contained in no small measure profound manifestations and admixtures of high ethical values and a transcendental sense of moral duty, codes of honour, political idealism, religious convictions, personal courage, remarkable selflessness, deep humanity, and a love of country that was light-years removed from Nazi chauvinism. The pre-history was also replete – how could it have been otherwise in the circumstances? – with disagreements, doubts, mistakes, miscalculations, moral dilemmas, short-sightedness, hesitancy, ideological splits, personal clashes, bungling organization, distrust – and sheer bad luck.

The origins of a *coup d'état* to eliminate Hitler dated back, as we saw in earlier chapters, to the Sudeten crisis of 1938. Hitler's determination to risk war with the western powers and court disaster for Germany had at that time prompted a number of highly-placed figures in the Army High Command, diplomatic service, and the Abwehr, together with a circle of their close contacts, to plot to remove him should he attack Czechoslovakia. Though fraught with difficulties, the conspiracy had, in fact, taken shape by the time that Chamberlain's readiness to come to terms with Hitler at Bad Godesberg, then at Munich, removed the opportunity and took the wind out of the sails of the plotters. Their planned action might, in any case, have failed to materialize. The following summer, as the threat of war loomed ever larger, the same band of individuals had attempted to revive the conspiracy that had faltered with the Munich Agreement. But the fainter flickerings of opposition a year after Munich had come to nothing – floundering on internal divisions, Hitler's continued popularity among the masses, and, not least, the loyalty (if at times appearing to waver – reluctant, but ultimately and decisively intact) of the army chiefs whose support for any coup was vital. The same ingredients would hamper the conspiracy against Hitler in immensely more difficult conditions during the war itself.

The Swabian joiner Georg Elser had, working alone, shared none of the hesitancy of those operating from within the power-echelons of the regime. He had acted incisively, as we saw earlier, in the Bürgerbräukeller on the night of 8 November 1939, and come within a whisker of sending Hitler into oblivion. Good fortune alone had saved Hitler on that occasion. But outside the actions of a lone assassin, with the left-wing underground resistance groups, though never eliminated, weak, isolated, and devoid of access to the corridors of power, the only hope of toppling Hitler thereafter lay with those who themselves occupied positions of some power or influence in the regime itself.

On the fringes of the conspiracy, the participation in Nazi rule in itself naturally created ambivalence. Breaking oaths of loyalty was no light matter, even for some whose dislike of Hitler was evident. Prussian values were here a double-edged sword: a deep sense of obedience to authority and service to the state clashed with equally profound feelings of duty to God and to country.[2] Whichever triumphed within an individual: whether heavy-hearted acceptance of service to a head of state regarded as legitimately constituted, however detested; or rejection of such allegiance in the interest of what was taken to be the greater good, should the head of state be leading the country to ruin; this was a matter for conscience and judgement.[3] It could, and did, go either way.

Though there were numerous exceptions to a broad generalization, generational differences played some part. The tendency was greater in a younger generation of officers, for example, than in those who had already attained the highest ranks of general or field-marshal, to entertain thoughts of active participation in an attempt to overthrow the head of state. This was implied in a remark by Stauffenberg himself, several months before his attempt on Hitler's life: 'Since the generals have up to now managed nothing, the colonels have now to step in.'[4] On the other hand, views on the morality of assassinating the head of state – in the midst of an external struggle of titanic proportions against an enemy whose victory threatened the very existence of a German state – differed fundamentally on moral, not simply generational, grounds. Any attack on the head of state contituted, of course, high treason. But in a war, distinguishing this from treachery against one's own country, from betrayal to the enemy, was chiefly a matter of individual persuasion and the relative weighting of moral values. And only a very few were in a position to accumulate detailed and first-hand experiences of gross inhumanity at the same time as possessing the means to bring about Hitler's removal. Even fewer were prepared to act.

Beyond ethical considerations, there was the existential fear of the awesome consequences – for the families as well as for the individuals themselves – of discovery of any complicity in a plot to remove the head of state and instigate a *coup d'état*. This was certainly enough to deter many who were sympathetic to the aims of the plotters but unwilling to become involved. Nor was it just the constant dangers of discovery and physical risks that acted as a deterrent. There was also the isolation of resistance. To enter into, even to flirt with, the conspiracy against Hitler meant acknowledging an inner distance from friends, colleagues, comrades, entry into a twilight world of immense peril, and of social, ideological, even moral isolation.

Quite apart from the evident necessity, in a terroristic police state, of minimizing risks through maximum secrecy, the conspirators were themselves well aware of their lack of popular support.[5] Even at this juncture, as the military disasters mounted and ultimate catastrophe beckoned, the fanatical backing for Hitler had by no means evaporated and continued, if as a minority taste, to show remarkable resilience and strength. Those still bound up with the dying regime, those who had invested in it, had committed themselves to it, had burnt their boats with it, were still true believers in the Führer, were likely to stop at nothing, as adversity mounted, in their unbridled retribution for any sign of opposition. But beyond the fanatics, there were many others who – naïvely, or after deep reflection – thought it not merely wrong, but despicable and treacherous, to undermine one's own country in war. Stauffenberg summed up the conspirators' dilemma a few days before he laid the bomb in the Wolf's Lair: 'It is now time that something was done. But the man who has the courage to do something must do it in the knowledge that he will go down in German history as a traitor. If he does not do it, however, he will be a traitor to his own conscience.'[6]

As this implies, the need to avoid a stab-in-the-back legend such as that which had followed the end of the First World War and left such a baleful legacy for the ill-fated Weimar Republic was a constant burden and anxiety for those who had decided – sometimes with a heavy heart – that Germany's future rested on their capacity to remove Hitler, violently or not, from the scene, constitute a new government, and seek peace terms. This was one important reason why, from 1938 onwards, the leading figures in the resistance fatefully awaited the 'right moment' – which never came. Fearful of cutting down a national hero who had just won scarcely imaginable triumphs (which, in some cases, they themselves had cheered, and were captivated by) they felt incapacitated as long as Hitler was chalking up one apparent success after another before the war, then in the wave of Blitzkrieg victories. But, also worried about the consequences of removing Hitler and seeming to stab the war effort in the back after a major disaster, the hesitancy continued when final victory had become no more than a chimera. Rather than controlling the moment for a strike, the conspirators let it rest on external contingencies that, in the nature of things, they could not orchestrate.

When the strike eventually came, with the invasion consolidated in the west and the Red Army pressing towards the borders of the Reich in the east, the conspirators themselves recognized that they had missed the chance to influence the possible outcome of the war through their action. As one of their key driving-forces, Major-General Henning von Tresckow, from late 1943 chief of staff of the 2nd Army in the southern section of the eastern front, put it: 'It's not a matter any more of the practical aim, but of showing the world and history that the German resistance movement at risk of life has dared the decisive stroke (*Wurf*). Everything else is a matter of indifference alongside that.'[7]

I

All prospects of opposition to Hitler had been dimmed following the astonishing chain of military successes between autumn 1939 and spring 1941. Then, following the promulgation of the notorious Commissar Law, ordering the liquidation of captured Red Army political commissars, it had been Colonel (as he was at the time) Henning von Tresckow, Field-Marshal von Bock's first staff officer at Army Group Centre, who had been instrumental in revitalizing thoughts of resistance among a number of front officers – some of them purposely selected on account of their anti-regime stance. Born in 1901, tall, balding, with a serious demeanour, a professional soldier, fervent upholder of Prussian values, cool and reserved but at the same time a striking and forceful personality, disarmingly modest, but with iron determination, Tresckow had been an early admirer of Hitler though had soon turned into an unbending critic of the lawless and inhumane policies of the regime.[8] Those whom Tresckow was able to bring to Army Group Centre included close allies in the emerging conspiracy against Hitler, notably Fabian von Schlabrendorff − six years younger than Tresckow himself, trained in law, who would serve as a liaison between Army Group Centre and other focal points of the conspiracy − and Rudolph-Christoph Freiherr von Gersdorff, born in 1905, a professional soldier, already an arch-critic of Hitler, and now located in a key position in the intelligence section of Army Group Centre.[9] But attempts to persuade Bock, together with the other two group commanders on the eastern front, Rundstedt and Leeb, to confront Hitler and refuse orders failed.[10] Any realistic prospect of opposition from the front disappeared again until late 1942. By then, in the wake of the unfolding Stalingrad crisis and seeing Hitler as responsible for the certain ruin of Germany, Tresckow was ready to assassinate him.[11]

During the course of 1942, a number of focal points of practically dormant opposition within Germany itself − army and civilian − had begun to flicker back to life. The savagery of the warfare on the eastern front and, in the light of the winter crisis of 1941−2, the magnitude of the calamity towards which Hitler was steering Germany, had revitalized the notions, still less than concrete, that something must be done. Beck, Goerdeler, Popitz, and Hassell − all connected with the pre-war conspiracy − met up again in Berlin in March 1942, but decided there were as yet few prospects. Even so, it was agreed that former Chief of Staff Beck would serve as a central point for the embryonic opposition. Meetings were held soon after with Colonel Hans Oster − head of the central office dealing with foreign intelligence in the Abwehr, the driving-force behind the 1938 conspiracy, who had leaked Germany's invasion plans to Holland in 1940 − and Hans von Dohnanyi, a jurist who had also played a significant part in the 1938 plot, and, like Oster, used his position in the foreign section of the Abwehr to develop good contacts to officers with oppositional tendencies.[12] Around the same time, Oster engineered a close link to a new and important recruit to the oppo-sitional groups, General Friedrich Olbricht, head of the General Army Office in Berlin and Fromm's deputy as commander of the home army. Olbricht, born in 1888 and a career soldier, was not one to seek the limelight. He epitomized the desk-general, the organizer, the military administrator. But he was unusual in his pro-Weimar attitude before 1933, and, thereafter − driven largely by Christian and patriotic feelings − in his consistent anti-Hitler stance, even amid the jubilation of the foreign-policy triumphs of the 1930s and the victories of the first phase of the war. His role would emerge as the planner of the *coup d'état* that was to follow upon the successful assassination of Hitler.[13]

Already as the Stalingrad crisis deepened towards the end of 1942,

Tresckow – later described by the Gestapo as 'without doubt one of the driving-forces and the "evil spirit" of the putschist circles', and allegedly referred to by Stauffenberg as his 'guiding master' (*Lehrmeister*) – was pressing for the assassination of Hitler without delay.[14] He had become convinced that nothing could be expected of the top military leadership in initiating a coup. 'They would only follow an order,' was his view.[15] He took it upon himself to provide the 'ignition (*Initialzündung*)', as the conspirators labelled the assassination of Hitler that would lead to their removal of the Nazi leadership and takeover of the state.[16] Tresckow had already in the summer of 1942 commissioned Gersdorff with the task of obtaining suitable explosives. The latter acquired and tested various devices, including British explosives intended for sabotage and for the French Resistance that had been captured following an ill-fated commando expedition to St Nazaire and Dieppe in 1942. Eventually, he and Tresckow settled on a small British magnetic device, a 'clam' (or type of adhesive mine) about the size of a book, ideal for sabotage and easy to conceal.[17] Olbricht, meanwhile, coordinated the links with the other conspirators in Berlin and laid the groundwork for a coup to take place in March. The plans to occupy important civilian and military positions in Berlin and other major cities were, in essence, along the lines that were to be followed in July 1944.[18]

One obvious problem was how to get close enough to Hitler to carry out an assassination. Hitler's movements were unpredictable. As we have had cause to note, he frequently – not just for security reasons – altered his plans at the last minute. Such an undependable schedule had in mid-February 1943 vitiated the intention of two officers, General Hubert Lanz and Major-General Hans Speidel, of arresting Hitler on an expected visit to Army Group B headquarters at Poltawa. The visit did not materialize. When Hitler suddenly decided to visit the front, on 17 February, it had been to Zaporozhye not Poltawa (which Army Group B had in any case by then left).[19] Hitler's personal security had, meanwhile, been tightened considerably.[20] He was invariably surrounded by SS bodyguards, pistols at the ready, and was always driven by his own chauffeur, Erich Kempka, in one of his own limousines which were stationed at different points in the Reich and in the occupied territories.[21] And Schmundt, Hitler's Wehrmacht adjutant, had told Tresckow and Gersdorff that Hitler wore a bullet-proof vest and hat. This helped persuade them that the possibilities of a selected assassin having time to pull out his pistol, aim accurately, and ensure that his shot would kill Hitler were not great. Nor was the chosen sharp-shooter, bearer of the Iron Cross with Oak Leaves Lieutenant-Colonel Georg Freiherr von

Boeselager, sure that he was mentally equipped to shoot down a person – even Hitler – in cold blood. It was an entirely different proposition, he felt, from firing at an anonymous enemy in war.[22]

Nevertheless, Boeselager made preparations for a group of officers, who had declared themselves ready to do so, to shoot Hitler on a visit which, it was hoped, he would soon pay to Army Group Centre headquarters at Smolensk. The visit eventually took place on 13 March. The plan to shoot him in the mess of Field-Marshal von Kluge, commander of Army Group Centre, was abandoned since there was a distinct possibility of Kluge and other senior officers being killed alongside Hitler. Given Kluge's wavering and two-faced attitude towards the conspiracy against Hitler, more cynical plotters might have thought the risk well worthwhile. As it was, they took the view that the loss of Kluge and other leading personnel from Army Group Centre would seriously weaken still further the shaky eastern front. The idea shifted to shooting Hitler as he walked the short distance back to his car from headquarters. But having infiltrated the security cordon around him and set up position to open fire, the assassination squad failed to carry out their plan. Whether this was because Hitler took a different route back to his car, or whether – the more likely explanation – the danger of killing Kluge and other officers from the Group was seen as too great, is unclear.[23]

Tresckow reverted to the original plan to blow up Hitler. During the meal at which, had the original plans been carried out, Hitler would have been shot, Tresckow asked one of the Führer's entourage, Lieutenant-Colonel Heinz Brandt, travelling in Hitler's plane, to take back a package for him to Colonel Hellmuth Stieff in Army High Command. This was in itself nothing unusual. Packages were often sent to and from the front by personal delivery when transport happened to be available. Tresckow said it was part of a bet with Stieff. The package looked like two bottles of cognac. It was, in fact, two parts of the British clam-bomb that Tresckow had put together.

Schlabrendorff carried the package to the aerodrome and gave it to Brandt just as he was climbing into Hitler's Condor ready for take-off. Moments before, Schlabrendorff had pressed the fuse capsule to activate the detonator, set for thirty minutes. It could be expected that Hitler would be blown from the skies shortly before the plane reached Minsk. Schlabrendorff returned as quickly as possible to headquarters and informed the Berlin opposition in the Abwehr that the 'ignition' for the coup had been undertaken. But no news came of an explosion. The tension among Tresckow's group was

palpable. Hours later, they heard that Hitler had landed safely at Rastenburg. Schlabrendorff gave the code-word through to Berlin that the attempt
had failed. Why there had been no explosion was a mystery. Probably the
intense cold had prevented the detonation. For the nervous conspirators,
ruminations about the likely cause of failure now took second place to the
vital need to recover the incriminating package. Tresckow rang up Brandt
to say a mistake had occurred, and he should hold on to the package. Next
morning, Schlabrendorff flew to Army High Command with two genuine
bottles of cognac, retrieved the bomb, retreated to privacy, cautiously
opened the packet with a razor-blade, and with great relief defused it. Mixed
with relief, the disappointment among the opposition at such a lost chance
was intense.[24]

Immediately, however, another opportunity beckoned. Gersdorff had the
possibility of attending the 'Heroes' Memorial Day', to take place on 21
March 1943 in Berlin. Gersdorff declared himself ready to sacrifice his own
life in order to blow up Hitler during the ceremony. Tresckow, for his part,
assured Gersdorff that the coup to follow Hitler's assassination would lead
to an agreement with the western powers for capitulation while continuing
the defence of the Reich in the east and introducing a democratic form of
government. With some difficulty, problems of ensuring that Gersdorff
would be close enough to Hitler to bring off the assassination, and problems
of establishing precisely what time the ceremonials would begin – given
security precautions, betrayal of this fact was in itself dubbed sufficient to
warrant the death penalty – were overcome. The timing of the attempt was
a third problem. The best fuse that Gersdorff could come up with lasted ten
minutes. The ceremony itself, in the glass-covered courtyard of the
Zeughaus, the old arsenal, on Unter den Linden, the beautiful tree-lined
boulevard running through the centre of Berlin, presented no possibility of
detonating an explosion in his close proximity. And once Hitler was outside,
inspecting the guard of honour at the war memorial on Unter den Linden,
laying the wreath, speaking to selected wounded soldiers, or conversing
with guests of honour, Gersdorff would have no cause to be near him. His
chance would have gone.

The attempt had to be made, therefore, while Hitler was visiting the
exhibition of captured Soviet war-booty, laid on to fill in the time between
the ceremony in the Zeughaus and the wreath-laying at the cenotaph.
Gersdorff positioned himself at the entry to the exhibition, in the rooms of
the Zeughaus. He raised his right arm to greet Hitler as the dictator came
by. At the same moment, with his left hand, he pressed the detonator charge

on the bomb. He expected Hitler to be in the exhibition for half an hour, more than enough time for the bomb to go off. But this year, Hitler raced through the exhibition, scarcely glancing at the material assembled for him, and was outside within two minutes. Gersdorff could follow Hitler no further. He sought out the nearest toilet and deftly defused the bomb.[25]

Once again, astonishing luck had accompanied Hitler. Whether it was concern about the possibility of an allied air-raid, which, as we saw in an earlier chapter, had been anticipated; whether Hitler's security advisers had given a hint of concern for his safety at a public appearance, given the uneasy atmosphere after Stalingrad, when, following the 'White Rose' protests of the Munich students Hans and Sophie Scholl and their friends, rumours of an attempt to overthrow the regime were circulating; or whether Hitler himself, ill-attuned to having to give a public performance in sensitive circumstances while the country was reeling from such a military disaster, had scant feeling for the ceremonials and simply wanted to get them over with: whatever the reason, yet another attempt, conscientiously planned despite the difficulties, and undertaken at notable risk, had failed. A new opportunity would not rapidly present itself.

The depressed and shocked mood following Stalingrad had probably also offered the best possible psychological moment for a coup against Hitler. A successful undertaking at that time might, despite the recently announced 'Unconditional Surrender' strategy of the Allies, have stood a chance of splitting them. The removal of the Nazi leadership and offer of capitulation in the west that Tresckow intended would at any rate have placed the western Allies in a quandary about whether to respond to peace-feelers.

Overtures by opposition groups to the western Allies had been systematically rebuffed long before this time. For example, for his pains in liaising with German churchmen belonging to the resistance who wanted to sound out the British government about their attitude towards a Germany without Hitler, Bishop George Bell of Chichester was described by Anthony Eden, the British Foreign Secretary, in words redolent of those once allegedly used by King Henry II to usher in the murder of Archbishop Thomas Becket in 1170, as a 'pestilent priest'.[26] Despite long-standing contacts with leading figures in the conspiracy – including Carl Goerdeler, Adam von Trott, and the radically-minded evangelical pastor Dietrich Bonhoeffer (who had spent some time in ministry at the German church in south London) – the resistance was regarded by the British war-leadership (and the Americans shared the view) as little more than a hindrance. A successful coup from within could, it was felt, endanger the alliance with the Soviet Union –

exactly the strategy which the conspirators were hoping to achieve – and would cause difficulties in establishing the post-war order in Germany. The key criterion was how far action by those within Germany who opposed Hitler would contribute to the Allied war effort. A British government internal memorandum written little over a month before Stauffenberg's bomb went off in Hitler's headquarters gave a clear answer: 'There is no initiative we can take vis-à-vis "dissident" German groups or individuals, military or civilian, which holds out the smallest prospect of affording practical assistance to our present military operations in the West.'[27]

Though prepared to distinguish between the Nazi leadership and the German people, Allied thinking was less ready to separate Hitler and his henchmen from his military leaders and from the Prussian traditions which, it was thought, had been a major cause of two world wars. Now, with the war turning remorselessly in their favour, the Allies were less than ever inclined to give much truck to an internal opposition which, it appeared, had claimed much but achieved nothing, and, furthermore, entertained expectations of holding on to some of the territorial gains that Hitler had made.[28]

This was indeed the case, certainly with some of the older members of the national-conservative group aligned to former Reich Price Commissar Carl Goerdeler whose break with Hitler had, as we have seen, already taken place in the mid-1930s. Goerdeler and those loosely aligned to him – notably former Chief of Staff Ludwig Beck, one-time German Ambassador in Rome Ulrich von Hassell, Prussian finance minister Johannes Popitz, and ex-Nazi enthusiast and Berlin professor of politics and economics (*Staat- und Wirtschaftswissenschaften*) Jens Jessen – despised the barbarism of the Nazi regime.[29] But they were keen to re-establish Germany's status as a major power, and continued to see the Reich dominating central and eastern Europe. Goerdeler, presumed to be the new Reich Chancellor in a post-Hitlerian government, had envisaged in early 1942 'a European federation of states under German leadership within 10 or 20 years' if the war could be ended and a 'sensible political system' put in place.[30] In summer 1943, despite the drastic deterioration of Germany's military situation, Goerdeler's incorrigible optimism still led him to put forward as his foreign-political aims: the restoration of the eastern borders of 1914 (meaning, of course, keeping the Polish Corridor, reacquired by Germany through such immeasurable barbarism); retention of Austria and the Sudetenland, along with Eupen-Malmedy and the South Tyrol (which even Hitler had not annexed); negotations with France over Alsace-Lorraine; undiminished German sovereignty; no reparations; and economic union in Europe (outside Russia).[31]

As regards the nature of a post-Nazi regime, the notions of the national conservatives, disdaining the plebiscitary and demagogic characteristics of what they saw as populist mass politics, were essentially (despite differences of emphasis) oligarchic and authoritarian. They favoured a restoration of the monarchy and limited electoral rights in self-governing communities, resting on Christian family values – the embodiment of the true 'national community' which the Nazis had corrupted.[32]

Among the most striking features of Goerdeler's lack of realism was his conviction, when it was put to him that Hitler would have to be forcefully removed from the scene, that he could be persuaded by reasoned argument to step down.[33] His expectation of an unbloody coup even led him to the idea of suggesting that he could eliminate Hitler through open debate if the military could provide him with the opportunity to address the Wehrmacht and the people.[34] It was as well that the letter, composed in May 1944, containing such a remarkable suggestion was sent back by Stieff and never passed to Chief of Staff Zeitzler.[35]

The notions of Goerdeler and his close associates, whose age, mentality, and upbringing inclined them to look back to the pre-1914 Reich for much of their inspiration, found little favour among a group of a younger generation (mainly born during the first decade of the twentieth century) which gained its common identity through outright opposition to Hitler and his regime. The group, whose leaders were mainly of aristocratic descent, came to be known as 'the Kreisau Circle', a term coined by the Gestapo and drawn from the estate in Silesia where the group held a number of its meetings. The estate belonged to one of its central figures, Helmuth James Graf von Moltke, born in 1907, trained in law, a great admirer of British traditions, a descendant of the famous Chief of the General Staff of the Prussian army in Bismarck's era.[36] The ideas of the 'Kreisau Circle' for a 'new order' after Hitler dated back in embryo to 1940, when they were first elaborated by Moltke and his close friend and relative Peter Graf Yorck von Wartenburg, three years older, also trained in law, a formative figure in the group, and with good contacts to the military opposition. Both had rejected Nazism and its gross inhumanity from an early stage. By 1942–3 they were drawing to meetings at Kreisau and in Berlin a number of like-minded friends and associates, ranging across social classes and denominational divisions, including the former Oxford Rhodes Scholar and foreign-policy spokesman of the group Adam von Trott zu Solz, the Social Democrat

Carlo Mierendorff, the socialist pedagogical expert Adolf Reichwein, the Jesuit priest Pater Alfred Delp, and the Protestant pastor Eugen Gerstenmaier.

Unlike the Goerdeler group, the Kreisau Circle drew heavily for its inspiration on the idealism of the German youth movement, socialist and Christian philosophies, and experiences of the post-war misery and rise of National Socialism. Moltke, Yorck, and their associates – unlike the Goerdeler group – had no desire to hold on to expectations of German hegemony on the continent. They looked instead to a future in which national sovereignty (and the nationalist ideologies which underpinned it) would give way to a federal Europe, modelled in part on the United States of America. They were well aware that major territorial concessions would have to be made by Germany, along with some form of reparation for the peoples of Europe who had suffered so grievously under Nazi rule. They saw an international tribunal to deal with war criminals as a basis for weaning the German people from its attachment to National Socialism. And they looked to a strong international organization to preserve equal rights for all countries of the world. Their concept of a new form of state rested heavily upon German Christian and social ideals, looking to democratization from below, through self-governing communities working on the basis of social justice, guaranteed by a central state that was little more than an umbrella organization for localized and particularized interests within a federal structure.[37]

Such notions were inevitably utopian. The 'Kreisau Circle' had no arms to back it, and no access to Hitler. It was dependent upon the army for action. Moltke, who opposed assassination, and Yorck, quite especially, pressed on a number of occasions for a coup to unseat Hitler. By 1943, Moltke's distrust of the German military leadership on account of its complicity in so much of the Nazi barbarism led him to advocate American military support for a new oppositional German government. Allied troops were to be parachuted into German cities to back a coup.[38]

Such an illusory hope still left out of the equation the initial step: how to remove Hitler, and who should do it. This, rather than utopian visions of a future social and political order, was the primary issue that continued to preoccupy Tresckow and his fellow officers who had committed themselves to the opposition. The problem became, if anything, more rather than less difficult during the summer and autumn of 1943. Any expectation that Manstein might commit himself to the opposition was wholly dashed in the summer. 'Prussian field-marshals do not mutiny,' was his lapidary response to Gersdorff's probings.[39] Manstein was at least honest and straightforward.

Kluge, by contrast, blew hot and cold – offering backing to Tresckow and Gersdorff, then retreating from it.[40] There was nothing to be gained from that quarter, though those in the opposition continued to persist in the delusion that Kluge was ultimately on their side.

There were other setbacks. Beck was meanwhile quite seriously ill. And Fritz-Dietlof Graf von der Schulenburg – a lawyer by training, who after initially sympathizing with National Socialism and holding a number of high administrative positions in the regime, had come to serve as a liaison between the military and civilian opposition – was interrogated on suspicion that he was involved in plans for a coup, though later released.[41] Others, including Dietrich Bonhoeffer, were also arrested, as the tentacles of the Gestapo threatened to entangle the leading figures in the resistance. Even worse: Hans von Dohnanyi and Hans Oster from the Abwehr were arrested in April, initially for alleged foreign currency irregularities, though this drew suspicion on their involvement in political opposition. The head of the Abwehr, Admiral Canaris, a professional obfuscater, managed for a time to throw sand in the eyes of the Gestapo agents. But as a centre of the resistance, the Abwehr had become untenable. By February 1944, its foreign department, which Oster had controlled, was incorporated into the Reich Security Head Office, and Canaris, dubious figure that he was for the opposition, himself placed under house arrest.[42]

Tresckow, partly while on leave in Berlin, was tireless in attempting to drive on the plans for action against Hitler. But in October, he was stationed at the head of a regiment at the front, away from his previously influential position in Army Group Centre headquarters. At the same time, in any case, Kluge was injured in a car accident and replaced by Field-Marshal Ernst Busch, an outright Hitler-loyalist, so that an assassination attempt from Army Group Centre could now be ruled out.[43] At this point, Olbricht revived notions, previously entertained but never sustained, of carrying out both the strike against Hitler and the subsequent coup, not through the front army, but from the headquarters of the reserve army in Berlin.[44] Finding an assassin with access to Hitler had been a major problem. Now, one was close at hand.

Claus Schenk Graf von Stauffenberg came from a Swabian aristocratic family. Born in 1907, the youngest of three brothers, he grew up under the influence of Catholicism – though his family were non-practising – and of the youth movement. He became particularly attracted to the ideas of the poet Stefan George, then held in extraordinary esteem by an impressionable circle of young admirers, strangely captivated by his vague, neo-conservative cultural mysticism which looked away from the sterilities of bourgeois existence towards a new élite of aristocratic aestheticism, godliness, and manliness.[45] Like many young officers, Stauffenberg was initially attracted by aspects of National Socialism – not least its renewed emphasis on the value of strong armed forces and its anti-Versailles foreign policy – but rejected its racial antisemitism and, after the Blomberg–Fritsch crisis of early 1938, was increasingly critical of Hitler and his drive to war. Even so, serving in Poland he was contemptuous of the Polish people, approved of the colonization of the country, and was enthusiastic about the German victory.[46] He was still more jubilant after the stunning successes in the western campaign, and hinted that he had changed his views on Hitler.[47]

The mounting barbarity of the regime nevertheless appalled him. And when he turned irredeemably against Hitler in the late spring of 1942, it was under the influence of incontrovertible eye-witness reports of massacres of Ukrainian Jews by SS men. Hearing the reports, Stauffenberg concluded that Hitler must be removed.[48] As some of his critics pointed out, it was, compared with others, somewhat late in the day that he was finally persuaded to join the oppositional conspiracy.[49] Serving in North Africa with the 10th Panzer Division, he was (as we noted) badly wounded in April 1943, losing his right eye, his right hand, and two fingers from his left hand. Soon after his discharge from hospital in August, speaking to Friedrich Olbricht about a new post as chief of staff in the General War Office (*Allgemeines Heeresamt*) in Berlin, he was tentatively asked about joining the resistance. There was little doubt what his answer would be. He had already come to the conclusion that the only way to deal with Hitler was to kill him.[50]

By early September, Stauffenberg had been introduced to the leading figures in the opposition. So far as it can be deduced, his political stance, once he had come to join the resistance, had little or nothing in common with that of the national-conservatives – Goerdeler's views he treated almost with disdain – and was closer to that of the Kreisau Circle.[51] But, like Tresckow, Stauffenberg was a man of action, an organizer more than a theoretician. He deliberated with Tresckow in autumn 1943 about the best way to assassinate Hitler and the related but separate issue of organizing the coup to follow. As a means of taking over the state, they came up with the idea of recasting an operational plan, code-named 'Valkyrie', already devised by Olbricht and approved by Hitler, for mobilizing the reserve army within Germany in the event of serious internal unrest. The recouched plan began by denouncing not anti-Nazi 'subversives', but putschists *within* the

Nazi Party itself – 'an unscrupulous clique of non-combat Party leaders' which 'has tried to exploit the situation to stab the deeply committed front in the back, and to seize power for selfish purposes', demanding the proclamation of martial law.[52] The aim of 'Valkyrie' had been to protect the regime; it was now transformed into a strategy for removing it.[53]

Unleashing 'Valkyrie' posed two problems. The first was that the command had to be issued by the head of the reserve army. This was General Friedrich Fromm, born in 1888 into a Protestant family with strong military traditions, a huge man, somewhat reserved in character, with strong beliefs in the army as the guarantor of Germany's status as a world-power. Fromm was no outright Hitler loyalist, but a fence-sitter who remained non-committal in his cautious desire to keep his options open and back whichever came out on top, the regime or the putschists – a policy which would eventually backfire upon him.[54] The other problem was the old one of access to Hitler. Tresckow had concluded that only an assassination attempt in Führer Headquarters could get round the unpredictability of Hitler's schedule and the tight security precautions surrounding him. The difficulty was to find someone prepared to carry out the attempt who had reason to be in Hitler's close proximity in Führer Headquarters.

Stauffenberg, who had brought new dynamism to the sagging momentum of the opposition, wanted a strike against Hitler by mid-November. But who would carry it out? Colonel Stieff, approached by Stauffenberg in October 1943, declined. The attempt had to be postponed. Colonel Joachim Meichßner from the Wehrmacht operational staff (*Wehrmachtführungsstab*) was subsequently asked, in spring 1944, if he might undertake it. He, too, declined.[55] In the interim, Stauffenberg had been introduced to Captain Axel Freiherr von dem Bussche, whose courage in action had won him the Iron Cross, First Class, among other decorations. Witnessing a mass shooting of thousands of Jews in the Ukraine in October 1942 had been a searing experience for Bussche, and opened him to any prospect of doing away with Hitler and his regime. Approached by Stauffenberg, he was prepared to sacrifice his own life by springing on Hitler with a detonated grenade while the Führer was visiting a display of new uniforms.

Bad luck continued to dog the plans. One such uniform display, in December 1943, had to be cancelled when the train carrying the new uniforms was hit in an air-raid and the uniforms destroyed. Before Bussche could be brought back for another attempt, he was badly wounded on the eastern front in January 1944, losing a leg and dropping out of consideration for Stauffenberg's plans.[56]

Lieutenant Ewald Heinrich von Kleist, son of the Prussian landowner and longstanding critic of Hitler Ewald von Kleist-Schmenzin, expressed himself willing to take over.[57] Everything was set for Hitler's visit to a uniform display in mid-February. But the display was once again cancelled.[58]

Yet another chance arose when Rittmeister Eberhard von Breitenbuch, orderly to Field-Marshal Busch (Kluge's successor as Commander-in-Chief of Army Group Centre) and already initiated in plans to eliminate Hitler, had the opportunity to accompany Busch to a military briefing at the Berghof on 11 March 1944. Breitenbuch was uncertain about an attempt with a bomb, but had declared himself ready to shoot Hitler in the head. His Browning pistol was in his trouser pocket, and ready to fire as soon as he came close to Hitler. But on this occasion, orderlies were not permitted in the briefing. Luck was still on Hitler's side.[59]

Even Stauffenberg began to lose heart – especially once the western Allies had established a firm footing on the soil of France. The Gestapo by now had the scent of the opposition; a number of arrests of leading figures pointed to the intensifying danger.[60] Would it not now be better to await the inevitable defeat? Would even a successful strike against Hitler be anything more than a largely empty gesture? Tresckow gave the answer: it was vital that the coup took place, that the outside world should see that there was a German resistance movement prepared at the cost of its members' lives to topple such an unholy regime.[61]

A last opportunity presented itself. On 1 July 1944, now promoted to colonel, Stauffenberg was appointed Fromm's chief of staff – in effect, his deputy. It provided him with what had been hitherto lacking: access to Hitler at military briefings related to the home army. He no longer needed look for someone to carry out the assassination. He could do it himself. That this was the only solution became more evident than ever when Stieff declined a second request from Stauffenberg to try to kill Hitler at the display of uniforms finally taking place at Klessheim on 7 July.[62]

The difficulty with Stauffenberg taking over the role of assassin was that he would be needed at the same time in Berlin to organize the coup from the headquarters of the reserve army.[63] The double role meant that the chances of failure were thereby enhanced. It was far from ideal. But the risk had to be taken.

On 6 July, Stauffenberg was present, for the first time in his capacity as chief of staff to Fromm, at two hour-long briefings at the Berghof. He had explosives with him. But, it seems, an appropriate opportunity did not present itself. Whatever the reason, at any rate, he made no attempt on this occasion. Impatient to act, Stauffenberg resolved to try at his next visit to the Berghof, five days later. But the absence of Himmler, whom the conspirators wanted to eliminate along with Hitler, deterred him.[64] Again, nothing happened. On 15 July, when he was once more at Führer Headquarters (now moved back to the Wolf's Lair in East Prussia), Stauffenberg was determined to act. Once more, nothing happened. Most probably, it seems, he had been unable to set the charge in time for the first of the three briefings that afternoon. While the second short briefing was taking place, he was telephoning Berlin to clarify whether he should in any case go through with the attempt in the absence of Himmler. And during the third briefing, he was himself directly involved in the presentation, which deprived him of all possibility of priming the bomb and carrying out the attack.[65] This time, Olbricht even issued the 'Valkyrie' order. It had to be passed off as a practice alarm-drill.[66] The error could not be repeated. Next time, the issue of the 'Valkyrie' order could not go out ahead of the assassination attempt. It would have to wait for Stauffenberg's confirmation that Hitler was dead. After the bungling of the opportunity on the 15th, the third time that he had taken such a high risk to no avail, Stauffenberg prepared for what he told his fellow conspirators, gathered at his home in Berlin's Wannsee district on the evening of 16 July, would be a last attempt.[67] This would take place during his next visit to the Wolf's Lair, in the briefing scheduled for 20 July.

II

After a two-hour flight from Berlin, Stauffenberg and his adjutant, Lieutenant Werner von Haeften, landed at Rastenburg at 10.15a.m. on 20 July. Stauffenberg was immediately driven the four miles to the Wolf's Lair. Haeften accompanied Major-General Stieff, who had flown in the same plane, to Army High Command, before returning later to Führer Headquarters. By 11.30a.m. Stauffenberg was in a pre-briefing, directed by Keitel, that lasted three-quarters of an hour. Time was pressing since Hitler's briefing, owing to the arrival of Mussolini that afternoon, was to take place half an hour earlier than usual, at 12.30p.m.

As soon as the meeting with Keitel was over, Stauffenberg asked where he could freshen up and change his shirt. It was a hot day, and an unremarkable request; but he needed to hurry. Haeften, carrying the briefcase containing the bomb, met him on the corridor. As soon as they were in the toilet, they began hastily to prepare to set the time-fuses in the two explosive devices they had brought with them, and to place the devices, each weighing around a kilogram, in Stauffenberg's briefcase. Stauffenberg set the first charge. The bomb could go off any time after quarter of an hour, given the hot and stuffy conditions, and would explode within half an hour at most. Outside, Keitel was getting impatient. Just then, a telephone call came from General Erich Fellgiebel, head of communications at Wehrmacht High Command and commissioned, in the plot against Hitler, with the vital task of blocking communications to and from the Führer Headquarters following an assassination attempt. Keitel's adjutant, Major Ernst John von Freyend, took the call. Fellgiebel wanted to speak to Stauffenberg and requested him to call back. There was no time for that. Freyend sent Sergeant-Major Werner Vogel to tell Stauffenberg of Fellgiebel's message, and to hurry him along. Vogel found Stauffenberg and Haeften busy with some object. On being told to hurry, Stauffenberg brusquely replied that he was on his way. Freyend then shouted that he should come along at once. Vogel waited by the open door. Stauffenberg hastily closed his briefcase. There was no chance of setting the time-fuse for the second device he and Haeften had brought with them. Haeften stuffed this, along with sundry papers, in his own bag. It was a decisive moment. Had the second device, even without the charge being set, been placed in Stauffenberg's bag along with the first, it would have been detonated by the explosion, more than doubling the effect. Almost certainly, in such an event, no one would have survived.[68]

The briefing, taking place as usual in the wooden barrack-hut inside the high fence of the closely guarded inner perimeter of the Wolf's Lair, had already begun when Stauffenberg was ushered in. Hitler, seated in the middle of the long side of the table nearest to the door, facing the windows, was listening to Major-General Adolf Heusinger, chief of operations at General Staff headquarters, describe the rapidly worsening position on the eastern front. Hitler absent-mindedly shook hands with Stauffenberg, when Keitel introduced him, and returned to Heusinger's report. Stauffenberg had requested a place as close as possible to the Führer. His hearing disability, together with the need to have his papers close to hand when he reported on the creation of a number of new divisions from the reserve army to help block the Soviet breakthrough into Poland and East Prussia, gave him a good excuse. Room was found for him on Hitler's right, towards the end of the table. Freyend, who had carried Stauffenberg's briefcase into the room, placed it under the table, against the outside of the solid right-hand table-leg.

No sooner had he arrived in the room, than Stauffenberg made an excuse to leave it. This attracted no special attention. There was much to-ing and fro-ing during the daily conferences. Attending to important telephone calls or temporarily being summoned away was a regular occurrence. Stauffenberg left his cap and belt behind to suggest that he would be returning. Once outside the room, he asked Freyend to arrange the connection for the call which he still had to make to General Fellgiebel. But as soon as Freyend returned to the briefing, Stauffenberg hung up and hurried back to the Wehrmacht adjutants' building, where he met Haeften and Fellgiebel. Lieutenant Ludolf Gerhard Sander, a communications officer in Fellgiebel's department, was also there. Stauffenberg's absence in the briefing had meanwhile been noted; he had been needed to provide a point of information during Heusinger's presentation. But there was no sinister thought in anyone's mind at this point. At the adjutancy, Stauffenberg and Haeften were anxiously making arrangements for the car that had been organized to rush them to the airfield. At that moment, they heard a deafening explosion from the direction of the barracks. Fellgiebel gave Stauffenberg a startled look. Stauffenberg shrugged his shoulders. Sander seemed unsurprised. Mines around the complex were constantly being detonated by wild animals, he remarked. It was around quarter to one.[69]

Stauffenberg and Haeften left for the airfield in their chauffeured car as expeditiously as could be done without causing suspicion. The alarm had still not been raised when Stauffenberg bluffed his way past the guards on the gate of the inner zone. He had greater difficulty leaving the outer perimeter. The alarm had by then been sounded. He had to telephone an officer, Rittmeister (captain of cavalry) Leonhard von Möllendorf, who knew him and was prepared to authorize his passage. Once out, it was full speed along the bending road to the airfield. On the way, Haeften hurled away a package containing the second explosive. The car dropped them 100 yards from the waiting plane, and immediately turned back. By 1.15p.m. they were on their way back to Berlin. They were firmly convinced that no one could have survived the explosion; that Hitler was dead.[70] Had they been able to plant the bomb in a concrete bunker, instead of in the wooden hut where the early-afternoon conferences were regularly held, they would have been right.

Hitler had been bent over the heavy oaken table, propped up on his elbow, chin in his hand, studying air reconnaissance positions on a map, when the bomb went off – with a flash of blue and yellow flame and an ear-splitting explosion. Windows and doors blew out. Clouds of thick smoke billowed up. Flying glass splinters, pieces of wood, and showers of paper and other debris flew in all directions. Parts of the wrecked hut were aflame. For a time there was pandemonium. Twenty-four persons had been in the briefing-hut at the time of the explosion. Some were hurled to the floor or blown across the room. Others had hair or clothes in flames. There were cries of help. Human shapes stumbled around – concussed, part-blinded, ear-drums shattered – in the smoke and debris, desperately seeking to get out of the ruins of the hut. The less fortunate lay in the wreckage, some very seriously injured.[71]

Eleven of those who had suffered the worst injuries were rushed to the field hospital, just over two miles away.[72] The stenographer, Dr Heinrich Berger, who had taken the full blast of the bomb, had both legs blown off and died later that afternoon. Colonel Heinz Brandt, Heusinger's right-hand man (and, as it transpired, connected with the conspiracy), lost a leg and died the next day, as did General Günther Korten, chief of the Luftwaffe's general staff, stabbed by a spear of wood. Hitler's Wehrmacht adjutant, Major-General Rudolf Schmundt, lost an eye and a leg, and suffered serious facial burns, eventually succumbing in hospital some weeks later. Of those in the barrack-hut, only Keitel and Hitler avoided concussion; and Keitel alone escaped burst ear-drums.[73]

Hitler had, remarkably, survived with no more than superficial injuries. After the initial shock of the blast, he established that he was all in one piece and could move. Then he made for the door through the wreckage, beating flames from his trousers and putting out the singed hair on the back of his head as he went. He bumped into Keitel, who embraced him, weeping and crying out: 'My Führer, you are alive, you are alive.'[74] Keitel helped Hitler, his uniform jacket torn, his black trousers and beneath them long white underwear in shreds, out of the building. But he was able to walk without difficulty.[75] He immediately returned to his bunker. Dr Morell was summoned urgently. Hitler had a swollen and painful right arm, which he could barely lift, swellings and abrasions on his left arm, burns and blisters on his hands and legs (which were also full of wood-splinters), and cuts to his forehead. But those, alongside the burst ear-drums, were the worst injuries he had suffered.[76] When Linge, his valet, panic-stricken, rushed in, Hitler was composed, and with a grim smile on his face said: 'Linge, someone has tried to kill me.'[77]

Below, Hitler's Luftwaffe adjutant, relatively lightly injured in the explosion, had been composed enough, despite the shock and the lacerations to his face through glass shards, to rush to the signals hut, where he demanded a block on all communications apart from those from Hitler, Keitel, and Jodl. At the same time, Below had Himmler and Göring summoned to Hitler's bunker. Then he made his way there himself.[78] Hitler was sitting in his study, relief written on his face, ready to show off – with a tinge of pride, it seemed – his shredded clothing.[79] His attention had already turned to the question of who had carried out the assassination attempt. According to Below, he rejected suggestions (which he appears initially to have believed) that the bomb had been planted by OT workers who were temporarily at Führer Headquarters to complete the reinforcement of the compound against air-raids.[80] By this time, suspicion had turned indubitably to the missing Stauffenberg. The search for Stauffenberg and investigation into the assassination attempt began around 2p.m., though it was not at that point realized that this had been the signal for a general uprising against the regime. Hitler's rage at the army leaders he had always distrusted mounted by the minute. He was ready to wreak terrible vengeance on those whom he saw as stabbing the Reich in the back in its hour of crisis.[81]

III

By this time, Stauffenberg was well on his way back to Berlin. The conspirators there were anxiously awaiting his return, or news of what had happened to him, hesitating to act, still unsure whether to proceed with 'Operation Valkyrie.'[82] The message that Fellgiebel had managed to get through, even before Stauffenberg had taken off from Rastenburg, to Major-General Fritz Thiele, communications chief at Army High Command, was less clear than he thought. It was that something terrible had happened; the Führer was still alive. That was all. There were no details. It was unclear whether the bomb had gone off, whether Stauffenberg had been prevented (as a few days earlier) from carrying out the attack, or whether Stauffenberg had been arrested, whether, in fact, he was even still alive. Further messages seeping through indicated that something had certainly happened in the Wolf's Lair, but that Hitler had survived.[83] Should 'Valkyrie' still go ahead? No contingency plans had been made for carrying out a coup if Hitler were still alive. And without confirmed news of Hitler's death, Fromm, in his position as commander of the reserve army, would certainly not give his approval for the coup. Olbricht concluded that to take any action before hearing definitive news would be to court disaster for all concerned. Vital time was lost. One of the plotters, Hans Bernd Gisevius, connected with the opposition since 1938 and by now an Abwehr agent based in Switzerland who had just returned to Germany, was later scathing about Olbricht's incompetence. 'Leaderless and mindless' was how he described the group in the Bendlerblock awaiting Stauffenberg's return.[84] Meanwhile, it had proved only temporarily possible to block communications from the Wolf's Lair. Soon after 4p.m. that afternoon, before any coup had been started, the lines were fully open again.[85]

Stauffenberg arrived back in Berlin between 2.45 and 3.15p.m. There was no car to meet him. His chauffeur was waiting at Rangsdorf aerodrome. But Stauffenberg's plane had flown to Tempelhof (or possible another Berlin aerodrome – this detail is not fully clear), and he had impatiently to telephone for a car to take him and Haeften to Bendlerstraße. It was a further delay. At such a crucial juncture, Stauffenberg did not reach the headquarters of the conspiracy, where tension was at fever-pitch, until 4.30p.m. Haeften had in the meantime telephoned from the aerodrome to Bendlerstraße. He announced – the first time the conspirators heard the message – that Hitler was dead.[86] Stauffenberg repeated this when he and Haeften arrived in Bendlerstraße. He had stood with General Fellgiebel outside the barrack-hut, he said, and seen with his own eyes first-aid men running to help and emergency vehicles arriving. No one could have survived such an explosion, was his conclusion.[87] However convincing he was for those anxious to believe his message, a key figure, General Fromm, knew otherwise. He had spoken to Keitel around 4p.m. and been told that the Führer had suffered only minor injuries. That apart, Keitel had asked where, in the meantime, Colonel Stauffenberg might be.[88]

Fromm refused outright Olbricht's request that he should sign the orders for 'Valkyrie'. But by the time Olbricht had returned to his room to announce Fromm's refusal, his impatient chief of staff Colonel Mertz von Quirnheim, a friend of Stauffenberg, and long closely involved in the plot, had already begun the action with a cabled message to regional military commanders, beginning with the words: 'The Führer, Adolf Hitler, is dead.'[89] When Fromm tried to have Mertz arrested, Stauffenberg informed him that, on the contrary, it was he, Fromm, who was under arrest.[90]

By now, several of the leading conspirators had been contacted and had begun assembling in the Bendlerstraße. Beck was there, already announcing that he had taken over command in the state; and that Field-Marshal Erwin von Witzleben, former commander-in-chief in France, and long involved in the conspiracy, was now commander-in-chief of the army.[91] General Hoepner, Fromm's designated successor in the coup, dismissed by Hitler in disgrace in early 1942 and forbidden to wear a uniform again, arrived around 4.30p.m. in civilian clothes, carrying a suitcase. It contained his uniform which he donned once more that evening.[92]

Scenes in the Bendlerstraße were increasingly chaotic. Conspiring to arrange a *coup d'état* in a police state is scarcely a simple matter. But even in the existential circumstances prevailing, much smacked of dilettante organization. Too many loose ends had been left dangling. Too little attention had been paid to small but important details in timing, coordination, and, not least, communications. Nothing had been done about blowing up the communications centre at Führer Headquarters or otherwise putting it permanently out of action.[93] No steps were taken to gain immediate control of radio stations in Berlin and other cities. No broadcast was made by the putchists. Party and SS leaders were not arrested. The master-propagandist, Goebbels himself, was left at bay. Among the conspirators, too many were involved in issuing and carrying out commands. There was too much uncertainty; and too much hesitation. Everything had been predicated upon killing Hitler. It had simply been taken for granted that if Stauffenberg succeeded in exploding his bomb, Hitler would be dead. Once that premiss was called into question, then disproved, the haphazard lines of a plan for the *coup d'état* rapidly unravelled. What was crucial, in the absence of confirmed news of Hitler's demise, was that there were too many regime-loyalists, and too many waverers, with too much to lose by committing themselves to the side of the conspirators.

Despite Stauffenberg's intense avowals of Hitler's death, the depressing news for the conspirators of his survival gathered strength. Beck declared that, whatever the truth of the matter, 'for me this man is dead', and his further actions would be determined by this.[94] But for the success of the plot, that was scarcely enough. By mid-evening, it was increasingly obvious to the insurrectionists that their coup had faltered beyond repair. 'A fine mess, this (*Schöne Schweinerei, das*),' Field-Marshal Witzleben had muttered to Stauffenberg, on his arrival around 8p.m. in Bendlerstraße.[95]

It rapidly became plain in Führer Headquarters that the assassination attempt was the signal for a military and political insurrection against the regime. By mid-afternoon, Hitler had given command of the reserve army to Himmler. And Keitel had informed army districts that an attempt on the Führer's life had been made, but that he still lived, and on no account were orders from the conspirators to be obeyed.[96] Loyalists could be found even in the Bendlerstraße, the seat of the uprising. The communications officer there, also in receipt of Keitel's order, was by the evening, as the conspirators were becoming more and more desperate, passing on the message that the orders he was having to transmit on their behalf were invalid.[97] Fromm's adjutants were meanwhile able to spread the word in the building that Hitler was still alive, and to collect together a number of officers prepared to challenge the conspirators, whose already limited and hesitant support, inside and outside Bendlerstraße, was by now rapidly draining away. Early instances where army units initially supported the coup dwindled once news of Hitler's survival hardened.[98]

This was the case, too, in Paris. The military commander there, General Karl Heinrich von Stülpnagel, and his subordinate officers had firmly backed the insurrectionists. But the supreme commander in the west, Field-Marshal von Kluge, vacillated as ever. In a vain call from Berlin, Beck failed to persuade him to commit himself to the rising. 'Kluge,' Beck said to Gisevius as he put down the receiver. 'There you have him!'[99] Once he learnt that the assassination attempt had failed, Kluge countered Stülpnagel's orders to have the entire SS, SD, and Gestapo in Paris arrested, dismissed the general, denounced his actions to Keitel, and later congratulated Hitler on surviving a treacherous attack on his life.[100]

By this time, the events in Berlin had reached their denouement. In the late morning, Goebbels had been hosting a speech about Germany's armaments position, attended by ministers, leading civil servants, and industrialists, given by Speer in the Propaganda Ministry. After the Propaganda Minister had closed the meeting, he had taken Walther Funk and Albert Speer back with him into his study to talk about mobilizing remaining resources within Germany. While they were talking, he was suddenly called to take an urgent telephone call from Führer Headquarters. Despite the swift block on communications, he had his own hot-line to FHQ which, evidently, at this point still remained open. The call was from Press Chief Otto Dietrich, who broke the news to Goebbels that there had been an attack on Hitler's life. This was within minutes of the explosion taking place.[101] There were few details at this stage, other than that Hitler was alive. Goebbels, told that OT workers had probably been responsible, angrily reproached Speer about the evidently over-casual security precautions that had been taken.[102]

The Propaganda Minister was unusually quiet and pensive over lunch. Somewhat remarkably, in the circumstances, he then retired for his usual afternoon siesta. He was awakened between 2 and 3p.m. by the head of his press office, Wilfried von Oven, who had just taken a phone-call from an agitated Heinz Lorenz, Dietrich's deputy. Lorenz had dictated a brief text –

drafted, he said, by Hitler himself – for immediate radio transmission. Goebbels was little taken with the terse wording, and remarked that urgency in transmitting the news was less important than making sure it was suitably couched for public consumption. He gave instructions to prepare an adequately massaged commentary. At this stage, the Propaganda Minister clearly had no idea of the gravity of the situation, that army officers had been involved, and that an uprising had been unleashed. Believing some breach of security had allowed unreliable OT workers to perpetrate some attack, he had been told that Hitler was alive. More than that he did not know. Even so, his own behaviour after first hearing the news, and then during the afternoon, when he attended to regular business and showed unusual dilatoriness in putting out the broadcast urgently demanded from Führer Headquarters, was odd. Possibly he had decided that any immediate crisis had passed, and that he would await further information before putting out any press communiqué. More probably, he was unsure of developments and wanted to hedge his bets.

Eventually, after this lengthy interval, further news from the Wolf's Lair ended his inaction. He rang Speer and told him to drop everything and rush over to his residence, close to the Brandenburg Gate. There he told Speer he had heard from Führer Headquarters that a full-scale military putsch in the entire Reich was under way. Speer immediately offered Goebbels his support in any attempt to defeat and crush the uprising. Within minutes, Speer noticed armed troops on the streets outside, ringing the building. By this time, it was early evening, around 6.30p.m.[103] Goebbels took one glance and disappeared into his bedroom, putting a little box of cyanide pills – 'for all eventualities' – in his pocket.[104] The fact that he had been unable to locate Himmler made him worried. Perhaps the Reichsführer-SS had fallen into the hands of the putschists? Perhaps he was even behind the coup? Suspicions were rife.[105] The elimination of such an important figure as Goebbels ought to have been a priority for the conspirators. Amazingly, no one had even thought to cut off his telephone. This, and the fact that the leaders of the uprising had put out no proclamation over the radio, persuaded the Propaganda Minister that all was not lost, even though he heard disquieting reports of troops moving on Berlin.[106]

The guard-battalion surrounding Goebbels's house was under the command of Major Otto-Ernst Remer, thirty-two years old at the time, a fanatical Hitler-loyalist, who initially believed the fiction constructed by the plotters that they were putting down a rising by disaffected groups in the SS and Party against the Führer. When ordered by his superior, the Berlin

City Commandant, Major-General Paul von Hase, to take part in sealing off the government quarter, Remer obeyed without demur.[107] He soon became suspicious, however, that what he had first heard was untrue; that he was, in fact, helping suppress not a putsch of Party and SS leaders against Hitler, but a military coup against the regime by rebellious officers. As luck had it, Lieutenant Hans Hagen, a National Socialist Leadership Officer (*NS-Führungsoffizier*) charged with inspiring Nazi principles among the troops, had that afternoon lectured Remer's battalion on behalf of the Propaganda Ministry.[108] Hagen now used his fortuitous contact to Remer to help undermine the conspiracy against Hitler. Hagen, through the mediation of Deputy Gauleiter of Berlin Gerhard Schach, persuaded Goebbels to speak directly to Remer, to convince him of what was really happening, and to win him over. Hagen then, through an intermediary, sought out Remer, played on the seeds of doubt in his mind about the action in which he was engaged, and talked him into disregarding the orders of his superior, von Hase, and going to see Goebbels. At this point, Remer was still unsure whether Goebbels was part of an internal party coup against Hitler. If he made a mistake, it could cost him his head. However, after some hesitation, he agreed to meet the Propaganda Minister.

Goebbels reminded him of his oath to the Führer. Remer expressed his loyalty to Hitler and the Party, but remarked that the Führer was dead. Consequently, he had to carry out the orders of his commander, Major-General von Hase. 'The Führer is alive!' Goebbels retorted. 'I spoke with him only a few minutes ago.' The uncertain Remer was visibly wavering. Goebbels offered to let Remer speak himself with Hitler. It was around 7p.m. Within minutes, the call to the Wolf's Lair was made. Hitler asked Remer whether he recognized his voice. Standing rigidly to attention, Remer said he did. 'Do you hear me? So I'm alive! The attempt has failed,' he registered Hitler saying. 'A tiny clique of ambitious officers wanted to do away with me. But now we have the saboteurs of the front. We'll make short shrift of this plague. You are commissioned by me with the task of immediately restoring calm and security in the Reich capital, if necessary by force. You are under my personal command for this purpose until the Reichsführer-SS arrives in the Reich capital!'[109] Remer needed no further persuasion. All Speer, in the room at the time could hear, was, 'Jawohl, my Führer . . . Jawohl, as you order, my Führer.' Remer was put in charge of security in Berlin to replace von Hase. He was to follow all instructions from Goebbels.[110]

Remer arranged for Goebbels to speak to his men. Goebbels addressed the guard battalion in the garden of his residence around 8.30p.m., and rapidly won them over.[111] Almost two hours earlier, he had put out a radio communiqué telling listeners of the attack on Hitler, but how the Führer had suffered only minor abrasions, had received Mussolini that afternoon, and was already back at his work.[112] For those still wavering, the news of Hitler's survival was a vital piece of information. Between 8 and 9p.m. the cordon around the government quarter was lifted.[113] The guard-battalion was by now needed for other duties: rooting out the conspirators in their headquarters in Bendlerstraße. The high-point of the conspiracy had passed. For the plotters, the writing was on the wall.

I V

Some were already seeking to extricate themselves even before Goebbels's communiqué broadcast the news of Hitler's survival.[114] By mid-evening, the group of conspirators in the Bendlerblock, the Wehrmacht High Command building in the Bendlerstraße, were as good as all that was left of the uprising. Remer's guard-battalion was surrounding the building. Panzer units loyal to the regime were closing in on Berlin's city centre. Troop commanders were no longer prepared to listen to the plotters' orders. Even in the Bendlerblock itself, senior officers were refusing to take orders from the conspirators, reminding them of the oath they had taken to Hitler which, since the radio had broadcast news of his survival, was still valid.[115]

A group of staff officers, dissatisfied with Olbricht's increasingly lame explanation of what was happening, and, whatever their feelings towards Hitler, not unnaturally anxious in the light of an evidently lost cause to save their own skins, became rebellious. Soon after 9p.m., arming themselves, they returned to Olbricht's room. While their spokesman, Lieutenant-Colonel Franz Herber, was talking to Olbricht, shots were fired on the corridor, one of which hit Stauffenberg in the shoulder. It was a brief flurry, no more. Herber and his men pressed into Fromm's office, where Colonel-General Hoepner, the conspirators' choice as commander of the reserve army, Mertz, Beck, Haeften, and the injured Stauffenberg also gathered. Herber demanded to speak to Fromm and was told he was still in his apartment (where he had been kept under guard since the afternoon). One of the rebel officers immediately made his way there, was admitted, and told Fromm what had happened. The guard outside Fromm's door had by now vanished. Liberated, Fromm returned to his office to confront the putschists. It was around 10p.m. when his massive frame appeared in the doorway of his office. He scornfully cast his eye over the utterly dispirited leaders of the insurrection. 'So, gentlemen,' he declared, 'now I'm going to do to you what you did to me this afternoon.'[116]

As Gisevius later pointed out, what the conspirators had done to Fromm had been to lock him in his room and give him sandwiches and wine.[117] Fromm was less naïve. He had his neck to save – or so he thought. He told the putchists they were under arrest and demanded they surrender all weapons. Beck asked to retain his 'for private use'. Fromm ordered him to make use of it immediately. Beck said at that moment he was thinking of earlier days. Fromm urged him to get on with it. Beck put the gun to his head, but only succeeded in grazing himself on the temple. Fromm offered the others a few moments should they wish to write any last words. Hoepner availed himself of the opportunity, sitting at Olbricht's desk; so did Olbricht himself. Beck, meanwhile, reeling from the glancing blow to his head, refused attempts to take the pistol from him, and insisted on being allowed another shot. Even then, he only managed a severe head-wound. With Beck writhing on the floor, Fromm left the room to learn that a unit of the guards battalion had entered the courtyard of the Bendlerblock. He knew, too, that Himmler, the newly appointed commander of the reserve army, was on his way. There was no time to lose. He returned to his room after five minutes and announced that he had held a court-martial in the name of the Führer. Mertz, Olbricht, Haeften, and 'this colonel whose name I will no longer mention' had been sentenced to death. 'Take a few men and execute this sentence downstairs in the yard at once,' he ordered an officer standing by. Stauffenberg tried to take all responsibility on his own shoulders, stating that the others had been merely carrying out his orders. Fromm said nothing, as the four men were taken to their execution, and Hoepner – initially also earmarked for execution, but spared for the time being following a private discussion with Fromm – was led out into captivity. With a glance at the dying Beck, Fromm commanded one of the officers to finish him off. The former Chief of the General Staff was unceremoniously dragged into the adjacent room and shot dead.[118]

The condemned men were rapidly escorted downstairs into the courtyard, where a firing-squad of ten men drawn from the guard-battalion was already waiting. To add to the macabre scene, the drivers of the vehicles parked in the courtyard had been ordered to turn their headlights on the little pile of sand near the doorway from which Stauffenberg and his fellow-conspirators emerged. Without ceremony, Olbricht was put on the sand-heap and promptly shot. Next to be brought forward was Stauffenberg. Just as the execution-squad opened fire, Haeften threw himself in front of Stauffenberg, and died first. It was to no avail. Stauffenberg was immediately placed again on the sand-heap. As the shots rang out, he was heard to cry: 'Long live holy Germany.' Seconds later, the execution of the last of the four, Mertz von Quirnheim, followed. Fromm promptly had a telegram dispatched, announcing the bloody suppression of the attempted coup and the execution of the ringleaders. Then he gave an impassioned address to those assembled in the courtyard, attributing Hitler's wondrous salvation to the work of providence. He ended with a three-fold 'Sieg Heil' to the Führer.

While the bodies of the executed men, along with Beck's corpse which had been dragged downstairs into the yard, were taken off in a lorry to be buried – next day Himmler had them exhumed and cremated – the remaining conspirators in the Bendlerblock (among them Fritz-Dietlof von der Schulenburg, Stauffenberg's brother Berthold, and Yorck von Wartenburg) were arrested. It was around half an hour after midnight.[119]

Apart from the lingering remnants of the coup in Paris, Prague, and Vienna, and apart from the terrible and inevitable reprisals to follow, the last attempt to topple Hitler and his regime from within was over.

V

Hours earlier on this eventful 20 July 1944, shortly after arriving back in his bunker following the explosion, Hitler had refused to contemplate cancelling the planned visit of the Duce, scheduled for 2.30p.m. that afternoon, but delayed half an hour because of the late arrival of Mussolini's train.[120] It was to prove the last of the seventeen meetings of the two dictators.[121] It was certainly the strangest. Outwardly composed, there was little to detect that Hitler had just escaped an attempt on his life. He greeted Mussolini with his left hand, since he had difficulty in raising his injured right arm.[122] He told the shocked Duce what had happened, then led him to the ruined wooden hut where the explosion had taken place. In a macabre scene, amid the devastation, accompanied only by the interpreter, Paul Schmidt, Hitler described to his fellow-dictator where he had stood, right arm leaning on the table as he studied the map, when the bomb went off. He showed him the singed hair at the back of his head. Hitler sat down on an upturned box. Schmidt found a still usable stool amid the debris for Mussolini. For a few moments, neither dictator said a word. Then Hitler, in a quiet voice, said:

'When I go through it all again . . . I conclude from my wondrous salvation, while others present in the room received serious injuries . . . that nothing is going to happen to me.' He was ever more convinced, he added, that it was given to him to lead their common cause to a victorious end.[123]

The same theme, that Providence had saved him, ran through Hitler's address which was transmitted by all radio stations soon after midnight. He had already inquired in mid-afternoon how quickly arrangements for a broadcast could be made, and been told that the earliest was 6p.m. That was unrealistic. The speech still had to be written, and the afternoon was taken up with Mussolini's visit. Preparations had to be made for the speech to be networked on all radio stations, and recorded. The equipment for the broadcast had to be brought by road from Königsberg. But the technical crew were not immediately available; they had gone off swimming in the Baltic.[124] Possibly, too, Hitler lost some interest in the idea during the diversions of the day. At any rate, it seems once more to have taken Goebbels's prompting to persuade him of the necessity of a brief address to the German people.[125] It was after midnight before the broadcast eventually took place, followed by addresses by Göring and Dönitz.[126]

Hitler said he was speaking to the German people for two reasons: to let them hear his voice, and know that he was uninjured and well; and to tell them about a crime without parallel in German history. 'A tiny clique of ambitious, unconscionable, and at the same time criminal, stupid officers has forged a plot to eliminate me and at the same time to eradicate (*auszu-rotten*) with me the staff practically of the German armed forces' leadership.' He likened it to the stab-in-the-back of 1918. But this time, the 'tiny gang of criminal elements' would be 'mercilessly eradicated (*unbarmherzig ausgerottet*)'. On three separate occasions he referred to his survival as 'a sign of Providence that I must continue my work, and therefore will continue it'.[127]

In fact, as so often in his life, it had not been Providence that had saved him, but luck: the luck of the devil.

15

NO WAY OUT

'Rather sacrifice everything, absolutely everything, for victory, than for Bolshevism . . . What would I still go to school for if I'm going to end up in Siberia? . . . But if we all wanted to think in this way, there would be no hope left. So, head high. Trust in our will and our leadership!!!'

A teenage girl's diary entry, September 1944

'It's always claimed that the Führer has been sent to us from God. I don't doubt it. The Führer was sent to us from God, though not in order to save Germany, but to ruin it. Providence has determined the destruction of the German people, and Hitler is the executor of this will.'

Reported opinion in the Stuttgart region,
November 1944

'If it doesn't succeed, I see no other possibility of bringing the war to a favourable conclusion.'

Hitler, to Speer, speaking in autumn 1944 of the
forthcoming Ardennes offensive

'We'll not capitulate. Never. We can go down. But we'll take a world with us.'

Hitler, to his Luftwaffe adjutant, Nicolaus von Below,
in the last days of December 1944

'Now I finally have the swine who have been sabotaging my work for years,' raged Hitler as details of the plot against him started to emerge. 'Now I have proof: the entire General Staff is contaminated.'[1] His long-standing, deep-seated distrust of his army leaders – an inevitable consequence of his ready acceptance of Keitel's fawning description of him following the triumph in France in 1940 as an unparalleled military genius, the 'greatest warlord of all time', together with the inability of the generals, in his eyes, to achieve final victory and, since the first Russian winter, to stave off the endless array of defeats – had found its confirmation. It now seemed blindingly obvious to him why his military plans had encountered such setbacks: they had been sabotaged throughout by the treachery of his army officers. 'Now I know why all my great plans in Russia had to fail in recent years,' he ranted. 'It was all treason! But for those traitors, we would have won long ago. Here is my justification before history' (an indication, too, that Hitler was consciously looking to his place in the pantheon of Teutonic heroes).[2] Goebbels, as so often, echoed Hitler's sentiments. 'The generals are not opposed to the Führer because we are experiencing crises at the front,' he entered in his diary. 'Rather, we are experiencing crises at the front because the generals are opposed to the Führer.'[3] Hitler was convinced of an 'inner blood-poisoning'. With leading positions occupied by traitors bent on destroying the Reich, he railed, with key figures such as General Eduard Wagner (responsible as Quartermaster-General for army supplies) and General Erich Fellgiebel (chief of signals operations at Führer Head-quarters) connected to the conspiracy, it was no wonder that German military tactics had been known in advance by the Red Army. It had been 'permanent treachery' all along. It was symptomatic of an underlying 'crisis in morale'. Action ought to have been taken sooner. It had been known, after all, for one and a half years that there were traitors in the army. But now, an end had to be made. 'These most base creatures who in the whole of history have worn the soldier's uniform, this rabble which has preserved itself from bygone times, must be got rid of and driven out.' Military recovery would follow recovery from the crisis in morale.[4] It would be 'Germany's salvation.'[5]

I

Vengeance was uppermost in Hitler's mind. There would be no mercy in the task of cleansing the Augean stables. Swift and ruthless action would be taken. He would 'wipe out and eradicate (*ausmerzen und ausrotten*)' the lot of them, he raged.[6] 'These criminals' would not be granted an honourable soldier's execution by firing-squad. They would be expelled from the Wehrmacht, brought as civilians before the court, and executed within two hours of sentence. 'They must hang immediately, without any mercy,' he declared.[7] He gave orders to set up a military 'Court of Honour', in which senior generals (including among others Keitel, Rundstedt – who presided – and Guderian) would expel in disgrace those found to have been involved in the plot.[8] Those subsequently sentenced to death by the People's Court, he ordered, were to be hanged in prison clothing as criminals.[9] He spoke favourably of Stalin's purges of his officers.[10] 'The Führer is extraordinarily furious at the generals, especially those of the General Staff,' noted Goebbels after seeing Hitler on 22 July. 'He is absolutely determined to set a bloody example and to eradicate a freemasons' lodge which has been opposed to us all the time and has only awaited the moment to stab us in the back in the most critical hour. The punishment which must now be meted out must have historic dimensions.'[11]

Hitler had been outraged at Colonel-General Fromm's peremptory action in having Stauffenberg and the other leaders of the attempted coup immediately executed by firing-squad. He gave orders forthwith that other plotters captured should appear before the People's Court.[12] The President of the People's Court, Roland Freisler, a fanatical Nazi who, despite early sympathies with the radical Left, had been ideologically committed to the *völkisch* cause since the early 1920s, saw himself – a classical instance of 'working towards the Führer' – pronouncing judgement as the 'Führer would judge the case himself'. The People's Court was, for him, expressly a 'political court'. Under his presidency, the number of death sentences delivered by the Court had risen from 102 in 1941 to 2,097 in 1944. It was little wonder that he had already gained notoriety as a 'hanging judge (*Blutrichter*)'.[13] Recapitulating Hitler's comments at their recent meeting, Goebbels remarked that those implicated in the plot were to be brought before the People's Court 'and sentenced to death'. Freisler, he added, 'would find the right tone to deal with them'.[14] Hitler himself was keen above all – perhaps remembering the leniency of the Munich court in 1924 which had allowed him to turn his trial following the failed putsch into a personal propaganda triumph – that the conspirators should be permitted 'no time for long speeches' during their defence. 'But Freisler will see to that,' he added. That's our Vyschinsky' – a reference to Stalin's notorious prosecutor in the show-trials of the 1930s.[15]

It took little encouragement from Goebbels to persuade Hitler that Fromm, Stauffenberg's direct superior officer, had acted so swiftly in an attempt to cover up his own complicity. Fromm had, in fact, already been named by Bormann in a circular to the Gauleiter in mid-evening of 20 July as one of those to be arrested as part of the 'reactionary gang of criminals' behind the conspiracy.[16] Following the suppression of the coup in the Bendlerblock and the swift execution of Stauffenberg, Olbricht, Haeften, and Mertz von Quirnheim, Fromm had made his way to the Propaganda Ministry, wanting to speak on the telephone with Hitler. Instead of connecting him, Goebbels had had Fromm seated in another room while he himself telephoned Führer Headquarters. He soon had the decision he wanted. Goebbels immediately had the former commander-in-chief of the Reserve Army placed under armed guard.[17] After months of imprisonment, a mockery of a trial before the People's Court, and a trumped-up conviction on grounds of alleged cowardice – despite the less-than-heroic motive of self-preservation that had dictated his role on centre-stage in the Bendlerblock on 20 July, he was no coward – Fromm would eventually die at the hands of a firing-squad in March 1945.[18]

In the confusion in the Bendlerblock late on the night of 20 July, it had looked for a time as if other executions would follow those of the coup's leaders (together with the assisted suicide of Beck). But the arrival soon after midnight of an SS unit under the command of Sturmbannführer Otto Skorzeny – the rescuer of Mussolini from captivity the previous summer – who had been dispatched to the scene of the uprising by Walter Schellenberg, head of SD foreign intelligence, along with the appearance at the scene of SD chief Ernst Kaltenbrunner and Major Otto Ernst Remer, newly appointed commander of the Berlin guards battalion and largely responsible for putting down the coup, blocked further summary executions and ended the upheaval.[19] Meanwhile, Himmler himself had flown to Berlin and, in his new temporary capacity as Commander-in-Chief of the Reserve Army, had given orders that no further independent action was to be taken against officers held in suspicion.[20]

Shortly before 4 a.m., Bormann was able to inform the Party's provincial chieftains, the Gauleiter, that the putsch was at an end.[21] By then, those arrested in the Bendlerstraße – including Stauffenberg's brother, Berthold, former civil-servant and deputy Police President of Berlin Fritz-Dietlof von der Schulenburg, leading member of the 'Kreisau Circle' Peter Graf Yorck von Wartenburg, Protestant pastor Eugen Gerstenmaier, and landholder and officer in the Abwehr Ulrich Wilhelm Graf Schwerin von Schwanenfeld – had been led off to await their fate.[22] Former Colonel-General Erich Hoepner, arrested by Fromm but not executed, and Field-Marshal Erwin von Witzleben, who had left the Bendlerstraße before the collapse of the coup, were also promptly taken into custody, along with a number of others who had been implicated.[23] Prussian Finance Minister Popitz, former Economics Minister Schacht, former Chief of Staff Colonel-General Halder, Major-General Stieff, and, from the Abwehr, Admiral Canaris and Major-General Oster were also swiftly arrested. Major Hans Ulrich von Oertzen, liaison officer for the Berlin Defence District (Wehrkreis III), who had given out the first 'Valkyrie' orders, blew himself up with a hand-grenade. Henning von Tresckow, the early driving-force behind the attempts to assassinate Hitler, killed himself in similar fashion at the front near Ostrow in Poland. General Wagner shot himself. General Fellgiebel refused to do so. 'You stand your ground, you don't do that,' he told his orderly. Well aware that his arrest was imminent, he spent much of the afternoon, remarkably, at the Wolf's Lair, even congratulated Hitler on his survival, and awaited his inevitable fate.[24]

Those who fell into the clutches of the Gestapo had to reckon with fearsome torture. It was endured for the most part with the idealism, even heroism, which had sustained them throughout their perilous opposition.[25] In the early stages of their investigations, the Gestapo managed to squeeze out remarkably limited information, beyond what they already knew, from those they so grievously maltreated. Even so, as the 'Special Commission, 20 July', set up on the day after the attempted coup under SS-Obersturmbannführer Georg Kießel and soon growing to include 400 officers, expanded its investigations, the numbers arrested rapidly swelled.

Kießel was soon able to report 600 persons taken into custody.[26] Almost all the leading figures in the various branches of the conspiracy were rapidly captured, though Goerdeler held out under cover until 12 August. Reports reached Hitler daily of new names of those implicated.[27] His early belief that it had been no more than a 'tiny clique' of officers which had opposed him had proved mistaken. The conspiracy had tentacles stretching further than he could have imagined. He was particularly incensed that even Graf Helldorf, Berlin Police President, 'Old Fighter' of the Nazi Movement, and a former SA leader, turned out to have been deeply implicated.[28] As the list lengthened, and the extent of the conspiracy became clear (all the more so following the remarkably full confession of Goerdeler, anxious to emphasize in the eyes of history the significance of the efforts of the opposition to remove Hitler and his regime), Hitler's fury and bitter resentment against the conservatives – especially the landed aristocracy – who had never fully accepted him mounted.[29] 'We wiped out the class struggle on the Left, but unfortunately forgot to finish off (*zur Strecke zu bringen*) the class struggle on the Right,' he was heard to remark.[30] But now was the worst possible time to encourage divisiveness within the people; the general showdown with the aristocracy would have to wait till the war was over.[31]

Even so, Himmler needed no prompting to take revenge against the families of the plotters, many of them from aristocratic backgrounds. He told the Gauleiter assembled in Posen a fortnight after the attempt on Hitler's life that he would act in accordance with the 'blood-vengeance (*Blutrache*)' traditions of old Germanic law in eradicating 'treasonable blood' throughout the entire clan of the traitors. 'The family of Graf Stauffenberg,' he promised, 'will be wiped out down to its last member.' The Gauleiter applauded. Claus von Stauffenberg's wife, brothers, their children, cousins, uncles, aunts, were all taken into custody. The families of others involved in the plot were similarly imprisoned. Only the end of the war vitiated the fulfilment of Himmler's intention.[32] A full-scale police operation ('*Gewitteraktion*' – 'Storm Action') in late August to round up opponents of the regime – indirectly rather than explicitly a consequence of the plot of 20 July – brought the arrest, in all, of over 5,000 persons.[33] The ferocity of the onslaught against all conceivable glimmers of opposition following the failed bomb-plot was certainly a show of the regime's continued untrammelled capacity for ruthless repression. But the utter ruthlessness now contained more than a mere hint of the desperation that indicated a regime whose days were numbered.

On 7 August, the intended show-trials began at the People's Court in

Berlin. The first eight – including Witzleben, Hoepner, Stieff, and Yorck – of what became a regular procession of the accused were each marched by two Gestapo men into a courtroom bedecked with swastikas, holding around 300 selected spectators (including the journalists hand-picked by Goebbels). There they had to endure the ferocious wrath, scathing contempt, and ruthless humiliation heaped on them by the red-robed president of the court, Judge Roland Freisler. Seated beneath a bust of Hitler, Freisler's face reflected in its contortions extremes of hatred and derision. He presided over no more than a base mockery of any semblance of a legal trial, with the death-sentence a certainty from the outset. The accused men bore visible signs of their torment in prison. To degrade them even in physical appearance, they were shabbily dressed, without collars and ties, and were handcuffed until seated in the courtroom. Witzleben was even deprived of braces or a belt, so that he had to hold up his trousers with one hand. The accused were not allowed to express themselves properly or explain their motivation before Freisler cut them short, bawling insults, calling them knaves, traitors, cowardly murderers. When, for instance, later in August, Graf Schwerin von Schwanenfeld tried to point out that his conscience had been wracked by the many murders he had witnessed in Poland, Freisler would stand none of it. 'Murders?' he screamed. 'You really are a low scoundrel. Are you breaking down under this rottenness?'[34] The order had been given – probably by Goebbels, though undoubtedly with Hitler's authorization – for the court proceedings to be filmed with a view to showing extracts in the newsreels as well as in a 'documentary' entitled 'Traitors before the People's Court' ('Verräter vor dem Volksgericht'). So loudly did Freisler shout that the cameramen had to inform him that he was ruining their sound recordings.[35] Nevertheless, the accused managed some moments of courageous defiance. For instance, after the death sentence had predictably been pronounced, General Fellgiebel uttered: 'Then hurry with the hanging, Mr President; otherwise you will hang earlier than we.' And Field-Marshal von Witzleben called out: 'You can hand us over to the hangman. In three months the enraged and tormented people will call you to account, and will drag you alive through the muck of the street.'[36] Such a black farce were the trials that even Reich Justice Minister Otto Georg Thierack, himself a fanatical Nazi who in his ideological ardour had by this time surrendered practically the last vestiges of a completely perverted legal system to the arbitrary police lawlessness of the SS, subsequently complained about Freisler's conduct.[37]

Once the verdicts had been pronounced, the condemned men were taken off, many of them to Plötzensee Prison in Berlin. On Hitler's instructions they were denied any last rites or pastoral care (though this callous order was at least partially bypassed in practice).[38] The normal mode of execution for civilian capital offences in the Third Reich was beheading.[39] But Hitler had reportedly ordered that he wanted those behind the conspiracy of 20 July 1944 'hanged, hung up like meat-carcasses'.[40] In the small, single-storey execution room, with white-washed walls, divided by a black curtain, hooks, indeed like meat-hooks, had been placed on a rail just below the ceiling. Usually, the only light in the room came from two windows, dimly revealing a frequently used guillotine. Now, however, certainly for the first groups of conspirators being led to their doom, the executions were to be filmed and photographed, as with the filming of the court proceedings presumably in line with Hitler's instructions or those of Goebbels, and the macabre scene was illuminated with bright lights, like a film studio. On a small table in the corner of the room stood a table with a bottle of cognac – for the executioners, not to steady the nerves of the victims. The condemned men were led in, handcuffed and wearing prison trousers. There were no last words, no comfort from a priest or pastor; nothing but the black humour of the hangman. Eye-witness accounts speak of the steadfastness and dignity of those executed. The hanging was carried out within twenty seconds of the prisoner entering the room. Death was not, however, immediate. Sometimes it came quickly; in other cases, the agony was slow – lasting more than twenty minutes. In an added gratuitous obscenity, some of the condemned men had their trousers pulled down by their executioners before they died. And all the time the camera whirred.[41] The photographs and grisly film were taken to Führer Headquarters. Speer later reported seeing a pile of such photographs lying on Hitler's map-table when he visited the Wolf's Lair on 18 August. SS-men and some civilians, he added, went into a viewing of the executions in the cinema that evening, though they were not joined by any members of the Wehrmacht.[42] Whether Hitler saw the film of the executions is uncertain; the testimony is contradictory.[43]

Most of the executions connected with the attempted coup of 20 July 1944 followed within the next weeks. Some took place only months later. By the time the blood-letting subsided, the death-toll of those directly implicated numbered around 200.[44] But it was Hitler's last triumph.

His initial euphoria at what he took to be his survival ordained by Providence, and at the explanation the 'treachery' of the plotters offered for the causes of Germany's military ill-fortune, soon evaporated. The reality of daily setbacks, crises, disasters was too strong even for Hitler to suppress completely. There was little respite. He rapidly had to turn his attention again to military affairs.

However, the Stauffenberg plot left its lasting mark on him. The injuries he had suffered in the bomb blast had been, as we noted, relatively super-ficial. As if to emphasize his own indestructibility and his manliness in surmounting pain, he made light of his injuries and even joked about them to his entourage.[45] But they were less trivial than Hitler himself implied. Blood was still seeping through the bandages from the skin wounds almost a fortnight after the bomb-attack.[46] He suffered sharp pain in especially the right ear, and his hearing was impaired.[47] He was treated by Dr Erwin Giesing, an ear, nose and throat specialist in a nearby hospital, then by Professor Karl von Eicken, who had removed a throat polyp in 1935 and was now flown in from Berlin. But the ruptured ear-drums, the worst injury, continued bleeding for days, and took several weeks to heal.[48] He thought for some time that his right ear would never recover.[49] The disturbance to his balance from the inner-ear injuries made his eyes turn to the right and gave him a tendency to lean rightwards when he walked. There was also frequent dizziness and malaise.[50] His blood pressure was too high.[51] He looked aged, ill, and strained.[52] Eleven days after the attack on his life, he told those present at the daily military briefing that he was unfit to speak in public for the time being; he could not stand up for long, feared a sudden attack of dizziness, and was also worried about not walking straight.[53] A few weeks later, Hitler admitted to his doctor, Morell, that the weeks since the bomb-attack had been 'the worst of his life' – adding that he had mastered the difficulties 'with a heroism no German could dream of.'[54] Strangely, the trembling in Hitler's left leg and hands practically disappeared following the blast.[55] Morell attributed it to the nervous shock. By mid-September, however, the tremor had returned.[56] By this time, the heavy daily doses of pills and injections could do nothing to head off the long-term deterioration in Hitler's health. At least as serious were the pyschological effects.

His sense of distrust and betrayal now reached paranoid levels. Outward precautions were swiftly taken. Security was at once massively tightened at Führer Headquarters.[57] At military briefings, all personnel were from now on thoroughly searched for weapons and explosives.[58] Hitler's food and medicines were tested for poison. Any presents of foodstuffs, such as choc-olates or caviar (which he was fond of), were immediately destroyed.[59] But the outward security measures could do nothing to alter the deep shock that some of his own generals had turned against him. According to Guderian, whom he appointed as successor to Zeitzler as Chief of the General Staff within hours of Stauffenberg's bomb exploding, 'he believed no one any more. It had already been difficult enough dealing with him; it now became a torture that grew steadily worse from month to month. He frequently lost all self-control and his language grew increasingly violent. In his intimate circle he now found no restraining influence . . .'[60]

Although Hitler stressed that his distrust of his military leaders had been vindicated, and though he had found the scapegoats he needed to explain to himself the setbacks on all fronts, he had never contemplated a plot to overthrow him being hatched by those close to the heart of the regime, especially by officers who, far from straining every sinew for Germany's victory, were doing all they could to undermine the war effort from within. In 1918, according to his distorted vision of the momentous weeks of defeat and revolution, enemies from within had stabbed in the back those fighting at the front. His entire life in politics had been aimed at reversing that disaster, and in eliminating any possible repetition in a new war. Now, a new variant of such treachery had emerged – led, this time, not by Marxist subversives at home threatening the military effort, but by officers of the Wehrmacht who had come close to undermining the war-effort on the home-front.[61] Suspicion had always been deeply embedded in Hitler's nature. But the events of 20 July now transformed the underlying suspicion into the most visceral belief in treachery and betrayal all around him in the army, aimed once more at stabbing in the back a nation engaged in a titanic struggle for its very survival.

Alongside the thirsting for brutal revenge, the failed bomb-plot gave a further mighty boost to Hitler's sense of walking with destiny. With 'Providence' on his side, as he imagined, his survival was to him the guarantee that he would fulfil his historic mission. It intensified the descent into pure messianism. 'These criminals who wanted to do away with me have no idea what would have happened to the German people,' Hitler told his secretaries. 'They don't know the plans of our enemies, who want to annihilate Germany so that it can never arise again. If they think that the western powers are strong enough without Germany to hold Bolshevism in check, they are deceiving themselves. This war must be won by us. Otherwise Europe will be lost to Bolshevism. And I will see to it that no one else can hold me back or eliminate me. I am the only one who knows the danger, and the only one who can prevent it.'[62] Such sentiments were redolent, through a distorting mirror, of the Wagnerian redeemer-figure, a hero who alone could save the holders of the Grail, indeed the world itself, from disaster – a latter-day Parsifal.

But, once more looking to his own place in history, and looking to the reasons why the path of destiny had led to mounting tragedy for Germany, instead of glorious victory, he found a further reason, beyond the treachery of his generals: the weakness of the people. If Speer can be believed, Hitler gave at this time an intimation that the German people might not deserve him, might have proved weak, have failed its test before history, and thus be condemned to destruction.[63] It was one of the few hints, whether in public or in private, amid the continued outpourings of optimism about the outcome of the war, that Hitler indeed contemplated, even momentarily, the possibility of total defeat.

Whatever the positive gloss he instinctively and insistently placed upon news of the latest setbacks as he continued to play the role of Führer to perfection, he was not devoid of understanding for the significance of the successful landing of the western Allies in Normandy, the dramatic collapse of the eastern front which left the Red Army in striking distance of the borders of the Reich itself, the ceaseless bombing that the Luftwaffe was powerless to prevent, the overwhelming Allied superiority in weaponry and raw materials, and gloomy reports of a mounting, critical fuel shortage. Kluge and Rommel had both urged Hitler to end the war which he could not win.[64] But he continued to dismiss out of hand all talk of suing for peace. The situation was 'not yet ripe for a political solution', he declared. 'To hope for a favourable political moment to do something during a time of severe military defeats is naturally childish and naïve,' he went on, during the military briefing session with his generals on 31 August 1944. 'Such moments can present themselves when you have successes.' But where were the successes likely to materialize? All he could point to was a feeling of certainty that at some point the Allied coalition would break down under the weight of its inner tensions. It was a matter of waiting for that moment, however tough the situation was.

'My task has been,' he continued, 'especially since 1941 under no circumstances to lose my nerve.' He lived, he said, just to carry out this struggle since he knew that it could only be won through a will of iron. Instead of spreading this iron will, the General Staff officers had undermined it, disseminating nothing but pessimism. But the fight would continue, if necessary even on the Rhine. He once more evoked one of his great heroes of history. 'We will under all circumstances carry on the struggle until, as Frederick the Great said, one of our damned opponents is tired of fighting any longer, and until we get a peace which secures the existence of the German nation for the next fifty or a hundred years and' – he was back at a central obsession – 'which, above all, does not defile our honour a second time, as happened in 1918.' This thought brought him directly to the bomb plot, and to his own survival. 'Fate could have taken a different turn,' he continued, adding with some pathos: 'If my life had been ended, it would have been for me personally, I might say, only a liberation from worries, sleepless nights, and severe nervous strain. In a mere fraction of a second you're freed from all that and have rest and your eternal peace. For the fact that I'm still alive, I nevertheless have to thank Providence.'[65]

They were somewhat rambling thoughts. But they were plain enough in meaning: a negotiated peace could not be considered except from a position of strength (which was in realistic terms unimaginable); the only hope was to hold out until the Allied coalition collapsed (but time, and the crass imbalance of material resources, were scarcely on Germany's side); his historic role, as he saw it, was to eradicate any possibility of a second capitulation on the lines of that of November 1918; he alone stood between Germany and calamity; but suicide would bring release for him (whatever the consequences for the German people) within a split second. In Hitler's extraordinary perspective, his historic task was to continue the fight to the point of utter destruction – and even self-destruction – in order to prevent another 'November 1918' and to erase the memory of that 'disgrace' for the nation. It was a task of infinitely greater honour than negotiating a peace from weakness – something which would bring new shame on himself and the German people. It amounted to scarcely less than a realization that the time for a last stand was approaching, and that no holds would be barred in a struggle likely to end in oblivion, where the only remaining monumental vision was the quest for historical greatness – even if Reich and people should go down in flames in the process.

This meant in turn that there was no way out. The failure of the conspiracy to remove Hitler took away the last opportunity of a negotiated end to the war. For the German people, it ensured the near total destruction of their country. Whatever the varied reactions to the events of 20 July and their aftermath, ordinary Germans were exposed over the next eight months to the laying waste of their cities in relentless bombing-raids against which there was as good as no defence, to the painful losses of loved ones fighting an obviously futile war against vastly superior enemy forces, to acute privations in the material conditions of their daily lives, and to intensified fear and repression at the hands of a regime that would stop at nothing. The horrors of a war which Germany had inflicted on the rest of Europe were rebounding – if, even now, in far milder form – on to the Reich itself.

With internal resistance crushed, and a leadership unable to bring victory, incapable of staving off defeat, and unwilling to attempt to find peace, only total military destruction could bring a release.

For Hitler's countless victims throughout Europe, the advances, impressive though they had been, of the Red Army in the east and the Anglo-American forces in the west and the south, were not yet nearly at the point where they could force an end to the war, and with it the immeasurable suffering inflicted by the Nazi regime. The human misery had, in fact, still not reached its peak. It would rise in crescendo in the months still to come.

II

Those who had risked their lives in the plot to assassinate Hitler were fully aware that they were acting without the masses behind them.[66] In the event of a successful coup, the conspirators had to hope that a rapid end to the war would win over the vast majority of the population – most of whom had at one time been admirers of Hitler – and that the emergence of a new 'stab-in-the-back-legend' (such as had poisoned German politics after the First World War) could be avoided.[67] If they were to fail, the plotters knew they would not have a shred of popular support, that their act would be seen as one of base treachery, and that they could expect to be regarded with nothing but outright ignominy by the mass of the population.

The Nazi leadership was, however, leaving nothing to chance. One Gauleiter, Siegfried Uiberreither, the Nazi leader in Styria, inquired within hours of Stauffenberg's bomb exploding whether public displays of support for Hitler were envisaged. He was told that 'loyalty rallies' were welcomed, and that, in the light of his request, instructions would soon be transmitted to all Gauleiter. These were sent the next day, encouraging huge open-air mass rallies 'in which the joy and satisfaction of the people at the wonderful salvation of the Führer' would be expressed.[68] Such rallies took place over the following days in towns and cities throughout Germany. Hundreds of thousands of ordinary citizens and Wehrmacht representatives 'spontaneously' gave voice to their shock and outrage at the 'foul attempt on the Führer's life (*das ruchlose Attentat gegen den Führer*)' and their relief and happiness that he had survived it.[69]

The sentiments were identical to those recorded in early soundings of opinion taken by the SD and passed on by the Chief of the Security Police Ernst Kaltenbrunner to Martin Bormann after the news of the assassination attempt had spread like wildfire. A first report, compiled on 21 July, announced uniform reactions throughout the German people of 'strongest consternation, shock, deep outrage, and fury'. Even, it was claimed, in districts or among sections of the population known to be critical of Nazism, such sentiments could be registered; not a single comment hinted at sympathy for the planned assassination. In some cities, women were said to have burst into tears in shops or on the streets when they heard what had happened. A remark commonly heard was: 'Thank God the Führer is alive.' Many were prepared to accept Hitler's own version in seeing his survival as a sign of Providence and an indication that, despite all setbacks, the war would end in victory. Very many people, the report added, connected 'mystical, religious notions with the person of the Führer'.[70]

People initially jumped to the conclusion that enemy agents were behind the assassination attempt – an assumption that triggered a new upsurge of hatred against the British.[71] After Hitler's speech – held so late at night that most people were already in bed, but repeated in the early afternoon of 21 July – the fury turned against those seen as traitors within. There was outrage that the attempt on the Führer's life had been carried out by officers of the Wehrmacht, something viewed (as Hitler himself saw it) as the treachery behind Germany's military disasters.[72] Full expectations of a ruthless 'cleansing' of the officer corps were placed in the 'strong man' Heinrich Himmler. Approving comments of Stalin's purges could be heard. And a speech by Robert Ley violently denouncing the aristocracy gave rise to widespread castigation of the 'high-ups', 'big noises', and 'monocle-chaps'. There was resentment that the burdens of 'total war' had not been spread evenly; that too many people had been able to avoid them. Such people needed to be forced into line, however tough the measures were to bring this about. Whatever sacrifices were needed to bring the war to a speedy and victorious end would then be willingly borne.[73]

The failure of the bomb-plot revived strong support for Hitler not only within Germany, but also among soldiers at the front. There was, for instance, a rise in expressions of faith in Hitler among prisoners-of-war captured by the western Allies in Normandy in late July.[74] And the military censor who had examined 45,000 letters of ordinary soldiers from the front in August 1944 commented on 'the high number of joyful expressions about the salvation of the Führer'.[75] There was no compulsion in letters back home even to refer to the attempt on Hitler's life. The pro-Hitler sentiment was doubtless genuine.

Four days after Stauffenberg's bomb had exploded, the SD reports still stressed the almost unanimous condemnation of the assassination attempt and the joy at the Führer's survival. There was now, however, a hint of other voices. 'Only in absolutely isolated cases,' it was said, 'was the attack not sharply condemned.' A woman in Halle had been arrested for expressing regret at the outcome of the bomb-attack. Another woman in Vienna had remarked that something like that was bound to happen because the war was lasting so long. But – so the SD claimed – even 'politically indifferent' sectors of the population reacted heatedly against such comments.[76]

The backlash of support for Hitler and ferocity of condemnation of those who had tried to kill the Führer, as mirrored in the SD's reports, had, as we have noted, been fully anticipated by the plotters themselves in the event of their failure. It highlighted the extensive reservoir of Hitler's popularity that still existed and could be tapped to bolster the regime at a critical time, despite the increasingly self-evident catastrophic course of the war. The Führer cult was far from extinguished.

But Hitler's popularity, as we have seen, had unquestionably waned over the previous two years. He had personally been drawn increasingly into the blame for the miseries of a war almost certain to end in defeat. It is hard to imagine, therefore, that the unanimity of feelings of joy at his survival recorded by the SD could have been an accurate reflection of the views of the German people as a whole. The SD was unquestionably registering widely expressed opinion, indeed indicating a real upsurge in pro-Hitler feeling. But the opinions the SD's informants were able to hear would doubtless have been those emanating in the main from regime-loyalists, Nazi fanatics, and those anxious to demonstrate their support or dispel any suspicions that they might be critical of Hitler. People with less positive views were well advised to keep them to themselves – at such a critical juncture quite especially.[77] As war-fortunes had worsened, punishment for incautious remarks had become more draconian. Expressing out loud in late July 1944 regret that Hitler was still alive was as good as suicidal. Some people did take risks. A Berlin tram conductor ventured a brief but pointed commentary on Goebbels's radio address on 26 July, in which the Propaganda Minister had castigated the plotters. 'It makes you want to throw up,' the tram conductor remarked.[78] He seems to have got away with it.

Critical sentiments could be expressed safely, however, only in privacy, or among trusted family or friends. One boy, for instance, just sixteen at the time, confided on 21 July 1944 in the remarkable diary that he kept in the attic of a house near Hamburg: 'Assassination attempt on Hitler! Yesterday, an attack on Hitler with explosives was carried out in his study.

Unfortunately, as if by a miracle the swine was unharmed . . . Last night at 1a.m. Hitler gave a speech on the radio. It's very noticeable that Hitler repeated six times that it's only a matter of "a tiny clique". But his extensive measures give the lie to these claims. You don't need to put in an entire army to wipe out "a tiny cabal".[79] The boy kept the diary to himself, not even showing it to his parents.

Another diary entry, from a one-time Hitler-loyalist whose former enthusiasm had turned cold, confined itself to the cynically ambiguous comment: 'Assassination attempt on the Führer. "Providence" has saved him, and therefore we can believe in victory.'[80] Letters to loved ones were also best 'coded' for safety. One well-educated German, for years a strong critic of Nazism, writing on 21 July from Paris to his Canadian wife in Germany, remarked about the events of the previous day: 'For some people it can hardly have been a good night, but we must be thankful that the affair ended as it did. For this war, as I have always pointed out, can only be brought to the desired conclusion by Adolf Hitler!'[81]

Signs that there were voices beyond the unanimous condemnation summarized by the SD, and that the silence of a large majority of the population was evocative, could even be found in official reports from provincial localities. One such report from Upper Bavaria frankly admitted that 'part of the population would have welcomed the success of the assassination attempt because in the first instance they would have hoped for an earlier end to the war from it'.[82] Another report relayed the perilous remark uttered by a woman, hidden in the gloom in the corner of a dark air-raid shelter: 'If only they'd have got him.'[83]

At the front, too, opinion about the bomb-plot was more divided than appearances suggested. Implying any regret that Hitler had survived was to court disaster. Letters home had to pass through the control of the censor and might be intercepted. It was safest to keep quiet. So it is remarkable that there was even a slight increase in criticism of the regime in August 1944, and even more telling that some letters risked extreme retribution for the sender. One soldier was lucky. His letter home on 4 August escaped the attention of the censor. It ran: 'You write in your letter of the attack on the Führer. Yes, we heard of it even on the same day. Unfortunately, the gents had bad luck. Otherwise there'd already be a truce, and we'd be saved from this mess.'[84] In other instances, the censor picked up similar bold comments. The death-sentence for the writer of the letter was then an almost certain consequence.[85]

As the reactions to the bomb-plot revealed, the bonds of the German people to Hitler, if greatly loosened, were far from broken in mid-1944. The failure of Stauffenberg's attempt had prompted an outpouring of support for Hitler which unquestionably strengthened the regime for a time. The feeling that to attempt to kill the head of state, and at a time when the nation was fighting for its very existence, was a heinous crime was far from confined to Nazi fanatics. The Catholic sector of the population, for instance, recognized for its lukewarm backing for a regime which since its inception had conducted its attritional campaign against the Church, was also prominently represented in the huge demonstrations of loyalty to Hitler in late July.[86] Both major denominations – important formative influences on opinion – condemned the attempt to kill Hitler even after the war.[87] And as late as the early 1950s, a third of those questioned in opinion surveys still criticized the attack on Hitler's life on 20 July 1944.[88] But above all, the voices captured by the SD in the first days after the assassination attempt were those of the dwindling masses of continued loyal believers in the Führer. They had spoken loudly for the last time. What proportion of the population (or even of a Nazi Party with a nominal membership by this time of over 8 million Germans)[89] they represented can only be guessed at; but they constituted by now almost certainly a minority – if still a controlling minority with massive repressive capacity.

Even some of the SD's own provincial stations were providing, within weeks of the explosion in the Wolf's Lair, blunt indicators of the collapse in Hitler's popularity. A devastating report on 8 August from the SD office in Stuttgart, for instance, began by stating that for the overwhelming majority of the population in that area it was not a question of whether Germany would win the war, but only whether they would be ruled by the Anglo-Americans or Russians. Beyond a small number of Party activists and a tiny section of the population, no one thought there would be a miracle. People read into Hitler's speech on the night after Stauffenberg's bomb-attack the exact opposite of what was intended. It was now plain, they said, that Göring, Goebbels, and other leading men in the regime had lied to them in claiming that time was on Germany's side, armaments production was rising, and the day of a return to the offensive backed by new, decisive weapons was close at hand. They had now heard in the Führer's own words that his work had been sabotaged for years. In other words, people were saying: 'The Führer is admitting that time has previously not been on our side, but running against us. If such a man as the Führer has been so thoroughly deceived,' the summary of prevailing opinion continued, 'then he is either not the genius that he has been depicted as, or, knowing that saboteurs were at work, he intentionally lied to the German people, which would be just as bad, for, with such enemies within, war-production could never have been raised, and we could never gain victory.' The consequence of such thoughts was made explicit: 'The most worrying aspect of the whole thing is probably that most comrades of the people, even those who up to now have believed unshakeably, have lost all faith in the Führer.'[90]

As the autumn wore on and Hitler, after his brief return for a final time to the centre of people's attention, again faded from most people's daily consciousness, attitudes against him in the same region hardened still further. On 6 November, the Stuttgart SD office recorded opinion which could in variants, it suggested, be frequently heard: 'It's always claimed that the Führer has been sent to us from God. I don't doubt it. The Führer was sent to us from God, though not in order to save Germany, but to ruin it. Providence has determined the destruction of the German people, and Hitler is the executor of this will.'[91]

Sometimes, irrational belief was all that was left. A teenage girl, writing in her diary at the end of August and in early September 1944, saw blow following blow in Germany's war effort: the attack on the Führer's life, advances of the western Allies, constant German retreat on the eastern front, the incessant bombing, and the collapse of the Reich's alliance-partners. 'On one side there is victory, which is becoming ever more doubtful, and on the other Bolshevism,' she wrote. 'But then: rather sacrifice everything, absolutely everything, for victory, than for Bolshevism. If that should come, then you shouldn't think further. What would I still go to school for if I'm going to end up in Siberia? What for? What for? A whole number of questions line up like this. But if we all wanted to think in this way, there would be no hope left. So, head high. Trust in our will and our leadership!!!'[92]

As this diary-entry suggests, the fear of Bolshevism was by now among the most central cohesive elements sustaining support for the German war effort and militating against any collapse of morale at home. Even so, as the news of defeats, destruction, and desertion of allies mounted without relief, and as losses of property and possessions, homes and loved ones piled misery on misery, the first signs of disintegration were visible. The German greeting, 'Heil Hitler', was increasingly replaced by 'Good morning', 'Good day', or, in south Germany, 'Grüß Gott'. The evacuation of the Aachen area – the old seat of Charlemagne's empire, where the Allies had broken through – in early September was accompanied by 'a more or less panic-type of flight by the German civilian population', according to a report to Himmler.[93] Wehrmacht reports from the western front spoke later in the month of mounting lack of discipline and indications of disintegration among the troops, with increasing numbers of desertions, reflected in a sharp rise in draconian punishment meted out by military courts.[94]

Some of the deserters in the west made their way to Cologne. This great city on the Rhine had by now been largely bombed into dereliction – though, amazingly, its magnificent Gothic cathedral was still standing – with much of its population evacuated. Amid the rubble and the ruins, in the cellars of burnt-out buildings, forms of opposition to the Nazi regime approaching partisan activity emerged. Here, heterogeneous groups of deserted soldiers, foreign workers – now forming around 20 per cent of the Reich's work-force and presenting the Nazi authorities with increasing worries about insurrection – members of dissident bands of disaffected youth (known picturesquely as 'Edelweiß Pirates'), and the Communist underground organization (infiltrated and smashed many times but always managing to replenish itself) blended together in the autumn of 1944 into short-lived but, for the regime, troublesome resistance. The Gestapo recorded some two dozen small resistance groups of up to twenty individuals, and one large body of around 120 persons. They stole food, broke into Wehrmacht camps and depots to get weapons, and organized minor forms of sabotage. It came on occasion to shoot-outs with camp guards and police. Their actions were politically directed: they killed, among others, several Gestapo men, including the head of the Cologne Gestapo, an SA man, and a Nazi Party functionary. In all, twenty-nine killings were attributed to them by the Gestapo. Attacks on the Hitler Youth and other Nazi formations by the 'Edelweiß Pirates' were commonplace. With the explosives they acquired, their intention was to blow up the Gestapo headquarters and the city's law-courts, and to shoot a leading attorney and several members of the Party organization.[95] Possibly, had the Allied advance in the west not slowed, the quasi-partisan activity in Cologne might have spread to other cities in the Rhine and Ruhr region. The problems of combating it would then have magnified. As it was, the Gestapo, aided by Wehrmacht units, was able to strike back with devastating effect in the autumn. The resistance groups did not give up without a fight. One group waged an armed battle for twelve hours before the ruined cellar which served as its 'fortress' was blown up. Another group defended itself with hand grenades and a machine-gun, finally breaking through a police cordon and escaping.[96] By the time the Gestapo were finished, however, some 200 members of the resistance groups had been arrested, the groups themselves totally destroyed, their leaders executed, and many other members imprisoned.[97]

Had the Stauffenberg bomb-plot succeeded, it is possible that the types of grass-roots political activism experienced in Cologne could have swelled into a revolutionary ferment from a base in western Germany. But many – and quite conflicting – scenarios could be imagined had Hitler been assassinated on 20 July. The actual outcome was that resistance from below – from Communists, Socialists, youth-rebels, foreign workers, deserted soldiers and others – was, whatever the continued courage of those involved, robbed of any prospect of success. The regime had been challenged internally. But the blow to its heart had not proved lethal. It now reacted with all the ferocity at its disposal. At least for the time being, it was able to regroup and reconsolidate, delaying the end for several more months, prolonging the agony of millions caught up in the intensifying maelstrom of death and destruction. Hitler and the Nazi leadership had survived. But there was no way leading from the self-destructive path on which they were embarked.

For the ordinary German, too, there was no way out. It was taken for granted that the regime was finished. The only hope was that the British and Americans would hold off the Bolsheviks. The most common reactions, as yet another war winter loomed, were apathy, resignation, fatalism. 'It's all the same to me. I can't judge the situation any longer. I'll just work further in my job, wait, and accept what comes' – this approach, reported by the regional agencies of the Propaganda Ministry in autumn 1944, was said to be prevalent not just with 'the man on the street', but also among Party members and even functionaries, some of whom were no longer wanting to wear their Party insignia.[98] It was a clear sign that the end was on the way.

III

The institutional pillars of the regime – the Wehrmacht, the Party, ministries of state, and the SS-controlled security apparatus – remained intact in the second half of 1944. And Hitler, the keystone bonding the regime's structure together, was still, paradoxically, indispensable to its survival while – by now even in the eyes of some close to the leadership – at the same time driving Germany inexorably towards perdition. The predictable rallying round Hitler following the July assassination attempt could not, therefore, for long conceal the fact that the regime's edifice was beginning to crumble as the Nazi empire throughout Europe shrivelled and the increasing certainty of a lost war made even some of those who had gained most from Nazism start looking for possible exit-routes. The aftermath of the bomb-plot saw the regime enter its most radical phase. But it was a radicalism that mirrored an increasingly desperate regime's reaction to internal as well as external crisis.

Hitler's own obvious reaction in the wake of the shock of Stauffenberg's bomb had been to turn to his firm loyalist base, the Party leadership, and to his most long-standing and trusted band of paladins. In the backs-to-the-wall atmosphere of the last months, the Party was to play a more dominant role than at any time since the 'seizure of power', invoking the overcoming of adversity in the 'time of struggle',[99] attempting to instil the 'fighting spirit of National Socialism' throughout the entire people in the increasingly vain attempt to combat overwhelming Allied arms and material superiority by little more than fanatical willpower.

As had invariably been the case in a crisis, Hitler had lost no time following the attempted coup on 20 July in ensuring the continued loyalty of the Gauleiter, the Party's provincial chieftains. Among them were some who had been among his most dependable lieutenants for close on two decades. Collectively, the Gauleiter constituted now, as before, a vital prop of his rule. His provincial viceroys were now, their Party positions enhanced through their extensive powers as Reich Defence Commissars, his insurance against any prospect of army-led unrest or possible insurrection in the regions. Bormann had sent out a string of circulars to the Gauleiter on 20 July and immediately thereafter, ensuring that they were well informed of the gravity of what had taken place and the steps taken to crush the uprising.[100] Within days, he was arranging a conference of the Reichsleiter and Gauleiter to take place in Posen on 3–4 August, as he put it 'to intensify the war effort'.[101] Speer, Himmler, Goebbels, and Bormann himself were among those to address the Party leaders. Speer was able to impress them with figures on armaments production – far greater than they had imagined and helping calm their nerves. Himmler fired them with a lengthy prehistory of the 'treachery' of 20 July, and with his plans for a thorough reorganiz-ation, 'according to National Socialist principles', of the Reserve Army, whose command Hitler had placed in his hands. Goebbels told them that the state and the army had caused the Führer only problems. 'That is going to end now,' he declared. 'The party will take over.'[102]

Next day, the Party leaders travelled to the Wolf's Lair. Hitler limply held out his uninjured left hand as he greeted each of them individually. They then trooped into the film-projection room where he addressed them about the consequences of the assassination attempt. He said nothing that he had not said to his closest circle immediately after the event. He told them he was necessary for the nation, which 'needs a man who does not capitulate under any circumstances but unswervingly holds high the flag of faith and confidence'. He would in the end settle with his enemies, he said. But the basis of this, he added, appealing, as always, to the support of his most trusted comrades, was to know that he had behind him 'absolute certainty, faithful trust, and loyal cooperation'. Once more, his words were sufficient to impress his audience and to bolster their morale.[103] This was crucial. Increasingly over the next months, as the threads of state administration started to fray and ultimately fell apart, the Party chieftains – especially those who acted as Reich Defence Commissars in their regions – were decisive in holding together in the provinces what was left of Nazi rule.[104]

Extended scope for propaganda, mobilization, and tightened control over the population – the overriding tasks of the Party as most people looked beyond the end of the regime and looming military defeat into an uncertain future – fell to the Reich Defence Commissars in the last desperate drive to maximize resources for 'total war'. The shortages of available men to be sent to the front, and workers for the armaments industries, had mounted alarmingly throughout the first half of 1944. Hitler's authorization in January to Fritz Sauckel, Plenipotentiary for Labour Deployment, to make up the manpower shortages through forced labour extracted from the occupied territories, while at the same time according Speer protection for the labour employed in his armaments plants in France had done nothing to resolve the difficulty and merely sharpened the conflict between Sauckel and Speer.[105] Apart from Speer, the SS, the Wehrmacht, and the Party had also proved adept at preventing any inroads into their personnel. Bormann had even presided over a 51 per cent increase in the number of 'reserved occupations', exempt from call-up, in the Party administration between May 1943 and June 1944.[106]

Meanwhile, the labour shortage had been greatly magnified through the double military disaster in June of the Allied landing in Normandy and the Red Army's devastating offensive on the eastern front. This had prompted Goebbels and Speer to link their efforts to persuade Hitler to agree to a drastic radicalization of the 'home front' to comb out all remaining manpower for the war effort.[107] Both had sent him lengthy memoranda in mid-July, promising huge labour savings to tide over the situation until new weaponry became available and the anti-German coalition broke up.[108] But before the Stauffenberg bomb, Hitler had, as we have noted, shown little readiness to comply with their radical demands. Whatever the accompanying rhetoric, and the undoubted feeling (which Goebbels's own propaganda had helped feed) among the under-privileged that many of the better-off were still able to escape the burdens of war, and were not pulling their weight in the national cause, such demands were bound to be unpopular in many circles, antagonize powerful vested interests, and also convey an impression of desperation. And, as the state administration rushed to point out, the gains might well be less than impressive; only one in twelve of those in the civil service who had not been called up was under forty-three, and more than two-thirds were over fifty-five years old.[109]

Hitler had told his Propaganda Minister as recently as June that the time was not ripe for 'a big appeal to total war in the true meaning of the word', that the crises would be surmounted 'in the usual way', but that he would be ready to introduce 'wholly abnormal measures' should 'more serious crises take place'.[110] Hitler's change of mind, directly following the failed assassination attempt, in deciding to grant Goebbels the new authority he had coveted, as Reich Plenipotentiary for the Total War Effort (*Reichsbevollmächtigter für den totalen Kriegseinsatz*), was a tacit admission that the regime was faced with a more fundamental crisis than ever before.

Goebbels's decisive action to put down the uprising on 20 July unquestionably weighed heavily in his favour when Hitler looked for the man to supervise the radicalization of the home front. And where before he had faced a hesitant Hitler, he was now pushing at an open door in his demands for draconian measures. The decision had in effect already been taken when, at a meeting of ministerial representatives along with some other leading figures in the regime two days after Stauffenberg's assassination attempt, head of the Reich Chancellery Lammers proposed the bestowing of wide-ranging powers on the Propaganda Minister to bring about the reform of the state and public life. Himmler was given extensive complementary powers at the same time to reorganize the Wehrmacht and comb out all remaining manpower.[111] The following day, 23 July, the regime's leaders, now joined by Göring, assembled at the Wolf's Lair, where Hitler himself, heavily leaning on Goebbels's memorandum of the previous week, confirmed the new role of the Propaganda Minister. Hitler demanded 'something fundamental' if the war were still to be won. Massive reserves were available, he claimed, but had not been deployed. This would now have to be done without respect to person, position, or office. He pointed to the Party in the early days, which had achieved 'the greatest historic success' with only a simple administrative apparatus. Goebbels noted with interest the change in Hitler's views since their previous meeting a month or so earlier. The assassination attempt and the events on the eastern front had produced clarity in his decisions, Goebbels noted in his diary.[112] To his own staff, the Propaganda Minister laconically remarked that 'it takes a bomb under his arse to make Hitler see reason'.[113]

Hitler's decree of 25 July, appointing Goebbels to his new position, indicated that the proposal for the establishment of a 'Reich Plenipotentiary for the Total War Effort' had come from Göring, in his long-standing (but wholly ineffectual) capacity as Chairman of the Ministerial Council for the Defence of the Reich.[114] In fact, the formulation had been suggested by Goebbels himself, then carefully drafted by Lammers, to save face for Göring, who had objected to the further diminution of his own authority and, as usual, been able to rely on Hitler's unwillingness to dent his prestige. Even so, the Reich Marshal retreated in high dudgeon to his East Prussian hunting estate at Rominten and could not be persuaded for weeks to return to the Wolf's Lair.[115] Goebbels relished his moment of triumph. He appeared to have finally achieved what he had desired for so long: control over the 'home front' with 'the most extensive plenipotentiary powers . . . that have up to now been granted in the National Socialist Reich', with rights – the decisive factor in his view – to issue directives to ministers and the highest-ranking governmental authorities.[116] To his staff, he spoke of having 'practically full dictatorial powers' within the Reich.[117]

However, nothing was ever quite what it seemed in the Third Reich. The decree itself limited Goebbels's powers in some respects. He could issue directives to the 'highest Reich authorities'. But only they could issue any consequential decrees and ordinances. And these had to be agreed with Lammers, Bormann, and Himmler (in the capacity he had adopted when becoming Interior Minister, as Plenipotentiary for Reich Administration). Any directives related to the Party itself had to have Bormann's support (and, behind Bormann, to correspond with Hitler's own wishes). Any unresolved objections to Goebbels's directives had to pass to Lammers for Hitler's own final decision. Beyond the wording of the decree itself, Hitler let Goebbels know that those authorities directly responsible to him – those involved in the rebuilding plans for Berlin, Munich, and Linz, his motor-vehicle staff, and the personnel of the Reich Chancellery, Presidential Chancellery, and Party Chancellery – were also excluded from the directives.[118] The Wehrmacht, under Himmler's authority, had been exempt from the outset.

Such restrictions on his powers left Goebbels's enthusiasm for his new task undimmed. In a radio address on 26 July, the day after his appointment, the Propaganda Minister conveyed the impression that, far from having its manpower reserves exhausted by five years of war, total mobilization was just beginning and would 'set free, all over the country, so many hands for both the front and the munition factories that it will not be too hard for us to master in sovereign fashion the difficulties that are bound to arise in the war from time to time'.[119] The belief that 'will' would overcome all problems was immediately put into action as Goebbels, with his usual forceful energy, unleashed a veritable frenzy of activity in his new role. The staff of fifty that he rapidly assembled from a number of ministries, most prominently from his own Propaganda Ministry, prided themselves on their unbureaucratic methods, swift decision-making, and improvisation. As his main agents in ensuring that directives were implemented in the regions, leaving no stone unturned in the quest to comb out all reserves of untapped labour, Goebbels looked to the Party's Gauleiter, bolstering their already extensive powers as Reich Defence Commissars. They could be relied upon, in his view, to reinvoke the spirit of the 'time of struggle', to ensure that bureaucracy did not get in the way of action. (In practice, the cooperation of the Gauleiter was assured as long as no inroads were made into the personnel of their own Party offices. Bormann ensured that they were well protected.)[120]

Behind the actionism of the Party, Goebbels also needed Hitler's backing. He ensured that this was forthcoming through a constant stream of bulletins on progress (*Führer-Informationen*), printed out on a 'Führer-Machine' – a typewriter with greatly enlarged characters which Hitler's failing eyesight could cope with[121] – recording successes and couching general recommendations (such as simplifying unnecessary bureaucratic paperwork) in such a way that, given Hitler's frame of mind, approval would be as good as automatic, thereby opening up yet further avenues for intervention.[122]

Nevertheless, Hitler did not give blanket approval to all measures suggested by Goebbels. He could rely upon Bormann to bring to his attention any proposals which his own still sharp antennae would tell him might have an unnecessarily harmful impact on morale, both at home and quite especially among soldiers at the front. He rejected, therefore, the Total War Plenipotentiary's proposals to save manpower in postal services by ending delivery of small parcels and private telegrams on the grounds that such changes would, for little return, be highly unpopular among families divided in war. Similarly, he blocked suggestions of ending supplies of newspapers and periodicals to the front because soldiers looked forward so much to reading them.[123]

Elsewhere, Goebbels encountered successful resistance to his proposals when Lammers and Göring combined to head off the suggestion to abolish the office of Minister President of Prussia along with the Prussian Finance Ministry (which had been deflected by Lammers the previous year, but now made enticing through the involvement of the Minister, Popitz, in the conspiracy against Hitler). Measured against the bureaucratic effort to transfer the business elsewhere, even the closure of the Prussian Finance Ministry proved counter-productive as a manpower-saving exercise. The complex problems of administrative reorganization which Lammers raised were the Minister Presidency to be abolished were eventually sufficient for Hitler to decide on its retention.[124]

An obvious problem was how the labour savings were to be redeployed. As Armaments Minister, Speer wanted to make use of the newly available labour in the factories under his control. Goebbels, on the other hand, saw his main task in freeing up new reserves for service at the front. The short-lived alliance between the two rapidly, therefore, came to grief. Speer saw his own powers now undermined by Goebbels, and by the Gauleiter who, spurred on by the Total War Plenipotentiary and seizing the new opportunities that the revitalization of the Party provided, intervened frequently and arbitrarily in his domain of armaments production. Matters came to a head over Goebbels's demand to conscript 100,000 men from the armaments industry. On 21 September, Speer presented Hitler with a lengthy letter setting out his demands for restriction of Party intervention in armaments questions.

Given both his personal standing with Hitler and the priority nature of his work, such a personal appeal by Speer would in the past have had a good chance of success. On this occasion, Hitler took the letter from Speer without comment, rang for his adjutant, and had it passed to Bormann who was asked, along with Goebbels who was in the Führer Headquarters at the time, for his views. It was as if, Speer wrote much later, Hitler was too weary to involve himself in such a difficult conflict.[125]

A few hours later, Speer was asked to Bormann's office nearby, where he met the head of the Party Chancellery, in shirt-sleeves and braces over his large stomach, and the more formally dressed diminutive Goebbels. Speer was no match for the new alliance, resting on mutual self-interest, controlling the Party, in charge of propaganda, calling on the principles of National Socialism, appealing to the Gauleiter – and with Hitler's ear. The discussion was heated. But Speer's references to his 'historic responsibility' and threats to resign did not impress. 'I think we have let this young man become somewhat too big,' Goebbels coolly noted in his diary. Bormann told Speer he had to accept Goebbels's decisions, and forbade any further recourse to Hitler. Goebbels informed Speer that he intended to make full use of the powers bestowed on him by Hitler. Discussion ended with Goebbels declaring that he would put the – wholly rhetorical – question to Hitler, as to whether he was prepared to dispense with the 100,000 men.[126]

Two days later, Hitler signed a proclamation by Speer to directors of armaments factories which, in the eyes of the Armaments Minister, granted most of the demands he had made in his letter. Hitler was typically appearing to grant both sides in a dispute what they wanted. But Speer recognized this was no victory over Bormann and Goebbels. Hitler was unwilling – Speer thought unable – to hold his Party leaders in check.[127] At any rate, he could do nothing to bring the conflict between two of his most important 'feudal' – and feuding – barons to a halt. The dispute rumbled on for weeks.[128] If there was no outright winner, the signs were plain enough that Speer's once unique influence on Hitler was on the wane. With a reversion to Party activism, on the other hand, the position of Goebbels as well as that of Bormann had been strengthened. And now, as before, all positions of power in the Third Reich still hinged on Hitler's favour.

Backed by this favour, Goebbels certainly produced a new, extreme austerity drive within Germany in the first weeks in his new office as Total War Plenipoteniary. In the cultural sphere, many theatres and art schools were closed, orchestras run down, the film industry drastically pruned of staff, three-quarters of the Reich Cultural Chamber axed. Big restrictions were imposed on printing, with many newspapers being shut down. Firms producing goods unnecessary for the war effort, such as toys or fashion items, were shut. Employment of domestic servants – most of them non-German – was tightly restricted, freeing up as many as 400,000 women for work (with an increase of registration age from forty-five to fifty-five years of age). Postal and railway services were cut back. Local government offices were forced to simplify administration and weed out their staff. From mid-August, leave was banned. Business and administration were working a minimum sixty-hour week. By October, 451,800 men had been made available for the war effort.[129]

The figures were deceptive. A large proportion of the men sifted out of the administration and economy were too old for military service. Goebbels was forced, therefore, to turn to fit men in reserved occupations – work thought essential for the war effort, including skilled employment in armaments factories or food production. Their replacement, where possible, by older, less fit, less experienced, less qualified workers was both administratively complicated and inefficient. The net addition of women workers numbered only little over quarter of a million. Many of the half a million mobilized overall replaced older women, or were tied to the home. There were only 271,000 more women in employment in September 1944 than there had been in May 1939. And, despite the draconian measures deployed, German men employed in industry had dropped by no more than 848,500 over the same period (more than compensated, numerically, by foreign workers), while even the much-purged administrative sector had only lost 17 per cent of its employees. The German economy was, in fact, only holding together at all because of the employment of foreign conscript labour – now accounting for 20.8 per cent of the work-force (a far higher percentage in agriculture). And although, partly through Goebbels's measures, it proved possible to send around a million men to the front between August and December 1944, German losses in the first three of those months numbered 1,189,000 dead and wounded.[130] Whatever the trumpeting by Goebbels of his achievements as Reich Plenipotentiary for the Total War Effort, the reality was that he was scraping the bottom of the barrel.

And among the most bizarre aspects of the 'total war' drive in the second half of 1944 was the fact that at precisely the time he was combing out the last reserves of manpower, Goebbels – according to film director Veit Harlan – was allowing him, at Hitler's express command, to commandeer 187,000 soldiers, withdrawn from active service, as extras for the epic colour film of national heroism, *Kolberg*, depicting the defence of the small Baltic town against Napoleon as a model for the achievements of total war. According to Harlan, Hitler as well as Goebbels was 'convinced that such a film was more useful than a military victory'.[131] Even in the terminal crisis of the regime, propaganda had to come first.

The evocation of heroic defence of the fatherland by the masses against the invading Napoleonic army – the myth enunciated in *Kolberg* – was put to direct use in the most vivid expression of the last-ditch drive to 'total war': the launching by Heinrich Himmler of the Volkssturm, or people's militia, on 18 October 1944, the 131st anniversary of the legendary defeat of Napoleon in the 'Battle of the Peoples' near Leipzig, when a coalition of forces under Blücher's leadership liberated German territory from the troops of the French Emperor once and for all.[132] The Volkssturm was the military embodiment of the Party's belief in 'triumph of the will'.[133] It was the Party's attempt to militarize the homeland, symbolizing unity through the people's participation in national defence, overcoming the deficiencies in weapons and resources through sheer willpower.

Suggestions of creating 'border protection' units in the east were put forward as early as mid-July by the Propaganda Ministry following the Red Army's advance into Lithuania.[134] But in the weeks following the attempt on Hitler's life, the initiative in this area was seized primarily by Martin Bormann. In readiness more to combat possible internal unrest than external invasion, Bormann sought in August the assistance of Himmler, as Commander of the Reserve Army, in arming Party functionaries. The Party had also taken over responsibility from the Luftwaffe for anti-aircraft and flak service. The threats from the borders produced new duties, again run by the Party, in digging fortifications, involving women as well as men in the hard manual labour.[135]

Though Goebbels continued to harbour the belief that he would incorporate in his 'total war' commission the organization of the 'Volkswehr' (People's Defence), as it was initially to be called, leaving the military aspects to the SA, Bormann and Himmler had come to an agreement to divide responsibility between them. Drafts for a decree by Hitler were put forward in early September. He eventually signed the decree on 26 September, though it was dated to the previous day.[136] It spoke of the 'final aim' of the enemy alliance as 'the eradication of the German person (*Ausrottung des deutschen Menschen*)'. This enemy must now be repulsed until a peace securing Germany's future could be guaranteed. To attain this end, Hitler's decree went on, in typical parlance, 'we set the total deployment of all Germans against the known total annihilatory will of our Jewish-international enemies'. In all Party Gaue, the 'German Volkssturm' was to be established, comprising all men capable of bearing weapons between the ages of sixteen and sixty. Training, military organization, and provision of weaponry fell to Himmler as Commander of the Reserve Army. Political and organizational matters were the province of Bormann, acting on Hitler's behalf.[137] Party functionaries were given the task of forming companies and battalions.[138] A total number of 6 million Volkssturm men was envisaged.[139] Each Volkssturm man had to swear an oath that he would be 'unconditionally loyal and obedient to the Führer of the Great German Reich Adolf Hitler', and would 'rather die than abandon the freedom and thereby the social future of my people'.[140]

The men called up had to provide their own clothing, as well as eating and drinking utensils, cooking equipment, a rucksack, and blanket.[141] And since munitions for the front were in short supply, the weaponry for the men of the Volkssturm was predictably miserable.[142] It was little wonder that the Volkssturm was largely unpopular, and widely seen as pointless on the grounds that the war was already lost. According to one reported comment, the Volkssturm had been called up because 'there is nothing more to oppose the assault of our enemies with than people and blood'. Another pointed out that the poster bearing the Führer's decree setting up the Volkssturm looked like notice of an execution – and indeed did announce an execution, 'the execution of the entire German people'.[143]

The fears, especially on the eastern front, were justified. Gauleiter Erich Koch reported severe losses among Volkssturm units in East Prussia already in October.[144] The losses were militarily pointless. They did not hold up the Red Army's advance by a single day. In all, approaching 175,000 citizens who were mainly too old, too young, or too weak to fight lost their lives in the Volkssturm.[145] The futility of the losses was a clear sign that Germany was close to military bankruptcy.

As the autumn of 1944 headed towards what would prove the last winter of the war, the fabric of the regime was still holding together. But the indications were that the threads were visibly starting to fray. The closing of the ranks which had followed Stauffenberg's assassination attempt had temporarily seen a revitalization of the *élan* of the Party. Hitler had, almost as a reflex, turned inwards to those he trusted. His distance, not just from the army leaders he detested, but also from the organs of state administration, started to extend immeasurably with his increased reliance on a diminishing number of his longstanding paladins. Bormann's position, dependent upon the combination of his role as head of the Party organization and, especially, his proximity to Hitler as the Führer's secretary and mouthpiece, guarding the portals and restricting access, was particularly strengthened. He was one of the winners from the changed circumstances after 20 July.[146] Another was Goebbels who, like Bormann, had seized the opportunity to enhance his own position of power as the Party increased its hold over practically all walks of life within Germany. Mobilization and control had been the essence of Party activity since the beginning. Now, as the regime tottered, the Party returned to its elements.

Speer was one of the losers in the aftermath of the bomb plot. He could no longer depend upon his special favour with Hitler. Without a Party base, he began to feel the cold. So, too, as the Party reasserted itself, did Lammers, the only point of coordination between the work of the various Reich ministries and Hitler. Though his relations with Bormann had never been free of tension, they had functioned after a fashion – and had sometimes formed the basis of a pragmatic alliance against other forces in the regime.[147] In autumn 1944, the balance in their positions had started to tip as Bormann's position strengthened. Contact between the two waned. More important still: Lammers lost his access to Hitler. The chief orchestrator of government business was no longer in a position to discuss that business with the head of state. In a letter to Bormann on 1 January 1945, Lammers, pointing to the early good cooperation, lamented the fact that his last audience with Hitler had been three months earlier, that he had had to give up at the end of October his quarters close to Hitler's field headquarters, and that Reich Ministers would inevitably have to seek other channels of approach to the Führer if he could not provide them. He had been, he bemoaned, often in the embarrassing situation that he had had to carry responsibility for decisions of the Führer which had simply been transmitted to him, without any possibility of his affecting them and bringing about a different outcome. His lament ended with a pathetic request to Bormann to arrange a brief audience with the Führer so that he could address the many issues which had accumulated in the meantime.[148] With the end of the regime in sight, Hitler had, it seemed obvious, little time for or interest in the normal business of government. Meanwhile, the work of the major offices of state could only fragment further.

Yet another development, from a most unlikely source, provides in retrospect – at the time it was still well concealed – the clearest indication that the regime was starting to teeter. Among the biggest beneficiaries of the failed coup of 20 July 1944 had been Reichsführer-SS Heinrich Himmler.[149] Hitler had given 'loyal Heinrich', his trusted head of the labyrinthine security organization, overall responsibility for uncovering the background to the conspiracy and for rounding up the plotters. And beyond his other extensive powers, Himmler had now also gained direct entrée into the military sphere as Commander of the Reserve Army, with a remit to undertake a full-scale reorganization. He was soon, as we have seen, also to have control over the people's militia, the Volkssturm. Yet at this very time, Himmler, conceivably now the most powerful individual in Germany after Hitler, was playing a double game, combining every manifestation of utmost loyalty with secret overtures to the West in the forlorn hope of saving not just his skin but his position of power in the event of the British and Americans eventually seeing sense and turning, with the help of his SS, to fend off the threat of Communism. In October, Himmler used an SS intermediary to put to an Italian industrialist with good connections in England a proposal to make twenty-five German divisions in Italy available to the Allies as a defence against Communism in return for a guarantee of the preservation of the Reich's territory and population. Both the British and the Americans rejected the overtures out of hand.[150] In this scenario, Hitler would have been dispensable. But it was pure self-delusion. Himmler was too centrally implicated in the most appalling facets of the Nazi regime to be taken seriously by the Allies as a prospective leader of a post-Hitlerian Germany. For Himmler, too, there was no way out. Without Hitler's backing, his power would evaporate like a breath in the chill morning air. This was as true in late 1944 as at any other time during the Third Reich.

Hitler's authority remained intact. But if they could have found an escape route by removing him or discarding him, there were now those among his closest paladins who would have followed it.

IV

Meanwhile, the vice around Hitler's Reich was tightening. Between June and September the Wehrmacht lost on all fronts well over a million men killed, captured, or missing. The losses of tanks, guns, planes, and other armaments were incalculable.[151] The war in the air was by now almost wholly one-sided. Fuel shortages left many German fighters unable to take to the air as the British and American bomber armadas wreaked havoc on German towns and cities with impunity by day as well as by night. The war at sea had also by this time been definitively lost by Germany. The U-boat fleet had never recovered from its losses in the second half of 1943, while Allied convoys could now cross the Atlantic almost unmolested. In the second half of 1944, only twelve ships, with a tonnage of 55,290 tons, were sunk in the northern Atlantic (with no losses at all in October). Another sixty-five ships – a tiny fraction of the overall Allied shipping crossing the seas – fell victim to German submarines off the shores of Britain. In all, 138 U-boats were lost over the same period.[152] In the meantime, the territories of the Nazi empire were shrinking markedly by the end of the summer following the advances of the Allies on both western and eastern fronts since June.

On the western front, Germany's military commanders had by then long viewed the continuation of the war as pointless. On replacing Rundstedt in early June, the weak and impressionable Kluge was easily persuaded by Hitler that the western commanders, especially Rommel, had been far too pessimistic in their judgement of the situation. After a two-day visit to the front, however, Kluge had been forced to admit that Rommel was right. In his letter to Hitler of 15 July, Rommel had explicitly stated that, heroically though the troops were fighting, 'the unequal struggle is heading for its end'. He felt, therefore, compelled to ask Hitler, he wrote, 'to draw the consequences from this position without delay'.[153] He let the leaders of the conspiracy against Hitler know that he would be prepared to join them if the demands for an end to the war were dismissed. Germany's most renowned field-marshal was never put to the test. Three days before Stauffenberg's bomb exploded, Rommel was seriously injured when his car skidded from the road after being strafed by an enemy aircraft.[154]

Five days after the assassination attempt on Hitler, 'Operation Cobra', the Allied attack southwards towards Avranches, began with a ferocious 'carpet-bombing' assault by over 2,000 aircraft, dropping 47,000 tons of bombs on an already weakened German panzer division in an area of only six or so square miles. It ended on 30 July with the taking of Avranches and the opening not only of the route to the Brittany coastal ports, but also to the exposed German flank towards the east, and to the heart of France.[155]

The significance of the loss of Avranches was still not fully appreciated when Hitler provided Jodl with his overview of the entire military situation on the evening of 31 July. Hitler was far from unrealistic in his assessment. He was well aware of how threatening the position was on all fronts, and how impossible it was in the current circumstances to combat the overwhelming Allied superiority in men and materials, above all in air-power. His main hope was to buy time. Weapon technology, more planes, and an eventual split in the Alliance would open up new opportunities.[156] He had to get some breathing-space in the west, he told his Luftwaffe adjutant, Nicolaus von Below, shortly after his briefing with Jodl. Then, with new panzer divisions and fighter formations, he could launch a major offensive on the western front. In common with many observers, Below had thought it more important to concentrate all forces against the Red Army in the east. Hitler replied that he could attack the Russians at a later point. But this could not be done with the Americans already in the Reich. (He led Below to believe at the same time that he feared the power of the Jews in the USA more than the power of the Bolsheviks.[157]) His strategy was, therefore, to gain time, inflict a major blow on the western Allies, hope for a split in the Alliance, and turn on the Russians from a new position of strength.

Hitler thought, so he told Jodl, that the eastern front could be stabilized, as long as additional forces could be mobilized. But a breakthrough by the enemy in the east, whether in East Prussia or Silesia, imperilling the home-land itself and bearing serious psychological consequences, would pose a critical danger.[158] Any destabilization on the eastern front would, he went on, affect the stance of the Balkan states – Turkey, Romania, Bulgaria, and Hungary. Preventive measures had to be taken. It was vital to secure Hungary, both for vital raw materials such as bauxite and manganese and for communications lines with south-eastern Europe. Bulgaria was essential to securing a hold on the Balkans and obtaining ore from Greece.[159] He also feared a British landing in the Balkans or on the Dalmatian islands, which Germany was scarcely in a position to ward off and which 'could naturally lead to catastrophic consequences'.[160]

On the Italian front, Hitler saw the greatest advantage in the tying down of significant Allied forces which could otherwise be deployed elsewhere. The withdrawal of German forces into the Apennines would remove tactical mobility, would still not prevent an Allied advance, and would leave only retreat to alpine defence positions as a possibility – thereby freeing up Allied troops for the western front. But as a last resort, he was prepared to give up Italy (and the entire Balkans), pull back German troops to the Alps, and withdraw his main forces for the vital struggle on the western front.[161]

This was for him the decisive theatre of war. The troops would not understand him remaining in East Prussia when valuable western parts of the Reich were threatened, and behind them the Ruhr – Germany's industrial heartland.[162] Preparations would have to be made to move Führer Head-quarters to the west.[163] Command would have to be centralized.[164] Kluge, supreme commander in the west, could not be left with the responsibility. So paranoid was Hitler by now about treachery within the army, that he told Jodl it would be necessary in such an event to avoid communicating such a plan to army command in the west – pointing to Stülpnagel's involvement in the plot against him – since it would probably be immediately betrayed to the enemy.[165]

Hitler pointed to what he saw as a decisive issue in the west. 'If we lose France as a war area (*Kriegsgebiet*), we lose the basis of the U-boat war.'[166] (Though, as we have noted, the U-boats were ineffective in the second half of 1944, Hitler was persuaded by Dönitz that new, improved submarines would soon be ready, and would be a vital weapon in the war against the western powers.[167]) In addition, essential raw materials – he singled out wolfram, important for steel production and electro-technical products – would be lost. If it were not so important to the war effort to hold on to France, he said, he would vacate the coastal areas – still vital for U-boat bases at Brest and St Nazaire – and pull back mobile forces to a more defensible line. But he saw no prospect at present of holding such a line with the forces available, wherever the line might be drawn. 'We've got to be clear,' he stated, 'that a change could come about in France only if we succeed – even for a certain time – in gaining air-supremacy.' But he drew the conclusion that, 'however bitter it might be at the moment', everything had to be done to hold back 'for the most extreme case' as a 'last reserve' whatever Luftwaffe divisions could be assembled in the Reich – though that could take weeks – to be deployed wherever it might be possible 'at the last throw of the dice (*wo die letzten Würfel fallen*)' to bring about a decisive shift in fortunes.[168]

Hitler was desperate to buy time. 'I can't operate myself,' he said, 'but I can make it colossally difficult for the enemy to operate in the depths of the area.' For this, it was essential to deprive the enemy of access to ports on the French coast, preventing the landing of troops, armaments, and provisions. (At this point only Cherbourg, with a much-damaged harbour, was in Allied hands.) Hitler was prepared, as he bluntly stated, 'simply to sacrifice certain troops' to this end. The ports were to be held, he emphasized, 'under all circumstances, with complete disregard for the people there, to make it impossible for the enemy to supply unlimited numbers of men'. Should this not happen, a breakthrough could come quickly. Along with this, in an early glimpse of what would become a 'scorched-earth' policy targeted finally at the Reich itself, all railway installations, including track and locomotives, were to be destroyed, as were bridges. The ports, too, were in the last resort to be destroyed if they could not be held. If the ports could be held for between six and ten weeks in the autumn, precious time would have been gained.[169]

Time was, however, not on Hitler's side. Learning of the gravity of the Allied capture of Avranches, he ordered – picking up on an operational plan that had been put forward by Kluge – an immediate counter-strike westwards from Mortain, initially intended to take place on 2 August, aimed at retaking Avranches and splitting the advancing American forces under General George S. Patton.[170] The counter-offensive, eventually launched on 7 August, proved disastrous. It lasted only a day, could not prevent some of Patton's troops from sweeping down into Brittany (where stiff defence, however, saw the garrison at Brest hold out until 19 September), and ended with the German forces in disarray but narrowly avoiding even worse calamity.[171]

On 15 August Hitler refused Kluge's request to pull back around 100,000 troops threatened with imminent disaster through encirclement near Falaise. When he was unable to reach Kluge that day – the field-marshal had entered the battle-zone itself in the heart of the 'Falaise pocket' and his radio had been put out of action by enemy fire – Hitler, well aware of Kluge's flirtation with the conspiracy against him and of his pessimism about the western front, jumped to the conclusion that he was negotiating a surrender with the western Allies.[172] It was, said Hitler, 'the worst day of his life'.[173] He promptly recalled Field-Marshal Model, one of his most trusted generals, from the eastern front, appointed him to take over from Kluge and dispatched him to western front headquarters. Until Model arrived, Kluge had not even been informed by Hitler that he was about to be dismissed. Hitler's peremptory handwritten note, handed over by Model and ordering Kluge back to Germany, ended with the threateningly ambiguous comment that the field-marshal should contemplate in which direction he wished to go. Model's arrival was unable to alter the plight of the German troops, but under his command – assisted by tactical errors of the Allied ground-forces commander, General Montgomery – it proved possible to squeeze out at the last minute some 50,000 men from the ever-closing 'Falaise pocket' to fight again another day, closer to home. As many again, however, were taken prisoner and a further 10,000 killed.[174]

Kluge must have reckoned with the near certainty that he would be promptly arrested, expelled from the Wehrmacht, and put before the People's Court for his connections with the plotters against Hitler.[175] On the way back to Germany on 19 August, in the vicinity of Metz, he asked his chauffeur to stop the car for a rest. Depressed, worn out, and in despair, he swallowed a cyanide pill.

The day before, he had written a letter to Hitler. The field-marshal, who (as Hitler knew) had had prior knowledge of the bomb-plot, and who had even the year before Stauffenberg's attempt shown sympathy for Tresckow and the oppositional group in Army Group Centre, used his dying words to praise Hitler's leadership. 'My Führer, I have always admired your greatness,' he wrote. 'You have led an honest, an entirely great struggle,' he continued, with reference to the war in the east. 'History will testify to that.' He then appealed to Hitler now to show the necessary greatness to bring to an end a struggle with no prospect of success in order to release the suffering of his people. This dying plea was as far as he would go to distance himself from the dictator's war leadership. He ended with a final vow of loyalty: 'I depart from you, my Führer, to whom I was inwardly closer than you perhaps imagined, in the consciousness of having carried out my duty to the very limits.'[176]

Hitler's direct reaction to the letter is not known.[177] But Kluge's suicide merely convinced him not only of the field-marshal's implication in the bomb-plot, but also that he had been trying to surrender his forces in the west to the enemy. Hitler found it difficult to comprehend, as he bitterly reflected. He had promoted Kluge twice, given him the highest honours, made him sizeable donations (including a cheque for RM250,000 tax-free on his sixtieth birthday, and a big supplement to his field-marshal's salary).[178] He was anxious to prevent any news seeping out about Kluge's alleged attempt to capitulate. It could seriously affect morale; it would certainly bring further contempt on the army. He let the generals know about Kluge's suicide. But for public consumption the field-marshal's death – from a heart-attack, it was said – was announced only after his body had lain in the church on his Brandenburg estate for a fortnight. Kluge's funeral was a quiet affair. Hitler had banned all ceremonials.[179]

On the day that Kluge had temporarily been out of contact, 15 August, the Allies undertook 'Operation Dragoon', the landing of troops on the French Mediterranean coast.[180] Quickly capturing Marseilles and Toulon, they pushed northwards, forcing Hitler reluctantly to agree to the withdrawal to the north of almost all his forces in southern France in the attempt to build a cohesive front along the upper Marne and Saône stretching to the Swiss border.[181] The end of the German occupation of France was now in sight. Though it would take several more weeks to complete, the symbolic moment arrived when, prompted by strikes, a popular uprising, and attacks by the French Resistance against the German occupiers, and by the eventual readiness of the German Commander, General Dietrich von Choltitz to surrender (despite orders from Hitler to reduce Paris to rubble if it could not be held),[182] the Allied Supreme Commander, General Dwight D. Eisenhower, gave a French division the honour of liberating the French capital on 24 August. The liberation was celebrated by enormous crowds two days later as they cheered the triumphal march down the Champs-Elysées of General Charles de Gaulle, leader of the Free French.[183] Bitter recriminations within the country against those French citizens who had collaborated with the occupiers were only momentarily held back in the joyous scenes.

By now, the western Allies had over 2 million men on the Continent.[184] Advancing into Belgium, they liberated Brussels on 3 September and next day captured the important port of Antwerp before the harbour installations could be destroyed. Only Cherbourg, of the major channel ports, had up to this point been in Allied hands, and supplies through that route were seriously hampered by the level of destruction. Antwerp was vital to the assault on Germany. But it was as late as 27 November before the Scheldt

65. Hitler viewing the Wehrmacht parade after laying a wreath at the cenotaph on Unter den Linden on 'Heroes' Memorial Day', 21 March 1943. Behind Hitler (*left to right*) are Göring, Keitel, Commander-in-Chief of the Navy Karl Dönitz, and Himmler. Shortly beforehand, a planned attempt to kill Hitler by opponents from within Army Group Centre had had to be aborted when the dictator's usual timetable on the day was altered without notice.

66. Hitler is saluted by the Party's 'Old Guard' in the Löwenbräukeller in Munich on 8 November 1943, the twentieth anniversary of the Beerhall Putsch. Göring is to Hitler's right. It was to be the last time that Hitler would appear in person at this symbolic ritual, a high point in the Nazi calendar.

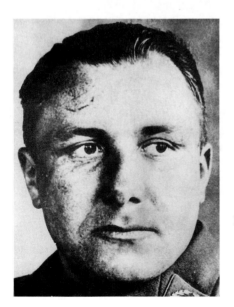

67. Martin Bormann, head of the Party Chancellery (following the flight of Rudolf Heß to Scotland in May 1941). From the beginning of the war onwards he was invariably at Hitler's side, and in April 1943 was officially appointed Secretary to the Führer. This proximity, together with his control of the Party, gave him great power.

68. Hitler and Goebbels, still capable of raising a smile despite military disasters and mounting domestic problems, photographed during a walk on the Obersalzberg above Berchtesgaden in June 1943.

69. (*left*) The Eastern Front in spring and autumn. A German vehicle bogged down in heavy mud.

70. (*above right*) The Eastern Front in winter. Tanks and armoured vehicles, unusable in the conditions, had to be dug in at strategic points to secure them against Soviet attacks.

71. The Eastern Front in summer. Limitless space. A Waffen-SS unit treks across seemingly unending fields.

72. (*top*) The 'Final Solution'. French Jews being deported in 1942. Frightened
faces peer out from behind the barbed-wire covering the slats of the railway-wagon.

73. The 'Final Solution'. Polish Jews forced to dig their own grave, 1942.

74. The 'Final Solution'. Incinerators at Majdanek with skeletons of camp-prisoners
murdered on the approach of the Red Army and liberation of the camp on
27 July 1944.

75. Hitler and Himmler take a wintry walk on the Obersalzberg in March 1944.

76. The 'White Rose' resistance group of Munich students. Christoph Probst (*left*) with Sophie and Hans Scholl in July 1942. On 22 February the following year, they were sentenced to death and beheaded on the same day for distributing leaflets in Munich University, in the wake of the disaster at Stalingrad, condemning the inhumanity of the Nazi regime.

77. (*above left*) The brilliant tank commander Heinz Guderian. Though he clearly recognized that Hitler was leading Germany to catastrophe, he condemned the attempt to assassinate him on 20 July 1944. A day later, Guderian was appointed Chief of the General Staff, retaining the position until his dismissal on 28 March 1945.

78. (*above right*) General Ludwig Beck, who, following his resignation – because of Hitler's insistence on risking war over Czechoslovakia – as Chief of the General Staff in 1938, became a central figure in the conservative resistance, committing suicide on 20 July 1944 after the failure of the bomb-plot.

79. (*right*) Colonel Claus Graf Schenk von Stauffenberg, the driving-force behind the conspiracy to kill Hitler on 20 July 1944, who took upon himself the responsibility both for carrying out the assassination in the Wolf's Lair and for directing the intended coup d'état in Berlin. On its failure, he was arrested and shot by a firing-squad late that night.

80. (*below*) Major-General Henning von Tresckow, one of the most courageous figures in the resistance, the inspiration of several plans, hatched within Army Group Centre, to kill Hitler in 1943. Stauffenberg regarded Tresckow as his mentor. This is one of the last photographs of him, taken in 1944. He committed suicide on 21 July on the Eastern Front on learning of the failure of the bomb-plot.

81. (*left*) Hitler, looking shaken, just after the assassination attempt on 20 July 1944.
82. (*right*) Hitler's trousers, shredded by the bomb-blast.

83. (*facing page, above*) Hitler greets Mussolini at Führer Headquarters – the last time they would meet – some three hours after Stauffenberg's bomb had exploded on 20 July 1944. Hitler had to shake hands with his left hand because his right arm had been slightly injured in the blast.

84. Grand-Admiral Dönitz professes the loyalty of the navy in a broadcast shortly after midnight on 21 July 1944, just after Hitler and Göring had spoken to the German people. Listening to Dönitz are Bormann (*left, next to Hitler*) and Jodl (*on Hitler's right, with bandaged head*).

85. An ageing Hitler, pictured at the Berghof in 1944.

86. Wonder-Weapons: a V1 flying-bomb is taken to its launch-pad.

87. (*left*) Wonder-Weapons: a V2 rocket, ready for launch at Cuxhaven.

88. (*right*) Wonder-Weapons: An American soldier stands alongside a Me 262 on the advance into Germany in April 1945. Hitler had for a long time insisted on having the jet-fighter designed as a bomber. When finally deployed as a fighter, it was far too late to be effective.

89. Scraping the barrel. Ill-equipped men of the 'German Volkssturm' – the people's militia proclaimed by Hitler on 18 October 1944, ordering all able-bodied men between 16 and 60 to take up arms – pictured during a swearing ceremony in Berlin in December 1944.

90. The last 'Heroes' Memorial Day', 11 March 1945. Hitler did not appear, leaving it to Göring (flanked by Dönitz on his left, and Keitel on his right) to lay the wreath at the cenotaph on Unter den Linden.

91. Women and children fleeing as the Red Army attacks Danzig in March 1945.

92. (*top*) Fantasy: In February 1945, with the Red Army within striking distance of
Berlin, Hitler ponders the model of the intended postwar rebuilding of his hometown
of Linz, designed for him by his architect Hermann Giesler.

93. Reality: Hitler, with his adjutant Julius Schaub, standing in the ruins of
the Reich Chancellery in Berlin in March 1945, a few weeks before his suicide.

estuary was secured and before the approaches to the harbour were fully cleared of mines.[185] In the interim, the Allied drive towards the German borders suffered a major setback with the serious losses suffered, especially by British troops, in ten days of bitter fighting in the combined airborne and land operation – 'Market Garden' – launched on 17 September, to seize the river crossings at Eindhoven, Nijmegen, and Arnhem.[186] Beyond supply problems, battle fatigue, and replacing the men lost, the Allied advance was stalling because of the stiff German defence, aided by shortened supply lines, redeployment of the men extricated from the Falaise Pocket, and reinforcements drawn from the east.[187] In the west, it was plain, despite the dramatic Allied successes since D-Day, the war was far from over.

In the east, following the Red Army's big summer offensive, the German network of alliances with Balkan countries started to unravel in August much as Hitler had feared. On 2 August, Turkey announced that it was breaking off relations with Germany. Economically, it meant the loss of chrome supplies.[188] Militarily, it was clear that Turkey would at some point join the Allies.[189] Three days later, on 5 August, Hitler, accompanied by Ribbentrop, Keitel, and Guderian, received Marshal Antonescu at the Wolf's Lair in a vain attempt to shore up the alliance with Romania.[190] : talks proceeded civilly enough. But Romania had already made peace ndings with the Allies. And forces were gathering in Bucharest aimed at ɔling Antonescu and taking Romania out of a war for which the country, ɔwing its severe battlefield losses at Stalingrad and in the Crimea, had long lost heart.[191] On 20 August, when the Soviets attacked Army Group South Ukraine, Romanian units deserted *en masse*, many of them joining the enemy and turning on their former allies. Reaching the Danube before the retreating Germans, Romanian troops closed the river-crossing. Sixteen German divisions, exposed to the onslaught of the Red Army, were totally destroyed.[192] It was a military calamity of the first order. Three days later, Antonescu was deposed following a coup in Bucharest. His successor, King Michael, sued for peace. Romania swapped sides, declaring war on Germany – and on Hungary (from which it now intended to regain the territory in Transylvania that it had been compelled to give up in 1940). The Red Army, joined by Romanian units, was now free to sweep across the Danube. The Wehrmacht, meanwhile, had lost 380,000 indispensable troops within a fortnight.[193]

Bulgaria, a country which since 1941 had played a careful diplomatic hand, was now hopelessly exposed. Soviet troops crossed its borders on 8 September (the USSR having declared war three days earlier), and on the same day Bulgaria rapidly switched sides and declared war on Germany.[194] The German control over the entire Balkan region now held by the most slender of threads. The collapse of Romania and Bulgaria, followed by rapid Soviet occupation, meant the urgent withdrawal of German troops from Greece was imperative. This began in September. In mid-October British airborne troops were able to occupy Athens. By that time, Tito's partisan army was on the verge of entry into Belgrade.[195] German troops were meanwhile engaged in the brutal suppression, finally accomplished by the end of October, of a rising, undertaken in the main by Soviet-inspired indigenous partisans alongside a sizeable minority of the 60,000-strong army, in the puppet state of Slovakia.[196] Most important of all, from Hitler's point of view, in the gathering mayhem in south-eastern Europe Hungary, his chief ally, but long wavering, had immediately following the volte-face in Romania begun urgent soundings for peace with the Soviet Union. The consequences would soon be felt with the German takeover of the country in mid-October.[197]

In these same critical weeks, Hitler was also losing a vital ally in northern Europe. The danger signals about Finland's position had been flashing brightly for months. The grave setbacks on the north of the German eastern front in the summer boosted the growing feeling in Finland that the country must extricate itself from its German alliance, and from the war. State President Risto Ryti resigned on 1 August and was replaced by the veteran war hero Marshal Carl Gustaf von Mannerheim. It was clear to the Nazi leadership that the next step for Mannerheim would be to seek an armistice with the Soviet Union.[198] It was to no avail that Hitler dispatched Colonel-General Ferdinand Schörner to Finland on 3 August in an attempt to stiffen Mannerheim's resolve; nor that Keitel was sent later in the month to Helsinki to bestow the Oak-Leaves to the Marshal's Knight's Cross.[199] On 2 September, Mannerheim informed Hitler that Finland was unable to continue the struggle. Relations were to be broken off immediately. German troops were to leave the country by 15 September. On 19 September, Finland signed an armistice with the Soviet Union.[200]

In these same momentous months, throughout the whole of August and September, the German leadership was also faced with suppressing the dangerous rising taking place in Warsaw. The rising had begun on 1 August, two days after tanks of the Red Army had pushed into the suburbs of Warsaw on the east of the Vistula and Soviet radio had encouraged the inhabitants of the city to rise against their occupiers. General Tadeusz Bor-Komorowski, head of the Polish underground army (around 25,000 strong) presumed the Red Army was poised to enter Warsaw, and wanted, with an eye on the future, to have the capital city liberated by Poles – and by Poles representing the exiled government based in London, not the 'Polish Committee for National Liberation' that Stalin had set up in Lublin. The uprising was not well planned. The Poles were aware that they could reckon with little help from the western powers. But they were unprepared to be left in the lurch by the Soviet Union. However, the Red Army halted at the Vistula and did not enter the city while Stalin – cynically conscious of containing hopes of Polish independence in a post-war order – neither aided the Poles nor, until it was too late, facilitated attempts by the British and Americans to supply the insurgents with weapons and munition.[201]

Unaware of Stalin's cynical ploy, the German Chief of Staff Guderian, fearing cooperation between the insurgents and the Red Army, asked Hitler to include Warsaw – still under the aegis of Hans Frank as Governor General – in the military zone of operations and place it thereby under Wehrmacht control.[202] Hitler refused. Instead, he handed over full responsibility for the crushing of the rising to SS chief Himmler. As soon as he had heard of the rising, Himmler had hastened to see Hitler. Himmler spoke shortly afterwards of how he had put the news of the rising to Hitler: 'I said, "Mein Führer, the time is disagreeable. Seen historically [however] it is a blessing that the Poles are doing it. We'll get through the five, six weeks. But by then Warsaw, the capital, the head, the intelligence of this former 16–17 million Polish people will be extinguished – this people that has blocked the east for us for 700 years and has always stood in our way ever since the first battle of Tannenberg. Then the Polish problem will historically no longer be a big problem for our children and for all who come after us, nor indeed for us." '[203]

Himmler now ordered the total destruction of Warsaw,[204] putting in SS-Obergruppenführer Erich von dem Bach-Zelewski, formerly involved in massacres of Jews in Russia and subsequently in charge of combating partisans on the eastern front, to suppress the rising with all the ruthlessness he needed. Over the next weeks, Bach directed a ferocious onslaught on the Polish insurgents, using as his spearhead the notoriously brutal Kaminski and Dirlewanger Brigades – SS units of around 6,000 men comprised in the former case of Russian ex-prisoners-of-war, many of them rabidly anti-Polish, in the latter of criminals and desperadoes drawn from the concentration camps.[205] Wild orgies of atrocities predictably followed as men, women, and children were slaughtered in their thousands while Warsaw burned. By the time General Bor surrendered on 2 October, the savage repression had left Polish civilian victims numbering around 200,000. German losses amounted to some 26,000 men killed, wounded, or missing.[206] On 11 October, Hans Frank received notification that all raw materials, textiles, and furniture left in Warsaw were to be removed before the smouldering remains of the city were razed to the ground.[207]

V

As the news from all parts of his empire turned from appalling to disastrous, Hitler fell ill. On 8 September, he complained to Morell, his doctor, of pressure around his right eye. In his notes, Morell indicated blood-pressure. Six days later, he recorded fluctuating blood-pressure 'following great agitation (*Aufregung*)'. Next day, 15 September, Morell noted: 'Complains of dizziness, throbbing head, and return of the tremor to his legs, particularly the left, and hands.' His left ankle was swollen. Again, 'much agitation (*viel Aufregungen*)' was registered by Morell.[208] The systolic blood-pressure, at 150mm, was not unduly high, though higher than it had been at the start of the month. In accordance with contemporary practice, Morell was less concerned with Hitler's diastolic blood-pressure, which he relatively seldom took. When he did, it was regularly too high, sometimes worryingly so.[209] It was an indication that Hitler had a cardiac problem, and an electrocardiogram on 24 September did indicate progressive arteriosclerosis (though no acute anginal danger).[210]

During the night before his cardiogram, Hitler's acute stomach spasms returned – as Morell indicated 'after great agitation' (probably in connection with the Allied airborne landing in Arnhem and Hitler's fury at the inadequacy of the Luftwaffe).[211] They were so bad the following night that Hitler was unable to get up in the morning – an extremely rare occurrence – and seemed unusually apathetic.[212] By 27 September, Morell pointed out to Hitler that his skin had a yellowish appearance – something Dr Giesing had noticed a few days earlier. Hitler refused to let Morell examine him.[213] But by now he was quite ill. The jaundice, accompanied by high temperature and severe stomach cramps, kept him in bed during the following days. It was 2 October, the day that Hitler was told of the death (following the injuries suffered in the bomb blast on 20 July) of his favourite adjutant, Rudolf Schmundt, that the yellow skin-colouring finally disappeared and Hitler felt well enough to get out of bed, dress himself, and make his way to the first situation briefing since he had fallen ill. He still seemed lifeless, however, to those in his company. It was the middle of the month before he felt himself again. By then, after eating little during his illness (when he was confined to a diet largely comprising mashed potatoes, oatmeal soup, and stewed fruit), he had lost sixteen pounds in weight.[214]

While Hitler was suffering from jaundice, Dr Giesing, the ear, nose, and throat specialist who had been brought in to treat him after Stauffenberg's bomb had exploded, began to be suspicious about Morell's treatment. He started to wonder whether the little black tablets that Hitler took each day on Morell's prescription, 'Dr Koester's Anti-Gas Pills', were in fact a contributory cause of the dictator's chronic stomach complaint rather than a satisfactory medicine for it. Whatever his concern for Hitler, Giesing's own ambitions to oust and displace Morell probably played a part in what he did next. He managed to lay hands on a number of the pills, had them analysed, and discovered that they contained strychnine. Giesing dosed himself with the pills and found they had mildly harmful effects – effects he associated with those on Hitler. Giesing made mention of his findings, and his suspicions, to Hitler's other attendant doctors, Dr Karl Brandt and Dr Hanskarl von Hasselbach, who passed on the sentiments to others in Hitler's entourage. When Hitler found out, he was furious. He announced his complete faith in Morell, and dismissed Brandt and Hasselbach, who had both been with him since the early years of his rule. Giesing, too, was requested to leave Hitler's service. Their replacement was one of Himmler's former staff doctors, SS-Obersturmbannführer Ludwig Stumpfegger.[215]

Morell's diagnoses and methods of treatment were indeed often questionable. Many of the innumerable tablets, medicines, and injections he prescribed for Hitler – which his valet Heinz Linge provided on demand from the medical chest that was always ready at hand[216] – were of dubious value, often useless, and in some instances even exacerbating the problem (particularly relating to the chronic intestinal disorder). But allegations that Morell was intentionally harming Hitler were misplaced. The fat, unctuously perspiring Morell was both physically unattractive and, in his privileged access to Hitler – becoming more extensive as the dictator's ailments mounted – provoked much resentment in the 'court circle'. That he visibly exploited the relationship to his patient to further his own power, influence, and material advantage simply magnified the ill-feeling towards Morell. But, whatever his considerable limitations as a medical practitioner, Morell was certainly doing his best for the Leader he so much admired and to whom he was devoted.

The hypochondriac Hitler was, in turn, dependent upon Morell. He needed to believe, and apparently did believe, that Morell's treatment was the best he could get, and was beneficial. In that way, Morell might indeed have been good for Hitler.[217] At any rate, Morell and his medicines were neither a major nor even a minor part of the explanation of Germany's plight in the autumn of 1944. That Hitler was poisoned by the strychnine and belladonna in the anti-gas pills or other medicaments, drugged on the opiates given him to relieve his intestinal spasms, or dependent upon the cocaine which formed 1 per cent of the ophthalmic drops prescribed by Dr Giesing for conjunctivitis, can be discounted. Whether Hitler took amphetamines to combat tiredness and sustain his energy is uncertain. That he was dependent upon them, even if he took them, cannot be proved; nor that his behaviour was affected by them.[218] Hitler's physical problems in autumn 1944, chronic though they were, had arisen from lifestyle, diet, lack of exercise, and excessive stress, on top of likely congenital weaknesses (which probably accounted for the cardiac problem as well as the Parkinson's Syndrome).[219] Mentally, he was under enormous strain, which magnified his deeply embedded extreme personality traits. His phobias, hypochondria, and hysterical reactions were probable indicators of some form of personality disorder or psychiatric abnormality. An element of paranoia underwrote his entire political 'career', and became even more evident towards the end. But Hitler did not suffer from any of the major pyschotic disorders. He was certainly not clinically insane.[220] If there was lunacy in the position Germany found itself in by the autumn of 1944, it was not the purported insanity of one man but that of the high-stakes 'winner-takes-all' gamble for Continental dominance and world power which the country's leaders – not just Hitler – backed by much of a gullible population had earlier been prepared to take, and which was now costing the country dearly and revealed as a high-risk policy without an exit-clause.

VI

That all ways out were closed off was made plain once again during these weeks. Hints had come from Japan in late August that Stalin might entertain ideas of a peace settlement with Hitler's Germany. Japan was interested in brokering such a peace, since it would leave Germany able to devote its entire war effort to the western Allies, thereby, it was hoped, draining the energies of the USA away from the Pacific. With massive casualties on the Soviet side, the territories lost since 1941 regained, and a presumed interest in Stalin wishing to harness what was left of German industrial potential for a later fight with the West, Tokyo thought prospects for a negotiated peace were not altogether negligible.[221] On 4 September, Oshima, the Japanese Ambassador in Berlin, travelled to East Prussia to put the suggestion to take up feelers with Stalin directly to Hitler. The response was predictable. Germany would soon launch a fresh counter-offensive with new weapons at its disposal. And there were, in any case, no signs that Stalin was entertaining thoughts of peace. Only a block on his advance might make him change his mind, Hitler realistically concluded. He wanted no overtures to be made by the Japanese for the present.[222]

Oshima evidently did not give up. Later in the month, he used the pretext of a discussion with Werner Naumann, State Secretary in the Propaganda Ministry, about the 'total war' effort to bring the suggestion of a separate peace with the Soviet Union to Goebbels's ears. He could be certain that by this route the proposal would again reach Hitler, perhaps with the backing of one who was known to carry influence at Führer Headquarters.

Naumann's report was plainly the first Goebbels had heard of the Japanese suggestion. The Propaganda Minister called the discussion between his State Secretary and the Japanese Ambassador 'quite sensational'.[223] Oshima told Naumann, according to Goebbels's summary, that Germany should make every attempt to reach a 'special peace'. Such an arrangement would be possible, he led Naumann to believe. He was frank about the Japanese interest, forced by its own problems in the war, in giving Germany a free hand in the west. He thought Stalin, a realist, would be open to suggestions if Germany were prepared to accept 'sacrifices', and criticized the inflexibility of German foreign policy. Goebbels noted that Oshima's proposal amounted to a reversal of German war policy, and was aware that the position of the pro-German Japanese Ambassador at home had been seriously weakened as the fortunes of war had turned. But, as Oshima had presumed, Goebbels immediately passed on the information to Bormann and Himmler, for further transmission to Hitler himself.[224]

Goebbels decided that more must be done. But rather than try to put the case verbally to Hitler, he decided to prepare a lengthy memorandum. By midnight on 20 September, after he had worked all afternoon and evening on it, the memorandum was ready. It was couched in the form of a letter to Hitler. Goebbels was evidently so pleased with it that he dictated the entire text for entry in his diary.

The letter was cleverly attuned to Hitler's mentality. The events of the summer had cast all their hopes overboard, he began. He pointed to the way Hitler had divided his opponents at the end of 1932 and beginning of 1933 in order to win a 'limited victory' on 30 January that then paved the way for the full conquest of power that was to follow. He drew an analogy with the need now to settle for something less than the original war aims in order to divide an alliance already showing distinct signs of fractiousness. Germany had never won a two-front war, he frankly pointed out. There was little prospect of coping with western and eastern enemies simultaneously. 'We can neither conclude peace with both sides at the same time nor in the long run successfully wage war against both sides at the same time,' he argued. He came to the main part of his case. Rehearsing what he had heard from Oshima, he suggested that Stalin's cold realism, knowing that he would sooner or later find himself in conflict with the west, offered an opening since the Soviet leader would not want either to exhaust his own military strength or allow the German armaments potential to fall into the hands of the western powers. He pointed to Japan's self-interest in brokering a deal. An arrangement with Stalin would provide new prospects in the west, and place the Anglo-Americans in a position where they could not indefinitely continue the war. 'What we would attain,' he stated, 'would not be the victory that we dreamed of in 1941, but it would still be the greatest victory in German history. The sacrifices that the German people had made in this war would thereby be fully justified.'

The danger in the east would not, it was true, be fully repelled. 'But we would stand armed for it in the future,' he claimed. The next words showed that Goebbels knew how difficult his task was if he were to alter Hitler's hitherto obdurate refusal to entertain any negotiations. 'You, my Führer, will reject all that perhaps as utopian,' he stated. But were it to be attained, it would mark in the eyes of the people 'the highest achievement of the German political art of war'. The war situation would be altered at one fell swoop. Germany would again have breathing space, freedom of movement, could regenerate itself and then, when necessary, 'dole out the blows which would decide the war'.[225]

Goebbels waited impatiently for Hitler's reactions to his memorandum. Eventually, he learnt that Hitler had read it, but then put it away without comment. A promised audience to discuss it with him never materialized.[226] Hitler's illness intervened. But in any case, there is no indication that Hitler took the slightest notice of his Propaganda Minister's suggestion. His own plans ran along quite different lines. The idea of a western offensive, which he had hatched in mid-August,[227] was taking concrete shape. He was contemplating a final attempt to turn the tide: using the last reserves of troops and weapons for an offensive through the Ardennes in late autumn or winter aimed at inflicting a significant blow on the western Allies by retaking Antwerp (depriving them of their major continental port) and even forcing them 'back into the Atlantic'.[228] 'A single breakthrough on the western front! You will see!' he told Speer. 'That will lead to a collapse and panic among the Americans. We'll drive through in the middle and take Antwerp. With that, they'll have lost their supply harbour. And there'll be a huge encirclement of the entire English army with hundreds of thousands of prisoners. Like it was in Russia!'[229]

The objective was to gain time to develop new weapons.[230] From a new position of strength, he could then turn against the Russians.[231] He was well aware that the 'miracle weapons' were, in their current state of deployment, incapable of bringing any decisive change in war fortunes, or of satisfying the exaggerated hopes that incessant propaganda had raised in them among the German public.[232] When he had first seen the prototypes of the V2, Hitler had envisaged 5,000 of the rockets being directed against Britain in a massive initial onslaught.[233] But when the eventual launch took place on 8 September, it proved possible only to dispatch twenty-five rockets in a period of ten days.[234] They were little more than a pin-prick in the Allied thrust against Nazi Germany. Even so, Hitler expected a great deal from the further deployment of the weapon.[235] By the end of the war, through the brutal exploitation of foreign workers, it had proved possible to aim over 3,000 V2s mainly at London, Antwerp, and Brussels. There was no defence against the missiles. Their terroristic effect was considerable, causing the deaths of 2,724 persons in England and many more in Belgium. Their military effect was, however, negligible.[236]

Meanwhile, the development of the one secret weapon certainly capable of affecting Germany's war fortunes, the atomic bomb, had been worked on since the start of the war (though with only slow progress). The research was given special support by Speer in 1942 but, despite his offer of increased funding, was still nowhere near completion and – though the German nuclear scientists were unaware of it – lagged far behind advances made in the USA. There had seemed no need to force research on such a weapon during the early, triumphant phase of the war. By the time of Speer's meeting with leading atomic scientists, including Otto Hahn and Werner Heisenberg, in mid-1942, a nuclear weapon was – as the Armaments Minister was told – theoretically possible but in practice several years off. Hitler, already aware in a general sense of the feasibility of an atomic bomb in the more distant future, took Speer's report as confirmation that he would never live to see its deployment, that it could play no part in the present war. Consequently, he took no great interest in it. By this time, in any case, the resources needed to deploy it were simply not available – and diminishing fast. It is as well, nevertheless, that the bomb was not on offer: Hitler would not have hesitated for an instant to drop it on London and Moscow.[237]

A key part of Hitler's strategy was the deployment of large numbers of fighters on the western front to regain the initiative in the air. He had emphasized this in his briefing with Jodl at the end of July.[238] In August, when Speer and Adolf Galland, the flying ace who headed the Luftwaffe's fighter arm, tried to persuade him to use the fighters in the Reich rather than at the western front, he had exploded in such a frenzy of rage that he had ordered a stop to all aircraft production in favour of total concentration on flak.[239] Speer had ignored the outburst of frustration. In September, fighter production reached a record 2,878 aircraft – a two-and-a-half-fold increase over production in January.[240] Hitler had his fighters.

Whether they would have any fuel was another question. Hitler knew that raw materials and fuel had sunk to perilous levels. Speer sent him a memorandum on 5 September pointing out that the loss of chrome from Turkey meant that the entire armaments production would grind to a halt within sixteen or so months, by 1 January 1946. Hitler took the news calmly.[241] It can only have encouraged him in the thought that there was nothing to lose, and that everything had to be staked on the new western offensive. He was also informed by Speer that the fuel situation was so critical that fighter squadrons were being grounded and army movements restricted. To make 17,500 tons of fuel – what had formerly been two-and-a-half days' production – available for the Ardennes offensive, delivery to other parts of the front had to be seriously curtailed.[242]

Together with Jodl, Hitler pored over maps of the Ardennes while lying on his sick-bed at the end of September.[243] He later told Goebbels that he had spent the weeks of his illness almost exclusively brooding over his revenge. Now he was well again, he could begin to put his intentions into effect.[244] It would be his final gamble. As he knew, it was a long shot. 'If it doesn't succeed,' he told Speer, 'I see no other possibility of bringing the war to a favourable conclusion.' 'But,' he added, 'we'll pull through.'[245]

From Hitler's perspective, there was no alternative. Even if the fronts could be stabilized, the shortages of fuel meant the war would be lost within months.[246] As his negative response to Oshima's proposal had shown, he would not entertain thoughts of suing for peace with Stalin from a position of weakness. He was equally dismissive of suggestions from Papen that soundings could be made towards peace in the west.[247] He *had* to regain the initiative – and this could only be achieved in the west. That was his thinking in autumn 1944. In Speer's view, Hitler knew that he was playing his last card.[248]

Before he could fully focus his attention on operational preparations for the coming offensive, a lingering remnant of the July bomb-plot momentarily detained him. Hitler had suspected since early August that Rommel had known about the plot against him.[249] This had been confirmed by the testimony of Lieutenant-Colonel Cäsar von Hofacker, a member of Stülpnagel's staff in Paris implicated in the plot, who had provided a written statement of Rommel's support for the conspiracy. Hitler showed the statement to Keitel and had Rommel summoned to see him. The field-marshal, recuperating from his injuries at home near Ulm, claimed he was not fit to travel. At this, Keitel wrote Rommel a letter, drafted by Hitler, suggesting he report to the Führer if innocent. Otherwise, he would face trial. He should weigh up the consequences and if necessary act on them. Hitler ordered the letter and Hofacker's incriminating statement to be taken to Rommel by General Wilhelm Burgdorf (Schmundt's replacement as his chief adjutant).

Burgdorf, accompanied by his deputy, General Ernst Maisel, drove to Rommel's home at Herrlingen on Saturday, 14 October, and handed over the letter together with Hofacker's statement. Rommel inquired whether Hitler was aware of the statement. He then requested a little time to think matters over. He did not take long. Hitler had given orders to Burgdorf that Rommel should be prevented from shooting himself – the traditional mode of suicide among officers – and should be offered poison so that the death could be attributed to brain damage following the car accident. Mindful of Rommel's popularity among the German public, Hitler offered him a state funeral with all honours. Faced with expulsion from the army, trial before the People's Court, certain execution, and inevitable recriminations for his family, Rommel took the poison.[250]

Hitler was represented by Rundstedt at the state funeral in the town hall at Ulm on 18 October. Rundstedt declared in his eulogy that Rommel's 'heart belonged to the Führer'. Addressing the dead field-marshal, he intoned: 'Our Führer and Supreme Commander sends you through me his thanks and his greetings.' For public consumption, Hitler announced the same day that Rommel had succumbed to his severe wounds following his car accident. 'With him, one of our best army leaders has passed away . . . His name has entered the history of the German people.'[251]

Another, more far-reaching, problem preoccupied Hitler in the middle of October: Hungary's attempt to defect from its alliance with Germany. Hitler had feared (and expected) this eventuality for weeks. The alliance with Hungary had become increasingly unstable across the summer. The defections of Romania and Bulgaria in August had then made it a matter of time before Hungary would seek to extricate itself from its dependence upon Germany. The feelers, known to German intelligence, put out both to the western allies and to the Soviet Union after Romania's defection gave a clear sign of the way things were moving. Another indicator, following the Romanian switch of sides, was the replacement by Admiral Horthy, the head of state, of the puppet Sztojay government, installed at German behest in March, by a military administration under General Geisa Lakatos directly answerable to him. At the beginning of October, Horthy had sent a delegation to Moscow to begin negotiations to take Hungary out of the war. A Soviet offensive driving forward on the Hungarian plains, beginning on 6 October, though fought off by German panzer divisions, gave the final impetus. Tough conditions laid down by Molotov, on behalf of the Allies, for Hungary to change sides, including an immediate declaration of war on Germany, were accepted by Horthy and signed by the Hungarian delegation in Moscow on 11 October. Their implementation had to await the coup being prepared in Budapest against the German forces in Hungary. Pressed by the Soviet Union to act, Horthy informed the German envoy Edmund Veesenmayer on 15 October that Hungary was leaving the German alliance and announced the armistice in a radio broadcast in the early afternoon.[252]

Hitler had not stood idly by while these developments were taking place. Both strategically, and also on account of its economic importance for foodstuffs and fuel supplies, everything had to be done to prevent Hungary going the way of Romania and Bulgaria. For weeks, Hitler had been preparing his own counter-coup in Budapest, aimed at ousting Horthy, replacing him with a puppet government under Ferencz Szalasi – fanatical leader of the radical Hungarian fascist Party, the Arrow Cross, a former discharged army officer who had subsequently served a three-year jail sentence – and thus ensuring that Hungary did not defect. Already in mid-September Otto Skorzeny, Hitler's leading troubleshooter (since his daring rescue of Mussolini a year earlier), had been called to the Wolf's Lair and told that Horthy was approaching the western Allies and the Russians with a view to an imminent separate peace, and was ready to throw himself on the mercy of the Kremlin. Hitler ordered Skorzeny to prepare an operational plan to seize by force the Citadel in Budapest – the fortress which was the residence of Horthy and his entourage – should Hungary betray its alliance with Germany.

Skorzeny immediately began detailed planning of the complex operation (which he dubbed 'Panzerfaust' – 'Bazooka') against the heavily fortified government quarter, with its labyrinth of subterranean passages. He was adamant that the action could only follow, not precede, a hostile act by Hungary against Germany.[253] Probably, German intelligence was aware of the Hungarian delegation's visit to Moscow. In any case, it was plain that events were rapidly reaching their denouement. The SS commander in Budapest, SS-Obergruppenführer Otto Winkelmann, pressed for urgent action. Hitler sent SS-Obergruppenführer von dem Bach-Zelewski, fresh from his brutal suppression of the rising in Warsaw, to Budapest to take charge of 'Panzerfaust'. Skorzeny had some initial difficulty in deflecting Bach-Zelewski from using the same crude brutality – including deployment of his massive 65cm mortar against the city of Budapest as earlier against Sevastopol and Warsaw – but eventually a more sophisticated approach was agreed.[254] This involved the kidnapping of Horthy's son, Nicklas (who, as German intelligence knew, had been working through Yugoslav contacts to promote a separate peace with the Soviet Union) in order to blackmail his father into abandoning intentions to defect. Skorzeny called the operation – a play on the name of Horthy's son – (Nicky) 'Mouse'.[255] In a daring ambush on the morning of Sunday, 15 October, Skorzeny's men, following a five-minute flurry of shooting with Hungarian bodyguards, carried off the younger Horthy, rolled up in a carpet, bundled him into a waiting lorry, whisked him to an airfield, and put him in a plane bound for Vienna and his eventual destination, Mauthausen concentration camp.[256]

Admiral Horthy was faced with the fact of his son's kidnap when Veesenmayer arrived for their prearranged meeting at noon. Veesenmayer told Horthy that at the first sign of 'treason', his son would be shot. The Regent's response was a combination of furious protestation and near nervous collapse. Neither were, of course, to any avail. But nor could German threats deter him, given the predicament he was in, from making his radio announcement two hours later of the separate peace with the Soviet Union. No sooner had he finished speaking than the radio building was seized by Arrow Cross men who put out a counter-declaration avowing Hungary's continuation of the fight against the Soviet Union on Germany's side. A little later Szalasi announced his takeover of power. That evening, the blackmail on Horthy came into full effect. He was told that if he resigned and formally handed over power to Szalasi, he would be given asylum in Germany, and his son would be freed; if not, the Citadel would be taken by force. Horthy buckled under the extreme pressure. He agreed to step down from office and make way for Szalasi. Skorzeny met little resistance when, accompanied by units of 'Panther' and 'Goliath' tanks, he entered the Citadel early next morning. Two days later, on 18 October, Horthy was on his way to Germany in a special train, accompanied by Skorzeny and a German army escort. He would spend the remainder of the war 'as the Führer's guest', in Schloß Hirschberg, near Weilheim, in Upper Bavaria. Under its new, fanatical fascist leadership, Hungary's fate remained tied to Germany's until the encircled defendants of Budapest gave up the struggle on 11 February 1945. Only a few hundred succeeded in breaking through to German lines. It was the end of Hitler's last remaining ally in south-eastern Europe.[257]

With the failure of Horthy's attempt to take Hungary out of the war, the final torment of the largest Jewish community still under German control began. As we noted earlier, Horthy had halted deportations – mainly to Auschwitz – in July. By that date, 437,402 Jews – more than half of the entire community – had been sent to their deaths.[258] By the time of the deposition of Horthy and takeover of power by Szalasi in mid-October, Himmler was halting the 'Final Solution' and terminating the killings at Auschwitz.[259] But the desperate labour shortage in Germany now led to plans to deploy Hungarian Jews as slave labourers in the underground assembly sites of V2 missiles. Without trains to transport them, they would have to walk. Within days of Szalasi taking over, tens of thousands of Jews – women as well as men – were being rounded up and, by the end of the month, beginning what for so many would turn into death marches as they succumbed to exhaustion, cold, and the torture of both Hungarian and SS guards. So high was the death rate among Jewish women, in fact, that Szalasi, probably concerned for his own skin as the war fortunes continued to worsen for Germany, stopped the treks in mid-November. Subsequent attempts of the SS to remove more Jews by rail were vitiated by lack of transport.[260] Meanwhile, for the 70,000 remaining Budapest Jews, crammed into a ghetto within range of Soviet guns, deprived of all property, terrorized and killed at will by Arrow Cross men, the daily nightmare continued until the surrender of the city in February. It is estimated that the bodies of some 10,000 Jews were lying unburied in the streets and houses of Budapest by that time.[261]

Meanwhile, on 21 October a delighted Hitler, recovered from his recent illness, was welcoming Skorzeny with outstretched arms as he led him into his dimly-lit bunker at the Wolf's Lair to hear the story of his triumph in Budapest and reward him with promotion to Obersturmbannführer. When

Skorzeny stood up to leave, Hitler detained him: 'Don't go, Skorzeny,' he remarked. 'I have perhaps the most important job in your life for you. So far very few people know of the preparations for a secret plan in which you have a great part to play. In December, Germany will start a great offensive, which may well decide her fate.' He proceeded to give Skorzeny a detailed outline of the military operation which would from now on occupy so much of his time: the Ardennes offensive.[262]

VII

Hitler had laid out his demands for an Ardennes offensive on 16 September. Guderian voiced grave misgivings because of the situation on the eastern front, the theatre for which he was directly responsible. Jodl warned of air supremacy and the likelihood of parachute landings. Hitler ignored them. He wanted, he said, 1,500 fighters by 1 November, when preparations for the offensive must be complete. The launch of the offensive would take place in bad weather, when enemy aircraft were badly handicapped. Enemy forces would be split and encircled. Antwerp would be taken, leaving the enemy without an escape route.[263]

By this time, the enemy was already on German soil in the west. Even by mid-September, American soldiers from the 1st US Army had penetrated the Westwall and reached the outskirts of Aachen. German rule in the city had been momentarily in disarray. The Party leaders had tried to organize a chaotic evacuation of the population, while the local Wehrmacht commander, General Gerd Graf von Schwerin, countered the order, dismissing it as 'stupid', and made preparations for surrender.[264] Schwerin had been peremptorily dismissed, and Hitler had issued orders that every inch of German soil should be defended by the most radical means; that nothing of value should be allowed to fall into enemy hands – a 'scorched earth' policy which prompted sharply varying responses even among Nazi leaders.[265] Rundstedt, reinstated on 5 September as Commander-in-Chief in the West, had declared, in his proclamation of Hitler's defence order, that every house was to be turned into a fortress, and that the destruction of German property and cultural monuments had to be carried out if it served defence needs.[266] In the event, Aachen had held out longer than had at first seemed likely. But after a month of heavy fighting in the area, the city was eventually surrounded by American forces on 13 October and, after a week of sustained bombardment, finally taken on 21 October.[267]

A few days earlier, on the very day that the Citadel in Budapest was capitulating to Skorzeny's men, the enemy had also burst into German territory in the east. On 16 October, the '3rd White Russian Front', led by General Ivan Tscherniakowski, had broken through into East Prussia as far as Nemmersdorf, Goldap – the first sizeable town in the province – and the fringes of Gumbinnen, heading for Königsberg.[268] The roads were full of refugees fleeing in panic from the oncoming Russians.[269] The Red Army was within striking reach of Führer Headquarters. Bormann told his wife that 'we would like rather more safety for the Führer – sixty or eighty kilometres are no distance for armoured cars'.[270] For the time being, however, Hitler resisted pressure to leave the Wolf's Lair. A move to the Berghof or to Berlin, he thought, would send the wrong signals to his fighting men at the front.[271] He gave strict instructions that there should be no talk of leaving. But the staff was reduced, while Schaub packed all Hitler's files and possessions, ready to depart at any moment.[272] It proved possible to delay the moment. Gumbinnen was recaptured – revealing horrifying scenes of atrocities (including untold cases of women raped and murdered, and houses plundered at will by Soviet troops). The Red Army was forced on the defensive in East Prussia. Goldap, too, was retaken by the Wehrmacht a fortnight or so later. The immediate danger was contained.[273]

When Nicolaus von Below, Hitler's Luftwaffe adjutant, returned to the Wolf's Lair on 24 October, after recuperating for several weeks from the effects of the bomb-blast on 20 July, he found the dictator heavily involved in preparations for the Ardennes offensive, expected to take place in late November or early December.[274] The big anxiety, as ever, was whether by then the Luftwaffe would be in any position to provide the necessary air cover. The failure of the Luftwaffe, Below was told by naval adjutant Karl-Jesko von Puttkamer, was still the 'number one topic', and there was permanent tension between Hitler and Göring.[275]

Already in September, Hitler had wanted to put the Luftwaffe in the hands of Colonel-General Robert Ritter von Greim, a First World War flying-ace, romantic nationalist, and fervent admirer of the Nazi leader since the early 1920s, who had later rapidly risen through the ranks and distinguished himself as a Luftwaffe commander, mainly on the eastern front. Though Greim would have had operational control, Hitler, characteristically, wanted to leave Göring, to whom he attached nothing but bitter recrimination for the failure of the Luftwaffe, in post as commander-in-chief.[276] Hitler's criticism of Göring was scathing. But, as Goebbels put it, he still held to the Reich Marshal with a 'real Nibelung loyalty'.[277] Despite

Göring's almost universal loss of prestige and popularity, the removal from office at this point of such a key figure in the regime could for Hitler only have been interpreted as a sign of weakness and desperation.[278] There could, therefore, be no question of discarding the Reich Marshal, whatever his failings. Greim was evidently more than aware of the impossible proposition being put to him, and was in no rush to accept. In any case, Göring's own objections appear to have persuaded Hitler that the idea had little chance of working. By the beginning of November, it had been dropped. As Greim told Below, everything would remain as it was – except for the appointment of General Karl Koller as Luftwaffe Chief of Staff in place of General Werner Kreipe (whom Hitler had refused to see for six weeks).[279] Göring had held on to his position. But he appeared listless, resigned, a shadow of his former ebullient self.[280]

None of this left Hitler deterred from his coming offensive, on which so much hinged. The rise in fighter production now gave him a fleet – at least nominally – of over 3,000 planes at his disposal, and the first Me262s were coming into service (though Hitler continued to place few hopes in them as fighters, instead of the bombers he had for so long demanded).[281] In reality, few of the planes could fly at any one time on account of the chronic lack of fuel.[282] Though he put the best face on it, Hitler was well aware that air-power was his weakest suit;[283] hence the constant tirades against Göring. The odds in the coming offensive were far more heavily stacked against him than he was prepared to acknowledge.

Immersed in military matters and facing calamity on all sides, Hitler was in no mood to travel through a war-weary Reich to address the Party's 'Old Guard' as usual on 8 November, the anniversary of the Putsch in 1923 and the most sacred date in the Nazi calendar. Goebbels had tried in September to persuade Hitler to speak to the German people again, at least through a brief radio broadcast. Hitler had agreed in principle, but wanted to await developments in Hungary. This was unintelligible to Goebbels. But the coup under preparation to prevent Hungary's defection was the only potential success in view for Hitler. And he evidently felt as always that he needed some success to proclaim if speaking to the German people, both to stir up morale at home and for consumption outside Germany.

Goebbels wanted an early broadcast, but, predictably, nothing came of the idea. Then Hitler's illness intervened and any hopes of a speech disappeared.[284] The dangers of a bombing-raid to coincide with a public speech as normal in the Löwenbräukeller in Munich probably also contributed to its cancellation this year. Instead, a pale shadow of the normal event was scheduled to take place for the first time not on the actual anniversary of the Putsch, but on the following Sunday, 12 November, in Munich. Its centrepiece was a proclamation by Hitler to be read out by Himmler. As Goebbels pointed out, this had nothing like the effect of hearing Hitler himself, particularly when read out in Himmler's cold diction.[285]

The proclamation itself, despite Goebbels's praise for its content and style, could only have been a disappointment for those hoping for news of some reversal of war fortunes or – the desire of most people – a hint that the war would soon be over. Hitler did not even refer directly to events at the front. A lengthy preamble reasserted the principles of National Socialism and drew the faintest of parallels between the current struggle and the crises the Party had mastered after 1923 and in gaining power ten years later. The fight for national survival against enemies intent upon the 'annihilation of our people [and] the eradication and thereby ending of its existence' was as usual underlined, as was the 'satanic will to persecution and destruction' of Jewry.[286] The 'salvation of Europe from the Bolshevik monster' could only be brought about by the German Reich under National Socialist leadership.[287] He went on to berate the 'betrayal on betrayal' that had beset Germany over the previous two years, saving his most poisonous bile for the 'criminals' within who had tried to stab Germany in the back.[288] He praised the bravery of the Wehrmacht and, quite especially, of the home front. He insisted that eventual triumph would come. And he made it clear that as long as he was alive, there would be no capitulation, no end to the fighting. His opponents were right in one thing, he said: 'As long as I live, Germany will not suffer the fate of the European states inundated by Bolshevism.'[289] He was, he said, 'unshakeable in his will to give the world to follow a no less praiseworthy example in this struggle than great Germans have given in the past'.[290] In this struggle, his own life was of no consequence. It was a veiled hint that what now remained for him to fight for was his place in history. The 'heroic' struggle he envisaged, one of Wagnerian proportions, ruled out any contemplation of capitulation, the shameful act of 1918. The fight to the last, it seemed clear, was destined to drag down to destruction the German people itself with the 'heroic' self-destruction of its warlord.

The warlord came close in the days following his speech, in fact, almost for the first time, even in private, to admitting the war was lost. His own end was now starting to occupy his mind. When Jodl recommended moving Führer Headquarters to Berlin, using the coming Ardennes offensive as an argument, Hitler stated that he would not leave East Prussia again.[291] Perhaps a renewed bout of illness, now affecting his throat, prompted his depressed mood.[292] It may also have encouraged him to agree with Bormann that the time had indeed finally come to move his headquarters from East Prussia, since it had been established that he needed a minor operation in Berlin to remove a polyp from his vocal cords.[293] On the afternoon of 20 November, Hitler and his entourage boarded his special train bound for Berlin and left the Wolf's Lair for good.

So little was Hitler a real presence for the German people by this time that, as Goebbels had to note, rumours were rife that he was seriously ill, or even dead.[294] Goebbels had the opportunity to speak at length with him at the beginning of December. He found him recovered from his stomach troubles, able to eat and drink normally again. He was also over the operation to his vocal cords, and his voice was back to normal.[295] Hitler told him he had come to Berlin to prepare for the coming attack in the West. Everything was prepared for a major blow to the Allies which would give him not just a military but also a political success. He said he had worked day and night on the plan for the offensive, also during his illness. Goebbels thought Hitler back to his old form.[296] They broke off their discussion in the afternoon, resuming it at midnight and carrying on until 5.30a.m.[297]

Hitler outlined the grandiose plan of the offensive. Antwerp would be taken within eight to ten days. The intention was to smash the entire enemy force to the north and south, then turn a massive rocket attack on London. A major success would have a huge impact on morale at home, and affect attitudes towards Germany abroad.[298] Hitler, in Goebbels's judgement, was like a man revived.[299] The prospect of a new offensive, and of regaining the initiative, had evidently worked on him like a drug.

Operational plans for the Ardennes offensive – known at the time as 'Watch on the Rhine', it was later changed to 'Autumn Mist' – had been worked out by the OKW in September and put to Hitler on 9 October. The objective of the operation – the sweep through the Eifel and Ardennes through Belgium to the Channel coast, taking Antwerp – was finalized at this point. The detailed plans of the offensive were outlined by Jodl to senior western commanders on 3 November. Sixteen divisions, eight of them armoured, would form the focal point of the attack. SS-Oberstgruppenführer Sepp Dietrich would lead the 6th SS-Panzer Army; General Hasso von Manteufel the 5th Panzer Army.[300] Without exception, the assembled military commanders thought the objective – the taking of Antwerp, some 125 miles away – quite unrealistic. The forces available to them were simply inadequate, they argued, especially in winter conditions.

At best, they claimed, a more limited objective – recovery of Aachen and the adjacent parts of the Westwall, with perhaps the base being laid for a later westward push – might be attained. Jodl ruled out the objections. He made clear to the commanders that limited gains would not suffice. Hitler had to be in a position, as a result of the offensive, to 'make the western powers ready to negotiate'. On 10 November, Hitler signed the order for the offensive which had been prepared by the OKW. He acknowledged in the preamble that he was prepared 'to accept the maximum risk in order to proceed with this operation'. The date was set for 27 November, then, in numerous postponements brought about by delays in assembling both equipment and army units engaged in fighting, eventually reset for 10 December.[301] Two further delays ensued before the date was finally fixed at 16 December.[302]

In preparation for the offensive, Hitler had left Berlin on the evening of 10 December and moved his headquarters to Ziegenberg, not far from Bad Nauheim, close to the western front. Bunkers and barracks had been constructed in a woodland area by the Organisation Todt earlier in the war. Rundstedt and his staff were quartered in a stately residence nearby.[303]

In two groups, on the day of his arrival, 11 December, and again the following day, Hitler spoke to his military commanders at the 'Adlerhorst' ('Eagle's Eyrie'), as the new headquarters were called, to brief them on the coming offensive. After a lengthy preamble giving his own account of the background to the war, he outlined his thinking behind the offensive. Psychological considerations, as always, were paramount for Hitler. War could only be endured as long as there was hope of victory. It was necessary, therefore, to destroy this hope through offensive action. A defensive strategy could not achieve this goal. It had to be followed by successful attack. 'I have striven, therefore, from the beginning to conduct the war wherever possible offensively,' he stated. 'Wars are finally decided through the recognition by one side or the other that the war as such can no longer be won. To get the enemy to realize this is therefore the most important task.'[304] If forced back on to the defensive, it was all the more important to convince the enemy that victory was not in sight. Hitler came to another unalterable premiss of his conduct of the war. 'It is also important to strengthen these psychological factors in letting no moment pass without making plain to the enemy that whatever he does he can never reckon with capitulation, never, never. That is the decisive point.'[305] He referred, almost inevitably, to the reversal of Frederick the Great's fortunes in the Seven Years War. Here, he had reached another constant in his thinking: the will of the heroic leader, which alone made triumph out of adversity possible when all around him despaired of success.

This brought him to the fragility (he thought) of the coalition he was facing. A few months earlier, he had castigated those who had plotted to bring him down for their naïvety in presuming that it was possible to split the Allies.[306] Now his view was that the Alliance comprised such heterogeneous elements with conflicting goals and interests diverging 'by the hour' that 'if a few really heavy blows were inflicted, it could happen any moment that this artificially sustained common front could suddenly collapse with a huge clap of thunder'.[307] The tensions between the Soviet and western Allies had, indeed, become more apparent during the second half of 1944. But Hitler was certainly rational enough to know that his own destruction, and that of the regime he headed, provided sufficient common ground to hold the coalition together until Germany's defeat. He knew, too, that neither the western Allies nor – despite what Oshima had told him – the Soviets would look for peace with Germany while they were militarily so totally in the ascendancy.

As the supreme propagandist of old, he could always summon up absolute conviction when addressing an audience and needing to persuade them that what he was proposing was the only alternative on offer. It had proved his greatest strength since the early 1920s. The hints of pessimism – or greater realism – to Below and others in the weeks before the Ardennes offensive, even though only momentary slips of his guard, suggest, however, that Hitler was well aware of the size of the gamble in the Ardennes. He had to take it because, indeed, from his perspective, there was no alternative way out. If the long-shot were to come off, he reasoned, and a serious defeat were to be inflicted on the western powers while new German weaponry started to come into operation and before the expected Soviet winter offensive could begin, then new options could open up. At any rate, the only alternative to the gamble, as he saw it, was to fight for every inch of German soil in a rearguard struggle certain ultimately to end not just in defeat but in Germany's total destruction – and his own. The gamble had to be taken.

'Operation Autumn Mist' – the Ardennes offensive – began in the early morning of 16 December. All possible reserves had been mustered. Around 200,000 German troops backed by 600 tanks were launched against a front comprising around 80,000 American soldiers with 400 tanks.[308] The weather was perfect for the German attack, with heavy cloud hindering enemy aircraft. The American forces were taken by surprise. Sepp Dietrich's SS-Panzer Army soon encountered strong defence on the north of the front and could make only slow progress. Manteuffel's 5th Panzer Army broke through in the south, however, and pressed forward in a deep cut of some sixty-five miles to within a few miles of the river Meuse, laying siege to the town of Bastogne, an important communications point. But aware that American troops were on their way to break the encirclement, Brigadier-General Anthony McAuliffe, commander of the trapped 101st Airborne Division, could offer a straightforward one-word answer to surrender demands: 'Nuts!'[309] Bastogne held out, tying down three German divisions in the process before eventually being relieved by General Patton's 3rd US Army.

Manteuffel's advance had meanwhile slowed, handicapped by difficult terrain, bad weather, broken bridges, and fuel shortages as well as increasingly stiff American resistance. On 24 December, the weather lifted, exposing the German troops to relentless air attacks by some 5,000 Allied aircraft. Troop movements could now only take place at night. Supply lines and German airfields were heavily bombed. German fighters suffered serious losses. Once Patton had broken through the German front to relieve Bastogne on 26 December, Manteuffel had to give up any hopes of advancing further. 'Operation Autumn Mist' had failed.[310]

Hitler was still not prepared, however, to bow to the inevitable. As a diversion, he ordered a subsidiary offensive in the north of Alsace ('Operation North Wind'). The aim was to cut off and destroy the American forces in the north-eastern corner of Alsace, enabling Manteuffel to continue the main offensive in the Ardennes.[311] Once more Hitler addressed the commanders of the operation. And once more he laid the stress on psychological motivation – the all-or-nothing nature of the struggle for Germany's existence. The problem Germany faced, he began, had to be solved, and would be solved – either to Germany's advantage, or by bringing the country's 'annihilation (Vernichtung)'. It was not, as in earlier wars, a case of an honourable peace being granted by the victors, should Germany be defeated. The war, he declared, would decide 'the existence of the substance of our German people'. Enemy victory 'must necessarily bolshevize Europe'. It was a matter not of alteration to the form of state, but of the very substance of the people. If not sustained, it would cease to exist. 'Elimination destroys such a race under certain circumstances for ever,' he stated.[312] They should not imagine, he added, that he was thereby contemplating for a second the loss of the war. He gave a glimpse of his own psychological motivation underpinning his all-or-nothing philosophy. 'I have never in my life come to know the term capitulation, and I am one of the men who have worked themselves up from nothing. For me, then, the situation that we find ourselves in is nothing new. The situation was for me at one time a quite different one, and much worse. I'm telling you this only so that you can judge why I pursue my goal with such fanaticism and why nothing can wear me down.'[313]

The rest of his address comprised the usual parade of historical parallels of the triumph of will over adversity – inevitably again including Frederick the Great – and, as always, an optimistic assessment of the chances of military success. As so often, he emphasized the importance of time, of striking without waiting for supposedly optimal conditions, and the dangers of waiting, seeing the moment pass, and conditions deteriorate. Again, he ruled out the impossibility of Germany fighting indefinitely a defensive war. For strategic and psychological reasons it was essential to return to the offensive, and to seize the initiative. The operation would be decisive, he claimed. Its success would automatically remove the threat to the southern part of the Ardennes offensive, and with that the Wehrmacht would have forced the enemy out of a half of the western front. 'Then we'll want to have a further look,' he added.[314]

One slip of the tongue seemed to reveal, however, his realization that the ambitious aim he had placed in the Ardennes offensive could no longer be attained; that he knew he could no longer force the Allies off the Continent; and that, therefore, defensive operations would have to continue in the west as in the east. He spoke at one point of 'the unshakeable (*das unverrückbäre*) aim' of the operation as producing merely 'in part (*halbwegs*)' a 'cleansing (*Bereinigung*)' of the situation in the west.[315] It implied that his speech to the commanders had been little more than the elevation of hope over reason.

'North Wind' began on New Year's Day. It was Hitler's last offensive – and his least effective. German troops were able to advance no more than about twenty kilometres, making a few minor gains and causing Eisenhower to pull back forces in the Strasbourg area for a time. But the offensive was too weak to have much effect. It proved possible to halt it without the Americans having to withdraw troops from the Ardennes. 'North Wind' had proved to be little more than a momentary stiff breeze.[316]

Even more devastating was the death-blow to the Luftwaffe, imparted on 1 January, the same day that 'North Wind' had commenced. It had finally proved possible to launch a German air-offensive – though with disastrous consequences. Around 800 German fighters and bombers engaged in mass attacks on Allied airfields in Northern France, Belgium, and Holland. They succeeded in destroying or seriously damaging almost 300 planes, limiting

Allied air-power for a week or more. But 277 German planes were also lost – a good number to flak from their own batteries around the V2 launch-sites. There was no possibility of the Luftwaffe recovering from such losses. It was effectively at an end.[317]

On New Year's Day 1945, German radios broadcast Hitler's traditional address to the German People. It held nothing new for them.[318] Hitler offered them not a sentence on the effect of 'wonder weapons', steps to counter the terror from the skies, or anything specific on military progress on the fronts. Above all, he gave no hint that the end of the war was near. He spoke only of its continuation in 1945 and until a final victory – which by now only dreamers could imagine – was attained. His audience had heard it all many times before: the reaffirmation that 'a 9 November in the German Reich will never repeat itself';[319] that Germany's enemies, led by 'the Jewish-international world conspiracy' intended to 'eradicate (auszurotten)' its people;[320] that Germany's plight had been caused by the weakness of its allies; that the combined effort of front and homeland showed the 'essence of our social community' and an indomitable spirit, incapable of destruction; and that 'the Jewish-international world enemy' would not only fail in its attempt 'to destroy (vernichten) Europe and eradicate (auszurotten) its peoples, but would bring about its own destruction (Vernichtung)'.[321]

Few remained convinced. Many, like some observers in the Stuttgart area, were probably ready to acknowledge that 'the Führer has worked for war from the very beginning'.[322] Far from being the genius of Goebbels's propaganda, such observers remarked, Hitler had 'intentionally unleashed this world conflagration in order to be proclaimed as the great "transformer of mankind"'.[323] It was belated recognition of the catastrophic impact of the leader they had earlier supported, cheered, eulogized. Their backing had helped to put him in the position where his power over the German state was total. By now, in the absence of either the ability or the readiness – especially since the events of 20 July – of those with access to the corridors of power to defy his authority, let alone oust him, this man quite simply held the fate of the German people in his own hands. He had again avowed, as he always had done, his adamant refusal to contemplate capitulation in any event. This meant that the suffering of the German people – and of the countless victims of the regime they had at one time so enthusiastically supported – had to go on. It would cease, it was abundantly clear, only when Hitler himself ceased to exist. And that could only mean Germany's total defeat, ruin, and occupation.

With the petering out of the Ardennes offensive, all hope of repelling the relentless advance from the west was gone. And in the east, the Red Army was waiting for the moment to launch its winter offensive. Hitler was compelled by 3 January to accept that 'continuation of the originally planned operation [in the Ardennes] no longer has any prospect of success'.[324] Five days later came the tacit acknowledgement that his last gamble had been a losing throw of the dice with his approval of the withdrawal of the 6th Panzer Army to the north-west of Bastogne, and next day, his order to pull back his SS panzer divisions from the front.[325] On 14 January, the day before Hitler left his headquarters on the western front to return to Berlin, the High Command of the Wehrmacht acknowledged that 'the initiative in the area of the offensive has passed to the enemy'.[326]

Hitler had stated categorically in his briefings before the Ardennes and Alsace offensives that Germany could not indefinitely sustain a defensive war. By now, he had used up his last precious reserves of manpower, lost untold quantities of weaponry, and exhausted his remaining divisions in an offensive that had cost the lives of about 80,000 German soldiers (at the same time weakening the eastern front and paving the way for the rapid inroads of the Red Army in the coming weeks).[327] He had also seen the remnants of the Luftwaffe devastated to the point of no return; while rapidly dwindling supplies of fuel and other supplies essential for the war effort held out in any case the prospect of continuing the struggle only for a few more months. The logic was plain: the last faint glimmer of hope had been extinguished, the last exit route cut off. Defeat was inevitable. Hitler had not lost touch with reality. He realized this. Below found him one evening after the failure of the offensive in his bunker after air-raid sirens had sounded, deeply depressed. He spoke of taking his own life since the last chance of success had evaporated. He was savage in his criticism of the failure of the Luftwaffe, and of the 'traitors' in the army. According to Below's later recollection, Hitler said: 'I know the war is lost. The superior power is too great. I've been betrayed. Since 20 July everything has come out that I didn't think possible. Precisely those were against me who have profited most from National Socialism. I spoilt them all and decorated them. That's the thanks. I'd like most of all to put a bullet through my head.' But, as so often, Hitler rapidly pulled himself together, saying: 'We'll not capitulate. Never. We can go down. But we'll take a world with us.'[328]

This was what kept him going. It had underpinned his political 'career' since the beginning. There would be no repeat of 1918: no stab-in-the-back; no capitulation. That – and his place in history as a German hero brought down by weakness and betrayal – was all that was left to him.

16

INTO THE ABYSS

'Then a man comes by on horseback, shouting in a loud voice. "Save yourselves, you who can. The Russians will be here in half an hour." We're overcome by a paralysing fear.'

Recollection of a German refugee in
East Prussia, referring to events of January 1945

'It was as if they were shooting at stray dogs . . . They didn't care and shot in every direction, without any consideration. We saw the blood on the white snow and carried on walking.'

Recollection of a Jewish prisoner on the forced
march from Auschwitz-Birkenau, January 1945

'It must be our ambition also in our times to set an example for later generations to look to in similar crises and anxieties, just as we today have to look to the past heroes of history. The year 1918 will therefore not repeat itself.'

Hitler, speaking to Goebbels, 11 March 1945

'For the last time, the Jewish-Bolshevik mortal enemy has set out with its masses on the attack. He is attempting to demolish Germany and to exterminate our people.'

Hitler's final proclamation to the soldiers
on the eastern front, 15 April 1945

'I've now finally given up hope that the war will be won. What an enormous guilt Hitler bears. If I can't see my family again, I don't want to live any longer. Above all, a quick death would be better for them than to be deported or otherwise tortured. I've buried one hope after another in this war. But now is the worst time. What will happen?'[1]

Similar sentiments to these, entrusted to his diary on 28 January 1945 by a young German soldier living in hiding in Hungary in daily fear of being retaken by the Russians from whom he had escaped the previous autumn, were shared by millions of ordinary Germans in the last months of the Third Reich. Without hope of the victory so long promised, often without hope of seeing homes and loved ones again, and in trepidation of a future in the hands of merciless conquerors, they now held Hitler, once their idol, personally to blame for the untold misery which had befallen them. What they had seen as such glorious triumphs of the years 1939–41 were long forgotten. So was the jubilation that had accompanied them. This acclaim, building upon the already existent massive popular support that he had gained through his 'triumphs' of the pre-war years, had helped to make Hitler's authority unassailable. His authority, most now plainly saw, had been used to follow disastrous policies which had directed the path to Germany's ruin.

How this could have come about was given to few, at this point, fully to comprehend. The same soldier, doubtless speaking once more for vast inarticulate masses, had a simple answer: 'The biggest mistake was the war with Russia. Whatever the courage and readiness for sacrifice, you can't take on an entire world . . . We just bit off too much to chew. Above all our leadership.'[2]

Disastrous policy it had certainly been that had taken Germany into war against the Soviet Union. But it had been no simple mistake. Rather, it had been deeply embedded as an objective since the 1920s in Hitler's own psyche and ideological drive. Germany could only survive by expanding eastwards, attaining 'living space' at the expense of the Soviet Union, winning it 'by the sword', and destroying the mortal danger of 'Jewish Bolshevism': that had been repeatedly his message since the mid-1920s. The destruction of Bolshevism had, beyond the obsession of a single individual, been transformed during the 1930s into the state ideology of the Nazi regime, a goal enthusiastically backed by the Nazi Party, the bulk of the state apparatus, and the leadership of the armed forces. Most ordinary Germans would have agreed, while fearing war, that Bolshevism marked the greatest threat to the nation's future. By the end of that decade, Hitler's ideological vision that had existed unchangingly from the time of *Mein Kampf* onwards had come sharply into focus; it had been transmuted from a distant, utopian goal into a conceivable, practical objective. As we saw, within weeks of the conquest of France, Hitler's eyes had turned to the east, to the war he *knew* he had one day to fight.

The second part of the soldier's simple explanation was closer to the mark. It had indeed been a goal pursued from the arrogance of power and the conceit of presumed innate superiority. It had amounted in reality to a colossal gamble with Germany's future as the stake. That Britain had still not been forced to terms and that the USA was a menacing presence in the wings, together with the perceived certainty that the USSR would prove an altogether more dangerous foe within a few years, meant – given Hitler's mentality – that the gamble could not be postponed. The military and political leaders of the Reich largely agreed. Most rational observers would have been careful not to stake much on the outcome. The peril ought to have seemed daunting. But, in the backwash of the triumph over France, and under the illusion that the 'inferiors' of the Soviet Union would be incapable of holding out for more than a few months against the might of the invincible Wehrmacht, not just Hitler, but the German army leadership, too, thought European hegemony was theirs for the taking. The hubris which had enveloped Hitler during the 1930s and had fed his quest for European domination was, however, now to meet its nemesis.

By the winter of 1941, it was obvious that the gamble had not paid off. By the following winter – the winter of Stalingrad – the consequences were already seen to be catastrophic. Germany had permanently lost the initiative. There was no longer any possibility of repeating the incisive, lightning campaigns that had brought the astonishing triumphs between 1939 and 1941.

Instead, a bitter and attritional defensive war, which Hitler was both temperamentally and in terms of military skill singularly ill-equipped to direct, had to be fought – and with increasingly stretched manpower and resources. Meanwhile, relentless bombing was reducing Germany's cities to ashes. And once the western Allies had established a firm hold on Continental soil in the summer of 1944, the writing was well and truly on the wall – at least for all who applied conventional military logic to the increasingly uneven contest.

The failure of the conspiracy in July 1944 to overthrow Hitler removed the last realistic hope within Germany of a negotiated end to a war which was by now inexorably leading to the eventual destruction of the German Reich. Thereafter, there was no possibility of altering the structures of power from within. Despite signs that they were starting to disintegrate, these structures – at their centre the undisputed authority of Hitler – remained intact until the final stages of the regime's death-agony. As a consequence, Hitler's power remained absolute and undiminished even as the regime staggered towards oblivion. And as long as Hitler survived, and until Germany was totally crushed, the war would continue.

This meant in turn that there was no possibility of an alternative to the calamitous escalation of death and destruction as Germany fell in ruins. It was not that alternatives were left uncontemplated. At one point or another, almost all the Nazi leaders below Hitler – Goebbels, Göring, Ribbentrop, and Himmler among them – entertained notions of exploring avenues for a separate peace with either the Russians or with the western Allies. Hitler dismissed all such ideas out of hand. He would only negotiate from a position of strength, following a military success, he repeatedly stated. The chances of such an option being open to him were, however, as good as non-existent. So, instead, he spoke tirelessly and incessantly of will overcoming adversity; of refusal to capitulate, of holding out until 'five minutes past midnight'. Meanwhile, Germany burned.

Time and again, his generals exhorted him to make tactical retreats, or to shore up key sectors of the fronts by giving up other areas for former conquest and withdrawing much-needed troops. Again, Hitler was invariably uncompromising in his refusal. The clashes with his military commanders – most of all with Chief of the General Staff Heinz Guderian – became ever more bitter. His stubborn unreasonableness appeared to confound all military logic. He seemed to have lost his grip on reality. It was as if he had a death-wish – not just for himself, but for Germany and its people; an invitation to nemesis.

That, indeed, was central to Hitler's own warped brand of logic. From his bitter experience of the last years of the First World War – encountering defeatism, sensing subversion at home, traumatized as he lay in the military hospital at Pasewalk by the news of unexpected defeat and revolution perpetrated by the hated Social Democrats, when all that had meaning for him had been shattered – he had been obsessed by treachery and betrayal. He had made it his life's mission to upturn the effects of that perceived 'stab-in-the-back' in 1918 and the national humiliation inflicted on the German nation by those he insisted on calling 'November criminals'. And he had staked his political existence on eliminating, whatever might come, any potential for a repeat of 1918, a recurrence of what he saw as a cowardly capitulation and consequent impotent exposure to the dictates of foreign powers. To this end, and based on a crude philosophy that will would overcome any obstacle, he felt justified in demanding total sacrifice from the German people under his rule. Again, according to his own view of the world, defeat would this time bring not another 'Diktat of Versailles' – however repulsive that had been – but the total destruction of Germany. There was, therefore, from this optic, no point in surrender. If victory could not be attained, then struggle to the last was all that was left. A place in history, to be recognized by future generations if not by the present for its heroic, epic qualities, was its imagined virtue.

Incapable of finding fault in himself – in his judgement, his strategy, his leadership – Hitler turned the blame for what had gone wrong more and more on the military professionals, the army leaders whom he had never fully trusted, who had never been fully imbued with the National Socialist spirit. And once some of these officers had tried to do away with him in the summer of 1944, his obsession with treachery reached paranoid levels. Attempts to reason with him on military or strategic grounds were increasingly futile – likely only to prompt furious outbursts about the worthlessness and betrayal of his army leaders. Only generals such as Schörner or Model, who combined high military skills with something approaching Hitler's own philosophy and acceptance of his ruthless and unbending demands of his troops, met with his favour. His refusal to accept that willpower alone could not overcome massive superiority of the enemy in numbers and equipment would cost countless thousands of his soldiers' lives in needless sacrifice. It mattered not to him. According to his remorselessly cruel logic, their weakness had condemned them. Their individual loss meant nothing in the nation's struggle for its very existence. And when the German people, despite heroic efforts, showed themselves, too, to be incapable of withstanding superior enemy might, he was prepared to accept that they deserved to go under. They had ultimately proved themselves weak; they had not matched up to his demands of them; they had been, as he told one of his generals, in the end, unworthy of him.[3]

This leadership, which had taken Germany into such a reckless gamble, which had stunned the world through triumphs derived from boldness, ruthlessness, and lack of compromise as long as it had held the whip-hand, and which had been founded on principles of 'all-or-nothing' struggle, was, therefore, not the leadership to seek or entertain a diplomatic way out once backs were to the wall. Indeed, as Hitler – less distant from reality than has often been presumed – fully realized, his own person was an outright obstacle to any form of negotiated armistice. His own days were numbered in the event both of a negotiated peace or total defeat. With nothing at stake for him personally, therefore, the principle of 'no capitulation' – meaning self-destruction for him, for the regime, and for the German Reich – was easy to uphold. When, almost two years earlier, Baldur von Schirach, the Gauleiter of Vienna, had expressed in frank terms his view that the war somehow had to be ended, an enraged Hitler had asked: 'How does he think that can come about? He knows only too well that there is no further way, unless I shoot myself in the head.'[4]

The 'either-or' dogmatism, the stubbornly principled refusal to entertain compromise or concession, had served him well and had invariably proved successful in his political 'career' as long as he was combating weak, divided, and irresolute opponents. But it was a massive and insuperable obstacle when enemy positions were strong and united, when initiative had been irretrievably lost, bargaining power was weakening by the day, and more flexible military tactics and more subtle political skills were desperately needed. Not just the scale of the monstrous crimes against humanity perpetrated by his regime eliminated the possibility of any search for a negotiated end to the war – which could conceivably have been attained by a different leadership despite the Allied demands for 'unconditional surrender' stipulated in 1943 at Casablanca. His character, and everything he had stood for since entering politics, also categorically ruled it out. Hitler's temperament, often revealed in crises on his way to attaining absolute power – in 1921, for instance, when he gained the Party leadership, in 1923, when forcing ahead the ill-fated putsch, or in 1932 when faced with the challenge of Gregor Strasser – inclined him to pose self-destruction as the alternative to having his own way. There was indeed a touch of the theatrical, the melodramatic, the hysterical about his threats of suicide. But they nevertheless reflected a genuine, deep-rooted trait of Hitler's character. His philosophy of life as 'struggle', his reduction of all elements of conflict to stark 'black' and 'white', 'either-or', his instinctively radical stance on all matters, precluded any thought of retreat or compromise, leaving only the threat of self-destruction as his alternative to domination of his will.

Thus a Wagnerian end implicitly beckoned. There would be no capitulation at any cost – even if this meant bringing down Valhalla.

I

Hitler was still reeling from the failure of the Ardennes offensive, his last big hope, when all hell broke loose on the eastern front. The Soviet offensive had started. The main thrust, from bridgeheads on the Vistula, south of Warsaw, was aimed at southern Poland, then on to the vital Silesian industrial belt, and the river Oder, the last barrier before Berlin. Marshal Ivan Konev's 1st Ukrainian Front began the attack on 12 January, following a five-hour artillery barrage, from the Baranov bridgehead on the southern Vistula. It was rapidly followed, farther to the north, from the bridgeheads at Polavy and Magnuszev, by an assault from Marshal Georgi Zhukov's 1st Belorussian Front. A secondary thrust, by the 2nd and 3rd Belorussian Fronts, from bridgeheads on the river Narev to the north of Warsaw, aimed at cutting off German troops in East Prussia.

The Red Army's superiority in numbers was overwhelming. In the vital central sector of the 900-kilometre front that stretched from the Carpathians to the Baltic, some 2,200,000 Soviet troops were arrayed against 400,000 on the German side. But at the key bridgeheads on the Vistula, from where the offensive was launched, the imbalance was massive. The German general staff calculated that it was 11 to 1 in infantry, 7 to 1 in tanks, and 20 to 1 in guns in favour of the Red Army.[5] Aware from the reports of General Reinhard Gehlen, head of 'Foreign Armies East' department, of the huge build-up of Soviet forces and of an impending offensive, Guderian had pleaded with Hitler at Christmas, when the Ardennes offensive had already lost impetus, to transfer troops to the east. Hitler had dismissed Gehlen's reports as enemy bluff, 'the greatest imposture since Ghengis Khan'.[6] When, on a further visit to Führer Headquarters at Ziegenberg on New Year's Day 1945, Guderian had wrung the release of four divisions out of Hitler, the Dictator insisted they be sent to Hungary, not to the centre of the eastern front where military intelligence was pointing to the looming peril.[7] On 9 January, Guderian had made a further trip to Ziegenberg to show Hitler diagrams and charts displaying the relative strength of forces in the vulnerable areas on the Vistula. Hitler, in a rage, rejected them as 'completely idiotic', and told Guderian that whoever had compiled them should be shut up in a lunatic asylum. Guderian defended Gehlen and stood his ground. The storm subsided as rapidly as it had blown up. But Hitler nevertheless contemptuously refused the urgent recommendations to evacuate parts of the Vistula and Narev, withdraw to more defensible positions, and transfer forces from the west to shore up these weak points of the front. Guderian remarked, prophetically: 'The Eastern Front is like a house of cards. If the front is broken through at one point, all the rest will collapse.' Hitler's reply was that 'The Eastern Front must help itself and make do with what it's got.' As Guderian later commented, it was an 'ostrich strategy'.[8]

A week later, on 16 January, with the Red Army already making massive advances, Hitler, now back in Berlin, was finally prepared to transfer troops from west to east. But Guderian was outraged to learn that Sepp Dietrich's 6th Panzer Army – brought back from the unsuccessful Ardennes campaign and forming the bulk of the new forces available – was to be sent to Hungary, where Hitler was hoping to force the Russians back across the Danube and relieve Budapest. With German synthetic oil-plants destroyed by air-raids in mid-January, retention of the Hungarian oil-fields and refineries was, for him, the vital consideration. Without them, he argued, the German war effort was doomed anyway.[9] Nor did Guderian have much success in trying to persuade Hitler to evacuate by sea over the Baltic the German troops in grave danger of being cut off in Courland, on the tip of Latvia, for redeployment on the eastern front. Dönitz had been instrumental in persuading Hitler that Courland was a vital coastal area for the new U-boats which, he claimed, were almost ready to be turned against the west.[10] The consequence was that 200,000 desperately needed troops were tied up in Courland until Germany's capitulation in May.[11]

As Guderian had predicted, the Wehrmacht was wholly incapable of blocking the Red Army's advance. By 17 January, the Soviet troops had steamrollered over the troops in their path. The way to the German frontier now lay open before them. Overhead, Soviet planes controlled the skies, strafing and bombing at will. Some German divisions were surrounded; others retreated westward as fast as they could go. Warsaw was evacuated by the remaining German forces on 17 January, driving Hitler into such a paroxysm of rage that, at a critical point of the advance when they were needed for vital military operations, he had several officers from the General Staff who had issued signals connected with the withdrawal from Warsaw arrested and – together with Guderian himself – interrogated for hours by the head of the Reich Security Head Office, Ernst Kaltenbrunner, and the chief of the Gestapo, Heinrich Müller.[12]

On 18 January, Soviet troops entered Budapest. The battles in the city would last until mid-February, bitter fighting around Lake Balaton and in other parts of Hungary for several weeks longer.[13] But however much weight Hitler attached to it, the uneven contest could have only one outcome. And Hungary formed little more than a sideshow to the major catastrophe for the Reich unfolding to the north, where Soviet troops encountered little serious opposition as they advanced at great speed through Poland. Lodz was taken. The towns of Kalisz and Posen in the Warthegau were already in their sights.[14] On 20 January, they crossed the German border in the Posen area and in Silesia.

Still further north, German forces were in disarray in the face of Soviet advances into East Prussia. Colonel-General Hans Reinhardt, commander of Army Group Centre which was defending East Prussia, was sacked by a raging Hitler for evacuating coastal positions when Soviet troops broke through on 26 January, cutting off two German armies. General Friedrich Hoßbach, commanding the 4th Army, was also peremptorily dismissed by a furious Hitler for ignoring orders to hold ground – and not consulting his Army Group about his decision – when faced with a hopeless position and in grave danger of encirclement.[15] In a wild temper, Hitler accused both Reinhardt and Hoßbach of treason.[16] But a change of personnel – the capable Austrian Colonel-General Lothar Rendulic in place of Reinhardt, and General Friedrich-Wilhelm Müller for Hoßbach – could do nothing to alter the disastrous German collapse in the face of hopeless odds, in East Prussia as on the rest of the eastern front. This proved equally true in Hitler's replacement on 17 January of Colonel-General Josef Harpe, made the scapegoat for the collapse of the Vistula front, by his favourite, Colonel-General Ferdinand Schörner, and his ill-judged appointment on 25 January of Reichsführer-SS Heinrich Himmler, in the teeth of Guderian's strident objections, to take command of the newly formed and hastily constituted Army Group Vistula which aimed to stave off the Soviet advance into Pomerania. The hope that 'triumph of the will' and the toughness of one of his most trusted 'hard' men would prevail rapidly proved ill-founded.[17] Himmler, backed by courageous but militarily inexperienced Waffen-SS officers, soon found that combating the might of the Red Army was a far stiffer task than rounding up and persecuting helpless political opponents and 'racial inferiors'. By mid-February, Hitler was forced to concede that Army Group Vistula was inadequately led. After a furious row with Guderian lasting two hours, Hitler suddenly backed down and assigned General Walther Wenck to Himmler's headquarters to take over effective command of the planned limited counter-offensive on the Oder in Pomerania. 'The General Staff has won a battle this day,' he declared.[18] The Reichsführer-SS's failure as a military commander would finally – and belatedly – be recognized by Hitler in his replacement by Colonel-General Gotthard Heinrici on 20 March.[19] It marked a significant point in the growing estrangement of Hitler and his SS chief.[20]

The catastrophe on the eastern front was by that time well-nigh complete. In the south, fired by the fanatical Nazi leadership of Gauleiter Karl Hanke, Breslau held out under siege until early May.[21] Glogau, to the north-west, also continued to resist. But the defiance was of little military significance. By the end of January, the key industrial region of Silesia was lost to Germany. By 23 January Russian troops had already reached the Oder between Oppeln and Ohlau; five days later, they crossed it at Steinau, south of Breslau.[22] Further north, Posen was encircled and most of the Warthegau lost.[23] Its Gauleiter, Arthur Greiser, one of Hitler's most brutal henchmen, who had imposed a reign of terror on the predominantly Polish population of his fiefdom, had already fled westwards, along with other Nazi leaders from the region, in an attempt – ultimately to prove futile – to save his own skin.[24] His flight, like that of other Party representatives, fuelled the anger and contempt of ordinary people at the behaviour of Nazi bigwigs.[25]

By the first days of February, Soviet troops had established a bridgehead over the Oder between Küstrin and Frankfurt an der Oder. Even now, Hitler, waving his fists in a frenzy of rage, refused to listen to Guderian's entreaties to evacuate forthwith the military outposts in the Balkans, Italy, Norway, and, especially, Courland to free up reserves to defend the capital.[26] All that Guderian could muster was poured into a short-lived German counter-offensive in Pomerania in mid-February. Easily fending this off, the Red Army occupied practically the whole of Pomerania during February and early March. Though the surrounded Königsberg was still holding out, most of East Prussia was by now also in Soviet hands.

The immense Soviet gains of January had by then been consolidated, and even extended. Zhuvov's men had advanced almost 300 miles since the middle of January. From the bridgehead on the Oder near Küstrin, Berlin lay open to attack, only forty or so miles away. The last obstacle *en route* to the capital had been surmounted. But the rapidity of the advance had meant that Soviet supply lines lagged behind. They needed to be assembled across the wrecked transport routes of a battered Poland. Soviet strategists reckoned, furthermore, that wet spring weather was certain to hamper military manoeuvres. And it was plain that the bloody battles in store to take Berlin would require detailed preparation. The final assault on the capital, they concluded, could wait for the time being.[27]

While this disaster of colossal proportions was unfolding on the eastern front, the Allies in the west were swiftly reasserting themselves after staving off the Ardennes offensive.[28] By early February, some 2 million American, British, Canadian, and French soldiers were ready for the assault on Germany.[29] The attack of the Canadian 1st Army, which began on 8 February south of Nijmegen in the Wesel direction, met stiff opposition and could at first advance only slowly, amid bitter fighting. But in the last week of the month, American troops to the south-west pushed rapidly forwards towards Cologne, reaching the Rhine south of Düsseldorf on 2 March and the outskirts of Cologne three days later. Hitler's dismissal – again – of Field-Marshal Gerd von Rundstedt, Commander-in-Chief in the West, who had tried in vain to persuade him to withdraw his forces behind the Rhine, and replacement on 10 March by Field-Marshal Albert Kesselring, the former tenacious defender of German positions in Italy, made no difference.[30]

Retreating German troops had blown up the Rhine bridges everywhere as they went – except Remagen, between Bonn and Koblenz, which was discovered intact, as the retreating Germans failed to detonate in time the explosives they had laid, and immediately secured by American forces of the 1st US Army under General Courtney H. Hodges on 7 March. With a bridgehead swiftly established, the last natural barrier in the way of the western Allies had been crossed. Within a fortnight, American troops had again crossed the Rhine, boldly using assault boats – the first time such a manoeuvre had been undertaken since Napoleon's era – at Oppenheim, south of Mainz, then rapidly erecting a pontoon bridge and consolidating their position on the right bank of the river.[31] By then, the banks of the Rhine between Koblenz and Ludwigshafen were under American control. Further north, Montgomery now enjoyed a staged moment of glory as, watched by Churchill and Eisenhower, his troops crossed the Lower Rhine on 23–4 March following a massive air and artillery assault on Wesel. The most serious German resistance had by now been largely overcome. A third of all the German forces arrayed on the western front had been lost since early February – 293,000 men captured, 60,000 killed or wounded. Hitler's insistence on refusing to concede any territory west of the Rhine, rather than retreating to fight from behind the river, as Rundstedt had recommended, had itself contributed significantly to the magnitude and speed of the Allied success.[32]

As German defences were collapsing on both eastern and western fronts and enemy forces prepared to strike at the very heart of the Reich, German cities as well as military installations and fuel plants were being subjected to the most ferocious bombing of the entire war. Pressed by the British Air Marshal Arthur Harris's Bomber Command, the American and British chiefs of staff had agreed by the end of January to exploit the shock of the Soviet offensive by extending the planned air-attacks on strategic targets – mainly oil-plants and transport interchanges – to include the area-bombing and destruction of Berlin, Leipzig, Dresden, and other cities in central and eastern Germany. The aim was to intensify the mounting chaos in the big urban centres in the east of the Reich, as thousands of refugees fled westwards from the path of the Red Army. In addition, the western Allies were keen to demonstrate to Stalin, about to meet Churchill and Roosevelt at Yalta, that they were lending support to the Soviet offensive in their bombing campaign. The result was to magnify massively the terror from the skies as the bombs rained down on near-defenceless citizens. Beyond the forty-three large-scale precision attacks on Magdeburg, Gelsenkirchen, Botrop, Leuna, Ludwigshafen, and other targeted installations that laid waste Germany's fuel production, massive raids directed at civilian centres of population turned German inner-cities into wastelands. Berlin was hit on 3 February by the most damaging raid it had suffered so far during the war, killing 3,000 and injuring a further 2,000 people. Some of its poorer inner-city areas suffered most. Ten days later, on the night of 13–14 February, the beautiful city of Dresden, the glittering cultural capital of Saxony, renowned for its fine china but scarcely a major industrial centre, and now teeming with refugees, was turned into a towering inferno as thousands of incendiaries and explosive bombs were dropped by waves of RAF Lancaster bombers (followed next day by a further massive raid by American B17s). At least 35,000 citizens are estimated to have lost their lives in the most ruthless display experienced of Allied air superiority and strength.[33] Other devastated cities included Essen, Dortmund, Mainz, Munich, Nuremberg, and Würzburg. In the last four and a half months of the war, 471,000 tons of bombs were dropped on Germany, double the amount during the entire year of 1943. In March alone, almost three times as many bombs were dispatched as during the whole of the year 1942.[34]

By that time, Germany – militarily and economically – was on its knees. But as long as Hitler lived, there could be no prospect of surrender.

II

The savage brutality inflicted on those they had conquered – most of all in the eastern parts of Europe – was now rebounding on the German people. In the last months they reaped the whirlwind of the unconstrained barbarism Hitler's regime had sown.

As news of the Red Army's advance spread like wildfire, East Prussia, Pomerania, Silesia, and other eastern regions were filled with panic-stricken refugees, often scarcely equipped to cope with the bitter cold, fleeing with or without their possessions by any means they could find, many of them on foot. 'The roads are full of refugees, carts, and pedestrians,' one eye-witness recalled. 'Now and then cars packed with people and suitcases go by, followed by envious looks from those on foot. Again and again there are jams. People are gripped by panic as the cry goes up: "The Russians are close!" People look at each other. That can't be possible. Then a man comes by on horseback, shouting in a loud voice: "Save yourselves, you who can. The Russians will be here in half an hour." We're overcome by a paralysing fear.'[35]

Another report, from Königsberg, where the main square was thronged with refugee-wagons, mainly driven by women, and a fearful population not daring to think of the future, described the scene on 26 January: 'It's night as we leave the house. On the old road to Pillau the wagon-wheels grind endlessly as they pass by. Alongside, people of every age and position pull their sledges or push fully-laden prams. No one looks back.'[36] One woman remarked: 'The Führer won't let us fall into Russian hands. He'll gas us instead.'[37] No one took any notice of such an extraordinary remark. Others discussed how much cyanide was needed to commit suicide; it was as if they were talking about what to have for the next meal.[38]

A boy fleeing from the collapsing front in Poland travelled, together with his mother and sister, for two days and two nights in an overcrowded train heading for Breslau. From the window of the train, he observed the bodies of German soldiers along the wayside, hanged with notices round their neck denouncing them as cowards and deserters, and roads full of slaughtered cattle which their owners had been unable to drive off.[39] A couple who managed to jump on the last train to leave from Breslau told of 'refugees who almost trampled each other to death, of bodies thrown out of unheated goods trains during the journey, of those trekking coming to a standstill on the streets, of mothers gone mad who did not want to believe that the babies they carried in their arms were already dead.'[40] Within days, Berlin was among the cities swarming with refugees from the east, bitter and angry. 'Those who have lost everything, also lose their fear,' as one account put it. The police, for the time being, did not intervene.[41]

Horror stories filtering out and exploited by propaganda about the treatment of the German population unable to leave before Soviet troops arrived intensified the panic.[42] 'The refugees arriving here from the eastern Gaue are bringing for the most part quite shattering news of the misery of the fleeing population which, partly in panic, has sought refuge within the Reich from the Bolsheviks,' was noted in a regional report from Lower Bavaria.[43] All too often the horror stories were true as soldiers of the Red Army, frequently drunk and out of control, wreaked vengeance for what had been done to their own people on the families who fell into their hands in orgies of plundering, rape, beatings, killings, and other forms of terrifying maltreatment.[44] One careful estimate suggests that as many as 1.4 million women were raped in the eastern territories – some 18 per cent of the female population of those regions. In East Prussia, the percentage may well have been much higher.[45]

Fear of capture by the Red Army was by no means confined to the civilian population. Reports reaching Himmler left no illusions of collapsing morale among German troops in the battle zones of the east. This was especially pronounced among the units hastily put together from 'stragglers (Versprengte)' – soldiers who had broken away from their original units as these had been broken up by enemy action or had scattered in disarray. Here, there was no semblance of corporate spirit or readiness to fight. Fear of atrocities and summary shooting on capture by the Red Army dominated; panic prevailed.[46] Robbery and plundering by German soldiers were also reported. Desertions were sharply on the increase. Retreats could be seen to be turning into routs. The last train to leave the West Prussian town of Bromberg carrying refugees westwards had many of its places snatched by armed soldiers at the expense of women and children who were left behind. Nazi Party functionaries were often also at the forefront of the rush to leave for safer havens.[47]

To combat the unmistakably growing signs of demoralization and disintegration, improvised courts to mete out summary punishment were established not just within the Wehrmacht but also for the civilian population.[48] The slightest utterance that smacked of defeatism could result in immediate and draconian retribution.[49] The terror which had earlier been 'exported' to the subjugated peoples under the Nazi jackboot was now being directed by the regime, in its death throes, at the German people themselves. It was the surest sign that, apart from ever-dwindling numbers of fanatics and the desperadoes with nothing to lose, the regime had forfeited any basis of mass support.

Even the threat of summary execution was insufficient to halt the evident signs of demoralization and war-weariness – especially noticeable in the western parts of the Reich. Appeals to heroism, sacrifice, holding out to the last man, fell largely on deaf ears. Most people, soldiers as well as civilians, wanted nothing more than to survive, and to see an end to the bombing, fighting, and suffering. They would have agreed with the scornful comment of a Berlin journalist: 'Hold out. Most stupid of all slogans. So, they'll hold out until they're all dead. There's no other salvation.'[50] In contrast to the situation on the eastern front, many – boosted by rumours of good treatment in districts captured by the Americans – were by now prepared to take their chances under the western Allies rather than to continue the struggle. 'The population is evidently waiting for the entry of the Americans,' ran a Wehrmacht report from the area around Mayen, a small town between Rhine and Mosel, 'and has sabotaged directly or indirectly all measures taken by German soldiers to defend places. As I observed myself, white flags were prepared, everything indicating Party membership was burned, and the fighting soldiers were urged to put on civilian clothing . . .' Similar reports came in from other districts in the Rhineland.[51]

In the south of the country it was little different. People in the Augsburg region were said to be following 'with horror the events in the east of the Reich, where the storm-flood of the Soviets surges over (*umbrandet*) the borders of the homeland.'[52] War-weariness, deeply downcast mood, great anxiety, and loss of any hope for a favourable outcome to the war were registered generally. The constant fear of air-raids plagued the nerves. 'Today was terrible with the planes (*Fliegern*)', one woman from the Black Forest noted in her diary in February. 'It's never been as bad. Almost the whole day they were flying backwards and forwards. We were terribly afraid. It can't go on like this for much longer.'[53] The despondency was maximized where devastating raids – such as the attack on Nuremberg on 2 January that destroyed 29,500 homes, killed 1,794 persons, and wiped out the medieval 'old town' – caused massive damage and loss of life.[54] In Dresden, bodies of the tens of thousands killed in the raid on 13–14 February – men, women, and children – were piled high and loaded on to any available lorry or cart. Tractors dug mass graves, but the dead could not be buried fast enough and the stench of rotting corpses forced the authorities to turn to mass cremations on the old market square – an unforgettable experience for those forced to witness it.[55]

One boy, deployed with others in the *Deutsches Jungvolk* – the preparatory organization for the Hitler Youth – to help in emergency clearance work after a raid on his small home-town in Thuringia, observed soldiers carrying out charcoaled corpses from a neighbouring burnt-out house. They were the first dead that he and his friends had seen in the war 'and we were so shocked that we lost all our courage'.[56] Even so, the Hitler Youth probably contained, outside the dwindling ranks of Party fanatics, most of the remaining idealists – reared on myths of heroism, ready to follow the call to the last, tirelessly serving as helpers on flak units, tending refugees, looking after the wounded, clearing up after air-raids, and trying ultimately to fend off Soviet tanks with bazookas. One boy, injured in an air-raid, managed to stand to attention when an officer came by, asking him if he was in pain: 'Yes, but that's not important,' he replied. 'Germany must be victorious.'[57]

Such voices were by now largely confined to the naïve and the blindly credulous. Fear of instant and ferocious reprisals made most people cautious in the extreme in their comments, other than to close friends and relatives. It was too early for inquests on the causes of the war, let alone for moral reflections. But, aware that the suffering and sacrifice demanded of them in the war had been immense, but in vain, they looked to assign blame. However camouflaged the language, it was obvious that this was directed at the Party leadership – and at Hitler himself.[58]

'Trust in the leadership shrinks ever more,' ran a summary, compiled in early March, of letters monitored by officials of the Propaganda Ministry, 'because the proclaimed counter-blow to liberate our occupied eastern provinces did not take place and because the manifold promises of an imminent shift in fortunes have proven incapable of fulfilment . . . Criticism of the upper leadership ranks of the Party and of the military leadership is especially bitter.'[59] Shortly afterwards, a report from the Propaganda Office in Halle-Merseburg – the sort of report usually keen to refrain from any hint of negativity – summed up the mood in that area in language which, however coded, could not disguise the extent of anti-Hitler feeling: 'Those who still unwaveringly and unshakeably trusted the words of the Führer that the historic shift in our favour would still take place in this year were said to have a very hard time in face of the doubters and miseries. Whatever the unshakeable faith in the Führer, people are not refraining from remarking that, for certain, the Führer could not be informed by the military authorities about the true situation, otherwise it would not have come to the present serious crisis.'[60]

A graphic illustration of feeling towards the man who had so recently been the focus of such unprecedented adulation arose in a remembrance ceremony on 11 March 1945 for the dead of the war around the memorial in Markt Schellenberg, a small alpine town lying within a few minutes' drive of Hitler's residence on the Berghof: 'When the leader of the Wehrmacht unit at the end of his speech for the remembrance called for a "Sieg Heil" for the Führer, it was returned neither by the Wehrmacht present, nor by the Volkssturm, nor by the spectators of the civilian population who had turned up. This silence of the masses,' commented an observer from the local police, 'had a depressing effect, and probably reflects better than anything the attitudes of the population.'[61]

In most people's eyes, Hitler, the leader so many of them had come close to adoring, was now hindering an end to their suffering. The perception was correct. He was also prolonging even now the end of the far greater suffering of Nazism's victims.

The torment of these victims – in prime place among them, as ever, the Jews – continued unabated. In contrast to the general 'mood of catastrophe', the few Jews remaining within Germany could at least begin cautiously to hope that the end of the regime would not be long delayed once the Soviet offensive had begun in mid-January. But the hopes were still hedged with anxiety that the mortally wounded regime could turn upon them at any moment, or that even at this late hour they would be deported.[62] When most of the small number of Jews still existing in Dresden and deemed fit for work were rounded up in mid-February for 'evacuation', they knew they had to interpret what lay before them as a 'march into death'.[63] One of those left behind remarked to Victor Klemperer, the former specialist in French literature at Dresden's technical university: 'We've only got a stay of execution of about eight days. Then they'll fetch us from our beds at six in the morning. It'll be no different for us than for the others.'[64] It was, as the remarks indicate, still a life ruled by the most acute fear. But the fate of the hundreds of thousands of Jews and others in the clutches of the SS in the camps in the east was infinitely more dreadful. Their lives continued to hang by a thread on the arbitrary whim of their persecutors as the rapid breakthrough of Soviet troops brought a final and terrible phase of their agony.

The death camps in Poland had been closed one after the other as the Red Army advanced, with hurried attempts made to conceal the evidence of genocide. But over 700,000 prisoners of differing nations, creeds, ethnic groups (prominent among them, of course, Jews) and political persuasions still remained incarcerated in the huge, sprawling web of concentration camps in Nazi-occupied Europe.[65] Over a third of them would die in the horrendous forced marches those in the eastern camps now had to endure as they were driven – starving, frozen, exhausted, eating snow to still the raging thirst – in terrible treks, five abreast, at gunpoint westwards through icy blizzards, and at punishing pace, by their merciless captors whose hatred showed no signs of diminishing even at this late stage.[66] There were mixed reactions among those who encountered the trekking columns on the streets, often adding to the crowds of refugees fleeing from the oncoming Red Army. Some – the merest ripple of humanitarianism in the unrelenting sea of cruelty – took pity on the prisoners, offering them titbits of food (which the guards prevented them from accepting). Others reacted with hostility to the human wrecks trudging by.[67] Seeing themselves as Hitler's victims did not even at this late hour necessarily offer an antidote to vindictiveness towards those persecuted by the regime. Frequently building upon pre-existing phobias and prejudice, the years of Nazi outpourings of hatred towards 'enemies of the state', towards Jews above all, had done their work.

In what was by far the biggest of the camps, the immense complex of terror at Auschwitz, not far from Kattowitz in Upper Silesia, some of the huge crematoria had been dismantled and blown up – one of them in a rising by Jewish prisoners – during autumn 1944.[68] But the horror continued without respite. There were still over 65,000 prisoners of numerous nationalities – the majority of them Jewish – in Auschwitz and its numerous subsidiary camps in mid-January 1945, as the Red Army approached. As desperate attempts were were made to cover up traces of unimaginable inhumanity, the arrangements to evacuate the camps were improvised with great haste. A last note smuggled out by two prisoners just before the clearance of the camps started gave a foretaste of what was to come: 'Now we are experiencing evacuation. Chaos. Panic among the SS – drunks . . . The intentions change from hour to hour since they don't know themselves what orders they will get . . . This sort of evacuation means the annihilation of at least half of the prisoners.'[69]

For five days, beginning on 17 January, long columns of emaciated, starving, and frozen prisoners left the camp complex and were driven westwards by SS guards in forced marches of up to 250 kilometres. Some 56,000 left on foot, another 2,200 were at the end of the evacuation sent by rail.[70] Hundreds too weak or sick to begin the marches were shot in the camps. The mortalities on the terrible journeys were predictably enormous. Those dropping by the wayside, unable to sustain the punishing pace, or attempting to escape were shot on the spot. Even stopping for the briefest of moments for the most basic human necessity was to risk incurring the wrath of the guards. 'It was as if they were shooting at stray dogs . . . They didn't care and shot in every direction, without any consideration. We saw the blood on the white snow and carried on walking.'[71] In one of the marches alone, around 800 prisoners were murdered by their SS guards.[72] After days of marching on starvation rations in freezing conditions, the survivors reached the more and more disastrously overcrowded concentration camp at Groß-Rosen in Lower Silesia.[73] Most were dispatched within a short time in open railway-wagons in journeys lasting up to two weeks in the midst of winter to more than ten other camps, including Mauthausen, Buchenwald, Dachau, and Sachsenhausen, and – in their tens of thousands – to Bergen-Belsen, near Celle in north-west Germany, now grossly overcrowded and rapidly descending into the depths of the hell-hole found by stunned and horrified British soldiers in April 1945.[74]

On 26 January, an SS unit blew up the last of the crematoria in Birkenau. The next day, the SS guards retreated in heavy fighting as Soviet troops liberated the 7,000 exhausted, skeleton-like prisoners they found in the Auschwitz camp-complex. They also found 368,820 men's suits, 836,244 women's coats and dresses, 5,525 pairs of women's shoes, 13,964 carpets, large quantities of children's clothes, toothbrushes, false teeth, pots and pans, and a vast amount of human hair.[75]

III

The man at the centre of the rapidly imploding system that had unleashed such unpredecented horror and misery boarded his special train at Ziegen-berg, his western headquarters, on the evening of 15 January 1945 and, with his regular entourage of orderlies, secretaries, and adjutants, left for Berlin. As one wit pointed out, Berlin was more practical as headquarters; it would soon be possible to travel from there both to the eastern and western front by suburban railway. Hitler was still able to raise a laugh.[76] But his hopes of military success in the west were definitively at an end. Trying to stave off the Soviet offensive in the east was now the urgent priority.[77] His departure had been prompted by Guderian's opposition to his order on 15 January to transfer the powerful Panzer Corps 'Großdeutschland' from

East Prussia to the vicinity of Kielce in Poland, where the Red Army was threatening to break through and expose the way forward through the Warthegau. Not only, Guderian pointed out, was the manoeuvre impossible to execute in time to block the Soviet advance; it would at the same time gravely weaken the defences of East Prussia just as the Soviet attack from the Narev was placing that province in the utmost peril. As it was, the 'Großdeutschland' troops sat in railway sidings while the Führer and his Chief of the General Staff argued on the telephone about their deployment. Hitler would not rescind his order. But the dispute helped to persuade him that he needed to direct affairs at closer quarters. It was time to move back to Berlin.[78]

His train, its blinds pulled down, pulled into the capital that night. Triumphant arrivals in Berlin were no more than distant memories. As his car made its way amid the rubble through unlit streets to the Reich Chancellery – now cold and dismal, its pictures, carpets, and tapestries removed to safety in view of the increasing air-raids on Berlin – few inhabitants of the city even knew he had returned; probably still fewer cared.[79] Hitler in any case had no wish to see them. The path to his portals was blocked for all but the few who had the requisite papers and passes to satisfy the intense scrutiny of SS guards armed with machine-guns and posted at a series of security checks. Even the Chief of the General Staff had to surrender his weapons and have his briefcase meticulously examined.[80]

Hitler was completely immersed during the next days in the events on the eastern front. His insistence on the troops standing fast and refusing to concede a metre of territory had proved successful in stemming what could have turned into a rout outside Moscow in December 1941. In the defensive campaigns of 1943 and 1944, it had been in the main costly and counter-productive. Now it was futile and disastrous. It brought daily confrontation with Chief of Staff Guderian. As we noted, Hitler's rage over the loss of Warsaw and over tactical withdrawals of his generals in East Prussia knew no bounds. Seemingly incapable of acknowledging the objective imbalances in forces and the tactical weaknesses which had left the Vistula front so exposed, he thought he scented betrayal at every point. Frequent rantings about the incompetence or treachery of his generals dragged out the twice-daily military briefings to inordinate length. Guderian reckoned that his trips from General Staff Headquarters at Zossen, south of Berlin, twice a day took up around three hours. A further four to six hours were consumed during the conferences themselves. From the Chief of Staff's point of view, it was time wasted.[81]

The regular clashes between Hitler and his one-time admirer Guderian reflected what were by now wholly and irreconcilably conflicting philosophies with no middle-ground between them. For Hitler, capitulation could not be contemplated, even if the price was the total destruction of Germany. For the Chief of Staff, the destruction of Germany must be prevented, even if the price was capitulation – at any rate, in the west. Guderian – and he was far from alone in this – saw the only hope of preventing the complete destruction of Germany as putting everything into blocking the Soviet onslaught and at the same time opening negotiations for an armistice with the West, however poor the bargaining base. Perhaps the West could be persuaded that it was in its own interests to prevent Russian dominance of a post-war Germany by accepting the surrender of the western parts of the country to enable the Reich to defend its eastern borders.

This was the proposition that Guderian outlined on 23 January to Dr Paul Barandon, the Foreign Ministry's new liaison with the army. It was a faint hope but, as Guderian noted, drowning men clutch at straws. He hoped that Barandon would engineer for him an audience with Ribbentrop, and that the Foreign Minister and he could approach Hitler immediately with a view to ending the war.[82] Barandon arranged the interview. Ribbentrop, when Guderian met him two days later, seemed shocked at the prospect of the Russians at the gates of Berlin within a few weeks. But he declared himself a loyal follower of the Führer, knew the latter's antipathy to any peace feelers, and was unwilling to support Guderian. As Guderian entered the briefing room that evening, he heard Hitler in a loud and agitated voice say: 'So when the Chief of the General Staff goes to see the Foreign Minister and informs him of the situation in the East with the object of securing an armistice in the West, he is doing neither more nor less than committing high treason!'[83] Ribbentrop had, of course, promptly reported to Hitler the content of his talks with Guderian. No action followed. But it was a warning shot across the bows. 'I forbid most decisively generalizations and conclusions about the overall situation,' Speer recalled Hitler ranting. 'That remains my business. Anyone in future claiming to another person that the war is lost will be treated as a traitor to his country with all the consequences for him and his family. I will act without respect for position and standing.' The head of the Security Police, Ernst Kaltenbrunner, from now on sat silently but menacingly in the background during the briefing sessions.[84]

In fact, despite this outburst – and Ribbentrop's refusal to entertain Guderian's suggestion – Hitler was aware in early 1945 of his Foreign Minister's extremely tentative feelers via Stockholm, Bern, and Madrid to the western Allies to end the war with Germany and join the fight against Bolshevism. He knew, too, of Ribbentrop's consideration of an alternative suggestion: approaching the Soviet Union to help crush Britain.[85] Hitler had first opposed any idea of peace feelers. Then he appeared to change his mind. 'Nothing will come of it,' Hitler told Ribbentrop. 'But if you really want, you can try it.'[86] However, not only was there no prospect of either the Soviets or the western Allies showing genuine readiness to enter peace negotiations at this stage; Ribbentrop knew that Hitler had not the slightest wish in pursuing them. A premiss of any peace-talks, as Hitler well realized, would have been his own removal. That in itself was sufficient to make him dismiss in fury any idea of negotiations.[87] As the Foreign Minister himself later remarked, Hitler 'regarded any peace feeler as a sign of weakness'. His soundings, so he said, merely 'showed that no serious peace talk was possible' as long as Hitler lived.[88]

This was equally plain to Goebbels. The Propaganda Minister was approached by Göring at the end of January, disconsolate at events in the east and despairing of Germany's military chances. Göring was prepared, he said, to use his Swedish contacts to put out feelers to Britain and sought the help of Goebbels in persuading Hitler that, since any overtures from Ribbentrop (regarded with utter contempt by the Reich Marshal as well as the Propaganda Minister) were doomed to failure, he should try this avenue. Goebbels was not encouraging. Privately, he was unwilling to push the case with Hitler since he ran the risk of losing the Führer's confidence which, he added pointedly, 'is indeed the entire basis of my work'. In any case, Göring could only act, he noted, with Hitler's approval 'and the Führer won't grant him such approval'. Göring thought Hitler too intransigent, and wondered whether he wanted a political solution at all. He did, replied Goebbels, but 'the Führer does not see such a possibility existing at present.'[89]

Hitler's lingering hopes, as ever, were in a split in the alliance against him. If Britain and the USA wanted to prevent a bolshevization of Europe, he told Goebbels, they would have to turn to Germany for help. The coalition had to break; it was a matter of holding out until the moment arrived.[90] Goebbels privately thought Hitler too optimistic.[91]

Jodl and Göring played to this illusion, however, at the military briefing on 27 January. However gloomy his attitude had been when speaking to Goebbels, in Hitler's presence Göring sang a different tune. The Soviet advance had unquestionably dashed British plans, he and Jodl reckoned. Göring thought that if things went much further they could expect a telegram from the British saying they were prepared to join forces to prevent a Soviet occupation of Germany. Hitler suggested the National Committee of Free Germany, the 'traitors' organization' based in Moscow and linked with General Seydlitz, from the 6th Army lost at Stalingrad, could come in useful. He had told Ribbentrop, he said, to filter a story to the British that the Soviets had trained up 200,000 Communists under the leadership of German officers, ready to march. The prospect of a Russian-led national government in Germany would be certain to stir up anxiety in Britain, he averred. The British did not enter the war to see 'the East come to the Atlantic', Göring added. Hitler commented: 'English newspapers are already writing bitterly: what's the point of the war?'[92]

He nevertheless saw no opening for overtures to his western enemies, when Goebbels tentatively broached the issue. In discussions with his Propaganda Minister on successive days at the end of January, appearing drained with fatigue, he reflected on the failure of the intended alliance with Britain. This might have been possible, he thought, had Chamberlain remained Prime Minister. But it had been totally vitiated by Churchill, 'the actual father of the war'.[93] On the other hand, he continued to express admiration for Stalin's brutal realism as a revolutionary who knew exactly what he wanted and had learnt his method of atrocities from Ghengis Khan. Here, too, Hitler dismissed any prospect of negotiations.[94] He berated, as always, the failings of his generals. He referred, as he had so frequently done, to the way crises in the Party before 1933 had been overcome, and how he was determined to withstand the crises of the war. 'He wanted,' he declared to Goebbels, 'to prove himself worthy of the great examples from history.' Should he succeed in transforming Germany's fortunes, thought the Propaganda Minister, without a trace of cynicism, he would be the man not only of the century, but of the millennium.[95]

Goebbels continued to find Hitler over-optimistic about the chances of staving off the Soviet advance.[96] Indeed, however pessimistic or fatalistic he was in dark moments, Hitler was as yet far from ready to give up the fight. He spoke of his aims in the forthcoming offensive in Hungary. Once he was again in possession of Hungarian oil, he would pour in additional divisions from Germany to liberate Upper Silesia. The whole operation would take around two months. The air of unreality did not escape Goebbels. It would take a great deal of luck to succeed, he noted.[97]

Goebbels had been 'astonished' that Hitler, after showing such repeated reluctance for two years to speak in public, had so readily taken up a suggestion to broadcast to the nation on 30 January, the twelfth anniversary of the 'seizure of power'.[98] Hitler presumably felt that at such a point of national crisis, with the enemy already deep inside the Reich, not to have spoken on such an important date in the Nazi calendar would have sent out the worst possible signals to the German people. It was imperative that he strengthen the will to fight, most of all on Germany's shrinking borders.

At any rate, his recorded speech, broadcast at 10p.m. that evening, amounted to little more than an attempt to stiffen morale, to appeal to fighting spirit, to demand the most extreme sacrifice in 'the most serious crisis for Europe in many centuries', and to emphasize his own will to fight on and refusal to contemplate anything other than victory. He referred, inevitably, to a 'Jewish-international world conspiracy', to 'Kremlin Jews', the 'spectre of asiatic Bolshevism', and of a 'storm-flood from inner Asia'. But the military disasters of the previous fortnight were not touched upon with a single word. And only a single sentence mentioned 'the horrible fate now taking place in the east, and eradicating people in their tens and hundreds of thousands in villages, in the marches, in the country, and in towns', which would eventually 'be fought off and mastered'.[99] The speech could have appealed to few beyond remaining diehards. Only two of a group of soldiers listening to the speech on the radio at their post in Bamberg rose to their feet and stood with outstretched right arms in the Nazi salute as the national anthem brought the broadcast to an end. The rest stayed sitting, and were soon voicing their criticism.[100] Goebbels professed himself satisfied with the speech and reckoned it had a significant impact on the German public.[101] Probably more realistic in its assessment of what proved to be the last time the German people heard Hitler's voice was a local SD report from southern Germany: 'Propaganda has not managed to strengthen belief in a positive change. Even the Führer's speech on 30 January was unable to remove the loudly voiced doubts (*die lauten Zweifel*).'[102] The once-revered Leader had little credibility left.

That same day, 30 January, Speer had a memorandum passed to Hitler. It told him that the war economy and armaments production were at an end. Following the loss of Upper Silesia, there was no possibility of meeting the needs of the front in munitions, weapons, and tanks. 'The material superiority of the enemy can, accordingly, no longer be compensated for by the bravery of our soldiers.' Hitler's cold response made plain that he did not take kindly to receiving such reports that smacked of defeatism. He forbade Speer to pass the memorandum to anyone, adding that conclusions from the armaments position were his alone to draw.[103] Short of the miracle for which he was still waiting, it must nevertheless have been obvious to

Hitler, as to all those around him, that Germany could last out neither economically nor militarily for much longer.

Speer, long after the events, posed the question why even at this point Hitler was not faced with any joint action from those with regular contact to him to demand an explanation of how he intended to bring the war to an end. (He gave no hint of what might have followed from such an unlikely scenario.) Göring, Himmler, Ribbentrop, and even in some ways Goebbels had, after all, been among the Nazi leaders who at one time or another had broached the question of peace overtures to the enemy, which Hitler had repeatedly dismissed out of hand. Now the end was near, and Germany was facing not just military defeat but total destruction. 'Surely something must happen,' Speer whispered to Dönitz during a briefing in early February, when further disasters were reported. Dönitz replied coolly that he was there only to represent the navy. The Führer would know what he was doing.[104]

The reply provided at the same time an answer to the question Speer raised many years later. There was no prospect of any united front against Hitler even now, and even among those who saw with crystal clarity the abyss looming before them. The aftermath of the plot against him the previous year had left none of his entourage in the slightest doubt of the ruthlessness with which he would turn on anyone seen as a threat. But the impossibility of any combined front against Hitler did not rest alone, or even primarily, on fear. The innermost structure of the regime had long depended upon the way Hitler could play off his paladins against each other. Their deep divisions and animosities were reconciled only in their unquestioning loyalty and adherence to the Leader, from whom all remaining shreds of power and authority were still drawn. The Führer cult was still far from dead in this inner part of the 'charismatic community'. Keitel, Jodl, and Dönitz, among the highest ranks of the military leaders, were still wholly bound to Hitler, their loyalty unshaken, their admiration undiluted. Göring, his prestige at rock-bottom, had long since lost all energy to undertake anything against Hitler, and certainly lacked the will to do so. The same was true of Ribbentrop, who was in any case devoid of friends within the Nazi hierarchy and held by most in contempt as well as loathing. Goebbels, Labour Front leader Robert Ley, and, not least, the Party leader in closest proximity to Hitler, Martin Bormann, were among the most radical supporters of his uncompromising line and remained wholly loyal. Speer, for his part, was – whatever his post-war feelings – one of the least likely to lead a fronde against Hitler, confront him with an ultimatum, or serve as focal point of a combined approach to put pressure on him. The scenario contemplated by Speer long after the events was, therefore, utterly inconceivable. The 'charismatic community' was compelled by its inner logic to follow the Leader on whom it had always depended – even when he was visibly taking it to perdition.

IV

The government quarter of Berlin, like much of the rest of the city, was already a dismal and depressing sight even before, in broad daylight on 3 February, a huge American fleet of bombers unleashed a new hail of destruction from the skies in the heaviest raid of the war on the Reich capital. The old Reich Chancellery, the neo-Baroque palace dating back to Bismarck's time, was ruined. The façade remained intact, but beyond one wing the building was now little more than an empty shell. The new Reich Chancellery, designed by Speer, also suffered a number of direct hits.[105] Bormann's headquarters in the Party Chancellery were severely damaged, and other buildings at the hub of the Nazi empire were demolished fully or in part. The whole area was a mass of rubble. Bomb craters pitted the Chancellery garden. For a time there was a complete power-failure, and water was available only from a water-cart standing in front of the Reich Chancellery.[106] But unlike most of the population in the bombed-out districts of Berlin and elsewhere, at least the leaders of the Third Reich could still find alternative shelter and accommodation, however modest by their standards.

His apartments in the Reich Chancellery largely gutted by incendiaries, Hitler now moved underground for much of the time, shuffling down the seemingly unending stone steps, flanked by bare concrete walls, that led to the claustrophobic, labyrinthine subterranean world of the Führer Bunker, a two-storey construction deep below the garden of the Reich Chancellery.[107] The enormous bunker complex had been deepened in 1943 – extending an earlier bunker (originally meant for possible future use as an air-raid shelter) dating from 1936 – and heavily reinforced during Hitler's stay at his western headquarters.[108] The complex was completely self-contained, with its own heating, lighting, and water-pumps run from a diesel generator.[109] Hitler had slept there since returning to Berlin.[110] From now on, it would provide a macabre domicile for the remaining weeks of his life.

The bunker was far removed from the palatial surrounds to which he had been accustomed since 1933. An attempt to retain a degree of splendour at least remained in the corridor leading up to his bunker, which had been converted into a type of waiting-room, laid with a red carpet, and provided with rows of elegant chairs lined against the walls, which were hung with paintings brought down from his apartments. From here, a small ante-room gave way to the curtained entrance to his study. This was a small room – around nine by twelve feet – and seemed oppressive. A door on the right opened on to his bedroom, which had doors leading into a small briefing room, into his bathroom, and a tiny dressing-room (and from there into what was to become Eva Braun's bedroom). A writing-desk, small sofa, a table, and three armchairs were squeezed into the study, making it cramped and uncomfortable. A large portrait of Frederick the Great entirely dominated the room, offering a constant reminder to Hitler of the seeming rewards for holding out when all appeared lost until the tide miraculously turned.[111] 'When bad news threatens to crush my spirit I derive fresh courage from the contemplation of this picture,' Hitler was heard to remark.[112]

At first, even after he had moved his living quarters into the bunker, Hitler continued to spend part of the day in the undamaged wing of the Reich Chancellery. He lunched each day with his secretaries behind closed curtains in a dingy room lit by electric light.[113] Since the operations room in the old Reich Chancellery building was no longer usable, the afternoon military conferences, usually beginning about 3p.m. and lasting two to three hours, were at this time held around the map-table in Hitler's imposing study in the New Reich Chancellery, with its polished floor, thick carpet, paintings, leather armchairs and couch, and – remarkably – still intact grey-curtained ceiling-high windows.[114] The circle of participants had by now been widened to include Bormann, Himmler, Kaltenbrunner, and often Ribbentrop. Afterwards, Hitler would usually drink a cup of tea with his secretaries and adjutants before returning to the safety of his underground abode.[115] For the evening meal his entourage trekked through kitchens and corridors, past machine rooms, ventilation shafts, and toilets, through two heavy iron gates, and down to the Führer Bunker.[116] The first time he ventured down to visit Hitler, Goebbels spoke of finding his way through the corridors 'just like in a maze of trenches'.[117] Over the next weeks, Hitler transferred almost all of his activities to the bunker, leaving it only for occasional snatches of fresh air to let Blondi out for a few minutes in the Chancellery garden or to take lunch with his secretaries above ground.[118] From then on, he seldom saw daylight. For him and his 'court', spending almost their entire existence in the confines of the underground headquarters, night and day lost most of their meaning.

Hitler's day usually began around this time with the sound of air-raid sirens in the late morning. Linge was instructed to wake him, if he were not already awake, at noon, sometimes as late as 1p.m.[119] Often – probably affected by the unholy concoctions of pills, potions, and injections he had daily (including stimulants as well as sedatives) – he had slept, so he claimed, for as little as three hours.[120] The air-raids made him anxious. He would immediately dress and shave. The outer appearance of the Führer had to be maintained. He could not face his entourage unshaven and in night clothes even during an air-raid. The afternoons were almost exclusively taken up with lunch and the first of the lengthy twice-daily military briefings. The evening meal, usually not beginning until eight o'clock, sometimes later, frequently dragged out until late in the evening. Hitler sometimes retired for an hour or two, sometimes taking a sleep until it was time for the second military briefing. By now, it was usually 1a.m. By the end of the briefing – invariably stressful in the extreme for all who attended, including Hitler himself – he was ready to slump on the sofa in his room. He was not too tired, however, to hold forth to his secretaries and other members of his close circle, summoned to join him for tea in the middle of the night. He would regale them, as he had done throughout the war, for up to two hours with banalities and monologues about the church, race problems, the classical world, or the German character.[121] After fondling Blondi and playing for a while with her puppy (which he had named 'Wolf'), he would at last allow his secretaries to retreat and finally retire himself to bed. It was by then, as a rule, according to Linge's planned schedule, around five o'clock in the morning, though in practice often much later.

A piece of pure escapism punctuated at this time Hitler's daily dose of gloom from the fronts: his visits to the model of his home-town Linz, his intended place of retirement, as it was to have been rebuilt at the end of the war, following a glorious German victory. The model had been designed by his architect Hermann Giesler (who had been commissioned by Hitler in autumn 1940 with the rebuilding of Linz), and was set up in February 1945 in the spacious cellar of the New Reich Chancellery. In January 1945, as the failure of the Ardennes offensive became apparent, as the eastern front caved in under the Red Army's assault, and as bombs rained down also on the Danube region in which Linz was situated, Giesler's office was repeatedly telephoned by Hitler's adjutants, and by Bormann. The Führer kept speaking of the model of Linz, they told Giesler; when would it be ready for him to inspect?

Giesler's team worked through the nights to meet Hitler's request. When the model was finally ready for him to see, on 9 February, Hitler was entranced. Bent over the model, he viewed it from all angles, and in different kinds of lighting. He asked for a seat. He checked the proportions of the different buildings. He asked about the details of the bridges. He studied the model for a long time, apparently lost in thought. While Giesler stayed in Berlin, Hitler accompanied him twice daily to view the model, in the afternoon and again during the night. Others in his entourage were taken down to have his building plans explained to them as they pored over the model.[122] Looking down on the model of a city which, he knew, would never be built, Hitler could fall into reverie, revisiting the fantasies of his youth, when he would dream with his friend Kubizek about rebuilding Linz.[123] They were distant days. It was soon back to a far harsher reality.

He spoke with Goebbels early in February about the defence of Berlin. They discussed the possible evacuation of some of the government offices to Thuringia. Hitler told Goebbels, however, that he was determined to stay in Berlin 'and to defend the city'.[124] Hitler was still optimistic that the Oder front could be held. Goebbels was more sceptical.[125] Hitler and Goebbels spoke of the war in the east as a historic struggle to save the 'European cultural world' from latter-day Huns and Mongols. Those would fare best who had burnt their boats and contemplated no compromises. 'At any rate even a thought of capitulation is never entertained among us,' noted Goebbels.[126] Even so, with Hitler still adamant that the coalition against him would collapse within the year, Goebbels recommended putting out feelers for an opening to the British. He did not embroider upon how this might be achieved. Hitler, as always, claimed the time was not conducive to such a move. Indeed, he feared that the British might turn to more draconian war methods, including the use of poison gas. In such an eventuality, he was determined to have large numbers of the Anglo-American prisoners in German hands shot.[127]

On the evening of 12 February, 'the Big Three' – Roosevelt, Stalin, and Churchill – put out a communiqué from Yalta on the Crimea, where they had been conferring for a week, spending much of the time on the post-war shape of Germany and Europe.[128] The communiqué left the Nazi leadership under no illusions about Allied plans for Germany: the country would be divided and demilitarized, its industry controlled, reparations paid; war criminals would be put on trial; the Nazi Party would be abolished. 'We know now where we are,' commented Goebbels.[129] Hitler was immediately informed. He seemed unimpressed.[130] He needed no further confirmation of his unchanging view that capitulation was pointless. The Allied leaders, he commented, 'want to separate the German people from its leadership. I've always said: there's no question of another capitulation.' After a brief pause, he added: 'History does not repeat itself.'[131]

The following night, the city centre of Dresden was obliterated. Hitler heard the news of the devastation stony-faced, fists clenched.[132] Goebbels, said to have been shaking with fury, immediately demanded the execution of tens of thousands of Allied prisoners-of-war, one for each citizen killed in air-raids.[133] Hitler was taken with the idea. Brutal German treatment of prisoners-of-war would, he was certain, prompt retaliation by the Allies. That would deter German soldiers on the western front from deserting.[134] Guderian recalled Hitler stating: 'The soldiers on the eastern front fight far better. The reason they give in so easily in the west is simply the fault of that stupid Geneva convention which promises them good treatment as prisoners. We must scrap this idiotic convention.'[135] It took the efforts of Jodl, Keitel, Dönitz, and Ribbentrop, viewing such a reaction as counter-productive, to dissuade him from such a drastic step.[136]

A few days later, Hitler summoned the Gauleiter, his most trusted Party viceroys, to the Reich Chancellery for what would prove to be a final meeting. The last time they had assembled was in early August of the previous year, shortly after Stauffenberg's attempt on Hitler's life. The present occasion was the twenty-fifth anniversary of the proclamation of the Party Programme in the Hofbräuhaus in Munich on 24 February 1920.

Hitler had frequently addressed the Gauleiter at moments of crisis during the past years. The real purpose of the present gathering was to rally the core of his support as the regime faced its gravest crisis. He had nothing resembling good news to impart. In the west, the Allies were pressing towards the Rhine. In the east, the counter-offensive launched a few days earlier in Pomerania offered no more than a fleeting ray of light in the deep gloom. Himmler's Army Group Vistula was encountering that very day a renewed assault from the Red Army. The absence of Erich Koch, whose East Prussian Gau was almost completely cut off by the Red Army, and Karl Hanke, besieged in Breslau, was a reminder of the fate of the eastern provinces. And the cluster of Gauleiter pressing Martin Mutschmann, Gauleiter of Saxony, for news about Dresden, or their Party comrades from the Rhineland about the failure of the Ardennes offensive and the fighting in the west, told its own tale.

Hitler's appearance, when he entered the hall at 2p.m. that afternoon, was a shock to many of the Gauleiter, who had not seen him for six months or so. His physical condition had deteriorated sharply even during the space of those six months. He was more haggard, aged, and bent than ever, shuffling in an unsteady gait as if dragging his legs. His left hand and arm trembled uncontrollably. His face was drained of colour; his eyes bloodshot, with bags underneath them; occasionally a drop of saliva trickled from the corner of his mouth.[137]

Bormann had warned the Gauleiter in advance not to raise any criticism.[138] There was, as ever, little likelihood of confrontation. But the sympathy at Hitler's outward appearance did deflect from the initial critical mood.[139] Perhaps playing on this, he gave up at one point an attempt to raise a glass of water to his mouth in a trembling hand, without spilling it, and made reference to his own debilitation. He spoke sitting down at a small table for an hour and a half, his notes spread out in front of him. He began, as so often, with the 'heroic' Party history. With present and future so bleak, he had come more and more to take refuge in the 'triumphs' of the past. He looked back now once more to the First World War, his decision to enter politics, and the struggle of National Socialism in the Weimar Republic. He lauded the new spirit created by the Party after 1933. But his audience did not want to hear of the distant past. They were anxious to know how, if at all, he would overcome the overwhelming crisis currently sweeping over them. As usual, he dealt only in generalities. He spoke of the approaching decisive hour of the war, which would determine the shape of the coming century. He pointed as usual to the 'new weapons', which would bring about the change in fortune, praising the jets and new U-boats. His main aim was to fire up his sturdiest supporters for a final effort, to stiffen their morale and enthuse them to fight to the end so that they in turn would stir up the people in their region to selfless sacrifice, indomitable defence, and refusal to capitulate. If the German people should lose the war, he declared (in a further demonstration of his unchanged social-Darwinism), then it would indicate that it did not possess the 'internal value (*inneren Wert*)' that had been attributed to it, and he would have no sympathy with this people. He tried to persuade the Gauleiter that he alone could judge the course of events correctly. But even in this circle, among the Party chieftains who for so many years had been the backbone of his power, few could share his optimism. His ability to motivate his closest supporters by the force of his rhetoric had dissolved.[140]

This was even more the case for the mass of the population, where the words of the greatest demagogue known to history had by this time been drained of all impact, and were generally regarded as little more than empty phrases, bearing the promise of nothing other than further suffering until the war could be ended. The anniversary of the promulgation of the Party Programme had, until 1942, been traditionally the date of a big speech by Hitler in the Festsaal of the Hofbräuhaus in Munich. In 1945, as in 1942 and 1943, Hitler confined himself to a proclamation. Read out by Hermann Esser, one of his Munich cronies from the early days of the Party, the proclamation was to prove Hitler's final public statement to the German people.

It amounted to no more than yet a further repeat of the long empty phrases of the old message. National Socialism alone had given the people the toughness to combat the threat to its very existence of an 'unnatural alliance', 'a diabolical pact between democratic capitalism and Jewish Bolshevism'. The atrocities of Bolshevism – 'this Jewish plague' – were now being experienced directly in the eastern parts of the Reich. Only 'extreme fanaticism and resolute steadfastness' could ward off the peril of 'this Jewish-Bolshevik annihilation of peoples and its west European and American pimps'. Weakness would and must perish. It was a 'duty to maintain the freedom of the German nation for the future' and – the unmistakable attempt to shore up fighting spirit through instilling fear – 'not to let German labour be shipped off to Siberia'. Its fanatical hatred for 'the destroyer of mankind' bolstered by the suffering it had endured, National Socialist Germany would continue the fight until 'the historical turning' came about. It would be that year. He ended on a note of pathos. His life had only the value it possessed for the nation. He wanted to share the suffering of the people, and almost regretted that the Berghof had not been bombed, which would have enabled him to share the sense of loss of possessions. (On this, the Allies were ready to oblige a few weeks later.) 'The life left to us,' he declared at the close, 'can serve only one command, that is to make good what the international Jewish criminals and their henchmen have done to our people.'[141]

A poignant commentary was voiced in the routine report of the SD station in Berchtesgaden, where once thousands of 'pilgrims' had poured in to try to catch a glance of the Führer during his stays at the Berghof. 'Among the overwhelming majority of people's comrades,' the report ran, 'the content of the proclamation whistled by like the wind in the empty boughs.'[142]

It was presumably Hitler's sensitivity to his public image that made him refuse Goebbels's request for a press report to shore up morale. He must have been alert to the inevitable derision that would be induced by reports of soldiers – by now many of them no more than boys – cheering him on a brief visit he and a small entourage had paid on 3 March to troops at

Wriezen, some forty miles north-east of Berlin, just behind the Oder front.[143] The news from the eastern front had left Hitler in a depressed mood, the shaking left hand more noticeable than ever, when the Propaganda Minister saw him the following evening. In Pomerania, Soviet tanks had broken through and were now outside Kolberg, on the Baltic. (When the town finally had to be evacuated later in the month, Goebbels suppressed the news because of the blatantly contradictory image of the nationalist epic colour-film he had had made on the town's stand against Napoleon, meant to stir modern-day defiance against the Red Army.)[144] Himmler, the commander of Army Group Vistula, responsible for Pomerania's defence, had taken to his sick bed – suffering, it seems, from nothing worse than a heavy cold on top of overwrought nerves – and retreated to the clinic at Hohenlychen, twenty or so kilometres north of Berlin, for convalescence. Hitler, as always, blamed the General Staff for the débâcle. He was still hopeful of blocking the Red Army's advance; Goebbels had his doubts. Further south, the Czech industrial areas were under dire threat. Without them, Goebbels could not see how minimal armaments demands could any longer be met.[145] Hitler hoped they could hold out, there and in Silesia, and inflict serious reverses on the Red Army with a counter-offensive – to prove the last of the war – beginning on 6 March.[146]

In the West, Hitler was still optimistic about holding the Rhine. In reality, US troops were on the verge of entering Cologne, and only days later would take the bridge at Remagen and secure a foothold across the mighty artery. Goebbels, ready as so often to counter Hitler's instinctive optimism with cautious hints of realism, pointed out that, should the western defences not hold, 'our last political war argument would collapse', since the Anglo-Americans would be able to penetrate to central Germany and would have no interest in any negotiations. The growing crisis in the Alliance remained a straw to clutch at. But Goebbels was aware that Germany might be prostrate before it materialized.

Hitler still thought Stalin more likely than the western powers to show interest in negotiations. Whereas Roosevelt and Churchill would have difficulties with public opinion, Stalin could ignore it in reversing his war-policy overnight. But, as always, Hitler emphasized that the basis of any 'special peace' could only be military success. Pushing the Soviets back and inflicting heavy losses on them would make them more amenable. A new division of Poland, the return of Hungary and Croatia to German sovereignty, and operational freedom against the West would, Hitler hoped, be the prize. Thereafter, his aim, according to Goebbels, was to 'continue the struggle against England with the most brutal energy'. Britain, he thought, turning on the country that had spurned his earlier advances, was the 'eternal trouble-causer (*Störenfried*) in Europe'. Sweeping it out of the Continent for good would bring Germany – at least for a while – some peace. Goebbels reflected that the Soviet atrocities were a handicap for Hitler's way forward. But he noted laconically that Europe had once survived the ravages of the Mongols: 'The storms from the east come and go, and Europe has to cope with them.'[147]

Goebbels remained the fervent devotee of Hitler that he had been for twenty years. Though often frustrated and critical behind his leader's back at what he saw as undue reluctance to take measures necessary to radicalize the home front, and weakness in personnel matters – particularly the repeated unwillingness to dismiss Göring and Ribbentrop (both of whom he saw as bearing undue responsibility for Germany's plight) – Goebbels never ceased to be enthused once more by Hitler after spending time in his company. For Goebbels, Hitler's determination and optimism shone through the 'desolate mood' of the Reich Chancellery. 'If anyone can master the crisis, then he can,' the Propaganda Minister remarked. 'No one else can be found who is anywhere near touching him.'[148]

But, though his personal subordination for the father-figure he had for so long revered remained, even Goebbels was no longer persuaded by Hitler's apparent confidence in turning the tide. He was anticipating the end, looking to the history books. Magda and the children would join him and stay in Berlin, come what may, he told Hitler. If the struggle could not be mastered, then at least it had to be sustained with honour, he wrote.[149] He was gripped by Thomas's Carlyle's biography, glorifying the heroism of Frederick the Great, and presented Hitler with a copy. He read out to him the passages relating the King's reward for his unbending resolution in circumstances of mounting despair during the Seven Years War by the sudden and dramatic upturn in his fortunes. Hitler's eyes filled with tears.[150] Hitler, too, was looking to his place in history. 'It must be our ambition,' he told Goebbels on 11 March, 'Heroes' Memorial Day', 'also in our times to set an example for later generations to look to in similar crises and pressures (*Belastungen*), just as we today have to look to the past heroes of history.'[151] The theme ran through his proclamation to the Wehrmacht that day. He declared it his 'unalterable decision . . . to provide the world to come with no worse example than bygone times have left us'. The sentence that followed encapsulated the essence of Hitler's political 'career': 'The year 1918 will therefore not repeat itself.'[152]

V

To rule this out, no price – even self-destruction – was too high. In his characteristic 'either-or' way of thinking, Hitler had invariably posed total destruction as the alternative to the total victory for which he had striven. Inwardly convinced that his enemies were intent on bringing about that total destruction – the Morgenthau Plan of 1944, envisaging the reduction of a defeated Germany to the status of an agricultural country with a pre-industrial economy, had given sustenance to this belief[153] – no measure was for him too radical in the fight for survival. Consistent only with his own warped and peculiar brand of logic, he was prepared to take measures with such far-reaching consequences for the German population that the very survival he claimed to be fighting for was fundamentally threatened. Ultimately, the continued existence of the German people – if it showed itself incapable of defeating its enemies – was less important to him than the refusal to capitulate.

Few, even of his closest acolytes, were ready to follow this self-destructive urge to the letter. Albert Speer was one of those looking to the future after a lost war – and after Hitler, the man whom he had revered, and who had given him his career, his route to power and influence. Perhaps the ambitious Speer was still hoping to have some part to play in a Germany without Hitler. At any rate, he knew the war was irredeemably lost. And he was looking – like Guderian in the military sphere – to save what could be saved of the economic substance of the country. He had no interest in a Germany going down in a maelstrom of destruction to satisfy the irrational and pointless principle of 'heroic' self-sacrifice rather than capitulation. He knew only too well that the preservation of Germany's material substance for a post-Hitler future had long been the aim of the leading industrialists with whom he had worked so closely.[154] He had hindered the implementation of Hitler's orders for the destruction of French industry. And in recent weeks, he had arranged with Colonel-General Heinrici in Upper Silesia, Field-Marshal Model in the Ruhr (now on the verge of being taken by the western Allies), and Colonel-General Guderian for the entire eastern front that factories, mines, railways, roads, bridges, waterworks, gasworks, power-stations, and other installations vital to the German economy should be spared destruction wherever possible.[155]

On 18 March, Speer passed to Below a memorandum he had drafted three days earlier. Below was to choose a favourable moment to hand it to

Hitler.[156] The memorandum stated plainly that the final collapse of the German economy would occur within four to eight weeks, after which the war could not be continued. The prime duty of those leading the country must be to do what they could for the civilian population. But detonating bridges, with the consequent major destruction of the transport infrastructure, would signify 'the elimination of all further possibility of existence (*Lebensmöglichkeit*) for the German people'. Speer concluded: 'We have no right, at this stage of the war, to undertake destruction which could affect the existence of the people . . . We have the duty of leaving the people every possibility of establishing a reconstruction in the distant future.'[157]

A strong hint of Hitler's likely response could be gleaned at the military briefing that evening, when the topic arose of evacuation of the local population from the combat zone in the Saar. Hitler's express order was that the complete evacuation should be undertaken forthwith. Consideration could not be given to the population.[158] A few hours after the briefing ended, just before Speer left for a tour of the threatened areas on the western front, Hitler summoned him. According to Speer's recollection, noted down ten days later, Hitler told him coldly that should the war be lost, the people would also be lost, and that there was no necessity of taking consideration of the basis even of its most primitive survival. The German people had proved the weaker in the struggle. Only those who were inferior would remain.[159]

Hitler had promised Speer a written reply to his memorandum. It was not long in coming, and was predictably the opposite of what Speer had recommended. Whatever the cost, in Hitler's view, intact vital installations for industrial production could not be allowed to fall into enemy hands as had happened in Upper Silesia and the Saar.[160] His decree of 19 March, headed 'Destructive Measures on Reich Territory', was consistent with a philosophy by now wholly at odds with Speer's. 'The struggle for the existence of our people,' his decree ran, 'compels the use of all means, also within the territory of the Reich, to weaken the fighting power of our enemy and its further advance. All possibilities of imparting directly or indirectly lasting damage to the striking power of the enemy must be exploited. It is an error to believe that undestroyed or only temporarily disabled transport, communications, industrial, and supplies installations can again be made operational for our own purposes at the recapture of lost territories. The enemy will leave us only scorched earth at its retreat and drop any consideration for the population. I therefore order: 1) All military transport, communications, industrial, and supplies installations as well as material assets within Reich territory, which the enemy can render usable immediately or within the foreseeable future are to be destroyed. 2) Those responsible for the implementation of this destruction are: military command authorities for all military objects, including transport and communications installations, the Gauleiter and Reich Defence Commissars for all industrial and supplies installations and other material assets. The troops are to provide the necessary aid to the Gauleiter and Reich Defence Commissars in the implementation of their task . . .'[161]

The decree was never put into practice. Though, initially, several Gauleiter – prominent among them Gauleiter Friedrich Karl Florian in Düsseldorf – were eager to carry out Hitler's orders to the letter, Speer was eventually successful in persuading them of the futility of the intended action. In any case, the Gauleiter agreed that it was in practice impossible to implement the order.[162] Model was one of the front-line military commanders also prepared to cooperate with Speer in keeping destruction of industrial plant to a minimum. By the end of March, with difficulty, Speer had managed to convince Hitler – aware though he was of the Armaments Minister's effective sabotage of his order – that he should be granted overall responsibility for implementing all measures for destruction. This took the key decisions out of the hands of the Gauleiter, Hitler's key representatives in the regions. It meant, as Hitler knew, that everything possible would be done to avoid the destruction he had ordered.[163]

The non-implementation of the 'scorched earth' order was the first obvious sign that Hitler's authority was beginning to wane, his writ ceasing to run. 'We're giving out orders in Berlin that in practice no longer arrive lower down, let alone can be implemented,' remarked Goebbels at the end of March. 'I see in that the danger of an extraordinary dwindling of authority.'[164]

Hitler continued to see himself as indispensable. 'If anything happens to me, Germany is lost, since I have no successor,' he told his secretaries. 'Heß has gone mad, Göring has squandered the sympathies of the German people, and Himmler is rejected by the Party,' was his assessment.[165]

Hitler had been absolutely dismissive of Göring's leadership qualities in 'turbulent times' in speaking to Goebbels in mid-February 1945. As 'leader of the nation', he was 'utterly unimaginable'.[166] Tirades about the Reich Marshal were commonplace. On one occasion, fists clenched, face flushed with anger, he humiliated Göring in front of all present at a military briefing, threatening to reduce him to the ranks and dissolve the Luftwaffe as a separate branch of the armed forces. Göring could only withdraw to the ante-room and swallow a few glasses of brandy.[167] But despite regular exposure to Goebbels's vitriol about the Reich Marshal and impassioned entreaties to dismiss him, Hitler persisted in his view that he had no suitable replacement.[168]

Hitler's attitude towards Himmler had also hardened. His blind fury at the retreat of divisions – including that specially named after him, the Leibstandarte-SS Adolf Hitler – of Sepp Dietrich's 6th Panzer Army in the face of heavy losses and imminent encirclement in bitter fighting on the Danube was directed at Himmler. The Reichsführer-SS was in despair at the breach with Hitler, symbolized in the order he was forced to carry to Dietrich commanding his four Waffen-SS divisions, among them the élite Leibstandarte Adolf Hitler, to remove their armbands in disgrace.[169] With Hitler now feeling betrayed even by his own SS commanders, Himmler's waning star sank steeply with his own evident failings as Commander of Army Group Vistula. Hitler held the Reichsführer-SS personally responsible for the failure to block the Soviet advance through Pomerania. He accused him of having immediately fallen under the influence of the General Staff – a heinous offence in Hitler's eyes – and even of direct disobedience of his orders to build up anti-tank defences in Pomerania. Blaming others as usual, he took the view that Pomerania could have been held if Himmler had followed his orders. He intended, he told Goebbels, to make plain to him at their next meeting that any repetition would lead to an irreparable breach.[170] Whether the rift was further deepened through rumours abroad – in fact, close to the truth – linking Himmler's name with peace soundings is unclear.[171] But there was no doubt that Himmler's standing with Hitler had slumped dramatically.[172] The Reichsführer-SS remained, for his part, both dismayed at the rupture in relations, and cautious in the extreme, aware that even now his authority hinged solely on Hitler's continued favour.[173] But after being relieved of his command of Army Group Vistula on 20 March, Himmler increasingly went his own way.

The circle of those Hitler trusted was diminishing sharply. At the same time, his intolerance of any contradiction of his views had become as good as absolute. The one remaining voice among his generals which had been increasingly outspoken in its criticism was that of General Guderian. Where Keitel spoke with so little authority that younger officers scornfully dubbed him the 'Reich Garage Attendant', and Jodl carefully attuned his briefings to Hitler's moods and anticipated his wishes, Guderian was terse, pointed, and frank in his remarks.[174] The conflicts, which had mounted since Christmas in their intensity, were ended abruptly at the end of March with

Guderian's dismissal. By that time, the final German offensive near Lake Balaton in Hungary, started on 6 March, had failed and the Soviets were marching on the last remaining oil reserves open to Germany; the Red Army had meanwhile cut off Königsberg in East Prussia, broken through at Oppeln in Upper Silesia, taken Kolberg on the Baltic coast, opened up German defences close to Danzig, and had surrounded the SS battalions fiercely defending the strategically important stronghold of Küstrin on the Oder. In the west, outside Guderian's sphere of responsibility, the news was at least as sombre. General Patton's 3rd US Army had taken Darmstadt and reached the River Main; and American tanks had entered the outskirts of Frankfurt. Hitler had not expected the western front to collapse so rapidly. As always, he smelled betrayal.[175] And, characteristically, he was now ready to make Guderian the scapegoat for the dire situation on the eastern front.[176]

Guderian had been expecting a stormy meeting when he arrived at Hitler's bunker on 28 March for the afternoon briefing. He was determined to continue his defence of General Theodor Busse against the accusation that he held responsibility for the failure of his 9th Army to relieve the encircled troops at Küstrin. But Hitler was not prepared to listen. He peremptorily adjourned the meeting, keeping only Keitel and Guderian back. Without demur, the Chief of Staff was told that his health problems demanded he take with immediate effect six weeks' convalescent leave. He was replaced by the more compliant General Hans Krebs.[177]

Reports were by now coming in from Kesselring's headquarters that the western front in the region of Hanau and Frankfurt am Main was showing serious signs of disintegration. White flags were being hoisted; women were embracing American soldiers as they entered; troops, not wanting to fight any longer, were fleeing from any prospect of battle or simply surrendering. Kesselring wanted Hitler to speak without delay to shore up the wavering will to fight. Goebbels agreed. Churchill and Stalin had both spoken to their nations at times of utmost peril. Germany's position was even worse. 'In such a serious situation, the nation cannot remain without an appeal from the highest authority,' Goebbels noted. He telephoned General Burgdorf, Hitler's chief Wehrmacht adjutant since Schmundt's death, and impressed upon him the need to persuade Hitler to speak to the German people.[178] Next day, walking for an hour among the ruins of the Reich Chancellery garden alongside the bent figure of Hitler, Goebbels tried to exert all his own influence in pleading with him to give a ten- or fifteen-minute radio address. Hitler did not want to speak, however, 'because at present he has nothing positive to offer'. Goebbels did not give up. Hitler finally agreed.

But Goebbels's evident scepticism proved justified.[179] A few days later, Hitler again promised to give his speech – but only after he had gained a success in the west. He knew he should speak to the people. But the SD had informed him that his previous speech – his proclamation on 24 February – had been criticized for not saying anything new. And Goebbels acknowledged that, indeed, he had nothing new to offer the people. The Propaganda Minister repeated his hope that Hitler would nevertheless speak to them. 'The people were waiting for at least a slogan,' he urged.[180] But Hitler had by now even run out of propaganda slogans for the people of Germany.

Goebbels remained puzzled – and, behind his admiration, irritated and frustrated – at Hitler's reluctance to take what the Propaganda Minister regarded as vital, radical steps even at this later hour to change Germany's fortunes. In this, he privately reflected, Frederick the Great had been far more ruthless. Hitler, by contrast, accepted the diagnosis of the problem. But no action followed. He took the setbacks and grave dangers, thought Goebbels, too lightly – at least, he pointedly added, in his presence; 'privately, he will certainly think differently.'[181] He was still confident of the split among the Allies he had so long been predicting. 'But it pains me,' Goebbels noted, 'that he is at present not to be moved to doing anything so that the political crisis in the enemy camp deepens. He doesn't change personnel, either in the Reich government or in the diplomatic service. Göring stays. Ribbentrop stays. All failures – apart from the second rank – are retained, and it would in my view be so necessary to undertake here in particular a change of personnel because this would be of such decisive importance for the morale of our people. I press and press; but I can't convince the Führer of the necessity of these measures that I put forward.' It was, Goebbels pointed out, 'as if he lived in the clouds.'[182]

Not only Hitler held on to a make-believe world. 'One day, the Reich of our dreams will emerge,' wrote Gerda Bormann to her husband. 'Shall we, I wonder, or our children, live to see it?' 'I have every hope that we shall!' jotted Martin, between the lines. 'In some ways, you know, this reminds me of the "Twilight of the Gods" in the Edda,' Gerda's letter continued '. . . The monsters are storming the bridge of the Gods; . . . the citadel of the Gods crumbles, and all seems lost; and then, suddenly a new citadel rises, more beautiful than ever before . . . We are not the first to engage in mortal combat with the powers of the underworld, and that we feel impelled, and are also able, to do so should give us a conviction of ultimate victory.'[183]

An air of unreality also pervaded, in part, the administrative machines of Party and state. Though, certainly, the state bureaucracy – now mostly removed from Berlin – was confronted with the actualities of a lost war in trying to cope with the acute problems of refugees from the east, housing the homeless from bomb-damaged cities, and ensuring that public facilities were kept running, much of what remained of civil administration – massively hampered through repeated breakdowns in postal and rail communications – had little to do with the everyday needs of the population.[184] The sober-minded and long-serving Finance Minister, Lutz Graf Schwerin von Krosigk, for instance, completed at the end of March his plans for tax reform – criticized by Goebbels (as if they were about to be implemented) for their 'unsocial' emphasis on consumer tax, which would affect the mass of the population, rather than income tax.[185] That much of the country was by this time under enemy occupation seemed irrelevant.

Meanwhile, Martin Bormann was still working feverishly on restructuring the Party to control the new, peacetime Germany that would emerge from the war.[186] And as the Reich shrank, lines of communication disintegrated, and directives became increasingly overtaken by events, he sent more circulars, decrees, and promulgations than ever – over 400 in the last four months of the war – cascading down to lower functionaries of the Party. 'Again a mass of new decrees and orders pour in from Bormann,' noted Goebbels on 4 April. 'Bormann has made a paper chancellery out of the Party Chancellery. Every day he sends out a mountain of letters and files which Gauleiter at present in the midst of the struggle can in practice not even read. In part, it's a matter of completely useless stuff of no value for the practical struggle.'[187] A Party bureaucracy in overdrive poured out regulations on provision of bread grain, small-arms training of women and girls, repair of railways and road communications, eking out additional food from wild vegetables, fruit, and mushrooms, and a host of other issues.[188]

Alongside such miscellanea went the constant demands and exhortations to hold out, whatever the cost. Bormann informed Party functionaries on 1 April that summary and draconian punishment for desertion awaited 'any scoundrel ... who does not fight to the the last breath'.[189] He detailed functionaries to work with Wehrmacht units in stiffening morale in areas close to the front and to set up quasi-guerrilla organizations such as the 'Freikorps Adolf Hitler' (drawn from the Party's functionaries) and the 'Werwolf' (to be made up largely of Hitler Youth members) to carry on the fight through partisan activity in the occupied areas of the Reich. German propaganda sought to convey the impression to the Allies that they were endangered by an extensively organized underground resistance movement. In practice, the 'Werwolf' was of scant military significance, and was mainly a threat, in its arbitrary and vicious retribution, to German citizens revealing any traces of 'defeatism'.[190]

On 15 April Bormann put out a circular to Political Leaders of the Party: 'The Führer expects that you will master every situation in your Gaue, if necessary with lightning speed and extreme brutality . . .'[191] Like more and more of his missives, it existed largely on paper. Correspondence to reality was minimal. It was a classic illustration of the continuing illusory and despairing belief in the triumph of will alone. But even the unconstrained and arbitary violence of a regime patently in its death-throes could not contain the open manifestations of disintegration. Ever fewer brown Party uniforms were to be seen on the streets. And ever more Party functionaries were disappearing into the ether as the enemy approached, looking more to self-preservation than to heroic last stands.[192] 'The behaviour of our Gau and District Leaders in the west has led to a strong drop in confidence among the population,' commented Goebbels. 'As a consequence, the Party is fairly played out in the west.'[193]

During early April, the last German troops pulled out of Hungary. Bratislava fell to the Red Army as it advanced on Vienna. To the north, the German troops cut off in Königsberg surrendered the city on 9 April. In the west, Allied troops pushed through Westphalia, taking Münster and Hamm. By 10 April, Essen and Hanover were in American hands. The vice was tightening on the Ruhr, Germany's battered industrial heartland. A sudden shaft of optimism penetrated the dense gloom enveloping Hitler's bunker: the news came through of the death on 12 April, at his winter retreat in Warm Springs, Georgia, of one of his greatest adversaries, and linchpin in the unholy coalition of forces against him, President Roosevelt.

Goebbels rang up, elated, to congratulate Hitler.[194] Two weeks earlier, the Propaganda Minister had been given a file of astrological material, including a horoscope of the Führer. It prophesied an improvement in Germany's military position in the second half of April. Goebbels's sole interest in the material, he said, was for propaganda purposes, to give people something to cling on to.[195] It served this purpose now, for the moment, for Hitler. 'Here, read this!' Hitler, looking revitalized and in an excited voice, instructed Speer. 'Here! You never wanted to believe it. Here! . . . Here we have the great miracle that I always foretold. Who's right now? The war is not lost. Read it! Roosevelt is dead!'[196] It seemed to him like the hand of Providence yet again. Goebbels, fresh from his reading of Carlyle's biography of Frederick the Great, reminded Hitler of the death of the Czarina Elisabeth that had brought a sudden change of fortune for the Prussian King in the Seven Years War. The artificial coalition enemies aligned against Germany would now break up. History was repeating itself.[197] Whether Hitler was as convinced as he seemed that the hand of Providence had produced the turning-point of the war is uncertain. One close to him in these days, his Luftwaffe adjutant Nicolaus von Below, thought him more sober at the news than Goebbels – whose cynical eye was, as always, directed at the possible propaganda advantages.[198]

Even for those who saw him at close quarters, it was difficult to be sure of Hitler's true feelings about the war. Field-Marshal Kesselring, who saw Hitler for the last time on 12 April, the day of Roosevelt's death, later recalled: '. . . He was still optimistic. How far he was play-acting it is hard to decide. Looking back, I am inclined to think that he was literally obsessed with the idea of some miraculous salvation, that he clung to it like a drowning man to a straw.'[199]

Whether genuine or contrived, Hitler's jubilation did not last long. On 13 April, the news was given to him that Vienna had been taken by the Red Army. The following day, American attacks succeeding in splitting German forces defending the Ruhr. Within three days, the fighting in the Ruhr was over. Field-Marshal Model, a long-standing favourite of Hitler, dissolved his encircled Army Group B rather than offer formal capitulation. It made no difference. Around 325,000 German troops and thirty generals gave themselves up to the Americans on 17 April. Model committed suicide four days later in a wooded area south of Duisburg.[200]

On 15 April, in anticipation of a new Soviet offensive – which he thought, probably taken in by Stalin's misinformation directed at the western Allies, would first sweep through Saxony to Prague to head off the Americans before tackling Berlin[201] – Hitler had issued a 'basic order' for the eventuality that the Reich might be split in two. He set up a supreme commander – in effect his military representative – to take full responsibility for the defence of the Reich in whichever part he himself was not situated should communications be broken. Great-Admiral Dönitz was designated for the northern zone, Field-Marshal Kesselring for the south.[202] The implication was that Hitler was keeping the option open of carrying on the fight from the south, in the fastness of the Bavarian Alps.

On the same day, Hitler issued what would turn out to be his last proclamation to the soldiers on the eastern front. It played heavily on the stories of Soviet atrocities. 'For the last time, the Jewish-Bolshevik mortal enemy has set out with its masses on the attack,' it began. 'He is attempting to demolish Germany and to exterminate our people. You soldiers from the

East know yourselves in large measure what fate threatens above all German women, girls, and children. While old men and children are murdered, women and girls are denigrated to barrack-whores. The rest are marched off to Siberia.' It went on to alert the troops to the slightest sign of treachery, particularly – the long-standing exaggeration of the influence of the National Committee for a Free Germany, established in Moscow by captured German officers – troops fighting against them in German uniforms receiving Russian pay. Anyone not known to them ordering a retreat was to be captured and 'if need be immediately dispatched, irrespective of rank'. The proclamation had its climax in the slogan: 'Berlin stays German, Vienna will be German again, and Europe will never be Russian.'[203]

It was to no avail. In the early hours of 16 April, a huge artillery barrage announced the launch of the awaited assault from the line of the Oder and Neisse rivers by over a million Soviet troops under Marshal Zhukov and Marshal Konev. The German defenders from the 9th Army and, to its south, the 4th Panzer Army fought tenaciously. The Soviets suffered some significant losses. For a few hours, the front held. But the odds were hopeless. During the afternoon, after renewed heavy artillery bombardment, the German line was broken north of Küstrin on the west bank of the Oder. The gap between the 9th Army and the 4th Panzer Army quickly widened. Soviet infantry poured through, rapidly followed by hundreds of tanks, and over the next two days extended and consolidated their hold in the area south of Frankfurt an der Oder. From then on the Oder front caved in completely. There could now be only one outcome. The Red Army drove on over and past the lingering defences. Berlin was directly in its sights.

General Busse's 9th Army was pushed back towards the south of the city. Hitler had ordered Busse to hold a line which his Army Group Commander, Colonel-General Heinrici, had thought exposed the 9th Army to encirclement. Ignoring Hitler's orders, Heinrici nevertheless commanded withdrawal westwards. By that time, only parts of Busse's army could evade imminent encirclement.[204] Meanwhile, the German General Staff was forced to flee from its headquarters in secure bunkers at Zossen to the Wannsee – its column of retreating vehicles mistaken by German planes for part of a Soviet unit and attacked from the air as they went.[205] To the north, the forces under Colonel-General Heinrici and SS-Obergruppenführer Felix Steiner were the last barrier to the ever more menacing prospect of encirclement of the city as the Red Army pushed through Eberswalde to Oranienburg. By 20 April, Soviet tanks had reached the outskirts of the capital. That afternoon, Berlin was under fire.[206]

The rumble of artillery fire could be plainly heard from the Reich Chancellery.[207] There, with the Red Army on the doorstep, and to the accompaniment of almost non-stop bombing by Allied planes, leading Nazis gathered for what they knew would be the last time – to celebrate Hitler's fifty-sixth birthday, and, in most cases, to say their farewells. It was the start of the last rites for the Third Reich.

17

EXTINCTION

'It's the only chance to restore personal reputation . . . If we leave the world stage in disgrace, we'll have lived for nothing.'

Hitler, hoping for a last military success, 25 April 1945

'Above all, I charge the leadership of the nation and their subjects with the meticulous observance of the race-laws and the merciless resistance to the universal poisoner of all peoples, international Jewry.'

Hitler's Political Testament, 29 April 1945

The atmosphere in the bunker on 20 April 1945, Hitler's fifty-sixth birthday, was more funereal than celebratory. There was no trace of the pomp and circumstance of earlier years. The gaunt ruins of the Reich Chancellery were themselves a stark reminder, if one was needed, that there was no cause for celebration. Hitler felt this himself. His birthday with the Russians at the gates of Berlin was – everything points to this – an embarrassment to him, and for all those who were obliged to offer him their birthday greetings.

Traditionally, Hitler's personal staff gathered to be the first to offer their congratulations on the stroke of midnight. This year, Hitler, in depressed mood, had already told his valet, Heinz Linge, that he did not want to receive his household; there were no grounds for congratulation. Linge was ordered to pass on the message. Predictably, this Führer order was ignored. Waiting in the ante-room, as midnight approached, to offer their formal congratulations were Chief Adjutant General Wilhelm Burgdorf, Himmler's liaison SS-Gruppenführer Hermann Fegelein (who had recently married Eva Braun's sister, Gretl), the long-serving factotum Julius Schaub, who had been a member of the 'household' since the mid-1920s, Hitler's adjutants NSKK-Oberführer Alwin-Broder Albrecht and SS-Sturmbannführer Otto Günsche, Ribbentrop's liaison Walter Hewel, and press officer Heinz Lorenz. Hitler, tired and dejected, said Linge should inform them that he had no time to receive them. Only following Fegelein's intercession with his sister-in-law Eva Braun (who had returned to the Reich Chancellery some weeks earlier, announcing she was staying with Hitler, and resisting all attempts to persuade her to leave)[1] did he concede, trudging down the assembled line of his staff to receive their murmured birthday greetings with a limp handshake and a vacant expression.[2] Further muted, almost embarrassed, congratulations followed from the military leaders attending the first briefing of the day. Afterwards, Hitler drank tea in his study with Eva Braun. It was approaching nine o'clock in the morning before he finally went to bed, only to be disturbed almost immediately by General Burgdorf with the news of a Soviet breakthrough and advance towards Cottbus, some sixty miles south-east of Berlin, on the southern part of the front. Hitler took the news standing in his nightshirt at the door of his bedroom, and told Linge he had not slept up to then and to waken him an hour later than normal, at 2p.m.[3]

After breakfasting, playing with his alsatian puppy for a while, and having Linge administer his cocaine eyedrops, he slowly climbed the steps into the Reich Chancellery park. Waiting with raised arms in the Nazi salute were delegations from the Courland army, from the SS-Division 'Berlin', and twenty boys from the Hitler Youth who had distinguished themselves in combat. Was this what Berlin's defence relied upon? one of Hitler's secretaries wondered.[4] Hitler muttered a few words to them, patted one or two on the cheek, and within minutes left them to carry on the fight against Russian tanks.

Bormann, Himmler, Goebbels, Reich Youth Leader Artur Axmann, and Dr Morell were among those in a further line waiting to be received at the door of the Chancellery's Winter Garden. Looking drained and listless, his face ashen, his stoop pronounced, Hitler went through the motions of a brief address. Not surprisingly, he was by now incapable of raising spirits.[5] Lunch with Christa Schroeder and senior secretary Johanna Wolf was a depressing affair.[6] Afterwards, he retraced his steps down into the bowels of the earth for the late afternoon briefing. He would not leave the bunker again alive.

By now, most of the leading figures in the Reich – at least, those in the Berlin vicinity – were assembled. Göring, Dönitz, Keitel, Ribbentrop, Speer, Jodl, Himmler, Kaltenbrunner, the new Chief of Staff General Hans Krebs, and others all presented their greetings. No one spoke of the looming catastrophe. They all swore their undying loyalty. Everyone noticed that Göring had discarded his resplendent silver-grey uniform with gold-braided epaulettes for khaki – 'like an American general', as one participant at the briefing remarked. Hitler passed no comment.[7]

I

The imminent assault on Berlin dominated the briefing. The news from the southern rim of the city was catastrophic. Göring pointed out that only a single road to the south, through the Bayerischer Wald, was still open; it could be blocked at any moment. His chief of staff, General Karl Koller, added that any later attempt to transfer the High Command of the Wehrmacht by air to new headquarters could be ruled out. Hitler was pressed from all sides to leave at once for Berchtesgaden. He objected that he could not expect his troops to fight the decisive battle for Berlin if he removed himself to safety. Keitel had told Koller before the briefing that Hitler was determined to stay in Berlin.[8] When greeting Hitler, Keitel had murmured words to the effect that they had confidence that he would take urgent decisions before the Reich capital became a battleground. It was a strong hint that Hitler and his entourage should leave for the south while there was still time. Hitler interrupted, saying: 'Keitel, I know what I want. I will fight on in front of, within, or behind Berlin.'[9] Nevertheless, Hitler now seemed indecisive. Increasingly agitated, he declared moments later that he would leave it to fate whether he died in the capital or flew at the last moment to the Obersalzberg.[10]

There was no indecision about Göring. He had sent his wife Emmy and daughter Edda to the safety of the Bavarian mountains more than two months earlier. He had written his will in February. Crate-loads of his looted art treasures from Carinhall, his palatial country residence in the Schorfheide, forty miles north of Berlin, had been shipped south in March. Half a million marks were transferred to his account in Berchtesgaden. By the time he arrived at the Reich Chancellery to pass on his birthday wishes to Hitler, Carinhall was mined with explosives; his own remaining belongings were packed and loaded on to lorries, ready to go on to the Obersalzberg.[11] Göring lost no time at the end of the briefing session in seeking out a private word with Hitler. It was urgent that he go to southern Germany, he said, to command the Luftwaffe from there. He needed to leave Berlin that very night. Hitler scarcely seemed to notice. He muttered a few words, shook hands absent-mindedly, and the first paladin of the Reich departed, hurriedly and without fanfare. It seemed to Albert Speer, standing a few feet away, to be a parting of ways that symbolized the imminent end of the Third Reich.[12]

It was the first of numerous departures. Most of those who had come to proffer their birthday greetings to Hitler and make avowals of their undying loyalty were waiting nervously for the moment when they could hasten from the doomed city. Convoys of cars were soon heading out of Berlin north, south, and west, on any roads still open. Dönitz left for the north, armed with Hitler's instructions – the implementation of the directive five days earlier on division of command should the Reich be geographically split – to take over the leadership in the north and continue the struggle. It was a sign of Dönitz's high standing with Hitler on account of his uncompromising support for the stance of fighting to the last, and of hopes for a continuation of the U-boat war, that he was given plenipotentiary powers to issue all relevant orders to State and Party, as well as to the Wehrmacht in the northern zone.[13] Himmler, Kaltenbrunner, and Ribbentrop soon followed. Speer left later that night in the direction of Hamburg, without any formal farewell.

Hitler, according to Julius Schaub's post-war testimony, was deeply disappointed at the desire of his paladins to leave the bunker in barely concealed haste. He gave no more than a perfunctory nod of valediction to those who, now that his power was as good as ended, were anxious to save what they could of themselves and their possessions.[14] By this time, most of the army top-brass had left. And Bormann had already told the remaining government ministers – Finance Minister Lutz Graf Schwerin-Krosigk, Transport Minister Julius Dorpmüller, Justice Minister Otto Georg Thierack, Minister for the Occupied Eastern Territories (a long redundant post) Alfred Rosenberg, Education Minister Bernhard Rust, and Labour Minister Franz Seldte – together with head of the Presidential Chancellery, the old survivor, Otto Meissner, to make hasty preparations to leave for the south, since the road would soon be blocked. Hitler's naval adjutant, Admiral Karl-Jesko von Puttkamer, was dispatched to the Obersalzberg to destroy important papers there.[15] His two older secretaries, Johanna Wolf and Christa Schroeder, were summoned to his study that evening and told to be ready to leave for the Berghof within the hour. Four days earlier, he had told them in confident tones: 'Berlin will stay German. We must just gain time.' Now, he said, the situation had changed so much in the past four days, that he had to break up his staff.[16]

The scene in the courtyard of the Reich Chancellery was near-chaotic as vehicles were stuffed with bags and suitcases, the rumble of artillery a reminder of how close the Red Army was as the cars hurried through the night, through clouds of smoke billowing from burning buildings, past shadowy ruins and Volkssturm men setting up street barricades, to waiting aeroplanes.[17] During the following three nights, some twenty flights were made from Gatow and Staaken aerodromes in Berlin, taking most of Hitler's staff to Berchtesgaden.[18]

Late in the evening, the remaining adjutants, secretaries, and his young Austrian diet cook, Constanze Manziarly, gathered in his room for a drink with Hitler and Eva Braun. There was no talk here of the war.[19] Hitler's youngest secretary, Traudl Junge, had been shocked to hear him admit for the first time in her presence earlier that day that he no longer believed in victory. *He* might be ready to go under; her own life, she felt, had barely begun. Once Hitler – early for him – had retired to his room, she was glad to join Eva Braun, and other bunker 'inmates', even including Bormann and Morell, in an 'unofficial' party in the old living room on the first floor of Hitler's apartment in the Reich Chancellery. In the ghostly surrounds of a room stripped of almost all its former splendour, with the gramophone scratching out the only record they could find – a schmaltzy pre-war hit called 'Red Roses Bring You Happiness' (*'Blutrote Rosen erzählen Dir vom Glück'*) – they laughed, danced, and drank champagne, trying to enjoy an hour or two of escapism – before a nearby explosion sharply jolted them back to reality.[20]

When Hitler was awakened at 9.30 next morning, it was to the news that the centre of Berlin was under artillery fire.[21] He was at first incredulous, immediately demanding information from Karl Koller, Luftwaffe chief of staff, on the position of the Soviet artillery battery. An observation post at Berlin's zoo provided the answer: the battery was no more than eight miles away in the suburb of Marzahn.[22] The dragnet was closing fast. The information scarcely helped to calm Hitler's increasingly volatile moods. As the day wore on, he seemed increasingly like a man at the end of his tether, nerves ragged, under intense strain, close to breaking point. Irrational reactions when a frenzy of almost hysterically barked-out orders proved impossible to implement or demands for information impossible to supply, point in this direction.

Soon, he was on the telephone again to Koller, this time demanding figures of German planes in action in the south of the city. Communications failures meant Koller was unable to provide them. Hitler rang once more, this time wanting to know why the jets based near Prague had not been operational the previous day. Koller explained that enemy fighters had attacked the airfields so persistently that the jets had been unable to take off. 'Then we don't need the jets any more. The Luftwaffe is superfluous,' Hitler had replied in fury. 'The entire Luftwaffe leadership should be hanged straight away!'[23]

II

The drowning man clutched at yet another straw. The Soviets had extended their lines so far to the north-east of Berlin that it opened up the chance, thought Hitler and Chief of Staff Krebs, for the Panzer Corps led by SS-Obergruppenführer Felix Steiner to launch a counter-attack with good chances of success. A flurry of telephone calls with more than a hint of near-hysteria assigned a motley variety of remaining units, including naval and Luftwaffe forces untrained in ground warfare and equipped only with small arms, to Steiner's command.[24] 'Every commander withholding forces has forfeited his life within five hours,' Hitler screamed at Koller. 'The commanders must know that. You yourself guarantee with your head that the last man is deployed.'[25] Any retreat to the west was strictly forbidden to Steiner's forces. Officers unwilling to obey were to be shot immediately. 'On the success of your assignment depends the fate of the German capital,' Hitler told Steiner – adding that the commander's life also hinged on the execution of the order.[26] At the same time, Busse's 9th Army, to the south of Berlin, was ordered to restabilize and reinforce the defensive line from Königswusterhausen to Cottbus. In addition, aided by a northward push of parts of Schörner's Army Group Centre, still doggedly fighting in the vicinity of Elsterwalde, around sixty miles south of Berlin, it was to attack and cut off Konev's tank forces that had broken through to their rear.[27] It was an illusory hope. But Hitler's false optimism was still being pandered to by some of the generals. His mood visibly brightened after hearing upbeat reports from his most recent field-marshal, Schörner (who had been promoted on 5 April), and from General Wenck about the chances of his newly constructed 12th Army attacking American forces on the Elbe.[28]

Colonel-General Heinrici, Commander of Army Group Vistula, was not one of the eternal optimists who played to Hitler's constant need for good news. He warned of encirclement if the 9th Army were not pulled back. He threatened resignation if Hitler persisted in his orders. But Hitler did persist; and Heinrici did not resign.[29] The general had implied to Speer days earlier that Berlin would be taken without serious resistance.[30] This thinking was anathema to Hitler. He told Jodl on the day his orders to Steiner and to the 9th Army went out: 'I will fight as long as I have a single soldier. When the last soldier deserts me, I will shoot myself.'[31] Late that night, he still exuded confidence in Steiner's attack. When Koller told him of the inadequacies of the Luftwaffe troops he had been compelled to supply to Steiner's forces,

Hitler replied: 'You will see. The Russians will suffer the greatest defeat, the bloodiest defeat in their history before the gates of the city of Berlin.'[32]

It was bravado. Two hours earlier, Dr Morell had found him drained and dejected in his study. The doctor and his medications, however little efficacious in an objective sense, had been for years an important psychological prop for Hitler. Now, Morell wanted to give him a harmless further dose of glucose. Without any forewarning, Hitler reacted in an uncontrollable outburst, accusing Morell of wanting to drug him with morphine. He knew, he said, that the generals wanted to have him drugged so that they could ship him off to Berchtesgaden. 'Do you take me for a madman?' Hitler railed. Threatening to have him shot, he furiously dismissing the quivering doctor.[33]

The storm had been brewing for days. It burst on the afternoon of 22 April, during the briefing that began at 3.30p.m. Even as the briefing began, Hitler looked haggard, stony-faced, though extremely agitated, as if his thoughts were elsewhere. He twice left the room to go to his private quarters.[34] Then, as dismaying news came through that Soviet troops had broken the inner defence cordon and were within Berlin's northern suburbs, Hitler was finally told – after a frantic series of telephone calls had elicited contradictory information – that Steiner's attack, which he had impatiently awaited all morning, had not taken place after all.[35] At this, he seemed to snap. He ordered everyone out of the briefing room, apart from Keitel, Jodl, Krebs, and Burgdorf.[36] Even for those who had long experience of Hitler's furious outbursts, the tirade which thundered through the bunker for the next half an hour was a shock. One who witnessed it reported that evening: 'Something broke inside me today that I still can't grasp.'[37] Hitler screamed that he had been betrayed by all those he had trusted. He railed at the long-standing treachery of the army. Now, even the SS was lying to him: after Sepp Dietrich's failure in Hungary, Steiner had not attacked. The troops would not fight, he ranted, the anti-tank defences were down. As Jodl added, he also knew that munitions and fuel would shortly run out.

Hitler slumped into his chair. The storm subsided. His voice fell to practically a whimper. The war was lost, he sobbed. It was the first time any of his small audience had heard him admit it. They were dumbstruck. He had therefore determined to stay in Berlin, he went on, and to lead the defence of the city. He was physically incapable of fighting himself, and ran the risk of falling wounded into the hands of the enemy. So he would at the last moment shoot himself. All prevailed upon him to change his mind. He should leave Berlin forthwith and move his headquarters to Berchtesgaden.

The troops should be withdrawn from the western front and deployed in the east. Hitler replied that everything was falling apart anyway. He could not do that. Göring could do it. Someone objected that no soldier would fight for the Reich Marshal. 'What does it mean: fight?' asked Hitler. 'There's not much more to fight for, and if it's a matter of negotiations the Reich Marshal can do that better than I can.'[38]

At this, Hitler, his face a deathly pallor, left the briefing room and retreated to his own quarters.[39] He sent for his remaining secretaries, Gerda Christian and Traudl Junge, and his dietician Constanze Manziarly. Eva Braun was also present as he told his staff they should get ready; a plane would take them south in an hour. 'It's all lost,' he said, 'hopelessly lost.' ('*Es ist alles verloren, hoffnungslos verloren.*') Somewhat to their own surprise, his secretaries found themselves rejecting the offer to leave and telling Hitler that they would stay with him in the bunker. Eva Braun had already told Hitler she was not leaving.[40]

Urgent telephone calls were meanwhile put through from Dönitz and Himmler. Neither could persuade him to change his mind. Ribbentrop arrived. He was not even allowed to see Hitler. Goebbels was also present.[41] Hitler, highly disturbed, had telephoned him around five o'clock, raving about treachery, betrayal, and cowardice. Goebbels hurried as fast as he could go to the bunker, and spoke a while alone with Hitler. He was able to calm him down. Goebbels emerged to announce that on the Führer's orders, he, his wife, and his children would be moving into the bunker and living there from now on.[42] For the Propaganda Minister, Hitler's decision was the logical consequence of his consistent stance; he saw it in full pathos as a historic deed which determined the heroic end in Berlin of a latter-day Siegfried, betrayed by all around him.[43]

For hard-headed military men like Karl Koller, the perspective was very different: Hitler was abandoning the German people at the time of their greatest need; he had renounced his responsibility to armed forces, state, and people at the most critical moment; it was dereliction of duty worse than many offences for which draconian retribution had been meted out.[44]

There were indeed serious practical considerations following from Hitler's hysterical behaviour. He had simply said he was staying in Berlin. The others should leave and go where they wanted.[45] He had no further orders for the Wehrmacht.[46] But he was still supreme commander. Who was now to give orders? Berlin was doomed for certain within a few days. So where were Wehrmacht Headquarters to be? How could forces simply be withdrawn from the western front without any armistice negotiations? After fruitless pleading with Hitler, Keitel decided to travel to the headquarters of General Wenck's 12th Army. Hitler had finally agreed to sign an order to Wenck to abandon his previous operational plans – defending against the Americans on the Elbe – and march on Berlin, linking up with the remnants of the 9th Army, still fighting to the south of the city. The aim was to cut off enemy forces to the south-west of the capital, drive forward 'and liberate (*freikämpfen*) again the Reich capital where the Führer resides, trusting in his soldiers'.[47] Wenck's army had been hastily put together at the beginning of April. It was inadequately armed; its panzer support was weak; and its troops were poorly trained.[48] They were outnumbered by the Soviet troops facing them, and possessed only a quarter of the weaponry.[49] What Wenck was supposed to do in the unlikely event of breaking through to the centre of Berlin – other than bringing out Hitler, if need be by force (as Keitel later put it) – was left entirely unclear.[50]

Hitler, his equilibrium now temporarily restored, was solicitous enough to make sure that Keitel was well fed before he set out on his journey. Jodl was meanwhile to take steps to ensure that part of the High Command of the Wehrmacht was immediately transferred to Berchtesgaden, while the remainder would be moved to the barracks at Krampnitz, near Potsdam. Hitler's overall direction would remain intact, maintained through telephone links to Krampnitz and Berchtesgaden. The regular briefings would continue, though with reduced personnel.[51]

In the bunker, meanwhile, Hitler had ordered Schaub to burn all the papers and documents in his private safe in the bunker. He was afterwards instructed to do the same in Munich and at the Berghof. After a perfunctory farewell from the master he had served for twenty years, he left Berlin and flew south.[52] The bunker company had by now shrunk.[53] Those left behind consoled themselves with drink. They referred to the bunker as 'the mortuary' and its inmates as 'a show house of living corpses'. Their main topic of conversation was when and how to commit suicide.[54]

Remarkably, Hitler had regained his composure by the next morning. He was still venting anger at troops that seemed to have evaporated into thin air. 'It's so disgraceful,' he fumed. 'When you think about it all, why still live!' But Keitel's news about his meeting with Wenck had provided yet another glimmer of hope. Hitler ordered all available troops, however ill-equipped, to be added to Wenck's army. Dönitz had already been cabled the previous evening to have all available sailors as the most urgent priority, overriding all naval concerns, flown to Berlin to join the 'German battle of fate (*deutsche Schicksalsschlacht*)' in the Reich capital. Telegrams were also dispatched to Himmler, and to Luftwaffe high command to send their remaining reserves to aid the reinforcement of Berlin. 'The enemy knows I'm here,' Hitler added, referring to Goebbels's proclamation to the Berlin people that day, telling them that the Führer would remain in the city to lead its defence.[55] They would concentrate all their efforts on taking the capital as soon as possible. But that, thought Hitler, gave him a chance to lure them into the trap of Wenck's army. Krebs reckoned they still had four days. 'In four days the business has to be decided,' agreed Hitler.[56]

That afternoon, Albert Speer arrived back in the bunker. He had had a tortuous ten-hour journey to cover only 100 or so miles from the Hamburg area. He had quickly given up an attempt to drive along roads choked with refugees desperate to leave Berlin by any route still open, and flew first to the airfield at Rechlin in Mecklenburg, then on to Gatow aerodrome in the west of Berlin. There, he picked up a Fieseler Storch light aircraft, eventually navigating a landing on the East-West Axis approaching the Brandenburg Gate, the wide boulevard on which he had triumphantly paraded six years earlier during Hitler's fiftieth birthday celebrations, now, its lampposts removed, converted into a makeshift landing-strip.[57] For weeks, as we have noted, Speer had been working with industrialists and generals to sabotage Hitler's 'scorched earth' orders. Only two days earlier, in Hamburg, he had recorded an address – never, in the event, broadcast, and probably made with more than one eye on embellishing his own prospects in a world after Hitler – urging an end to the pointless destruction. But despite the growing alienation, Speer could still not break free of Hitler. The emotional bonds remained strong. After his unsung departure on the evening of Hitler's birthday, the former Armaments Minister felt unhappy at ending their special relationship without an appropriate farewell. That was the reason for his wholly unnecessary, extremely hazardous flight back into the cauldron.[58]

On his way to Hitler's room in the bunker, he encountered Bormann. Not anxious to end his own days in the bunker catacombs, the Secretary to the Führer implored Speer to use his influence to persuade Hitler to leave for the south. It was still just possible. In a few more hours it would be too late. Speer gave a non-committal reply. He was then ushered in to see Hitler, who, as Bormann had foreseen, lost no time in asking Speer's opinion whether he should stay in Berlin or fly to Berchtesgaden. Speer did not hesitate. It would be better to end his life as Führer in the Reich capital than in his 'weekend house', he said. Hitler looked tired, apathetic, resigned, burnt out. He had decided to stay in Berlin, he murmured. He had just wanted to hear Speer's opinion. As the previous day, he said he would not fight. There was the danger that he would be captured alive. He was also anxious to avoid his body falling into the hands of his enemy to be displayed as a trophy. So he had given orders to have his body burnt. Eva Braun would die alongside him. 'Believe me, Speer,' he added, 'it will be easy to end my life. A brief moment, and I am freed from everything, released from this miserable existence.'[59]

Minutes later, in the briefing – by now a far smaller affair,[60] over much more quickly, and, because of communications difficulties, often lacking precise, up-to-date intelligence – Hitler, immediately after speaking of his imminent death and cremation, was again trying to exude optimism. Only now did Speer realize how much of an act the role of Führer had always been.[61]

All at once, there was a commotion in the corridor. Bormann hurried in with a telegram for Hitler. It was from Göring. The report of the momentous meeting the previous day, which Koller had personally flown to Berchtesgaden to deliver verbally, had placed the Reich Marshal in a quandary. Koller had helped persuade a hesitant Göring that, through his actions, Hitler had in effect given up the leadership of state and Wehrmacht. As a consequence, the edict of 29 June 1941, nominating Göring as his successor in the event of his incapacity to act, ought to come into force. Göring was still unsure. He could not be certain that Hitler had not changed his mind; and he worried about the influence of his arch-enemy, Bormann. Eventually, Koller suggested sending a telegram. Göring agreed. Koller, advised by Lammers, drafted its careful wording, cautiously stipulating that, had Göring not heard by ten o'clock that evening, he would presume that the terms of the succession law would come into operation, and that he would take over the entire leadership of the Reich. He would take immediate steps, he told Koller, to surrender to the western powers, though not to the Russians.

His telegram to Hitler (with a copy to Below, the Luftwaffe adjutant still in the bunker) gave no inkling of disloyalty.[62] But, as Göring had feared, Bormann was immediately at work to place the worst possible construction upon it. Hitler seemed at first unconcerned, or apathetic. But when Bormann produced another telegram from Göring, summoning Ribbentrop to see him immediately, should he have received no other directive from Hitler or himself by midnight, it was an easy matter to invoke the spectre of treachery once more. Bormann was pushing at an open door. For months, as we have had cause to note, Goebbels (and Bormann himself) had been the most prominent among those urging Hitler to dismiss Göring, portrayed as an incompetent, corrupt, drug-taking sybarite, single-handedly responsible for the débâcle of the Luftwaffe and the air-superiority of the Allies which they saw as so decisive for Germany's plight. Given Hitler's extreme volatility, as the events of the previous day had demonstrated only too plainly, the uncontrolled torrent of rage at Göring's ruination of the Luftwaffe, his corruption, and his morphine addiction was utterly predictable.

Savouring his victory, Bormann swiftly drew up a telegram, stripping Göring of his rights of succession, accusing him of treason, but refraining from further measures if the Reich Marshal resigned all his offices forthwith on health grounds. Göring's agreement was received within half an hour.[63] But that evening, the once most powerful man in the Reich after Hitler was nevertheless put under house-arrest, the Berghof surrounded by SS guards.[64] Hitler's power was fading fast; but it was not yet finally at an end.

Late that night, before leaving the bunker, Speer sat in Eva Braun's room, drinking a bottle of Moët et Chandon and eating cakes and sweets. Eva seemed calm and relaxed. She told Speer that Hitler had wanted to send her back to Munich, but she had refused; she had come to Berlin to end it. At three in the morning, Hitler appeared. Speer felt emotional at saying farewell. He had flown back to the bunker precisely for this purpose. It was, for him, a poignant moment. Hitler proffered a weak handshake. 'You're going then. Good. Good-bye.' That was all.[65]

Another visitor besides Speer had arrived in the bunker unannounced the previous evening: General Helmuth Weidling, commander of the 56th Panzer Corps, attached to the 9th Army fighting to the south-east of Berlin. Communications had been lost with him since the evening of 20 April, and Hitler had ordered him arrested for desertion.[66] Astonishingly, he had made his way back to Berlin, and into the Führer Bunker to protest his innocence. Hitler was impressed. Next morning, he made Weidling responsible for Berlin's defence, replacing Colonel Ernst Kaether, who had held the post for all of two days.

It was a daunting assignment. Weidling had at his disposal units rapidly patched together, comprising 44,600 soldiers, along with 42,500 Volkssturm men (whose fighting capabilities were severely limited on account both of their age and their miserable equipment), around 2,700 boys from the Hitler Youth, and a few hundred other 'combatants' from the Labour Service and *Organisation Todt*, assigned to defend the bridges that Wenck's relieving army would have to cross. A further 5,500 sailors had been promised by Dönitz, but were not yet available. Facing them, and closing in on the city by the hour, were some 2½ million combat troops in crack divisions of the

Red Army. Weidling knew from the start that his task was an impossible one.[67]

The news from the ever-narrowing fronts around Berlin was meanwhile becoming ever grimmer. By midday on 24 April, Soviet troops from Zhukov's and Konev's armies had met up in the southern suburbs of the city. The encirclement of Busse's 9th Army was complete. Hopes of it fighting its way through to the west to join Wenck's 12th Army – still only in the preparatory stage of its march on the capital – were now illusory. Reports were reaching the Reich Chancellery of bitter street fighting in eastern and southern districts of the capital. Several districts to the north were already in Soviet hands, and the Nauen road, the last main road to the west, was blocked by T34 tanks. Tempelhof aerodrome, close to the city centre, had been bombarded by Soviet artillery since lunchtime. By the evening, Gatow airfield on the banks of the Havel to the west of Berlin had also come under heavy shelling. The East-West Axis, where Albert Speer had landed the previous day, was in practice now Berlin's last remaining thin artery of non-telephonic communication with the outside world.

By dawn next morning, areas close to the city centre had started to come under persistent and intense artillery fire. Around midday, the spearhead of Konev's army, skirting round Berlin to the south, met up with forward units from Zhukov's army, heading round the city to the north, at Ketzin in the west. Berlin was as good as encircled. About the same time, Soviet and American troops were smoking cigarettes together at Torgau, on the Elbe, in central Germany. The Reich was now cut in two.[68]

Symbolically – there was absolutely no military purpose to the operation (other than striking at the possible focus of continued Nazi guerrilla warfare after formal cessation of hostilities from what transpired to be a mythical 'National Redoubt') – Hitler's alpine palace, the Berghof, above Berchtesgaden, had been reduced to smouldering ruins by RAF bombers that morning.[69]

In his ever more isolated and beleaguered underground lair, with communications rapidly worsening, and with operational charts increasingly out of date and almost immediately overtaken by events, Hitler was still sure that he knew best. 'The situation in Berlin looks worse than it is,' he stated, with apparent confidence, on 25 April, having not ventured out of doors for five days. He ordered the city combed for all possible last reserves of manpower to throw into the fray and help prepare the ground from within for the arrival of Wenck.[70] By this time, Wenck had made some advance towards the lakes south of Potsdam. But parts of his army were still engaged in combat with the Americans to the west, on the Elbe north of Wittenberg. And only remnants were by now left of the 9th Army, which was to have joined forces with him.[71] With what he had at his disposal, Wenck had only the remotest chance of reaching Berlin.

But Wenck was now the only hope. Hitler was still looking for one final victory, one last chance to turn the tables on his enemies. Even now, he clung to the belief that the Alliance against him would fall apart if he could deliver a stinging blow to the Red Army. 'I think the moment has come when out of self-preservation-drive the others will confront in any case this hugely swollen proletarian Bolshevik colossus and moloch . . . If I can be successful here and hold the capital, perhaps the hope will grow among the English and Americans that they could maybe still face this whole danger together with a Nazi Germany. And the only man for this is me,' he asserted.[72]

His comments to Goebbels that day were in part still apparently directed at convincing himself that his decision not to go to southern Germany and to stay in Berlin was the right one. 'I'd regard it as a thousand times more cowardly to commit suicide on the Obersalzberg than to stand and fall here,' he stated. 'They shouldn't say: "You, as the Führer . . ." I'm only the Führer as long as I can lead. And I can't lead through sitting somewhere on a mountain, but have to have authority over armies that obey. Let me win a victory here, however difficult and tough, then I've a right again to do away with the sluggish elements who are constantly causing an obstruction. Then I'll work with the generals who've proved themselves.'[73]

More than anything, Hitler's words were aimed at his place in history. Even now, Hitler – egged on, naturally, by Goebbels – remained the propagandist, looking to image. Whether leading to glorious victory, or sacrificial self-destruction, the last stand in the bunker was necessary for prestige purposes. It never occurred to him to question the continued slaughter of soldiers and civilians to that end. 'Only here can I attain a success,' he told Goebbels, '. . . and even if it's only a moral one, it's at least the possibility of saving face and winning time.'[74] 'Only through a heroic attitude can we survive this hardest of times,' he went on. If he won the 'decisive battle' he would be 'rehabilitated'. It would prove by example that he had been right in dismissing generals for not holding their ground.

And if he were to lose, then he would have perished 'decently', not like some 'inglorious refugee sitting in Berchtesgaden and issuing useless orders from there'. He saw, he said, 'a possibility of repairing history' through gaining a success. 'It's the only chance to restore personal reputation . . . If we leave the world stage in disgrace, we'll have lived for nothing. Whether you continue your life a bit longer or not is completely immaterial. Rather end the struggle in honour than continue in shame and dishonour a few months or years longer.' Goebbels, with Frederick the Great's exploits at the famous Battle of Leuthen – the Prussian King's epic victory in 1757 over an Austrian army far superior in numbers – tripping once more from his tongue, summed up the 'heroic' alternatives: 'If all goes well, then it's in any case good. If things don't go well and the Führer finds in Berlin an honourable death and Europe were to become bolshevized, then in five years at the latest the Führer would be a legendary personality and National Socialism would have attained mythical status (ein Mythos) . . .'[75]

III

Not everyone in the maze of tunnels below the Reich Chancellery was looking to share the 'heroic' end that Hitler and Goebbels were contemplating. 'I don't want to die with that lot down there in the bunker,' thirty-one-year-old Major Bernd von Freytag-Loringhoven, Krebs's tall adjutant, uttered. 'When it comes to the end, I want my head above ground and free.'[76] Even the SS guards from Hitler's bodyguard were anxiously asking about Wenck's progress, consoling themselves with drink when off duty, and looking for possible exit-routes from what looked more and more like a certain underground grave. In the streets above, despite the threat – often carried out – of summary execution by 'flying courts-martial' for 'defeatism', let alone desertion, many elderly Volkssturm men, aware of the utter futility of carrying on such a hopeless unequal fight and looking to avoid a pointless 'hero's' death, sought any opportunity at the approach of Soviet troops to melt away and try to rejoin families taking what refuge they could in cellars and bunkers.[77]

Amid the burning ruins of the great city, living conditions were deteriorating rapidly. Food was running out. The water-supply system had broken down. The old, infirm, wounded, women and children, injured soldiers, refugees, all clung on to life in the cellars, in packed shelters, and in underground stations as hell raged overhead.[78]

As communications increasingly petered out – the lines to Jodl at OKH headquarters went dead for a time in the course of the evening[79] – 'intelligence' of troop movements in the city was gathered for the once-mighty Army High Command in the bunker by using the telephone directory to ring numbers at random. 'Excuse me, madam, have you seen the Russians?' ran the question. 'Yes,' would come a reply, 'half an hour ago two of them were here. They were part of a group of about a dozen tanks at the crossroads.'[80]

Despite the uneven contest, the regular troops, mostly insufficiently trained and badly equipped, often down to their last reserves of ammunition, continued the bitter struggle in Berlin's streets. By the evening of 26 April, Soviet soldiers were close to Alexanderplatz, the very heart of the city. The Reich Chancellery in the government district, under heavy fire all day, was now less than a mile away.

A fresh moment of excitement gripped the inmates of the bunker during the early evening: the unexpected arrival of the wounded Colonel-General of the Luftwaffe Robert Ritter von Greim, propped up by his glamorous female companion, twenty years his junior, the flying-ace and test pilot Hanna Reitsch. Both were fervent, long-standing admirers of Hitler. Greim had been summoned two days earlier to Berlin.[81] He and Reitsch had had to risk an extremely hazardous flight from Munich. Greim's foot had been injured when their Fieseler Storch had been hit by artillery fire on approach to the centre of Berlin, and Reitsch had grabbed the controls and brought the plane down safely on the East-West Axis. They had then requisitioned a car to bring them to the Reich Chancellery. Propped up by Reitsch, the wounded Greim now limped painfully into the bunker. He still did not know why he had come.

Once his foot had been bandaged, Hitler came in to tell him. After railing at Göring's 'betrayal', Hitler informed Greim that he was promoting him to Field-Marshal and appointing him as the new head of the Luftwaffe. It could all have been done by telephone. Instead, Greim had had to risk life and limb to receive the news in person. And, it seemed likely, he and Reitsch were now doomed to end their lives in the bunker. But far from being infuriated or depressed, or both, Greim and Reitsch were exhilarated. They begged to stay in the bunker with Hitler. They were given phials of poison, should the worst happen. But Hitler persuaded Greim that all was not lost. 'Just don't lose faith,' Koller heard Greim say, when he telephoned the bunker. 'It'll all come to a good end. The meeting with the Führer and his vigour have given me extraordinary new strength. It's like the fountain of youth (*Jungbad*) here'. Koller thought it sounded more like a mad-house.[82]

The briefing sessions were by this time much reduced in size and changed in character. Krebs was now the only senior military figure present. Goebbels had joined since taking up residence in the bunker. Hitler Youth Leader

Axmann, General Weidling (responsible for the defence of Berlin), Vice-Admiral Voß (Dönitz's liaison), Colonel Nicolaus von Below (the long-serving Luftwaffe adjutant), and SS-Brigadeführer Wilhelm Mohnke, just appointed by Hitler as commandant of the government quarter of Berlin (which had been dubbed 'The Citadel') were also present.

Discussion at the first meeting on 27 April, in the early hours, centred on the prospects of Wenck breaking through. He had reached the outskirts of Potsdam. But he had only three divisions at his disposal. He desperately needed reinforcements. The chances of Busse's beleaguered 9th Army forcing their way north-westwards to join him were now slim in the extreme. But there were still hopes that troops under Lieutenant-General Rudolf Holste, to the north-west of Berlin, might fight their way south to link up with Wenck. Time was short. Krebs reported heavy street-fighting in the heart of the city. The Soviets had advanced on Alexanderplatz. They would soon have Potsdamer Platz in their sights; and that was where the bunker was situated. 'May God let Wenck come!' intoned Goebbels. 'A dreadful situation crosses my mind,' he added, grimly. 'Wenck is located at Potsdam, and here the Soviets are pressing on Potsdamer Platz!' 'And I'm not in Potsdam, but in Potsdamer Platz,' commented Hitler, laconically.'

His assessment of the situation was realistic: Wenck's three divisions were not enough. They might suffice to take Potsdam, but they were only infantry divisions, lacking panzer support, and not capable of breaking their way through the Soviet tank units. Voß breathed encouragement. 'Wenck will get here, my Führer! It's only a question of whether he can do it alone.' It was enough for Hitler to lapse into a new reverie. 'You've got to imagine. That'll spread like wildfire through the whole of Berlin when it's known: a German army has broken through in the west and established contact with the Citadel (*Festung*).' The Soviets, he thought, had suffered great losses, were suffering even more in the intense house-to-house fighting, and could only throw more troops into exposed forward positions. The thought sufficed: he had convinced himself that the situation was not wholly bleak. The constant explosions had kept him awake in recent nights. But he would sleep better tonight, he said. He only wanted to be awakened 'if a Russian tank is standing in front of my cabin' so that he had time to do what was necessary.[83]

The second briefing of the day began with Mohnke announcing that the first enemy tanks had managed to penetrate to the Wilhelmsplatz, the heart of the government quarter. They had been repulsed – on this occasion – but time was running out. Krebs reckoned the bunker residents had no more than about twenty-four to twenty-six hours; the link-up between the armies of Wenck and Busse had to take place within that time if there was to be any hope. Hitler inwardly knew, however, that this would not happen. He repeatedly bemoaned 'the catastrophic mistake' of the 9th Army, which he blamed for ignoring his orders and trying to penetrate the Soviet lines in the wrong direction. The faint hopes from the remaining forces in the north, those of Holste and Steiner (in whom Hitler had lost all confidence days earlier), were now also – realistically, if not in dreams – largely abandoned.

Despite a desperate plea from Keitel to throw everything into the relief of Berlin, Jodl had diverted the hard-pressed units of Holste and Steiner to fend off Soviet forces to the north of the capital. It was tantamount to giving up on Berlin.[84] Bormann scathingly commented in his diary, in remarks pointedly directed at Reichsführer-SS Himmler's recognized reluctance to deploy Steiner's SS corps to help save Berlin: 'The divisions marching to our relief are held up by Himmler-Jodl! *We* will stand and fall with the Führer: loyal into death. Others believe they have to act "from *higher* insight". They sacrifice the Führer, and their lack of loyalty – shame on them – matches their "feeling of honour".'[85]

Hitler and Goebbels relapsed into reminiscences. They were prompted by Mohnke's remark, entirely without irony: 'We haven't quite brought about what we wanted in 1933, my Führer!' Hitler's explanation – it had scarcely been in his mind at the time – was that he had come to power too early. A year or more later, at Hindenburg's death, would have been the right time. To bring about a complete revolution, the old system needed to have revealed itself as utterly bankrupt. As it was, he had been forced to compromise with Hugenberg, Schleicher – not much of a compromise since the former Reich Chancellor had, in fact, been murdered by Hitler's henchmen at the time of the 'Röhm affair' in 1934 – and other pillars of the old order. By the time of Hindenburg's death, Hitler went on, the determination to rid himself of the conservatives had lessened, and the work of reconstruction was under way. 'Otherwise, thousands would have been eliminated at that time,' he declared. 'It could have happened, if I had come to power through an express will of the people' – presumably meaning a presidential election – 'or through a putsch. You regret it afterwards that you are so good,' he concluded.

This took the discussion inexorably once more back into pathos and an evocation of 'heroism'. He was staying in Berlin, Hitler said, 'so that I have more moral right to act against weakness . . . I can't constantly threaten others if I run away myself from the Reich capital at the critical hour . . .

I've had the right to command in this city. Now I must obey the commands of fate. Even if I could save myself, I won't do it. The captain also goes down with his ship.' Voß, predictably, picked up the metaphor. Pathos and emotion got the better of him, too. 'Here in the Reich Chancellery it's just like the command-bridge of a ship,' he implausibly ruminated. 'One thing here applies to all. We don't want to get away.' (He would, ultimately, like most of the others, nevertheless seek to flee the bunker at the last moment.) 'We belong together. It's only a matter of being an upright community.'[86]

IV

The news trickling in during the day could scarcely have been worse. Wenck's troops, without assistance from the 9th Army (whose encirclement was by now accepted as practically a foregone conclusion), had been pushed back south of Potsdam. There was a 'doomsday' mood in the bunker, alleviated only by copious supplies of alcohol and food from the Reich Chancellery cellars.[87] Hitler told Below he had decided to give Weidling, the Commandant of Berlin, the order to break out. All his staff should go, as well as Bormann and Goebbels. He would stay behind and die in the capital. By evening, amid worsening news, he had changed his mind. An attempt to break out would be useless. He gave Below a poison-capsule, should it come to 'a difficult situation'.[88]

The fate of the encircled 9th Army, with its eleven divisions almost four times as strong as the forces at Wenck's disposal, took Hitler back, like a long-playing record, at the third briefing of the day to what he saw as constant disobedience and disloyalty in the army. Only Schörner, commander of Army Group Centre, was singled out for praise as 'a true warlord'. Dönitz, too, stood in high favour for holding to his promise to send naval units to the defence of Berlin, and to Hitler's personal protection. The faint hope in Wenck was still not totally extinguished. But Hitler was looking to the last stand in the 'Citadel'. Firm command and reliable troops for the defence of the 'Citadel' were vital. His fear of capture surfaced again. 'I must have the absolute certainty,' he said, following news that enemy tanks had for a short time forced their way into Wilhelmstraße, 'that I will not be dragged out through some crafty trick by a Russian tank.' He saw it as only a question of time before the Soviets brought up heavy artillery to shell the 'Citadel' from close range. 'It's a matter then of a heroic struggle for a last small island,' he commented. 'If the relief doesn't arrive, we have to be clear: it's no bad end to a life to fall in the struggle for the capital of your Reich.'[89]

Not everyone was willing to join a suicide pact. Hermann Fegelein, the swashbuckling, womanizing, cynical opportunist who had risen to high position in the SS through Himmler's favour then sealed his bonds to Hitler's 'court' through marrying Eva Braun's sister, had disappeared from the bunker. His absence was noticed on 27 April. And that evening he was discovered in civilian clothes in his apartment in Charlottenburg, allegedly with a woman friend, worse for wear from drink, and with a good deal of money in bags packed for departure.[90] He rang Eva Braun to have his sister-in-law intercede. (It seems, in fact, that he may have been more attracted to Eva Braun than he was to her sister; and that he had been in touch with her beforehand from his apartment, attempting to persuade her to leave the bunker before it was too late.[91]) But it was to no avail. He was hauled back into the Reich Chancellery that evening in deep disgrace, stripped of his epaulettes and collar flashes, reduced to the ranks, and kept in an improvised cell until Hitler was ready to see him.[92]

In the early hours of 28 April, despairing calls were made from the bunker to Keitel and Jodl urging all conceivable effort to be made to relieve Berlin as absolute priority. Time was of the essence. There were at most forty-eight hours, it was thought. 'If no help comes within that time, it will be too late,' Krebs told Keitel. 'The Führer passes that on again!!!'[93] From Wenck, there was nothing but silence.

As so often, the bunker inmates thought they smelled the scent of disloyalty and treason. Bormann telegraphed Puttkamer that evening: 'Instead of spurring on the troops who should liberate us with orders and appeals, the men in authority are silent. Loyalty has given way to disloyalty. We remain here. The Reich Chancellery is already a heap of ruins.'[94] In his desk diary, the entry was of high treason and betrayal of the country.[95]

An hour later, the suspicions seemed dramatically confirmed. Heinz Lorenz appeared in the bunker. He had just picked up a message from Reuters, sent by the BBC in London and confirmed in Stockholm. He gave one copy to Bormann, whom he found sitting with Goebbels and Hewel. The other copy he handed to Linge to pass on to Hitler. It confirmed the truth of a disturbing story broadcast in the morning news of Radio Stockholm, relayed to Hitler in mid-afternoon, though initially seeming to lack substance: that the Reichsführer-SS, Heinrich Himmler, had offered to surrender to the western Allies, but that this had been declined. Hitler had at first received the news, late that afternoon, of Himmler's discussions about capitulation 'with complete contempt'.[96] He had immediately telephoned Admiral Dönitz, who had said he knew nothing of it. Dönitz then in turn contacted Himmler, who categorically denied the report and recommended ignoring it rather than putting out a denial on the radio.[97] But Hitler continued to brood on it. Perhaps he was expecting something of the sort. His distrust of Himmler had grown in recent weeks. The disobedience, as he saw it, of Sepp Dietrich in Hungary and of Felix Steiner in the failure to attempt the relief of Berlin, showed, it seemed, that even the SS were now disloyal to him. As the day wore on, so it appeared to Below, Hitler's bitterness towards Himmler mounted.[98]

And now it all fell into place: the earlier story had been correct, and Himmler's denial a lie. More than that: the Reuter report had added that 'Himmler had informed the western Allies that he could implement an unconditional surrender and support it.'[99] It amounted to an implication that the Reichsführer-SS was now *de facto* head of state, that Hitler had been disempowered.[100] This was a bombshell. This could on no account be tolerated. This was base treason.

Whether Hitler had earlier been aware of Himmler's tentative feelers towards the western powers through the intermediacy of Count Folke Bernadotte, Vice-President of the Swedish Red Cross and a close relative of the King of Sweden, is uncertain.[101] The Reichsführer's dealings with Bernadotte had stretched back some two months. SS-Brigadeführer Walter Schellenberg, head of the Foreign Intelligence Service in the Reich Security Main Office, had instigated the meetings and acted as intermediary.[102] Bernadotte's initial aim had been to bargain for the release of prisoners – particularly Scandinavians – from concentration camps.[103] From Himmler's point of view, urged on by Schellenberg, Bernadotte offered a possible opening to the West.[104] As Germany's military situation had drastically deteriorated, Himmler, still hesitant and evidently under great nervous strain, had become more amenable to gestures at humanitarian concessions aimed at showing himself in as good a light as possible. Like most Nazi leaders, he was looking to survive, not throw himself on the funeral pyre in the Berlin *Götterdämmerung*. In March, he had agreed, in contravention of Hitler's wishes, to allow concentration camps to be handed over to the approaching enemy, not destroyed. He had conceded the release of small numbers of Jews and other prisoners, to be sent to Switzerland and Sweden.[105] At his second meeting with Bernadotte at the beginning of April, he had also consented to let Danish and Norwegian women and the sick in camps be taken to Sweden.[106] At the same time, he still regarded the camp prisoners as his 'hostages' – bargaining counters in any negotiations with the West.[107]

Bernadotte had brushed aside Schellenberg's suggestion – almost certainly prompted by Himmler – that he might sound out Eisenhower about the possibility of a surrender in the West. Such a proposition, Bernadotte had pointed out, had to come from the Reichsführer himself.[108] Himmler was, however, in a state of chronic indecision as well as extreme nervous tension. He saw clearly the writing on the wall; the war was irredeemably lost. But he was well aware that Hitler would take Germany down into perdition with him rather than capitulate. Himmler, in common with most Nazi leaders, wanted to save his own skin. And he still hankered after some role in a post-Hitler settlement. As dogmatic as Hitler in the fight against Bolshevism, he harboured the notable illusion that the enemy might overlook his part in monstrous crimes against humanity because of his value to the continuation of the struggle against the mortal enemy not just of Germany, but also of the West. He could not, however, even now free himself from his bonds with Hitler. He still hankered after Hitler's favour, and was distressed at the way he had fallen into discredit after his failure as commander of Army Group Vistula. Not least: now, as before, he feared Hitler.[109]

A third meeting with Bernadotte on 21 April, at which the Reichsführer-SS looked extremely drawn and in a highly nervous state, made no progress on the issue of overtures to the West. Himmler still remained ultra-cautious, unwilling to risk any initiative.[110] Possibly, as Schellenberg later suggested, he had already decided by lunchtime on 22 April that the time had come to act, though this seems doubtful.[111] What certainly convinced him was the news which Fegelein telephoned through to him from the Führer-Bunker that day of Hitler's extraordinary fit of pent-up fury and his uncontrolled tirade against treachery on all sides – not least directed at the SS on account of Steiner's failure to launch the ordered counter-offensive – culminating in his announcement that he would stay and die in Berlin.[112] At this, Himmler's indecision evaporated.

On 23 April, Count Bernadotte had agreed, somewhat reluctantly, to Schellenberg's suggestion to meet Himmler for a fourth time that evening. The meeting took place in the Swedish Consulate in Lübeck, eerily lit by candles because of a power cut. 'Hitler is very probably already dead,' Himmler began. At any rate, his end could be no more than a few days away. Before now, his oath of loyalty had prevented him from acting, Himmler went on. But with Hitler dead or on the verge of death, the situation was different. He now had a free hand. There could be no surrender to the Soviet Union. He was, and always would be, the sworn enemy of Bolshevism. He insisted that the struggle against Bolshevism must continue. But he was ready to declare Germany defeated by the western powers, and begged Bernadotte to pass his offer of capitulation to General Eisenhower in order to prevent further senseless destruction. Still by candlelight, Himmler drafted a letter to Sweden's Foreign Minister, to be handed to him by Bernadotte, and passed on to the western Allies.[113]

Himmler, like Göring (if in a different way), had taken the news of Hitler's outburst on 22 April to imply the Führer's effective abdication. Like Göring, Himmler was soon to be disabused of such presumption. His immediate instinct, however, now that his own decision had been clarified, was to build a cabinet, invent (at Schellenberg's suggestion) the name for a new party – the 'Party of National Concentration (*Nationale Sammlungspartei*)' – and ponder whether he should bow or shake hands when he met Eisenhower.[114] It apparently never occurred to him that his offer of capitulation might be turned down. But that outcome – as good as certain to all beyond the perimeters of the detached mental world of Nazi leaders at this juncture – was precisely what had happened by the time, during the course of the afternoon of 28 April, the sensational news filtered out of the Reichsführer-SS's willingness to capitulate.[115]

For Hitler, this was the last straw. That his 'loyal Heinrich', whose SS had as its motto 'my honour is loyalty', should now stab him in the back: this was the end. It was the betrayal of all betrayals. The bunker reverberated to a final elemental explosion of fury. All his stored-up venom was now poured out on Himmler in a last paroxysm of seething rage. It was, he screamed, 'the most shameful betrayal in human history.'[116]

When the outburst subsided, Hitler retired to his rooms with Goebbels and Bormann for a lengthy discussion. As soon as he reappeared, he sent for the imprisoned Fegelein and subjected him to a fearsome verbal assault. Fegelein's recent disappearance now appeared to have sinister significance: joining the base treachery of the Reichsführer-SS. Hitler's paranoid suspicions were running riot. Possibly Himmler was plotting to assassinate him; or to hand him over to the enemy. And Fegelein was part of the plot. After the merest formalities in a hastily improvised 'court martial', Fegelein was summarily sentenced to death, immediately taken out, put in front of a firing-squad and executed.[117] For some of the bunker inmates, there was a sense of shock that one from within the 'inner circle' was guilty of such 'betrayal', and had been so peremptorily dispatched. For Hitler, it was the closest he could come to revenge on the Reichsführer-SS himself.

V

By now, Soviet troops had forced their way into Potsdamer Platz and streets in the immediate vicinity of the Reich Chancellery. They were no more than a few hundred yards away. A breakdown in communications for most of the day had left the bunker inmates desperate for any news of Wenck's army (which remained, hemmed in, south of Potsdam).[118] In the prevailing climate within the bunker, even the lapdog Keitel and the ever-reliable Jodl were now coming under suspicion of treachery for not bringing about the relief of Berlin.[119]

Soon after midnight, following Fegelein's execution, Hitler commissioned Greim to deploy the Luftwaffe in making every effort to aid Wenck through attacks on Soviet positions blocking his route to Berlin. It was the faintest of faint hopes. He had a second commission for Greim – one, if anything, even more important. Greim was to leave Berlin and fly to Dönitz in Plön to ensure that the traitor, Himmler, was arrested – better still, liquidated forthwith.[120] To this end, an Arado 96 training plane had been ordered to Berlin from Rechlin and, astonishingly, had defied all odds in touching down on the East-West Axis. Protesting their wish to stay with Hitler in the bunker, Greim, on crutches and far from recovered from his injured foot, and his companion Hanna Reitsch nonetheless accepted the commission, were driven in an armoured vehicle to the plane, waiting close to the Brandenburg Gate, managed to take off, and, even more remarkably, to negotiate the heavy Soviet anti-aircraft fire to fly to Rechlin, from where they later flew to Plön. The perilous journey was pointless. The few planes Greim was able to order into the defence of Berlin made not the slightest difference. And by the time he reached Dönitz's headquarters, the Grand Admiral had nothing to gain by having Himmler arrested, let alone shot. Even avoiding death in the bunker was no consolation to Greim and Reitsch. 'It is the greatest sorrow of our lives that we were not permitted to die with the Führer,' they chorused some days later. 'One should kneel in reverence at the altar of the Fatherland and pray.'[121]

After Greim and Reitsch had left, Hitler became calmer. It was time to make preparations. As long as Hitler had had a future, he had ruled out marriage. His life, he had said, was devoted to Germany. There was no room for a wife. It had also been politically inconvenient. No one outside the inner circle was to know of Eva Braun's existence. She had been forced to accept that she was no more than an appendage, there when Hitler wanted her to be, stored well out of sight for the rest of the time. But she had chosen to come to the bunker. And she had refused Hitler's own entreaties to leave. She had committed herself to him once and for all, when others were deserting. The marriage now cost him nothing. He did it simply to please Eva Braun, to give her what she had wanted more than anything at a moment when marrying him was the least enviable fate in the world.

Eva Braun had dropped a hint earlier in the day that this would be her wedding night.[122] Now, following the departure of Greim and Reitsch, not long after midnight on 29 April, in the most macabre surroundings, with the bunker shaking from nearby explosions, Hitler and Eva Braun exchanged married vows in the conference-room in front of one of Goebbels's minor officials, city councillor Walter Wagner, dressed in Nazi uniform with a Volkssturm armband, who had been brought to the bunker in an armoured car to conduct the bizarre ceremony. Goebbels and Bormann were witnesses. The rest of the staff waited outside to congratulate the newly wedded couple. Champagne, sandwiches, and reminiscences – with somewhat forced joviality – of happier days followed.[123]

Just before the wedding ceremony, Hitler had asked his youngest secretary, Traudl Junge, to go with him to the room where his military conferences took place. It had been about 11.30p.m. when he said that he wanted her to take down some dictation. She was still wondering what this might be at such a late hour when, leaning on the table, he started to dictate his last will and testament.[124]

He began with a brief Private Testament. He referred first to his marriage to Eva Braun, and her decision to come to Berlin and die at his side. He disposed of his possessions to the Party – or, should it no longer exist, to the state; he still hoped his collection of paintings would go to a gallery in Linz; and he appointed Martin Bormann as executor to see that relatives and his long-serving staff had some reward for their support.[125]

He came to the more significant part. 'This is my political testament,' he declared. Traudl Junge paused for a moment, expectantly. But she had heard it all before.[126] His last words for posterity were a piece of pure self-justification. The rhetoric is instantly recognizable, redolent of *Mein Kampf* and countless speeches; the central idea of the responsibility of international Jewry for the death, suffering, and destruction in the war remained unchanged, even as he himself now looked death in the face. 'It is untrue that I or anyone else in Germany wanted the war in 1939,' he dictated. 'It was desired and instigated exclusively by those international statesmen who were either of Jewish descent or who worked for Jewish interests . . .

Centuries will pass away, but out of the ruins of our towns and cultural monuments the hatred will ever renew itself against those ultimately responsible whom we have to thank for everything: international Jewry and its helpers.' The conspiracy theory continued unabated. He attributed the rejection of his proposal on the eve of the attack on Poland partly to the business interests of 'leading circles in English politics', partly to the 'influence of propaganda organized by international Jewry'.

He came to a key passage – an oblique reference to the 'Final Solution' – relating once more to the fulfilment of the 'prophecy' of 1939: 'I also left no doubt that, if the nations of Europe are again to be regarded as mere blocks of shares of these international money and finance conspirators, then that race, too, which is really guilty of this murderous struggle, will be called to account: Jewry! I further left no one in doubt that this time millions of children of Europe's aryan peoples would not die of hunger, millions of grown men would not suffer death, and hundreds of thousands of women and children not be burnt and bombed to death in the towns, without the real culprit having to atone for his guilt, even if by my more humane means.'[127]

Despite all its setbacks, the six-year struggle, he went on, would one day go down in history as 'the most glorious and valiant manifestation of a nation's will to existence'. He himself could not forsake Berlin. The forces there were too small to hold out against the enemy and – the inevitable side-swipe against those deemed to have betrayed him – 'our own resistance is gradually devalued by deluded and characterless subjects'. He would choose death at the appropriate moment.

Again, he gave an indication of his own fear of what he saw as the still dominant power of the Jews: 'I do not wish to fall into the hands of enemies who, for the amusement of their whipped-up masses, will need a spectacle arranged by Jews.'

A renaissance of National Socialism, he avowed, would eventually emerge from the sacrifice of the soldiers and his own death alongside them. He ended with an exhortation to continue the struggle. He begged the heads of the armed forces to instil the spirit of National Socialism in the troops. His long-standing scapegoat, the officer corps of the army, did not even now go unscathed: 'May it at some time be part of the concept of honour of the German officer – as is already the case in our navy – that the surrender of a district or a town is impossible and that above all the leaders have to proceed here with a shining example in most loyal fulfilment of their duty unto death.'[128]

In the second part of his Testament, Hitler went through the charade of nominating a successor government for what was left of the Reich. The tone was vindictive. Göring and Himmler were formally expelled from the Party and from all their offices for the damage they had done through negotiating with the enemy 'without my knowledge and against my wishes', for attempting to take power in the state, and for disloyalty to his person. Nor was there any place in the new government for Speer. The new head of state and head of the armed forces was Grand Admiral Dönitz – less of a surprise than at first sight, given his specially high standing in Hitler's eyes in the closing phase of the war, and in view particularly of the responsibility he had already been given a few days earlier for Party and state affairs as well as military matters in the northern part of the country. Significantly, however, Dönitz was not to inherit the title of Führer. Instead, the title of Reich President, dropped in 1934 on Hindenburg's death, was reinvented. Goebbels, who had been pressing for so long for full control over internal affairs, was rewarded for his loyalty by being appointed Chancellor of a Reich that scarcely any longer existed. Bormann, another who had proved his loyalty, was made Party Minister. Goebbels – who, together with Bormann, kept bringing Fräulein Junge the names of further ministers for typing in the list[129] – probably engineered the dismissal at this late point of his old adversary Ribbentrop, and his replacement as Foreign Minister by Arthur Seyß-Inquart. Hitler's favourite general, Schörner, was to be Commander of the Army, while Gauleiter Karl Hanke, still holding out in Breslau, was to take over from Himmler as Reichsführer-SS and Chief of the German Police. The tough Munich Gauleiter, Paul Giesler, was made Interior Minister, with Karl-Otto Saur replacing Speer as Minister for Armaments. The pointless job of Propaganda Minister fell to Goebbels's State Secretary, Werner Naumann. Old survivors included Schwerin-Krosigk (Finance), Funk (Economics), Thierack (Justice), and Herbert Backe (Agriculture). Hitler commissioned them with continuing the task – 'the work of coming centuries' – of building up a National Socialist State. 'Above all,' the Political Testament concluded, 'I charge the leadership of the nation and their subjects (*Gefolgschaft*) with the meticulous observance of the race-laws and the merciless resistance to the universal poisoner of all peoples, international Jewry.'[130]

It was turned 4a.m. when Goebbels, Bormann, Burgdorf, and Krebs signed the Political Testament, and Nicolaus von Below added his signature to the Private Testament.[131]

Hitler, looking weary, took himself off to rest. He had completed the winding-up order on the Third Reich. Only the final act of self-destruction remained.

For Fräulein Junge, however, the night's secretarial duties were not yet over. Soon after Hitler had retired, Goebbels, in a highly emotional state, white-faced, tears running down his cheeks, appeared in the ante-room, where she was finishing her work. He asked her to draft his own coda to Hitler's will. Hitler, he said, had ordered him to leave Berlin as a member of the new government. But 'if the Führer is dead, my life is meaningless', he told her.[132] Of all the Nazi leaders, Goebbels was the one who for weeks had assessed with some realism the military prospects, had repeatedly evoked the imagery of heroism, looking to his own place in the pantheon of Teutonic heroes, and had accordingly brought his wife and children to the bunker to die alongside their adored Leader in a final act of *Nibelungentreue*. It was, therefore, utterly consistent when he now dictated: 'For the first time in my life, I must categorically refuse to obey an order of the Führer.' His wife and children joined him in this refusal. He would, he continued, lose all self-respect – quite apart from the demands of personal loyalty – were he to 'leave the Führer alone in his hour of greatest need'. Betrayal was in his mind, as in that of his master. 'In the delirium of treachery, which surrounds the Führer in these critical days of the war,' he had Fräulein Junge type, 'there have to be at least a few who stay unconditionally loyal to him even unto death, even if this contradicts a formal, objectively well-founded order which finds expression in his Political Testament.' Consequently, he – together with his wife and children (who, were they old enough to judge, would be in agreement) – were firmly resolved not to leave the Reich capital 'and rather at the Führer's side to end a life which for me personally has no further value if it cannot be used in the service of the Führer and by his side'. It was 5.30a.m. before this last act in the nocturnal drama closed.[133]

VI

The mood in the bunker now sank to zero-level. Despair was now written on everyone's face. All knew it was only a matter of hours before Hitler killed himself, and wondered what the future held for them after his death.[134] There was much talk of the best methods of committing suicide.[135] Secretaries, adjutants, and any others who wanted them had by now been given the brass-cased ampoules containing prussic acid supplied by Dr Ludwig

Stumpfegger, the SS surgeon who had joined the 'court' the previous October.[136] Hitler's paranoia stretched now to doubts about the capsules. He had shown his alsatian bitch Blondi more affection in recent years than any human being, probably including even Eva Braun. Now, as the end approached, he had the poison tested on Blondi. Professor Werner Haase was summoned from his duties in the nearby public air-raid shelter beneath the new Reich Chancellery building nearby. Shortly before the afternoon briefing on 29 April, aided by Hitler's dog-attendant, Sergeant Fritz Tornow, he forced open the dog's jaws and crushed the prussic acid capsule with a pair of pliers. The dog slumped in an instant motionless to the ground. Hitler was not present. However, he entered the room immediately afterwards. He glanced for a few seconds at the dead dog. Then, his face like a mask, he left without saying anything and shut himself in his room.[137]

The bunker community had by this time dwindled still further. Three emissaries – Bormann's adjutant, SS-Standartenführer Wilhelm Zander, Hitler's army adjutant Major Willi Johannmeier, and Acting Press Chief Heinz Lorenz – had left that morning as couriers on a perilous, and fruitless, mission to deliver copies of the Testament to Dönitz, Schörner, and the Nazi Party's Headquarters, the 'Brown House' in Munich.[138] By this time, normal telephone communications had finally broken down, though naval and Party telegraph wires remained usable, with difficulty, to the end.[139] But dispatch runners brought reports that Soviet troops had brought up their lines to a mere 400–500 metres from the Reich Chancellery. The Berlin Commandant General Weidling informed Hitler that they had begun a concentrated attack on the 'Citadel'; resistance could only be sustained for a short time.[140] Three young officers, Major Bernd von Loringhoven (Krebs's adjutant), his friend Gerhard Boldt (the Chief of Staff's orderly), and Lieutenant-Colonel Rudolf Weiß (General Burgdorf's adjutant) decided to try a last chance to escape from their predestined tomb. They put it to Krebs that they should break out in the attempt to reach Wenck. He agreed; so, following the midday conference, did Hitler. As he shook hands wearily with them, he said: 'Give my regards to Wenck. Tell him to hurry or it will be too late.'[141]

That afternoon, Below too, who had been a member of Hitler's 'household' since 1937, decided to try his luck. He asked if Hitler would permit him to attempt to get through to the west. Hitler readily agreed. Below left late that night, bearing a letter from Hitler to Keitel which, from Below's memory of it (the letter itself was destroyed), repeated his praise for the navy, his attribution of blame for the Luftwaffe's failure exclusively to

Göring, and his condemnation of the General Staff together with the disloyalty and betrayal which had for so long undermined his efforts. He could not believe, he said, that the sacrifices of the German people had been in vain. The aim had still to be the winning of territory in the East.[142]

By this time, Hitler had learned that Mussolini had been captured and executed by Italian partisans. Whether he was told the details – how Mussolini was hanged upside down in a square in Milan, together with his mistress Clara Petacci, and stoned by a mob – is uncertain. If he did learn the full gory tale, it could have done no more than confirm his anxiety to take his own life before it was too late, and to prevent his body from being seized by his enemies.[143] During the late-evening briefing, General Weidling had told Hitler that the Russians would reach the Reich Chancellery no later than 1 May.[144] There was little time remaining.

Nevertheless, Hitler undertook one last attempt to ascertain the possibilities of relief, even at this late hour. With nothing heard throughout the day of Wenck's progress (or lack of it), he cabled five questions to Jodl in the most recent OKW headquarters in Dobbin at eleven o'clock that evening, asking in the tersest fashion where Wenck's spearheads were, when the attack would come, where the 9th Army was, where Holste's troops were, and when *their* attack might be expected.[145]

Keitel's reply arrived shortly before 3a.m. on 30 April: Wenck's army was still engaged south of the Schwielow Lake, outside Potsdam, and unable to continue its attack on Berlin. The 9th Army was encircled. The Korps Holste had been forced on to the defensive.[146] Keitel added, below the report: 'Attacks on Berlin not advanced anywhere.'[147] It was now plain beyond any equivocation: there would be no relief of the Reich capital.

Hitler had, in fact, already given up. Before 2a.m. he had said goodbye to a gathering of around twenty to twenty-five servants and guards. He mentioned Himmler's treachery and told them that he had decided to take his own life rather than be captured by the Russians and put on show like an exhibition in a museum. He shook hands with each of them, thanked them for their service, released them from their oath to him, and hoped they would find their way to the British or Americans rather than fall into Russian hands. He then went through the same farewell ceremony with the two doctors, Haase and Schenck, and the nurses and assistants, who had served in the emergency hospital established below the New Reich Chancellery.[148]

At dawn, Soviet artillery opened up intensive bombardment of the Reich Chancellery and neighbouring buildings. Hitler inquired soon afterwards of the commandant of the 'Citadel', SS-Obergruppenführer Mohnke, how long he could hold out. He was told for one to two days at most.[149] In the last briefing, in the late morning, Berlin's commandant, General Weidling, was even more pessimistic. Munition was fast running out; air-supplies had dried up and any replenishment was out of the question; morale was at rock-bottom; the fighting was now in a very small area of the city. The battle for Berlin would in all probability, he concluded, be over that evening. After a long silence, Hitler, in a tired voice, asked Mohnke's view. The 'Citadel' commandant concurred. Hitler wearily levered himself out of his chair. Weidling pressed him for a decision on whether, in the event of a total ammunitions failure, the remaining troops could attempt to break out. Hitler spoke briefly with Krebs, then gave permission – which he confirmed in writing – for a break-out to be attempted in small numbers. As before, he rejected emphatically a capitulation of the capital.[150]

He sent for Bormann. It was by now around noon. He told him the time had come; he would shoot himself that afternoon. Eva Braun would also commit suicide. Their bodies were to be burnt. He then summoned his personal adjutant, SS-Sturmbannführer Otto Günsche. He did not want to be put on display in some waxworks in Moscow, he said. He commissioned Günsche with making the arrangements for the cremation, and for ensuring that it was carried out according to his instructions. Hitler was calm and collected. Günsche, less calm, immediately rushed to telephone Hitler's chauffeur, Erich Kempka, to obtain as much petrol as was available. He impressed upon him the urgency. The Soviets could reach the Chancellery garden at any time.[151]

Hitler took lunch as usual around 1p.m. with his secretaries, Traudl Junge and Gerda Christian, and his dietician Fräulein Manziarly. Eva Braun was not present. Hitler was composed, giving no hint that his death was imminent. Some time after the meal had ended, Günsche told the secretaries that Hitler wished to say farewell to them. They joined Martin Bormann, Joseph and Magda Goebbels, General Burgdorf and General Krebs, and others from the 'inner circle' of the bunker community. Looking more stooped than ever, Hitler, dressed as usual in his uniform jacket and black trousers, appeared alongside Eva Braun, who was wearing a blue dress with white trimmings.[152] He held out his hand to each of them, muttered a few words, and, within a few minutes and without further formalities, returned to his study.

Eva Braun went into Magda Goebbels's room with her. Magda, on whom three days earlier Hitler had pinned his own Golden Party Badge – a signal token of esteem for one of his most fervent admirers – was in a tearful state.

She was conscious not only that this was the end for the Führer she revered but that within hours she would be taking, as well as her own life, the lives of her six children, still playing happily in the corridors of the bunker. Highly agitated, Magda immediately reappeared, asking Günsche to speak to Hitler again. Hitler somewhat grudgingly agreed and went in to see Magda. It was said that she begged him a last time to leave Berlin. The response was predictable and unemotional. Inside a minute, Hitler had retreated behind the doors of his study for the last time. Eva Braun followed him almost immediately. It was shortly before half-past three.[153]

For the next few minutes, Goebbels, Bormann, Axmann (who had arrived too late to say his own farewell to Hitler) and the remaining members of the bunker community waited. Günsche stood on guard outside Hitler's room.[154] The only noise was the drone of the diesel ventilator. In the upstairs part of the bunker, Traudl Junge chatted with the Goebbels children as they ate their lunch.[155]

After waiting ten minutes or so, still without a sound from Hitler's room, Linge took the initiative. He took Bormann with him and cautiously opened the door. In the cramped study, Hitler and Eva Braun sat alongside each other on the small sofa. Eva Braun was slumped to Hitler's left. A strong whiff of bitter almonds – the distinctive smell of prussic acid – drifted up from her body. Hitler's head drooped lifelessly. Blood dripped from a bullet-hole in his right temple. His 7.65mm Walther pistol lay by his foot.[156]

EPILOGUE

'Europe has never known such a calamity to her civilisation and nobody can say when she will begin to recover from its effects.'

Manchester Guardian, 2 May 1945

Hitler was dead. Only the last obsequies remained. They would not detain the inhabitants of the bunker for long. The man who, living, had dominated their existence to the last was now merely a corpse to be disposed of as rapidly as possible. With the Russians at the portals of the Reich Chancellery, the bunker inmates had thoughts other than their dead leader on their minds.

Within minutes of the deaths being established, the bodies of Adolf Hitler and his wife of a day and a half, Eva Braun, were wrapped in the blankets that Heinz Linge, Hitler's valet, had quickly fetched. The corpses were then lifted from the sofa and carried through the bunker, up twenty-five feet or so of stairs, and into the garden of the Reich Chancellery. Linge, helped by three SS guards, brought out the remains of Hitler, head covered by the blanket, his lower legs protruding. Martin Bormann carried out Eva Braun's body into the corridor, where Erich Kempka, Hitler's chauffeur, relieved him of his burden. Otto Günsche, Hitler's personal adjutant, and commissioned with overseeing the burning of the bodies, then took over on the stairs and carried Eva Braun up into the garden. He laid the bodies side by side, Eva Braun to Hitler's right, on a piece of flat, open, sandy ground only about three metres from the door down to the bunker. It was impossible to look around for any more suitable spot. Even this location, close to the bunker door, was extremely hazardous, since an unceasing rain of shells from the Soviet barrage continued to bombard the whole area, including the garden itself. General Hans Krebs, Hitler's last Chief of the General Staff, Wilhelm Burgdorf, his Wehrmacht adjutant, Joseph Goebbels, newly-appointed Chancellor of what was left of the Reich, and Martin Bormann, now designated Party Minister, had followed the small cortège and joined the extraordinary funeral party witnessing the macabre scene.

A good store of petrol had been gathered in the bunker in readiness. Kempka had himself provided, at Günsche's request, as much as 200 litres. More was stored in the bunker's machine-room. The petrol was now swiftly poured over the bodies. Nonetheless, as the hail of shells continued, setting the funeral pyre alight with the matches Goebbels supplied proved difficult. Günsche was about to try with a grenade, when Linge managed to find some paper to make a torch. Bormann was finally able to get it burning, and either he or Linge hurled it on to the pyre, immediately retreating to the safety of the doorway. Someone rapidly closed the bunker door, leaving open only a small crevice, through which a ball of fire was seen to erupt around the petrol-soaked bodies. Arms briefly raised in a final 'Heil Hitler' salute, the tiny funeral party hurriedly departed underground, away from the danger of the exploding shells. As the flames consumed the bodies in a suitably infernal setting, the end of the leader whose presence had a mere few years earlier electrified millions was witnessed by not a single one even of his closest followers.[1]

Neither Linge nor Günsche, the two men entrusted by Hitler with the disposal of the bodies, returned to ensure that the task was complete. One of the guards in the Chancellery garden, Hermann Karnau, later testified (though, like a number of the witnesses in the bunker, he gave contradictory versions at different times) that, when he revisited the cremation site, the bodies had been reduced to little more than ashes, which collapsed when he touched them with his foot.[2] Another guard, Erich Mansfeld, recalled that he had viewed the scene together with Karnau around 6p.m. Karnau had shouted to him that it was all over. When they went across together, they found two charcoaled, shrivelled, unrecognizable bodies ('*zwei verkohlte, zusammengeschrumpfte Leichen, die nicht mehr zu identifizieren waren*').[3] Günsche himself told of commissioning, around half an hour after returning from the cremation, two SS men from Hitler's bodyguard, Hauptsturm-führer Ewald Lindloff and Obersturmführer Hans Reisser, with ensuring that the remains of the bodies were buried. Lindloff later reported that he had carried out the order. The bodies, he said, had been already thoroughly burnt ('*schon verkohlt*') and were in a 'shocking state (*scheußlichem Zustand*)', torn open – Günsche presumed – in the heavy bombardment of the garden. Reisser's involvement was not needed. Günsche told him, an hour and a half after giving him the order, that Lindloff had already carried it out. It was by this time no later than 6.30p.m. on 30 April.[4]

There had been little left of Hitler and Eva Braun for Lindloff to dispose of. Their few mortal remains joined those of numerous other unidentifiable bodies (or parts of them), some from the hospital below the New Reich Chancellery, which had rapidly been thrown into bomb-craters in the vicinity of the bunker exit during the previous days. The intense bombardment which continued for a further twenty-four hours or so played its own part in destroying and scattering the human remains strewn around the Chancellery garden.[5]

When the Soviet victors arrived there on 2 May they immediately began a vigorous search for the bodies of Hitler and Eva Braun. Nine days later, they showed the dental technician Fritz Echtmann, who had worked for Hitler's dentist, Dr Johann Hugo Blaschke, since 1938, a cigar-box containing part of a jaw-bone and two dental bridges. He was able to identify from his records one of the bridges as that of Hitler, the other as Eva Braun's. The lower jaw-bone, too, was Hitler's. It was almost certainly all that they were able to identify of the former Dictator of Germany. The earthly remains of Adolf Hitler, it appears, were contained in a cigar-box.

I

The bunker inmates were now finally free to think of their own survival. Even while the bodies still burned in the Chancellery garden above, they had forgotten their views of self-immolation alongside their leader and were agreeing to do what he had always and explicitly ruled out: seek a last-minute arrangement with the Soviet Union. An emissary was sent out under a white flag to try to engineer a meeting of General Krebs (who, as a former military attaché in Moscow, had the advantage of speaking fluent Russian) with Marshal Zhukov. At 10p.m. that evening, Krebs went over the Soviet lines bearing a letter from Goebbels and Bormann.

It was an anxious night for those incarcerated in the bunker. And when Krebs returned around 6a.m. next morning it was only to report that the Soviet side insisted upon unconditional surrender and demanded a declaration to that effect by 4p.m. that afternoon, 1 May.[6]

This was the end. It was time for final preparations – on the sole remaining principle of save what can be saved. At 10.53a.m., a telegram for Dönitz arrived in Plön: 'Testament in force. I'll come to you as quickly as possible. Until then, in my view, hold back from publication. Bormann.'[7] Earlier that morning, more than nine hours after the grotesque scene in the Chancellery garden, the Grand Admiral, still believing Hitler was alive, had telegraphed an expression of his continued unconditional loyalty to the bunker.[8] Only now did he realize that Hitler was dead. This was confirmed in a further telegram – the last to leave the bunker – dictated by Goebbels and arriving at Plön at 3.18p.m. that afternoon.[9] Neither the Wehrmacht nor the German people were as yet aware of Hitler's death. When they were finally told, seven hours later, in a broadcast at 10.26p.m. that night, it was, typically, with a double distortion of the truth: that Hitler had died that afternoon – it was the previous day – and that his death had taken place in combat 'at his post in the Reich Chancellery, while fighting to his last breath against Bolshevism'. In his proclamation to the Wehrmacht, Dönitz spoke of the Führer's 'heroic death'. The Wehrmacht's report stated that he had fallen 'at the head of the heroic defenders of the Reich capital'.[10] The delay in informing Dönitz had plainly been to allow Bormann and Goebbels the final opportunity of a negotiated surrender to the Red Army without consulting the new head of state. The untruth relayed by Dönitz to the Wehrmacht and German people was to prevent a predictable response by the troops, had they been aware of Hitler's suicide, that the Führer had deserted them at the last.[11] This was, in fact, precisely the message which General Helmuth Weidling, the German commander in Berlin, conveyed to his troops when ordering them, in the early hours of 2 May, to cease fighting. 'On 30.4.45 the Führer took his own life and thereby abandoned those who had sworn him loyalty,' ran the order. 'At the Führer's command you believe that you must still fight for Berlin, although the lack of heavy weaponry and munitions, and the overall situation shows the struggle to be pointless . . . In agreement with the High Command of the Soviet troops, I therefore demand you end the fighting immediately.'[12]

By then, the drama in the bunker was finally over. Most of those still entombed below the Reich Chancellery had spent the afternoon and evening of 1 May planning their break-out. Goebbels was not among them. Along with his wife, Magda, he was now making arrangements for their own suicides – and for taking the lives of their six children. In the early evening, Magda summoned Helmut Gustav Kunz, adjutant to the head doctor in the SS medical administration (*Sanitätsverwaltung*) in the Reich Chancellery, and asked him to give each of the children – Helga, Hilde, Hellmut, Holde, Hedda, and Heide, aged between twelve and four – a shot of morphine. It was about 8.40p.m. when Kunz carried out the request. Once they had fallen into a drugged sleep, Dr Ludwig Stumpfegger, Hitler's own physician at the end, crushed a phial of prussic acid in the mouth of each of the children.

Later that evening, as Wilhelm Mohnke, commandant of the 'Citadel', gave orders for the mass break-out from the bunker, Goebbels instructed his adjutant, Günther Schwägermann, to take care of the burning of his and Magda's bodies. He gave him the silver-framed signed photograph of Hitler that for so many years had stood on his desk as a memento. Then he and his wife, after saying their brief farewells, climbed the stairs to the Chancellery garden, and bit on the prussic acid capsules. An SS orderly fired two shots into the bodies to make sure.[13] Far less petrol was available for the unceremonious cremation than had been saved for burning the bodies of Hitler and Eva Braun. Soviet troops had little difficulty in identifying the corpses when they entered the Chancellery garden next day.[14]

Krebs, Burgdorf, and Franz Schädle, head of Hitler's escort (*Begleitkommando*), also chose to end their lives in the bunker before the Russians arrived. The rest of the company sought their luck late that evening in the mass escape, undertaken in groups. The underground railway tunnel brought them to Friedrichstraße station, a few hundred yards to the north of the ruined Reich Chancellery. But once on the surface, in the burning hell of Berlin, with shells falling all around, confusion took over. The groups found themselves split up in the chaos. Individuals took what chances they could. A few, including the secretaries Gerda Christian, Traudl Junge, and Else Krüger, managed, remarkably, to make their way through to the west. Most, among them Otto Günsche and Heinz Linge, fell into Soviet hands and years of misery and maltreatment in Moscow prisons. Most of the others were killed seeking a route to safety, or took the last decision left to them. Prominent among the latter were Hitler's constant right hand during the war years, Martin Bormann, and his doctor, Ludwig Stumpfegger. Both had given up their hopes of escape and, rather than fall into Soviet hands, had swallowed poison in the early hours of 2 May 1945 in Berlin's Invalidenstraße.[15]

II

Outside Berlin, the winding-up orders on the Third Reich were meanwhile in the process of being served. However, they were carried out by the new Dönitz regime – based in Flensburg in the north of Schleswig-Holstein – with great reluctance, and only under the evident compulsion of the hopeless military situation. At the end of the First World War, disastrous though the defeat had been, it had proved possible to save the existence of the Reich and the German army. The basis for the hopes of national rebirth had been laid. Dönitz held to the illusion that this much might be achieved a second time.[16] Even at this late hour, he was hoping through the offer of partial capitulation to the west to avoid total and unconditional surrender on all fronts, at the same time sustaining, with western backing, the German Reich to form, alongside the western powers, a common front against Bolshevism. For this, he needed to gain time – also to allow withdrawal to the west of as many as possible of the Wehrmacht troops still engaged in bitter fighting against the Red Army. He was ready to sanction, therefore, the German capitulation in northern Italy on 2 May, which had already been agreed between Himmler's former right-hand man Karl Wolff and OSS chief Allen Dulles on the day before Hitler's suicide. He also reluctantly conceded on 4 May a further partial capitulation involving German troops in north-west Germany, Holland, and Denmark. In the south, where the Americans reached Munich on the day of Hitler's death, Innsbruck on 3 May, and Linz – Hitler's home town – four days later, Kesselring negotiated the surrender of the German divisions in the northern Alps on the 5th and in Austria on 7 May.[17] Dönitz did not, however, include in the partial capitulation the German troops further east, still fighting in Yugoslavia.[18]

The Grand Admiral's hopes of rescuing the remnants of Hitler's Reich were visible in his choice of cabinet. Though he rejected Himmler's overtures for inclusion, and turned his back, too, on Ribbentrop, he retained several members of Hitler's cabinet, among them Albert Speer, while foreign affairs and the direction of the cabinet were placed in the hands of the long-standing finance minister Schwerin von Krosigk, who, it was presumed, would appear unsullied by the worst crimes of Nazism. He made no changes in the High Command of the Wehrmacht. Hitler's mainstays, Keitel and Jodl, were left in post. The Nazi Party was neither banned nor dissolved. Pictures of Hitler still adorned the walls of government offices in Flensburg. One of the few concessions that Dönitz made was the reintroduction of the military salute in the Wehrmacht to replace the 'Heil Hitler' greeting. But military courts continued to hand out death-sentences even as the last rites on the Third Reich were being pronounced.[19]

The tactics employed by Dönitz were at least successful in enabling an estimated 1.8 million German soldiers to avoid Soviet captivity by surrendering to the western Allies – though at a high cost of continuing bloodshed and suffering before the fighting could be finally terminated. While the eastern front had since 1941 been the main theatre of war, under a third of the 10 million or so German prisoners-of-war fell into Soviet hands.[20] But Dönitz's intentions of a one-sided, partial capitulation to win the West at this late stage to the defence against Bolshevism cut little ice with Allied leaders. When his envoy (and successor as Commander-in-Chief of the Navy) Admiral Hans-Georg von Friedeburg journeyed with a delegation to Rheims, Eisenhower's headquarters, hoping to seal an agreement with the western Allies amounting to a capitulation to the west, but not to the Soviet Union, Eisenhower was having none of it. He insisted on a full and unconditional surrender on all fronts. Accordingly, on 6 May, Dönitz sent Jodl to Rheims on seemingly the same mission – to persuade the West to accept German surrender, but to avoid total capitulation – though this time with powers to agree to a complete capitulation (following final authorization from Flensburg) and instructions to gain maximum time – at least four days – in order to bring back the largest German fighting unit still in combat, Army Group Centre, across American lines. Eisenhower remained unmoved. He insisted on the capitulation being signed that very day, 6 May, with effect from midnight on 9 May, and threatened a renewal of air-raids if the agreement were not forthcoming. Jodl was given half an hour to think it over. After difficulties in communication with Flensburg, Dönitz, faced with no alternative, eventually conceded his authorization in the early hours. At 2.41a.m. on 7 May, in the presence of representatives of all four of the Allied powers, the capitulation was signed, stipulating a complete ending of all German military engagements by the end of the following day.[21]

The document to which the signatures were appended was, however, a shortened version of the original text of surrender, agreed by all the Allies. It was, in fact, regarded by the OKW leadership as 'not final', and to be replaced by 'a general capitulation treaty' still to be signed. Meanwhile, the order had gone out to bring back as many troops and as speedily as possible to the west for surrender to the British and Americans.[22] At Stalin's insistence, Allied representatives assembled once more, on 9 May, just after midnight, this time at Karlshorst on the outskirts of Berlin, headquarters of Marshal Zhukov, to sign the full document of capitulation. Since the terms agreed at Rheims had already come into effect a few minutes earlier, the document was dated 8 May.[23] Keitel, Friedeburg, and Colonel-General Hans-Jürgen Stumpff (representing the Commander-in-Chief of the Luftwaffe, Ritter von Greim) signed from the German side. Zhukov, the British Air-Marshal Arthur W. Tedder (representing Eisenhower), the French General Jean de Lattre de Tassigny, and the US General Carl Spaatz signed for the Allies.[24]

The last Wehrmacht report, on 9 May 1945, retained a tone of pride, speaking of 'the unique achievement of front and homeland' which would 'in a later, just verdict of history find its final appreciation'. These words, hollow for millions, followed the declaration: 'On command of the Grand Admiral the Wehrmacht has stopped the fight which had become hopeless. The struggle lasting almost six years is accordingly at an end.'[25]

Hitler's war was over. The reckoning was about to begin.

III

Many of those bearing heaviest responsibility, after Hitler, for the terrible suffering of the previous years and the deep pall of sorrow left behind escaped full retribution. Suicide, Hitler had always said, was easy. Some of his leading henchmen now followed his example. Heinrich Himmler, the embodiment of police terror, captured by the British under false identity and wearing the uniform of a Wehrmacht sergeant, crunched a phial of potassium cyanide in his prison cell at Lüneburg on 23 May as soon as his true identity had been established.[26] Robert Ley, the stridently antisemitic head of the German Labour Front, captured by American troops in the mountains of the Tyrol, strangled himself in the lavatory of his prison cell at Nuremberg on 24 October while awaiting trial.[27] Arrested by US forces near Berchtesgaden on 9 May 1945, Hermann Göring, for so long Hitler's designated successor until his abrupt dismissal in the last days of the Third Reich, also committed suicide – cheating the hangman awaiting his presence next day on the late evening of 15 October 1946 after being convicted on all charges, including crimes against humanity, at the International Military Tribunal in Nuremberg.[28]

Others among the regime's leaders, unwilling or unable to end their own lives, suffered the fate imposed upon them by the Tribunal and were hanged at Nuremberg. Convicted for crimes against humanity – in all but one case war crimes, and in some instances conspiracy to commit or actual commission of crimes against peace – the warmongering former Foreign Minister Joachim von Ribbentrop; chief of the High Command of the Wehrmacht Wilhelm Keitel; head of the Operations Department of the Wehrmacht and Hitler's chief military adviser Alfred Jodl; Nazi ideological guru and Reich Minister for the Occupied Eastern Territories Alfred Rosenberg; Reich Minister of the Interior (until his removal from office in 1943) Wilhelm Frick; Hitler's key man in Vienna at the time of the Anschluß and later Reich Commissar in the Netherlands Arthur Seyß-Inquart; Labour Plenipotentiary who presided over the slave-labour programme Fritz Sauckel; Heydrich's fearsome successor as head of the RSHA Ernst Kaltenbrunner; Governor-General of Poland and leading Nazi lawyer Hans Frank; and the former Gauleiter of Franconia, leading Jew-baiter Julius Streicher were executed on 16 October 1946.[29] Few mourned them.

Albert Speer, the Armaments Minister whose hands were barely less dirty than Sauckel's in the exploitation of forced labour, was one of those fortunate to escape the hangman's noose. Like the last head of state Admiral Dönitz, Economics Minister Walther Funk, Foreign Minister (until his replacement by Ribbentrop in 1938) Konstantin von Neurath, head of the navy Erich Raeder, long-time Hitler Youth leader and Gauleiter of Vienna Baldur von Schirach, and (until his flight to Scotland in 1941) deputy head of the Nazi Party Rudolf Heß, Speer was given a long prison sentence. Funk, Neurath, and Raeder were released early on health grounds. Dönitz, Speer, and Schirach left prison each after serving the full sentence – in Speer's case to become a celebrity, best-selling author, and pundit on the Third Reich with a belated guilt complex as his trademark. Heß was to commit suicide in 1987, still serving a life-sentence in Spandau prison in Berlin.[30]

Among second-ranking Nazis implicated in the regime's most heinous crimes, the most notorious, the manager of the 'Final Solution' Adolf Eichmann, was to be dramatically abducted from Argentina by Israeli agents, tried in Jerusalem, and hanged in 1962. The commandant of Auschwitz Rudolf Höß, the butcher of the Warsaw ghetto Jürgen Stroop, the terror of the Poles in the Warthegau Gauleiter Arthur Greiser, and his scarcely less fanatical counterpart in Danzig-West Prussia Albert Forster were all hanged at earlier dates after trials in Poland. The Poles proved more humanitarian than their previous tormentors in commuting, on account of his poor health, the death-sentence on the notably (even by Nazi standards) cruel and brutal former Gauleiter of East Prussia Erich Koch to a term of life-imprisonment.[31]

Many implicated in crimes against humanity escaped lightly. Hinrich Lohse, former Reich Commissar in the Baltic, was released in 1951 on grounds of ill-health after serving only three years of a ten-year sentence. He died peacefully in his home town in 1964.[32] Wilhelm Koppe, SS leader in the Warthegau and alongside Greiser the instigator of Chelmno extermination camp, where over 150,000 Jews lost their lives, was able to prosper under a pseudonym as the director of a chocolate factory in Bonn until the 1960s. When discovered and arraigned for his part in mass murder in Poland he was deemed unfit to stand trial, eventually dying in his bed in 1975.[33] Countless others, who in 'working towards the Führer' had exercised positions of great power, often determining life or death (including doctors implicated in the 'euthanasia action') and lining their own pockets at the same time through boundless corruption and ruthless careerism, were able wholly or in part to avoid serious retribution for their actions – in some cases building successful post-war careers for themselves.[34]

Few of those forced to account for their actions under Hitler showed remorse or contrition, let alone guilt. With scant exception, they showed themselves, when called to book, incapable of acknowledging their own contribution to the remorseless slide into barbarism during the Nazi era. Alongside the inevitable lies, distortions, and excuses often went, it seems, a psychological block on recognizing responsibility for their actions. It amounted to a self-deception that mirrored the total collapse of their value-system and the demolition of the idealized image of Hitler to which they had clung for so many years – which, indeed, had usually underpinned or at least given justification for their motivation. They had been content for years to see their power, careers, ambitions, aspirations depend solely on Hitler. Now, it was in a perverse sense logical that their own plight would be attributed solely to what they saw as Hitler's lunacy and criminality. From being the revered leader whose utopian vision they had eagerly followed, Hitler was now the scapegoat who had betrayed their trust and seduced them through the brilliance of his rhetoric into becoming helpless accomplices to his barbaric plans.

Such a psychology applied not merely to many of those most heavily incriminated in the Nazi experiment to determine who should inhabit this planet. Countless ordinary Germans were now prepared to find an explanation for or defence of their own actions (or lack of action) in the alleged seductive powers of Hitler – a leader promising salvation but in the end delivering damnation. Alternatively, they looked to a level of totalitarian terror that had left them with no alternative but to follow orders of which they disapproved. Both reponses were wide of the mark.

Hitler's regime, as we have had ample cause to acknowledge, was – certainly for most of its twelve-year duration – no narrowly based tyranny imposing its will upon the hostile masses of the population. And, until the 'running amok'[35] of the last phase of the war, the terror – at least within Germany – had been specifically targeted at defined racial and political enemies, not random and arbitrary, while the level of at least partial consensus in all reaches of society had been extensive. Generalizations about the mentalities and behaviour of millions of Germans in the Nazi era are bound to be of limited application – apart, perhaps, from the generalization that, for the great mass of the population, the figurative colours to look for are less likely to be stark black and white than varying and chequered shades of grey. Even so, it remains the case that, collectively, the inhabitants of a highly modern, sophisticated, pluralistic society which, following a lost war, was experiencing deep-seated national humiliation, economic bankruptcy, acute social, political, and ideological polarization, and a generally perceived – both by those with power and by the overwhelming mass of the population – complete failure of a discredited political system, had been prepared in increasing numbers to place their trust in the chiliastic vision of a self-professed political saviour. Once, as can now more easily be seen, a series of relatively cheap and easy (though in reality exceedingly dangerous) national triumphs had been achieved, still further vast numbers were prepared to swallow their doubts and to believe in the destiny of their great leader. Moreover, these triumphs, however much they were portrayed by propaganda as attributable to the achievements of one man, had been brought about not only with huge mass acclaim, but also with a very high level of support from almost all of the non-Nazi élite-groups – business, industry, civil service, above all the armed forces – which controlled practically all the avenues of power outside the upper echelons of the Nazi Movement itself. Though the consensus was in many respects a shallow one, resting upon differing degrees of backing for the various strands of the overall ideological vision which Hitler embodied, it offered nevertheless until the middle of the war an extremely wide and potent platform of support for Hitler to build upon and exploit.

The rise from the depths of national degradation to the heights of national greatness seemed for so many (as propaganda never ceased to trumpet) to be a near-miracle – a work of redemption brought about by the unique genius of the Führer. Hitler's power was able thereby to draw on strong elements of pseudo-religious belief translated into the mysticism of national salvation and rebirth – emanating in part no doubt from declining institutional religion and from the psychologically needed substitution in some quarters for the quasi-religious associations with the monarchy – which also compensated in some ways for the many negative aspects of everyday life under Nazi rule. Even to the very end there were intelligent individuals prepared to exempt Hitler from knowledge of the atrocities committed in Poland and Russia – and to attach blame instead to Himmler.[36] The Führer cult, accepted not only by millions of believers but pandered to in their own interests by all in positions of authority and influence, even if they were often inwardly critical or sceptical, enabled Hitler's power to shake off all constraints and become absolute. By the time realization dawned that the road to riches was proving the road to ruin, the personalized rule of the leader was out of control. Hitler was by now – though this had not always been so – incapable of being checked by the splintered parts of an increasingly fragmented regime bound together largely by the commitment to the ruler himself and, increasingly, fear of the alternative: Bolshevism. The road to perdition lay open, but – other than the courageous attempts by small groups or individuals which ultimately failed through bad luck even more than through bad planning – there was by now little alternative but to follow this road.

The price to be paid – by the German people, above all by the regime's untold numbers of victims inside and outside Germany – was beyond calculation. The material price was immense. Writing to *The Times* on 12 November 1945, the left-wing British Jewish publisher Victor Gollancz described his impressions in Düsseldorf: 'I am never likely to forget the unspeakable wickedness of which the Nazis were guilty. But when I see the swollen bodies and living skeletons in hospitals here and elsewhere . . . then I think, not of Germans, but of men and women. I am sure I should have the same feelings if I were in Greece or Poland. But I happen to be in Germany, and write of what I see here.'[37] The moral price was, if anything, even more immeasurable. Decades would not fully erase the simple but compelling sentiment painted in huge letters at the scene of Hitler's annual celebration of the 1923 Putsch, the Feldherrnhalle in Munich, in May 1945: 'I am ashamed to be a German.'[38] 'Europe has never known such a calamity to her civilization and nobody can say when she will begin to recover from its effects,' was the telling and at the same time prophetic comment of one

British newspaper only three days after the suicide in the bunker.[39] The trauma which was Hitler's lasting legacy was only just beginning.

Never in history has such ruination – physical and moral – been associated with the name of one man. That the ruination had far deeper roots and far more profound causes than the aims and actions of this one man has been evident in the preceding chapters. That the previously unprobed depths of inhumanity plumbed by the Nazi regime could draw upon wide-ranging complicity at all levels of society has been equally apparent. But Hitler's name justifiably stands for all time as that of the chief instigator of the most profound collapse of civilization in modern times. The extreme form of personal rule which an ill-educated beerhall demagogue and racist bigot, a narcissistic, megalomaniac, self-styled national saviour was allowed to acquire and exercise in a modern, economically advanced, and cultured land known for its philosophers and poets, was absolutely decisive in the terrible unfolding of events in those fateful twelve years.

Hitler was the main author of a war leaving over 50 million dead and millions more grieving their lost ones and trying to put their shattered lives together again. Hitler was the chief inspiration of a genocide the like of which the world had never known, rightly to be viewed in coming times as a defining episode of the twentieth century. The Reich whose glory he had sought lay at the end wrecked, its remnants to be divided among the victorious and occupying powers. The arch-enemy, Bolshevism, stood in the Reich capital itself and presided over half of Europe. Even the German people, whose survival he had said was the very reason for his political fight, had proved ultimately dispensable to him.

In the event, the German people he was prepared to see damned alongside him proved capable of surviving even a Hitler. Beyond the repairing of broken lives and broken homes in broken towns and cities, the searing moral imprint of Hitler's era would remain. Gradually, nevertheless, a new society, resting in time, mercifully, on new values, would emerge from the ruins of the old. For in its maelstrom of destruction Hitler's rule had also conclusively demonstrated the utter bankruptcy of the hyper-nationalistic and racist world-power ambitions (and the social and political structures that upheld them) that had prevailed in Germany over the previous half a century and twice taken Europe and the wider world into calamitous war.

The old Germany was gone with Hitler. The Germany which had produced Adolf Hitler, had seen its future in his vision, had so readily served him, and had shared in his hubris, had also to share his nemesis.

GLOSSARY OF TERMS AND ABBREVIATIONS

ADAP	*Akten zur Deutschen Auswärtigen Politik 1918–1945. (Serie D: 1.9.37–11.12.41; Serie E: 1941–1945)*
Anatomie	Hans Buchheim, Martin Broszat, Hans-Adolf Jacobsen, and Helmut Krausnick, *Anatomie des SS-Staates*, 2 vols., Olten and Freiburg im Breisgau, 1965
AO	Auslandsorganisation (Foreign Organisation of the Nazi Party)
APZ	*Aus Politik und Zeitgeschichte* (Beilage zur Wochenzeitung 'Das Parlament')
BA	Bundesarchiv (German Federal Archives, Berlin)
BA/MA	Bundesarchiv/Militararchiv (German Federal Archives/Military Archives, Potsdam)
BDC	Berlin Document Center
BHStA	Bayerisches Hauptstaatsarchiv (Bavarian Main State Archive)
CD	*Ciano's Diary 1939–1943*, ed. Malcolm Muggeridge, London/Toronto, 1947
CP	*Ciano's Diplomatic Papers*, ed. Malcolm Muggeridge, London, 1948
DAF	Deutsche Arbeitsfront (German Labour Front)
DBFP	*Documents on British Foreign Policy, 1919–1939, 2nd Series, 1929–1938, 3rd Series, 1938–1939*, London, 1947–61
DBS	*Deutschland-Berichte der Sozialdemokratischen Partei Deutschlands, 1934–1940*, 7 vols, Frankfurt am Main, 1980
DGFP	*Documents on German Foreign Policy, 1918–1945, Series C (1933–1937), The Third Reich: First Phase; Series D (1937–1945)*, London, 1957–66
Domarus	Max Domarus (ed.), *Hitler. Reden und Proklamationen 1932–1945*, 2 vols., in 4 parts, Wiesbaden, 1973
DRZW	*Das Deutsche Reich und der Zweite Weltkrieg*, 6 vols. so far published, ed. Militargeschichtliches Forschungsamt, Stuttgart, 1979–
DTB Frank	*Das Diensttagebuch des deutschen Generalgouverneurs in Polen 1939–1945*, ed. Werner Präg and Wolfgang Jacobmeyer, Stuttgart, 1975
DZW	*Deutschland im zweiten Weltkrieg*, 6 vols., ed. Autorenkollektiv, East Berlin, 1974–85

FHQ	Führerhauptquartier (Führer Headquarters)
Gestapo	Geheime Staatspolizei (Secret State Police)
GG	*Geschichte und Gesellschaft*
GS	Gendarmerie-Station (police station)
GStA	Geheimes Staatsarchiv (Bayerisches Hauptstaatsarchiv, Abt.II, Munich)
Halder Diary	*The Halder War Diary 1939-1942*, ed. Charles Burdick and Hans-Adolf Jacobsen, London, 1988
Halder KTB	*Generaloberst Halder: Kriegstagebuch*, ed. Hans-Adolf Jacobsen, 3 vols., Stuttgart, 1962-4
HJ	Hitlerjugend (Hitler Youth)
HZ	*Historische Zeitschrift*
IfZ	Institut für Zeitgeschichte, München (Institute of Contemporary History, Munich)
IMG	*Der Prozeß gegen die Hauptkriegsverbrecher vor dem Internationalen Militärgerichtshof, Nürnberg, 14.November 1945-1. Oktober 1946*, 42 vols., Nuremberg, 1947-9 (= IMT: *Trial of the Major War Criminals before the International Military Tribunal, Nuremberg*)
IML/ZPA	Institut für Marxismus-Leninismus, Zentrales Parteiarchiv (East Berlin, GDR)
Irving, *HW*	David Irving, *Hitler's War*, London, 1977
IWM	Imperial War Museum
JCH	*Journal of Contemporary History*
JK	Eberhard Jäckel and Axel Kuhn (eds.), *Hitler. Sämtliche Aufzeichnungen 1905-1924*, Stuttgart, 1980
JMH	*Journal of Modern History*
Keitel	*Generalfeldmarschall Keitel. Verbrecher oder Offizier? Erinnerung, Briefe, Dokumente des Chefs OKW*, ed. Walter Görlitz, Göttingen/Berlin/Frankfurt, 1961
Koeppen	Aufzeichnungen des persönlichen Referenten Rosenbergs Dr. Koeppen über Hitlers Tischgespräche 1941, Bundesarchiv R6/34a, Fols.1-82 (Notes of Dr Werner Koeppen, liaison of Alfred Rosenberg at FHQ, on Hitler's 'table talk', 1941)
KPD	Kommunistische Partei Deutschlands (Communist Party of Germany)
KTB OKW	*Kriegstagebuch des Oberkommandos der Wehrmacht (Wehrmachtsführungsstab)*, ed. Percy Ernst Schramm, 4 vols. (in six parts), Frankfurt am Main, 1961-5
LB Darmstadt	*Lagebesprechungen im Führerhauptquartier. Protokollfragmente aus Hitlers militärischen Konferenzen 1942-1945*, ed. Helmut Heiber, abridged edn, Berlin/Darmstadt/Vienna, 1962
LB Stuttgart	*Hitlers Lagebesprechungen – Die Protokollfragmente seiner militärischen Konferenzen 1942-1945*, ed. Helmut Heiber (unabridged text), Stuttgart, 1962
LBYB	*Leo Baeck Institute Yearbook*
LR	Landrat (head of district state administration)

MadR	*Meldungen aus dem Reich. Die geheimen Lageberichte des Sicherheitsdienstes der SS 1938–1945*, ed. Heinz Boberach, 17 vols., Herrsching, 1984
MK	Adolf Hitler, *Mein Kampf*, 876–880th reprint, Munich, 1943
MK Watt	Adolf Hitler, *Mein Kampf*, London, 1969, trans. by Ralph Manheim, with an introduction by D. C. Watt, paperback edition, London, 1973
Monologe	*Adolf Hitler: Monologe im Führerhauptquartier 1941–1944. Die Aufzeichnungen Heinrich Heims*, ed. Werner Jochmann, Hamburg, 1980
NA	National Archives, Washington
Nbg-Dok.	Nürnberg-Dokumente (Documents in evidence at the Nuremberg Trials)
NCA	*Nazi Conspiracy and Aggression*, ed. Office of the United States Chief of Counsel for Prosecution of Axis Criminality, 9 vols. and 2 supplementary vols., Washington DC, 1946–8
N & P	Jeremy Noakes and Geoffrey Pridham (eds.), *Nazism, 1919–1945. A Documentary Reader*, 4 vols., Exeter, 1983–98
NSDAP	Nationalsozialistische Deutsche Arbeiterpartei (Nazi Party)
NSKK	Nationalsozialistisches Kraftfahrerkorps (Nazi Drivers' Corps)
NSV	Nationalsozialistische Volkswohlfahrt (Nazi Welfare Organisation)
OKH	Oberkommando des Heeres (High Command of the Army)
OKW	Oberkommando der Wehrmacht (High Command of the Wehrmacht (armed services))
OSS	Office of Strategic Services (US intelligence organization)
OT	Organisation Todt
PRO	Public Record Office (London, and Belfast)
RAF	Royal Air Force
RGBl	*Reichsgesetzblatt*
RP	Regierungspräsident (Government President, head of regional state administration)
RSA	*Hitler. Reden, Schriften, Anordnungen: Februar 1925 bis Januar 1933*, ed. Institut für Zeitgeschichte, 5 vols. in 12 parts, Munich/London/New York/Paris, 1992–8
RSHA	Reichssicherheitshauptamt (Reich Security Head Office)
SA	Sturmabteilung (Storm Troop)
SD	Sicherheitsdienst (Security Service)
Sopade	Sozialdemokratische Partei Deutschlands (exiled SPD executive based in Prague (1933–8), then Paris (1938–40), and from 1940 onwards in London)
SPD	Sozialdemokratische Partei Deutschlands (Social Democratic Party of Germany)
SS	Schutzstaffeln (Protection Squads)
StA	Staatsarchiv
Staatsmänner I	*Staatsmänner und Diplomaten bei Hitler. Vertrauliche Aufzeichnungen 1939–1941*, ed. Andreas Hillgruber, Munich, 1969
Staatsmänner II	*Staatsmänner und Diplomaten bei Hitler. Vertrauliche Aufzeichnungen 1942–1944*, ed. Andreas Hillgruber, Frankfurt am Main, 1970
StdF	Stellvertreter des Führers (Führer's Deputy)

TBJG   *Die Tagebücher von Joseph Goebbels. Teil I, Aufzeichnungen 1923–1941*, 9 vols. (vols. 6–9 so far published), *Teil II, Diktate 1941–1945*, 15 vols., ed. Elke Fröhlich, Munich etc., 1993–8

Tb Irving   *Der unbekannte Dr Goebbels. Die geheimen Tagebücher 1938*, ed. David Irving, London, 1995

Tb Reuth   *Joseph Goebbels. Tagebücher 1924–1945*, 5 vols., ed. Ralf Georg Reuth, Munich/Zurich, 1992

Tb Spiegel   Extracts from Goebbels's diary published in *Der Spiegel*, 29/1992, 104–28, 30/1992, 100–109, 31/1992, 102–12, 32/1992, 58–75

TWC   *Trials of War Criminals before the Nuernberg Military Tribunals under Control Council Law No. 10*, 15 vols., Nuremberg, October 1946-April 1949

US   United States

VB   *Völkischer Beobachter* (main Nazi newspaper)

VfZ   *Vierteljahreshefte für Zeitgeschichte*

völkisch   racial-nationalist

Weinberg I   Gerhard L. Weinberg, *The Foreign Policy of Hitler's Germany. Diplomatic Revolution in Europe, 1933–36*. Chicago/London, 1970

Weinberg II   Gerhard L. Weinberg, *The Foreign Policy of Hitler's Germany. Starting World War II, 1937–1939*, Chicago/London, 1980

Weinberg III   Gerhard L. Weinberg, *A World at Arms. A Global History of World War II*, Cambridge, 1994

Weisungen   *Hitlers Weisungen für die Kriegführung 1939–1945. Dokumente des Oberkommandos der Wehrmacht*, ed. Walther Hubatsch, Munich, 1965

NOTES

INTRODUCTION: 1936: HITLER TRIUMPHANT

1. Max Domarus (ed.), *Hitler. Reden und Proklamationen 1932–1945*, Wiesbaden, 1973, 596–7.

2. See Hermann Weber, 'Die KPD in der Illegalität', in Richard Löwenthal and Patrik von zur Muhlen (eds.), *Widerstand und Verweigerung in Deutschland 1933 bis 1945*, Berlin/Bonn, 1984, 83–101, here 93.

3. Weber, 83.

4. It had, in effect, to be a 'resistance of servants of the state' ('*Widerstand der Staatsdiener*'). Hans Mommsen, 'Der Widerstand gegen Hitler und die deutsche Gesellschaft', in Jürgen Schmädeke and Peter Steinbach (eds.), *Der Widerstand gegen den Nationalsozialismus. Die deutsche Gesellschaft und der Widerstand gegen Hitler*, Munich, (1985), 1986, 9.

5. See Carl Dirks and Karl-Heinz Janßen, *Der Krieg der Generäle. Hitler als Werkzeug der Wehrmacht*, Berlin, 1999, ch.1.

6. *Akten der Reichskanzlei. Die Regierung Hitler. Teil I, 1933/34*, ed. Karl-Heinz Minuth, Boppard am Rhein, 1989, i.50; trans. *Documents on German Foreign Policy, 1918–1945, Series C (1933–1937). The Third Reich: First Phase*, London, 1957–66 (=*DGFP*), C, I, 37, No.16.

7. Hans Müller (ed.), *Katholische Kirche und Nationalsozialismus*, Munich, 1965, 88–9, Kundgebung der Fuldaer Bischofskonferenz vom 28.3.1933. And see Ernst-Wolfgang Böckenförde, 'Der deutsche Katholizismus in Jahre 1933. Eine kritische Betrachtung', *Hochland*, 53 (1960–61), 215–39; Ernst-Wolfgang Böckenförde, 'Der deutsche Katholizismus im Jahre 1933. Stellungnahme zu einer Diskussion', *Hochland*, 54 (1961–2), 217–45; and Hans Buchheim, 'Der deutsche Katholizismus im Jahr 1933', *Hochland*, 53 (1960–61), 497–515.

8. Guenter Lewy, *The Catholic Church and Nazi Germany*, London, 1964, 206.

9. *Deutschland-Berichte der Sozialdemokratischen Partei Deutschlands 1934–1940*, 7 vols., Frankfurt am Main, 1980 (=*DBS*), iii. 308, 2 April 1936, report for March 1936. See also Bernd Stöver, *Volksgemeinschaft im Dritten Reich. Die Konsensbereitschaft der Deutschen aus der Sicht sozialistischer Exilberichte*, Düsseldorf, 1993, 182–3, 303.

10. In 1933, the first 100,000 '*Volksempfänger*' were put on the market. By the end of 1939, three and a half million had been sold, and almost three-quarters of German households possessed a wireless set. (Z. A. B. Zeman, *Nazi Propaganda*, Oxford, (1964), 1973, 49.)

11. See Hermann Weiß, 'Ideologie der Freizeit im Dritten Reich. Die NS-Gemeinschaft "Kraft durch Freude"', *Archiv für Sozialgeschichte*, 33 (1993), 289–303.

12. Ulrich Herbert, 'Good Times, Bad Times: Memories of the Third Reich', in Richard Bessel (ed.), *Life in the Third Reich*, Oxford, 1987, 97–110.

13. *DBS*, iii.308, 2 April 1936, report for March 1936.

14. See, on this point, Martin Broszat, 'Soziale Motivation und Führer-Bindung des Nationalsozialismus', *Vierteljahreshefte für Zeitgeschichte (VfZ)*, 18 (1970), 392–409.

15. See Fritz Stern, *The Politics of Cultural Despair*, Berkeley/Los Angeles, 1961.

16. Oswald Spengler, *Der Untergang des Abendlandes*, 2 vols., Vienna/Munich, 1918–22 (English translation published in New York, 1926). And see Michael Biddis, 'History as Destiny: Gobineau, H. S. Chamberlain, and Spengler', *Transactions of the Royal Historical Society*, 6th Series, 7 (1997), 73–100, here especially 87–97.

17. See, for example, George L. Mosse, *The Crisis of German Ideology. Intellectual Origins of the Third Reich*, (1964), London, 1966, Part III; Detlev J. K. Peukert, *Die Weimarer Republik. Krisenjahre der Klassischen Moderne*, Frankfurt am Main, 1987, especially ch.9; and Michael H. Kater, *Different Drummers: Jazz in the Culture of Nazi Germany*, New York/Oxford, 1992.

18. See the strains of such a mentality in Kurt Sontheimer, *Antidemokratisches Denken in der Weimarer Republik*, 3rd edn, Munich, 1992; and the cultural framework for such thought in Peter Gay, *Weimar Culture. The Outsider as Insider*, (1968), London, 1988, ch.4.

19. For a reassessment of the scale of antisemitic violence during the Weimar Republic, see Dirk Walter, *Antisemitische Kriminalität und Gewalt. Judenfeindschaft in der Weimarer Republik*, Bonn, 1999. Donald L. Niewyk, *The Jews in Weimar Germany*, Baton Rouge, 1980, ch.III, emphasizes, rather, the exceptionality of violence, but the prevalence (if uneven in manifestation) of anti-Jewish prejudice. Sarah Gordon, *Hitler, Germans, and the 'Jewish Question'*, Princeton, 1984, ch.1–2, also plays down the extent of anti-Jewish violence and the role of antisemitism in the rise of Nazism. Daniel J. Goldhagen, *Hitler's Willing Executioners. Ordinary Germans and the Holocaust*, New York, 1997, ch.1–3, in a highly contentious interpretation, sees 'eliminatory' antisemitism as ubiquitous in Germany already in the nineteenth century and the Weimar Republic as a logical continuation and accentuation of pre-existing proto-genocidal traits widespread in German society.

20. For Hitler's first written statement on antisemitism, in September 1919, see Eberhard Jäckel and Axel Kuhn (eds.), *Hitler. Sämtliche Aufzeichnungen 1905–1924*, Stuttgart, 1980, 88–90.

21. See Woodruff D. Smith, *The Ideological Origins of Nazi Imperialism*, New York/Oxford, 1986.

22. See Dirks and Janßen, ch.1; and Karl-Heinz Janßen, 'Politische und militärische Zielvorstellungen der Wehrmachtführung', in Rolf-Dieter Müller and Hans-Erich Volkmann (eds.), *Die Wehrmacht: Mythos und Realität*, Munich, 1999, 75–84.

CHAPTER 1: CEASELESS RADICALIZATION

1. See Gerhard L. Weinberg, *The Foreign Policy of Hitler's Germany, vol.i, Diplomatic Revolution in Europe, 1933–36*, Chicago/London, 1970, (= Weinberg I), ch.11.

2. *DGFP*, C, V, 355–63, No.242; Paul Schmidt, *Statist auf diplomatischer Bühne 1923–45. Erlebnisse des Chefdolmetschers im Auswärtigen Amt mit den Staatsmännern Europas*, Bonn, 1953, 329–30, 332–4 (where Schmidt misdates the flight to London to present the plan to the end of April, not March); Domarus, 617–18.

3. Weinberg I, 254–7.

4. *DGFP*, C, V, 514, No.312; Schmidt, 334–5.

5. See Weinberg I, 272–3.

6. Thomas Jones, *A Diary with Letters, 1931–1950*, Oxford, 1954, 191 (30 April 1936).

7. Domarus, 621 and n.121.

8. Heinz Höhne, *Die Zeit der Illusionen. Hitler und die Anfänge des 3. Reiches 1933 bis 1936*,

Düsseldorf/Vienna/New York, 1991, 347; Richard D. Mandell, *The Nazi Olympics*, London, 1972, 93–4, 142–3.

9. Höhne, 345.

10. Albert Speer, *Erinnerungen*, Frankfurt am Main/Berlin, 1969, 94, where the architect's name is mistakenly given as Otto March (the father of Werner).

11. Arnd Krüger, *Die Olympischen Spiele 1936 und die Weltmeinung*, Berlin, 1972, 63; Mandell, 39, 125 (where it is pointed out that the stadium was only a twentieth of the enormous sporting complex, of a size equivalent to that of the city of Berlin itself in the late seventeenth century), 292.

12. Mandell, 141–50.

13. See Leni Riefenstahl, *A Memoir*, New York, 1993, 190–206. For a description of the film, *Olympiade*, see David Welch, *Propaganda and the German Cinema, 1933–1945*, Oxford, 1983, 112–21.

14. Mandell, 227–9; Riefenstahl, 193.

15. Baldur von Schirach, *Ich glaubte an Hitler*, Hamburg, 1967, 217–18.

16. *Chips. The Diaries of Sir Henry Channon*, ed. Robert Rhodes James, London, 1967, 110–11. See also Joachim von Ribbentrop, *The Ribbentrop Memoirs*, London, 1954, 63–4; William E. Dodd and Martha Dodd (eds.), *Ambassador Dodd's Diary, 1933–1938*, London, 1941, 346; Schmidt, 337–8; Mandell, 156–8.

17. Mandell, 206–7; Höhne, 352.

18. Höhne, 352. The racial, as well as nationalist, overtones had been obvious in German reactions to the unexpected victory of the heavyweight boxing hero Max Schmeling over the presumed invincible 'Black Bomber', Joe Louis, in New York on 18 June 1936. Goebbels, listening to the fight at 3.00a.m., noted in his diary: 'In the 12th round, Schmeling knocks out the negro. Wonderful. A dramatic, exciting fight. Schmeling has fought and won for Germany. The white man over the black man, and the white man was a German.' (*Die Tagebücher von Joseph Goebbels. Sämtliche Fragmente, Teil I, Aufzeichnungen 1924–1941*, 4 Bde., ed. Elke Fröhlich, Munich etc., 1987 (*TBJG*), vol.2, 630 (20 June 1936); and see Mandell, 117–21.

19. Kruger, 200.

20. Krüger, 201; Mandell, 138–9.

21. Krüger, 196.

22. Hohne, 351–2. The US Ambassador Dodd was not among them. He thought the propaganda had pleased the Germans, but had 'had a bad influence on foreigners'. (Dodd, 349. Most eyewitnesses appear to have had a far more favourable impression.)

23. William Shirer, *Berlin Diary, 1934–1941*, Sphere Books edn, London, 1970, 58 (16 August 1936).

24. Viktor Klemperer, *Ich will Zeugnis ablegen bis zum letzten. Tagebücher 1933–1941*, 2 vols., ed. Walter Nowojski and Hadwig Klemperer, Darmstadt, 1998, i.293 (13 August 1936).

25. Melita Maschmann, *Fazit. Mein Weg in die Hitler-Jugend*, 5th paperback edn, Munich, 1983, 30–31.

26. Dieter Petzina, *Autarkiepolitik im Dritten Reich. Der nationalsozialistische Vierjahresplan*, Stuttgart, 1968, 35.

27. Petzina, 37.

28. Hjalmar Schacht, *Abrechung mit Hitler*, Berlin/Frankfurt am Main, 1949, 61–2; and see Höhne, 375.

29. *Das Deutsche Reich und der Zweite Weltkrieg*, 6 vols. so far published, ed. Militärgeschichtliches Forschungsamt, Stuttgart, 1979 (=*DRZW*), i.431–3.

30. Niedersächsisches Staatsarchiv, Oldenburg, Best.131 Nr.303, Fol.131v.

31. See Höhne, 373.

32. Petzina, 46.

33. Stefan Martens, *Herman Göring. 'Erster Paladin des Führers' und 'Zweiter Mann im Reich'*, Paderborn, 1985, 68–9; Petzina, 35–40; Höhne, 377–8.

34. Petzina, 39.

35. *Der Prozeß gegen die Hauptkriegsverbrecher vor dem Internationalen Militärgerichtshof. Nürnberg, 14. November 1945–1 Oktober 1946*, 42 vols. (=IMG) ix.319; Arthur Schweitzer, *Big Business in the Third Reich*, Bloomington, 1964, 544; Petzina, 40; Martens, 69.

36. IMG, ix.319; Petzina, 35–40; Martens, 69; Alfred Kube, *Pour le mérite und Hakenkreuz. Hermann Göring im Dritten Reich*, Munich, 1986, 140–41.

37. Carl Vincent Krogmann, *Es ging um Deutschlands Zukunft 1932–1939*, Leoni am Starnberger See, 1976, 272.

38. *TBJG*, I/2, 607 (3 May 1936).

39. See *TBJG*, I/2, 701 (20 October 1936): '*Die Energie bringt er mit, ob auch die wirtschaftl. Kenntnis und Erfahrung? Wer weiß! Immerhin wird er viel Wind machen.*' After the war, Göring himself acknowledged that it had been his task, in confronting the raw-materials difficulties, to deploy his energy 'not as an expert, but as a driving-force (*Treiber*)' (*IMG*, ix.319).

40. Höhne, 379; Petzina, 44–5; Peter Hayes, *Industry and Ideology. IG Farben in the Nazi Era*, Cambridge, 1987, 150ff.; *DRZW*, i.278ff.

41. Höhne, 380; Berenice Carroll, *Design for Total War. Arms and Economics in the Third Reich*, The Hague/Paris, 1968, ch.7.

42. Cit. Kube, 152.

43. Kube, 152–3; Höhne, 380.

44. See Alfred Sohn-Rethel, *Ökonomie und Klassenstruktur des deutschen Faschismus*, Frankfurt am Main, 1973, 139–41, for Göring's reminders to Hitler in autumn 1935 about his coming war against the Soviet Union.

45. Marquess of Londonderry (Charles S. H. Vane-Tempest-Stewart), *Ourselves and Germany*, London, 1938, 94–103. Lord Londonderry's personal papers in the Public Record Office, Belfast, contain a description of his visit to Germany (D3099/2/19/8, 9A–9B), but deal only in the briefest terms with his interview with Hitler. The account which formed the basis for his printed comments appears to be missing from the file. In the audience he granted Londonderry, Hitler was, of course, trying to impress upon his guest the need for Britain to develop close links with Germany. (As the Londonderry papers show, the German leadership greatly overestimated his influence at the time within Britain.) But this does not meant that Hitler's feelings about Bolshevism were not genuine. In fact, Londonderry was little moved by them, pointing out that the Bolshevik danger was seen as far less important in Britain. He was more interested in the colonial question. On the Londonderry visit, see also Schmidt, 338–42.

46. *TBJG*, I/2.622 (9 June 1936).

47. *TBJG*, I/2.644 (17 July 1936).

48. Nicholas Mosley, *Beyond the Pale: Sir Oswald Mosley, 1933–1980*, London, 1983, 72. On the Mitford sisters, see Robert Skidelsky, *Oswald Mosley*, London, 1981, 340–41; and Richard Griffiths, *Fellow Travellers of the Right. British Enthusiasts for Nazi Germany, 1933–9*, London, 1980, 171ff.

49. *TBJG*, I/2, 646 (22 July 1936). Goebbels found the Mitfords 'boring as ever' (I/2, 646 (21 July 1936)).

50. See Paul Preston, *Franco. A Biography*, London, 1993, 159; Hans-Adolf Jacobsen, *Nationalsozialistische Außenpolitik 1933–1938*, Frankfurt am Main/Berlin, 1968, 422–4.

51. Höhne, 356–7.

52. Preston, 128ff.

53. Preston, 140–58.

54. Kube, 163–6. And see Weinberg I, 289–90.

55. Kube, 164.

56. Hans-Henning Abendroth, 'Deutschlands Rolle im Spanischen Bürgerkrieg', in Manfred Funke (ed.), *Hitler, Deutschland und die Mächte. Materialien zur Außenpolitik des Dritten Reiches*, Düsseldorf, 1978, 471–88, here 472–3; Preston, 158–9.

57. Abendroth, 474.

58. *DGFP*, D, III, 10–11, No.10, Memorandum of the Director of the Political Department of the Foreign Office, Dr Hans Heinrich Dieckhoff, 25 July 1936. According to Kube, 164, Bohle and Heß tried to take up the matter with the Foreign Office, and almost certainly, too, with Göring.

59. Abendroth, 474.

60. *DGFP*, D, III, 6–7, No.4; Abendroth, 474–5.

61. Implied in the account of Kube, 164–5.

62. Abendroth, 475.

63. Kube, 165, n.11.

64. See Abendroth, 476–9.

65. Suggested by Martens, 66.

66. Preston, 159.

67. Abendroth, 475, citing a communication to him from Bernhardt. Kube, 165 claims that Hitler's decision was in support of Göring's 'economic concept'. Wolfgang Schieder, 'Spanischer Bürgerkrieg und Vierjahresplan', in Wolfgang Michalka (ed.), *Nationalsozialistische Außenpolitik*, Darmstadt, 1978, 325–59, also emphasizes Göring's role and the centrality of economic motives. Martens, 66, on the other hand, argues convincingly – along Abendroth's lines – that Hitler took the decision alone, and that Göring was at first hesitant, indeed shocked at hearing of the decision. Serious economic involvement in Spain only dated from October 1936, when the first substantial military supplies also began. Göring claimed at Nuremberg that he had pressed Hitler, who was still thinking it over, to provide the support, both to combat the spread of Communism and to give him the opportunity to try out the Luftwaffe (*IMG*, ix.317; and see Kube, 165 n.12). But by the time Göring pressed for action, Hitler was no longer thinking it over; his mind was already made up. Göring's intentional or unintentional misrepresentation at Nuremberg was presumably aimed, as elswhere in his testimony, at bolstering his self-importance. Alternatively, as Preston suggests (814 n.64), Göring may have conflated two separate meetings with Hitler. Even so, Göring's claim that he was influential in shaping Hitler's original decision to intervene stands in contradiction to other evidence on the taking of the decision.

68. Abendroth, 475.

69. Ribbentrop, 59–60.

70. Ribbentrop, 60.

71. Abendroth, 476; Preston, 159–61; see also Schieder, 'Spanischer Bürgerkrieg', 342ff.; and the careful analysis (concluding that economic considerations were secondary to ideological in the initial decision by Hitler to involve Germany in support for Franco) by Christian Leitz, 'Nazi Germany's Intervention in the Spanish Civil War and the Foundation of HISMA/ROWAK', in Paul Preston and Ann L. Mackenzie (eds.), *The Republic Besieged: Civil War in Spain, 1936–1939*, Edinburgh, 1996, 53–85.

72. *TBJG*, I/2, 648 (27 July 1936), dealing as always with the events of the previous day.

73. Martens, 66.

74. *TBJG*, I/2, 671 (23 September 1936); Höhne, 363. The Republican side in the Civil War also attracted external support, particularly from the Soviet Union and from the International Brigades volunteer forces organized by the Comintern and individual Communist parties, in which some 60,000 men fought the nationalist insurgents. British and French statesmen were concerned at Soviet involvement in Spain, fearing, as Anthony Eden, the British Foreign Secretary put it in September 1937, that as a consequence 'Communism would get its clutches into Western Europe'. Cit. Denis Smyth, ' "We Are With You": Solidarity and Self-interest in Soviet Policy towards Republican Spain, 1936–1939', in Preston and Mackenzie, 87–105, here 105.

75. This is implied by Kube, 164–5, though the argument, so far as Hitler's motivation is concerned, seems overstretched.

76. Domarus, 638; *TBJG*, I/2, 675 (9 September 1936).

77. *TBJG*, I/2, 743 (2 December 1936).

78. *TBJG*, I/2, 726 (15 November 1936).

79. Kube, 153-4. Göring informed Hitler verbally of the finalized raw-material plans on 15 August (Petzina, 49).

80. Petzina, 47-8; Richard J. Overy, *Goering: the Iron Man*, London, 1984, 45-6; Gerhard Ritter, *Carl Goerdeler und die deutsche Widerstandsbewegung*, Stuttgart, 1956, 80-82. For a sketch of Goerdeler, see Hermann Weiß (ed.), *Biographisches Lexikon zum Dritten Reich*, Frankfurt am Main, 1998, 153-5.

81. In his official biography of Göring, Erich Gritzbach, *Hermann Göring. Werk und Mensch*, Munich, 1938, 160, remarked that 'after days of quiet work at the Berghof, on 2 September the Führer gives the Minister President [Göring] detailed directives about the reconstruction of the National Socialist economy which will determine the life of Germany for the present and the future'. Hitler's memorandum was read out to government ministers at a meeting on 4 September (*IMG*, xxxvi.489ff., Doc.EC-416).

82. Wilhelm Treue, 'Hitlers Denkschrift zum Vierjahresplan 1936', *VfZ*, 3 (1955), 184-210, here 184; *DGFP*, C, V, 853 n.1, No.490.

83. Petzina, 48, 52. According to Hans Kehrl, *Krisenmanager im Dritten Reich*, Dusseldorf, 1973, 86, Göring was forbidden to pass on the document or even to read it out to his closest staff. Overy, *Goering*, 46, has a third copy given to Fritz Todt, engaged in building the Autobahnen. The evidence for this is unclear. Speer's note attached to his copy of the memorandum (Treue, 184) remarked that there were only three copies, one of which he had received in 1944. If Todt had received a copy, it might have been expected to have remained in the files of his ministry, which Speer took over in 1942.

84. Treue, 'Denkschrift', 204-5; Engl. transl. in *DGFP*, C, V, 853-6, Doc. 490; and Jeremy Noakes and Geoffrey Pridham (eds.), *Nazism, 1919-1945. A Documentary Reader*, vol.2, Exeter, 1984, 281-9.

85. Petzina, 51; Hayes, 155-65, especially 164.

86. Kube, 154-5 and n.22.

87. Treue, 206-7, 209-10; Engl. transl. in *DGFP*, C, V, 856-8, 860-61, Doc.490.

88. Kube, 156.

89. Kube, 156-7.

90. Kube, 156.

91. *TBJG*, I/2, 727 (15 November 1936).

92. Kube, 157.

93. Kube, 158, citing post-war testimony of Lammers and Friedrich Gramsch, State Secretary to Göring in the office of the Four-Year Plan.

94. *Reden des Führers am Parteitag der Ehre 1936*, Munich, 1936, 48-52; Domarus, 637-8; Kube, 155 and n.24.

95. Kube, 156-7.

96. A warning against equating the Four-Year Plan with the Stalinist Five-Year Plans is, however, appropriate, as noted by Hans Mommsen, 'Reflections on the Position of Hitler and Göring in the Third Reich', in Thomas Childers and Jane Caplan (eds.), *Reevaluating the Third Reich*, New York/London, 1993, 86-97, here 92.

97. Kube, 157-8.

98. See Griffiths, 206-7, 218-19, 268-9. Among the prominent British visitors who met Hitler during 1936 were Lord Londonderry (former Air Minister), David Lloyd George (highly respected former Prime Minister), and Thomas Jones (former senior civil servant and Deputy Secretary to the Cabinet, and a close associate of the current Prime Minister, Stanley Baldwin).

99. Wolfgang Michalka, *Ribbentrop und die deutsche Weltpolitik, 1933-1940. Außenpolitische Konzeptionen und Entscheidungsprozesse im Dritten Reich*, Munich, 1980, 155, for the mandate.

Hitler told Ribbentrop towards the end of July that he wanted him to become the next ambassador in London (See *TBJG*, I/2, 646 (22 July 1936)). Disappointed not to have been made State Secretary in the Foreign Office, Ribbentrop delayed making the appointment public until 11 August (Michael Bloch, *Ribbentrop*, London, 1994, 97–9). Ribbentrop's own misleading version in his post-war testimony at Nuremberg was that he had personally asked Hitler to withdraw an earlier appointment as State Secretary in the Foreign Office, and to send him as Ambassador to London (IMG, x.267; and Ribbentrop, 60–61).

100. *Ciano's Diplomatic Papers*, ed. Malcolm Muggeridge, London, 1948 (= CP), 44. Mussolini was sure that Ribbentrop would achieve nothing (*CP*, 46).

101. See the memoirs of Ribbentrop's secretary during his time in London, Reinhard Spitzy, *So haben wir das Reich verspielt. Bekenntnisse eines Illegalen*, Munich, 1986, 101–3; Weinberg I, 275; Bloch, 100, 110, 111–34 (and note to 111 attributing the appellation to cartoonist David Low); Michalka, *Ribbentrop*, 157–8, for Ribbentrop's lengthy absences.

102. Josef Henke, 'Hitlers England-Konzeption – Formulierung und Realisierungsversuche', in Funke, 584–603, here 592; Speer, 86; Fritz Wiedemann, *Der Mann, der Feldherr werden wollte*, Velbert/Kettwig, 1964, 152, 156 and 153–6 for the Duke of Windsor's visit to the Berghof on 22 October 1937. According to Wiedemann (p.156) Hitler thought the Duke the most intelligent prince he had met, and that it was no wonder, because he was so pro-German, that he had been forced to abdicate.

103. Bloch, 122–3. Awkwardly for the readiness of Hitler and Ribbentrop to portray Winston Churchill as the arch-warmonger and leading exponent of anti-German sentiment in Britain, Churchill had been a staunch supporter of the King throughout the abdication crisis.

104. Cit. Jonathan Wright and Paul Stafford, 'Hitler, Britain, and the Hoßbach Memorandum', *Militärgeschichtliche Mitteilungen*, 42 (1987), 94, from BA, ZSlg., 101. Nr. 31 (Dertinger report). The deteriorating relations between Britain and Germany during the second half of 1936 and in 1937 are thoroughly examined by Josef Henke, *England in Hitlers politischem Kalkül, 1935–1939*, Boppard am Rhein, 1973, 49–107 and – emphasizing the significance of the colonial question – Klaus Hildebrand, *Vom Reich zum Weltreich. Hitler, NSDAP und koloniale Frage 1919–1945*, Munich, 1969, 491–548. See also Dietrich Aigner, *Das Ringen um England*, Munich/Esslingen, 1969, 302–20.

105. Weinberg I, 264.

106. *DGFP*, C, V, 756–60, No.446.

107. Weinberg I, 268–71. On the background to the Agreement, see Jürgen Geyl, *Austria, Germany, and the Anschluss, 1931–1938*, London/New York/Toronto, 1963, ch.V.

108. Geyl, 133–4.

109. Höhne, 364. Mussolini's decision to intervene in Spain was independent of Hitler's. The initial limited aid followed a similar pattern, though Italian involvement soon escalated to a level far greater than that of Germany. See Paul Preston, 'Mussolini's Spanish Adventure: From Limited Risk to War', in Preston and Mackenzie, 21–51.

110. See Preston, *Franco*, 243–4.

111. Treue, 205.

112. *CP*, 44, 47; Höhne, 364; Pierre Milza, *Mussolini*, Paris, 1999, 695–7.

113. Manfred Funke, 'Die deutsch-italienischen Beziehungen – Antibolschewismus und außenpolitische Interessenkonkurrenz als Strukturprinzip der "Achse"', in Funke, 823–46, here 834–5; Hohne, 364. Mussolini had expressed his own approval of the agreement between Austria and Germany – one he had suggested to Schuschnigg – at his meeting with Frank on 23 September (*CP*, 45).

114. *CP*, 56.

115. *CP*, 59.

116. *CP*, 57.

117. *CP*, 56–60; Jens Petersen, *Hitler-Mussolini. Die Entstehung der Achse Berlin-Rom 1933–1936*, Tübingen, 1973, 491; Höhne, 364–5.

118. *CP*, 60; Petersen, 492; Elizabeth Wiskemann, *The Rome-Berlin Axis. A History of the Relations between Hitler and Mussolini*, New York/London, 1949, 68.

119. Treue, 205.

120. *CP*, 58.

121. Despite his racial disparagement of the Japanese as merely capable of 'bearing', not 'creating', culture, Hitler had encouraged Ribbentrop in 1933, according to the latter's testimony at Nuremberg (*IMG*, x.271), to explore closer relations with Japan, predominantly on ideological grounds. See John Fox, *Germany and the Far Eastern Crisis, 1931–1938. A Study in Diplomacy and Ideology*, Oxford, 1982, 175–6; and Theo Sommer, *Deutschland und Japan zwischen den Mächten 1935–1940. Vom Antikominternpakt zum Dreimächtepakt*, Tübingen, 1962, 21–2; and, for Hitler's race-views on Japan, *MK*, 319. The first soundings to Japan were made in January 1935 (Bernd Martin, 'Die deutsch-japanischen Beziehungen während des Dritten Reiches', in Funke, 454–70, here 460).

122. For the Dienststelle Ribbentrop, see Hans-Adolf Jacobsen, 'Zur Struktur der NS-Außenpolitik 1933–1945', in Funke, 137–85, here 162–4.

123. Fox, 182–3, suggests this was only in autumn 1935.

124. Martin, 459; Fox, 185; Hartmut Bloß, 'Deutsche Chinapolitik im Dritten Reich', in Funke, 407–29, here especially 409–11.

125. Martin, 460; Fox, 177.

126. Fox, 180–81.

127. Martin, 461–2 and n.34, 40; Weinberg I, 344–5; Fox, 199–204. The planned *coup d'état* by junior officers followed elections in February 1936 with an outcome which did not satisfy the army, engaged in conflict with the navy over allocation of resources and strategic planning for expansion. The conflict lasted into the summer before a compromise gave equal weight to the navy's pressure for expansion to the south and the army's strong preference for a continental policy looking to expand northwards. Eventually, adventurist elements in the government were able to advance towards a pact, but the disruption following the army revolt held matters up for some time.

128. Höhne, 368; Martin, 464 n.54 for Italy's joining on 6 November 1937.

129. See Weinberg I, 347.

130. Domarus, 668.

131. *IMG*, xxv.404, 409, Doc. 386-PS.

132. *Die kirchliche Lage in Bayern nach den Regierungspräsidentenberichten 1933–1943*, vol.i, ed. Helmut Witetschek, Mainz, 1966, 193.

133. Domarus, 668; Nicolaus von Below, *Als Hitlers Adjutant 1937–1945*, Mainz, 1980, 15.

134. Schmidt, 348.

135. Schmidt, 342–6. See also the extensive account of Lloyd George's visit by Thomas Jones, who accompanied him on his trip to Germany and noted how impressed he was with Hitler (Jones, 241–52). Just over a year later, Lloyd George wrote to a friend: 'I have never doubted the fundamental greatness of Herr Hitler . . . I have never withdrawn one particle of the admiration which I personally felt for him . . . I only wish we had a man of his supreme quality at the head of affairs in our country today.' Cit. Martin Gilbert, *Britain and Germany between the Wars*, London, 1964, 102. And see Winston S. Churchill, *The Second World War. Vol.i: The Gathering Storm*, London 1948, 224–5: 'No one was more completely misled than Mr Lloyd George, whose rapturous accounts of his conversations make odd reading today. There is no doubt that Hitler had a power of fascinating men . . .'

136. Schmidt, 350; *TBJG*, I/3, 119, 142 (21 April 1937, 12 May 1937). See Lansbury's comment in a private letter written on 11 May 1937: '. . . A soft word, a tiny recognition of Hitler's position by diplomats, would make all the difference . . . He will *not* go to war unless pushed into it by others.

He knows how a European war will end.' Cit. Gilbert, 102. Lansbury had roundly condemned Hitler in the book he had published the previous year (George Lansbury, *My England*, London, n.d. (1936), 193–6).

137. Schmidt, 349–50.

138. André François-Poncet, *Souvenirs d'une ambassade à Berlin, Septembre 1931–Octobre 1938*, Paris, 1946, 262.

139. Cit. Ludwig Volk, 'Kardinal Faulhabers Stellung zur Weimarer Republik und zum NS-Staat', *Stimmen der Zeit*, 177 (1966), 173–95, here 187.

140. Henry Picker, *Hitlers Tischgespräche im Führerhauptquartier 1941–1942*, ed. Percy Ernst Schramm, Stuttgart, 1963, 478 (26 July 1942).

141. August Kubizek, *Adolf Hitler, mein Jugendfreund*, 5th edn, Graz/Stuttgart, 1989, 275.

142. Christa Schroeder, *Er war mein Chef. Aus dem Nachlaß der Sekretärin von Adolf Hitler*, ed. Anton Joachimsthaler, Munich/Vienna (1985), 4th edn, 1989, 47, 60.

143. Schroeder, 54, 58.

144. Below, 20.

145. Schroeder, 269.

146. Schroeder, 55–6.

147. See Schroeder, 269 and 78: 'Before dictation I didn't exist for him, and I doubt that he often saw me sitting at the typewriter.'

148. Below, 31. Hermann Döring, who referred to himself as 'manager' (*Verwalter*) of the Berghof, spoke of Hitler as 'extremely strict' (*'unwahrscheinlich streng'*) about cleanliness and organization, and the atmosphere as tense when he was present, with everyone alert to his rapid changes of mood (BBC Archives, London, 'The Nazis: A Warning from History', transcript of roll 242, pp.22, 27–9).

149. Schroeder, 269.

150. Schroeder, 78, 81.

151. Schroeder, 38–9, 58, 289–90, n.18.

152. Schroeder, 326 n.99.

153. Schroeder, 55. See Willi Schneider, 'Hitler aus nächster Nähe', 7 *Tage. Illustrierte Wochenschrift aus dem Zeitgeschehen*, Nr.42, 17 October 1952- Nr.1, 2 January 1953, here Nr.42, 8, for Hitler's high expectations and Kannenberg's nervousness.

154. Below, 10, 28; Schroeder, 269.

155. Schroeder, 37–46; Below, 29–30.

156. Below, 18, 29–32.

157. Schroeder, 48.

158. Below, 29, 31. The Reich Chancellery had been renovated by Troost and Speer after 1933. The Neue Reichskanzlei was begun by Speer in 1938 and completed on 7 January 1939.

159. Below, 29, 31–2; Schroeder, 47.

160. Below, 20.

161. Gitta Sereny, *Albert Speer: His Battle with the Truth*, London, 1995, 113.

162. Below, 32.

163. Below, 28–9, 32.

164. Schroeder, 79.

165. Below, 32–3.

166. *TBJG*, I/3, 378 (22 December 1937).

167. Below, 33.

168. Below, 33–4.

169. Domarus, 606.

170. Below, 22–3; see Schroeder, 170–96. And for Hitler's dislike of Berlin, see *Tb* Irving, 268 (25 July 1938).

171. Schroeder, 317 n.326.

172. Heinrich Hoffmann, *Hitler was my Friend*, London, 1955, 162–3.

173. Schroeder, 167.

174. Sereny, 109.

175. See Sereny, 110. Enthused by Resi Iffland as Brünnhilde in the Bayreuth performance of Wagner's *Götterdämmerung*, Hitler had told Goebbels that summer of 'his preference for large women' (*TBJG*, I/3, 221 (1 August 1937)).

176. Nerin E. Gun, *Eva Braun-Hitler. Leben und Schicksal*, Velbert/Kettwig, 1968, 74–8; Werner Maser, *Adolf Hitler. Legende, Mythos, Wirklichkeit*, 3rd paperback edn, Munich, 1973, 325–69; John Toland, *Adolf Hitler*, London, 1976, 375–7.

177. Gun, 78–9; Maser, 362–3, 368–9, 369n.; Toland, 377–8.

178. Domarus, 677; Speer, 87–93, especially 90.

179. In August 1938, after a lengthy conversation with Hitler about his marital problems with Magda, Goebbels would note in his diary: 'The Führer is like a father to me' (*TBJG*, I/6, 44 (16 August 1938).

180. *TBJG*, I/3, 266 (14 September 1937).

181. See Sereny, 109, 138–9, 156; and Joachim C. Fest, *Speer. Eine Biographie*, Berlin, 1999, 459ff.

182. *TBJG*, I/3, 221 (1 August 1937).

183. Sereny, ch.5.

184. See Gerhard Weinberg (ed.), *Hitlers Zweites Buch. Ein Dokument aus dem Jahr 1928*, Stuttgart, 1961, 129–30 for his views on the USA. In his view, only a strong, racially purified Germany, built up on the principles of National Socialism, could combat the USA in the contest for world hegemony that would inevitably occur in the distant future. See also Milan Hauner, 'Did Hitler want a World Dominion?', *JCH*, 13 (1978), 15–32, especially 24.

185. See *TBJG*, I/3, 104, 115, 119, 236, 261, 316, 321, 325 (10 April 1937, 17 April 1937, 20 April 1937, 15 August 1937, 10 September 1937, 28 October 1937, 2 November 1937, 4 November 1937). See in general on Hitler's monumental building plans, and their connection with his utopian goals of domination, Jochen Thies, *Architect der Weltherrschaft. Die 'Endziele' Hitlers*, Düsseldorf, 1976; and Jochen Thies, 'Hitlers European Building Programme', *JCH*, 13 (1978), 413–31.

186. *TBJG*, I/3, 119 (20 April 1937). Hitler had revealed his schemes for the rebuilding, including the gigantic hall, a few days earlier (*TBJG*, I/3, 115 (17 April 1937)).

187. *TBJG*, I/3, 236, 316 (15 August 1937, 28 October 1937).

188. *TBJG*, I/3, 261 (10 September 1937).

189. David Irving, *The Secret Diaries of Hitler's Doctor*, paperback edn, London, 1990, 31.

190. Irving, *Doctor*, 34.

191. Irving, *Doctor*, 35.

192. Irving, *Doctor*, 30, 36.

193. Irving, *Doctor*, 38.

194. *TBJG*, I/3, 177, 224 (18 June 1937, 3 August 1937).

195. Irving, *Doctor*, 38.

196. Irving, *Doctor*, 18.

197. Domarus, 745.

198. Domarus, 661–768; Milan Hauner, *Hitler. A Chronology of his Life and Time*, London, 1983, 116–23.

199. Domarus, 667. Following his speech, the Reichstag, without formalities, unanimously renewed the Enabling Act for a further four years (Domarus, 676). In this same speech, Hitler advanced the German demand for colonies (Domarus, 673). The colonial question would be raised on a number of occasions during 1937 (see, for example, *TBJG*, I/3, 46 (16 February 1937)), but largely for tactical reasons. (See Domarus, 759.) Hitler told Goebbels that he had consciously included colonial demands in his proclamation to the Reich Party Rally in order to demonstrate greater assertiveness

to the outside world (*TBJG*, I/3, 258 (8 September 1937). His unchanged interest was not in the reacquisition of colonial territory in Africa, but in a continental empire in eastern Europe. See Hildebrand, *Vom Reich zum Weltreich*, 501–2; Klaus Hildebrand, *Das vergangene Reich. Deutsche Außenpolitik von Bismarck bis Hitler 1871–1945*, Stuttgart, 1995, 640; and Hauner, *Hitler*, 120 for Hitler's reported comments in *The Times*, 13 September 1937, on the colonial question.

200. Domarus, 690.

201. Domarus, 705–6.

202. Domarus, 765. For Hitler's plans for Berlin, see Speer, 87–90; Thies, *Architekt*, 95–8. The metaphor of a 'thousand-year Reich' was a play on the chiliastic religious traditions of the coming heavenly Reich associated with millenarian mystics such as Joachim di Fiore. Wolfgang Benz, Hermann Graml, and Hermann Weiß (eds.), *Enzyklopädie des Nationalsozialismus*, Stuttgart, 1997, 435, 757; Cornelia Schmitz-Berning, *Vokabular des Nationalsozialismus*, Berlin, 1998, 607.

203. Domarus, 715–32, here 717.

204. For Hitler's use of the term in this speech, see Domarus, 730.

205. Domarus, 728, 731.

206. Schroeder, 78–9.

207. *TBJG*, I/3, 45 (16 February 1937).

208. See Ian Kershaw, *Popular Opinion and Political Dissent in the Third Reich: Bavaria, 1933–1945*, Oxford, 1983, 216.

209. On the struggle over denominational schools, see, especially, Franz Sonnenberger, 'Der neue "Kulturkampf". Die Gemeinschaftsschule und ihre historischen Voraussetzungen', in Martin Broszat, Elke Fröhlich, and Anton Grossmann (eds.), *Bayern in der NS-Zeit, vol.3, Herrschaft und Gesellschaft im Konflikt*, Munich/Vienna, 1981, 235–327; see also Kershaw, *Popular Opinion*, 209ff.

210. Kershaw, *Popular Opinion*, ch.5; John Conway, *The Nazi Persecution of the Churches, 1933–1945*, London, 1968, 206–13; Edward N. Peterson, *The Limits of Hitler's Power*, Princeton, 1969, especially ch.5 and 8; Elke Frohlich, 'Der Pfarrer von Mömbris', in Martin Broszat and Elke Fröhlich (eds.), *Bayern in der NS-Zeit, vol.6, Die Herausforderung des Einzelnen. Geschichten über Widerstand und Verfolgung*, Munich/Vienna, 1983, 52–75.

211. For the trials and the orchestrated campaign of defamation against the Catholic clergy, see Hans Günter Hockerts, *Die Sittlichkeitsprozesse gegen katholische Ordensangehörige und Priester 1936/1937*, Mainz, 1971. The trials and publicity were often counter-productive in strongly Catholic regions. See Kershaw, *Popular Opinion*, 196.

212. *TBJG*, I/3, 5 (5 January 1937), 10 (14 January 1937), 37–8 (9 February 1937).

213. See Conway, 206–7, where the reasons for Hitler's decision are regarded as unclear. Goebbels's diary entries indicate that he, not Hitler, took the initiative, and that Hitler eagerly seized upon the suggestion for elections as a way out of the problem, to end the damaging discord. It proved a miscalculation. See Conway, 206–13.

214. *TBJG*, I/3, 55 (23 February 1937). Hitler indicated again to Goebbels in June that he was considering the separation of Church and State. Goebbels added that the clergy would do well not to provoke the Fuhrer any further (*TBJG*, I/3, 181 (22 June 1937)). However, Hitler was concerned that in the event of a separation of church and state Protestantism would then be destroyed and provide no counter-weight against the Vatican (*TBJG*, I/3, 359 (7 December 1937). See Hans Günter Hockerts, 'Die nationalsozialistische Kirchenpolitik im neuen Licht der Goebbels-Tagebücher', *APZ*, 30 July 1983, B30, 23–8, here 29.

215. *TBJG*, I/3, 77 (13 March 1937).

216. *TBJG*, I/3, 97, 105 (2 April 1937, 10 April 1937).

217. *TBJG*, I/3, 129, 143, 156–7, 162 (1 May 1937, 12 May 1937, 29 May 1937, 2 June 1937).

218. *TBJG*, I/3, 119 (21 April 1937).

219. Conway, 209. 'We've got the swine and won't let him go again,' noted Goebbels (*TBJG*, I/3, 195 (4 July 1937); see also 194, 196, 198 (3 July 1937, 6 July 1937, 10 July 1937)). Hitler's order for the detention of Niemöller (Conway, 209) was almost certainly sanction for actions requested by the Gestapo. Niemöller's fundamental opposition to Nazism had undergone a pronounced course of development since his initial enthusiasm in 1933. For most Protestant clergy, opposition on church matters was compatible with conformity – often enthusiastic approval – in other areas of Nazi policy. See the contributions by Gunther van Norden, 'Widerstand in den Kirchen', and Helmut Gollwitzer, 'Aus der Bekennenden Kirche', in Löwenthal and Mühlen, *Widerstand und Verweigerung* 111–28, 129–39; the critical assessment by Shelley Baranowski, *The Confessing Church, Conservative Elites, and the Nazi State*, Lewiston/Queenston, 1986; and, for the penetration of the thinking even of prominent Protestant theologians by Nazi ideas, Robert P. Ericksen, *Theologians under Hitler*, New Haven/London, 1985.

220. *TBJG*, I/3, 258 (8 September 1937).

221. In the event, the exclusion was carried out by police decrees since a law would have drawn too much public attention. *TBJG*, I/3, 354 (3 December 1937).

222. *TBJG*, I/3, 351 (30 November 1937).

223. Hildegard von Kotze and Helmut Krausnick (eds.), '*Es spricht der Führer*'. *7 exemplarische Hitler-Reden*, Gütersloh, 1966, 147–8.

224. David Bankier, 'Hitler and the Policy-Making Process on the Jewish Question', *Holocaust and Genocide Studies*, 3 (1988), 1–20, here 15.

225. Domarus, 727–30; Uwe Dietrich Adam, *Judenpolitik im Dritten Reich*, Düsseldorf, 1972, 173; Saul Friedländer, *Nazi Germany and the Jews. The Years of Persecution, 1933–39*, London, 1997, 184–5.

226. Otto Dov Kulka, '"Public Opinion" in National Socialist Germany and the "Jewish Question"', *Zion*, 40 (1975), 186–290 (text in Hebrew, abstract in English, documentation in German), 272–3. And see Michael Wildt, *Die Judenpolitik des SD 1935 bis 1938. Eine Dokumentation*, Munich, 1995; and Lutz Hachmeister, *Der Gegenforscher. Die Karriere des SS-Führers Alfred Six*, Munich, 1998, ch.V. The SD had originally been established under the direction of Reinhard Heydrich in 1931 to carry out surveillance on the Nazi Party's political opponents. Much of this was undertaken by the Gestapo after 1933, when the SD's main role increasingly centred upon the gathering of information and production of reports on ideological 'enemies' (such as the Churches), the 'Jewish Question', and soundings of opinion.

227. Kulka, 274. See also BA, R58/991, Fols.71a-c, Vermerk of SD Abt. II 112, 7 April 1937. The SD's work was assisted by volunteers, such as the expert in Hebrew – a long-standing party member – who, while in Leipzig, had on his own initiative put together a register of all 'full-, three-quarter, half-, and quarter-Jews' in the area and now proposed to do the same for Upper Silesia, then for the whole of Silesia. He also offered to teach Hebrew to SD members. It was recommended that the SD should make use of his offer. BA, R58/991, Fol.46. See also Friedländer, 197ff.

228. The numbers of Jews emigrating from Germany had, in fact, not fluctuated massively since the first massive wave of emigration in 1933, despite the varying intensity of Nazi persecution. In 1937, there was even a decline compared with the rate of the previous year. By the Nazis' own standards, emigration pressure had not been adequate; more than two-thirds of the Jewish population of 1933 still remained in Germany. According to the statistics of the Reichsvertretung der deutschen Juden, the organization established in 1933 to coordinate and represent Jewish interests in the ever-worsening conditions, 37,000 Jews fled the country in 1933, 23,000 in 1934, 21,000 in 1935, 25,000 in 1936, and 23,000 in 1937. Werner Rosenstock, 'Exodus 1933–1939. A Survey of Jewish Emigration from Germany', *LBYB*, 1 (1956), 373–90, here 377; Herbert A. Strauss, 'Jewish Emigration from Germany. Nazi Policies and Jewish Responses (I)', *LBYB*, 25 (1980), 313–61, here 326, 330–32.

229. Adam, 172–4.

230. Karl A. Schleunes, *The Twisted Road to Auschwitz. Nazi Policy toward German Jews, 1933–1939*, Urbana/Chicago/London, 1970, 159–60.

231. Hermann Graml, *Reichskristallnacht. Antisemitismus und Judenverfolgung im Dritten Reich*, Munich, 1988, 167.

232. Adam, 174ff.

233. See Martin Broszat, *Der Staat Hitlers. Grundlegung und Entwicklung seiner inneren Verfassung*, Munich, 1969, 432–3.

234. *TBJG*, I/3, 26 (28 January 1937). He spoke again in late February of his expectation that the showdown would follow in five or six years' time (*TBJG*, I/3, 55 (23 February 1937)).

235. *TBJG*, I/3, 25–6 (28 January 1937). Frick came back to his notions of Reich Reform, but, despite Blomberg's support, found no favour with Hitler. Frick had raised the issue in connection with a law of 26 January 1937 to regulate the regional government and administration of Greater Hamburg, which he saw as a step to more comprehensive Reich Reform (Günter Neliba, *Wilhelm Frick. Der Legalist des Unrechtsstaates: Eine politische Biographie*, Paderborn etc., 1992, 149).

236. *TBJG*, I/3, 158–9 (31 May 1937); Domarus, 696–7. According to Goebbels, Hitler was sorely disappointed in Raeder and Blomberg, who would have been satisfied with diplomatic protests (*TBJG*, I/3, 162 (2 June 1937)). Naval intelligence, which only reported the incident to Hitler at lunchtime on 30 May, though the news had come in on the Saturday evening, was seen as having failed miserably. Goebbels thought that Raeder would not be long in office (*TBJG*, I/3, 158 (31 May 1937), 162 (2 June 1937)). The American journalist William Shirer was informed that Hitler had been 'screaming with rage all day' and wanted to declare war on Spain (Shirer, 63). Goebbels – possibly echoing Hitler's own opinion – expressed the view soon afterwards that Blomberg was weak and 'a puppet in the hands of his officers'. Hitler's own anger at Wehrmacht officers wanting to intervene in police matters, 'where they understood not the slightest thing', was also mentioned in the same entry (*TBJG*, I/3, 181 (22 June 1937)). By September, Göring, too, was expressing anger at the Wehrmacht leadership, which Goebbels saw on the way to becoming a 'state within a state' (*TBJG*, I/3, 257 (8 September 1937)). See also Goebbels's comments along the same lines, *TBJG*, I/3, 316, 322 (28 October 1937, 2 November 1937), after Hitler, in a rage, had criticized monarchical tendencies in the Wehrmacht.

237. *TBJG*, I/3, 211 (24 July 1937).

238. *TBJG*, I/3, 221 (1 August 1937).

239. *TBJG*, I/3, 370 (15 December 1937), for the view that the Russian threat was at least partially removed through the Japanese victory over China.

240. *TBJG*, I/3, 198 (10 July 1937).

241. *TBJG*, I/3, 378 (22 December 1937); see also 385 (28 December 1937).

242. *TBJG*, I/3, 351 (30 November 1937).

243. See Wright and Stafford, 'Hitler, Britain, and the Hoßbach Memorandum', 100 and 120 n.167.

244. *TBJG*, I/3, 200 (13 July 1937). See also Goebbels's own comments (p.252) on 3 September 1937.

245. *TBJG*, I/3, 177 (18 June 1937). Goebbels was still sceptical after the effusive expressions of mutual friendship following Mussolini's state visit in September (*TBJG*, I/3, 283 (29 October 1937), 285 (1 October 1937)).

246. Schneider, Nr.42, 8, where the elaborate organization of the receptions for Mussolini in Munich and Berlin is also described.

247. Domarus, 737; Hauner, *Hitler*, 121.

248. *TBJG*, I/3, 281 (28 September 1937). See also 282–3 (29 November 1937), 284–5 (1 October 1937).

249. *Joseph Goebbels. Tagebücher 1924–1945*, 5 vols., ed. Ralf Georg Reuth, Munich, 1992 (*Tb* Reuth), iii.1100, n.88. See Norbert Schausberger, 'Österreich und die nationalsozialistische Anschluß-Politik', in Funke, 728–56, here 744–8.

250. Schausberger, 'Österreich', 746.

251. Schausberger, 'Österreich', 744; Geyl, 157.

252. *TBJG*, I/3, 201 (13 July 1937).

253. *TBJG*, I/3, 223 (3 August 1937).

254. *TBJG*, I/3, 266 (14 September 1937). In October, Hitler hinted to the Aga Khan that Austria, Czechoslovakia, Danzig, and the Corridor figured in German revisionism (Schmidt, 382).

255. *TBJG*, I/3, 369 (15 December 1937).

256. Gerhard L. Weinberg, *The Foreign Policy of Hitler's Germany. Starting World War II, 1937–1939*, Chicago/London, 1980 (= Weinberg II), 289, and 287, where it is pointed out that foreign visitors were also starting to expect action against Austria in the near future. The economic gains from the seizure of assets in Austria were an attractive proposition with the German armaments economy under strain (Schausberger, in Funke, 744–8; and the fuller account in Norbert Schausberger, *Der Griff nach Österreich. Der Anschluß*, Vienna/Munich, 1978, ch.6).

257. *TBJG*, I/3, 223 (3 August 1937).

258. *TBJG*, I/3, 223 (3 August 1937).

259. Wright/Stafford, 102.

260. *TBJG*, I/3, 307 (20 October 1937). 'This temporary state must disappear,' (*Dieser Saisonstaat muß weg*) he had entered in his diary the previous day (306 (19 October 1937)).

261. *TBJG*, I/3, 327 (6 November 1937).

262. Jost Dülffer, *Weimar, Hitler und die Marine. Reichspolitik und Flottenbau 1920–1939*, Düsseldorf, 1973, 446–7.

263. Kube, 195. Klaus-Jürgen Müller, in his *Das Heer und Hitler. Armee und nationalsozialistisches Regime 1933–1940*, (1969), 2nd edn, Stuttgart, 1988, 243; and *General Ludwig Beck. Studien und Dokumente zur politisch-militärischen Vorstellungswelt und Tätigkeit des Generalstabschefs des deutschen Heeres 1933–1938*, Boppard am Rhein, 1980, 249, has Hitler summoning the meeting.

264. Friedrich Hoßbach, *Zwischen Wehrmacht und Hitler 1934–1938*, Wolfenbüttel/Hanover, 1949, 219; Wright/Stafford, 82, for the second part of the meeting dealing with rearmament questions. Following the discussion of the raw materials issue, new allocations to the navy were agreed. Instead of 45,000 tons of steel, the navy would receive its full complement of 75,000 tons. (Dülffer, *Marine*, 447; Hoßbach, 219; Weinberg II, 41; Wright/Stafford, 123 n.200 on Hitler speaking from notes.)

265. Walter Bußmann, 'Zur Entstehung und Überlieferung der "Hoßbach-Niederschrift"', *VfZ*, 16 (1968), 373–84, here 377; Wright/Stafford, 82.

266. *IMG*, xxv, 402–13, Doc. 386-PS. Hoßbach, 217–20, relates how he made the notes on the meeting. And see Müller, *Heer*, 243ff.; Muller, *Beck*, 249ff.; Dülffer, *Marine*, 448–51; Hermann Gakenholz, 'Reichskanzlei 5. November 1937', in Richard Dietrich and Gerhard Oestreich (eds.), *Forschungen zu Staat und Verfassung. Festgabe für Fritz Hartung*, Berlin, 1958, 459–74. Bußmann, Wright/Stafford, and Bradley F. Smith, 'Die Überlieferung der Hoßbach-Niederschrift im Lichte neuer Quellen', *VfZ*, 38 (1990), 329–36, have removed any doubts about the authenticity of the document.

267. See Wright/Stafford, 84.

268. See Weinberg II, 39 n.74 for the generally understood notion that Austria would be taken over from the outside, and Papen's comments to a Hungarian minister in Vienna in May that both Austria and Czechoslovakia would disappear. Hitler's view that little was to be gained at that time by a rapprochement with Britain, and his strong preference for close ties with Italy, figured in the confidential reports on press briefings by Georg Dertinger and Dr Hans Joachim Kausch. See Wright/Stafford, 91–5.

269. Wright/Stafford, 82–4.

270. Hoßbach, 219; Müller, *Heer*, 244; Wright/Stafford, 85.

271. Bussmann, 378.

272. Weinberg II, 39.

273. Müller, *Beck*, 501.

274. *IMG*, xxv. 412–13; Müller, *Heer*, 244; Wright/Stafford, 99; Gackenholz, 469–72. Hoßbach, 219, recalled that the meeting became heated in the exchanges between Blomberg and Fritsch on the one hand and Göring on the other, with Hitler saying little. According to Muller, 244 (though without source for the assertion), the discussion with Göring concerned above all the technical questions of armaments issues. In Hoßbach's record of the meeting, Göring's only intervention was to suggest cutting down Germany's military involvement in Spain in the light of Hitler's comments (*IMG*, xxv.413).

275. Wright/Stafford, 99.

276. Wright/Stafford, 103.

277. IMG, xiv, 44–5; Erich Raeder, *Mein Leben von 1935 bis Spandau 1955*, Tübingen/Neckar, 1957, 149–50; Müller, *Heer*, 245; Dülffer, 450 n.56. But Raeder's testimony at Nuremberg and his memoirs are often unreliable (Dülffer, *Marine*, 450 n.56; Weinberg II, 40; Wright/Stafford, 101, 107; Gackenholz, 470). Göring, Raeder claimed, had told him before the meeting that Hitler's remarks were solely aimed at stirring the army to speed up rearmament. (Göring also declared at Nuremberg that this was the purpose of the meeting (Wright/Stafford, 77).) He was expecting, therefore, some exaggeration for effect.

278. Müller, *Heer*, 246 n.193.

279. Müller, *Beck*, 254.

280. Müller, *Beck*, 498–501 (text), 254–61 (commentary).

281. Gackenholz, 471; Müller, *Heer*, 246.

282. Müller, *Heer*, 247 (Neufassung des Aufmarschplanes 'Grün', 21 December 1937). Blomberg stated after the war that he and Fritsch had wanted to express their doubts about the possibility of implementing Hitler's plans in the light of the opposition of Britain and France, but added that those present at the meeting agreed when leaving the room that Hitler's remarks were not to be taken seriously (IMG, xl, 406). This was probably an indirect reference to an exchange of views with Raeder, who was of the same opinion.

283. Karl-Heinz Janßen and Fritz Tobias, *Der Sturz der Generäle. Hitler und die Blomberg-Fritsch-Krise 1938*, Munich, 1994, 38; Speer, 83.

284. Janßen/Tobias, 35. For the film *Hitlerjunge Quex*, see Welch, 59–74.

285. Janßen/Tobias, 59–60.

286. Janßen/Tobias, 34–5.

287. Janßen/Tobias, 16. At the end of 1944, Blomberg was to send Hitler a letter expressing his disgust and shame at the military plot against him (*TBJG*, II/14, 333 (2 December 1944)).

288. Janßen/Tobias, 30.

289. Janßen/Tobias, 38–41.

290. Janßen/Tobias, 27–8.

291. Janßen/Tobias, 56–7 (where it is convincingly argued that the call did not come from the Gestapo, as often presumed).

292. Janßen/Tobias, 45–7, 51.

293. Janßen/Tobias, 27, 51–2.

294. Wiedemann, 112.

295. *TBJG*, I/3, 414 (26 January 1938).

296. Hoßbach, 124.

297. *TBJG*, I/3, 415–16 (27 January 1938).

298. Janßen/Tobias, 54–5; *TBJG*, I/3, 419 (29 January 1938).

299. Janßen/Tobias, 86–8, 91, 93–7.

300. Hoßbach, 127; Hans Bernd Gisevius, *Bis zum bittern Ende* (single vol. edn), Zürich, n.d. (1954?), 258; Janßen/Tobias, 90. This speaks directly against the well-versed argument that Fritsch's

dismissal was a consequence of his objections to Hitler's remarks at the meeting on 5 November 1937, noted by Hoßbach. For this interpretation, see Peter Graf Kielmansegg, 'Die militärisch-politische Tragweite der Hoßbach-Besprechung', *VfZ*, 8 (1960), 268–75.

301. Janßen/Tobias, 86–7.

302. Gerhard Engel, *Heeresadjutant bei Hitler 1938–1943. Aufzeichnungen des Majors Engel*, ed. Hildegard von Kotze, Stuttgart, 1974, 20–21. Engel's notes, though having the appearance of contemporary diary entries, were, in fact, compiled after the war, taken both from memory and, he claimed, from notes made at the time but subsequently lost. Since Engel was in Hitler's immediate entourage for a period of five years, his notes remain of value though should not be taken as an authentic diary record.

303. Hoßbach, 125–7; Gisevius, *Bis zum bittern Ende*, (single vol. edn), 258–61; Janßen/Tobias, 99.

304. Hoßbach, 126–7; Wiedemann, 117–18.

305. Hoßbach, 127; Janßen/Tobias, 100.

306. Wiedemann, 117–18. See *TBJG*, I/3, 417 (28 January 1938): 'He was thus able to prepare himself. Who knows here what's true and false! In any case, the situation is impossible. It's being further investigated. But after that Fritsch will also have to go.'

307. Hoßbach, 127–8; Janßen/Tobias, 101–2.

308. Janßen/Tobias, 102–3.

309. Hoßbach, 128–9; Below, 65; *Generalfeldmarschall Keitel. Verbrecher oder Offizier? Erinnerungen, Briefe, Dokumente des Chefs OKW*, ed. Walter Gorlitz, Göttingen/Berlin/Frankfurt am Main, 1961 (=Keitel), 104ff.

310. Janßen/Tobias, 91. Schmidt had been in custody since 1935, and was sentenced in December 1936 to seven years' imprisonment for numerous cases of blackmail and infringement of the laws on homosexuality. His criminal record stretched back to 1929. Janßen/Tobias, 91–2 and 277 n.33.

311. Janßen/Tobias, 104–5.

312. See the account of the extraordinary meeting in Hoßbach, 129–30; also Janßen/Tobias, 106.

313. Janßen/Tobias, 108.

314. Goebbels wrote: 'Here is word against word: that of a homosexual blackmailer against that of the head of the army. And the Führer does not trust Fritsch any longer' (*TBJG*, I/3, 421 (30 January 1938)).

315. Janßen/Tobias, 109–16, especially 113–14.

316. *TBJG*, I/3, 421 (30 January 1938).

317. Janßen/Tobias, 120–21. A second HJ boy was also looked after by Fritsch for a month (Janßen/Tobias, 101).

318. Janßen/Tobias, 122–3.

319. *TBJG*, I/3, 417 (28 January 1938).

320. The idea of separate ministries for the branches of the armed forces possibly came initially from Raeder (Janßen/Tobias, 126). As late as 31 January, Hitler and Goebbels were still discussing possible successors to Fritsch, with the Propaganda Minister favouring Beck (*TBJG*, I/3, 423 (1 February 1938)).

321. Janßen/Tobias, 125–6. See Hoßbach, 132 n.1 (the post-war comments by Fritsch's defender, Graf v.d. Goltz, of a conversation he had had in June 1945 with Blomberg); see also Keitel, 105 n.184; Below, 67.

322. Janßen/Tobias, 128–32. The sarcastic comment about Himmler was made after the war while in British internment by Field-Marshal Ewald von Kleist.

323. Janßen/Tobias, 126–7.

324. *IMG*, xxviii.358, Doc. 1780-PS, Jodl-Tagebuch; Keitel, 106–9; Janßen/Tobias, 127. Keitel and Jodl worked out the organizational structure (Janßen/Tobias, 136). Blomberg's recommendation of Keitel had scarcely been enthusiastic. Hitler had asked who was in charge of Blomberg's staff.

Blomberg mentioned Keitel's name, but dismissed the possibility of using him. 'He's nothing but the man who runs my office,' he said. 'That's exactly the man I am looking for,' Hitler replied (Walter Warlimont, *Inside Hitler's Headquarters, 1939–1945*, London, 1964, 13).

325. Janßen/Tobias, 136.

326. Müller, *Heer*, 636.

327. Janßen/Tobias, 140.

328. *TBJG*, I/3, 424 (1 February 1938). Hitler had hinted to Keitel and Brauchitsch that the reshuffle was aimed at heading off the negative impression that could be prompted abroad at the departure of Blomberg and Fritsch (Keitel, 112).

329. *TBJG*, I/3, 423–4 (1 February 1938).

330. *IMG*, xxviii.362, Doc.1780-PS, Jodl-Tagebuch (31 January 1938): '*Führer will die Scheinwerfer von der Wehrmacht ablenken, Europa in Atem halten . . . Schußnig* [sic] *soll nicht Mut fassen sondern zittern.*'

331. Janßen/Tobias, 150; Domarus, 783, has sixty military posts, including fourteen generals, as well as Blomberg and Fritsch. General Liebmann remarked of the senior army officers removed, that there could be no doubt that they were all figures who in some way were 'uncomfortable' ('*unbequem*') for the Party (*IfZ*, ED 1, Fol.416, Liebmann memoirs).

332. Janßen/Tobias, 199–200. Brauchitsch told the generals that he had accepted the post 'only unwillingly and with considerable reservations' ('*nur widerstrebend und unter erheblichen Bedenken*') (*IfZ*, ED 1, Fol.416, Liebmann memoirs).

333. *TBJG*, I/3, 424 (1 February 1938).

334. Lothar Gruchmann, 'Die "Reichsregierung" im Führerstaat. Stellung und Funktion des Kabinetts im nationalsozialistischen Herrschaftssystem', in Günther Doeker and Winfried Steffani (eds.), *Klassenjustiz und Pluralismus*, Hamburg, 1973, 187–223, here 200–201.

335. Janßen/Tobias, 154.

336. *TBJG*, I/3, 431 (5 February 1938); Domarus, 783. Hitler told his generals on 5 February that, for prestige reasons both at home and abroad, he could not possibly disclose the real reason for Blomberg's dismissal (*IfZ*, ED 1, Fol.415, Liebmann memoirs).

337. Janßen/Tobias, 79. Hitler's view of Blomberg, as disclosed to his generals in early February 1938, was less favourable. He described him as a weak character ('*einen schwachen Charakter*') who in every critical situation, especially during the occupation of the Rhineland, had lost his nerve (*IfZ*, ED 1, Fol.415, Liebmann memoirs).

338. Janßen/Tobias, 182.

339. Janßen/Tobias, 148.

340. Janßen/Tobias, 247–9.

341. Domarus, 728.

342. *DBS*, v.9–22; and see Ian Kershaw, *The 'Hitler Myth'. Image and Reality in the Third Reich*, Oxford, (1987), paperback edn, 1989, 129–30.

343. *TBJG*, I/3, 434 (6 February 1938).

344. Towards the end of 1944, in the wake of the bomb-plot against him, Hitler would once more refer to the Fritsch case. He was, according to Goebbels, more convinced than ever that Fritsch had been the head of the generals' conspiracy – in its early stages – 'and that the indictment against him for homosexuality was in the last resort correct' (*TBJG*, II/14, 333 (2 December 1944)).

345. IfZ, ED 1, Fol.416, Liebmann memoirs: '*Der Eindruck dieser Eröffnungen – sowohl der über Blomberg, wie der über Fritsch, war geradezu niederschmetternd, besonders deshalb, weil Hitler beide Sachen so dargestellt hatte, dass über die tatsächliche Schuld kaum noch ein Zweifel bestehen konnte. Wir alle hatten das Gefühl, dass das Heer – im Gegensatz zur Marine, Luftwaffe und Partei – einen vernichtenden Schlag erlitten hatte.*' See also Janßen/Tobias, 153 and 294 n.31 for the date of 5 February and not, as Liebmann, Fol.416, has it, the 4th.

346. *TBJG*, I/3, 434 (6 February 1938). In speaking to the generals, Hitler had mentioned that

during the Rhineland crisis, when Blomberg's nerve had deserted him, of all his advisers only the 'thick-skulled Swabian Neurath' had been in favour of holding out. ('*Von allen seinen Beratern sei damals nur der "dickschädelige Schwabe Neurath" für Durchhalten gewesen.*') (IfZ, ED 1, Liebmann memoirs, Fol.415.) Neurath was able to be so sanguine about the plans to remilitarize the Rhineland because the Foreign Office had received accurate intelligence indicating that the French would not resort to military action in such an event (Zach Shore, 'Hitler, Intelligence, and the Decision to Remilitarize the Rhine', *JCH*, 34 (1999), 5–18).

347. *TBJG*, I/3, 434 (6 February 1938).

348. Domarus, 792–804, here especially 796–7, 799–800.

349. Domarus, 797. See Janßen/Tobias, 157.

CHAPTER 2: THE DRIVE FOR EXPANSION

1. Plainly implied in numerous speeches in the later 1920s, emphasizing Germany's 'lack of space' (*Raumnot*) equivalent to the needs of its population, man's eternal struggle for existence and survival of the fittest, and analogies with the eastern colonization during the Middle Ages or the attainment and defence of the British Empire. See e.g. *Hitler. Reden, Schriften, Anordnungen: Februar 1925 bis Januar 1933*, ed. Institut für Zeitgeschichte, 5 vols. in 12 parts, Munich/London/New York/Paris, 1992–8 (=*RSA*), II/2, 447 (6 August 1927), 546 (16 November 1927), 554 (21 November 1927), 733 (3 March 1928), 778 (17 April 1928).

2. Adolf Hitler, *Mein Kampf* [= *MK*], 876–880th reprint, Munich, 1943, 742; trans. Adolf Hitler, *Mein Kampf*, London, 1969, trans. by Ralph Manheim, with an introduction by D. C. Watt (= *MK* Watt), 597.

3. One country with no illusions about Hitler was the Soviet Union. At his meeting with the United States' Ambassador to the Soviet Union, Joseph E. Davies, on 4 February 1937, the People's Commissar for Foreign Affairs, Maxim M. Litvinov, had commented 'that Hitler's policy had not changed from that which he had announced in his book *Mein Kampf*; that he was dominated by a lust for conquest and for the domination of Europe; that he could not understand why Great Britain could not see that once Hitler dominated Europe he would swallow the British Isles also'. In Davies's view, Litvinov 'seemed to be very much stirred about this and apprehensive lest there should be some composition of differences between France, England, and Germany' (Joseph E. Davies, *Mission to Moscow*, New York, 1941, 59–60).

4. See Dirks and Janßen, 58–72, for a summary of the Wehrmacht's aims in the rearmament programme.

5. Werner Maser, *Adolf Hitler. Legende-Mythos-Wirklichkeit*, 3rd paperback edn, Munich/Esslingen, (1971), 1976, 374, 455–6; Gerhard L. Weinberg, 'Hitler's Private Testament of May 2, 1938', in *JMH*, 27 (1955), 415–19, here 415. In 1942, Hitler referred to his testament four years earlier and his fears at the time that he had cancer (Picker, 222 (29 March 1942)).

6. *IMG*, xxviii.367, Doc. 1780-PS (Jodl-Tagebuch).

7. See Gerhard Botz, *Der 13. März 38 und die Anschluß-Bewegung. Selbstaufgabe, Okkupation und Selbstfindung Österreichs 1918–1945*, 5–14; Bruce F. Pauley, *Hitler and the Forgotten Nazis. A History of Austrian National Socialism*, London/Basingstoke, 1981, 4–10.

8. Walther Hofer (ed.), *Der Nationalsozialismus. Dokumente 1933–1945*, Frankfurt am Main (1957), 1974, 28.

9. *MK*, 1; *MK* Watt, 3.

10. See Kube, 233, where it is suggested that this arose from internal rivalries in the Austrian party, and was also an indication that Göring had received no equivalent commission from Hitler to operate in Austrian affairs and was acting quasi-independently.

11. Weinberg II, 278–9.

12. Weinberg II, 122; Martens, 122.

13. Borthwick Institute, York, Papers of 1st Earl of Halifax, 410.3.6, 'Conversation with Herr Hitler – 19th November 1937', Fols.13, 16; 410.3.3 (vi), 'Lord Halifax's Diary. Visit of the Lord President to Germany, 17th to 21st November, 1937', Fol.9; Confidential Memo., Fol.4. Hitler, Halifax noted in his diary (Fol.12), struck him 'as very sincere, and as believing everything he said'. Halifax's notes made in the train *en route* from Berlin to Calais on 21 November (Fol.1) stated: 'Unless I am wholly deceived, the Germans, speaking generally, from Hitler to the man in the street, do want friendly relations with Great Britain. There are no doubt many who don't: and the leading men may be deliberately throwing dust in our eyes. But I don't think so . . .' See also The Earl of Halifax, *Fulness of Days*, London, 1957, 187.

14. Weinberg II, 288.

15. *Akten zur Deutschen Auswärtigen Politik 1918–1945* (=*ADAP*) D, I, No.80, 106; *DGFP*, D, I, 80, 129–31; *TBJG*, I/3, 369 (15 December 1937); Weinberg II, 287–8; Kube, 241.

16. Weinberg II, 289.

17. Kube, 216.

18. See Kube, 212–14.

19. See Kube, 235–6 for Göring's emphasis on political and military, not just economic motives for Anschluß.

20. Stefan Martens, 'Die Rolle Hermann Görings in der deutschen Außenpolitik', in Franz Knipping and Klaus-Jürgen Müller (eds.), *Machtbewußtsein in Deutschland am Vorabend des Zweiten Weltkrieges*, Paderborn, 1984, 75–92, here 80; Kube, 216, 224ff.

21. Kube, 225–7, 229–30, Schmidt, 352–3.

22. Kube, 232, 236–7.

23. Franz von Papen, *Memoirs*, London, 1952, 401.

24. Papen, 401; and see Kube, 238–9.

25. Kube, 240. Halifax had been 'immensely entertained' at meeting Göring, whose personality he found 'frankly attractive', like a combination of 'film star, great landowner . . . Prime Minister, party-manager, head gamekeeper . . .' (Borthwick Institute, Halifax Papers, 410.3.3 (vi), Fol.21, Diary of Halifax's visit to Germany; an abbreviated version of his meeting with Göring is in Halifax, 190–91).

26. Martens, *Göring*, 122.

27. *TBJG*, I/3.369 (15 December 1937). 'Papen unfolds a plan to bring down Schuschnigg,' Goebbels recorded. 'The cat doesn't leave the mouse alone. But that's good. Schuschnigg is getting too strong and cheeky (*frech*)'.

28. Papen, 408–9; Franklin D. Roosevelt Library, Hyde Park, New York, John Toland Collection, Tape 53, Side B (Toland interview with Kurt Schuschnigg, 11 September 1971). Kurt Schuschnigg, *Austrian Requiem*, London, 1947, 18, dates Papen's approach to early 1938. But in his subsequent interview, he makes clear that the invitation to Berchtesgaden, passed on by Papen in January, followed an earlier approach.

29. Papen, 409–10.

30. Papen, 412; Weinberg II, 289–91. On 26 January, Papen told Schmidt that Hitler would like Schuschnigg to come to Berchtesgaden on 15 February (Papen, 410). When, precisely, the date for the meeting was altered is unclear. But Papen was sent to Vienna to confirm it on 5 February, the day after he had been dismissed as ambassador to Vienna. Papen claimed he had again recommended the meeting, after initially suggesting one at the time that the Austrian police confiscated the papers of Gauleiter Tavs – revealing the plans for actions to provoke German intervention – at the raid on the Vienna party headquarters (Papen, 408–9). The raid took place on 25 January (Pauley, 195–6; Weinberg II, 288). Papen had then issued an invitation to Schuschnigg, endorsed by Hitler, on 27 January (Pauley, 195). This was the invitation to the rearranged meeting, which Papen implausibly claimed Hitler had forgotten and had to be reminded of (Papen, 408). The original invitation, again

at Papen's suggestion and with Hitler's approval, had been agreed to by the Austrian chancellor on 8 January (Weinberg II, 289).

31. Pauley, 196; Weinberg II, 288.

32. Weinberg II, 278, 290; Papen, 413.

33. Weinberg II, 290.

34. Keppler's report to Hitler, describing the terms agreed on 2 February between Schuschnigg and Seyß-Inquart, is in *'Anschluß' 1938. Eine Dokumentation*, ed. Dokumentationsarchiv des österreichischen Widerstandes, Vienna, 1988, 149–50. See also Papen, 411–12, 420; Weinberg II, 292.

35. Papen, 418, 420.

36. Papen, 413. However, according to his later testimony, Schuschnigg, aware that the Blomberg–Fritsch affair had created serious tension between Hitler and the army, had mistakenly taken the news that three generals would be in attendance as an indication that they would be exerting a restraining influence (Franklin D. Roosevelt Library, Hyde Park, New York, John Toland Collection, Tape 53, Side B (Toland interview with Kurt Schuschnigg, 11 September 1971)).

37. Below, 84.

38. Papen, 413. Below, 84 for Hitler's tension at the visit.

39. Kurt Schuschnigg, *Ein Requiem in Rot-Weiß-Rot*, Zurich, 1946, 38.

40. Schuschnigg, *Ein Requiem*, 40–2.

41. Papen, 414–17. For the terms, see *DGFP*, D, I, No.294–5, 513–17; see also Gehl, 174.

42. Papen, 420. Schuschnigg was given three days to comply (Schuschnigg, *Ein Requiem*, 49; Papen, 420; Below, 85). Hitler had retired to the Obersalzberg to prepare his speech (Below, 83).

43. Below, 85; Papen, 415.

44. Keitel, 177; Papen, 417.

45. Papen, 418–19; Schuschnigg, *Ein Requiem*, 49.

46. Papen, 420; Domarus, 790; Schuschnigg, *Ein Requiem*, 51–2.

47. Keitel, 178 and n.26. Jodl and Canaris were involved with Keitel in setting up the manoeuvres. See *IMG*, xxviii.367 (Doc.1780-PS, Jodl-Tagebuch), entry for 13 February 1938.

48. Keitel, 178.

49. Below, 85.

50. *Tb* Reuth, 1208 (16 February 1938).

51. Below, 85; *Tb* Reuth, 1209 (16 February 1938).

52. *Der unbekannte Dr Goebbels. Die geheimen Tagebücher 1938*, ed. David Irving (= *Tb* Irving), London, 1995, 53 (17 February 1938); *Der Spiegel* (= *Tb* Spiegel), 31/1992, 102.

53. Below, 86.

54. Domarus, 803.

55. *ADAP*, D, I, Dok.328, p.450; Kube, 243; Pauley, 198.

56. Papen, 403–4; Pauley, 194–201; also Weinberg II, 288–90.

57. Domarus, 801. The speech had been toned down somewhat from its draft (Pauley, 203).

58. Pauley, 202–4.

59. Papen, 422–3; John Toland, *Adolf Hitler*, London, 1977, 438–9.

60. Weinberg II, 294.

61. Domarus, 804.

62. Nevile Henderson, *Failure of a Mission. Berlin, 1937–1939*, London, 1940, 116–17.

63. Pauley, 205. Hitler had demanded a plebiscite in his meeting with Henderson on 3 March – though, of course, only on his terms (Henderson, 116–17).

64. Pauley, 206; Dieter Wagner and Gerhard Tomkowitz, *Ein Volk, ein Reich, ein Führer. The Nazi Annexation of Austria, 1938*, London, 1971, 15–19, 25–6. The relevant section of Schuschnigg's speech, proclaiming the referendum, is printed in *'Anschluß' 1938*, 221–2. See also Galeazzo Ciano, *Tagebücher 1937/38*, Hamburg, 1949, 121–3, entries for 9–10 March 1938.

65. Below, 89; see also Domarus, 818, for Hitler's *post facto* comments to Ward Price, a journalist on the *Daily Mail* who had interviewed him a number of times in earlier years, in Linz on 12 March, that he had acted because of Schuschnigg's betrayal, which he had at first not believed. Hitler told the Reichstag on 18 March that he thought the rumours of the referendum were 'fantastic' and 'incredible' (Domarus, 829).

66. *Tb* Irving, 97 (10 March 1938); *Tb* Spiegel, 31/1992, 102–3.

67. *Tb* Irving, 97–8 (10 March 1938); *Tb* Spiegel, 31/1992, 103, 105.

68. Helmut Michels, *Ideologie und Propaganda. Die Rolle von Joseph Goebbels in der national-sozialistischen Außenpolitik bis 1939*, Frankfurt am Main etc., 1992, 380.

69. *Tb* Irving, 98 (10 March 1938); *Tb* Spiegel, 31/1992, 105; see also David Irving, *Goebbels: Mastermind of the Third Reich*, London, 1996, 242–3; Wagner and Tomkowitz, 68–9.

70. Kube, 244.

71. Janßen/Tobias, 175–6.

72. *Tb* Irving, 99 (11 March 1938); *Tb* Spiegel, 31/1992, 105.

73. *IMG*, x.566; Keitel, 178 and n.27; Wagner and Tomkowitz, 51–5.

74. *Tb* Irving, 99–100 (11 March 1938); *Tb* Spiegel, 31/1992, 105; *Tb* Reuth, 1212–13 (11 March 1938); Irving, *Goebbels*, 243.

75. *Tb* Reuth, 1213 (11 March 1938).

76. *Tb* Irving, 101 (12 March 1938); *Tb* Spiegel, 31/1992, 106.

77. Papen, 427; Kube, 244 n.87. The dramatic events of 11 March are meticulously described in Ulrich Eichstädt, *Von Dollfuss zu Hitler. Geschichte des Anschlusses Österreichs 1933–1938*, Wiesbaden, 1955, 378–422.

78. *ADAP*, D. I, 468–70, no.352 (quotation, 469).

79. *IMG*, xxxiv, 336–7, Doc.102-C; Domarus, 809.

80. Papen, 428.

81. *IMG*, ix. 333; trans. *Trials of War Criminals before the Nuernberg Military Tribunals*, 12 vols., Nuremberg, 1946–9, xii.735.

82. *IMG*, ix. 333. See Papen, 438: 'The course of events in the Reich Chancellery on March 11, 1938, revealed the extent to which Goering had become the dominating personality among those who advocated the "total" solution.'

83. *IMG*, xvi.131–2; *Tb* Irving, 101–2 (12 March 1938); *Tb* Spiegel, 31/92, 106; Toland, 444; Pauley, 208.

84. *IMG*, xxxi.355–6, 358, 361, Doc. 2949-PS; *Nazi Conspiracy and Aggression*, ed. Office of the United States Chief of Counsel for Prosecution of Axis Criminality, Washington, 1946–8, v.629–31, 635; *Tb* Irving, 101–3 (12 March 1938); *Tb* Spiegel, 31/92, 106–7. Goebbels does not mention the demand to withdraw the plebiscite, and has Göring reporting that all demands were met, then posing a further – and almost identical – ultimatum for half an hour later. His own entry appears garbled.

85. Pauley, 208.

86. *NCA*, v.970, 982, Doc.3254-PS; see also *IMG*, xvi.199 (testimony of Michael Skubl, pointing out Seyß's embarrassed stance, and the impression he gave of being led rather than leading).

87. *Tb* Irving, 103 (12 March 1938); *Tb* Spiegel, 31/92, 107; *Tb* Reuth, 1214 (12 March 1938).

88. See Below, 89, who was told on returning to the Reich Chancellery on the early evening of 11 March that the next day 'Austria will be coordinated'.

89. *DBFP*, Series 3, I, 13, Doc. 25.

90. Geyl, 189.

91. *Tb* Reuth, 1214 (12 March 1938).

92. *Tb* Reuth, 1214 (12 March 1938).

93. Below, 89–90.

94. Shirer, *Berlin Diary* 82–3.

95. Pauley, 211. The Nazi Party in Austria had by this time around 164,000 members, more than twice as many as in 1933, when the NSDAP had been outlawed. With the Party proscribed, and in the absence of free elections, the level of its overall support in the population on the eve of the Anschluß can only be estimated. But in 1932, in regional elections, the NSDAP had already won around a fifth of the vote. See Gerhard Botz, 'Austria', in Detlef Mühlberger (ed.), *The Social Basis of European Fascist Movements*, London/New York/Sydney, 1987, 242–80, here 251. Assuming more than a doubling by 1938, in line with the level of increase in Party membership, it could be guessed that Nazi supporters (of differing levels of commitment) formed at least two-fifths of the population by the time the Anschluß crisis broke. Gerhard Botz's estimate of 25–35 per cent of the population who were enthusiasts for the Anschluß in 1938 may be too low (Gerhard Botz, *Der 13.März 38 und die Anschluß-Bewegung. Selbstaufgabe, Okkupation und Selbstfindung Österreichs 1918–1945*, Vienna, 1978, 27).

96. *Tb* Reuth, 1214 (12 March 1938); Pauley, 213; text in Domarus, 81 n.120.

97. *TWC*, xii.729.

98. Pauley, 213; Kube, 246; *Tb* Irving, 103 (12 March 1938); *Tb* Spiegel, 31/92, 107; Eichstädt, 411.

99. Keitel, 178; Papen, 430. Jodl had found Brauchitsch on the night of 11 March 'in a completely desolate mood' (*'in einer vollkommen desolaten Stimmung'*), fearing international repercussions (*IMG*, xv.442; Keitel, 178, n.27).

100. *IMG*, xxxi.369, Doc. 2949–PS; Domarus, 813; and see *Tb* Spiegel, 107, for Goebbels's reaction.

101. Domarus, 811.

102. Shirer, 83.

103. Pauley, 214; Toland, 450.

104. Keitel, 179.

105. *Tb* Irving, 104 (13 March 1938); *Tb* Spiegel, 31/92, 107; Domarus, 814 ('Freundschaftsbesuch' in DNB-Meldung, 12 March 1938). The official version had German troops crossing the border at 8a.m. (Domarus, 814).

106. Domarus, 814, has Hitler landing at 10a.m.; Keitel, 179 has a 6a.m. departure from Berlin; Below, 91, has Hitler leaving at 8 and landing at 10.

107. Below, 91; Keitel, 179. For Bock, see the sketches by Horst Mühleisen, 'Fedor von Bock – Soldat ohne Fortune', in Ronald Smelser and Enrico Syring (eds.), *Die Militärelite des Dritten Reiches*, Berlin/Frankfurt am Main, 1995, 6–82, and Samuel W. Mitcham Jr, 'Generalfeldmarschall Fedor von Bock', in Gerd R. Ueberschär (ed.), *Hitlers militärische Elite. Von den Anfängen des Regimes bis Kriegsbeginn*, Darmstadt, 1998, 37–44; and *Generalfeldmarshall Fedor von Bock. The War Diary, 1939–1945*, ed. Klaus Gerbet, Atglen PA, 1996, 16–17.

108. *Tb* Irving, 104 (13 March 1938); *Tb* Spiegel, 31/92, 107. See Papen, 438, for Hitler's orders for draft legislation to be prepared to make him head of both states in personal union.

109. Domarus, 816–17.

110. Below, 91; *Tb* Irving, 106 (13 March 1938); *Tb* Spiegel, 31/92, 107; Domarus, 817; Wagner and Tomkowitz, 194–5.

111. Below, 91.

112. Below, 92.

113. Heinz Guderian, *Panzer Leader*, New York (1952), Da Capo Press edn, 1996, 50–56, here 56.

114. Domarus, 817–18 and n.139; Wagner and Tomkowitz, 198–201.

115. *Tb* Irving, 107 (14 March 1938); *Tb* Spiegel, 31/92, 107. Gerhard Botz, *Nationalsozialismus in Wien. Machtübernahme und Herrschaftssicherung 1938/39*, 3rd edn, Buchloe, 1988, 71, suggests that delays in getting the troops to Vienna and the wish to be sure of reactions abroad were responsible for the postponement of Hitler's arrival in Vienna. But Guderian, who was in charge of the motorized units to enter Austria, later corrected the widely read, but misleading, account of military inefficiency and tank breakdowns, allegedly prompting fury from Hitler, as the reason (Guderian, 54–5; Churchill, i.242 (who probably derived his information from a usually well-

informed British witness of events in Vienna, G. E. R. Gedye, *Fallen Bastions. The Central European Tragedy*, London, 1939, 315–16. Gedye had been the *Daily Telegraph*'s correspondent in Austria for twelve years)).

116. See Schroeder, 85; Below, 92.

117. Below, 92.

118. Domarus, 819.

119. As suggested by David Irving, *Führer und Reichskanzler. Adolf Hitler 1933–1945*, Munich/ Berlin, 1989, 91.

120. Schuschnigg was by this time, while nominally free, in effect under house arrest. See Schuschnigg, *Austrian Requiem*, 59–60.

121. Franz Jetzinger, *Hitlers Jugend*, Vienna, 1956, 131–3, 136 (photo); Domarus, 821; Below, 93, for the visit to Leonding.

122. Domarus, 821; there is no record of any prior telephone conversation with Mussolini (see Keitel, 179, n.32), though it is likely that the telegram followed such a call, to ensure the Duce's approval for the final step of full Anschluß.

123. Domarus, 822.

124. Below, 92; Domarus, 820–21 for the law. A first draft had already been drawn up before Stuckart left Berlin (Erwin A. Schmidl, *März 38. Der deutsche Einmarsch in Österreich*, Vienna, 1987, 214).

125. Kube, 248 and n.118. Stuckart flew at midday on 13 March to Vienna to discuss the draft with Keppler and representatives of the Austrian government (Schmidl, 214).

126. '*Anschluß' 1938*, 330–31.

127. *Tb* Irving, 107, 108–9 (14–15 March 1938); *Tb* Spiegel, 31/92, 107, 110, entry for 14 March (dealing with events of the previous day) has 'The Anschluß is practically there. The Führer is staying in Linz on Sunday' ('*Der Anschluß ist praktisch da. Der Führer bleibt Sonntag in Linz*'). The entry for 15 March (reporting on 'yesterday') has: 'Anschluß completed. Election on 10 April ... The Austrian armed forces under the Führer's command' ('*Anschluß vollzogen. Am 10.April Wahl . . . Die österreichische Wehrmacht dem Führer unterstellt*'). This suggests that the signing of the Anschluß legislation took place in the evening of 13 March.

128. Account of the decision for the Anschluß based on Below, 92; Leonidas E. Hill (ed.), *Die Weizsäcker-Papiere 1933–1950*, Frankfurt am Main/Berlin/Vienna, 1974, 124 (26 March 1938); Domarus, 820–21; Schmidl, 214–15; '*Anschluß' 1938*, 328ff; Irving, *Führer*, 91.

129. Kube, 248–9; David Irving, *Göring. A Biography*, London, 1989, 210–11. The frequently cited version – see, for example, Toland, 452; Irving, *Führer*, 91; Wagner and Tomkowitz, 211 – of Göring sending an intermediary to Linz with the suggestion of moving to full Anschluß and Hitler agreeing, rests on a single piece of doubtful testimony, and reflects Göring's embellishment of his own role. (See Kube, 248 n.117.) Papen, influenced by Göring's Nuremberg testimony, also stated that Hitler moved to Anschluß at Goring's insistence (Papen, 438).

130. Domarus, 821; Below, 92; Pauley, 219–20.

131. Below, 92–3; Domarus, 822; Gedye, 318; Botz, *Wien*, 72.

132. Botz, *Wien*, 119.

133. Domarus, 822.

134. Gedye, 318.

135. Below, 93; Schroeder, 85; Domarus, 822; Gedye, 318–19; Botz, *Wien*, 73.

136. Keitel, 180.

137. Botz, *Wien*, 69–71.

138. Botz, *Wien*, 73–4.

139. Botz, *Wien*, 55–8.

140. Domarus, 823; Botz, *Wien*, 75.

141. Domarus, 824; Wagner and Tomkowitz, 226–9.

142. Papen, 432–3. Papen says the meeting lasted an hour. Botz, *Wien*, 76, 120, 523 n.19, claims it was no longer than a quarter of an hour. Hitler's tight schedule would not have allowed for Papen's lengthier audience.

143. Papen, 433; Botz, *Wien*, 120.

144. Botz, *Wien*, 123; Lewy, 212.

145. Domarus, 825; Botz, *Wien*, 122.

146. Domarus, 825–6; Botz, *Wien*, 76, 523 n.19.

147. Domarus, 830.

148. Domarus, 832–50.

149. BA, R55/445, 'Wahlparole Nr.8', 1 April 1938.

150. Domarus, 850.

151. BA, R55/445, 'Rundspruch Nr.69. Tagesparole vom 11. April 1938, betr. die Kommentierung des Wahlergebnisses'. ['*Ein solches, beinahe 100 prozentiges Wahlergebnis ist gleichzeitig ein Ruhmesblatt für alle Wahlpropagandisten.*']

152. See Botz, *Der 13.März 38*, 24–6, and, especially, Botz, *Wien*, ch.II; Ernst Hanisch, *Nationalsozialistische Herrschaft in der Provinz. Salzburg im Dritten Reich*, Salzburg, 1983, 52–71, for the vote in Austria; also Helmut Auerbach, 'Volksstimmung und veroffentlichte Meinung', in Knipping and Müller, 273–93, here 279. One example, cited by Auerbach (279 n.33), of ballot-rigging was the case in the Konstanz area where thirty-two voting slips containing 'Nein' votes had been counted as 'Ja'. (See Jörg Schadt (ed.), *Verfolgung und Widerstand unter dem Nationalsozialismus in Baden. Die Lageberichte der Gestapo und des Generalstaatsanwalts Karlsruhe 1933–1940*, Stuttgart, 1976, 270.)

153. *Tb* Irving, 123 (20 March 1938); *Tb* Spiegel, 31/92, 110.

154. Papen, 438.

155. Botz, *Wien*, 57.

156. Gerhard Botz, 'Die Ausgliederung der Juden aus der Gesellschaft. Das Ende des Wiener Judentums unter der NS-Herrschaft (1938–1943)', in Gerhard Botz, Ivar Oxaal, and Michael Pollak (eds.), *Eine zerstörte Kultur. Jüdisches Leben und Antisemitismus in Wien seit dem 19. Jahrhundert*, Buchloe, 1990, 285–312, here 289–90; Gedye, 307–9.

157. Gedye, 295.

158. Carl Zuckmayer, *Als wärs ein Stück von mir. Erinnerungen*, Frankfurt am Main (1966), 1971, 61.

159. George Clare, *Last Waltz in Vienna. The Destruction of a Family, 1842–1942*, Pan Books edn, London, 1982, 177–8.

160. Botz, *Wien*, 55; Gedye, 300–302; Wagner and Tomkowitz, 160–61.

161. Gedye, 305, 307, 313.

162. See Hans Safrian, *Eichmann und seine Gehilfen*, Frankfurt am Main, 1995, ch.1, especially 36ff.; Wildt, 52–4.

163. Janßen/Tobias, 190–94, quotation 194.

164. Cit. Kershaw, '*Hitler Myth*'. 130–31; and see Auerbach in Knipping and Müller, 278.

165. See Karl Stadler, *Österreich 1938–1945 im Spiegel der NS-Akten*, Vienna/Munich, 1966, ch.2; Botz, *Wien*, 355–64, 475–82; Tim Kirk, *Nazism and the Working Class in Austria. Industrial Unrest and Political Dissent in the National Community*, Cambridge, 1996, ch.2.

166. See Kershaw, '*Hitler Myth*', 124–32.

167. The German minority had indeed suffered some forms of economic and bureaucratic discrimination at the hands of the Czechs, though seldom of a serious nature before the Nazi takeover of power in Germany had given a new edge to ethnic tensions – mainly stirred up by the Sudeten Germans. Even then, Nazi propaganda within and outside the Sudetenland contrived to exaggerate the alleged maltreatment of the German population. See Ronald M. Smelser, *The Sudeten Problem 1933–1938. Volkstumspolitik and the Formulation of Nazi Foreign Policy*, Folkestone, 1975, 8–9,

214ff.; and, especially, the contemporary observations on the nature and degree of the discrimination against the German minority – described as 'easily the most privileged in the whole of Europe' – in Gedye, 396: 'At no time politically persecuted, always arrogantly conscious of the backing of Germany's sixty-six millions, its real grounds of complaint were limited to certain economic disabilities – which were in part politically necessary because of German disloyalty to the Republic – and to petty officiousness practised by some of the local Czech officials . . . Their minor grievances had been continually exaggerated, inflated, and trumpeted abroad by the German propaganda machine because they were an instrument to forward the German plans for hegemony in Eastern Europe.'

168. Helmut Groscurth, *Tagebücher eines Abwehroffiziers 1938–1940*, ed. Helmut Krausnick and Harold C. Deutsch, Stuttgart, 1970, 111–12 (4 September 1938).

169. Wiedemann, 171.

170. *IMG*, xxxiv.732–47, Doc.175-C.

171. *IMG*, xxxiv.745–7. See also *ADAP*, D, VII, 547ff. The term 'living space' was not understood by Beck and the army leadership in the same way that Hitler deployed it. But the vagueness of the concept meant such dangerous overlaps were possible. See Muller, *Heer*, 250 and n.215.

172. See Timothy W. Mason, *Arbeiterklasse und Volksgemeinschaft. Dokumente und Materialien zur deutschen Arbeiterpolitik 1936–1939*, Opladen, 1975, ch.XII.

173. Müller, *Beck*, 521; Klaus-Jürgen Müller, 'The Structure and Nature of the National Conservative Opposition in Germany up to 1940', in H. W. Koch (ed.), *Aspects of the Third Reich*, London, 1985, 132–78, here 159.

174. See Kube, Ch.VII.

175. See Hans Bernd Gisevius, *To the Bitter End*, Cambridge, Mass., 1947, 275–326; Erich Kordt, *Nicht aus den Akten . . . Die Wilhelmstraße in Frieden und Krieg. Erlebnisse, Begegnungen und Eindrücke 1928–1945*, Stuttgart, 1950, 232–57; Müller, in Koch, *Aspects*, 156ff.; Hans Rothfels, *The German Opposition to Hitler. An Assessment*, London, 1970, 56–63; and, especially, Harold C. Deutsch, *The Conspiracy against Hitler in the Twilight War*, Minneapolis, 1968, ch.1; and Peter Hoffmann, *Widerstand-Staatsstreich-Attentat. Der Kampf der Opposition gegen Hitler*, (1969), 4th edn, Munich/Zurich, 1985, ch.IV.

176. For Beck, see above all Muller, *Beck*, ch.6. Müller's interpretation of Beck gave rise to strong criticism from Peter Hoffmann, 'Generaloberst Ludwig Becks militärpolitisches Denken', *HZ*, 234 (1982), 101–21, who saw in Müller's treatment an undue emphasis on opportunism at the expense of stress on ethical motivation; and a sharp riposte from Klaus-Jurgen Müller, 'Militarpolitik nicht Militaropposition!', *HZ*, 235 (1982), 355–71. For Canaris, see Heinz Höhne, *Canaris – Patriot im Zwielicht*, Munich, 1976.

177. On Weizsäcker, see Rainer A. Blasius, *Für Großdeutschland – gegen den großen Krieg. Staatssekretär Ernst Freiherr von Weizsäcker in den Krisen um die Tschechoslowakei und Polen 1938/39*, Cologne/Vienna, 1981; and Rainer A. Blasius, 'Weizsäcker kontra Ribbentrop: "München" statt des großen Krieges', in Knipping and Muller, 93–118. As with Beck, Weizsäcker's motives have been differently interpreted. Leonidas E. Hill, the editor of Weizsäcker's papers, underlines the State Secretary's emphasis on a peaceful evolution to Germany's position as a world power (Leonidas E. Hill, 'Alternative Politik des Auswartigen Amtes bis zum 1. September 1939', in Jürgen Schmadeke and Peter Steinbach (eds.), *Der Widerstand gegen den Nationalsozialismus. Die deutsche Gesellschaft und der Widerstand gegen Hitler*, Munich/Zurich, 1985, 664–90, here 669–78). Blasius, in contrast, stresses Weizsäcker's affinity with Hitler's expansionist aims, though growing opposition to a war which he is certain will bring catastrophe on Germany.

178. See Ritter, ch.10; Klemens von Klemperer, *German Resistance against Hitler. The Search for Allies Abroad, 1938–1945*, Oxford, 1992, 86–101; Patricia Meehan, *The Unnecessary War. Whitehall and the German Resistance to Hitler*, London, 1992, 86–7, 102–3, 122ff.

179. A term used by the Regierungspräsident of Niederbayern and the Oberpfalz in his report of 8

September 1938, GStA, MA 106673. The SD's annual report for 1938 also spoke of a 'war psychosis' (*Meldungen aus dem Reich. Die geheimen Lageberichte des Sicherheitsdienstes der SS 1938–45*, 17 vols, ed. Heinz Boberach, Herrsching, 1984 (=*MadR*), ii.72–3).

180. See Kershaw, '*Hitler Myth*', 132–9; and Auerbach, in Knipping and Müller, 28off.

181. Bloch, 175.

182. *Weizsäcker-Papiere*, 136; *ADAP*, D, II, No. 374, 473; Blasius, in Knipping, 101.

183. Henderson thought another crisis like that on 21 May would push him over the edge (*DBFP*, Series 3, II, Appendix 1, 649, 651, 653, and Doc.823, 284).

184. *Tb* Irving, 123 (20 March 1938).

185. *IMG*, xxviii.372.

186. Weinberg II, 318; see also 366–70; Gerhard L. Weinberg, 'The May Crisis, 1938', *JMH*, 29 (1957), 213–25, especially 225; and Donald Cameron Watt, 'Hitler's visit to Rome and the May Weekend Crisis: A Study in Hitler's Response to External Stimuli', *JCH*, 9 (1974), 23–32 (and Weinberg's criticism of Watt's interpretation, in Weinberg II, 366 n.210).

187. See, for this term – derived from the analysis of Nazi rule by Franz Neumann, *Behemoth. The Structure and Practice of National Socialism*, London, 1942 (see his comments on 296, 382–3) – Peter Huttenberger, 'Nationalsozialistische Polykratie', *GG*, 2 (1976), 417–42.

188. Müller, *Heer*, 327; Müller, *Beck*, 350–51.

189. Klaus-Jürgen Müller, *Armee, Politik und Gesellschaft in Deutschland 1933–1945*, Paderborn, 1979, 43–4.

190. Even reports from oppositional sources made plain that, while opinion was divided on the likelihood and the outcome of war, extensive nazified sections of the population remained firmly behind Hitler. (See *DBS*, v.684–90, report for July 1938, drawn up on 24 August 1938.)

191. Weinberg II, 328, 363–4.

192. Weinberg II, 341, 352ff.

193. Weinberg II, 322–3.

194. Weinberg II, 343.

195. Weinberg II, 348; quotation from Lord Halifax to Henderson, 19 March 1938.

196. Weinberg II, 325. For the exaggeration of grievances in German propaganda, see Gedye, 396.

197. *Tb* Irving, 91 (7 March 1938); and see Irving, *Goebbels*, 242.

198. Weinberg II, 334.

199. *IMG*, xxviii.372. The British Prime Minister Neville Chamberlain had himself 'likened Germany to a boa constrictor that had eaten a good meal and was trying to digest the meal before taking anything else' (cit. Weinberg II, 302).

200. *ADAP*, D, II, 157, No.106; and see Smelser, 217ff.

201. *DGFP*, D, II, 242, No.135.

202. *DGFP*, D, II, 198, No.197; Weinberg II, 335.

203. Weinberg II, 321; and see Michels, 382, for Goebbels's propaganda during the Sudeten crisis.

204. See his views as recorded in Hoßbach's memorandum of the meeting on 5 November 1937 (*DGFP*, D, I, 29–39, especially 32–4, No.19; Weinberg II, 317, 336).

205. See Hitler's 'Denkschrift zur Frage unserer Festungsanlagen' of 1 July 1938 in Otto-Wilhelm Förster, *Das Befestigungswesen*, Neckargemünd, 1960, Anlage 13, 123–48; also John D. Heyl, 'The Construction of the Westwall, 1938: An Exemplar for National Socialist Policymaking', *Central European History*, 14 (1981), 63–78; and Weinberg II, 318.

206. See Weinberg II, 337.

207. Keitel, 182. Keitel dates the meeting to 20 April. But for the correct date of 21 April see *IMG*, xxv.415–18, Doc.388-PS; Domarus, 851 (and 851–2 for Schmundt's notes); and Weinberg II, 337–8 and n.91.

208. Domarus, 851–2; Weinberg II, 338.

209. Keitel, 183; *DGFP*, D, II.300–303, here 300, No.175.

210. Müller, *Beck*, 510 (full text pp.502–12); Müller, *Heer*, 301ff.

211. Keitel, 184; Müller, *Heer*, 305.

212. Keitel, 184–5; Below, 105–6; Weinberg II, 318, 371; and see Franz W. Seidler, *Fritz Todt. Baumeister des Dritten Reiches*, Munich, 1986, ch.4. I am grateful to Steven F. Sage for sharing some insights into Todt and his work, which will be re-evaluated in his forthcoming study, and letting me see an unpublished paper he had compiled on Todt. The army's planning for the Westwall had looked to the construction of large, well-provisioned underground fortresses mirroring the French Maginot Line. This clashed with Hitler's conception of a far greater number of relatively simple fortified gun-sites and anti-tank structures, aimed heavily at deterrent effect. (See Heyl, 64–5.)

213. See Below, 106.

214. *Monologe*, 344 (16 August 1942).

215. Schmidt, 390; Bloch, 181.

216. Ciano, *Tagebücher 1937/1938*, 156–9 (entries for 3–9 May 1938); Eugen Dollmann, *Dolmetscher der Diktatoren*, Bayreuth, 1963, 37–8; Wiedemann, 140.

217. Schmidt, 392–3; Wiedemann, 141–2; Ciano, *Tagebücher*, 156, note. There are minor discrepancies between the reliable description of Schmidt and that of Wiedemann (who does not mention the performance of *Aïda*, and has Hitler inspecting a Nazi formation following a glittering dinner attended not by the King, but by the Crown Prince).

218. Bloch, 181.

219. Ciano, *Tagebücher*, 157 (entry for 6 May 1938); Bloch, 182; see also Schmidt, 394.

220. Domarus, 861; and see Schmidt, 394–5.

221. *DGFP*, D, I, 1108–10, No.761–2; Weinberg II, 340.

222. *DGFP*, D, I, 1110, No.762; Weinberg II, 309.

223. Politisches Archiv, Auswärtiges Amt, Bonn, Pol.2a 1 (6936), Bd.16, Deutsch-italienische pol. Beziehungen, Jan.-Sept. 1938. ('*Was sudetendeutsche Frage anlangt, so ergaben Unterhaltungen ohne weiteres, daß Italiener für unsere Anteilnahme am sudetendeutschen Schicksal Verständnis haben.*')

224. *Weizsäcker-Papiere*, 127–8.

225. See the accounts in Bloch, 183–5; Weinberg II, 367–9; Weinberg, 'May Crisis', and Watt, 'Hitler's Visit to Rome'.

226. Boris Celovsky, *Das Münchener Abkommen 1938*, Stuttgart, 1958, 209 and n.2.

227. Schmidt, 395–6.

228. *DBFP*, Ser.3, I, 332–3, 341, Nos.250, 264.

229. *DGFP*, D, II, 315–17, No.186.

230. Bloch, 185.

231. Bloch, 185; Weinberg II, 369.

232. *IMG*, xxviii.372. For the suggestion that the timing of Hitler's order of 30 May was not caused by the May Crisis, but rested on his deliberations of 20 April, see Weinberg II, 366, and 337 n.87, and 370 n.219, for the dating of Jodl's diary entry to June–July.

233. Keitel, 185 (on Hitler's return to Berlin; he brings it in direct relation with new directions for 'Green'). See also Hitler's public statements, indicating his response to the 'Czech provocation', in speeches on 12 September 1938 and 30 January 1939 (Domarus, 868–9).

234. Wilhelm Treue (ed.), 'Rede Hitlers vor der deutschen Presse (10. November 1938)', *VfZ*, 6 (1958), 175–91, here 183.

235. Wiedemann, 126; Dülffer, *Marine*, Düsseldorf, 1973, 466.

236. Dulffer, *Marine*, 471–4. Hitler demanded the building of six heavy battleships – the beginnings of the later Z-Plan – saying to Raeder that he needed a 'risk fleet' in order to reach terms with Great Britain ('. . . *daß er eine Risikoflotte haben müsse, ohne die es nicht zu einem Ausgleich mit England kommen werde*'). (IfZ, ZS–41, Admiral a.D. Werner Fuchs, 16 December 1951, Fol.16.) Raeder was

well aware in 1938 of the hopelessness (*Aussichtslosigkeit*) of a war at sea against the British Navy (BA/MA, PG/34566, Akten des Oberbefehlshabers der Kriegsmarine, Großadmiral Erich Raeder, 'Aus der Unterrichtung des Amtschefs A am 12.7.38 . . .') The navy leadership saw the six battleships as the minimum over the following six years for an eventual conflict with Britain which would involve, taking account of the British Empire and other nations, war against a third to a half of the entire world (BA/MA, PG 34566, Admiral Rolf Carls, 'Stellungnahme zur "Entwurfstudie" Seekriegführung gegen England', September 1938).

237. Wiedemann, 128.

238. *NCA*, i.520–51, Doc.PS–3037; Wiedemann, 127.

239. Muller, *Beck*, 512–20 (and also 290ff.).

240. *IMG*, xxv.433–9, here 433–4, Doc.388–PS; *DGFP*, D, II, 358–64, here 358, No.221.

241. *ADAP*, D, II, 377–80 (quotation, 377), No.282; *DGFP*, D, II, 473–7, here 473, No.282.

242. Michael Geyer, 'Restorative Elites, German Society, and the Nazi Pursuit of War', in Richard Bessel (ed.), *Fascist Italy and Nazi Germany. Comparisons and Contrasts*, Cambridge, 1996, 134–64, here 163; see also *Das Deutsche Reich und der Zweite Weltkrieg* (= *DRZW*), ed. Militärgeschichtliches Forschungsamt, 6 vols. so far published, Stuttgart, i.644ff.

243. Muller, *Beck*, 521–37 (and 289–97).

244. Müller, *Beck*, 523–5.

245. Müller, *Heer*, 313.

246. Müller, *Heer*, 313–14. See Janßen/Tobias, 206–19, for the inaccuracy of the rumours that Brauchitsch had been 'bought' by Hitler through a sizeable bribe to assist in the costs incurred through divorcing his wife in order to remarry. Brauchitsch's subservience to Hitler was not purchased; it came naturally.

247. Müller, *Heer*, 314.

248. Muller, *Armee*, Dok.115, S.259–61 (Halder's report on Hitler's speech); Below, 103–5; Janßen/Tobias, 237ff.; Weinberg II, 385; Müller, *Beck*, 297; Muller, *Heer*, 315; IfZ, ED 1, Fol.416–17, 'Persönliche Erlebnisse des Generals d.Inf. a.D. Curt Liebmann in den Jahren 1938/39' (compiled in November 1939).

249. Janßen/Tobias, 240.

250. Müller, *Beck*, 298–300.

251. Muller, *Beck*, 300–301 (and n.88 for a date after 16 June for the concluding discussion).

252. Muller, *Beck*, 307–8, 537–62. Beck imagined Brauchitsch issuing Hitler in the second half of September with a collective protest of the top military leadership and refusal to collaborate in a war against Czechoslovakia (Müller, *Beck*, 558). See also Muller, *Heer*, 315–33.

253. Muller, *Beck*, 552.

254. Muller, *Heer*, 333–5 and n.138, 337; Muller, *Beck*, 542–50, for the text of Beck's memorandum of 16 July 1938. See also the account of the meeting (misdated to 3 August 1938) in General Liebmann's memoirs, IfZ, ED 1, Fol.418.

255. Müller, *Heer*, 335–7.

256. Müller, *Heer*, 337.

257. Below, 112.

258. Below, 113.

259. Anton Hoch and Hermann Weiß, 'Die Erinnerungen des Generalobersten Wilhelm Adam', in Wolfgang Benz (ed.), *Miscellanea: Festschrift für Helmut Krausnick zum 75. Geburtstag*, Stuttgart, 1980, 32–62, here 54. Adam's account is to be preferred to one in which Hitler's fury was directed at Beck's criticism of the Westwall (Muller, *Heer*, 338).

260. Below, 113.

261. IfZ, ED 1, Liebmann Memoirs, Fol.417–18; Müller, *Heer*, 339; Keitel, 186–7; Below, 115.

262. Müller, *Heer*, 339.

263. Muller, *Heer*, 333, 339–40; Muller, *Beck*, 310–11.

264. Muller, *Heer*, 340; Muller, *Beck*, 557.

265. Müller, *Beck*, 311, 580.

266. See Müller, *Beck*, 311. For extensive analysis of Beck's position and radicalization during the summer of 1938, see Müller, *Heer*, ch.7.

267. Klemperer, 96–101; Meehan, 141ff.

268. Kube, 269.

269. Weinberg II,383 and n.18.

270. Wiedemann, 166; Müller, *Beck*, 557, 559; Bloch, 188–9; Weinberg II, 383.

271. Wiedemann, 166, 235–6; Bloch, 188–9; Weinberg II,383.

272. *TWC*, xii.798–9. Hitler and Goring had told naval chiefs much the same in July (BA/MA, PG/34566, Akten des Oberbefehlshabers der Kriegsmarine, Großadmiral Erich Raeder, 'Aus der Unterrichtung des Amtschefs A am 12.7.38 . . .').

273. Ernst von Weizsäcker, *Erinnerungen*, Munich/Leipzig/Freiburg i.Br., 1950, 192 (and for his quoted words, 165).

274. Cit. Blasius in Knipping and Müller, 118.

275. Irving, *Führer*, 118–19 (with examples, but no sources). See also Broszat, *Staat Hitlers*, 418.

276. Below, 112, 114–15.

277. *TBJG*, I/6, 49 (19 August 1938).

278. Cit. Irving, *Führer*, 127.

279. Text in Förster, *Befestigungswesen*, 123–48, here especially 132, 137, 143; and see Keitel, 185–6, for Hitler's intended fortifications on the Westwall.

280. Irving, *Fuhrer*, 128; Mason, *Arbeiterklasse*, 106, 556, 667, 849.

281. Hoch and Weiß, 55.

282. *TBJG*, I/6, 59 (26 August 1938).

283. *TBJG*, I/6, 61–2 (28 August 1938).

284. *TBJG*, I/6, 63 (30 August 1938).

285. *TBJG*, I/6, 68 (1 September 1938).

286. Muller, *Beck*, 538–9, 544–5, 561.

287. Shirer, 102.

288. *TBJG*, I/6, 65 (31 August 1938), 68 (1 September 1938).

289. See Kershaw, '*Hitler Myth*', 133ff.; Auerbach in Knipping and Müller, 282–3.

290. BA/MA, RW19/41, WWI VII (Munich, 9 September 1938).

291. Groscurth, 105 n.29; Smelser, 231–2.

292. Bloch, 191; Weinberg II, 421, 428; Klemperer, 101ff.; Meehan, 149ff.

293. *DBFP*, Ser.3, II, 195–6, No.727 (and see also 220–21, No.752).

294. Weinberg II, 418–20; Smelser, 235.

295. Smelser, 235.

296. Smelser, 236–7.

297. Groscurth, 104 and n.26.

298. Groscurth, 111.

299. Groscurth, 104.

300. Groscurth, 107.

301. Groscurth, 112.

302. Groscurth, 112 and n.62; Smelser, 234–5.

303. *DGFP*, D/II, 686–7, No.424; and see Bloch, 191.

304. Groscurth, 113–15.

305. Groscurth, 109.

306. Groscurth, 107.

307. Groscurth, 109.

308. Groscurth, 112.

309. Cit. Weinberg II, 423 n.195.

310. Domarus, 900–905 (especially 904–5); Shirer, 104–5 for reactions.

311. Schmidt, 401.

312. Shirer, 104–5.

313. At a meeting with his military leaders at Nuremberg on September 9–10, the target day was confirmed as that stated in Plan Green (1 October) (*DGFP*, D, II, 727–30, No.448 (notes of Schmundt); Smelser, 238).

314. Smelser, 237.

315. Weinberg II, 426–9.

316. *TBJG*, I/6, 91 (15 September 1938); Groscurth, 118.

317. Schmidt, 401; Keith Feiling, *The Life of Neville Chamberlain*, London, 1946, 364.

318. He confessed to 'some slight sinking when I found myself flying over London and looking down thousands of feet at the houses below', but he was soon enjoying 'the marvellous spectacle of ranges of glittering white cumulus clouds stretching away to the horizon below me', before experiencing 'more nervous moments when we circled down over the aerodrome' in Munich after passing through some turbulence when 'the aeroplane rocked and bumped like a ship in a sea'. (Birmingham University Library, Chamberlain Collection, NC 18/1/1069, letter of Neville Chamberlain to his sister Ida, 19 September 1938.)

319. Birmingham University Library, Chamberlain Collection, NC 18/1/1069, letter of Neville Chamberlain to his sister Ida, 19 September 1938.

320. Schmidt, 401–7; *DGFP*, D, II, 787–98, No.487; *DBFP*, Ser.3, II, 342–51, No.896. According to Chamberlain's notes of the meeting (*DBFP*, Ser.3, II, 338–41, No.895, here 340), his reply to Hitler had been: 'If the Führer is determined to settle this matter by force without even waiting for a discussion between ourselves to take place, what did he let me come here for? I have wasted my time.'

321. Schmidt, 406, blames it on Ribbentrop. As Weinberg II points out, however, 433 and n.235, it appears that Ribbentrop was acting on Hitler's orders. See *DGFP*, D, II, 830–31, no.532.

322. Weinberg II, 433.

323. Weizsäcker, *Erinnerungen*, 184.

324. *Weizsäcker-Papiere*, 143.

325. *TBJG*, I/6, 94 (17 September 1938); Below, 123. Keitel, 189, claimed that Hitler was not satisfied at the outcome. This assertion is left unsupported, and contradicts the impressions of Weizsäcker and Below.

326. Below, 123. Keitel's own account – since he had been present at the Berghof, but not at the actual talks – must have drawn upon Hitler's own description and diminished the role played by Chamberlain. Hitler, reported Keitel, had threatened the cancellation of the naval pact, at which Chamberlain had 'collapsed' (*zusammengesackt*). The Führer had added that he was ready for anything, and had twenty years' advantage over the British Prime Minister. To spare Chamberlain the long journey to Berchtesgaden, he agreed to meet him in Godesberg. He was prepared to travel to London but would be exposed there to insults of the Jews. 'There is a determination to march,' Keitel concluded. (Groscurth, 120 and n.102–3.)

327. Weinberg II, 438.

328. Birmingham University Library, Chamberlain Collection, NC 18/1/1069, letter of Neville Chamberlain to his sister Ida, 19 September 1938.

329. Weinberg II, 437–44.

330. *TBJG*, I/6, 94 (17 September 1938).

331. *TBJG*, I/6, 99 (19 September 1938).

332. *TBJG*, I/6, 101 (20 September 1938).

333. *TBJG*, I/6, 98 (18 September 1938).

334. Groscurth, 120 and n.104; Weinberg II, 434.

335. See Goebbels's report on Hitler's thinking in *TBJG*, I/6, 113 (26 September 1938).

336. *TBJG*, I/6, 101 (20 September 1938), 103 (21 September 1938), 105 (22 September 1938).

337. *TBJG*, I/6, 103 (21 September 1938).

338. Schmidt, 407.

339. Shirer, 113. For references to Hitler as the 'carpet-biter' in the middle of the war, see Kershaw, '*Hitler Myth*', 187.

340. Schmidt, 407–9.

341. Schmidt, 409–11.

342. Schmidt, 412.

343. *TBJG*, I/6, 105 (22 September 1938).

344. Schmidt, 412.

345. Schmidt, 413–14.

346. *TBJG*, I/6, 113 (26 September 1938).

347. See Weizsäcker, *Erinnerungen*, 184; *Weizsäcker-Papiere*, 143.

348. Below's recollection differed somewhat. According to his later account, Hitler did not believe that the Czechs would fall into line with British and German demands. Therefore, he would continue with Plan Green, aimed at the occupation of the whole of Czechoslovakia. Hitler had told his military leaders that this would be his favourite solution. The talks with Chamberlain had confirmed his impression that Britain and France would not intervene militarily. (Below, 126.)

349. Weinberg II, 449.

350. Schmidt, 415; Henderson, 159; *DBFP*, Ser.3, II, 554–7 (quotation, 555), No.1118, where Kirkpatrick's note reads: 'If France and England decided to strike, let them strike. He did not care a farthing.'

351. Domarus, 933, has 20,000; Shirer, 116, has 15,000.

352. Shirer, 116.

353. *TBJG*, I/6, 116 (27 September 1938).

354. Domarus, 928.

355. Domarus, 930–32.

356. Domarus, 932 (and see also 927).

357. Domarus, 932.

358. Domarus, 932–3; Shirer, 116–17.

359. Henderson, 160; Schmidt, 416–17.

360. Henderson, 160; Schmidt, 417.

361. Schmidt, 416.

362. Henderson, 160–61; Groscurth, 125–6, n.130–31 (for Weizsäcker's authorship); Schmidt, 417; Weinberg, II, 451 and n.294 for the timing of the decision to write to Chamberlain being taken before the military demonstration that afternoon; *DGFP*, D, II, 966–8, No.635; *DBFP*, Ser.3, II, 576–8, No.1144.

363. Henderson, 161.

364. Below, 127.

365. Shirer, 117; and see Wiedemann, 175–6.

366. *TBJG*, I/6, 119 (29 September 1938).

367. Below, 127.

368. Schmidt, 417; Shirer, 117. See also *Weizsäcker-Papiere*, 145; Engel, 39–40; Ruth Andreas-Friedrich, *Schauplatz Berlin. Ein deutsches Tagebuch*, Munich, 1962, 5–6; and Marlis Steinert, *Hitlers Krieg und die Deutschen. Stimmung und Haltung der deutschen Bevölkerung im Zweiten Weltkrieg*, Düsseldorf/Vienna, 1970, 77–9.

369. *Weizsäcker-Papiere*, 170.

370. Groscurth, 125 (27 September 1938) and n.127.

371. Himmler, as Weizsäcker subsequently implied, also favoured war. (See Weizsäcker, *Erin-*

nerungen, 191.) The growth of his SS empire was predicated upon German expansion. But his involvement in foreign-policy deliberations was minimal.

372. Groscurth, 128 (28 September 1938).

373. Kube, 273–5.

374. Neville Chamberlain, *The Struggle for Peace*, London, 1939, 275; Groscurth, 125 n.129.

375. Chamberlain, 299; Schmidt, 420.

376. Henderson, 162–3.

377. *DBFP*, Ser.3, II, 587, no.1159; Feiling, 372–3.

378. Henderson, 162.

379. Weizsäcker, *Erinnerungen*, 186–7.

380. Henderson, 162–3.

381. Schmidt, 418.

382. Henderson, 163; *TBJG*, I/6, 119 (29 September 1938).

383. André François-Poncet, *Als Botschafter im Dritten Reich. Die Erinnerungen des französischen Botschafters in Berlin September 1931 bis Oktober 1938*, Mainz/Berlin, 1980, 378; Schmidt, 418–19.

384. Schmidt, 420; Henderson, 164.

385. Schmidt, 420.

386. Henderson, 164.

387. *TBJG*, I/6, 119 (29 September 1938).

388. Henderson, 164–6; *DBFP*, 3rd Ser., 11. 597, No.1180; Weinberg II, 453–6 for the diplomatic background to Mussolini's decision. Goebbels (*TBJG*, I/6, 119 (29 September 1938)) mistakenly remarks that the idea for the Four-Power Conference was Hitler's.

389. *Chips*, 171; see also Harold Nicolson, *Diaries and Letters, 1930–1964*, New York, 1980, 138; Jones, 410–11; *Diaries of Sir Alexander Cadogan*, 109; Richard Lamb, *The Ghosts of Peace, 1935–1945*, Salisbury, 1987, 86. Chamberlain himself commented a few days later: 'That the news of the deliverance should come to me in the very act of closing my speech in the House was a piece of drama that no work of fiction saw surpassed' (University of Birmingham Library, Chamberlain Papers, NC 18/1/1070, letter of Neville Chamberlain to his sister, Hilda, 2 October 1938). The Labour and Liberal leaders were warm in their approval of Chamberlain's decision to go to Munich, though they were aware that any settlement would mean the cession of the Sudetenland to Germany. Conservative critics, including Winston Churchill and Anthony Eden were silent. Only one Member of Parliament – a Communist – protested. (Roy Douglas, 'Chamberlain and Appeasement', in Wolfgang J. Mommsen and Lothar Kettenacker (eds.), *The Fascist Challenge and the Policy of Appeasement*, London, 1983, 79–88, here 86–7.)

390. *TBJG*, I/6, 120 (29 September 1938).

391. Schmidt, 421. See Celovsky, ch.10, especially 460ff., for a detailed account of the course of the conference and its results; also Keith Eubank, *Munich*, Norman, Oklahoma, 1963, 207–22.

392. University of Birmingham Library, Chamberlain Papers, NC 18/1/1070, letter of Neville Chamberlain to his sister, Hilda, 2 October 1938.

393. Description of the conference proceedings from Schmidt, 421–4. See also *DBFP*, 3rd Ser., 11, 630–5, No.1227; Henderson, 166–8. For the authorship of the proposal attributed to Mussolini, see Schmidt, 423, Weinberg II, 457; Kube, 273; and Blasius, *Für Deutschland*, 68.

394. Henderson, 166.

395. Schmidt, 421.

396. Schmidt, 424.

397. Henderson, 167.

398. *TBJG*, I/6, 122 (30 September 1938).

399. *TBJG*, I/6, 122 (1 October 1938).

400. Groscurth, 128 (29 September 1938) and n.142; Weizsäcker, *Erinnerungen*, 187–8; Schmidt, 425–6.

401. Schmidt, 425–6; see Below, 129 (a distorted account). Kube, 276 n.86; Michalka, *Ribbentrop*, 240 n.2; Josef Henke, *England*, 187–204, for Hitler's negative reactions to Munich.

402. University of Birmingham Library, Chamberlain Papers, NC 18/1/1070, letter of Neville Chamberlain to his sister, Hilda, 2 October 1938.

403. Schmidt, 425; *DBFP*, 3rd Ser., 11, 635–50, No.1228.

404. See Henderson, 174–5.

405. *IMG*, xxvi.343, Doc.798-PS.

406. Kube, 275–8, 299ff.

407. Henke, *England*, 188.

408. According to Below, Hitler's Wehrmacht adjutant Major Engel reported at the time that he had found Halder slumped across his desk when the announcement of the Munich Conference was made. Below was incredulous, since he was aware that Halder had been against mobilization, and only, he said, understood following the post-war revelations about his connections with a plot to depose Hitler how the Munich Agreement had pulled the rug from under his feet (Below, 130). For Halder's connections with the emergent opposition to Hitler, and for his behaviour during the Sudeten crisis, see Hoffmann, 109–29; Christian Hartmann, *Halder. Generalstabschef Hitlers 1938–1942*, Paderborn etc., 1991, 99–116; and also Gerd R. Ueberschär, *Generaloberst Franz Halder. Generalstabschef, Gegner und Gefangener Hitlers*, Göttingen, 1991, 33–4. On Munich and the failure of the coup plans, see Gisevius, *Bis zum bittern Ende*, 326; Klemperer, 109–10; and Hoffmann, 128–9. For the internal divisions of those opposed to war, and the coup plans, see Müller, in Koch, *Aspects*, 163–72.

409. University of Birmingham Library, Chamberlain Papers, NC 18/1/1070, letter of Neville Chamberlain to his sister, Hilda, 2 October 1938, where the euphoric scenes in the streets as he was driven from the aerodrome at Heston to Buckingham Palace, then in Downing Street, are described. See also *The Diaries of Sir Alexander Cadogan, 1938–1945*, ed. David Dilks, London, 1971, 111; Winston S. Churchill, *The Second World War. Vol.1: The Gathering Storm*, London etc., 1948, 286. For Chamberlain's immediate regret at having used such a phrase while swept away by emotion on his return, see Nicolson, 140; Halifax, 198–9.

410. *Manchester Guardian*, 1 October 1938.

411. Gisevius, *Bis zum bittern Ende*, 326; Müller, in Koch, *Aspects*, 171. See also Ritter, 204; Ulrich von Hassell, *Die Hassell-Tagebücher 1938–1944. Aufzeichnungen vom Andern Deutschland*, ed. Friedrich Freiherr Hiller von Gaertringen, Berlin, 1988, 54–7.

412. Kershaw, *'Hitler Myth'*, 138; Auerbach in Knipping and Müller, 284–6; Steinert, 79; Below, 129.

413. Treue, 'Rede Hitlers vor der deutschen Presse', 182.

CHAPTER 3: MARKS OF A GENOCIDAL MENTALITY

1. For the sphere of competence of the Party's central office, see, especially, Peter Longerich, *Hitlers Stellvertreter. Führung der Partei und Kontrolle des Staatsapparates durch den Stab Heß und die Partei-Kanzlei Bormann*, Munich etc., 1992; and Dietrich Orlow, *The History of the Nazi Party, vol.2, 1933–1945*, Newton Abbot, 1973.

2. Bernd Wegner, *Hitlers Politische Soldaten: Die Waffen-SS 1933–1945*, Paderborn, 1982, 114–15.

3. See Weizsäcker, *Erinnerungen*, 188, 191.

4. Bradley F. Smith and Agnes F. Peterson (eds.), *Heinrich Himmler. Geheimreden 1933 bis 1945*. Frankfurt am Main/Berlin/Vienna, 1974, 37 (speech to SS-Gruppenführern, 8 November 1938). See also Peter Padfield, *Himmler. Reichsführer-SS*, London, 1991, 238.

5. The term '*Reich*kristallnacht' was an ironic reference, alluding not simply to the amount of

broken crystal-glass littering the streets in the centre of Berlin and other cities, but also to the obvious orchestration of the destruction from above, despite the propaganda line that there had been a spontaneous outburst of the people's anger against the Jews (Graml, *Reichskristallnacht*, 35).

6. Fundamental studies are those of Helmut Genschel, *Die Verdrängung der Juden aus der Wirtschaft im Dritten Reich*, Göttingen, 1966; and Avraham Barkai, *Vom Boykott zur 'Entjudung'. Der wirtschaftliche Existenzkampf der Juden im Dritten Reich 1933–1943*, Frankfurt am Main, 1987. See also Avraham Barkai, 'Schicksalsjahr 1938', in Walter H. Pehle (ed.), *Der Judenpogrom 1938. Von der 'Reichskristallnacht' zum Völkermord*, Frankfurt am Main, 1988, 94–117, 220–24; and Günter Plum, 'Wirtschaft und Erwerbsleben', in Wolfgang Benz (ed.), *Die Juden in Deutschland 1933–1945. Leben unter nationalsozialistischer Herrschaft*, Munich, 1988, 268–313.

7. Graml, *Reichskristallnacht*, 170.

8. Graml, *Reichskristallnacht*, 171–5.

9. *IMG*, xxvii, 163.

10. Graml, *Reichskristallnacht*, 171; Peter Hanke, *Zur Geschichte der Juden in München zwischen 1933 und 1945*, Munich, 1967, 204–5; Baruch Z. Ophir and Falk Wiesemann (eds.), *Die jüdischen Gemeinden in Bayern 1918–1945. Geschichte und Zerstörung*, Munich, 1979, 50.

11. Ophir and Wiesemann, 211; Fritz Nadler, *Eine Stadt im Schatten Streichers*, Nuremberg, 1969, 8–10, and Bild 2.

12. Gordon, 153.

13. Bankier, 'Hitler', 8.

14. Examples include pressure from Heß to include Mischlinge (part-Jews) in the discriminatory legislation, demands from the NS Lawyers' League (NS-Rechtswahrerbund) to exclude Jewish lawyers, and the successful complaint by the Reich Doctors' Leader Gerhard Wagner to Hitler that Jewish doctors were still allowed to practise in Germany. (Adam, *Judenpolitik* 167–70; Bankier, 'Hitler', 15; Wildt, 45; Longerich, *Hitlers Stellvertreter*, 214–16.)

15. See Raul Hilberg, *The Destruction of the European Jews*, (1961), Viewpoints edn, New York, 1973, 60ff.; Karl A. Schleunes, *The Twisted Road to Auschwitz. Nazi Policy Toward German Jews, 1933–1939*, Urbana/Chicago/London, 1970, 160–64, 222–3; Barkai, 'Schicksalsjahr', 96–109; Barkai, *Boykott*, ch.3; Friedländer, 243; Harold James, 'Die Deutsche Bank und die Diktatur', in Lothar Gall et al., *Die Deutsche Bank 1870–1995*, Munich, 1995, pt.II, especially 347–51.

16. Michael H. Kater, *Doctors under Hitler*, Chapel Hill/London, 1989, 198–201; Barkai, *Boykott*, 133–4.

17. Victor Klemperer, *Ich will Zeugnis ablegen bis zum letzten. Tagebücher 1933–1941*, ed. Walter Nowojski and Hadwig Klemperer, (1995), 10th edn, Darmstadt, 1998, 415 (12 July 1938).

18. One poignant account, among the many, of the impact of the rapidly deteriorating conditions on a single family is that of Peter Gay, *My German Question. Growing Up in Nazi Berlin*, New Haven/London, 1998, here especially 119–23.

19. The role of denunciation in helping to enforce and drive on anti-Jewish policy has been examined by Robert Gellately, *The Gestapo and German Society. Enforcing Racial Policy, 1933–1945*, Oxford, 1990.

20. See especially, Wildt, 35ff., and Dok.9–32; also, the files relating to Eichmann's Department II.112, in BA, R58/991–5; and Hachmeister, ch.V.

21. *Tb* Irving, 169–70 (23 April 1938).

22. See Magnus Brechtken, *'Madagaskar für die Juden'. Antisemitische Idee und politische Praxis 1885–1945*, Munich, 1997, especially chs.II–III.

23. According to the SD's figures, some 370,000 Jews still remained in the 'Old Reich' territory on 1 January 1938 – almost three-quarters of the recorded figure in 1933. Taking account of an estimated 200–250,000 Jews who found themselves on German territory after the annexations of Austria and the Sudetenland, there were by late summer 1938 – even taking account of the forced

emigration that year – probably more Jews in Nazi hands than there had been at the time of Hitler's takeover of power (*MadR*, ii.21–2, 27–9).

24. Zionists had contacted Eichmann in February 1937 in the hope of encouraging more favourable arrangements for allowing Jews to emigrate to Palestine. Feivel Polkes, an emissary of the Haganah, a Jewish underground military organization, was authorized to come to Berlin and meet Eichmann for discussions about easing restrictions on the transfer of foreign currency in order to facilitate emigration. Polkes left empty-handed, but subsequently invited Eichmann to visit the Middle East. With his superior, Herbert Hagen, Eichmann left for Palestine in early November 1937. Unrest in Palestine prevented any meeting taking place there, but Eichmann and Hagen met Polkes again in Cairo. On his return, Eichmann reported negatively to Heydrich on Polkes's proposals for subsidizing Jewish emigration to Palestine. By then, in any case, fears in the Nazi leadership of the dangers of helping erect a Jewish state in Palestine had grown rapidly. Hitler himself had intervened to order the suspension of negotiations for further transfer agreements between Germany and Palestine. (BA, R58/954, Fols.11–66 (Hagen's report); Schleunes, 207–11; Jochen von Lang, *Das Eichmann-Protokoll. Tonbandaufzeichnungen der israelischen Verhöre*, Berlin, 1982, 31–5, 43–6; Wildt, 44. And see Francis R. Nicosia, *The Third Reich and the Palestine Question*, Austin/London, 1985.)

25. Wildt, 44.

26. Wildt, 32–3.

27. Wildt, 33.

28. Wildt, 60.

29. *TBJG*, I/3, 490 (25 July 1938).

30. See Christian Gerlach, 'Die Wannsee-Konferenz, das Schicksal der deutschen Juden und Hitlers politische Grundsatzentscheidung, alle Juden Europas zu ermorden', *Werkstattgeschichte*, 18 (1997), 7–44, here 27.

31. *Tb* Irving, 214 (25 May 1938). Economics Minister Walther Funk was brought into the discussions by Goebbels.

32. Wildt, 55–6.

33. *Tb* Irving, 214 (25 May 1938), 253 (2 July 1938).

34. Goebbels stated in his diary again in late July that 'the Führer approves how I am going about things (*mein Vorgehen*) in Berlin' (*Tb* Irving, 268 (26 July 1938)).

35. Wildt, 55–6.

36. *TBJG*, I/3, 463 (22 June 1938); *Tb* Irving, 246–7 and n.1; Wildt, 57.

37. Wildt, 55.

38. See Kulka, 'Public Opinion', xliv.

39. See Graml, *Reichskristallnacht*, 174.

40. Graml, *Reichskristallnacht*, 174; Barkai, 'Schicksalsjahr', 101.

41. Wildt, 99; Kulka, 'Public Opinion', 274–5.

42. Graml, *Reichskristallnacht*, 9–12; Helmut Heiber, 'Der Fall Grünspan', *VfZ*, 5 (1957), 134–72, here 134–9; Rita Thalmann and Emmanuel Feinermann, *Crystal Night: 9–10 November 1938*, London, 1974, 26–42; Anthony Read and David Fisher, *Kristallnacht. Unleashing the Holocaust*, London, 1989, 1–6, 33–55; Lionel Kochan, *Pogrom: 10 November 1938*, London, 1957, 34–49. The deportation of the Polish Jews had been set in motion by the actions of the Polish government, banning the return of Polish Jews living abroad. See Sybil Milton, 'The Expulsion of Polish Jews from Germany, October 1938 to July 1939: A Documentation', *LBYB*, 29 (1984), 166–99; Sybil Milton, 'Menschen zwischen Grenzen: Die Polenausweisung 1938', *Menora: Jahrbuch für deutsch-jüdische Geschichte 1990*, 184–206; and H. G. Adler, *Der verwaltete Mensch. Studien zur Deportation der Juden aus Deutschland*, Tübingen, 1974, 91–105. Grynszpan later successfully deployed the argument that he had had a homosexual relationship with vom Rath to prevent the show-trial which the Nazi regime had intended from taking place. See Heiber, 'Der Fall Grünspan', 148ff., demonstrating the implausibility of this as a genuine motive for the shooting. Hans-Jürgen Döscher,

Reichskristallnacht. Die November-Pogrome 1938, Frankfurt am Main, 1988, 62–3, attempts to revive the argument that vom Rath's killing did in fact arise from a homosexual relationship with Grynszpan, though this remains no more than speculation. Döscher's case rests heavily upon the fact that the bar to which Grynszpan went to load his revolver on the morning of 7 November was known as a haunt of homosexuals, and that, when he went to the embassy, Grynszpan did not ask for the Ambassador, but for 'a legation secretary' to whom – vom Rath – he was ushered in with little prior formality. The ambassador at the time, Johannes Graf von Welczek, recalled after the war, however, returning from his morning walk and meeting Grynszpan outside the embassy, where Grynszpan, not knowing whom he was addressing, asked how he might see the Ambassador and was directed to the porter of the building (Heiber, 'Der Fall Grünspan', 134–5).

43. Graml, *Reichskristallnacht*, 13.

44. Hermann Graml, *Der 9. November 1938. 'Reichskristallnacht', Beilage zur Wochenzeitung 'Das Parlament'*, No.45, 11 November 1953, here 6th edn, Bonn, 1958 (Schriftenreihe der Bundeszentrale für Heimatdienst), 17–23; Graml, *Reichskristallnacht*, 12–16.

45. *TBJG*, I/6, 178 (9 November 1938); *Tb* Irving, 407 (9 November 1938).

46. *TBJG*, I/6, 180 (10 November 1938); *Tb* Irving, 409 (10 November 1938).

47. *TBJG*, I/6, 180 (10 November 1938); the alternative reading of the last word in *Tb* Irving, 409 (10 November 1938): 'Now it's good' ('*Nun aber ist es gut*'), can almost certainly be discounted, even if the text remains difficult to decipher at this point. Close comparison of the handwriting, especially in adjacent passages, gives '*gar*' as the best reading. I am grateful to Elke Frohlich for advice on this point.

48. IfZ, ZS-243, Bd.I (Heinrich Heim), Fol.27: statement of former SA-Gruppenführer Max Jüttner. See also Irving, *Goebbels*, 274.

49. Adam, *Judenpolitik*, 206; Domarus, 966ff. for the speech.

50. Uwe Dietrich Adam, 'Wie spontan war der Pogrom?', in Pehle 74–93, here 76. It seems highly unlikely, as often claimed, that Hitler heard of vom Rath's death for the first time shortly before nine o'clock that evening during the meal at the Old Town Hall in Munich. Vom Rath had by then been dead for several hours. The Foreign Office had been informed of vom Rath's imminent death already that morning. A telegram from Dr Brandt to Hitler, notifying him of vom Rath's death at 4.30p.m., arrived in Berlin at 6.20p.m. It could be surmised (and would be supported by the testimony of Below) that Hitler heard the news that afternoon (that the telegram followed a telephone communication. (See Below, 136.) The German News Agency (DNB) circulated the news to newspaper editors by 7.00p.m. (Ralf Georg Reuth, *Goebbels*, Munich, 1990, 395 – according to Irving, *Goebbels*, 273 and 612 n.22, though without supporting source, even as early as 5.00p.m.). The Foreign Office dispatched a telegram of sympathy to vom Rath's father at 7.40p.m. The above chronology (except where otherwise stated) is taken from Hans-Jürgen Döscher, 'Der Tod Ernst vom Raths und die Auslösung der Pogrome am 9. November 1938 – ein Nachwort zur "Reichskristallnacht"', *Geschichte in Wissenschaft und Unterricht*, 41 (1990), 619–20. If indeed the stories are correct – see Adam, in Pehle, 77, 92 – that the telegram announcing vom Rath's death was delivered to Hitler during the meal in the Old Town Hall as late as 8.45p.m., it can only, therefore, have been for effect. It seems in the light of this probable that some degree of pre-planning between Goebbels and Hitler took place between vom Rath's shooting on 7 November and the discussion in the Old Town Hall prior to Goebbels's speech on the night of 9 November. See Adam, in Pehle, 91–2; Döscher, 'Der Tod Ernst vom Raths', 620. See also Döscher, 'Reichskristallnacht', 79.

51. Below, 136.

52. *IMG*, xxxii.20–29 (Doc.3063–PS, Report of the Party Court, Feb.1939); *IMG*, xx.320–21 (Eberstein testimony); Graml, *Reichskristallnacht*, 17–18; Graml, *Der 9. November 1938*, 23ff.

53. *TBJG*, I/6, 180 (10 November 1938); *Tb* Irving, 409 (10 November 1938). According to the Party Court's assessment of the pogrom and its aftermath, sent on 13 February 1939 to Goring, 'the Fuhrer had decided after his [Goebbels's] account, that such demonstrations [as had occurred in

the Gaue of Kurhessen and Magdeburg-Anhalt] were neither to be prepared nor organized by the Party. But if they arose spontaneously, they were not to be countered' (*IMG*, xxxii.21).

54. *TBJG*, I/6, 180 (10 November 1938). Away from Munich, among Party leaders who had not been present at Goebbels's speech, there were some initial attempts to ignore the encouragement to unleash pogroms. See *IMG*, xx.48–9, for the instructions – only partially obeyed – of Gauleiter Karl Kaufmann (Hamburg) to prevent the 'action' being carried out in his Gau. See also Graml, *Reichskristallnacht*, 24–6; Graml, *Der 9. November 1938*, 30–35; Irving, *Goebbels*, 612 n.33. Goebbels had not been content to have his message conveyed only by telephone. At 12.30 and 1.40a.m. on 10 November, he cabled Gau Propaganda Offices to ensure as much Party coordination as possible (*IMG*, xxxii.21–2; Graml, *Der 9. November 1938*, 27).

55. *TBJG*, I/6, 180 (10 November 1938); *Tb* Irving, 409 (10 November 1938). For the pogrom in Munich, see Hanke, 214ff.

56. According to a note dictated by Himmler at 3.00a.m. on 10 November (*IMG*, xxi.392), and the subsequent account of his chief adjutant, SS-Gruppenführer Karl Wolff (IfZ, ZS-317, Bd.II, Fol.28), Himmler was in Hitler's apartment in Prinzregentenplatz at the time. Wolff said he had learned of the 'action' around 11.20p.m. – presumably at the same time as Heydrich – and had then immediately driven to Hitler's private apartment. Heydrich was contacted at 11.15p.m. by Stapo Munich. He gave out a first order on the wearing of civilian clothing at 0.20a.m. (Adam, in Pehle, 77; Kurt Patzold and Irene Runge, *Kristallnacht. Zum Pogrom 1938*, Cologne, 1988, 113–14).

57. *IMG*, xxi.392; IfZ, ZS-317, Bd.II, Fol.28.

58. Pätzold/Runge, 113–14.

59. *IMG*, xxxi. 516–18; Patzold/Runge, 114–16; Adam, in Pehle, 77–9; Graml, *Reichskristallnacht*, 21, 33; Thalmann, 59–61.

60. *IMG*, xv, 377 (Doc.734–PS).

61. Peter Longerich, *Die braunen Bataillone. Geschichte der SA*, Munich, 1989, 230–37; Pätzold/Runge, 112–13, 116–18.

62. Milton Mayer, *They Thought they were Free. The Germans 1933–45*, Chicago, 1955, 16–20.

63. Adam, in Pehle, 74–5.

64. Goebbels does not specify which synagogue it was. But Munich newspaper reports of the pogrom-night refer to the old synagogue in Herzog-Rudolf-Straße in flames. The interior of the synagogue for east-European Jews in Reichenbachstraße was also set on fire, but the building itself was not burnt down. The main synagogue in Herzog-Max-Straße had been demolished in the summer. See Wolfgang Benz, 'Der Rückfall in die Barbarei. Bericht uber den Pogrom', in Pehle, 28; Hanke, 214; and Ophir and Wiesemann 50, 52.

65. The figure of 20–30,000 Jews to be arrested was mentioned in the instructions sent by telegram by Gestapo chief Heinrich Müller just before midnight (*IMG*, xxv.377). This was after Himmler and Hitler had met in the latter's apartment in Prinzregentenplatz in Munich, when the SS leader had sought clarification of directions. These preliminary instructions, passed on by Himmler to Müller, were amplified only once the SS chief had returned from the midnight swearing-in of SS recruits. On his return, Himmler immediately saw Heydrich, who put out more elaborate instructions to the Gestapo by telegram at 1.20 a.m. (*IMG*, xxxi.516–18). The number of Jews was not specified in this later telegram. It was emphasized that, in particular, well-off and healthy male Jews were to be arrested and taken to concentration camps (Patzold/Runge, 113–16).

66. *TBJG*, I/6, 180–81 (10 November 1938); *Tb* Irving, 409–10 (10 November 1938).

67. *TBJG*, I/6, 181 (10 November 1938); *Tb* Irving, 411 (10 November 1938).

68. Benz, in Pehle, 32. The 'action' nevertheless continued in various places until 13 November, when it eventually petered out. The 'stop' orders can be seen in Pätzold/Runge, 127–9.

69. *TBJG*, I/6, 182 (11 November 1938); *Tb* Irving, 411 (11 November 1938).

70. *TBJG*, I/6, 182 (11 November 1938); *Tb* Irving, 411 (11 November 1938).

71. See the description, one among many, in Gay, 132–6.

72. Pätzold/Runge, 136 (Heydrich's report), but the figures are an underestimate (Graml, *Reichskristallnacht*, 32).

73. Günter Fellner, 'Der Novemberpogrom in Westösterreich', in Kurt Schmid and Robert Streibel (eds.), *Der Pogrom 1938. Judenverfolgung in Österreich und Deutschland*, Vienna, 1990, 34–41, here 39.

74. Elisabeth Klamper, 'Der "Anschlußpogrom" ', in Schmid and Streibel, 25–33, here 31.

75. Graml, *Reichskristallnacht*, 32.

76. This is the compelling suggestion of Peter Loewenberg, 'The Kristallnacht as a Public Degradation Ritual', *LBYB*, 32 (1987), 309–23.

77. Monika Richarz (ed.), *Jüdisches Leben in Deutschland. Selbstzeugnisse zur Sozialgeschichte 1918–1945*, Stuttgart, 1982, 323–35. See also the testimony, along similar lines, provided in Loewenberg, 314.

78. See on this Loewenberg, especially 314, 321–3.

79. *IMG*, xxxii.27.

80. Wiener Library, London, PIId/15, 151, 749; Thomas Michel, *Die Juden in Gaukönigshofen/Unterfranken (1550–1942)*, Wiesbaden, 1988, 506–19.

81. See Walter Tausk, *Breslauer Tagebuch 1933–1940*, East Berlin, 1975, 181–2; Richarz, 326–7 (testimony of Hans Berger); Kershaw, *Popular Opinion*, 265.

82. Maschmann, *Fazit*, 58.

83. *DBS*, v.1204–5.

84. See Wiener Library, London, 'Der 10. November 1938' (typescript of collected short reports of persecuted Jews, compiled in 1939 and 1940); and see Kershaw, *Popular Opinion*, 265ff.

85. GStA, Munich, Reichsstatthalter 823, cit. in Ian Kershaw, 'Antisemitismus und Volksmeinung. Reaktionen auf die Judenverfolgung', in Martin Broszat and Elke Fröhlich (eds.), *Bayern in der NS-Zeit, Bd.II: Herrschaft und Gesellschaft im Konflikt*, Munich, 1979, 281–348, here 332.

86. StA Amberg, BA Amberg 2399, GS Hirschau, 23 November 1938, cit. Kershaw, 'Antisemitismus und Volksmeinung', 333. For reactions in general of the public to the pogrom and its aftermath, see: Kershaw, *Popular Opinion*, 263ff.; Ian Kershaw, 'Indifferenz des Gewissens. Die deutsche Bevölkerung und die "Reichskristallnacht" ', *Blätter für deutsche und internationale Politik*, 11 (1988), 1319–30; Kulka, 'Public Opinion', xliii-iv, 277–86; David Bankier, *The Germans and the Final Solution. Public Opinion under Nazism*, Oxford, 1992, 85ff.; Hans Mommsen and Dieter Obst, 'Die Reaktion der deutschen Bevölkerung auf die Verfolgung der Juden 1933–1943', in Hans Mommsen and Susanne Willems (eds.), *Herrschaftsalltag im Dritten Reich. Studien und Texte*, Düsseldorf, 1988, 374–485, here 388ff.; William S. Allen, 'Die deutsche Öffentlichkeit und die "Reichskristallnacht" – Konflikte zwischen Werthierarchie und Propaganda im Dritten Reich', in Detlev Peukert and Jürgen Reulecke (eds.), *Die Reihen fast geschlossen. Beiträge zur Geschichte des Alltags unterm Nationalsozialismus*, Wuppertal, 1981, 397–411.

87. *IMG*, xiii.131 (Funk testimony); Adam, in Pehle, 79–80; Adam, *Judenpolitik*, 208.

88. *IMG*, ix.312–13 (Göring testimony). Göring's account has to be treated with care (despite being followed by Adam, *Judenpolitik*, 208, Read/Fisher, 146, Adam, in Pehle, 80, and other accounts). It was self-servingly unreliable and inaccurate, especially with regard to alleged meetings with Hitler and Goebbels in Berlin on the afternoon of 10 November. Göring claimed to have berated Hitler as soon as the Führer returned himself to Berlin, late on the morning of 10 November, about Goebbels's irresponsibility. Hitler, Göring recalled, was equivocal. He 'made some excuses, but agreed with me on the whole that these things should and could not happen'. This was consonant with Hitler's continued attempts to distance himself from the events of the previous night. However, if the discussion between Göring and Hitler on 10 November took place at all, then it must have been by telephone. For, contrary to Göring's recollection, Hitler did not return to Berlin that morning, but stayed in Munich and had lunch with Goebbels – *TBJG*, I/6, 182 (11 November 1938). I am grateful to Karl Schleunes for alerting me to inconsistencies in Göring's testimony.

89. *IMG*, ix.313–14; *TBJG*, I/6, 182 (11 November 1938) for the lunchtime meeting in the Osteria. For Hitler's comments on the envisaged economic measures against Jews in the Four-Year-Plan Memorandum, see Treue, 'Denkschrift', *VfZ*, 3 (1955), 210; see also Barkai, 'Schicksalsjahr', in Pehle, 99.

90. Adam, *Judenpolitik*, 217.

91. Minutes of the meeting: *IMG*, xxviii.499–540 (Doc. 1816-PS); imposition of the 'fine', 537ff. An abbreviated version is printed in Pätzold/Runge, 142–6; summaries are given in Adam, *Judenpolitik*, 209–11; Read/Fisher, ch.9; Schleunes, 245–50; Graml, *Reichskristallnacht*, 177–9.

92. Pätzold-Runge, 146–8; see Adam, *Judenpolitik*, 209–12.

93. *TBJG*, I/6, 185 (13 November 1938).

94. Adam, *Judenpolitik*, 205; Reuth, *Goebbels*, 393–4; Graml, *Reichskristallnacht*, 176. For the affair, see Helmut Heiber, *Joseph Goebbels*, Berlin, 1962, 275–80. But Heiber goes too far in his speculation that this was a vital motive in Goebbels's initiative in unleashing the pogrom.

95. Graml, *Reichskristallnacht*, 183.

96. Gay, ch.8.

97. Konrad Kwiet and Helmut Eschwege, *Selbstbehauptung und Widerstand. Deutsche Juden im Kampf um Existenz und Menschenwürde 1933–1945*, Hamburg, 1984, 143.

98. Gay, 140–41.

99. Bob Moore, *Refugees from Nazi Germany in the Netherlands, 1933–1940*, Dordrecht, 1986, 87–8. See also Dan Michman, 'Die jüdische Emigration und die niederländische Reaktion zwischen 1933 und 1940', in Kathinka Dittrich and Hans Würzner (eds.), *Die Niederlande und das deutsche Exil 1933–1940*, Königstein/Ts., 1982, 73–90, especially 76, 89–90.

100. Martin Gilbert, *The Holocaust. The Jewish Tragedy*, London, 1986, 75.

101. Friedländer, 303–4.

102. *IMG*, xxxii.415 (Doc.3575-PS; summary of Goring's address to the Reich Defence Council, 18 November 1938); in the longer extracts of the minutes, in Mason, *Arbeiterklasse*, 907–37, here 925–6, Goring says: 'Gentlemen. The finances look very critical . . . Now, through the billion that the Jews have to pay, an improvement has taken place . . .'

103. Adam, *Judenpolitik*, 213–16.

104. Müller, *Heer*, 385–7.

105. Nicholas Reynolds, 'Der Fritsch-Brief vom 11. Dezember 1938', *VfZ*, 28 (1980), 358–71, here 362–3, 370.

106. *JK*, 89 (Doc.61).

107. Adam, *Judenpolitik*, 228; Wildt, 60.

108. Peter Longerich (ed.), *Die Ermordung der europäischen Juden. Eine umfassende Dokumentation des Holocaust 1941–1945*, Munich, 1989, 83.

109. Adam, *Judenpolitik*, 217–19.

110. Below, 136; IfZ, ZS-317, Bd.II, Fol.28 (Wolff); IfZ, ZS-243, Bd.I (for the comment of Hitler's adjutant Brückner, that Hitler was said to have fallen into a rage when told of the burning of the synagogue in Munich). See also Irving, *Goebbels*, 277, 613 and David Irving, *The War Path. Hitler's Germany, 1933–9*, London, 1978, 164–5, for Hitler's alleged surprise at, or condemnation of, the events.

111. *IMG*, xxi.392.

112. Below, 136. Below's account is very sympathetic to Hitler. Below thought Hitler knew nothing about what was going on. He also mentions Schaub's remark that Goebbels somehow had his finger in the pie. This was something of an understatement. According to Goebbels's own account, Schaub had been in his element when the pair of them had gone together after midnight to the Artists' Club (*TBJG*, I/6, 181 (10 November 1938); *Tb* Irving, 410 (10 November 1938)). Below's chronology is also inaccurate. He gives the impression that Hitler's entourage heard of the destruction on their return from the midnight swearing-in of the SS recruits. But Hitler had been informed before he

had set out for this (*IMG*, xxi.392; IfZ, ZS-317 (Wolff), Bd.II, Fol.28; Adam, in Pehle, 78).

113. Speer, *Erinnerungen*, 126.

114. Hans-Günther Seraphim (ed.), *Das politische Tagebuch Alfred Rosenbergs 1934/35 und 1939/40*, Munich, 1964, 81 (6 February 1939).

115. Müller, *Heer*, 385–6; Erich Raeder, *Mein Leben*, Tübingen, 2 vols., 1956–7, ii.133–4.

116. *TBJG*, I/6, 180 (10 November 1938); *Tb* Irving, 409 (10 November 1938).

117. IfZ, ZS-243, Bd.I (Heim), Fol.27 (statement by Jüttner); Irving, *Goebbels*, 274.

118. *TBJG*, I/6, 189–90 (17 November 1938); *Tb* Irving, 417 (17 November 1938). See also Irving, *Goebbels*, 282.

119. See, for a contrasting interpretation, Irving, *Goebbels*, 276–7. The post-war explanation of Heinrich Heim (a lawyer and civil servant employed in Hess's office, later an adjutant of Martin Bormann, and commissioned by him to make notes of Hitler's 'table-talk' monologues) was that Goebbels had regarded the casual remark by Hitler 'that the demonstrators (for the time being only relatively harmless) should not be severely dealt with' (*'dass man die Demonstranten (vorläufig nur relativ harmlose!) nicht scharf anpacken soll'*), as a licence (*Freibrief*), and believed therefore that he was 'certainly acting along the lines of what his master wanted' (*'bestimmt im Sinne seines Herrn zu handeln'*) (IfZ, ZS-243, Bd.I (Heim), Fol.29).

120. For Goebbels's 'anger' at the burning of the Munich synagogue and other outrages in publicly berating his Gau Propaganda Leaders at the station in Munich on returning to Berlin, see IfZ, ZS-243, Bd.I (Heim), Fol.28 (post-war statement of Werner Naumann, later State Secretary in the Propaganda Ministry); and see Irving, *Goebbels*, 280.

121. Domarus, 973; Treue, 'Rede Hitlers vor der deutschen Presse (10. November 1938)', 175ff. Nor had Hitler given any indication, despite vom Rath's perilous condition at the time and the menacing antisemitic climate, of any intended action when he had spoken to the 'old guard' of the Party at the Bürgerbräukeller on the evening of 8 November. Domarus, 966ff. for the speech. The point is made by Adam, *Judenpolitik*, 206.

122. Below, 137.

123. *MK*, 772; *MK* Watt, 620.

124. *IMG*, xxviii.538–9.

125. *Das Schwarze Korps*, 27 October 1938, p.6.

126. *Das Schwarze Korps*, 3 November 1938, p.2. And see Kochan, 39.

127. Graml, *Reichskristallnacht*, 185.

128. *ADAP*, D, IV, Dok.271, 293–5 (quotation, 293); Graml, *Reichskristallnacht*, 184; Adam, *Judenpolitik*, 234, n.4. Pirow had raised the possibility of an international loan to finance Jewish emigration and the notion of settling Jews in a former German colony such as Tanganyika – a proposal rejected out of hand by Hitler. See Graml, *Reichskristallnacht*, 182–3 (and n.4–5) for emigration as a policy, and 184–5 for the hostage notion. For the latter, see also the remarks of Hans Mommsen, 'Die Realisierung des Utopischen: Die "Endlosung der Judenfrage" im "Dritten Reich" ', *GG*, 9 (1983), 381–420, here 396.

129. *ADAP*, D, IV, Dok.158, 170; Graml, *Reichskristallnacht*, 186; Adam, *Judenpolitik*, 235. It appears that his association of the Jews with the November Revolution of 1918 had also been reinforced at this time. Hitler referred vaguely to 'threats from others' to destroy the Reich in his annual speech to the party faithful on the anniversary of the proclamation of the Party Programme, on 24 February 1939, and immediately followed this by stating: 'The year 1918 will never repeat itself in German history' (Domarus, 1086). For Hitler's 'November Syndrome', see Tim Mason, 'The Legacy of 1918 for National Socialism', in Anthony Nicholls and Erich Mathias, *German Democracy and the Triumph of Hitler*, London, 1971, 215–39.

130. Birger Dahlerus, *Der letzte Versuch. London-Berlin. Sommer 1939*, Munich, 1948, 126 (recording Hitler's comment to him on 1 September 1939); *Documents concerning German-Polish Relations and the Outbreak of Hostilities between Great Britain and Germany on September 3, 1939*, London,

1939, 129, no.75 (Hitler to Henderson, 28 August 1939); Domarus, 1238 (Hitler's speech to his military leaders, 22 August 1939).

131. *Das Schwarze Korps*, 24 November 1938, p.1; also cit. in Graml, *Reichskristallnacht*, 187.

132. Hans Mommsen, 'Hitler's Reichstag Speech of 30 January 1939', *History and Memory*, 9 (1997), 147–61, emphasizes above all (see especially 157–8) the propaganda component of the speech. He places the speech in its context of the talks between George Rublee, the American Chairman of the Intergovernmental Committee for Refugees (charged by President Roosevelt with trying to find a way out of the crisis of Jewish refugees from Nazi Germany) and Helmut Wohltat, one of Göring's close associates on the Four-Year Plan and on Jewish emigration. The negotiations were aimed at financing the emigration of 150,000 Jews within three years through an international loan of one and a half million Reich Marks. In Mommsen's view (151), Hitler's speech was 'a rhetorical gesture designed to put pressure on the international community' to accept the Reich's blackmailing demand. He stresses (154) the need felt by Hitler 'to promise effective measures on the part of the government in order to calm down the extreme antisemitic activities which endangered the emigration scheme that Göring and Schacht had worked out'. It seems doubtful, however, that Hitler was as serious about the Rublee-Wohltat scheme as Mommsen implies, and not altogether convincing to suggest (156) that it is 'difficult to believe that [Hitler's] inclination to exaggerate the issues involved was more than mere camouflage'.

133. Domarus, 1058.

134. Eberhard Jäckel, 'Hitler und der Mord an europäischen Juden', in Peter Märthesheimer and Ivo Frenzel (eds.), *Im Kreuzfeuer: Der Fernsehfilm Holocaust. Eine Nation ist betroffen*, Frankfurt am Main, 1979, 151–62, here 160–61.

CHAPTER 4: MISCALCULATION

1. Michael Jabara Carley, *1939: the Alliance that Never Was and the Coming of World War II*, Chicago, 1999, 77–9.

2. Donald Cameron Watt, *How War Came. The Immediate Origins of the Second World War, 1938–1939*, London, (1989), Mandarin paperback edn, 1991, 101–4. Generally, on Oster's role in the resistance to Hitler (though not mentioning this episode), see Romedio Galeazzo Reichsgraf von Thun-Hohenstein, *Der Verschwörer. General Oster und die Militäropposition*, Berlin, 1982.

3. Watt, *How War Came*, 40, 101, and see ch.6 passim.

4. John de Courcy, *Searchlight on Europe*, London, 1940, 87; Watt, *How War Came*, 59–64; Weinberg II, 474–8.

5. Courcy, 85–8.

6. Weinberg II, 476–8; Watt, *How War Came*, 64.

7. See also Weinberg II, 467–8.

8. Weinberg II, 479ff.; Watt, *How War Came*, 41.

9. Weinberg II, 481–3; Watt, *How War Came*, 65.

10. Watt, *How War Came*, 66. The Poles initially took the ideas to be Ribbentrop's own. But it seems plain that the German Foreign Minister was acting as Hitler's mouthpiece. See Joachim von Ribbentrop, *Zwischen London und Moskau. Erinnerungen und letzte Aufzeichnungen*, ed. Annelies von Ribbentrop, Leoni am Starnberger See, 1953, 154–5.

11. Weinberg II, 484, and see 503.

12. *DGFP*, D, V, 125, no.99, 141, no.110 (12 November 1938, 5 December 1938). The Polish foreign minister Josef Beck was, in fact, somewhat less intransigent at first than others in the Polish government, but there was little prospect from the outset of any flexibility on Danzig and the Corridor. (See Weinberg II, 501.)

13. Domarus, 1065.

14. Watt, *How War Came*, 69; *DBFP*, 3, IV, 80, no.82, Shepherd to Halifax, 6 February 1939. According to Shepherd's memorandum, Hitler's meeting with his military leaders had taken place on 21 January 1939.

15. Watt, *How War Came*, 70.

16. *DGFP*, D, IV, 529, No.411.

17. See Dülffer, 471–88 and especially 492ff. for the genesis of the Z-Plan; *DRZW*, i.465–73; and Charles S. Thomas, *The German Navy in the Nazi Era*, London, 1990, 179–80. See Weinberg II, 503 for plans to settle with France and Great Britain before turning to the east, and Keitel, 196–7, for the 'Ostwall'.

18. *TBJG*, I/6, 158 (24 October 1938).

19. Irving, *Göring*, 241.

20. Keitel, 196.

21. Keitel, 196–7.

22. In a memorandum of 3 September 1939 'on the outbreak of war', Raeder wrote: 'Today the war against England-France has broken out, which, according to previous comments of the Führer we did not need to reckon with before around 1944.' He went on to outline the battle-fleet that would have been ready at the turn of the year 1944–5. He then added: 'As far as the navy is concerned, it is obviously in autumn 1939 still nowhere near sufficiently ready for the great struggle against England.' ('*Am heutigen Tage ist der Krieg gegen England-Frankreich ausgebrochen, mit dem wir nach den bisherigen Äusserungen des Führers nicht vor etwa 1944 zu rechnen brauchten ... Was die Kriegsmarine anbetrifft, so ist sie selbstverständlich im Herbst 1939 noch keineswegs für den grossen Kampf mit England hinreichend gerüstet.*) (BA/MA, PG/33965; and see Thomas, 187). I am grateful to Prof. Meir Michaelis for providing me with a copy of this memorandum. For remarks on the inadequate state of the army at the outbreak of war, see IfZ, F34/1, 'Erinnerungen von Nikolaus v. Vormann über die Zeit vom 22.8–27.9.1939 als Verbindungsoffizier des Heeres beim Führer und Obersten Befehlshaber der Wehrmacht', Fol.56.

23. Martens, *Göring*, 169–70.

24. Watt, *How War Came*, ch.4; for divisions over policy towards Poland among Hitler's entourage, 68. For Göring's diminishing influence on the direction of foreign policy at this time, to the benefit of his arch-rival Ribbentrop, see Kube, 299ff.; and for Ribbentrop, Bloch, ch.XI.

25. In his comments to his armed forces' leaders on 23 May 1939, Hitler, though by this time bent on destroying Poland in the near future, again indicated that the armaments programme would only be completed in 1943 or 1944, pointing to the West as the main enemy (*DGFP*, D, VI, 575–80, Doc.433; and see the retrospective comments of Raeder in his memorandum of 3 September 1939, BA/MA, PG/33965 (quoted above in note 22)).

26. See *DRZW*, i.349–68; and also Bernd-Jürgen Wendt, 'Nationalsozialistische Großraumwirtschaft zwischen Utopie und Wirklichkeit – Zum Scheitern einer Konzeption 1938/39', in Knipping and Müller, 223–45, especially 239ff., for the mounting problems in the economy and the collapse of prospects of an alternative economic strategy to the ideologically determined aim of acquiring 'living space'.

27. R. J. Overy, *War and Economy in the Third Reich*, Oxford, 1994, 108–9, 196–7 (and 93ff. for the Reichswerke Hermann Goring); *DRZW*, i.323–31.

28. Tim Mason, *Nazism, Fascism, and the Working Class. Essays by Tim Mason*, ed. Jane Caplan, Cambridge, 1995, 109.

29. Goring's speech (Mason, *Arbeiterklasse*, 908–33, Dok.152) gave an overview of the major problems facing the German economy in shortages of labour and raw materials, inefficient production, and precarious finances; quotation, 925.

30. *TBJG*, I/6, 219 (13 December 1938).

31. See the speech by Schacht of 29 November 1938: *IMG*, xxxvi.582–96, especially 587–8, Doc.611-EC.

32. *IMG*, xxxvi.365ff., Doc.EC-369. See Mason, *Nazism*, 108, for inflationary pressures building up by 1939. It would be important not to exaggerate their actual seriousness by that date. Even so, though stringent controls and repression had held inflation in check until then, the dangers in an increase in Reichsbank notes in circulation from 3.6 billion Reich Marks in 1933 to 5.4 in 1937, rising sharply to 8.2 billion in 1938 and 10.9 billion in 1939 were obvious. (Willi A. Boelcke, *Die Kosten von Hitlers Krieg*, Paderborn etc., 1985, 32. See also Dietrich Eichholtz, *Geschichte der deutschen Kriegswirtschaft 1939–1945*, Bd.I, 1939–1941, East Berlin, 1984, 30.)

33. Hjalmar Schacht, *My First Seventy-Six Years*, London, 1955, 392–4 (quotation, 392).

34. Mason, *Nazism*, 106–7.

35. See BA, R43II/194, 213b, for numerous complaints of Darré.

36. Mason, *Nazism*, 111; Timothy W. Mason, *Sozialpolitik im Dritten Reich. Arbeiterklasse und Volksgemeinschaft*, Opladen, 1977, 226ff.; J. E. Farquharson, *The Plough and the Swastika. The NSDAP and Agriculture in Germany, 1928–45*, London/Beverly Hills, 1976, 196ff.; Gustavo Corni, *Hitler and the Peasants, Agrarian Policy of the Third Reich, 1930–1939*, New York/Oxford/Munich, 1990, ch.10; Gustavo Corni and Horst Giest, *Brot-Butter-Kanonen. Die Ernährungswirtschaft in Deutschland unter der Diktatur Hitlers*, Berlin, 1997, 280–97; Kershaw, *Popular Opinion*, 55–61.

37. Mason, *Nazism*, 111. The investment in new farm machinery had indeed risen by 25.8 per cent during the first six years of Nazi rule, with a high point in 1938. But mechanization was progressing slowly in international comparison. Whereas there was a tractor for every 325 hectares of arable in Germany, the ratio was 1:95 in Great Britain and 1:85 in the USA and Canada. Two-thirds of German farmers still sowed their fields by hand; many used oxen and horses for ploughing. (Corni and Giest, 308.)

38. Corni and Giest, 286–7, 294; Corni, 227–9; Farquharson, 199–200.

39. See Kershaw, *Popular Opinion*, 286. Some 300,000 Polish prisoners-of-war were put to work on the land in Germany by the end of 1939, together with around 40,000 civilian workers (Ulrich Herbert, *Fremdarbeiter. Politik und Praxis des 'Ausländer-Einsatzes' in der Kriegswirtschaft des Dritten Reiches*, Berlin/Bonn, 1985, 68).

40. Mason, *Sozialpolitik*, 215–26; reports of the Reichstreuhänder der Arbeit for the last quarter of 1938 and first quarter of 1939, emphasizing the difficulties, are printed in Mason, *Arbeiterklasse*, 847–55, Dok.147, 942–59, Dok.156. Numerous reports from the Defence Districts, pointing out the problems in armaments manufacture, can be seen in BA/MA, RW 19/40, 54, 56.

41. See the analyses by Mason, *Sozialpolitik*, 241, 245, 295, 313ff. Tim Mason, 'The Workers' Opposition in Nazi Germany', *History Workshop Journal*, 11 (1981), 120–37; Timothy W. Mason, 'Die Bandigung der Arbeiterklasse im nationalsozialistischen Deutschland. Eine Einleitung', in Carola Sachse *et al.*, *Angst, Belohnung, Zucht und Ordnung. Herrschaftsmechanismen im Nationalsozialismus*, Opladen, 1982, 11–53; and also Michael Voges, 'Klassenkampf in der "Betriebsgemeinschaft". Die "Deutschland-Berichte" der Sopade (1934–40) als Quelle zum Widerstand der Industrie-Arbeiter im Dritten Reich', *Archiv für Sozialgeschichte*, 21 (1981), 329–84; and also Kershaw, *Popular Opinion*, 98–110. Even given the usual paranoia, Gestapo reports did not give the regime's leaders the impression that the widespread discontent among industrial workers was being translated into any serious political threat from the Communist or Socialist underground resistance. See examples of reports in Mason, *Arbeiterklasse*, 856–7, Dok.148, 960–61, Dok.157; in BA, R58/446, 582, 584, 719; and in IML/ZPA, St3/64, St3/184, PSt3/153.

42. Mason, *Nazism*, 113.

43. The argument, advanced – in sophisticated fashion – by Mason in his various works, for economic determinants (within the regime's ideological framework) shaping a social crisis and leaving Hitler with no alternative other than to risk war before Germany was ready for it, has encountered widespread criticism. See, particularly, Jost Dülffer, 'Der Beginn des Krieges 1939: Hitler, die innere Krise und das Mächtesystem', *GG*, 2 (1976), 443–70; Ludolf Herbst, 'Die Krise des nationalsozialistischen Regimes am Vorabend des Zweiten Weltkrieges und die forcierte

Aufrustung. Eine Kritik', *VfZ*, 26 (1978), 347–92; and Richard Overy, 'Germany, "Domestic Crisis", and War in 1939', *Past and Present*, 116 (1987), 138–68. Mason, *Nazism*, ch.9, contains the author's response.

44. Below, 138.

45. *TBJG*, I/6, 158 (24 October 1938).

46. Below, 138.

47. *DGFP*, D, IV, 99–100, No.81; Keitel, 195–6.

48. See Weinberg II, 468–9.

49. *TBJG*, I/6, 296 (23 March 1939).

50. *IMG*, xii.580: '*Der Kerl hat mir meinen Einzug nach Prag versiebt.*'

51. Watt, *How War Came*, 142; Weinberg II, 469.

52. See, for example, the entry in *TBJG*, I/6, 113 (26 September 1938).

53. Courcy, 94–5.

54. See Bernd-Jürgen Wendt, *Großdeutschland. Außenpolitik und Kriegsvorbereitung des Hitler-Regimes*, Munich, 1987, 166–7; Watt, *How War Came*, 195.

55. Gedye, 371.

56. Courcy, 94–7. The economic motive was probably not in itself sufficient. But Weinberg II, 469, n.16, seems in danger of underestimating its importance.

57. Wendt, *Großdeutschland*, 166; Watt, *How War Came*, 195.

58. Weinberg II, 479.

59. Courcy, 92–3.

60. Below, 138.

61. Courcy, 85–9.

62. Irving, *Göring*, 240–42; Watt, *How War Came*, 142–3.

63. See Watt, *How War Came*, 143–7, for Slovakia.

64. Weinberg II, 485.

65. *DGFP*, D, V, 361–6, No.272.

66. *Weizsäcker-Papiere*, 150. And see Jutta Sywottek, *Mobilmachung für den totalen Krieg. Die propagandistische Vorbereitung der deutschen Bevölkerung auf den Zweiten Weltkrieg*, Opladen, 1976, 187.

67. Watt, *How War Came*, 146.

68. *ADAP*, D, V, 127–32, Nr.119; Weinberg II, 497–8.

69. Weinberg II, 498. According to Below, it was following the failure of his visit to Warsaw that Ribbentrop began to contemplate a link with Russia to prevent Poland looking for support to Britain (Below, 146).

70. Weinberg II, 498–9 and n.140.

71. Watt, *How War Came*, 143; hinted at also in Weinberg II, 497–8.

72. BA, NS 11/28, Fols.55–62: quotations, Fol.58 ('*dass unser Deutschland, unser Deutsches Reich einmal die dominierende Macht Europas sein wird*'); Fol.61 ('*den Geist unserer jetzigen Zeit, den Geist der Weltanschauung, die heute Deutschland beherrscht . . . ein zutiefst soldatischer Geist . . .*'); Fol.60 ('*Es ist mein unerschütterliche Wille, dass die deutsche Wehrmacht die stärkste Wehrmacht der ganzen Welt wird*').

73. Below, 144; Irving, *Führer*, 164; Irving, *War Path*, 173ff.

74. IfZ, F19/10, 'Hitlers Rede vor dem Offiziersjahrgang 1938 am 25.1.1939 in der Reichskanzlei (geheim)': '*Und wenn dieser Aufbau – sagen wir – in 100 Jahren endgültig in sich gefestigt sein wird, und eine neue tragende Gesellschaftsschichte abgegeben haben wird, dann wird das Volk – das ist meine Überzeugung – das als erstes diesen Weg beschritt, die Anwartschaft besitzen, auf die Herrschaft Europas . . .*' (Fol.25, and see also esp. Fols.8–9, 15–16, 19, 24). A different copy of the text is in BA, NS 11/28, Fols. 63–85, quotations Fols. 68 ('*Prinzipien der demokratischen,*

parlamentarischen, pazifistischen, defätistischen Mentalität'), 75 ('*Brutalität, d.h. das Schwert, wenn alle anderen Mittel versagen*'), 84 (as above). See also Irving, *Führer*, 165.

75. BA, NS 11/28, Fols.86–119; quotations: Fols.114–15 ('*Verstehen Sie eines, meine Herren, die grossen Erfolge der letzten Zeit sind uns nur deswegen geworden, weil ich die Gelegenheiten wahrgenommen habe . . .*' '*Ich habe mir vorgenommen, die deutsche Frage zu losen, d.h. das deutsche Raumproblem zu lösen. Nehmen Sie es zur Kenntnis, dass, solange ich lebe, dass dieser Gedanke mein ganzes Dasein beherrschen wird. Seien Sie weiter der Überzeugung, dass, sowie ich glaube, in irgendeinem Augenblick einen Schritt hiervorwärts zu kommen, dass ich dann augenblicklich immer handeln werde, dass ich dabei auch vor dem Äussersten nie zurückschrecken werde . . .*'); Fol.119 ('*Seien Sie daher nicht überrascht, wenn auch in den kommenden Jahren bei jeder Gelegenheit irgendein deutsches Ziel zu erreichen versucht wird, und stellen Sie sich dann, bitte sehr, im gläubigsten Vertrauen hinter mich . . .*'). See also, for summary notes of the speech, IfZ, ED 57, Irving-Sammlung, 'Wiedergabe von Notizen einer Ansprache Hitlers an Offiziere der Wehrmacht am 10.2.1939'; brief extracts from the text are printed in Jost Dülffer, 'Der Einfluß des Auslandes auf die nationalsozialistische Politik', in Erhard Forndran, Frank Golczewski, and Dieter Riesenberger (eds.), *Innen- und Außenpolitik unter nationalsozialistischer Bedrohung*, Opladen, 1977, 295–313, here 304; Wolfgang Michalka (ed.), *Das Dritte Reich. Dokumente zur Innen- und Außenpolitik*, Bd.1, Munich, 1985,267–8; and Irving, *Führer*, 165–6. See also Below, 145. In a fourth speech, to newly qualified officers, held on 11 March 1939 in Berlin, Hitler repeated themes of his speeches in January and February, including the need for 'living space', the heroism and racial value of the German people, the failure of its leadership in 1918, the qualities of the new state he had led since 1933, and the historical precedents for a master-race dominating an inferior people (BA, NS 11/28, Fols. 120–46).

76. *TBJG*, I/6, 247 (3 February 1939).

77. *TBJG*, I/6, 246 (1 February 1939).

78. Watt, *How War Came*, 147–9.

79. *TBJG*, I/6, 280 (11 March 1939); see also Irving, *Goebbels*, 288–9.

80. Below, 151; Irving, *Göring*, 244.

81. Keitel, 200.

82. *TBJG*, I/6, 283 (13 March 1939).

83. Below, 151; Irving, *Goebbels*, 290; Watt, *How War Came*, 152.

84. *TBJG*, I/6, 283–4 (13 March 1939).

85. *TBJG*, I/6, 285 (14 March 1939); *DGFP*, D, IV, 243–5, Doc.202.

86. Watt, *How War Came*, 150.

87. *TBJG*, I/6, 285–6 (14 March 1939, 15 March 1939).

88. Schmidt, 435; Watt, *How War Came*, 144, 152; Toland, 515.

89. *TBJG*,I/6,287 (15 March 1939); Keitel, 200. According to Keitel, Hácha's arrival was announced to Hitler around 10.00p.m. He had only been expected in late evening (Below, 151), though photographs of the Czech President inspecting a guard of honour outside the station in Berlin in daylight suggest that he had actually arrived in the city no later than about 7.00p.m. (Domarus, 1093 n.263).

90. Keitel, 200. For Hitler's relaxed attitude during the evening, see Below, 152.

91. Schmidt, 435–6.

92. *DGFP*, D, IV, 263–9, Doc. 228; Otto Meissner, *Staatssekretär unter Ebert-Hindenburg-Hitler. Der Schicksalsweg des deutschen Volkes von 1918 bis 1945, wie ich ihn erlebte*, Hamburg, 1950, 476; Keitel, 201; Schmidt, 437; Below, 150–53.

93. Keitel, 201.

94. Keitel (200–201) claimed Hácha had no knowledge. But, according to Schmidt, Hácha had been told by Mastny on arrival in Berlin that troops had crossed near Ostrau (Schmidt, 437); and

Goebbels pointed out that the purpose of sending some troops into Czech territory was to exert further pressure on Hácha (*TBJG*, 286 (15 March 1939)).

95. Keitel, 201.

96. Irving, *Göring*, 245.

97. Schmidt, 438–9.

98. Schmidt, 439; *DGFP*, D, IV, 263–9, No.228.

99. Schroeder, 88.

100. Below, 153; Keitel, 202; Domarus, 1097.

101. Schroeder, 88; Below, 153–4; Schneider, Nr.47, 21 November 1952, 8; *TBJG*, I/6, 293 (20 March 1939), where Goebbels noted that Hitler thought the people of Prague had 'behaved quite neutrally', and that more could not have been expected of them.

102. Schroeder, 88–9.

103. *Reichsgesetzblatt* (=*RGBl*) 1939, I, 485–8, quotation 485; Below, 154.

104. Below, 154.

105. *TBJG*, I/6, 293 (20 March 1939); Below, 155; Domarus, 1103.

106. See Below, 154, 156.

107. StA München, NSDAP 126, report of the Kreisleiter of Aichach, Upper Bavaria, 31 March 1939: '*Die Menschen freuten sich über die großen Taten des Führers und blicken vertrauensvoll zu ihm auf. Die Nöte und Sorgen des Alltags sind aber so groß, daß bald wieder die Stimmung getrübt wird.*'

108. Below, 156. Speer, 162, remarked on the depressed mood in Germany and the worries about the future. See also, for reactions to the latest coup, Kershaw, '*Hitler Myth*', 139–40.

109. *DBS*, vi.279. Analysts at Sopade headquarters, by now moved from Prague to Paris, concluded that, in the light of Hitler's broken promises and so many occasions in which to recognize the true essence of the Nazi regime, 'If the world . . . allows itself to be deceived, then it alone is to blame . . . For this system, there is no right other than that of the stronger' (*DBS*, vi.372–3).

110. Andreas-Friedrich, *Schauplatz Berlin*, 32.

111. Eva Sternheim-Peters, *Die Zeit der großen Täuschungen. Mädchenleben im Faschismus*, Bielefeld, 1987, 361–2.

112. *DBS*, vi.278.

113. Chamberlain, *Struggle*, 413–20, quotation 418.

114. Courcy, 98.

115. Cit. Weinberg II, 542–3.

116. Weinberg II, 545–6.

117. *DGFP*, D, IV, 99–100, No.81.

118. Domarus, 510–11, 1029, n.49a, 1109; Benz, Graml, and Weiß, *Enzyklopädie*, 582; Watt, *How War Came*, 156.

119. See Weinberg II, 536.

120. Domarus, 1109, *How War Came*, 156–7.

121. *TBJG*, I/6, 296 (23 March 1939).

122. *TBJG*, I/6, 297 (23 March 1939); Domarus, 1109–10.

123. Domarus, 1110–14. There appears to be no evidence for the assertion by Watt, *How War Came*, 157, that Hitler came on land sea-sick from his stay on the *Deutschland*.

124. *TBJG*, I/6, 297 (23 March 1939).

125. *TBJG*, I/6, 296 (23 March 1939). Hitler had been taking it for granted for a few months that the former colonies would be returned to Germany (Weinberg II, 512–13). The issue was at best, however, of secondary importance to him, and his somewhat vague presumption was that the colonial question would be solved perhaps in the later 1940s when Germany was the master of the European continent and when the battle-fleet was ready (Klaus Hildebrand, *Deutsche Außenpolitik 1933–1945. Kalkül oder Dogma?*, Stuttgart etc., 1971, 78–9).

126. *DGFP*, D, VI, 70–72, No. 61.

127. *DBFP*, Ser. 3, IV, 463–4, No. 485.

128. Watt, *How War Came*, 158–9.

129. Below, 157; *DGFP*, D, VI, 117–19 (quotation, 117), No. 99. Hitler's stance is not compatible with the post-war claim – on the basis of dubious evidence – that he had already decided upon the military occupation of Poland as early as 8 March, when he spoke to leaders of business, the Party, and the military (Dietrich Eichholtz and Wolfgang Schumann (eds.), *Anatomie des Krieges. Neue Dokumente über die Rolle des deutschen Monopolkapitals bei der Vorbereitung und Durchführung des zweiten Weltkrieges*, East Berlin, 1969, 204–5, Dok.88 (based on reports sent to President Roosevelt on 19 September 1939 by William Christian Bullitt, the United States Ambassador in Paris)).

130. *TBJG*, I/6, 300 (25 March 1939).

131. Domarus, 1115–16; Watt, *How War Came*, 160–61.

132. As in Domarus, 1116. Hitler was, however, displeased with Ribbentrop's clumsy alienation of the Poles, which threatened to do just what he wanted to avoid and drive them into the arms of the British (Bloch, 220).

133. *TBJG*, I/6, 302 (28 March 1939).

134. Watt, *How War Came*, 160–61.

135. Weinberg II, 554–5.

136. *DBFP*, Ser.3, IV, 553, No.582. For the background, and the shifts in the British stance towards Germany in spring 1939, though inclined to interpret them as a continuation by other means of existing policy (as Chamberlain himself saw it), aimed at preserving the status quo in Eastern Europe and maintaining Britain's status as a world power, rather than a change of direction, see Simon Newman, *March 1939: the British Guarantee to Poland. A Study in the Continuity of British Foreign Policy*, Oxford, 1976, stressing the role of Halifax in urging the Guarantee on Chamberlain. For greater emphasis upon the Guarantee as a decisive turning-point, if not intended as such, in British policy, see A. J. P. Taylor, *The Origins of the Second World War*, (1961), Penguin edn, Harmondsworth, 1964, 253. It is tempting to agree with P. M. H. Bell, *The Origins of the Second World War in Europe*, London, 1986, 252–5, that the simplest explanation for the Guarantee is probably the best: Hitler's invasion of Czechoslovakia had sharply altered opinion in Britain, including Chamberlain's own. There had to be a significant shift in policy. Chamberlain now fully realized the extent to which he had been duped; how the Munich Agreement, which he regarded as his own achievement, had been no more than a major deception. A balanced assessment of Chamberlain's attempts to appease then deter Hitler in 1938–9 can be found in R. A. C. Parker, *Chamberlain and Appeasement. British Policy and the Coming of the Second World War*, London, 1993, here especially 204ff.

137. Domarus, 1128–9. The communiqué of the meeting between Chamberlain and Beck on 5 April 1939 is in *DBFP*, Ser.3, V, 35, No.10 (and see 50, No.17 n.2, referring to the text of the speech in Parliamentary Debates, 5th Series, House of Commons, vol.345, Cols.2996–9). For the firm resolution and false optimism in Warsaw that followed the announcement, see Shirer, 131. British guarantees for Romania, Greece, and Turkey and the beginning of serious negotiations with the Soviets followed (Watt, *How War Came*, 193; see also Weinberg II, 556).

138. Gisevius, *Bis zum bittern Ende*, 1946, vol.2, 127: '*Denen werde ich einen Teufelstrank brauen.*' Gisevius was reporting what he had been told by Admiral Canaris, present when Hitler made the remark.

139. Goebbels anticipated Hitler's response: 'So Beck has fallen after all into the Lords' trap. Poland will perhaps some day have to pay a high price for that.' – *TBJG*, I/6, 313 (10 April 1939).

140. See Dirks/Janßen, 83–4.

141. Domarus, 1119–27, especially 1120, 1125. The speech was not allowed to be transmitted live, presumably to allow the text to be edited if need be (which it was not). The orders, allegedly from

Hitler himself, preventing a live broadcast were issued at such short notice that they came through to William Shirer only after Hitler had already begun to speak. The abrupt end to the broadcast of the speech, and its replacement by music, led to immediate queries from New York about whether Hitler had been assassinated (Shirer, 130).

142. Walter Warlimont, *Inside Hitler's Headquarters, 1939–45,* (1962), Presidio paperback edn, Novato, n.d. (1964), 19–20. For the text: Walther Hubatsch (ed.), *Hitlers Weisungen für die Kriegführung. Dokumente des Oberkommandos der Wehrmacht,* (1962), Munich, 1965, 19–22 (= *Weisungen*) ; and see Müller, *Heer,* 390–92.

143. Domarus, 1130; Below, 159.

144. *DGFP,* D, VI, 223–8, Doc.185; Domarus, 1131–3. *Weisungen,* 22; *IMG,* xxxiv. 388–91, Doc.120-C ('Fall-Weiß'), 429–42, Doc.126-C.

145. *Weisungen,* 22.

146. Hoffmann, 122.

147. Though Poland was aiming to modernize its armed forces, its defence budget in the years 1935–9 amounted to no more than 10 per cent of that of the Luftwaffe alone for the single year of 1939. Andrzej Suchcitz, 'Poland's Defence Preparations in 1939', in Peter D. Stachura (ed.), *Poland between the Wars, 1918–1939,* London, 1998, 109–36, here 110.)

148. Christian Hartmann and Sergej Slutsch, 'Franz Halder und die Kriegsvorbereitungen im Frühjahr 1939. Eine Ansprache des Generalstabschefs des Heeres', *VfZ,* 45 (1997), 467–95, quotations 480, 482–3, 488–90, 495; for the dating to the second half of April, 469–70.

CHAPTER 5: GOING FOR BROKE

1. Speer, 163–4; Domarus, 1144; *TBJG,* I/6, 322 (20 April 1939); Below, 160; Schroeder, 92–4. And see Kurt Pätzold, 'Hitlers fünfzigster Geburtstag am 20. April 1939', in Dietrich Eichholtz and Kurt Pätzold (eds.), *Der Weg in den Krieg. Studien zur Geschichte der Vorkriegsjahre (1935/36 bis 1939),* East Berlin, 1989, 309–43.

2. Domarus, 1146. Henderson, 214, for his recall (and 220 for his return on 25 April).

3. *TBJG,* I/6, 323 (21 April 1939); Domarus, 1145–6; Below, 161; Schroeder, 94.

4. Fritz Terveen, 'Der Filmbericht über Hitlers 50. Geburtstag. Ein Beispiel nationalsozialistischer Selbstdarstellung und Propaganda', *VfZ,* 7 (1959), 75–84, here 82.

5. *TBJG,* I/6, 323 (21 April 1939).

6. *DBS,* vi.435–54.

7. Ilse McKee, *Tomorrow the World,* London, 1960, 27.

8. See Kershaw, *Popular Opinion,* 106, 148–9, 222, for examples.

9. Domarus, 1178; see also Sebastian Haffner, *Anmerkungen zu Hitler,* Munich, 1978, 43–5.

10. *MadR,* ii.160–61.

11. *MadR,* ii.293.

12. GStA, Reichsstatthalter 563, 'Die Lage der bayerischen Landwirtschaft im Frühjahr 1939', Fol.13; see Kershaw, *Popular Opinion,* 61.

13. *MadR,* ii.159, 161, 292, 295.

14. *MadR,* ii.157.

15. BA/MA, RW19/68, 'Zusammenfassender Überblick', 31 January 1939, Fol.119.

16. BA/MA, RW19/56, Wehrwirtschaftsinspektion VI, June 1939.

17. BA/MA, RW19/56, Wehrwirtschaftsinspektion VI, July 1939.

18. See the references in Ch.5 n. 41. Though it never posed any serious danger to the regime, the illegal oppositional activity of the Left, especially the Communists, never ceased and appears to have intensified in the years immediately before the war. See Klaus Mammach, 'Widerstandsaktionen und oppositionelles Verhalten', in Eichholtz and Pätzold, 403–34.

19. BA, R43II/194, Fol.103.

20. IfZ, Doc. NG-5428.

21. BA, R43II/528. Lammers also regularly brought the reports of the Reich Labour Minister to Hitler's attention in the years 1935-7, but ceased to do so after 5 January 1938 (R43II/533).

22. BA, R43II/195, Fol.182.

23. See Speer, 229.

24. See Mason, *Sozialpolitik*, ch.1.

25. Treue, 'Hitlers Rede vor der deutschen Presse', 188-9.

26. Wiedemann, 90.

27. Domarus, 1317.

28. See Below, 162.

29. Schneider, 24 October 1952, 8.

30. See Thies, *Architekt*; and Jost Dülffer, Jochen Thies, and Josef Henke (eds.), *Hitlers Städte. Baupolitik im Dritten Reich. Eine Dokumentation*, Cologne, 1978.

31. See Martin Broszat and Klaus Schwabe (eds.), *Die deutschen Eliten und der Weg in den Zweiten Weltkrieg*, Munich, 1989, especially 61-71 (Hitler); 133 (industry's worries about war); 224-5 (role of diplomats); 285-90 (position of the military after Munich); 383ff. (agrarians' hopes from expansion).

32. See Fritsch's remark to von Hassell in December 1938: 'This man – Hitler – is Germany's fate for better or worse. If it is now into the abyss,' which Fritsch thought likely, 'he will drag us all down with him. There's nothing to be done' (Hassell, 71). The remarks betray little recognition of the part Fritsch and those like him had played in placing Hitler in such a position.

33. *CD* 78, for the length of the speech.

34. Domarus, 1137-8.

35. Below, 161.

36. Domarus, 1173.

37. Domarus, 1148-79 (for the text of the speech; Roosevelt 'answers', 1166-79); Shirer, 133, for the laughter of the deputies.

38. Schneider, Nr.48, 28.22.52, 8.

39. Below, 162. See also Shirer, 133, who thought Hitler's reply 'rather shrewd' in playing to the sympathies of the appeasers.

40. Shirer, 133.

41. Domarus, 1158-9.

42. Watt, *How War Came*, 196-7; Dirks/Janßen, 94ff.

43. Domarus, 1161-3.

44. Weinberg II, 560 and n.87, and see 561 and n.90. The avoidance of further negotiations from this date favours the interpretation that Hitler had decided to solve the 'Polish Question' by force. (For differing positions on this point, see Müller, *Heer*, 391, and Henke, *England*, 242-5.) It is not consonant with the view that he still believed that the Poles could be coerced into accepting his terms. (Watt, *How War Came*, 196.)

45. Müller, *Heer*, 392 and n.73; see also Weinberg II, 558 and n.78.

46. Müller, *Heer*, 390-91 and n.67.

47. Müller, 392. Halder had reservations (393-6), but, in discussions with Beck, one of his arguments about the lack of prospect of opposition was that Danzig was unquestionably a German city (395-6). See also Below, 175; also, Hartmann/Slutsch, 'Franz Halder und die Kriegsvorbereitungen im Frühjahr 1939' for Halder's aggressive speech to military leaders in April 1939, cited in the previous chapter.

48. Dulffer, *Marine*, 507, 510, 529-30. According to Below, 163, those present were expecting a discussion of '*Fall Weiß*' ('Case White'), the plan for the attack on Poland.

49. Weinberg II, 576.

50. Brauchitsch claimed after the war to remember Hitler's words at this point: 'I would have to be an idiot to slide into a war on account of Poland like the incapable lot (*die Unfähigen*) of 1914' (*IMG*, xx.623).

51. *IMG*, xxxvii.546–56, Doc.079-L; *DGFP*, D, VI, 574–80 (quotations 576–80); Domarus, 1196–1201; Below, 163–4 for reactions. See also Weinberg II, 579–83.

52. Mario Toscano, *The Origins of the Pact of Steel*, Baltimore, 1967, 367 (and chs. 4-5 for the genesis and significance of the pact).

53. *CD*, 46.

54. Weinberg II. 565–6.

55. *DGFP*, D, VI, 450–52, No.341; see also Bloch, 225; and Toscano, *Pact of Steel*, 307–34; and, for Hitler's comment on Ribbentrop, *CD*, 91.

56. By 1939, Sweden and Norway supplied 54 per cent of Germany's imports of iron-ore, with 13 per cent coming from France, 8 per cent from Luxemburg, and most of the remainder from Spain, North Africa, and Newfoundland (Lotte Zumpe, *Wirtschaft und Staat in Deutschland 1933 bis 1945*, East Berlin, 1980, 175).

57. Weinberg II, 581, 584–93, and, a more negative assessment, Bloch, 223. For the level of economic penetration of the Balkan countries, see also Alan S. Milward, 'Fascism and the Economy', in Walter Laqueur (ed.), *Fascism. A Reader's Guide*, Harmondsworth 1979, 409–53, here 440–41; and George W. F. Hallgarten and Joachim Radkau, *Deutsche Industrie und Politik von Bismarck bis in die Gegenwart*, Reinbek bei Hamburg, 1981, 330–32. Wendt, *Großdeutschland*, 167–9, 245–8, indicates the continued serious deficiencies for the German economy in 1939 despite such penetration.

58. Bloch, 235. According to Below, 155, Hitler had also begun to play with such ideas following the occupation of Czechoslovakia. At this point, Hitler was, he himself later claimed, unsure whether to strike first in the east or in the west (Domarus, 1422–3 (from Hitler's speech to military leaders on 23 November 1939)).

59. See Ribbentrop, *Zwischen London und Moskau*, 171; Wolfgang Michalka, *Ribbentrop und die deutsche Weltpolitik 1933–1940. Außenpolitische Konzeptionen und Entscheidungsprozesse im Dritten Reich*, Munich, 1979, 278–9; and Wolfgang Michalka, 'From the Anti-Comintern Pact to the Euro-Asiatic Bloc: Ribbentrop's Alternative Concept to Hitler's Foreign Policy Programme', in Koch, *Aspects*, 267–84, here 275–8.

60. Weinberg II, 550–53, 568–77; Alan Bullock, *Hitler and Stalin. Parallel Lives*, London, 1991, 676–7; Bloch, 235; Geoffrey Roberts, *The Unholy Alliance. Stalin's Pact with Hitler*, London, 1989, 109–19; Watt, *How War Came*, ch.13. Carley, *1939: the Alliance that Never Was*, examines in detail the failings of the French and British negotiations with the USSR.

61. Roberts, 151–4.

62. *Ribbentrop Memoirs*, 109. For Stalin's speech, Roberts, 118; Weinberg II, 550. Ribbentrop (if his recollections were accurate) was reading too much into Stalin's speech. Stalin was, in fact, keeping his options open by indicating that the Soviet Union intended to keep its distance from any war among capitalist-imperialist states (Weinberg II, 550).

63. Peter Kleist, *Die europäische Tragödie*, Gottingen, 1961, 52.

64. *DGFP*, D, VI, 266–7 (here 266), No.215.

65. Gustav Hilger and Holger G. Meyer, *The Incompatible Allies: A Memoir-History of German-Soviet Relations 1918–1941*, New York, 1953, 293–7. Hilger believed that Litvinov had been dismissed because he had pressed for an understanding with Britain and France, while Stalin had been more inclined to look to Germany. See also Bloch, 236; and Weinberg II, 570–72, for the change of Soviet foreign minister. Hitler referred to the significance of the dismissal of Litvinov in his speech to his generals on 22 August 1939 (Winfried Baumgart, 'Zur Ansprache Hitlers vor den Führern der Wehrmacht am 22. August 1939. Eine quellenkritische Untersuchung', *VfZ*, 16 (1968), 120–49, here 145), and in his letter to Mussolini of 25 August 1939 (Domarus, 1254).

66. Kleist, 58.

67. Weinberg II, 573–4.

68. Below, 170.

69. Bloch, 236; Weinberg II, 573.

70. Weinberg II, 574; Bloch, 236.

71. *DGFP*, D, VI, 589–93, 597–8, Nos.441, 446 (quotation, 598).

72. *DGFP*, D, VI, 790, 810, 813, Nos. 570, 583, 588.

73. Weinberg II, 604–5; Bullock, *Hitler and Stalin*, 678; Bloch, 237.

74. *DGFP*, D, VI, 755–6 (quotation 755), No.700.

75. *DGFP*, D, VI, 1006–9, No.729; and Anthony Read and David Fisher, *The Deadly Embrace*, London, 1988, 122–6.

76. *DGFP*, D, VI, 1047–8 (here 1048), No.757.

77. *DGFP*, D, VI, 1059–62 (here 1060), 1067–8, Nos.766, 772.

78. *DGFP*, D, VI, 1006–9, 1015–16, 1047–8, Nos.729, 736, 757; *Weizsäcker-Papiere*, 157 (entry for 30 July 1939); Weinberg II, 605.

79. *DGFP*, D, VI, 1059–62, No.766. Molotov had been 'unusually open' (1059) and twice mentioned 'well-known demands on Poland' (1060–61).

80. Weinberg II, 604.

81. *CP*, 300, 304; *DGFP*, D, VII, 39–49 (quotation, 47), No.43.

82. Domarus, 1217.

83. Keitel, 206; Domarus, 1214; Irving, *Führer*, 190.

84. Below, 166–9.

85. Below, 172–4.

86. Domarus, 1217–19.

87. Schneider, Nr.44, 31 October 1952.

88. Kubizek, 282–6.

89. *CD*, 91 (21 May 1939). Ciano had found Hitler well, but looking older, with more wrinkled eyes. He remarked on Hitler's insomnia.

90. Schneider, Nr.43, 24 October 1952, 1,8. See also Sereny, *Speer*, 193–5.

91. Seraphim, *Rosenberg-Tagebuch*, 81 (6 February 1939). Rosenberg's opinion that Goebbels was so disliked was based, to go from the context of his remarks, on the Propaganda Minister's use of his power for the sexual exploitation of young women hoping for career-advancement. In conversation with Himmler, Rosenberg also went on to criticize Goebbels for the damage to the state caused by the 'Reichskristallnacht' pogrom.

92. See Martens, 178ff., 199; Kube, 312; Irving, *Göring*, 247–54.

93. Sereny, 206.

94. Weizsäcker, *Erinnerungen*, 234.

95. Weinberg II, 583–4 and n.199.

96. Steinert, 84ff.; Ian Kershaw, 'Der Überfall auf Polen und die öffentliche Meinung in Deutschland', in Ernst Willi Hansen, Gerhard Schreiber, and Bernd Wegner (eds.), *Politischer Wandel, organisierte Gewalt und nationale Sicherheit. Beiträge zur neueren Geschichte Deutschlands und Frankreichs. Festschrift für Klaus-Jürgen Müller*, Munich, 1995, 237–50, here 239–45.

97. *DBS*, vi.407ff.

98. McKee, 27.

99. StA Bamberg, K8/III, 18473, BA Ebermannstadt, no date (end of July 1939).

100. *DBS*, vi.275.

101. *DBS*, vi.561.

102. *DBS*, vi.818.

103. *DBS*, vi.409ff.

104. Herbert S. Levine, *Hitler's Free City. A History of the Nazi Party in Danzig, 1925–39*, Chicago/London, 1973, 151; and Weinberg II, 584 n.208.

105. Carl J. Burckhardt, *Meine Danziger Mission 1937-1939*, Munich, 1962, 254-5 for the customs crisis.

106. Burckhardt, 255-6.

107. See Herbert S. Levine, 'The Mediator: Carl J. Burckhardt's Efforts to Avert a Second World War', *JMH*, 45 (1973), 439-55, here 453-5.

108. Burckhardt, 261-3; and see Paul Stauffer, *Zwischen Hofmannsthal und Hitler. Carl J. Burckhardt: Facetten einer aussergewöhnlichen Existenz*, Zurich, 1991, 141ff., who points out (152-3) that news of the 'secret' meeting was deliberately leaked in advance, almost certainly on Hitler's initiative, in an attempt to demonstrate his openness to dialogue with the west, to the French journalist (known to have sympathized in the past with Nazi Germany) Bertrand de Jouvenel.

109. Burckhardt, 264. The 'Eagle's Nest', built at a height of almost 2,000 metres, some 800 metres higher up than the Berghof itself, was actually no 'Tea House'. Hitler's 'Tea House', the regular goal of his afternoon walks, lay below the Berghof. The name 'Teehaus' was a corruption of the official name D-Haus (Diplomaten-Haus), which betrayed the intention of making the maximum impression upon selected important foreign visitors. It had been designed by Bormann, with plans reaching back to 1936, as a present for Hitler's fiftieth birthday. Around 3,500 men worked on it and, by the time that it was finished in summer 1938, it had cost some 30 million Reich Marks. During most of the war years it was empty and unused. (Ernst Hanisch, *Der Obersalzberg: das Kehlsteinhaus und Adolf Hitler*, Berchtesgaden, 1995, 18-21; Below, 124. See the impressions of François-Poncet, *Als Botschafter*, 395-7.)

110. Below, 124.

111. Schneider, Nr.46, 14 November 1952, 8; Speer, 176.

112. At his first visit to the 'Eagle's Nest' the previous summer, Hitler had mentioned that he would take up there visitors he wanted especially to honour or impress (Below, 124).

113. Schneider, Nr.46, 14 November 1952, 8.

114. Burckhardt, 264-70; English text in *DBFP*, Ser.3, VI, 691-6, No. 659, (quotations, 694-5). See Watt, *How War Came*, 332, for the description of Ironside. The Ironside suggestion was also advanced by Weizsäcker, and by Henderson, but it was eventually decided in London that he would not be an appropriate person to send (Meehan, 232-3, 235). The British Embassy in Paris had warned the Foreign Office that it might be damaging to good relations between France and Britain were the Ironside proposal to be accepted without consultation with the French (Stauffer, 154).

115. Burckhardt met, in the house of his mother in Basel, Roger Makins from the British Foreign Office and Pierre Arnal of the Quai d'Orsay already on 13 August. Makins's report on the meeting (*DBFP*, Ser.3, VI, 691-5, No.659) was largely dictated by Burckhardt, and was translated into German for *Meine Danziger Mission*, 264ff. (Stauffer, 141, 179, 182).

116. *DBFP*, Ser.3, VI, 696, No.659; Stauffer, 140-41.

117. *The Diaries of Sir Alexander Cadogan*, 195.

118. *DBFP*, Ser.3, VI, 697-8, No.659; Watt, *How War Came*, 435. Makins's report, later reproduced by Burckhardt in his book, did not include remarks by Hitler which the High Commissioner added in his memoirs, written more than twenty years later, claiming, somewhat remarkably, that they had not struck him at the time: 'Everything that I undertake is directed against Russia. If those in the West are too stupid and too blind to understand this, then I shall be forced to come to an understanding with the Russians to beat the West, and then, after its defeat, turn with all my concerted force against the Soviet Union. I need the Ukraine, so that no one will starve us out as they did in the last war' (Burckhardt, 272; trans. Klaus Hildebrand, *The Foreign Policy of the Third Reich*, London, 1973, 88). Hildebrand and others have taken it for granted that the comments were intended to carry weight in London. There is, however, no indication that they were passed on, even unofficially. Neither Halifax in his memoirs, nor Cadogan in his diaries, refers to the remarks. Despite the passage finding its way into practically every account of Burckhardt's meeting with Hitler, it is not surprising that many doubts have been raised about its authenticity. It seems on

first impression inherently unlikely that Hitler would have made such comments, knowing that Burckhardt was meant to report the content of the conversation to the western powers at a time when discussions for a pact with the Russians were at such a delicate stage and when those between the Soviet Union and the western democracies were still dragging on. An extant copy of Burckhardt's own sparse notes of Hitler's comments, undated but allegedly from the day of his meeting with the Nazi leader, does indicate that Hitler, having stated he was not bluffing and would strike hard, did remark that 'he would only temporarily come to an arrangement with Russia, then after victory [over] the West attack with entire force on account of Ukraine!! Grain, timber!' (cit. Stauffer, 188). The original is, however, not contained in Burckhardt's papers (Stauffer, 308 n.33) and, so it seems, has never been seen. Though Stauffer, after careful inquiry (178–201), is prepared to grant the benefit of doubt as regarding the authenticity of the document (189–90), a question-mark must remain until the original – allegedly held in a bank-vault – is produced. Burckhardt produced no compelling reason why he omitted to mention Hitler's remark to Makins. If the document is taken to be authentic, the best gloss is perhaps that Hitler's remarks struck Burckhardt as, in essence, uttered in the heat of the moment, nothing different from that which Hitler had written in *Mein Kampf*, and consequently uninteresting to the western governments. Hitler had spoken earlier in the meeting of the need for land in the east and the need to secure grain and timber, and the near repetition of the point perhaps made little mark on Burckhardt at the time. In any event, his published version of the remarks must be regarded as a later embellishment on Burckhardt's part – not the only one in his published memoirs.

119. *CP*, 297–9.

120. *CD*, 124.

121. *CP*, 299–303. Just over a week later, on 20 August, the former head of the London branch of the German News Agency, Fritz Hesse, was conveying to the British Government, on the authorization of Ribbentrop, the impression not simply of Hitler's determination to resolve the Danzig issue, come what may, but – probably to be seen as bluff – of his awareness 'that if war should break out between Germany and Poland Great Britain will be in it'. (Josef Henke, 'Hitler und England Mitte August 1939. Ein Dokument zur Rolle Fritz Hesse in den deutsch-britischen Beziehungen am Vorabend des Zweiten Weltkrieges', *VfZ*, 21 (1973), 231–42, especially 240 and (for the quotation) 241. Henke (and Hesse himself, as he later stated) regarded the remarks as a genuine reflection of Hitler's views at the time, not as a tactical calculation – see 236 and n.20.) The claims made by Hesse in his book, *Fritz Hesse, Das Spiel um Deutschland*, Munich, 1953, about the importance of his role as an intermediary between the German and British governments in the last weeks of peace are greatly exaggerated.

122. *CD*, 124.

123. *DGFP*, D, VII, 39–49 (48–9 for the interruption in the talks), 58–9, Nos. 43, 50; *CP*, 302.

124. *DGFP*, D, VII, 68–9, No.62; Bloch, 240; Read and Fisher, *The Deadly Embrace*, 193–4.

125. Bloch, 240. *Ribbentrop Memoirs*, 109–10, suggest that the Foreign Minister had himself proposed Göring. Since the two were arch-rivals, this sounds inherently unlikely. Ribbentrop's comment that he knew nothing at this time of Hitler's intention to attack Poland is not credible.

126. Bloch, 241–4.

127. *DGFP*, D, VII, 142–8, 152–3, Nos.131, 135. It was agreed on 19 August and signed, after some further delay from the Moscow end, at 2 a.m. on 20 August.

128. *DGFP*, D, VII, 134, No.125; Read and Fisher, *The Deadly Embrace*, 214.

129. That Hitler was planning to attack Poland by the end of August or beginning of September had been known to Stalin since June (Dmitri Volkogonov, *Stalin. Triumph and Tragedy*, (1991), Rocklin Ca., 1996, 357). The frenetic diplomatic activity in Berlin in mid-August was an indicator to Stalin and Molotov that the date of the invasion was close (Weinberg II, 608). Bloch, 244, states (without source) that Stalin and Molotov knew that Hitler was intending to invade on 26 August.

130. *DGFP*, D, VII, 156–7, No.142.

131. Hoffmann, *Hitler Was My Friend*, 102. Speer's account, 176, differs in detail, recording Hitler's reactions on receiving the telegram (for which see Domarus, 1233).

132. Steinert, 85–6. And see Schmidt, 449; Shirer, 145.

133. Baumgart, 142 (the comment written in November 1939 of General Liebmann), and 145 n.100, citing Rundstedt's recollections in testimony at Nuremberg on 19 June 1946; see also Below, 181.

134. *TBJG*, I/7, 72 (22 August 1939).

135. *TBJG*, I/7, 72 (24 August 1939): '*Wir sind in Not und fressen da wie der Teufel Fliegen.*'

136. Seraphim, *Rosenberg-Tagebuch*, 89–90 (22 August 1939).

137. See *DBS*, vi.985–6.

138. *DBS*, vi.988.

139. Hoffmann, *Hitler Was My Friend*, 103.

140. *TBJG*, I/7, 73 (23 August 1939).

141. Watt, *How War Came*, 466.

142. Cit. Werner Maser, *Der Wortbruch. Hitler, Stalin und der Zweite Weltkrieg*, (1994), 4th edn, Munich, 1997, 59–60.

143. Watt, *How War Came*, 467–70.

144. Meehan, 233–4. Halifax stressed only the importance of the effect on morale.

145. Watt, *How War Came*, 463.

146. The order to attend the meeting was delivered to General Liebmann on the morning of 21 August (Baumgart, 141).

147. Below, 181.

148. Baumgart, 144 n.97, 148.

149. Baumgart, 144 n.97. Some present later claimed that they were there in uniform. The most contemporary accounts, however, mention civilian clothes. Below, 180, confirms this.

150. Baumgart, 142.

151. Baumgart, 143 and n.93–6, 148.

152. Baumgart, 143 and n.96.

153. Baumgart, 148 n.111. The notes were handwritten headings, according to Below, 181.

154. Baumgart, 120.

155. Baumgart, 122–8. For the significance of the document, its authenticity, and the authorship of the best version (that of Canaris), see Baumgart's article, and his reply, 'Zur Ansprache Hitlers vor den Führern der Wehrmacht am 22.August 1939 (Erwiderung)', *VfZ*, 19 (1971), 301–4, to Hermann Böhm, 'Zur Ansprache Hitlers vor den Führern der Wehrmacht am 22.August 1939', *VfZ*, 19 (1971), 294–300.

156. *IMG*, xxvi, 338–44, Doc. 798-PS; *DGFP*, D, VII, 200–204 (quotations 204), No.192; Baumgart, 149 and n.113 for the timing and lunchtime break, 135–6, n.67. Also Below, 181.

157. For the time, Baumgart, 126, 149 n.113. Below recalled that he spoke for about two hours. (Below, 180). Baumgart, 132–3 n.53, 55 for operational talks, and reference to Halder and Warlimont; Below, 181.

158. On the different interpretations of what Hitler meant by this phrase, see Baumgart, 133 and n.57.

159. *IMG*, xxvi, 523–4, Doc.1014-PS; *DGFP*, D, VII, 205–6, No.205–6 (quotations, 205).

160. Baumgart, 146.

161. Baumgart, 146.

162. Below, 181, thought the Soviet pact had silenced some sceptics.

163. Baumgart, 148. For Hitler's insistence that the West would not intervene, see IfZ, F34/1, Vormann Memoirs, Fols.42–3.

164. Hassell, 71.

165. Below, 181–2.

166. Baumgart, 143 n.96, 146; Schmidt, 449–50; Bloch, 246.

167. Schmidt, 455. Hoffmann's account of the visit to Moscow (*Hitler Was My Friend*, 103–14) is inaccurate and self-important. The signs are that Stalin was, in fact, less than happy at Hoffmann's photographic interference and did not welcome the publicity (*Ribbentrop Memoirs*, 114).

168. Based on *Ribbentrop Memoirs*, 110–13, and Schmidt, 450–52. Both are variedly inaccurate on the time of arrival and first talks; see Bloch, 247. Though Schulenburg had been in Moscow for years, it was the first time that he had spoken to Stalin.

169. Below, 182.

170. Below, 183. Speer, 177, gives a distorted version of the incident, which is also graphically described by the 'manager' (*Verwalter*) at the Berghof, Herrmann Döring, BBC-Archive, 'The Nazis: A Warning from History', Transcript, Roll 244, Fols. 30–37. Speer recalled after the war that no one hearing Hitler was shocked by his remarks about the shedding of much blood, and that Germany would have to plunge into the abyss with him if the war was not won. Speer himself was taken, so he recalled, by 'the grandeur of the historical hour' (Albert Speer, *Spandau. The Secret Diaries*, Fontana edn, London, 1977, 40–41 (entry for 21 December 1946)).

171. Schmidt, 452–3; Below, 183; *Ribbentrop Memoirs*, 113. A telegram containing just those words followed within two hours (*DGFP*, D, VII, 220, 223, Nos. 205, 210).

172. *Ribbentrop Memoirs*, 113; Schmidt, 454. Hoffmann's account, *Hitler Was My Friend*, 109–11, cannot be trusted.

173. Bloch, 249 (contradicting Ribbentrop's own claim, *Ribbentrop Memoirs*, 113, that they were signed before midnight).

174. *TBJG*, I/7, 75 (24 August 1939).

175. Below, 183.

176. Watt, *How War Came*, 463, 465. Sumner Welles, Acting Secretary of State in the USA, was told on 22 August by Joseph E. Davies, former US Ambassador in Moscow, that news of the non-aggression pact was 'not unexpected' (Davies, 453–4).

177. *The Diaries of Sir Alexander Cadogan*, 200.

178. Nicolson, 154.

179. *Chips*, 208–9.

180. N. J. Crowsen (ed.), *Fleet Street, Press Barons, and Politics: the Journals of Collin Brooks, 1932–1940*, Camden Soc., 5th Ser., vol.11, London, 1998, 252.

181. Roberts, 174; Allan Merson, *Communist Resistance in Nazi Germany*, London, 1985, 212–13.

182. Heinz Kühnrich, 'Der deutsch-sowjetische Nichtangriffsvertrag vom 23. August 1939 aus der zeitgenossischen Sicht der KPD', in Eichholtz and Pätzold, 517–51, here 519 (quotation), 529.

183. Below, 184.

184. See *TBJG*, I/7, 74–7 (24 August 1939, 25 August 1939) for the uncertainty of Goebbels who, at this time on the Berghof, was probably echoing Hitler's own sentiments.

185. *Documents concerning German-Polish Relations and the Outbreak of Hostilities between Great Britain and Germany on September 3, 1939*, London, 1939, 96–8, No.56; *DBFP*, 3rd Ser., VII, 170–71 (here 171), No.207; *DGFP*, D, VII, 215–16, No.200; Henderson, 256.

186. *Documents*, 99, No.57; *DBFP*, 3rd Ser., VII, 161–3 (here 162), No.200; see Henderson, 247–8, 256–7, 301–5.

187. *Documents*, 99–100, No.57; *DBFP*, 3rd Ser., VII, 161–3 (here 163), No.200; *DGFP*, D, VII, 210–16, No.200; Domarus, 1244–7.

188. *DBFP*, 3rd Ser. VII, 201–2 (quotation 201), No.248.

189. *Documents*, 100–101, No.58; *DBFP*, 3rd Ser., VII, 201–2 (here 202), No.248; *DGFP*, D, VII, 210–16, No.200; Henderson, 257; Domarus, 1249–50.

190. Domarus, 1247–8; *DBFP*, 3rd Ser., VII, 177–9 (here, 178), No.211.

191. Weizsacker, *Erinnerungen*, 252.

192. *TBJG*, I/7, 76 (25 August 1939); Below, 187; Watt, *How War Came*, 464–5. And see Hitler's remarks to Reich Press Chief Otto Dietrich: 'No democratic government can survive such a defeat

and embarrassment as Chamberlain and Daladier have had inflicted on them through our Moscow treaty.' (cit. Peter Kleist, *Zwischen Hitler und Stalin*, Bonn, 1950, 66. ('*Keine demokratische Regierung kann sich halten, der eine solche Niederlage und zugleich Blamage zuteil geworden ist, wie Chamberlain und Daladier durch unseren Moskauer Vertrag.*')) The speeches of Chamberlain and Halifax can be found in *Documents*, 107–18.

193. *Ribbentrop Memoirs*, 116.

194. *Documents*, 120–22, No.68; *DBFP*, 3rd Ser., VII, 227–31, Nos.283–4; Henderson, 259; Schmidt, 458–9; Domarus, 1256–7.

195. *Documents*, 122–3, No.69; *DBFP*, 3rd Ser., VII, 230, No.284; Domarus, 1257.

196. Henderson, 259. See also *DBFP*, 3rd Ser., VII, 235, 239, Nos.286, 293.

197. *TBJG*, I/7, 77 (26 August 1939).

198. *IMG*, xxviii.389, Doc.1780-PS (Jodl's diary, 23 August 1939) for the time set for the operation. Hitler took the decision to go ahead at 3.02p.m. on 25 August and various subsidiary orders to army units followed (Franz Halder, *Kriegstagebuch. Tägliche Aufzeichnungen des Chefs des Generalstabes des Heeres 1939–1942*, ed. Arbeitskreis für Wehrforschung Stuttgart, 3 vols., Stuttgart, 1962–4 (= *Halder KTB*), i.33 (26 August 1939); Vormann, in IfZ, F34/1, Fol.24). Saturday – a day favoured by Hitler for the withdrawal from the League of Nations, the introduction of conscription, the reoccupation of the Rhineland, and the Anschluß – was possibly chosen since it delayed the likely response time of the British government. (See Domarus, 1239 and n.654. See also Weinberg II, 634; Walther Hofer, *Die Entfesselung des Zweiten Weltkrieges*, Frankfurt am Main, 1964, 274; Hermann Graml, *Europas Weg in den Krieg. Hitler und die Mächte 1939*, Munich, 1990, 287 (and 277ff. for a detailed account of the developments during the last days of August.)

199. Weinberg II, 633–4.

200. Below, 178.

201. *Generaloberst Halder, Kriegstagebuch. Bd. I: Vom Polenfeldzug bis zum Eride der Westoffensive (14.8.1939–30.6.1940)*, ed. Hans-Adolf Jacobsen, Stuttgart, 1962 [= *Halder KTB*], 26 (22 August 1939); *The Halder War Diary, 1939–1942*, ed. Charles Burdick and Hans-Adolf Jacobsen, London, 1988 (the abridged English translation of *Halder KTB* = *Halder Diary*), 32; *DGFP*, D, VII, 557–9, Appendix I (extracts from Halder's diary); Domarus, 1239.

202. Below, 182.

203. *TBJG*, I/7, 77 (26 August 1939).

204. Henderson, 258; *Halder KTB*, i.31 (25 August 1939), mentions the lifting of telephone restrictions on Britain and France by Canaris. *TBJG*, I/7, 79–80 (27 August 1939), refers to the introduction of ration cards, though not yet for bread and potatoes. See Shirer, 148, 150 for grumbling at the ration cards.

205. *Halder KTB*, i. 31–3 (25–6 August 1939), IfZ, F34/1, Vormann, Fols.24–5.

206. *Halder KTB*, i. 31 (25 August 1939), 39 (28 August 1939); IfZ, F34/1, Vormann, Fols. 26–8.

207. Müller, *Heer*, 416–17.

208. *Halder KTB*, i. 33 (26 August 1939), 39 (28 August 1939); Engel, 59 and n.160.

209. Domarus, 1254–5.

210. Weinberg II, 630–31.

211. *DGFP*, D, VII, 285–6, No.271. Mussolini remarked that he had been preparing for war in 1942.

212. Schmidt, 462.

213. *TBJG*, I/7, 78 (26 August 1939). See Halder's remark: 'Führer rather gone to pieces' ('*Führer ziemlich zusammengebrochen*'), *Halder KTB*, i.34 (26 January 1939). According to Vormann, Hitler walked up and down the room in a state of agitation speaking to this and that person. To Vormann, he said: 'We now have to be sly, sly as foxes' (' "*Schlau müssen wir jetzt sein, schlau wie die Füchse*" ') (IfZ, F34/1, Vormann, Fol.26).

214. IfZ, F34/1, Vormann, Fol.43: 'The refusal of Mussolini was felt on all sides to be treachery and

most harshly condemned' (' . . . *war die Absage Mussolinis allseitig als Verrat empfunden und schärfstens verurteilt worden*'). See also Below, 187–9, where, however, Hitler, despite the 'hard words' against his ally, did not doubt Mussolini's loyalty.

215. IfZ, F34/1, Vormann, Fols.26–8; *Ribbentrop Memoirs*, 117. On the effect on Hitler's prestige, Muller, *Heer*, 420 and n.206.

216. Schmidt, 462.

217. Schmidt, 459–61; *IMG*, x.240; Robert Coulondre, *Von Moskau nach Berlin 1936–1939. Erinnerungen des französischen Botschafters*, Bonn, 1950, 421–4; Weinberg II, 634 and n.32; Hofer, *Entfesselung*, 275; Graml, *Europas Weg*, 288–9.

218. Weinberg II, 635.

219. *Ribbentrop Memoirs*, 116–17. There is no corroborative support for Ribbentrop's unlikely claim that, learning of the British–Polish pact, he had persuaded Hitler to halt the attack on Poland (Domarus, 1259; Schmidt, 459; Weinberg II, 637–8; and for Ribbentrop's claim see also Bloch, 253). Below, 187, seems directly drawn from Ribbentrop's memoirs and cannot be taken as supportive evidence. Brauchitsch – 'not unjustifiably', in Engel's view – also claimed to have persuaded Hitler to postpone the attack (Engel, 59 (26 August 1939)). Goebbels makes it plain in his diary notes that it was the news from Mussolini that was decisive in the change of plan (*TBJG*, I/7, 78 (26 August 1939)).

220. A point made by Weinberg II, 635.

221. *Ribbentrop Memoirs*, 117; Bloch, 254.

222. Domarus, 1261.

223. *IMG*, iii.280.

224. Dahlerus, 53–6.

225. Domarus, 1261.

226. Domarus, 1264–5; *CD*, 135.

227. *CD*, 135; *DGFP*, D, VII, 324–6, No.320.

228. *TBJG*, I/7, 80, 82–3 (28 August 1939, 29 August 1939).

229. Domarus, 1265–6.

230. Engel, 60 (27 August 1939, 29 August 1939).

231. Dahlerus, 56.

232. *DBFP*, 3rd Ser., VII, 283–4, Annex 1 to Doc.349.

233. Dahlerus, 56–66 (quotation, 66: '*Sein ganzes Verhalten machte den Eindruck eines völlig Anormalen*').

234. Dahlerus, 69–70.

235. Dahlerus, 78–9.

236. *DBFP*, 3rd Ser., VII, 318–20, 321–2, Nos.402, 406.

237. *DBFP*, 3rd Ser., VII, 324, No.411, and, especially, 328, No.420.

238. *TBJG*, I/7, 80 (28 September 1939).

239. Groscurth, 187 (27 August 1939).

240. *Halder KTB*, i. 40 (28 August 1939).

241. *TBJG*, I/7, 81 (28 August 1939). Goebbels was evidently getting a preview on 27 August of the talk Hitler would give the next day.

242. *Halder KTB*, i. 38 (28 August 1939), trans. *Halder Diary*, 37.

243. *Documents*, 128, No.75; *DBFP*, 3rd Ser., VII, 330–32, 351–5, Nos.426, 455.

244. Henderson, 262.

245. *Documents*, 128–31, here 129, No.75; *DBFP*, 3rd Ser., VII, 352, No.455.

246. *DBFP*, 3rd Ser., VII, 330, No.426; Alan Bullock, *Hitler. A Study in Tyranny*, (1952), Harmondsworth, 1962, 541.

247. *Documents*, 126–8, No.74; *DBFP*, 3rd Ser., VII, 321, No.426.

248. Henderson, 262.

249. *TBJG*, I/7, 83 (29 August 1939).

250. *TBJG*, I/7, 84 (30 August 1939). The plebiscite idea formed part of the proposals read out by Ribbentrop at his meeting with Henderson late on the evening of 30 August (*Documents*, 146, No.92).

251. IfZ, ED 100, Irving-Sammlung, Hitler-Dokumentation, Bd.20, Aug. 1939; Irving, *Führer*, 222–3; Irving, *War Path*, 255–6.

252. Henderson, 263. Shirer, 150–54, remarked on how few people, and those with grim, silent faces, had been there the previous evening when Henderson went to the Reich Chancellery.

253. Henderson, 265; *Documents*, 138, No.79 (text, 135–7, no.78); *DBFP*, 3rd Ser., VII, 374–5 (here 374), No.490, 388–90 (here, 390), No.502; Domarus, 1285–7.

254. Henderson, 267.

255. *Documents*, 138–9, No.80; *DBFP*, 3rd Ser., VII, 376–7 (here 376), No.493.

256. *Documents*, 140, No.82; *DBFP*, 3rd Ser., 400–401 (here 401), No.520.

257. Schmidt, 465.

258. Dahlerus, 99–100.

259. *Documents*, 139, Nos.81–2; *DBFP*, 3rd Ser., VII, 391, 400–401, Nos.504, 520; Henderson, 268–9.

260. Domarus, 1289.

261. Domarus, 1290 and n.809 for Hitler's use of 'Führer' alone after decrees from now on (though not consistently).

262. Dieter Rebentisch, *Führerstaat und Verwaltung im Zweiten Weltkrieg. Verfassungsentwicklung und Verwaltungspolitik 1939–1945*, Stuttgart, 1989, 117–32; also Broszat, *Staat*, 382.

263. Schmidt, 465–9, here 467–8.

264. Henderson, 270–71; *Documents*, 142–3, No.89, 145–6, no.92; *DBFP*, 3rd Ser., VII, 413–14, 432–3, Nos.543, 574; text of Hitler's offer, Domarus, 1291–3. Schmidt claimed that Ribbentrop did not read the terms too quickly, though Henderson had noted that in his report to Halifax immediately after the meeting (*Documents*, 145, No.92 (*DBFP*, 3rd Ser., VII, 432–3, No.574)). For Hitler's order to Ribbentrop not to hand out the terms, see *IMG*, x. 311.

265. *Documents*, 146, No.92; *DBFP*, 3rd Ser., VII, 433, No.574.

266. Henderson, 271.

267. Schmidt, 469.

268. *TBJG*, I/7, 86 (31 August 1939).

269. Domarus, 1297; Henderson, 275, 277; *TBJG*, I/7, 87 (1 September 1939).

270. Dahlerus, 107.

271. *Halder KTB*, i. 46 (30 August 1939).

272. *Halder KTB*, i. 47 (31 August 1939).

273. *Halder KTB*, i. 46 (30 August 1939).

274. *IMG*, xxxiv, 456–9, Doc.126-C; *Weisungen*, 23–5.

275. *Halder KTB*, i. 47–8 (31 August 1939), trans. *Halder Diary*, 43 (31 August 1939). See also Groscurth, 195, n.441 for the timing of the transmission of the attack order, passed on by Brauchitsch at 16.20 hours. *TBJG*, I/7, 87 (1 September 1939) notes that at midday Hitler gave the order to attack 'in the night approaching 5a.m.'.

276. *IMG*, ix.313 (Ribbentrop testimony).

277. *TBJG*, I/7, 87 (1 September 1939).

278. *TBJG*, I/7, 88 (1 September 1939).

279. Henderson, 276; *Ribbentrop Memoirs*, 125; Josef Lipski, *Diplomat in Berlin 1933–1939*, ed. Waclaw Jedrzejewicz, New York/London, 1968, 609–10; Irving, *Führer*, 225; Irving, *War Path*, 260.

280. Domarus, 1305–6.

281. Heinz Höhne, *The Order of the Death's Head. The Story of Hitler's SS*, London, 1969, 238–44. In the most spectacular of the 'incidents', the attack on the Gleiwitz radio station, Polish uniforms were not used (as some post-war testimony claimed), and were not necessary. An SS guard had already taken over the watch on the station to ensure the success of the operation when, as pre-arranged, five SD men dressed in civilian clothes entered the building to carry out the attack (Jürgen Runzheimer, 'Der Überfall auf den Sender Gleiwitz im Jahre 1939', *VfZ*, 10 (1962), 408–26).

282. Shirer, 152.

283. StA Bamberg, K8/III, 18473, LR Ebermannstadt, 31 August 1939. See also *DBS*, vi.980–83; Steinert, 91ff.; Wolfram Wette, 'Zur psychologischen Mobilmachung der deutschen Bevölkerung 1933–1939', in Wolfgang Michalka (ed.), *Der Zweite Weltkrieg. Analysen-Grundzüge-Forschungsbilanz*, Munich-Zurich, 1989, 205–23, here 220; and *DRZW*, i.142.

284. Horst Rohde, 'Kriegsbeginn 1939 in Danzig – Planungen und Wirklichkeit', in Michalka (ed.), *Der Zweite Weltkrieg*, 462–81, here 462, 472–7, 479 n.1; Levine, 153; Domarus, 1307–8. It should have been the cruiser *Königsberg*, but that ship had developed engine trouble (Levine, *Hitler's Free City*, 152). See Baumgart, 147, for Liebmann's report of the conversation he overheard between Raeder and Hitler following the meeting on the Berghof on 22 August. Raeder remarked that the *Schleswig-Holstein* would probably be sunk by Polish coastal batteries with the loss of 300 or so sea-cadets. Hitler replied with a dismissive wave of the hand. In fact, the attack on the Westerplatte did not go according to plan. The Luftwaffe had to intervene before the Westerplatte was finally taken on the afternoon of 1 September, by which time the Germans had lost between 40 and 50 men (Rohde, 474–5).

285. *Halder KTB*, i.52 (1 September 1939), trans. *Halder Diary*, 47.

286. Levine, *Hitler's Free City*, 153.

287. Domarus, 1308.

288. Shirer, 156. See Henderson's impressions, 287–91; and those of Dahlerus, 123–4.

289. Domarus, 1311, cit. *Neue Zürcher Zeitung*, 1 September 1939.

290. Shirer, 156; Domarus, 1316 and n.901. Below, 195 contradicts Shirer's impressions, stating that Hitler was received with far more cheering than usual, which broke out repeatedly through his speech. Shirer's contemporary account is probably to be preferred. Hellmuth Groscurth, a rooted opponent of Hitler in the Abwehr, noted in his diary: '10.00a.m. Reichstag speech. Terrible impression everywhere' (Groscurth, 196).

291. Domarus, 1315; text of speech 1312–17. As regards the timing of the start of hostilities, Hitler appears simply to have made a mistake (Rohde, 479 n.1).

292. Dahlerus, 124–5.

293. See the references to Mussolini's peace efforts in Chamberlain's speeches in the House of Commons on 1 and 2 September 1939: *Documents*, 161, No.105, 172, No.116; *DBFP*, 3rd Ser., VII, 501–2, 507–8, Nos. 700, 710; and Weinberg II, 640–41.

294. Domarus, 1319; *DGFP*, D, VII, 485–9, Nos. 504, 505, 507. In the evening of 3 September, Hitler thanked Mussolini for his efforts and explained why Germany was now at war with Great Britain and France (*DGFP*, D, VII, 538–9, No.565).

295. Dahlerus, 125–6. And see Hofer, *Entfesselung*, 392–3.

296. Sir Alexander Cadogan, Permanent Under-Secretary at the British Foreign Office, was brisk in his reply when Dahlerus telephoned him on the early afternoon of 1 September, after his meeting with Hitler (Dahlerus, 127; *DBFP*, 3rd Ser., VII, 479–80, Nos.651–2). Cadogan had already noted in his diary on 28 August that the 'masses of messages from Dahlerus . . . don't amount to much unless one can infer from them that Hitler has cold feet' (*The Diaries of Sir Alexander Cadogan*, 203). Dahlerus's frantic last efforts to engineer a visit by Göring to London were no more than whistling in the wind (Dahlerus, 136–7). In an interview on BBC-TV on 14 September 1997, Sir Frank Roberts (then a prominent diplomat in the Foreign Office, later, in the 1960s, British Ambassador to Moscow, then Bonn), who took the call from Dahlerus on the morning of 3 September, after the British ultimatum had been issued, recalled that he had not thought it worth passing on the message to the Foreign Secretary, Lord Halifax.

297. *DGFP*, VII, 527–8, No.558; *DBFP*, 3rd Ser., IX, 539, App.IV; Weinberg, ii.649–50.

298. Henderson, 278–9; *Documents*, 168–9, No.109–11; *DBFP*, 3rd Ser., VII, 492, No.682.

299. *Documents*, 175, No.118; *DBFP*, 3rd Ser., VII, 521, 535, Nos.732, 757.

300. Schmidt, 472; Henderson, 284.

301. *Documents*, 175, No.118; *DBFP*, 3rd Ser., VII, 535, No.757; German reply, *DBFP*, 3rd Ser., VII, 539–41, No.766; Domarus, 1336–8.

302. *Documents*, 179, No.120.

303. *Halder KTB*, 1.58 (3 September 1939); *TBJG*, I/7, 91 (4 September 1939); *DBFP*, 3rd Ser., VII, 538, No.764.

304. See IfZ, F34/1, Vormann, Fol.56.

305. Schmidt, 473. Doubts have been expressed about the accuracy of Schmidt's account (Gerhard L. Weinberg, 'Hitler and England, 1933–1945: Pretense and Reality', *German Studies Review*, 8 (1985), 299–309, here 306). Certainly, Schmidt's memoirs contain errors. However, Schmidt was present on the occasion, and Hitler's response was short enough and striking enough for the interpreter to have remembered it correctly, even several years later. What might, perhaps, be justifiably doubted is whether Schmidt grasped Hitler's meaning; whether Hitler was not simply asking Ribbentrop in practical terms about what the next step would be. The reported response (Schmidt, 473) of the Foreign Minister, 'I presume that the French will hand us a similar-sounding ultimatum in the next hour,' points in this direction.

306. *Documents*, 157, No.105.

307. L.B. Namier, *Conflicts. Studies in Contemporary History*, London, 1942, 57.

308. Klemperer, 112–29; Watt, *How War Came*, 390–94; Meehan, especially ch.7; Lamb, 105–8. Some of the clearest warnings of the need for Britain to take a firm stand against Hitler were passed on in the spring and summer by Lieutenant-Colonel von Schwerin, head of the 'Foreign Armies West' section of the Army High Command's Intelligence Department. The Foreign Office was, however, largely dismissive of his information. 'As usual the German army trusts us to save them from the Nazi regime,' was the minute of one prominent diplomat, Frank K. Roberts (Klemperer, 119). I am grateful to R. A. C. Parker for referring me to reports on Schwerin in PRO, FO 371/22990 and FO 371/22968.

309. Gisevius, *Bis zum bittern Ende*, 1946, ii.138. Gisevius did not claim these were Oster's exact words, but was adamant that they represented his meaning.

310. Gisevius, *Bis zum bittern Ende*, 1946; ii.140.

311. See Muller, *Heer*, 414–19.

312. Watt, *How War Came*, 394–404.

313. See Kube, 319; Martens, 199–200; Irving, *Goring*, 268, 272.

314. Bloch, 261. Similar thoughts were current in Berlin on the very day of the British declaration (Shirer, 159).

315. According to Hoffmann, *Hitler Was My Friend*, 115–16, the photographer found Hitler at the height of the crisis in August 1939 slumped in his chair in the Reich Chancellery, just after a visit by Ribbentrop, bitterly criticizing the Foreign Office. 'I knew, of course, exactly what he meant,' Hoffmann wrote. 'Again and again I had myself heard Ribbentrop, with an aplomb and self-confidence out of all proportion to his knowledge and his faulty powers of judgment, assure Hitler that Britain was degenerate, that Britain would never fight, that Britain would certainly never go to war to pull someone else's chestnuts out of the fire . . .'

316. IfZ, F34/1, Vormann, 43: '*Hitler glaubte nicht an einen Krieg mit den Westmächten, weil er nicht daran glauben wollte. Wie weit Ribbentrop mitverantwortlich war für diesen Glauben, wird sich wohl kaum mehr feststellen lassen. Aus der Verschiedenheit der beiden Charaktere und auf Grund der ganzen Atmosphare im Führerhauptquartier [sic] möchte ich jedoch schließen, daß die Initiative bei Hitler gelegen hat, und der im Grund weiche Ribbendrop, der sowieso keine eigene Meinung vertrat, es für angebracht und zweckmäßig hielt, ihn in dieser Einstellung zu bestärken . . .*'

317. See Himmler's diary entry of 28 August 1939, where Hitler was pondering his next step in the Polish crisis. Hitler said he wanted to think about it overnight. He had his clearest thoughts between 5.00 and 6.00a.m. (IfZ, ED 100, Irving-Sammlung, Hitler-Dokumentation, 1939 Bd.20; Irving, *Führer*, 222–3).

318. See the comment of army liaison officer Nikolaus v. Vormann, on what he regarded as characteristic for Hitler: 'On problems that bothered him, he spoke until he was clear about them. Just as others need paper, pencil, and the peace of a study to order and clarify their thoughts sitting at a desk, he needed to speak to an audience' (IfZ, F34/1, Vormann, Fol.47) ('*Über Probleme, die ihn beschäftigten, sprach er sich klar. Wie andere Papier und Bleistift und die Ruhe eines Arbeitszimmers brauchen, um am Schreibtisch ihre Gedanken zu ordnen und zu klaren, brauchte er einen Zuhörerkreis, vor dem er sprechen konnte*').

319. See Speer, 178–9, for his little contact.

320. Gisevius, *Bis zum bittern Ende*, 1946, ii.135.

321. Weizsäcker, *Erinnerungen*, 254–5.

322. Weizsäcker, *Erinnerungen*, 255.

323. *DBFP*, 3rd Ser., VII, 201–2 (quotation 201), No.248. The remark was made on 23 August.

324. IfZ, F34/1, Vormann, Fol.44 (29 August): '*Ich bin jetzt 50 Jahre alt, noch im Vollbesitz meiner Kraft. Die Probleme müssen von mir gelöst werden, und ich kann nicht mehr warten. In einigen Jahren bin ich dazu rein körperlich und vielleicht auch geistig nicht mehr im Stande . . .*'

325. Weinberg II, 629.

326. See Weinberg II, 654.

327. See Dahlerus, 126.

328. IfZ, F34/1, Vormann, Fols.31, 34.

329. *Weizsäcker-Papiere*, 162 (entry for 29 August 1939): '*Ich habe in meinem Leben immer va banque gespielt*'.

330. *TBJG*, I/7, 92 (4 September 1939).

CHAPTER 6: LICENSING BARBARISM

1. See Broszat, *Staat*, 380–81.

2. Mason, *Sozialpolitik*, 26.

3. Schroeder, 98; Jochen von Lang, *Der Sekretär. Martin Bormann: Der Mann, der Hitler beherrschte*, Frankfurt am Main, 1980, 149.

4. Below, 205.

5. Below, 204.

6. Lang, 149; Irving, *Hitler's War*, London etc., 1977 (Irving, *HW*), 3.

7. Cit. Broszat, *Staat*, 392 n.

8. Below, 203.

9. Below, 207.

10. *Halder KTB*, i.61; trans. *Halder Diary*, 50.

11. Gerhard L. Weinberg, *A World at Arms. A Global History of World War II*, Cambridge, 1994 (= Weinberg III), 51.

12. Keitel, 216–17; Below, 205.

13. Keitel, 216, mentions visits to the front every other day from morning until late at night.

14. Schroeder, 98–9.

15. *Halder KTB*, i.80 (20 September 1939). See also Groscurth, 207–8: 'German blood helped the Russians and Bolshevism to the effortless advance.' See also Below, 206; Irving, *HW*, 19.

16. Below, 206; Irving, *HW*, 19–20.

17. Below, 207; Irving, *HW*, 24.

18. *DRZW*, ii.133. Czeslaw Madajczyk, *Die Okkupationspolitik Nazideutschlands in Polen 1939–1945*, East Berlin, 1987, 4, has 400,000. According to Weinberg III, 57 (no source), a million Polish soldiers had entered either German or Russian captivity.

19. *DRZW*, ii.133. Jörg K. Hoensch, *Geschichte Polens*, Stuttgart, 1983, S.280, has 66,300 dead, and 134,000 wounded. See also Christian Jansen/Arno Weckbecker, 'Eine Miliz im "Weltanschauungskrieg": der "Volksdeutsche Selbstschutz" in Polen 1939/40', in Michalka, *Der Zweite Weltkrieg*, 482–500, here 484. The figures do not include those murdered by the SS Einsatzkommandos or the Selbstschutz, etc. Madajczyk, 4, gives 66,000 dead and 133,000 wounded.

20. *DRZW*, ii.133. Madajczyk, *Okkupationspolitik*, 4 (no source), gives figures of 16,000 German dead and 28,000 wounded. On 6 October 1939, Hitler announced 10,572 dead, 30,322 wounded, and 3,409 men missing as of 30 September. (Domarus, 1381. Groscurth, 211 (29 September 1939) gave an interim figure, between 1 and 24 September, of 5,450 dead and 22,000 wounded.)

21. Groscurth, 265–6; Janßen/Tobias, 248–9. The evidence demonstrates that his death was not, as often surmised (and immediately hinted at by Heydrich), in effect suicide. See also Groscurth, 210–11; Keitel, 219.

22. Cit. Janßen/Tobias, 247.

23. Domarus, 1367; Below, 207.

24. Groscurth, 209–10 (25 September 1939); Janßen/Tobias, 250.

25. Janßen/Tobias, 251.

26. *RSA*, IIA, 'Außenpolitische Standortbestimmung nach der Reichstagswahl Juni-Juli 1928' (first published as Gerhard Weinberg (ed.), *Hitlers Zweites Buch. Ein Dokument aus dem Jahr 1928*, Stuttgart, 1961), 37.

27. See Martin Broszat, *Nationalsozialistische Polenpolitik*, (1961), Fischer paperback edn, Frankfurt am Main, 1965, 11–15.

28. *Halder KTB*, i.65 (7 September 1939).

29. Groscurth, 357; *Halder KTB*, i.72 (12 September 1939).

30. Groscurth, 357; Broszat, *Polenpolitik*, 16.

31. Domarus, 1362 (speech, 1354–66); Broszat, *Polenpolitik*, 16.

32. Broszat, *Polenpolitik*, 16–17.

33. Seraphim, *Rosenberg-Tagebuch*, 99 (19 September 1939); *Weisungen*, 34 (Weisung Nr.5, 30 September 1939).

34. Domarus, 1391 (text of the speech, 1377–93).

35. Broszat, *Polenpolitik*, 29–35.

36. Broszat, *Polenpolitik*, 36–41.

37. Mason, *Arbeiterklasse*, 1074–83, for the War Economy Decree; Max Seydewitz, *Civil Life in Wartime Germany. The Story of the Home Front*, New York, 1945, 58–9; Steinert, 97.

38. Shirer, 157.

39. Shirer, 159.

40. Shirer, 164.

41. Shirer, 165.

42. Shirer, 173.

43. *DBS*, vi.965ff.

44. *DBS*, vi.1032.

45. Ortwin Buchbender and Reinhold Sterz (eds.), *Das andere Gesicht des Krieges. Deutsche Feldpostbriefe 1939–1945*, Munich, 1982, 41.

46. See Shirer, 173.

47. *MadR*, ii.331.

48. See Kershaw, 'Hitler Myth', 143–6.

49. See Broszat, *Polenpolitik*, 41ff.; Madajczyk, *Okkupationspolitik*, 14–18, 186ff.

50. In his discussion with Army Commander-in-Chief Brauchitsch on 22 September, Heydrich

agreed to withdraw the order – which had come, it was claimed, directly from Hitler's train – to shoot insurgents without trial (Groscurth, 360–61).

51. Heydrich demanded, in his discussion with Brauchitsch on 22 September, that they be immediately arrested and deposited in concentration camps (Groscurth, 361–2).

52. Helmut Krausnick and Hans-Heinrich Wilhelm, *Die Truppe des Weltanschauungskrieges. Die Einsatzgruppen der Sicherheitspolitzei und des SD 1938–1942*, Stuttgart, 1981, 19–106, esp.44ff., 63, 69; Helmut Krausnick, 'Judenverfolgung', in Hans Buchheim *et al.*, *Anatomie des SS-Staates*, Olten-Freiburg im Breisgau, 1965, ii.348–9; Madajczyk, *Okkupationspolitik*, 14ff., 187; Benz, Graml, and Weiß, *Enzyklopädie*, 524 (entry on 'Intelligenzaktion'). The terror against the Polish population was far from confined to the German zone of occupation. After the Soviet Union had occupied the eastern part of Poland on 17 September, the NKVD (Stalin's secret police, which sustained links at the time with the SS), arrested and deported to the Arctic or Central Asia an estimated 315,000–330,000 Poles, and in the spring of 1940 perpetrated the infamous massacre of thousands of captured Polish officers, later discovered in the Katyn Forest, near Smolensk (Norman Davies, *Europe. A History*, Oxford, 1996, 1002–5 (where the number of 1–2 million deportees is given, following the figures claimed by the Polish exiled government during the war)). The most detailed analysis of the expulsions and closest estimates of the numbers involved is provided by Günther Häufele, 'Zwangsumsiedlungen in Polen 1939–1941. Zum Vergleich sowjetischer und deutscher Besatzungspolitik', in Dittmar Dahlmann and Gerhard Hirschfeld (eds.), *Lager, Zwangsarbeit, Vertreibung und Deportation. Dimensionen der Massenverbrechen in der Sowjetunion und in Deutschland 1933 bis 1945*, Essen, 1999, 515–33, here 526 and 521 for the estimated 11,000 victims of the Katyn 'executions'.

53. Helmut Krausnick, 'Hitler und die Morde in Polen', *VfZ*, 11 (1963), 196–209, here 196–7.

54. Jansen/Weckbecker, 'Miliz', 483.

55. Jansen/Weckbecker, 'Miliz', 484.

56. Hilarius Breitinger, *Als Deutschenseelsorger in Posen und im Warthegau 1934–1945. Erinnerungen*, Mainz, 1984, 30–38; Jansen/Weckbecker, 'Miliz', 484.

57. Madajczyk, *Okkupationspolitik*, 12–13; Broszat, *Polenpolitik*, 50–51. The exiled Polish government in London, citing the report of an Englishwoman who had lived in Bromberg and had been there on the so-called 'Bloody Sunday' of 3 September, implied that nothing untoward had happened that day and that it had been purely a German invention (*The German New Order in Poland*, London, n.d. (1941), 131).

58. Broszat, *Polenpolitik*, 51.

59. Broszat, *Polenpolitik*, 51 and 180 n.78 (for the later claim by Hitler's Army Adjutant Gerhard Engel that the dictator had personally given the order to exaggerate the number of victims); Madajczyk, *Okkupationspolitik*, 12–13, and n.23. See also Breitinger, 38–42, and, for a detailed examination of the myth launched by German propaganda, Karol Marian Pospieszalski, 'The Case of the 58,000 "Volksdeutsche". An Investigation into Nazi Claims Concerning Losses of the German Minority in Poland before and during 1939', in *Documenta Occupationis*, ed. Instytut Zachodni, vol.vii, 2nd edn, Poznan, 1981.

60. Jansen/Weckbecker, 'Miliz', 484.

61. Broszat, *Polenpolitik*, 51.

62. Jansen/Weckbecker, 'Miliz', 486. A full analysis of the role of the 'Volksdeutscher Selbstschutz' is provided in the book by the same authors: Christian Jansen and Arno Weckbecker, *Der 'Volksdeutsche Selbstschutz' in Polen 1939/40*, Munich, 1992, especially, for the atrocities perpetrated by the organization, 111–59.

63. Jansen/Weckbecker, 'Miliz', 486.

64. Jansen/Weckbecker, 'Miliz', 487–8; Madajczyk, *Okkupationspolitik*, 14.

65. Cit. Jansen/Weckbecker, 'Miliz', 490.

66. Broszat, *Polenpolitik*, 32.

67. Jansen/Weckbecker, 'Miliz', 491.

68. Jansen/Weckbecker, 'Miliz', 496; Madajczyk, *Okkupationspolitik*, 14.

69. Groscurth, 201 (8 September 1939) and n.476, including the recollection that Hitler had made the same complaints as Heydrich on the same day to Keitel.

70. *Halder KTB*, i.79 (19 September 1939). See Broszat, *Polenpolitik*, 20, for the first use of 'Flurbereinigung' in the notes of Canaris's talk with Keitel on 12 September.

71. *Halder KTB*, i.67 (10 September 1939); Groscurth, 203 (11 September 1939).

72. IfZ, Nuremberg Documents, PS-3047, Serie II, Blatt 2, 'Aktenvermerk über die Besprechung im Führerzug am 12.9.1939 in Ilnau'; Groscurth, 358; also cit. Broszat, *Polenpolitik*, 20; Jansen-Weckbecker, 'Miliz', 494.

73. Groscurth, 202 (9 September 1939).

74. *IMG*, xxvi.255–7, Doc.686-PS; Broszat, *Polenpolitik*, 22 and 175, n.35.

75. Broszat, *Polenpolitik*, 21–2; also printed in Kurt Pátzold (ed.), *Verfolgung, Vertreibung, Vernichtung. Dokumente des faschistischen Antisemitismus 1933 bis 1942*, Leipzig, 1983, 239–40 (misdated to 27 September); and *Europa unterm Hakenkreuz: Die faschistische Okkupationspolitik in Polen (1939–1945)*, Dokumentenauswahl und Einleitung von Werner Röhr *et al.*, East Berlin, 1989, 119–20 (and 120–22 for the instructions issued the same day to the commanders of the Einsatzgruppen). The SD's 'Jewish Department' II 112 had already begun collecting detailed data early in May on the Jewish population in Poland, building up a card-index which, in the event of its deployment, could be passed on to an Einsatzkommando. (I am most grateful to Professor Dan Michmann, Bar-Ilan, Israel, for passing to me a copy of the relevant document, taken from BA, R 58/954. See also Dan Michmann, 'Preparing for Occupation? A Nazi Sicherheitsdienst Document of Spring 1939 on the Jews of Holland', *Studia Rosenthaliana*, 32 (1998), 173–80, here 177.)

76. Seraphim, *Rosenberg-Tagebuch*, 98–9. Unlike Heydrich, Hitler evidently envisaged the eastern fortifications beyond the General Government, but excluding the area of Jewish settlement. Heydrich depicted it as running along the line of the German provinces.

77. *TBJG*, I/7, 147 (10 October 1939). Hitler's contempt for the Poles was, as he told Mussolini several months later, bolstered by his impressions of Poland during the campaign (Andreas Hillgruber (ed.), *Staatsmänner und Diplomaten bei Hitler. Vertrauliche Aufzeichnungen 1939–1941*, Munich, 1969 (= *Staatsmänner* I) 46–7 (18 March 1940)).

78. Domarus, 1283; Broszat, *Polenpolitik*, 23.

79. The meeting was apparently occasioned by a complaint by Hans Frank about his military superiors (Krausnick/Wilhelm, *Truppe*, 85).

80. General Governor Frank later, on 30 May 1940, justified the liquidation of a Polish ruling stratum in the notorious 'AB-Aktion' – the '*Außerordentliche Befriedungsaktion*' ('Extraordinary Pacification Action'), camouflage for the liquidation of mainly political opponents and criminals in the General Government between May and July 1940 – by recourse to a directive from Hitler (Krausnick, *Morde*, 203; Müller, *Heer*, 453).

81. *IMG*, xxvi.378–9 (quotation, 379), Doc.864-PS; *Documenta Occupationis*, vol.vi, ed. Instytut Zachodni, Poznan, 1958, 27–30; Broszat, *Polenpolitik*, 25.

82. *IMG*, xxvi.381, Doc.864-PS; *Documenta Occupationis*, vi.29; Krausnick/Wilhelm, *Truppe*, 86.

83. Though doubts are implied in Irving, *HW*, 12.

84. Krausnick, *Morde*, 206–7.

85. Groscurth, 358; Müller, *Heer*, 428. Brauchitsch's wishes, outlined to Heydrich on 22 September, for 'no over-hasty elimination of the Jews', to back the Führer's order of priority for economic matters, and for 'ethnic-political movements' only after the end of military operations, also indicate his broad knowledge of the 'ethnic-cleansing' programme. Heydrich told him explicitly on this occasion that, as far as economic concerns went, no consideration could be made for nobility, clergy, teachers, and legionaries: 'But those weren't many – a few thousand,' he said (Groscurth, 361).

86. *Documenta Occupationis*, vol.v, ed. Instytut Zachodni, Poznan, 1952, 40.

87. Krausnick/Wilhelm, *Truppe*, 76–7; Omer Bartov, *Hitler's Army. Soldiers, Nazis, and War in the Third Reich*, New York/Oxford, 1991, 62–7. Marcel Reich-Ranicki, the German literary critic, of Polish-Jewish descent, described the plundering and sadistic behaviour of German soldiers in Warsaw in autumn 1939, which he witnessed at first hand, as 'the pleasure of the hunt'. Freed of any constraints they might have felt at home, they were subject to no control, and could simply 'let rip' (Marcel Reich-Ranicki, *Mein Leben*, Stuttgart, 1999, 178ff., especially 183–4).

88. Krausnick/Wilhelm, *Truppe*, 77–8 (quotation from the amnesty decree, 82).

89. Krausnick/Wilhelm, *Truppe*, 80.

90. Krausnick/Wilhelm, *Truppe*, 84; Broszat, *Polenpolitik*, 34 (for the complaint by Gauleiter Forster).

91. *TBJG*, I/7, 153 (14 October 1939).

92. Krausnick/Wilhelm, *Truppe*, 87.

93. Broszat, *Polenpolitik*, 34–5.

94. See Müller, *Heer*, 437–50, for the complaints of Blaskowitz and Ulex.

95. Krausnick/Wilhelm, *Truppe*, 97–8, 102–3; Ernst Klee, Willi Dreßen, and Volker Rieß (eds.), *'Schöne Zeiten'. Judenmord aus der Sicht der Täter und Gaffer*, Frankfurt am Main, 1988, 14–15; Hans-Adolf Jacobsen, *1939–1945, Der Zweite Weltkrieg in Chronik und Dokumenten*, 5th edn, Darmstadt, 1961, 606–8; Müller, *Heer*, 448–9.

96. See Muller, *Heer*, 428ff.

97. IfZ, MA 1564/24, Nuremberg Documents, NOKW-1799; text printed in Krausnick/Wilhelm, *Truppe*, 103–4 and n.425; Brauchitsch's comments came a day after Blaskowitz's final report, and five days after the complaint of Ulex.

98. Engel, 68; Krausnick, *Morde*, 204, n.42.

99. Krausnick/Wilhelm, *Truppe*, 103.

100. Müller, *Heer*, 451, n.152.

101. Cit. Krausnick/Wilhelm, *Truppe*, 106; Klaus-Jürgen Müller, 'Zu Vorgeschichte und Inhalt der Rede Himmlers vor der höheren Generalität am 13.März 1940 in Koblenz', *VfZ*, 18 (1970), 95–120, here 108. See Albert Zoller, *Hitler privat. Erlebnisbericht seiner Geheimsekretärin*, Düsseldorf, 1949, 195, for Himmler's comments, evidently in the same context: 'The person of the Führer must on no account be brought into connection with [the atrocities in Poland]. I accept full responsibility.'

102. IfZ, ZS 627, (Gen. Wilhelm Ulex) Fol.124: '*Ich tue nichts, was der Führer nicht weiß.*' See also Krausnick/Wilhelm, *Truppe*, 105; Krausnick, *Morde*, 205; Müller, *Heer*, 451. Irving, *HW*, 13n., casts doubt on the veracity of Ulex's recollection, on the grounds that no one else present on the occasion subsequently referred to these words.

103. Broszat, *Polenpolitik*, 41.

104. *TBJG*, I/7, 157 (17 October 1939). For the production and content of the film, see the detailed study of Stig Hornshøh-Møller, *'Der ewige Jude'. Quellenkritische Analyse eines antisemitischen Propagandafilms*, Institut für den Wissenschaftlichen Film, Göttingen, 1995.

105. *TBJG*, I/7, 173 (29 October 1939); quotation, 177 (2 November 1939). Hitler took a direct interest in the film. He had suggestions to make when Goebbels spoke to him again about the development of the film in mid-November (*TBJG*, I/7, 201 (19 November 1939). Fritz Hippler, head of the film department in the Propaganda Ministry and producer of the film, claimed in his memoirs long after the war that Goebbels had told him when commissioning film of the Polish ghettos that the Führer wanted all the Jews resettled in Madagascar or elsewhere, and that the film was required for archival purposes (Hornshøh-Møller, *'Der ewige Jude'*, 16; Fritz Hippler, *Die Verstrickung*, Dusseldorf, 1981, 187). Goebbels's language on the Poles resembled that of Hitler: 'Drive over Polish roads. That's already Asia. We'll have a lot to do to germanize this area' (*TBJG*, I/7, 177 (2 November 1939)).

106. Michael Burleigh, *Germany turns Eastwards. A Study of Ostforschung in the Third Reich*, Cambridge, 1988, especially ch.4.

107. *Documenta Occupationis*, v.2–28; Broszat, *Polenpolitik*, 26–7.

108. See Götz Aly and Susanne Heim, *Vordenker der Vernichtung. Auschwitz und die deutschen Pläne für eine neue europäische Ordnung*, Frankfurt am Main, 1993.

109. For a brief sketch of Greiser's personality and career, see Ian Kershaw, 'Arthur Greiser – Ein Motor der "Endlösung" ', in Ronald M. Smelser, Enrico Syring, and Rainer Zitelmann (eds.), *Die Braune Elite II*, Darmstadt, 1993, 116–27. Greiser's motor-boat licence from 1930 is in his file in NA, IRR, Box 69, XE 000933, NND 871063, Folder 3. By then he had already joined the Party, because, he was said to have stated (letter in the file to Greiser from Rolf-Heinz Höppner, 22 November 1943), 'that this was the only thing that could still save him' (*'dass dies das einzige sei, was ihn noch retten könne'*). His political enemies later claimed that he was engaged at the time in currency smuggling.

110. Cit. Kershaw, 'Greiser', 118.

111. Burckhardt, 78.

112. Burckhardt, 79.

113. Cit. Kershaw, 'Greiser', 125.

114. Rebentisch, 163–88, here especially 183.

115. Cit. Kershaw, 'Greiser', 125.

116. Cit. Kershaw, 'Greiser', 123.

117. Archiwum Panstowe Poznan, Best. Schutzpolizei Posen, Bd.7, S.1, Dienstabt. Jarotschin, 15 October 1939, Dienstbefehl Nr.1.

118. Dienstbefehl, Nr. 5, 20 March 1940.

119. Information kindly provided by Stanislaw Nawrocki, Director of the Archiwum Panstowe Poznan, 25 September 1993. The figures relate to the situation in 1942–3.

120. Cit. Krausnick/Wilhelm, *Truppe*, 626–7, cit. BA R43 II/1549, Bormann to Lammers, 20 November 1940.

121. See Broszat, *Polenpolitik*, 200, n.45.

122. Broszat, *Polenpolitik*, ch.5.

123. See Ian Kershaw, 'Improvised Genocide? The Emergence of the "Final Solution" in the "Warthegau" ', *Transactions of the Royal Historical Society*, 6th Ser., 2 (1992), 51–78. It was no accident that the first extermination unit, Chelmno, to begin operations, at the beginning of December 1941, was situated in the 'Warthegau'.

124. Ernst Klee (ed.), *Dokumente zur 'Euthanasie'*, Frankfurt am Main, 1985, 85; Ernst Klee, *'Euthanasie' im NS-Staat. Die 'Vernichtung lebensunwerten Lebens'*, Frankfurt am Main, 1983, 100; facsimile in Michael Burleigh and Wolfgang Wippermann, *The Racial State. Germany, 1933–1945*, Cambridge, 1991, 143. Philipp Bouhler was Head of the Chancellery of the Fuhrer of the NSDAP, responsible for dealing with the voluminous correspondence addressed to Hitler as Party Leader. Dr Rudolf Brandt had since 1934 been Hitler's personal doctor. (Benz, Graml, and Weiß, *Enzyklopädie*, 51–2, 54–5.)

125. Lothar Gruchmann, 'Euthanasie und Justiz im Dritten Reich', *VfZ*, 20 (1972), 235–79, here 241; Lothar Gruchmann, *Justiz im Dritten Reich 1933–1940. Anpassung und Unterwerfung in der Ära Gürtner*, Munich, 1990, 502, and 497–534 for the reactions of the judicial authorities to the 'euthanasia action'; Burleigh and Wippermann, 143; Jeremy Noakes, 'Philipp Bouhler und die Kanzlei des Fuhrers der NSDAP: Beispiel einer Sonderverwaltung im Dritten Reich', in Dieter Rebentisch and Karl Teppe (eds.), *Verwaltung contra Menschenführung im Staat Hitlers. Studien zum politisch-administrativen System*, Gottingen, 1986, 208–36, here 229.

126. Gruchmann, 'Euthanasie', 241, 254.

127. Gruchmann, 'Euthanasie', 247–50; Klee, *Dokumente*, 86–7.

128. Klee, *Dokumente*, 86–7; Gruchmann, 'Euthanasie', 241–2.

129. Gruchmann, 'Euthanasie', 242.

130. Gruchmann, 'Euthanasie', 254.

131. Gruchmann, 'Euthanasie', 255; Gruchmann, *Justiz*, 511–13; Susanne Willems, *Lothar Kreyssig. Vom eigenen verantwortlichen Handeln. Eine biographische Studie zum Protest gegen die Euthanasieverbrechen in Nazi-Deutschland*, Göttingen, n.d. (1996), 137–61.

132. The background of 'racial hygiene' and eugenics ideas, and their transportation into the Third Reich, is thoroughly dealt with by Hans-Walter Schmuhl, *Rassenhygiene, Nationalsozialismus, Euthanasie. Von der Verhütung zur Vernichtung 'lebensunwerten Lebens', 1890–1945*, Göttingen, 1987; Robert N. Proctor, *Racial Hygiene. Medicine under the Nazis*, Cambridge, Mass., 1988; and Paul Weindling, *Health, Race, and German Politics between National Unification and Nazism, 1870–1945*, Cambridge, 1989.

133. Klee, *'Euthanasie'*, 19–28; Schmuhl, 115–25; Burleigh, *Death*, 15ff.; Gruchmann, 'Euthanasie', 235–6; Robert Jay Lifton, *The Nazi Doctors. Medical Killing and the Psychology of Genocide*, New York, 1986, ch. 2.

134. Michael Burleigh, *Death and Deliverance. 'Euthanasia' in Germany, c.1900–1945*, Cambridge, 1994, ch.1, especially 24, 33, 38–9; and 53–4. See also Hans Ludwig Siemen, 'Reform und Radikalisierung. Veränderungen der Psychiatrie in der Weltwirtschaftskrise', in Norbert Frei (ed.), *Medizin und Gesundheitspolitik in der NS-Zeit*, Munich, 1991, 191–200; Michael Burleigh, 'Psychiatry, German Society, and the Nazi "Euthanasia" Programme', in Michael Burleigh, *Ethics and Extermination. Reflections on Nazi Genocide*, Cambridge, 1997, 113–29; Schmuhl, 121, 147, 192–3; and Hilde Steppe, ' "Mit Tränen in den Augen haben wir dann diese Spritzen aufgezogen". Die Beteiligung von Krankenschwestern und Krankenpflegern an den Verbrechen gegen die Menschlichkeit', in Hilde Steppe (ed.), *Krankenpflege im Nationalsozialismus*, 7th edn, Frankfurt am Main, 1993, 137–74, especially 146ff. The sharp caesura of 1933, discernible in the shift towards pro-euthanasia views that followed, is well brought out in Michael Schwarz, ' "Euthanasie"-Debatten in Deutschland (1895–1945)', *VfZ*, 46 (1998), 617–65, especially 621–2, 643ff. The bureaucratic administration of the 'euthanasia action' is thoroughly examined by Henry Friedlander, *The Origins of Nazi Genocide. From Euthanasia to the Final Solution*, Chapel Hill/London, 1995.

135. Kurt Nowak, 'Widerstand, Zustimmung, Hinnahme. Das Verhalten der Bevölkerung zur "Euthanasie" ', in Frei, *Medizin und Gesundheitspolitik*, 235–51; Schwarz, 639–43, 647–9.

136. *MK*, 279–80; transl. *MK Watt*, 232.

137. *RSA*, III.2, 347.

138. *RSA*, III.2, 348.

139. Klee, *'Euthanasie'*, 46–7.

140. Burleigh, *Death*, 97.

141. Cit. Gruchmann, 'Euthanasie', 235.

142. Gruchmann, 'Euthanasie', 236. See also Cardinal Faulhaber's public warnings in 1934 of the dangers in possible moves towards euthanasia (Klee, *'Euthanasie'*, 53).

143. Gruchmann, 'Euthanasie', 236–7.

144. Cit. Gruchmann, 'Euthanasie', 238; IfZ, 2719/61, Fols.28–9: 'Aktenvermerk zu dem Ermittlungsverfahren gegen Professor Dr Werner Heyde und Rechtsanwalt Dr Gerhard Bohne (Stand vom 1.1.1961)'. Hitler had already indicated to Wagner the previous year his readiness to override the law in preventing the prosecution of any doctor accused of carrying about terminating a pregnancy where one of the partners suffered from hereditary illness (Gruchmann, 'Euthanasie', 239–40).

145. Klee, *'Euthanasie'*, 53.

146. Burleigh, *Death*, 187.

147. Burleigh, *Death*, 184, 188.

148. Klee, *'Euthanasie'*, 66ff.

149. Klee, *'Euthanasie'*, 63; Burleigh, *Death*, ch.2.

150. Klee, 'Euthanasie', 62.

151. Cit. Klee, 'Euthanasie', 63.

152. Noakes, 'Bouhler', 210–11.

153. Noakes, 'Bouhler', 221.

154. Albert Krebs, *Tendenzen und Gestalten der NSDAP. Erinnerungen an die Frühzeit der Partei*, Stuttgart, 1959, 142, 197; Orlow, 59.

155. For biographical sketches, see Hans-Walter Schmuhl, 'Philipp Bouhler – Ein Vorreiter des Massenmordes', in Smelser, Syring, and Zitelmann (eds.), *Die braune Elite II*, 39–50; Robert Wistrich, *Wer war wer in Dritten Reich*, Munich, 1983, 29; Weiß, *Biographisches Lexikon*, 51–2.

156. Noakes, 'Bouhler', 211–12, 234.

157. Noakes, 'Bouhler', 223–4.

158. Noakes, 'Bouhler', 223.

159. Noakes, 'Bouhler', 226.

160. Noakes, 'Bouhler', 225–7.

161. Burleigh, *Death*, 94–5.

162. Gitta Sereny, *Into that Darkness. An Examination of Conscience*, Pan Books edn, London, 1977, 65; Burleigh, *Death*, 93.

163. Noakes, 'Bouhler', 227; Burleigh, *Death*, 98; Udo Benzenhöfer, *Der gute Tod? Euthanasie und Sterbehilfe in Geschichte und Gegenwart*, Munich, 1999, 114–18. Udo Benzenhöfer, 'Der Fall "Kind Knauer"', *Deutsches Ärzteblatt*, 95, Heft 19, 8 May 1998, 54–5, was able to identify the child concerned, which was born on 20 February and died on 25 July 1939. See also Ulf Schmidt, 'Reassessing the Beginning of the "Euthanasia" Programme', *German History*, 17 (1999), 543–50.

164. Noakes, 'Bouhler', 227; Gruchmann, 'Euthanasie', 240. Hitler's doctor, Theo Morell, prepared a memorandum during the summer of 1939 on the need for a 'euthanasia' law, and spoke to Hitler, probably on the basis of this memorandum about it, though at what precise date is unclear (Burleigh, *Death*, 98).

165. Sereny, *Into that Darkness*, 64ff., here 68; Klee, *Dokumente*, 40–46, 146–51; Udo Benzenhöfer and Karin Finsterbuch, *Moraltheologie pro 'NS-Euthanasie'. Studien zu einem 'Gutachten' (1940) von Prof. Joseph Mayer mit Edition des Textes*, Hannover, 1998.

166. Noakes, 'Bouhler', 227–8.

167. Gruchmann, 'Euthanasie', 241.

168. Noakes, 'Bouhler', 228.

169. Bert Honolka, *Die Kreuzelschreiber. Ärzte ohne Gewissen: Euthanasie im Dritten Reich*, Hamburg, 1961, 35. Broszat, *Staat*, 399, suggests only about fifty doctors and technicians knew the full extent of the 'action'. The German names for the dummy-organizations involved were, respectively: 'Reichsarbeitsgemeinschaft der Heil- und Pflegeanstalten'; 'Gemeinnützige Krankentransportgesellschaft'; and 'Gemeinnützige Stiftung für Anstaltspflege'.

170. Honolka, 37.

171. Honolka, 33.

172. Burleigh/Wippermann, *The Racial State*, 148.

173. Klee, 'Euthanasie', 95–8, 112–15, 192–3; Schmuhl, 240–42; Götz Aly, 'Endlösung'. *Volkerverschiebung und der Mord an den europäischen Juden*, Frankfurt am Main, 1995, 114–26; Benzenhofer, *Der gute Tod?*, 118–19.

174. Gruchmann, 'Euthanasie', 244 and n.33; Burleigh/Wippermann, *The Racial State*, 153.

175. Including the killings which continued in asylums despite the 'stop decree', the thousands more later killed in the so-called 'wild' euthanasia and the '14f13' programme that continued down to the end of the war, the thousands of 'euthanasia' victims who were killed in Poland, the Soviet Union, and other occupied territories, and the children murdered in the 'Child Euthanasia' programme (which was not halted by the 'stop decree'), it is possible to reach estimates as high as a

further 90,000 to add to the 70,000 or more of the T4 'action'. (Klee, '*Euthanasie*', 345ff.; Burleigh/ Wippermann, *The Racial State*, 144, 148; Benzenhöfer, *Der gute Tod?*, 129.)

176. Above based on Deutsch, 42–67, 81–91, 105–7, Ch.VI; and see Gisevius, *To the Bitter End*, 419–29.

177. Mommsen, 'Widerstand', 9, speaks of 'a resistance of state servants' ('*einen Widerstand der Staatsdiener*').

178. Deutsch, 188–9.

179. Gisevius, *To the Bitter End*, 376–402; Kordt, 359–77; Deutsch, 189–253, and Ch.VII; Müller, *Heer*, Ch.XI.

180. See Peter Hoffmann, 'Maurice Bavaud's Attempt to Assassinate Hitler in 1938', in George L. Mosse, *Police Forces in History*, Beverly Hills, 1975, 173–204, for the hare-brained schemes of the Swiss student Maurice Bavaud. For Hitler's security, see Hoffmann, 'Hitler's Personal Security', in the same volume, 151–71, and Peter Hoffmann, *Hitler's Personal Security*, London, 1979. Left-wing resistance groups had by this time inevitably dwindled greatly in size since the early years of the regime, when tens of thousands of people had been involved in various forms of illegal activity. A minute fraction of the working class was now involved. Networks of friends and trusted contacts frequently formed the base. (See Detlev J. K. Peukert, 'Working-Class Resistance: Problems and Options', in David Clay Large (ed.), *Contending with Hitler. Varieties of German Resistance in the Third Reich*, Cambridge, 1991, 35–48, here 41–2; and Martin Broszat, 'A Social and Historical Typology of the German Opposition to Hitler', in the same volume, 25–33, here 27–9.) Secretly maintaining such networks of like-minded opponents of the regime, exchanging views, and keeping up morale was often an end in itself for Social Democrats. (William Sheridan Allen, 'Die sozialdemo-kratische Untergrundbewegung: Zur Kontinuität der subkulturellen Werte', in Schmädeke and Steinbach, 849–66, especially 857ff.) For the Communists, a difficult phase, with much disillusion-ment and disarray at the grass-roots of the underground resistance-movement, had begun with the conclusion of the Nazi-Soviet Pact in August. (Detlev Peukert, *Die KPD im Widerstand. Verfolgung und Untergrundarbeit an Rhein und Ruhr 1933 bis 1945*, Wuppertal, 1980, 329ff.)

181. *Weizsäcker-Papiere*, 164: '... wäre man der peinlichen Entscheidung überhoben, wie man denn England militärisch zu Boden zwingen kann'.

182. The sixty-five French divisions available for an assault on Germany from the West in September 1939 had massively outnumbered the Wehrmacht units, which were so heavily committed in Poland. But they were never sent into action. (*DRZW*, ii.18–19, 270. See also Andreas Hillgruber, *Hitlers Strategie. Politik und Kriegführung 1940–1941*, (1965), 3rd edn, Bonn, 1993, 34–5, 53.)

183. See Domarus, 1369–70, for Hitler's suggestion to the Swedish intermediary Dahlerus on 26 September that he would guarantee security for Britain and France, needed peace to cultivate – a task requiring at least fifty years – the newly-won territories in Poland (a state which would not be allowed to be recreated), and could offer Britain peace within fourteen days without loss of face. As usual, this 'generosity' was coupled with threats. He had destroyed Poland within three weeks. The British (*Engländer*) should reflect on what could happen to them within three months. If they wanted a long war, Germany would hold out and reduce England to a heap of rubble. Some of these sentiments were repeated in Hitler's Reichstag speech of 6 October. (See Domarus, 1388ff.)

184. Irving, *HW*, 25. The British War Cabinet put out the announcement on 9 September that it expected a three-year war to quell rumours that British action depended upon events in Poland (*The Diaries of Sir Alexander Cadogan*, 215 and n).

185. *DRZW*, ii.240.

186. Below, 210. He had already learned from Schmundt on 8 September that Hitler was intending to attack France as soon as possible. Hitler, according to Below, spoke about this to his closest military advisers on a number of occasions during the following days and was determined to launch the attack in October or November.

187. *Halder KTB*, i.86–90 (27 September 1939); trans. *Halder Diary*, 62–6.

188. *DRZW*, II.238.

189. Warlimont, 37.

190. Seraphim, *Rosenberg-Tagebuch*, 99 (29 September 1939).

191. Domarus, 1392.

192. Domarus, 1390.

193. Domarus, 1389, 1393.

194. Domarus, 1393.

195. Chamberlain asked who stood in the way of genuine peace in Europe, and answered his own rhetorical question: 'It is the German Government, and the German Government alone' (cit. *Diaries of Sir Alexander Cadogan*, 223). All unofficial feelers in the following months met with a similar response.

196. *Halder KTB*, i. 99 (7 October 1939); Müller, *Heer*, 475.

197. *Halder KTB*, i. 100 (9 October 1939); Müller, *Heer*, 476.

198. Cit. Müller, *Heer*, 476.

199. Warlimont, 50; Müller, *Heer*, 476.

200. *Halder KTB*, i. 101–3 (10 October 1939); Müller, *Heer*, 476; Hans-Adolf Jacobsen, *Dokumente zur Vorgeschichte des Westfeldzuges 1939–1940*, Göttingen/Berlin/Frankfurt, 1956, 4–20, Nr.3, S.4ff., here, 15, 19. See also *DRZW*, ii.239; and Hillgruber, *Strategie*, 45–6. Hitler remained convinced that he had been correct in his views when he referred to the memorandum in December 1944. (Helmut Heiber (ed.), *Lagebesprechungen im Führerhauptquartier. Protokollfragmente aus Hitlers militärischen Konferenzen 1942–1945*, Deutsche Buch-Gemeinschaft edn, Berlin/Darmstadt/Vienna, 1963 (=*LB* Darmstadt), 284.)

201. *Halder KTB*, i. 101 (10 October 1939).

202. *Weisungen*, 37–8.

203. Weizsäcker, *Erinnerungen*, 268.

204. *Halder KTB*, i. 107 (16 October 1939, mistakenly dated the following day).

205. *Halder KTB*, i.111 (22 October 1939); Jacobsen, *Vorgeschichte*, 41 (for confirmation on 27 October 1939).

206. *TBJG*, I/7, 150 (12 October 1939).

207. *TBJG*, I/7, 153 (14 October 1939). '*Die Engländer müssen durch Schaden klug werden.*'

208. *TBJG*, I/7, 164 (22 October 1939).

209. Groscurth, 385; and see Müller, *Heer*, 493.

210. *TBJG*, I/7, 180 (3 November 1939).

211. *TBJG*, I/7, 184 (7 November 1939). The Treaty of Westphalia (1648) ended the religious and political conflicts of the Thirty Years War, but did so by weakening the central authority of the Holy Roman Empire to the advantage of the individual states. Territorial concessions had also to be made to France and Sweden, while Switzerland and the Netherlands finally established their independence of the Reich. That the settlement was anathema to Hitler is plain to see.

212. *TBJG*, I/7, 187 (9 November 1939).

213. Dülffer, *Marine*, 541ff.

214. Göring had continued in the first weeks of the war to put out unofficial feelers through Dahlerus towards a possible settlement with Britain (Irving, *Göring*, 274–8). The British Foreign Office was dismissive and, on 19 October, diplomatically told Dahlerus to bring the contact to an end (*Diaries of Sir Alexander Cadogan*, 223–6).

215. *Halder KTB*, i.105 (14 October 1939).

216. Müller, *Heer*, 480 and n.59; Weizsäcker, *Erinnerungen*, 269–70.

217. Müller, *Heer*, 480.

218. Müller, *Heer*, 481.

219. Müller, *Heer*, 485.

220. Muller, *Heer*, 485–6.

221. Hoffmann, *Widerstand*, 167–8; Müller, *Heer*, 516–17 (with doubts about whether later conspiracy details were not intermingled with the plans of 1939 in the post-war account of this document). For the Abwehr group see Deutsch, 81ff.

222. Müller, *Heer*, 490–96.

223. Deutsch, 16–17.

224. Hoffmann, *Widerstand*, 166; Muller, *Heer*, 500–501.

225. Hoffmann, *Widerstand*, 172–3; Müller, *Heer*, 502, 507–8. On Halder's ambivalent opposition in autumn 1939, see also Hartmann, *Halder*, 162–72; Ueberschär, *Halder*, 35–45.

226. Hoffmann, *Widerstand*, 173–4.

227. Müller, *Heer*, 518–20.

228. Deutsch, 226–9; Müller, *Heer*, 520–21; Hoffmann, *Widerstand*, 177; *Halder KTB*, i. 120 (5 November 1939); *IMG*, xx.628; Groscurth, 224 (5 November 1939); Keitel, 225; Warlimont, 58; Below, 213; Engel, 66–7.

229. *Halder KTB*, i. 120 (5 November 1939); trans. *Halder Diary*, 78.

230. Hoffmann, *Widerstand*, 178.

231. Groscurth, 225, 305 (5 November 1939).

232. Hoffmann, *Widerstand*, 178.

233. Groscurth, 226, 306 (7 November 1939).

234. Hoffmann, *Widerstand*, 178–80, 182–3; Müller, *Heer*, 524–46; Gisevius, *Bis zum bittern Ende*, 1946 edn, 120–22.

235. The number of postponements is given in Hauner, *Hitler*, 147.

236. Groscurth, 227 (9 November 1939); Gisevius, *To the Bitter End*, 393–4 (where Gisevius states that he initially thought Himmler was behind the assassination attempt, and comments that Helldorf, the Berlin Police Chief, knew no more than what he had seen in the newspapers); Hoffmann, *Widerstand*, 181. Gisevius (396–411) eventually came to the realization that it was the work of a single man.

237. Zoller, 181.

238. *TBJG*, I/7, 188 (9 November 1939).

239. *TBJG*, I/7, 197 (17 November 1939), 201 (19 November 1939).

240. Lothar Gruchmann (ed.), *Autobiographie eines Attentäters. Johann Georg Elser. Aussage zum Sprengstoffanschlag im Bürgerbräukeller, München, am 8. November 1939*, Stuttgart, 1970, 13–14; Hoffmann, *Widerstand*, 181.

241. Most early accounts of the attempt (with the exception of that of Gisevius) took it for granted that Elser had been the 'front-man' for a plot. (See, e.g., Bullock, *Hitler*, 566–7, where it is stated that the attempt was organized by the Gestapo). That Elser had planned and carried out the attempt alone was first convincingly demonstrated by Anton Hoch, 'Das Attentat auf Hitler im Münchener Burgerbräukeller 1939', *VfZ*, 17 (1969), 383–413. The article presented an accurate description of Elser's background and motivation, as well as his preparation of the bomb-attack, testing the veracity of Elser's own statement to the police (printed in Gruchmann, *Elser*, on which the following account rests).

242. Gruchmann, *Elser*, 27. He had been born in 1903 in Hermaringen (Württemberg).

243. Gruchmann, *Elser*, 9, 20–22, 76–8, 80–84, 146, 165, n.64.

244. Gruchmann, *Elser*, 84–101, 104–6, 121–4, 131, 146–53.

245. Gruchmann, *Elser*, 9; Domarus, 1404.

246. Domarus, 1405.

247. Domarus, 1405–14; see *TBJG*, I/7, 187–8 (9 November 1939).

248. Gruchmann, *Elser*, 9; Domarus, 1414–15. Hitler had travelled to Munich by air, but a return flight could not be guaranteed to leave on time because of weather conditions.

249. Domarus, 1414–15; Gruchmann, *Elser*, 8–9.

250. Zoller, 181; Below, 214.

251. *Der Völkische Beobachter* (=*VB*), 10 November 1939 ('Die wunderbare Errettung des Führers').

252. Gruchmann, *Elser*, 9–10.

253. Gruchmann, *Elser*, 7–8, 13ff., 18–20.

254. Mason, *Arbeiterklasse*, 961ff., 1050ff., 1196, 1205.

255. Mason, *Arbeiterklasse*, 1086ff., 1183ff., 1233–4.

256. Kershaw, *Popular Opinion*, 298–301.

257. See Kershaw, '*Hitler Myth*', 144–5.

258. Friedrich Percyval Reck-Malleczewen, *Tagebuch eines Verzweifelten*, Frankfurt am Main, 1971, 68.

259. *MadR*, iii.499. And see *HM* and n.88.

260. *DBS*, vi.1024–5 (2 December 1939).

261. *IMG*, xxvi.327–36, Doc.789-PS; Domarus, 1422; *DGFP*, D, 8, 439–46, here 440, No.384, 'Memorandum of a Conference of the Führer with the Principal Military Commanders, November 23, 1939'.

262. Domarus, 1422; *DGFP*, D, 8, 441, No.384.

263. Domarus, 1423; *DGFP*, D, 8, 441, No.384.

264. Domarus, 1423; *DGFP*, D, 8, 442, No.384.

265. Domarus, 1424; *DGFP*, D, 8, 442, No.384.

266. Domarus, 1424; *DGFP*, D, 8, 443, No.384.

267. Domarus, 1424; *DGFP*, D, 8, 443, No.384.

268. Domarus, 1425; *DGFP*, D, 8, 444, No.384.

269. This echoed the comments he had made several weeks earlier, immediately after returning from Poland, on 27 September (*Halder KTB*, i. 88 (27 September 1939)).

270. Domarus, 1426; *DGFP*, D, 8, 445, No.384. See also Hillgruber, *Strategie*, 28–9.

271. Domarus, 1425, 1426; *DGFP*, D, 8, 444–5, No.384.

272. Domarus, 1426; *DGFP*, D, 8, 445–6, No.384.

273. Domarus, 1426; *DGFP*, D, 8, 446, No.384.

274. *LB* Darmstadt, 287.

275. Domarus, 1426; *DGFP*, D, 8, 446, No.384.

276. Domarus, 1427; *DGFP*, D, 8, 446, No.384.

277. *Halder KTB*, i.132 (23 November 1939), for Hitler's reference to the 'Geist von Zossen'; *IMG*, xx.628 (statement of von Brauchitsch, 9 August 1946).

278. Müller, *Heer*, 547–9, 550.

279. *TBJG*, I/7, 228 (12 December 1939).

280. *Halder KTB*, i. 154 (10 January 1940), 157 (13 January 1940), 161 (18 January 1940), 165–7 (20 January 1940), 167–9 (21 January 1940); Hans-Adolf Jacobsen, *Fall Gelb. Der Kampf um den deutschen Operationsplan zur Westoffensive 1930*, Wiesbaden, 1957, 93.

281. See Hilberg, 137ff.; Aly, 29ff.

282. *TBJG*, I/7, 220–21 (5 December 1939).

CHAPTER 7: ZENITH OF POWER

1. *TBJG*, I/7, 273 (16 January 1940).

2. *Halder KTB*, i.93 for the pessimistic report of Major-General Georg Thomas, head of the Defence Economy and Armaments Office at the OKW, on economic shortages and the inability to satisfy the needs of the armed forces for months to come; *DRZW*, ii.242; Hillgruber, *Strategie*, 54, referring to the basic plan, aimed at a long war, approved by the British cabinet on 9 September 1939.

3. *DRZW*, ii.235–6; Hillgruber, *Strategie*, 40.

4. Hillgruber, *Strategie*, 38–9. Nevertheless, the Luftwaffenführungsstab (Luftwaffe Operations

Staff) pressed in autumn 1939 for bombing-raids on Britain to be launched before the end of the year – targeting harbours to damage shipping and supplies – before British aerial defences could be built up (*DRZW*, ii.333, 336).

5. *DRZW*, ii.193.

6. *DRZW*, ii.239, 266; Hillgruber, *Strategie*, 34–40, 48, and (for the Z-Plan, which, on 11 July 1940, Hitler agreed to recommence) 148.

7. *IMT*, xv.385–6 (Jodl testimony); Jacobsen, *Fall Gelb*, 4–5; Hillgruber, *Strategie*, 34, 53. The British Expeditionary Force, initially comprising a mere 152,000 men, began moving to France only on 4 September and was purely defensive in composition – without armoured division, inadequate in communications, equipment, and training, and with little air power (*The Oxford Companion to the Second World War*, ed. I. C. B. Dear and M. R. D. Foot, Oxford, 1995, 154–5).

8. *DRZW*, ii.236–7. See *Staatsmänner*, i.45, for Hitler's account to Mussolini (on 18 March 1940) of how weak the German forces were on the western front at the outbreak of war, though he added that the Westwall would have provided an impenetrable barrier to an allied attack. Germany's munitions were sufficient for a third of the available divisions for fourteen days of fighting, with reserves sufficient for a further fourteen days (*Halder KTB*, 1.99 (8 October 1939)).

9. Jacobsen, *Fall Gelb*, 18–21.

10. Hillgruber, *Strategie*, 41–5, 48.

11. Hillgruber, *Strategie*, 32, 45–6. See also Andreas Hillgruber, 'Der Faktor Amerika in Hitlers Strategie 1938–1941', *Aus Politik und Zeitgeschichte. Beilage zur Wochenzeitung 'Das Parlament'*, B19/66 (11 May 1966), 3–21, especially 8ff.

12. *DGFP*, D, VIII, 604–9 (especially 608), Doc.504; Hillgruber, *Strategie*, 30 n.13.

13. *DGFP*, D, VIII, 871–80 (especially 876), Doc.663; Hillgruber, *Strategie*, 30 n.13. See William Carr, *Poland to Pearl Harbor. The Making of the Second World War*, London, 1985, 113–14, for further comments along these lines, which Carr is prepared to see as an indication that Hitler's views on Russia were undergoing a metamorphosis.

14. *TBJG*, I/7, 269–70 (13 January 1940). A fortnight earlier, he had referred to Stalin as 'a typical Asiatic Russian'. Bolshevism had eliminated the westernized leadership stratum capable of activating 'this giant colossus', he had said. Germany could be content that Moscow had its hands full, but would know how to deal with any attempt by Bolshevism to move westwards (*TBJG*, I/7, 250 (29 December 1939)).

15. Jacobsen, 4–21 (Hitler's 'Denkschrift und Richtlinien über die Führung des Krieges im Westen'), here 7.

16. *TBJG*, I/7, 270 (13 January 1940).

17. See Hillgruber, *Strategie*, 43–4, for the misreading of British motives, and, for the personalized elements of the conflict, John Lukacs, *The Duel. Hitler vs. Churchill: 10 May–31 July 1940*, Oxford, 1992; John Strawson, *Churchill and Hitler*, London, 1997, Ch.5.

18. Hillgruber, *Strategie*, 16.

19. *DRZW*, ii.193, 195–6.

20. Hillgruber, *Strategie*, 49–50.

21. *DRZW*, ii.190–92.

22. For the raid, see Churchill, 1.506–8. Norwegian gunboats did not intervene. The *Altmark* was left grounded in the Jösing Fjord as the *Cossack*, with the rescued prisoners on board, made good its escape. Norwegian protests at the entry into their territorial waters were brushed aside by the British Government, which could register a needed boost in morale.

23. Below, 221–2. On the planning of the campaign, see Walther Hubatsch, *'Weserübung'. Die deutsche Besetzung von Dänemark und Norwegen 1940*, Göttingen/Berlin/Frankfurt, 2nd edn, 1960, ch.2, 39ff.; and Michael Salewski, *Die deutsche Seekriegsleitung 1935–1945, Bd.1: 1935–1941*, Frankfurt am Main, 1970, 176ff.; *Lagevorträge des Oberbefehlshabers der Kriegsmarine vor Hitler 1939–1945*, ed. Gerhard Wagner, Munich, 1972, 82, 85ff.

24. *DRZW*, ii.197–8; *Weisungen*, 54–7.

25. *DRZW*, ii.198; see *Halder KTB*, i.218 (3 March 1940).

26. *Weisungen*, 57; *DRZW*, ii.200.

27. Churchill had suggested the mining operation as early as the previous September. Problems about infringement of Scandinavian neutrality and divisions within the British government and between the British and the French had led to the postponement of any action before – without realizing the imminence of 'Weser Exercise' – the decision to mine Narvik was taken in early April. The British aim had been both to interrupt the iron-ore supplies to Germany, and also to provoke German retaliation thereby justifying British landings in Scandinavia (*DRZW*, ii.204–11).

28. *DRZW*, ii.202.

29. *TBJG*, I/8, 41–2 (9 April 1940). Two days later, Hitler was talking of the aim being a '*nordgermanischer Staatenbund*' – effectively with Denmark and Norway as German puppet states under military 'protection' (*TBJG*, I/8, 47 (11 April 1940)).

30. Churchill, i.524 for the Swedish reports.

31. Lothar Gruchmann, *Der Zweite Weltkrieg. Kriegführung und Politik*, (1967), 4th edn, Munich, 1975, 56.

32. Based on: *DRZW*, ii.212–25; Weinberg III, 116–19; Lukacs, *Duel*, 32–5; Gruchmann, *Zweiter Weltkrieg*, pt.I, Ch.4; R. A. C. Parker, *Struggle for Survival. The History of the Second World War*, Oxford, 1990, 25; Churchill, i.528–92.

33. Warlimont, 75–8.

34. Warlimont, 76, 79–80.

35. *DRZW*, ii.247–8.

36. A point made by Lukacs, *Duel*, 22.

37. *DRZW*, ii.248. The following rests above all on Hans-Adolf Jacobsen, 'Hitlers Gedanken zur Kriegführung im Westen', *Wehrwissenschaftliche Rundschau*, 5 (1955), 433–46; and Jacobsen, *Fall Gelb*, 66ff., 107ff., esp.112ff.

38. This version was, in fact, captured after a German officer's plane was forced to land in Belgium. See Jacobsen, *Fall Gelb*, 93–9.

39. *DRZW*, ii.250–51.

40. IfZ, MA 444/3, 'Grundsätzlicher Befehl', 11 January 1940; Domarus, 1446.

41. Engel, 75.

42. *DRZW*, ii.252.

43. *DRZW*, ii.254. François Delpla, *La ruse nazi. Dunkerque – 24 mai 1940*, Paris, 1997, 120 and nn.30–31, could find no reference to the term in contemporary documents. He attributed it to Churchill, who wrote after the war of 'the German scythe-cut' (Winston S. Churchill, *The Second World War, vol.ii, Their Finest Hour*, London etc., 1949, 74). Its first usage in scholarly literature, he suggested, was by Jacobsen in *Fall Gelb*, published in 1957.

44. *Weisungen*, 53; Jacobsen, *Vorgeschichte*, 64–8; *DRZW*, ii.253 (map).

45. Schmidt, 488–9; *CD*, 223.

46. *Staatsmänner*, i.47.

47. *Staatsmänner*, i.48.

48. Above based on *Staatsmänner*, i.37–59; Schmidt, 488–91; *CD*, 223–5; *CP*, 361–5.

49. *CD*, 224–5.

50. *TBJG*, I/7, 356 (19 March 1940), 357 (20 March 1940).

51. *TBJG*, I/7, 358 (20 March 1940).

52. As pointed out by Lukacs, 221.

53. *TBJG*, I/8, 66 (21 April 1940).

54. *TBJG*, I/8, 73 (25 April 1940).

55. Hillgruber, *Strategie*, 58.

56. *DRZW*, ii.283–4; Below, 228.

57. Below, 228–9.

58. *DRZW*, ii.282.

59. *DRZW*, ii.266–7.

60. Schroeder, 101–2, 349–50, n. 196; Below, 229–30.

61. Below, 231.

62. *DRZW*, ii.284–96; Weinberg III, 125–30; Gruchmann, *Zweiter Weltkrieg*, pt.1, ch.5; Parker, *Struggle*, 27ff.; Churchill, ii.66–104.

63. See *DRZW*, ii.296 for Rundstedt's post-war self-exculpatory view. See also Guenther Blumentritt, *Von Rundstedt. The Soldier and the Man*, London, 1952, 74–8. Churchill recognized, even writing in the late 1940s, the misleading nature of the German generals' accounts (Churchill, ii.68–70). See also, on the 'halt order', Gruchmann, *Zweiter Weltkrieg*, 63; Weinberg III, 130–31; Parker, *Struggle*, 35–6; Irving, *HW*, 120–22; Charles Messenger, *The Last Prussian. A Biography of Field Marshal Gerd von Rundstedt, 1875–1953*, London etc., 1991, 113–20; Lukacs, *Duel*, 90–97. Delpla, *La ruse*, here especially 290–92 (also François Delpla, *Hitler*, Paris, 1999, 326–7) is alone in interpeting the 'halt order' as part of a complex diplomatic manoeuvre, involving Göring and Dahlerus, to hold the British to ransom and force them to end the war on German terms.

64. Schroeder, 105–6 (where Hitler's comment is dated to the day that he learned of the French armistice offer – 17 June).

65. Below, 232.

66. *IMG*, xxviii.433, Doc.1809-PS (Jodl-Tagebuch); Hans-Adolf Jacobsen (ed.), *Dokumente zum Westfeldzug 1940*, Göttingen/Berlin/Frankfurt, 1960, 73–86; Jacobsen, *1939–1945. Der Zweite Weltkrieg*, 146; Hans-Adolf Jacobsen, *Dünkirchen. Ein Beitrag zur Geschichte des Westfeldzuges 1940*, Neckargemünd, 1958, 70–122, especially 94–5. Jodl repeated after the war that the notion that Hitler refused to send the tanks on to Dunkirk was a 'legend'. Hitler, he stated, had hesitated to adopt Brauchitsch's recommendation to do this because the terrain was not suitable for tanks and the risk was too great that the tanks would not be available for the thrust to the south. However, he left the decision to the local commanders, who chose not to deploy the tanks against Dunkirk (IfZ, ZS 678 (Generaloberst Alfred Jodl), 'Hitler, eine militärische Führerpersönlichkeit. Ein Gespräch mit Generaloberst Jodl von Freg.Kapt. Meckel', May-July 1946, Fol.3).

67. Below, 232–3.

68. *Halder KTB*, 1.319 (25 May 1940).

69. *IMG*, xxviii.434, Doc.1809-PS (Jodl-Tagebuch); Jacobsen, 1939–45, 146–7; Below, 233.

70. *Halder KTB*, 1.318–19 (24 May 1940, 25 May 1940).

71. *DRZW*, ii.297.

72. *Halder KTB*, 1.318 (24 May 1940); Below, 232.

73. *DGFP*, D, 9, 484, No.357.

74. *DRZW*, ii.296; Weinberg III, 130–31.

75. *Halder KTB*, i.320–21 (26 May 1940).

76. In fact, General Sir John Gort, the commander of the British Expeditionary Force, had ordered the evacuation only at 7 p.m. on 26 May, and as few as 8,000 troops were evacuated during the following twenty-four hours (Lukacs, *Duel*, 96–7). The evacuation continued for another week. Dunkirk fell only on 4 June.

77. See Lukacs, *Duel*, 97ff., for Churchill's political isolation during the days of the evacuation, and the pressure of those wanting to sue for terms, articulated above all by Lord Halifax.

78. Below, 233; Schroeder, 102.

79. See Eugen Weber, *The Hollow Years. France in the 1930s*, New York/London, 1996, 272–9.

80. Weinberg III, 131; Below, 233–4.

81. *DRZW*, ii.307; *Oxford Companion*, 414.

82. Schroeder, 106. Trick photography later turned Hitler's characteristic gesture of raising his leg and slapping his thigh into a jig for joy (Lukacs, *Duel*, 142).

83. *CD*, 263–4, 268.

84. Below, 234; Domarus, 1527–8.

85. Lukacs, *Duel*, 139.

86. *CD*, 267 (18–19 June 1940).

87. *CD*, 266–7; Schmidt, 495.

88. *TBJG*, I/8, 202 (3 July 1940).

89. *Churchill and Roosevelt: The Complete Correspondence, vol.1*, ed. Warren Kimball, Princeton, 1984, 49–51, Doc.C-17x (quotation, 49).

90. Schmidt, 495; *CD*, 266–7; Domarus, 1528.

91. *IMG*, xxviii.431, Doc. 1809-PS (Jodl-Tagebücher).

92. *TBJG*, II/4, 492 (10 June 1942).

93. Schmidt, 497–502; Keitel, 235–6; Domarus, 1529–30. And see Eberhard Jäckel, *Frankreich in Hitlers Europa. Die deutsche Frankreichpolitik im Zweiten Weltkrieg*, Stuttgart, 1966, 38–40. Hitler gave orders for the railway carriage and memorial to the French victory to be brought back to Berlin. The monument to Marshal Foch, the French hero of the First World War, was to be left untouched. The carriage was pulled through the Brandenburg Gate on 'Heroes' Memorial Day' (*Heldengedenktag*) 1941, then put on display in the Lustgarten. (*Tb* Reuth, 1438, n.105.)

94. *TBJG*, I/8, 186 (22 June 1940).

95. *DRZW*, ii.316–19.

96. Domarus, 1533.

97. Speer, 185–6.

98. Below, 235; Schroeder, 106 and 351 n.202. Hitler had already at the beginning of the month paid one visit to the battlefields, taking in the Langemarck Monument and Vimy Ridge (*TBJG*, I/8, 154 (4 June 1940), 159 (6 June 1940); Below, 235).

99. Without indicating any source, Irving, *HW*, 131, Hauner, 152, and an editorial note to Schroeder, 351 n.203, date the visit to 23 June; Giesler, 387, to 24 June. But both Schroeder, 106, and Below, 235, place the visit after, not before, the trip to the battlefields. Speer, 186, dates the visit to 'three days after the commencement of the armistice', which would be 28 June. This is the date given by Domarus, 1534, referring to newspaper reports of 30 June 1940 on the visit.

100. Speer, 186–7.

101. *Monologe*, 116 (29 October 1941).

102. Speer, 187.

103. *TBJG*, I/8, 202 (3 July 1940).

104. Speer, 187. In autumn 1941 he told the guests at the evening meal, despite mixed impressions of the city's beauty, that he had been glad that it had not been necessary to destroy it (*Monologe*, 116 (29 October 1941)).

105. *TBJG*, I/8, 202 (3 July 1940). England could be defeated in four weeks, Hitler had told Goebbels. See Schroeder, 105, for Hitler indicating on the very night that the armistice came into effect that he was going to make a speech (which she took to be a last appeal to England), and that if they did not comply he would proceed against them 'unmercifully'. Schroeder dates her letter, however, 20 June 1940 – five days before the ceasefire. Below also indicated Hitler's presumption that his 'offer' would be turned down (Below, 236).

106. Zoller, *Hitler privat*, 141; Below, 237; *TBJG*, I/8, 209–10 (7 July 1940).

107. StA Neuburg an der Donau, vorl.LO A5, report of the Kreisleiter of Augsburg-Stadt, 10 July 1940.

108. GStA, MA 106683, report of the Regierungspräsident of Schwaben, 9 July 1940.

109. See Kershaw, 'Hitler Myth', 155–6. Goebbels's comment that the people were thirsting for war with England (*TBJG*, I/8, 205 (5 July 1940)) was on this occasion not far wide of the mark.

110. Below, 237.

111. Weinberg III, 145–6; Lukacs, *Duel*, 172–3. Hitler had assured the French, in the terms of the

armistice, that he had no intention of deploying their fleet for war purposes and had allowed the French fleet to remain armed (Domarus, 1532; *TBJG*, I/8, 210 (7 July 1940)).

112. *TBJG*, I/8, 210 (7 July 1940).

113. *CD*, 275 (7 July 1940); *CP*, 375–9. Hitler's words were partly directed at Britain, since he was aware that what he said to Ciano would find its way to the British (Below, 239).

114. Lukacs, *Duel*, 173.

115. *TBJG*, I/8, 213 (9 July 1940).

116. Hillgruber, *Strategie*, 168; Karl Klee (ed.), *Dokumente zum Unternehmen 'Seelöwe'. Die geplante deutsche Landung in England 1940*, Göttingen/Berlin/Frankfurt, 1959, 238–9.

117. Klee, *Dokumente zum Unternehmen 'Seelöwe'*, 239–40; Karl Klee, *Das Unternehmen 'Seelöwe'*, Göttingen/Berlin/Frankfurt, 1958, 58–9; Below, 236.

118. *DRZW*, ii.371. See Jodl's Memorandum of 30 June 1940 in *IMG*, xxviii.301–3, Doc.1776-PS. Jodl had seen landings only as a last resort, and if air-superiority was assured.

119. Thomas, *German Navy*, 195.

120. Klee, *Dokumente*, 240–41; BA/MA, PG/31320, Handakten Raeder, Denkschrift, 11 June 1940 (kindly drawn to my attention by Meir Michaelis); see Thomas, *Navy*, 192.

121. Lukacs, *Duel* 180–81; Below, 239–40.

122. Klee, *Unternehmen*, 72. Invasion scares had been prevalent in Britain for weeks by this time. Churchill deliberately kept the scare running to build up fighting morale, though doubting personally the seriousness of the invasion threat (John Colville, *Downing Street Diaries 1939–1955*, London, 1985, 192). I am grateful for this reference to Tilman Remme. Churchill had received an insight into German naval thinking about an invasion in June (Churchill, ii.267).

123. *Halder KTB*, II, 19–22 (13 July 1940). Apart from 'Sealion', Hitler discussed with Halder proposals put forward by the army leadership for demobilization of some units. Evidently contemplating the likelihood of new military engagements in the near future, Hitler would only agree to disbanding fifteen divisions – subsequently (*Halder KTB*, ii.20 (13 July 1940), 27 (19 July 1940); *DRZW*, ii. 371; *DRZW*, iv.9, 261–2) raised to seventeen – instead of an intended thirty-five divisions, with the bulk of the remaining personnel to be sent on leave and therefore be made available for speedy recall. The initial plans in mid-June 1940 had foreseen the disbanding of forty divisions (*DRZW*, iv.260).

124. *Halder KTB*, ii.21 (13 July 1940), trans. *Halder Diary*, 227. See also Below, 240. By 'others', Hitler meant the Soviet Union (Hillgruber, *Strategie*, 155 n.53).

125. As a wave of fear of fifth-columnists mounted in Britain once the German western offensive had begun, Mosley and his wife Diana (*née* Mitford), a long-standing admirer of Hitler, were placed in internment (Skidelsky, 449ff.).

126. Engel, 85 (15 July 1940).

127. Below, 240.

128. *Weisungen*, 71.

129. Blumentritt, 85–7; and see Messenger, 125–7.

130. Domarus, 1539.

131. Below, 240–41; Shirer, *Berlin Diary*, 356.

132. Engel, 85–6 (22 July 1940). BA, R43II/1087a contains records relating to handsome gifts during the war of estates to Keitel, Guderian, Reichenau, Leeb, and others.

133. Below, 237, 240 (for the feeling that Brauchitsch did not deserve promotion).

134. Shirer, *Berlin Diary*, 355–6.

135. *TBJG*, I/8, 229 (20 July 1940).

136. William L. Shirer, *This is Berlin. Reporting from Nazi Germany 1938–40*, London, 1999, 35.

137. Shirer, *Berlin Diary*, 357.

138. Domarus, 1558.

139. Domarus, 1558 (text of the speech, 1540–59).

140. Below, 242; *CD*, 277 (19 July 1940); Domarus, 1560.

141. Lukacs, *Duel*, 193ff.

142. *CP*, 381.

143. *TBJG*, I/8, 231 (21 July 1940).

144. For the following: *Halder KTB*, ii.30–33 (22 July 1940); trans. *Halder Diary*, 230–32; Klee, *Dokumente*, 245–6. And see *DRZW*, ii.370.

145. For continued considerations of the need to discuss terms with Hitler, see John Charmley, *Churchill: the End of Glory. A Political Biography*, London/New York, 1993, 422–32; and Lukacs, *Duel*, 97ff. Ribbentrop's plan to engage the Duke of Windsor, then in Portugal, as a go-between to groups in Britain prepared to entertain peace, presumably with the aim of bringing the Duke back to the throne at the expense of his brother, George VI, ended with the departure of the Windsors on 1 August to the Bahamas, where the Duke, from Churchill's standpoint out of harm's way, took up the position as Governor. (Hillgruber, *Strategie*, 153–4; Walter Schellenberg, *Schellenberg*, Mayflower edn, 1965, 67–80.)

146. *Halder KTB*, ii.30–33 trans. *Halder Diary*, 230–32 (22 July 1940). According to Below, Hitler had commented at the beginning of July that he wanted to avoid war with England because a showdown with Russia was unavoidable (Below, 236). A month earlier than this, on 2 June, he was reported to have remarked in conversation with von Rundstedt that with England, he imagined, now ready for peace he could start to settle the account with Bolshevism (Warlimont, 113; Walter Ansel, *Hitler Confronts England*, Durham NC, 1960, 175–6).

147. Speer, 188.

148. See Hitler's reported comments to Rundstedt and Jodl about the attack on Bolshevism (Warlimont, 111, 113). And see Bernd Stegemann, 'Hitlers Kriegsziele im ersten Kriegsjahr 1939/40. Ein Beitrag zur Quellenkritik', *Militargeschichtliche Mitteilungen*, 27 (1980), 93–105, here especially 99.

149. *Halder KTB*, i.358 (16 June 1940); 372 (25 June 1940); *DRZW*, iv.9; Carr, *Poland*, 115.

150. *Halder KTB*, ii.6 and n.1 (3 July 1940); trans. *Halder Diary*, 220–21. Halder had already spoken about preparations to a small number of his planning staff in mid-June (Dirks/Janßen, 131).

151. *TBJG*, I/8, 232 (22 July 1940).

152. *TBJG*, I/8, 234 (24 July 1940); Domarus, 1562.

153. Kubizek, 287–90.

154. *Halder KTB*, ii.43 (30 July 1940).

155. *DRZW*, ii.371.

156. *Halder KTB*, ii.45–6 (30 July 1940).

157. IfZ, ZS 678, Generaloberst Alfred Jodl, 'Hitler, eine militarische Führerpersönlichkeit', Summer, 1946, Fol.5: '*Das Heer hatte von den Absichten des Führers schon erfahren, als diese noch im Stadium der Erwägung waren. Es wurde deshalb ein Operationsplan entworfen, noch ehe der Befehl dazu erging.*' IfZ, ZS 97, Major-General Bernhard v. Loßberg, Fol.10 (Letter of Loßberg, 7 September 1956). Loßberg also pointed out (Fol.15, letter of 16 September 1956) that a further feasibility study (by Major-General Marcks, see Jacobsen, *1939–1945*, 164–7) from the OKH General Staff was already submitted by 5 August, although Hitler had only spoken to Jodl for the first time about the Russian campaign on 29 July. And already by 20 August, operational plans were so far advanced that General Quarter-Master Eduard Wagner was in a position to report to Halder on planning for troop supplies (Eduard Wagner, *Der Generalquartiermeister. Briefe und Tagebuchaufzeichnungen des Generalquartiermeisters des Heeres General der Artillerie Eduard Wagner*, ed. Elisabeth Wagner, Munich/Vienna, 1963, 261–3, especially 263). According to Jodl, in a further post-war statement (IfZ, MA 1564–1 Nuremberg Document NOKW-065, a ten-page statement by Jodl, dated 26 September 1946, here pp.9–10 (Frames 0654–5)), Hitler was concerned about the Russian threat to the Romanian oil-fields. However, the feasibility studies over the next

weeks completely ruled out any early move. Preparations could not be completed in under four months and by that time it would be winter when, Jodl's staff reckoned, military operations in the east would be impossible. For the time being, the idea of an attack on the Soviet Union was shelved. But Warlimont was commissioned in August with working out improvements aimed at speeding up troop concentration in the east. Then in November, Hitler passed on to Jodl the order that all sections of the Wehrmacht should start planning for an operation against Russia. (See also Lukacs, *Duel*, 213–14.) As Loßberg pointed out, the later operational plans bore a strong resemblance to the feasibility studies of summer 1940 for what he had dubbed – after his small son – 'Operation Fritz' and was later renamed 'Barbarossa'. (IfZ, ZS 97, Fols.10–11, 14–15.)

158. According to Warlimont's later account, Jodl checked the doors and windows were closed before telling them that Hitler had decided to rid the world of Bolshevism 'once and for all' by a surprise attack on Russia the following May (Warlimont, 111).

159. Warlimont, 111–12.

160. Warlimont, 112. See also Lukacs, *Duel*, 214.

161. *Halder KTB*, ii.46–50 (31 July 1940); trans. *Halder Diary*, 241–5.

162. *Halder KTB*, ii.6 (3 July 1940).

163. Hillgruber, *Strategie*, 213–14.

164. *Weisungen*, 75–6.

165. *DRZW*, ii.378, 382. Below, 244, has fighters in action from the 8th.

166. Below, 244. Churchill, ii.Ch.XVI, provides a graphic description of the 'Battle of Britain'.

167. *DRZW*, ii.386 (and, for Göring's directive of 2 August 1940, aimed initially at destroying the British fighter-arm in the London area before major attacks on the capital, 380 and nn.50–51).

168. Steinert, 367 and n.160.

169. Below, 244.

170. Domarus, 1580.

171. Below, 244. For the 'Blitz', see Churchill, ii. Ch.XVII-XVIII.

172. Hillgruber, *Strategie*, 174.

173. *Halder KTB*, ii.128–9 (7 October 1940); Hillgruber, *Strategie*, 177.

174. Hillgruber, *Strategie*, 175–6.

175. *Halder KTB*, ii.98–100 (14 September 1940); *DRZW*, ii.389.

176. Below, 246.

177. Domarus, 1585.

178. *DRZW*, ii.396; Below, 245. The city centre of Coventry (including the cathedral) was destroyed. The dead numbered 380, the injured 865. Twelve armaments factories were also damaged, though not put out of production. British decoding of German signals had forewarned the RAF of a major attack on cities in the Midlands and had even indicated Coventry as the main target. However, the air-defence of Coventry was woeful. Almost all the fleet of over 500 German bombers reached the target. Only one plane was certainly brought down (*Oxford Companion*, 275; Churchill, ii.332–3).

179. Klee, *Unternehmen*, 205; Domarus, 1586 n.505; Jacobsen, *1939–1945*, 172; and see Hillgruber, *Strategie*, 175–6.

180. Carr, *Poland*, 103; Lukacs, *Duel*, 225–7.

181. A term coined by Hans Mommsen, *Beamtentum im Dritten Reich*, Stuttgart, 1966, 98 n.26; and Hans Mommsen, 'Nationalsozialismus', in *Sowjetsystem und demokratische Gesellschaft. Eine vergleichende Enzyklopädie*, ed. C.D. Hernig, 7 vols, Freiburg etc., 1966–72, vol.4, column 702. For critical assessments, see Hermann Weiß, 'Der "schwache" Diktator. Hitler und der Führerstaat', in Wolfgang Benz, Hans Buchheim, and Hans Mommsen (eds.), *Der Nationalsozialismus. Studien zur Ideologie und Herrschaft*, Frankfurt am Main, 1993, 64–77; Manfred Funke, *Starker oder schwacher Diktator? Hitlers Herrschaft und die Deutschen. Ein Essay*, Düsseldorf, 1989; and Ian Kershaw, *The Nazi Dictatorship. Problems and Perspectives of Interpretation*, London, (1985), 4th edn, 2000, Ch.4.

182. Broszat, *Staat*, 382, notes that radicalization of political content and disintegration of governmental form went hand in hand.

183. The following relies upon Rebentisch, 117–28, and Broszat, *Staat*, 382–3.

184. Hitler put out a decree to that effect on 5 June 1940 (Broszat, *Staat*, 382).

185. Gruchmann, ' "Reichsregierung" im Fuhrerstaat', 202; Rebentisch, 290 and n.24, 371–3.

186. Rebentisch, 291.

187. Rebentisch, 291, 331ff. See Frank's post-war comment on the recognitions of the 'social Darwinism' at the root of Hitler's encouragement of conflict and struggle: '. . . I associated with my struggle the personal ambition to achieve; not to value myself lower than a Himmler or Bormann; and, trusting in the tactic of the Fuhrer, giving broad scope to the political "Darwinism" of selection among his underlings as they fought among themselves, to be firmly confident of proving victorious in this struggle' (Hans Frank, *Im Angesicht des Galgens. Deutung Hitlers und seine Zeit auf Grund eigener Erlebnisse und Erkenntnisse*, Munich/Grafelfing, 1953, 195).

188. Rebentisch, 290–91.

189. See Reinhard Bollmus, *Das Amt Rosenberg und seine Gegner. Studien zum Machtkampf im nationalsozialistischen Herrschaftssystem*, Stuttgart, 1970, ch.6, 236ff., especially 245; Rebentisch, 284.

190. For the term, see Hans Mommsen, 'Der Nationalsozialismus. Kumulative Radikalisierung und Selbstzerstörung des Regimes', in *Meyers Enzyklopädisches Lexikon*, Bd.16, Mannheim, 1976, 785–790 (though Mommsen plays down ideology as a driving-force).

191. See also Rebentisch, 164, 338.

192. See Rebentisch, 132ff.; Peter Hüttenberger, *Die Gauleiter. Studie zum Wandel des Machtgefüges in der NSDAP*, Stuttgart, 1969, 152ff.; and Karl Teppe, 'Der Reichsverteidigungskommissar. Organisation und Praxis in Westfalen', in Rebentisch and Teppe, *Verwaltung contra Menschenführung*, 278–301.

193. Nineteen *Gauleitertagungen* were held during the course of the war (Rebentisch, 290 and n.26). I am most grateful to Martin Moll for letting me see a detailed study, as yet unpublished, which he has undertaken: 'Die Tagungen der Reichs- und Gauleiter der NSDAP: Ein verkanntes Instrument zur Koordinierung im "Ämterchaos" des Dritten Reiches?'

194. Schirach, 298.

195. See Orlow, 268–72.

196. See Longerich, *Hitlers Stellvertreter*, ch.VIII.

197. Rebentisch, 246–51.

198. Cit. Rebentisch, 251.

199. Rebentisch, 206ff., 247, 251; Huttenberger, *Gauleiter*, 138ff.

200. For the administrative confusion and tangled reins of control in occupied Poland, see Norman Rich, *Hitler's War Aims. The Establishment of the New Order*, London, 1974, 72–3.

201. See Rebentisch, 248–50 for Forster and Greiser; also Kershaw, 'Greiser'. Forster's remark about Himmler – '*Wenn ich so aussehen würde wie Himmler, würde ich von Rasse überhaupt nicht reden*' – is cited in Hüttenberger, 181 (from testimony provided to the RSHA in 1943 in the dispute between Himmler and Forster) and by Jochen von Lang, *Der Adjutant. Karl Wolff: Der Mann zwischen Hitler und Himmler*, Munich, 1985, 147.

202. Ruth Bettina Birn, *Die Höheren SS- und Polizeiführer. Himmlers Vertreter im Reich und in den besetzten Gebieten*, Düsseldorf, 1986, 197–205. Martyn Housden, 'Hans Frank – Empire Builder in the East, 1939–41', *European History Quarterly*, 24 (1994), 367–93, here especially 376–8, is inclined to play down Frank's subordination to the SS. On the figure of Hans Frank, see Christoph Kleßmann, 'Der Generalgouverneur Hans Frank', *VfZ*, 19 (1971), 245–60; Christoph Kleßmann, 'Hans Frank – Parteijurist und Generalgouverneur in Polen', in Ronald Smelser and Rainer Zitelmann (eds.), *Die braune Elite*, Darmstadt, 1989, 41–51; and Joachim C. Fest, *The Face of the Third Reich*, Harmondsworth, 1972, 315–31.

203. See Herbert, *Fremdarbeiter*, 115ff.

204. See Christopher Browning, 'Nazi Resettlement Policy and the Search for a Solution to the Jewish Question, 1939–1941', in Christopher Browning (ed.), *The Path to Genocide. Essays on Launching the Final Solution*, Cambridge, 1992, 3–27. Aly, '*Endlösung*', 14ff., emphasizes the interconnection of resettlement plans and genocide, which his study examines.

205. Aly, 60–62.

206. See Seev Goschen, 'Eichmann und die Nisko-Aktion im October 1939', *VfZ*, 29 (1981), 74–96, especially 72, 82, 86; Safrian, 68ff.

207. Aly, 62–4.

208. Goschen, 91ff; Safrian, 78–81.

209. *Faschismus-Getto-Massenmord. Dokumentation über Ausrottung und Widerstand der Juden in Polen während des zweiten Weltkrieges*, ed. Jüdisches Historisches Institut Warschau, Frankfurt am Main, n.d. [1961], 42–3.

210. *Faschismus*, 43–6; Hilberg, 137ff.; Kershaw, ' "Warthegau" ', 56–7.

211. See Ernst Klee and Willi Dreßen (eds.), '*Gott mit uns*'. *Der deutsche Vernichtungskrieg im Osten 1939–1945*, Frankfurt am Main, 1989, 12–13; *The New German Order in Poland*, 220ff., 230–31; *Faschismus*, 53.

212. *Faschismus*, 46.

213. Glowna Komissa Badni Zbrodni Hitlerowskich w Polsce Archiwum Warsaw [War Crimes Archive], Process Artura Greisera, File 27, Fol.167.

214. See *Faschismus*, 52–3.

215. Aly, 84–5. As we noted in the previous chapter, patients in asylums in Stettin and other localities on the Pomeranian coast had been murdered the previous autumn to make accommodation available for almost 50,000 ethnic Germans transported there from Latvia. (See Aly, '*Endlösung*', 65.)

216. Aly, 85.

217. Pätzold, *Verfolgung*, 262.

218. Browning, *Path*, 32.

219. Lucjan Dobroszycki (ed.), *The Chronicle of the Lodz Ghetto, 1941–1944*, New Haven/London, 1984, xxxix.

220. Browning, *Path*, 35.

221. Werner Präg and Wolfgang Jacobmeyer (eds.), *Das Diensttagebuch des deutschen Generalgouverneurs in Polen 1919–1945*, Stuttgart, 1975 (=*DTB Frank*), 261–4 (31 July 1940).

222. Kershaw, ' "Warthegau" ', 58.

223. *DTB Frank* (31 July 1940), 261; *Faschismus*, 57–8.

224. Wildt, 32–3.

225. Brechtken, 16, 32ff.; and Leni Yahil, 'Madagascar – Phantom of a Solution for the Jewish Question', in Bela Vago and George L. Mosse (eds.), *Jews and Non-Jews in Eastern Europe*, New York, 1974, 315–34, here 315–19, where consideration by the Polish government in the later 1930s of Madagascar as an area to resettle Jews, leading to talks with the French government about the proposal, is also outlined. On 5 March 1938, Heydrich instructed Eichmann to prepare a memorandum indicating that emigration could no longer, partly for financial reasons, be regarded as a solution to the 'Jewish Question', and that it was therefore necessary 'to find a foreign-political solution as had already been negotiated between Poland and France' ('*und dass man darum herantreten muss, eine außenpolitische Lösung zu finden, wie sie bereits zwischen Polen und Frankreich verhandelt wurde*'). An arrow pointed to 'Madagaskar-Projekt' written in the margin. (Cit. Yahil, 'Madagascar', 321.)

226. Christopher Browning, *The Final Solution and the German Foreign Office*, New York/London, 1978, 35.

227. Richard Breitman, *The Architect of Genocide. Himmler and the Final Solution*, London,

1991, 122. The French Foreign Minister Georges Bonnet had reported in late 1938 that, if other governments participating in the Evian Committee were prepared to contribute, France 'would consider the settlement in Madagascar and New Caledonia of 10,000 persons', though these were not to be of German origin. (Brechtken, 204. And see Yahil, 'Madagascar', 319.)

228. *IMG*, xxviii.539, 1816–PS (Minutes of meeting of 12 November 1938); Yahil, 'Madagascar', 322; Breitman, *Architect*, 122.

229. Breitman, *Architect*, 121, mentions Hitler speaking to Jodl on 20 May about demanding the return of German colonies as part of a settlement with Britain and (276 n.24) Himmler already working out plans for a colonial police.

230. Helmut Krausnick, 'Denkschrift Himmlers über die Behandlung der Fremdvölkischen im Osten (Mai 1940)', *VfZ* 5 (1957), 194–8, here 197. For the significance of Himmler's remarks on extermination, as regards the Jews, see the interpretation of Breitman, *Architect*, 121 and n.

231. Breitman, *Architect*, 118 and 275–6 n.11. Aly, 140, has 25 June, but this seems an error.

232. Krausnick, 'Denkschrift', 197 (transl., *N&P*, iii.932).

233. Hans-Jürgen Döscher, *Das Auswärtige Amt in Dritten Reich. Diplomatie im Schatten der 'Endlösung'*, Berlin, 1987, 215; see also Yahil, 'Madagascar', 325; Browning, *Final Solution*, 36; Breitman, *Architect*, 123.

234. Döscher, *Das Auswärtige Amt*, 219–20.

235. Browning, *Final Solution*, 37.

236. Döscher, *Das Auswärtige Amt*, 217–18.

237. Döscher, *Das Auswärtige Amt*, 217. See Lukacs, *Duel*, 142 n.

238. Döscher, *Das Auswärtige Amt*, 218–19; Yahil, 'Madagascar', 326; Browning, *Final Solution*, 40–41.

239. Schmidt, 495.

240. *CP*, 374; see also *CD* (18–19 June 1940), where Ribbentrop is reported to have said 'that there is a German project to round up and send the Jews to Madagascar'.

241. *Lagevorträge*, 107 (20 June 1940); Brechtken, 230; Browning, *Path*, 18. According to the note of the meeting with Raeder, Hitler spoke, remarkably, of 'French responsibility' for the Jews to be deported to Madagascar. Raeder suggested exchanging Madagascar for the northern part of Portuguese Angola. Hitler said he would have the suggestion tested. The exchange hints at superficial interest in the Madagascar proposal.

242. *DTB Frank*, 252; Aly, 146–7 (and n.35); and *Faschismus*, 57.

243. John P. Fox, 'German Bureaucrat or Nazified Ideologue? Ambassador Otto Abetz and Hitler's Anti-Jewish Policies 1940–44', in Michael Graham Fry (ed.), *Power, Personalities, and Policies. Essays in Honour of Donald Cameron Watt*, London, 1992, 175–232, here 184; Döscher, *Das Auswärtige Amt*, 216; Breitman, *Architect*, 128. The meeting took place on 3 August.

244. *TBJG*, I/8, 276 (17 August 1940).

245. Goebbels thought the film was finished, but within three days had to rework it (*TBJG*, I/7, 264 (9 January 1940), 268 (12 January 1940); Hornshøh-Møller, 19).

246. *TBJG*, I/8, 159 (6 June 1940).

247. *TBJG*, I/8, 236 (25 July 1940).

248. Breitman, *Architect*, 131–2.

249. Pätzold, *Verfolgung*, 271–5; Hilberg, 392.

250. Breitman, *Architect*, 135.

251. *IMG*, xxxix, 425–9, Doc. 172-USSR; *DTB Frank*, 302 (6 November 1940); Breitman, *Architect*, 142–3. Frank was also told by Hitler that he would have to accept more Poles deported to his area from the incorporated territories. Their standard of living was immaterial.

252. Breitman, *Architect*, 137; Hilberg, 166; Ulrich Herbert, 'Labour and Extermination: Economic Interest and the Primacy of Weltanschauung in National Socialism', *Past and Present*, 138 (1993), 144–95, here 158ff.

253. Breitman, *Architect*, 139.

254. *DTB Frank*, 318–20 (11 January 1941); Breitman, *Architect*, 143.

255. *IMG*, xxviii.301, Doc.1776-PS; Klee, *Dokumente*, 298; Hillgruber, *Strategie*, 178.

256. Michalka, 'From the Anti-Comintern Pact', 282; Hillgruber, *Strategie*, 179; Carr, *Poland*, 117.

257. Carr, *Poland*, 107.

258. Domarus, 1588–9; Carr, *Poland*, 107–8; Michalka, 'From the Anti-Comintern Pact', 281–3; Bloch, 303–6; Weinberg III, 168–9, 182, 248.

259. Hillgruber, *Strategie*, 188–92.

260. Hillgruber, *Strategie*, 189–90; and see Carr, *Poland*, 117.

261. Hillgruber, *Strategie*, 190.

262. Bloch, 308–10.

263. *CP*, 395–9; Bloch, 307.

264. *CD*, 296 (4 October 1940).

265. *CD*, 297 (12 October 1940); *CP*, 398.

266. Bloch, 311.

267. *Staatsmänner*, i.124–33; and see Jäckel, *Frankreich*, 105–17.

268. Bloch, 310.

269. *Halder KTB*, ii.133 (11 October 1940); *Weizsäcker-Papiere*, 221 (21 October 1940).

270. Preston, *Franco*, 393.

271. Schmidt, 510–11, claimed that Franco's train was an hour late. In fact, it was eight minutes late (Preston, *Franco*, 394).

272. Schmidt, 511.

273. The following account is based upon *Staatsmänner* I, 133–40 (quotation, 138); and Schmidt, 511–14. Schmidt, 511, conveys the misleading impression that he was present throughout the talks. In fact, another German interpreter was used on this occasion since Schmidt did not command fluent Spanish. Schmidt was in the party at Hendaye, however, and almost certainly drew up the (incomplete) record of the discussion for the Foreign Office. He was, therefore, thoroughly versed in the course of the talks, and his account accords well with the contemporary notes of the Spanish interpreter, Baron de las Torres. On the meeting, see, especially, Paul Preston, 'Franco and Hitler: the Myth of Hendaye 1940', *Contemporary European History*, 1 (1992), 1–16, here 9–10; and Preston, *Franco*, 394–400. The misleading impression given by Schmidt is pointed out in David Wingeate Pike, 'Franco and the Axis Stigma', *JCH*, 17 (1982), 369–406, here 377–9.

274. See Samuel Hoare, *Ambassador on Special Mission*, London, 1946, 92–5, for the general view in diplomatic circles that Spanish claims on north Africa had been the major stumbling-block in the discussions.

275. Cit. Preston, 'Hendaye', 10 and n.32 (the reported comment of the Spanish interpreter, Baron de las Torres, on 26 October 1940).

276. Cit. Preston, 'Hendaye', 12.

277. Schmidt, 514; Bloch, 311–12.

278. *CP*, 401–2.

279. *Halder KTB*, ii.158 (1 November 1940); trans. *Halder Diary*, 272. Halder was noting comments passed on by Hitler's Army adjutant, Gerhard Engel.

280. Schmidt, 514–16.

281. François Delpla, *Montoire. Les premiers jours de la collaboration*, Paris, 1996, ch.16, and Delpla, *Hitler*, 337–8, places a more positive gloss on the outcome of the talks, from Hitler's point of view, especially in terms of the propaganda impression intended to be conveyed abroad that Germany was indomitable on the continent of Europe.

282. *Staatsmänner*, i.149; *Halder KTB*, ii.157–8 (1 November 1940); *CP*, 401; and see Jäckel, *Frankreich*, 121.

283. Schmidt, 516; Below, 249. Hitler's disappointment was implicit in the comments passed on by Engel and noted by Halder. (*Halder KTB*, ii.158 (1 November 1940).)

284. Below, 250.

285. Schmidt, 516–17; Engel, 88 (28 October 1940).

286. *CP*, 399–404; Schmidt, 517.

287. *CP*, 402.

288. Engel, 89–90 (4 November 1940), and n.272.

289. Carr, *Poland*, 98–9, 118–19; Martin van Creveld, *Hitler's Strategy 1940–1941. The Balkan Clue*, Cambridge, 1973, 69–72; and see Robert Cecil, *Hitler's Decision to Invade Russia 1941*, London, 1975, Ch.VI–VII.

290. *Weisungen*, 81, Directive No.18, Section 5 (12 November 1940).

291. Carr, *Poland*, 120.

292. *Weizsäcker-Papiere*, 224 (15 November 1940). The Molotov visit is well described in Read and Fisher, *Deadly Embrace*, ch.46, 510ff. The following account draws on Schmidt, 526–36, and the official texts of the discussions: *Staatsmänner* I, 166–93; *ADAP*, D, XI.1, 455–61, 462–72, Nos.326, 328.

293. Carr, *Poland*, 121.

294. *Staatsmänner* I, 193; *ADAP*, D, XI.1, 472–8, No.329.

295. *ADAP*, D, XI.2, 597–8, No.404; Carr, *Poland*, 121; Weinberg III, 201; Bloch, 316.

296. Bloch, 316.

297. Hillgruber, *Strategie*, 356 and n.21 (Engel communication of 10 April 1964).

298. Engel, 91 (15 November 1940).

299. Below, 253.

300. Fedor von Bock, *The War Diary 1939–1945*, ed. Klaus Gerbet, Atglen PA, 1996, 193–4 (3 December 1940); Hillgruber, *Strategie*, 361 n.50. The translation of part of the passage from Bock's diary – '*zumal ein wirksames Eingreifen Amerikas dann durch Japan, das nun den Rücken frei hat, erschwert wird*' ('especially since an effective intervention by America would be complicated by Japan, which would keep our rear free') – mistakenly implies that the implication of eliminating the Soviet Union would be that Germany's, not Japan's, rear would be unexposed.

301. *Halder KTB*, ii.209–14 (5 December 1940); trans. *Halder Diary*, 292–8. Hitler amended the operational plan when Jodl presented it to him on 17 December in one significant element. He insisted that strong mobile units from the centre of the front swing northwards from the Warsaw region to ensure the destruction of Soviet forces in the north and subsequently occupy Leningrad and Kronstadt. Only thereafter were operations aimed at Moscow to be undertaken. (*Kriegstagebuch des Oberkommandos der Wehrmacht (Wehrmachtführungsstab)*, ed. Percy Ernst Schramm (=*KTB OKW*) Bd.I: 1. *August 1940–31. Dezember 1941*, Frankfurt am Main, 1965, 233.)

302. *Halder KTB*, ii.227–8 (13 December 1940).

303. *KTB OKW*, 1.996; Hillgruber, *Strategie*, 363.

304. *Weisungen*, 96 (18 December 1940).

305. The Army High Command had until December 1940 used the code-name 'Otto' for its operational plan for the east (*Halder KTB*, ii.210, 214 (5 December 1940)). The Wehrmachtführungs-stab, however, had used the designation 'Fritz', coined by Loßberg, who (see above n.157) named the operation after his son, for its own campaign-plan. The latter term was then given by Jodl to the draft directive No.21 for the 'eastern operations' on 12 December 1940, before being altered to 'Barbarossa' five days later. (*KTB OKW*, 1.226, 233. And see B. Whaley, *Codeword Barbarossa*, Cambridge, Mass., 1973, 16–18; Barry A. Leach, *German Strategy against Russia 1939–1941*, Oxford, 1973, 79, 82, 258; Dirks/Janßen, ch.9). Confusingly, 'Otto-Programm' was also used by the Army for the programme to develop rail and roads in the east (*Halder KTB*, ii.133 n.3, 210 n.6, 381).

306. *KTB OKW*, i.257–8; Hillgruber, *Strategie*, 364–5.

307. Below, 259.

308. *Halder KTB*, ii.283; trans. *Halder Diary*, 320 (17 February 1941); Hillgruber, *Strategie*, 365.

CHAPTER 8: DESIGNING A 'WAR OF ANNIHILATION'

1. Below, 252, 254. He probably exaggerates (259, 279–80) the extent of reservation about the attack on the USSR. See Irving, *HW*, 181–2, and Irving, *Göring*, 307–9, for Göring's initial objections (in November 1940) on economic, not moral, grounds – emphasizing Germany's dependence on Soviet grain and oil – but rapid capitulation to Hitler's arguments. Göring's preferred strategy would have been, acting together with the Italians and Spanish, to force the British out of the Mediterranean and the Middle East, and to occupy North Africa and the Balkans.

2. IfZ, F37/3 (1940–41), Kreisleitertagung am 28.11.1940, quotations Fols.290–91 (pp.18–19 of speech). In the earlier part of his speech, Himmler had stated (Fol.277) that Hitler was not interested in destroying the English people and their Empire (*'Dem Führer lag nichts an der Vernichtung des englischen Volkes und Imperiums'*), but that the British had refused his offers of peace. The Führer would prefer not to undertake a landing in England, but would do so the following spring if the last resistance was not broken. He saw Britain's future, after its collapse, residing in a probable merger (*'Fusion'*) with America (Fols.279–82). Himmler went on to depict his vision of the future development of the European continent under German domination, before coming to the question of Russia.

3. Hofer, *Der Nationalsozialismus*, 194.

4. *IMG*, xxxiv.469, Doc.134-C (Hitler's comments on 20 January 1941); and, for Hitler's comments on 20 June 1941 (as noted by General Thomas) on the need to secure all territories needed for the defence economy, *IMG*, xxvii.220–21, Doc.1456-PS; see also Norman Rich, *Hitler's War Aims. Vol.1: Ideology, the Nazi State, and the Course of Expansion*, London, 1973, 207; and Carr, *Poland*, 122–5.

5. See Breitman, *Architect*, ch.7.

6. Engel, 92 (18 December 1940).

7. *DRZW*, iv.244; Leach, 159–65; Hillgruber, *Strategie*, 501–4.

8. Leach, 140.

9. *Halder KTB*, ii.261 (28 January 1941); trans. *Halder Diary*, 314.

10. Leach, 141.

11. Bock, *Diary*, 197–8 (1 February 1941); Leach, 141.

12. Leach, 142–3.

13. Below, 262.

14. Leach, 143–5.

15. *KTB OKW*, i.339–40 (1 March 1941); *DRZW*, iv. 244; Leach, 159–61.

16. *Halder KTB*, ii.319 (17 March 1941); Leach, 162–3.

17. Engel, 92–3 (entry for 17 January 1941); Hillgruber, *Strategie*, 504 (where Engel's entry is misdated to 17 March 1941); Leach, 163.

18. *CD*, 328–9 (16 January 1941, 18 January 1941), for Mussolini's unease at the visit; Domarus, 1654.

19. *CP*, 417–20. For the visit and Mussolini's reaction, see MacGregor Knox, *Mussolini Unleashed 1939–1941. Politics and Strategy in Fascist Italy's Last War*, Cambridge, (1982) 1986 paperback edn, 279–81; Milza, 791.

20. *CD*, 329 (entry dated 18 January 1941 in text, but actually covering the dates 18–21 January 1941, here referring to 19 January 1941). For the authenticity of the diaries, despite some touching up in 1943, see Knox, 291–2.

21. *CD*, 330 (entry dated 18 January 1941, but relating here to 20 January 1941).

22. *IMG*, xxxiv.469, Doc. 134-C.

23. *CD*, 330 (entry dated 18 January 1941, but relating to 21 January 1941).

24. *CD*, 331 (22 January 1941).

25. For scorn in the population directed at Italian war-efforts in Greece and North Africa, see Steinert, 171.

26. *TBJG*, I/9, 114 (29 January 1941); see also 153 (22 February 1941) for growing doubts about Mussolini, and 197–8 (21 March 1941) for further complaints about the Italian leadership and military capability.

27. *TBJG*, I/9, 118 (31 January 1941) for Hitler's criticism of the Italians.

28. See Gruchmann, *Der Zweite Weltkrieg*, 107, for the military defeats and numbers of prisoners; and Knox, 251ff., for the disastrous campaigns.

29. Irving, *HW*, 200.

30. *KTB OKW*, i.284 (28 January 1941).

31. Domarus, 1666.

32. *CP*, 421–30 (here 428). See Preston, *Franco*, 421–2, for the extraordinary 'shopping-list' of military equipment put together by the Spanish General Staff – so exorbitant that it was dismissed in Berlin as a pretext to avoid entering the war.

33. *TBJG*, I/9, 121 (1 February 1941).

34. *TBJG*, I/9, 119 (31 January 1941), 121 (1 February 1941).

35. *TBJG*, I/9, 121 (1 February 1941).

36. Domarus, 1661 n.50.

37. *TBJG*, I/9, 121 (1 February 1941).

38. Domarus, 1663.

39. Domarus, 1663 n.54; and see Jäckel, 'Hitler und der Mord', 151–62, here 160–62.

40. Domarus, 1659. He also remarked, in a different context, in his speech, that neither he nor the Duce were Jews or 'doers of business' (*Geschäftemacher*), and that their handshake was genuine (Domarus, 1661).

41. Aly, 269.

42. Hornshøh-Møller, 187; and see 2–3, 18–19, 179–81, 295–6. At a preview for an invited audience on 1 March 1940, the extract of Hitler's speech, which had only recently been incorporated into the film, provoked a spontaneous burst of applause. The film was first shown in public at the 'UFA-Palast' in Berlin on 28 November 1940. (Møller, 18–19, 33.)

43. For the nature of the Engel 'diary' entries, only seemingly contemporary, see Engel, 12–13.

44. Engel, 94–5. See Breitman, *Architect*, 155 n., for reasons to accept this testimony, despite its contentious nature.

45. Aly, 273.

46. See Aly, 268–79.

47. Gerhard Botz, *Wohnungspolitik und Judendeportation 1938–1945. Zur Funktion des Antisemitismus als Ersatz nationalsozialistischer Sozialpolitik*, Vienna, 1975, 108–9, 197; *IMG*, xxix.176, Doc.1950-PS.

48. *TBJG*, I/9, 193 (18 March 1941).

49. Aly, 212–15; Breitman, *Architect*, 151–2.

50. Aly, 217–18.

51. Aly, 219–25; Safrian, 96–8.

52. Aly, 269; Breitman, *Architect*, 152 and 285 n.33.

53. Cit. Aly, 269.

54. Aly, 269.

55. Cit. Aly, 269; Breitman, *Architect*, 152 and 205 n.33.

56. *DTB* Frank, 332–3 (17 March 1941), 336–7 (25 March 1941); Breitman, *Architect*, 156.

57. Breitman, *Architect*, 156 and 285 n.33.

58. Breitman, *Architect*, 146.

59. *IMG*, iv.535–6 (statement of Erich von dem Bach-Zelewski, 7 January 1946); Krausnick/ Wilhelm, 115; Breitman, *Architect*, 147.

60. Krausnick/Wilhelm, 141.

61. Breitman, *Architect*, 147–8.

62. Cit. Christian Streit, *Keine Kameraden. Die Wehrmacht und die sowjetischen Kriegsgefangenen 1941–1945*, Stuttgart, 1978, 28. This is the first documentary evidence hinting at the order for annihilation in the eastern campaign.

63. It was taken to Hitler at the Berghof at the end of a quiet month when, according to one who experienced the atmosphere there at first hand, it was scarcely noticeable that Germany was at war (Below, 262).

64. *KTB OKW*, i.341 (3 March 1941); trans. amended from Warlimont, 150–51; Krausnick/ Wilhelm, 115; Breitman, *Architect*, 148–9; Streit, 30.

65. Warlimont, 152–3; *Anatomie*, 198–201, here especially 199.

66. Cit. Aly, 270. The GPU was the State Political Executive, the successor body to the Cheka, the notorious secret police of the Tsars, then of the Bolsheviks.

67. Aly, 270–22.

68. In a paper as yet unpublished, 'From Barbarossa to Wannsee. The Role of Reinhard Heydrich', Eberhard Jäckel (to whom I am most grateful for the opportunity to consult it) puts a compelling case for viewing Heydrich, not Himmler (as does Richard Breitman in his *The Architect of Genocide*), as the chief 'architect' of the Final Solution.

69. *Halder KTB*, ii.320 (17 March 1941); trans. *Halder Diary*, 339.

70. Streit, 31.

71. Warlimont, 158–60; *Anatomie des SS-Staates*, ii.172, 202–3 (Doc.2). Negotiations involving the General-Quartermaster Eduard Wagner and the SS leadership about the arrangements for the 'special commission' of the Reichsführer-SS in the east were under way in early March (*Anatomie*, ii.171–2). According to Walter Schellenberg, he himself was involved in deliberations with Wagner, and in turning them into 'an expression of the Führer's will' (Schellenberg, 92; see Streit, 31–2 and 310 n.19 (for contradictions in Schellenberg's testimony)). Wagner's meeting with Heydrich turned upon establishing a demarcation line between police and military spheres of responsibility for the liquidation of captured political commissars, and was prompted by the Wehrmacht's concern that Heydrich would greatly widen the scope of his own powers (Jörg Friedrich, *Das Gesetz des Krieges. Das deutsche Heer in Rußland 1941–1945. Der Prozeß gegen das Oberkommando der Wehrmacht*, Munich/Zurich, 2nd edn, 1995, 289–92).

72. *DRZW*, iv.416–17.

73. *Halder KTB*, ii.335–7 (30 March 1941); trans. *Halder Diary*, 345–6. According to Halder's post-war testimony, Hitler justified his ideological warfare in the East by alluding to the fact that the USSR had not signed the Geneva Convention of 27 July 1928 relating to the treatment of prisoners-of-war. (*IMG*, vii.396–7 (statement by Halder on 31 October 1945). See also *Anatomie*, ii.174; and Streit, 36.)

74. *IMG*, xx.635 (testimony by Brauchitsch on 9 August 1946); see also Leach, 153; and Streit, 35.

75. Warlimont, 162. His explanation, that they had not followed Hitler's diatribe or grasped the meaning of what he was saying, is scarcely credible.

76. Cit. Domarus, 1683, n.134.

77. Cit. *Anatomie*, ii.175–6; trans., *Anatomy of the SS State*, London, 1968, 516.

78. *Anatomie*, ii.176, 211–12.

79. *Anatomie*, ii.211.

80. See Jürgen Förster, 'The German Army and the Ideological War against the Soviet Union', in Gerhard Hirschfeld (ed.), *The Policies of Genocide. Jews and Soviet Prisoners of War in Nazi Germany*, London, 1986, 15–29, here 17. See also Streit, ch.III; Manfred Messerschmidt, *Die*

Wehrmacht im NS-Staat. Zeit der Indoktrination, Hamburg, 1969, 390–411; and Helmut Krausnick, 'Kommissarbefehl und "Gerichtsbarkeitserlaß Barbarossa" in neuer Sicht', *VfZ*, 25 (1977), 682–738, especially 717ff., 737.

81. Förster, 'German Army', 19; Streit, 36ff.

82. *Anatomie*, ii.178–9, 215–18.

83. Forster, 'German Army', 19. See, on its genesis, Streit, 44–9.

84. *Anatomie*, ii.225–7; trans., *Anatomy of the SS State*, 532. (Italics in the original.)

85. Streit, 50–51.

86. Engel, 102–3 (10 May 1941); *Anatomie*, ii.177; *DRZW*, iv.446; Bodo Scheurig, *Henning von Tresckow. Ein Preusse gegen Hitler*, Frankfurt am Main/Berlin, 1987, 113–14. On reports of the order being implemented by different units, see Krausnick, 'Kommissarbefehl', 733–6. According to the most meticulous, if still provisional, statistical analysis yet made, between a half and two-thirds of front divisions implemented the order. (Detlef Siebert, 'Die Durchführung des Kommissarbefehls in den Frontverbänden des Heeres. Eine quantifierende Auswertung der Forschung'. I am most grateful to Detlef Siebert for providing me with a copy of this as yet unpublished paper.)

87. *Anatomie*, ii.177.

88. Leach, 154–5. It has been surmised, however, with some justification that Bock's objections were primarily levelled against the decree limiting military jurisdiction, issued a day after the decree on treatment of 'political functionaries' (*Anatomie*, ii.174–5).

89. *DRZW*, iv. 24, 446. For Küchler's support of 'severe measures undertaken' in Poland (where he had nonetheless criticized the brutality of the SS) in the interests of a 'final *völkisch* solution' of 'an ethnic struggle raging for centuries on the eastern border', see Streit, 55–6.

90. *DRZW*, iv. 24, 446. For a brief sketch of the career of the enigmatic Hoepner, see Samuel W. Mitcham, Jr and Gene Mueller, 'Generaloberst Erich Hoepner', in Gerd R. Ueberschär (ed.), *Hitlers militärische Elite. Bd.2, Vom Kriegsbeginn bis zum Weltkriegsende*, Darmstadt, 1998, 93–9.

91. See Arno J. Mayer, *Why did the Heavens not Darken? The 'Final Solution' in History*, New York, 1988, 212.

92. As Ulrich von Hassell put it, shortly before the campaign began: 'Brauchitsch and Halder have already gone along with Hitler's manoeuvre of transferring the odium of incendiarism (*Mordbrennerei*) to the army from the SS, which up to now had alone been burdened with it' (Hassell, 257 (15 June 1941)).

93. *CP*, 432 (25 March 1941).

94. *Staatsmänner* I, 234.

95. *Staatsmänner* I, 236; Irving, *HW*, 217, for Abwehr reports of growing anti-government feeling in Yugoslavia.

96. Keitel, 260.

97. *DRZW*, iii.419.

98. Hillgruber, *Strategie*, 337; *DRZW*, iii.418.

99. *Weisungen*, 80.

100. *DRZW*, iii.421.

101. *Weisungen*, 94.

102. *Weisungen*, 95; *DRZW*, iii. 423.

103. *DRZW*, iii.422.

104. See Creveld, 96ff.

105. Creveld, 134–5.

106. *DRZW*, iii.418 n.10; Domarus, 1623–4.

107. Domarus, 1670; Hauner, *Hitler*, 158.

108. Weinberg, iii.216.

109. *DRZW*, iii.438–40.

110. *DRZW*, iii.442ff.; Creveld, 139ff.

111. Keitel, 261.

112. *TBJG*, I/9, 210 (29 March 1941).

113. *IMG*, xxviii.22, Doc.1746-PS (Hitler's speech to his military leaders); IfZ, ED 100, Sammlung-Irving, Hewel-Diary, entry for 27 March 1941; Irving, *HW*, 218.

114. Below, 265.

115. Peter Bor, *Gespräche mit Halder*, Wiesbaden, 1950, 180. See also Heidemarie Schall-Riancour, *Aufstand und Gehorsam. Offizierstum und Generalstab im Umbruch. Leben und Wirken von Generaloberst Franz Halder, Generalstabschef 1938–1942*, Wiesbaden, 1972, 159. Creveld, 145, points out that preliminary preparations for a preventive attack on Yugoslavia had been undertaken months earlier, so that the army was not caught as unawares as post-war accounts sometimes claimed.

116. *Halder KTB*. ii.330–31 (27 March 1941); Below, 265. Ribbentrop was also present.

117. *IMG*, xxviii.23, Doc.1746-PS; *KTB OKW*, 1.368 (27 March 1941).

118. Keitel, 262.

119. *Weisungen*, 124–6; Below, 265.

120. Keitel, 262; *DRZW*, iii.448ff.

121. *DRZW*, iii.451. Initially, the attacks on Greece ('Marita') and Yugoslavia ('Directive 25') were foreseen as separate operations, starting at different dates in early April. On 29 March it was decided to link the operations. According to the new timetable, the bombing of Belgrade and beginning of 'Marita' were put back from 1 to 5 April then, on 3 April, postponed for twenty-four hours (Creveld, 154).

122. *TBJG*, I/9, 211 (29 March 1941). This was the first time that Goebbels had referred to 'Barbarossa' in his diary (*Tb* Reuth, 1546, n.46).

123. Schmidt, 539–40, 542.

124. Schmidt, 536–9.

125. Irving, *HW*, 220.

126. The thinking in Tokyo differed sharply on this point. It was presumed that an attack on Singapore would be precisely the step to bring the USA into the war in support of Britain (*Staatsmänner*, I, 255 and n.5). Hitler reckoned with conflict between Germany and the USA – but not before the conquest of the USSR had given him the basis to undertake such a contest (*Staatsmänner*, I, 256 n.7; and see Andreas Hillgruber, 'Hitler und die USA', in Otmar Franz (ed.), *Europas Mitte*, Gottingen/Zurich, 1987, 125–44, here 134).

127. Carr, *Poland*, 146.

128. Schmidt, 540–42; *Staatsmänner*, i., 244 n.16. According to Schmidt, Hitler himself gave a broad hint on Matsuoka's departure following his return to Berlin that conflict between Germany and the Soviet Union could not be excluded (Schmidt, 548). By this date, American cryptanalysts had broken Japanese diplomatic codes and were able to read the increasing number of messages, following Matsuoka's visit, passed to Tokyo by the Japanese Ambassador in Berlin, General Oshima Hiroshi. By mid-April 1941, US intelligence had detailed information on the forthcoming German invasion of the USSR, and was passing the information to the Russians. (Carl Boyd, *Hitler's Japanese Confidant. General Oshima Hiroshi and MAGIC Intelligence, 1941–1945*, Kansas, 1992, 18–21.)

129. *Staatsmänner*, I, 245 and n.18. At the lunch given for Matsuoka on 28 March, Hitler commented in an aside to the Japanese Ambassador Oshima that should the USSR attack Japan Germany would not hesitate to attack the Soviet Union (Andreas Hillgruber, 'Japan und der Fall "Barbarossa". Japanische Dokumente zu den Gesprächen Hitlers und Ribbentrops mit Botschafter Oshima von Februar bis Juni 1941', *Wehrwissenschaftliche Rundschau*, 18, 1968, 312–36, here 315–16).

130. *Staatsmänner* I, 240–47.

131. *Staatsmänner* I, 248.

132. *Staatsmänner* I, 262.

133. *CP*, 436 (20 April 1941).

134. *Staatsmänner* I, 256–7.

135. *TBJG*, I/9, 248 (15 April 1941). Stalin had made demonstrative gestures of friendship towards Germany immediately following Matsuoka's departure from Moscow, embracing the German ambassador and military attaché and declaring that Russia and Germany would march together to their goal (*TBJG*, I/9, 247 (14 April 1941); Schmidt, 548–9).

136. *TBJG*, I/9, 230 (6 April 1941).

137. *TBJG*, I/9, 229 (6 April 1941); Domarus, 1686.

138. Hitler had spoken extensively about this on his visit to Linz in mid-March (*TBJG*, I/9, 185 (13 March 1941). By mid-May, Goebbels was noting how much the transformation of Linz into a cultural capital was costing. 'But the Führer attaches so much value to it,' he added (*TBJG*, I/9, 318 (17 May 1941). Hitler would often repeat in future his intention of making Linz a cultural centre, and his criticism of Vienna. (See *TBJG*, II/4, 407 (30 May 1942); Picker, 377 (29 May 1942) and 493–4 (10 June 1942).)

139. *TBJG*, I/9, 231 (6 April 1941).

140. *TBJG*, I/9, 231 (6 April 1941); text of the proclamation, Domarus, 1687–9.

141. Domarus, 1689.

142. *TBJG*, I/9, 230 (6 April 1941); and in his speech to military leaders on 27 March 1941 (Domarus, 1677).

143. *DRZW*, iv.423.

144. Below, 268–9; Keitel, 263; Domarus, 1691 n.155 (where it is stated that the engine was kept under steam in case of air-attack, though without a source-reference).

145. Below, 268.

146. Below, 271; Keitel, 263–4; Domarus, 1692–3.

147. Domarus, 1692.

148. Keitel, 263.

149. Creveld, 158–66; *DRZW*, iii.458ff.

150. Creveld, 165–6; Gruchmann, *Der Zweite Weltkrieg*, 112.

151. Gruchmann, *Der Zweite Weltkrieg*, 112; Weinberg III, 221.

152. *TBJG*, I/9, 234 (8 April 1941). Hitler gushed about his admiration for the classical world, whereas he hated Christianity 'because it had crippled everything noble about humanity'. He applauded the grandeur of classical architecture, 'its clarity, brightness, and beauty', and disliked the 'gloominess and indistinct mysticism' of Gothic architecture.

153. Creveld, 163. Jodl reported that the joint surrender had been grotesque (*TBJG*, I/9, 279 (29 April 1941)).

154. Gruchmann, *Der Zweite Weltkrieg*, 113–14; Weinberg III, 222.

155. Keitel, 263, mistakenly says five weeks.

156. Creveld, 167.

157. Gruchmann, *Der Zweite Weltkrieg*, 115; Creveld, 170.

158. Creveld, 170; Gruchmann, *Der Zweite Weltkrieg*, 115.

159. Domarus, 1692, 1708; Kershaw, '*Hitler Myth*', 158–60.

160. *Weisungen*, 97.

161. *Halder KTB*, ii.210, 214 (5 December 1940); and see Creveld, 151.

162. *IMG*, xxviii.23, Doc. 1746-PS.

163. *KTB OKW*, i.411–12 (28 May 1941); *Halder KTB*, 387 (30 April 1941); Hillgruber, *Strategie*, 507; Domarus, 1696.

164. *Hitlers politisches Testament. Die Bormann-Diktate vom Februar und April 1945*, Hamburg, 1981, 88 (17 February 1945). No authentic German text of the misnamed 'Testament' has ever come to light, though the comments certainly have the ring of Hitler about them.

165. See Hillgruber, *Strategie*, 506 n.26, who points out that Hitler's comments served only the interests of his reputation for posterity.

166. Leach, 166; Hillgruber, *Strategie*, 506.

167. Hillgruber, *Strategie*, 506 and n.26.

168. Hillgruber, *Strategie*, 506–7.

169. Leach, 166.

170. Irving, *HW*, 233.

171. Domarus, 1709.

172. Schmidt, 549.

173. Schmidt, 549; and see *TBJG*, I/9, 309 (13 May 1941).

174. Rainer F. Schmidt, 'Der Heß-Flug und das Kabinett Churchill', *VfZ*, 42 (1994), 1–38, here 12–13.

175. Peter Padfield, *Hess. The Führer's Disciple*, London, 1991, 193–211.

176. Winston S. Churchill, *The Second World War. Vol.III: The Grand Alliance*, London etc., 1950, 43; James Douglas-Hamilton, *Motive for a Mission. The Story behind Hess's Flight to Britain*, London, 1971, 157ff., quotation 163; Colville, 306–7; John Costello, *Ten Days that Saved the West*, London, 1991, 417–19; Padfield, *Hess*, 213–17, quotation 217; James Leasor, *Rudolf Hess: the Uninvited Envoy*, London, 1962, ch.1–2, 7; J. Bernard Hutton, *Hess: the Man and his Mission*, London, 1970, 1ff., 49–52.

177. Padfield, *Hess*, 218–19, 225; *Diaries of Sir Alexander Cadogan*, 377. Cadogan was hugely irritated by what he saw as an unwelcome distraction caused by Heß. 'Heß is the bane of my life and all my time is wasted,' he noted on 14 May (*Diaries*, 378). 'If only the parachute had failed to open, he would be a happier and more efficient man,' he told close colleagues; 'the handling of the whole business is difficult but very important psychologically' (Colville, 388 (14 May 1941).

178. According to some versions, Hitler was still in bed when Pintsch arrived, though he dressed remarkably quickly (Heinz Linge, 'Kronzeuge Linge. Der Kammerdiener des "Führers"', *Revue*, Munich, November 1955-March 1956, 60; Below, 273). Linge later, however, contradicted his first account, indicating that, though not wanting to be wakened before midday, Hitler was already dressed when Pintsch arrived (Heinz Linge, *Bis zum Untergang. Als Chef des persönlichen Dienstes bei Hitler*, hrsg. von W. Maser, Munich/Berlin, 1980, 141–2). According to Engel, he was present – something disputed by Linge, *Bis zum Untergang*, 142 n. – while the Führer was discussing military matters when Pintsch was ushered into the Berghof. Angry at being disturbed, Hitler initially refused to see Pintsch, but eventually, with a bad grace, agreed to do so (Engel, 103 (11 May 1941)). General Karl Bodenschatz, Göring's representative, claimed after the war to have been alone with Hitler when Pintsch handed over the missive from Heß around 11a.m. (*IfZ*, ZS 10, Karl Bodenschatz, Fol.32 (Interview with David Irving, 30 November 1970)); Irving, *HW*, 244; Schmidt, 'Der Heß-Flug', 5 n.20. Hitler himself apparently recalled, mistakenly, in April 1942 that he had received the news from Heinz Lorenz, Press Chief Dietrich's representative at Fuhrer HQ, while taking tea by the fireside (Picker, 282 (19–20 April 1942)).

179. Engel, 103 (11 May 1941). Linge, 'Kronzeuge', 60, in a scene he claimed he would never forget, has Hitler apparently calm as he read the letter, and only on Bormann's arrival falling into a rage and thumping his fist on the table.

180. Speer, 189. Speer's details are, however, not always accurate. He has Pietsch instead of Pintsch for Hess's adjutant, and Leitgen also being present, which he was not. He has Goebbels and Himmler being summoned, and Bormann doing the telephoning. Neither Himmler nor Goebbels were there in the first round. Goebbels was not informed until the following day.

181. A package from Heß had, in fact, so Hitler told his military chiefs a few days later, been delivered to the Berghof the previous evening, but, presuming it was no more than routine Party administrative material from the Deputy Führer, he had simply not bothered to open it (*Halder*

KTB, ii.414 (15 May 1941)). See also Irving, *HW*, 144. There is no obvious reason why Hitler would have made this up. But, since the letters have not survived, the precise content and how the Saturday evening package (left unopened until the Sunday) and the Sunday letter which came via Pintsch related to each other is unclear. The longer letter, which Hitler had not bothered to open, appears to have been a fourteen-page memorandum with the suggestions for peace that he intended to put to the British. The shorter letter, which so appalled Hitler when he read it, apparently began by saying that by the time the letter was received, its author would be in England. (According to Bodenschatz, who claimed to have read it, this letter was only about two pages long. – IfZ, ZS 10, Fol.32.) Heß handed this letter over to Pintsch immediately before taking off from the airfield at Haunstetten (David Irving, *Rudolf Heß – ein gescheiterter Friedensbote? Die Wahrheit über die unbekannten Jahre 1941–1945*, Graz/Stuttgart, 1987, 89–90, 100). Heß told the Duke of Hamilton that he had made three previous attempts, but bad weather had intervened. It was, however, also the case that he needed far greater navigational detail than he had initially thought (Irving, *Heß*, 91–2).

182. Domarus, 1711; Irving, *Heß*, 90, both resting on the post-war testimony at Nuremberg of Hildegard Fath, one of Heß's secretaries: Eidesstattliche Erklärung, undatiert, ND Beweisstuck, Heß-13, IWM FO 645, Box Nr.31, Nr.3 – cit. Irving, *Heß*, 444, note to p.89.

183. Engel, 103–4 (11 May 1941).

184. Below, 273.

185. Hewel's diary entry speaks of 'great agitation (*Große Erregung*)' when Pintsch delivered the letter. Ribbentrop and Göring were summoned. Hitler broke off his talks with Darlan. When Göring arrived that evening and was put in the picture by Bodenschatz, he was also 'very agitated (*sehr erregt*)'. Hewel also described the atmosphere of the lengthy discussion in the hall between Hitler, Ribbentrop, Göring, and Bormann as 'very agitated (*sehr erregt*).' 'Many combinations (*Viele Kombinationen*)', the diary-entry ends (IfZ, ED 100, Irving-Sammlung, Hewel-Tagebuch (entry for 11 May 1941)).

186. Martin Moll (ed.), '*Führer-Erlasse*' *1939–1945*, Stuttgart, 1997, 172; Domarus, 1716; Longerich, *Hitlers Stellvertreter*, 149–50.

187. See Orlow, ii.334.

188. See Longerich, *Hitlers Stellvertreter*, 154ff., especially 178–9.

189. IfZ, ED 100, Hewel-Tagebuch, Irving-Sammlung, entry for 12 May 1941; Ilse Heß, *England-Nürnberg-Spandau. Ein Schicksal in Bildern*, Leoni am Starnberger See, 1952, 130; Irving, *HW*, 246; Domarus, 1713 n.215, 1714. *Halder KTB*, ii.414 (15 May 1941), conveys the mistaken impression that Göring and Udet had thought it probable that Heß would reach his target. According to Hewel, their initial view was that he would not; but Hitler overrode them.

190. Below, 273–4; IfZ, ED 100, Hewel-Tagebuch, Irving-Sammlung, entry for 12 May 1941: 'Day full of agitation. Inquiries about Heß's flight. The Führer decides on publishing. Section that it was an act of madness pushed through by Führer.' ('*Sehr erregter Tag. Untersuchungen über Hess's Flug. Der Führer entschließt sich zur Veröffentlichung. Passus, daß es sich um eine Wahnsinnstat handelt, wird von F[ührer] durchgesetzt.*')

191. Domarus, 1714.

192. *TBJG*, I/9, 309 (13 May 1941).

193. *TBJG*, I/9, 311 (14 May 1941).

194. Domarus, 1716.

195. *TBJG*, I/9, 309 (13 May 1941).

196. *TBJG*, I/9, 309–10 (13 May 1941). And see Below, 274. The following day – after he had seen Hitler – he wrote that it had been necessary to bring out the communiqué of 12 May and to attribute the affair to Heß's delusions. 'How else could it have been explained?' he asked (*TBJG*, I/9, 311 (14 May 1941)).

197. *TBJG*, I/9, 311 (14 May 1941).

198. *Kriegspropaganda 1939–1941. Geheime Ministerkonferenzen im Reichspropagandaminister-ium*, ed. Willi A. Boelcke, Stuttgart, 1966, 728–36 (13, 14, 15 May 1941); Rudolf Semmler, *Goebbels – the Man Next to Hitler*, London, 1941, 32–3 (14 May 1941); Orlow, II.332.

199. *TBJG*, I/9, 311 (14 May 1941). Heß was, in fact, officially the third man in the Reich, having been designated in September 1939 as Hitler's successor after Göring in the event of his death (Domarus, 1709).

200. *TBJG*, I/9, 312–13 (14–15 May 1941).

201. Kershaw, *'Hitler Myth'*, 167.

202. GStA, MA 106671, report of the Regierungspräsident of Oberbayern, 10 June 1941: '. . . der Monat der Gerüchte'.

203. See Kershaw, *'Hitler Myth'*, 164.

204. *TBJG*, I/9, 313–14 (15 May 1941).

205. *TBJG*, I/9, 315 (16 May 1941).

206. Hans-Jochen Gamm, *Der Flüsterwitz im Dritten Reich*, Munich, 1972, 36; *The Berlin Diaries 1940–1945 of Marie 'Missie' Vassiltchikov*, London, 1985, 51 (18 May 1941), and 50–51 for other Heß jokes.

207. Kershaw, *'Hitler Myth'*, 160ff., 166–7.

208. See Hewel's description of the meeting, IfZ, ED 100, Irving-Sammlung, Hewel-Tagebuch, entry for 13 May 1941: 'Chief and Goring on the mountain. 4 o'clock all Reichsleiter and Gauleiter up there. Bormann reads out Heß's letters. Dramatic meeting. Great emotion. Führer comes, speaks very personally, analyses deed as such and proves mental disturbance through illogicality . . . Very moving demonstration. Sympathy. "The Führer is spared nothing."' ('*Chef und Göring auf dem Berg. 4 Uhr alle Reichsleiter und Gauleiter oben. Bormann verliest Heß' Briefe. Dramatische Versammlung. Große Ergriffenheit. Führer kommt, spricht sehr persönlich, analysiert Tat als solche und beweist Geistesgestörtheit an Unlogik. . . . Sehr ergreifende Kundgebung. Mitleid. "Dem Führer bleibt auch nichts erspart."'*)

209. Cit. Fest, *Face*, 292.

210. IfZ, MA 120/5, Fol.480, 'Rede Hans Franks über Wirkung des Englandflugs von Rudolf Heß': '*Der Führer war so vollkommen erschüttert, wie ich das eigentlich noch nicht erlebt habe.*' 'I was absolutely dismayed (*Ich war geradezu entsetzt*),' Frank wrote after the war, in prison in Nuremberg (Frank, 411).

211. Robert M. W. Kempner, *Das Dritte Reich im Kreuzverhör. Aus den Vernehmungsprotokollen des Anklägers*, Düsseldorf, 1984, 107–9 (testimony of Gauleiter Ernst Wilhelm Bohle).

212. *TBJG*, I/9, 312 (14 May 1941).

213. Kempner, 106.

214. R. Schmidt, 5 n.20, points out that the bugging of Bodenschatz's conversations with other former high-ranking officers of the Luftwaffe while he was in British captivity has undermined his evidence, and thereby the testimony on which so many have relied to claim that Hitler was implicated. Julius Schaub, Hitler's longstanding adjutant and general factotum, was convinced, in post-war testimony, that Hitler knew nothing of Heß's flight. (IfZ, ZS 137, Julius Schaub, Vernehmung, 12 March 1947, Fol.14).

215. See R. Schmidt, 5 n.20.

216. Costello tries to make the case for a British Secret Service plot. But for criticism, see R. Schmidt, 5 n.20. I am most grateful to Ted Harrison for the opportunity to read his, as yet, unpublished essay '". . . wir wurden schon viel zu oft hereingelegt"'. Mai 1941: Rudolf Heß in englischer Sicht', a thorough investigation of British intelligence and the Heß affair, which plainly demonstrates the absence of any plan to lure Heß to Britain, or prior knowledge that he was coming.

217. After the war, Göring poured scorn on the notion that Hitler had been behind the Heß flight. Would he have sent him on such a lone mission without the slightest preparation, he asked? Had he wanted to deal with Britain, semi-official channels through neutral countries (as had been the

case with Dahlerus) were open to him, and he, Göring, could through his connections have organized this within forty-eight hours (Irving, *Göring*, 323).

218. Cit. R. Schmidt, 14.

219. R. Schmidt, 15–16.

220. See also R. Schmidt, 26–7 for Heß's third interrogation with Lord Simon and Kirkpatrick on 9 June. Here, too, Heß explicitly denied any knowledge of his escapade by Hitler. See also National Archives, NND 881102, US intelligence report on Heß, 28 Oct. 1941: 'Hess has always insisted that Hitler had no knowledge of his flight.'

221. See Schmidt, 26.

222. Padfield, *Hess*, xiii for 'Fräulein Anna' and xiv for other unflattering nicknames. Sir John Simon concluded from his interrogation of Heß on 10 June 'that Heß's position and authority in Germany have declined and that if he could bring off the coup of early peace on Hitler's terms he would confirm his position . . . and render an immense service to his adored Master and to Germany' (cit. Schmidt, 28).

223. NA, NND-881102; Irving, *HW*, 246–7 and n.2. Harrison, 'Rudolf Heß' (unpubl. typescript, 2–4), points out that the British counter-intelligence organization MI5 had received on 2 November 1940 a letter from Albrecht Haushofer to Hamilton, dated 23 September and intercepted by British censors. This referred to a previous letter of July 1939, and suggested a meeting with Hamilton in Lisbon, or elsewhere on the periphery of Europe. MI5 discussed the letter with the Secret Service, with a view to using Hamilton to ply the Germans with misinformation. Hamilton himself was not consulted about the idea until some months later. Meanwhile, the original of the letter went missing. Hamilton's cagey response to the proposal left the British authorities hesitant about proceeding. It was at this point that Heß arrived.

224. *Diaries of Sir Alexander Cadogan*, 379, expressing Cadogan's impatience with Churchill's initial line, that Heß had come on a peace-mission, which he thought corresponded too closely with what German propaganda was saying. Churchill, in a furious temper, only bowed next day, 15 May, to pressure from Cadogan and other advisers to refrain from a public statement on the Heß affair. Massively relieved that the British had not acted as he would have done in making maximum propaganda capital out of the affair – 'the only but also dreadful danger for us' – Goebbels remarked that 'it seems as if a guardian angel is again standing near us', witheringly concluding that 'we're dealing with dim dilettantes (*mit doofen Dilettanten*) over there. What we would do if it were the other way round!' (*TBJG*, I/9, 315 (16 May 1941).

225. See R. Schmidt, 24.

226. R. Schmidt, 29.

227. Irving, *Göring*, 316–17, 327; Irving, *HW*, 221n.

228. R. Schmidt, 10; Gabriel Gorodetsky, 'Churchill's Warning to Stalin. A Reappraisal', *The Historical Journal*, 29 (1986), 979–90. For information reaching Stalin on the German military build-up, and his awareness of a coming invasion, see Valentin Falin, *Zweite Front. Die Interessenkonflikte in der Anti-Hitler-Koalition*, Munich, 1995, 193–5.

229. R. Schmidt, 18–19. Harrison, 'Rudolf Heß' (unpubl. typescript, 22–3), plays down the intent, emphasizing instead the confusion in the British Foreign Office and the missed propaganda opportunity, while acknowledging the enormous concern and misinterpretation which ensued in the Soviet leadership.

230. R. Schmidt, 34–6.

231. Stalin was still suspicious about the Heß affair, believing it had been a plot to involve Britain and Germany entering the war together against the Soviet Union, some three years later (Churchill, iii.49).

232. R. Schmidt, 32, 36. Such moves do not provide evidence of a prior intention on the part of the Soviet Union to attack Germany – the notorious 'preventive war theory'. See Chapter 9 n.4, below.

233. *Weisungen*, 139–40; Domarus, 1719–20; *Oxford Companion*, 571.

234. Elizabeth-Anne Wheal and Stephen Pope, *The Macmillan Dictionary of the Second World War*, 2nd edn, London, 1995, 57–9, contains a summary description of the sinking of the *Bismarck*. A vivid account is provided by Churchill, iii.Ch.XVII.

235. Hewel recorded the 'very depressed mood (*sehr deprimierte Stimmung*)' among the Nazi leadership on account of the fate of the *Bismarck*. Hitler was 'endlessly sad (*unendlich traurig*)', and had 'immeasurable anger at the navy leadership (*Maßlose Wut auf Seekriegsleitung*)' for failure to adopt the correct tactics and unnecessary exposure of the *Bismarck*. (IfZ, ED 100, Irving-Sammlung, Hewel-Tagebuch, entries for 26 May, especially, 27 May, and 31 May 1941. See also Raeder, *Mein Leben*, ii.269–71; *Lagevorträge*, 239 (6 June 1941); Irving, *HW*, 254, 258.)

236. Christopher R. Browning, *Ordinary Men. Reserve Police Battalion 101 and the Final Solution in Poland*, New York, 1992, 11.

237. *Anatomie*, ii.176–82, 206ff.

238. Krausnick/Wilhelm, 141–50; Höhne, *Death's Head*, 328–30.

239. Höhne, *Death's Head*, 328.

240. Krausnick/Wilhelm, 148.

241. Ulrich Herbert, ' "Generation der Sachlichkeit". Die völkische Studentenbewegung der frühen zwanziger Jahre in Deutschland', in Frank Bajohr, Werner Johe and Uwe Lohalm (eds.), *Zivilisation und Barbarei*, Hamburg, 1991, 115–44, especially 137–8.

242. Krausnick/Wilhelm, 148–9.

243. Höhne, *Death's Head*, 330.

244. *TBJG*, I/9, 346 (31 May 1941).

245. Domarus, 1722.

246. *CD*, 352 (1 June 1941).

247. IfZ, ED 100, Irving-Sammlung, Hewel-Tagebuch, entry for 2 June 1941; Irving, *HW*, 262. Hitler told Goebbels just before the invasion that Mussolini had been broadly orientated during their Brenner meeting (*TBJG*, I/9, 395 (22 June 1941)).

248. *CD*, 352 (2 June 1941).

249. Hitler, noted Goebbels on the day that 'Barbarossa' began, had nothing but contempt for Heß, who had caused the Party and the Wehrmacht enormous damage and ought to have been shot, had he not been mad (*TBJG*, I/9, 395–6 (22 June 1941)).

250. *CP*, 442.

251. *Staatsmänner* I, 260–76.

252. *CD*, 352 (1 June 1941); *CP*, 441; *Staatsmänner* I, 262–3.

253. *Staatsmänner* I, 264–6, 269–72, 276.

254. See Schmidt, 550.

255. Domarus, 1722.

256. *CD*, 352 (2 June 1941).

257. IfZ, ED 100, Irving-Sammlung, Hewel-Tagebuch, entry for 3 June 1941; Irving, *HW*, 262; Bernd Martin, *Deutschland und Japan im Zweiten Weltkrieg*, Göttingen, 1969, 97 n.13; Boyd, 21.

258. *Staatsmänner* I, 277–91.

259. *Staatsmänner* I, 279, 285, 289 and n.39.

260. *Staatsmänner* I, 280 n.14, 288 n.36, 289 n.39.

261. *Staatsmänner* I, 284–90.

262. *Staatsmänner* I, 291.

263. Below, 277.

264. *Halder KTB*, 455 (14 June 1941). Despite this apparent confidence, he had, in fact, only three days earlier issued Directive 32, laying out operational plans for continuing the struggle against the British position in the Mediterranean, North Africa, and the Middle East (*Weisungen*, 151ff.).

265. Below, 277.

266. Below, 278.

267. The following from *TBJG*, I/9, 377–80 (16 June 1941).

268. Below, 272–3. Goebbels was himself aware of accurate rumours and a good deal of tension both at home and abroad about the impending 'action' (*TBJG*, I/9, 372 (14 June 1941), 387 (19 June 1941)).

269. BA/MA, RW 20–13/9, 'Geschichte der Rüstungs-Inspektion XII', Fol.156: '*Die Konzentration zahlreicher Truppen in den Ostgebieten hatte zwar die Vermutung aufkommen lassen, als bereiten sich dort bedeutungsvolle Ereignisse vor, jedoch glaubte wohl der überwiegende Teil des deutschen Volkes an keine kriegerische Auseinandersetzung mit der Sowjet-Union.*'

270. *TBJG*, I/9, 380 (16 June 1941).

271. *TBJG*, I/9, 387 (19 June 1941); *Tb* Reuth, 1606 has 800,000. Goebbels had noted some days earlier that 30 million leaflets had been prepared in the Propaganda Ministry for distribution about the war in the east (*TBJG*, I/9, 366–7 (12 June 1941)).

272. Below, 278; *TBJG*, I/9, 395 (22 June 1941). Goebbels suggested a few alterations.

273. Below, 178–9; *TBJG*, I/9, 395 (22 June 1941).

274. *TBJG*, I/9, 395–6 (22 June 1941).

275. According to *KTB OKW*, 1.408 (22 June 1941), the attack began at 3a.m. Domarus, 1733, has it beginning at 3.05a.m.; *DRZW*, iv.451, states that it began between 3.00 and 3.30, noting (n.1) that the variations in time arose from the differing point of sunrise along such a lengthy front. *TBJG*, I/9, 396 (22 June 1941), has '3.30. Now the guns are thundering.'

276. *TBJG*, I/9, 396 (22 June 1941); *Tb* Reuth, 1611 n.128.

277. Domarus, 1727.

278. Domarus, 1731.

279. Domarus, 1732.

280. Domarus, 1735–6.

281. *DGFP*, D, XII, 1066–9, No.660, quotation 1069.

CHAPTER 9: SHOWDOWN

1. *TBJG*, II/1, 36–7 (9 July 1941); Domarus, 1732. Hitler was by summer 1942 sufficiently aware that the parallel was being drawn that he had 'experts' counter the talk by declaring that Napoleon really only commenced his march into Russia on 23 June (Picker, 462 (19 July 1942)).

2. *DRZW*, iv.72, 75; Leach, 192; Omer Bartov, 'From Blitzkrieg to Total War: Controversial Links between Image and Reality', in Kershaw and Lewin, 158–84, here 165 (who points out that the Luftwaffe deployed significantly fewer aircraft than in the Western campaign); Hartmut Schustereit, *Vabanque: Hitler's Angriff auf die Sowjetunion 1941 als Versuch, durch den Sieg im Osten den Westen zu bezwingen*, Herford, 1988, 30–41. A detailed evaluation of the rival forces and the early military operations is provided by David M. Glantz (ed.), *The Initial Period of War on the Eastern Front, 22 June–August 1941*, London, 1993; see 29–31 for Soviet troop dispositions and deployment on 22 June 1941.

3. *DRZW*, iv.Beiheft, maps 5, 7; Domarus, 1744 for the fall of Minsk, reported on 10 July.

4. See above all Gerd R. Ueberschär and Lev A. Bezymenskij (eds.), *Der deutsche Überfall auf die Sowjetunion. Die Kontroverse um die Präventivkriegsthese*, Darmstadt, 1988, here especially VIII–IX, 59, 100–101, and, for the plan of Timoshenko and Zhukov, 186–93. See also Gabriel Gorodetsky, 'Stalin und Hitlers Angriff auf die Sowjetunion. Eine Auseinandersetzung mit der Legende vom deutschen Präventivschlag', *VfZ*, 37 (1989), 645–72; and Bianka Pietrow, 'Deutschland im Juni 1941 – ein Opfer sowjetischer Aggression? Zur Kontroverse über die Präventivkriegsthese', *GG*, 14 (1988), 116–35. Stalin had in a speech on 5 May warned a large audience of graduates from Soviet military academies that war was imminent. But the belated discovery of a text of the speech, of which all copies were thought lost, has disproved those reports suggesting that Stalin was advocating a preventive war against Germany. See Lev A. Bezymenskıj, 'Stalıns Rede vom 5. Maı 1941 – neu dokumentiert', in Ueberschär and Bezymenskij, 131–44; also *DGFP*, D, XII, 964–5, No.593; Alexander Werth, *Russıa at War 1941–1945*, New York (1964), 1984, 122–3; John Erickson, *The Road to Stalıngrad. Stalin's War with Germany*, London, (1975), Phoenix paperback edn, 1998, 82; Falin, 194–7; Weinberg III, 203–4, Bullock, *Hıtler and Stalin*, 791, 798–9, 807.

5. Bullock, *Hitler and Stalin*, 791–3.

6. Volkogonov, 411–13.

7. Bernd Bonwetsch, 'Stalin, the Red Army, and the "Great Patriotic War"', in Kershaw and Lewın, 185–207, here 188, 193–5; and see Glantz, *Initial Period*, 31.

8. Soviet captives numbered some 3.8 million by the end of 1941, and 5.25 million by the end of the war (*DRZW*, ıv.727 (586 n.523 for slightly different figures for the numbers captured by late 1941)). At least 2½ mıllıon died in German captivity, apart from a minimum of 140,000 liquidated immediately on capture (*DRZW*, iv.730; Streit, ch.VII). Goebbels spoke in mid-December of 900,000 already dead of hunger, exhaustion, and illness, with many more certain to die ın the next weeks and months (*TBJG*, II.2, 484 (12 December 1941)). Shortly before this, Göring had spoken to Ciano of cannibalism in the Russian prison-of-war camps (*CP*, 464–5 (24–27 November 1941)).

9. Bonwetsch, 189.

10. See Streit, ch.VI; *DRZW*, iv.Teıl II, Kap.VII; Omer Bartov, *The Eastern Front, 1941–45, German Troops, and the Barbarisation of Warfare*, New York, 1986, Ch.4.

11. Volkogonov, 413; Irving, *HW*, 286–7.

12. *IMG*, xxxviii. 86–94, Doc. 221-L; Klee and Dreßen, *'Gott mit uns'*, 23 (meetıng of 16 July 1941). For the Wehrmacht's brutal struggle against the partisans, see Hannes Heer, 'Die Logik des Vernıchtungskriegs. Wehrmacht und Partisanenkampf', in Hannes Heer and Klaus Naumann (eds.), *Vernıchtungskrıeg. Verbrechen der Wehrmacht 1941 bis 1944*, Hamburg, 1995, 104–38; Hannes Heer, 'Kıllıng Fields: the Wehrmacht and the Holocaust in Belorussia, 1941–1942', *Holocaust and Genocide Studies*, 11 (1997), 79–101; Lutz Klınkhammer, 'Der Partisanenkrieg der Wehrmacht 1941–1944' and Timm C. Richter, 'Die Wehrmacht und der Partısanenkrieg ın den besetzten Gebieten der Sowjetunion', both in Müller and Volkmann, *Dıe Wehrmacht*, 815–36, 837–57.

13. *TBJG*, I/9, 398 (23 June 1941).

14. Below, 253, 281.

15. Domarus, 1743 for the name 'Wolf'; Schroeder, 111.

16. Below, 281–2; Warlimont, 172–3; Alfons Schulz, *Drei Jahre ın der Nachrıchtenzentrale des Führerhauptquartiers*, Stein am Rheın, 1996, 30–31, 39ff.; Hitler's succession decree relating to Görıng in Domarus, 1741.

17. Schroeder, 116, 120–21; Below, 282–3. Schroeder implies that the second brıefing of the day, as later ın the war, was late in the evening. But Below is precise in stıpulating that it took place during the early weeks of the campaign at 6 p.m.

18. Schroeder, 115.

19. Schroeder, 120–21.

20. Schroeder, 113.

21. Below, 282–3, 285.

22. *IMG*, xv, 325. See also Picker, 374 (28 May 1942), where life at FHQ was referred to by Picker as a 'monastic existence (*Klösterdasein*)'.

23. Schroeder, 119, 121–2.

24. Schroeder, 111–12. Goebbels remarked on the swarms of mıdges ın the area when he first visited FHQ on 8 July 1941 (*TBJG*, II/1, 30 (9 July 1941)).

25. Schroeder, 112.

26. Schroeder, 125.

27. Below, 283.

28. Schroeder, 113–14. For similarly optimistic notions from the OKW and Ribbentrop around this time, see Irving, *HW*, 282. In the earlier version of her memoirs, noted by Zoller, Hitler allegedly added that he would build a reservoir (*Staubecken*) on the site of Moscow (Zoller, 143).

29. Schroeder, 120.

30. *TBJG*, II/1, 30 (9 July 1941).

31. *TBJG*, II/1, 35 (9 July 1941).

32. *TBJG*, II/1, 32–5 (9 July 1941).

33. Schroeder, 113.

34. *Staatsmänner* I, 293. Oshima was impressed by what he heard of German progress in the war and recommended to his government that Japan quickly strike against the Soviet Union in the east (Boyd, 27).

35. Schroeder, 114.

36. Below, 283; Domarus, 1740.

37. *TBJG*, I/9, 412 (30 June 1941); Domarus, 1740 n.323.

38. *TBJG*, I/9, 412, 415–16 (30 July 1941), 415–16 (1 July 1941), 426 (5 July 1941).

39. Willi A. Boelcke (ed.), *Wollt Ihr den totalen Krieg? Die geheimen Goebbels-Konferenzen 1939–1943*, Munich, 1969, 235–7; *Tb* Reuth, 1623 n.144. And see Wolfram Wette, 'Die propagandistische Begleitmusik zum deutschen Überfall auf die Sowjetunion am 22. Juni 1941', in Gerd R. Ueberschär and Wolfram Wette (eds.), *'Unternehmen Barbarossa'. Der deutsche Überfall auf die Sowjetunion 1941. Berichte, Analysen, Dokumente*, Paderborn, 1984, 111–29, here especially 118–19.

40. See *TBJG*, II/1, 30–9 (9 July 1941): 'The Fuhrer is blazing about the Bolshevik leadership clique which intended to invade Germany, and thus Europe, and at the last moment, with the Reich weakened, to carry out the attempt to bolshevize the continent that had been planned since 1917' (31). 'The preventive war is always still the surest and mildest, if there is certainty that the enemy will in any case attack at the first best opportunity; and that was the case with Bolshevism' (33). 'Without doubt [the Kremlin] wanted this autumn, when we had no further possibility of aggressive action against Russia on account of the weather, to occupy Romania. Through this the Kremlin would have cut off our petroleum supply' (38). Hitler told his entourage in mid-September: 'It needed the greatest strength to take the decision last year for the attack on Bolshevism. I had to reckon that Stalin would go over to the attack in the course of this year. It was necessary to move as soon as at all possible. The earliest date was June 1941.' (*Monologe*, 60–61 (17–18 September 1941).)

41. *DRZW*, iv.461.

42. Leach, 200.

43. Leach, 202.

44. *KTB OKW*, i.1021; *DRZW*, iv.487; Leach, 201.

45. *Halder KTB*, iii, 38; trans. *Halder Diary*, 446–7 (3 July 1941).

46. *Monologe*, 39 (5–6 July 1941).

47. 'Aufzeichnungen des persönlichen Referenten Rosenbergs Dr Koeppen uber Hitlers Tischgespräche 1941' (= Koeppen), Fol. 15 (19 September 1941). In fact, as the hopes of the Volkswagenwerk of returning to production of cars for civilian use dimmed over the summer and autumn of 1941, the campaign in the east demanded the production of more and more tanks. (See Hans Mommsen and Manfred Grieger, *Das Volkswagenwerk und seine Arbeiter im Dritten Reich*, Düsseldorf, 1996, 453, 460ff.)

48. *Monologe*, 39 (5–6 July 1941).

49. Koeppen, Fol.9 (10 September 1941).

50. Koeppen, Fol.12 (19 September 1941). Goebbels reported Hitler's intention on 18 August as the starvation of St Petersburg (Leningrad) and Kiev. Once Leningrad had been put under siege and the bombardment had taken place, ran Hitler's plan, 'there would probably not be much left of this city' (*TBJG*, II/1, 260–61 (19 August 1941)).

51. *Monologe*, 48 (27 July 1941).

52. Koeppen, Fol.28 (23 September 1941).

53. *Monologe*, 38 (5 July 1941).

54. Koeppen, Fol.12 (19 September 1941).

55. Koeppen, Fol.28 (24 September 1941).

56. *Monologe*, 42 (11–12 July 1941).

57. In September, Hitler commented that it would be a mistake to educate the native population. All this would achieve would be the sort of semi-knowledge that leads to revolution. (*Monologe*, 63 (17–18 September 1941); Koeppen, Fol.12 (18 September 1941).

58. *Monologe*, 48 (27 July 1941).

59. *Monologe*, 54–5 (8–11 August 1941).

60. *Monologe*, 51 (1–2 August 1941).

61. *Monologe*, 54 (8–11 August 1941).

62. *Monologe*, 55 (8–11 August 1941). He repeated the sentiments in similar words a month later. 'The Russian territory (*Raum*) is our India,' he stated, 'and just as the English rule it with a handful of people, so we will govern this, our colonial territory' (*Monologe*, 62–3 (17–18 September 1941)); Koeppen, Fol.12 (18 September 1941).

63. A month after these comments in mid-August, Hitler enthused about the capture of the iron-ore district of Kriwoi-Rog, whose productive capacity, he claimed, removed all worries about covering demand (Koeppen, Fol.10 (17 September 1941)).

64. *Monologe*, 58 (19–20 August 1941).

65. *Monologe*, 63 (17–18 September 1941).

66. *Monologe*, 62 (17–18 September 1941).

67. *Monologe*, 69–71 (25 September 1941).

68. *Monologe*, 66 (23 September 1941).

69. *Monologe*, 67 (23 September 1941); Koeppen, Fol.29 (23 September 1941).

70. *Monologe*, 68 (25 September 1941). On 27–28 September, he spoke of the aim of fighting war 'on the edges' of German territory (*Monologe*, 72). Hitler had referred earlier to a 'living wall' to protect the new east 'against the mid-Asian masses' (*Monologe*, 55 (8–11 August 1941)). See also Rolf-Dieter Muller, *Hitlers Ostkrieg und die deutsche Siedlungspolitik*, Frankfurt am Main, 1991, 23–4.

71. *Monologe*, 71 (25–6 September 1941).

72. *Monologe*, 71 (25–6 September 1941).

73. *Monologe*, 58 (19–20 August 1941).

74. *Monologe*, 72 (27–8 September 1941).

75. *Monologe*, 65 (22–3 September 1941).

76. *Monologe*, 65 (22–3 September 1941).

77. An overemphasis on Hitler's 'modernity' runs through the interpretation of Rainer Zitelmann, *Hitler. Selbstverständnis eines Revolutionärs*, Hamburg/Leamington Spa/New York, 1987. See also Rainer Zitelmann, *Adolf Hitler. Eine politische Biographie*, Göttingen, 1989, and his essay 'Die totalitäre Seite der Moderne', in Michael Prinz and Rainer Zitelmann (eds.), *Nationalsozialismus und Modernisierung*, Darmstadt, 1991, 1–20. For strong criticism of such an emphasis, see Hans Mommsen, 'Nationalsozialismus als vorgetäuschte Modernisierung', in Walter H. Pehle (ed.), *Der historische Ort des Nationalsozialismus. Annäherungen*, Frankfurt am Main, 1990, 11–46; Norbert Frei, 'Wie modern war der Nationalsozialismus?', *GG*, 19 (1993), 367–87, here especially 374ff.; Axel Schildt, 'NS-Regime, Modernisierung und Moderne. Anmerkungen zur Hochkonjunktur einer andauernden Diskussion', *Tel Aviver Jahrbuch für deutsche Geschichte*, 23 (1994), 3–22, here especially 11ff.

78. *Monologe*, 57 (8–11 August 1941).

79. *Monologe*, 64 (17–18 September 1941).

80. *IMG*, xxxviii, 86–94, quotation 87–8, Doc. 221-L; *DGFP*, 3, 13, 149–56, No.114; extracts in Klee and Dreßen, *Gott mit uns*, 22–3. See also Alexander Dallin, *German Rule in Russia 1941–1945. A Study of Occupation Policies*, (1957), 2nd edn, Basingstoke/London, 1981, 84, 123, 204; and Eberhard Jackel, 'Hitlers doppeltes Kernstuck', in Roland G. Foerster (ed.), *'Unternehmen Barbarossa'. Zum historischen Ort der deutsch-sowjetischen Beziehungen von 1933 bis Herbst 1941*, Munich, 1993, 14–22, here 14–18.

81. *IMG*, xxix, 235–7, 1997-PS.

82. *CP*, 465 (24–7 November 1941); Klee and Dreßen, *Gott mit uns*, 23; Halder *KTB*, ii.335–8 (30 March 1941); *IMG*, xxxi.135–7, 126-EC. The plans for mass deportation were in the process of being worked out for the 'General Plan for the East'. See Helmut Heiber (ed.), 'Der Generalplan Ost', *VfZ*, 6 (1958), 281–325; Czeslaw Madajczyk (ed.), *Vom Generalplan Ost zum Generalsiedlungsplan*, Munich etc., 1994; Mechtild Rößler and Sabine Schleiermacher (eds.), *Der 'Generalplan Ost'. Hauptlinien der nationalsozialistischen Planungs- und Vernichtungspolitik*, Berlin, 1993.

83. Dallin, ch.3, especially 56ff.

84. Dallin, 84, 123–4. Civilian rule was established in the occupied territories in August and September 1941 (Dallin, 85).

85. Koeppen, Fols.12–13 (18 September 1941).

86. Dallin, 185ff.

87. Dallin, 203ff.

88. *Halder KTB*, iii.10 (24 June 1941).

89. *Halder KTB*, iii.15 (25 June 1941); trans. *Halder Diary*, 424.

90. *Halder KTB*, iii.20 (27 June 1941), 25 (29 June 1941), 29 (30 June 1941), 34–5 (2 July 1941), 39 (3 July 1941).

91. *Halder KTB*, iii.39 (3 July 1941); trans. *Halder Diary*, 448.

92. *DRZW*, iv.212–13; Leach, 53, 99; Dirks/Janßen, 137ff.

93. *DRZW*, iv.219–42; Leach, 99–118, 250–69. See above, Chapter 7, n.157, for Loßberg's post-war claim to have begun work on the strategic study already in early July 1940, and without any formal request to do so. In his post-war memoirs, Bernhard von Loßberg, *Im Wehrmachtführungsstab. Bericht eines Generalstabsoffiziers*, Hamburg, 1950, 104–8, Loßberg makes no mention of this.

94. See *Halder KTB*, ii.463–9, 'Aufmarschanweisung OKH vom 31.1.1941 "Barbarossa"' (Leach, 263–9 (OKH Deployment Directive, 'Barbarossa', 31 January 1941). The Directive was discussed by Halder and Brauchitsch with the three Army Group Commanders on 31 January 1941, then issued on 19 February 1941 (*Halder KTB*, ii.264 n.1, 266 (31 January 1941, 2 February 1941). Mention of Moscow was confined to a single sentence: 'In the event of a sudden unexpected collapse of enemy resistance in northern Russia, the abandonment of the turning movement and an immediate thrust towards Moscow could be considered' (*Halder KTB*, ii.465; trans. Leach, 264).

95. *Weisungen*, 98–9 (No.21, 18 December 1940). Hitler's significant amendment to the original plan of attack had been conveyed to Jodl on 17 December 1940, the day before the issuing of Directive No.21 for 'Barbarossa' (*KTB OKW*, 1.233).

96. *Halder KTB*, iii.24–5 (29 June 1941).

97. *KTB OKW*, 1.1020; *DRZW*, iv.486–7; and see Warlimont, 182.

98. *DRZW*, iv.487.

99. Leach, 197.

100. *DRZW*, iv.487; Leach, 216.

101. *KTB OKW*, i.1030 (during Hitler's visit to Leeb in Army Group North on 21 July). See also Warlimont, 186; *DRZW*, iv.495.

102. *Weisungen*, 166 (23 July 1941); *DRZW*, iv.490; Leach, 198.

103. *KTB OKW*, i.1030; *Halder KTB*, iii.103–7 (23 July 1941), especially 104 and n.1, 106 (quotation); *DRZW*, iv.491.

104. *Weisungen*, 165; *DRZW*, iv.689–93; Leach, 204. Hitler's Directive No.33 of 19 July 1941,

'Continuation of the War in the East', had, however, indicated that air-raids supporting the army on the south-eastern front, not on Moscow, were the first priority (*Weisungen*, 164–5). Göring later described the raids on Moscow as 'prestige attacks', prompted by sarcastic remarks by Hitler casting doubt on whether the Luftwaffe had a single squadron with the courage to raid Moscow (*DRZW*, iv.693).

105. Leach, 205.

106. *Halder KTB*, iii.151 (4 August 1941). Under 'Losses (*Verluste*)' Halder noted 46,470 officers and men dead, 11,758 missing, and 155,073 injured.

107. Leach, 205–7, 210.

108. Leach, 207.

109. *KTB OKW*, i.1033.

110. *DRZW*, iv.493.

111. *KTB OKW*, i.1037, 1040.

112. Warlimont, 185; Leach, 208.

113. *KTB OKW*, i.1040; *DRZW*, iv.495–6; Leach, 209.

114. *Halder KTB*, iii. 134 (30 July 1941); trans. *Halder Diary*, 490.

115. *Weisungen*, 168–9; *DRZW*, iv.495; Leach, 209.

116. *DRZW*, iv.495–6.

117. *DRZW*, iv. 499–500.

118. *Halder KTB*, iii.170 (11 August 1941); trans. *Halder Diary*, 506.

119. *Weisungen*, 173; and see DRZW, iv.503; Warlimont, 187.

120. *DRZW*, iv.504.

121. *TBJG*, II/1, 258 (19 August 1941). Hitler's own – exaggerated – view was that he had not been ill since he was sixteen years old (*Monologe*, 190 (9–10 January 1942)).

122. Irving, *Doctor*, 87–8; Irving, *HW*, 293–5.

123. *TBJG*, II/1, 260–3 (19 August 1941).

124. Laurence Rees, *War of the Century. When Hitler Fought Stalin*, London, 1999, 52–6; Volkogonov, 412–13.

125. *TBJG*, II/1, 266 (19 August 1941).

126. *KTB OKW*, ii.1055–9; *DRZW*, iv.505.

127. Adolf Heusinger, *Befehl im Widerstreit. Schicksalsstunden der deutschen Armee 1923–1945*, Tübingen/Stuttgart, 1950, 132–5; Warlimont, 189 (whose translation has been used).

128. *KTB OKW*, i.1061–3 (Halder's memorandum, and Hitler's order); *Halder KTB*, iii.192 (22 August 1941), trans. *Halder Diary*, 514; Warlimont, 190.

129. *KTB OKW*, i.1065; *Halder KTB*, iii.193 (22 August 1941); *DRZW*, iv.506; Warlimont, 190–91.

130. *KTB OKW*, ii.1063–8 (Hitler's 'Study'); *DRZW*, iv.505–6.

131. *Halder KTB*, iii.193 (22 August 1941); trans. *Halder Diary*, 515; and see Bock, 290–91 (23 August 1941), and Hartmann, 283.

132. Above from Guderian, 198–202.

133. Hartmann, 283–4; Halder's reaction to Guderian's change of mind in *Halder KTB*, iii.194–5 (24 August 1941).

134. Bock, 291 (24 August 1941); Hartmann, 284 n.57.

135. A point made by Warlimont, 191.

136. *DRZW*, iv.514, 516, 516 n.252; Leach, 222 (slightly different figures).

137. Leach, 222.

138. *DRZW*, iv.516; Warlimont, 193, on agreement now on the necessity of reaching Moscow before the winter.

139. In fact, once the German blockade set in, around 2.5 million civilians would be practically trapped – apart from a path over the iced Lake Ladoga – in the city over an exceptionally icy winter and beyond. (The siege would finally be raised only at the end of January 1944.) With supply routes

cut off, famine conditions quickly took hold. Horses and stray dogs were rapidly consumed. Bread and gruel were in exceedingly short supply. Most people had to resort to root vegetables and, when they dried up, an unholy concoction made from peat and paper. An estimated 850–950,000 are estimated to have succumbed to starvation, cold, and illness. (Osobyi Arkhiv (Sonderarchiv), Moscow, 500–1–25, 'Ereignismeldung UdSSR Nr.191', 10 April 1942, Fols.264–70; *Oxford Companion*, 683–6; Richard Overy, *Russia's War*, London, 1997, 105–11.)

140. *TBJG*, II/1, 481–3 (24 September 1941).

141. *TBJG*, II.1, 486 (24 September 1941).

142. *TBJG*, II/1, 482 (24 September 1941). In fact, Hitler was hoping to be able to withdraw a good number of divisions after attaining the next military goals. Halder had decided as early as 8 July to make winter arrangements for an occupying rather than a combat force in the Soviet Union (*Halder KTB*, iii.53 (8 July 1941); Dallin, 62).

143. An attached cover-note by Keitel of 1 September states that Hitler had approved the Memorandum. Its circulation was restricted on Hitler's orders to the Commanders-in-Chief of the branches of the Wehrmacht, and the Reich Foreign Minister (Ribbentrop). Chief of Staff Halder presumably saw it only several days after its initial distribution, since he noted extracts in his diary entry for 13 September. (*ADAP*, D, XIII, 345–53, quotation 352, No. 265; *DGFP*, D, 13, 422–33, quotation 431, No.265; *Halder KTB*, iii.226–9; *DRZW*, iv.507; Warlimont, 192–3.)

144. *Halder KTB*, iii.205 (29 August 1941).

145. *DRZW*, IV. 571.

146. See Leach, 220, 222.

147. Bonwetsch, 203ff. (though the change was only gradual, and from 1942 onwards). For an emphasis, diluting the blame attached exclusively to Stalin, on the structural weaknesses in the Red Army in 1941, but rapid remedial action taken, see Jacques Sapir, 'The Economics of War in the Soviet Union during World War II', in Kershaw and Lewin, 208–36, here 216–19. See also David M. Glantz and Jonathan M. House, *When Titans Clashed. How the Red Army stopped Hitler*, Kansas, 1995, 65ff.

148. Leach, 234–7 (and see also pp.118–23) for above.

149. Leach, 212, 223–4. Whether Soviet determination to stand and defend Moscow, backed by utterly ruthless butchery of those attempting to flee, would have been sustainable had Stalin fled from the capital might, however, be doubted. And such an eventuality was close in mid-October, when a special train was waiting under steam at one of Moscow's stations ready to carry the Soviet dictator out of the city. Stalin seems to have pondered the likely consequences for morale, however, and decided to stay. (Volkogonov, 434–5; Edvard Radzinsky, *Stalin*, New York, 1996, 482–3; Rees, *War of the Century*, 71–4; Bonwetsch, 189; Glantz and House, 81; Heinz Magenheimer, *Hitler's War. German Military Strategy, 1940–1945*, London, 1998, 117–18. For a guide through the labyrinth of interpretations, see Rolf-Dieter Müller and Gerd R. Ueberschär, *Hitler's War in the East 1941–1945. A Critical Assessment*, Providence/Oxford, 1997, 85–104, especially 99ff.)

150. See Leach, 238–41.

151. Hauner, *Hitler*, 151–2.

152. Hauner, *Hitler*, 166–8. For Udet, whose death was attributed by the regime to an accident while testing a new aeroplane, see Wistrich, 280.

153. Rebentisch, 374.

154. Lang, *Der Sekretär*, 464.

155. Rebentisch, 374.

156. Steinert, 206–8.

157. Boelcke, *Wollt Ihr*, 236.

158. Steinert, 209–13; Boelcke, *Wollt Ihr*, 234–44; Seydewitz, 70–72.

159. Heinrich Breloer (ed.), *Mein Tagebuch. Geschichten vom Überleben 1939–1947*, Cologne, 1984, 63.

160. Breloer, 63.

161. StA Bamberg, K8/III, 18475, report of the Landrat of Ebermannstadt, 1 July 1941: '*Nicht das geringste Verständnis besteht für die Verwirklichung von Weltherrschaftsplanen . . . Die überarbeiteten und abgewirtschafteten Männer und Frauen sehen nicht ein, warum der Krieg noch weiter nach Asien und Afrika hineingetragen werden muß.*'

162. StA Bamberg, K8/III, 18475, report of the Landrat of Ebermannstadt, 30 August 1941; printed in Martin Broszat, Elke Fröhlich, and Falk Wiesemann (eds.), *Bayern in der NS-Zeit. Soziale Lage und politisches Verhalten der Bevölkerung im Spiegel vertraulicher Berichte*, Munich/Vienna, 1977, 152.

163. Steinert, 213–14.

164. StA Munich, LRA 61618, report of Gendarmerie-Posten Mittenwald, 24 May 1941 ('*schlecht und kriegsmüde*'); report of Gendarmerie-Kreisführer Mittenwald, 28 November 1941 ('. . . *die sich stetig steigernden großen und kleinen Alltagssorgen . . .*').

165. Conway, 259–60, 383–6.

166. For Bormann's increasing intervention in Church matters during the war, see Longerich, *Hitlers Stellvertreter*, 250ff.

167. Kershaw, *Popular Opinion*, 332–4; E. D. R. Harrison, 'The Nazi Dissolution of the Monasteries: a Case Study', *English Historical Review*, 109 (1994), 323–55, here 336–41.

168. GStA Munich, Epp-Akten 157, Reichsstatthalter Epp to Lammers, 23 December 1941: '*Staatsminister Wagner wollte mit seinem Kruzifixerlaß auf seine Weise der von Reichsleiter Bormann herausgegebenen Lehre, daß Nationalsozialismus und Christentum unvereinbare Gegensätze seien, sichtbare Auswirkung verschaffen . . .*'

169. Landratsamt Traunstein, IV-7-177, anonymous letter to the Landrat of the Landkreis Traunstein, 20 September 1941: '*Die Söhne unserer Stadt stehen im Osten im Kampf gegen den Bolshewismus. Viele aus ihnen geben dafür ihr Leben. Wir können nicht verstehen, dass man uns gerade in dieser schweren Zeit das Kreuz aus den Schulen nehmen will.*'

170. See Kershaw, *Popular Opinion*, 340–57; Heinrich Huber (ed.), *Dokumente einer christlichen Widerstandsbewegung. Gegen die Entfernung der Kruzifixe aus den Schulen 1941*, Munich, 1948.

171. Cit. Kershaw, '*Hitler Myth*', 178.

172. Landratsamt Parsberg 939, report of the Landrat of Parsberg, 19 September 1941: 'Durchführung des Kreuzerlasses in Parsberg': '. . . *das will der Führer nicht und er weiss bestimmt nichts von dieser Kreuzentfernung*'.

173. StA Munich, LRA 31933, anonymous letter (undated but received on 2 October 1941) to the Bürgermeister of Ramsau, Landkreis Berchtesgaden: '*Braune Hemden trägt Ihr von Oben, Innen raus seid Bolschewisten u. Juden sonst könnt Ihr nicht handeln des Führers Rücken . . .*' (grammar and punctuation as in the original).

174. See Kershaw, *Popular Opinion*, 340; Lutz Lemhöfer, 'Gegen den gottlosen Bolschewismus. Zur Stellung der Kirchen zum Krieg gegen die Sowjetunion', in Ueberschär and Wette, 131–9, here 135–6.

175. This was the implication of the interpretation by Peter Hüttenberger, 'Vorüberlegungen zum "Widerstandsbegriff"', in Jürgen Kocka (ed.), *Theorien in der Praxis des Historikers*, Göttingen, 1977, 117–34.

176. Klee, 'Euthanasie', 290.

177. Klee, 'Euthanasie', 324–5.

178. Klee, 'Euthanasie', 206ff., 289–91.

179. Honolka, 84–90; Klee, 'Euthanasie', 286–7.

180. Klee, 'Euthanasie', 334.

181. Klee, 'Euthanasie', 334, 486–7 n.127.

182. Heinz Boberach (ed.), *Berichte des SD und der Gestapo über Kirchen und Kirchenvolk*, Mainz, 1971, 570–71.

183. Harrison, 'Dissolution', 349–50.

184. Cit. Harrison, 'Dissolution', 350; Peter Löffler (ed.), *Bischof Clemens August Graf von Galen. Akten, Briefe und Predigten, vol.2, 1939–1946*, Mainz, 1988, 864–6.

185. Harrison, 'Dissolution', 352; see also Löffler, 874–83; and Ludwig Volk, 'Episkopat und Kirchenkampf', in Dieter Albrecht (ed.), *Katholische Kirche und Nationalsozialismus. Ausgewählte Aufsätze von Ludwig Volk*, Mainz, 1987, 94.

186. Klee, *Dokumente*, 193–8; trans. *N & P*, iii.1036–9.

187. Harrison, 'Dissolution', 352; Lewy, 253.

188. Papen, 481–2.

189. See Harrison, 'Dissolution', 325–6.

190. Picker, 260 (7 April 1942).

191. Bernhard Stasiewski, 'Die Kirchenpolitik der Nationalsozialisten im Warthegau 1939–1945', *VfZ*, 7 (1959), 46–74, here 65.

192. Papen, 481–2.

193. Klee, 'Euthanasie', 335.

194. Klee, 'Euthanasie', 335.

195. *TBJG*, II/2, 33 (1 October 1941).

196. *TBJG*, II/1, 239 (15 August 1941). Goebbels referred to the possibility of linking the 'debate' to the film justifying 'euthanasia', *Ich klage an* (*I Accuse*), which he had commissioned and was now almost ready for release. See Welch, *Propaganda and the German Cinema*, 121ff. for the content of the film, first shown in Berlin on 29 August 1941.

197. Klee, 'Euthanasie', 339; Eugen Kogon et al. (eds.), *Nationalsozialistische Massentötungen durch Giftgas. Eine Dokumentation*, Frankfurt am Main, 1983, 62.

198. Aly, 314–15.

199. The above based on Aly, 313, 316.

200. Klee, 'Euthanasie', 340–41.

201. *TBJG*, I/9, 119 (31 January 1941).

202. Klee, 'Euthanasie', 340–41.

203. Klee, 'Euthanasie', 345ff., 417ff.

204. *TBJG*, II/1, 484 (24 September 1941).

205. The aim was to destroy the Soviet Army Group of Marshal Timoschenko before the onset of winter and, only once that was achieved, to advance on Moscow. (*Weisungen*, 174–8. For the military developments, see *DRZW*, iv.568ff.)

206. *TBJG*, II/2, 44 (3 October 1941).

207. Domarus, 1756.

208. Domarus, 1757.

209. *TBJG*, II/2, 50 (4 October 1941).

210. *TBJG*, II/2, 50–1 (4 October 1941).

211. *TBJG*, II/2, 51 (4 October 1941).

212. *TBJG*, II/2, 52 (4 October 1941). During the coming fortnight, Stalin would come close to fleeing from Moscow and, according to one piece of anecdotal evidence, did contemplate – if this is accurate, for a second time, following such considerations in July – putting feelers out to Germany for peace-terms (Rees, *War of the Century*, 55–6).

213. *TBJG*, II/2, 54 (4 October 1941).

214. Hewel's diary entry notes for the afternoon of 3 October: '. . . With the Führer to the Sportpalast. Great speech – impromptu. Tremendously rapt. Directly afterwards to the train and back to Headquarters.' ('. . . *mit dem F[ührer] zum Sportpalast. Ganz große Rede – aus dem Stehgreif. Unerhört andachtsvoll. Direkt anschließend zum Zug und zurück ins Hauptquartier.*' (IfZ, ED 100. And see Irving, *HW*, 319.)

215. *TBJG*, II/2, 55 (4 October 1941).

216. Domarus, 1759.

217. Domarus, 1763.

218. *TBJG*, II/2, 55–6 (4 October 1941).

219. Koeppen, Fol.36 (Midday, 4 October 1941); *TBJG*, II/2, 56 (4 October 1941).

220. *TBJG*, II/2, 53, 56 (4 October 1941).

221. *TBJG*, II/2, 56 (4 October 1941).

222. *TBJG*, II/2, 55 (4 October 1941).

223. *TBJG*, II/2, 56 (4 October 1941).

224. See Irving, *HW*, 318.

225. *Halder KTB*, iii.266 (4 October 1941), 268 (5 October 1941).

226. *DRZW*, iv.574, where it is pointed out that the fighting-power, with many of the units scarcely rested and having suffered serious losses, was not up to that of the force of 22 June. See also Koeppen, 32 (2 October 1941).

227. *DRZW*, iv.765; see also 575ff.; Below, 292, has over 660,000 prisoners.

228. IfZ, ED 100 (Hewel diary), entry for 7 October 1941: 'Viaz'ma taken. Ring round Timoschenko army closed. Jodl: Most decisive day of the Russian war. Comparison with Königgrätz'. ('*Wiasma genommen. Ring um Timoschenko-Armee geschlossen. Jodl: Entscheidenster Tag des Russenkrieges. Vergleich mit Königgrätz*'.) For the confidence of Army Group Centre and of Halder, see *DRZW*, iv.576.

229. Wagner, *Der Generalquartiermeister*, 204.

230. Koeppen, Fols.45–6 (8–9 October 1941).

231. *Monologe*, 77 (10–11 October 1941). By early December, Hitler was admitting that the Wehrmacht had no satisfactory defence against the heavy Soviet tanks (*TBJG*, II.2, 467 (10 December 1941); Below, 297.)

232. Koeppen, Fol. 48 (16 October 1941).

233. Koeppen, Fol. 37 (4 October 1941).

234. Koeppen, Fol. 40 (5 October 1941).

235. *Monologe*, 78 (13 October 1941).

236. Koeppen, Fols. 51–2 (17 October 1941).

237. Bock, 337 (21 October 1941).

238. Koeppen, Fol. 57 (19 October 1941).

239. See Koeppen, Fols. 53, 57, 62 (18 October 1941, 19 October 1941, 23 October 1941). Goebbels comments several times on the bad weather: e.g. *TBJG*, II/2, 96 (11 October 1941); 152 (21 October 1941); 204 (30 October 1941), where he remarks that 'the weather situation has made almost our entire operations in the east impossible'. See also *DRZW*, iv.578–82 for deterioration in the weather and the growing transport and supplies crisis; and for the suggestion that the bad weather was not unseasonally early, Domarus, 1770, n.439.

240. Koeppen, Fol. 72 (26 October 1941).

241. Below, 294.

242. *TBJG*, II/2, 215 (1 November 1941).

243. *Halder KTB*, iii.58 (9 July 1941), 142 (2 August 1941); E. Wagner, 206–7 (letters of 12 and 20 October). Trains with winter equipment had been standing in sidings near Breslau and Cracow since the end of August, but frozen engines and shortage of wagons were among the reasons why supplies to the front could not be sustained. (E. Wagner, 206n., 266–7. See also Irving, *HW*, 333, 851; Leach, 212.)

244. *TBJG*, II/2, 213 (1 November 1941).

245. *TBJG*, II/2, 214–18 (1 November 1941).

246. *DRZW*, iv.578 for military optimism in mid-October, 584–5 for unrealistic expectations. See also Irving, *HW*, 339.

247. *DRZW*, iv.585.

248. Domarus, 1771–81 for the text of the speech. The Bürgerbräukeller had still not been repaired since the attack on Hitler's life there two years earlier (Domarus, 1771 n.446).

249. *TBJG*, II/2, 259 (10 November 1941).

250. Domarus, 1775.

251. Domarus, 1776.

252. Domarus, 1778.

253. *TBJG*, II/2, 261–2 (10 November 1941); Orlow, ii.270–71; Johannes Volker Wagner, *Hakenkreuz über Bochum*, Bochum, 1983, 206.

254. Hitler had declared in his speech the previous day that 'a November 1918 will never repeat itself in Germany! It cannot repeat itself. Everything is possible except one thing: that Germany will ever capitulate!' (Domarus, 1778).

255. *TBJG*, II/2, 262 (10 November 1941).

256. *TBJG*, II/2, 262–3 (10 November 1941), quotation 263.

257. The journey took so long because the Special Train did not travel at night (Koeppen, Fol. 80 (6 November 1941)).

258. Guderian, 245–8.

259. *DRZW*, iv.586, gives losses of 277,000 men by 16 October, with a replacement available of 151,000 men.

260. Guderian, 247.

261. *DRZW*, iv.586–7, 591–2.

262. *DRZW*, iv.587–8. See also Hartmann, 292–3.

263. See Engel, 113–16 (12 November 1941, 16 November 1941, 22 November 1941, 24 November 1941) for Hitler's uncertainty.

264. *DRZW*, iv.590–91.

265. Engel, 116 (25 November 1941).

266. *TBJG*, II/2, 336–7 (22 November 1941). The British Army had begun its counter-offensive on 18 November.

267. *TBJG*, II/2, 337 (22 November 1941).

268. *TBJG*, II/2, 338 (22 November 1941).

269. *TBJG*, II/2, 364 (25 November 1941).

270. *MadR*, ix.3120 (5 January 1942).

271. *TBJG*, II/2, 403 (30 November 1941).

272. Halder *KTB*, iii.315 (28 November 1941); *KTB OKW*, i.781 (28 November 1941); Irving, *HW*, 342.

273. *TBJG*, II/2, 398–9 (30 November 1941).

274. *TBJG*, II/2, 399–401 (30 November 1941).

275. *TBJG*, II/2, 401 (30 November 1941).

276. *TBJG*, II/2, 403 (30 November 1941).

277. Seidler, *Fritz Todt*, 356. This contrasted with Hitler's view, as expressed to Goebbels on 21 November, that the entry of the USA into the war posed no acute threat and could not alter the situation on the Continent (*TBJG*, II/2, 339 (22 November 1941)).

278. Walter Rohland, *Bewegte Zeiten. Erinnerungen eines Eisenhüttenmannes*, Stuttgart, 1978, 78; Seidler, 356–7.

279. *TBJG*, II/2, 404 (30 November 1941). By this time, the casualties – dead, wounded, missing – on the eastern front had risen sharply, now amounting since the starting of 'Barbarossa' to 743,112 persons, or 23 per cent of the eastern army (*Halder KTB*, iii.318 (30 November 1941)).

280. *Halder KTB*, iii.319 (30 November 1941).

281. *Halder KTB*, iii.322 (1 December 1941).

282. *Halder KTB*, iii.322 (1 December 1941).

283. *Halder KTB*, iii.325 (3 December 1941); Domarus, 1787.

284. Irving, *HW*, 349–50.

285. Guderian, 258–60.

286. Irving, *HW*, 350.

287. Irving, *HW*, 352, has (without source) Heinz Lorenz, a press officer in FHQ, bursting in with the news – just announced on an American radio station – towards midnight. The Japanese attack at Pearl Harbor took place in the early morning of Sunday, 7 December, local time, and was over by 9.45a.m. – evening in central Europe. Churchill heard of the attack shortly after 9p.m. (Churchill, iii.537). A junior officer in FHQ at the time stated from memory many years later that an orderly had brought a telegram from Berlin with the news during the evening meal, shortly before 8p.m. (though the date given, 9 December, is plainly erroneous). (Unpublished notes (25 April 1997) and taped interview with Hans Mommsen of Wolfgang Brocke, a Leutnant in the Technischer Kriegsverwaltungsrat who had served on the staff of the Führer-Begleitbataillon in FHQ since 22 June 1941. I am grateful to Hans Mommsen for giving me access to this material.

288. *TBJG*, II.2, 455 (9 December 1941). The Japanese Embassy in Berlin had initially reported the sinking of two battleships (*Virginia* and *Oklahoma*) and two cruisers (*KTB OKW*, i.803). In fact, the attack proved less of a military disaster in the long run than imagined at the time. The battleship *Arizona* was blown up, seven others grounded, and ten other ships sunk or damaged. Over 2,400 American servicemen were killed and a further 1,100 wounded. But the two aircraft carriers with the Pacific fleet were not in the harbour at the time and escaped. Most of the ships could be repaired. All the battleships except the *Arizona* returned to service (and contributed to later American naval victories). Most of the crew members survived and continued in service (Weinberg III, 260–61).

289. Weinberg III, 261.

290. Churchill, iii. 537–43 (quotation 538).

291. IfZ, ED 100, Hewel-Tagebuch, entry for 8 December 1941: '*Wir können den Krieg garnicht verlieren. Wir haben jetzt einen Bundesgenossen, der in 3 000 Jahren nicht besiegt worden ist ...*' Hitler remarked, a few days later (entry for 16 December 1941): 'Strange, that with the help of Japan we will destroy the positions of the white race in East Asia and that England fights against Europe with the Bolshevik swine.' ('*Seltsam, daß wir mit Hilfe Japans die Positionen der weißen Rasse in Ostasien vernichten und daß England mit den bolshewistischen Schweinen gegen Europa kämpft.*')

292. See Eberhard Jäckel, 'Die deutsche Kriegserklärung an die Vereinigten Staaten von 1941', in Friedrich J. Kroneck and Thomas Oppermann (eds.), *Im Dienste Deutschlands und des Rechts: Festschrift für Wilhelm G. Grewe*, Baden-Baden, 1981, 117–37, here 137.

293. *TBJG*, II.2, 457 (9 December 1941).

294. Saul Friedländer, *Prelude to Downfall: Hitler and the United States, 1939–1941*, New York, 1967, 285.

295. Friedländer, *Prelude*, 304.

296. Friedländer, *Prelude*, 304–5.

297. *TBJG*, II/2, 339 (22 November 1941).

298. Jäckel, 'Kriegserklärung', 126.

299. *DGFP*, D, 13, 806, No.487.

300. *DGFP*, D, 13, 813–14, No.492.

301. *IMG*, xxxv.320–23, Doc. D-656; Friedländer, *Prelude*, 306; Jäckel, 'Kriegserklärung', 127–8. Oshima concluded, from his discussion with Ribbentrop, that 'there are indications at present that Germany would not refuse to fight the United States if necessary' (Boyd, 35).

302. Friedländer, *Prelude*, 306.

303. *Staatsmänner* I, 256–7 and n.9; and see *CP*, 436 (20 April 1941). Hitler had commented in May that Japan held the key to the USA (IfZ, ED 100, Hewel diary, entry for 22 May 1941).

304. Eberhard Jäckel, *Hitler in History*, Hanover/London, 1984, 80. In the original German version of the essay, Jäckel dates Ribbentrop's comment to Oshima to 2 December ('Kriegserklärung', 30).

Ribbentrop again expressed the willingness of the German government to fight the USA (Boyd, 36).

305. Jäckel, 'Kriegserklärung', 130–31; Domarus, 1788–9.

306. *DGFP*, D, 13, 958–9, No.546; Jäckel, 'Kriegserklärung', 131–2; Jäckel, *Hitler in History*, 81.

307. Jäckel, 'Kriegserklärung', 132–4.

308. *TBJG*, II/2, 346 (22 November 1941). He intended to follow it with a few weeks of recuperation at the Berghof. Given the situation on the eastern front, he evidently abandoned all thoughts of this.

309. *TBJG*, II/2, 453 (8 December 1941). See Below's comment, after speaking with Hitler on 9 December: 'He trusted that America in the foreseeable future, also compelled by the conflict with Japan, would not be able to intervene in the European theatre of war' (Below, 296).

310. *IMG*, xxxv.324, Doc.657-D; Friedländer, *Prelude*, 308.

311. *TBJG*, II/2, 468 (10 December 1941); 476 (11 December 1941).

312. *TBJG*, II/2, 476 (11 December 1941).

313. Domarus, 1793; *TBJG*, II.2, 463 (10 December 1941); Below, 295.

314. *TBJG*, II/2, 463–4 (10 December 1941). Halder had learned from Dr Hasso von Etzdorf, Ribbentrop's liaison man at the OKH, on 7 December, the very day of Pearl Harbor, that Japanese conflict with the USA was 'possibly imminent' (*'Möglich, daß Konflikt mit Amerika bevorsteht'*) (*Halder KTB*, iii.332 (7 December 1941); trans. *Halder Diary*, 582). Despite the growing awareness that war between Japan and the USA could be imminent, the Japanese had not revealed any operational plans. Ribbentrop was still hoping, two days before Pearl Harbor, that the Americans would instigate it with some act of aggression (Friedländer, *Prelude*, 307; and see Carr, *Poland*, 169).

315. *TBJG*, II/2, 469 (10 December 1941).

316. *TBJG*, II/2, 463, 468 (10 December 1941).

317. *TBJG*, II/2, 476 (11 December 1941).

318. Weizsäcker, *Erinnerungen*, 328.

319. Weinberg II, 262; Friedländer, *Prelude*, 308; *TBJG*, II/2, 464 (10 December 1941). According to Wolfgang Brocke, then an officer attached to FHQ, though commenting more than fifty years after the events, declaring war on the USA was Hitler's immediate reaction on hearing the news of Pearl Harbor (Brocke, unpubl. notes (25 April 1997) and taped interview; see above n.287).

320. Jäckel, 'Kriegserklärung', 136–7.

321. Friedländer, *Prelude*, 309.

322. Weizsäcker, *Erinnerungen*, 328.

323. *TBJG*, II/2, 485 (12 December 1941). Text in Domarus, 1794–2111.

324. *TBJG*, II/2, 485 (12 December 1941); Domarus, 1800 and n.533.

325. Halder gave figures for total losses on the eastern front by 30 November (not counting sick) as 743,112 men, including 156,475 dead. *Halder KTB*, iii.318 (30 November 1941) and (iii.319) mentions a shortage of 340,000 men for the eastern army. On 5 January 1942 (iii.374), he states that total losses in the east between 22 June and 31 December 1941 numbered 830,903 men (173,722 dead), 26 per cent of the eastern army complement of 3.2 million men.

326. Domarus, 1801ff., here 1804. See also 1803, 1808 for specific allegations of Jews behind Roosevelt.

327. Domarus, 1808–10.

328. *TBJG*, II/2, 504 (14 December 1941).

329. See Philipp Gassert, *Amerika im Dritten Reich. Ideologie, Propaganda und Volksmeinung 1933–1945*, Stuttgart, 1997, 316–22; and Kershaw, 'Hitler Myth', 176.

330. See, for example, his revealing remarks in *TBJG*, II/2, 477 (11 December 1941), and 482–3, 486 (12 December 1941).

331. *TBJG*, II/2, 465 (10 December 1941). Three days later, Hitler was voicing similar sentiments. Naturally, the events in the east were painful, was his assessment, but 'nothing could be changed

about that', and he hoped to reach the prescribed line of defence without serious losses (*TBJG*, II/2, 493 (13 December 1941)).

332. *TBJG*, II/2, 466 (10 December 1941).

333. *TBJG*, II/2, 467 (10 December 1941).

334. *TBJG*, II/2, 468 (10 December 1941).

335. *TBJG*, II/2, 475–6 (11 December 1941).

336. See *TBJG*, II/2, 483 (12 December 1941).

337. *TBJG*, II/2, 475–6 (11 December 1941).

338. *TBJG*, II/2, 494 (13 December 1941).

339. *TBJG*, II/2, 494–5 (13 December 1941).

340. *TBJG*, II/2, 495–7 (13 December 1941).

341. *TBJG*, II/2, 497 (13 December 1941).

342. *TBJG*, II/2, 498 (13 December 1941).

343. *TBJG*, II/2, 499 (13 December 1941).

344. *TBJG*, II/2, 499–500 (13 December 1941).

345. *TBJG*, II/2, 500 (13 December 1941); Domarus, 1812. Goebbels was amused that Hitler, in presenting the award to Oshima, forgot its name (*TBJG*, II/2, 506 (14 December 1941)). Oshima told Hitler of Japan's aims to strike at India after taking Singapore. Hitler, repeating in general terms much of what he had said to Goebbels and the Gauleiter about a spring offensive, spoke of a German advance to the Caucasus on account of oil, and then into Iraq and Iran, but did not commit himself to the synchronized attack on India which Oshima had hinted at. Hitler repeated that Moscow was for him of little significance. (*Staatsmänner* I, 337–43).

346. Below, 298, for Hitler's arrival back in the Wolfsschanze.

347. *Halder KTB*, iii. 335 (8 December 1941).

348. *Halder KTB*, iii.336 (9 December 1941); *DRZW*, iv.606.

349. *DRZW*, iv.609.

350. *DRZW*, iv.609–10.

351. *DRZW*, iv. 610.

352. *Halder KTB*, iii.346 (15 December 1941); *DRZW*, iv.608.

353. *DRZW*, iv.608.

354. *Halder KTB*, iii.348 (15 December 1941); Warlimont, 212.

355. *Halder KTB*, iii.332 (7 December 1941).

356. Bock, 391 (13 December 1941); *DRZW*, iv.611. Bock's diary entry suggests, however, that he was taken aback by Hitler's order to prohibit a withdrawal, and regarded his exhortation to close gaps by use of reserves as illusory, since he had no reserves (Bock, 394–5 (16 December 1941)).

357. Bock, 395 (16 December 1941); *DRZW*, iv.610.

358. Guderian, 262–3.

359. *DRZW*, iv.612.

360. *Halder KTB*, iii.350 (16 December 1941).

361. *DRZW*, iv.607 n.592.

362. Bock, 396–9 (16–19 December 1941); *Halder KTB*, iii.354 (18 December 1941); Below, 298 (referring to 18 December 1941); *DRZW*, iv.612 and n.608. Within weeks Bock, evidently having made a remarkable recovery, was given the command of Army Group South (*DRZW*, iv.612 n.608, 646).

363. Engel, 115 (22 November 1941).

364. *Halder KTB*, iii.285 (10 November 1941).

365. *Halder KTB*, iii.322 (1 December 1941).

366. Engel, 115 (22 November 1941).

367. Engel, 117 (6 December 1941); *Halder KTB*, iii.332 (7 December 1941).

368. Engel, 117 (6 December 1941); Irving, *HW*, 351, 854.

369. Engel, 115 (22 November 1941); 117 (7 December 1941); Below, 297 (referring to 9 December 1941).

370. See Bock, 395 (16 December 1941). Three months later, speaking to Goebbels, Hitler attributed much of the blame for the winter crisis to Brauchitsch. He showed nothing but contempt for his former Army Commander-in-Chief, whom he described as a 'coward' and wholly incapable (*TBJG*, II/3, 510 (20 March 1942)). Why he had retained such an unsatisfactory army chief so long in post, Hitler did not explain.

371. Below, 298; Engel, 115 (22 November 1941); 117 (6 December 1941). For biographical sketches of Kesselring, see Samuel J. Lewis, 'Albert Kesselring – Der Soldat als Manager', in Smelser/Syring, 270–87; Elmar Krautkrämer, 'Generalfeldmarschall Albert Kesselring', in Ueberschär, *Hitlers militärische Elite*, i.121–9; Shelford Bidwell, 'Kesselring', in Correlli Barnett (ed.), *Hitler's Generals*, London, 1989, 265–89. In *The Memoirs of Field-Marshal Kesselring*, (1953), London, 1997, the change of army leadership in December 1941 is not mentioned.

372. Franz Halder, *Hitler als Feldherr. Der ehemalige Chef des Generalstabes berichtet die Wahrheit*, Munich, 1949, 45: '*Das bißchen Operationsführung kann jeder machen.*'

373. See *Halder KTB*, iii.354 and n.3 (19 December 1941); *DRZW*, iv.613 n.610, 614; Hartmann, 303.

374. Domarus, 1813–15.

375. A point also made in *DRZW*, iv.619.

376. Domarus, 1815.

377. *TBJG*, II/2, 554 (21 December 1941); *Tb* Reuth, 1523, n.224.

378. Kershaw, '*Hitler Myth*', 176.

379. Hans-Adolf Jacobsen, *Der Weg zur Teilung der Welt, Politik und Strategie von 1939–1945*, Koblenz/Bonn, 1977, 134–5; Wolfgang Michalka (ed.), *Das Dritte Reich. Bd.2: Weltmachtanspruch und nationaler Zusammenbruch 1939–1945*, Munich, 1985, 66–7; trans. (slightly amended) *N & P*, iii.827–8.

380. *DRZW*, iv.614.

381. *DRZW*, iv.614–15; Guderian, 264, and 269–70 for conflict with Kluge; see also Below, 298, for Kluge's influence. Bock and Guderian had also clashed in early September, to the extent that Bock had asked on 4 September for the tank commander's replacement. See Bock, 298–306 (31 August–6 September 1941). Bock thought Guderian an 'outstanding and brave commander', but 'headstrong' (Bock, 304–5 (4–5 September 1941)).

382. Guderian, 265–8.

383. Guderian, 270.

384. *Halder KTB*, iii.369 (29 December 1941), iii.376–7 (8 January 1942), iii.386 (15 January 1942); Warlimont, 223.

385. See Irving, *HW*, 366; and also Leach, 225–6.

386. For the constant conflict between Hitler and Kluge during this period, see *Halder KTB*, iii.370–385 (30 December 1941–14 January 1942).

387. Schroeder, 126–8; Irving, *HW*, 354–5.

388. *Halder KTB*, iii.385, 388 (14 January 1942, 19 January 1942); *KTB OKW*, ii.1268–9 (15 January 1942).

389. Willi Boelcke (ed.), *Deutschlands Rüstung im Zweiten Weltkrieg. Hitlers Konferenzen mit Albert Speer 1942–1945*, Frankfurt am Main, 1969, 126–30, here 127.

390. Warlimont, 223; *TBJG*, II/3, 511 (20 March 1942), 517 (21 March 42); *CD*, 461 (29 April 1942).

391. Halder, *Hitler als Feldherr*, 46–7; Guenther Blumentritt, 'Moscow', in *The Fatal Decisions*, London, 1956, 29–74, here 67; John Strawson, *Hitler as Military Commander*, London, 1971, 147. Alan Clark, *Barbarossa. The Russian-German Conflict 1941–45*, (1965) New York, 1985, 182–3, exaggerates the point in describing the 'stand-still' order as 'Hitler's finest hour', when his 'complete mastery of the detail even of a regimental action' saved the German army.

392. The most thorough analysis of the winter crisis, Klaus Reinhardt, *Die Wende vor Moskau. Das Scheitern der Strategie Hitler im Winter 1941/42*, Stuttgart, 1972, 221–2, acknowledges that Hitler's decision corresponded with the views of Bock and his subordinate commanders, and that 'the claim that Hitler's order initially saved the eastern front is as such correct (*die Behauptung, daß Hitlers Befehl die Ostfront zunächst gerettet habe, an sich richtig [ist]*)'. He adds, however, that the inability to provide reinforcements meant that the rigidity of the order, given the existing troop placements, also proved a weakness, and that more flexibility would have allowed the consolidation of a more defensible position.

393. William Carr, *Hitler. A Study in Personality and Politics*, London, 1978, 96.

394. *TBJG*, II/3, 501, 509, 512 (20 March 1942).

395. Hitler had said on 27 November to the Danish Foreign Minister, Erik Scavenius, that if the German people was not strong enough, then it deserved to be destroyed 'by another, stronger power'. It was the first of a number of occasions on which he would use such characteristic social-Darwinist phraseology, offering to his own mind justification for a German defeat. (See *Staatsmänner* I, 329 and n.7.)

396. *Monologe*, 179 (5 January 1942).

397. *Monologe*, 183–4 (7 January 1942).

398. *Monologe*, 193 (10 January 1942).

399. Indeed, it has been suggested that 'no rational man in early 1942 would have guessed at the eventual outcome of the war' (Richard Overy, *Why the Allies Won*, London, 1995, 15).

400. See Klaus Reinhardt, 'Moscow 1941. The Turning-Point', in John Erikson and David Dilks (eds.), *Barbarossa. The Axis and the Allies*, Edinburgh, 1994, 207–24.

401. See Churchill, iii.341–2; Weinberg III, 284–5.

402. See *Monologe*, 184 (7 January 1942) for Hitler's expression of contempt.

CHAPTER 10: FULFILLING THE 'PROPHECY'

1. See also the remarks in Mommsen, 'Realisierung', 417–18.

2. Klee, Dreßen, and Rieß, '*Schöne Zeiten*', 148, cit. a letter of Gendarmerie-Meister Fritz Jacob, 29 October 1941, on his keenness to be sent to the east.

3. *DTB* Frank, 386 (entry for 17 July 1941, referring to a statement by Hitler of 19 June).

4. *TBJG*, iv.705 (20 June 1941).

5. See Philippe Burrin, *Hitler and the Jews. The Genesis of the Holocaust*, (1989), London, 1994, 98–100, for evidence that a 'territorial solution' was what was envisaged at this time.

6. Müller, 96. See Heiber, 'Der Generalplan Ost', 297–324, especially 299–301, 307–9; Czeslaw Madajczyk, 'Generalplan Ost', *Polish Western Affairs*, 3 (1962), 3–54, here especially 3. In his lengthy memorandum of 27 April 1942, assessing the plan that had been drawn up in autumn 1941 in the RSHA, Dr Erhard Wetzel, head (*Dezernent*) of the department of racial policy in the Ostministerium, thought the figure of 31 million too low, and reckoned that 46–51 million would have to be removed. Himmler had initially wanted the 'construction of the east (*Ostaufbau*)' completed in twenty years (Heiber, 298 n.16). For the date of the commissioning of the Plan (24 June 1941), see the letter of 15 July 1941 from Prof. Dr Konrad Meyer, SS-Standartenführer and head of the planning department of the Reich Commission for the Strengthening of Germandom, to Himmler in Dietrich Eichholtz, 'Der "Generalplan Ost". Über eine Ausgeburt imperialistischer Denkart und Politik (mit Dokumenten)', *Jahrbuch für Geschichte*, 26 (1982), 217–74, here 256. See also Robert L. Koehl, *RKFDV: German Resettlement and Population Policy 1939–1945. A History of the Reich Commission for the Strengthening of Germandom*, Cambridge, Mass., 1957, 147–51.

7. Warlimont, 150.

8. Longerich, *Ermordung* 116–18; Krausnick/Wilhelm, 164.

9. Alfred Streim, *Die Behandlung sowjetischer Kriegsgefangener im 'Fall Barbarossa'*, Heidelberg/Karlsruhe, 1981, 89 n.333.

10. Krausnick/Wilhelm, 163; Klee, Dreßen, and Rieß, *'Schöne Zeiten'*, 52.

11. Osobyi Arkhiv, Moscow, 500–1–25, Fols.119–20: 'Gesamtaufstellung der im Bereich des EK.3 bis zum 1.Dez.1941 durchgeführten Exekutionen'. Of the total of 138,272 persons 'executed' by the same Einsatzkommando (including 55,556 women, and 34,464 children), registered by the same Einsatzkommando in a handwritten summary (in the same file, Fol.128) of 9 February 1942, no fewer than 136,421 were Jews.

12. See Krausnick/Wilhelm, 627; Streim, 88–9.

13. Burrin, 106–7.

14. Krausnick/Wilhelm, 196.

15. Christoph Dieckmann, 'Der Krieg und die Ermordung der litauischen Juden', in Ulrich Herbert (ed.), *Nationalsozialistische Vernichtungspolitik 1939–1945. Neue Forschungen und Kontroversen*, Frankfurt am Main, 1998, 292–329, here 292–3, and 295–306. See also Dina Porat, 'The Holocaust in Lithuania. Some Unique Aspects', in David Cesarani (ed.), *The Final Solution. Origins and Implementation*, London, 1996, 159–74.

16. The encouragement of 'self-cleansing efforts of anti-Communist and anti-Jewish circles (*Selbstreinigungsbestrebungen antikommunistischer oder antijüdischer Kreise*)' had been verbally stipulated by Heydrich in his briefing in Berlin on 17 June, then laid down in writing in written orders to the chiefs of the four Einsatzgruppen on 29 June, and incorporated in the instructions to the Higher SS and Police Leaders on 2 July. (Osobyi Arkhiv, Moscow, 500–1–25, Fols.387, 391, 393.)

17. Klee, Dreßen, and Rieß, *'Schöne Zeiten'*, 32–41. And see Laurence Rees, *The Nazis. A Warning from History*, London, 1997, 179–81. At the end of August, instructions went to the chiefs of the Einsatzgruppen to prevent gatherings of spectators, including Wehrmacht officers, to view the 'executions'. (Osobyi Arkhiv, Moscow, 500–1–25, Fol.424 (RSHA IV – Müller – to Einsatzgruppen A–D, 30 August 1941).)

18. Klee, Dreßen, and Rieß, *'Schöne Zeiten'*, 36, 38.

19. Gerald Fleming, *Hitler und die Endlösung. 'Es ist des Führers Wunsch . . .'*, Wiesbaden/Munich, 1982, 86. For the reporting system of the Einsatzgruppen, using Enigma codes, see Richard Breitman, *Official Secrets. What the Nazis Planned. What the British and Americans Knew*, London, 1998, Ch.4.

20. *TBJG*, II/1, 213 (11 August 1941).

21. *TBJG*, II/2, 221–2 (2 November 1941).

22. Klee and Dreßen, *'Gott mit uns'*, 101ff.

23. See Krausnick/Wilhelm, Ch.IVB, 205–78, especially 223–43; *DRZW*, iv.1044ff.; Streit, 109–27; and see Omer Bartov, 'Operation Barbarossa and the Origins of the Final Solution', in Cesarani, *Final Solution*, 119–36.

24. Klee and Dreßen, *'Gott mit uns'*, 102–3.

25. Klee and Dreßen, *'Gott mit uns'*, 106.

26. *IMG*, xxxv.85–6, Doc.411–D; Klee and Dreßen, *'Gott mit uns'*, 39–40. And see *DRZW*, iv.1050–2; Krausnick/Wilhelm, 258–61 and Gerd Ueberschär and Wolfgang Wette (eds.), *'Unternehmen Barbarossa'. Der deutsche Überfall auf die Sowjetunion*, Paderborn, 1984, 373–4.

27. *DRZW*, iv.1052–3.

28. *IMG*, xxxiv.129–32 (quotation, 130–31), Doc.4064-PS; Klee and Dreßen, *'Gott mit uns'*, 41–2.

29. Heer, 'Killing Fields', 87–90; Richter, 844–6; and see Theo J. Schulte, *The German Army and Nazi Policies in Occupied Russia*, Oxford/New York/Munich, 1989, esp. ch.6,9.

30. Stalin had called for partisan warfare in his speech of 3 July (Volkogonov, 413). But organized partisan units did not take shape before autumn 1941. The ruthless German attempts to combat the spread of partisan warfare intensified from then on.

31. *DRZW*, iv.1044 (and see 1041–4).

32. See *DRZW*, iv.1054.

33. *DRZW*, iv.1047.

34. *DRZW*, iv.1048.

35. See Bartov, *Hitler's Army*, ch.4; Bartov, *Barbarisation*, ch.3–4; Bartov, 'Operation Barbarossa', 124–31.

36. Buchbender and Sterz, 73, letter 101; Bartov, *Hitler's Army*, 153.

37. Bartov, *Hitler's Army*, 155. German text in Omer Bartov, *Hitlers Wehrmacht. Soldaten, Fanatismus und die Brutalisierung des Krieges*, Reinbek bei Hamburg, 1995, 232: 'Jeder hier, selbst der Zweifler, weiß heute, daß der Kampf gegen diese Untermenschen, die von den Juden bis zur Raserei aufgehetzt wurden, nicht nur notwendig war, sondern auch gerade zum rechten Zeitpunkt kam. Unser Führer hat Europa vor dem sicheren Untergang bewahrt.'

38. Bartov, *Barbarisation*, 120ff.

39. Burrin, 110.

40. Osobyi Arkhiv, Moscow, 500–1–25, Fol.94: 'Tätigkeits- und Lagebericht Nr.6 der Einsatzgruppen der Sicherheitspolizei und des SD in der UdSSR (Berichtszeit vom 1.–31 October 1941)': 'Als Vergeltungsmaßnahme für die Brandstiftungen in Kiew wurden sämtliche Juden verhaftete und am 29. und 30.9 insgesamt 33 771 Juden exekutiert.'

41. Klee, Dreßen, and Rieß, *'Schöne Zeiten'*, 66–70; Klee and Dreßen, *'Gott mit uns'*, 117–36; Mayer, *Why Did the Heavens Not Darken?*, 267–8.

42. Burrin, 104–5, 110–13; Christopher Browning, 'Hitler and the Euphoria of Victory. The Path to the Final Solution', in Cesarani, *Final Solution*, 137–47, here 140–43. The instructions were interpreted differently by the leaders of the various killing squads. Plainly they did not amount to a blanket order to kill all Jews without discrimination. (Christian Gerlach, *Krieg, Ernährung, Völkermord. Forschungen zur deutschen Vernichtungspolitik im Zweiten Weltkrieg*, Hamburg, 1998, 63ff., 261.)

43. Burrin, 110.

44. Burrin, 113. For the extension of the killing, see Peter Longerich, *Politik der Vernichtung. Eine Gesamtdarstellung der nationalsozialistischen Judenverfolgung*, Munich/Zurich, 1998, 352–410.

45. Burrin, 104.

46. Krausnick/Wilhelm, 160; Streim, 74–80.

47. See Burrin, 102ff.; Streim, 83–4; Longerich, *Politik*, 310–51.

48. Browning, *Path*, 106. For the composition of the Einsatzgruppen, see Krausnick/Wilhelm, 141–50, 281–93; Longerich, *Politik*, 302–10. A good proportion of the leaders were SS men with university backgrounds, some with doctorates in law (Krausnick-Wilhelm, 282–3). The members of the battalions of the Ordnungspolizei, an organization whose leadership, like that of the Sicherheitspolizei (Security Police), was dominated by the SS, were in the main young career-policemen, and ideologically trained. (See Longerich, *Politik*, 305–10 (with criticism of Goldhagen, Ch.6, for the latter's emphasis on randomly selected, non-ideologically trained, recruits who were 'ordinary Germans'; and indicating, too, that they were less 'ordinary men' than Browning, *Ordinary Men*, 45–8 and ch.18, claimed).)

49. Browning, *Path*, 106: by June 1942 there were 165,000 members of the units, and by January 1943 the number had risen to a staggering 300,000. See also Browning, 'Hitler and the Euphoria of Victory', 138ff.; and, especially, Yehoshua Büchler, 'Kommandostab Reichsführer-SS: Himmler's Personal Murder Brigades in 1941', *Holocaust and Genocide Studies*, I/1 (1986), 11–26.

50. *Der Dienstkalender Heinrich Himmlers 1941/42*, ed. Peter Witte et al., Hamburg, 1999, 195 and n.14; *Justiz und NS-Verbrechen. Sammlung deutscher Strafurteile wegen nationalsozialistischer Tötungsverbrechen 1945–1966*, vol.20, Amsterdam, 1979, 435–6, No.580 a-51-2 (trial of Karl Wolff); Burrin, 105.

51. Browning, 'Hitler and the Euphoria of Victory', 140–41; and see Longerich, *Politik*, 362–9.

52. *Dienstkalender*, 184–5; Browning, *Path*, 105.

53. *IMG*, xxxviii, 86–94, Doc.221-L; Klee and Dreßen, '*Gott mit uns*', 23.

54. Moll, '*Führer-Erlasse*', 188–9; Longerich, *Politik*, 362–3; Breitman, *Architect*, 183–4.

55. Browning, 'Hitler and the Euphoria of Victory', 140.

56. IfZ, EW 100, Tagebuch Walther Hewel 1941, 10 July 1941; and see Irving, *HW*, 291: '*Ich fühle mich wie Robert Koch in der Politik. Der fand den Bazillus [der Tuberkulose* – these two words crossed out by Hewel] *und wies damit der ärztlichen Wissenschaft neue Wege. Ich entdeckte den Juden als den Bazillus und das Ferment aller [menschl.* – crossed out by Hewel] *gesellschaftlichen Dekomposition. Ihr Ferment. Und eines habe ich bewiesen, daß ein Staat ohne Juden leben kann. Daß Wirtschaft, Kultur, Kunst etc etc ohne Juden bestehen kann und zwar besser. Das ist der schlimmste Schlag, den ich den Juden versetzt habe.*'

57. *Staatsmänner* I, 304 and n.2, 295.

58. *Staatsmänner* I, 306–7.

59. *Staatsmänner* I, 309–10.

60. Pätzold, *Verfolgung*, 295–6.

61. Eichmann confirmed after the war that the document had been drawn up in the RSHA and merely signed by Göring (Rudolf Aschenauer (ed.), *Ich, Adolf Eichmann*, Leoni, 1980, 479). Göring's desk diary indicates that he had an appointment to see Heydrich on 31 July between 6.15 and 7.15p.m. (Hermann Weiß, 'Die Aufzeichnungen Hermann Görings im Institut für Zeitgeschichte', *VfZ*, 31 (1983), 365–8, here 366–7).

62. *IMG*, xxvi, 266–7, Doc. 710-PS; Longerich, *Ermordung*, 78.

63. Aly, 270–71, 307.

64. Aly, 271; Burrin, 116.

65. The only evidence linking the document with Hitler is tenuous. Over a year later, the Foreign Office expert on anti-Jewish policy, Martin Luther, claimed to have heard Heydrich mention at the Wannsee Conference, on 20 January 1942, that he had received the commission from Göring on Hitler's instructions (Gerald Fleming, *Hitler and the Final Solution*, Oxford, 1986, 46n.13). There is no supporting evidence, either from the minutes or from others attending the Conference, for Heydrich's alleged remark. (See Burrin, 116; Breitman (who accepts Luther's comment), 193 and 296 n.27.) Eberhard Jäckel, in an as yet unpublished paper on Heydrich's role in the development of extermination policy which he kindly allowed me to see, presumes it to be 'very unlikely that Göring gave his signature without instruction from or at least approval by Hitler'. Since the 'mandate' was essentially confirming powers which Heydrich already possessed – if (which was its purpose) now establishing more plainly for others his primacy in planning a 'final solution of the Jewish Question' – it remains unclear why Hitler's explicit involvement was necessary.

66. See Burrin, 116ff.; Aly, 271–3, 307; Mommsen, 'Realisierung', 409.

67. Aly, 307.

68. NA, T175, Roll 577, Frame 366337, Report of SD-Hauptaußenstelle Bielefeld, 5 August 1941. I am most grateful to Prof. Otto Dov Kulka (Jerusalem) for referring me to this report.

69. *TBJG*, II/2, 218 (12 August 1941).

70. 'Das Reichsministerium des Innern und die Judengesetzgebung. Aufzeichnungen von Dr. Bernhard Lösener', *VfZ*, 9 (1961), 262–311, here 303.

71. 'Das Reichsministerium des Innern und die Judengesetzgebung', 302–3. There is no doubt that this was an accurate reflection of Goebbels's own views. On 7 August, he had written in his diary, in the context of reports of typhus in the Warsaw ghetto: 'The Jews have always been carriers of infectious diseases. They should be either packed into (*zusammenpferchen*) a ghetto and left to themselves, or liquidated' (*TBJG*, II/1, 189 (7 August 1941)).

72. 'Das Reichsministerium des Innern und die Judengesetzgebung', 303.

73. 'Das Reichsministerium des Innern und die Judengesetzgebung', 303–4.

74. *TBJG*, II/1, 258–9, 261 (19 August 1941).

75. *TBJG*, II/1, 265–6, 269 (19 August 1941). Tobias Jersak, 'Die Interaktion von Kriegsverlauf

und Judenvernichtung', *HZ*, 268 (1999), 311–49, here 349–52, argues that Hitler had already, when meeting Goebbels, taken the fundamental decision that the Jews of Europe were to be physically destroyed. But the evidence that Hitler dramatically changed policy towards the Jews, taking a fundamental decision for their destruction at this point, while suffering a nervous breakdown, under the impact of the realization that his strategic plan for rapidly defeating the Soviet Union had failed, and recognizing that following the signing of the Atlantic Charter by Roosevelt and Churchill he would inevitably be soon fighting the USA, is not persuasive. Hitler's view of the Atlantic Charter (as expressed to Goebbels) was, moreover, predictably dismissive (*TBJG*, II/1, 263 (19 August 1941)).

76. *TBJG*, II/1, 278 (20 August 1941).

77. Fleming, *Hitler und die Endlösung*, 79.

78. NA, T175, Roll 577, reports of SD-Außenstelle Höxter, 25 September 1941, SD-Hauptaußenstelle Bielefeld, 30 September 1941; *MadR*, ix.3245–8; Steinert, 239–40; Ian Kershaw, 'German Popular Opinion and the "Jewish Question", 1939–1943: Some Further Reflections', in Arnold Paucker (ed.), *Die Juden im nationalsozialistischen Deutschland*, Tübingen, 1986, 366–86, here 373; Bankier, 134.

79. Andreas-Friedrich, 53 (entry for 19 September 1941, the day the decree on the wearing of the Yellow Star came into effect).

80. Klemperer, i.671 (20 September 1941), 673 (25 September 1941).

81. Inge Deutschkron, *Ich trug den gelben Stern*, (1978), 4th edn, Cologne, 1983, 87.

82. Bankier, 124–30.

83. Bankier, 127.

84. *Faschismus*, 250–52; Aly, 336–7; Fox, 'Abetz', 198–201.

85. Aly, 335–6, 338; see also Burrin, 118–19.

86. Christopher R. Browning, *Fateful Months. Essays on the Emergence of the Final Solution*, New York/London, 1985, 26; Browning, *The Final Solution and the German Foreign Office*, 58.

87. An inference of Aly, 306.

88. Overy, *Russia's War*, 232–3; Robert Service, *A History of Twentieth-Century Russia*, London, 1998, 276–7; Robert Conquest, *The Nation Killers. The Soviet Deportation of Nationalities*, London, 1970, 59–66, 107–9.

89. Longerich, *Politik*, 429.

90. *TBJG*, II/2, 385 (9 September 1941).

91. H.D. Heilmann, 'Aus dem Kriegstagebuch des Diplomaten Otto Bräutigam', in *Biedermann und Schreibtischtäter. Materialien zur deutschen Täter-Biographie*, ed. Götz Aly, Berlin, 2nd edn, 1989, 123–87, here 144–5 (entry for 14 September 1941); Adler, 176–7; Peter Witte, 'Two Decisions concerning the "Final Solution to the Jewish Question": Deportations to Lodz and Mass Murder in Chelmno', *Holocaust and Genocide Studies*, 9 (1995), 293–317, here 330; see also Burrin, 122; Longerich, *Politik*, 429–30.

92. Adler, 176–7; Witte, 'Two Decisions', 330; Eberhard Jäckel, *Hitlers Herrschaft. Vollzug einer Weltanschauung*, (1986), Stuttgart, 1988, 116; Burrin, 122; Longerich, *Politik*, 430 and 699 n.45.

93. Koeppen, Fol.21 (Bericht Nr.34, Blatt 2–3, 20 September 1941). Koeppen was almost certainly uninformed at this point of the steps which had by then already been taken two days earlier. His entry probably, therefore, reflects his understanding of Hitler's stance several days earlier. (See Longerich, *Politik*, 431.)

94. The emphasis placed on the Atlantic Charter as the cause of a fundamental shift in Hitler's policy towards the Jews, allegedly bringing the decision for the 'Final Solution', by Jersak, 341ff., 349ff., (see above, n.75) seems exaggerated.

95. See Longerich, *Politik*, 431–2.

96. See *Halder KTB*, iii.226 (13 September 1941), for the OKW memorandum of 13 September 1941, approved by Hitler, indicating for the first time that the war was likely to last over the winter.

The victory at Kiev temporarily restored Hitler's confidence, a few days later, that an early end to the campaign was in prospect (TBJG, II/1, 481–2 (24 September 1941)).

97. *Dienstkalender*, 211.

98. Longerich, 430; Witte, 'Two Decisions', 330; *Dienstkalender*, 213 and n.57.

99. Longerich, *Ermordung*, 157. The figure of 60,000 Jews was the same as that mentioned in at least two earlier references to deportation – that of the Viennese Jews in the winter of 1940–41, and by Eichmann at a meeting in the Propaganda Ministry in March. It seems to have been plucked from thin air. The actual number agreed on, following hard bargaining between Eichmann and the regional authorities in the Warthegau, was 20,000 Jews and 5,000 Gypsies, whom Eichmann seems to have accommodated in the demands for deportation following pressure from the local Nazi authorities in the Burgenland. (Saffrian, 115–19; Michael Zimmermann, 'Die nationalsozialistische Lösung der Zigeunerfrage', in Herbert, *Vernichtungspolitik*, 235–62, here 248–9.) As Zimmermann (237–8) points out, the murder of the Gypsies took place without Hitler ever showing notable interest in the 'Gypsy question'; nor was a pre-existing programme for their persecution and extermination devised, either by Himmler or Heydrich. (Michael Zimmermann, *Verfolgt, vertrieben, vernichtet. Die nationalsozialistische Vernichtungspolitik gegen Sinti und Roma*, Essen, 1989, 82–3, where the numbers of Roma and Sinti murdered is estimated at between 220,000 and 500,000.)

100. The connections with genocide have been well brought out by Gerlach, *Krieg, Ernährung, Völkermord*, 167–257; and Christian Gerlach, 'Deutsche Wirtschaftsinteressen, Besatzungspolitik und der Mord an den Juden in Weißrußland, 1941–1943', in Herbert, *Vernichtungspolitik*, 263–91.

101. See Herbert, 'Labour and Extermination', 167ff., for the sensitivity of the labour question in the unfolding of anti-Jewish policy at this juncture.

102. *TBJG*, II/1, 481–2 (24 September 1941).

103. Burrin, 123–4, sees it as such. Eichmann, whose testimony while in Israeli custody many years later was shaky on chronology, claimed to have been told by Heydrich two to three months after the beginning of the Russian campaign of the Führer's order for the physical extermination of the Jews. (Lang, *Eichmann-Protokoll*, 69; see Browning, *Fateful Months*, 23–6.) Höß, the Commandant of Auschwitz, recalled being told by Himmler in summer 1941 of Hitler's decision. But his memory was as at least as fallible as Eichmann's on detail and much, if not all, of what he said appears better to fit 1942 than 1941. (*Kommandant in Auschwitz. Autobiographische Aufzeichnungen des Rudolf Höß*, (1963), Munich, 4th edn, 1978, 157. And see Browning, *Fateful Months*, 22–3; Burrin, 170 n.15.) Breitman, *Architect*, 189–90, accepts the testimony for the timing of Hitler's decision, as does Graml, *Reichskristallnacht*, 228–9. The view that Höß's testimony referred to 1941 is, however, convincingly rejected by Karin Orth, 'Rudolf Höß und die "Endlösung der Judenfrage". Drei Argumente gegen deren Datierung auf den Sommer 1941', *Werkstattgeschichte*, 18 (1997), 45–57.

104. Longerich, *Politik*, 475.

105. John L. Heinemann, *Hitler's First Foreign Minister. Constantin Freiherr von Neurath, Diplomat and Statesman*, Berkeley/Los Angeles/London, 1979, 209–11.

106. *TBJG*, II.i.480–81 (24 September 1941).

107. *TBJG*, II.i.485 (24 September 1941).

108. *TBJG*, II.ii.169 (24 October 1941). It was the first of nine batches of deportation from Berlin before a temporary halt at the end of January 1942 because of transport problems (*Tb Reuth*, 1710, n.209).

109. *TBJG*, II.ii.194–5 (28 October 1941).

110. *TBJG*, II.ii.309 (18 November 1941).

111. *Das Reich*, 16 Nov. 1941: 'Die Juden sind schuld!': '. . . Es bewahrheitet sich an ihnen [den Juden] auch die Prophezeihung, die der Führer am 30. Januar 1939 im Deutschen Reichstag aussprach . . . Wir erleben eben den Vollzug dieser Prophezeihung, und es erfüllt sich damit am

Judentum ein Schicksal, das zwar hart, aber mehr als verdient ist. Mitleid oder Bedauern ist da gänzlich unangebracht . . .' A lengthy extract from the article, including this passage, is printed in Hans-Heinrich Wilhelm, 'Wie geheim war die "Endlösung" ', in Benz, *Miscellanea*, 131–48, here 137–8 (136 for *Das Reich*'s circulation figures); and see Reuth, *Goebbels*, 491. As the passage indicates, Goebbels, unlike Hitler, dated the 'prophecy' of 1939 correctly.

112. Irving, *Goebbels*, 379.

113. *MadR*, viii.3007 (20 November 1941).

114. *TBJG*, II/2, 352 (23 November 1941).

115. *TBJG*, II/2, 340–1 (22 November 1941). Hitler also recommended – obviously responding to a point close to the Propaganda Minister's heart – Goebbels to tread carefully with regard to Jewish 'mixed-marriages', especially in artistic circles. He was of the opinion that such marriages were dying out anyway with the passage of time, and that it was not necessary to lose any sleep about them. Fifteen months later, Goebbels would ignore such a recommendation. But a week-long protest of hundreds of wives would eventually halt the planned deportation of their Jewish husbands. (See Nathan Stoltzfus, *Resistance of the Heart*, New York/London, 1996.)

116. See Martin Broszat, 'Hitler und die Genesis der "Endlösung". Aus Anlaß der Thesen von David Irving', *VfZ*, 25 (1977), 739–75, here especially 752–3, 755–6.

117. Raul Hilberg, 'Die Aktion Reinhard', in Eberhard Jäckel and Jurgen Rohwer (eds.), *Der Mord an den Juden im Zweiten Weltkrieg. Entschlußbildung und Verwirklichung*, Stuttgart, 1985, 125–36, here 126; Longerich, *Politik*, 457; Aly, 342–7; Christian Gerlach, 'Failure of Plans for an SS Extermination Camp in Mogilev, Belorussia', *Holocaust and Genocide Studies*, 11 (1997), 60–78.

118. For the significance of local and regional initiatives in the unfolding of genocide in Poland, see Dieter Pohl, *Von der 'Judenpolitik' zum Judenmord. Der Distrikt Lublin des Generalgouvernements 1939–1944*, Frankfurt am Main, 1993; Dieter Pohl, *Nationalsozialistische Judenverfolgung in Ostgalizien. Organisation und Durchführung eines staatlichen Massenverbrechens*, Munich, 1996; Dieter Pohl, 'Die Ermordung der Juden im Generalgouvernement', in Herbert, *Vernichtungspolitik*, 98–121; Thomas Sandkühler, *'Endlosung' in Galizien. Der Judenmord in Ostpolen, und die Rettungsinitiativen von Berthold Beitz*, Bonn, 1996; Thomas Sandkühler, 'Judenpolitik und Judenmord im Distrikt Galizien, 1941–1942', in Herbert, *Vernichtungspolitik*, 122–47; also Longerich, *Politik*, 457–8; Kershaw, 'Improvised Genocide?', especially 74ff.

119. See Browning, *Fateful Months*, ch.3 ('The Development and Production of the Nazi Gas Van').

120. *Kommandant in Auschwitz*, 159; Danuta Czech, *Kalendarium der Ereignisse im Konzentrationslager Auschwitz-Birkenau 1939–1945*, Reinbek bei Hamburg, 1989, 117–18; Yehuda Bauer, *A History of the Holocaust*, New York etc., 1982, 214–15; Leni Yahil, *The Holocaust. The Fate of European Jewry, 1932–1945*, New York/Oxford, 1990, 365; Browning, *Fateful Months*, 29; Gerald Fleming, 'The Auschwitz Archives in Moscow', *Jewish Quarterly* (Autumn, 1991), 9–12, here 9. Jean-Claude Pressac, *Les Crématoires d'Auschwitz. La Machinerie du Meurtre de Masse*, Paris, 1993, 26ff., especially 34, 101 n.107, 113–14, dates the gassing of the Soviet prisoners to December, rather than 3 September, the date given by Czech and most other historians. See Longerich, *Politik*, 444–5, 457 and 704 n.114.

121. BDC, SS-HO, 1878: '. . . *Es bestehe auf jeden Fall die Gefahr, daß vor allem von Seiten der Wirtschaft in zahlreichen Fällen Juden als unentbehrliche Arbeitskräfte reklamiert würden und daß sich niemand bemühe, an Stelle der Juden andere Arbeitskräfte zu bekommen. Dies würde aber den Plan einer totalen Aussiedlung der Juden aus den von uns besetzten Gebieten zunichte machen . . .'*

122. Browning, *Fateful Months*, 30–31; Breitman, *Architect*, 200; Longerich, *Politik*, 455.

123. See *Faschismus*, 269–70.

124. See Yitzhak Arad, *Belzec, Sobibor, Treblinka. The Operation Reinhard Death Camps*, Bloomington/Indianapolis, 1987. The name appears to have been taken from the State Secretary in the Reich Finance Ministry, Fritz Reinhardt, and hinted at the regime's interest in the material outcome of the mass murder of around 1.75 million Jews (mainly from Poland). When account was

rendered, money and valuables worth around 180 million Reich Marks were placed in the Deutsche Reichsbank for the future use of the SS. Mistakenly, SS men involved in the 'Action' attributed the name to Reinhard Heydrich (Benz, Graml, and Weiß, *Enzyklopädie*, 354–5).

125. *Faschismus*, 374–7; *Kommandant in Auschwitz*, 157–8; Lang, *Eichmann-Protokoll*, 76–7; Browning, *Fateful Months*, 24; Breitman, *Architect*, 203.

126. Kershaw, 'Improvised Genocide?', 63, 65–6.

127. *Faschismus*, 278; Kershaw, 'Improvised Genocide?', 71, 73; Longerich, 451–2.

128. BDC, Personalakte Arthur Greiser, Brandt to Koppe, 14 May 1942: '*Der letzte Entscheid muß ja in dieser Angelegenheit vom Führer gefallt werden.*'

129. BDC, Personalakte Arthur Greiser, Greiser to Himmler, 21 November 1942: '*Ich für meine Person glaube nicht, daß der Führer in dieser Angelegenheit noch einmal befragt werden muß umso mehr, als er mir bei der letzten Rücksprache erst bezüglich der Juden gesagt hat, ich möchte mit diesen nach eigenem Ermessen verfahren.*'

130. Kershaw, 'Improvised Genocide?', 65ff., 70–74.

131. Hilberg, *Destruction*, 232; Longerich, *Politik*, 461–5.

132. *TBJG*, II.2, 503 (14 December 1941). See Burrin, 124–5, and Ulrich Herbert, 'Die deutsche Militärverwaltung in Paris und die Deportation der französischen Juden', in Herbert, *Vernichtungspolitik*, 170–208, here 185–93, for the background to the deportation of the French Jews; and Leni Yahil, 'Some Remarks about Hitler's Impact on the Nazis' Jewish Policy', *Yad Vashem Studies*, 23 (1993), 281–93, here 288–9, for Hitler's role in the moves leading to the deportation.

133. Krausnick/Wilhelm, 566–70 (Jeckeln testimony), quotation 566; Fleming, *Hitler und die Endlösung*, 87–104; Longerich, *Politik*, 464.

134. Gerlach, 'Wannsee', 7–44, here 17; Longerich, *Politik*, 463.

135. Gerlach, 'Wannsee', 12; Fleming, *Hitler und die Endlösung*, 88 and n.184, 103–4; Longerich, *Politik*, 464.

136. Longerich, *Politik*, 466.

137. A point emphasized by Eberhard Jäckel in his hitherto unpublished paper on Heydrich's role in the genesis of the 'Final Solution'.

138. Longerich, *Politik*, 466.

139. *IMG*, xxix, 145, Doc. PS-1919.

140. Koeppen, 42 (6 October 1941).

141. *Monologe*, 99; Koeppen, 60–61 (21 October 1941).

142. Himmler visited FHO nineteen times – more frequently than any other guest – between July 1941 and January 1942 (Bullock, *Hitler and Stalin*, 800–801).

143. Koeppen, 71 (25 October 1941).

144. *Monologe*, 106. The translation of the passage in *Hitler's Table Talk, 1941–1944*, London, 1953, 87, is not wholly accurate, and includes a phrase – 'Terror is a salutary thing' – not found in the German text.

145. Himmler had spoken on 1 August about driving female Jews into the Pripet marshes. The SS had done this, but the swamps had proved too shallow for drowning (Burrin, 111–12; Browning, *Path*, 106).

146. It is difficult to see why Irving, *HW*, 331, infers from the comments that Hitler did not favour the extermination of the Jews.

147. *Monologe*, 130.

148. *Monologe*, 130–31; Koeppen, 78 (5 November 1941).

149. Domarus, 1772–3.

150. *Monologe*, 148; Picker, 152.

151. Kershaw, 'Improvised Genocide?', 66 n.71 for the conflicting evidence about the precise date of the commencement of the gassing; and for the extermination at Chelmno, see above all Adalbert Rückerl (ed.), *NS-Vernichtungslager im Spiegel deutscher Strafprozesse*, Munich, 1977, Part 2.

152. *TBJG*, II.2, 498–9 (13 December 1941). Though Hitler's extreme comments undoubtedly gave further impetus to the gathering momentum of genocide, Gerlach, 'Wannsee', 28, in my view goes too far in seeing his speech to the Gauleiter as the announcement of a 'basic decision' to murder all the Jews in Europe. See also Kershaw, *Nazi Dictatorship*, 2000, 126–30.

153. *IMG*, xxvii.270, Doc.PS-1517; and see Gerlach, 'Wannsee', 24.

154. *DTB* Frank, 457–8 (16 December 1941); trans., slightly amended, *N & P*, iii.1126–7, Doc.848.

155. *IMG*, xxxii.435–7, Docs. PS-3663, PS-3666 (quotation, 437).

156. *Dienstkalender*, 294. It is extremely unlikely that the entry can be equated in the way Gerlach, 'Wannsee', 22 interprets it, with a 'basic decision' to extend the extermination from Soviet Jewry to the rest of Europe, seeing European Jews in general as 'imaginary partisans'. As far as is known, Hitler did not use the term 'partisan' in connection with Jews in the Reich or in western Europe. (See Longerich, *Politik*, 467 and 712 n.234.)

157. The following is taken from the minutes of the Conference: Longerich, *Ermordung*, 83–92; trans., *N & P*, iii.1127–34, Doc.849. See Eichmann's comments on the minutes during his interrogation in Jerusalem in 1961 in Longerich, *Ermordung*, 92–4.

158. See Jeremy Noakes, 'The Development of Nazi Policy towards the German-Jewish "Mischlinge" 1933–1945', *LBYB*, 34 (1989), 291–354, here 341ff.

159. Longerich, *Ermordung*, 93.

160. Longerich, *Politik*, 470–71.

161. Longerich, *Ermordung*, 91.

162. Longerich, *Politik*, 514–15.

163. *Dienstkalender*, 73.

164. Domarus, 1829. Hitler had also issued a threat to those seeking through 'Jewish hatred' to bring about destruction through the war in his 'New Year's Appeal' (Domarus, 1821). Two weeks later, Hitler spoke to Goebbels of the Jews deserving the catastrophe that was befalling them. 'With the destruction of our enemies they will also experience their own destruction,' Goebbels reported Hitler as saying (*TBJG*, II/3, 320 (15 February 1942)).

165. *MadR*, 3235.

166. Martin Broszat and Norbert Frei (eds.), *Das Dritte Reich im Überblick. Chronik-Ereignisse-Zusammenhänge*, Munich/Zurich, 1989, 270, give the date of 17 March for the beginning of the mass killing in Belzec. The decision to exterminate most of the Jews of the districts of Lublin and Galicia had probably been taken at the beginning of March (Longerich, *Politik*, 513).

167. *TBJG*, II/3, 513 (20 March 1942).

168. *TBJG*, II/3, 561 (27 March 1942).

CHAPTER 11: LAST BIG THROW OF THE DICE

1. Schroeder, 129.

2. *TBJG*, II/3, 501–2 (20 March 1942).

3. *TBJG*, II/3, 511 (20 March 1942).

4. Schroeder, 129–30.

5. *TBJG*, II/3, 513 (20 March 1942). The absence of any genuinely personal contact with Hitler was underlined by Gerda Daranowski, one of his secretaries, who nevertheless still thought well of him many years after the war. (Library of Congress, Washington, Adolf Hitler Collection, tape C-63A (interview with John Toland, 26 July 1971).)

6. Koeppen, Fol. 67 (24 October 1941).

7. Guderian, 266.

8. Breloer, 100 (29 January 1942).

9. Adolf Görtz, *Stichwort: Front. Tagebuch eines jungen Deutschen 1938—1942*, 2nd edn, Leipzig, 1987, 139.

10. *MadR*, ix.3225, 29 January 1942).

11. Ernest K. Bramsted, *Goebbels and National Socialist Propaganda 1925—1945*, Michigan, 1965, 222—3; Kershaw, '*Hitler Myth*', 180—81 and n.40; Robert Edward Herzstein, *The War that Hitler Won. The Most Infamous Propaganda Campaign in History*, London, 1979, 429, for the success of the film.

12. For the plainly intended parallels indicated by Goebbels himself, Hitler's pleasure at the film, and the impact upon him of the characterization of Frederick the Great, see *TBJG*, II/3, 499, 506 (20 March 1942).

13. Seidler, chs.3—4.

14. Seidler, 239; Alan S. Milward, 'Fritz Todt als Minister fur Bewaffnung und Munition', *VfZ*, 1966, 46; Alan S. Milward, *Die deutsche Kriegswirtschaft 1939—1945*, Stuttgart, 1966, 56.

15. Seidler, 273.

16. Seidler, 262—3; Mommsen, *Volkswagenwerk*, 544—5.

17. Seidler, 352ff.

18. Overy, *War and Economy*, 354—5; Seidler, 256.

19. Overy, *War and Economy*, ch.11, especially 352ff.; Hans-Ulrich Thamer, *Verführung und Gewalt. Deutschland 1933—1945*, Berlin, 1986, 716; Ludolf Herbst, *Das nationalsozialistische Deutschland 1933—1945*, Frankfurt am Main, 1996, 410.

20. Seidler, 256—60.

21. Seidler, 258, 265.

22. Seidler, 260, 365—6.

23. Jürgen Thorwald, *Die ungeklärten Fälle*, Stuttgart, 1950, 144—5.

24. Seidler, 367—9; Max Müller, 'Der Tod des Reichsministers Dr Fritz Todt', and Reimer Hansen, 'Der ungeklärte Fall Todt', *Geschichte in Wissenschaft und Unterricht*, 18 (1967), 602—5.

25. Seidler, 375ff., Thorwald, 133—54. I am grateful to Steven Sage for a summary preview of the research he is undertaking on Fritz Todt. He sees the air-crash as arranged at Hitler's behest.

26. Below, 305—6; Hans Baur, *Ich flog Mächtige der Erde*, Kempten, 1956, 216; see also *TBJG*, II/3, 299, 306 (13 February 1941).

27. Seidel, 377ff.; Speer, 209; Fest, *Speer*, 181-2. Speer's own account is unreliable and, in the published version of his memoirs (*Erinnerungen*, 205ff.), greatly touched-up. (See Sereny, *Speer*, 274—83; Seidler, 366—7.) In the Speer Papers (pen-pictures of Nazi leaders, drawn up in 1946, and kindly made available to me by Gitta Sereny) AH/I/Bl.4, Albert Speer claimed that he was by chance in FHQ at the time of Todt's crash. Speer initially asked Todt whether he could make use of the free seat in the plane to fly to Munich, backing out of the flight, scheduled for 8a.m., after talking to Hitler until the early hours. (Matthias Schmidt, *Albert Speer: Das Ende eines Mythos. Speers wahre Rolle im Dritten Reich*, Bern/Munich, 1982, 75.)

28. Schroeder, 132.

29. Sereny, *Speer*, 104ff.

30. Speer, 210; Seidler, 832.

31. Seidler, 403—4; Speer, 210; Speer Papers, AH/I/Bl.4.

32. Speer, 210; Sereny, *Speer*, 276—7; Seidler, 382.

33. Speer, 211, 215, 217; Overy, *War and Economy*, 355; Herbst, *Das nationalsozialistische Deutschland*, 410.

34. Domarus, 1836—40; Thorwald, 148.

35. Speer, 217.

36. Dietrich Eichholtz, *Kriegswirtschaft 1939—1945, Bd.II 1941—1943*, East Berlin, 1985, 265, 308ff.; Overy, *War and Economy*, 366—7.

37. *TBJG*, II.3, 299 (13 February 1942), 303, 308 (14 February 1942), 311—12, 318 (15 February

1942). See also Irving, *HW*, 367–8, 371–2; Domarus, 1841 n.73. The German delight was soon tempered by the news that the *Scharnhorst* and *Gneisenau* had run on to mines laid by the RAF. The *Scharnhorst* was out of action for months; the *Gneisenau* was bombed while under repair and incapable of further deployment (Weinberg III, 358).

38. *TBJG*, II.3, 321 (15 February 1941); Below, 307.

39. *Staatsmänner* II, 48 (11 February 1942). Hitler had said on 18 December in the Wolfsschanze: 'I didn't want that in East Asia. For years I said to every Englishman: "You'll lose East Asia if you begin a conflict in Europe"' (*Monologe*, 156). He was rumoured to be unenthusiastic about the Japanese successes and have remarked that he would most like to send twenty divisions to the English to repel 'the Yellows' (Hassell, 305 (22 March 1942)). Over a year later he would ruminate wistfully on 'whether the white man can sustain his superiority at all in the long run in the face of the enormous human reservoirs in the east' (*TBJG*, II/6, 236 (8 May 1943)).

40. Schroeder, 132.

41. *TBJG*, II/3, 514 (20 March 1942).

42. Schroeder, 131.

43. *TBJG*, II/3, 319 (15 February 1942).

44. Domarus, 1842.

45. Below, 306.

46. Domarus, 1851.

47. Domarus, 1850. Hitler repeated the claim in his Reichstag speech on 26 April. In fact, the previous winter, of 1940–41, had been colder in the east (Domarus, 1871 and n.181; see also 1872 and n.183).

48. Domarus, 1850.

49. *MadR*, ix.3486–8 (19 March 1942); Steinert, 283–5. See also *TBJG*, II/3, 479 (16 March 1942), on the basis of SD reports: 'The German people is in the main concerned with the foodstuffs situation.' As a consequence 'interest in military events dies away somewhat'.

50. *TBJG*, II/3, 488 (18 March 1942), 496 (19 March 1942).

51. *TBJG*, II/3, 479 (16 March 1942).

52. *TBJG*, II/3, 496 (19 March 1942).

53. *TBJG*, II/3, 497 (19 March 1942).

54. *TBJG*, II/3, 489 (18 March 1942), 496 (19 March 1942).

55. *TBJG*, II/3, 494 (19 March 1942).

56. *TBJG*, II/3, 484 (17 March 1942).

57. *TBJG*, II/3, 495 (19 March 1942).

58. *TBJG*, II/3, 499 (20 March 1942).

59. *TBJG*, II/3, 503 (20 March 1942). Clearly, however, Hitler detested being reminded of poor morale. Only a few days later he noted on a report on the decline in mood which had been presented to him: 'If it were decisive, what people always say, everything would long since have been lost. The true bearing of the people lies much deeper and rests on a very firm inner bearing. If that were not the case, all the achievements of the people would be inexplicable' (Picker, 206 (25 March 1942)).

60. *TBJG*, II/3, 504 (20 March 1942); Weiß, *Biographisches Lexikon*, 457–9.

61. For the capitulation of justice to the police-state, see especially Martin Broszat, 'Zur Perversion der Strafjustiz im Dritten Reich', *VfZ*, 6 (1958), 390–443; and Broszat, *Staat*, ch.10, especially 421–2. Thierack was appointed Reich Minister of Justice on 20 August 1942 (Wistrich, *Wer war wer*, 272).

62. *TBJG*, II/3, 505 (20 March 1942); Irving, *HW*, 366.

63. *TBJG*, II/3, 506 (20 March 1942).

64. *MadR*, ix.3526–9 (26 March 1942); Steinert, 287–9.

65. Picker, 222–5, here 225 (29 March 1942).

66. Domarus, 1857, 1859–60; Rebentisch, 419; Ralph Angermund, *Deutsche Richterschaft 1919–1945. Krisenerfahrung, Illusion, politische Rechtsprechung*, Frankfurt am Main, 1990, 249–50. For further interventions by Hitler in sentencing, see Rebentisch, 399 and n.83; Broszat, *Staat*, 418. It has been estimated that there were some 25–30 cases between 1939 and 1942 in which Hitler imposed the death sentence instead of a lesser penalty (Jeremy Noakes and Geoffrey Pridham, *Documents on Nazism 1919–1945*, London, 1974, 276). The supine behaviour of Schlegelberger in the Schlitt case stood in contrast to the readiness, remarkable in the circumstances, of Gauleiter Rover of Oldenburg, to take up with Hitler on 2 May the complaint of the President of the Higher Regional Court in Oldenburg and persuade him that he had been mistaken in presuming the sentence on Schlitt had been too lenient. Röver was left to convey Hitler's regrets to the Oldenburg judges. His fury was directed at those who had 'misled' him. (Domarus, 1881; Angermund, 250.)

67. Picker, 199 (22 March 1942).

68. *TBJG*, II/4, 162–3 (24 April 1942).

69. Gruchmann, *Der Zweite Weltkrieg*, 197; Steinert, 286; Below, 308.

70. *TBJG*, II/4, 174 (26 April 1942).

71. *TBJG*, II/4, 176 (26 April 1942).

72. *TBJG*, II/4, 175–6 (26 April 1942).

73. See also Picker, 294–5 (25 April 1942) for an extended account of Hitler's comments on vegetarianism at the lunchtime gathering.

74. *TBJG*, II/4, 177 (26 April 1942).

75. *TBJG*, II/4, 180 (27 April 1942).

76. *TBJG*, II/4, 181 (27 April 1942).

77. *TBJG*, II/4, 183–4 (27 April 1942). Picker's account of the midday conversation deals solely with the question of the political comments of actors, particularly of Emil Jannings. Goebbels's own account of the lunchtime session makes plain that this was only an unimportant subsidiary theme. (Picker, 296; *TBJG*, II/4, 185–6 (27 April 1942).)

78. *TBJG*, II/3, 561 (27 March 1942).

79. *TBJG*, II/4, 184 (27 April 1942).

80. *TBJG*, II/4, 183 (27 April 1942).

81. *TBJG*, II/4, 186–7 (27 April 1942).

82. Domarus, 1865–74.

83. Domarus, 1874–5.

84. Rebentisch, 420–21.

85. *RGBl*, 1942, I.247. See also Rebentisch, 421 and n.154 (for Lammers's insertion); and Max Domarus, *Der Reichstag und die Macht*, Wurzburg, 1968, 149–51.

86. Domarus, 1877.

87. *MadR*, x.3673–4 (27 April 1941); 3685–8 (30 April 1942); Steinert, 289.

88. *MadR*, x.3686–7; Steinert, 289–92; Angermund, 248–9; Klaus Oldenhage, 'Justizverwaltung und Lenkung der Rechtsprechung im Zweiten Weltkrieg', in Rebentisch and Teppe, 100–20, here 114–15.

89. Cit. Oldenhage, 115.

90. Steinert, 289–90.

91. Picker, 298–9 (26 April 1942); *TBJG*, II/4, 188 (27 April 1942).

92. StA Neuburg an der Donau, vorl.LO 30/35, KL Nördlingen, 11 May 1942: '*Verzagte Gemüter . . . scheinen nur von einer Stelle der Rede des Führers beeindruckt worden zu sein: als der Führer von den Vorbereitungen zum Winterfeldzug 42/43 sprach. Je mehr die Grausamkeit und Härte des Winterkampfes im Osten der Heimat voll bewußt geworden ist, umso mehr ist die Sehrsucht nach einem Ende gestiegen. Nun aber ist das Ende noch nicht absehbar – darunter leiden viele Frauen und Mütter.*'

93. The 'Osteria Bavaria' was in Schellingstraße 62, in the 'Party district' of Munich (Domarus, 1878, n.198).

94. Picker, 299–300 (27 April 1942).

95. Picker, 300–303 (29 April 1942). Hitler praised Furtwangler for making the Berlin Philharmonic a far superior orchestra to the Vienna Philharmonic, despite smaller subsidies. For an assessment of the relationship with the regime of Walter, Knappertsbusch, Furtwängler, and – a rapidly rising star combining musical brilliance with ruthless career-opportunism – Herbert von Karajan, see Michael H. Kater, *The Twisted Muse. Musicians and their Music in the Third Reich*, New York/ Oxford, 1997, 40–46, 55–61, 93–4, 114–16, 195–203. Richard J. Evans, *Rereading German History 1800–1996. From Unification to Reunification*, London, 1997, 187–93, offers a necessary corrective to the uncritical treatment of Furtwängler in Fred K. Prieberg, *Trial of Strength: Wilhelm Furtwängler and the Third Reich*, London, 1992, and Sam H. Shirakawa, *The Devil's Music Master: the Controversial Life and Career of Wilhelm Furtwängler*, New York, 1992.

96. *CD*, 461 (29 April 1942); Schmidt, 562.

97. *Staatsmänner* II, 65 (29 April 1942).

98. *CP*, 481–4 (29–30 April 1942); *CD*, 461–2 (29 April 1942); Schmidt, 562–3.

99. *CD*, 462–3 (dated 29 April 1942, though refers to both meetings, and here to the meeting on 30 April 1942).

100. *CD*, 463–4.

101. Andreas Hillgruber and Jürgen Förster (eds.), 'Zwei neue Aufzeichnungen über "Führer-Besprechungen" aus dem Jahre 1942', *Militärgeschichtliche Mitteilungen*, 11 (1972), 109–26, here 116.

102. Rommel's offensive was launched on 26 May against the numerically superior British forces of the 8th Army at Gazala in Libya, on the Mediterranean coast between Benghazi and Tobruk (Gruchmann, *Der Zweite Weltkrieg*, 183; Weinberg III, 350). The invasion of Malta was never to take place. The summer of 1942 proved to be the height of the siege of the island. (See *Oxford Companion*, 713–16.)

103. *Staatsmänner* II, 79 (30 April 1942); Hillgruber and Förster, 114–21.

104. Picker, 304 (1 May 1942).

105. *Weisungen*, 215.

106. *Weisungen*, 213–19; *Halder KTB*, iii.420 (28 March 1942).

107. *IMG*, vii.290 (Testimony of Field-Marshal Friedrich Paulus).

108. See the comments of Bernd Wegner, 'Hitlers zweiter Feldzug gegen die Sowjetunion. Strategische Grundlagen und historische Bedeutung', in Michalka, *Der Zweite Weltkrieg*, 652–66, here 659.

109. Hartmann, 314–16; Wegner, 'Hitlers zweiter Feldzug', 657.

110. Wegner, 'Hitlers zweiter Feldzug', 660.

111. Wegner, 'Hitlers zweiter Feldzug', 658–9.

112. Hartmann, 313 (on the basis of figures compiled on 2 April 1942; see 314 n.14).

113. Wegner, 'Hitlers zweiter Feldzug', 654.

114. *Halder KTB*, iii.430–32 (21 April 1942).

115. Hartmann, 314.

116. Overy, *Why the Allies Won*, 66.

117. *Halder KTB*, iii.442–4 (15–19 May 1942).

118. *Halder KTB*, iii.449–50 (28 May 1942).

119. Hartmann, 320 (and see n.58 for criticism of Irving's interpretation, giving all credit to Hitler, and claiming Halder had subsequently altered his diary entry); Below, 310.

120. Domarus, 1883; *TBJG*, II/4, 344 (23 May 1942).

121. *TBJG*, II/4, 354 (24 May 1942).

122. *TBJG*, II/4, 354, 360–61 (24 May 1942). At lunch the previous day, Hitler had already launched

into further scathing attacks on the judiciary (Picker, 371–2 (22 May 1942)); *TBJG*, II/4, 343 (23 May 1942).

123. *TBJG*, II/4, 357 (24 May 1942).

124. *TBJG*, II/4, 358–9, 362 (24 May 1942).

125. *TBJG*, II/4, 360 (24 May 1942).

126. *TBJG*, II/4, 361 (24 May 1942).

127. *TBJG*, II/4, 355 (24 May 1942).

128. *TBJG*, II/4, 355–7 (24 May 1942).

129. *TBJG*, II/4, 358–9, 361 (24 May 1942).

130. *TBJG*, II/4, 362–4 (24 May 1942).

131. Domarus, 1887–8; see also Picker, 493–504.

132. *TBJG*, II/4, 401 (30 May 1942).

133. *TBJG*, II/4, 402 (30 May 1942).

134. *TBJG*, II/4, 406 (30 May 1942). At his meeting with Mussert on 10 December 1942, Hitler would make plain that he envisaged, in the future new European order, the Netherlands, like Belgium, while not being treated as a conquered country, having no independence and being incorporated into a 'Greater German Reich' ('*groß-germanisches Reich*'). Hitler explicitly mentioned the incorporation of Austria as an indicator of what he had in mind. (Hillgruber and Förster, 121–6, here 125.)

135. Charles Wighton, *Heydrich. Hitler's Most Evil Henchman*, London, 1962, 268ff.; Charles Whiting, *Heydrich. Henchman of Death*, London, 1999, 141–7; M. R. D. Foot, *Resistance. European Resistance to Nazism 1940–45*, London, 1976, 204–6; *Oxford Companion*, 1018–22.

136. Foot, *Resistance*, 206, puts the death-toll of the reprisals at 2,000; Whiting, 159ff.; *Tb* Reuth, 1800, n.66.

137. *TBJG*, II/4, 405 (30 May 1942). Baum and his colleagues were arrested, tortured, sentenced to death, and executed. On the attempt, see Merson, 243; Arnold Paucker, *Deutsche Juden im Widerstand 1933–1945. Tatsachen und Probleme, Beiträge zum Widerstand 1933–1945*, ed. Gedenkstatte Deutscher Widerstand, Berlin, 1999, 21; Wolfgang Benz and Walter H. Pehle (eds.), *Lexikon des deutschen Widerstandes*, Frankfurt am Main, 1994, 225–7. Hitler had given Goebbels permission to have 500 Jewish 'hostages' arrested, and to respond to any further attempts by shootings. (Goebbels let the leaders of the Jewish community in Berlin know that 100–150 Jews would be shot for any new attempt. He also had a number of Jews in Sachsenhausen concentration camp shot. *TBJG*, 4, 432 (2 June 1942).) At the same time, Hitler had commissioned Goebbels – probably at the Propaganda Minister's own prompting – to 'see to it as quickly as possible that the Berlin Jews are evacuated'. But Speer had objected that replacements needed first to be found for the Jews working in the armaments industry (351 (24 May 1942)). See also 386 (28 May 1942), where Goebbels referred to the list of Jewish hostages he had had drawn up, and numerous arrests he had caused to be made, after the sabotage attempt at the exhibition.

138. *TBJG*, II/4, 393 (29 May 1942).

139. *TBJG*, II/4, 405 (30 May 1942). Goebbels repeated at the end of his summary of Hitler's remarks that he had been practically in total agreement with what the Führer had said (*TBJG*, II/4, 410 (30 May 1942)).

140. *TBJG*, II/4, 361 (24 May 1942).

141. *TBJG*, II/4, 405 (30 May 1942).

142. *TBJG*, II/4, 406 (30 May 1942). For another version of Hitler's comments on the Jews that lunchtime, claiming they were indeed Asiatic, not European, see Picker, 378 (29 May 1942). In speaking over supper to his entourage in his headquarters near Vinnitsa in late July of the removal of the Jews, Hitler, describing them as 'enemy number one', once more mentioned the prospect of removing them to Madagascar 'or some other Jewish national state' – plans which had been abandoned in 1940 (Picker, 471 (24 July 1942)).

143. *IMG*, xxix.582, Doc. 2233-PS ('Die Weisung der Judenvernichtung kommt von hoherer Stelle'). Goebbels noted, after speaking to Frank on 23 May about Jewish policy in the General Government, that it was 'no trifling matter (*nicht von Pappe*)', but that Frank could take little credit for it because the Führer had appointed an SS-State Secretary (Krüger) at his side who took his orders from Himmler. This was necessary since 'Jewish and ethnic policy must above all follow unified guidelines'. (*TBJG*, II/4, 352 (24 May 1942).) In his post-war memoirs, Frank was adamant that Hitler was responsible for the order to murder the Jews. See Frank, 391–2.

144. BDC, SS-HO, 933: RFSS to Berger, 28 July 1942: '*Verbot einer Verordnung über den Begriff "Jude"*'. '*Die besetzten Ostgebiete werden judenfrei. Die Durchführung dieses sehr schweren Befehls hat der Führer auf meine Schultern gelegt.*' For frequent recourse by those connected with the 'Final Solution' to an order by or wish of Hitler, see Fleming, *Hitler und die Endlösung*, 62ff.

145. BDC, SS-HO/1220, Chef des OKW, 16 December 1942, betr. Bandenbekämpfung; SS-HO/1238, Reichsführer-SS, 29 December 1942: 'Meldungen an den Führer über Bandenbekämpfung, Meldung Nr.51, Rußland-Sud, Ukraine, Bialystok. Bandenbekämpfungserfolge vom 1.9 bis 1.12.1942'. Himmler's handwritten note at the top indicates that he presented the report to Hitler on 31 December 1942.

146. See Walter Laqueur, *The Terrible Secret. Suppression of the Truth about Hitler's 'Final Solution'*, Harmondsworth, 1982, 15n., 17–18; Steinert, 257. Raul Hilberg, *Die Vernichtung der europäischen Juden*, revised trans. edn, Frankfurt am Main, 1990, iii.1283–4, has an unduly complex explanation of the excision of the explicit language by Himmler. The Reichsführer, he suggests, was keen to boast of his 'achievements'. But he faced a problem. Speer and the Commander of the Reserve Army, General Fritz Fromm, had criticized Himmler and queried with Hitler himself the RSHA's statistics on arrests of Jews who, they claimed, were needed for the armaments industry. Himmler's way round his problem was to have a statistical report drawn up for Hitler, but to present it in camouflaged language. Irving, *HW*, 392, 503–4, 871, takes the view that the Korherr report was doctored to prevent Hitler knowing about the killing operations.

147. See Mommsen, 'Realisierung', 414–17.

148. *TBJG*, II/3, 561 (27 March 1942).

149. In his speech to the Reichs- and Gauleiter after Rover's death, Hitler indicated that he had little interest in overseas colonies, stating instead: 'Our colonial territory lies in the East' (*TBJG*, II/4, 363 (24 May 1942)).

150. Irving uses this to allege that Hitler did not know of the 'Final Solution'; see *HW*, 327 and 850–51 (n. to 326).

151. Laqueur, 18 refers to Himmler's chief of staff, Karl Wolff, denying in his post-war trial that his boss had ever mentioned mass murder to him. Himmler's chief adjutant, Werner Grothmann, indicated similarly in an interview long after the war that he had never heard Himmler discuss the 'Final Solution' (Franklin D. Roosevelt Library, Hyde Park, New York, Toland Papers, C-58, I/T2/S1/10, taped interview with John Toland, 7 October 1971). Once – if the much later account of a telephonist in Fuhrer Headquarters is to be trusted – the Reichsführer-SS did inadvertently break the code. He was, it was recalled, overheard on the line in mid-May 1942 telling Bormann he had good news for the Führer from Auschwitz that again 20,000 Jews had been 'liquidated' there. He immediately corrected the word to 'evacuated'. But Bormann angrily reminded him that such reports, as arranged, were only to be sent to him by SS courier for passing on to the Fuhrer (Schulz, 98). The veracity of the account is impossible to check. That Hitler was sent frequent reports by SS courier sounds doubtful; as does Himmler's slip of the tongue. The date, too, seems early, since the routine and systematic mass extermination in Auschwitz only began in July 1942 (Longerich, *Politik*, 515).

152. Domarus, 1446: 'Grundsatzlicher Befehl', 11 January 1940; Laqueur, 18–19. The number of persons with indirect or partial knowledge was of course far wider.

153. This was given as a reason, in autumn 1942, why Gauleiter Greiser should not proceed with

his aim to exterminate 30,000 Poles suffering from incurable tuberculosis (Kershaw, 'Improvised Genocide?', 72).

154. See Steinert, 252-7, including (257) reference to Bormann's secret circular to Gauleiter, informing them on Hitler's behalf, that 'in public treatment of the Jewish question all discussion of a future complete solution (*Gesamtlösung*) must cease. It can however be mentioned that the Jews are conscripted en bloc for appropriate deployment of labour.'

155. *IMG*, xxvii.270-73, here 270, Doc. 1517-PS, Alfred Rosenberg: 'Vermerk über Unterredung beim Führer am 14.12.41'.

156. Steinert, 252-3.

157. *IMG*, xxix. 145, 1919-PS; *Anatomie*, i.329; ii.446-7.

158. See Jackel, 'Hitler und der Mord an den europäischen Juden', 161.

159. See note 144 above: BDC, SS-HO, 933: RFSS to Berger, 28 July 1942: 'Verbot einer Verordnung über den Begriff "Jude" '.

160. See *TBJG*, II/4, 402 (30 May 1942) for the 'psychological pressure' during the winter on account of 'the unsuccessful Napoleonic adventure'.

161. See Kershaw, *Popular Opinion*, 365, 368-9.

162. See *TBJG*, II/4, 482, 489 (10 June 1942).

163. S. W. Roskill, *The War at Sea*, London, 1954, 1956, 1960, i.599ff., 614, ii.467ff., 475, iii.364ff. See also Overy, *Why the Allies Won*, 47 (with different figures), 49, 52.

164. Gruchmann, *Der Zweite Weltkrieg*, 183; Weinberg III, 350 (who gives the number of British troops captured as 28,000); *DRZW*, vi.623-33; Winston S. Churchill, *The Second World War. Vol.IV, The Hinge of Fate*, London etc., 1951, 371-8.

165. Weinberg III, 350-51.

166. Below, 312; Irving, *HW*, 399; Weinberg III, 350-51.

167. *TBJG*, II/4, 416 (31 May 1942). Hitler repeated that the attacks would be on 'cultural centres', since those on military and economic targets had hardly been worthwhile. The appointment of Air Marshal Arthur Harris as Commander-in-Chief of the RAF's Bomber Command on 23 February had sharply intensified the British strategy of 'area bombing', aimed at demoralization of the population living in the centres of German cities (Overy, *Why the Allies Won*, 112-13).

168. *TBJG*, II/4, 422 (1 June 1942); 431 (2 June 1942).

169. Below, 311-12.

170. *Kriegstagebuch des Oberkommandos der Wehrmacht (Wehrmachtführungsstab), Bd.II: 1.Januar 1942-31.Dezember 1942*, ed. Andreas Hillgruber, Frankfurt am Main, 1963 (=KTB OKW, ii.), ii/1, 395-6 (1 June 1942); Bock, 490 (1 June 1942); Picker, 381 (1 June 1942).

171. Picker, 381 (2 June 1942).

172. *TBJG*, II/4, 489 (10 June 1942).

173. A military alliance, rather than a formal pact, had been arrived at in spring 1941. The Finns had initially put out a declaration of neutrality on the day of the German attack on the Soviet Union, though Hitler's own proclamation the same day had pointed out that German soldiers at the northern point of the front were fighting alongside Finnish divisions. Immediate Soviet attacks on Finland led to a Finnish declaration of war on 25 June 1941. (See *DRZW*, iv.Ch.VI, pts.1-4, especially 390ff., 400-404.)

174. Bernd Wegner, 'Hitlers Besuch in Finnland. Das geheime Tonprotokoll seiner Unterredung mit Mannerheim am 4. Juni 1942', *VfZ*, 41 (1993), 122 n.23; Domarus, 1889.

175. Wegner 'Hitlers Besuch in Finnland', 122-3, 127.

176. Wegner 'Hitlers Besuch in Finnland', 124, 128; Domarus, 1889.

177. Wegner, 'Hitlers Besuch in Finnland', 126 and (for the text) 130-37.

178. Wegner, 'Hitlers Besuch in Finnland', 127.

179. Wegner, 'Hitlers Besuch in Finnland', 125-6 and n.40, 134 n.74. For the 'preventive war' legend, and the way it was exploited by Nazi propaganda, see above, Ch.9, notes 4, 39.

180. Wegner, 'Hitlers Besuch in Finnland', 128.

181. *TBJG*, II/4, 489 (10 June 1942).

182. Wegner, 'Hitlers Besuch in Finnland', 129.

183. *TBJG*, II/4, 450 (5 June 1942). Daluege rang Goebbels at 10a.m. to say that Heydrich had died a half an hour earlier. Presumably, he had first rung FHQ. But Hitler, as Goebbels pointed out, could not make any decision about the state funeral since he was in Finland and not expected back until the evening. So he must already have left FHQ when the news arrived. He landed in Finland at 11.15a.m. (Domarus, 1889). Whether Hitler was informed during his six-hour visit to Finland, or learnt of Heydrich's death only on return (Domarus, 1890) is uncertain.

184. Picker, 386 (4 June 1942). Hitler referred here, as on an earlier occasion, on 3 May 1942 (Picker, 306–8), to attempts on his own life. Hitler repeated, when in Berlin for Heydrich's funeral, that he had warned him only to travel in an armour-plated car (*TBJG*, II/4, 486 (10 June 1942)).

185. *TBJG*, II/4, 486 (10 June 1942).

186. *TBJG*, II/4, 492 (10 June 1942).

187. See *DRZW*, vi.868ff. for the unfolding of the campaign.

188. *Halder KTB*, iii.462 (21 June 1942).

189. Overy, *Why the Allies Won*, 66.

190. *Halder KTB*, iii.467 (28 June 1942).

191. *Halder KTB*, iii.469 (1 July 1942); Domarus, 1895–6.

192. Bock, 512–14 (3 July 1942).

193. *Halder Diary*, 632–9 (3–13 July 1942); Bock, 525–6 (13 July 1942); Below, 312. In his talk with Bock on 3 July, Hitler had made fun of the English for sacking generals when something went wrong and thereby undermining the freedom of decision in the army (Bock, 513 (3 July 1942)).

194. See Domarus, 1897, n.312.

195. Domarus, 1897; Hauner, *Hitler*, 179, for the return to Rastenburg on 1 November.

196. Schroeder, 135–41; *Halder KTB*, iii.483 (16 July 1942); Below, 313. Picker found the Ukraine an attractive area (Picker, 465 (22 July 1942)). Below, who had mentioned that Hitler disliked the heat and the flies in the summer of 1942, referred to the Vinnitsa headquarters during the second sojourn there in late February and early March 1943 as 'pleasant' (Below, 331). Goebbels, however, visiting FHQ in that period, found the location 'desolate (*trostlos*)' TBJG, II/7, 501 (9 March 1943).

197. Below, 313; Picker, 461 (19 July 1942).

198. Picker, 457–77 (18–26 July 1942).

199. Below, 313.

200. *Halder KTB*, iii.492 (28 July 1942), 493–4 (30 July 1942), 494–5 n.1; *KTB OKW*, ii/2, 1285; Irving, *HW*, 405–6.

201. Hartmann, 325.

202. Below, 313.

203. See Bernd Wegner, 'Vom Lebensraum zum Todesraum. Deutschlands Kriegführung zwischen Moskau und Stalingrad', in Jürgen Förster (ed.), *Stalingrad. Ereignis-Wirkung-Symbol*, Munich/Zürich, 1992, 17–37, here 19.

204. Cit. Hartmann, 326 n.90. Ninety per cent of the Soviet Union's oil came from Baku and the north Caucasian oil-fields (Wegner, 'Vom Lebensraum zum Todesraum', 19).

205. Wegner, 'Vom Lebensraum zum Todesraum', 21, for the scepticism, but the lack of a convincing alternative on the part of the generals.

206. Wegner, 'Hitler zweiter Feldzug', 660; Wegner, 'Vom Lebensraum zum Todesraum', 29.

207. *Weisungen*, 227. Marshal Semyon Timoshenko was the Red Army's senior general, commonly regarded at this point as the Soviet Union's most competent military commander. He had, however, presided over the loss of a quarter of a million men, together with their tanks and artillery, in the battle for Kharkov in spring, and was recalled to Moscow on 23 July, returning to a field-command, this time on the north-west front, only in October (*Oxford Companion*, 1108–9).

208. Hartmann, 325.

209. *Weisungen*, 227-9; see Hartmann, 326.

210. Hartmann, 328-9; *DRZW*, vi.953ff.

211. *Halder KTB*, iii.489 (23 July 1942), trans. *Halder Diary*, 646; Hartmann, 328.

212. Cit. Hartmann, 328.

213. Overy, *Why the Allies Won*, 67.

214. *Halder KTB*, iii.503-7 (12-19 August 1942); Hartmann, 329.

215. *Halder KTB*, iii.501 (9 August 1942); Speer, 252; *DRZW*, vi.942-3; Wegner, 'Vom Lebensraum zum Todesraum', 30; Irving, *HW*, 414.

216. *TBJG*, ii/5, 353-4 (20 August 1942).

217. This is what Speer later claimed (Speer, 252).

218. *Halder KTB*, iii.508 (22 August 1942); Below, 313; Domarus, 1905.

219. Speer, 253.

220. *DRZW*, vi.965; Hartmann, 329.

221. *Halder KTB*, iii.509 (23 August 1942).

222. See Hartmann, 329.

223. *Halder KTB*, iii.511 (26 August 1942).

224. Warlimont, 251 (dating the meeting to 8 August); *Halder KTB*, iii.501 (7 August 1942); *DRZW*, vi.908; Irving, *HW*, 415.

225. Below, 314; *DRZW*, vi.898-906; Irving, *HW*, 416-18.

226. Hartmann, 330.

227. Heusinger, 200-201; trans. amended from Warlimont, 251-2.

228. Engel, 125 (4 September 1942); see also Warlimont, 251-2, 618 n.21; Erich von Manstein, *Lost Victories*, (1955), London, 1982, 261-2. Though his diary entry is misdated, and is a post-war reconstruction, there seems no obvious reason to doubt the authenticity of Engel's record. Heusinger's account (Heusinger, 201, also misdated) of Hitler's further response is less insulting than what was actually said. Heusinger accepted after the war that he had deliberately avoided publishing Hitler's worst insult. (See Hartmann, 331-2 and nn.14, 17.)

229. Engel, 125 (4 September 1942). Halder, recognizing that he could no longer cope with Hitler's operational leadership, appears, in fact, consciously to have been working towards the second half of July at provoking his own dismissal, aware that a conventional resignation would not be acceptable (*DRZW*, vi.954).

230. Engel, 126 n.395.

231. Engel, 124 (27 August 1942). This and a further entry for the same date are misdated by Engel (see 124 n.389) and repeated almost verbatim (126) under the date 7 September 1942.

232. Engel, 124 (27 August 1942).

233. Engel, 126 (8 September 1942). According to her later testimony, Jodl told his second wife, Luise, that 'he had never witnessed such an outbreak of fury' in Hitler. (Franklin D. Roosevelt Library, Hyde Park, New York, Toland Tapes, II/T1/S2/3 (interview, in English, with John Toland, 7 November 1970).)

234. Below, 315.

235. Warlimont, 256; *Halder KTB*, iii.518-19 (8 September 1942).

236. Engel, 125 (27 August 1942).

237. Irving, *HW*, 422.

238. Engel, 125 (27 August 1942). See his similar comments, 128 (18 September 1942).

239. Engel, 127 (8 September 1942).

240. Warlimont, 256; Below, 315.

241. Engel, 127 (18 September 1942). For Hitler's lack of trust in his generals, see Engel 127-9 (14-30 September 1942).

242. Warlimont, 257-8.

243. Warlimont, 258.

244. Below, 316.

245. Warlimont, 259; Below, 315. Zeitzler was a close friend of Schmundt (Warlimont, 259). See Hartmann, 337–9, for a description of Zeitzler and his belief in Hitler. Hitler had pointed out to Goebbels some weeks earlier how impressed he had been by Zeitzler's work in the west (*TBJG*, II/5, 353 (20 August 1942)).

246. Warlimont, 260.

247. Hartmann, 339.

248. *Halder KTB*, iii.528 (24 September 1942). Halder was far from pessimistic about overall developments in the war. (See *Weizsäcker-Papiere*, 303 (30 September 1942).)

249. Hartmann, 339.

250. *KTB OKW*, ii/I, 669 (2 September 1942).

251. *Halder KTB*, iii.514 (31 August 1942).

252. *Halder KTB*, iii.521 (11 September 1942); *DRZW*, vi.982; Wegner, 'Vom Lebensraum zum Todesraum', 32.

253. Wegner, 'Vom Lebensraum zum Todesraum', 32–3.

254. Below, 318; Domarus, 1924–5.

255. *DRZW*, vi.684–7; Wegner, 'Vom Lebensraum zum Todesraum', 30–31; Irving, *HW*, 419; Domarus, 1924.

256. See Weinberg III, 351, 355–6, 361–2.

257. Below, 317.

258. *TBJG*, II/5, 594 (29 September 1942). For a repeat of these remarks and criticism of the behaviour of the Munich population during the raid, *TBJG*, II/5, 604 (30 September 1942).

259. *TBJG*, II/5, 358 (20 August 1942).

260. Steinert, 316; Kershaw, *'Hitler Myth'*, 185.

261. Below, 317; Irving, *HW*, 427.

262. *TBJG*, II/5, 370 (20 August 1942). The date appears to have been fixed only late in September (*TBJG*, II/5, 584 (28 September 1942).

263. *TBJG*, II/5, 594–5 (29 September 1942). See also 596 for Goebbels's scepticism; and Domarus, 1912, for the DNB summary of the speech.

264. Below, 318.

265. IfZ, ED 100, Irving-Sammlung, Hitler-Dokumentation, Bd. 1942 (Sept.-Okt.), from NA T78/317/1567ff., Führerrede zum Ausbau des Atlantikwalles am 29.Sept. 1942. See Irving, *HW*, 428–9.

266. Domarus, 1913–24.

267. Domarus, 1915; *MadR*, xi.4259 (1 October 1942).

268. Domarus, 1920.

269. Domarus, 1914, 1916.

270. *TBJG*, II/6, 42 (2 October 1942).

271. *TBJG*, II/5, 357 (20 August 1942).

272. *TBJG*, II/6, 46–7 (2 October 1942); and see also *TBJG*, II/5, 354 (20 August 1942).

273. *TBJG*, II/6, 48–9 (2 October 1942).

274. Wegner, 'Vom Lebensraum zum Todesraum', 33; and see Engel, 129–30 (2–3, 10 October 1942).

275. *TBJG*, II/5, 356 (20 August 1942).

276. *DRZW*, vi.987–8; Wegner, 'Vom Lebensraum zum Todesraum', 33.

277. *DRZW*, vi.988–93; Wegner, 'Vom Lebensraum zum Todesraum', 34.

278. Engel, 129 (10 February 1942).

279. *DRZW*, vi.993–4; Wegner, 'Vom Lebensraum zum Todesraum', 34.

280. Domarus, 1916.

281. Below, 319; Manfred Kehrig, 'Die 6.Armee im Kessel von Stalingrad', in Forster, *Stalingrad*, 76–110, here 76–9.

282. Domarus, 1931.

283. Below, 320–21; 1929–30; Irving, *HW*, 439–42 (who draws the comparison with the fate of Generals Hoepner and Sponeck the previous January).

284. On 1 November Hitler had transferred his headquarters from Vinnitsa back to the Wolf's Lair in East Prussia, where his entourage were pleased to find that bright and spacious wooden barracks had been added to the gloomy bunkers to which they had all been earlier confined. He had left his headquarters for Berlin, then Munich, on 6 November (Below, 321).

285. German views on the eastward-bound convoy from Gibraltar varied between seeing it as carrying provisions for Malta or heading for Tripolitania to attack Rommel from the rear. The Italian General Staff more realistically presumed that the objective was the occupation of French bases in North Africa. Mussolini and Ciano expected no resistance from the French (*CD*, 520 (7 November 1942)).

286. The first American fighting units to be engaged in the north African theatre of war were bombing crews relocated from India to the Egyptian front in the wake of the Tobruk disaster (Weinberg III, 356).

287. Below, 321–2; Engel, 134 (8 November 1942).

288. Below, 321–2.

289. Domarus, 1937.

290. *TBJG*, II/6, 254 (9 November 1942).

291. *TBJG*, II/6, 257–9 (9 November 1942).

292. *TBJG*, II/6, 259 (9 November 1942).

293. Domarus, 1935.

294. Domarus, 1938.

295. Domarus, 1937; Jäckel, 'Hitler und der Mord an den europäischen Juden', 161.

296. Steinert, 318–19; Kershaw, 'Hitler Myth', 186–9.

297. Engel reported that Hitler's speech had been the subject of much discussion at Führer Headquarters. He and others, he said, had been 'disgusted' that Hitler had spoken so optimistically 'with his audience in mind (*berechnet auf Zuhörerkreis*)' (Engel, 134 (10 November 1942)).

298. *TBJG*, II/6, 259–60 (9 November 1942).

299. *TBJG*, II/6, 261, 263 (9 November 1942).

300. *TBJG*, II/6, 258–9, 261–2 (9 November 1942).

301. *CD*, 521 (9 November 1942); 522 (10 November 1942).

302. *CD*, 522 (9 November 1942).

303. *CD*, 522 (10 November 1942); Schmidt, 576.

304. Domarus, 1945–9.

305. *Weisungen*, 220–21 (Directive No.42, 29 May 1942).

306. Below, 322–3.

307. Below, 323; *DRZW*, vi.997; Irving, *HW*, 455.

308. Gruchmann, *Der Zweite Weltkrieg*, 191; Kehrig, 'Die 6.Armee', 80–81; *DRZW*, vi.997–1009, 1018–21; and, fundamental especially for the Soviet side, Erickson, ch.10. There were also more than 30,000 soldiers of other nationalities, 10,000 of them Romanians, encircled (Kehrig, 'Die 6.Armee', 90).

309. Below, 323–4.

310. Manfred Kehrig, *Stalingrad. Analyse und Dokumentation einer Schlacht*, Stuttgart, 1974, 163; Kehrig, 'Die 6.Armee', 82; *DRZW*, vi.1024.

311. *KTB OKW*, ii/I, 84, ii/II, 1006 (22 November 1942); Kehrig, *Stalingrad. Analyse und Dokumentation*, 183; Kehrig, 'Die 6.Armee', 85; *DRZW*, vi.1025.

312. Below, 324. Both those close to Hitler and those who later castigated his direction of the war

concurred many years after the events that he accepted Göring's assurances that the troops at Stalingrad could be sustained from the air. (Franklin D. Roosevelt Library, Hyde Park, New York, Toland Tapes, T1-S1, interview of Adolf Heusinger by John Toland, 30 March 1970; 68-1, interview of Otto Günsche by John Toland, 26 March 1971.) For the dreadful weather conditions in Stalingrad in November, at times dipping to as low as minus eighteen degrees Celsius, see Antony Beevor, *Stalingrad*, London, 1998, 214, 230, 232.

313. Kehrig, *Stalingrad. Analyse und Dokumentation*, 219; Kehrig, 'Die 6.Armee', 86; *DRZW*, vi.1025-6; Gruchmann, *Zweiter Weltkrieg*, 192.

314. Kehrig, *Stalingrad. Analyse und Dokumentation*, 220; Kehrig, 'Die 6.Armee', 87; *DRZW*, vi.1028-9.

315. Gruchmann, *Der Zweite Weltkrieg*, 192.

316. Kehrig, *Stalingrad. Analyse und Dokumentation*, 224; Kehrig, 'Die 6.Armee', 87-8; Manstein, 315; *DRZW*, vi.1032. Manstein's own post-war account of Stalingrad (Manstein, 289-366) showed, naturally enough, his own actions in the best possible light. Hitler (almost exclusively), though to some extent Göring (for his unrealistic claims to relieve Stalingrad by air), and Paulus (for errors in not attempting to break out while there was still time) were held responsible for the débâcle. While Hitler's disastrous leadership and overriding culpability are undeniable, it was accepted by a strong critic of Hitler's direction of the war, former Army Operations Chief Adolf Heusinger, long after the war, that Manstein had to share some of the blame for the catastrophe. (Franklin D. Roosevelt Library, Hyde Park, New York, Toland Tapes, T1-S1, interview of Adolf Heusinger by John Toland, 30 March 1970.) See also the critical assessments by Joachim Wieder and Heinrich Graf von Einsiedel (eds.), *Stalingrad. Memories and Reassessments*, (1962), London, 1997, 148-78; Beevor, 308-10; and, especially, *DRZW*, vi.1060-3. Less critical of Manstein is Geoffrey Jukes, *Hitler's Stalingrad Decisions*, Berkeley/Los Angeles/London, 1985, 106-47, where, however, Hitler's disastrous role is portrayed within an increasingly overloaded process of decision-making, not just on the Stalingrad front.

317. Manstein, 316; *DRZW*, vi.1033.

318. Kehrig, *Stalingrad. Analyse und Dokumentation*, 386ff.; Kehrig, 'Die 6.Armee', 97-8; *DRZW*, vi.1033-4.

319. Below, 324; Gruchmann, *Der Zweite Weltkrieg*, 192-3. For Hoth's attempt, *DRZW*, vi.1035ff.

320. According to *KTB OKW*, ii/2, 1168 (21 December 1942), Manstein had stated at the briefing that the 6th Army could advance a maximum of 30 kilometres; Kehrig, 'Die 6.Armee', 99; Kehrig, *Stalingrad. Analyse und Dokumentation*, 334; *DRZW*, vi.1048.

321. Kehrig, *Stalingrad. Analyse und Dokumentation*, 406-7; Kehrig, 'Die 6.Armee', 99-100.

322. *KTB OKW*, ii/2, 1168 (21 December 1942).

323. Kehrig, *Stalingrad. Analyse und Dokumentation*, 407; Kehrig, 'Die 6.Armee', 100; *DRZW*, vi.1048.

324. Kehrig, *Stalingrad. Analyse und Dokumentation*, 410; Kehrig, 'Die 6.Armee', 100; *DRZW*, vi.1048-9.

325. Gruchmann, *Der Zweite Weltkrieg*, 193.

326. Kehrig, *Stalingrad. Analyse und Dokumentation*, 431-2; Kehrig, 'Die 6.Armee', 101.

327. Gruchmann, *Der Zweite Weltkrieg*, 193.

328. Below, 324.

329. Kehrig, 'Die 6.Armee', 102; Manstein, 373.

330. Weinberg III, 441; Below, 329.

331. Irving, *Göring*, 372-3.

332. Weinberg III, 434, 436.

333. Irving, *Göring*, 373.

334. See *The Rommel Papers*, ed. B.H. Liddell Hart, London, 1953, 368-9.

335. *Staatsmänner* II, 160–81 (18 December 1942), 190–6 (19 December 1942, 20 December 1942), here especially 165, 168–70, 195 (*'kriegsentscheidend'*).

336. *CD*, 536 (18 December 1942).

337. *CD*, 535 (18 December 1942); *Staatsmänner* II, 169–70 (18 December 1942).

338. *Staatsmänner* II, 192 (19 December 1942).

339. William Craig, *Enemy at the Gates. The Battle for Stalingrad*, London, 1973, 295–6; Beevor, 313.

340. Craig, 293.

341. Kershaw, *'Hitler Myth'*, 191; Buchbender/Sterz, 99. For graphic accounts of the terrible conditions of the doomed army in its last weeks, see Beevor, especially ch. 19–22; and Craig, 259–381.

342. Buchbender/Sterz, 102. Goebbels's plans for an edition of last letters from soldiers at Stalingrad had to be abandoned when it transpired that most of them contained sentiments far from the heroic tone required. (Steinert, 328. See *Letzte Briefe aus Stalingrad*, Frankfurt am Main/Heidelberg, 1950, 5–6 (pointing out that only 2 per cent of the letters were favourably disposed towards the leadership of the war)).

343. *Letzte Briefe*, 21.

344. *Letzte Briefe*, 14.

345. *Letzte Briefe*, 25.

346. *Letzte Briefe*, 16–17.

347. Below, 326.

348. Below, 325–7.

349. The above based on Kehrig, 'Die 6.Armee', 104–6; Below, 327; Gruchmann, *Der Zweite Weltkrieg*, 194; *DRZW*, vi.1056–7.

350. Boelcke, *Wollt ihr*, 422.

351. Boelcke, *Wollt ihr*, 425–6; Steinert, 327. For Goebbels's pressure for a reorientation of press and OKW propaganda, see *TBJG*, II/7, 164, 180 (23 January 1943).

352. *TBJG*, II/7, 162, (23 January 1943).

353. *TBJG*, II/7, 169, 173 (23 January 1943).

354. *TBJG*, II/7, 162, 168–9 (23 January 1943).

355. *TBJG*, II/7, 166 (23 January 1943).

356. *TBJG*, II/7, 162, 168 (23 January 1943).

357. *TBJG*, II/7, 162–3, 171–2 (23 January 1943).

358. *TBJG*, II/7, 175 (23 January 1943).

359. Kehrig, 'Die 6.Armee', 107; *DRZW*, vi.1057–8.

360. Domarus, 1974.

361. Kehrig, *Stalingrad. Analyse und Dokumentation*, 531; Kehrig, 'Die 6.Armee', 108; Gruchmann, *Der Zweite Weltkrieg*, 194; *DRZW*, vi.1059–60.

362. Kehrig, 'Die 6.Armee', 108.

363. Domarus, 1975.

364. This had been arranged at Goebbels's visit to FHQ on 22 January (*TBJG*, II/7, 173 (23 January 1943); the text is in Domarus, 1976–80).

365. Domarus, 1979.

366. Kehrig, 'Die 6.Armee', 108.

367. Domarus, 1981.

368. Kehrig, 'Die 6.Armee', 109. The splitting of the two pockets in Stalingrad, completed on 26 January, had led to a break in communications between them from the following day. Paulus commanded the larger, southern pocket (*LB* Darmstadt, 72 n.76). According to Lew Besymenski, who acted as interpreter at Paulus's first interrogation after capture, the newly elevated field-marshal insisted on recognition of his new rank, denied that he had surrendered (claiming he had been

'surprised' by his assailants, although he had engaged in lengthy prior negotiations), and refused to sanction the capitulation of his men (despite his own surrender) as 'unworthy of a soldier'. (' "Nein, nein, das ist nicht mehr meine Pflicht". Lew Besymenski über Stalingrad und seine Erlebnisse mit Generalfeldmarschall Paulus', *Der Spiegel*, 37/1992, 170–71.)

369. Gruchmann, *Der Zweite Weltkrieg*, 194; Kehrig, 'Die 6.Armee', 109.

370. *LB* Darmstadt, 73 (1 February 1943).

371. *LB* Darmstadt, 72.

372. *LB* Darmstadt, 73.

373. *LB* Darmstadt, 74 and n.84, 79.

374. *LB* Darmstadt, 77, 79–80. Paulus entered Soviet captivity with the remainder of his troops, and was eventually released in 1953. In 1944 he provided support from Moscow for the 'National Committee of Free Germany', the organization initiated by the Soviet leadership and comprising exiled German Communists and prisoners-of-war, which sought – largely in vain – to subvert morale at the front among German troops and to incite resistance to the Nazi regime. Ernst Nolte, *Der europäische Bürgerkrieg. Nationalsozialismus und Bolschewismus*, Berlin, 1987, 114–23 (especially 115), 528–9, 564 n.24, 596 n.36, used Hitler's comments on rats in the Lubljanka prison as part of a speculative hypothesis that his paranoid antisemitism arose out of his acute and lasting horror at Bolshevik atrocities in the years immediately following the Russian Revolution. This assertion was then incorporated in the construction of his heavily criticized interpretation positing Bolshevism, and 'class genocide', as the prior agent of a causal nexus leading ultimately to the Nazi 'race genocide' against the Jews. (See Ernst Nolte, 'Vergangenheit, die nicht vergehen will', in '*Historikerstreit*'. *Die Dokumentation der Kontroverse um die Einzigartigkeit der nationalsozialistischen Judenvernichtung*, 2nd edn, Munich/Zurich, 1987, 39–47.

375. Domarus, 1985.

376. Kershaw, '*Hitler Myth*', 192.

377. Nadler, 73, 76.

378. *MadR*, xii.4720 (28 January 1943), 4750–1 (4 February 1943), 4760–1 (8 February 1943).

379. Goebbels acknowledged that the criticism was now also directed at Hitler (*TBJG*, II/7, 266 (5 February 1943).

380. Hassell, 347 (14 February 1943).

381. *MadR*, xii.4720 (28 January 1943).

382. GStA, Munich, MA 106671, report of the Regierungspräsident of Oberbayern, 10 March 1943: '*Der Stalingrad-Mörder*'.

383. Hassell, 348–9 (14 February 1943); Gisevius, *To the Bitter End*, 464ff.; Ritter, 350ff.; Hoffmann, 346ff., Joachim Fest, *Staatsstreich. Der lange Weg zum 20. Juli*, Berlin, 1994, 199–205.

384. Inge Scholl, *Die Weiße Rose*, Frankfurt am Main, 1952, 108; ('*Kommilitonen! Kommilitoninnen! Erschüttert steht unser Volk vor dem Untergang der Männer von Stalingrad. Dreihundertdreißigtausend deutsche Männer hat die geniale Strategie des Weltkriegsgefreiten sinn- und verantwortungslos in Tod und Verderben gehetzt. Führer, wir danken dir!*'); also printed in Hinrich Siefken (ed.), *Die Weiße Rose und ihre Flugblätter*, Manchester, 1994, 32. This was the sixth and final broadsheet. The fifth, produced between 13 and 29 January, is printed (wrongly dated to 18 February 1943) alongside other texts related to the 'White Rose' in Peter Steinbach and Johannes Tuchel (eds.), *Widerstand in Deutschland 1933–1945. Ein historisches Lesebuch*, Munich, 1994, 236–7 (trans. in N & P, iv.457) and reproduced in facsimile in Siefken, *Die Weiße Rose und ihre Flugblätter*, 88–9 (see 20–1 for dating). See also J. P. Stern, 'The White Rose', in Hinrich Siefken (ed.), *Die Weiße Rose. Student Resistance to National Socialism 1942/43. Forschungsergebnisse und Erfahrungsberichte*, Nottingham, n.d. (1991), 11–36.

385. Benz and Pehle, *Lexikon*, 318–19.

386. See IfZ, ED 100, Irving-Sammlung, Traudl Junge Memoirs, Fol.79: Hitler was on the evening of the news of the fall of Stalingrad 'a tired old man (*ein müder alter Herrn*)', and the mood at

headquarters reminded her of a visit to a cemetery on a rainy November day. See also Irving, *HW*, 480. According to Speer, 264, after the capitulation Hitler never referred to Stalingrad again.

387. *TBJG*, II/7, 171 (23 January 1943).

388. Schroeder, 130; *TBJG*, II/7, 171 (23 January 1943).

389. See Irving, *HW*, 480.

390. Below, 326.

391. Below, 329–30.

392. *TBJG*, II/7, 285 (8 February 1943).

393. *TBJG*, II/7, 293 (8 February 1943).

394. *TBJG*, II/7, 285–6 (8 February 1943); also 287–8, 293–5.

395. *TBJG*, II/7, 288–9 (8 February 1943).

396. *TBJG*, II/7, 287 (8 February 1943).

397. Below, 327.

398. *TBJG*, II/7, 287 (8 February 1943).

399. *TBJG*, II/7, 291–2 (8 February 1943).

400. *TBJG*, II/7, 290–2, 294 (8 February 1943).

401. *TBJG*, II/7, 295–6 (8 February 1943).

402. *TBJG*, II/7, 295–7, (8 February 1943).

403. *TBJG*, II/7, 292 (8 February 1943).

404. TBJG, II/7, 296 (8 February 1943).

405. The speech had been postponed from 14 March (*RGBl*, 1943 I, 137; Domarus, 1998). Hitler indicated at the beginning of his speech (Domarus, 1999) that the postponement had been caused by the crisis on the eastern front. This had – temporarily – been ended by the retaking of Kharkov (which the Red Army had regained in February) on 14–15 March (*KTB OKW*, ii/2, 209 (14 March 1943), 214–15 (15 March 1943).

406. *TBJG*, II/7, 593–4, 607, 611 (20 March 1943).

407. *TBJG*, II/7, 610 (20 March 1943).

408. Kershaw, '*Hitler Myth*', 196–7. The figures probably seemed far too low because most people conflated them with the total casualties. In Halder's last note of casualties on the eastern front before he left office, he gave the total killed for the period between 22 June 1941 and 10 September 1942 as 336,349, and the total losses (killed, wounded, missing) as 1,637,280 (*Halder KTB*, iii.522 (15 September 1942). The figure for dead provided by Hitler in March 1943 was, therefore, less outlandish than it seemed to his audience. Many presumed Hitler was referring only to dead on the eastern front, not in all theatres of war. But the eastern front in any case accounted for the vast proportion of those killed in action.

409. Kershaw, '*Hitler Myth*', 207–10.

CHAPTER 12: BELEAGUERED

1. Iring Fetscher, *Joseph Goebbels im Berliner Sportpalast 1943. 'Wollt ihr den totalen Krieg?'*, Hamburg, 1998, 95, 98; Hofer, *Der Nationalsozialismus*, 251. The text of the speech is printed in Helmut Heiber (ed.), *Goebbels-Reden*, 2 Bde., Düsseldorf, 1971, 1972 (Bd.1:1932–1939; Bd.2: 1939–1945), ii.172–208; and Fetscher, 63–98; and analysed in Fetscher, 104–22, and Günter Moltmann, 'Goebbels' Rede zum totalen Krieg am 18. Februar 1943', *VfZ*, 12 (1964), 13–43 (background to speech, 13–29, analysis 30–43); English trans., Günter Moltmann, 'Goebbels' Speech on Total War, February 18, 1943', in Hajo Holborn (ed.), *Republic to Reich. The Making of the Nazi Revolution*, Vintage Books edn, New York, 1973, 298–342. See also Reuth, *Goebbels*, 518ff.; Irving, *Goebbels*, 421ff. Fetscher, pt.II, offers a thorough analysis of the reception of the speech abroad.

2. Boelcke, *Wollt Ihr*, 445–6. See also, for the aims of the speech, Fetscher, 107–8.

3. Boelcke, *Wollt Ihr*, 25.

4. For conflicting interpretations, see Moltmann, 'Goebbels' Speech', 310–14; and Irving, *HW*, 421, 659 n.11.

5. *TBJG*, II/7, 373 (19 February 1943).

6. Moltmann, 'Goebbels' Speech', 311, 313–14; *TBJG*, II/7, 508 (9 March 1943).

7. See Mason, *Sozialpolitik*, ch.1. Moltmann, 'Goebbels' Speech', 305, refers to Göring's opposition to 'total war' measures in 1942.

8. See Stephen Salter, 'The Mobilisation of German Labour, 1939–1945. A Contribution to the History of the Working Class in the Third Reich', unpubl. D.Phil. thesis, Oxford, 1983, 29–38, 48–56, 73–4, emphasizing the concern to avoid damage to morale and political tension on the home front; and Dörte Winkler, 'Frauenarbeit versus Frauenideologie. Probleme der weiblichen Erwerbstätigkeit in Deutschland 1930–1945', *Archiv für Sozialgeschichte*, 17 (1977), 99–126, here 116–20, acknowledging the morale question but stressing the decisive role of Hitler's ideological objections.

9. Moltmann, 'Goebbels' Speech', 306–7.

10. On the rival power-blocs of Sauckel and Speer, contesting control of labour deployment, see Walter Naasner, *Neue Machtzentren in der deutschen Kriegswirtschaft 1942–1945*, Boppard am Rhein, 1994, pts.1–2.

11. *TBJG*, II/7, 561 (16 March 1943).

12. He was empowered to issue directives but not binding decrees, and Hitler reserved to himself the right to decide where objections were raised to Goebbels's directives (Rebentisch, 516–17).

13. *TBJG*, II/8, 521 (24 June 1943).

14. *TBJG*, II/8, 265 (10 May 1943).

15. Speer, 315. In fact, Hitler seemed remarkably cool and businesslike rather than outwardly friendly towards Eva Braun in overheard telephone conversations in the Wolfsschanze (Schulz, 90–91).

16. Schroeder, 130.

17. *TBJG*, II/8, 265 (10 May 1943).

18. Speer, 259.

19. Moltmann, 'Goebbels' Speech', 312; Hauner, *Hitler*, 181–7; Domarus, 1999–2002 (21 March 1943), 2050–9 (8 November 1943).

20. Hauner, *Hitler*, 181–7.

21. TBJG, II/ 9, 160 (25 July 1943).

22. Rebentisch, 463.

23. *Monologe*, 221–2 (24 January 1942); Rebentisch, 466 and n.295.

24. Rebentisch, 466–70.

25. Rebentisch, 470–72.

26. Rebentisch, 473 and n.318. Vast rebuilding projects for Berlin and Linz were among the other fantasy-schemes Hitler had in mind.

27. Rebentisch, 475.

28. Rebentisch, 477.

29. Steinert, 356.

30. Speer, 234–5.

31. See Dörte Winkler, *Frauenarbeit im Dritten Reich*, Hamburg, 1977, 114–21, for Hitler's attitude to the Women's Service Duty (*Frauendienstpflicht*).

32. *IMG*, xxv.61, 63–4, Doc. 016-PS (Sauckel's statement of 20 April 1942).

33. See, for the figures, *Sozialgeschichtliches Arbeitsbuch III. Materialien zur Statistik des Deutschen Reiches 1914–1945*, ed. Dietmar Petzina, Werner Abelshauser, and Anselm Faust, Munich, 1978, 85. By 1944, foreign workers would account for 26.5 per cent of the total labour force in Germany, and no less than 46.5 per cent of those working in agriculture (Herbert, *Fremdarbeiter*, 270).

34. Rebentisch, 478.

35. Moll, 311–13; Michalka, *Das Dritte Reich*, ii.294–5 (Doc.169). For the impact of the decree, see especially Ludolf Herbst, *Der Totale Krieg und die Ordnung der Wirtschaft. Die Kriegswirtschaft im Spannungsfeld von Politik, Ideologie und Propaganda 1939–1945*, Stuttgart, 1982, 207–31.

36. Salter, 'Mobilisation', 76–81; Stephen Salter, 'Class Harmony or Class Conflict? The Industrial Working Class and the National Socialist Regime 1933–1945', in Jeremy Noakes (ed.), *Government, Party, and People in Nazi Germany*, Exeter, 1980, 76–97, here 90–91; Winkler, 'Frauenarbeit versus Frauenideologie', 118–20.

37. Rebentisch, 478.

38. Rebentisch, 479.

39. Speer, 265.

40. Speer, 266; Rebentisch, 480.

41. Speer, 268; Rebentisch, 479 and n.332.

42. See Rebentisch, 481ff.

43. Speer, 270–71.

44. *TBJG*, II/7, 444–5 (1 March 1943); Speer, 272.

45. *TBJG*, II/7, 450 (2 March 1943).

46. *TBJG*, II/7, 452 (2 March 1943).

47. *TBJG*, II/7, 452–3 (2 March 1943).

48. Speer, 270–71.

49. *TBJG*, II/7, 452 (2 March 1943).

50. *TBJG*, II/7, 454 (2 March 1943).

51. *TBJG*, II/7, 454 (2 March 1943).

52. *TBJG*, II/7, 456 (2 March 1943). A withering critique – with negligible results – of the Party and the urgency of its reform had been compiled in 1942 by either Gauleiter Carl Röver, or (more probably) his successor as Gauleiter of Weser-Ems, Paul Wegener. (See Peterson, 25–6; and Orlow, ii.352–5.)

53. *TBJG*, II/7, 456–7 (2 March 1943).

54. *TBJG*, II/7, 456–8 (2 March 1943); Speer, 273, 275.

55. Speer, 271.

56. *TBJG*, II/8, 98 (12 April 1943).

57. *TBJG*, II/8, 521 (24 June 1943).

58. *TBJG*, II/7, 456 (2 March 1943).

59. Speer, 271 and 553 n.5.

60. Rebentisch, 460, 498. Bormann's influence was indeed great, and growing. Above all, his proximity to Hitler and control of the access of others (with important exceptions) to the Führer, in addition to his leadership of the Party, gave him his unique position of power. But in 1943, Lammers was able for the most part to hold his own, and come to a working arrangement with Bormann, in matters relating to the state administration. Later, his own access to Hitler was increasingly circumscribed by Bormann, whose power was at its peak in the final phase of the Third Reich (Rebentisch, 459–63, 531). Even then, however, Bormann had no independent power, but remained, as Lammers put it, 'a true interpreter of Adolf Hitler's directives' (cit. Rebentisch, 83, n.182 (and see also 498)).

61. Speer, 274; *TBJG*, II/7, 501–2 (9 March 1943).

62. *TBJG*, II/7, 503 (9 March 1943); Speer, 275.

63. *TBJG*, II/7, 505–6, 512 (9 March 1943).

64. *TBJG*, II/7, 507 (9 March 1943).

65. Speer, 275–6; *TBJG*, II/7, 516 (9 March 1943).

66. *TBJG*, II/7, 576–7 (18 March 1943); Speer, 276.

67. Rebentisch, 495.

68. Speer, 278 (claiming it arose from Göring's morphine addiction). A medical examination by the Americans in 1945 revealed Göring's dependence on dihydro-codeine, whose effects and level of addiction were only a fraction of those of morphine (Irving, *Göring*, 476).

69. Irving, *Göring*, 383.

70. Speer, 279.

71. *TBJG*, II/9, 549–50 (21 September 1943).

72. Rebentisch, 482–3.

73. Rebentisch, 483–4.

74. Rebentisch, 485–6.

75. Rebentisch, 486–7.

76. Rebentisch, 489–90. According to one report, from Vienna, of 84,000 who had reported there under the 'combing-out action', closures had yielded only 3,600 men, of whom a mere 384 were useful for the armed forces (Rebentisch, 490).

77. See Steinert, 332ff.

78. StA Würzburg, SD/13, report of SD-Außenstelle Bad Kissingen, 22 April 1943: '*Das Ansehen der NSDAP wurde durch ein[e] Einschaltung der Partei bei der Geschäftsschließung und dem Arbeitseinsatz in der Provinz stark beeinträchtigt. Gerüchtweise verlautet, daß Vg. welche durch Schließungen wie auch durch Verluste von Angehörigen heimgesucht wurden, Führerbilder in ihrer Wohnung heruntergerissen und zertrümmert hätten.*'

79. For a brief sketch of Weber's character and career, see *München – Hauptstadt der Bewegung*, ed. Münchner Stadtmuseum, 1993, 231–2. Weber is the subject of a documentary-novel written with much insight by Herbert Rosendorfer, *Die Nacht der Amazonen. Roman*, dtv edn, Munich, 1992.

80. All the above rests on Rebentisch, 490–92.

81. Guderian, 288.

82. See Churchill, IV, ch.xxxviii for a description of the conference and 615 for Churchill's surprise. The surprise was somewhat disingenuous. As Churchill admitted, and the minutes of the war cabinet of 20 January showed, he had already before the Casablanca Conference approved the notion of stipulating a demand for 'unconditional surrender'. For the implications – often exaggerated – of the demand for 'Unconditional Surrender', see Gruchmann, *Der Zweite Weltkrieg*, 342–4; Weinberg, III.482; *Oxford Companion*, 1174–6.

83. Below, 330; and see also 329, 339 for Hitler's repeated recourse to the 'unconditional surrender' demand to reinforce his view that any suggestion of capitulating or searching for a negotiated peace was pointless. Goebbels, on the other hand, made no mention of it during his 'total war' speech and little or no use of it in the direction of propaganda. (See Gruchmann, *Der Zweite Weltkrieg*, 344; Irving, *HW*, 478 n.4.)

84. Below, 329; Manstein, 406–13; Gruchmann, *Der Zweite Weltkrieg*, 238.

85. Guderian, 302.

86. Eberhard Schwarz, *Die Stabilisierung der Ostfront nach Stalingrad: Mansteins Gegenschlag zwischen Donez und Dnieper im Frühjahr 1943*, Diss. Köln, 1981, 325–6; Below, 330–31; Guderian, 302; Weinberg III, 457–9.

87. Below, 332.

88. Warlimont, 312.

89. *TBJG*, II/7, 593 (20 March 1943).

90. Guderian, 306.

91. *Kriegstagebuch des Oberkommandos der Wehrmacht (Wehrmachtführungsstab), Band III: 1. Januar 1943–31. Dezember 1943*, ed. Walther Hubatsch, Frankfurt am Main, 1963 (= *KTB OKW*, iii) pt.2, 1420–2 (Operationsbefehl Nr.5, Weisung für die Kampfführung der nächsten Monate an der Ostfront vom 13.3.1943). See also Manstein, 443–6; and Weinberg III, 601.

92. *KTB OKW*, iii/2, 1425–8 (Operationsbefehl Nr.6, Zitadelle, 15.4.43), quotation 1425.

93. Domarus, 2009; Manstein, 447.

94. Guderian, 306.

95. For brief portraits of Model, see Joachim Ludewig, 'Walter Model – Hitlers bester Feldmarschall?', in Smelser and Syring, 368–87; Samuel W. Mitcham, Jr and Gene Mueller, 'Generalfeldmarschall Walter Model', in Ueberschär, *Hitlers militärische Elite*, ii.153–60; and Carlo D'Este, 'Model', in Barnett, 318–33.

96. Guderian, 306.

97. Guderian, 308–9.

98. See *LB* Darmstadt, 197–8 (26 July 1943).

99. Timothy Mulligan, 'Spies, Cyphers, and "Zitadelle". Intelligence and the Battle of Kursk', *JCH*, 22 (1987), 235–60; Glantz and House, 162–6.

100. Warlimont, 308, 311.

101. Warlimont, 307.

102. Warlimont, 308–10. Hitler was aware that Kesselring was 'an enormous optimist (*ein kolossaler Optimist*)', and that he needed to be careful not to be blinded by this optimism (*LB* Darmstadt, 95–6 (20 May 1943)).

103. Warlimont, 312.

104. Below, 333–4.

105. So Hitler told Goebbels, almost a month later (*TBJG*, II/8, 225 (7 May 1943)). The meetings at Klessheim took place between 7 and 10 April (Hauner, *Hitler*, 182–3).

106. Schmidt, 563.

107. *TBJG*, II/8, 225 (7 May 1943).

108. Dollmann, 35–7; see also Irving, *HW*, 504–6.

109. *TBJG*, II/7, 225 (7 May 1943).

110. Domarus, 2003–8.

111. *Staatsmänner* II, 214–33, especially 217–24, 228–33 (quotations 215, 233).

112. *Staatsmänner* II, 234–63, quotation 238.

113. Nuremberg and Fürth were about four miles apart in the region of Middle Franconia, and had been linked in 1835 by Germany's first stretch of railway. Nuremberg's tradition as a 'Freie Reichsstadt' (Free Imperial City) in the days of the Holy Roman Empire, the 'German' virtues associated with the city through Wagner's *Meistersinger von Nürnberg*, and, in the Nazi era, its standing as the 'City of the Reich Party Rallies (*Stadt der Reichsparteitage*)' all contributed (together with the extreme antisemitic climate influenced by the Jew-baiting Gauleiter, Julius Streicher) to singling it out for Hitler as an especially 'German' city. Fürth, by contrast, had, until the late nineteenth century, had the largest Jewish population in Bavaria, coming to epitomize for the Nazis a 'Jewish town'. In fact, by the time that Hitler came to power the proportion of Jews in the population of Fürth (2.6 per cent) was scarcely greater than that of Nuremberg (1.8 per cent). By 1939, the relative proportions had dwindled, respectively, to 1.0 per cent and 0.6 per cent (Ophir/ Wiesemann, 179, 203).

114. Hillgruber, *Staatsmänner* II, 256–7.

115. *TBJG*, II/7, 515 (9 March 1943).

116. Hilberg, *Vernichtung*, iii.1283–5; Fleming, *Hitler und die Endlösung*, 148–53; Gerald Reitlinger, *The Final Solution*, (1953), Sphere Books edn, London, 1971, 534–5.

117. Hilberg, *Destruction*, 323. For the uprising, see Yisrael Gutman, *The Jews of Warsaw 1939– 1943. Ghetto, Underground, Revolt*, London, 1982, ch.14. The length of time it took to crush the uprising was a reflection, as Gutman shows, of the extent to which the German occupying forces had underestimated the activities and tenacity of the Jewish underground in the ghetto.

118. *TBJG*, II/8, 104 (14 April 1943).

119. *TBJG*, II/8, 114–15 (17 April 1943). Hitler let Goebbels know a few days later that he wished to talk with him about the future treatment of the 'Jewish Question', of which he had very high

hopes (II.8, 165 (25 April 1943)). For Goebbels's exploitation of Katyn for propaganda purposes, see Bramsted, 330–32; Reuth, *Goebbels*, 526–7; and David Welch, *The Third Reich. Politics and Propaganda*, London, 1993, 112–13. Reports of the Katyn massacres by the Bolsheviks had the effect, however, of provoking comment about the killing of the Jews by the Germans. See the entry in the diary of Hassell, 365 (15 May 1943), indicating knowledge of gassing of hundreds of thousands in specially built chambers (*Hallen*). And see also Steinert, 255; Lawrence D. Stokes, 'The German People and the Destruction of the European Jews', *Central European History*, 6 (1973), 167–91, here 186–7; Bankier, 109; Kershaw, *Popular Opinion*, 365–7; and Kulka, ' "Public Opinion" ', 289 (for the telling report from the Gauleitung of Upper Silesia pointing out wall-daubings in the area comparing Katyn and Auschwitz).

120. *TBJG*, II/8, 235, 237 (and see 229) (8 May 1943). Hitler returned on several occasions to emphasize the vital role to be played by antisemitic propaganda in discussions with Goebbels during the following days (*TBJG*, II/8, 261 (10 May 1943), 297–90 (13 May 1943)).

121. *TBJG*, II/8, 105 (14 April 1943), 225 (7 May 1943).

122. *TBJG*, II/8, 236 (8 May 1943).

123. *Deutschland im Zweiten Weltkrieg*, ed. Wolfgang Schumann et al., 6 vols., East Berlin, 1974–84, iii.411–13.

124. *TBJG*, II/8, 236, 238 (8 May 1943).

125. *TBJG*, II/8, 224 (7 May 1943).

126. *TBJG*, II/8, 229, 233–40 (8 May 1943).

127. Warlimont, 313; Domarus, 2014; Weinberg III, 446; Gruchmann, *Der Zweite Weltkrieg*, 221.

128. Karl Doenitz, *Memoirs. Ten Years and Twenty Days*, (1958), New York, 1997, 299ff., 342ff.; Thomas, 218, 226–7. On taking office Dönitz had, however, changed his mind about scrapping the battleships and was successful in persuading Hitler to retain them (Doenitz, 371ff.; Thomas, 227).

129. *TBJG*, II/7, 239 (8 May 1943).

130. *Lagevorträge*, 510 (5 June 1943): 'Niederschrift uber die Besprechung des Ob.d.M. beim Führer am 31.5.43 auf dem Berghof.'

131. Doenitz, 341; Roskill, ii.470; Thomas, 230–31.

132. Winston S. Churchill, *The Second World War. Volume V, Closing the Ring*, London etc., 1952, 6–10; Overy, *Why the Allies Won*, 50–9; *Oxford Companion*, 68–9, 1168–9.

133. Weinberg III, 594.

134. Warlimont, 317–19.

135. *LB* Darmstadt, 97–8 (20 May 1943).

136. *LB* Darmstadt, 100–101.

137. *LB* Darmstadt, 104–6.

138. Warlimont, 331.

139. *TBJG*, II/8, 300 (15 May 1943), 314 (17 May 1943), 337 (21 May 1943), 351 (23 May 1943).

140. Below, 339.

141. *TBJG*, II/8, 492–8 (19 May 1943).

142. Kershaw, 'Hitler Myth', 202–3.

143. *TBJG*, II/8, 527–8 (25 June 1943). Hitler thought, as he had said before on occasion, that it was not so bad that the inner-cities had been destroyed. Most of the industrial cities had been badly laid out and constructed. The British air-raids gave the opportunity for grandiose rebuilding schemes after the war.

144. *TBJG*, II/8, 533 (25 June 1943).

145. *TBJG*, II/8, 291 (13 May 1943).

146. *TBJG*, II/8, 287 (13 May 1943).

147. *TBJG*, II/8, 288 (13 May 1943).

148. *TBJG*, II/8, 288 (13 May 1943).

149. *TBJG*, II/8, 290 (13 May 1943).

150. *The Stroop Report. The Jewish Quarter of Warsaw Is No More*. A facsimile edition and translation of the official Nazi report on the destruction of the Warsaw Ghetto, introd. by Andrzej Wirth, (1960), London, 1980, (unpaginated), entry for 16 May 1943.

151. Broszat, *Nationalsozialistische Polenpolitik*, 164–71; Madajczyk, *Okkupationspolitik*, 422–8; Irving, *HW*, 528–9. Hitler expressed on several occasions his dissatisfaction with Frank, and thought of replacing him with Greiser. But, as so often, he took no decision, and ultimately pointed out that Frank's task in the General Government was so difficult that it was beyond anyone to accomplish. (See *TBJG*, II/8, 226 (7 May 1943), 251 (9 May 1943), 535 (25 June 1943).)

152. IfZ, MA 316, Frames 2615096–8, 'Vortrag beim Führer am 19.6.1943 auf dem Obersalzberg: "Bandenkampf und Sicherheitslage" ', quotation Frame 2615097; Fleming, *Hitler und die Endlösung*, 33. That the suggestion came from Himmler is supported by the similar wording of his letter to Hans Frank some weeks earlier, on 26 May, when he wrote: 'The evacuation also of the last 250,000 Jews, which will without doubt provoke unrest for some weeks, must despite all the difficulties be completed as rapidly as possible' (IfZ, MA 330, Frames 2654157–8, 'Einladung des Generalgouverneurs an den Reichsführer-SS Heinrich Himmler zu Besprechung', 26 May 1943; 2654162–3, Antwortschreiben Himmlers, 26 May 1943 (quotation, 2654162: '*Die Evakuierung auch der letzten 250,000 Juden, die für Wochen noch ohne Zweifel Unruhe hervorrufen wird, muß trotz aller Schwierigkeiten so rasch wie möglich vollzogen werden*').

153. Schirach, 288; *TBJG*, II/8, 265 (10 May 1943), 458 (11 June 1943).

154. Schirach, 289.

155. Schirach, 290–91.

156. Schirach, 291–2.

157. Schirach, 292–4; also *Monologe*, 403–6, for a watered-down version; *TBJG*, II/8, 538–41 (25 June 1943), describing Frau von Schirach as behaving like a 'silly goose (*dumme Pute*)'; Hoffmann, *Hitler Was My Friend*, 190–91; Below, 340 (who does not mention the incident with the Jewish women); Henriette von Schirach, *Der Preis der Herrlichkeit. Erlebte Zeitgeschichte*, (1956), Munich/ Berlin, 1975, 8–10.

158. Guderian, 310.

159. Guderian, 311.

160. Warlimont, 333–4.

161. *TBJG*, II/8, 531–2 (25 June 1943).

162. Domarus, 2021; see also Irving, *HW*, 532–3.

163. Below, 340.

164. See *LB Stuttgart*, 269–75, 297–8, 309–12, 338–40, 364–8 (midday and evening briefings, 25 July 1943), where it is apparent that tank production figures were lower than those Hitler had expected; Guderian, 306–9; Manstein, 448–9; Earl F. Ziemke, *Stalingrad to Berlin: the German Defeat in the East*, Washington, 1968, 130–32, 135–73; John Erickson, *The Road to Berlin*, Boulder, Colorado, 1983, 86, 97ff., 135; Ernst Klink, *Das Gesetz des Handelns: Die Operation 'Zitadelle' 1943*, Stuttgart, 1966, 140–44, 196; Weinberg III, 601–3; Gruchmann, *Der Zweite Weltkrieg*, 239; Overy, *Why the Allies Won*, 86–97; Overy, *Russia's War*, ch.7, especially 203–12; Glantz and House, 166–7; Irving, *HW*, 533. Accounts of the battle give differing numbers of tanks involved. Ziemke, 101, has 4,000 Soviet and 3,000 German tanks. *DZW*, iii.545, numbers the Soviet tanks at 2,700; see also Erickson, *Road to Berlin*, 144–5; and Klink, 205.

165. Guderian, 311; and see Manstein, 448.

166. Below, 341; Manstein, 448–9; Weinberg III, 603.

167. Guderian, 312.

168. Warlimont, 334.

169. Below, 341; Warlimont, 335–8; Weinberg III, 594; Irving, *HW*, 534–5; *Oxford Companion*, 1001–3. Looking back in 1944, Mussolini himself remarked on the poor morale of the Italian troops in Sicily prior to the Allied landing (Benito Mussolini, *My Rise and Fall*, (1948), New York, 1998, two vols. in one, ii.25.

170. Warlimont, 336–7.

171. *Staatsmänner* II, 287–300; Baur, *Ich flog Mächtige der Erde*, 245–6; Warlimont, 339.

172. Based on: *Staatsmänner* II, 286–300; IfZ, ED 100, Irving-Sammlung, Hitler-Dokumentation (1943), extracts from Mussolini's diary, Auswärtiges Amt, Serial 715/263729–32, 263755–8 (in Italian, and in German translation); Mussolini, ii.49–51; Irving, *HW*, 541–2; Denis Mack Smith, *Mussolini*, Paladin edn, London, 1985, 341–2; Warlimont, 339–40; Schmidt, 340; Domarus, 2022–3.

173. IfZ, MA 460, Frames 2567178–81. Himmler was informed on 19 July and cabled Bormann without delay. See also Irving, *HW*, 543; and Meir Michaelis, *Mussolini and the Jews. German Italian Relations and the Jewish Question in Italy 1922–1945*, Oxford, 1978, 339–40.

174. *LB* Darmstadt, 148 and n.207 (25 July 1943); *TBJG*, II/9, 157 (25 July 1943); Below, 342.

175. Mussolini, ii.55–67; Mack Smith, 342–5; Domarus, 2023 and n.250. See also Hans Woller, *Die Abrechnung mit dem Faschismus in Italien 1943 bis 1948*, Munich, 1996, 9–35.

176. Mussolini, ii.68–81; Mack Smith, 346–9.

177. *LB* Darmstadt, 148–9. The extremist Roberto Farinacci was only one of the forces behind calling the Council meeting. The faction around the more moderate Dino Grandi intended to use the meeting to pave the way for ending Italy's involvement in the war, (See *LB* Darmstadt, 148 n.207 (25 July 1943); Mack Smith, 344.)

178. *LB* Darmstadt, 153 (25 July 1943).

179. *LB* Darmstadt, 156–7, 160.

180. *LB* Darmstadt, 149–50, 158.

181. *LB* Darmstadt, 160.

182. *LB* Darmstadt, 159–61.

183. *TBJG*, II/9, 166 (26 July 1943).

184. *TBJG*, II/9, 169 (27 July 1943).

185. *LB* Darmstadt, 168–70 (26 July 1943).

186. *TBJG*, II/9, 169 (27 July 1943).

187. *LB* Darmstadt, 171 (26 July 1943).

188. *TBJG*, II/9, 174 (27 July 1943).

189. *MadR*, xiv, 5560–2 (2 August 1943).

190. *TBJG*, II/9, 169–74 (27 July 1943).

191. *LB* Darmstadt, 173–96 (26 July 1943).

192. *LB* Darmstadt, 206 (26 July 1943).

193. *TBJG*, II/9, 177 (27 July 1943), 185 (28 July 1943).

194. *TBJG*, II/9, 179–80 (27 July 1943).

195. *TBJG*, II/9, 185 (27 July 1943).

196. Warlimont, 373.

197. Warlimont, 373; Irving, *HW*, 550.

198. Domarus, 2026. 'The Will to Power' ('*Der Wille zur Macht*') was the title of the work – intended as a systematic statement of his philosophy – which was left unfinished at Nietzsche's death.

199. *LB* Darmstadt, 133 n.179; Broszat-Frei, 278; Weinberg III, 616; Churchill, v.459–60; Martin Middlebrook, *The Battle of Hamburg: Allied Bomber Forces against a German City in 1943*, New York, 1981, 252ff. (for reports from citizens of Hamburg), 322ff. for an assessment of the raid. For popular opinion and the difficulties facing the propaganda machine, see Gerald Kirwin, 'Allied Bombing and Nazi Domestic Propaganda', *European History Quarterly*, 15 (1985), 341–62, here 350–51.

200. *LB* Darmstadt, 136 (25 July 1943).

201. *MadR*, xiv.5562–3 (2 August 1943).

202. Speer, 296.

203. *TBJG*, II/9, 205–6 (2 August 1943).

204. *TBJG*, II/9, 229 (6 August 1943).

205. Warlimont, 375–7, 379; *Oxford Companion*, 1001, 1003.

206. In fact, having rejected Kesselring because of his lack of reputation, compared with that of Rommel, Hitler eventually came, in the autumn, to prefer the optimism of the former and give him overall command in Italy (*LB* Darmstadt, 186 (26 July 1943) and n.258; Warlimont, 386).

207. Warlimont, 374–8; Irving, *HW*, 554–5, 559–60.

208. *TBJG*, II/8, 535 (25 June 1943).

209. Himmler had seen Hitler or Bormann with unusual frequency from the day after the fall of Mussolini until his appointment as Reich Minister of the Interior. Hitler had decided upon the appointment at the latest by 16 August, when Lammers began drawing up the necessary documents for a change of minister. Though for months Frick's fall had seemed predestined – prevented only by Hitler's notorious unwillingness for prestige reasons to make changes in personnel in the leading echelons of the regime – Himmler's appointment was plainly an improvised reaction to the potential internal threat in Germany in the wake of the crisis in Italy. Goebbels and Bormann had both harboured pretensions to succeed Frick. Evidently, the determining factor in favour of Himmler was not administrative – he made few changes in this sphere – but control over the instruments of repression. (For the circumstances of Himmler's appointment, see especially Birgit Schulze, 'Himmler als Reichsinnenminister', unpubl. Magisterarbeit, Ruhr-Universität Bochum, 1981, 16–23; also Rebentisch, 499–500; Jane Caplan, *Government without Administration. State and Civil Service in Weimar and Nazi Germany*, Oxford, 1988, 318–19; Peter Diehl-Thiele, *Partei und Staat im Dritten Reich. Untersuchungen zum Verhältnis von NSDAP und allgemeiner innerer Staatsverwaltung*, Munich, 2nd edn, 1971, 196–7.)

210. Domarus, 2028–9.

211. *TBJG*, II/9, 458 (10 September 1943); Irving, *HW*, 561.

212. Manstein, 458–67; Below, 346; Domarus, 2029, 2032–3; Irving, *HW*, 562–3.

213. Below, 346; *TBJG*, II/9, 449–50 (9 September 1943), 457 (10 September 1943)).

214. Goebbels was telephoned by Hitler before 7p.m., within an hour of the BBC broadcasting the news of the capitulation, and told to come to FHQ that very night. Plans to fly were vitiated by dense mist – it had poured down that day – so by 9.20p.m. he had left on the night train to East Prussia (*TBJG*, II/9, 449–50, 454 (10 September 1943), 455, 457 (10 September 1943)).

215. *TBJG*, II/9, 455–6 (10 September 1943).

216. *TBJG*, II/9, 458 (10 September 1943); Warlimont, 380; Irving, *HW*, 564.

217. *TBJG*, II/9, 460 (10 September 1943).

218. Warlimont, 381; Below, 346; Weinberg III, 599; *Oxford Companion*, 573, 588.

219. See *TBJG*, II/9, 456 (10 September 1943).

220. Irving, *HW*, 567–8.

221. Below, 347, who says Hitler ruled out entirely any accommodation with the western powers; *TBJG*, II/9, 464, where his preference for overtures to Britain is recorded, 466–7 (10 September 1943); see also 566 (23 September 1943). For the possible Soviet interest in a separate peace at this time, see Weinberg III, 609–11.

222. Domarus, 2034–9 (10 September 1943).

223. Goebbels was delighted at its impact (*TBJG*, II/9, 489–90, 493–4 (12 September 1943), 499 (13 September 1943)); for the SD's monitoring, see Kershaw, '*Hitler Myth*', 211.

224. *TBJG*, II/9, 468, 473, 475, 483–4, 485–7 (10 September 1943).

225. Warlimont, 385–6; *TBJG*, II/9, 460–61, 464–5 (10 September 1943).

226. *TBJG*, II.9, 500–501 (13 September 1943); Below, 346–7; Otto Skorzeny, *Geheimkommando Skorzeny*, Hamburg, 1950, 135–51.

227. *TBJG*, II/9, 567–8 (23 September 1943).

228. Below, 347.

229. Mack Smith, 350–58; Woller, 45ff.

230. *TBJG*, II/9, 561, 563, 565–7 (23 September 1943).

231. Warlimont, 388; Weinberg III, 606; Irving, *HW*, 565–7; Glantz and House, 172–3. Manstein, 450–86, outlines the Soviet advance and German rearguard action from his own perspective.

232. Manstein, 486–7; and see Irving, *HW*, 578–9.

233. Weinberg III, 605–7 (for the above military developments).

234. *IMG*, xxxiiii.68–9, Doc. 4024-PS, Globocnik's report to Himmler of 4 November 1943. See also Leon Poliakov and Josef Wulf, *Das Dritte Reich und die Juden. Dokumente und Aufsätze*, 2nd edn, Berlin, 1955, 44–5; Hilberg, *Vernichtung*, iii.1299; Fleming, *Hitler und die Endlösung*, 71 n.132.

235. Leni Yahil, *The Rescue of Danish Jewry. Test of a Democracy*, Philadelphia, 1969, 285ff.; Herbert, *Best*, 363–4, 367; Ulrich Herbert, 'Die deutsche Besatzungspolitik in Dänemark im 2. Weltkrieg und die Rettung der dänischen Juden', *Tel Aviver Jahrbuch für deutsche Geschichte*, 23 (1994), 93–114; Hilberg, *Vernichtung*, ii.586–96; Longerich, *Politik*, 555–60.

236. Michaelis, 360–70; Hilberg, *Vernichtung*, ii.714–15; John Cornwell, *Hitler's Pope. The Secret History of Pius XII*, London, 1999, 298–318. Odilo Globocnik, who had organized 'Action Reinhardt' in the General Government, had been appointed Higher SS and Police Leader in Istria at the end of August. Some of the key experts on gassing, formerly with the T4 'euthanasia action', had gone with him. It looks, therefore, as if the intention was to set up an extermination unit for the Italian Jews (*N & P*, iii.1168). For reflections on different Italian and German behaviour towards Jews, see Jonathan Steinberg, *All or Nothing. The Axis and the Holocaust 1941–43*, London/New York, 1991, 168–80, 220–41.

237. *IMG*, xxix.145–6, Doc.908; trans., slightly amended, *N & P*, iii.1199–1200; partial extract, Michalka, *Das Dritte Reich*, ii.256–7.

238. Fleming, *Hitler und die Endlösung*, 73–4.

239. *TBJG*, II/10, 72 (7 October 1943).

240. Smith and Peterson, *Himmler. Geheimreden*, 169 (entire text of the speech, 162–83; typescript, BDC, o.238 I – H. Himmler; handwritten notes, BDC, o–238 III – H.Himmler); Fleming, *Hitler und die Endlösung*, 74–5.

241. Irving, *HW*, 575–6.

242. Domarus, 2045.

243. Domarus, 2050–59. The speech was recorded for radio transmission that evening. Hitler had a written text for the first part, but improvised much of the second. This necessitated Goebbels, with Hitler's permission, cutting 'a few somewhat awkward formulations' from the broadcast version (*TBJG*, II/10, 262 (9 November 1943)).

244. Broszat/Frei, 278.

245. Kershaw, '*Hitler Myth*', 211–13.

246. Domarus, 2054–5.

247. *Weisungen*, 270.

248. *LB* Darmstadt, 218–19 (20 December 1943).

CHAPTER 13: HOPING FOR MIRACLES

1. Domarus, 2073 (text of the Proclamation, 2071–4).

2. Domarus, 2075 (text of the Daily Command, 2074–6).

3. Domarus, 2076.

4. Speer referred, in a series of short reflections on Nazi leaders which he wrote in captivity directly after the end of the war, to Hitler's increased emphasis on 'Fate', attributing it to his manic overwork

and loss of ability to detach himself from events and think freely. (Speer Papers, AH/II, Bl.13. I am grateful to Gitta Sereny for giving me access to this material in her possession.)

5. *TBJG*, II/12, 421 (7 June 1944).

6. This was the opinion, immediately after the war, of Albert Speer, who wrote that Hitler remained inwardly 'convinced of his mission (*von seiner Mission . . . überzeugt*)', and that the war could not be lost (Speer Papers, AH/II, Bl.14). Below, 361, however, wondered whether Hitler's over-optimism represented his true feelings. That Hitler had since autumn 1942 harboured no illusions about the outcome of the war is strongly argued in a hitherto unpublished paper, which he kindly made available to me, by Bernd Wegner, 'Hitler, der Zweite Weltkrieg und die Choreographie des Untergangs'.

7. Speer Papers, AH/II, Bl.1–11.

8. See, among numerous witnesses of this, *TBJG*, II/13, 142 (23 July 1944). Goebbels himself thought Hitler had become old and gave an impression of frailty.

9. *KTB OKW*, iv, ed. Percy Ernst Schramm, pt.2, 1701–2. Though Schramm's description dates from several months later, he points out that the deterioration in Hitler's appearance had been a steady progression. For a similar description, by Werner Best, referring to 30 December 1943, see Ernst Günther Schenck, *Patient Hitler. Eine medizinische Biographie*, Düsseldorf, 1989, 390–91.

10. Schenck, 190–215; Irving, *Doctor*, 66ff., 259–70; Fritz Redlich, *Hitler. Diagnosis of a Destructive Prophet*, New York/Oxford, 1999, 237–54, 358–62.

11. Redlich, 224–5.

12. Ellen Gibbels, 'Hitlers Nervenkrankheit. Eine neurologisch-psychiatrische Studie', *VfZ*, 42 (1994), 155–220; also Redlich, 232–3; Schenk, 426–38.

13. Redlich, 276.

14. Speer Papers, AH/Schl., Bl.2, for Speer's view of Hitler as a 'demonic phenomenon (*in seiner dämonischen Erscheinung*)', and one of the 'eternally inexplicable historical natural phenomena (*eines dieser immer unerklärlichen geschichtlichen Naturereignisse*)'.

15. After the first weeks of the year at the Wolf's Lair, he repaired to the Berghof, where he stayed, with no more than a day or two's absence, until he left his alpine retreat for the last time on 14 July 1944. He then returned to the Wolf's Lair until his final departure from there on 20 November. After staying for three weeks in Berlin, he moved on 10 December to his field headquarters in the West, the Adlerhorst (Eagle's Nest), which had been constructed in 1939–40 at Ziegenberg, near Bad Nauheim, where he oversaw the Ardennes offensive and remained until January 1945 (Hauner, *Hitler*, 187–95; *Das Große Lexikon des Zweiten Weltkriegs*, ed. Christian Zentner and Friedemann Bedürftig, Munich, 1988, 13, 204).

16. Hitler, who had announced his intention of giving the speech only two days earlier, was, according to Goebbels, in good form. The Propaganda Minister thought he would persuade Hitler to allow a broadcast version of the speech, but evidently did not succeed in this (*TBJG*, II/11, 332, 347–8 (23 February 1944, 25 February 1944)). Nor was there a report, or even an announcement of the speech, in the *VB* (*Tb* Reuth, v.1994, n.38). But Domarus, 2088–9, was mistaken in thinking that Hitler had let the entire event drop that year.

17. GStA Munich, MA 106695, report of the Regierungspräsident of Oberbayern, 7 August 1944: '*Lieber ein Ende mit Schrecken als ein Schrecken ohne Ende!*'

18. These were, for example, Jodl's sentiments when he addressed a gathering of Gauleiter in February in Munich (*TBJG*, II/11, 345–6 (25 February 1944)). Goebbels followed in like vein at a meeting of Propaganda Leaders in Berlin a few days later (*Tb* Reuth, v.1996, n.41).

19. Below, 357.

20. Below, 352.

21. Below, 357.

22. 'Freies Deutschland', established in September 1943, blended together the organizations

'Nationalkomitee "Freies Deutschland"' (NKFD), which had been set up in July 1943 by the Soviet leadership and comprised largely German Communist emigrés and prisoners-of-war, and the 'Bund Deutscher Offiziere' (Federation of German Officers), headed by General Walter von Seydlitz-Kurzbach (one of the Sixth Army's senior commanders who had been captured with Paulus at Stalingrad). (Benz, Graml, and Weiß, *Enzyklopädie*, 408, 596–7.)

23. See Waldemar Besson, 'Zur Geschichte des nationalsozialistischen Führungsoffiziers (NSFO)', *VfZ*, 9 (1961), 76–116; Gerhard L. Weinberg, 'Adolf Hitler und der NS-Führungsoffizier (NSFO)', *VfZ*, 12 (1964), 443–56; Volker R. Berghahn, 'NSDAP und "geistige Führung" der Wehrmacht 1939–1943', *VfZ*, 17 (1969), 17–71; and Messerschmidt, 441ff. For Hitler's order of 22 December 1943, see Besson, 94; and for the response in the army, Below, 356. The mandate to create a corps of National Socialist Leadership Officers was given to General Hermann Reinecke. Their task was to spread commitment to the National Socialist ideology through lectures and indoctrination. By the end of 1944, there were around 1,100 full-time and 47,000 part-time 'Leadership Officers', most of them in the reserve. (Benz, Graml, and Weiß, *Enzyklopädie*, 608.)

24. Manstein, 500–503, quotation 503; Domarus, 2076–7.

25. Manstein, 504.

26. Manstein, 505; Domarus, 2077.

27. Guderian, 326–7, quotation 327.

28. Irving, *Doctor*, 126, mentions around 105 generals as present on the basis of Morell's diary.

29. IfZ, F19/3, 'Ansprache des Führers an die Feldmarschälle und Generale am 27.1.1944 in der Wolfsschanze', 56–7 (for new U-Boats); quotation, 63 ('...*daß niemals auch nur der leiseste Gedanke einer Kapitulation kommen kann, ganz gleich, was auch geschehen möge*). Irving, *HW*, 598; IfZ, ED 100, Irving-Sammlung, Hitler-Dokumentation (1944), extract from Nachlaß von Salmuth (undated, but from 27 March 1946, according to Irving, *HW*, 881); cold atmosphere: Manstein, 511; *TBJG*, II/11, 368 (29 February 1944), report to Goebbels by Schmundt.

30. IfZ, F19/3, 'Ansprache des Führers an die Feldmarschälle und Generale am 27.1.1944 in der Wolfsschanze', 48 ('*In der letzten Konsequenz müßte ich, wenn ich als oberster Führer jemals verlassen sein würde, als Letztes um mich das gesamte Offizierkorps haben, das müßte dann mit gezogenem Degen um mich geschart stehen...*'; differing (inaccurate) wording in Manstein, 511, and Domarus, 2080 (based on Linge), and in Traudl Junge, unpubl. memoirs, IfZ, ED 100, Irving-Sammlung, Fol.106.

31. IfZ, F19/3, 'Ansprache des Führers an die Feldmarschälle und Generale am 27.1.1944 in der Wolfsschanze', 49 ('*So wird es auch sein, mein Führer!*'); Manstein, 511 (with slightly different wording, both of Hitler's remark and his own interjection).

32. IFZ, F19/3, 'Ansprache des Führers an die Feldmarschälle und Generale am 27.1.1944 in der Wolfsschanze', 49 ('*Das ist schön! Wenn das so sein wird, dann werden wir diesen Krieg nie verlieren können – niemals, da kann sein, was sein will. Denn die Nation wird dann mit der Kraft in den Krieg gehen, die notwendig ist. Ich nehme das sehr gern zur Kenntnis, Feldmarschall von Manstein!*'). Manstein, 512, inaccurately quotes Hitler's words, and states that Hitler then somewhat abruptly concluded his speech. In fact almost a fifth of the speech was still to come at this point.

33. On hearing of the incident, Goebbels was not inclined to take it seriously (*TBJG*, II/11, 249 (6 February 1944)). He altered his view some weeks later after Schmundt had described what had happened, referring then to Manstein's 'stupid interjection' (*blöder Zwischenruf*), made 'in rather provocative fashion (*in ziemlich provozierender Form*)'. Schmundt recalled that the meeting had taken place in a glacial atmosphere (*in einer eisigen Kühle*). Goebbels noted that Hitler's relationship with his generals was 'somewhat poisoned (*etwas vergiftet*)' (*TBJG*, II/11, 368 (29 February 1944)).

34. Manstein, 512.

35. Below, 360.

36. Manstein, 510–11.

37. Manstein, 512.

38. See Irving, HW, 881 note, from Schmundt's diary, where the interruption and tension of late were noted in connection with Manstein's retirement.

39. TBJG, II/11, 205–6, 208 (31 January 1944).

40. Domarus, 2082–6.

41. TBJG, II/11, 273–4 (10 February 1944).

42. MadR, 16, 6299 (4 February 1944).

43. On 21 December 1943, Hitler had made Goebbels head of the newly-founded Reichsinspektion der zivilen Luftkriegsmaßnahmen (Reich Inspectorate of Civilian Air-War Measures) (Moll, 380).

44. TBJG, II/11, 401 (4 March 1944).

45. TBJG, II/11, 402 (4 March 1944).

46. TBJG, II/12, 406–7 (6 June 1944).

47. Speer, 372; Irving, HW, 531.

48. Below, 363–4.

49. TBJG, II/12, 354–5 (24 May 1944).

50. Speer, 374–8, quotation 377.

51. TBJG, II/11, 247 (6 February 1944).

52. Speer, 378; Heinz Dieter Hölsken, Die V-Waffen. Entstehung-Propaganda-Kriegseinsatz, Stuttgart, 1984, 142.

53. Irving, HW, 609.

54. TBJG, II/11, 247 (6 February 1944). Jodl told the Gauleiter later that month that the retaliation would finally begin in mid-April (TBJG, II/11, 347 (25 February 1944).

55. Irving, 609.

56. Below, 363.

57. Below, 363; and see Hoffmann, Security, 229–32, 241–4.

58. Hauner, 188; Irving, HW, 607; both have Hitler leaving on 23 Feb., but Morell's diary records that he took the train on the evening of 22 February (Irving, Doctor, 129). TBJG, II/11, 332 (23 March 1944), for Hitler's notification that he would speak in Munich. Goebbels, in referring to Hitler's intention to come to Munich, offered an implicit criticism in the very next lines of his diary entry by noting that it would be good if the Führer were to visit Berlin or another city that had suffered from the bombing. So far he had not visited a single such city, and 'that cannot be sustained in the long run'.

59. Schenck, 352, 391; Irving, Doctor, 128–9; Redlich, 346; TBJG, II/11, 297 (16 February 1944).

60. Irving, Doctor, 131–2; Redlich, 228–9, 346; Schenck, 308.

61. Irving, Doctor, 131; Redlich, 346; Schenck, 382ff.

62. TBJG, II/11, 346–7 (25 February 1944).

63. TBJG, II/11, 347–8 (25 February 1944).

64. Irving, Doctor, 129; TBJG, II/11, 349 (25 February 1944).

65. TBJG, II/11, 408–9 (4 March 1944); Irving, Doctor, 129; Irving, HW, 608. For the building of the underground passages, see Josef Geiss, Obersalzberg. The History of a Mountain, Berchtesgaden, n.d. (1955), 147–56; and Hanisch, 35. By 1944, British intelligence had built up a surprisingly detailed knowledge of the layout of the Berghof, devised with the intention of a possible assassination attempt there on Hitler. (Operation Foxley: the British Plan to Kill Hitler, London, 1998, 87ff. (for security arrangements), 100–101 (for the air-raid shelters).)

66. TBJG, II/11, 389 (3 March 1944).

67. Hauner, Hitler, 194. The armistice between Finland and the Allies was concluded on 19 September 1944: German troops had to leave Finland within two weeks.

68. TBJG, II/11, 397–8 (4 March 1944).

69. The amphibious landing had taken the German forces by surprise. But the Allied commanders had not seized the opportunity to advance, and the consolidation of their position allowed Kesselring time to marshal no fewer than six divisions to surround the Allied perimeter. Heavy fighting

continued throughout February, and it was spring before the Allies, by now heavily reinforced, were able to break out. Allied losses totalled over 80,000 men (with some 7,000 killed); German losses were estimated at 40,000 (including around 5,000 killed). (Churchill, V. ch. xxvii; Parker, *Struggle for Survival*, 188–91; Weinberg III, 661; Gruchmann, *Der Zweite Weltkrieg*, 231; *Oxford Companion*, 45–6.)

70. *TBJG*, II/11, 399–400 (4 March 1944).

71. *TBJG*, II/11, 400 (4 March 1944).

72. *TBJG*, II/11, 401 (4 March 1944).

73. *TBJG*, II/11, 403 (4 March 1944).

74. Gruchmann, *Der Zweite Weltkrieg*, 248–9; Bloch, 398–9; Weinberg III, 671–2; Irving, *HW*, 611.

75. Warlimont, 412; Gruchmann, *Der Zweite Weltkrieg*, 249; Irving, *HW*, 611.

76. Schmidt, 587.

77. Gruchmann, *Der Zweite Weltkrieg*, 249. When they met again on 23 March, Hitler told Antonescu – something the Romanian leader had long been waiting to hear – that Germany was renouncing its commitment to the territorial settlement of 30 August 1940 on account of Hungary's disloyalty, but requested him to keep this confidential for the time being. The announcement of this step which Hitler promised Antonescu never materialized (*Staatsmänner* II, 391–2).

78. Warlimont, 413.

79. Bloch, 399.

80. Schmidt, 587–8.

81. Domarus, 2091; also IfZ, ZS Eichmann 807, Fol.2703 (Eichmann-Prozeß, Beweisdokumente: Horthys Aussage am 4.März 1948 über Treffen mit Hitler in Klessheim).

82. Schmidt, 587–9; also Irving, *HW*, 612–13; Bloch, 399–400.

83. When speaking to his party leaders on 17 April, Hitler told them that raw materials and manpower would be available from Hungary. 'In particular,' noted Goebbels, 'he wants to put the 700,000 Jews in Hungary to activity useful for our war purposes' (*TBJG*, II/12, 137 (18 April 1944)). Even before his party leaders, Hitler held to the fiction that the Jews were being put to work (though the wording, as Goebbels reported it, was ambiguous). In fact, more than half of them were deported within three months to Auschwitz.

84. Longerich, *Ermordung*, 322–4.

85. Randolph L. Braham, *The Destruction of Hungarian Jewry. A Documentary Account*, New York, 1963, vol.1, 399 (facsm., 13 June 1944).

86. Hilberg, *Destruction*, 547. And see *Staatsmänner* II, 462–6, for Hitler's comments to the new Hungarian premier Sztojay at Klessheim on 7 June 1944.

87. Goebbels (*TBJG*, II/11, 515 (20 March 1944)), recorded the meeting taking place at Klessheim, but Manstein (531, 533), who was present, wrote of being summoned to the Obersalzberg, and the meeting taking place there.

88. *TBJG*, II/11, 368 (29 February 1944), 454–5 (11 March 1944); II/12, 128 (18 April 1944).

89. See above, note 22.

90. Manstein, 532. Hitler had been particularly pleased that Manstein, his most openly critical field-marshal, had signed the declaration (*TBJG*, II/11, 475 (14 March 1944)).

91. Manstein, 532; *TBJG*, II/11, 515 (20 March 1944).

92. Manstein, 536–43. Goebbels, when he heard about it, was dismayed at the weakening of the western front. So, he had heard, was Jodl. According to his own remarkable logic, the more the Soviets advanced, the better the German political situation would be, since the western allies would then see their own peril from Bolshevik expansion. Should, however, a western invasion succeed, then the Reich would indeed be in a 'fateful situation' (*TBJG*, II/11, 568–9 (28 March 1944). See also 556–7 (26 March 1944) and 564 (27 March 1944) for Goebbels's strong criticism of Manstein then, typically, acceptance of Hitler's volte-face.)

93. Gruchmann, *Der Zweite Weltkrieg*, 250.

94. Manstein, 544.

95. *TBJG*, II/11, 589 (31 March 1944), II/12, 33 (1 April 1944); Manstein, 544–6. The passage in *Tb* Reuth, v.2030–1 (31 March 1944), deviates from the entries in *TBJG*.

96. *Weisungen*, 289.

97. Gruchmann, *Der Zweite Weltkrieg*, 251–2.

98. Parker, *Struggle for Survival*, 194.

99. *TBJG*, II/12, 128 (18 April 1944); Irving, *HW*, 624.

100. *TBJG*, II/12, 129–30 (18 April 1944).

101. *TBJG*, II/11, 472 (14 March 1944).

102. Domarus, 2090; *TBJG*, II/11, 456 (11 March 1944).

103. *TBJG*, II/12, 132 (18 April 1944).

104. *TBJG*, II/12, 134–40 (here, 136).

105. *TBJG*, II/12, 126 (18 April 1944), for Goebbels's reporting to him on poor mood.

106. *TBJG*, II/12, 155 (20 April 1944).

107. *TBJG*, II/12, 167 (22 April 1944).

108. Kershaw, 'Hitler Myth', 214.

109. *VB* (Suddeutsche Ausgabe), 20 April 1944, printed in Hans Mommse and Susanne Willems (eds.), *Herrschaftsalltag im Dritten Reich: Studien und Texte*, Düsseldorf, 1988, 88–9: '*Niemals hat das deutsche Volk so gläubig zu seinem Führer aufgeschaut wie in den Tagen und Stunden, da ihm die ganze Schwere dieses Kampfes um unser Leben bewußt wurde . . .*'

110. Below, 367; *TBJG*, II/12, 160 (21 April 1944); Irving, *HW*, 619.

111. Below, 367–8; *TBJG*, II/12, 168 (22 April 1944), 191 (27 April 1944), 194–5 (27 April 1944); Domarus, 2099.

112. *Staatsmänner* II, 418ff.; trans. *N & P*, iii.868.

113. Speer, 336–47; Sereny, *Speer*, 409–28.

114. Speer, 344.

115. Speer, 347–8.

116. Speer, 348–54; also Below, 368–9; and Sereny, *Speer*, 428–30; Fest, *Speer*, 282–9.

117. IfZ, ED 100, Irving-Sammlung, Hitler-Dokumentation, 1944 (copy of Göring's comments on the need to increase bomber production, at a meeting on 23 May 1944 on the Obersalzberg, attended by Speer, Milch, Koller, and others); Irving, *HW*, 626–8.

118. Irving, *HW*, 580; Irving, *Göring*, 410–11; Carr, *Hitler*, 80.

119. Speer, 372–3.

120. IfZ, ED 100, Irving-Sammlung, Hitler-Dokumentation, 1944: former Major-General Galland's post-war testimony at Hitler's explosion on learning that the Me262, despite Messerschmitt's promise (as he saw it) was being produced as a fighter. For Göring's anger – reflecting Hitler's anger with him – at his advisers at Messerschmitt for what he took to be misleading advice (also from Messerschmitt himself to Hitler) on the practicality of producing the jet-bomber, see IfZ, ED 100, Irving-Sammlung, Hitler-Dokumentation, 1944, 'Stenographische Niederschrift über die Besprechung beim Reichsmarschall am 24.Mai 1944', 1–4. The file also contains a copy (from BA, NS6/152) of a note for Bormann of 21 October 1944, relating to Hitler's commission in the previous October to develop the Me262 as a bomber and his expectation that it would be used to repulse an invasion in the west. The note stated: 'On account of the failure of the Luftwaffe, the type Me262, now developed as a bomber, was not ready on time.' ('*Infolge Versagens der Luftwaffe wurde der nunmehr als Bomber entwickelte Typ Me 262 nicht rechtzeitig fertig*'). Also in the file are extracts from a further meeting on construction of the Me262 on 25 May. See also Below, 370–71; Irving, *HW*, 628–30.

121. Speer, 357–60. Hitler agreed to the transfer on 4 June.

122. Hans-Heinrich Wilhelm, 'Hitlers Ansprache vor Generalen und Offizieren am 26. Mai 1944', *Militärgeschichtliche Mitteilungen*, 2 (1976), 123–70, here 134.

123. Wilhelm, 'Hitlers Ansprache', 135, 167 n.74; IfZ, MA-316, Bl.2614608–46, Rede des Reichs-führers-SS am 24.5.44 in Sonthofen vor den Teilnehmern des politisch-weltanschaulichen Lehrgangs (Generale), quotation Bl.2614639 (and printed in Himmler: *Geheimreden*, 203): '*Eine andere Frage, die maßgeblich für die innere Sicherheit des Reiches und Europa war, ist die Judenfrage gewesen. Sie wurde nach Befehl und standesmäßiger Erkenntnis kompromißlos gelöst.*'

124. Wilhelm, 'Hitlers Ansprache', 136.

125. Wilhelm, 'Hitlers Ansprache', 146–7.

126. Wilhelm, 'Hitlers Ansprache', 155.

127. Wilhelm, 'Hitlers Ansprache', 156; see also 168 n.77. See also Wilhelm, 'Wie geheim war die "Endlösung"?', 131–48, here 134–6.

128. Wilhelm, 'Hitlers Ansprache', 157.

129. Wilhelm, 'Hitlers Ansprache', 161.

130. Below, 370; Speer, 359; *Monologe*, 406–12. Goebbels remarked, after discussions with Albert Bormann on arrival at the Berghof on 5 June: 'Up here only the top leadership notices something of the war; the middle and lower leadership are rather apathetic towards it' (*TBJG*, II/12, 405 (6 June 1944)).

131. *TBJG*, II/12, 405 (6 June 1944); Below, 372.

132. *TBJG*, II/12, 408 (6 June 1944).

133. *Weisungen*, 291–2.

134. *TBJG*, II/12, 407 (6 June 1944).

135. Speer, 363–4; *TBJG*, II/12, 407 (6 June 1944).

136. Below, 373.

137. *TBJG*, II/12, 410, 413 (6 June 1944).

138. *TBJG*, II/12, 414–15 (6 June 1944); and see Dieter Ose, *Entscheidung im Westen. Der Oberbefehlshaber west und die Abwehr der alliierten Invasion*, Stuttgart, 1982, 101–2.

139. Irving, *HW*, 884. According to the *KTB* Ob West H 11–10/10 (copy in IfZ, ED 100, Irving-Sammlung, Hitler-Dokumentation, 1944), page 7, the sighting of around 100 warships west of Le Havre and in the Barfleur area offered final confirmation, at 6.42a.m., that it was the beginning of the invasion.

140. German intelligence failed miserably in the build-up to the landing. Later analysis suggested that about four-fifths of reports on the coming invasion from Abwehr agents, received before 6 June, were inaccurate. The *OKW* seems, in addition, to have been dismissive of reports reaching it at the beginning of June and indicating an imminent invasion. (See Irving, *HW*, 884, and IfZ, ED 100, Irving-Sammlung, Hitler-Dokumentation, 1944, for cables of 2–3 June 1944 from the SD warning of imminent invasion on the basis of detected coded radio messages to French resistance groups.)

141. Weinberg III, 686.

142. Weinberg III, 688.

143. Irving, *HW*, 638, 883–4. Rundstedt had requested the release 'for all eventualities (*für alle Fälle*)' of the two reserve divisions based between the Loire and Seine at 4.45a.m. (*KTB* Ob West H 11–10/10 (copy in IfZ, ED 100, Irving-Sammlung, Hitler-Dokumentation, 1944), page 4. See also *KTB OKW*, iv.1, 311–12.)

144. Speer, 364–5.

145. This was only partially accurate. It had, in fact, been Rommel who had placed greatest stress on the possibility of a landing in Normandy, whereas Hitler, while not excluding this, had been more inclined to follow Rundstedt in presuming the landing would take place in the Pas de Calais, at the shortest sea-crossing over the Straits of Dover (Gruchmann, *Der Zweite Weltkrieg*, 291).

146. Here, too, Hitler was over-optimistic. The weather on 6 June, though cloudy and windy, had improved from that of the day before (when it had been bad enough to cause 'Operation Overlord' to be postponed). While the German defenders thought the weather too bad for an invasion,

Eisenhower had adjudged that it was just good enough. (Parker, *Struggle for Survival*, 197; Weinberg III, 684.)

147. *TBJG*, II/12, 418–19 (7 June 1944); Below, 374; Linge, 'Kronzeuge', Bl.42.

148. Based on Gruchmann, *Der Zweite Weltkrieg*, 291–2; Parker, *Struggle for Survival*, 197–8; Weinberg III, 686–8; Winston S. Churchill, *The Second World War*, vol.6: *Triumph and Tragedy*, London etc., 1954, 6; *Oxford Companion*, 853. The accounts give differing numbers of ships engaged in the landings. Parker, *Struggle for Survival*, 197, has 2,727 vessels approaching, multiplying to 6,939 as the smaller landing craft left their parent ships. Gruchmann, *Der Zweite Weltkrieg*, 291, has 5,134 ships and vehicles (*Fahrzeuge*). *Oxford Companion* speaks of nearly 7,000 ships and landing-craft, including 1,213 naval warships. Parker's figure for ships on approach has been used.

149. Weinberg III, 686, 688.

150. Irving, *Göring*, 426–7; see also Parker, *Struggle for Survival*, 196.

151. Parker, *Struggle for Survival*, 198–9; Weinberg III, 687.

152. Weinberg III, 688.

153. See Speer, 366.

154. Speer, 366; Irving, *HW*, 641 (with slightly different figures from those of Speer); *TBJG*, II/12, 479 (17 June 1944).

155. Speer, 366; Hölsken, *V-Waffen*, 132. Göring had tried to blame the initial failure of the V1 on Milch. When Hitler, changing his tune completely, now demanded increased production, Göring predictably attempted to claim the credit.

156. Weinberg III, 691.

157. *Die Wehrmachtberichte 1939–1945*, Cologne, 1989, iii.128ff.: 'Southern England and the area of London were last night and this morning bombed (*belegt*) with new explosives of the heaviest caliber.' See also Domarus, 2106; and Tb Reuth, v.2058, n.125 for Dietrich's propaganda.

158. *TBJG*, II/12, 480 (17 June 1944), 491–2 (18 June 1944). Goebbels's dampening of expectations is mentioned in Elke Fröhlich, 'Hitler und Goebbels im Krisenjahr 1944', *VfZ*, 38 (1990), 196–224, here 217–18; and Reuth, *Goebbels*, 542–4. For the disappointed mood and the propaganda failure over the V1, see especially Gerald Kirwin, 'Waiting for Retaliation. A Study in Nazi Propaganda Behaviour and German Civilian Morale', *JCH*, 16 (1981), 565–83.

159. Irving, *HW*, 642.

160. Below, 375; Linge, 'Kronzeuge', Bl.42; Domarus, 2106; Speer, 366; Irving, *HW*, 641.

161. Hans Speidel, *Invasion 1944. Ein Beitrag zu Rommels und des Reiches Schicksal*, Tübingen/Stuttgart, 1949, 113–14.

162. Below, 375.

163. Speidel, 114–17.

164. Speidel, 118; Below, 375.

165. Speer, 366.

166. *LB* Stuttgart, 573–4; Weinberg III, 688.

167. Weinberg III, 687-9.

168. Below, 375-6.

169. *TBJG*, II/12, 463 (14 June 1944), 517 (22 June 1944).

170. *TBJG*, II/12, 516–18 (22 June 1944).

171. *TBJG*, II/12, 518–19 (22 June 1944).

172. *TBJG*, II/12, 519–21 (22 June 1944), quotation 521.

173. *TBJG*, II/12, 521–2, 527 (22 June 1944), quotation 522.

174. *TBJG*, II/12, 523–6 (22 June 1944).

175. IfZ, F19/3, Hitler's speech, 22 June 1944 (quotations, page 7: '. . . *daß das Ende im Falle des Nachgebens immer die Vernichtung ist, auf die Dauer die restlose Vernichtung*'); 'Vorsehung', page 12, and his comment on page 47: '*Ich habe das Leben schon im Weltkrieg als Geschenk der*

Vorsehung aufgefaßt. Ich konnte so oft tot sein und bin nicht tot. Das ist also schon ein Geschenk gewesen'; '*Der Jude ist weg . . .*', page 39; '*Niemals wird dieser neue Staat kapitulieren*', page 67); see also, especially, 55, 59, and 62 ('*Wir kämpfen hier für die deutsche Zukunft, um Sein oder Nichtsein*').

176. Below, 376. The speech was frequently interrupted by applause, and was followed by shouts of '*Heil*' (IfZ, F19/3, page 70). Hitler was in much less good form when he spoke on 26 June – the military situation had worsened during the previous four days – to about 100 leading representatives of the armaments industry, to try to assuage them about Party interference in the economy. During this speech, there was barely applause, and Hitler's vague philosophizing did not come across well. The attempt, which Speer had hoped would rouse the morale of the assembled businessmen, did not succeed. (The text is printed in von Kotze, 35–68; and see Speer, 369–71.)

177. *TBJG*, II/12, 524 (22 June 1944). Goebbels had been more sceptical. Heavy bombing attacks against German rear areas began on the night of 21–22 June; the main attacks commenced the following day (Glantz and House, 204).

178. *DZW*, vi.35–6; Glantz and House, ch.13.

179. Gruchmann, *Der Zweite Weltkrieg*, 252; Weinberg III, 704; David Glanz, *Soviet Military Deception in the Second World War*, London/Totowa NJ, 1989, 362–79, here 463, 467ff.; *DZW*, vi.33.

180. Irving, *HW*, 643–4.

181. Hans-Adolf Jacobsen and Jürgen Rohwer, *Entscheidungsschlachten des Zweiten Weltkrieges*, Frankfurt am Main, 1960, 452.

182. *TBJG*, II/12, 538–9, 542 (24 June 1944).

183. *Weisungen*, 281–5. The principle of the twelve bastions created in the theatre of Army Group Centre, with three divisions assigned to each of the strongholds, was to suck in the Red Army, tying them down, then building the basis for a successful counter-operation. The tactic backfired drastically in the Soviet offensive of June 1944.

184. Below, 377–8.

185. See *DZW*, vi.34.

186. Gruchmann, *Der Zweite Weltkrieg*, 253.

187. Gruchmann, *Der Zweite Weltkrieg*, 253; Weinberg III, 706–8; Below, 378. The Soviet offensive in the Centre, South, and North is extensively described in *DZW*, vi.30–52, 52–70, 70–81.

188. Wistrich, *Wer war wer*, 188; Gruchmann, *Der Zweite Weltkrieg*, 253; *DZW*, vi.41.

189. Speidel, 127; Guderian, 334; Irving, *HW*, 649–51.

190. Domarus, 2110.

191. Guderian, 334.

192. Below, 378; Irving, *HW*, 648; Wistrich, *Wer war wer*, 301; Domarus, 2130.

193. Below, 378.

194. Below, 379.

195. Below, 380.

196. Below, 380.

197. Domarus, 2118. See Peter Hoffmann, *Stauffenberg. A Family History, 1905–1944*, Cambridge, 1995, ch.9, especially 179–80, for Stauffenberg's involvement in the North African campaign that led to his serious injuries, sustained on 7 April 1943, and 253–4 for his presence at the briefings on 6 and 11 July 1944.

198. Domarus, 2121; Hoffmann, *Stauffenberg*, 256–60; Hoffmann, *Widerstand*, 469–75.

199. Witnesses gave differing times for the explosion, between 12.40 and 12.50p.m. (Hoffmann, *Widerstand*, 493, 817 n. 43).

CHAPTER 14: LUCK OF THE DEVIL

1. The most wide-ranging anthology of essays on resistance is Jürgen Schmädeke and Peter Steinbach (eds.), *Der Widerstand gegen den Nationalsozialismus*, Munich/Zürich, 1985. Among the numerous guides through the labyrinth of the literature and moral debates on resistance are Gerd R. Ueberschar (ed.), *Der 20.Juli 1944. Bewertung und Rezeption des deutschen Widerstandes gegen das NS-Regime*, Cologne, 1994; Ulrich Heinemann, 'Arbeit am Mythos. Neuere Literatur zum bürgerlich-aristokratischen Widerstand gegen Hitler und zum 20.Juli 1944 (Teil I)', *GG*, 21 (1995), 111–39; and Ulrich Heinemann and Michael Kruger-Charlé, 'Arbeit am Mythos. Der 20.Juli 1944 in Publizistik und wissenschaftlicher Literatur des Jubiläumsjahres 1994 (Teil II)', *GG*, 23 (1997), 475–501. The most detailed and thoroughly researched description of the conspiracies against Hitler remains that of Hoffmann, *Widerstand*, on which this chapter frequently relies. A shorter, stylish account is that of Fest, *Staatsstreich*. Short descriptions of the personnel can be found in Peter Steinbach and Johannes Tuchel, *Lexikon des Widerstandes 1933–1945*. Munich, 1994. Problems of concepts and terminology, not entered into here, can be followed in the entries in Benz and Pehle; also in Ian Kershaw, *The Nazi Dictatorship. Problems and Perspectives of Interpretation*, 4th edn, London, 2000, ch.8.

2. For reflections on the role of Prussian ideals – seen as a 'determining motive (*bestimmendes Motiv*)' within the resistance to Hitler – see Hans Mommsen, 'Preußentum und Nationalsozialismus', in Wolfgang Benz, Hans Buchheim, and Hans Mommsen (eds.), *Der Nationalsozialismus. Studien zur Ideologie und Herrschaft*, Frankfurt am Main, 1993, 29–41, here 37, 41.

3. The mixture of motives within the wartime conspiracy is briefly surveyed by Peter Hoffmann, 'Motive', in Schmädeke und Steinbach, 1089–96; and more extensively in Theodore S. Hamerow, *On the Road to the Wolf's Lair. German Resistance to Hitler*, Cambridge, Mass./London, 1997. The moral dimension is assessed by Robert Weldon Whaley, *Assassinating Hitler: Ethics and Resistance in Nazi Germany*, London/Ontario, 1993. See also the compilation put together in the 1950s by Annedore Leber, *Conscience in Revolt*, London, 1957, and the more recent collection of texts: Peter Steinbach and Johannes Tuchel, *Widerstand in Deutschland*, Munich, 1994.

4. Joachim Kramarz, *Claus Graf Stauffenberg. 15. November, 1907–20. Juli 1944: Das Leben eines Offiziers*, Frankfurt am Main, 1965, 131; Hoffmann, *Stauffenberg*, 183.

5. See Hans Mommsen, 'Social Views and Constitutional Plans of the Resistance', in Hermann Graml *et al.*, *The German Resistance to Hitler*, (1966), London, 1970, 55–147, here 59, for perceptions by Pater Alfred Delp and Adam von Trott of lack of popular support for a putsch. Over seven years after the events, General Klaus Uebe was adamant that the mass of the rank-and-file troops rejected any notion of a move by officers against Hitler (IfZ, ZS 164, Klaus Uebe, 3 January 1952).

6. Kramarz, 201.

7. Fabian von Schlabrendorff, *Offiziere gegen Hitler*, (1946), revised edn, Berlin, 1984, 109.

8. Scheurig, *Tresckow*, especially ch.4; also Fest, *Staatsstreich*, 177; Whaley, 48–9, 54, 56.

9. Scheurig, *Tresckow*, 111–12.

10. Scheurig, *Treskow*, 110ff.; Fest, *Staatsstreich*, 177–80.

11. Fest, *Staatsstreich*, 193–4.

12. Hassell, 307 (28 March 1942).

13. Helena P. Page, *General Friedrich Olbricht. Ein Mann des 20.Juli*, Bonn/Berlin, 1992, 206.

14. Fest, *Staatsstreich*, 194; quotation, *Spiegelbild einer Verschwörung. Die Kaltenbrunner-Berichte an Bormann und Hitler über das Attentat vom 20.Juli 1944. Geheime Dokumente aus dem ehemaligen Reichssicherheitshauptamt*, ed. Archiv Peter für historische und zeitgeschichtliche Dokumentation, Stuttgart, 1961, 368.

15. Thun-Hohenstein, 224, citing Hermann Kaiser, Tagebuch v.3 February 1943. The entry was not

included in the extracts from Kaiser's diary published in 'Neue Mitteilungen zur Vorgeschichte des 20.Juli', *Die Wandlung*, 1 (1945/46), 530–34. But see also Kaiser's diary entry for 31 March 1943 in Annedore Leber and Freya Gräfin von Moltke, *Für und wider Entscheidungen in Deutschland 1918–1945*, Frankfurt, 1961, 203: 'A discussion arises about discipline and obedience of the leadership and Fromm says, in a hundred cases one must be 100 per cent obedient. Olbricht opposes this: one must be able to say no once in 99 cases. Fromm retorts vehemently in favour of unconditional obedience . . .' ('*Es kommt Gespräch über Disziplin und Gehorsam der Führung auf und Fromm sagt, in hundert Fällen müsse man 100ig gehorsam sein. Olbricht dagegen: Man müsse bei 99 Fällen einmal nein sagen können. Fromm erwidert heftig, für unbedingten Gehorsam . . .*') Kaiser's involvement in the opposition is thoroughly dealt with by Ger van Roon, 'Hermann Kaiser und der deutsche Widerstand', *VfZ*, 24 (1976), 259–86.

16. For use of the term, see, e.g., Hoffmann, *Widerstand*, 350.

17. Hoffmann, *Widerstand*, 341–2.

18. Hoffmann, *Widerstand*, 343–6, 350; Fest, *Staatsstreich*, 194–5.

19. Hoffmann, *Widerstand*, 348–9.

20. See Hoffmann, *Hitler's Personal Security*, 111ff.

21. Hoffmann, *Widerstand*, 351; Hoffman, *Hitler's Personal Security*, ch.5–9.

22. Hoffmann, *Widerstand*, 347.

23. Hoffmann, *Widerstand*, 347, 351.

24. Schlabrendorff, 67–75; Hoffmann, *Widerstand*, 352–3; Fest, *Staatsstreich*, 196–7.

25. Rudolf-Christoph Frhr. v. Gersdorff, *Soldat im Untergang. Lebensbilder*, Frankfurt etc., 1979, 128–32; Hoffmann, *Widerstand*, 353–60.

26. Meehan, 337; and see Klemperer, 287. Henry II had allegedly used the words, 'Will no one rid me of this turbulent priest?' at which four knights from his entourage rode to Canterbury to murder the Archbishop, Thomas Becket. The formation of Bishop Bell's attitude towards the Nazi regime during the 1930s can be traced in Andrew Chandler (ed.), *Brethren in Adversity. Bishop George Bell, the Church of England, and the Crisis of German Protestantism, 1933–1939*, Woodbridge, 1997.

27. In Lothar Kettenacker (ed.), *Das 'Andere Deutschland' im Zweiten Weltkrieg. Emigration und Widerstand in internationaler Perspektive*, Stuttgart, 1977, 203.

28. British attitudes are critically explored in Lothar Kettenacker, 'Die britische Haltung zum deutschen Widerstand während des Zweiten Weltkriegs', in Kettenacker, 49–76 (and see the documentation in the same volume, 164–217); and Richard Lamb, 'Das Foreign Office und der deutsche Widerstand 1938–1944', in Klaus-Jürgen Muller and David N. Dilks (eds.), *Großbritannien und der deutsche Widerstand 1933–1944*, Paderborn etc., 1994, 53–81. For differing evaluations of the Allies' uncompromising stance, see Fest, *Staatsstreich*, 212–13; and Heinemann/Kruger-Charlé, 492–3. The variety of ideas on foreign policy within the resistance is explored by Hermann Graml, 'Resistance Thinking on Foreign Policy', in Graml et al., *German Resistance*, 1–54.

29. For brief surveys of the 'Goerdeler Group', see Ger van Roon, *Widerstand im Dritten Reich. Ein Überblick*, Munich, (1979), 7th revised edn, 1998, ch.8; and Benz/Pehle, *Lexikon des deutschen Widerstandes*, 217–22.

30. Graml, 'Resistance Thinking', 27. And see Goerdeler's foreign policy plans put forward in 1941 in *Germans against Hitler: July 20, 1944*, 5th edn, ed. Bundeszentrale für politische Bildung, Bonn, 1969, 55–60.

31. Hoffmann, *Widerstand*, 372–3; Goerdeler put forward a similar programme in May 1944 (Christian Müller, *Stauffenberg*, Düsseldorf, 1970, 393).

32. Mommsen, 'Social Views', 60; Mommsen, 'Der Widerstand gegen Hitler und die deutsche Gesellschaft', 9, 11; and Hans Mommsen, 'Verfassungs- und Verwaltungsreformpläne der Widerstandsgruppen des 20.Juli 1944', in Schmädeke and Steinbach, 570–97; Roon, *Widerstand*, 135–9; Fest, *Staatsstreich*, 147–57.

33. Hoffmann, *Widerstand*, 373.

34. *Spiegelbild*, 178.

35. *Spiegelbild*, 56, 112; Fest, *Staatsstreich*, 234.

36. See Helmuth James von Moltke, *Letters to Freya, 1939–1945. A Witness against Hitler*, London, 1991; and Michael Balfour and Julian Frisby, *Helmuth von Moltke. A Leader against Hitler*, London, 1972.

37. See Ger van Roon, *Neuordnung im Widerstand. Der Kreisauer Kreis innerhalb der deutschen Widerstandsbewegung*, Munich, 1967; Ger van Roon, 'Staatsvorstellungen des Kreisauer Kreises', in Schmädeke and Steinbach, 560–9; Roon, *Widerstand*, 155–7; Hans Mommsen, 'Der Kreisauer Kreis und die kunftige Neuordnung Deutschlands und Europas', *VfZ*, 42 (1994), 361–77; Benz/Pehle, *Lexikon des deutschen Widerstandes*, 247–52.

38. Roon, *Widerstand*, 157–8.

39. Gersdorff, 134ff. (quotation, 135).

40. Hoffmann, *Widerstand*, 361.

41. For the important intermediary role of Schulenburg, see Ulrich Heinemann, *Ein konservativer Rebell. Fritz-Dietlof von der Schulenburg und der 20.Juli*, Berlin, 1990, 142ff. (149–50 for his temporary arrest).

42. Hoffmann, *Widerstand*, 363–6; Heinz Hohne, *Canaris – Patriot im Zwielicht*, Munich, 1976, 529; and, for the enigmatic role played by Canaris, see, apart from his biography of the Abwehr chief, also Heinz Höhne, 'Canaris und die Abwehr zwischen Anpassung und Opposition', in Schmädeke and Steinbach, 405–16.

43. Hoffmann, *Widerstand*, 373.

44. Fest, *Staatsstreich*, 218.

45. Hoffmann, *Stauffenberg*, ch.1–2; Michael Baigent and Richard Leigh, *Secret Germany: Claus von Stauffenberg and the Mystical Crusade against Hitler*, London, 1994, ch.5; and see Mosse, 209–11; and Roon, *Widerstand*, 180.

46. Hoffmann, *Stauffenberg*, 115–16.

47. Hoffmann, *Stauffenberg*, 132.

48. Hoffmann, *Stauffenberg*, 133, 151. For assessments of the varied attitudes towards Jews and antisemitism among those involved in resistance to the Nazi regime, see Christoph Dipper, 'Der deutsche Widerstand und die Juden', *GG*, 9 (1983), 349–80; Christoph Dipper, 'Der Widerstand und die Juden', in Schmadeke and Steinbach, 598–616; and Hans Mommsen, 'Der Widerstand gegen Hitler und die nationalsozialistische Judenverfolgung' (as yet unpublished, but kindly made available to me by Hans Mommsen). As could hardly otherwise be expected, strains of antisemitism – for the most part traditional resentments, far removed from the extremes of Nazi genocidal mentalities – are not infrequently encountered, especially among the older and more conservative sectors of the opposition. At opposite poles in the resistance, not least as regards attitudes towards the Jews, were Oster and Groscurth, who revealed no signs of antisemitism, and Wolf Heinrich Graf von Helldorf (the rabidly antisemitic Berlin police-chief and former SA leader) and Arthur Nebe (head of a murderous Einsatzgruppe, responsible for the deaths of tens of thousands of Jews). The mounting atrocities against the Jewish population in the occupied eastern territories were unquestionably, as in Stauffenberg's case, a strong – though for the most part, it seems, not the decisive – motive in engaging in the conspiracy to kill Hitler. Yet, ambiguities almost inevitably remain: even among the courageous front officers of Army Group Centre, there seems to have been at least initial approval for the ruthless war against partisans and 'bandits' which was to a large extent coterminous with the growing genocidal assault on the Jews. (See Heinemann/Krüger-Charlé, 499 and n.99.)

49. Gisevius, *To the Bitter End*, 508, for a somewhat unflattering picture of Stauffenberg.

50. Eberhard Zeller, *Geist der Freiheit. Der Zwanzigste Juli*, 4th edn, Munich, 1963, 244; Roon, *Widerstand*, 179–83.

51. Ritter, 366–7; Fest, *Staatsstreich*, 222; Hoffmann, *Widerstand*, 396; Roon, *Widerstand*, 184.

52. *Germans against Hitler*, 131.

53. Roon, *Widerstand*, 178–9; Hoffmann, *Widerstand*, 374ff., especially 386–7; Fest, *Staatsstreich*, 222–4.

54. For a character sketch, see Bernhard R. Kroener, 'Friedrich Fromm – Der "starke Mann im Heimatkriegsgebiet" ', in Smelser/Syring, 171–86.

55. Hoffmann, *Widerstand*, 397–8.

56. Hoffmann, *Widerstand*, 398–405. For Bussche, see the brief portrait from personal acquaintance in Marion Gräfin Dönhoff, *'Um der Ehre willen'. Erinnerungen an die Freunde vom 20.Juli*, (1994) 2nd edn, Berlin, 1996, 67–76.

57. Kleist first asked Stauffenberg for time to think it over. He asked his father, hoping he would advise against it. His father replied without hesitation: 'Yes, you must do it. Whoever fails in such a moment will never again be happy in his lifetime.' (Bodo Scheurig, *Ewald von Kleist-Schmenzin. Ein Konservativer gegen Hitler. Biographie*, Berlin/Frankfurt am Main, 1994.) The father would eventually pay for his opposition with his life; the son would survive the Nazi regime.

58. Hoffmann, *Widerstand*, 405–6.

59. Hoffmann, *Widerstand*, 407–10.

60. Roon, *Widerstand*, 188–9.

61. See, for the reference, above, note 7.

62. Hoffmann, *Widerstand*, 406; Fest, *Staatsstreich*, 243.

63. Roon, *Widerstand*, 187.

64. Hoffmann, *Widerstand*, 469; Fest, *Staatsstreich*, 242–3, 246.

65. Hoffmann, *Widerstand*, 471–5.

66. Roon, *Widerstand*, 189; Hoffmann, *Widerstand*, 471–2; Fest, *Staatsstreich*, 250–52.

67. Roon, *Widerstand*, 189–90; Fest, *Staatsstreich*, 252–3.

68. Hoffmann, *Widerstand*, 486–8; Fest, *Staatsstreich*, 258–9.

69. Hoffmann, *Widerstand*, 489–91, 493. Fest, *Staatsstreich*, 261, has 12.40p.m. Below, 381, and some other witnesses suggest that time, others (e.g., in his much later second set of memoirs, Linge, 225, who, however, is frequently unreliable with detail) a slightly later time. Benz, Graml, and Weiß, *Enzyklopädie des Nationalsozialismus*, 814, give the precise time of 12.42p.m., though without source. According to the summary of the evidence in Hoffmann, *Widerstand*, 817 n.43, the explosion can not be timed more precisely than between 12.40 and 12.50p.m. Sander's comment about explosions occurring as a result of animals setting off mines was later echoed by Hitler's secretary Christa Schroeder (Schroeder, 147). Hitler's valet, Heinz Linge, stated much later that he initially thought Hitler's dog had set off a mine (Linge, *Bis zum Untergang*, 224). Since, however, Linge was close to the hut where the explosion took place, this sounds contrived.

70. Hoffmann, *Widerstand*, 491–3; Hoffmann, *Stauffenberg*, 267.

71. Hoffmann, *Widerstand*, 493–5; Fest, *Staatsstreich*, 261; Irving, *HW*, 662–3; Below, 381; Schroeder, 147; Irving, *Doctor*, 145.

72. Below, 381.

73. Hoffmann, *Widerstand*, 496–7; *Spiegelbild*, 83

74. Speer, 399; *TBJG*, II/13, 139 (23 July 1944).

75. Below, 381; Schroeder, 148; Hoffmann, *Widerstand*, 496.

76. Irving, *Doctor*, 146–8 (where Hitler's pulse and blood-pressure are said to have risen, but not excessively, following the attack); Below, 381; Schroeder, 148; *TBJG*, II/13, 139 (23 July 1944); Redlich, 204–5; Schenck, 317–18. Morell told Paul Schmidt, the interpreter, that afternoon that Hitler's pulse had been quite normal following the explosion (Schmidt, 593).

77. Linge, *Bis zum Untergang*, 225.

78. Below, 382; Hoffmann, *Widerstand*, 498–501; Irving, *Goring*, 430.

79. Schroeder, 148. Hitler asked Christa Schroeder, so she later wrote, to send the tattered coat and

trousers to Eva Braun for safe keeping. One of Hitler's other secretaries, Gerda Christian (Daranowski before her marriage in February 1943), later recalled that Hitler had been calm when he spoke to them on the evening after the attempt on his life. (Library of Congress, Washington, Toland Tapes, C-63B, interview with John Toland, 26 July 1971.)

80. Below, 382; see also Speer, 391; and Reuth, *Goebbels*, 548.

81. *TBJG*, II/13, 141 (23 July 1944); Below, 382; Linge, *Bis zum Untergang*, 229; Schroeder, 148–9; Hoffmann, *Widerstand*, 597. According to the account compiled by Linge in the 1950s, he heard from a telephonist that Stauffenberg had left the barracks in a direction from which it could be concluded that he was leaving the Führer Headquarters, and had this information conveyed to Hitler (Linge, 'Kronzeuge', Bl.83). Since Stauffenberg left the barrack-hut without cap and belt, heading in the direction of the adjutants' building, well away from any exit from the compound and in the opposite direction to the airfield, this seems like a later elaboration by Linge, designed to play up his own role.

82. Hoffmann, *Widerstand*, 506ff.

83. Hoffmann, *Widerstand*, 509 and 823 n.88.

84. Gisevius, *To the Bitter End*, 546.

85. Hoffmann, *Widerstand*, 506–11; Roon, *Widerstand*, 192. Himmler had ordered the communications block lifted around 3p.m.. Full clearance was only attained around an hour later. (Hoffmann, *Widerstand*, 504, 510–11. See also *Spiegelbild*, 330.)

86. Hoffmann, *Widerstand*, 511, 823–6 (notes 93, 95).

87. Hoffmann, *Widerstand*, 519 and 833 n.122. That Stauffenberg had seen a person carried from the briefing hut covered in Hitler's cloak, presuming that it was the Führer, as he (and later Fellgiebel) claimed (Fest, *Staatsstreich*, 261; Hoffmann, *Stauffenberg*, 267), seems, however, unlikely. The adjutancy, where they heard the explosion, was some distance – around 200 metres (Hoffmann, *Widerstand*, 490) – from the hut. There were other buildings, and trees, which would have obscured the view. And it is doubtful that, following the explosion and when time was of the essence, Stauffenberg and Haeften would have hesitated long enough before hurrying away to await the first casualties being carried from the hut. It is possible that they caught a glimpse of someone being taken from the hut as they drove away. Whether, in the mêlée, it was feasible to ascertain that he was draped in Hitler's cloak, seems doubtful.

88. Gisevius, *To the Bitter End*, 545; Hoffmann, *Widerstand*, 513–14.

89. Hoffmann, *Widerstand*, 514; Hoffmann, *Stauffenberg*, 269.

90. Gisevius, *To the Bitter End*, 546–7; Hoffmann, *Widerstand*, 519–20; Hoffmann, *Stauffenberg*, 270.

91. Hoffmann, *Widerstand*, 520–24.

92. Hoffmann, *Widerstand*, 520, 607, 609.

93. A point criticized by Gisevius, *To the Bitter End*, 545.

94. In the German version, Gisevius has the following account of Beck's words: '*Gleichgültig, was jetzt verbreitet werde, gleichgültig sogar, was wahr sei, für ihn, Beck, sei die Entscheidung gefallen. Er fordert die Herren auf, sich mit ihm solidarisch zu erklären. "Für mich ist dieser Mann tot. Davon lasse ich mein weiteres Handeln bestimmen."* ' ('Whatever is now being said, whatever is even true, for him, Beck, the decision has been taken. He calls upon the gentlemen to declare in solidarity with him: "For me, this man is dead. I will let my further actions be determined by this."') (Gisevius, *Bis Zum Bittern Ende*, 1946, ii.382.) The English version – Gisevius, *To the Bitter End*, 557 – differs: '. . . It did not matter at all whether Hitler was dead or still living. A "leader" whose immediate entourage included those who opposed him to the extent of attempting assassination must be considered morally dead.'

95. Gisevius, *To the Bitter End*, 558; Hoffmann, *Widerstand*, 615.

96. Fest, *Staatsstreich*, 269.

97. Roon, *Widerstand*, 194.

98. See Hoffmann, *Widerstand*, 529ff.; Fest, *Staatsstreich*, 270–71; Roon, *Widerstand*, 195.

99. Gisevius, *To the Bitter End*, 558.

100. Hoffmann, *Widerstand*, 581ff.; Fest, *Staatsstreich*, 283–91.

101. The only way to reconcile the differing accounts of Speer, 391 and Wilfried von Oven, *Mit Goebbels bis zum Ende*, 2 vols., Buenos Aires, 1950, ii, 59ff., is to presume that there were two phone-calls from Führer Headquarters, the first from Otto Dietrich very soon after the attack, the second between 2 and 3p.m. from Heinz Lorenz. This seems accepted by Oven in his second, later account (after the publication of Speer's memoirs) (Wilfried von Oven, 'Der 20.Juli 1944 – erlebt im Hause Goebbels', in *Verrat und Widerstand im Dritten Reich*, *Nation Europa*, 28 (1978), 43–58, here 47ff.). Goebbels referred to a telephone call at midday – mentioning that two of his ministerial colleagues (Funk and Speer) were with him – in his radio address on 26 July about the assassination attempt (Heiber, *Goebbels-Reden*, ii.342–3; see also Reuth, *Goebbels*, 548). It seems unlikely that in this telephone-call, minutes after the bomb-blast, as Irving, *Goebbels*, 471, suggests (placing the call, though without apparent supporting evidence, at 1p.m., and from Lorenz, not Dietrich), a request was passed on from Hitler for an immediate broadcast to make plain that he was alive and well. More probably, this request came in a subsequent call, in mid-afternoon, as Oven states (See Reuth, *Goebbels*, 550; Irving, *Goebbels*, 471, 473, for conflicting accounts). Linge, 'Kronzeuge', Bl.84, referred to difficulties in reaching Goebbels that afternoon, and that the telephone link was finally established at 4.30p.m.. In his account, this was the telephone-call in which Hitler spoke to Remer. This call, however, was made around 7p.m. (See Hoffmann, *Widerstand*, 597; Reuth, *Goebbels*, 550–2. Here, as in other points of detail, Linge is unreliable.)

102. Speer, 391.

103. Hoffmann, *Widerstand*, 593, 595.

104. Speer, 392–3.

105. Speer, 393–4. The unease about Himmler was not altogether ungrounded. Himmler had been aware since at least autumn 1943 of 'some sort of dark plans' brewing and, with Hitler's permission, had taken up contact with Popitz and, through him, other members of the conspiracy. The intermediary role was played by Himmler's lawyer, Dr Carl Langbehn, who, as Himmler knew, had sympathized with the opposition since before the war. Himmler was obviously playing a double game. On the one hand, he was careful to demonstrate his loyalty to Hitler, pointing out to the dictator that should any rumours reach him over his contact with the opposition, he should know that his motives were beyond question. Hitler acknowledged that he had complete trust in the Reichsführer. On the other hand, Himmler was well aware that the regime's days were numbered and that Hitler presented a block on any room for manoeuvre. He wanted to keep his options open, and to maintain a possible escape route should it prove necessary (Speer, 390; Ritter, 360–62; Hoffmann, *Widerstand*, 367–8; and Hedwig Maier, 'Die SS und der 20. Juli 1944', *VFZ*, 14 (1966), 299–316, here especially 311–14). It seems, nevertheless, doubtful that Himmler had an inkling of specific plans to topple Hitler on 20 July. It has been suggested that he was slow to act, leaving the Wolf's Lair belatedly, and only appearing around midnight to take charge of putting down the coup (Padfield, *Himmler*, 498–514). But he was prompt enough in addressing security issues at FHQ directly following the attempt, where he appeared with his entourage within an hour of the bomb exploding (Hoffmann, *Widerstand*, 503, 824). He was required to accompany Hitler at the visit of Mussolini later that afternoon, which delayed his departure for Berlin. Probably, too, he waited to confer with the head of the Security Police, Ernst Kaltenbrunner, at that very time *en route* to the Wolf's Lair, before leaving for the Reich capital. On arrival in Berlin, some time would have been taken up with coordinating the crushing of a military uprising whose ramifications, at that time, were still uncertain.

106. Speer, 393.

107. See Remer's account in: Hans Adolf Jacobsen (ed.), *Spiegelbild einer Verschwörung. Die Opposition gegen Hitler und der Staatsstreich vom 20.Juli 1944 in der SD-Berichterstattung.*

Geheime Dokumente aus dem ehemaligen Reichssicherheitshauptamt, 2 vols., Stuttgart, 1984, II.637ff.; also Hoffmann, *Widerstand*, 528, 594–5.
108. Hoffmann, *Widerstand*, 528.
109. Otto Ernst Remer, *20.Juli 1944*, Hamburg, 1951, 12; repeated with minor variations in Otto Ernst Remer, *Verschwörung und Verrat um Hitler. Urteil eines Frontsoldaten*, Preußisch-Oldendorf, 1981, 33. Similar wording is given by Linge, 'Kronzeuge', Bl.84. Linge was, he said, in the room as Hitler spoke. See also Jacobsen, *Spiegelbild*, 639. It is unlikely that Hitler immediately promoted Remer to colonel, as Linge, 'Kronzeuge', Bl.84, claimed. (See Hoffmann, *Widerstand*, 597 and 854 n.343.)
110. Speer, 394–5; Hoffmann, *Widerstand*, 594–8. See also Gisevius, *To the Bitter End*, 563–4; Remer, *20.Juli 1944*, Hamburg, 1951, 12; Remer, *Verschwörung und Verrat um Hitler*, 33–4; and Hagen's report, *Spiegelbild*, 12–15.
111. *Germans against Hitler*, 147, for the time.
112. Domarus, 2127 gives the time of the broadcast, at Hitler's bidding, as 6.30p.m.; Speer, 395–6, recalls the broadcast as 'towards seven o'clock in the evening'; Reuth, *Goebbels*, 550, gives the time of the broadcast as 6.45p.m..
113. Hoffmann, *Widerstand*, 599.
114. Hoffmann, *Widerstand*, 608, 613.
115. Hoffmann, *Widerstand*, 616.
116. Hoffmann, *Widerstand*, 620–26; Fest, *Staatsstreich*, 277–9.
117. Gisevius, *To the Bitter End*, 570.
118. *IMG*, xxxiii.417–18, Doc.3881–PS; Gisevius, *To the Bitter End*, 570–71 (with some textual variation); Zeller, 397–8; Hoffmann, *Widerstand*, 623–5; Fest, *Staatsstreich*, 279–80.
119. Hoffmann, *Widerstand*, 623ff.; Fest, *Staatsstreich*, 280–81; Hoffmann, *Stauffenberg*, 276–7.
120. Schroeder, 148; Domarus, 2123.
121. Domarus, 2124; Schmidt, 595.
122. Schmidt, 593. Linge's remark, *Bis zum Untergang*, 229, that Hitler had his right arm in a sling conflicts with Schmidt's, 593, that he noticed nothing untoward in Hitler's appearance before he used his left hand to shake hands with Mussolini and it became apparent that he had difficulty in raising his right arm. The photograph of Hitler inspecting the ruined barrack-room with Mussolini is taken at the wrong angle to be conclusive, but nevertheless does not suggest that Hitler had his arm in a sling. When he gave his radio address in the early hours of the following morning, his arm was not in a sling. (See the photographs in Fest, *Staatsstreich*, 265, 278.)
123. Schmidt, 594.
124. Hoffmann, *Widerstand*, 501–2.
125. Below, 383.
126. Schroeder, 149; *Germans against Hitler*, 180, has about 1a.m..
127. Domarus, 2127–9.

CHAPTER 15: NO WAY OUT

1. Schroeder, 148–9; Zoller, 186.
2. Speer, 399–400; trans., Albert Speer, *Inside the Third Reich*, Sphere Books edn, London, 1971, 525.
3. *TBJG*, II/13, 206 (3 August 1944).
4. *LB Darmstadt*, 246–8.
5. Schroeder, 148. The phrase is also used in Bormann's telegram to the Gauleiter at 9.20p.m. on the evening of 20 July (*The Bormann Letters. The Private Correspondence between Martin Bormann and his Wife from January 1943 to April 1945*, ed. H. R. Trevor-Roper, London, 1954, 63).

6. Speer, 400; trans., Speer, *Inside*, 525.

7. Zeller, 538 n.11, cit. W. Scheidt, 'Gespräche mit Hitler', *Echo der Woche*, 7 October 1949, p.5: '*Die müssen sofort hängen ohne jedes Erbarmen.*' Scheidt was on the staff of Major-General Walther Scherff, the official historian in Hitler's Headquarters (who was injured in the explosion on 20 July 1944), and heard the words at one of the military briefings following the assassination attempt, when he was deputizing for Scherff.

8. Guderian, 345–7, indicates that he was ordered to attend, and did so reluctantly and as infrequently as possible.

9. *TBJG*, II/13, 212 (3 August 1944). The military 'Court of Honour' met for the first time on 4 August 1944. On this and three subsequent sittings (14 and 24 August, 14 September), a total of fifty-five officers were expelled from the army (*Germans against Hitler*, 196–8).

10. Speer, 399; Schroeder, 149.

11. *TBJG*, II/13, 141 (23 July 1944). Goebbels added the comment (142): 'The Führer is resolved to eradicate root and branch the entire clan of generals which has opposed us in order to break down the wall which has been artificially erected by this generals' clique between the army on the one side and Party and people on the other.'

12. Below, 383; Linge, *Bis zum Untergang*, 232.

13. For a brief biographical summary, see Weiß, *Biographisches Lexikon*, 130–31.

14. *TBJG*, II/13, 141 (23 July 1944).

15. Zeller, 538 n.11, cit. Scheidt, 'Gespräche mit Hitler' (see above n.7): '*Und das wichtigste ist, daß sie keine Zeit zu langen Reden erhalten dürfen. Aber der Freisler wird das schon machen. Das ist unser Wyschinski.*' Goebbels discussed with Hitler at the beginning of August, a few days before the trials before the People's Court were to begin, how they should proceed. No lengthy speeches in defence would be permitted, it was determined. The sessions would not be public, but Goebbels would ensure that first-class journalists were present to cover the trials and produce reports on them for public consumption. He undertook to speak directly to Freisler to explain how the trials were to proceed. Hitler himself was keen that background details which cast negative light on the plotters should be brought out. He was also anxious that the fiction should be held to that the plotters had been no more than a small clique, and that there should be no sweeping attacks on the officer class as such, on the army, or on the aristocracy (which would be dealt with at a later date) (*TBJG*, II/13, 214 (3 August 1944)). Propaganda directives had emphasized in the immediate aftermath of the failed *coup d'état* that the conspirators had been only a tiny group, and that there was to be no criticism levelled at the Wehrmacht and its officers as a whole (Steinert, 473–4).

16. *Bormann Letters*, 62–3.

17. Speer, 397–8.

18. Kroener, 183–4. Fromm's execution appears specifically to have been ordered by Hitler, probably at Goebbels's prompting, after the Propaganda Minister had brought up the case again on 5 March 1945, pointing out that Fromm deserved to die 'because he had behaved in such cowardly fashion in face of the enemy, namely the putschists of 20 July', and that no death penalty could be expected under the current leadership of the People's Court (*TBJG*, II/15, 425 (5 March 1945); Speer, 450; Linge, *Bis zum Untergang*, 232).

19. See Otto Skorzeny, *Skorzeny's Special Missions*, London (1957), 1997, 113–19.

20. *Bormann Letters*, 65.

21. *Bormann Letters*, 64–5.

22. *Spiegelbild*, 23; Hoffmann, *Widerstand*, 625–6. Gerstenmaier was later sentenced to seven years in a penitentiary; the others were executed.

23. *Spiegelbild*, 16; Hoffmann, *Widerstand*, 629–30.

24. Hoffmann, *Widerstand*, 630–4; Below, 384.

25. See especially Schlabrendorff, 132–40; also Hoffmann, *Widerstand*, 642–3; Fest, *Staatsstreich*, 296–8.

26. Hoffmann, *Widerstand*, 628; Ritter, 420; Fest, *Staatsstreich*, 294.

27. Below, 385.

28. *Berlin Diaries* 204; Ted Harrison, 'Der "Alte Kämpfer" Graf Helldorf im Widerstand', *VfZ*, 45 (1997), 385–423, here 421.

29. Below, 385; Ritter, 411-24; Fest, *Staatsstreich*, 306–11.

30. Schroeder, 149.

31. *TBJG*, II/13, 214 (3 August 1944). Robert Ley was firmly told not to repeat the vicious attacks on the aristocracy which he had made in populist speeches.

32. 'Die Rede Himmlers vor den Gauleitern am 3. August 1944', ed. Theodor Eschenburg, *VfZ*, 1 (1953), 357–94, here 385: '*Die Familie Graf Stauffenberg wird ausgelöscht werden bis ins letzte Glied.*' See also Hoffmann, *Widerstand*, 639–41; Fest, *Staatsstreich*, 305–6.

33. Hoffmann, *Widerstand*, 635.

34. Cit. Dieter Ehlers, *Technik und Moral einer Verschwörung. Der Aufstand am 20. Juli 1944*, Bonn, 1964, 28: '"Morde? . . . Sie sind ja ein schäbiger Lump! Zerbrechen Sie unter der Gemeinheit?"'; trans. *Germans against Hitler*, 198–200. See also Zeller, 461–2, and *Germans against Hitler*, 211. For a description of the courtroom, see Oven, *Mit Goebbels*, ii.113, entry for 10 August 1944.

35. *Germans against Hitler*, 198, 211; Reuth, *Goebbels*, 599–60.

36. Zeller, 463–4: '*Dann beeilen Sie sich mit dem Aufhängen, Herr Präsident, sonst hängen Sie eher als wir*' (Fellgiebel). '*Sie können uns dem Henker überantworten. In drei Monaten zieht das empörte und gequälte Volk Sie zur Rechenschaft und schleift Sie bei lebendigem Leibe durch den Kot der Straßen*' (Witzleben); trans., *Germans against Hitler*, 201.

37. *Germans against Hitler*, 201; *TBJG*, II/13, 225 (4 August 1944).

38. *Germans against Hitler*, 210.

39. Beheading by axe had been the traditional practice of execution in much of Germany, including Prussia, and was continued in the early years of Hitler's rule. In some states (Bavaria, Württemberg, Baden, Saxony, Thuringia, Bremen, Oldenburg, and Hesse), however, the guillotine was used. Discussion in legal circles (including letters sent from the general public to the Reich Ministry of Justice recommending variants of gruesomely inhumane capital punishment) eventually culminated in a decision by Hitler in 1936 to standardize execution by the guillotine throughout Germany. The wild escalation in the number of executions during the war led, however, by 1942–3 to the increasing use of hanging as a cheap and simple alternative. Shooting of condemned prisoners now also took place as the search for speedy new methods of execution grew and as the complete collapse of established legal practice gathered pace. (See Richard J. Evans, *Rituals of Retribution. Capital Punishment in Germany 1600–1987*, Oxford, 1996, ch.15–16, here especially 651–60, 710–20.)

40. Cit. Ehlers, 113: '*Ich will, daß sie gehängt werden, aufgehängt wie Schlachtvieh.*'

41. Based on the eye-witness accounts in *Germans against Hitler*, 211–12, and the evidence collected by Hoffmann, *Widerstand*, 649–50, and 971–3, note 111.

42. Speer, 404.

43. According to Speer's later claim, Hitler watched it over and again (Toland, 818, cit. Speer's interview for *Playboy*, June 1971). Luftwaffe adjutant Below remarked, on the other hand, that Hitler showed little interest in the photographs of the executions, which were bandied about Führer Headquarters in repulsive fashion by SS-Gruppenführer Hermann Fegelein, Himmler's liaison officer at the Wolf's Lair (Below, 385). Walter Frentz, Hitler's cameraman, based at Führer Headquarters and frequently a guest at the evening monologues, also claimed, long after the war, that the films had arrived there, but that Fegelein was the only one to have seen them (Hoffmann, *Widerstand*, 872).

44. Hoffmann, *Widerstand*, 652, 864–5, note 33, 874, note 123; and see *Germans against Hitler*, 202–9, 214–19.

45. See Irving, *Doctor*, 151–2. He told his military entourage at the end of the month that he ought

to have spent ten to fourteen days in bed, but had carried on working at least eight hours a day (*LB* Darmstadt, 271 (31 July 1944)).

46. Irving, *Doctor*, 154.

47. Irving, *Doctor*, 150.

48. Redlich, 204–6; Schenck, 302, 318; Irving, *Doctor*, 152–3; *LB* Darmstadt, 270 (31 July 1944) (where Hitler ruled out flying for at least a further eight days until his ears were healed); *TBJG*, II/13, 209 (3 August 1944), 232 (5 August 1944).

49. *Bormann Letters*, 68.

50. Redlich, 205.

51. Irving, *Doctor*, 150; *TBJG*, II/13, 213 (3 August 1944).

52. Irving, *Doctor*, 149 (Giesing's impressions), 157 (those of Lieutenant-General Werner Kreipe); *TBJG*, II/13, 209 (3 August 1944) (Goebbels's impressions); and see Schenck, 394–5.

53. *LB* Darmstadt, 270 (31 July 1944).

54. Schenck, 250, cit. Morell's diary entry of 3 October 1944; Redlich, 205.

55. Irving, *Doctor*, 153 (Morell diary entry for 29 July 1944); *LB* Darmstadt, 217 (31 July 1944).

56. Irving, *Doctor*, 160; Redlich, 205.

57. Hoffmann, *Security*, 253–4; Zoller, 186.

58. *TBJG*, II/13, 210 (3 August 1944); Warlimont, 442.

59. Zoller, 186.

60. Guderian, 342, and 339–40 for his appointment.

61. See *TBJG*, II/13, 207 (3 August 1944), where Goebbels writes that propaganda must play its part in preventing an inverted version of the 1918 stab-in-the-back. Then, in his view, the home-front had subverted the military effort; now, the military had threatened to undermine the home-front.

62. Schroeder, 149.

63. *IMG*, xvi. 541; Speer, 403.

64. *KTB OKW*, iv. 2, 1572–6.

65. *LB* Darmstadt, 275–7, 280; *LB* Stuttgart, 609–20.

66. See above, Ch. 14, note 5.

67. Propaganda directives immediately after the putsch attempt referred specifically to it as a failed 'stab-in-the-back' (see Steinert, 475).

68. Steinert, 472–3.

69. BA, R55/614, R55/678, ' "Treukundgebungen" nach den 20.7.44; insbes. Berichte über einzelne Veranstaltungen und Stimmung nach dem Attentat'; Imperial War Museum, London (= IWM), 'Aus deutschen Urkunden 1935–1945', unpublished collection of captured documents, n.d., c.1945–6, 289–92 (instructions from the Reich Propaganda Ministry to Gauleiter and Gau Propaganda Offices, regarding 'Treukundgebungen anläßlich des mißlungenen Attentates auf den Fuhrer'); *MadR*, xvii.6684–6 (28 July 1944); Steinert, 476ff.; Michael Balfour, *Propaganda in War, 1939–1945*, London, 1979, 388.

70. *Spiegelbild*, 1–3. For the utterly contrasting reactions – based on newspaper reports and rumour – of remaining, anxiety-ridden Jews in Dresden, see the entries in Klemperer, ii.548–54 (21–28 July 1944).

71. In fact, British plans to assassinate Hitler had been formulated only a few weeks earlier than Stauffenberg's attempt on the dictator's life. Among the arguments used by staff officers within the British subversive agency, Special Operations Executive, to oppose a British assassination attempt – which, in any case, was almost a dead letter at the very time it was conceived – was the view that it would prove counter-productive in stirring up support for Hitler (and thereby making a post-war settlement more difficult). It was also felt 'that, from the strictly military point of view, it was almost an advantage that Hitler should remain in control of German strategy, having regard to the blunders that he has made' (*Operation Foxley*, 14–15, 30–31).

72. *Spiegelbild*, 4–7.

73. *Spiegelbild*, 8–11.

74. M.I. Gurfein and Morris Janowitz, 'Trends in Wehrmacht Morale', *Public Opinion Quarterly*, 10 (1946), 78–84, here 81; Balfour, *Propaganda*, 389. See also Breloer, 334, for a letter sent from one German prisoner-of-war in Texas to Hitler, congratulating him on his survival, and a diary entry from 21 July 1944 stating: 'I don't think I'm wrong when I say in such a sad hour for all of us: "Germany stands or falls in this struggle with the person of Adolf Hitler . . ." If this attack on Adolf Hitler had been successful, I am convinced that our homeland would now be in chaos.'

75. Buchbender and Sterz, 21–2.

76. *Spiegelbild*, 8–11.

77. See, for example, Andreas-Friedrich, 103 (entry for 31 July 1944), where she was denounced to the Gestapo for a derogatory remark about Hitler by a Party member sitting close by in a Berlin café. 'Since the 20 July all organs of the Nazis are inclined to sense a putschist in every German citizen,' she wrote. She narrowly escaped recriminations following the denunciation.

78. *Berlin Diaries*, 203.

79. Breloer, 132–3.

80. Breloer, 69.

81. Elisabeth Hoemberg, *Thy People, My People*, London, 1950, 161.

82. GStA, Munich, MA 106695, report of the Regierungspräsident of Oberbayern, 7 August 1944: '. . . *ein Teil der Bevölkerung das Gelingen des Attentats in erster Linie deshalb begrüßt hätte, weil er sich davon eine frühere Beendigung des Krieges erhoffte.*'

83. StA, Munich, LRA 29656, report of the SD-Außenstelle Berchtesgaden, 3 August 1944: '*Ja, wenn's ihn nur erwischt hätte.*'

84. Buchbender and Sterz, 146.

85. See Buchbender and Sterz, 24, 147–8. The censor's report showed negative comments – on matters in general, not specifically on Hitler – in 25 per cent of the letters checked, an increase on the previous month. A statistic from the end of November 1944 indicates that 9,523 members of the Wehrmacht had been shot for offences including indiscipline, subversion, and sabotage following usually perfunctory court-martial proceedings. How many had been picked up by negative remarks in letters cannot be established. Comments related to the attempt on Hitler's life, it can be safely surmised, would have been a minuscule proportion (Buchbender and Sterz, 20–25).

86. Steinert, 482.

87. Steinert, 479.

88. *Jahrbuch der öffentlichen Meinung 1947–1955*, ed. Elisabeth Noelle and Erich Peter Neumann, Allensbach, 1956, 138.

89. Michael Kater, *The Nazi Party. A Social Profile of Members and Leaders, 1919–1945*, Oxford, 1983, 263 (Figure 1).

90. IWM, 'Aus deutschen Urkunden 1935–1945', 264, report of SD-Leitabschnitt Stuttgart, 8 August 1944: '*Mit anderen Worten würde das heißen: Der Führer gibt zu, daß die Zeit bisher nicht für uns, sondern gegen uns gearbeitet hat. Wenn sich also ein Mann wie der Führer einer solch gewaltigen Täuschung hingegeben hat, . . . so wäre er entweder nicht das Genie, für das er immer hingestellt wird, oder aber, er hatte in Kenntnis der Tatsache, daß Saboteurs am Werk sind, das deutsche Volk vorsätzlich belogen, was ebenso schlimm wäre, denn mit solchen Feinden im eigenen Haus könnte die Kriegsproduktion niemals gesteigert werden, könnten wir niemals siegen. . . . Das Bedenklichste an der ganzen Sache ist wohl, daß die meisten Volksgenossen, auch diejenigen, die bisher unerschütterlich glaubten, jeden Glauben an den Führer verloren haben.*'

91. IWM, 'Aus deutschen Urkunden', 276, report of SD-Leitabschnitt Stuttgart, 6 November 1944: '*Es wird immer wieder behauptet, der Führer sei uns von Gott gesandt worden. Ich bezweifle es nicht. Der Führer wurde uns von Gott gesandt, aber nicht um Deutschland zu retten, sondern um*

Deutschland zu verderben. Die Vorsehung hat beschlossen, das deutsche Volk zu vernichten und Hitler ist der Vollstrecker dieses Willens.'

92. Breloer, 219–20.

93. Steinert, 498.

94. Manfred Messerschmidt, 'Krieg in der Trümmerlandschaft. "Pflichterfüllung" wofür?', in Ulrich Borsdorf and Mathilde Jamin (eds.), *Über Leben im Krieg. Kriegserfahrungen in einer Industrieregion 1939–1945*, Reinbeck bei Hamburg, 1989, 169–78, here 173.

95. Matthias von Hellfeld, *Edelweißpiraten in Köln*, 2nd edn, Cologne, 1983, especially 9–14, 38–59; Detlev Peukert, *Die Edelweißpiraten. Protestbewegungen jugendlicher Arbeiter im Dritten Reich*, Cologne, 1980, 103–15; *Widerstand und Verfolgung in Köln 1933–1945*, ed. Historisches Archiv der Stadt Köln, Cologne, 1974, 394–7.

96. *Widerstand und Verfolgung in Köln*, 396.

97. See Peukert, *Die KPD im Widerstand*, 388–400; Merson, 293–5; *Widerstand und Verfolgung in Köln*, 394–7.

98. Cit. Steinert, 499–500, 515.

99. Oven, *Mit Goebbels*, ii.109, entry for 5 August 1944, and Goebbels's speech to the Gauleiter in Posen two days earlier (Heiber, *Goebbels Reden*, ii.360–404, here 370, 372–3, 377–8) for his comparison with the Strasser crisis in 1932; also Orlow, ii.463.

100. *Bormann Letters*, 61–5; Orlow, ii.462 and n.282.

101. *Bormann Letters*, 69. Bormann wrote, in this letter to his wife dated 26 July, that the Gauleiter conference would be on 1–2 August. In fact, it took place on 3–4 August.

102. TBJG, II/13, 221–3 (4 August 1944); Speer, 402; 'Die Rede Himmlers', 357–94; Goebbels's speech of 3 August in Heiber, *Goebbels Reden*, ii.360–404, quotation 396: '*das muß jetzt Schluß sein! Jetzt nimmt die Partei diese Entwicklung in die Hand*'; Orlow, ii.463–4.

103. Domarus, 2138–9; Speer, 402–3.

104. See Teppe, 278–301, here 299–301.

105. See Speer, 322–4, 333–4; Rebentisch, 412–13; Herbert, *Fremdarbeiter*, 252–5.

106. Rebentisch, 528.

107. Fröhlich, 'Hitler und Goebbels im Krisenjahr 1944', 195–224, here 205–6; Rebentisch, 512–14; Eleanor Hancock, *National Socialist Leadership and Total War 1941–45*, New York, 1991, 127–36; Wolfgang Bleyer, 'Pläne der faschistischen Führung zum totalen Krieg im Sommer 1944', *Zeitschrift für Geschichtswissenschaft*, 17 (1969), 1312–29. Speer seems to have been galvanized into action by the head of his Planning Office, Hans Kehrl, who saw the time as ripe following Goebbels's article in *Das Reich* on 30 June 1944, pressing for the rigorous squeezing out of all remaining labour reserves. (See Kehrl's letter to Speer of 10 July 1944, in Bleyer, 'Pläne der faschistischen Führung', 1315–16.)

108. Bleyer, 'Pläne der faschistischen Führung', 1317–25 (Speer Memoranda from 12 and 20 July 1944); Peter Longerich, 'Joseph Goebbels und der totale Krieg: eine unbekannte Denkschrift des Propagandaministers vom 18. Juli 1944', *VfZ*, 35 (1987), 289–314, text of Memorandum, 305–14; Hancock, 129, 133; Fröhlich, 'Hitler und Goebbels im Krisenjahr 1944', 206.

109. Rebentisch, 514.

110. *TBJG*, II/12, 521 (22 June 1944).

111. The text is in Bleyer, 'Pläne der faschistischen Führung', 1326–9. See also *TBJG*, II/13, 135–6 (23 July 1944); Rebentisch, 515; Hancock, 137–8; Longerich, 'Joseph Goebbels und der totale Krieg', 304–5; Fröhlich, 'Hitler und Goebbels im Krisenjahr 1944', 206–7.

112. *TBJG*, II/13, 154 (24 July 1944).

113. Rudolf Semmler (real name: Semler), *Goebbels – the Man Next to Hitler*, London, 1947, 147 (entry for 23 July 1944).

114. *RGBl*, 1944, I, Nr.34, 161–2.

115. Irving, *Göring*, 433; Fröhlich, 'Hitler und Goebbels im Krisenjahr 1944', 207. For Rominten

(and Göring's other residences – he had ten at various times, apart from Carinhall, his main home, and special trains and yachts at his disposal), see Volker Knopf and Stefan Martens, *Görings Reich. Selbstinszenierungen in Carinhall*, Berlin, 1999, 158–9.

116. *TBJG*, II/13, 153–6 (24 July 1944).

117. Oven, *Mit Goebbels*, ii.94, entry for 25 July 1944.

118. Rebentisch, 516–17; Hancock, 138.

119. Text in Heiber, *Goebbels Reden*, ii.342–59, quotation 353: '*Es wird im Lande sowohl für die Front wie für die Rüstungsproduktion so viel Kräfte frei machen, daß es uns nicht allzu schwerfallen dürfte, der Schwierigkeiten, die die Kriegslage immer wieder mit sich bringen wird, in souveräner Weise Herr zu werden.*' (Trans. amended from Seydewitz, 274.)

120. Orlow, ii.470.

121. According to the former housekeeper at his Munich apartment, Frau Anni Winter, Hitler's sight had deteriorated sharply, requiring him to have five pairs of increasingly strong spectacles in as many years (IfZ, ZS 194, Bl.3).

122. Rebentisch, 518–20.

123. Rebentisch, 521.

124. Rebentisch, 522.

125. Speer, 406.

126. Speer, 405–7; *TBJG*, II/13, 525–7 (20 September 1944).

127. Speer, 407.

128. See Speer, 575 n.5; and Rebentisch, 520.

129. Hancock, 152–5, 287 n.27. See also *DZW*, vi.222–37; Herbst, *Der Totale Krieg*, 343–7; Seydewitz, 275–9; Steinert, 505–6; Klaus Mammach, *Der Volkssturm. Bestandteil des totalen Kriegseinsatzes der deutschen Bevölkerung 1944/45*, East Berlin, 1981, 17–20.

130. Hancock, 157–8.

131. Harlan was also able to use the powers granted to him by Goebbels to acquire the services for his film of 4,000 sailors, training to counter Allied attacks on U-boats, as well as 6,000 horses. He was allowed to spend what he wanted. He put the costs of the film at around 8½ million marks – eight times as much as a good film normally cost to make. (Veit Harlan, *Im Schatten meiner Filme. Selbstbiographie*, Gütersloh, 1966, 184, 187–8. And see Welch, *Propaganda and the German Cinema*, 221ff., here 234.)

132. Mammach, 39; Franz W. Seidler, '*Deutscher Volkssturm*'. *Das letzte Aufgebot 1944/45*, Munich, 1989, 45–9; Padfield, *Himmler*, 540–3. Text of Himmler's speech at the first 'roll-call' of the Volkssturm in Bartenstein (East Prussia), on 18 October 1944, in IfZ, MA 315, frames 261420ff.

133. Hitler had, in fact, in referring in 1937 to the reasons why he had had to 'annihilate' Ernst Röhm and other SA leaders three years earlier, explicitly rejected 'the so-called levée en masse' and the notion 'that soldiers can be created only through the mobilisation of, let's say, enthusiasm' (Domarus, 424, 2150, n.312).

134. Mammach, 32; Hancock, 141.

135. Mammach, 24–9.

136. *RGBl*, 1944, I, Nr.53, 253–4; Mammach, 32–3.

137. Mammach, 168–70.

138. Mammach, 171.

139. Mammach, 57.

140. Mammach, 54.

141. Mammach, 186–7.

142. Mammach, 65–8.

143. See Mammach, 43–51, here 47, 50.

144. Mammach, 72–3.

145. Benz, Graml, and Weiß, *Enzyklopädie*, 788.

146. Longerich, *Hitlers Stellvertreter*, 171, seems to underplay this.

147. See Rebentisch, 423–63, referring largely to the 1941–3 period.

148. *IMG*, xxxv, 494–502, Doc.753-D (with Bormann's reply of 5 January 1945, putting it down largely to 'misunderstandings'). See Rebentisch, 426; Longerich, *Hitlers Stellvertreter*, 171–2; Gruchmann, 'Die "Reichsregierung" im Fuhrerstaat', 211, 223 n.115; Broszat, *Staat*, 394–5; Lang, *Der Sekretar*, 309–10, 490; Dieter Rebentisch, 'Hitlers Reichskanzlei zwischen Politik und Verwaltung', in Rebentisch and Teppe, 65–99, here 96; Diehl-Thiele, 256–7.

149. Padfield, *Himmler*, 514, even describes him as 'undoubtedly the chief beneficiary of the failed putsch'.

150. Padfield, *Himmler*, 543ff.

151. Weinberg III, 750; *DZW*, vi.78–9. Total losses since the beginning of the war were, by 1 October 1944, 2,748,034 men killed, injured, missing, or captured.

152. *DZW*, vi.183; Weinberg III, 750 (where the October losses are given as only one merchant ship). The total lost to U-boats in the last months of 1944 amounted to 321,732 tons of shipping, only about 2.3 per cent of the 14 million tons of Allied shipping launched the previous year (*Oxford Companion*, 69).

153. *KTB OKW*, iv/2, 1573.

154. Hoffmann, *Widerstand*, 433–4, 478, 480, 741 n.112, 786 n.155; Gruchmann, *Der Zweite Weltkrieg*, 295.

155. Weinberg III, 692–3; Gruchmann, *Der Zweite Weltkrieg*, 295–6. On the military details: John Prados, 'Cobra: Patton's Offensive in France, Summer 1944', in Albert A. Nofi (ed.), *The War against Hitler. Military Strategy in the West*, Conshohoken, PA, 1995, 133–55.

156. In the briefing, Hitler asserted that if he could use another 800 fighters there and then, 'the entire crisis that we have would be immediately overcome' (*LB Darmstadt*, 245). In a subsequent military briefing, on 31 August, Hitler said there would always be moments when the tensions became too great to sustain an alliance. 'Coalitions in world history have always at some point collapsed. Now we have to wait for the moment, however hard it is' (*LB Darmstadt*, 276).

157. Below, 386–7. Hitler eventually gave orders to prepare for a western offensive to take place in November on 19 August, when he told Keitel, Jodl, and Speer to prepare to raise 25 new divisions for the attack. (IfZ, MA 1360, frame 6217521: 'Notiz Keitels uber Besprechung mit General der Artillerie Buhle vom 24. August 1944', in which Buhle communicated Hitler's thoughts; Irving, *HW*, 689 and 889, n. to 689. See also Guderian, 364, where the aim was registered as defeating the western powers and throwing them back into the Atlantic.)

158. *LB Darmstadt*, 243, 245, 253.

159. *LB Darmstadt*, 249.

160. *LB Darmstadt*, 250.

161. *LB Darmstadt*, 244, 250, 260.

162. Hitler correctly guessed what would have been Montgomery's preference – a strike into the Ruhr. Eisenhower prevailed in his judgement that the attack on Germany should follow on a broad front along the Rhine. (See *LB Darmstadt*, 252, n.331; Weinberg III, 697–700.)

163. *LB Darmstadt*, 251, 253, 258, 262–3.

164. *LB Darmstadt*, 253, 255.

165. *LB Darmstadt*, 251, also 258–9, 264.

166. *LB Darmstadt*, 244.

167. Weinberg III, 721. Donitz had persuaded Hitler to give priority to building two new U-boat types, Type XXI and the smaller Type XXIII, faster than their predecessors and equipped with schnorkel and radar, allowing them to remain for long periods submerged and to detect enemy aircraft. Shortage of skilled labour and materials, along with disruption caused by bombing, hindered production so that, while the Americans expected 300 new U-boats in service by the end of 1944, only 180 were actually produced by the end of the war. (Parker, *Struggle for Survival*, 211;

see also Thomas, 244–5; Peter Padfield, *Dönitz: the Last Führer*, New York, 1984, 387 (for Dönitz's comments to Hitler on 16 December about the need for the new U-boats); and Doenitz, *Memoirs*, 424ff., 432–3 for his retrospective views on the U-boat campaign in late 1944 and early 1945.)

168. *LB* Darmstadt, 244–5.

169. *LB*, Darmstadt, 254–5, 259, 268. The lack of ports for the landing of men and provisions was indeed a hindrance to the Allies during the autumn. Only Cherbourg, much destroyed, was initially in their hands. The surrender of Dieppe and Ostend, and the capture of Brest, Le Havre, Boulogne and Calais made things somewhat easier by October. But the shortage of big dock cranes remained a serious handicap until Antwerp, taken by the British on 4 September, became fully operational, once the Scheldt estuary had been taken, in late November (*LB* Darmstadt, 253, n.335; Weinberg III, 693). For Hitler's exchange of telegrams with the commander of the German garrison at St Malo, taken in mid-August, see Domarus, 2142. Hitler told the commander (Colonel von Aulock) that every day he held out was of profit for the German war effort. The commander promised to fight to the last man. Hitler thanked him and his 'heroic men', and said the commander's name would go down in history.

170. Irving, *HW*, 683–4; Weinberg III, 693; Parker, *Struggle for Survival*, 202.

171. Gruchmann, *Der Zweite Weltkrieg*, 296–7; Weinberg III, 692–4; Parker, *Struggle for Survival*, 200–2; Irving, *HW*, 683–9.

172. *LB* Darmstadt, 273. Irving, *HW*, 696 and n.6, 889–90, notes to 687 and 696, regards Hitler's suspicions as justified, and is followed in this by Richard Lamb, 'Kluge', in Correlli Barnett (ed.), *Hitler's Generals*, London, 1990, 394–409, here 407. The evidence assembled seems, however, tenuous. And it seems doubtful whether Kluge would have had the courage for such a step. Colonel von Gersdorff, who had been deeply involved in the attempts at Army Group Centre to kill Hitler, claimed he had pleaded in vain with Kluge at this time to enter into negotiations with the enemy. Gersdorff had said the decision was the sort which had faced 'all great men in world history'. Kluge's answer was: 'Gersdorff, Field-Marshal v. Kluge is not a great man.' (Cit. Gersdorff, 151–2. For Hitler's awareness of Kluge's connections with the resistance group, see Guderian, 341; *TBJG* II/13, 208, 210 (3 August 1944).)

173. *LB* Darmstadt, 273.

174. Gene Mueller, 'Generalfeldmarschall Gunther von Kluge', in Ueberschär, *Hitlers militärische Elite*, I, 130–57, here 134; Peter Steinbach, 'Hans Günther von Kluge – Ein Zauderer im Zwielicht', in Smelser and Syring, *Die Militärelite des Dritten Reiches*, 288–324, here 318–19. For Montgomery's errors, see Weinberg III, 689–90, 693–4, 725.

175. Hitler remarked in a military briefing on 31 August that the suspicions were such that, had he not committed suicide, Kluge would have been immediately arrested (*LB* Darmstadt, 272).

176. Dieter Ose, *Entscheidung im Westen. Der Oberbefehlshaber West und die Abwehr der allierten Invasion*, Stuttgart, 2nd edn, 1985, 340, Anlage 18.

177. Despite the doubts of Steinbach, 'Kluge', 320, and Mueller, 'Kluge', 135, it is clear that Hitler did receive Kluge's letter. See *TBJG*, II/13, 372 (31 August 1944), and Irving, *HW*, 696.

178. *LB* Darmstadt, 279 and n.383.

179. *LB* Darmstadt, 280. See also Irving, *HW*, 696.

180. See Weinberg III, 761; *Oxford Companion*, 418–22.

181. Gruchmann, *Der Zweite Weltkrieg*, 299.

182. Domarus, 2143; *DZW*, vi.424–5; *KTB OKW*, iv/1, 358–60.

183. Gruchmann, *Der Zweite Weltkreig*, 297–9; Weinberg III, 694–5.

184. Ronald Heifermann, *World War II*, London, 1973, 229.

185. Weinberg III, 700.

186. The military aspects are assessed in Phil Kosnett and Stephen B. Patrick, 'Highway to the Reich: Operation Market-Garden, 17–26 September 1944', in Nofi, 156–77.

187. *DZW*, vi.112–18; Gruchmann, *Der Zweite Weltkrieg*, 302–5; Weinberg III, 701–2; Parker,

Struggle for Survival, 206–8; Heifermann, 229–30. Around 17,000 men were lost by the western Allies in the fighting in the second half of September. German losses were 3,300 troops. British losses alone numbered between 12,000 and 13,000 (*DZW*, vi.116).

188. Weinberg III, 752.

189. See *TBJG*, II/13, 204, 209 (3 August 1944). Turkey did not, in fact, declare war on Germany until 1 March 1945 (Domarus, 2136).

190. Guderian, 364–5; Irving, *HW*, 681.

191. Weinberg III, 713.

192. Guderian, 367.

193. Weinberg III, 714.

194. Weinberg III, 714–15.

195. Gruchmann, *Der Zweite Weltkrieg*, 274–5; Weinberg III, 716–17; *DZW*, vi.90–95.

196. Erickson, *Road to Berlin*, 290–307; Weinberg III, 712; *DZW*, vi.86–90.

197. Weinberg III, 715.

198. *TBJG*, II/13, 204 (3 August 1944).

199. Domarus, 2142–3; Gruchmann, *Der Zweite Weltkrieg*, 258.

200. Gruchmann, *Der Zweite Weltkrieg*, 258–9.

201. Gruchmann, *Der Zweite Weltkrieg*, 254–6; Weinberg III, 710–11.

202. Guderian, 355.

203. Himmler's speech to Wehrkreis Commanders of 21 September 1944, in Smith/Petersen, *Himmler. Geheimreden*, 246; trans. (slightly amended), Padfield, *Himmler*, 524. In the handwritten notes he made for his speech to Wehrkreis commanders in Jägerhöhe on 21 September 1944, Himmler jotted: 'General Bor in Warsaw rejects surrender. Then the population dies with him.' ('*General Bor in Warschau lehnt Übergabe ab, dann stirbt Bevölkerung mit.*') (IfZ, MA 315, frames 2584103ff. (quotation, frame 2584105).)

204. Himmler stated this in his address to the Wehrkreis commanders on 21 September (see Padfield, *Himmler*, 524). For the order to raze Warsaw by Hitler on 11 October, see *IMG*, xii.88, cit. Dok. USSR-128 (=PS-3305); also Padfield, *Himmler*, 524–5; and Guderian, 358.

205. Guderian, 356; Hohne, *Death's Head*, 502; Padfield, *Himmler*, 524–5; Benz, Graml, and Weiß, *Enzyklopädie*, 440, 539, for the Dirlewanger and Kaminski units. See also, Hellmuth Auerbach, 'Konzentrationslagerhaftlinge im Fronteinsatz', in Benz, *Miscellanea. Festschrift für Helmut Krausnick*, 63–83, here especially 66–7.

206. Padfield, *Himmler*, 527; *DZW*, vi.61. Gruchmann, *Der Zweite Weltkrieg*, 257, has lower figures for both Polish and German losses.

207. *IMG*, xii.88; Guderian, 358.

208. Schenck, 148; Irving, *Doctor*, 160; also Redlich, 207.

209. Schenck, 337–8, 342–3.

210. Schenck, 329, 333–6; Irving, *Doctor*, 161–2, 252–6; Redlich, 224–5, 368–9. Schenck, 336–7. dismisses suggestions that Hitler might have at any point suffered a heart attack, as has sometimes been claimed (e.g. in Hauner, *Hitler*, 193, and Toland, 822).

211. Schenck, 148. Below, 389, attributed Hitler's physical collapse to the news that Himmler had just given him of the involvement by Canaris, Goerdeler, Oster, Dohnanyi, and Beck in plotting against him as early as 1938–9. But Himmler gave that information to Hitler on 26 September, as Below notes (see also Irving, *HW*, 710–11); Hitler's severe stomach spasms had begun in the night of 23–4 September, as Morell's diary indicates. For Hitler's 'agitation' over Arnhem and the failure of the Luftwaffe, see Irving, *HW*, 706–8.

212. Irving, *Doctor*, 163; Irving, *HW*, 712; Below, 389.

213. Schenck, 148–9; Irving, *Doctor*, 164; Irving, *HW*, 712; Redlich, 207.

214. Schenck, 44, 150–3; Irving, *Doctor*, 164–8, 172–3.

215. Irving, *Doctor*, 169–79; Redlich, 209.

216. Linge, *Bis zum Untergang*, 161.

217. See Redlich, 244–52 for a balanced assessment of Morell. Far more critical is Schenck, 287–8.

218. Redlich, 237–44. Schenck, 196–215, assesses the numerous medicines given to Hitler. See also Irving, *Doctor*, 259–70. Leonard L. Heston and Renate Heston, *The Medical Casebook of Adolf Hitler*, London, 1979, build up an implausible theory of Hitler's dependency upon amphetamines as the basis of his irrationality. (See Redlich, 240–42 for a critique.)

219. See Redlich, 233; and Schenck, 325ff. and Redlich, 224–5 for cardiovascular problems.

220. Redlich, 332–41.

221. Ingeborg Fleischhauer, *Die Chance des Sonderfriedens. Deutsch-sowjetische Geheimgespräche 1941–1945*, Berlin, 1986, 265ff.; Ziemke, *Stalingrad to Berlin*, 404–5; and Martin, *Deutschland und Japan im Zweiten Weltkrieg*, 195ff.

222. *IMG*, xvi.533 (Speer's testimony of 20 June 1946); Boyd, 158–9; Irving, *HW*, 891 (note to 699). It is unclear why Weinberg III, 720, thinks 'there is some evidence that in the fall of 1944 Hitler for the first time seriously considered a possibility he had hitherto always dismissed out of hand'.

223. *TBJG*, II/13, 524 (20 September 1944).

224. *TBJG*, II/13, 524–5 (20 September 1944). Word of Oshima's proposal had evidently by this time spread further than Goebbels's own ministry. The following day, Goebbels castigated in his diary entry a speech, held in private to a select audience, by Labour Front leader Robert Ley which reported on the Oshima initiative and indicated that peace with Moscow was to be expected in the near future (*TBJG*, II/13, 535 (21 September 1944)).

225. *TBJG*. II/13, 536–42 (23 September 1944). The rest of his letter was an attack on Ribbentrop, his old adversary, as the man least likely to be capable of bringing about the skilful manoeuvre needed, and a disclaimer that he himself had any ambitions other than to serve Hitler, whose genius in successfully guiding this 'greatest war in our history' to victory and securing a happy future for the German people he did not doubt for a second.

226. *TBJG*, II/13, 556 (24 September 1944), 562 (25 September 1944); *TBJG* II/14, 83–4 (12 October 1944).

227. See Irving, *HW*, 689.

228. Below, 390; Guderian, 364.

229. Speer, 423.

230. Below, 390.

231. Below, 386–7.

232. Speer, 417–19. And see Kirwin, 'Waiting for Retaliation', for the expectations.

233. Speer, 377. Even this would have carried an explosive load of less than half that of a single combined British and American bombing sortie towards the end of the war (Speer, 572, n.9).

234. Speer, 378.

235. Below, 390.

236. Gruchmann, *Der Zweite Weltkrieg*, 284–5; *DZW*, vi.176.

237. Speer, 239–43; Mark Walker, *German National Socialism and the Quest for Nuclear Power 1939–1949*. Cambridge, 1989, 77–8 and ch.4, especially 136–7, and 155; Mark Walker, 'Legenden um die deutsche Atombombe', *VfZ*, 38 (1990), 45–74, here 53; Monika Renneberg and Mark Walker (eds.), *Science, Technology, and National Socialism*, Cambridge, 1994, 2; Kristie Macrakis, *Surviving the Swastika. Scientific Research in Nazi Germany*, New York/Oxford, 1993, 173–4, 244 n.41.

238. *LB* Darmstadt, 245.

239. Speer, 415–17.

240. Speer, 578 n.21.

241. Speer, 414.

242. Speer, 414–15.

243. Irving, *Doctor*, 166.

244. *TBJG*, II/14, 117 (29 October 1944).

245. Speer, 423.

246. Speer, 413.

247. Domarus, 2141 (in response to Papen's offer to take soundings via Spain).

248. Speer, 423.

249. *TBJG*, II/13, 208, 210 (3 August 1944). See also his negative comments about Rommel on 31 August in *LB* Darmstadt, 273–5.

250. Keitel, 332; Domarus, 2155; Speidel, *Invasion*, 178ff.; Hoffmann, *Widerstand*, 651–2; Fest, *Staatsstreich*, 313–14.

251. Domarus, 2157.

252. Gruchmann, *Der Zweite Weltkrieg*, 275–6 (and see Irving, *HW*, 722–3).

253. Skorzeny, 126, 130, 132, 134.

254. Skorzeny, 134–5.

255. Skorzeny, 133–5.

256. Skorzeny, 136–8.

257. See Gruchmann, *Der Zweite Weltkrieg*, 275–8; Irving, *HW*, 719–24; *DZW*, vi.531–2; Hilberg, *Destruction*, 552–4.

258. Hilberg, *Destruction*, 546.

259. Hilberg, *Destruction*, 552.

260. Hilberg, *Destruction*, 553 and n.1035.

261. Hilberg, *Vernichtung*, ii.925–6.

262. Skorzeny, 146.

263. IfZ, F29, diary of General Werner Kreipe, Luftwaffe Chief of Staff, Fol.21. See also Guderian, 370–71; Irving, *HW*, 705. Guderian's warnings that an offensive in the west would seriously weaken the defences in the east would all too soon prove prophetic. (See Weinberg III, 770.)

264. *TBJG*, II/13, 498, 500–501 (17 September 1944). See also Irving, *HW*, 706.

265. Warlimont, 478. For the varying views of Goebbels, Speer, and Stuckart from the Reich Ministry of the Interior, see *TBJG*, II/13, 491 (16 September 1944), 501 (17 September 1944). The failure of relations between the Party and the Wehrmacht in the first critical days of the Allied advance on Aachen prompted Hitler's directives of 19 and 20 September, ordering the continuation of the activities of Party and civil administration in operational areas, also within the Reich itself, and stipulating the duties of the Gauleiter/Reich Defence Commissars. (*Weisungen*, 337–41; Warlimont, 478–9.)

266. *TBJG*, II/13, 553 (24 September 1944).

267. Gruchmann, *Der Zweite Weltkrieg*, 306.

268. Gruchmann, *Der Zweite Weltkrieg*, 260; *TBJG*, II/14, 89 (23 October 1944).

269. Below, 391.

270. *Bormann Letters*, 139 (25 October 1944).

271. *Bormann Letters*, 138 (24 October 1944); Schroeder, 150.

272. *TBJG*, II/14, 93 (24 October 1944). See also *TBJG*, II/14, 88 (23 October 1944), Schroeder, 150; and Irving, *HW*, 725.

273. Below, 391; *TBJG*, II/14, 110 (26 October 1944); Irving, *HW*, 726, 893 note. Hitler was keen to make use of the atrocities for propaganda purposes. (See Jodl's note arising from the military briefing on 25 October 1944 in IfZ, Nbg.-Dok., 1787-PS, 496: 'Russian atrocities in the occupation of East Prussian territory must be spread by Wehrmacht propaganda. Photographs, questioning of witnesses, factual reports etc. for this. Where are the [Wehrmacht] propaganda companies?' ('*Russische Greueltaten bei der Besetzung ostpreußischen Gebiets müssen durch Wpr verbreitet werden. Dazu Aufnahmen. Zeugenvernehmung, Tatsachenberichte usw. Wo bleiben die Prop.-Kompanien?*')) Whatever the propaganda exploitation, there can be no doubt that horrific atrocities were indeed perpetrated by soldiers of the Red Army. In military terms, the short-lived capture of

Gumbinnen and Goldap (at high cost) provided Soviet forces with valuable experience to prepare their later full-scale assault on East Prussia. (Glantz and House, 228–9, 365–6 (n.34).)

274. *KTB OKW*, iv/1, 439, 442–3; Warlimont, 480; Below, 391–2.

275. Below, 390.

276. See *TBJG*, II/13, 582 (28 September 1944); Irving, *HW*, 708; Samuel W. Mitcham Jr, 'General-feldmarschall Robert Ritter von Greim', in Ueberschär, *Hitlers militärische Elite*, II, 72–7.

277. *TBJG*, II/14, 328 (2 December 1944).

278. In discussion with Goebbels, one of the Reich Marshal's main detractors, Hitler defended Göring and pointed to his earlier services in building up the Luftwaffe (*TBJG*, II/13, 213 (3 August 1944)). Sentimentality is, however, unlikely to have been the real reason for holding on to Göring. Issues of public image were more weighty.

279. Below, 394; Irving, *HW*, 708, 714, 728; Mitcham, 76.

280. *TBJG* II/13, 582 (28 September 1944); Irving, *HW* 728. See also Irving, *Göring*, 438–45.

281. *TBJG*, II/14, 330 (2 December 1944).

282. Speer, 578. n.21; Irving, *Göring*, 442, 444. Hitler cut Below short when the latter advocated the exclusive use of the Me262s as fighters (Below, 393). Despite his insistence on their production as bombers, the first fifty fighters began operations in mid-October (Irving, *Göring*, 442).

283. See his comments in his military briefing on 28 December 1944 (*LB Darmstadt*, 314); also his hints in this direction in the briefing on 12 December (*LB Darmstadt*, 294). He told Goebbels at the beginning of December that German arms were superior to those of the Allies in all areas except that of the Luftwaffe, and that there was no prospect of overcoming *this* inferiority in the near future (*TBJG*, II/14, 330 (2 December 1944)).

284. *TBJG*, II/13, 503–4 (17 September 1944), 510 (18 September 1944).

285. *TBJG*, II/14, 193 (10 November 1944), 210 (13 November 1944).

286. Domarus, 2162. The words '*Ausrottung*' ('eradication') and '*Vernichtung*' ('annihilation') were used on numerous occasions during the proclamation.

287. Domarus, 2163.

288. Domarus, 2165–6.

289. Domarus, 2165.

290. Domarus, 2167.

291. Below, 395. For further indications of despondency, see Irving, *HW*, 893, note to 726, and 894, note to 739.

292. *TBJG*, II/14, 210 (13 November 1944), 217 (16 November 1944). For Hitler's general ill-health, throat problems, nervous tension about the coming offensive, and irritability in November 1944, see Schenk, 256–62; Irving, *Doctor*, 187–97 (from Morell's diary).

293. Below, 395; Schenck, 320–23; Irving, *Doctor*, 194–7; Irving, *HW*, 734. The operation was carried out on 22 November. For a week, he could speak only in a whisper (Below, 396).

294. *TBJG* II/14, 316 (2 December 1944).

295. *TBJG*, II/14, 317 (2 December 1944).

296. *TBJG*, II/14, 318–19 (2 December 1944).

297. *TBJG*, II/14, 322 (2 December 1944).

298. *TBJG*, II/14, 323–4 (2 December 1944).

299. *TBJG*, II/14, 321 (2 December 1944). Linge recalled Hitler's short-lived revitalization at the beginning of the offensive (Linge, *Bis zum Untergang*, 250).

300. For Dietrich, see Charles Messenger, *Hitler's Gladiator. The Life and Times of Oberstgruppen-führer der Waffen-SS Sepp Dietrich*, London, 1988; James T. Weingartner, 'Josef "Sepp" Dietrich – Hitlers Volksgeneral', in Smelser and Syring, *Die Militärelite des Dritten Reiches*, 113–28; William T. Allbritton and Samuel W. Mitcham, Jr, 'SS-Oberstgruppenführer und Generaloberst der Waffen-SS Joseph (Sepp) Dietrich', in Ueberschär, *Hitlers militärische Elite*, ii.37–44. I am grateful to Dr Chris Clarke for letting me see a sketch of Dietrich's character and career, 'Josef

"Sepp" Dietrich: Landsknecht im Dienste Hitlers', forthcoming in Ronald Smelser and Enrico Syring (eds.), *Die SS: Elite unter dem Totenkopf. 30 Lebensläufe*, Paderborn etc., 2000, 119–33. Both Dietrich and Manteuffel are the subjects of a brief pen-picture by Franz Kurowski, 'Dietrich and Manteufel', in Barnett, *Hitler's Generals*, 411–37.

301. Warlimont, 480–83 (quotations, 482, 482–3; code-names of the operation, 480, 490); *KTB OKW*, iv/1, 439.

302. Warlimont, 485.

303. Below, 396; Domarus, 2171, n.377.

304. *LB Darmstadt*, 290–91 (12 December 1944).

305. *LB Darmstadt* 291.

306. *LB Darmstadt* 277 (31 August 1944).

307. *LB Darmstadt* 292.

308. Weinberg III, 766.

309. Stephen B. Patrick, 'The Ardennes Offensive: An Analysis of the Battle of the Bulge, December 1944', in Nofi, 206–24, here 217; *Oxford Companion*, 114.

310. Guderian, 380–81; Warlimont, 490–91; Gruchmann, *Der Zweite Weltkrieg*, 310–12; Weinberg III, 766–8; Heifermann, 232–4.

311. *LB Darmstadt*, 302–3; Gruchmann, *Der Zweite Weltkrieg*, 313.

312. *LB Darmstadt*, 295–6 (28 December 1944).

313. *LB Darmstadt*, 297.

314. *LB Darmstadt*, 315.

315. *LB Darmstadt*, 305.

316. Gruchmann, *Der Zweite Weltkrieg*, 313–14; *LB Darmstadt*, 316 n.428.

317. Gruchmann, *Der Zweite Weltkrieg*, 312; Weinberg III. 769.

318. Even reports from the Reich Propaganda Offices throughout Germany, invariably hesitant about conveying anything other than the rosiest-coloured views, mentioned disappointment about the speech (BA, R55/612, 'Echo zur Führerrede', Fols.20–21). Goebbels, in evident irritation, scored through the offending passages of the summary report drawn up for him. Newspaper reports of the speech struck Jewish readers in Dresden by the absence of any mention whatsoever of the western offensive (Klemperer, ii.637 (5 January 1945)).

319. Domarus, 2180.

320. Domarus, 2180, 2182.

321. Domarus, 2184.

322. IWM, 'Aus deutschen Urkunden', 277, report of SD-Leitabschnitt Stuttgart, 9 January 1945: '*Der Fuhrer habe also von allem Anfang an auf den Krieg hingearbeitet.*'

323. IWM, 'Aus deutschen Urkunden', 67, report of the SD-Leitabschnitt Stuttgart, 12 January 1945: '. . . *er hätte bewußt diesen Weltbrand entfacht, um als großer "Verwandler der Menschheit" proklamiert zu werden.*'

324. *KTB OKW*, iv/2, 1345; Warlimont, 494.

325. *KTB OKW*, iv/2, 1346–7; also 1352–4.

326. Warlimont, 494; *KTB OKW*, iv/2, 1353 (heading of the section dealing with military events between 14 and 28 January 1945).

327. Weinberg III, 769.

328. Below, 398.

CHAPTER 16: INTO THE ABYSS

1. Breloer, 359–60.

2. Breloer, 359 (entry for 22 January 1945).

3. Hitler was reported to have stated this explicitly, in addressing Colonel-General Carl Hilpert, Commander-in-Chief of Army Group Courland, on 18 April 1945: 'If the German people loses the war, it will have shown itself as not worthy of me.' ('*Wenn das deutsche Volk den Krieg verliert, hat es sich meiner als nicht würdig erwiesen.*') (*KTB OKW*, iv/1, 68 (introduction by Percy Ernst Schramm, citing a written account of Hitler's meeting with Hilpert by Dr W. Heinemeyer, then responsible for compiling the War Diary of Army Group Courland).)

4. Below, 340, with reference to the visit to the Berghof on 24 June 1943 of Baldur and Henriette von Schirach, which ended in their premature departure after angering Hitler.

5. Guderian, 382; and see Gruchmann, *Der Zweite Weltkrieg*, 414; Parker, *Struggle for Survival*, 217; *DZW*, vi.502–3. At the beginning of 1945, the German army had some 7.5 million men at its disposal. Of its 260 divisions, seventy-five were placed on the eastern front between the Carpathians and the Baltic, where the Soviet offensive was forecast. Apart from the seventy-six divisions in the west, a further twenty-four were deployed in Italy, seventeen were located in Norway and Denmark protecting U-boat bases and Swedish iron-ore supplies, ten were in Yugoslavia, twenty-eight defended oil and bauxite supplies from Hungary, and thirty were cut off in Memel and the Courland (Gruchmann, *Der Zweite Weltkrieg*, 414).

6. Guderian, 383.

7. Guderian, 385.

8. Guderian, 386–8. Speaking privately to Goebbels a few days after the Soviet breakthrough, Hitler did not blame it primarily on a failure of the military leadership. He pointed to the unavoidable thinness of the defences around the Baranov bridgehead because of the need to take troops to the west for the Ardennes offensive, and to Hungary to secure oil supplies (*TBJG*, II/15, 193 (23 January 1945)).

9. Guderian, 393–4, 417. Göring, who found the weakness of German defences at the Baranov bridgehead incomprehensible, given the prior intelligence that the offensive could be expected there, was critical, in discussion with Goebbels, about Hitler's decision to attempt a counter-attack on Hungary. Goebbels thought Hitler's approach was correct because of the urgent need of fuel (*TBJG*, II/15, 251 (28 January 1945)).

10. Guderian, 394–5, 412–13; Gerhard Boldt, *Hitler's Last Days. An Eye-Witness Account*, (1947), Sphere Books edn, London, 1973, 50–53; Michael Salewski, *Die deutsche Seekriegsleitung 1933–1945, Bd.II: 1942–1945*, Munich, 1975, 493, 496, 520–35; Weinberg III, 721, 782; and Gerhard L. Weinberg, 'German Plans for Victory, 1944–1945', in Gerhard L. Weinberg (ed.), *Germany, Hitler, and World War II*, Cambridge, 1995, 274–86, here 284–5.

11. *DZW*, vi.525.

12. Guderian, 396–8.

13. *DZW*, vi.529–36.

14. Guderian, 398.

15. *DZW*, vi.510–12; Guderian, 400–401; Gruchmann, *Der Zweite Weltkrieg*, 416.

16. Guderian, 400.

17. Goebbels underlined Himmler's difficulties, since his 'army group exists in practice only on paper'. He thought Hitler's optimism about holding the line in the east misplaced (*TBJG*, II/15, 231 (26 January 1945)).

18. Guderian, 415.

19. For the above, see Guderian, 403–4, 414–15, 422.

20. 'The Führer is very dissatisfied with him,' Goebbels noted on 12 March 1945 (*TBJG*, II/15, 480). See also Below, 406.

21. For a description of conditions within Breslau in February 1945, see Siegfried Knappe and Ted Brusaw, *Soldat. Reflections of a German Soldier, 1936–1949*, New York, 1992, 299–312.

22. Gruchmann, *Der Zweite Weltkrieg*, 416.

23. Guderian, 402, 405, 417.

24. Orlow, ii.478. Goebbels, contemptuous of Greiser's flight, after having misinformed Hitler about the imminence of the fall of Posen, recommended ruthless punishment (*TBJG*, II/15, 232 (26 January 1945). See also *TBJG*, II/15, 205, 210 (24 January 1945), 214, 219, 223 (25 January 1945), 241 (27 January 1945).) Hitler took no action. It transpired from what he told Goebbels, and from a conversation Goebbels had with Bormann, that Greiser had been instructed by Hitler to leave Posen – as it turned out quite prematurely. (Greiser claimed after the war that Hitler had ordered him to go to Frankfurt an der Oder as Reich Governor and that he left his post in the Warthegau on 20 January (NA, Washington, NND 871063: arrest report on Greiser, 17 May 1945; Special Interrogation Report, 1 June 1945)). The town remained for a further eight days in German hands, but the refugee columns fleeing from the Red Army received no support from the Party (*TBJG*, II/15, 190, 193 (23 January 1945), 261–2 (29 January 1945)). Greiser was to be put on trial after the war in Warsaw, sentenced to death, and publicly hanged in Poznan on 14 July 1946.

25. See BA, R55/622, Fols.181–2, a survey, dated 9 March 1945, of letters sent to Reich Propaganda Offices, which stated: 'The "Greiser case" is doing the rounds and is supplemented by reports from refugees about the failure of the NSDAP in the evacuation of entire Gaue.' ('*Der "Fall Greiser" macht überall die Runde und wird durch die Berichte der Flüchtlinge über das Versagen der NSDAP bei der Evakuierung ganzer Gaue ergänzt.*') One passage cited from an anonymous letter held to the old fable: 'If the Fuhrer knew how he is deceived everywhere, he would have swept through long ago.' ('*Wenn der Führer wußte, wie er überall hintergangen wird, hätte er längst dazwischengefegt.*')

26. Guderian, 412; Gruchmann, *Der Zweite Weltkrieg*, 417–18. See Speer's description of the heated arguments between Hitler and Guderian over evacuating the troops from Courland (Speer, 428).

27. Parker, *Struggle for Survival*, 218; Weinberg III, 801; Gruchmann, *Der Zweite Weltkrieg*, 420.

28. The following passages are based on Gruchmann, *Der Zweite Weltkrieg*, 420–25; Weinberg III, 811–13; Parker, *Struggle for Survival*, 219–20; DZW, vi. 537–58.

29. Weinberg III, 811.

30. Gruchmann, *Der Zweite Weltkrieg*, 423–4. Hitler told Kesselring that he was confident of holding the eastern front on which all depended. The urgent demand was to hold the western front until reinforcements from the east, new fighters and other new weapons could be employed in great numbers, and until Dönitz could make the new U-boats tell. 'So it was,' he concluded, 'once again a battle for time!' (Albert Kesselring, *The Memoirs of Field-Marshal Kesselring*, (1953), Greenhill Books edn, London, 1997, 237–9 (quotation, 239)). On Rundstedt's dismissal, see Blumentritt, 277–9; Messenger, 228–9.

31. John Toland, *The Last 100 Days*, London, 1966, 256; *LB* Darmstadt, 339 n.451.

32. Gruchmann, *Der Zweite Weltkrieg*, 424.

33. DZW, vi.583–5; *Oxford Companion*, 311–12.

34. DZW, vi.586; Gruchmann, *Der Zweite Weltkrieg*, 280, 414. Postwar Allied estimates reckoned that a third of the German population suffered directly from the bombing, around 14 million people losing property, up to 20 million being deprived of electricity, gas, or water at some time, 5 million being forced to evacuate. A quarter of homes had been damaged. Some 305,000 people had been killed. (*United States Strategic Bombing Survey*, vol.4, New York/London, 1976, 7–10.)

35. *Die Vertreibung der deutschen Bevölkerung aus den Gebieten östlich der Oder-Neiße*, repr. Munich, 1984, Bd.1, 28.

36. Hans Graf von Lehndorff, *Ostpreußisches Tagebuch. Aufzeichnungen eines Arztes aus den Jahren 1945–1947*, Munich (1967), 15th edn, 1985, 18, 22.

37. Lehndorff, 18.

38. Lehndorff, 24–5.

39. Johannes Steinhoff, Peter Pechel and Dennis Showalter, *Voices from the Third Reich: an Oral History*, (1989), New York, 1994, 420.

40. Ursula von Kardorff, *Berliner Aufzeichnungen 1942–1945*, Munich (1976), 2nd edn, 1982, 228. See also the description of a woman's flight from Breslau in January 1945, accompanied by her two

small children and elderly parents, in Margarete Dörr, 'Wer die Zeit nicht miterlebt hat . . .'. Frauenerfahrungen im Zweiten Weltkrieg und in den Jahren danach, 3 vols., Frankfurt/New York, 1998, ii.455–60.

41. Andreas-Friedrich, 126.

42. See the initial scepticism about the stories in Kardorff, 229. For anxiety in Dresden, see Klemperer, ii.645–6.

43. GStA, Munich, MA 106696, report of the Regierungspräsident of Niederbayern and Oberpfalz, 10 March 1945: 'Die aus den Ostgauen hier eintreffenden Flüchtlinge bringen zum großen Teil recht erschütternde Nachrichten von dem Elend der flüchtenden Bevölkerung, die zum Teil panikartig ins Innere des Reiches vor den Bolschewisten geflüchtet ist.' Goebbels wrote in his diary of 'indescribable misery' among the refugee treks from the east, adding two days later that reports on Bolshevik atrocities could only be released for publication abroad since they would give rise to panic among the refugees if published within Germany (TBJG, II/15, 190 (23 January 1945), 216 (25 January 1945)).

44. See, among many examples, Die Vertreibung, Bd.2, 159–64, 224–34; Kathe von Normann, Tagebuch aus Pommern 1945/46, Munich (1962), 5th edn, 1984, 12ff. Dörr, ii.406–24.

45. Barbara Johr, 'Die Ereignisse in Zahlen', in Helke Sander and Barbara Johr (eds.), Befreier und Befreite. Krieg, Vergewaltigungen, Kinder, Munich, 1992, 46–72, here 47–8, 58–9. I am grateful to Detlef Siebert for referring me to this essay.

46. Cit. Steinert, 547.

47. Steinert, 547–50.

48. Steinert, 550–51; text of Thierack's decree of 15 February 1945 and Hitler's order of 9 March 1945 in Rolf-Dieter Müller and Gerd R. Ueberschär, Kriegsende 1945. Die Zerstörung des Deutschen Reiches, Frankfurt am Main, 1994, 161–4.

49. See the example in Rees, The Nazis, 231–4.

50. Kardorff, 231.

51. Cit. Steinert, 559.

52. GStA, Munich, MA 106695, report of the Regierungspräsident of Schwaben, 7 February 1945: 'Mit Schrecken verfolgt die Bevölkerung die Ereignisse im Osten des Reiches, wo die Sturmflut der Sowjets die Grenzen der Heimat umbrandet . . .'

53. Dörr, 'Wer die Zeit nicht miterlebt hat . . .'. Frauenerfahrungen, 1.156.

54. GStA, Munich, MA 106696, report of the Regierungspräsident of Oberfranken and Mittelfranken, 8 February 1945.

55. Based on a report compiled ten years after the events by the Geschäftsführer des Interministeriellen Luftkriegsauschusses der Reichsregierung in Berlin 1943–5, Theodor Ellgering, cit. in Müller and Ueberschär, Kriegsende 1945, 158–61. See also the description of the bombing in Klemperer, ii.661–72.

56. Friedmann Behr, Mein Jahr 1945, East Berlin, 1988, 15: 'Wir sahen die ersten Toten des Krieges und erschraken so sehr, daß uns aller Mut verließ.'

57. Cit. Maschmann, 169: 'Ja, aber das ist nicht wichtig. Deutschland muß siegen.'

58. See Klemperer, ii.676, for comments following the raid on Dresden.

59. BA, R55/622, Fol.181, 'Briefübersicht Nr.10', 9 March 1945: 'Das Vertrauen in die Führung schwindet immer mehr, weil der angekündigte Gegenschlag zur Befreiung unserer besetzten Ostprovinzen ausblieb und sich die manigfachen Versprechungen auf eine bevorstehende Wende als unerfüllbar erwiesen haben. . . . Besonders hart ist die Kritik an der oberen Führerschicht der Partei und der militärischen Führung.'

60. BA, R55/601. Fol.295–6, Tätigkeitsbericht, 21 March 1945: 'Diejenigen, die noch nach wie vor unbeirrbar und unerschütterlich auf die Worte des Führers vertrauten, daß noch in diesem Jahre die geschichtliche Wende zu unserem Gunsten eintrete, hätten gegenüber den Zweiflern und Miesmachern einen sehr schweren Stand. Bei allem unerschütterlichen Vertrauen in den Führer

scheue man sich jedoch nicht zu äußern, daß der Führer bestimmt nicht durch die militärischen Stellen über die wirkliche Lage unterrichtet sein könne, sonst wäre es nicht zu der jetzigen schweren Krise gekommen.' Goebbels referred even in late January to the 'deeply depressing' reports from the regional Propaganda Offices, the loss of hope of any new weapons turning the tide, and severe criticism of the leadership for being unprepared to combat the Soviet offensive (*TBJG*, II/15, 230 (26 January 1945)).

61. StA, Munich, report of the Landrat of Berchtesgaden, 4 April 1945: '*Als der Führer der Wehrmachtseinheit am Schluß seiner zu der Feier gehaltenen Rede ein "Sieg-Heil" auf den Führer ausbrachte, wurde es weder von der angetretenen Wehrmacht, dem Volkssturm noch von der als Zuschauer erschienenen Zivilbevölkerung erwidert. Dieses Schweigen der Masse wirkte geradezu drückend und spiegelt wohl am besten die tatsächliche Einstellung des Volkes.*' The comment was passed on by the Regierungspräsident of Oberbayern in his report of 7 April 1945: GStA, Munich, MA 106695.

62. See Klemperer, ii.646, 658, 661, 675, 677; and also Monika Richarz (ed.), *Jüdisches Leben in Deutschland. Bd.3. Selbstzeugnisse zur Sozialgeschichte 1918–1945*, Stuttgart, 1982, 471.

63. Klemperer, ii.658 (13 February 1945).

64. Klemperer, ii.661 (13 February 1945).

65. Martin Broszat, 'Nationalsozialistische Konzentrationslager 1933–1945', in Buchheim *et al.* (eds.), *Anatomie des SS-Staates*, ii.159–60; Daniel Blatman, 'Die Todesmärsche', in Ulrich Herbert, Karin Orth, and Christoph Dieckmann (eds.), *Die nationalsozialistischen Konzentrationslager. Entwicklung und Struktur*, 2 vols., Göttingen, 1998, ii.1063–92, here 1066; and, especially, for the concentration camps in the last year of Nazi rule, Karin Orth, *Das System der nationalsozialistischen Konzentrationslager. Eine politische Organisationsgeschichte*, Hamburg, 1999, 222ff. Around half a million of the prisoners were men, some 200,000 women; they were guarded by about 40,000 SS men.

66. See a first-hand account of the horror in Richarz, 443–53 (account of Paul Heller). See also Blatman, especially 1085–7; Goldhagen, 330; Orth, 278ff., 285–6; Schmuel Krakowski, 'The Death Marches in the Period of the Evacuation of the Camps', and Yehuda Bauer, 'The Death-Marches, January–May 1945', both in Michael Marrus (ed.), *The Nazi Holocaust: Historical Articles on the Destruction of European Jews*, Westport, 1989, vol.9, 476–90 (here, especially, 480–83), and 491–511; and 'Death Marches', in *Encyclopaedia of the Holocaust*, ed. Israel Gutmann, New York, 1990, 348–54.

67. Goldhagen, 365, 587 n.23; Isabell Sprenger, 'Das KZ Groß-Rosen in der letzten Kriegsphase', in Herbert *et al.*, *Die Konzentrationslager*, ii.1113–27, here 1120–21.

68. Czech, *Kalendarium* 898–900, 933, 940–41, 948–9, 952–3, 957–8; Pressac, *Les Crématoires d'Auschwitz*, 93.

69. Cit. Czech, 967.

70. Andrej Strzelecki, 'Der Todesmarsch der Häftlinge aus dem KL Auschwitz', in Herbert *et al.*, *Konzentrationslager*, ii.1093–1112, here 1097–8; Orth, 276–9.

71. Cit. in Blatman, 1078–9.

72. Czech, 982.

73. See, for this camp, Sprenger, especially 1118 ff.; and also Orth, 279–81.

74. Based on Czech, 966–95; Herbert *et al.*, *Konzentrationslager*, ii.1063–1138 (contributions by Blatman, Strzelecki, Sprenger, and Kolb); Eberhard Kolb, 'Bergen-Belsen', in Martin Broszat (ed.), *Studien zur Geschichte der Konzentrationslager*, Stuttgart, 1970, 130–53, here 147ff.; and Eberhard Kolb, *Vom 'Aufenthaltslager' zum Konzentrationslager 1943 bis 1945*, Göttingen, 1985, 39ff. See also Hilberg, *Destruction*, 631–3; Goldhagen, ch.13; Martin Gilbert, *The Holocaust. The Jewish Tragedy*, London, 1987, chs.40–41; Martin Gilbert, *Atlas of the Holocaust*, London, 1982, 215ff.

75. Hilberg, 632.

76. IfZ, ED 100, Irving-Sammlung, Traudl Junge Memoirs, 123; Pierre Galante and Eugen Silianoff,

Last Witnesses in the Bunker, London, 1989, 137 (testimony of Traudl Junge); Below, 400; Domarus, 2189.

77. Hitler blamed the eastern offensive for the failure of his own offensive in the west (*TBJG*, II/15, 197 (23 January 1945), 217 (25 January 1945)).

78. Guderian, 392–3.

79. Boldt, 36, for description of Reich Chancellery; IfZ, ZS 2235, Traudl Junge, Fol.2 (Interview with David Irving, 29 June 1968), comments that the blinds were down on the train, and the route for the cars from the station to the Reich Chancellery passed through streets which had been relatively little destroyed. Awareness that Hitler was back in the capital might have given citizens further cause for anxiety about the likelihood of intensified air-raids, as soon as the Allies knew of his presence there.

80. Boldt, 36–7.

81. Guderian, 409.

82. Guderian, 401–2.

83. Guderian, 404–5.

84. Speer, 431.

85. Hansjakob Stehle, 'Deutsche Friedensfühler bei den Westmächten im Februar/März 1945', *VfZ*, 30 (1982), 538–55; Reimer Hansen, 'Ribbentrops Friedensfühler im Frühjahr 1945', *Geschichte in Wissenschaft und Unterricht*, 18 (1967), 716–30; Ingeborg Fleischhauer, *Die Chance des Sonderfriedens. Deutsch-sowjetische Geheimgespräche 1941–1945*, Berlin, 1986, 267–75; Werner von Schmieden, 'Notiz betreffend den deutschen Friedensfühler in der Schweiz Anfang 1945', IfZ, ZS 604 (30 June 1947); Weinberg III, 783–4.

86. Schmidt, 587. According to Goebbels, in mid-January, Ribbentrop wanted to put out feelers to the British, but Hitler prohibited him from doing so (*TBJG*, II/15, 199 (23 January 1945)). Hitler did not give Ribbentrop 'official authorization' for his soundings (*IMG*, x.218; Hansen, 'Ribbentrops Friedensfühler', 718–19).

87. Schmidt, 587. According to Schmidt, Ribbentrop's own interest diminished immediately when he learnt that his removal from office was also a precondition.

88. *The Ribbentrop Memoirs*, 170, 173. Speer pointed to Hitler's vague hints at peace-feelers in early 1945. He had the impression, however, that Hitler 'was far more concerned to create an atmosphere of the utmost irreconcilability, leaving no way open' (Speer, 433). The secret dealings which Karl Wolff, head of the police in northern Italy and formerly the chief of Himmler's personal staff, opened up in Zürich in February 1945 with Allen W. Dulles, head of the United States' Office of Strategic Services (OSS) in Europe, were aimed primarily at saving Wolff's skin (ultimately, in this, proving successful) but, beyond that, at offering to deliver surrender of German forces in Italy – which did eventually capitulate prematurely, on 2 May 1945 – as part of a ploy to split the western Allies from the Soviet Union. The feelers were almost certainly put out with Himmler's knowledge, looking to an 'arrangement' which would bypass Hitler's implacable hostility to a negotiated end to the war by dispensing with the Führer in an attempt to rescue what was possible of the SS's power by linking forces with the West in the fight against Bolshevism. (See Padfield, *Himmler*, 572–7.)

89. *TBJG*, II/15, 251–2 (28 January 1945).

90. *TBJG*, II/15, 232 (26 January 1945).

91. *TBJG*, II/15, 255 (28 January 1945).

92. *LB* Stuttgart, 860–61 (27 January 1945). See *TBJG*, II/15, 259 (29 January 1945) for Goebbels's summary of the tenor of reports from British newspapers, asking whether British war aims had been upturned by the mounting Soviet threat.

93. *TBJG*, II/15, 253 (28 January 1945).

94. *TBJG*, II/15, 254–5 (28 January 1945); also *TBJG*, II/15, 220 (25 January 1945).

95. *TBJG*, II/15, 264–5 (29 January 1945). As so often, Goebbels had a few days earlier compared Hitler with Frederick the Great during the Seven Years War (*TBJG*, II/15, 221 (25 January 1945)).

96. *TBJG*, II/15, 273 (30 January 1945).

97. *TBJG*, II/15, 275 (30 January 1945).

98. *TBJG*, II/15, 256 (28 January 1945).

99. Text of speech in Domarus, 2195–8; quotations, 2195, 2197. According to Traudl Junge, Hitler railed in private about the appalling stories of Soviet barbarity coming from the eastern regions, repeatedly declaring: 'It cannot and must not be that these cultureless beasts inundate Europe. I'm the last bulwark against this danger.' ('*Es kann und darf nicht sein, dass diese kulturlosen Bestien Europa überschwemmen. Ich bin das letzte Bollwerk gegen diese Gefahr.*') (IfZ, ED 100, Irving-Sammlung, Traudl Junge Memoirs, 125; Galante, 139 (with a loose translation).) Bormann wrote of the 'Russian atrocities' in a letter to his wife of 30 January, telling her that 'the Bolsheviks are ravaging everything', and 'regard ordinary rape as just a joke, and mass shootings – particularly in the rural districts – as an everyday occurrence' (*Bormann Letters*, 164).

100. Joachim Günther, *Das letzte Jahr. Mein Tagebuch 1944/45*, Hamburg, 1948, 453–4.

101. *TBJG*, II/15, 285 (31 January 1945); 301–2 (2 February 1945), where Goebbels admitted that 'in intellectual circles' there was disappointment over the absence of any assessment of the likely development in the east.

102. StA Neuburg an der Donau, vorl. Slg. Schum. Anh.3, SD-Außenstelle Friedberg, 3 February 1945: '*Die Propaganda hat es nicht fertiggebracht, den Glauben an eine positive Wendung zu stärken. Selbst die Führerrede zum 30.Januar vermochte nicht die lauten Zweifel zu beseitigen.*'

103. Speer, 431–2. Guderian was mistaken in believing that Hitler had locked it away in his safe unread (Guderian, 407).

104. Speer, 434.

105. According to Bormann (*Bormann Letters*, 168), the New Reich Chancellery was not usable for the time being. However, Goebbels had discussions with Hitler in the large study there on 12 February and described the New Reich Chancellery as 'still completely undestroyed' (*TBJG*, II/15, 371 (13 February 1945)).

106. See a description of the damage in *Bormann Letters*, 168; also Schroeder, 197, 199; *TBJG*, II/15, 306 (5 February 1945), 320 (6 February 1945), 327 (7 February 1945); IfZ, ED 100, Irving-Sammlung, Traudl Junge Memoirs, 123; Galante, 138 (Junge); Boldt, 35; Anton Joachimsthaler, *Hitlers Ende. Legenden und Dokumente*, Augsburg, 1999, 58–60.

107. See Ada Petrova and Peter Watson, *The Death of Hitler: the Final Words from Russia's Secret Archives*, London, 1995, 84; Boldt, 73; Joachimsthaler, 47ff.

108. Schroeder, 197, 378 n.364; IfZ, ED 100, Irving-Sammlung, Traudl Junge Memoirs, 123; Galante, 137 (Junge); Joachimsthaler, 46–7, 65ff.

109. Joachimsthaler, 48, 75–7.

110. *TBJG*, II/15, 200 (23 January 1945).

111. Descriptions were provided by Hitler's secretaries Christa Schroeder, Traudl Junge, and Johanna Wolf. See Schroeder, 197–8; IfZ, ED 100, Irving-Sammlung, Traudl Junge Memoirs, 124–5; Galante (Junge), 138; Joachimsthaler, 73–81.

112. Guderian, 416.

113. Schroeder, 197, and 59–60, 318 n.75 for descriptions of the Old Reich Chancellery (Radziwill Palais).

114. Below, 405; Boldt, 37–8 (giving the impression that the meetings were still held in the undamaged wing of the Old Reich Chancellery).

115. Below, 403–4.

116. Schroeder, 197; IfZ, ED 100, Irving-Sammlung, Traudl Junge Memoirs, 124; Galante, 138 (Junge).

117. *TBJG*, II/15, 320 (6 February 1945); see also 371 (13 February 1945).

118. IfZ, ED 100, Irving-Sammlung, Traudl Junge Memoirs, 123; Galante, 138 (Junge); Irving, *Doctor*, 216–17.

119. See the appointments diary kept by Heinz Linge, and preserved for the period 14 October 1944–28 February 1945, IfZ, F19/14, Fols.450–77 (for February 1945). The following description of Hitler's daily routine is based on this appointments diary and Schroeder, 198–9.

120. For his medications, see Redlich, 243, 358–62; Irving, *Doctor*, 208ff.; Maser, 401–6; Heston, 82–9; Schenck, 446–50. Hitler, looking drained, told Goebbels in January that his working day was around 16–18 hours, and ran through the night (*TBJG*, II/15, 262 (29 January 1945)). Two months later, he informed Goebbels that he had had two hours sleep during the previous twenty-four hours (*TBJG*, II/15, 644 (31 March 1945)).

121. These were similar themes to the 'table talk' monologues of the earlier war years, noted down by Heim, Picker, and Koeppen. In 1951, a further series of monologues, allegedly by Hitler, dictated to Bormann, came to light (seventeen from February 1945, a last one on 2 April). The tone of the monologues is unmistakably that of Hitler. The themes are familiar, as are the rambling style and the discursive dips into history. There is talk, among other topics: of Churchill's responsibility (influenced by Jews) for the war; of Britain's rejection of German peace-offers which would have enabled the destruction of Bolshevism and saved the British Empire; of an unnatural coalition aiming to destroy Germany, a will to exterminate which gave the German people no other choice but to continue the struggle; of the example of Frederick the Great; of the need for eastward expansion, not the quest for colonies; of exposing to the world 'the Jewish peril' and of his warning to Jews on the eve of the war; of the timing and necessity of the war against the Soviet Union; of the difficulties caused for Germany by Italy's weakness and blunders; of regrets that Japan did not enter the war against Russia in 1941, and the inevitability that the United States would enter the war against Germany; of the missed chance of going to war in 1938, which would have given Germany an advantage; of time always being against Germany; of being compelled to wage war as Europe's last hope; and of the need to uphold the racial laws, and claim on gratitude for having eliminated Jews from Germany and central Europe. The monologues have a self-justificatory ring to them. They are intended for posterity, establishing a place in history. They have a reflective readiness – unusual, if not unique, for Hitler – to contemplate responsibility for errors, for example, in policy towards Italy and Spain.

The monologues were not, as those from 1941–4 were, the product of musings during meals attended by others in his entourage, or during the 'tea hours' with his secretaries. Neither a secretary nor anyone else mentioned them at the time, or apparently knew they were being compiled. Gerda Christian (formerly Daranowski), writing to Christa Schroeder long after the war, did not regard them as authentic, though she accepted that they could be a compilation of Hitler's thoughts in the last months. She ruled out a possibility of Hitler summoning Bormann to dictate to him, pointing out from her own recollection how he hated verbatim accounts on paper of what he had said casually (Schroeder, 257). The main problem with the authenticity of the text is that no reliable and certifiable German version exists. It is impossible, therefore, to be certain. A great deal has to be taken on trust; and even then no safe mechanism for checking is available.

The original document containing the monologues was said to have been entrusted on 17 April 1945 by Martin Bormann to Walther Funk, Reich Minister for Economics, to remove from Berlin for safe keeping in a bank vault in Bad Gastein. While serving his term of imprisonment in Spandau after the Nuremberg Trials, fearing further incrimination should the document be discovered, Funk, it was claimed, commissioned a friend, Hans Rechenberg, with the destruction of the document. Rechenberg, the account continues, kept his promise in a literal sense; but he made a photocopy, and in 1951 handed it to François Genoud, a Swiss lawyer who had meanwhile acquired control over copyright matters pertaining to Bormann, Goebbels, and other Nazi leaders. Funk, after release from Spandau, authorized Genoud to seek out Hugh Trevor-Roper with a view to arranging publication outside Germany of the document. After the meeting with Trevor-Roper, according to Genoud, the photocopy was handed back to Funk. It thereafter went missing. Remarkably, it seems, no copy of the copy had been made before returning it. Genoud had made a French translation (*La testament politique de Hitler. Notes recueillies par Martin Bormann*, Paris, 1959), and in 1958 had had a translation back into German made from the French version. According to Genoud, this was at Funk's wish, since he wished to compare the texts. Funk then allegedly corrected the re-translation in accordance with the still existing copy of the original, 'so that', in Genoud's words, 'a practically authentic text, coming from this time, exists'. An English edition, with an introduction by Trevor-Roper, was published in 1961 (François Genoud (ed.), *The Testament of Adolf Hitler. The Hitler-Bormann Documents. February–April 1945, with an Introduction by H. R. Trevor-Roper*, London, 1961). This English version contains a very loose and untrustworthy translation of the German text – itself not guaranteed to be identical with any long-lost original or the lost copy of that original – which was eventually published only in 1981 (*Hitlers politisches Testament. Die Bormann Diktate von Februar und April 1945, mit einem Essay von Hugh R. Trevor-Roper und einem Nachwort von André François-Poncet*, Hamburg, 1981). Further examination of the text in the meantime – though this was not mentioned by the German publishers – by Professor Eduard Baumgarten had established that the translation back into German from the French (carried out by a Dutchman) contained between the lines a second German text, written in the hand of François Genoud. The available German text is, therefore, at best a construct; neither the original nor the copy of that original exists. Baumgarten tended, since the content was consonant with Hitler's thinking and expression, to accept the authenticity of the text. There is, however, no proof and, therefore, no reliable German text whose authenticity can be placed beyond question. (Institut für Zeitgeschichte (ed.), *Wissenschaftsfreiheit und ihre rechtlichen Schranken. Ein Kolloquium*, Munich/Vienna, 1978, 45–51 (comments of François Genoud, Eduard Baumgarten, and Martin Broszat).)

122. Hermann Giesler, *Ein anderer Hitler. Erlebnisse, Gespräche, Reflexionen*, Leoni, 1977, 478–80. For the date of the unveiling of the model, Irving, *HW*, 478–80, 483.

123. See Kubizek, especially 97–110. Hitler was still dreaming when he told Goebbels, following his viewing of the Linz model, that modern technology would allow for a swift rebuilding of German cities after the war, and that housing capacity would be restored within five years (*TBJG*, II/15, 379 (13 February 1945)).

124. *TBJG*, II/15, 321 (6 February 1945). He repeated this to Goebbels a few days later, though the Propaganda Minister noted that it could not be publicized since, otherwise, every future air-raid on Berlin would be attributed to the decision (*TBJG*, II/15, 370 (12 February 1945)).

125. *TBJG*, II/15, 320 (6 February 1945), 337 (8 February 1945), 365 (12 February 1945).

126. *TBJG*, II/15, 323 (6 February 1945).

127. *TBJG*, II/15, 368 (12 February 1945).

128. See Weinberg III, 802–9.

129. *TGJG*, II/15, 381–2 (13 February 1945).

130. Below, 402.

131. Speer, 433.

132. Giesler, 482.

133. Semmler, 183; Reuth, *Goebbels*, 581–2; Irving, *Goebbels*, 502.

134. *LB* Stuttgart, 902–3 (2 March 1945).

135. Guderian, 427 (trans. slightly amended); *LB* Stuttgart, 905 n.2. And see *TBJG*, II/15, 617, 620 (28 March 1945).

136. Jodl's summary for Hitler of advantages and disadvantages of leaving the Geneva Convention argued that the way would then be clear for Allied usage of gas and chemical warfare at a time when they enjoyed obvious air-superiority; also that there were more German prisoners in Allied hands than Allied prisoners-of-war in Germany, so that massive retaliation would also be to Germany's disadvantage. (*IMG*, xxxv.181–6, Doc.606-D. See also *IMG*, ix.434, x.342, xiii.517–18, xvi.542, xviii.397–8, and xxxiiii.641–4, Doc.158-C.)

137. Descriptions by Dr Giesing, in mid-February, and Percy Ernst Schramm a month later: Maser,

394–5, cit. Giesing report of 12 June 1945, 175ff.; Percy Ernst Schramm, *Hitler als militärischer Führer. Erkenntnisse und Erfahrungen aus dem Kriegstagebuch des Oberkommandos der Wehrmacht*, Frankfurt am Main, 1962, 134ff.; *KTB OKW*, iv/2, 1701–2. See also Irving, *HW*, 772–3; Irving, *Doctor*, 211.

138. Rudolf Jordan, *Erlebt und erlitten. Weg eines Gauleiters von München bis Moskau*, Leoni am Starnberger See, 1971, 253.

139. Below, 402. Goebbels had remarked in his diary, early in February, that the Gauleiter had not been taking central directions from Berlin seriously and were running things in their own way (*TBJG*, II/15, 311 (5 February 1945)).

140. Jordan, 251–8; Karl Wahl, '. . . *es ist das deutsche Herz'. Erlebnisse und Erkenntnisse eines ehemaligen Gauleiters*, Augsburg, 1954, 384–92 (where the meeting is wrongly dated to 25 February); Below, 402; Martin Moll, 'Die Tagungen der Reichs- und Gauleiter der NSDAP: Ein verkanntes Instrument der Koordinierung im "Amterchaos" des Dritten Reiches?', typescript, 60–61 (with best thanks to Dr Moll for the opportunity to see this valuable, as yet unpublished, paper); Irving, *HW*, 772–3; Toland, *Adolf Hitler*, 855 (based on oral testimony in 1971 of three Gauleiter present). The formal communiqué of the meeting confined itself to stating that Hitler had imparted to the Gauleiter 'the guidelines for the victorious continuation of the struggle, for the comprehensive organization of all forces of resistance, and for the ruthless deployment of the Party in the fateful struggle of the German people' (Domarus, 2207). In individual cases, Hitler was nevertheless even now able to rouse new hope. According to Christa Schroeder, Albert Forster, Gauleiter of Danzig-West Prussia, came to Berlin in March 1945 determined to tell Hitler the unvarnished truth about the desolate situation in Danzig. He came out of his audience reinvigorated, saying 'he has told me he will save Danzig, and about that there can be no more doubt' (Schroeder, 74).

141. Domarus, 2203–6. Domarus (2202, n.71, 2088) mistakenly thought the occasion had been dropped altogether in 1944. In fact, Hitler had given a speech on that occasion (24 February 1944), which Goebbels had described as 'extraordinarily fresh' (*TBJG*, II/11, 347 (25 February 1944)). In 1942, the Gauleiter of Munich and Upper Bavaria, Adolf Wagner, had read out a proclamation by Hitler (*TBJG*, II/3, 371 (25 February 1942)); in 1943, Hermann Esser read out the proclamation (*TBJG*, II/7, 412 (25 February 1943)).

142. StA Munich, LRA 29656, report of the SD-Außenstelle Berchtesgaden, 7 February 1945: '. . . *während bei der überwiegenden Zahl der Volksgenossen der Inhalt der Proklamation vorbeirauschte wie der Wind in leerem Geäst'*. Other reports underlined the impression that Hitler's address had been unable to lift the mood and found no echo among the mass of the population (GStA, Munich, MA 106695, reports of the Regierungspräsident of Oberbayern, 7 March 1945, 7 April 1945). Some reports from mid-February noted that hope of a miracle was now confined to belief in Hitler himself (Volker Berghahn, 'Meinungsforschung im "Dritten Reich": Die Mundpropaganda-Aktion der Wehrmacht im letzten Kriegshalbjahr', *Militärgeschichtliche Mitteilungen*, 1 (1967), 83–119, here 105.

143. *TBJG*, II/15, 420 (5 March 1945); Irving, *Doctor*, 212. Hitler, it seems, eventually did allow the pictures to appear in the press and newsreel, though, accommodating the delay, the impression was given that the visit had taken place on 'Heroes' Memorial Day', 11 March 1945. Domarus, 2211 and Hauner, *Hitler*, 200, give this as the date of Hitler's last visit to the front, while Irving, *HW*, 776, has 15 March 1945 (possibly based on Below, 405, who has 15 February, though presumably in error for 15 March). Goebbels was with Hitler for several hours on the evening of 11 March, though there was no mention of a second visit to the Oder front that day. He referred to the new edition of the newsreel, shown that evening, containing scenes of Hitler's visit to the front, though this presumably refers to the Wriezen visit, not any subsequent one (*TBJG*, II/15, 479, 487). Among captured soldiers on the western front, trust in Hitler had fallen by March 1945 to 31 per cent, half of what it had been in January (Gurfein and Janowitz, 81).

144. *TBJG*, II/15, 542 (19 March 1945).

145. *TBJG*, II/15, 420–21, 423 (5 March 1945), 450 (8 March 1945). Goebbels first noted that Himmler had an infection; then that he had suffered an angina attack. Guderian was told that the Reichsführer had been laid low with influenza, but found him 'in apparently robust health' on a visit to the Hohenlychen sanatorium (Guderian, 421). See also Felix Kersten, *The Kersten Memoirs 1940–1945*, London, 1956, 276–7; Padfield, *Himmler*, 567.

146. *TBJG*, II/15, 421–2 (5 March 1945). Sepp Dietrich, in whose leadership in Hungary Hitler was pinning such hopes, had been highly critical of Hitler's repeated interventions, down to company level, in military matters, leaving his commanders no room for manoeuvre (*TBJG*, II/15, 404 (3 March 1945)).

147. *TBJG*, II/15, 421–4 (5 March 1945), quotations 422, 424, 486 (12 March 1945).

148. *TBJG*, II/15, 426–7 (5 March 1945).

149. *TBJG*, II/15, 425–6 (5 March 1945).

150. H. R. Trevor-Roper, *The Last Days of Hitler*, (1947), Pan Books edn, London, 1973, 140.

151. *TBJG*, II/15, 383–4 (28 February 1935), 419 (5 March 1945), quotation 479 (12 March 1945). See also 557 (21 March 1945), 570 (22 March 1945).

152. Domarus, 2212.

153. Named after the Secretary of the US Treasury, Henry Morgenthau Jr, the plan envisaged dividing Germany into two and 'pastoralizing' the country. It was initially adopted both by Roosevelt and Churchill, and, though effectively discarded in the light of strong opposition from their advisers, was finally put to rest only in the post-war settlement at Potsdam in July-August 1945 (Churchill, vi.138–9; Weinberg III, 796–7; *Oxford Companion*, 758–9).

154. See Herbst, *Der Totale Krieg*, 345–7 (and Pt.V in general), for post-war planning within German industry in the last months of the regime. See also Neil Gregor, *Daimler-Benz in the Third Reich*, New Haven/London, 1998, 100–108; and Dietrich Eichholtz and Wolfgang Schumann, *Anatomie des Krieges*, East Berlin, 1969, 484–6.

155. Speer, 440–42, 581 n.5; Guderian, 422–3.

156. Speer, 443. Speer, 448, refers to his memorandum of 18 March. He suggests elsewhere, however, that he himself handed the memorandum to Hitler, and after midnight on 19 March (Speer, 445). Below, 404, writes of Speer passing the memorandum to him.

157. *IMG*, xli.420–25 (quotation, 424–5), Beweisstück Speer, Doc.23; *IMG*, xvi.546–7 (Speer testimony); and see also Speer, 443, 582 n.6; Guderian, 423; Below, 404–5.

158. Speer, 444–5.

159. Speer, 446 and 583 n.8. Domarus, 2214 and n.106 points out that Speer's recollection probably did not match Hitler's comment exactly. According to Speer, Hitler had stated that 'the future belongs exclusively to the stronger people of the east' – a phrase he is otherwise not known to have used, and which stood in contradiction to his belief in the primitivity of the Soviet population.

160. See Irving, *HW*, 784.

161. *IMG*, xli.430–31, Doc. Beweisstück Speer-25; *Weisungen*, 348–9.

162. Speer, 453; *TBJG*, II/15, 612–13 (28 March 1945).

163. See *IMG*, xli.425–37, Docs. Beweisstuck Speer-24, -28, -29; Speer, 450–64; Guderian, 424. According to Guderian, 426, Hitler was by this time reluctant to see Speer and hear his pessimistic views about the war. He told Goebbels of his anger at Speer's comments, and how he had let himself be influenced by industrialists. He intended replacing him with Saur (*TBJG*, II/15, 619–20 (28 March 1945), 645 (31 March 1945).)

164. *TBJG*, II/15, 613 (28 March 1945).

165. Schroeder, 209.

166. *TBJG*, II/15, 369 (12 February 1945).

167. Boldt, 86–7.

168. See, e.g., *TBJG*, II/15, 425 (5 March 1945), 569–71 (22 March 1945), 618–19 (28 March 1945).

169. Walter Schellenberg, *Schellenberg*, Mayflower Paperback edn, London, 1965, 175; Trevor-Roper, 133 and n.1; *TBJG*, II/15, 613–14 (28 March 1945); Gruchmann, *Der Zweite Weltkrieg*, 434; Padfield, *Himmler*, 577. Dietrich did not carry out the order, but was even so not dismissed by Hitler – an indication that the order had been issued in enraged frustration. (Weingartner, 124. And see n.146 above.)

170. *TBJG*, II/15, 480 (12 March 1945). Himmler experienced the displeasure at first hand when he had his next audience with Hitler on 15 March. (*TBJG*, II/15, 521 (16 March 1945). See also Padfield, *Himmler*, 569.)

171. *TBJG*, II/15, 525 (17 March 1945); and see also 532–3 (18 March 1945), 634 (30 March 1945).

172. See *TBJG*, II/15, 649 (31 March 1945).

173. See Guderian, 426.

174. See Boldt, 40–46 for the comparison (40, for the description of Keitel).

175. *TBJG*, II/15, 567 (22 March 1945), 615–16 (28 March 1945).

176. *TBJG*, II/15, 648 (31 March 1945). Hitler blamed Guderian, at the same time, for the winter crisis of 1941–2.

177. Guderian, 428–9, and see, for Krebs, 415–16.

178. *TBJG*, II/15, 606–7 (27 March 1945).

179. *TBJG*, II/15, 614–15, 617, 622–3 (28 March 1945); also 643 (31 March 1945), 678 (4 April 1945).

180. *TBJG*, II/15, 648 (31 March 1945).

181. *TBJG*, II/15, 616 (28 March 1945).

182. *TBJG*, II/15, 621 (28 March 1945).

183. *Bormann Letters*, 177–8 (7 February 1945).

184. See Rebentisch, 530.

185. *TBJG*, II/15, 613 (28 March 1945).

186. Orlow, ii.479–80.

187. *TBJG*, II/15, 677 (4 April 1945).

188. Rebentisch, 529; Longerich, *Hitlers Stellvertreter*, 201–2.

189. Cit. Kurt Patzold and Manfred Weißbecker, *Geschichte der NSDAP 1920–1945*, Cologne, 1981, 379.

190. Benz, Graml, and Weiß, *Enzyklopädie*, 802–4. For Goebbels's criticism of both 'Werwolf' and 'Freikorps Adolf Hitler' – a brainchild of Robert Ley – see *TBJG*, II/15, 637–8 (30 March 1945).

191. Cit. Longerich, *Hitlers Stellvertreter*, 202.

192. See Pätzold/Weißbecker, 377; Orlow, ii.482.

193. *TBJG*, II/15, 672 (4 April 1945).

194. Trevor-Roper, 140–43.

195. *TBJG*, II/15, 638–9 (30 March 1945).

196. Speer, 467.

197. Trevor-Roper, 140–42; Speer, 467.

198. Below, 408.

199. Kesselring, 265.

200. Gruchmann, *Der Zweite Weltkrieg*, 429; Ludewig, 383–4.

201. See Gruchmann, *Der Zweite Weltkrieg*, 433; Parker, *Struggle for Survival*, 221; Weinberg III, 820–21; Irving, *HW*, 790; Boldt, 113. As a consequence, Hitler had removed a number of divisions from Army Group Vistula and transferred them to Army Group Centre and Army Group South.

202. *Weisungen*, 355–6.

203. *Weisungen*, 357–8.

204. Gruchmann, *Der Zweite Weltkrieg*, 436; *DZW*, vi.696–7; Irving, *HW*, 801–2.

205. *KTB OKW*, iv/2, 1438–9.

206. *DZW*, vi.686–703; Gruchmann, *Der Zweite Weltkrieg*, 435–7; see Below, 409–10.

207. Schroeder, 200; IfZ, ED 100, Irving-Sammlung, Traudl Junge Memoirs, Fol.126; Galante, 14 (Junge).

CHAPTER 17: EXTINCTION

1. Below, 407–8, refers to Eva Braun's return in late March. Schroeder, 168, has February, as does (without any precise indication of the date) Gun, *Eva Braun-Hitler*, 181. Speer noted (Speer, 468) that she came to Berlin 'surprisingly and without being summoned' in the first half of April. Irving, *HW*, 793 (without source reference) gives a specific date, 15 April. Joachimsthaler, 472 n.23 (also without source reference), provides an equally specific – but different – date: 7 March.

2. Based on Linge, *Bis zum Untergang*, 270–72; and also IfZ, ZS 194, the post-war recollections of Hitler's Munich housekeeper, Anni Winter, Fol.4, noting what she had been told by the wife of Hitler's major-domo, Arthur Kannenberg. According to this account, Hitler had needed assistance in walking when leaving his room to meet his staff.

3. Linge, *Bis zum Untergang*, 272.

4. IfZ, ED 100, Irving-Sammlung, Traudl Junge Memoirs, Fol.126: '*20.April 1945 – Hitlers Geburtstag!... Die ersten russischen Panzer standen vor Berlin. Der Donner der Infanteriegeschütze drang bis in das Gebiet der Reichskanzlei. Der Führer empfing die Glückwünsche seiner Getreuen. Alle kamen, drückten ihm die Hand, gelobten Treue, und versuchten, ihn zum Verlassen der Stadt zu bewegen.... Draussen im Park dekorierte er Hitlerjungen. Kinder waren es, die sich ausgezeichnet hatten im Kampf gegen russische Panzer. Wollte er sich auf diese Verteidigung verlassen?...*' ('20 April 1945 – Hitler's birthday. The first Russian tanks were on the approaches to Berlin. The thunder of infantry guns could even be heard in the Reich Chancellery. The Führer received the congratulations of his loyal supporters. All came, shook his hand, vowed loyalty, and tried to persuade him to leave the city ... Outside in the park, he decorated boys from the Hitler Youth. They were children who had distinguished themselves in the fight against Russian tanks. Did he want to depend upon this defence?...)' See also Galante, 141 (Junge), with some inaccuracy in translation.

5. Linge, *Bis zum Untergang*, 273–4; Speer, 477; Keitel, 342; Joachimsthaler, 139–41.

6. Schroeder, 200.

7. Speer, 477; Linge, *Bis zum Untergang*, 274.

8. Karl Koller, *Der letzte Monat. Die Tagebuchaufzeichnungen des ehemaligen Chefs des Generalstabes der deutschen Luftwaffe vom 14. April bis 27. Mai 1945*, Mannheim, 1949, 16–17.

9. Keitel, 343.

10. Speer, 477; Below, 410–11; Boldt, 116.

11. Irving, *Göring*, 452–9; for Carinhall's fate after the end of the war, see Knopf and Martens, *Görings Reich*, 145ff.

12. Speer, 477–8; Below, 410; Linge, *Bis zum Untergang*, 274; Koller, 18; Irving, *Göring*, 459–60.

13. Joachimsthaler, 140–41. *Weisungen*, 357, does not make clear that this additional order followed five days after the initial directive.

14. Cit. Joachimsthaler, 140.

15. Michael A. Musmanno Collection, Duquesne University, Pittsburgh, interview with Admiral Karl-Jesko von Puttkamer, 3 April 1948, FF53, Fols.8–10; Franklin D. Roosevelt Library, Hyde Park, New York, Toland Tapes, V/8/3; Below, 410–11; Speer, 478; Joachimsthaler, 139.

16. Schroeder, 200.

17. Schroeder, 203.

18. Joachimsthaler, 143. One plane, carrying Wilhelm Arndt, one of his servants, and remaining personal possessions of Hitler and Eva Braun, crashed near Börnersdorf in Saxony. See also Robert Harris, *Selling Hitler*, London, 1986, 29–32.

19. Below, 411.

20. IfZ, ED 100, Irving-Sammlung, Traudl Junge Memoirs, Fols. 126–8; Galante, 141–2 (Junge). Traudl Junge vigorously defended her version long after the war against those who denied that there had been any such jollifications (Library of Congress, Toland Tapes, C-86). Gerda Daranowski Christian (Tape C-64) stated that there had been no parties in the bunker itself, which was in any case too cramped for such events; but Junge had described a gathering above ground, in the partly ruined Reich Chancellery.

21. This was the news that he promptly imparted to Luftwaffe Chief of Staff Karl Koller: 'Early in the morning Hitler rang. "Do you know that Berlin is under artillery fire? The city centre." ('*Am frühen Morgen ruft Hitler an. "Wissen Sie, daß Berlin unter Artilleriefeuer liegt? Das Stadtzentrum."*)' (Koller, 20; also *KTB OKW*, iv.2, 1685 (entry of 21 April 1945)).

22. Koller, 20–21.

23. Koller, 21.

24. Koller, 22–3, 26.

25. Koller, 23.

26. Cit. *DZW*, vi.705; Joachimsthaler, 146.

27. *DZW*, vi.705; Joachimsthaler, 146; Boldt, 117–18.

28. Keitel, 344–5.

29. *DZW*, vi.705.

30. Speer, 471, 479.

31. 'Die Vernehmung des Generaloberst Jodl durch die Sowjets', *Wehrwissenschaftliche Rundschau*, 11 (1966), 534–42, here 535: '*Ich werde so lange kämpfen, solange ich noch einen Soldaten habe. Wenn mich der letzte Soldat verläßt, werde ich mich erschießen.*'

32. Koller, 25. See also the telegram sent to Mussolini on 21 April, speaking of 'the spirit of dogged contempt of death', in which the German people would halt the assault of 'Bolshevism and the troop of Jewry' set upon 'plunging our continent into chaos' (Domarus, 2226).

33. Cit. Irving, *Doctor*, 219. See also IfZ, ED 100, Irving-Sammlung, Traudl Junge Memoirs, Fol. 143.

34. Keitel, 346.

35. Koller, 27–8.

36. Below, 411.

37. Koller, 29, comments of Eckhard Christian.

38. Joachimsthaler, 150–51 (photocopy of a report – 'Meldung über Führerlage am 22.4.1945' – by Oberleutnant Hans Volck, adjutant of Major-General Eckhard Christian, from 25 April 1945, containing an extract from notes of General Karl Koller's discussion with Jodl of 23 April 1945, dated 25 April 1945), and 148–54 (post-war accounts); Koller, 28–33; Keitel, 346–8; and 'Die Vernehmung von Generalfeldmarschall Keitel durch die Sowjets', *Wehrwissenschaftliche Rundschau*, 11 (1966), 651–62, here 656 (for Hitler's angry ejection of Keitel from the room, and Keitel's remark to Jodl: 'That's the collapse' ('*Das ist der Zusammenbruch*'); IfZ, ED 100, Irving-Sammlung, Traudl Junge Memoirs, Fols.130–32; Galante, 2–3 (Junge); Boldt, 121–3. See also Trevor-Roper, 157ff.

39. Joachimsthaler, 152 (account of Schaub); IfZ, ED 100, Irving-Sammlung, Traudl Junge Memoirs, Fols.131–2, describes Hitler standing in the small ante-chamber to his room 'motionless. His face has lost all expression, his eyes are dim. He looks like his own death-mask.' ('*In dem kleinen Vorraum vor seinem Zimmer steht Hitler regungslos. Sein Gesicht hat jeden Ausdruck verloren, die Augen sind erloschen. Er sieht aus wie seine eigene Totenmaske.*')

40. IfZ, ED 100, Irving-Sammlung, Traudl Junge Memoirs, Fols.131–2, 137 (slightly revised text); Galante, 2–3 (Junge, with inaccurate translation). In a letter to her sister, Gretl Braun-Fegelein, the next day, 23 April, Eva stated that Hitler had 'lost all hope of a desirable conclusion (*Der Führer selbst hat jeden Glauben an einen glücklichen Ausgang verloren*)', and that they would not let themselves be captured alive. She made arrangements to pass some of her jewellery to Gretl, and also asked her to destroy some private letters, including an envelope addressed to the Führer. (NA, Washington, NND 901065, Folder 5, text and translation of letter from Eva Braun to Gretl Braun Fegelein, 23 April 1945.)

41. Joachimsthaler, 150 (Volck report).

42. Reuth, *Goebbels*, 599–600.

43. See Linge, *Bis zum Untergang*; 275.

44. Koller, 29–30.

45. Koller, 29.

46. Linge, *Bis zum Untergang*, 275.

47. *KTB OKW*, iv/2, 1454.

48. Joachimsthaler, 156.

49. *DZW*, vi.711.

50. This idea was in any case already next day given up by Keitel, after speaking to Jodl, as impractical (Keitel, 352).

51. Keitel, 348; *KTB OKW*, iv/2, 1454.

52. Michael A. Musmanno Collection, Duquesne University, Pittsburgh, interview with Julius Schaub (March, 1948), FF39a, Fols.2–3, 7; Amtsgericht Laufen, Verfahren des Amtsgerichts Berchtesgaden zur Todeserklärung bzw. Feststellung der Todeszeit von Adolf Hitler, testimony of Otto Günsche, 19–21.6.56, Bl.9; Joachimsthaler, 157 (testimony of Günsche and Schaub); Below, 411; Michael A. Musmanno, *Ten Days to Die*, London, 1951, 32. Traudl Junge (IfZ, ED 100, Irving-Sammlung, Traudl Junge Memoirs, Fol.139; Galante, 3 (Junge)), stated that Schaub flew out that day (22 April). (Earlier in her text (Fol.133), Junge had '*am nächsten Morgen*' (i.e. 23 April) for packing a chest with documents and Schaub reluctantly leaving to fly south.) Schaub repeated in his Musmanno interview that he left on 25 April.

53. Below, 412; IfZ, ED 100, Irving-Sammlung, Traudl Junge Memoirs, Fol.133; Galante, 3 (Junge); Joachimsthaler, 158.

54. Michael A. Musmanno Collection, Duquesne University, Pittsburgh, testimony of Major Bernd von Loringhoven, 14 March 1948, FF51, Fol.41 (quotations in English); Joachimsthaler, 152. See also Koller, 29.

55. *KTB OKW*, iv/2, 1454; Boldt, 123; Domarus, 2228; Joachimsthaler, 160–61.

56. ' ". . . warum dann überhaupt noch leben!" Hitlers Lagebesprechungen am 23., 25. und 27. April 1945', *Der Spiegel*, 10 January 1966, 32–46, here 32–3. The typescripts of the briefings (*Lagebesprechungen*) are contained in PRO, WO208/3791, Fols.89–111.

57. The initiative for this had come from Goebbels in mid-March. (*LB* Darmstadt, 343–5 (23 March 1945).)

58. Speer, 479–81. And see Sereny, *Albert Speer*, 517–19, 523–33; Fest, *Speer*, 360–65.

59. Speer, 482–3.

60. Once Keitel had departed, only General Krebs, Chief of the General Staff, supported by his junior officers Major Bernd Freiherr von Freytag-Loringhoven and Captain Gerhard Boldt, and Wehrmacht adjutant General Burgdorf remained of the military advisers. Liaison with Dönitz continued to be maintained through Admiral Voß; Below provided the links with the Luftwaffe. (Keitel, 348–9; Below, 412. See also Trevor-Roper, 181, for the personnel remaining in the bunker after 25 April.)

61. Speer, 483–4.

62. Koller, 35–40. Text: Below, 412; Domarus, 2228 n.165; Joachimsthaler, 162.

63. Speer, 485–6; Lang, *Der Sekretär*, 329–30.

64. Koller, 42–3; Schroeder, 210–11.

65. Speer, 487–8.

66. Keitel, 366; Irving, *HW*, 803.

67. Joachimsthaler, 163–4; Irving, HW 811–12. For Weidling's account of his meeting with Hitler, see 'Der Endkampf in Berlin (23.4–2.5.1945)', Wehrwissenschaftliche Rundschau, 12/I (1962), 40–52, 111–18, 169–74, here 43. He found Hitler, face like a 'smiling mask (gleich einer lachelnden Maske)', both hands and one of his legs constantly trembling, hardly able to rise from his seat.

68. Joachimsthaler, 164–7; Boldt, 142–5. Towards the end of March, Eisenhower had changed the strategic plan of the western Allies. Concerned about the possibility of prolonged fighting even once the war had ended, centred on notions of a 'National Redoubt' in the Alps, probably with its headquarters at the Berghof, he made no attempt to advance on Berlin but, instead, directed US forces to the south of the capital into Saxony, into what had been foreseen as the Soviet zone after the war. It was as part of this advance that soldiers from the 1st US Army met Konev's troops on 25 April at Torgau.

69. For a description, see Schroeder, 211–12; also Koller, 49, 51.

70. 'Hitlers Lagebesprechungen', Der Spiegel, 1966, 34.

71. Keitel, 356.

72. 'Hitlers Lagebesprechungen', Der Spiegel, 1966, 34 (and 37–8 for similar comments). See also Boldt, 145–6 for Hitler's reaction to news of what turned out to be minor disagreements between Soviet and American commanders when they met at Torgau.

73. 'Hitlers Lagebesprechungen', Der Spiegel, 1966, 37.

74. 'Hitlers Lagebesprechungen', Der Spiegel, 1966, 34.

75. 'Hitlers Lagebesprechungen', Der Spiegel, 1966, 37–9.

76. Boldt, 150.

77. Boldt, 149.

78. Boldt, 157.

79. Joachimsthaler, 168.

80. Boldt, 153.

81. Koller, 48; Hanna Reitsch, Fliegen – Mein Leben, Stuttgart, 1951, 292ff. (and for the following); also NA, Washington, NND 901065, Folder, 2, US interrogation of Hanna Reitsch, 8 October 1945, Fols. 1–14; and PRO, London, WO208/4475, Fols.7–8 of undated (1945?) intelligence report on Hanna Reitsch.

82. Koller, 60–61; Trevor-Roper, 186–91; Below, 413–14; NA, Washington, NND 901065, Folder, 2, US interrogation of Hanna Reitsch, 8 October 1945, Fol. 4.

83. 'Hitlers Lagebesprechungen', Der Spiegel, 1966, 40–2.

84. KTB OKW, iv/2, 1460; Joachimsthaler, 171–2.

85. Lew Besymenski, Die letzten Notizen von Martin Bormann. Ein Dokument und sein Verfasser, Stuttgart, 1974, 230–31.

86. 'Hitlers Lagebesprechungen', Der Spiegel, 1966, 42–4.

87. Boldt, 160.

88. Below, 414.

89. 'Hitlers Lagebesprechungen', Der Spiegel, 1966, 44–5.

90. Linge, Bis zum Untergang, 277.

91. Joachimsthaler, 442ff., especially 464ff.; Schroeder, 167–9.

92. Joachimsthaler, 464–5; Trevor-Roper, 191–5; Boldt, 167.

93. KTB OKW, iv/2, 1461–2 (quotation 1462).

94. Cit. Trevor-Roper, 198; Lang, Der Sekretär, 334; Olaf Groehler, Das Ende der Reichskanzlei, East Berlin, 1974, 29 (none with source reference). See also Bormann's entry for 28 April in his desk diary: 'Our Reich Chancellery is turned into a heap of ruins (Unsere RK [Reichskanzlei] wird zum Trümmerhaufen)' (Besymenski, Die letzten Notizen, 230–1). Trevor-Roper noted that Bormann sent the message to Puttkamer at Munich. But Puttkamer's own later accounts give no indication that he flew to Munich, and suggest that his destination was Salzburg, before travelling to Berchtesgaden. (Michael A. Musmanno Collection, Duquesne University, Pittsburgh, interview with Admiral

Karl-Jesko von Puttkamer, 3 April 1948; FF53, Fols.8–10; Franklin D. Roosevelt Library, Hyde Park, New York, Toland Tapes, V/8/3.) If indeed the message was sent to Munich, it must have sent on the Party's telegraph line and been relayed from Munich – presumably from a Party Headquarters on its last legs – to Puttkamer in Berchtesgaden.

95. Besymenski, *Die letzten Notizen*, 230–3.

96. Below, 415.

97. *KTB OKW*, iv/2, 1463. Domarus, 2232 appears to conflate the two separate reports, that of the afternoon and that of the evening.

98. Below, 415. Below is confused in the chronology of Fegelein's escapade in connection with the news of Himmler's behaviour, but his comments otherwise fit the differing responses to the afternoon and evening reports.

99. Cit. Joachimsthaler, 182–3; and Groehler, *Das Ende der Reichskanzlei*, 30. See also Trevor-Roper, 198, 202; Boldt, 169; Below, 415.

100. This was the trigger to Hitler's explosion. See the letter to Wenck (though never reaching him) from Bormann, referring to Himmler's 'proposal to the Anglo-Americans which delivers our people unconditionally to the plutocrats. A change can only by brought about by the Führer himself, and only by him.' ('... hat der Reichsführer SS Himmler den Anglo-Amerikanern einen Vorschlag gemacht, der unser Volk bedingungslos den Plutokraten ausliefert. Eine Wende kann nur vom Führer selbst herbeigeführt werden und nur von ihm!') Cit. Groehler, *Das Ende der Reichskanzlei*, 31; Joachimsthaler, 185; and Olaf Groehler, *Die Neue Reichskanzlei. Das Ende*, Berlin, 1995, 60 (where it is referred to as a cable from Krebs and Bormann to Wenck, dispatched in the evening, not in the early hours).

101. See Below, 406.

102. The main first-hand accounts are Schellenberg, 170–87 (though touched up from the original diary; see Irving, *HW*, 610 n.4); and Graf Folke Bernadotte, *Das Ende. Meine Verhandlungen in Deutschland im Frühjahr 45 und ihre politischen Folgen*, Zurich/New York, 1945. See also, for the Bernadotte dealings, Hesse, *Das Spiel um Deutschland*, 384–5, 429; Kleist, *Die europäische Tragödie*, 247–52; Kersten, 14–19 (introduction by H. R. Trevor-Roper) and 272–90; Trevor-Roper, 144–7, 155–6, 162–4, 170–3, 199–202; Padfield, *Himmler*, 565–96.

103. Padfield, *Himmler*, 565.

104. Padfield, *Himmler*, 566.

105. Padfield, *Himmler*, 567; Kersten, 276–83 (though of dubious authenticity; see Irving, HW, xx).

106. Padfield, *Himmler*, 578.

107. See Padfield, *Himmler*, 582, 585.

108. Padfield, *Himmler*, 578.

109. See Kersten, 278, 281; Guderian, 426; Padfield, *Himmler*, 567, 571, 579–80.

110. Padfield, *Himmler*, 591. Arrangements were discussed at the meeting for a Red Cross convoy to transport a number of Jewish women from Ravensbrück concentration camp. This had followed a remarkable rendezvous at 2a.m. that morning at the home of his masseur, Felix Kersten, between Himmler and a representative of the World Jewish Congress in New York, Norbert Masur, who had travelled to Germany incognito and under promise of safe conduct. Himmler, accompanied by his adjutant Rudolf Brandt, and Schellenberg, had agreed to release female Jews held in Ravensbruck, providing this was kept secret and they were described as Poles. He also consented that no further Jews would be killed, and to hold to his promise to hand over the concentration camps intact to the Allies (Kersten, 284–90; Padfield, *Himmler*, 590).

111. Schellenberg, 181–2.

112. Padfield, *Himmler*, 593; Trevor-Roper, 171.

113. Bernadotte, *Das Ende*, 79–85; Schellenberg, 182–5; Trevor-Roper, 171–2; Padfield, *Himmler*, 593–4.

114. Padfield, *Himmler*, 595; Trevor-Roper, 172, 200–201; Bernadotte, 85.

115. Padfield, *Himmler*, 595–6.

116. Boldt, 170; see also IfZ, ED 100, Irving-Sammlung, Traudl Junge Memoirs, Fols.152–3; Galante, 11 (Junge); Trevor-Roper, 202.

117. Trevor-Roper, 203–4, 277–8; Joachimsthaler, 183, 465; Padfield, 596–7; Below, 415 (who conflates events); Erich Kempka, *Die letzten Tage mit Adolf Hitler*, Preußisch Oldendorf, 1975, 78–83 (with inaccuracies); Boldt, 170; IfZ, ED 100, Irving-Sammlung, Traudl Junge Memoirs, Fol.153; Galante, 11–12 (Junge); Hans Baur, *Hitler at my Side*, Houston, 1986, 187–8 (with inaccuracies); Linge, *Bis zum Untergang*, 278; Koller, 95.

118. Joachimsthaler, 181 (and 174 for the communications interruption).

119. Boldt, 171.

120. Boldt, 170; Trevor-Roper, 205; Reitsch, 303–4 (without mentioning the commission concerning Himmler).

121. Koller, 93. Hanna Reitsch described her and Greim's departure from the bunker, and her confrontation with Himmler about his betrayal of Hitler in her interview with US interrogators on 8 October 1945, NA, Washington, NND 901065, Folder 2, Fols.10–13.

122. Amtsgericht Laufen, Verfahren des Amtsgerichts Berchtesgaden zur Todeserklärung bzw. Feststellung der Todeszeit von Adolf Hitler, testimony of Gertraud Junge, 24 February 1954, Bl.4; Michael A. Musmanno Collection, Duquesne University, Pittsburgh, interview with Gertraud Junge, 7 February 1948, FF25, Fol.31; Joachimsthaler, 188. Whatever the hints, Junge only fully learned of the marriage to Eva Braun when Hitler dictated his Private Testament to her. (Musmanno interview, 32; IfZ, ED 100, Irving-Sammlung, Traudl Junge Memoirs, Fol.156; Galante, 16.) Gerda Daranowski Christian commented on the surprise caused by the wedding (PRO, WO208/3791, Fol.190 (Interrogation, 25 April 1946, where, however, her chronology of events is wayward); and Library of Congress, Toland Tapes, C-64 (interview with John Toland, 26 July 1971).)

123. Below, 415–16; IfZ, ED 100, Irving-Sammlung, Traudl Junge Memoirs, Fol.156; Galante, 13, 16 (Junge, with inaccuracies), 17–18 (Gunsche); Joachimsthaler, 185–9; Linge, *Bis zum Untergang*, 281–3; Kempka, 84–6; Boldt, 171–2; Baur, 186 (brief and inaccurate); Trevor-Roper, 207–8; Musmanno, 197ff. In her 1954 testimony (Amtsgericht Laufen, Verfahren des Amtsgerichts Berchtesgaden zur Todeserklärung bzw. Feststellung der Todeszeit von Adolf Hitler, testimony of Gertraud Junge, 24 February 1954, Bl.4), Traudl Junge stated that Hitler's dictation of his testament had begun shortly before midnight, before the wedding. Joachimsthaler, 185, follows her in this in speaking of the wedding 'towards midnight'. But in her earlier testimony for Musmanno (Michael A. Musmanno Collection, Duquesne University, Pittsburgh, interview with Gertraud Junge, 7 February 1948, FF25, Fols.32–6), she had said that, while the dictation of the testament – from which that she learnt from the private will (which he dictated first) that he intended to marry Eva Braun – began about 11.30p.m., it then took two to three hours for her to type up the wills (political and private), and that the wedding took place while she was doing this. In her later testimony (IfZ, ED 100, Irving-Sammlung, Traudl Junge Memoirs, Fols.152–4), she wrote of being awakened in the middle of the night while preparations for the wedding were being made. As Trevor-Roper (207 n.1) points out, when Greim and Reitsch spoke to Koller as late as 8 May they knew nothing of the nocturnal marriage (Koller, 95). It was, therefore, after they had left the bunker. Joachimsthaler, 183, accepts that Greim and Reitsch left after midnight. The date of the wedding certificate itself is 29 April, indicating that the ceremony was completed after, not before, midnight (Joachimsthaler, 186–7). The wedding was probably, therefore, not before 1a.m. Copy of the wedding certificate in PRO, WO208/3790, Fols.151–2; Joachimsthaler, 186–7 (photostat).

124. IfZ, ED 100, Irving-Sammlung, Traudl Junge Memoirs, Fol.155 (where the impression is given that the dictation began later in the night); Amtsgericht Laufen, Verfahren des Amtsgerichts Berchtesgaden zur Todeserklärung bzw. Feststellung der Todeszeit von Adolf Hitler, testimony of Gertraud Junge, 24 February 1954, Bl.4; Michael A. Musmanno Collection, Duquesne University,

Pittsburgh, interview with Gertraud Junge, 7 February 1948, FF25, Fol.32; Galante, 13 (Junge); Joachimsthaler, 188–9; Musmanno, 202ff.

125. Joachimsthaler, 192 (text photostat); Domarus, 2240–41. In her early post-war testimony, Traudl Junge made clear that Hitler dictated first the private and then afterwards the political testament. (Michael A. Musmanno Collection, Duquesne University, Pittsburgh, interview with Gertraud Junge, 7 February 1948, FF25, Fol. 32; Amtsgericht Laufen, Verfahren des Amtsgerichts Berchtesgaden zur Todeserklärung bzw. Feststellung der Todeszeit von Adolf Hitler, testimony of Gertraud Junge, 24 February 1954, Bl.4.) In her later memoirs, she implied that the political testament came first (IfZ, ED 100, Irving-Sammlung, Traudl Junge Memoirs, Fol.155; Galante, 13).

126. IfZ, ED 100, Irving-Sammlung, Traudl Junge Memoirs, Fol.155; Galante, 13.

127. The grammar of this passage is garbled in the original: '*Ich habe weiter keinen darüber im Unklaren gelassen, dass dieses Mal nicht nur Millionen Kinder von Europaern der arischen Volker verhungern werden, nicht nur Millionen erwachsener Manner den Tod erleiden und nicht nur Hunderttausende an Frauen und Kindern in den Städten verbrannt und zu Tode bombardiert werden dürften, ohne dass der eigentlich Schuldige, wenn auch durch humanere Mittel, seine Schuld zu bussen hat.*' ('I further left no one in doubt that this time not only millions of children . . . would die. . . without the real culprit having to atone . . .') (Werner Maser (ed.), *Hitlers Briefe und Notizen. Sein Weltbild in handschriftlichen Dokumenten*, Dusseldorf, 1973, 360–61; Joachimsthaler, 190; trans. NCA, vi.260.)

128. Maser, *Hitlers Briefe und Notizen*, 356–66; Joachimsthaler, 190–91; Domarus, 2236–7; trans. (slightly amended), NCA, vi.260–61.

129. Amtsgericht Laufen, Verfahren des Amtsgerichts Berchtesgaden zur Todeserklärung bzw. Feststellung der Todeszeit von Adolf Hitler, testimony of Gertraud Junge, 24 February 1954, Bl.4; Michael A. Musmanno Collection, Duquesne University, Pittsburgh, interview with Gertraud Junge, 7 February 1948, FF25, Fol. 35; Joachimsthaler, 189.

130. Maser, *Hitlers Briefe und Notizen*, 368–75; Joachimsthaler, 191–2; Domarus, 2238–9; trans. (amended), NCA, vi.262–3, Doc.3569-PS. The copy of the private and political testaments in PRO, WO208/3781, Fols.90–105, was the one which Heinz Lorenz had been given to carry out of the bunker, and was found, when he was captured, sewn into his shoulder pads (PRO, WO208/3789, Fol.69).

131. Traudl Junge claimed in 1954 that she finished work on Hitler's will, carried out while the wedding celebrations continued, only around 5a.m. (Amtsgericht Laufen, Verfahren des Amtsgerichts Berchtesgaden zur Todeserklärung bzw. Feststellung der Todeszeit von Adolf Hitler, testimony of Gertraud Junge, 24 February 1954, Bl.4). In 1948, she had stated that the typing of the wills had taken two to three hours, putting the completion time, therefore, no later than 3a.m. (Michael A. Musmanno Collection, Duquesne University, Pittsburgh, interview with Gertraud Junge, 7 February 1948, FF25, Fol.35. See also Joachimsthaler, 189. The document itself gives the time of 4a.m. for the signing).

132. IfZ, ED 100, Irving-Sammlung, Traudl Junge Memoirs, Fols.152–3 ('*Wenn der Führer tot ist, ist mein Leben sinnlos*'); Galante, 16 (Junge).

133. NA, Washington, NND 901065, Folder 2; printed in Joseph Goebbels, *Tagebücher 1945. Die letzten Aufzeichnungen*, Hamburg, 1977, 555–6.

134. Below, 416.

135. Linge, *Bis zum Untergang*, 279–80.

136. Amtsgericht Laufen, Verfahren des Amtsgerichts Berchtesgaden zur Todeserklärung bzw. Feststellung der Todeszeit von Adolf Hitler, testimony of Otto Günsche, 19–21 June 1956, Bl.8; Kempka, 80; Trevor-Roper, 227 (Junge). Joachimsthaler, 250–9, convincingly argues that the poison was not cyanide, as most of the bunker inmates themselves thought, but the more effective prussic acid capsules, produced in thousands by the criminal police, and causing death within a fraction of a second.

137. Amtsgericht Laufen, Verfahren des Amtsgerichts Berchtesgaden zur Todeserklärung bzw.

Feststellung der Todeszeit von Adolf Hitler, testimony of Otto Günsche, 19–21 June 1956, Bl.8–9; Joachimsthaler, 194–7; IfZ, ED 100, Irving-Sammlung, Traudl Junge Memoirs, Fol.153; Galante, 12 (Junge); Kempka, 84.

138. Trevor-Roper, 218–21; Domarus, 2241 and n.214–16.

139. Trevor-Roper, 221; Joachimsthaler, 176–81.

140. Joachimsthaler, 193–4.

141. Boldt, 172–5.

142. Trevor-Roper, 224–5; Domarus, 2242.

143. Domarus, 2242; Trevor-Roper, 226.

144. Trevor-Roper, 223–4.

145. *KTB OKW*, iv/2, 1466; Joachimsthaler, 199 (photostat).

146. *KTB OKW*, iv/2, 1467; Joachimsthaler, 201–2 (photostat, where it is clear that the cable, with the time given as 1a.m., was in fact dispatched at 2.57a.m.).

147. Joachimsthaler, 202. Keitel, 368, has another version, for which there is no other evidence and is presumably a distortion from memory: 'No further hope of relief of Berlin and reopening of access from west; suggest break-out via Potsdam to Wenck; alternatively flight of Führer to southern region.' The effect of the telegram seems to have been to reinvoke accusations of betrayal, now even in Keitel. (See Trevor-Roper, 228–9 (though the original text for Bormann's cable to Dönitz does not survive and Trevor-Roper gives no source).)

148. Amtsgericht Laufen, Verfahren des Amtsgerichts Berchtesgaden zur Todeserklärung bzw. Feststellung der Todeszeit von Adolf Hitler, testimony of Erwin Jakubeck, 23 November 1954; Michael A. Musmanno Collection, Duquesne University, Pittsburgh, interview with Gertraud Junge, 7 February 1948, FF25, Fols.38, 41; Joachimsthaler, 201–4, 217; Trevor-Roper, 227 and 275 (where the leave-taking is misdated to 29 April). One guard later testified that he had witnessed a farewell ceremony for Hitler's close entourage during the night of 29–30 April. (Joachimsthaler, 201 (Kölz testimony)). He must have been confusing this with the farewell gathering of around twenty to twenty-five mainly servants and guards. Hitler bade farewell to his 'household' only shortly before his suicide, next afternoon.

149. Joachimsthaler, 206.

150. 'Der Endkampf in Berlin', *Wehrwissenschaftliche Rundschau*, 12/I (1962), 118, 169–70.

151. Joachimsthaler, 210–15 (with justifiable criticisms of Kempka's reliability); Kempka, 90–92. In his testimony of 20 June 1945, Kempka stated that Günsche had telephoned about 2.30p.m., telling him to come to the Führer bunker and to bring 200 litres of petrol (David Irving Microfilm Collection (Microform Academic Publishers, East Ardsley, Wakefield), Third Reich Documents, Group 7/13, 'Erklarung von Herrn Erich Kempka über die letzten Tage Hitlers').

152. Junge, often inaccurate with detail, recollected (IfZ, ED 100, Irving-Sammlung, Traudl Junge Memoirs, Fol.159; Galante, 20) that Eva Braun wore a black dress trimmed with pink roses, one that Hitler especially liked. Linge and Günsche, two of the first to enter the suicide scene, both mentioned independently that she wore a blue dress with white trimmings. (Amtsgericht Laufen, Verfahren des Amtsgerichts Berchtesgaden zur Todeserklärung bzw. Feststellung der Todeszeit von Adolf Hitler, testimony of Heinz Linge, 8–10 February 1956, Bl.6; testimony of Otto Günsche, 19–21 June 1956, Bl.5; Joachimsthaler, 230, 232.)

153. Amtsgericht Laufen, Verfahren des Amtsgerichts Berchtesgaden zur Todeserklärung bzw. Feststellung der Todeszeit von Adolf Hitler, testimony of Heinz Linge, Bl.4–5; testimony of Otto Günsche, 19–21 June 1956, Bl.3–5; testimony of Gertraud Junge, Bl.5; Joachimsthaler, 217–19, 221–2 (Junge, Christian, Jakubeck, Linge, and, especially, Gunsche testimony); PRO, WO208/3791, Fol.192, Interrogation report on Gerda Christian, 2 April 1946; Michael A. Musmanno Collection, Duquesne University, Pittsburgh, interview with Gertraud Junge, 7 February 1948, FF25, Fols.45–8; IfZ, ED 100, Irving-Sammlung, Traudl Junge Memoirs, Fols.158–9; Galante, 20–22 (Junge, Günsche); Linge, *Bis zum Untergang*, 284–6 (with inaccuracies, and see Joachimsthaler,

222–4 for Linge's unreliability as a witness); Günsche testimony in James P. O'Donnell and Uwe Bahnsen, *Die Katakombe. Das Ende in der Reichskanzlei*, Stuttgart, 1975, 210 (also in Galante, 21–2); Library of Congress, Washington, Toland Tapes, C-64, interview with Gerda Daranowski Christian, 26 July 1971. Reuth, 608; Trevor-Roper, 230. Kempka, 90, has Eva Braun present at the lunch. He himself was not present; those who were – Traudl Junge and Gerda Daranowski Christian – independently commented on Eva Braun's absence. Baur, 191–2, and 1955 testimony in Joachimsthaler, 225–6, is unreliable in detail.

154. Amtsgericht Laufen, Verfahren des Amtsgerichts Berchtesgaden zur Todeserklärung bzw. Feststellung der Todeszeit von Adolf Hitler, testimony of Otto Gunsche, Bl.4; Galante, 22 (Günsche). He had been told to wait ten minutes before entering.

155. Amtsgericht Laufen, Verfahren des Amtsgerichts Berchtesgaden zur Todeserklärung bzw. Feststellung der Todeszeit von Adolf Hitler, testimony of Otto Gunsche, 19–21 June 1956, Bl.5; testimony of Heinz Linge, 8–10 February 1956, Bl.5; Joachimsthaler, 230, 232 (Linge, Gunsche); testimony of Gertraud Junge, 24 February 1954, Bl.5; Michael A. Musmanno Collection, Duquesne University, Pittsburgh, interview with Gertraud Junge, 7 February 1948, FF25, Fols.47–8; IfZ, ED 100, Irving-Sammlung, Traudl Junge Memoirs, Fol.159; Galante, 21 (Junge).

156. Amtsgericht Laufen, Verfahren des Amtsgerichts Berchtesgaden zur Todeserklarung bzw. Feststellung der Todeszeit von Adolf Hitler, testimony of Otto Günsche, 19–21 June 1956, Bl.5–6, 8–9; testimony of Heinz Linge, 8–10 February 1956, Bl.5–8; Joachimsthaler, 230, 232. The meticulous study of the testimony and forensic evidence by Joachimsthaler, 229–73, dispels doubt about the manner of death. The earliest accounts emanating from the bunker were that Hitler had shot himself and Eva Braun had taken poison. Below (who had left before the suicides) heard this as early as 6 May related by one of the guards attached to the bunker (PRO, London, WO208/3781, Fol.5, interrogation of Nicolaus von Below, n.d. (but covering letter is of 22 June 1946)). Hugh Trevor-Roper was given the same information by Erich Kempka and Artur Axmann, who saw the bodies in situ, as well as by Martin Bormann's secretary Else Krüger. (PRO, WO208/3790, Fol.54 (Trevor-Roper's handwritten note, on a chronology of events during the last days in the bunker).) The key witnesses give no indication that a shot was heard – counter to some of the unreliable stories (e.g. Michael A. Musmanno Collection, Duquesne University, Pittsburgh, interview with Gertraud Junge, 7 February 1948, FF25, Fol.48; IfZ, ED 100, Irving-Sammlung, Traudl Junge Memoirs, Fol.159; Galante, 21, testimony of Junge). The intentionally misleading account of Hitler's death by cyanide poisoning put about by Soviet historians – see, especially, Lev Bezymenski, *The Death of Adolf Hitler. Unknown Documents from Soviet Archives*, London, 1968, can be dismissed. Equally redundant are the findings of Petrova and Watson, *The Death of Hitler*. The earliest suggestion that Hitler had poisoned, not shot, himself appears to have come from the reported testimony from around an hour after the shooting by Sergeant Fritz Tornow, who had helped poison Hitler's alsatian, and said he had detected a similar odour in the room after the suicides (though he had not been in the room before the removal of the bodies) (PRO, London, WO208/3790, Fol.128 (where he is named Tornoff), testimony of Willi Otto Müller, 4 February 1946). Hitler's pilot, Hans Baur, claimed on release from prison in Moscow in 1949 that Hitler had taken poison, then shot himself through the head. But Baur was not present at the time of the deaths, and his evidence is in any case unreliable in several respects. (See Joachimsthaler, 225, 260.) Artur Axmann, who had seen the bodies, also testified on 16 October 1947 that Hitler had first taken poison and then shot himself through the mouth (PRO, WO208/4475, Fol.39). He repeated this in his interview with Musmanno on 7 January 1948 ((Michael A. Musmanno Collection, Duquesne University, Pittsburgh, interview with Artur Axmann, 7 January 1948, FF1, Fols.28–32, 44), saying he had the information from Günsche, which the latter explicitly denied (Joachimsthaler, 236–7). Axmann's claim contradicted, moreover, his earlier testimony from 1946 (see below). Neither of the surviving witnesses to the scene immediately following the deaths – Linge and Günsche – who saw the bodies in situ suggested that Hitler had poisoned himself; and there was no trace of the acrid smell of bitter almonds on his body (in distinction to that of Eva Braun). This negative evidence in itself also rules out the faint possibility that he both took poison and shot himself. The speed at which prussic acid acts would itself render it virtually impossible for Hitler to have crushed the ampoule of poison and then shot; and if the poison could have been swallowed a split-second after the shooting, the spasms incurred would have caused the blood to splatter on the shoulder and immediate surrounds, which did not happen. (On this, see Joachimsthaler, 269–70 and, including a few lines not to be found in the German original, the English version of his book, *The Last Days of Hitler. The Legends, the Evidence, the Truth*, London, 1996, 179–80.) The forensic evidence also eliminates the story, first put round by Artur Axmann, though based on hearsay evidence without substance, that Hitler shot himself in the mouth. Axmann had in his earliest testimony, in fact, explicitly ruled out a shot through the mouth and claimed (as Günsche had done) that Hitler had shot himself through the right temple (PRO, WO208/3790, Fol.125 (Axmann Interrogation, 14 January 1946)). Notions that Hitler was given a *coup de grâce* by Linge or Günsche – a further surmise of Bezymenski – are utterly baseless. The 'theories' of Hugh Thomas, *Doppelgänger: The Truth about the Bodies in the Berlin Bunker*, London, 1995 – that Hitler was strangled by Linge, and that the female body burned was not that of Eva Braun, who escaped from the bunker, belong in fairyland.

EPILOGUE

1. This and what follows is based on Joachimsthaler, chs.5–7, the most reliable and detailed examination of the cremation of Hitler and Eva Braun, providing, in addition (347ff.), compelling reasons for utmost scepticism towards the Soviet claims to have recovered the remains of Hitler's body and to have performed an autopsy on it. (For this, see Bezymenski, *Death of Adolf Hitler*, and, for an early expression of scepticism, the review of Bezymenski's book by Hugh Trevor-Roper, 'The Hole in Hitler's Head', *Sunday Times*, 29 September 1968.) It also rests upon the testimony of Heinz Linge and Otto Günsche, given in Berchtesgaden in 1954 (Linge) and 1956 (Günsche), together with several other witnesses to Hitler's end. I am grateful to Frau A. Regnauer, Director of the Amtsgericht Laufen, for permission to see this material. I would also like to thank Professor Robert Service (St Antony's College, Oxford) for translating for me part of one of Günsche's interrogations in Moscow (Osobyi Arkhiv (= Special Archive), Moscow, 130–0307, Fol.282). Even apart from forensic issues, it is remarkable that, had they possessed Hitler's remains, the Soviet authorities never indicated this, let alone showed the remains, to Linge, Günsche, and other witnesses from the bunker whom they held in captivity for up to ten years. Instead, in countless hours of grilling them in highly inhumane fashion, including taking them back to Berlin in 1946 to reconstruct the scene in the bunker – aimed at ascertaining whether Hitler had in fact committed suicide – they continued to insist, despite consistent testimony from independent witnesses to the contrary, that Hitler was still alive. According to Linge (Amtsgericht Laufen, Fol.9), he was repeatedly interrogated about whether Hitler was alive or dead, whether he could have flown out of Berlin, and whether he had been substituted by a 'double'. When Linge asked his interrogators during the visit to Berlin whether they had Hitler's corpse in their possession, he was told (Fol.10) that they had found many corpses but did not know whether Hitler's was among them. Stalin himself also appears persistently in the immediate post-war years – not just for propaganda purposes – to have disbelieved stories of Hitler's death. The opening of Soviet archives following the end of the Cold War brought a flurry of new 'revelations' about Hitler's end and the location of his remains, which were allegedly dug up on the orders of Soviet chief Leonid Brezhnev on the night of 4–5 April 1970 by five officers of the KGB from a plot of land near a garage in Magdeburg, and burnt. The remains had, it was said, been buried there along with those of Eva Braun, the Goebbels family, and (probably) General Hans Krebs in 1946 and were now to be exhumed because of the danger of discovery through

building work on the site. (See 'Hitlers Höllenfahrt', *Der Spiegel*, 14/1995, 170–87, 15/1995, 172–86; also Norman Stone, 'Hitler, ein Gespenst in den Archiven', *Frankfurter Allgemeine Zeitung*, 19 April 1995; Alexander Lesser, 'Russians wanted to sell "Hitler skull" story', *Jerusalem Report*, 11 March 1993; 'Kremlin "secretly burned Hitler's remains"', *Guardian*, 4 April 1995; 'Secret of Hitler's ashes revealed in Soviet archive', *New York Post*, 27 January 2000.) The Soviet evidence was most extensively examined in Petrova and Watson, and was also the subject of a BBC TV documentary, optimistically entitled 'Hitler's Death: The Final Report', in April 1995. Apart from the jawbone, however, the only additional alleged remains of Hitler that have come to light are part of a skull discovered in 1946 (which has never been conclusively identified as Hitler's). It is unclear how this skull related to the remains purported to have been found in May 1945 and exhumed – presumably headless – in Magdeburg in 1970. If, of course, the Soviets never had Hitler's body in the first place, the post-Cold War revelations of the disposal of his remains have no standing. Whichever remains they buried in Magdeburg then dug up and burnt, it is unlikely that they were those of Hitler. In any event, the matter is chiefly of relevance to interpretations of Soviet post-war actions rather than to a study of Hitler's life.

2. Joachimsthaler, 334.

3. Joachimsthaler, 335.

4. Joachimsthaler, 339, 346–7, 349.

5. Joachimsthaler, 356–7; Galante, 162 (Günsche).

6. Joachimsthaler, 274–6; Trevor-Roper, 238–9.

7. Joachimsthaler, 280–81.

8. Joachimsthaler, 277–8.

9. Joachimsthaler, 281–3.

10. Domarus, 2250 and notes 250, 252; Joachimsthaler, 282–3.

11. Trevor-Roper, 240–41.

12. Joachimsthaler, 284–5; see also 278–80.

13. Trevor-Roper, 241–3; Reuth, *Goebbels*, 613–14; Irving, *Goebbels*, 531–3.

14. See Joachimsthaler, 350.

15. Trevor-Roper, 243–7; Lang, *Der Sekretär*, 340–50, 436–40. The skeletons were uncovered during work on a building site in 1972. It was possible to identify Bormann and Stumpfegger with almost total certainty through dental records and pathological examination.

16. Müller and Ueberschär, *Kriegsende 1945*, 101. And see Doenitz, *Memoirs*, ch.22.

17. *DZW*, vi.748–58.

18. Müller and Ueberschär, *Kriegsende* 103.

19. *DZW*, vi.775–8; Müller and Ueberschär, *Kriegsende*, 103.

20. Müller and Ueberschär, *Kriegsende*, 107–8.

21. Müller and Ueberschär, *Kriegsende*, 178–9 (Dok.19); *KTB OKW*, vi, 1478–84.

22. *KTB OKW*, vi, 1482.

23. The signing took place according to western European time at 11.16p.m. on 8 May; according to central European time (German summer time) at 0.16a.m. on 9 May (Domarus, 2252, n.259).

24. *KTB OKW*, vi, 1485–6; Müller and Ueberschär, *Kriegsende*, 180–81 (Dok.20).

25. *KTB OKW*, vi, 1281–2; Müller and Ueberschär, *Kriegsende*, 181 (Dok.21).

26. Padfield, *Himmler*, 611.

27. Douglas M. Kelley, *22 Cells in Nuremberg*, (1947), New York, 1961, 125–6; Ronald Smelser, *Robert Ley. Hitler's Labor Front Leader*, Oxford/New York/Hamburg, 1988, 292–7.

28. Irving, *Göring*, 504–11; Kelley, 61.

29. Michale R. Marrus, *The Nuremberg War Crimes Trial 1945–46. A Documentary History*, Boston New York, 1997, 57–70; 258–61.

30. Marrus, 258–60. For the pyschology behind Speer's guilt-complex, see especially the aptly entitled book by Gitta Sereny, *Albert Speer: His Battle with the Truth*.

31. Wistrich, *Wer war wer*, 64, 73, 98, 141, 159, 268; Weiß, *Biographisches Lexikon*, 107, 125, 161, 228, 270, 451.

32. Wistrich, *Wer war wer*, 177–8; Weiß, *Biographisches Lexikon*, 304–5.

33. Kershaw, 'Improvised Genocide', 78.

34. For the post-war careers of many of those involved in the 'euthanasia action', see Ernst Klee, *Was sie taten – Was sie wurden. Àrzte, Juristen und andere Beteiligte am Kranken- oder Judenmord*, Frankfurt am Main, 1986.

35. For use of the term, see Hans Mommsen, *Von Weimar nach Auschwitz. Zur Geschichte Deutschlands in der Weltkriegsepoche*, Stuttgart, 1999, 247.

36. Klemperer, ii.766.

37. Victor Gollancz, *In Darkest Germany. The Record of a Visit*, London, 1947, 28.

38. Klemperer, ii.790.

39. *Manchester Guardian*, 2 May 1945.

LIST OF WORKS CITED

Abendroth, Hans-Henning, 'Deutschlands Rolle im Spanischen Bürgerkrieg', in Manfred Funke (ed.), *Hitler, Deutschland und die Mächte. Materialien zur Außenpolitik des Dritten Reiches*, Düsseldorf, 1978, 471–88.

Adam, Uwe Dietrich, *Judenpolitik im Dritten Reich*, Düsseldorf, 1972.

—— 'Wie spontan war der Pogrom?', in Walter H. Pehle (ed.), *Der Judenpogrom. Von der 'Reichskristallnacht' zum Völkermord*, Frankfurt am Main, 1988, 74–93.

Adler, H. G., *Der verwaltete Mensch. Studien zur Deportation der Juden aus Deutschland*, Tübingen, 1974.

Adolf Hitler: Monologe im Führerhauptquartier 1941–1944. Die Aufzeichnungen Heinrich Heims, ed. Werner Jochmann, Hamburg, 1980.

Aigner, Dietrich, *Das Ringen um England*, Munich/Esslingen, 1969.

Akten der Reichskanzlei. Die Regierung Hitler. Teil I, 1933–34, ed. Karl-Heinz Minuth, Boppard am Rhein, 1989.

Akten zur Deutschen Auswärtigen Politik 1918–1945. (Serie D: 1.9.37–11.12.41; Serie E: 1941–1945).

Allbritton, William T., and Mitcham, Samuel W. Jr, 'SS-Oberstgruppenführer und Generaloberst der Waffen-SS Joseph (Sepp) Dietrich', in Gerd Ueberschär (ed.), *Hitlers militärische Elite, Bd. II. Vom Kriegsbeginn zum Weltkriegsende*, Darmstadt, 1998, 37–44.

Allen, William Sheridan, 'Die deutsche Öffentlichkeit und die "Reichskristallnacht" – Konflikte zwischen Werthierarchie und Propaganda im Dritten Reich', in *Die Reihen fast geschlossen. Beiträge zur Geschichte des Alltags unterm Nationalsozialismus*, Wuppertal, 1981, 397–411.

—— 'Die sozialdemokratische Untergrundbewegung: Zur Kontinuität der subkulturellen Werte', in Jürgen Schmädeke and Peter Steinbach (eds.), *Der Widerstand gegen den Nationalsozialismus. Die deutsche Gesellschaft und der Widerstand gegen Hitler*, Munich/Zurich, 1985, 859–66.

Aly, Götz, *'Endlösung'. Völkerverschiebung und der Mord an den europäischen Juden*, Frankfurt am Main, 1995.

Aly, Götz, and Heim, Susanne, *Vordenker der Vernichtung. Auschwitz und die deutschen Pläne für eine neue europäische Ordnung*, Frankfurt am Main, 1993.

Anatomie des SS-Staates, incl. contributions by Hans Buchheim *et al.*, Olten/Freiburg i. Br., 1965.

Anatomy of the SS State, London, 1968.

Andreas-Friedrich, Ruth, *Schauplatz Berlin. Ein deutsches Tagebuch*, Munich, 1962.

Angermund, Ralph, *Deutsche Richterschaft 1919–1945. Krisenerfahrung, Illusion, politische Rechtsprechung*, Frankfurt am Main, 1990.

'Anschluß' 1938. Eine Dokumentation, ed. Dokumentationsarchiv des Österreichischen Widerstandes, Vienna, 1988.

Ansel, Walter, Hitler Confronts England, Durham NC, 1960.

Arad, Yitzhak, Belzec, Sobibor, Treblinka. The Operation Reinhard Death Camps, Bloomington/Indianapolis, 1987.

Aschenauer, Rudolf (ed.), Ich, Adolf Eichmann, Leoni am Starnberger See, 1980.

Auerbach, Hellmuth, 'Konzentrationslagerhäftlinge im Fronteinsatz', in Wolfgang Benz (ed.), Miscellanea: Festschrift für Helmut Krausnick zum 75. Geburtstag, Stuttgart, 1980, 63–83.

—— 'Volksstimmung und veröffentlichte Meinung', in Franz Knipping and Klaus-Jürgen Müller (eds.), Machtbewußtsein in Deutschland am Vorabend des Zweiten Weltkrieges, Paderborn, 1984, 273–93.

Baigent, Michael, and Leigh, Richard, Secret Germany: Claus von Stauffenberg and the Mystical Crusade against Hitler, London, 1994.

Balfour, Michael, Propaganda in War, 1939–1945, London, 1979.

Balfour, Michael, and Frisby, Julian, Helmuth von Moltke. A Leader against Hitler, London, 1972.

Bankier, David, 'Hitler and the Policy-Making Process on the Jewish Question', Holocaust and Genocide Studies, 3 (1988), 1–20.

—— The Germans and the Final Solution. Public Opinion under Nazism, Oxford, 1992.

Baranowski, Shelley, The Confessing Church, Conservative Elites, and the Nazi State, Lewiston/Queenston, 1986.

Barkai, Avraham, Vom Boykott zur 'Entjudung'. Der wirtschaftliche Existenzkampf der Juden im Dritten Reich 1933–1943, Frankfurt am Main, 1987.

—— 'Schicksalsjahr 1938', in Walter H. Pehle (ed.), Der Judenpogrom 1938. Von der 'Reichskristallnacht' zum Völkermord, Frankfurt am Main, 1988, 94–117, 220–24.

Barnett, Correlli (ed.), Hitler's Generals, paperback edn, London, 1990.

Bartov, Omer, The Eastern Front, 1941–45, German Troops, and the Barbarisation of Warfare, New York, 1986.

—— Hitler's Army. Soldiers, Nazis, and War in the Third Reich, New York/Oxford, 1991.

—— Hitlers Wehrmacht. Soldaten, Fanatismus und die Brutalisierung des Krieges, Reinbek bei Hamburg, 1995.

—— 'Operation Barbarossa and the Origins of the Final Solution', in David Cesarani (ed.), The Final Solution. Origins and Implementation, London, 1996, 119–36.

—— 'From Blitzkrieg to Total War: Controversial Links between Image and Reality', in Ian Kershaw and Moshe Lewin (eds.), Stalinism and Nazism: Dictatorships in Comparison, Cambridge, 1997, 158–84.

Bauer, Yehuda, A History of the Holocaust, New York etc., 1982.

—— 'The Death-Marches, January–May 1945', in Michael Marrus (ed.), The Nazi Holocaust: Historical Articles on the Destruction of European Jews, vol. 9, Westport, 1989, 491–511.

Baumgart, Winfried, 'Zur Ansprache Hitlers vor den Führern der Wehrmacht am 22. August 1939. Eine quellenkritische Untersuchung', VfZ, 16 (1968), 120–49.

—— 'Zur Ansprache Hitlers vor den Führern der Wehrmacht am 22. August 1939 (Erwiderung)', VfZ, 19 (1971), 301–4.

Baur, Hans, Ich flog Mächtige der Erde, Kempten, 1956.

—— Hitler at My Side, Houston, 1986.

Beevor, Antony, Stalingrad, London, 1998.

Behr, Friedmann, Mein Jahr 1945, East Berlin, 1988.

Bell, P. M. H., The Origins of the Second World War in Europe, London, 1986.

Below, Nicolaus von, Als Hitlers Adjutant 1937–1945, Mainz, 1980.

Benz, Wolfgang, 'Der Rückfall in die Barbarei. Bericht über den Pogrom', in Walter H. Pehle (ed.),

Der Judenpogrom. Von der 'Reichskristallnacht' zum Völkermord, Frankfurt am Main, 1988, 13–51.

Benz, Wolfgang, *et al.* (eds.), *Miscellanea: Festschrift für Helmut Krausnick zum 75. Geburtstag*, Stuttgart, 1980.

Benz, Wolfgang, and Pehle Walter H. (eds.), *Lexikon des deutschen Widerstandes*, Frankfurt am Main, 1994.

Benz, Wolfgang, Graml, Hermann, and Weiß, Hermann (eds.), *Enzyklopädie des Nationalsozialismus*, Stuttgart, 1997.

Benzenhöfer, Udo, *Der gute Tod? Euthanasie und Sterbehilfe in Geschichte und Gegenwart*, Munich, 1999.

—— 'Der Fall "Kind Knauer" ', *Deutsches Ärtzeblatt*, 95, Heft 19 (8 May 1998), B 954–5.

Benzenhofer, Udo, and Finsterbuch, Karin, *Moraltheologie pro 'NS-Euthanasie'. Studien zu einem 'Gutachten' (1940) von Prof. Joseph Mayer mit Edition des Textes*, Hannover, 1998.

Berghahn, Volker R., 'Meinungsforschung im "Dritten Reich": Die Mundpropaganda-Aktion der Wehrmacht im letzten Kriegshalbjahr', *Militärgeschichtliche Mitteilungen*, 1 (1967), 83–119.

—— 'NSDAP und "geistige Führung" der Wehrmacht 1939–1943', *VfZ*, 17 (1969), 17–71.

The Berlin Diaries 1940–1945 of Marie 'Missie' Vassiltchikov, London, 1985.

Bernadotte, Graf Folke, *Das Ende. Meine Verhandlungen in Deutschland im Frühjahr 45 und ihre politischen Folgen*, Zurich/New York, 1945.

Besson, Waldemar, 'Zur Geschichte des nationalsozialistischen Führungsoffiziers (NSFO)', *VfZ*, 9 (1961), 76–116.

Besymenski, Lew, *Die letzten Notizen von Martin Bormann. Ein Dokument und sein Verfasser*, Stuttgart, 1974.

Bezymenski, Lev, *The Death of Adolf Hitler. Unknown Documents from Soviet Archives*, London, 1968.

Bezymenskij, Lev A., 'Stalins Rede vom 5. Mai 1941 – neu dokumentiert', in Gerd R. Ueberschär and Lev A. Bezymenskij (eds.), *Der deutsche Überfall auf die Sowjetunion. Die Kontroverse um die Präventivkriegsthese*, Darmstadt, 1988, 131–44.

Biddis, Michael, 'History as Destiny: Gobineau, H. S. Chamberlain, and Spengler', *Transactions of the Royal Historical Society*, 6th Series, 7 (1997), 73–100.

Bidwell, Shelford, 'Kesselring', in Correlli Barnett (ed.), *Hitler's Generals*, London, 1989, 265–89.

Birn, Ruth Bettina, *Die Höheren SS- und Polizeiführer. Himmlers Vertreter im Reich und in den besetzten Gebieten*, Düsseldorf, 1986.

Blasius, Rainer A., *Für Großdeutschland – gegen den großen Krieg. Staatssekretär Ernst Freiherr von Weizsacker in den Krisen um die Tschechoslowakei und Polen 1938/39*, Cologne/Vienna, 1981.

—— 'Weizsacker kontra Ribbentrop: "München" statt des großen Krieges', in Franz Knipping and Klaus-Jürgen Müller (eds.), *Machtbewußtsein in Deutschland am Vorabend des Zweiten Weltkrieges*, Paderborn, 1984, 93–118.

Blatman, Daniel, 'Die Todesmärsche', in Ulrich Herbert, Karin Orth and Christoph Dieckmann (eds.), *Die nationalsozialistischen Konzentrationslager. Entwicklung und Struktur*, vol. 2, Göttingen, 1998, 1063–92.

Bleyer, Wolfgang, 'Pläne der faschistischen Führung zum totalen Krieg im Sommer 1944', *Zeitschrift für Geschichtswissenschaft*, 17 (1969), 1312–29.

Bloch, Michael, *Ribbentrop*, London, 1994.

Bloß, Hartmut, 'Deutsche Chinapolitik im Dritten Reich', in Manfred Funke (ed.), *Hitler, Deutschland und die Machte. Materialien zur Außenpolitik des Dritten Reiches*, Düsseldorf, 1978, 407–29.

Blumentritt, Guenther, *Von Rundstedt. The Soldier and the Man*, London, 1952.

—— 'Moscow', in *The Fatal Decisions*, London, 1956, 29–74.

Boberach, Heinz (ed.), *Berichte des SD und der Gestapo über Kirchen und Kirchenvolk*, Mainz, 1971.

Bock, Fedor von, *The War Diary 1939–1945*, ed. Klaus Gerbet, Atglen PA, 1996.

Böckenförde, Ernst-Wolfgang, 'Der deutsche Katholizismus im Jahre 1933. Eine kritische Betrachtung', *Hochland*, 53 (1961–2), 215–39.

—— 'Der deutsche Katholizismus im Jahre 1933. Stellungnahme zu einer Diskussion', *Hochland*, 54 (1961–62), 217–45.

Boelcke, Willi A. (ed.), *Deutschlands Rüstung im Zweiten Weltkrieg. Hitlers Konferenzen mit Albert Speer 1942–1945*, Frankfurt am Main, 1969.

—— (ed.), *Wollt Ihr den totalen Krieg? Die geheimen Goebbels-Konferenzen 1939–1943*, Munich, 1969.

—— *Die Kosten von Hitlers Krieg*, Paderborn etc., 1985.

Böhm, Hermann, 'Zur Ansprache Hitlers vor den Führern der Wehrmacht am 22. August 1939', *VfZ*, 19 (1971), 294–300.

Boldt, Gerhard, *Hitler's Last Days. An Eye-Witness Account*, Sphere Books edn (1947), London, 1973.

Bollmus, Reinhard, *Das Amt Rosenberg und seine Gegner. Studien zum Machtkampf im national-sozialistischen Herrschaftssystem*, Stuttgart, 1970.

Bonwetsch, Bernd, 'Stalin, the Red Army, and the "Great Patriotic War" ', in Ian Kershaw and Moshe Lewin (eds.), *Stalinism and Nazism: Dictatorships in Comparison*, Cambridge, 1997, 185–207.

Bor, Peter, *Gespräche mit Halder*, Wiesbaden, 1950.

The Bormann Letters: The Private Correspondence between Martin Bormann and his Wife from January 1943 to April 1945, ed. H.R. Trevor-Roper, London, 1954.

Botz, Gerhard, *Wohnungspolitik und Judendeportation 1938–1945. Zur Funktion des Antisemitismus als Ersatz nationalsozialistischer Sozialpolitik*, Vienna, 1975.

—— *Der 13. März 38 und die Anschluß-Bewegung. Selbstaufgabe, Okkupation und Selbstfindung Österreichs 1918–1945*, Vienna, 1978.

—— 'Austria', in Detlef Mühlberger (ed.), *The Social Basis of European Fascist Movements*, London/New York/Sydney, 1987, 242–80.

—— *Nationalsozialismus in Wien. Machtübernahme und Herrschaftssicherung 1938/39*, 3rd edn, Buchloe, 1988.

—— 'Die Ausgliederung der Juden aus der Gesellschaft. Das Ende des Wiener Judentums unter der NS-Herrschaft (1938–1943)', in Gerhard Botz, Ivar Oxaal and Michael Pollack (eds.), *Eine zerstörte Kultur. Jüdisches Leben und Antisemitismus in Wien seit dem 19. Jahrhundert*, Buchloe, 1990, 285–312.

Boyd, Carl, *Hitler's Japanese Confidant. General Oshima Hiroshi and MAGIC Intelligence, 1941–1945*, Kansas, 1992.

Braham, Randolph L., *The Destruction of Hungarian Jewry. A Documentary Account*, New York, 1963.

Bramsted, Ernest K., *Goebbels and National Socialist Propaganda 1925–1945*, Michigan, 1965.

Brechtken, Magnus, *'Madagaskar für die Juden'. Antisemitische Idee und politische Praxis 1885–1945*, Munich, 1997.

Breitinger, Hilarius, *Als Deutschenseelsorger in Posen und im Warthegau 1934–1945. Erinnerungen*, Mainz, 1984.

Breitman, Richard, *The Architect of Genocide. Himmler and the Final Solution*, London, 1991.

—— *Official Secrets. What the Nazis Planned. What the British and Americans Knew*, London, 1998.

Breloer, Heinrich (ed.), *Mein Tagebuch. Geschichten vom Überleben 1939–1947*, Cologne, 1984.

Broszat, Martin, 'Zur Perversion der Strafjustiz im Dritten Reich', *VfZ*, 6 (1958), 390–443.

—— *Nationalsozialistische Polenpolitik*, Fischer paperback edn, (1961), Frankfurt am Main, 1965.

—— 'Nationalsozialistische Konzentrationslager 1933–1945', in *Anatomie des SS-Staates*, incl. contributions by Hans Buchheim *et al.*, Olten/Freiburg i. Br., 1965, ii. 9–160.

—— *Der Staat Hitlers. Grundlegung und Entwicklung seiner inneren Verfassung*, Munich, 1969.

—— 'Soziale Motivation und Führer-Bindung des Nationalsozialismus', *VfZ*, 18 (1970), 392–409.

—— 'Hitler und die Genesis der "Endlösung". Aus Anlaß der Thesen von David Irving', *VfZ*, 25 (1977), 739–75.

—— 'A Social and Historical Typology of the German Opposition to Hitler', in David Clay Large (ed.), *Contending with Hitler. Varieties of German Resistance in the Third Reich*, Cambridge, 1991, 25–33.

Broszat, Martin, Fröhlich, Elke, and Wiesemann, Falk (eds.), *Bayern in der NS-Zeit. Soziale Lage und politisches Verhalten der Bevölkerung im Spiegel vertraulicher Berichte*, Munich/Vienna, 1977.

Broszat, Martin, and Frei, Norbert (eds.), *Das Dritte Reich im Überblick. Chronik-Ereignisse-Zusammenhänge*, Munich/Zurich, 1989.

Broszat, Martin, and Schwabe, Klaus (eds.), *Die deutschen Eliten und der Weg in den Zweiten Weltkrieg*, Munich, 1989.

Browning, Christopher R., *The Final Solution and the German Foreign Office*, New York/London, 1978.

—— *Fateful Months. Essays on the Emergence of the Final Solution*, New York/London, 1985.

—— 'Nazi Resettlement Policy and the Search for a Solution to the Jewish Question, 1939–1941', in Christopher Browning (ed.), *The Path to Genocide. Essays on Launching the Final Solution*, Cambridge, 1992, 3–27.

—— *Ordinary Men. Reserve Police Battalion 101 and the Final Solution in Poland*, New York, 1992.

—— 'Hitler and the Euphoria of Victory. The Path to the Final Solution', in David Cesarani (ed.), *The Final Solution. Origins and Implementation*, London, 1996, 137–47.

Buchbender, Ortwin, and Sterz, Reinhold (eds.), *Das andere Gesicht des Krieges. Deutsche Feldpostbriefe 1939–1945*, Munich, 1982.

Buchheim, Hans, 'Der deutsche Katholizismus im Jahr 1933', *Hochland*, 53 (1960–61), 497–515.

Buchler, Yehoshua, 'Kommandostab Reichsführer-SS: Himmler's Personal Murder Brigades in 1941', *Holocaust and Genocide Studies*, I/1 (1986), 11–26.

Bullock, Alan, *Hitler. A Study in Tyranny*, (1952), Harmondsworth, 1962.

—— *Hitler and Stalin. Parallel Lives*, London, 1991.

Burckhardt, Carl J., *Meine Danziger Mission 1937–1939*, Munich, 1962.

Burleigh, Michael, *Germany Turns Eastwards. A Study of Ostforschung in the Third Reich*, Cambridge, 1988.

—— *Death and Deliverance. 'Euthanasia' in Germany, c. 1900–1945*, Cambridge, 1994.

—— 'Psychiatry, German Society, and the Nazi "Euthanasia" Programme', in Michael Burleigh (ed.), *Ethics and Extermination. Reflections on Nazi Genocide*, Cambridge, 1997, 113–29.

Burleigh, Michael, and Wippermann, Wolfgang, *The Racial State. Germany 1933–1945*, Cambridge, 1991.

Burrin, Philippe, *Hitler and the Jews. The Genesis of the Holocaust*, (1989), London, 1994.

Bussmann, Walter, 'Zur Entstehung und Überlieferung der "Hoßbach-Niederschrift" ', *VfZ*, 16 (1968), 373–84.

Caplan, Jane, *Government without Administration. State and Civil Service in Weimar and Nazi Germany*, Oxford, 1988.

Carley, Michael Jabara, *1939: the Alliance that Never Was and the Coming of World War II*, Chicago, 1999.

Carr, William, *Hitler. A Study in Personality and Politics*, London, 1978.

——— *Poland to Pearl Harbor. The Making of the Second World War*, London, 1985.

Carroll, Berenice, *Design for Total War. Arms and Economics in the Third Reich*, The Hague/Paris, 1968.

Cecil, Robert, *Hitler's Decision to Invade Russia 1941*, London, 1975.

Celovsky, Boris, *Das Münchener Abkommen 1938*, Stuttgart, 1958.

Cesarani, David (ed.), *The Final Solution. Origins and Implementation*, London, 1996.

Chamberlain, Neville, *The Struggle for Peace*, London, 1939.

Chandler, Andrew (ed.), *Brethren in Adversity. Bishop George Bell, the Church of England, and the Crisis of German Protestantism, 1933–1939*, Woodbridge, 1997.

Charmley, John, *Churchill: the End of Glory. A Political Biography*, London/New York, 1993.

Chips. The Diaries of Sir Henry Channon, ed. Robert Rhodes James, London, 1967.

Churchill, Winston S., *The Second World War. Vol. 1: The Gathering Storm*, London etc., 1948.

——— *The Second World War. Vol. 2: Their Finest Hour*, London etc., 1949.

——— *The Second World War. Vol. 3: The Grand Alliance*, London etc., 1950.

——— *The Second World War. Vol. 4: The Hinge of Fate*, London etc., 1951.

——— *The Second World War. Vol. 5: Closing the Ring*, London etc., 1952.

——— *The Second World War. Vol. 6: Triumph and Tragedy*, London etc., 1954.

Churchill and Roosevelt: The Complete Correspondence, vol. 1, ed. Warren Kimball, Princeton, 1984.

Ciano, Galeazzo, *Tagebücher 1937/38*, Hamburg, 1949.

Ciano's Diary, 1939–1943, ed. Malcolm Muggeridge, London, 1947.

Ciano's Diplomatic Papers, ed. Malcolm Muggeridge, London, 1948.

Clare, George, *Last Waltz in Vienna. The Destruction of a Family, 1842–1942*, Pan Books edn, London, 1982.

Clark, Alan, *Barbarossa. The Russian–German Conflict 1941–45*, New York (1965), 1985.

Clarke, Chris, 'Josef "Sepp" Dietrich: Landsknecht im Dienste Hitlers', in Ronald Smelser and Enrico Syring (eds.), *Die SS: Elite unter dem Totenkopf. 30 Lebensläufe*, Paderborn etc., 2000, 119–33.

Colville, John, *Downing Street Diaries 1939–1955*, London, 1985.

Conquest, Robert, *The Nation Killers. The Soviet Deportation of Nationalities*, London, 1970.

Conway, John, *The Nazi Persecution of the Churches, 1933–1945*, London, 1968.

Corni, Gustavo, *Hitler and the Peasants, Agrarian Policy of the Third Reich, 1930–1939*, New York/Oxford/Munich, 1990.

Corni, Gustavo, and Gies, Horst, *Brot-Butter-Kanonen. Die Ernährungswirtschaft in Deutschland unter der Diktatur Hitlers*, Berlin, 1997.

Cornwell, John, *Hitler's Pope. The Secret History of Pius XII*, London, 1999.

Costello, John, *Ten Days That Saved the West*, London, 1991.

Coulondre, Robert, *Von Moskau nach Berlin 1936–1939. Erinnerungen des französischen Botschafters*, Bonn, 1950.

Courcy, John de, *Searchlight on Europe*, London, 1940.

Craig, William, *Enemy at the Gates. The Battle for Stalingrad*, London, 1973.

Creveld, Martin van, *Hitler's Strategy 1940–1941. The Balkan Clue*, Cambridge, 1973.

Crowsen, N. J. (ed.), *Fleet Street, Press Barons, and Politics: the Journals of Collin Brooks, 1932–1940*, Camden Soc., 5th Ser., vol. 11, London, 1998.

Czech, Danuta, *Kalendarium der Ereignisse im Konzentrationslager Auschwitz-Birkenau 1939–1945*, Reinbek bei Hamburg, 1989.

Dahlerus, Birger, *Der letzte Versuch. London-Berlin. Sommer 1939*, Munich, 1948.

Dallin, Alexander, *German Rule in Russia 1941–1945. A Study of Occupation Policies*, (1957), 2nd edn, Basingstoke/London, 1981.

Das Deutsche Reich und der Zweite Weltkrieg, ed. Militärgeschichtliches Forschungsamt, 6 vols. so far published, Stuttgart, 1979–.

'Das Reichsministerium des Innern und die Judengesetzgebung. Aufzeichnungen von Dr Bernhard Lösener', *VfZ*, 9 (1961), 262–311.

Davies, Joseph E., *Mission to Moscow*, New York, 1941.

Davies, Norman, *Europe. A History*, Oxford, 1996.

Delpla, François, *Montoire. Les premiers jours de la collaboration*, Paris, 1996.

—— *La ruse nazi. Dunkerque: 3–4 mai 1940*, Paris, 1997.

—— *Hitler*, Paris, 1999.

D'Este, Carlo, 'Model', in Correlli Barnett (ed.), *Hitler's Generals*, London, 1989, 318–33.

Deutsch, Harold C., *The Conspiracy against Hitler in the Twilight War*, Minneapolis, 1968.

Deutschkron, Inge, *Ich trug den gelben Stern*, (1978), 4th edn, Cologne, 1983.

Deutschland-Berichte der Sozialdemokratischen Partei Deutschlands 1934–1940, 7 vols, Frankfurt am Main, 1980.

Deutschland im zweiten Weltkrieg, ed. Wolfgang Schumann *et al.*, 6 vols., East Berlin, 1974–84.

The Diaries of Sir Alexander Cadogan, 1938–1945, ed. David Dilks, London, 1971.

Dieckmann, Christoph, 'Der Krieg und die Ermordung der litauischen Juden', in Ulrich Herbert (ed.), *Nationalsozialistische Vernichtungspolitik 1939–1945. Neue Forschungen und Kontroversen*, Frankfurt am Main, 1998, 292–329.

Diehl-Thiele, Peter, *Partei und Staat im Dritten Reich. Untersuchungen zum Verhältnis von NSDAP und allgemeiner innerer Staatsverwaltung*, 2nd edn, Munich, 1971.

Das Diensttagebuch des deutschen Generalgouverneurs in Polen 1939–1945, ed. Werner Präg and Wolfgang Jacobmeyer, Stuttgart, 1975.

Der Dienstkalender Heinrich Himmlers 1941/42, ed. Peter Witte *et al.*, Hamburg, 1999.

Dipper, Christoph, 'Der deutsche Widerstand und die Juden', *GG*, 9 (1983), 349–80.

—— 'Der Widerstand und die Juden', in Jürgen Schmädeke and Peter Steinbach (eds.), *Der Widerstand gegen den Nationalsozialismus. Die deutsche Gesellschaft und der Widerstand gegen Hitler*, (1985), Munich, 1986, 598–616.

Dirks, Carl, and Janßen, Karl-Heinz, *Der Krieg der Generäle. Hitler als Werkzeug der Wehrmacht*, Berlin, 1999.

Dobroszycki, Lucjan (ed.), *The Chronicle of the Lodz Ghetto, 1941–1944*, New Haven/London, 1984.

Documenta Occupationis, ed. Instytut Zachodni, vol. v, Poznan, 1952.

Documents Concerning German-Polish Relations and the Outbreak of Hostilities between Great Britain and Germany on September 3, 1939, London, 1939.

Documents on German Foreign Policy, 1918–1945, Series C (1933–1937). The Third Reich: First Phase; Series D (1937–1945), London, 1957–66.

Dodd, William E., and Dodd, Martha (eds.), *Ambassador Dodd's Diary, 1933–1938*, London, 1941.

Doenitz, Karl, *Memoirs. Ten Years and Twenty Days*, (1958), New York, 1997.

Dollmann, Eugen, *Dolmetscher der Diktatoren*, Bayreuth, 1963.

Domarus, Max, *Der Reichstag und die Macht*, Würzburg, 1968.

—— (ed.), *Hitler. Reden und Proklamationen 1932–1945*, 2 vols. in 4 parts, Wiesbaden, 1973.

Dönhoff, Marion Gräfin, *'Um der Ehre willen'. Erinnerungen an die Freunde vom 20. Juli*, (1994), 2nd edn, Berlin, 1996.

Dörr, Margarete, *'Wer die Zeit nicht miterlebt hat . . .'. Frauenerfahrungen im Zweiten Weltkrieg und in den Jahren danach*, 3 vols., Frankfurt/New York, 1998.

Döscher, Hans-Jürgen, *Das Auswärtige Amt im Dritten Reich. Diplomatie im Schatten der 'Endlösung'*, Berlin, 1987.

—— *Reichskristallnacht. Die November–Pogrome 1938*, Frankfurt am Main, 1988.

—— 'Der Tod Ernst vom Raths und die Auslösung der Pogrome am 9. November 1938 – ein

Nachwort zur "Reichskristallnacht" ', *Geschichte in Wissenschaft und Unterricht*, 41 (1990), 619–20.

Douglas, Roy, 'Chamberlain and Appeasement', in Wolfgang J. Mommsen and Lothar Kettenacker (eds.), *The Fascist Challenge and the Policy of Appeasement*, London, 1983, 79–88.

Douglas-Hamilton, James, *Motive for a Mission. The Story behind Hess's Flight to Britain*, London, 1971.

Dülffer, Jost, *Weimar, Hitler und die Marine. Reichspolitik und Flottenbau 1920–1939*, Düsseldorf, 1973.

—— 'Der Beginn des Krieges 1939: Hitler, die innere Krise und das Mächtesystem', *GG*, 2 (1976), 443–70.

—— 'Der Einfluß des Auslandes auf die nationalsozialistische Politik', in Erhard Forndran, Frank Golczewski and Dieter Riesenberger (eds.), *Innen- und Außenpolitik unter nationalsozialistischer Bedrohung*, Opladen, 1977, 295–313.

Dülffer, Jost, Thies, Jochen, and Henke, Josef (eds.), *Hitlers Städte. Baupolitik im Dritten Reich. Eine Dokumentation*, Cologne, 1978.

Ehlers, Dieter, *Technik und Moral einer Verschwörung. Der Aufstand am 20. Juli 1944*, Bonn, 1964.

Eichholtz, Dietrich, 'Der "Generalplan Ost". Uber eine Ausgeburt imperialistischer Denkart und Politik (mit Dokumenten)', *Jahrbuch für Geschichte*, 26 (1982), 217–74.

—— *Geschichte der deutschen Kriegswirtschaft 1939–1945, Bd. I: 1939–1941*, East Berlin, 1984.

—— *Geschichte der deutschen Kriegswirtschaft 1939–1945, Bd II: 1941–1943*, East Berlin, 1985.

Eichholtz, Dietrich, and Pätzold, Kurt (eds.), *Der Weg in den Krieg. Studien zur Geschichte der Vorkriegsjahre (1935/36 bis 1939)*, East Berlin, 1989.

Eichholz, Dietrich, and Schumann, Wolfgang (eds.), *Anatomie des Krieges. Neue Dokumente über die Rolle des deutschen Monopolkapitals bei der Vorbereitung und Durchführung des zweiten Weltkrieges*, East Berlin, 1969.

Eichstädt, Ulrich, *Von Dollfuss zu Hitler. Geschichte des Anschlusses Österreichs 1933–1938*, Wiesbaden, 1955.

Encyclopaedia of the Holocaust, ed. Israel Gutmann, New York, 1990.

'Der Endkampf in Berlin (23.4–2.5.1945)', *Wehrwissenschaftliche Rundschau*, 12/I (1962), 40–52, 111–18, 169–74.

Engel, Gerhard, *Heeresadjutant bei Hitler 1938–1943*, ed. Hildegard von Kotze, Stuttgart, 1974.

Ericksen, Robert P., *Theologians under Hitler*, New Haven/London, 1985.

Erickson, John, *The Road to Berlin*, Boulder, Colorado, 1983.

—— *The Road to Stalingrad. Stalin's War with Germany*, (1975), Phoenix paperback edn, London, 1998.

Eubank, Keith, *Munich*, Norman, Oklahoma, 1963.

Europa unterm Hakenkreuz: Die faschistische Okkupationspolitik in Polen (1939–1945). Dokumentenauswahl und Einleitung von Werner Rohr et al., East Berlin, 1989.

Evans, Richard J., *Rituals of Retribution. Capital Punishment in Germany 1600–1987*, Oxford, 1996.

—— *Rereading German History 1800–1996. From Unification to Reunification*, London, 1997.

Falin, Valentin, *Zweite Front. Die Interessenkonflikte in der Anti-Hitler-Koalition*, Munich, 1995.

Farquharson, J. E., *The Plough and the Swastika. The NSDAP and Agriculture in Germany, 1928–45*, London/Beverly Hills, 1976.

Faschismus-Getto-Massenmord. Dokumentation über Ausrottung und Widerstand der Juden in Polen während des zweiten Weltkrieges, ed. Jüdisches Historisches Institut Warschau, (1961), Frankfurt am Main, n.d.

Feiling, Keith, *The Life of Neville Chamberlain*, London, 1946.

Fellner, Günter, 'Der Novemberpogrom in Westösterreich', in Kurt Schmid and Robert Streibel (eds.), *Der Pogrom 1938. Judenverfolgung in Österreich und Deutschland*, Vienna, 1990, 34–41.

Fest, Joachim C., *The Face of the Third Reich*, Harmondsworth, 1972.

—— *Hitler. Eine Biographie*, Frankfurt am Main/Berlin/Vienna, 1976 edn.

—— *Staatsstreich. Der lange Weg zum 20. Juli*, Berlin, 1994.

—— *Speer. Eine Biographie*, Berlin, 1999.

Fetscher, Iring, *Joseph Goebbels im Berliner Sportpalast 1943. 'Wollt ihr den totalen Krieg?'*, Hamburg, 1998.

Fleischhauer, Ingeborg, *Die Chance des Sonderfriedens. Deutsch-sowjetische Geheimgespräche 1941–1945*, Berlin, 1986.

Fleming, Gerald, *Hitler und die Endlösung. 'Es ist des Führers Wunsch . . .'*, Wiesbaden/Munich, 1982.

—— *Hitler and the Final Solution*, Oxford, 1986.

—— 'The Auschwitz Archives in Moscow', *Jewish Quarterly*, autumn 1991, 9–12.

Foot, M. R. D., *Resistance. European Resistance to Nazism 1940–45*, London, 1976.

Förster, Jürgen, 'The German Army and the Ideological War against the Soviet Union', in Gerhard Hirschfeld (ed.), *The Policies of Genocide. Jews and Soviet Prisoners of War in Nazi Germany*, London, 1986, 15–29.

—— *Stalingrad. Ereignis-Wirkung-Symbol*, Munich/Zurich, 1992.

Förster, Otto-Wilhelm, *Das Befestigungswesen*, Neckargemünd, 1960.

Fox, John P., *Germany and the Far Eastern Crisis, 1931–1938. A Study in Diplomacy and Ideology*, Oxford, 1982.

—— 'German Bureaucrat or Nazified Ideologue? Ambassador Otto Abetz and Hitler's Anti-Jewish Policies 1940–44', in Michael Graham Fry (ed.), *Power, Personalities, and Policies. Essays in Honour of Donald Cameron Watt*, London, 1992, 175–232.

François-Poncet, André, *Souvenirs d'une ambassade à Berlin, Septembre 1931–Octobre 1938*, Paris, 1946.

—— *Als Botschafter im Dritten Reich. Die Erinnerungen des französischen Botschafters in Berlin September 1931 bis Oktober 1938*, Mainz/Berlin, 1980.

Frank, Hans, *Im Angesicht des Galgens. Deutung Hitlers und seiner Zeit auf Grund eigener Erlebnisse und Erkenntnisse*, Munich/Gräfelfing, 1953.

Frei, Norbert (ed.), *Medizin und Gesundheitspolitik in der NS-Zeit*, Munich, 1991.

—— 'Wie modern war der Nationalsozialismus?', *GG*, 19 (1993), 367–87.

Friedlander, Henry, *The Origins of Nazi Genocide. From Euthanasia to the Final Solution*, Chapel Hill/London, 1995.

Friedländer, Saul, *Prelude to Downfall: Hitler and the United States, 1939–1941*, New York, 1967.

—— *Nazi Germany and the Jews. The Years of Persecution, 1933–39*, London, 1997.

Friedrich, Jörg, *Das Gesetz des Krieges. Das deutsche Heer in Rußland 1941–1945. Der Prozeß gegen das Oberkommando der Wehrmacht*, 2nd edn, Munich/Zurich, 1995.

Fröhlich, Elke, 'Hitler und Goebbels im Krisenjahr 1944. Aus den Tagebüchern des Reichspropagandaministers', *VfZ*, 38 (1990), 196–224.

—— 'Der Pfarrer von Mömbris', in Martin Broszat and Elke Fröhlich (eds.), *Bayern in der NS-Zeit, vol. 6, Die Herausforderung des Einzelnen. Geschichten über Widerstand und Verfolgung*, Munich/Vienna, 1983, 52–75.

Funke, Manfred, 'Die deutsch-italienischen Beziehungen: Antibolschewismus und außenpolitische Interessenkonkurrenz als Strukturprinzip der "Achse" ', in Manfred Funke (ed.), *Hitler, Deutschland und die Mächte. Materialien zur Außenpolitik des Dritten Reiches*, Düsseldorf, 1978, 823–46.

—— (ed.), *Hitler, Deutschland und die Mächte. Materialien zur Außenpolitik des Dritten Reiches*, Düsseldorf, 1978.

——— Starker oder schwacher Diktator? Hitlers Herrschaft und die Deutschen. Ein Essay, Düsseldorf, 1989.

Gakenholz, Hermann, 'Reichskanzlei 5. November 1937', in Richard Dietrich and Gerhard Oestreich (eds.), Forschungen zu Staat und Verfassung. Festgabe für Fritz Hartung, Berlin, 1958, 459–74.

Galante, Pierre, and Silianoff, Eugen, Last Witnesses in the Bunker, London, 1989.

Gamm, Hans-Jochen, Der Flüsterwitz im Dritten Reich, Munich, 1972.

Gassert, Philipp, Amerika im Dritten Reich. Ideologie, Propaganda und Volksmeinung 1933–1945, Stuttgart, 1997.

Gay, Peter, Weimar Culture. The Outsider as Insider, London (1968), 1988.

——— My German Question. Growing Up in Nazi Berlin, New Haven/London, 1998.

Gedye, G. E. R., Fallen Bastions. The Central European Tragedy, London, 1939.

Geiss, Josef, Obersalzberg. The History of a Mountain, (1955), Berchtesgaden, n.d.

Gellately, Robert, The Gestapo and German Society. Enforcing Racial Policy, 1933–1945, Oxford, 1990.

Generalfeldmarschall Fedor von Bock. The War Diary, 1939–1945, ed. Klaus Gerbet, Atglen PA, 1996.

Generalfeldmarschall Keitel. Verbrecher oder Offizier? Erinnerungen, Briefe, Dokumente des Chefs OKW, ed. Walter Görlitz, Göttingen/Berlin/Frankfurt am Main, 1961.

Genschel, Helmut, Die Verdrängung der Juden aus der Wirtschaft im Dritten Reich, Göttingen, 1966.

Gerlach, Christian, 'Die Wannsee-Konferenz, das Schicksal der deutschen Juden und Hitlers politische Grundsatzentscheidung, alle Juden Europas zu ermorden', Werkstattgeschichte, 18 (1997), 7–44.

——— 'Failure of Plans for an SS Extermination Camp in Mogilev, Belorussia', Holocaust and Genocide Studies, 11 (1997), 60–78.

——— Krieg, Ernährung, Völkermord. Forschungen zur deutschen Vernichtungspolitik im Zweiten Weltkrieg, Hamburg, 1998.

——— 'Deutsche Wirtschaftsinteressen, Besatzungspolitik und der Mord an den Juden in Weißrußland, 1941–1943', in Ulrich Herbert (ed.), Nationalsozialistische Vernichtungspolitik 1939–1945. Neue Forschungen und Kontroversen, Frankfurt am Main, 1998, 263–91.

The German New Order in Poland, (1941), London, n.d.

Germans against Hitler: July 20, 1944, 5th edn, Bonn, 1969.

Gersdorff, Rudolf-Christoph, Frhr v., Soldat im Untergang. Lebensbilder, Frankfurt etc., 1979.

Geyer, Michael, 'Restorative Elites, German Society, and the Nazi Pursuit of War', in Richard Bessel (ed.), Fascist Italy and Nazi Germany. Comparisons and Contrasts, Cambridge, 1996, 134–64.

Geyl, Jürgen, Austria, Germany, and the Anschluss, 1931–1938, London/New York/Toronto, 1963.

Gibbels, Ellen, 'Hitlers Nervenkrankheit. Eine neurologisch-psychiatrische Studie', VfZ, 42 (1994), 155–220.

Giesler, Hermann, Ein anderer Hitler. Erlebnisse, Gespräche, Reflexionen, Leoni am Starnberger See, 1977.

Gilbert, Martin, Britain and Germany between the Wars, London, 1964.

——— Atlas of the Holocaust, London, 1982.

——— The Holocaust. The Jewish Tragedy, Fontana Paperback edn, London, 1987.

Gisevius, Hans Bernd, Bis zum bittern Ende, Bd. II: Vom Münchener Abkommen zum 20. Juli 1944, 2nd edn, Zurich, 1946.

——— To the Bitter End, Cambridge, Mass., 1947.

——— Bis zum bittern Ende, single vol. edn, Zurich, n.d. [1954?].

Glantz, David M., Soviet Military Deception in the Second World War, London/Totowa NJ, 1989.

—— (ed.), *The Initial Period of War on the Eastern Front, 22 June-August 1941*, London, 1993.

Glantz, David M., and House, Jonathan, *When Titans Clashed. How the Red Army Stopped Hitler*, Kansas, 1995.

Goebbels, Joseph, *Tagebücher 1945. Die letzten Aufzeichnungen*, Hamburg, 1977.

—— *Goebbels-Reden*, 2 Bde. (Bd. 1: 1932–1939; Bd. 2: 1939–1945), ed. Helmut Heiber, Düsseldorf, 1971–2.

Goldhagen, Daniel J., *Hitler's Willing Executioners. Ordinary Germans and the Holocaust*, New York, 1997.

Gollancz, Viktor, *In Darkest Germany. The Record of a Visit*, London, 1947.

Gollwitzer, Helmut, 'Aus der Bekennenden Kirche', in Richard Löwenthal and Patrik von zur Mühlen (eds.), *Widerstand und Verweigerung in Deutschland 1933 bis 1945*, Berlin/Bonn, 1984, 129–39.

Gordon, Sarah, *Hitler, Germans and the 'Jewish Question'*, Princeton, 1984.

Gorodetsky, Gabriel, 'Churchill's Warning to Stalin. A Reappraisal', *Historical Journal*, 29 (1986), 979–80.

—— 'Stalin und Hitlers Angriff auf die Sowjetunion. Eine Auseinandersetzung mit der Legende vom deutschen Praventivschlag', *VfZ*, 37 (1989), 645–72.

Görtz, Adolf, *Stichwort: Front. Tagebuch eines jungen Deutschen 1938–1942*, 2nd edn, Leipzig, 1987.

Goschen, Seev, 'Eichmann und die Nisko-Aktion im Oktober 1939', *VfZ*, 29 (1981), 74–96.

Graml, Hermann, *Der 9. November 1938. 'Reichskristallnacht'*, Beilage zur Wochenzeitung 'Das Parlament', No. 45, 11 Nov. 1953, Schriftenreihe der Bundeszentrale für Heimatdienst, 6th edn, Bonn, 1958.

—— 'Resistance Thinking on Foreign Policy', in Hermann Graml et al., *The German Resistance to Hitler*, (1966), London, 1970, 1–54.

—— *Reichskristallnacht. Antisemitismus und Judenverfolgung im Dritten Reich*, Munich, 1988.

—— *Europas Weg in den Krieg. Hitler und die Mächte 1939*, Munich, 1990.

Graml, Hermann, et al., *The German Resistance to Hitler*, (1966), London, 1970.

Gregor, Neil, *Daimler-Benz in the Third Reich*, New Haven/London, 1998.

Griffiths, Richard, *Fellow Travellers of the Right. British Enthusiasts for Nazi Germany, 1933–9*, London, 1980.

Gritzbach, Erich, *Hermann Göring. Werk und Mensch*, Munich, 1938.

Groehler, Olaf, *Das Ende der Reichskanzlei*, East Berlin, 1974.

—— *Die Neue Reichskanzlei. Das Ende*, Berlin, 1995.

Groscurth, Helmut, *Tagebücher eines Abwehroffiziers 1938–1940*, ed. Helmut Krausnick and Harold C. Deutsch, Stuttgart, 1970.

Das Große Lexikon des Zweiten Weltkriegs, ed. Christian Zentner and Friedemann Bedurftig, Munich, 1988.

Gruchmann, Lothar (ed.), *Autobiographie eines Attentäters. Johann Georg Elser. Aussage zum Sprengstoffanschlag im Bürgerbräukeller, München, am 8. November 1939*, Stuttgart, 1970.

—— 'Euthanasie und Justiz im Dritten Reich', *VfZ*, 20 (1972), 235–79.

—— 'Die "Reichsregierung" im Führerstaat. Stellung und Funktion des Kabinetts im nationalsozialistischen Herrschaftssystem', in Günter Doeker and Winfried Steffani (eds.), *Klassenjustiz und Pluralismus*, Hamburg, 1973, 187–223.

—— *Der Zweite Weltkrieg. Kriegführung und Politik*, (1967), 4th edn, Munich, 1975.

—— *Justiz im Dritten Reich 1933–1940. Anpassung und Unterwerfung in der Ära Gürtner*, Munich, 1990.

Guderian, Heinz, *Panzer Leader*, Da Capo Press edn, New York, (1952), 1996.

Gunther, Joachim, *Das letzte Jahr. Mein Tagebuch 1944/45*, Hamburg, 1948.

Gun, Nerin E., *Eva Braun-Hitler. Leben und Schicksal*, Velbert/Kettwig, 1968.

Gurfein, M. I., and Janowitz, Morris, 'Trends in Wehrmacht Morale', *Public Opinion Quarterly*, 10 (1946), 78–84.

Gutman, Yisrael, *The Jews of Warsaw 1939–1943. Ghetto, Underground, Revolt*, London, 1982.

Hachmeister, Lutz, *Der Gegenforscher. Die Karriere des SS-Führers Alfred Six*, Munich, 1998.

Häufele, Günther, 'Zwangsumsiedlungen in Polen 1939–1941. Zum Vergleich sowjetischer und deutscher Besatzungspolitik', in Dittmar Dahlmann and Gerhard Hirschfeld (eds.), *Lager, Zwangsarbeit, Vertreibung und Deportation. Dimensionen der Massenverbrechen in der Sowjetunion und in Deutschland 1933 bis 1954*, Essen, 1999, 515–33.

Haffner, Sebastian, *Anmerkungen zu Hitler*, Munich, 1978.

Halder, Franz, *Hitler als Feldherr. Der ehemalige Chef des Generalstabes berichtet die Wahrheit*, Munich, 1949.

—— *Kriegstagebuch. Tägliche Aufzeichnungen des Chefs des Generalstabes des Heeres 1939–1942, Bd. I. Vom Polenfeldzug bis zum Ende der Westoffensive (14.8.1939–30.6.1940)*, ed. Hans-Adolf Jacobsen, Stuttgart, 1962.

—— *Kriegstagebuch. Tägliche Aufzeichnungen des Chefs des Generalstabes des Heeres 1939–1942, Bd. II. Von der geplanten Landung in England bis zum Beginn des Ostfeldzuges (1.7.1940–21.6.1941)*, ed. Hans-Adolf Jacobsen, Stuttgart, 1963.

—— *Kriegstagebuch. Tägliche Aufzeichnungen des Chefs des Generalstabes des Heeres 1939–1942, Bd. III: Der Rußlandfeldzug bis zum Marsch auf Stalingrad (22.6.1941–24.9.1942)*, ed. Hans-Adolf Jacobsen, Stuttgart, 1964.

The Halder War Diary, 1939–1942, ed. Charles Burdick and Hans-Adolf Jacobsen, London, 1988, abridged English translation.

Halifax, Earl of, *Fulness of Days*, London, 1957.

Hallgarten, George W. F., and Radkau, Joachim, *Deutsche Industrie und Politik von Bismarck bis in die Gegenwart*, Reinbek bei Hamburg, 1981.

Hamerow, Theodore S., *On the Road to the Wolf's Lair. German Resistance to Hitler*, Cambridge, Mass./London, 1997.

Hancock, Eleanor, *National Socialist Leadership and Total War 1941–45*, New York, 1991.

Hanisch, Ernst, *Nationalsozialistische Herrschaft in der Provinz. Salzburg im Dritten Reich*, Salzburg, 1983.

—— *Der Obersalzberg: das Kehlsteinhaus und Adolf Hitler*, Berchtesgaden, 1995.

Hanke, Peter, *Zur Geschichte der Juden in München zwischen 1933 und 1945*, Munich, 1967.

Hansen, Reimer, 'Der ungeklärte Fall Todt', *Geschichte in Wissenschaft und Unterricht*, 18 (1967), 602–5.

—— 'Ribbentrops Friedensfühler im Frühjahr 1945', *Geschichte in Wissenschaft und Unterricht*, 18 (1967), 716–30.

Harlan, Veit, *Im Schatten meiner Filme. Selbstbiographie*, Gütersloh, 1966.

Harris, Robert, *Selling Hitler*, London, 1986.

Harrison, E. D. R., 'The Nazi Dissolution of the Monasteries: a Case Study', *English Historical Review*, 109 (1994), 323–55.

—— 'Der "Alte Kämpfer" Graf Helldorf im Widerstand', *VfZ*, 45 (1997), 385–423.

—— '"... wir wurden schon viel zu oft hereingelegt". Mai 1941: Rudolf Heß in englischer Sicht', unpublished essay.

Hartmann, Christian, *Halder. Generalstabschef Hitlers 1938–1942*, Paderborn, 1991.

Hartmann, Christian, and Sergej Slutsch, 'Franz Halder und die Kriegsvorbereitungen im Frühjahr 1939. Eine Ansprache des Generalstabschefs des Heeres', *VfZ*, 45 (1997), 467–95.

Hassell, Ulrich von, *Die Hassell-Tagebücher 1938–1944. Aufzeichnungen vom Andern Deutschland*, ed. Friedrich Freiherr Hiller von Gaertringen, Berlin, 1988.

Haufele, 'Zwangsumsiedlungen in Polen 1939–1941. Zum Vergleich sowjetischer und deutscher

Besatzungspolitik', in Dittmar Dahlmann and Gerhard Hirschfeld (eds.), *Lager, Zwangsarbeit, Vertreibung und Deportation. Dimensionen der Massenverbrechen in der Sowjetunion und in Deutschland 1933 bis 1945*, Essen, 1999.

Hauner, Milan, 'Did Hitler want a World Dominion?', *JCH*, 13 (1978), 15–32.

—— *Hitler. A Chronology of his Life and Time*, London, 1983.

Hayes, Peter, *Industry and Ideology. IG Farben in the Nazi Era*, Cambridge, 1987.

Heer, Hannes, 'Die Logik des Vernichtungskriegs. Wehrmacht und Partisanenkampf', in Hannes Heer and Klaus Naumann (eds.), *Vernichtungskrieg. Verbrechen der Wehrmacht 1941 bis 1944*, Hamburg, 1995, 104–38.

—— 'Killing Fields: the Wehrmacht and the Holocaust in Belorussia, 1941–1942', *Holocaust and Genocide Studies*, 11 (1997), 79–101.

Heiber, Helmut, 'Der Fall Grünspan', *VfZ*, 5 (1957), 134–72.

—— (ed.), 'Der Generalplan Ost', *VfZ*, 6 (1958), 281–325.

—— *Joseph Goebbels*, Berlin, 1962.

Heifermann, Ronald, *World War II*, London, 1973.

Heilmann, H. D., 'Aus dem Kriegstagebuch des Diplomaten Otto Bräutigam', in Götz Aly (ed.), *Biedermann und Schreibtischtäter. Materialien zur deutschen Täter-Biographie*, 2nd edn, Berlin, 1989, 123–87.

Heinemann, John L., *Hitler's First Foreign Minister. Constantin Freiherr von Neurath, Diplomat and Statesman*, Berkeley/Los Angeles/London, 1979.

Heinemann, Ulrich, *Ein konservativer Rebell. Fritz-Dietlof von der Schulenberg und der 20. Juli*, Berlin, 1990.

—— 'Arbeit am Mythos. Neuere Literatur zum bürgerlich-aristokratischen Widerstand gegen Hitler und zum 20. Juli 1944 (Teil I)', *GG*, 21 (1995), 111–39.

Heinemann, Ulrich, and Michael Kruger-Charlé, 'Arbeit am Mythos. Der 20. Juli 1944 in Publizistik und wissenschaftlicher Literatur des Jubiläumsjahres 1994 (Teil II)', *GG*, 23 (1997), 475–501.

Hellfeld, Matthias von, *Edelweißpiraten in Köln*, 2nd edn, Cologne, 1983.

Henderson, Nevile, *Failure of a Mission. Berlin, 1937–1939*, London, 1940.

Henke, Josef, *England in Hitlers politischem Kalkül: 1935–1939*, Boppard am Rhein, 1973.

—— 'Hitler und England Mitte August 1939. Ein Dokument zur Rolle Fritz Hesses in den deutsch-britischen Beziehungen am Vorabend des Zweiten Weltkrieges', *VfZ*, 21 (1973), 231–42.

—— 'Hitlers England-Konzeption: Formulierung und Realisierungsversuche', in Manfred Funke (ed.), *Hitler, Deutschland und die Mächte. Materialien zur Außenpolitik des Dritten Reiches*, Düsseldorf, 1978, 584–603.

Herbert, Ulrich, *Best. Biographische Studien über Radikalismus, Waltanschanung und Vernunft 1903–1989*, Bonn, 1996.

—— *Fremdarbeiter. Politik und Praxis des 'Ausländer-Einsatzes' in der Kriegswirtschaft des Dritten Reiches*, Berlin/Bonn, 1985.

—— 'Good Times, Bad Times: Memories of the Third Reich', in Richard Bessel (ed.), *Life in the Third Reich*, Oxford, 1987, 97–110.

—— ' "Generation der Sachlichkeit". Die völkische Studentenbewegung der frühen zwanziger Jahre in Deutschland', in Frank Bajohr, Werner Johe and Uwe Lohalm (eds.), *Zivilisation und Barbarei*, Hamburg, 1991, 115–44.

—— 'Labour and Extermination: Economic Interest and the Primacy of Weltanschauung in National Socialism', *Past and Present*, 138 (1993), 144–95.

—— 'Die deutsche Besatzungspolitik in Dänemark im 2. Weltkrieg und die Rettung der dänischen Juden', *Tel Aviver Jahrbuch für deutsche Geschichte*, 23 (1994), 93–114.

—— (ed.), *Nationalsozialistische Vernichtungspolitik 1939–1945. Neue Forschungen und Kontroversen*, Frankfurt am Main, 1998.

—— 'Die deutsche Militarverwaltung in Paris und die Deportation der französischen Juden', in

Ulrich Herbert (ed.), *Nationalsozialistische Vernichtungspolitik 1939–1945. Neue Forschungen und Kontroversen*, Frankfurt am Main, 1998, 170–208.

Herbert, Ulrich, Karin Orth and Christoph Dieckmann (eds.), *Die nationalsozialistischen Konzentrationslager. Entwicklung und Struktur*, 2 vols., Göttingen, 1998.

Herbst, Ludolf, 'Die Krise des nationalsozialistischen Regimes am Vorabend des Zweiten Weltkrieges und die forcierte Aufrüstung. Eine Kritik', *VfZ*, 26 (1978), 347–92.

—— *Der Totale Krieg und die Ordnung der Wirtschaft. Die Kriegswirtschaft im Spannungsfeld von Politik, Ideologie und Propaganda 1939–1945*, Stuttgart, 1982.

—— *Das nationalsozialistische Deutschland 1933–1945*, Frankfurt am Main, 1996.

Herzstein, Robert Edward, *The War that Hitler Won. The Most Infamous Propaganda Campaign in History*, London, 1979.

Heß, Ilse, *England-Nürnberg-Spandau. Ein Schicksal in Bildern*, Leoni am Starnberger See, 1952.

Hesse, Fritz, *Das Spiel um Deutschland*, Munich, 1953.

Heston, Leonard L., and Heston, Renate, *The Medical Casebook of Adolf Hitler*, London, 1979.

Heusinger, Adolf, *Befehl im Widerstreit. Schicksalsstunden der deutschen Armee 1923–1945*, Tübingen/Stuttgart, 1950.

Heyl, John D., 'The Construction of the Westwall, 1938: An Exemplar for National Socialist Policymaking', *Central European History*, 14 (1981), 63–78.

Hilberg, Raul, *The Destruction of the European Jews*, Viewpoints edn, New York, (1961), 1973.

—— 'Die Aktion Reinhard', in Eberhard Jäckel and Jürgen Rohwer (eds.), *Der Mord an den Juden im Zweiten Weltkrieg. Entschlußbildung und Verwirklichung*, Stuttgart, 1985, 125–36.

—— *Die Vernichtung der europäischen Juden*, revised transl. edn, Frankfurt am Main, 1990.

Hildebrand, Klaus, *Vom Reich zum Weltreich. Hitler, NSDAP und koloniale Frage 1919–1945*, Munich, 1969.

—— *Deutsche Außenpolitik 1933–1945. Kalkül oder Dogma?*, Stuttgart etc., 1971.

—— *The Foreign Policy of the Third Reich*, London, 1973.

—— *Das vergangene Reich. Deutsche Außenpolitik von Bismarck bis Hitler 1871–1945*, Stuttgart, 1995.

Hilger, Gustav, and Meyer, Holger G., *The Incompatible Allies: A Memoir-History of German-Soviet Relations 1918–1941*, New York, 1953.

Hill, Leonidas E. (ed.), *Die Weizsäcker-Papiere 1933–1950*, Frankfurt am Main/Berlin/Vienna, 1974.

—— 'Alternative Politik des Auswärtigen Amtes bis zum 1. September 1939', in Jürgen Schmädeke and Peter Steinbach (eds.), *Der Widerstand gegen den Nationalsozialismus. Die deutsche Gesellschaft und der Widerstand gegen Hitler*, Munich/Zurich, 1985, 664–90.

Hillgruber, Andreas, 'Der Faktor Amerika in Hitlers Strategie 1938–1941', *Aus Politik und Zeitgeschichte Beilage zur Wochenzeitung 'Das Parlament'*, B19/66 (11 May 1966), 3–21.

—— 'Japan und der Fall "Barbarossa". Japanische Dokumente zu den Gesprächen Hitlers und Ribbentrops mit Botschafter Oshima von Februar bis Juni 1941', *Wehrwissenschaftliche Rundschau*, 18 (1968), 312–36.

—— (ed.), *Staatsmänner und Diplomaten bei Hitler. Vertrauliche Aufzeichnungen 1939–1941*, Munich, 1969.

—— (ed.), *Staatsmänner und Diplomaten bei Hitler. Zweiter Teil. Vertrauliche Aufzeichnungen über Unterredungen mit Vertretern des Auslandes 1942–1944*, Frankfurt am Main, 1970.

—— 'Hitler und die USA', in Otmar Franz (ed.), *Europas Mitte*, Göttingen/Zurich, 1987, 125–44.

—— *Hitlers Strategie. Politik und Kriegführung 1940–1941*, (1965), 3rd edn, Bonn, 1993.

Hillgruber, Andreas, and Förster, Jürgen (eds.), 'Zwei neue Aufzeichnungen über "Führer-Besprechungen" aus dem Jahre 1942', *Militärgeschichtliche Mitteilungen*, 11 (1972), 109–26.

Hippler, Fritz, *Die Verstrickung*, Düsseldorf, 1981.

Hitler, Adolf, *Mein Kampf*, 876–880th reprint, Munich, 1943.

—— *Mein Kampf*, London, 1969, English transl. by Ralph Manheim, with an introduction by D. C. Watt.

Hitler. *Reden, Schriften, Anordnungen: Februar 1925 bis Januar 1933*, ed. Institut für Zeitgeschichte, 5 vols. in 12 parts, Munich/London/New York/Paris, 1992–8.

'Hitlers Höllenfahrt', *Der Spiegel*, 14/1995, 170–87, 15/1995, 172–86.

Hitlers Lagebesprechungen im Führerhauptquartier. Die Protokollfragmente seiner militärischen Konferenzen 1942–1945, ed. Helmut Heiber, Stuttgart 1962.

Hitlers politisches Testament. Die Bormann Diktate vom Februar und April 1945, mit einem Essay von Hugh R. Trevor-Roper und einem Nachwort von André François-Poncet, Hamburg, 1981.

Hoare, Samuel, *Ambassador on Special Mission*, London, 1946.

Hoch, Anton, 'Das Attentat auf Hitler im Münchener Burgerbräukeller 1939', *VfZ*, 17 (1969), 383–413.

Hoch, Anton, and Weiß, Hermann, 'Die Erinnerungen des Generalobersten Wilhelm Adam', in Wolfgang Benz (ed.), *Miscellanea: Festschrift für Helmut Krausnick zum 75. Geburtstag*, Stuttgart, 1980, 32–62.

Hockerts, Hans Günter, *Die Sittlichkeitsprozesse gegen katholische Ordensangehörige und Priester 1936/1937*, Mainz, 1971.

Hoemberg, Elisabeth, *Thy People, My People*, London, 1950.

Hoensch, Jörg K., *Geschichte Polens*, Stuttgart, 1983.

Hofer, Walther, *Die Entfesselung des Zweiten Weltkrieges*, Frankfurt am Main, 1964.

—— (ed.), *Der Nationalsozialismus. Dokumente 1933–1945*, Frankfurt am Main (1957), 1974.

Hoffmann, Heinrich, *Hitler Was My Friend*, London, 1955.

Hoffmann, Peter, 'Maurice Bavaud's Attempt to Assassinate Hitler in 1938', in George L. Mosse (ed.), *Police Forces in History*, Beverly Hills, 1975, 173–204.

—— 'Hitler's Personal Security', in George L. Mosse (ed.), *Police Forces in History*, Beverly Hills, 1975, 151–71.

—— *Hitler's Personal Security*, London, 1979.

—— 'Generaloberst Ludwig Becks militärpolitisches Denken', *HZ*, 235 (1982), 101–21.

—— *Widerstand-Staatsstreich-Attentat. Der Kampf der Opposition gegen Hitler*, 4th edn, Munich/Zurich (1969), 1985.

—— 'Motive', in Jurgen Schmädeke and Peter Steinbach (eds.), *Der Widerstand gegen den Nationalsozialismus. Die deutsche Gesellschaft und der Widerstand gegen Hitler*, Munich/Zurich, 1985, 1089–96.

—— *Stauffenberg. A Family History, 1905–1944*, Cambridge, 1995.

Höhne, Heinz, *The Order of the Death's Head. The Story of Hitler's SS*, London, 1969.

—— *Canaris – Patriot im Zwielicht*, Munich, 1976.

—— 'Canaris und die Abwehr zwischen Anpassung und Opposition', in Jürgen Schmädeke and Peter Steinbach (eds.), *Der Widerstand gegen den Nationalsozialismus. Die deutsche Gesellschaft und der Widerstand gegen Hitler*, (1985), Munich, 1986, 405–16.

—— *Die Zeit der Illusionen. Hitler und die Anfänge des 3. Reiches 1933 bis 1936*, Düsseldorf/Vienna/New York, 1991.

Hölsken, Heinz Dieter, *Die V-Waffen. Entstehung-Propaganda-Kriegseinsatz*, Stuttgart, 1984.

Honolka, Bert, *Die Kreuzelschreiber. Ärtze ohne Gewissen: Euthanasie im Dritten Reich*, Hamburg, 1961.

Hornshøj-Møller, Stig, *'Der ewige Jude'. Quellenkritische Analyse eines antisemitischen Propagandafilms*, Institut für den Wissenschaftlichen Film, Göttingen, 1995.

Hoßbach, Friedrich, *Zwischen Wehrmacht und Hitler 1934–1938*, Wolfenbüttel/Hannover, 1949.

Housden, Martyn, 'Hans Frank – Empire Builder in the East, 1939–41', *European History Quarterly*, 24 (1994), 367–93.

Hubatsch, Walther, 'Weserübung'. Die deutsche Besetzung von Dänemark und Norwegen 1940, 2nd edn, Göttingen/Berlin/Frankfurt, 1960.

—— (ed.), Hitlers Weisungen für die Kriegführung 1939–1945. Dokumente des Oberkommandos der Wehrmacht, (1962), Munich, 1965.

Huber, Heinrich (ed.), Dokumente einer christlichen Widerstandsbewegung. Gegen die Entfernung der Kruzifixe aus den Schulen 1941, Munich, 1948.

Hüttenberger, Peter, Die Gauleiter. Studie zum Wandel des Machtgefüges in der NSDAP, Stuttgart, 1969.

—— 'Nationalsozialistische Polykratie', GG, 2 (1976), 417–42.

—— 'Vorüberlegungen zum "Widerstandsbegriff"', in Jürgen Kocka (ed.), Theorien in der Praxis des Historikers, Göttingen, 1977, 117–34.

Hutton, J. Bernard, Hess: the Man and his Mission, London, 1970.

Institut für Zeitgeschichte (ed.), Wissenschaftsfreiheit und ihre rechtlichen Schranken. Ein Kolloquium, Munich/Vienna, 1978.

Irving, David, Hitler's War, London etc., 1977.

—— The War Path. Hitler's Germany, 1933–9, London, 1978.

—— Rudolf Heß – ein gescheiterter Friedensbote? Die Wahrheit über die unbekannten Jahre 1941–1945, Graz/Stuttgart, 1987.

—— Führer und Reichskanzler. Adolf Hitler 1933–1945, Munich/Berlin, 1989.

—— Göring. A Biography, London, 1989.

—— The Secret Diaries of Hitler's Doctor, paperback edn, London (1983), 1990.

—— (ed.), Der unbekannte Dr. Goebbels. Die geheimen Tagebücher 1938, London, 1995.

—— Goebbels: Mastermind of the Third Reich, London, 1996.

Jäckel, Eberhard, Frankreich in Hitlers Europa. Die deutsche Frankreichpolitik im Zweiten Weltkrieg, Stuttgart, 1966.

—— 'Hitler und der Mord an europäischen Juden', in Peter Märthesheimer and Ivo Frenzel (eds.), Im Kreuzfeuer: Der Fernsehfilm Holocaust. Eine Nation ist betroffen, Frankfurt am Main, 1979, 151–62.

—— 'Die deutsche Kriegserklärung an die Vereinigten Staaten von 1941', in Friedrich J. Kroneck and Thomas Oppermann (eds.), Im Dienste Deutschlands und des Rechts: Festschrift für Wilhelm G. Grewe, Baden-Baden, 1981, 117–37.

—— Hitler in History, Hannover/London, 1984.

—— Hitlers Herrschaft. Vollzug einer Weltanschauung, (1986), Stuttgart, 1988.

—— 'Hitlers doppeltes Kernstück', in Roland G. Foerster (ed.), 'Unternehmen Barbarossa'. Zum historischen Ort der deutsch-sowjetischen Beziehungen von 1933 bis Herbst 1941, Munich, 1993, 14–22.

—— 'From Barbarossa to Wannsee. The Role of Reinhard Heydrich', unpublished essay.

Jäckel, Eberhard, and Axel Kuhn (eds.), Hitler. Sämtliche Aufzeichnungen 1905–1924, Stuttgart, 1980.

Jacobsen, Hans-Adolf, 'Hitlers Gedanken zur Kriegführung im Westen', Wehrwissenschaftliche Rundschau, 5 (1955), 433–46.

—— Dokumente zur Vorgeschichte des Westfeldzuges 1939–1940, Göttingen/Berlin/Frankfurt, 1956.

—— Fall Gelb. Der Kampf um den deutschen Operationsplan zur Westoffensive 1930, Wiesbaden, 1957.

—— Dünkirchen. Ein Beitrag zur Geschichte des Westfeldzuges 1940, Neckargemünd, 1958.

—— (ed.), Dokumente zum Westfeldzug 1940, Göttingen/Berlin/Frankfurt, 1960.

—— 1939–1945. Der Zweite Weltkrieg in Chronik und Dokumenten, (1959), 5th edn, Darmstadt, 1961.

—— Nationalsozialistische Außenpolitik 1933–1938, Frankfurt am Main/Berlin, 1968.

—— *Der Weg zur Teilung der Welt, Politik und Strategie von 1939–1945*, Koblenz/Bonn, 1977.

—— 'Zur Struktur der NS-Außenpolitik 1933–1945', in Manfred Funke (ed.), *Hitler, Deutschland und die Mächte. Materialien zur Außenpolitik des Dritten Reiches*, Düsseldorf, 1978, 137–85.

—— (ed.), *Spiegelbild einer Verschwörung. Die Opposition gegen Hitler und der Staatsstreich vom 20. Juli 1944 in der SD-Berichterstattung. Geheime Dokumente aus dem ehemaligen Reichssicherheitshauptamt*, 2 vols., Stuttgart, 1984.

Jacobsen, Hans-Adolf, and Rohwer, Jürgen, *Entscheidungsschlachten des Zweiten Weltkrieges*, Frankfurt am Main, 1960.

Jahrbuch der öffentlichen Meinung 1947–1955, ed. Elisabeth Noelle and Erich Peter Neumann, Allensbach, 1956.

James, Harold, 'Die Deutsche Bank und die Diktatur', in Lothar Gall, *et al.* (ed.), *Die Deutsche Bank 1870–1995*, Munich, 1995, 315–408.

Jansen, Christian, and Weckbecker, Arno, *Der 'Volksdeutsche Selbstschutz' in Polen 1939/40*, Munich, 1992.

—— 'Eine Miliz im "Weltanschauungskrieg": der "Volksdeutsche Selbstschutz in Polen 1939/40', in Wolfgang Michalka (ed.), *Der Zweite Weltkrieg. Analysen-Grundzüge-Forschungsbilanz*, Munich/Zurich, 1989, 482–500.

Janßen, Karl-Heinz, 'Politische und militärische Zielvorstellungen der Wehrmachtführung', in Rolf-Dieter Müller and Hans-Erich Volkmann (eds.), *Die Wehrmacht: Mythos und Realität*, Munich, 1999, 75–84.

Janßen, Karl-Heinz, and Tobias, Fritz, *Der Sturz der Generäle. Hitler und die Blomberg-Fritsch-Krise 1938*, Munich, 1994.

Jersak, Tobias, 'Die Interaktion von Kriegsverlauf und Judenvernichtung', *HZ*, 268 (1999), 311–49.

Jetzinger, Franz, *Hitlers Jugend*, Vienna, 1956.

Joachimsthaler, Anton, *The Last Days of Hitler. The Legends, the Evidence, the Truth*, London, 1996.

—— *Hitlers Ende. Legenden und Dokumente*, (1994), Augsburg, 1999.

Johr, Barbara, 'Die Ereignisse in Zahlen', in Helke Sander and Barbara Johr (eds.), *Befreier und Befreite. Krieg, Vergewaltigungen, Kinder*, Munich, 1992, 46–72.

Jones, Thomas, *A Diary With Letters, 1931–1950*, Oxford, 1954.

Jordan, Rudolf, *Erlebt und erlitten. Weg eines Gauleiters von München bis Moskau*, Leoni am Starnberger See, 1971.

Jukes, Geoffrey, *Hitler's Stalingrad Decisions*, Berkeley/Los Angeles/London, 1985.

Justiz und NS-Verbrechen, Sammlung deutscher Strafurteile wegen nationalsozialistischer Tötungsverbrechen 1945–1966, vol. 20, Amsterdam, 1979.

[Kaiser, Hermann], 'Neue mitteilungen zur Vorgeschichte des 20. Juli', *Die Wandlung*, 1 (1945/46), 530–34, extracts from Kaiser's diary.

Kardorff, Ursula von, *Berliner Aufzeichnungen 1942–1945*, (1976), 2nd edn, Munich, 1982.

Kater, Michael H., *The Nazi Party. A Social Profile of Members and Leaders 1919–1945*, Oxford, 1983.

—— *Doctors under Hitler*, Chapel Hill, London, 1989.

—— *Different Drummers: Jazz in the Culture of Nazi Germany*, New York/Oxford, 1992.

—— *The Twisted Muse. Musicians and their Music in the Third Reich*, New York/Oxford, 1997.

Kehrig, Manfred, *Stalingrad. Analyse und Dokumentation einer Schlacht*, Stuttgart, 1974.

—— 'Die 6. Armee im Kessel von Stalingrad', in Jürgen Förster (ed.), *Stalingrad. Ereignis-Wirkung-Symbol*, Munich/Zurich, 1992, 76–110.

Kehrl, Hans, *Krisenmanager im Dritten Reich*, Düsseldorf, 1973.

Kelley, Douglas M., *22 Cells in Nuremberg*, (1947), New York, 1961.

Kempka, Erich, *Die letzten Tage mit Adolf Hitler*, Preußisch Oldendorf, 1975.

Kempner, Robert M. W., *Das Dritte Reich im Kreuzverhör. Aus den Vernehmungsprotokollen des Anklägers*, Düsseldorf, 1984.

Kershaw, Ian, 'Antisemitismus und Volksmeinung. Reaktionen auf die Judenverfolgung', in Martin Broszat and Elke Fröhlich (eds.), *Bayern in der NS-Zeit, Bd. II: Herrschaft und Gesellschaft im Konflikt*, Munich, 1979, 281–348.

—— *Popular Opinion and Political Dissent in the Third Reich: Bavaria, 1933–1945*, Oxford, 1983.

—— 'German Popular Opinion and the "Jewish Question", 1939–1943: Some Further Reflections', in Arnold Paucker (ed.), *Die Juden im nationalsozialistischen Deutschland*, Tübingen, 1986, 366–86.

—— 'Indifferenz des Gewissens. Die deutsche Bevölkerung und die "Reichskristallnacht" ', *Blätter für deutsche und internationale Politik*, 11 (1988), 1319–30.

—— *The 'Hitler Myth'. Image and Reality in the Third Reich*, paperback edn, Oxford, (1987), 1989.

—— 'Improvised Genocide? The Emergence of the "Final Solution" in the "Warthegau" ', *Transactions of the Royal Historical Society*, 6th Series, 2 (1992), 51–78.

—— 'Arthur Greiser – Ein Motor der "Endlösung" ', in Ronald Smelser, Enrico Syring and Rainer Zitelmann (eds.), *Die braune Elite II*, Darmstadt, 1993, 116–27.

—— 'Der Überfall auf Polen und die öffentliche Meinung in Deutschland', in Ernst Willi Hansen, Gerhard Schreiber and Bernd Wenger (eds.), *Politischer Wandel, organisierte Gewalt und nationale Sicherheit. Beiträge zur neueren Geschichte Deutschlands und Frankreichs. Festschrift für Klaus-Jürgen Müller*, Munich, 1995, 237–50.

—— *The Nazi Dictatorship. Problems and Perspectives of Interpretation*, (1985), 4th edn, London, 2000.

Kershaw, Ian, and Lewin, Moshe (eds.), *Stalinism and Nazism: Dictatorships in Comparison*, Cambridge, 1997.

Kersten, Felix, *The Kersten Memoirs 1940–1945*, London, 1956.

[Kesselring, Albert], *The Memoirs of Field-Marshal Kesselring*, (1953), Greenhill Books edn, London, 1997.

Kettenacker, Lothar (ed.), *Das 'Andere Deutschland' im Zweiten Weltkrieg. Emigration und Widerstand in internationaler Perspektive*, Stuttgart, 1977.

—— 'Die britische Haltung zum deutschen Widerstand während des Zweiten Weltkriegs', in Lothar Kettenacker (ed.), *Das 'Andere Deutschland' im Zweiten Weltkrieg. Emigration und Widerstand in internationaler Perspektive*, Stuttgart, 1977, 49–76.

Kielmansegg, Peter Graf, 'Die militärisch-politische Tragweite der Hoßbach-Besprechung', *VfZ*, 8 (1960), 268–75.

Kirk, Tim, *Nazism and the Working Class in Austria. Industrial Unrest and Political Dissent in the National Community*, Cambridge, 1996.

Kirwin, Gerald, 'Waiting for Retaliation. A Study in Nazi Propaganda Behaviour and German Civilian Morale', *JCH*, 16 (1981), 565–83.

—— 'Allied Bombing and Nazi Domestic Propaganda', *European History Quarterly*, 15 (1985), 341–62.

Klamper, Elisabeth, 'Der "Anschlußpogrom" ', in Kurt Schmid and Robert Streibel (eds.), *Der Pogrom 1938. Judenverfolgung in Österreich und Deutschland*, Vienna, 1990, 25–33.

Klee, Ernst, *'Euthanasie' im NS-Staat. Die 'Vernichtung lebensunwerten Lebens'*, Frankfurt am Main, 1983.

—— (ed.), *Dokumente zur 'Euthanasie'*, Frankfurt am Main, 1985.

—— *Was sie taten – Was sie wurden. Ärzte, Juristen und andere Beteiligte am Kranken- oder Judenmord*, Frankfurt am Main, 1986.

Klee, Ernst, Dreßen, Willi, and Rieß, Volker (eds.), *'Schöne Zeiten'. Judenmord aus der Sicht der Täter und Gaffer*, Frankfurt am Main, 1988.

Klee, Ernst, and Dreßen, Willi (eds.), *'Gott mit uns'. Der deutsche Vernichtungskrieg im Osten 1939–1945*, Frankfurt am Main, 1989.

Klee, Karl, *Das Unternehmen 'Seelöwe'*, Göttingen/Berlin/Frankfurt, 1958.

—— (ed.), *Dokumente zum Unternehmen 'Seelöwe'. Die geplante deutsche Landung in England 1940*, Göttingen/Berlin/Frankfurt, 1959.

Kleist, Peter, *Zwischen Hitler und Stalin*, Bonn, 1950.

—— *Die europäische Tragödie*, Göttingen, 1961.

Klemperer, Klemens von, *German Resistance against Hitler. The Search for Allies Abroad, 1938–1945*, Oxford, 1992.

Klemperer, Victor, *Ich will Zeugnis ablegen bis zum letzten. Tagebücher 1933–1941*, ed. Walter Nowojski and Hadwig Klemperer, (1995), 10th edn, 2 vols., Darmstadt, 1998.

Kleßmann, Christoph, 'Der Generalgouverneur Hans Frank', *VfZ*, 19 (1971), 245–60.

—— 'Hans Frank – Parteijurist und Generalgouverneur in Polen', in Ronald Smelser and Rainer Zitelmann (eds.), *Die braune Elite*, Darmstadt, 1989, 41–51.

Klink, Ernst, *Das Gesetz des Handelns: Die Operation 'Zitadelle' 1943*, Stuttgart, 1966.

Klinkhammer, Lutz, 'Der Partisanenkrieg der Wehrmacht 1941–1944', in Rolf-Dieter Müller and Hans-Erich Volkmann (eds.), *Die Wehrmacht: Mythos und Realität*, Munich, 1999, 815–36.

Knappe, Siegfried, and Brusaw, Ted, *Soldat. Reflections of a German Soldier, 1936–1949*, New York, 1992.

Knipping, Franz, and Müller, Klaus-Jurgen (eds.), *Machtbewußtsein in Deutschland am Vorabend des Zweiten Weltkrieges*, Paderborn, 1984.

Knopf, Volker, and Martens, Stefan, *Görings Reich. Selbstinszenierungen in Carinhall*, Berlin, 1999.

Knox, MacGregor, *Mussolini Unleashed 1939–1941. Politics and Strategy in Fascist Italy's Last War*, (1982), paperback edn, Cambridge, 1986.

Koch, H. W. (ed.), *Aspects of the Third Reich*, London, 1985.

Kochan, Lionel, *Pogrom: 10 November 1938*, London, 1957.

Kocka, Jurgen (ed.), *Theorien in der Praxis des Historikers*, Göttingen, 1977.

Koehl, Robert L., *RKFDV: German Resettlement and Population Policy 1939–1945. A History of the Reich Commission for the Strengthening of Germandom*, Cambridge, Mass., 1957.

Kogon, Eugen, *et al.* (eds.), *Nationalsozialistische Massentötung durch Giftgas. Eine Dokumentation*, Frankfurt am Main, 1983.

Kolb, Eberhard, 'Bergen-Belsen', in Martin Broszat (ed.), *Studien zur Geschichte der Konzentrationslager*, Stuttgart, 1970, 130–53.

—— *Bergen-Belsen. Vom 'Aufenthaltslager' zum Konzentrationslager 1943–1945*, Göttingen, 1985.

Koller, Karl, *Der letzte Monat. Die Tagebuchaufzeichnungen des ehemaligen Chefs des Generalstabes der deutschen Luftwaffe vom 14. April bis 27. Mai 1945*, Mannheim, 1949.

Kommandant in Auschwitz. Autobiographische Aufzeichnungen des Rudolf Hoß, (1963), 4th edn, Munich, 1978.

Kordt, Erich, *Nicht aus den Akten ... Die Wilhelmstraße in Frieden und Krieg. Erlebnisse, Begegnungen und Eindrücke 1928–1945*, Stuttgart, 1950.

Kosnett, Phil, and Patrick, Stephen B. 'Highway to the Reich: Operation Market-Garden, 17–26 September 1944', in Albert A. Nofi (ed.), *The War against Hitler. Military Strategy in the West*, Conshokoken, PA, 1995, 156–77.

Kotze, Hildegard von, and Krausnick, Helmut (eds.), *'Es spricht der Führer'. 7 exemplarische Hitler-Reden*, Gutersloh, 1966.

Krakowski, Schmuel, 'The Death Marches in the Period of the Evacuation of the Camps', in Michael Marrus (ed.), *The Nazi Holocaust: Historical Articles on the Destruction of European Jews*, vol. 9, Westport, 1989, 476–90.

Kramarz, Joachim, *Claus Graf Stauffenberg. 15. November, 1907–20. Juli 1944: Das Leben eines Offiziers*, Frankfurt am Main, 1965.

Krausnick, Helmut, 'Denkschrift Himmlers über die Behandlung der Fremdvölkischen im Osten (Mai 1940)', *VfZ*, 5 (1957), 194–8.

—— 'Hitler und die Morde in Polen', *VfZ*, 11 (1963), 196–209.

—— 'Judenverfolgung', in Hans Buchheim *et al.*, *Anatomie des SS-Staates*, Olten/Freiburg i. Br., 1965, ii. 283–448.

—— 'Kommissarbefehl und "Gerichtsbarkeitserlaß Barbarossa" in neuer Sicht', *VfZ*, 25 (1977), 682–738.

Krausnick, Helmut, and Wilhelm, Hans-Heinrich, *Die Truppe des Weltanschauungskrieges. Die Einsatzgruppen der Sicherheitspolizei und des SD 1938–1942*, Stuttgart, 1981.

Krautkrämer, Elmar, 'Generalfeldmarschall Albert Kesselring', in Gerd R. Ueberschär (ed.), *Hitlers militärische Elite. Bd. I: Von den Anfängen des Regimes bis Kriegsbeginn*, Darmstadt, 1998, 121–9.

Krebs, Albert, *Tendenzen und Gestalten der NSDAP. Erinnerungen an die Frühzeit der Partei*, Stuttgart, 1959.

'Kremlin "secretly burned Hitler's remains"', *Guardian*, 4 April 1995.

Kriegspropaganda 1939–1941. Geheime Ministerkonferenzen im Reichspropagandaministerium, ed. Willi A. Boelcke, Stuttgart, 1966.

Kriegstagebuch des Oberkommandos der Wehrmacht (Wehrmachtführungsstab), Bd. I: 1. August 1940–31. Dezember 1941, ed. Percy Ernst Schramm, Frankfurt am Main, 1965.

—— *Bd. II: 1. Januar 1942–31. Dezember 1942*, ed. Andreas Hillgruber, Frankfurt am Main, 1963.

—— *Bd. III: 1. Januar 1943–31. Dezember 1943*, ed. Walther Hubatsch, Frankfurt am Main, 1963.

—— *Bd. IV: 1. Januar 1944–22. Mai 1945*, ed. Percy Ernst Schramm, Frankfurt am Main, 1961.

Kroener, Bernhard R., 'Friedrich Fromm – Der "starke Mann im Heimatkriegsgebiet"', in Ronald Smelser and Enrico Syring (eds.), *Die Militärelite des Dritten Reiches*, Berlin/Frankfurt am Main, 1995, 171–86.

Krogmann, Carl Vincent, *Es ging um Deutschlands Zukunft 1932–1939*, Leoni am Starnberger See, 1976.

Krüger, Arnd, *Die Olympischen Spiele 1936 und die Weltmeinung*, Berlin, 1972.

Kube, Alfred, *Pour le mérite und Hakenkreuz. Hermann Göring im Dritten Reich*, Munich, 1986.

Kubizek, August, *Adolf Hitler, mein Jugendfreund*, 5th edn, Graz/Stuttgart, 1989.

Kühnrich, Heinz, 'Der deutsch-sowjetische Nichtangriffsvertrag vom 23. August 1939 aus der zeitgenössischen Sicht der KPD', in Dietrich Eichholtz and Kurt Pätzold (eds.), *Der Weg in den Krieg. Studien zur Geschichte der Vorkriegsjahre (1935/36 bis 1939)*, East Berlin, 1989, 517–51.

Kulka, Otto Dov, '"Public Opinion" in National Socialist Germany and the "Jewish Question"', *Zion*, 40 (1975), 186–290 (text in Hebrew, abstract in English, documentation in German).

Kurowski, Franz, 'Dietrich and Manteufel', in Correlli Barnett (ed.), *Hitler's Generals*, London, 1990, 411–37.

Kwiet, Konrad, and Eschwege, Helmut, *Selbstbehauptung und Widerstand. Deutsche Juden im Kampf um Existenz und Menschenwürde 1933–1945*, Hamburg, 1984.

Lagebesprechungen im Führerhauptquartier. Protokollfragmente aus Hitlers militärischen Konferenzen 1942–1945, ed. Helmut Heiber, Deutsche Buch-Gemeinschaft edn (abridged edn), Berlin/Darmstadt/Vienna, 1963.

Lagevorträge des Oberbefehlshabers der Kriegsmarine vor Hitler 1939–1945, ed. Gerhard Wagner, Munich, 1972.

Lamb, Richard, *The Ghosts of Peace, 1935–1945*, Salisbury, 1987.

—— 'Kluge', in Correlli Barnett (ed.), *Hitler's Generals*, London, 1990, 394–409.

—— 'Das Foreign Office und der deutsche Widerstand 1938–1944', in Klaus-Jürgen Müller and David N. Dilks (eds.), *Großbritannien und der deutsche Widerstand 1933–1944*, Paderborn etc., 1994, 53–81.

Lang, Jochen von, *Der Sekretär. Martin Bormann: Der Mann, der Hitler beherrschte*, Frankfurt am Main, 1980.

—— *Das Eichmann-Protokoll. Tonbandaufzeichnungen der israelischen Verhöre*, Berlin, 1982.

—— *Der Adjutant. Karl Wolff. Der Mann zwischen Hitler und Himmler*, Munich, 1985.

Lansbury, George, *My England*, (1936), London, n.d.

Laqueur, Walter, *The Terrible Secret. Suppression of the Truth about Hitler's 'Final Solution'*, Harmondsworth, 1982.

Large, David Clay (ed.), *Contending with Hitler. Varieties of German Resistance in the Third Reich*, Cambridge, 1991.

Leach, Barry A., *German Strategy against Russia 1939–1941*, Oxford, 1973.

Leasor, James, *Rudolf Hess: the Uninvited Envoy*, London, 1962.

Leber, Annedore, *Conscience in Revolt*, London, 1957.

Leber, Annedore, and Moltke, Freya Gräfin von, *Für und wider Entscheidungen in Deutschland 1918–1945*, Frankfurt am Main, 1961.

Lehndorff, Hans Graf von, *Ostpreußisches Tagebuch. Aufzeichnungen eines Arztes aus den Jahren 1945–1947*, (1967), 15th edn, Munich, 1985.

Leitz, Christian, 'Nazi Germany's Intervention in the Spanish Civil War and the Foundation of HISMA/ROWAK', in Paul Preston and Ann L. Mackenzie (eds.), *The Republic Besieged: Civil War in Spain, 1936–1939*, Edinburgh, 1996, 53–85.

Lemhöfer, Lutz, 'Gegen den gottlosen Bolschewismus. Zur Stellung der Kirchen zum Krieg gegen die Sowjetunion', in Gerd R. Ueberschär and Wolfram Wette (eds.), *'Unternehmen Barbarossa'. Der deutsche Überfall auf die Sowjetunion 1941. Berichte, Analysen, Dokumente*, Paderborn, 1984, 131–9.

Lesser, Alexander, 'Russians wanted to sell "Hitler skull" story', *Jerusalem Report*, 11 March 1993.

Letzte Briefe aus Stalingrad, Frankfurt am Main/Heidelberg, 1950.

Levine, Herbert S., *Hitler's Free City. A History of the Nazi Party in Danzig, 1925–39*, Chicago/London, 1973.

—— 'The Mediator: Carl J. Burckhardt's Efforts to Avert a Second World War', *JMH*, 45 (1973), 439–55.

Lewis, Samuel J., 'Albert Kesselring – Der Soldat als Manager', in Ronald Smelser and Enrico Syring (eds.), *Die Militärelite des Dritten Reiches*, Berlin/Frankfurt am Main, 1995, 270–87.

Lewy, Guenter, *The Catholic Church and Nazi Germany*, London, 1964.

Lifton, Robert Jay, *The Nazi Doctors. Medical Killing and the Psychology of Genocide*, New York, 1986.

Linge, Heinz, 'Kronzeuge Linge. Der Kammerdiener des "Führers"', *Revue, Munich*, November 1955–March 1956.

—— *Bis zum Untergang. Als Chef des persönlichen Dienstes bei Hitler*, Munich/Berlin, 1980.

Lipski, Josef, *Diplomat in Berlin 1933–1939*, ed. Waclaw Jedrzejewicz, New York/London, 1968.

Loewenberg, Peter, 'The Kristallnacht as a Public Degradation Ritual', *LBYB*, 32 (1987), 309–23.

Löffler, Peter (ed.), *Bischof Clemens August Graf von Galen. Akten, Briefe und Predigten, vol. 2: 1939–1946*, Mainz, 1988.

Londonderry, Marquess of (Charles S. H. Vane-Tempest-Stewart), *Ourselves and Germany*, London, 1938.

Longerich, Peter, 'Joseph Goebbels und der totale Krieg: eine unbekannte Denkschrift des Propagandaministers vom 18. Juli 1944', *VfZ*, 35 (1987), 289–314.

—— *Die braunen Bataillone. Geschichte der SA*, Munich, 1989.

—— (ed.), *Die Ermordung der europäischen Juden. Eine umfassende Dokumentation des Holocaust 1941–1945*, Munich/Zurich, 1989.

—— *Hitlers Stellvertreter. Führung der Partei und Kontrolle des Staatsapparates durch den Stab Heß und die Partei Kanzlei Bormann*, Munich etc., 1992.

—— *Politik der Vernichtung. Eine Gesamtdarstellung der nationalsozialistischen Judenverfolgung*, Munich/Zurich, 1998.

Loßberg, Bernhard von, *Im Wehrmachtführungsstab. Bericht eines Generalstabsoffiziers*, Hamburg, 1950.

Löwenthal, Richard, and Mühlen, Patrik von zur (eds.), *Widerstand und Verweigerung in Deutschland 1933 bis 1945*, Berlin/Bonn, 1984.

Ludewig, Joachim, 'Walter Model – Hitlers bester Feldmarschall?', in Ronald Smelser and Enrico Syring (eds.), *Die Militärelite des Dritten Reiches*, Berlin/Frankfurt am Main, 1995, 368–87.

Lukacs, John, *The Duel. Hitler vs. Churchill: 10 May–31 July 1940*, Oxford, 1992.

Macrakis, Kristie, *Surviving the Swastika. Scientific Research in Nazi Germany*, New York/Oxford, 1993.

Madajczyk, Czeslaw, 'Generalplan Ost', *Polish Western Affairs*, 3 (1962), 3–54.

—— *Die Okkupationspolitik Nazideutschlands in Polen 1939–1945*, East Berlin, 1987.

—— (ed.), *Vom Generalplan Ost zum Generalsiedlungsplan*, Munich etc., 1994.

Magenheimer, Heinz, *Hitler's War. German Military Strategy, 1940–1945*, London, 1998.

Maier, Hedwig, 'Die SS und der 20. Juli 1944', *VfZ*, 14 (1966), 299–316.

Mammach, Klaus, *Der Volkssturm. Bestandteil des totalen Kriegseinsatzes der deutschen Bevölkerung 1944/45*, East Berlin, 1981.

—— 'Widerstandsaktionen und oppositionelles Verhalten', in Dietrich Eichholtz and Kurt Pätzold (eds.), *Der Weg in den Krieg. Studien zur Geschichte der Vorkriegsjahre (1935/36 bis 1939)*, East Berlin, 1989, 403–34.

Mandell, Richard D., *The Nazi Olympics*, London, 1972.

Manstein, Erich von, *Lost Victories*, (1955), London, 1982.

Marrus, Michael R., *The Nuremberg War Crimes Trial 1945–46. A Documentary History*, Boston/New York, 1997.

Martens, Stefan, 'Die Rolle Hermann Görings in der deutschen Außenpolitik', in Franz Knipping and Klaus-Jürgen Müller (eds.), *Machtbewußtsein in Deutschland am Vorabend des Zweiten Weltkrieges*, Paderborn, 1984, 75–92.

—— *Hermann Göring. 'Erster Paladin des Führers' und 'Zweiter Mann im Reich'*, Paderborn, 1985.

Martin, Bernd, *Deutschland und Japan im Zweiten Weltkrieg. Vom Angriff auf Pearl Harbor bis zur deutschen Kapitulation*, Göttingen, 1969.

—— 'Die deutsch-japanischen Beziehungen während des Dritten Reiches', in Manfred Funke (ed.), *Hitler, Deutschland und die Mächte. Materialien zur Außenpolitik des Dritten Reiches*, Düsseldorf, 1978, 454–70.

Maschmann, Melita, *Fazit. Mein Weg in die Hitler-Jugend*, 5th edn, Munich, 1983.

Maser, Werner (ed.), *Hitlers Briefe und Notizen. Sein Weltbild in handschriftlichen Dokumenten*, Düsseldorf, 1973.

—— *Adolf Hitler. Legende-Mythos-Wirklichkeit*, (1971), 3rd edn, Munich/Esslingen, 1976.

—— *Der Wortbruch. Hitler, Stalin und der Zweite Weltkrieg*, (1994), 4th edn, Munich, 1997.

Mason, Timothy W., 'The Legacy of 1918 for National Socialism', in Anthony Nicholls and Erich Mathias (eds.), *German Democracy and the Triumph of Hitler*, London, 1971, 215–39.

—— *Arbeiterklasse und Volksgemeinschaft. Dokumente und Materialien zur deutschen Arbeiterpolitik 1936–1939*, Opladen, 1975.

—— *Sozialpolitik im Dritten Reich. Arbeiterklasse und Volksgemeinschaft*, Opladen, 1977.

—— 'The Workers' Opposition in Nazi Germany', *History Workshop Journal*, 11 (1981), 120–37.

—— 'Die Bändigung der Arbeiterklasse im nationalsozialistischen Deutschland. Eine Einleitung', in Carola Sachse, et al. (eds.), *Angst, Belohnung, Zucht und Ordnung. Herrschaftsmechanismen im Nationalsozialismus*, Opladen, 1982, 11–53.

—— *Nazism, Fascism, and the Working Class. Essays by Tim Mason*, ed. Jane Caplan, Cambridge, 1995.

Mayer, Arno J., *Why did the Heavens Not Darken? The 'Final Solution' in History*, New York, 1988.

Mayer, Milton, *They Thought They Were Free. The Germans 1933–45*, Chicago, 1955.

McKee, Ilse, *Tomorrow the World*, London, 1960.

Meehan, Patricia, *The Unnecessary War. Whitehall and the German Resistance to Hitler*, London, 1992.

Meissner, Otto, *Staatssekretär unter Ebert-Hindenberg-Hitler. Der Schicksalsweg des deutschen Volkes von 1918 bis 1945, wie ich ihn erlebte*, Hamburg, 1950.

Meldungen aus dem Reich. Die geheimen Lageberichte des Sicherheitsdienstes der SS 1938–1945, ed. Heinz Boberach, 17 vols., Herrsching, 1984.

Merson, Allan, *Communist Resistance in Nazi Germany*, London, 1985.

Messenger, Charles, *Hitler's Gladiator. The Life and Times of Oberstgruppenführer der Waffen-SS Sepp Dietrich*, London, 1988.

—— *The Last Prussian. A Biography of Field Marshal Gerd von Rundstedt, 1875–1953*, London etc., 1991.

Messerschmidt, Manfred, *Die Wehrmacht im NS-Staat. Zeit der Indoktrination*, Hamburg, 1969.

—— 'Krieg in der Trümmerlandschaft. "Pflichterfüllung" wofür?', in Ulrich Borsdorf and Mathilde Jamin (eds.), *Über Leben im Krieg. Kriegserfahrung in einer Industrieregion 1939–1945*, Reinbeck bei Hamburg, 1989, 169–78.

Michaelis, Meir, *Mussolini and the Jews. German Italian Relations and the Jewish Question in Italy 1922–1945*, Oxford, 1978.

Michalka, Wolfgang, *Ribbentrop und die deutsche Weltpolitik 1933–1940. Außenpolitische Konzeptionen und Entscheidungsprozesse im Dritten Reich*, Munich, 1979.

—— (ed.), *Das Dritte Reich. Dokumente zur Innen- und Außenpolitik*, vol. 1, Munich, 1985.

—— (ed.), *Das Dritte Reich. Bd 2: Weltmachtanspruch und nationaler Zusammenbruch 1939–1945*, Munich, 1985.

—— 'From the Anti-Comintern Pact to the Euro-Asiatic Bloc: Ribbentrop's Alternative Concept to Hitler's Foreign Policy Programme', in H. W. Koch (ed.), *Aspects of the Third Reich*, London, 1985, 267–84.

Michel, Thomas, *Die Juden in Gaukönigshofen/Unterfranken (1550–1942)*, Wiesbaden, 1988.

Michels, Helmut, *Ideologie und Propaganda. Die Rolle von Joseph Goebbels in der nationalsozialistischen Außenpolitik bis 1939*, Frankfurt am Main etc., 1992.

Michman, Dan, 'Die jüdische Emigration und die niederländische Reaktion zwischen 1933 und 1940', in Kathinka Dittrich and Hans Würzner (eds.), *Die Niederlande und das deutsche Exil 1933–1940*, Königstein/Ts., 1982, 73–90.

—— 'Preparing for Occupation? A Nazi Sicherheitsdienst Document of Spring 1939 on the Jews of Holland', *Studia Rosenthaliana*, 32 (1998), 173–80.

Middlebrook, Martin, *The Battle of Hamburg: Allied Bomber Forces against a German City in 1943*, New York, 1981.

Milton, Sybil, 'The Expulsion of Polish Jews from Germany, October 1938 to July 1939. A Documentation', *LBYB*, 29 (1984), 166–99.

—— 'Menschen zwischen Grenzen: Die Polenausweisung 1938', *Menora: Jahrbuch für deutsch-jüdische Geschichte*, (1990), 184–206.

Milward, Alan S., 'Fritz Todt als Minister für Bewaffnung und Munition', *VfZ*, 14 (1966), 40–58.

—— *Die deutsche Kriegswirtschaft 1939–1945*, Stuttgart, 1966.

—— 'Fascism and the Economy', in Walter Laqueur (ed.), *Fascism. A Reader's Guide*, Harmondsworth, 1979, 409–53.

Milza, Pierre, *Mussolini*, Paris, 1999.

Mitcham, Samuel W., Jr, 'Generalfeldmarschall Fedor von Bock', in Gerd R. Ueberschär (ed.), *Hitlers militärische Elite. Bd. 1: Von den Anfängen des Regimes bis Kriegsbeginn*, Darmstadt, 1998, 37–44.

—— 'Generalfeldmarschall Robert Ritter von Greim', in Gerd Ueberschär (ed.), *Hitlers militärische Elite, Bd. 2. Vom Kriegsbeginn zum Weltkriegsende*, Darmstadt, 1998, 72–9.

Mitcham, Samuel W., Jr, and Mueller, Gene, 'Generaloberst Erich Hoepner', in Gerd R. Ueberschär (ed.), *Hitlers militärische Elite. Bd. 2: Vom Kriegsbeginn bis zum Weltkriegsende*, Darmstadt, 1998, 93–9.

—— 'Generalfeldmarschall Walter Model', in Gerd R. Ueberschär (ed.), *Hitlers militärische Elite. Bd. 2: Vom Kriegsbeginn bis zum Weltkriegsende*, Darmstadt, 1998, 153–60.

Moll, Martin (ed.), *'Führer-Erlasse' 1939–1945*, Stuttgart, 1997.

—— 'Die Tagungen der Reichs- und Gauleiter der NSDAP: Ein verkanntes Instrument zur Koordinierung im "Ämterchaos" des Dritten Reiches?', unpublished paper.

Moltke, Helmuth James von, *Letters to Freya, 1939–1945. A Witness against Hitler*, London, 1991.

Moltmann, Günter, 'Goebbels' Rede zum totalen Krieg am 18. Februar 1943', *VfZ*, 12 (1964), 13–43.

—— 'Goebbels' Speech on Total War, February 18, 1943', in Hajo Holborn (ed.), *Republic to Reich. The Making of the Nazi Revolution*, Vintage Books edn, New York, 1973, 298–342.

Mommsen, Hans, *Beamtentum im Dritten Reich*, Stuttgart, 1966.

—— 'Nationalsozialismus', in C. D. Hernig (ed.), *Sowjetsystem und demokratische Gesellschaft. Eine vergleichende Enzyklopädie*, 7 vols., Freiburg etc., 1966–72, vol. 4, column 702.

—— 'Social Views and Constitutional Plans of the Resistance', in Hermann Graml et al., *The German Resistance to Hitler*, (1966), London, 1970, 55–147.

—— 'Der Nationalsozialismus. Kumulative Radikalisierung und Selbstzerstörung des Regimes', in *Meyers Enzyklopädisches Lexikon*, vol. 16, Mannheim, 1976, 785–90.

—— 'Die Realisierung des Utopischen: Die "Endlösung der Judenfrage" im "Dritten Reich"', *GG*, 9 (1983), 381–420.

—— 'Der Widerstand gegen Hitler und die deutsche Gesellschaft', in Jürgen Schmädeke and Peter Steinbach (eds.), *Der Widerstand gegen den Nationalsozialismus. Die deutsche Gesellschaft und der Widerstand gegen Hitler*, Munich (1985), 1986, 3–23.

—— 'Verfassungs- und Verwaltungsreformpläne der Widerstandsgruppen des 20. Juli 1944', in Jürgen Schmädeke and Peter Steinbach (eds.), *Der Widerstand gegen den Nationalsozialismus. Die deutsche Gesellschaft und der Widerstand gegen Hitler*, Munich (1985), 1986, 570–97.

—— 'Nationalsozialismus als vorgetäuschte Modernisierung', in Walter H. Pehle (ed.), *Der historische Ort des Nationalsozialismus. Annäherung*, Frankfurt am Main, 1990, 11–46.

—— 'Reflections on the Position of Hitler and Göring in the Third Reich', in Thomas Childers and Jane Caplan (eds.), *Reevaluating the Third Reich*, New York/London, 1993, 86–97.

—— 'Preußentum und Nationalsozialismus', in Wolfgang Benz, Hans Buchheim and Hans Mommsen (eds.), *Der Nationalsozialismus. Studien zur Ideologie und Herrschaft*, Frankfurt am Main, 1993, 29–41.

—— 'Der Kreisauer Kreis und die künftige Neuordnung Deutschlands und Europas', *VfZ*, 42 (1994), 361–77.

—— 'Hitler's Reichstag Speech of 30 January 1939', *History and Memory*, 9 (1997), 147–61.

—— *Von Weimar nach Auschwitz. Zur Geschichte Deutschlands in der Weltkriegsepoche*, Stuttgart, 1999.

—— 'Der Widerstand gegen Hitler und die nationalsozialistische Judenverfolgung', unpublished paper.

Mommsen, Hans, and Grieger, Manfred, *Das Volkswagenwerk und seine Arbeiter im Dritten Reich*, Düsseldorf, 1996.

Mommsen, Hans, and Obst, Dieter, 'Die Reaktion der deutschen Bevölkerung auf die Verfolgung der Juden 1933–1943', in Hans Mommsen and Susanne Willems (eds.), *Herrschaftsalltag im Dritten Reich. Studien und Texte*, Düsseldorf, 1988, 374–485.

Mommsen, Hans, and Willems, Susanne (eds.), *Herrschaftsalltag im Dritten Reich: Studien und Texte*, Düsseldorf, 1988.

Moore, Bob, *Refugees from Nazi Germany in the Netherlands, 1933–1940*, Dordrecht, 1986.

Mosley, Nicholas, *Beyond the Pale: Sir Oswald Mosley, 1933–1980*, London, 1983.

Mosse, George L., *The Crisis of German Ideology. Intellectual Origins of the Third Reich*, (1964), London, 1966.

Mueller, Gene, 'Generalmarschall Günther von Kluge', in Gerd R. Ueberschär (ed.), *Hitlers militärische Elite*, vol. 1, Darmstadt, 1998, 130–37.

Mühleisen, Horst, 'Fedor von Bock – Soldat ohne Fortune', in Ronald Smelser and Enrico Syring (eds.), *Die Militärelite des Dritten Reiches*, Berlin/Frankfurt am Main, 1995, 66–82.

Müller, Christian, *Stauffenberg*, Düsseldorf, 1970.

Müller, Hans (ed.), *Katholische Kirche und Nationalsozialismus*, Munich, 1965.

Müller, Klaus-Jürgen, 'Zu Vorgeschichte und Inhalt der Rede Himmlers vor der höheren Generalität am 13. März 1940 in Koblenz', *VfZ*, 18 (1970), 95–120.

—— *Armee, Politik und Gesellschaft in Deutschland 1933–1945*, Paderborn, 1979.

—— (ed.), *General Ludwig Beck, Studien und Dokumente zur politisch-militärischen Vorstellungswelt und Tätigkeit des Generalstabschefs des deutschen Heeres 1933–1938*, Boppard am Rhein, 1980.

—— 'Militärpolitik nicht Militäropposition!', *HZ*, 235 (1982), 355–71.

—— 'The Structure and Nature of the National Conservative Opposition in Germany up to 1940', in H. W. Koch (ed.), *Aspects of the Third Reich*, London, 1985, 132–78.

—— *Das Heer und Hitler. Armee und nationalsozialistisches Regime 1933–1940*, 2nd edn, Stuttgart, (1969), 1988.

Müller, Max, 'Der Tod des Reichsministers Dr Fritz Todt', *Geschichte in wissenschaft und Unterricht*, 18 (1967), 602–5.

Müller, Rolf-Dieter, *Hitlers Ostkrieg und die deutsche Siedlungspolitik*, Frankfurt am Main, 1991.

Müller, Rolf-Dieter, and Gerd R. Ueberschär, *Kriegsende 1945. Die Zerstörung des Deutschen Reiches*, Frankfurt am Main, 1994.

—— *Hitler's War in the East 1941–1945. A Critical Assessment*, Providence/Oxford, 1997.

Müller, Rolf-Dieter, and Volkmann, Hans-Erich (eds.), *Die Wehrmacht: Mythos und Realität*, Munich, 1999.

Mulligan, Timothy, 'Spies, Cyphers, and "Zitadelle". Intelligence and the Battle of Kursk', *JCH*, 22 (1987), 235–60.

München – Hauptstadt der Bewegung, ed. Münchener Stadtmuseum, Munich, 1993.

Musmanno, Michael A., *Ten Days to Die*, London, 1951.

Mussolini, Benito, *My Rise and Fall*, (1948), two vols. in one, New York, 1998.

Naasner, Walter, *Neue Machtzentren in der deutschen Kriegswirtschaft 1942–1945*, Boppard am Rhein, 1994.

Nadler, Fritz, *Eine Stadt im Schatten Streichers*, Nuremberg, 1969.

Namier, L. B., *Conflicts. Studies in Contemporary History*, London, 1942.

Nazi Conspiracy and Aggression, ed. Office of the United States Chief of Counsel for Prosecution of Axis Criminality, 9 vols. and 2 supplementary vols., Washington, 1946–8.

' "Nein, nein, das ist nicht mehr meine Pflicht". Lew Besymenski über Stalingrad und seine Erlebnisse mit Generalfeldmarschall Paulus', *Der Spiegel*, 37/1992, 170–71.

Neliba, Günter, *Wilhelm Frick. Der Legalist des Unrechtsstaates: Eine politische Biographie*, Paderborn etc., 1992.

Neumann, Franz, *Behemoth. The Structure and Practice of National Socialism*, London, 1942.

Newman, Simon, *March 1939: the British Guarantee to Poland. A Study in the Continuity of British Foreign Policy*, Oxford, 1976.

Nicolson, Harold, *Diaries and Letters, 1930–1964*, New York, 1980.

Nicosia, Francis R., *The Third Reich and the Palestine Question*, Austin/London, 1985.

Niewyk, Donald L., *The Jews in Weimar Germany*, Baton Rouge, 1980.

Noakes, Jeremy, 'Phillip Bouhler und die Kanzlei des Fuhrers der NSDAP: Beispiel einer Sonderverwaltung im Dritten Reich', in Dieter Rebentisch and Karl Teppe (eds.), *Verwaltung contra Menschenführung im Staat Hitlers. Studien zum politisch-administrativen System*, Göttingen, 1986, 208–36.

—— 'The Development of Nazi Policy towards the German-Jewish "Mischlinge" 1933–1945', *LBYB*, 34 (1989), 291–354.

Noakes, Jeremy, and Geoffrey Pridham (eds.), *Documents on Nazism 1919–1945*, London, 1974.

—— (eds.), *Nazism 1919–1945: A Documentary Reader*, 4 vols., Exeter, 1983–98.

Nofi, Albert A. (ed.), *The War against Hitler. Military Strategy in the West*, Conshokoken PA, 1995.

Nolte, Ernst, *Der europäische Bürgerkrieg. Nationalsozialismus und Bolschewismus*, Berlin, 1987.

—— 'Vergangenheit, die nicht vergehen will', in '*Historikerstreit'. Die Dokumentation der Kontroverse um die Einzigartigkeit der nationalsozialistischen Judenvernichtung*, 2nd edn, Munich/Zurich, 1987, 39–47.

Norden, Günter van, 'Widerstand in den Kirchen', in Richard Löwenthal and Patrik von zur Mühlen (eds.), *Widerstand und Verweigerung in Deutschland 1933 bis 1945*, Berlin/Bonn, 1984, 111–28.

Normann, Käthe von, *Tagebuch aus Pommern 1945/46*, (1962), 5th edn, Munich, 1984.

Nowak, Kurt, 'Widerstand, Zustimmung, Hinnahme. Das Verhalten der Bevölkerung zur "Euthanasie" ', in Norbert Frei (ed.), *Medizin und Gesundheitspolitik in der NS-Zeit*, Munich, 1991, 235–51.

O'Donnell, James P., and Bahnsen, Uwe, *Die Katakombe. Das Ende in der Reichskanzlei*, Stuttgart, 1975.

Oldenhage, Klaus, 'Justizverwaltung und Lenkung der Rechtsprechung im Zweiten Weltkrieg', in Dieter Rebentisch and Karl Teppe (eds.), *Verwaltung contra Menschenführung im Staat Hitlers. Studien zum politisch-administrativen System*, Göttingen, 1986, 208–36.

Operation Foxley: the British Plan to Kill Hitler, London, 1998.

Ophir, Baruch Z., and Wiesemann, Falk (eds.), *Die jüdischen Gemeinden in Bayern 1918–1945. Geschichte und Zerstörung*, Munich, 1979.

Orlow, Dietrich, *The History of the Nazi Party, vol. 2: 1933–1945*, Newton Abbot, 1973.

Orth, Karin, 'Rudolf Höß und die "Endlösung der Judenfrage". Drei Argumente gegen deren Datierung auf den Sommer 1941', *Werkstattgeschichte*, 18 (1997), 45–57.

—— *Das System der nationalsozialistischen Konzentrationslager. Eine politische Organisationsgeschichte*, Hamburg, 1999.

Ose, Dieter, *Entscheidung im Westen. Der Oberbefehlshaber West und die Abwehr der alliierten Invasion*, Stuttgart, 1982.

Oven, Wilfried von, *Mit Goebbels bis zum Ende*, 2 vols., Buenos Aires, 1950.

—— 'Der 20. Juli 1944 – erlebt im Hause Goebbels', *Verrat und Widerstand im Dritten Reich, Nation Europa*, 28 (1978), 43–58.

Overy, Richard J., *Goering: the Iron Man*, London, 1984.

—— 'Germany, "Domestic Crisis", and War in 1939', *Past and Present*, 116 (1987), 138–68.

—— *War and Economy in the Third Reich*, Oxford, 1994.

—— *Why the Allies Won*, London, 1995.

—— *Russia's War*, London, 1997.

The Oxford Companion to the Second World War, ed. I.C.B. Dear and M.R.D. Foot, Oxford, 1995.

Padfield, Peter, *Dönitz: the Last Führer*, New York, 1984.

—— *Himmler. Reichsführer-SS*, London, 1991.

—— *Hess. The Führer's Disciple*, London, 1991.

Page, Helena P., *General Friedrich Olbricht. Ein Mann des 20. Juli*, Bonn/Berlin, 1992.

Papen, Franz von, *Memoirs*, London, 1952.

Parker, R. A. C., *Struggle for Survival. The History of the Second World War*, Oxford, 1990.

—— *Chamberlain and Appeasement. British Policy and the Coming of the Second World War*, London, 1993.

Patrick, Stephen B., 'The Ardennes Offensive: An Analysis of the Battle of the Bulge, December 1944', in Albert A. Nofi (ed.), *The War against Hitler. Military Strategy in the West*, Conshokoken, PA, 1995, 206–24.

Pätzold, Kurt (ed.), *Verfolgung, Vertreibung, Vernichtung. Dokumente des faschistischen Antisemitismus 1933 bis 1942*, Leipzig, 1983.

—— 'Hitlers fünfzigster Geburtstag am 20. April 1939', in Dietrich Eichholtz and Kurt Patzold (eds.), *Der Weg in den Krieg. Studien zur Geschichte der Vorkriegsjahre (1935/36 bis 1939)*, East Berlin, 1989, 309–43.

Patzold, Kurt, and Runge, Irene, *Kristallnacht. Zum Pogrom 1938*, Cologne, 1988.

Pätzold, Kurt, and Weißbecker, Manfred, *Geschichte der NSDAP 1920–1945*, Cologne, 1981.

Paucker, Arnold, *Deutsche Juden im Widerstand 1933–1945. Tatsachen und Probleme, Beitrage zum Widerstand 1933–1945*, ed. Gedenkstatte Deutscher Widerstand, Berlin, 1999.

Pauley, Bruce F., *Hitler and the Forgotten Nazis. A History of Austrian National Socialism*, London/Basingstoke, 1981.

Pehle, Walter H. (ed.), *Der Judenpogrom. Von der 'Reichskristallnacht' zum Völkermord*, Frankfurt am Main, 1988.

Petersen, Jens, *Hitler-Mussolini. Die Entstehung der Achse Berlin-Rom 1933–1936*, Tübingen, 1973.

Peterson, Edward N., *The Limits of Hitler's Power*, Princeton, 1969.

Petrova, Ada, and Watson, Peter, *The Death of Hitler: the Final Words from Russia's Secret Archives*, London, 1995.

Petzina, Dieter, *Autarkiepolitik im Dritten Reich. Der nationalsozialistische Vierjahresplan*, Stuttgart, 1968.

Peukert, Detlev J. K., *Die Edelweißpiraten. Protestbewegungen jugendlicher Arbeiter im Dritten Reich*, Cologne, 1980.

—— *Die KPD im Widerstand. Verfolgung und Untergrundarbeit an Rhein und Ruhr 1933 bis 1945*, Wuppertal, 1980.

—— *Die Weimarer Republik. Krisenjahre der Klassischen Moderne*, Frankfurt am Main, 1987.

—— 'Working-Class Resistance: Problems and Options', in David Clay Large (ed.), *Contending with Hitler. Varieties of German Resistance in the Third Reich*, Cambridge, 1991, 35–48.

Picker, Henry, *Hitlers Tischgespräche im Führerhauptquartier 1941–1942*, ed. Percy Ernst Schramm, Stuttgart, 1963.

Pietrow, Bianka, 'Deutschland im Juni 1941 – ein Opfer sowjetischer Aggression? Zur Kontroverse über die Praventivkriegsthese', *GG*, 14 (1988), 116–35.

Pike, David Wingeate, 'Franco and the Axis Stigma', *JCH*, 17 (1982), 369–406.

Plum, Gunter, 'Wirtschaft und Erwerbsleben', in Wolfgang Benz (ed.), *Die Juden in Deutschland 1933–1945. Leben unter nationalsozialistischer Herrschaft*, Munich, 1988, 268–313.

Pohl, Dieter, *Von der 'Judenpolitik' zum Judenmord. Der Distrikt Lublin des Generalgouvernements 1939–1944*, Frankfurt am Main, 1993.

—— *Nationalsozialistische Judenverfolgung in Ostgalizien. Organisation und Durchführung eines staatlichen Massenverbrechens*, Munich, 1996.

—— 'Die Ermordung der Juden im Generalgouvernement', in Ulrich Herbert (ed.), *Nationalsozial-*

istische Vernichtungspolitik 1939–1945. Neue Forschungen und Kontroversen, Frankfurt am Main, 1998, 98–121.

Poliakov, Leon and Wulf, Josef, *Das Dritte Reich und die Juden. Dokumente und Aufsätze*, 2nd edn, Berlin, 1955.

Porat, Dina, 'The Holocaust in Lithuania. Some Unique Aspects', in David Cesarani (ed.), *The Final Solution, Origins and Implementation*, London, 1996, 159–74.

Pospieszalski, Karol Marian, 'The Case of the 58,000 "Volksdeutsche". An Investigation into Nazi Claims Concerning Losses of the German Minority in Poland before and during 1939', in Instytut Zachodni (ed.), *Documenta Occupationis*, 2nd edn, vol. vii, Poznan, 1981.

Prados, John, 'Cobra: Patton's Offensive in France, Summer 1944', in Albert A. Nofi (ed.), *The War against Hitler. Military Strategy in the West*, Conshokoken, PA, 1995, 133–55.

Pressac, Jean-Claude, *Les Crématoires d'Auschwitz. La Machinerie du Meurtre de Masse*, Paris, 1993.

Preston, Paul, 'Franco and Hitler: the Myth of Hendaye 1940', *Contemporary European History*, 1 (1992), 1–16.

—— *Franco. A Biography*, London, 1993.

—— 'Mussolini's Spanish Adventure: From Limited Risk to War', in Paul Preston and Ann L. Mackenzie (eds.), *The Republic Besieged: Civil War in Spain 1936–1939*, Edinburgh, 1996, 21–51.

Preston, Paul and Mackenzie, Ann L. (eds.), *The Republic Besieged: Civil War in Spain 1936–1939*, Edinburgh, 1996.

Prieberg, Fred K., *Trial of Strength: Wilhelm Furtwängler and the Third Reich*, London, 1992.

Proctor, Robert N., *Racial Hygiene. Medicine under the Nazis*, Cambridge, Mass., 1988.

Der Prozeß gegen die Hauptkriegsverbrecher vor dem Internationalen Militärgerichtshof, 42 vols., Nuremberg, 14 November 1945–1 October 1946.

Radzinsky, Edvard, *Stalin*, New York, 1996.

Raeder, Erich, *Mein Leben von 1935 bis Spandau 1955*, 2 vols., Tübingen, 1957.

Read, Anthony, and Fisher, David, *The Deadly Embrace. Hitler, Stalin, and the Nazi-Soviet Pact, 1939–1941*, New York/London, 1988.

—— *Kristallnacht. Unleashing the Holocaust*, London, 1989.

Rebentisch, Dieter, 'Hitlers Reichskanzlei zwischen Politik und Verwaltung', in Dieter Rebentisch and Karl Teppe (eds.), *Verwaltung contra Menschenführung im Staat Hitlers. Studien zum politisch-administrativen System*, Göttingen, 1986, 65–99.

—— *Führerstaat und Verwaltung im Zweiten Weltkrieg. Verfassungsentwicklung und Verwaltungspolitik 1939–1945*, Stuttgart, 1989.

Rebentisch, Dieter, and Teppe, Karl (eds.), *Verwaltung contra Menschenführung im Staat Hitlers. Studien zum politisch-administrativen System*, Gottingen, 1986.

'Die Rede Himmlers vor den Gauleitern am 3. August 1944', ed. Theodor Eschenburg, *VfZ*, 1 (1953), 357–94.

Reden des Führers am Parteitag der Ehre 1936, Munich, 1936.

Redlich, Fritz, *Hitler. Diagnosis of a Destructive Prophet*, New York/Oxford, 1999.

Rees, Laurence, *The Nazis. A Warning from History*, London, 1997.

—— *War of the Century. When Hitler Fought Stalin*, London, 1999.

Reich-Ranicki, Marcel, *Mein Leben*, Stuttgart, 1999.

Reinhardt, Klaus, *Die Wende vor Moskau. Das Scheitern der Strategie Hitler im Winter 1941/42*, Stuttgart, 1972.

—— 'Moscow 1941. The Turning-Point', in John Erickson and David Dilks (eds.), *Barbarossa. The Axis and the Allies*, Edinburgh, 1994, 207–24.

Reitlinger, Gerald, *The Final Solution*, (1953), Sphere Books edn, London, 1971.

Reitsch, Hanna, *Fliegen – Mein Leben*, Stuttgart, 1951.

Remer, Otto Ernst, *Verschwörung und Verrat um Hitler. Urteil eines Frontsoldaten*, Preußisch-Oldendorf, 1981.

Renneberg, Monika, and Mark Walker (eds.), *Science, Technology, and National Socialism*, Cambridge, 1994.

Reuth, Ralf Georg, *Goebbels*, Munich, 1990.

—— (ed.), *Joseph Goebbels. Tagebücher*, 5 vols., Munich/Zurich, 1992.

Reynolds, Nicholas, 'Der Fritsch-Brief vom 11. Dezember 1938', *VfZ*, 28 (1980), 358–71.

Ribbentrop, Joachim von, *Zwischen London und Moskau. Erinnerungen und letzte Aufzeichnungen*, ed. Annelies von Ribbentrop, Leoni am Starnberger See, 1953.

—— *The Ribbentrop Memoirs*, London, 1954.

Rich, Norman, *Hitler's War Aims. Vol 1: Ideology, the Nazi State, and the Course of Expansion*, London, 1973.

—— *Hitler's War Aims. Vol. 2: The Establishment of the New Order*, London, 1974.

Richarz, Monika (ed.), *Jüdisches Leben in Deutschland. Bd. 3. Selbstzeugnisse zur Sozialgeschichte 1918–1945*, Stuttgart, 1982.

Richter, Timm C., 'Die Wehrmacht und der Partisanenkrieg in den besetzten Gebieten der Sowjetunion', in Rolf-Dieter Müller and Hans-Erich Volkmann (eds.), *Die Wehrmacht: Mythos und Realität*, Munich, 1999, 837–57.

Riefenstahl, Leni, *A Memoir*, New York, 1993.

Ritter, Gerhard, *Carl Goerdeler und die deutsche Widerstandsbewegung*, Stuttgart, 1956.

Roberts, Geoffrey, *The Unholy Alliance. Stalin's Pact with Hitler*, London, 1989.

Rohde, Horst, 'Kriegsbeginn 1939 in Danzig – Planungen und Wirklichkeit', in Wolfgang Michalka (ed.), *Der Zweite Weltkrieg. Analysen-Grundzüge-Forschungsbilanz*, Munich/Zürich, 1989, 462–81.

Rohland, Walter, *Bewegte Zeiten. Erinnerungen eines Eisenhüttenmannes*, Stuttgart, 1978.

The Rommel Papers, ed. B. H. Liddell Hart, London, 1953.

Roon, Ger van, *Neuordnung im Widerstand. Der Kreisauer Kreis innerhalb der deutschen Widerstandsbewegung*, Munich, 1967.

—— 'Hermann Kaiser und der deutsche Widerstand', *VfZ*, 24 (1976), 259–86.

—— 'Staatsvorstellungen des Kreisauer Kreises', in Jürgen Schmädeke and Peter Steinbach (eds.), *Der Widerstand gegen den Nationalsozialismus. Die deutsche Gesellschaft und der Widerstand gegen Hitler*, (1985), Munich, 1986, 560–69.

—— *Widerstand im Dritten Reich. Ein Überblick*, (1979) 7th edn, Munich 1998.

Rosenstock, Werner, 'Exodus 1933–1939. A Survey of Jewish Emigration from Germany', *LBYB*, 1 (1956), 373–90.

Roskill, S. W., *The War at Sea*, 3 vols., London, 1954, 1956, 1960.

Rößler, Mechtild, and Schleiermacher, Sabine (eds.), *Der 'Generalplan Ost'. Hauptlinien der nationalsozialistischen Planungs- und Vernichtungspolitik*, Berlin, 1993.

Rothfels, Hans, *The German Opposition to Hitler. An Assessment*, London, 1970.

Rückerl, Adalbert (ed.), *NS-Vernichtungslager im Spiegel deutscher Strafprozesse*, Munich, 1977.

Runzheimer, Jürgen, 'Der Überfall auf den Sender Gleiwitz im Jahre 1939', *VfZ*, 10 (1962), 408–26.

Safrian, Hans, *Eichmann und seine Gehilfen*, Frankfurt am Main, 1995.

Salewski, Michael, *Die deutsche Seekriegsleitung 1935–1945. Bd. 1: 1935–1941*, Frankfurt am Main, 1970.

—— *Die deutsche Seekriegsleitung 1933–1945, Bd. II: 1942–1945*, Munich, 1975.

Salter, Stephen, 'Class Harmony or Class Conflict? The Industrial Working Class and the National Socialist Regime 1933–1945', in Jeremy Noakes (ed.), *Government, Party, and People in Nazi Germany*, Exeter, 1980, 76–97.

—— 'The Mobilisation of German Labour, 1939–1945. A Contribution to the History of the

Working Class in the Third Reich', unpublished D.Phil thesis, Oxford University, 1983.

Sandkühler, Thomas, *'Endlösung' in Galizien. Der Judenmord in Ostpolen und die Rettungsinitiativen von Berthold Beitz*, Bonn, 1996.

——'Judenpolitik und Judenmord im Distrikt Galizien, 1941–1942', in Ulrich Herbert (ed.), *Nationalsozialistische Vernichtungspolitik 1939–1945. Neue Forschungen und Kontroversen*, Frankfurt am Main, 1998, 122–47.

Sapir, Jacques, 'The Economics of War in the Soviet Union during World War II', in Ian Kershaw and Moshe Lewin (eds.), *Stalinism and Nazism: Dictatorships in Comparison*, Cambridge, 1997, 208–36.

Schacht, Hjalmar, *Abrechnung mit Hitler*, Berlin/Frankfurt am Main, 1949.

——*My First Seventy-Six Years*, London, 1955.

Schadt, Jörg (ed.), *Verfolgung und Widerstand unter dem Nationalsozialismus in Baden. Die Lageberichte der Gestapo und des Generalstaatsanwalts Karlsruhe 1933–1940*, Stuttgart, 1976.

Schall-Riancour, Heidemarie, *Aufstand und Gehorsam. Offizierstum und Generalstab im Umbruch. Leben und Wirken von Generaloberst Franz Halder, Generalstabschef 1938–1942*, Wiesbaden, 1972.

Schausberger, Norbert, *Der Griff nach Österreich. Der Anschluß*, Vienna/Munich, 1978.

——'Österreich und die nationalsozialistische Anschluß-Politik', in Manfred Funke (ed.), *Hitler, Deutschland und die Mächte. Materialien zur Außenpolitik des Dritten Reiches*, Düsseldorf, 1978, 728–56.

Schellenberg, Walter, *Schellenberg*, Mayflower Paperback edn, London, 1965.

Schenck, Ernst Günther, *Patient Hitler. Eine medizinische Biographie*, Düsseldorf, 1989.

Scheurig, Bodo, *Henning von Tresckow. Ein Preusse gegen Hitler*, Frankfurt am Main/Berlin, 1987.

——*Ewald von Kleist-Schmenzin. Ein Konservativer gegen Hitler*, Berlin/Frankfurt am Main, 1994.

Schieder, Wolfgang, 'Spanischer Bürgerkrieg und Vierjahresplan', in Wolfgang Michalka (ed.), *Nationalsozialistische Außenpolitik*, Darmstadt, 1978, 325–59.

Schildt, Axel, 'NS-Regime, Modernisierung und Moderne. Anmerkungen zur Hochkonjunktur einer andauernden Diskussion', *Tel Aviver Jahrbuch für deutsche Geschichte*, 23 (1994), 3–22.

Schirach, Baldur von, *Ich glaubte an Hitler*, Hamburg, 1967.

Schirach, Henriette von, *Der Preis der Herrlichkeit. Erlebte Zeitgeschichte*, (1956), Munich/Berlin, 1975.

Schlabrendorff, Fabian von, *Offiziere gegen Hitler*, (1946), revised edn, Berlin, 1984.

Schleunes, Karl A., *The Twisted Road to Auschwitz. Nazi Policy Toward German Jews, 1933–1939*, Urbana/Chicago/London, 1970.

Schmädeke, Jürgen, and Peter Steinbach (eds.), *Der Widerstand gegen den Nationalsozialismus. Die deutsche Gesellschaft und der Widerstand gegen Hitler*, (1985), paperback edn Munich/Zurich, 1986.

Schmidl, Erwin A., *März 38. Der deutsche Einmarsch in Österreich*, Vienna, 1987.

Schmidt, Matthias, *Albert Speer: Das Ende eines Mythos. Speers wahre Rolle im Dritten Reich*, Bern/Munich, 1982.

Schmidt, Paul, *Statist auf diplomatischer Bühne 1923–45. Erlebnisse des Chefdolmetschers im Auswärtigen Amt mit den Staatsmännern Europas*, Bonn, 1953.

Schmidt, Rainer F., 'Der Heß-Flug und das Kabinett Churchill', *VfZ*, 42 (1994), 1–38.

Schmidt, Ulf, 'Reassessing the Beginning of the "Euthanasia" Programme', *German History*, 17 (1999), 543–50.

Schmitz-Berning, Cornelia, *Vokabular des Nationalsozialismus*, Berlin, 1998.

Schmuhl, Hans-Walter, *Rassenhygiene, Nationalsozialismus, Euthanasie. Von der Verhütung zur Vernichtung 'lebensunwerten Lebens', 1890–1945*, Göttingen, 1987.

——'Philipp Bouhler – Ein Vorreiter des Massenmordes', in Ronald Smelser, Enrico Syring and Rainer Zitelmann (eds.), *Die braune Elite II*, Darmstadt, 1993, 39–50.

Schneider, Willi, 'Hitler aus nächster Nähe', 7 *Tage. Illustrierte Wochenschrift aus dem Zeitgeschehen*, 17 Oct. 1952–2 Jan. 1953.

Scholl, Inge, *Die Weiße Rose*, Frankfurt am Main 1952.

Schramm, Percy Ernst, *Hitler als militärischer Führer. Erkenntnisse und Erfahrungen aus dem Kriegstagebuch des Oberkommandos der Wehrmacht*, Frankfurt am Main, 1962.

Schroeder, Christa, *Er war mein Chef. Aus dem Nachlaß der Sekretärin von Adolf Hitler*, ed. Anton Joachimsthaler, (1985), 4th edn, Munich/Vienna, 1989.

Schulte, Theo J., *The German Army and Nazi Policies in Occupied Russia*, Oxford/New York/Munich, 1989.

Schulz, Alfons, *Drei Jahre in der Nachrichtenzentrale des Führerhauptquartiers*, Stein am Rhein, 1996.

Schulze, Birgit, 'Himmler als Reichsinnenminister', unpubl. Magisterarbeit, Ruhr-Universität Bochum, 1981.

Schuschnigg, Kurt, *Ein Requiem in Rot-Weiß-Rot*, Zurich, 1946.

—— *Austrian Requiem*, London, 1947.

Schustereit, Hartmut, *Vabanque: Hitler's Angriff auf die Sowjetunion 1941 als Versuch, durch den Sieg im Osten den Westen zu bezwingen*, Herford, 1988.

Schwarz, Eberhard, 'Die Stabilisierung der Ostfront nach Stalingrad: Mansteins Gegenschlag zwischen Donez und Dnieper im Frühjahr 1943', unpublished dissertation, Cologne, 1981.

Schwarz, Michael, ' "Euthanasie"-Debatten in Deutschland (1895–1945)', *VfZ*, 46 (1998), 617–65.

Schweitzer, Arthur, *Big Business in the Third Reich*, Bloomington, 1964.

'Secret of Hitler's ashes revealed in Soviet archive', *New York Post*, 27 January 2000.

Seidler, Franz W., *Fritz Todt. Baumeister des Dritten Reiches*, Munich/Berlin, 1986.

—— '*Deutscher Volkssturm*'. *Das letzte Aufgebot 1944/45*, Munich, 1989.

Semmler, Rudolf, *Goebbels – the Man Next to Hitler*, London, 1947.

Seraphim, Hans-Günter (ed.), *Das politische Tagebuch Alfred Rosenbergs 1934/35 und 1939/40*, Munich, 1964.

Sereny, Gitta, *Into That Darkness. An Examination of Conscience*, Pan Books edn, London, 1977.

—— *Albert Speer: His Battle with the Truth*, London, 1995.

Service, Robert, *A History of Twentieth-Century Russia*, London, 1998.

Seydewitz, Max, *Civil Life in Wartime Germany. The Story of the Home Front*, New York, 1945.

Shirakawa, Sam H., *The Devil's Music Master: the Controversial Life and Career of Wilhelm Furtwängler*, New York, 1992.

Shirer, William L., *Berlin Diary, 1934–1941*, Sphere Books edn, London, 1970.

—— *This is Berlin. Reporting from Nazi Germany 1938–40*, London, 1999.

Shore, Zach, 'Hitler, Intelligence, and the Decision to Remilitarize the Rhine', *JCH*, 34 (1999), 5–18.

Siebert, Detlef, 'Die Durchführung des Kommissarbefehls in den Frontverbänden des Heeres. Eine quantifierende Auswertung der Forschung', unpublished paper.

Siefken, Hinrich (ed.), *Die Weiße Rose und ihre Flugblätter*, Manchester, 1994.

Siemen, Hans Ludwig, 'Reform und Radikalisierung. Veranderung der Psychiatrie in der Weltwirtschaftskrise', in Norbert Frei (ed.), *Medizin und Gesundheitspolitik in der NS-Zeit*, Munich, 1991, 191–200.

Skidelsky, Robert, *Oswald Mosley*, London, 1981.

Skorzeny, Otto, *Skorzeny's Special Missions*, London (1957), 1997.

Smelser, Ronald M., *The Sudeten Problem 1933–1938. Volkstumspolitik and the Formulation of Nazi Foreign Policy*, Folkestone, 1975.

—— *Robert Ley. Hitler's Labor Front Leader*, Oxford/New York/Hamburg, 1988.

Smelser, Ronald M., and Zitelmann, Rainer (eds.), *Die braune Elite*, Darmstadt, 1989.

Smelser, Ronald M., Syring, Enrico, and Zitelmann, Rainer (eds.), *Die braune Elite II*, Darmstadt, 1993.

Smelser, Ronald M., and Syring, Enrico (eds.), *Die Militarelite des Dritten Reiches. 27 biographische Skizzen*, Berlin/Frankfurt am Main, 1995.

Smith, Bradley F., 'Die Überlieferung der Hoßbach-Niederschrift im Licht neuer Quellen', *VfZ*, 38 (1990), 329–36.

Smith, Bradley F., and Agnes F. Peterson (eds.), *Heinrich Himmler. Geheimreden 1933 bis 1945*, Frankfurt am Main/Berlin/Vienna, 1974.

Smith, Denis Mack, *Mussolini*, Paladin edn, London, 1985.

Smith, Woodruff D., *The Ideological Origins of Nazi Imperialism*, New York/Oxford, 1986.

Smyth, Denis, ' "We Are With You": Solidarity and Self-Interest in Soviet Policy towards Republican Spain, 1936–1939', in Paul Preston and Ann L. Mackenzie (eds.), *The Republic Besieged: Civil War in Spain, 1936–1939*, Edinburgh, 1996, 87–105.

Sohn-Rethel, Alfred, *Ökonomie und Klassenstruktur des deutschen Faschismus*, Frankfurt am Main, 1973.

Sommer, Theo, *Deutschland und Japan zwischen den Mächten 1935–1940. Vom Antikominternpakt zum Dreimächtepakt*, Tübingen, 1962.

Sonnenberger, Franz, 'Der neue "Kulturkampf". Die Gemeinschaftsschule und ihre historischen Voraussetzungen', in Martin Broszat, Elke Frohlich and Anton Grossmann (eds.), *Bayern in der NS-Zeit, vol. 3: Herrschaft und Gesellschaft im Konflikt*, Munich/Vienna, 1981, 235–327.

Sontheimer, Kurt, *Antidemokratisches Denken in der Weimarer Republik*, 3rd edn, Munich, 1992.

Sozialgeschichtliches Arbeitsbuch, III: Materialien zur Statistik des Deutschen Reiches 1914–1945, ed. Dietmar Petzina, Werner Abelshauser and Anselm Faust, Munich, 1978.

Speer, Albert, *Erinnerungen*, Frankfurt am Main/Berlin, 1969.

—— *Inside the Third Reich*, Sphere Books edn, London, 1971.

—— *Spandau. The Secret Diaries*, Fontana edn, London, 1977.

Speidel, Hans, *Invasion 1944. Ein Beitrag zu Rommels und des Reiches Schicksal*, Tübingen/Stuttgart, 1949.

Spengler, Oswald, *Der Untergang des Abendlandes*, 2 vols., Vienna/Munich, 1918–22.

Spiegelbild einer Verschwörung. Die Kaltenbrunner-Berichte an Bormann und Hitler über das Attentat vom 20. Juli 1944. Geheime Dokumente aus dem ehemaligen Reichssicherheitshauptamt, ed. Archiv Peter für historische und zeitgeschichtliche Dokumentation, Stuttgart, 1961.

Spitzy, Reinhard, *So haben wir das Reich verspielt. Bekenntnisse eines Illegalen*, Munich, 1986.

Sprenger, Isabell, 'Das KZ Groß-Rosen in der letzten Kriegsphase', in Ulrich Herbert, Karin Orth and Christoph Dieckmann (eds.), *Die nationalsozialistischen Konzentrationslager. Entwicklung und Struktur*, vol. 2, Göttingen, 1998, 1113–27.

Stadler, Karl, *Österreich 1938–1945 im Spiegel der NS-Akten*, Vienna/Munich, 1966.

Stasiewski, Bernhard, 'Die Kirchenpolitik der Nationalsozialisten im Warthegau 1939–1945', *VfZ*, 7 (1959), 46–74.

Stauffer, Paul, *Zwischen Hofmannsthal und Hitler. Carl J. Burckhardt: Facetten einer ausserge-wöhnlichen Existenz*, Zurich, 1991.

Stegemann, Bernd, 'Hitlers Kriegsziele im ersten Kriegsjahr 1939/40. Ein Beitrag zur Quellenkritik', *Militärgeschichtliche Mitteilungen*, 27 (1980), 93–105.

Stehle, Hansjakob, 'Deutsche Friedensfühler bei den Westmächten im Februar/März 1945', *VfZ*, 30 (1982), 538–55.

Steinbach, Peter, 'Hans Günther von Kluge – Ein Zauderer im Zwielicht', in Ronald Smelser and Enrico Syring (eds.), *Die Militärelite des Dritten Reiches*, Berlin/Frankfurt am Main, 1995, 288–324.

Steinbach, Peter, and Tuchel, Johannes (eds.), *Widerstand in Deutschland 1933–1945. Ein historisches Lesebuch*, Munich, 1994.

—— *Lexikon des Widerstandes 1933–1945*, Munich, 1994.

Steinberg, Jonathan, *All or Nothing. The Axis and the Holocaust 1941–43*, London/New York, 1991.

Steinert, Marlis, *Hitlers Krieg und die Deutschen. Stimmung und Haltung der deutschen Bevölkerung im Zweiten Weltkrieg*, Düsseldorf/Vienna, 1970.

Steinhoff, Johannes, Pechel, Peter, and Showalter, Dennis, *Voices from the Third Reich: an Oral History*, (1989), New York, 1994.

Steppe, Hilde, ' "Mit Tränen in den Augen haben wir dann diese Spritzen aufgezogen". Die Beteiligung von Krankenschwestern und Krankenpflegern an den Verbrechen gegen die Menschlichkeit', in Hilde Steppe (ed.), *Krankenpflege im Nationalsozialismus*, 7th edn, Frankfurt am Main, 1993, 137–74.

Stern, Fritz, *The Politics of Cultural Despair*, Berkeley/Los Angeles, 1961.

Stern, J. P., 'The White Rose', in Hinrich Siefken (ed.), *Die Weiße Rose. Student Resistance to National Socialism 1942/43. Forschungsergebnisse und Erfahrungsberichte*, (1991), Nottingham, n.d., 11–36.

Sternheim-Peters, Eva, *Die Zeit der großen Täuschungen. Mädchenleben im Faschismus*, Bielefeld, 1987.

Stokes, Lawrence D., 'The German People and the Destruction of the European Jews', *Central European History*, 6 (1973), 167–91.

Stoltzfus, Nathan, *Resistance of the Heart*, New York/London, 1996.

Stone, Norman, 'Hitler, ein Gespenst in den Archiven', *Frankfurter Allgemeine Zeitung*, 19 April 1995.

Stöver, Bernd, *Volksgemeinschaft im Dritten Reich. Die Konsensbereitschaft der Deutschen aus der Sicht sozialistischer Exilberichte*, Düsseldorf, 1993.

Strauss, Herbert A., 'Jewish Emigration from Germany. Nazi Policies and Jewish Responses (I)', *LBYB*, 25 (1980), 313–61.

Strawson, John, *Hitler as Military Commander*, London, 1971.

—— *Churchill and Hitler*, London, 1997.

Streim, Alfred, *Die Behandlung sowjetischer Kriegsgefangener im 'Fall Barbarossa'*, Heidelberg/Karlsruhe, 1981.

Streit, Christian, *Keine Kameraden. Die Wehrmacht und die sowjetischen Kriegsgefangenen 1941–1945*, Stuttgart, 1978.

The Stroop Report. The Jewish Quarter of Warsaw Is No More. A facsimile edition and translation of the official Nazi report on the destruction of the Warsaw Ghetto, intro. by Andrzej Wirth (1960), London, 1980.

Strzelecki, Andrej, 'Der Todesmarsch der Häftlinge aus dem KL Auschwitz', in Ulrich Herbert, Karin Orth and Daniel Blatman (eds.), *Die nationalsozialistischen Konzentrationslager. Entwicklung und Struktur*, vol. 2, Göttingen, 1998, 1093–1112.

Suchcitz, Andrzej, 'Poland's Defence Preparations in 1939', in Peter D. Stachura (ed.), *Poland between the Wars, 1918–1939*, London, 1998, 109–36.

Sywottek, Jutta, *Mobilmachung für den totalen Krieg. Die propagandistische Vorbereitung der deutschen Bevölkerung auf den Zweiten Weltkrieg*, Opladen, 1976.

Die Tagebücher von Joseph Goebbels. Sämtliche Fragmente, Teil I.: Aufzeichnungen 1924–1941, 4 Bde, ed. Elke Fröhlich, Munich, 1987.

Die Tagebücher von Joseph Goebbels. Teil I, Aufzeichnungen 1923–1941, 9 vols. (vols. 6–9 so far published), Teil II, Diktate 1941–1945, 15 vols., ed. Elke Fröhlich, Munich etc., 1993–8.

Tausk, Walter, *Breslauer Tagebuch 1933–1940*, East Berlin, 1975.

Taylor, A. J. P., *The Origins of the Second World War*, (1961), Penguin edn, Harmondsworth, 1964.

Teppe, Karl, 'Der Reichsverteidigungskommissar. Organisation und Praxis in Westfalen', in Dieter

Rebentisch and Karl Teppe (eds.), *Verwaltung contra Menschenführung im Staat Hitlers. Studien zum politisch-administrativen System*, Göttingen, 1986, 278–301.

Terveen, Fritz, 'Der Filmbericht über Hitlers 50. Geburtstag. Ein Beispiel nationalsozialistischer Selbstdarstellung und Propaganda', *VfZ*, 7 (1959), 75–84.

The Testament of Adolf Hitler. The Hitler–Bormann Documents, February-April 1945, with an Introduction by H. R. Trevor-Roper, London, 1961.

La testament politique de Hitler. Notes receuillies par Martin Bormann, ed. François Genoud, Paris, 1959.

Thalmann, Rita, and Feinermann, Emmanuel, *Crystal Night: 9–10 November 1938*, London, 1974.

Thamer, Hans-Ulrich, *Verführung und Gewalt. Deutschland 1933–1945*, Berlin, 1986.

Thies, Jochen, *Architekt der Weltherrschaft. Die 'Endziele' Hitlers*, Düsseldorf, 1976.

—— 'Hitler's European Building Programme', *JCH*, 13 (1978), 413–31.

Thomas, Charles S., *The German Navy in the Nazi Era*, London, 1990.

Thomas, Hugh, *Doppelgänger: The Truth about the Bodies in the Berlin Bunker*, London, 1995.

Thorwald, Jürgen, *Die ungeklärten Fälle*, Stuttgart, 1950.

Thun-Hohenstein, Romedio Galeazzo Reichsgraf von, *Der Verschwörer. General Oster und die Militäropposition*, Berlin, 1982.

Toland, John, *The Last 100 Days*, London, 1966.

—— *Adolf Hitler*, London, 1977.

Toscano, Mario, *The Origins of the Pact of Steel*, Baltimore, 1967.

Treue, Wilhelm (ed.), 'Hitlers Denkschrift zum Vierjahresplan 1936', *VfZ*, 3 (1955), 184–210.

—— 'Rede Hitlers vor der deutschen Presse (10. November 1938)', *VfZ*, 6 (1958), 175–91.

Trevor-Roper, H. R., *The Last Days of Hitler*, (1947), Pan Books edn, London, 1973.

—— 'The Hole in Hitler's Head', *Sunday Times*, 29 September 1968 (review of Bezymenski's *Death of Adolf Hitler*).

Trials of War Criminals before the Nuernberg Military Tribunals, 12 vols., Nuremberg, 1946–9.

Ueberschar, Gerd R., *Generaloberst Franz Halder. Generalstabschef, Gegner und Gefangener Hitlers*, Göttingen, 1991.

—— (ed.), *Der 20. Juli 1944. Bewertung und Rezeption des deutschen Widerstandes gegen das NS-Regime*, Cologne, 1994.

—— (ed.), *Hitlers militärische Elite*, 2 vols., Darmstadt, 1998.

Ueberschar, Gerd R., and Wette, Wolfgang (eds.), *'Unternehmen Barbarossa'. Der deutsche Überfall auf die Sowjetunion*, Paderborn, 1984.

Ueberschàr, Gerd R., and Bezymenskij, Lev A. (eds.), *Der deutsche Überfall auf die Sowjetunion. Die Kontroverse um die Praventivkriegsthese*, Darmstadt, 1988.

United States Strategic Bombing Survey, vol. 4, New York/London, 1976.

'Die Vernehmung des Generaloberst Jodl durch die Sowjets', *Wehrwissenschaftliche Rundschau*, 11 (1966), 534–42.

'Die Vernehmung von Generalfeldmarschall Keitel durch die Sowjets', *Wehrwissenschaftliche Rundschau*, 11 (1966), 651–62.

Die Vertreibung der deutschen Bevölkerung aus den Gebieten östlich der Oder-Neiße, vol. 1, Munich, 1984.

Voges, Michael, 'Klassenkampf in der "Betriebsgemeinschaft". Die "Deutschland-Berichte" der Sopade (1934–40) als Quelle zum Widerstand der Industrie-Arbeiter im Dritten Reich', *Archiv für Sozialgeschichte*, 21 (1981), 329–84.

Volk, Ludwig, 'Kardinal Faulhabers Stellung zur Weimarer Republik und zum NS-Staat', *Stimmen der Zeit*, 177 (1966), 173–95.

—— 'Episkopat und Kirchenkampf', in Dieter Albrecht (ed.), *Katholische Kirche und Nationalsozialismus. Ausgewählte Aufsätze von Ludwig Volk*, Mainz, 1987.

Volkogonov, Dmitri, *Stalin. Triumph and Tragedy*, (1991) Rocklin, Ca., 1996.

Wagner, Dieter, and Tomkowitz, Gerhard, *Ein Volk, ein Reich, ein Führer. The Nazi Annexation of Austria, 1938*, London, 1971.

Wagner, Eduard, *Der Generalquartiermeister. Briefe und Tagebuchaufzeichnungen des Generalquartiermeisters des Heeres General der Artillerie Eduard Wagner*, ed. Elisabeth Wagner, Munich/Vienna, 1963.

Wagner, Johannes Volker, *Hakenkreuz über Bochum*, Bochum, 1983.

Wahl, Karl, '. . . *es ist das deutsche Herz'. Erlebnisse und Erkenntnisse eines ehemaligen Gauleiters*, Augsburg, 1954.

Walker, Mark, *German National Socialism and the Quest for Nuclear Power 1939–1949*, Cambridge, 1989.

——'Legenden um die deutsche Atombombe', *VfZ*, 38 (1990), 45–74.

Walter, Dirk, *Antisemitische Kriminalität und Gewalt. Judenfeindschaft in der Weimarer Republik*, Bonn, 1999.

Warlimont, Walter, *Inside Hitler's Headquarters, 1939–45*, (1964), Presidio paperback edn, Novato, n.d.

' ". . . warum dann überhaupt noch leben!". Hitlers Lagebesprechungen am 23., 25. und 27. April 1945', *Der Spiegel*, 10. January 1966, 32–46.

Watt, Donald Cameron, 'Hitler's Visit to Rome and the May Weekend Crisis: A Study in Hitler's Response to External Stimuli', *JCH*, 9 (1974), 23–32.

——*How War Came. The Immediate Origins of the Second World War, 1938–1939*, (1989), Mandarin paperback edn, London, 1991

Weber, Eugen, *The Hollow Years. France in the 1930s*, New York/London, 1996.

Weber, Hermann, 'Die KPD in der Illegalität', in Richard Löwenthal and Patrik von zur Mühlen (eds.), *Widerstand und Verweigerung in Deutschland 1933 bis 1945*, Berlin/Bonn, 1984, 83–101.

Wegner, Bernd, *Hitlers Politische Soldaten: Die Waffen-SS 1933–1945*, Paderborn, 1982.

——'Hitlers zweiter Feldzug gegen die Sowjetunion. Strategische Grundlagen und historische Bedeutung', in Wolfgang Michalka (ed.), *Der Zweite Weltkrieg. Analysen-Grundzüge-Forschungsbilanz*, Munich/Zurich, 1989, 652–66.

——'Vom Lebensraum zum Todesraum. Deutschlands Kriegführung zwischen Moskau und Stalingrad', in Jürgen Förster (ed.), *Stalingrad. Ereignis-Wirkung-Symbol*, Munich/Zurich, 1992, 17–37.

——'Hitlers Besuch in Finnland. Das geheime Tonprotokoll seiner Unterredung mit Mannerheim am 4. Juni 1942', *VfZ*, 41 (1993), 117–37.

——'Hitler, der Zweite Weltkrieg und die Choreographie des Untergangs', unpublished paper.

Weinberg, Gerhard L., 'Hitler's Private Testament of May 2, 1938', *JMH*, 27 (1955), 415–19.

——'The May Crisis, 1938', *JMH*, 29 (1957), 213–25.

——(ed.), *Hitlers Zweites Buch. Ein Dokument aus dem Jahr 1928*, Stuttgart, 1961.

——'Adolf Hitler und der NS-Führungsoffizier (NSFO)', *VfZ*, 12 (1964), 443–56.

——*The Foreign Policy of Hitler's Germany*, vol. I: *Diplomatic Revolution in Europe, 1933–36*, Chicago/London, 1970.

——*The Foreign Policy of Hitler's Germany*, vol. II: *Starting World War II, 1937–1939*, Chicago/London, 1980.

——'Hitler and England, 1933–1945', *German Studies Review*, 8 (1985), 299–309.

——*A World at Arms. A Global History of World War II*, Cambridge, 1994.

——'German Plans for Victory, 1944–1945', in Gerhard L. Weinberg (ed.), *Germany, Hitler, and World War II*, Cambridge, 1995, 274–86.

Weindling, Paul, *Health, Race, and German Politics between National Unification and Nazism, 1870–1945*, Cambridge, 1989.

Weingartner, James T., 'Josef "Sepp" Dietrich – Hitlers Volksgeneral', in Ronald Smelser and

Enrico Syring (eds.), *Die Militärelite des Dritten Reiches*, Berlin/Frankfurt am Main, 1985, 113–28.

Weiß, Hermann, 'Die Aufzeichnungen Hermann Gorings im Institut für Zeitgeschichte', *VfZ*, 31 (1983), 365–8.

—— 'Der "schwache" Diktator. Hitler und der Führerstaat', in Wolfgang Benz, Hans Buchheim and Hans Mommsen (eds.), *Der Nationalsozialismus. Studien zur Ideologie und Herrschaft*, Frankfurt am Main, 1993, 64–77.

—— 'Ideologie der Freizeit im Dritten Reich. Die NS-Gemeinschaft "Kraft durch Freude" ', *Archiv für Sozialgeschichte*, 33 (1993), 289–303.

—— (ed.), *Biographisches Lexikon zum Dritten Reich*, Frankfurt am Main, 1998.

Weizsäcker, Ernst von, *Erinnerungen*, Munich/Leipzig/Freiburg i. Br., 1950.

Welch, David, *Propaganda and the German Cinema, 1933–1945*, Oxford, 1983.

—— *The Third Reich. Politics and Propaganda*, London, 1993.

Wendt, Bernd-Jürgen, 'Nationalsozialistische Großraumwirtschaft zwischen Utopie und Wirklichkeit – Zum Scheitern einer Konzeption 1938/39', in Franz Knipping and Klaus-Jurgen Müller (eds.), *Machtbewußtsein in Deutschland am Vorabend des Zweiten Weltkrieges*, Paderborn, 1984, 223–45.

—— *Großdeutschland. Außenpolitik und Kriegsvorbereitung des Hitler-Regimes*, Munich, 1987.

Werth, Alexander, *Russia at War 1941–1945*, (1964), New York, 1984.

Wette, Wolfram, 'Die propagandistische Begleitmusik zum deutschen Überfall auf die Sowjetunion am 22. Juni 1941', in Gerd R. Ueberschär and Wolfram Wette (eds.), *'Unternehmen Barbarossa'. Der deutsche Überfall auf die Sowjetunion 1941. Berichte, Analysen, Dokumente*, Paderborn, 1984, 111–29.

—— 'Zur psychologischen Modbilmachung der deutschen Bevölkerung 1933–1939', in Wolfgang Michalka (ed.), *Der Zweite Weltkrieg. Analysen-Grundzüge-Forschungsbilanz*, Munich/Zurich, 1989, 205–23.

Whaley, B., *Codeword Barbarossa*, Cambridge, Mass., 1973.

Whaley, Robert Weldon, *Assassinating Hitler: Ethics and Resistance in Nazi Germany*, London, Ontario, 1993.

Wheal, Elizabeth-Anne, and Pope, Stephen, *The Macmillan Dictionary of the Second World War*, 2nd edn, London, 1995.

Whiting, Charles, *Heydrich. Henchman of Death*, London, 1999.

Widerstand und Verfolgung im Köln 1933–1945, ed. Historisches Archiv der Stadt Köln, Cologne, 1974.

Wiedemann, Fritz, *Der Mann, der Feldherr werden wollte*, Velbert/Kettwig, 1964.

Wieder, Joachim, and Einsiedel, Heinrich Graf von (eds.), *Stalingrad. Memories and Reassessments*, (1962), London, 1997.

Wighton, Charles, *Heydrich. Hitler's Most Evil Henchman*, London, 1962.

Wildt, Michael, *Die Judenpolitik des SD 1935 bis 1938. Eine Dokumentation*, Munich, 1995.

Wilhelm, Hans-Heinrich, 'Hitlers Ansprache vor Generalen und Offizieren am 26. Mai 1944', *Militärgeschichtliche Mitteilungen*, 2 (1976), 123–70.

—— 'Wie geheim war die "Endlösung"?', in Wolfgang Benz (ed.), *Miscellanea: Festschrift für Helmut Krausnick zum 75. Geburtstag*, Stuttgart, 1980, 131–48.

Willems, Susanne, *Lothar Kreyssig. Vom eigenen verantwortlichen Handeln. Eine biographische Studie zum Protest gegen die Euthanasieverbrechen in Nazi-Deutschland*, (1996), Göttingen, n.d.

Winkler, Dörte, 'Frauenarbeit versus Frauenideologie. Probleme der weiblichen Erwerbstätigkeit in Deutschland 1930–1945', *Archiv für Sozialgeschichte*, 17 (1977), 99–126.

—— *Frauenarbeit im Dritten Reich*, Hamburg, 1977.

Wiskemann, Elizabeth, *The Rome-Berlin Axis. A History of the Relations between Hitler and Mussolini*, New York/London, 1949.

Wistrich, Robert, *Wer war wer im Dritten Reich*, Munich, 1983.

Witetschek, Helmut (ed.), *Die kirchliche Lage in Bayern nach den Regierungspräsidentenberichten 1933–1945*, vol. 1, Mainz, 1966.

Witte, Peter, 'Two Decisions concerning the "Final Solution to the Jewish Question": Deportations to Lodz and Mass Murder in Chelmno', *Holocaust and Genocide Studies*, 9 (1995), 293–317.

Woller, Hans, *Die Abrechnung mit dem Faschismus in Italien 1943 bis 1948*, Munich, 1996.

Wright, Jonathan, and Stafford, Paul, 'Hitler, Britain, and the Hoßbach Memorandum', *Militärgeschichtliche Mitteilungen*, 42 (1987), 77–123.

Yahil, Leni, *The Rescue of Danish Jewry. Test of a Democracy*, Philadelphia, 1969.

—— 'Madagascar – Phantom of a Solution for the Jewish Question', in Bela Vago and George L. Mosse (eds.), *Jews and Non-Jews in Eastern Europe*, New York, 1974, 315–34.

—— *The Holocaust. The Fate of European Jewry, 1932–1945*, New York/Oxford, 1990.

—— 'Some Remarks about Hitler's Impact on the Nazis' Jewish Policy', *Yad Vashem Studies*, 23 (1993), 281–93.

Zeller, Eberhard, *Geist der Freiheit. Der Zwanzigste Juli*, Munich, 1963.

Zeman, Z. A. B., *Nazi Propaganda*, Oxford (1964), 1973.

Ziemke, Earl F., *Stalingrad to Berlin: the German Defeat in the East*, Washington, 1968.

Zimmermann, Michael, *Verfolgt, vertrieben, vernichtet. Die nationalsozialistische Vernichtungspolitik gegen Sinti und Roma*, Essen, 1989.

—— 'Die nationalsozialistische Losung der Zigeunerfrage', in Ulrich Herbert (ed.), *Nationalsozialistische Vernichtungspolitik 1939–1945. Neue Forschungen und Kontroversen*, Frankfurt am Main, 1998, 235–62.

Zitelmann, Rainer, *Hitler. Selbstverständnis eines Revolutionärs*, Hamburg/Leamington Spa/New York, 1987.

—— *Adolf Hitler. Eine politische Biographie*, Göttingen, 1989.

—— 'Die totalitäre Seite der Moderne', in Michael Prinz and Rainer Zitelmann (eds.), *Nationalsozialismus und Modernisierung*, Darmstadt, 1991, 1–20.

Zoller, Albert, *Hitler privat. Erlebnisbericht seiner Geheimsekretärin*, Düsseldorf, 1949.

Zuckmayer, Carl, *Als wärs ein Stück von mir. Erinnerungen*, (1966), Frankfurt am Main, 1971.

Zumpe, Lotte, *Wirtschaft und Staat in Deutschland 1933 bis 1945*, East Berlin, 1980.

INDEX